THE
CAMBRIDGE
ECONOMIC HISTORY

GENERAL EDITORS: M. M. POSTAN, Professor of Economic History in the University of Cambridge, and H. J. HABAKKUK, Chichele Professor of Economic History in the University of Oxford

VOLUME III

THE
CAMBRIDGE
ECONOMIC HISTORY
OF EUROPE

VOLUME III
ECONOMIC ORGANIZATION AND
POLICIES IN THE MIDDLE AGES

EDITED BY

M. M. POSTAN

Professor of Economic History in the
University of Cambridge

E. E. RICH

Vere Harmsworth Professor of Imperial and Naval
History in the University of Cambridge

AND

EDWARD MILLER

Lecturer in History in the University of Cambridge

CAMBRIDGE

AT THE UNIVERSITY PRESS

1963

PUBLISHED BY
THE SYNDICS OF THE CAMBRIDGE UNIVERSITY PRESS

Bentley House, 200 Euston Road, London, N.W.1
American Branch: 32 East 57th Street, New York 22, N.Y.
West African Office: P.O. Box 33, Ibadan, Nigeria

Printed in Great Britain by The Broadwater Press Ltd, Welwyn Garden City, Hertfordshire

PREFACE

The plans for this volume laid down by the initiators of the series—Sir John Clapham and Eileen Power—were given their final shape some eight years ago; the contributors were chosen and their contracts signed in the following year; but, despite the considerable interval, the present volume has had to go to press without three of the chapters originally scheduled.

Of the missing chapters, that on the economic policies of east European states fell victim to the difficulties of academic communication with Russian scholars in the early and middle fifties; that of the organization of transport had to be given up owing to the resignation of another author for health reasons. But the most important gap is caused by the withdrawal of the writer designated for the chapter on money and currency. This was a chapter which the editors hoped to make into one of the cornerstones of the volume, and which in their view was well worth waiting for. Unfortunately the field of monetary history is thinly held, and the hour was so late when the original contributor withdrew that the editors had to renounce all hope of recommissioning the chapter. All they were able to do was to provide a short appendix listing the coins and currencies mentioned in the volume and giving, where possible, their rates of exchange.

According to Sir John Clapham's and Eileen Power's plans the third medieval volume was intended to deal with the aspects of medieval economic history purposely left out of the first two volumes, and in the first place with economic policies and policy-making institutions. What suggested this division of matter was that, in the past, economic policies unduly dominated the story of economic history. The development of industry, trade and agriculture, and that of population and land usage, were not only discussed in close relation to corresponding policies and regulations, but were often seen through the eyes of regulating and policy-making authorities. Thus viewed, the history of agriculture tended to be wholly absorbed into that of the manor, and the history of trade and industry into that of towns and gilds. To correct this bias the planners of the series decided in the first place to devote the agricultural volume to the various economic and social processes in the countryside and correspondingly to reduce the space occupied by the institutional problems of the manor, and, secondly, so to divide the story of industry and trade as to make it possible for the contributors to the second volume to devote themselves wholly to trade as an economic activity. This meant postponing to the third volume the discussions of economic policies, of policy-making institutions, and of the related problems of commercial and industrial organization and economic theory.

This plan has in fact been consummated in this volume. The readers will find in it two main groups of chapters: one dealing with the development of commercial organization and of the institutions from which economic policies issued, i.e. towns, gilds, markets, fairs and commercial firms; the other concerned with the economic policies of municipalities, gilds and state governments, with taxation and with state and municipal finance. The chapter on economic doctrines provides a summary of the ideas which dominated economic thought and to some extent provided the policy-makers with guiding objects and criteria. In this grouping of chapters, some naturally occupy focal positions. Thus Mr Hibbert's subject—that of the economic policies of medieval town governments—naturally places his chapter in the very centre of the section concerned with urban institutions and policies. Similarly Mr Miller's contribution to the subject of state policies—and more especially his introductory observations—have been designed to give unity to the various contributions to this topic. In the preparation of this section Mr Miller has been assigned the role which Marc Bloch played in Volume I by assembling and editing the chapters and sub-chapters concerned with European agrarian economy at its prime.

Whether this division and arrangement of the matter is preferable to the conventional method of presentation in which economic policies and institutions dominate the story of trade and industry, is for readers and critics to judge. It has undoubtedly added to the difficulties of editors and contributors in that it prevented them from drawing on ready-made and easily accessible versions of medieval economic history. It has not made it any easier to place proper emphasis on some of the really 'basic' problems of economic history, such as population, prices, or formation of capital. On the other hand it enabled the contributors to the second volume to place the problems of commercial development in their proper economic and social setting, and the writers of the third to discuss policy and organization in relation to political and constitutional developments which do not commonly enter into the ken of economic history. Moreover, separate treatment of the 'basic' topics is not incompatible with the Clapham–Power plan, and the editors hope to deal with them when the second edition of these volumes is called for.

It will be noticed that, in enforcing their general plan, the editors did nothing to enforce a common attitude to certain fundamental problems of medieval development. If the preceding volume, the second, happens to exhibit, with a few inconspicuous exceptions, a common attitude to the chronology and phasing of medieval development, this is wholly due to the unplanned and unsolicited community of views among the contributors. In the present volume the great majority of the contributors also share common assumptions about the direction and the rhythm of medieval economic development. In one important instance, however, that of Professor Cipolla's sub-chapter, these assumptions are questioned, and a disagreement with Professor Lopez's views in the second volume is implied. The editors have done nothing to conceal or even to reconcile this conflict and have left it to the readers to judge the case by the cogency of the argument and the evidence cited in its support. The editors have also refrained from interference in several less fundamental matters. Thus the authors have been given freedom to decide the internal arrangements—i.e. frequency and the hierarchy of sections and sub-sections—within each chapter. The editors have also refused to interfere drastically with the manner in which the authors have presented their bibliographies. The subjects of individual chapters are disparate; some cover the whole of western Europe, others are regional; some deal with well-worn topics abundantly served by books and articles, others tread new ground hardly traversed by earlier writers. The bibliographies therefore differ in both length and arrangement. But, every care has been taken to make the references to books and articles uniform in accordance with scholarly practice prevailing in this country.

M. M. P.

CONTENTS

Chapter III. Markets and Fairs

By O. Verlinden, Professor in the University of Brussels

PART II. POLICIES

Chapter IV. The Economic Policies of Towns

By A. B. Hibbert, Lecturer in the University of Cambridge

Chapter V. The Gilds

By Sylvia L. Thrupp, Associate Professor in the University of Chicago

CHAPTER VI. The Economic Policies of Governments

CHAPTER VII. Public Credit, with Special Reference to North-Western Europe

By E. B. FRYDE, Lecturer in the University College of Wales, Aberystwyth; and
M. M. FRYDE, Lecturer in Columbia University, New York

CHAPTER VIII. Conceptions of Economy and Society

By GABRIEL LE BRAS, Dean of the Faculty of Law
and Economic Science, University of Paris

TABLES

TABLES

PART I
ORGANIZATION

CHAPTER I
The Rise of the Towns

I. *Introduction*

A human community whose members are predominantly engaged in agriculture is unlikely to exceed a village in importance. A concentration of an urban character presupposes, in fact, the presence of a population whose resources are of quite a different order.

There are towns which, from the economic point of view, operate essentially as consumers. They obtain the means of purchasing the consumption goods their inhabitants require from dues derived from a variety of external sources, or receive these dues directly in kind. This was the position of such political and religious centres as Imperial Rome and Papal Rome. It was the position, too, of many *civitates* in the early Middle Ages, formerly Roman administrative centres with active populations of merchants and craftsmen, but now devitalized and inhabited primarily by clerical communities living on the produce of episcopal and abbatial domains.

Nevertheless, town-dwellers normally have an economic function as producers, not, of course, in agriculture, but in trade and in industry. In such cases, towns are at once producers and consumers.

In this chapter the history of the town will be studied in relation to economic history. We shall consider it in some measure from its beginnings, bearing in mind that in the Carolingian period the towns, as centres of population, were of slight importance. It should not be forgotten, however, that what then existed in the way of towns, and what in large measure would serve as the basis for later development, was inherited from earlier times. The decline of the Roman towns becomes evident at various periods from the fall of the Empire onwards, earlier in the north, later and less completely in the Mediterranean countries. In the north, where they were more scattered, there emerged alongside of them, at the time of the urban renaissance at the end of the early Middle Ages, a greater number of new formations than in the Mediterranean basin; this was the case in England and still more so in the Low Countries. As for that part of Germany beyond the Rhine which had not formed part of the Roman Empire, the town was completely unknown in ancient times.

It is from the ninth century onwards that the formation of concentrations of an urban character is attested in western and southern Europe—from England to Italy, in Germany as well as in France. The movement becomes more marked and continues over the centuries, before coming to an abrupt end in the fourteenth century as a consequence of causes which we shall have the opportunity of examining later. From this time on, and for a period of four to five centuries up to the Industrial Revolution, the modification undergone by the map and the demography of the European towns was to be considerably slower than formerly.

The object of this chapter will be to study what forces stimulated this movement towards urban concentration so characteristic of the Middle Ages. It is to Henri Pirenne that the credit belongs for showing, in the vast syntheses which he devoted to the origin of the towns, that they were the result of an economic phenomenon of general significance, the renaissance of trade in western Europe.

Pirenne's theory has been subjected in the course of the last quarter of a century to many criticisms. These criticisms have generally arisen in regard to particular cases, which often relate to towns of secondary importance. Too often they have overlooked the fact that it is a question of explaining a general phenomenon and of accounting in the first instance for what took place in the case of the oldest and largest towns. We think, therefore, that in the following pages we may adhere in the main to Pirenne's opinion while modifying it in some degree. The present chapter is mainly based on the historical literature relating to England, France, the Low Countries and Spain. However, H. Ammann's general survey of Spanish towns, which appeared a short time before this study was due to go to press, reveals that urban developments in that country were not only closely related to those of other western countries, but were also marked by features equally ancient.

Among those towns which are at once producers and consumers a distinction must be made according to their radius of action. Trade between towns and the world about them, which is an indispensable condition of their existence, may come about on two different levels. One town will draw its supplies entirely from the surrounding rural district and will supply only this latter area with the products of its handicrafts; another town, on the contrary, will engage in long-distance trade and ultimately also in an export industry, and the profits thus realized will allow it to draw the food and raw materials it needs, not merely from its environs but also from distant regions. The distinction is an old one: contemporary writers were already aware of it. St Thomas Aquinas contrasts the town whose food-supplies are assured by the fertility of the surrounding territory (*regionis fertilitatis abunde omnia producentis*) with the town which depends upon trade to satisfy its needs (*mercationis usus, ex quo ibidem necessaria vitae ex diversis partibus adducuntur*).

It is not always easy to assign a given town to one of these two categories: every urban centre engaged in long-distance trade also had transactions with the neighbouring countryside, and it would be difficult, moreover, to find a town whose symbiosis with its immediate hinterland excluded all contact with more distant economic regions. For the purposes of this study, however, it will suffice to distinguish the predominant features.

Logically, one would expect to see the type of town with a restricted radius of trade appear first of all. This represents, indeed, the simplest phenomenon and it might seem that the more complicated ones ought to have evolved only subsequently. Such a theory has naturally appealed to theoretical economists. Put forward by Hildebrand about the middle of the nineteenth century, taken up by Schmoller, then brilliantly systematized by Karl Bücher, it enjoyed an enormous success in Germany. According to Bücher, medieval Germany is to be seen as divided into a great number of cells with a radius in the west of the country of four or five hours of walking time, and six or eight in the east; of these cells the towns themselves would form the nuclei. The maximum distance separating the peasants from the nearest town would be such that, having gone to market to sell their products, they could return home by evening.

To some extent, this picture corresponds to reality, but does so principally in the parts of Germany beyond the Rhine, located far from the sea or from any other great commercial highway. For other regions and, in particular, for Italy and the Low Countries, it is not valid. From the very outset the Venetians took to voyaging overseas; at a very early date, too, merchants from the first urban concentrations located upon the Scheldt, the Meuse and the Waal (Rhine) are found sailing up the Thames or paying tolls at Coblenz.

In the case of towns with a limited radius of trade their differentiation from the countryside was the result of a slow and protracted process. In towns engaged in long-distance trade, on the contrary, the establishment of a concentrated group of merchants quickly stimulated the immigration of craftsmen anxious to work for this assured clientele, and they were soon followed by workers who provided the merchants with manufactured goods capable of feeding their trade. While the population of the first type of town grew slowly and only within limits imposed by the potentialities of the surrounding rural area, that of the second group snowballed. It is primarily these latter towns which will engage our attention.

II. *Roman Survivals*

In the Roman Empire, the *civitates*, the administrative centres of districts of the same name, were the principal centres of urban life. The Church having copied its organization from that of the Empire, the term *civitas* from the fifth century onwards designated also the diocese, while at the same time coming more and more to denote especially the old chief town, the centre of a diocese and generally also of a county.

It is known that, with the exception of a few towns located near the frontier, such as Tongres, the Roman cities of the early Empire were not fortified. They became so only after the Germanic invasions in the middle of the third century. The town walls then constructed continued to protect them until well after the fall of the Empire, in England as well as on the continent. On the frontiers of Christendom, at León, they resisted in 846 the attacks of the Moslems. In the Carolingian Empire, the security which prevailed under Charlemagne caused their upkeep to be neglected. Thus the fortifications finally fell into ruins, but the Norse invasions from the middle of the ninth century onwards and those of the Hungarians in the tenth necessitated their restoration or their reconstruction. With rare exceptions, their circumference was not enlarged at this juncture.

Within the walls urban life waned on the morrow of the Germanic invasions. This was the case even in the extreme south of Gaul. Although it is true that, even up to the beginning of the eighth century, the Mediterranean still preserved its character as a great artery of communications, the main profits from the activity which was carried on went to the Orientals and not, for example, to the inhabitants of the cities of the Narbonnaise established near its shores. It is certain, however, that the decline was more rapid and more complete in the cities of northern Gaul than in those of the Midi or of Italy. In this respect it is most instructive to compare the Roman plans and the modern plans of Turin, on the one hand, and of Tongres and Trier on the other. All three towns were at the outset characterized by the chequerboard arrangement of their streets so typical of the Roman or Latin settlements. This lay-out is still easily recognizable in a modern plan of Turin, while at Tongres and at Trier the present arrangement of the streets bears no resemblance to that of the Roman period. The fact is that a part at least of Turin survived uninterruptedly as an inhabited centre, while Tongres and Trier were practically deserted, for some time at least, during the early Middle Ages.

The area of the cities allows an estimate of their population to be made, or at least, since this area is known, their population in the Roman period can be inferred from the number of inhabitants in the eighteenth century. Thus Rheims, the largest city of *Belgica Secunda*, with an area of more than 20 hectares, may have had 5,800 inhabitants; Senlis, the smallest, with 6 hectares 38 ares, could not have had more than 400. In the ninth century these figures must have been still lower.

While the total population declined, the ecclesiastical element assumed greater importance. At Lyons, in the first half of the ninth century, the religious establishments alone sheltered from 300 to 350 people. This predominance of the clerical element was reflected in the tenure of the land. Certainly in the sixth and seventh centuries frequent reference was still being made to lands belonging to the fisc or to free proprietors of various social categories, but ecclesiastical property—episcopal, capitular, abbatial—became increasingly predominant. The evolution was completed by the end of the tenth century.

The consequence was that the lay population was greatly reduced and the free element within that population became progressively smaller. There is scarcely any trace any longer, as there had been in the fifth and sixth centuries, of merchants, craftsmen or of private individuals who lived on the revenue of lands located outside the city walls. In the Rhineland cities, surviving records of gifts of lands indicate the existence of free laymen and are at the same time a sign of their disappearance. Their place was partially taken by the non-free servants of the great landed estates whose headquarters lay within the walls. Some cities had as many as ten or even twenty of these headquarters.

If we leave aside the data provided by topography, demography or social history and come to the direct evidence deriving from economic history, the general impression of a contraction in the material necessities of life is confirmed, although the range of variation between towns is very wide.

It is apparently in northern Italy that the towns, or at least a number of them, survived best the transition from Antiquity to the Middle Ages. Pavia was certainly the most favoured as well as being the city about which most is known. A simple *municipium* in the Roman period, it profited from its political importance under the Ostrogoths and the Lombards. There survived a class of merchants and a population of craftsmen, the organization of which, under the control of the government, is revealed by a tenth-century text: it was at this time also that its precinct must have been enlarged.

The fate of the ports was generally less happy. Genoa no doubt retained its prosperity after the occupation of the city by the Goths. Even when the Lombards invaded northern Italy the city could still play a role as intermediary between the Byzantine and barbarian worlds. It was, however, conquered about 642 by the Lombard king, Rothari, and this time its commercial activity was obliterated for centuries.

The destiny of Marseilles was not cut short so abruptly. Only gradually did the advance of the Moslems in the Mediterranean basin paralyse its trade. But if the activity of its port did not completely disappear in the eighth, ninth and tenth centuries, it none the less ceased to be, for Gaul, the open door to the East. As for the cities of the Narbonnaise, it was precisely when they were subjugated by the Moslems in the second and third quarters of the eighth century that their trade collapsed.

Reverting to the interior of these lands, one notes that a few cities retained for a relatively long period an economic life of some importance: thus at Lyons a colony of Jewish merchants seems to have survived until the ninth century. On the other hand, in the cities of Paris, Verdun, Cambrai and Trier, the eastern merchants who continued to carry on a certain economic activity there do not seem to have carried on beyond the Merovingian period. Further north, the textile and glass industries which flourished in the Late Empire in the cities of *Belgica Secunda*, leave no trace after the fifth century.

Finally, as far as England is concerned, the little we know of the Roman cities of that country before the Norse invasions suggests that the population they had managed to retain found its livelihood primarily in agriculture.

Besides the cities, there existed other centres of Roman origin, similarly fortified but smaller, to which, from the Late Imperial period onwards, the name of *castrum* was given. This appellation frequently survived the fall of the Empire. Like the cities, the *castra* lost their vitality, but like them, these fortified localities later became the eventual starting-points of new commercial and industrial centres.

In the ninth century, the evolution outlined in the preceding pages was almost completed. The cities were reduced to organisms of a very special type: they had no, or almost no, free population living by trade and industry; they enjoyed no autonomy whatever. Rare indeed were those in which there existed the elements of an economy heralding the future. Various, apparently new, developments must not mislead us on this point. The weekly markets which were established, in some places outside, elsewhere within, the town wall were the scene of local transactions only; the presence of a mint did not necessarily imply a very complex commercial economy; and, finally, the storehouses where the bishop or other landed proprietor accumulated his crops only catered for the needs of a domanial economy.

III. *The New Fortifications*

The walls of the Roman cities and *castra* were not adequate to ensure security during the successive periods of anarchy through which Europe passed after the fall of the Roman Empire. New fortifications were constructed as a defence against the invasions of the Moslems, the Norsemen and the Magyars. In many cases they were the starting-points of medieval towns.

This phenomenon is somewhat rare in Italy where cities were numerous, where urban life had remained more vigorous than elsewhere and where the counts had established themselves in the shelter of the old ramparts. There is, however, a well-known exception which must be highlighted because of its great importance, namely that of the Venetian lagoon. Here, where the populations of the Po valley found a refuge from the time of the fifth-century invasions onwards, *tribuni* built castles at Torcello and in the neighbouring islands. Peasants sought protection beneath their ramparts. In the ninth century the doges effected an integration of the island population about their palace on the Rialto and thus permanently founded the town of Venice. With this exception, it can be said that in Italy the new fortifications—those for example constructed in the tenth century to protect the country against the incursions of the Magyars—attracted a mercantile population only to a very limited extent.

In northern Europe the situation was very different. At the time of the Norse invasions, from the middle of the ninth century onwards, it was evident that the royal power was incapable of protecting the population. It was its local representatives, the counts, who organized resistance on their own account. They erected fortifications which generally bear the name of *castrum* or *castellum* in the texts, but which must not be confused with the *castra* of the Roman period. They consisted primarily of an enclosure formed of earthworks and palisades and surrounded by moats. Some *castra* were very small in area; for example, that of Bruges did not exceed 1·5 hectares. They were entirely occupied by the count's administrative buildings arranged around a square or market place: the count's house, storehouses, chapel, courthouse. The character of these *castra* was even less truly urban than that of the cities which had fallen into decay. They were primarily centres of public and domanial administration. From the economic point of view they were settlements of consumers. Other *castra*, such as those of Ghent or Middelburg (Zeeland), covered greater areas: the former 5·6 hectares, the latter 3·14 hectares. They seem to have been conceived at the outset as refuges to which the population of the countryside came temporarily to seek safety in time of danger. Later, the space not occupied by the elements devoted to the business of the castle was covered, like the *portus* which grew up beside the *castrum*, with houses inhabited by merchants and craftsmen.

With the *castra* must be linked the newly fortified abbeys. Some of them, built in the immediate vicinity of a city, such as St Géry near Cambrai, gave rise to communities which ended by fusing with it. In other cases, when the city walls were so dilapidated that they no longer offered any protection, it was around, and under the protection of, the neighbouring fortified abbey that the medieval town developed; this phenomenon is seen at Arras where the abbey of St Vaast overshadowed the episcopal city. Finally, some fortified abbeys gave birth to urban concentrations independent of any city; this happened in the case of St Bertin, or rather that of its dependency, the church of St Omer, the starting-point of the city of the same name (France, dep. Pas-de-Calais).

In England, too, many defensive works were thrown up, and particularly during the reign of Alfred the Great (871–99), with the object of resisting the attacks of the Norsemen. These fortifications bore the name of *burhs*. They were either simple forts, or else previously existing communities which were now surrounded for the first time by defences. This latter type had an area several times that of the largest Flemish *castra*. Thus the mercantile or industrial population which came and sought protection there was able to establish itself within the ramparts. This Anglo-Saxon *burh* was at the same time a *port*—the texts expressly say so—in contrast to the situation in Flanders where the *portus* lay alongside the *castrum* and for a long time remained separate.

In Germany beyond the Rhine, where ancient cities were unknown, the fortifications were all new creations. The terms *castellum* and *burg* here describe the newly founded ecclesiastical cities no less than the fortifications of a purely lay character.

IV. *The Merchant Class Before the Urban Renaissance*

In the Merovingian period, several cities in Gaul contained settlements of foreign merchants, either Orientals—generally designated under the name of Syrians—or Jews. In the Carolingian period the former had completely disappeared. Nor is there much evidence any longer of the presence of professional merchants in the episcopal towns. Yet, texts attest the existence of *negociatores* engaged full-time in their profession. Some were Jews, some Christians. Among both groups there were some who made—and who were, moreover, required to make—in the course of their peregrinations an appearance at court at intervals of one or two years in order to supply it with goods, and in particular with luxury goods. The Carolingian princes in return accorded them protection. The first traces of this policy are found in Lombardy in the legislation of Aistulf (749–56).

It would seem that, at the beginning of this period of transition, the Jews formed the most important group among the professional merchants and that they were in several senses of the word pioneers. Moreover, their ranks were regularly swollen by reinforcements from eastern Europe. In contrast to their practice in the later Middle Ages, they devoted themselves in the main not to trafficking in money but to trade in goods. Their importance is revealed particularly by the account of the Arab postmaster, Ibn Kordadbeh, written between 854 and 874, which lists the four routes followed by the Jewish merchants trading between Asia and western Europe.

Among Christian merchants, only one ethnic group within the Empire is designated by name: the Frisians. They too, like the Jews, settled along the highways they followed, despite the importance during the whole of this period of the base which they had established at Dorstad. When merchant elements established themselves in the Altstadt of Cologne the texts distinguish among them two groups separate from the rest, the Jews and the Frisians.

If, at the outset, the Christian merchants did not show to much advantage, they soon had at their disposal an almost limitless source of recruitment. From the mass of the population originally engaged in agriculture, there emerged everywhere individuals driven to seek a livelihood, and even wealth, by their enterprising spirit and by their shrewd ability to profit by circumstances. Whereas the Jews founded settlements only in a small number of places, the Christians, above all in Germany, not only set up alongside them, but established themselves elsewhere on their own at the very beginnings of the great majority of the towns. Even at an early stage one can detect signs of that move to drive the Jews back to the periphery of economic life which was to continue in Europe until the end of the Middle Ages.

V. *The Permanent Establishment of the Merchants in the Towns*

The immigration of the merchants into the embryonic towns is a phenomenon which continued for centuries. The birth of trading towns is spread over the greater part of the Middle Ages and the first centres of urban life were relatively few. They are encountered above all in two zones of the west: in the south, in Italy, and certain other coastal regions of the Mediterranean; in the north, along the Scheldt, Meuse and Rhine, facing England.

In the south, the development of colonies of merchants continued without interruption from the very beginning of the renaissance of maritime traffic. In the north there are more ups and downs in their history.

Even though one must beware of attaching too much importance to Bede's words, in which he describes London as *multorum emporium populorum terra marique venientium*, one is none the less struck by the fact that long before the Norse invasions several places in the north of Europe are termed *portus*, a name which necessarily implies commercial activity. This is true of Dinant and of Huy on the Meuse, of Cambrai and of Valenciennes on the Scheldt. Dorstad, at the point at which the Rhine divides into the Lek and the Kromme Rijn, and Quentowic, at the mouth of the Canche, were already flourishing at the end of the Merovingian period. Later additions to this list were Rouen on the Seine, Amiens on the Somme, Tournai and Ghent, both on the Scheldt, the last named locality being styled *portus* in a text of 850–75. On the Meuse appeared Maastricht, Namur and, above all, Verdun, known for the profitable slave-trade its merchants conducted with Spain.

In the ninth century the first place was still held by Quentowic and by Dorstad. The first town commanded the greater part of the continental traffic with England. Dorstad was the main commercial centre of the Frisians. This trading people founded new colonies along the Rhine: thus they may claim the credit for the creation of the merchant city of Mainz where in 866 we hear of a quarter inhabited by Frisians and located at the confluence of the Rhine and Main.

To the localities already enumerated may perhaps be added a certain number of the places referred to by the word *wik*, whether this element formed part of their names (*Schleswig*, beginning of ninth century, *Bardowiek*, 985) or whether they were merely described as such (Winchester, where a *wicgerefa* is reported in 847). The term must have a meaning analogous to that of *portus*, since about 900 it can be seen slowly yielding place to the latter, both in England and in the Low Countries. According to the attractive interpretation of W. Vogel, when a place was described as *wik* in the ninth century, the word apparently signified a 'place where itinerant merchants usually obtain merchandise, where surplus produce is collected, whether this *entrepôt* was founded by landowners or by merchants'. It appears, however, from the most recent researches, that some of these *wiks* were also permanently inhabited, at least by a few merchants.

The development of the commercial centres in north-western Europe was interrupted by the Norse and Magyar invasions. Some of them, like Quentowic and Dorstad, were permanently destroyed by this storm. In any case, it became imperative to ensure that in future colonies were established in the shelter of some fortification or other. It is most significant that the *portus*, which existed in the ninth century on the Scarpe, a tributary of the Scheldt, in a locality called Lambres, disappeared with the Norse invasions, and that the new *portus* which appeared in the same district in the tenth century, and which one day would become Douai, was established at some distance from the first, at the foot of a *castellum* which had made its appearance in the meantime. The lack of security which continued to reign after the invasions obliged the merchants to take into account not merely the geographical advantages of the site, but also the protection it offered. In most cases, however, the merchants' routes were precisely those which it was important to bar against armies.

We have seen above how the cities lost their urban nature while at the same time generally retaining their walls. When they were repopulated from the end of the Carolingian period onwards, it was generally within the fortified wall that the merchants and the immigrants who came in their wake established themselves, provided that the space sufficed. If it did not, they rapidly overflowed, as at Strasbourg, or alternatively they deliberately established themselves outside the ancient enclosure, as at Verdun, where there existed from 985 onwards a fortified merchant quarter (*negotiatorum claustrum*). According to most recent investigations a number of new urban centres, other than Roman cities, made their appearance in the west of France, above all in the eleventh century. Urban development there was at that time as important as in Flanders and Italy, even if not equally intensive.

In England, likewise, a great number of medieval towns were Roman cities given a new lease of life. Here again the population generally established itself within the restored ramparts. On the other hand, as we have seen, the English *ports* were settlements of traders which had established themselves within recently fortified localities, and hence differed from the continental *portus* which lay alongside the *castra*. In the case of the latter in the Low Countries, as Pirenne has emphasized, the medieval town was born not of the *bourg* but of the *faubourg* which in the end absorbed the primitive military nucleus.

The new centres of urban life made their appearance in successive waves. In Flanders, St Omer, Ghent, Douai, Bruges and Arras were followed by Ypres only at the beginning of the twelfth century. The Brabant towns were equally far behind.

In France the Oise basin underwent, about the same time, a profound transformation: merchants and usurers are reported at this period in Laon, Soissons, Rheims, Senlis, Noyon. At the same time, too, the ports lying along the Atlantic became the centres of an intensive maritime trade: Bayonne commanded the traffic with Spain, Bordeaux that with England; La Rochelle came to the forefront in the thirteenth century as a result of its export of wine and salt to the northern countries.

It was in Germany above all that the number of towns increased notably in the course of the twelfth and thirteenth centuries. Their location was again frequently determined by the sites of castles, many of which continued to be built. A good number of these towns still corresponded closely to the type previously studied. This is true of Freiburg-im-Breisgau (1120), of the 'old town' of Brunswick (*c.* 1100–20), of Lübeck (definitely founded in 1158) and in general of the future Hanseatic towns. Other German towns of this period come into the category of towns with a limited radius of exchange, about which we shall have more to say later. Among the latest merchant towns are to be noted those of Holland, and particularly Amsterdam, which was to have such a remarkable future. The locality is mentioned for the first time in 1275; it acquired town status in 1306. It did not grow up in the neighbourhood of a fortified pre-urban nucleus. Emerging three or four centuries after Ghent or Bruges, as a result of similar commercial needs but in a society less exposed to violence, its organization bore the stamp of a new age.

VI. *The Contour of the First Towns*

Meagre as our information is about the beginnings of towns whose first nucleus was a cluster of merchants, some features of their physical aspect can be clearly delineated.

The first point to notice is that the sites on which the new towns grew up did not immediately shed their rural character. They sheltered not only the merchants and craftsmen who gathered in them but also people whose prime occupation was still agriculture. Both the character and the lay-out of the dwellings, especially on the fringes of the community, were still influenced by its hybrid character. These features persisted for a long time: in a town like Paris, which grew rapidly by reason of its triple character as capital, commercial centre and university town, they had not disappeared at the end of the twelfth century.

It may be said that, from the outset, all towns had at least one market. In the case of the ancient cities it was to be found either inside or outside the walls in the immediate neighbourhood of a town gate. In the case of the towns arising from the juxtaposition of a *portus* and a *castrum*, as so frequently happened in the Low Countries, a market was likewise gener-ally found under the very walls of the *castrum* and in front of the gate which joined it to the *portus*. It must therefore have been demarcated from the outset. This oldest type of market served essentially to provision the urban population. It was generally described as a fish market, but was certainly used also for the sale of other goods and particularly of meat. Frequently, however, a meat market was established subsequently on a part of the site of the old market.

Trading towns of late formation were often distinguished from the older towns by the fact that they were founded according to plans drawn up in advance. The plans of these towns often reveal a regularity which bears witness to their artificial character. On the other hand, everything indicates that the older cities, those of Flanders for example, took shape quite spontaneously.

For a long time the concept of a town implied a fortified place or a place requiring fortifications. Even when the merchant community grew up around the foot of a *castrum* it soon felt the need to surround it-self with defensive works. It was the town wall which presented the most tangible and striking demarcation between town and open country.

At first these defensive works were still very primitive. They comprised mounds of earth, moats and palisades. 'Incapable of resisting a formal attack,' says Pirenne, 'their only use was to prevent robbers from the countryside breaking into the town.' Normally, it was only from the beginning of the twelfth century that the *suburbia*—as the *portus* built on to the *castra* were frequently called—were surrounded with real stone walls.

The problem of urban fortifications leads to that of the origin of the words *burgus* and *burgensis*. The Germanic term *burg* appears to have originally designated a small non-fortified settlement. It was apparently introduced into Gaul after the Invasions. It established itself in the valleys of the Loire and the Rhône, where we find it frequently in the ninth century, and spread during the tenth and the eleventh centuries all over Gaul and Italy. By now it had come to designate mainly the agglomerations formed round abbeys and suburbs of cities. It is this connotation which determined that of the *burgensis*, i.e. an inhabitant of a *burgus*, followed by that of the *bourgeois*. In its country of origin, Germany, the term *burgus* changed its meaning between the sixth and the seventh centuries. There, in the sense of a fortification devoid of any urban character, it entered into the place-names of a number of localities, some of which were later to develop into towns. In the eleventh century, especially in Germany, the term could also be used in the sense of *civitas*. It was not until the beginning of the twelfth century that the meaning of the term preserved in the Latin countries was adopted again in Germany.

With this change of meaning may be linked that undergone by the word *castrum* itself, which in Flanders from the beginning of the twelfth century is met not only in its original meaning, but also in that of trading suburb (unfortified), and is even applied to the entity composed of a comital fortress and the suburb attached to it. It recalls also the exact synonymy pointed out by W. Vogel between *burgrecht* in Upper Germany and *wicbeld* in Lower Germany as designating the town law. This is explained by the fact that *burg* and *wik* had an identical meaning. Both seem to have been proper designations for a place of refuge or even simply a concentration of people and goods, without necessarily conveying the idea of a locality fortified by a wall.

VII. *The Origins of Capital*

Our views about the origins of the class of merchants will also determine those we entertain about the origins of the capital they employed. To postulate that the merchants were *parvenus* is to assume at the same time that their initial capital was limited, so limited in fact that it was within reach of anybody. If, on the other hand, it can be established that the merchants were former landed proprietors or domanial officials, then it would follow that from the outset they had employed in commerce fairly considerable sums derived either from the sale of lands or from accumulated revenue from land.

This latter view was maintained by Rodbertus and Bücher, and subsequently systematized by Sombart who stressed the role played by the accumulation of ground-rents. The theory, after enjoying an initial success, was seriously shaken by the fact that Strieder demonstrated its absurdity in a concrete instance, that of the Augsburg financiers at the end of the Middle Ages and the beginning of modern times. The proof is particularly relevant because it rests upon abundant documentation, the interpretation of which cannot seriously be doubted. It cannot, however, be immediately assumed that the formation of commercial capital at the beginning of the history of the towns followed the same pattern as at Augsburg in the fifteenth century. Reasoning by analogy is dangerous and in fact the documentation bearing upon the period which concerns us, although meagre, suggests rather a great deal of variety.

It is possible that a part of the capital of the Jewish merchants in the early Middle Ages came from landed property. The Jews, in fact, in the fifth, sixth and seventh centuries owned extensive lands in Spain as well as in Italy and Gaul. When Roman law gave way to national laws they were obliged to sell out (sixth to eighth centuries) and devote themselves to trade. But it was commercial profits which augmented this capital in the eighth and ninth centuries, and which also increased the somewhat limited capital resources brought by the Jews who came from eastern Europe.

From the Carolingian period onwards the capital in the hands of Christian merchants assumed an increasing predominance. The origin of this capital in actual fact is still more obscure. In Venice, it presents a problem closely linked to the controversial question of the origin of the patriciate of the lagoon town. The possibility cannot be excluded *a priori* that landed proprietors coming from the mainland had converted their real estate into liquid wealth so that they might take up trade. It is nevertheless certain that from very remote times, much earlier than the formation of the town of Venice (which can be placed at the beginning of the ninth century), wealth sufficient to give a man a start in large-scale commerce had been accumulated by other methods in the hands of the inhabitants of the lagoons. The export of salt produced along the Adriatic coast was one of its principal sources. The services rendered by the Venetian ships to the exarch of Ravenna was another. Finally, it is worth noting that the information we have about Venetian fortunes allows us in several cases to affirm that the element of real property they include was acquired in part out of profits derived from trade.

In the case of Genoa, on the other hand, it can be suggested with some degree of certainty that it was the noble landed proprietors who first laid out important capital sums in trade. Their outlay was derived not only from the proceeds of the sale of lands or from the accumulation of revenues from land, but also from booty and plunder accruing from the sea war against the infidel. The capital thus formed was mainly entrusted by them to the seafarers of the town actively engaged in commerce, who were themselves able rapidly to increase their initial investments, though more by the remuneration they received for their services than by commercial profit in the proper sense.

Trade in the northern countries has given rise to similar conflicting theses. As we have seen, Pirenne considered the first merchants who established themselves in the town to be men without roots, dwelling on the margin of normal society. Strenuous efforts have been made to belittle the evidence he adduces. Yet the total amount of evidence he brought together, quite apart from the well-known example of St Godric of Finchale, is most impressive.[1] It would be wrong to think that these cases were necessarily exceptional, that they were described simply because they were peculiar. On the contrary, it is surprising that they have been preserved in such great number: in fact, at this time in the northern countries, the pen was wielded exclusively by members of the clergy who did not speak of merchants unless a purely fortuitous circumstance had brought them into contact with religion and the Church. It was because Godric, against all expectation and unlike the great majority of his kind, died a holy man, that a *Vita* was devoted to him at a time when his peers were consigned to oblivion. It was because he had stolen a chalice from St Bavon and had later made restitution of the equivalent after having used it as capital and multiplied this initial investment several times over to his own profit, that a pre-eleventh-century merchant found his place in the *Miracula* of the Ghent abbey. It can, however, be granted on the evidence of certain relatively late texts that persons whose existence was originally linked with landed property were later caught up in the movement and were enabled to engage in trade because they could dispose of funds derived from the sale of lands or from the accumulation of revenues from land.

VIII. *The Status of Individuals Within the Town*

The population which survived in the ancient cities did not escape the increasing encroachments upon personal liberty which occurred in the Carolingian period. In the episcopal towns of northern France the number of free men seems to have diminished considerably in the ninth and

---

[1] See his article *Les périodes de l'histoire sociale du capitalisme* (see bibliography), 26–30.

C

tenth centuries. It probably remained higher in Provence and the Rhine-land.

On the other hand, the movement towards a revival of trade, which became more marked from the same period onwards, was calculated to prepare the way for an extension of liberty in the urban communities. 'Liberty', writes Pirenne, 'is a necessary and universal attribute of the townsman.' Yet it must be observed that even for the merchants it was originally a *de facto* rather than a *de jure* liberty; that it was, at the outset, peculiar to these merchants; and that it was not fully realized in a good many towns of an ecclesiastical character.

There was no presumption of serfdom. Even if of servile origin, the merchant who came and established himself in a locality where he was unknown was considered free. This liberty, as Pirenne again remarked, was not claimed by the merchants. They were allowed it because it was impossible to prove that they had no right to it. They would have abandoned it had this course been more profitable to them. We shall see one example which proves this clearly. But once the advantages of freedom had become obvious it was recognized as a desirable and normal condition for the merchant class. The towns at first sheltered people whose status imposed upon them dues and services towards one lord or other. That, however, did not prevent them from embarking upon economic activity of a specifically urban character. They included persons originating from estates near to the town who came thither to seek a livelihood, either by working to satisfy the day-to-day needs of the population collected there or by making goods which could be sold abroad by the merchants. At the outset their legal status remained unaffected, but the custom expressed in the adage *Stadtluft macht frei* slowly gained ground and finally prevailed. In general, it was agreed that residence for a year and a day in a town set a serf free.

It may be noted, however, that in a number of cities in the north of ancient Gaul, and also in many new towns founded in the domains of important churches, a considerable part of the population was granted a status from the legal point of view apparently irreconcilable with liberty but in practice very much akin to it. From very remote times many individuals had placed themselves under the protection of the patron saint of the local church, had become in other words 'serfs' of that saint. From the financial point of view this 'serfdom' was limited to the payment of a few pence yearly. On the other hand, it entailed very real advantages (exemption from the toll and, later, competence to sit on the local tribunal) which must have made it something to be sought after. It did not in the least interfere with the liberty of the church serfs to come and go at will, to conclude contracts, etc., so that they were able without any let or hindrance to take up trade. At Tournai, Amiens, Laon, Arras and Worms they comprised a large proportion of the population; at Mons, a city which originated on the land of an abbey, they still formed, in 1293, 93% of the taxpayers whose fortune exceeded 30 livres. Broadly speaking, however, they were far from including the whole body of merchants. An incident which occurred in 1122 at Arras throws considerable light on the motives which might exert an influence on the extension or restriction of this class and, at the same time, upon the attitude of those concerned towards this problem of liberty. A number of free townsmen wanted to have themselves inscribed as serfs of St Vaast so that they might profit by exemption from the toll levied by the abbey in the town market. At the request of the abbot, the count of Flanders had formally to forbid them to do so.

Finally, to round off this glimpse of the condition of the townsfolk, it may be recorded that in certain Rhine cities the *ministeriales*, that servile aristocracy, were one of the sources—albeit a late one—of the urban middle class. It was from *c.* 1200 onwards that at Strasbourg, for example, the *ministeriales* escaped from dependence upon the bishop to merge with the patriciate. The evolution was completed a century later.

IX. *The Status of Town Land*

The ground within the town played an important role in the new economy associated with the emergence of the urban classes. To understand this role one must first consider the legal status of the land.

It is possible that in certain towns in Germany, such as Cologne or Münster, there survived remnants of the *altfreie Gemeinde*, the *freien Hofstätten* which went back to Germanic antiquity. It cannot, however, be proved with any degree of certainty, and the phenomenon, if it existed, is of wholly secondary importance.

This apart, it may be said that the inhabitants of the towns which emerged or re-emerged in the Carolingian period established themselves on land belonging to a lord, whether that lord was an ecclesiastic—bishop, chapter or abbot—or a layman, i.e. a territorial prince or even a king.

The new inhabitants paid a rent in respect of their occupation of the land: they thus possessed a kind of tenure which is described as free tenure (*freie Leihe*), or urban tenure. This tenure is found throughout western Europe, although naturally under widely differing names: *bourgage* (Normandy), burgage tenure (England), *Weichbild* (northern Germany), *Burgrecht* (southern Germany), *jus forense*, *Marktrecht*. It was distinguished from manorial tenure (*Leihe nach Hofrecht*), which carried heavier obligations. The essential difference lies in the fact that the latter involved the tenant in personal dependence. It subjected him, according to Rietschel, to manorial obligations and jurisdiction. Moreover, the alienability of free urban tenements was much easier than in the case of demesne tenure: the tenant might transfer them without the intervention and even without the agreement of the proprietor. It is also worth noting that the right of lineal relatives to recover land sold by a kinsman (*retrait lignager*), which often interfered with the alienation of tenements, was abolished in certain towns.

One may ask whether, at the outset, manorial tenure existed in the towns and whether it gradually evolved into free urban tenure. Gobbers, Hoeniger and Des Marez were of this opinion, which was disputed, however, by Rietschel. It may well have been the case in certain ancient cities, and this evolution may be likened to another which is more clearly distinguishable: in some places jurisdiction over the land within the towns was exercised successively by the seignorial landlord alone, by the seignorial landlord conjointly with the town magistrature and, finally, by the latter alone.

In the great majority of cases, however (and there are some relatively late examples, such as the 'founded towns', like Freiburg-im-Breisgau for which full information is available), freehold tenure appears from the start with all its characteristic features.

In certain towns a further step towards liberty was achieved. The ground-rent finally disappeared so that the urban tenement became an urban alod. This was the case at Ghent, where the ground-rent ceased to be levied between 1038 and 1120, probably in the second half of the eleventh century. Sometimes, as at Dortmund and Duisburg, the seigneur gave up levying it; sometimes, as at Tournai, it seems that the tenants refused to pay it. Elsewhere again it was bought out *in toto* by the town, as at Arras, or in other cases by individuals. There were instances, for example in certain English towns, where the total return became so insignificant that it was not worth collecting. In some towns, where the rich had succeeded in acquiring direct ownership of the majority of the plots of town land by redeeming the rent on their own behalf, as at Ghent, the ownership of an urban alod became the distinctive attribute of the patrician class.

The terms used to designate urban freeholds in various European countries have been enumerated above. It seems that it was frequently these very terms themselves which served to designate urban law. Thus at Leiden in Holland, *in poortrecht uitgeven* means 'to establish a burgage tenement'. There was therefore an intimate connection between the two: in some towns the grant of burgage tenement even involved a pledge by the new citizen to engage in commerce. Is there any wonder if thereafter free tenure was looked upon as a contract likely to be extremely beneficial to commercial activity?

The features which characterized urban ground-rents were that they were moderate and fixed. In fact, because of the decline in the value of money, their real level continually fell. Since a tenement essentially represented land on which buildings could be erected, and since the growth of towns continued to be very rapid down to the beginning of the fourteenth century, the ground-rent soon became insignificant in comparison with the value of the land. Then again, as we have seen, the tenant could freely dispose of his holding.

The tenant could sell his holding or his house, could let them or could pledge them (to secure a short-term loan). He could also—and this was apparently the most common use to which it was put—charge his holding with a new rent. This became one of the principal ways in which a merchant could acquire capital needed for his trade.

Conversely, the purchase of rent charges on property became the common method of investment for every individual or corporate body wanting to ensure a fixed and steady return on capital. The credit market was primarily supplied with funds by merchant families retiring from trade after making their fortune and by religious and charitable institutions.

In those towns where the original ground-rent disappeared and where town alods were established to the advantage of a small number of burgess proprietors, as at Ghent, many of these alods were re-subjected to rents. They thus became urban tenures, the proprietor of which was now not the former feudal landlord, but a patrician. The new tenants could thus utilize their 'secondary' tenures exactly as those of other towns did their 'primary' ones.

The increase in the value of land, coupled with the impossibility of terminating joint possession without the consent of all the parties concerned, frequently resulted in the subdivision of property and urban rents to an incredible degree. At Cologne fractional house ownership has been recorded of the order of 1/70, 5/160 and even 1/672, and at Ghent even more minute fractions of taxable property are attested.

The increase in the value of land did not necessarily continue indefinitely. When a town was declining economically, as frequently happened in the period of contraction at the end of the Middle Ages, it could happen that the value of the charges on a tenement exceeded that of the buildings erected on it. This was already the case at Bruges in 1466 at a time when the decline of the town was still far from evident. To remedy the situation Philip the Good took special measures, which were extended by Charles V in 1529 to the whole of Flanders.

X. *Types of Towns other than Trading Towns*

The trading towns engaged in long-range exchanges necessarily occupy the chief place in this chapter. It was these towns which set in motion the process of urban development; they, too, became the most important centres. They owed this greater destiny to the larger resources they derived from long-distance trade. Around the primitive nucleus formed by the merchants there gathered an artisan population working to meet local and regional needs; like a chemical precipitate, the presence of this nucleus brought about the division of labour between the town and the country. In many cases the trading towns became the seats of export industries capable of supplying their trade; hence emerged a second class of artisans, working essentially for the export trade. Their numbers might, in some cases, amount to more than half the town population.

Other types of towns to which allusion was made at the beginning of this chapter must not, however, be ignored.

We may first consider those towns, with a dual role as producers and consumers, whose radius of action did not extend beyond the immediately neighbouring countryside. Here there was neither a merchant class engaged in distant trade nor an artisan class occupied with the manufacture of woollen goods or of other products intended for a foreign clientele. The population was composed, in the main, of artisans working for the local and regional market, exchanging their products for the raw materials and foodstuffs provided for them by the agricultural population.

Towns of this type were numerous, especially from the thirteenth century onwards, not only in those countries which were relatively backward from an economic point of view, such as central Germany, but even in certain principalities of the Low Countries: Hainault, Namur, Liège and above all Luxembourg. These towns grew up where they did, as was the case with the trading towns, because of geographical advantages and considerations of safety, but the consumer nucleus, elsewhere made up of a group of merchants, was generally provided here by a small military, administrative or ecclesiastical community.

In many cases, too—and this was especially true in central Germany—the authority from which this community emanated deliberately encouraged the concentration of craftsmen in a precise locality by the creation of a 'market' and by the protection it accorded to that market. It is improbable that anyone would now think of maintaining the old idea that the towns, even those of the type studied here, owed their origin to the markets established in such great numbers in the ninth and tenth centuries, or even that town law was simply the continuation of the law of the market. In actual fact, the notion of market to which we allude here does not correspond to *mercatus*, the weekly market, but—and Pirenne already stressed this point—to *forum*, the permanent site for transactions which the town as such constituted. This market was not in fact limited to the more or less rectangular-shaped place designated by the same name. In several towns founded by the dukes of Zähringen it was the main street which served this purpose. Obviously, what mattered was to centralize transactions within a prescribed area, both in order to do away with competition and to facilitate supervision.

This centralization of transactions within a deliberately licensed place was much more frequent in Germany than elsewhere and, moreover, spread there to quite a number of trading towns engaged in long-range exchanges. The example of Lübeck—which is thereby distinguished from, *inter alia*, the Flemish towns—is conclusive in this respect: there the products of artisan industry were disposed of as a rule in the market, and this system reflected a deliberate policy on the part of the patrician founders of the town who were the proprietors of the places of sale and derived therefrom considerable revenues.

Nevertheless, it is primarily with the class of towns having a limited trade radius that the concession of market privileges is connected. Ottonian charters authorizing the erection of a market and the collection of a toll in that market were numerous. At that time it was the bishops and the religious houses who were the principal beneficiaries and who thereby assumed complete control of the regulation of trade in the emerging towns. In the course of the following centuries the process of founding markets shifted more and more towards the east and at the same time the proportion of laymen among the lords of markets gradually increased.

From the foregoing observations it follows that, in a general way at least, within towns having a limited radius of trade the participation of the seigneur in urban economic life was much greater than in the trading towns properly so called. Monopolies of wine and oven belonged to the seigneur and from these monopolies derived a supervision which was to extend by the end of the Middle Ages to the whole range of economic activity. It was in virtue of these rights, too, that the seigneur built the butchery or town market-hall or hired out the market stalls. The different proportions of autonomy and of seignorial intervention in economic affairs are evident, however, if we compare even two such comparatively similar groups of towns in regard to their commercial character as those of Flanders and Brabant: the initiative of the prince was much more marked in the latter than in the former.

We can deal more quickly with those towns whose function as consumers was not balanced, from the economic point of view, by a more or less equivalent function as producers. In this category can be placed the political and religious capitals, military towns, university towns. It goes without saying that this type of town rarely occurs in a pure state. Generally speaking a town which can be included from one point of view under this heading was at the same time, to a certain extent, a centre of commerce and industry or the home at least of a body of craftsmen.

In medieval Paris we can distinguish first of all the capital city owing its rank to the initiative of Clovis; the trading city of which, amongst other things, the hanse of the *marchands de l'eau* is evidence; and the university city whose men of learning thronged the left bank of the Seine and the Petit-Pont leading to it. These three elements combined to form the largest urban concentration known in medieval western Europe. But if its role as a consumer derived from its population, its role as a producer remained much inferior, despite the importance and the special character given to its industry by the presence of the court.

The episcopal cities for their part continued to draw their subsistence from outside, even though to a varying degree they made some return for this in the form of industrial products or commercial services. Some, in fact, whose geographical situation was unfavourable, remained untouched by the rebirth of town life: this is true of Thérouanne in Artois, which perpetuated right to the end of the Middle Ages, almost in its pure state, the type of early medieval city. Others, more favoured, often the seat of an important bishopric, such as Liège, saw a numerous group of money-lenders, as well as a class of artisans working to satisfy local and regional needs, gather around their ecclesiastical population. Others again, like Arras, developed into the commercial and industrial type of town, which in this case acquired almost complete predominance over the ecclesiastical city.

Finally, we must say a word or two about one last category of towns, which, indeed, scarcely deserved that name. These were small concentrations whose inhabitants followed occupations of an essentially agricultural character. They were very numerous in Germany, in a great part of Italy (but not in Tuscany) and in the south-west of France (including the *bastides*). Their pseudo-urban character was due to the fact that their lord wanted either to turn them into military strong-points by surrounding them with walls, or to emancipate them by granting them urban rights. They offer little of interest, however, either from the industrial and commercial point of view, or as consumers, and so they will not be considered in the remainder of this survey.

XI. *The Town Constitutions*

In the first period of its existence, the town was distinguished from the surrounding district only in its demographic and economic aspects. From the legal standpoint it scarcely differed. It did not yet answer to

Pirenne's eminently satisfactory definition of the medieval town 'as it appears from the twelfth century onwards': 'a commune living, under the shelter of its surrounding fortifications, on trade and industry and possessing rights, an administration and its own distinctive system of law which conferred upon it a privileged corporate status'. There are grounds therefore, for distinguishing, as G. Des Marez did, a pre-constitutional period and a constitutional period in the urban history of the Middle Ages.

Writers, and especially nineteenth-century writers, who have concerned themselves with medieval towns have generally paid more attention to their institutions than to their economic history. In the present survey, on the other hand, the study of their legal and administrative organization can occupy only a limited place. Yet some reference to this aspect must be made because a knowledge of it is indispensable to an understanding of certain facts in the economic realm.

From the middle of the nineteenth century many scholars, for the most part Germans, strove to elucidate the origins of the town constitutions. Most of them confined themselves to a very limited field of study. Sometimes the constitution of the town—in the case of episcopal towns which subsequently became the *Freistädte*—was considered to be the result of a struggle waged by an *Altfreigemeinde* to avoid being reduced to serfdom by a lord (Arnold); sometimes an explanation of the formation of the urban middle classes was found in manorial law (Nitzsch); sometimes the autonomy of the towns was explained by the sworn communes, which were associated with the gilds (Gierke). Or yet again the town constitution was held to derive from that of the Germanic mark (von Maurer), the *Stadtgemeinde* from the *Landgemeinde* (von Below), the town privilege from the market privilege (Sohm), or the town peace from the peace of the seignorial *burgen* to which the towns were attached (Rietschel and Keutgen).

The great achievement of Pirenne was not only to demonstrate the insufficiency and inexactitude of these different theories, but also to develop new views which could be applied to the whole of western Europe. He was the first to stress the fact that the town constitutions were new phenomena, a response to profound changes of an economic and social nature, in particular the rebirth of trade and the formation of a solidly grouped merchant class. He showed how the communal movement was the result of a threefold series of causes: the need to confer upon the territory of the town its own particular peace, the need to band together in order to free this territory and those who dwelt there from oppressive obligations, and the need to create a tax system capable of ensuring the defence of the town.

We have used the word commune in the wide sense in which Pirenne himself liked to employ it. 'All medieval towns', he wrote, 'were, in the legal sense of the word, communes. All were, in fact, corporate bodies endowed with their own rights and recognized as such by the public powers. Some authors, however, reserve the name of communes for those towns alone which received either from their lord or from the king a charter of liberty conceding to them a more or less extensive autonomy.' It may be added that, before the thirteenth century, the sense which contemporary writers accorded to the term was still more restricted. According to Petit-Dutaillis's definition of it, in France at this time 'to grant a commune to the burgesses or to a group of burgesses of a town was to allow them to form an association and to band themselves together by oath.' It is important, however, to draw attention to the fact that the burgesses frequently set up a commune without awaiting the authorization of the lord and that, even if this authorization was refused, they none the less frequently persisted in their attitude. For greater clarity, therefore, the meaning of the term commune must, when necessary, be defined more accurately, when it is not used in the most general sense, by the addition, according to the individual case, of the qualification 'sworn' or 'revolutionary'. In the present survey, however, it is not essential to stress whether or not in a given case the constitution of a commune was preceded by the taking of an oath or was effected with the consent of the lord. What is important is to bear in mind the characteristics of the association and of the organs which enabled it to secure its objects.

The degree of autonomy attained by the communes varied considerably. In some cases it was limited to administration, police and finances. In others it was also of a legal nature and in others again it resulted in complete independence.

The method and the extent of emancipation were influenced by two factors: whether the lord of a town was an ecclesiastic or a layman and by the greater or less degree of effectiveness retained by the royal power in the different countries of Europe. The lay lords showed a better understanding of the profit which commercial activity could bring to their treasuries and the potential advantage of the rise of the middle classes for their own political power; they were less restrained than were the bishops by ethical scruples or by conservative prejudices in their relations with the merchant class whose brilliant future they fully understood. As for royal weakness, it was in Italy that this was most evident; then followed, in descending order, Germany, France and England. In the Low Countries, the territorial princes had to all intents and purposes already taken the place of the king everywhere at the time when the question of the emancipation of the towns arose.

Thus it was in the northern half of Italy that the towns managed to achieve their ideal of autonomy most completely. The struggle is first visible in the cities of the Po plain where an attack was made upon the imperial bishops. Milan revolted by 1057. The first communal magistrates, the consuls, who are found at Lucca and Pisa about 1081, appear in Milan in 1094. This institution spread by 1128 at the latest to Provence and, about the same time, to the Narbonnaise. In the towns of the French Midi the magistratures were at first filled by petty nobility of landed origin; the urban middle class, as a result of its rise in the economic scale, began to replace that nobility in the second half of the century, but the emancipation of the towns was halted by the territorial expansion of the French Crown. As for the Lombard towns, they secured recognition of their territorial sovereignty by the Peace of Constance (1183); but the anarchy which threatened them as a result of the rivalry between the patrician families forced them to have recourse to the authority of a *podestà* chosen from outside their population. This measure proving insufficient, recourse had to be had subsequently to a still more pronounced form of personal authority: out of the function of captain of the people or *mercanzia* was born the *signoria*. In the fifteenth century northern Italy was divided into a series of city-states, placed under the quasi-sovereignty of tyrant-lords.

The evolution at Florence, although revealing similar characteristics to those which occurred in the plain of Lombardy, did not reach the same conclusion: the town was able to maintain its liberty up to the end of the Middle Ages. The middle class there had acquired power by the middle of the thirteenth century and gradually less and less well-to-do classes gained a share of it. Venice, which enjoyed a quasi-independence *vis-à-vis* Byzantium and for which, therefore, the question of emancipation did not arise, remained on the contrary subject to the power of a class of great merchants and wealthy shipowners whose ranks were closed to newcomers from 1297 onwards. Venice's great rival, Genoa, through its *compagna* composed of the leading families of the town and identified shortly after 1100 with the commune, freed itself from feudal trammels. Here, however, in contrast to what happened at Venice, the patriciate was destroyed by private wars. These troubles led on two occasions in the fifteenth century to foreign domination. The re-liberated town found a stable regime only after the transmission of the principal powers of state to the *Casa di San Giorgio*, an organism composed of the rich middle-class creditors of the state.

In Germany the revolt of the Worms burgesses against their bishop in 1073 was the signal for a long struggle which spread to all the ecclesiastical cities. There was not one of them where, on one occasion or another, a bishop did not have to leave his residence to escape from trouble; and in Saxony the prelates nearly all ended by choosing a new domicile for themselves. Generally speaking the struggle ended in the fifteenth

century, in most of the Rhine cities, in a compromise which ensured autonomy for the middle classes. The monarchy looked upon this emancipation of the towns with a favourable eye: the immediate dependence of
the towns upon the imperial Crown was likely to ensure for the latter a
support against the forces which tended to dismember it. The weakening
of the royal power, however, after the Great Interregnum (1254–73) prevented the monarch from keeping them in a strict dependence. The
Reichsstädte, the originally imperial towns, became almost independent
republics which served the sovereign as allies rather than as subjects.

In the Low Countries the towns did not succeed in winning complete
autonomy. They did not cease to form part of the territorial principalities within which they had sprung up. Their institutions had a mixed
character, half princely, half urban. This duality is seen in the southern
part of the Low Countries in two different forms, represented principally by Flanders and the principality of Liège. In Flanders, about the
year 1100, the towns were removed from the jurisdiction of the *échevins*
of the castellanies and granted their own *échevins*, in principle nominated
by the prince and supervised by his representative, but chosen from the
local patrician class. These judges, who quickly assumed an administrative role as well, were therefore both princely and urban in character. In
the Liège towns, duality continued to be manifested by the simultane-
ous existence of two magistratures: the prince's tribunal (the *échevinage*)
administered justice properly speaking, and the tribunal of the commune
(the *corps des jurés*) watched over the application of the municipal statutes.
In Brabant, the town institutions, which were later than those of Flanders
or of the district of Liège, were primarily based on those of the latter. In
Holland, finally, urban laws, like urban institutions, were copied from
the models provided by various Brabant towns. The constitutions of the
towns were rather the result of the initiative of the prince, who created
ex nihilo an organization which had seemed to give such happy results in
the neighbouring principalities.

The north of France, where the main towns were almost all ecclesiastical cities, was the particular home of the sworn and even of the revolutionary communes. The oldest, ephemeral it is true, was set up at Cambrai, on the border of the Low Countries (1077). It was followed by those
of St Quentin (1080), Beauvais (*c.* 1099), Noyon (1108–9), Laon (1115),
Soissons (1115–18). The movement even spread to the countryside.
There the formation of rural communes is seen in the regions of Laon
and Soissons, above all between 1184 and 1216. This expansion, however, came to an end about 1223. These rural communes were intensely
disliked by the conservative classes. The attitude of the monarchs varied
according to the needs of their policy: hesitant under Louis VI and VII,
it was favourable under Philip Augustus and Louis VIII, only to be-

come hostile under their successors. When the royal authority showed itself sympathetic it was primarily because the concession of communes opened up the possibility of ensuring the assistance of the town militias. From the point of view of town emancipation, however, the sworn communes were not necessarily more independent than the ordinary 'free towns'.

It is understandable that the king accorded no autonomy to Paris, his capital, by far the most important town in France and even in western Europe. Here everything depended directly on the king. It was he who had established the market, he who regulated commerce and industry, and the burgesses were *his* burgesses.

The Scandinavian invasions had tended to bring about in England a judicial and administrative distinction between the fortified centres and the countryside. The existence in the second half of the tenth century of an embryonic court of justice peculiar to the boroughs may be conjectured, although the only direct proof before the Conquest is the existence of the *husting* of London. Then again, a community, represented by the *seniores* or the *sapientes*, is already discernible before 1066. From the Conquest to 1191, the date of the departure of Richard I for the Crusade, the tendency towards autonomy is revealed above all by the development of the gilds, by the elaboration of the notion of 'free borough' which implied at least the existence of burgage tenure, and lastly by the acquisition of the *firma burgi*, that is to say, the right of the burgesses to take over the collection of the revenues which the king derived from the town and which up till then his sheriff had been responsible for raising. The first known case of a town farming its revenues directly from the king is provided by Lincoln in 1130. Henry II granted this favour sparingly. The English town in his reign enjoyed nothing like the autonomy of the continental communes. In the royal towns, the reeves, who levied the revenues there and presided over the portmoot, originally a court of justice, seem to have been nominated by the king or by the sheriff. Only the gild, in theory a purely economic body, could ensure—unofficially—some autonomy to the town. (It should be noted that some towns, such as London, Norwich and Colchester, were denied this institution.)

The situation changed considerably under Henry II's sons, Richard I and John Lackland. The boroughs acquired at that time a true corporate existence: henceforth they were governed by elected reeves and by a newly created official, also elected, the mayor, borrowed no doubt from the continental communes. The portmoot, moreover, became more independent. The appearance of a common seal ultimately conferred upon the community a corporate legal status. Thus was born a type of constitution which was to last more or less intact until 1835.

From the above analysis it can be seen that too much importance should not be attached to the grant of urban charters. The setting of town privileges down in writing and their approbation in due form by the prince were not indispensable to the existence of a free community. Generally speaking small towns were more interested in obtaining this sort of guarantee than important towns. Thus in more than one region the older charters duly issued and sealed by the prince are those for small and not for the large centres. The charters, moreover, were incomplete: far from setting out the whole of the town privilege they often recorded only the provisions about which there was some doubt or argument.

XII. *The Urban Patriciate*

In connection with the medieval towns, and often, too, with those of the modern period, it has become customary to speak of a town 'patriciate'. The term is, of course, borrowed from the history of ancient Rome and is not found in medieval texts. Not all authors apply the term in absolutely the same way. Their definitions, however, generally emphasize the following characteristics: the term is applied to a socially coherent, well-to-do stratum of the town population which tended to organize itself, from the political point of view, as a closed and privileged class. The only idea in this definition with economic connotations is that of affluence. Since affluence can have very varied sources, it is clear that the concept of a 'patriciate' is not properly an economic concept.

The urban patriciate viewed throughout western, central and southern Europe presents considerable diversity. It is impossible to give an overall picture of it. It is even difficult to separate its different manifestations sufficiently accurately into types because a sufficient number of good monographs is not yet available. We must limit ourselves, therefore, to indicating a certain number of divergent cases.

In the first place some essential differences may be pointed out which will enable a distinction to be made between several categories of patriciate. It may be noted first of all that Italy was distinctive in that the nobility there lived not only in the countryside, as in the northern countries, but also in the towns. Thus, while in the north the noble element in the composition of the patriciate is almost negligible, it is an essential ingredient south of the Alps. A second observation is connected with the degree of development of the towns and with the extent of their industrial or commercial character. In those centres which scarcely deserve the name of town, by reason of their small size or because from the economic point of view they differed but little from their rural surroundings, a ruling class composed primarily of proprietors living on income from their land was able to establish itself. This is a phenomenon frequently encountered in trans-Rhenian Germany. On the other hand, in the large commercial and industrial cities, it is the merchant element which is primarily involved.

It is with the trading towns in north-western Europe, where the purely economic factor was most fully operative, that this survey must start.

In those towns which had emerged spontaneously at an early date but which lacked at first their own institutions, it seems that there were not originally any great differences of wealth or any real social distinctions. It was only gradually that wealth enabled a group of merchants to emerge from the mass as a ruling class. From the beginning of the eleventh century (as at Tiel) or in any case from the second half of that century (at Valenciennes, St Omer) we see them organized in gilds. These associations, which no doubt concerned themselves also with the economic interests of their members, had primarily a social aim. Through the *potationes*, which assumed such an important place in their lives, they helped greatly to draw these newly rich members of the population together and to give them a class feeling. The same applied also in the twelfth century to the *Richerzeche* of Cologne, which brought together members of families engaged in trade but also called upon them to take their seat regularly in the magistrature.

It was, however, only in the thirteenth century that the patriciate took definite shape in the northern towns; that is to say, it tended at this time to close its ranks against those who still sought to climb the social ladder and strove to reserve for its current members and for their descendants the advantages it had already acquired. It was at this time, too, that the Gild Merchant finally closed its doors to the craftsman.

The patriciate was careful to adopt some outward sign which would emphasize in the eyes of the world the line of demarcation which separated it from the mass of the population. In some towns, such as Ghent (and likewise at Cologne) it was outright proprietorship of a parcel of town land which characterized the burgess *optimo jure*. Thanks to his *hereditas*, the patrician of the Flemish town was considered better able to meet financial obligations than the citizen of the second rank, his testimony had greater value, he could even exercise his authority to accord confirmation to private transactions (*juridiction gracieuse*); and it was from members of this class of *viri hereditarii* that the magistrature was drawn.

We should beware of applying indiscriminately to other towns these features derived from one well-studied case. The ways in which they could apply might vary indefinitely. Yet it is nevertheless true that in this type of town certain dominant features can be isolated. The patrician there is normally a merchant or a descendant of merchants. In the industrial centres he is often at the same time the entrepreneur, who puts out work in the export industry. As a sideline he can also engage in financial dealings. He consolidates his wealth by investing a part of his

profits in real estate and rents within the town as well as in the country.
He sits on the bench of town magistrates and as such enacts by-laws, fixes
the scale of industrial wages, administers the town finances. These features are not all necessarily combined in the person of one and the same
man, but it is usual to find that one member of a family is mentioned as a
merchant, another as a money-changer, a third as a magistrate.

In the second half of the thirteenth century a number of patricians are
found retiring from business, either because they cannot adapt themselves to changes in economic life or simply because they want to enjoy
their wealth. Thereafter they live on their estates and investments and are
described as *otiosi* (French, *oiseux*; Dutch, *ledichgangers*).

Certain groups of northern towns, although they belong to the type
described above, present special features. Thus, the Hanseatic towns like
Lübeck, and with them their patrician class, preserved a more markedly
commercial character than the Flemish towns, which with the exception
of Bruges developed increasingly into the industrial type of town.

In other towns, such as Dinant, the transformation of the merchant
entrepreneurs into *rentiers* seems to have occurred earlier than in Flanders.
In this Meuse town, the prosperity of which was based on the copper industry, the patriciate was composed solely of *otiosi*: they alone could be
named as mayors or as magistrates. It is still possible, however, to prove
that some among them were former merchant copper-beaters.

As the patriciate became a closed body there arose in many towns a
tendency for it to subdivide into somewhat artificial groups of families
(French, *lignages*; Dutch, *geslachten*; German, *Geschlechter*). Frequently
this innovation had no other aim than that of facilitating the sharing out
of the urban magistratures among the patrician families.

In the northern towns the patriciate displayed the same social tendencies, which are often self-contradictory; political oppression and industrial exploitation of the common people, solicitude for the outcast
which finds practical expression in the foundation of hospitals and charitable institutions, quarrels between families and private wars which entail
the formation of factions even among the artisans (Cologne, Ratisbon),
conspicuous expenditure, disorders caused by youthful sowers of wild
oats (London, Ghent); and, more than anything else, the desire to live
nobly.

To the north of the Alps, in fact, where the nobility did not live in the
towns, the urban patricians none the less exhibited a tendency to merge
with the aristocracy. Many of them gave their richly dowered daughters
in marriage to nobles; others served on horseback in the army, had their
own seals, or acquired fiefs (Paris, Flanders).

From the day when the patriciate became a closed class there was a
group of newly-rich who, despite their wealth, necessarily continued to

belong to the common people. At Cologne a *plebeius nummatus* is already recorded at the beginning of the twelfth century. At the end of the thirteenth century at Ghent the very wealthy Wouter van der Meer was not a patrician because he had not managed to acquire ownership of a plot of town land, that is, of a *hereditas*.

In the fourteenth century the economic and political fortunes of the patriciate differed in the various categories of towns. On the North Sea and Baltic coasts of Germany, where trade still flourished, the merchant class was continually replenished and remained in power. In Flanders, where active trade disappeared towards the end of the thirteenth century, the dominating role of the great merchant came to an end: the old patriciate, closed to newcomers, collapsed at the time of the popular revolution of 1302.

A glance at the Italian towns shows how the conjunction of the nobility and the upper strata of the commoner class gave rise to situations which are not only more complicated than those in the northern countries, but also differ from town to town.

At Genoa the patriciate was formed mainly by the nobility or more exactly by those of 'viscountly' lineage whose wealth originally consisted of landed property. In the course of the eleventh century they converted their real estate, at least in part, into liquid resources, or used the income from their land, as well as the booty they derived from the maritime war against the Saracens, for commercial ventures. In this way they were gradually brought together with the merchant elements which took to large-scale trade and which progressively broke away from the commoner class to which they had originally belonged. These two groups came to be united in the *compagna*, an organization comparable to the gilds of the northern countries and which, not long after 1100, was identified with the commune. From the political point of view, however, the nobility long remained privileged. It retained power until its internal dissensions allowed the commoner class on two occasions, in 1257 and from 1339 onwards, to impose on the state leaders of its own choice.

The distant origins of the Venetian patriciate are not so clear. Some consider that it, too, sprang from landed proprietors turned merchants and hence comparable to the Genoese nobles; others that it was a class of great merchants, and therefore similar in its origins to the patriciates of the northern towns; others again prefer to compromise between the two theories. What is certain is that this class, which in the thirteenth century devoted itself to maritime trade and which was regularly rejuvenated by new accessions, closed its ranks in 1297 to form a politically privileged class. Those families which subsequently managed to rise to wealth through trade no longer had access to power.

Florence presented a completely different picture. Here there is no

D

rapprochement whatever between the landed nobility and the merchant element of the *popolo*. The nobility did nothing to adapt itself to specifically urban functions. Nor had the elements which provided the economic drive any intention of leaving the lower class. They preferred to make use of it and thus succeeded in depriving the nobility, in the second half of the thirteenth century, of its political privileges. It is difficult to say exactly, in this case, to which class the appellation of patriciate is properly to be applied.

XIII. *The Democratic Revolution*

The patrician rule in the medieval towns corresponded by and large to the era of commercial and industrial expansion. Similarly, the popular regime which many towns experienced subsequently was more or less contemporaneous with the contracted economy which characterized the last centuries of the Middle Ages. Probably there is not a strictly causal relationship between these latter phenomena. It is none the less true that they must have exercised a reciprocal influence: contraction without any doubt led to economic control, of which the crafts, which constituted the nucleus of the popular movements, made themselves the instruments; similarly, control necessarily accentuated contraction. It is therefore important, if one wishes to weigh the causes and effects of economic phenomena at the end of the Middle Ages, to determine also the momentum and the intensity of the so-called 'democratic' movements which emerged at this time in nearly all parts of western Europe.

They first come to light in certain towns in Italy.[1] At Milan, for example, by the end of the twelfth century, the lower classes were grouped in an organization which took its place beside those of the upper and lower nobility and that of the merchants. These classes were not, of course, represented as such in the government of the town. It is none the less true that the way to the greatest honours was soon open even to the members of the lower class. At Siena, Piacenza and Arezzo the lower class acquired a political organization by the second half of the thirteenth century. In a good many towns the crafts became an integral part of the constitution of the state but their role was often a passive rather than an active one. At Pisa, for example, while securing their own participation in political affairs alongside the representatives of the merchant class, they were forced to suffer the interference and the supervision of the state in their economic activity. At Genoa and at Venice, commercial interests were so preponderant that the artisans never managed to play a true

---

[1] It may be noted that, even though the crafts were the professional associations of the artisans, they did not always assume the role of political groupings of the lower class. In Italy this role was sometimes played by the local military fraternities.

political role. At Genoa, it is true, some offices were reserved in the end for persons descended from the *populus*, but the crafts were not represented as such in political life; at Venice the crafts were closely subjected to the state, which from 1264 onwards interfered in their internal organization. Florence is almost unique in that the crafts really triumphed in the political sphere. From 1267 to 1292 they arrogated to themselves the right to participate in increasing numbers—seven, twelve, finally twenty-one—in the direction of the state. But this political organization, which was based entirely upon the craft organization, did not imply that the poorest elements could assert themselves. In Florence, in fact, the merchant entrepreneurs kept the direction of the crafts in their own hands; the artisans of the manufacturing industries had no say in the affairs of their own *arte*. The riot of the Ciompi (1378) modified this state of affairs only temporarily.

In the towns of the Low Countries the social struggles were at least as intense as in Italy. The appearance in 1225 of an impostor, who passed himself off as Count Baldwin IX who had died in 1205 as Emperor of Constantinople, stirred the common folk of Flanders. In 1253, a Liège patrician, Henri of Dinant, assumed the leadership of the crafts and tried, but without lasting success, to overthrow the government of the *majores*. In 1280 a more or less general rising of the lower class in the towns of Flanders, which was suppressed with difficulty, found an echo in the north and east of France where unrest broke out in Arras, Rouen, Lens and Dijon. In Flanders and in Brabant, however, the starting-point of the future crafts must be sought in the supervision exercised by the town authority in industrial and commercial affairs; it is within the framework of the organization thus created that the artisans sought to undertake corporate action. They were materially helped by the fact that the military organization of the towns at the end of the thirteenth century was based on the crafts, and the craftsmen sometimes found an opportunity to pursue within their charitable and religious confraternities a clandestine political activity. The crafts had not advanced far in the direction of emancipation and autonomy in Flanders, however, when in 1302 the victory of Courtrai, where the town workers (*communiers*) crushed the French forces favourable to the patrician class, suddenly brought their efforts to a successful conclusion. For a moment it even seemed that in several towns magistratures composed solely of craft-members, both those engaged in large-scale industry and those who worked for local and regional needs, would maintain themselves in power. A reaction, however, set in, especially from 1320 onwards. In the end, after a series of movements which were sometimes numerous and violent, and especially so at Ghent, a state of equilibrium was reached and political power was shared between the different classes, the patriciate, the textile workers, and the 'small crafts', these last being either brought together in a single organization or divided into several groupings. A similar constitution is also found in a town like Dinant in the episcopal principality of Liège, the prosperity of which likewise depended upon an export industry, in particular the manufacture of copper articles. In certain episcopal towns, such as Utrecht or Liège, where there were no major industries, it was the small corporations of craftsmen which dominated the political picture. Finally, in the Brabant towns, where the patriciate displayed greater vitality than in Flanders, the final triumph of the crafts occurred much later; at Brussels as late as 1423.

In the south-west of Germany, again, more or less the same situation is found as in the Low Countries. Here, too, the crafts acquired a share of power, either because their representatives were admitted to the town council or because a new municipal body was created, composed of delegates from the lower classes. The case of Cologne is somewhat different. There the patriciate exercised a real tyranny in the course of the fourteenth century, a situation which was the cause of a rising of the weavers in 1371 and later, in 1396, of the overthrow of the system of rule by a few leading families. But the new regime which followed was based only theoretically on the artisans' organizations; in fact, power remained in the hands of a few families. In the towns of northern Germany, where commercial interests were predominant, the merchant class, by continually introducing new blood, preserved all its vitality and succeeded in maintaining itself in power.

In the towns of northern France special magistratures composed of *jurés* representing the 'community' are found from the beginning of the fourteenth century; they watched over the public interests by attending the presentation of the town accounts or by taking part in the administration of the town. The term 'community' (*communitas*) here, as in Flanders, designated to an increasing extent not the whole body of citizens, but the lesser townsmen as opposed to the patriciate.

England experienced a different political evolution. There the stronger royal power always mitigated class antagonisms. Town administration remained more open in the thirteenth and fourteenth centuries to the generality of the burgesses. The crafts which developed there from the twelfth century onwards could not have the same aspirations as on the continent. It was only when, in the fourteenth and fifteenth centuries, there was a tightening up which tended to reserve the magistratures to an oligarchy, that a reaction set in: in some towns of northern England the crafts intervened and succeeded in ensuring for themselves a participation in the government of the towns.

XIV. *Town Populations*

For a full appreciation of the economic role played by the towns in the Middle Ages, as centres of both consumption and production, we need to know the number of their inhabitants; and to know this not only at one date but at different dates, so that a population curve can be drawn; further, we need to know the percentage which this population represented in relation to that of the surrounding countryside for each century.

This information is far from available. A complete census exists only for a very few towns. In general an estimate has to be based upon lists of hearths for hearth taxes, registers of the *taille* and muster rolls. The notion of hearth, however, often degenerated into a fiscal fiction; and there was no consistent definition of an able-bodied man liable for muster. As a result the coefficient by which figures derived from these sources must be multiplied in order to obtain figures of population is often uncertain. Where such calculations are available, they mostly relate, like the censuses, to the fourteenth and fifteenth centuries.

One will indeed be lucky to arrive at satisfactory figures for two or more points of time during the Middle Ages, and so be in a position to establish some sort of tentative curve. Generally speaking, one will have to be content with what is known about the general trend of population movements in western Europe in the Middle Ages: it seems certain that there was a fairly steady increase from 1000 to *c.* 1300 and that in the course of the fourteenth and fifteenth centuries the population suffered a series of drastic reductions as a result of great famines or epidemics, in particular those which followed in the wake of the Black Death (1347–51). In the intervals between these recessions, the disasters were apparently repaired, so that about 1500 the population may have been as numerous as it was *c.* 1300. These views of the broad trends, which are valid for the total population, are also valid for the towns, subject to the reservation that the increase for the period 1000–1300 was much more marked than in the countryside. This is shown by the multiplication of parishes and by the increase in the areas enclosed by the walls. In the Low Countries, for example, the first period of town fortification took place at the end of the eleventh century and during the twelfth. In many towns a second surrounding wall was planned or constructed between 1250 and 1350. The area it enclosed was much greater than that protected by the old ramparts. This difference however is not a true measure of the real increase of population: it must have been thought about 1300 that the population would continue to grow at the same pace and it was no doubt thought prudent to take account of this possibility. This expectation, however, was not realized. Frequently, from the fourteenth century onwards the population and the inhabited area did not appreciably change, and in many towns there long remained within the new walls spaces which had not been built up.

As with population trends and absolute figures of population, satisfactory information is also lacking about the relation between urban and total population. It must be admitted, however, that the concentration of the population in the towns could not exceed a certain limit and that in the fourteenth century this limit had been reached nearly everywhere. It could vary according to whether the town concerned belonged to one or other of the principal types which we have previously studied. For a town not engaged in large-scale trade and export industry this limit was determined by the extent to which the products of its craftsmen could be absorbed by the surrounding countryside, and by the amount of victuals and raw materials which the latter could provide. A town engaged in long-distance trade and having an export industry could, on the other hand, reach a population figure relatively greater in relation to the countryside, since it was able to import from distant regions supplies which it paid for by its exports.

With these reservations, various concrete facts may be given. In Brabant, a region for which four hearth-tax returns are available for the second half of the fifteenth century, the towns, both great and small, accounted for about one-third of the total hearths. This proportion tended to increase and did so solely as a result of the growth of the great towns. In Flanders, which was even more industrialized than Brabant, the proportion was certainly not less. A percentage exceeding 50% was reached by the towns of the county of Holland at the beginning of the sixteenth century. This situation is explained by very special circumstances: these towns lived on fishing and on river and sea traffic and could easily draw their supplies from afar.

In northern and central Italy it seems that the urban population, which increased between the eleventh and thirteenth centuries, lost its relative importance in the fifteenth century, although in southern Italy at the same period it still seems to show a relative increase.

Finally, a few absolute figures for the main towns of western Europe. They are not all equally reliable but they provide none the less an order of size.

The largest towns were found in Italy. Before the middle of the fourteenth century four towns there numbered more than 50,000 inhabitants: Milan, Venice, Naples and Florence, and probably also a fifth, Palermo, in the course of the thirteenth century. Some of these may even have reached or nearly reached a total of 100,000 inhabitants. The Black Death represented an enormous setback. In the fifteenth century the three first named seem more or less to have repaired their losses, while

Florence lagged behind. Genoa, Bologna and Rome must be placed about the 50,000 mark.

In the Low Countries, the other centre of intensive town life, the largest town was Ghent: it exceeded 56,000 inhabitants in the middle of the fourteenth century. Bruges may have numbered 35,000 about 1340. Ypres had about 10,700 in 1412, but at that time its industry had been in decay for a century; at the beginning of the fourteenth century it may well have sheltered double this number. In Brabant, Louvain did not exceed 20,000 souls in the fifteenth century, and Brussels 40,000. Antwerp itself in 1374 was only a town of some 18,000 inhabitants; the great expansion was to take place only in the sixteenth century (50,000 in 1526, 100,000 in 1566). As for Holland, where the town population was relatively numerous but spread over a great number of centres, the four most populous places (Leiden, Amsterdam, Delft and Haarlem) barely numbered 10,000 to 12,000 each at the dawn of modern times (1514).

For France, the hearth returns of 1328 provide important data. Nevertheless, the figure they give for Paris, 61,098 hearths, when multiplied by the coefficient $3 \cdot 5$, is completely inadmissible; on the other hand, a figure of 80,000 inhabitants is perfectly plausible. Toulouse, a large provincial town, may have had about 24,000.

For Germany, the most recent comprehensive survey is that of H. Ammann. We reproduce here the principal data accepted by him. Cologne, with barely 40,000 inhabitants, far surpassed all the other towns. Among those in the 20,000 class were, in southern Germany, Metz, Strasbourg, Nuremberg, Augsburg, as well as Vienna and Prague; in northern Germany, Lübeck, Magdeburg and, at a later date, Danzig. Six other towns appear to have exceeded 10,000 inhabitants, while 200 others, with 2,000 to 10,000, are to be included in the category which, for Germany, is to be regarded as towns of average size.

In England, London far exceeded the other towns. From the evidence of the poll-tax of 1377 it may be inferred that it had a population of 35,000 to 45,000 inhabitants. York and Bristol followed with figures between 10,000 and 14,000.

About the same time the Iberian peninsula may have had four towns with a population over 35,000: Barcelona, Cordoba, Seville and Granada.

The documentation available to the demographer does not generally allow him to go beyond estimates of the kind just set out. Almost invariably he is prevented from tackling more complex problems. At the most, it may be deduced from various sources that the number of females was often greater than that of males, 12 or 13 to 10 for example. It seems, too, that the number of unattached individuals (single persons) was greater the more industrialized the town. Finally, it seems certain that the birth rate, probably fairly high, was compensated by a death rate equally high; so that the growth of the towns must have been the result of an immigration coming no doubt, in large measure, from the surrounding countryside, but also, to some extent, from fairly distant regions.

XV. *Conclusion*

The urban movement in medieval times was a social phenomenon due primarily to economic causes and one which, in its turn, caused profound changes in the economic structure of the Western world.

The demand for goods, whether primary goods or luxury goods, accompanied by considerable differences in the level of prices, brought about a new circulation of men and goods in the long static society of the early Middle Ages. The emergence of the towns, and in particular of the trading towns, which initiated the urban movement, was due to the appearance of these commercial currents.

The foundation of the future towns was laid at the moment when the merchants felt the necessity to establish themselves in groups in places which they intended to make the focal points of their activity. The localization of urban life, as it was established from the Carolingian and post-Carolingian period onwards, was determined by the conditions of security and travel which existed at that time.

Around the first economically active nuclei composed of merchants soon congregated populations of artisans. Among the latter, some laboured with a view to satisfying the daily needs of the local population. In a great number of towns their ranks were swollen by groups of craftsmen working for industries whose products flowed far afield. For these latter it was a matter of necessity that they should establish themselves near to merchants who procured them their raw materials and disposed of their products and who, in many cases, also assumed in relation to them the character of real entrepreneurs. The merchants were, in fact, in some cases up to 1300, in others throughout the whole Middle Ages, the driving force in all economic activity. The circulation of goods which they ensured stimulated, up to the extreme limits permitted by the conditions of the period, economic specialization and consequently, too, the concentration of population in the urban centres.

From the moment when the towns were constituted as geographical units enjoying special legal privileges, conditions were created which allowed a still greater mobility of men and goods: essentially these conditions were liberty of person, the prerogative of all those who were attracted into the town precinct, and the freedom of urban land, of which the most notable outward sign was the emergence of free tenure. In Italy the nobility, in closer contact with the merchants, liquidated landed property and thereby intensified commercial activity. Conversely, throughout the whole of western Europe, the merchants invested part of the wealth they acquired in land within the towns as well as in the countryside.

The towns, once they had acquired their own constitution and had become independent political entities, often tried through their town privilege to consolidate their prosperity and their preponderance over the surrounding countryside, which had originally resulted from the free interplay of economic forces. In the same way, within the towns, the ruling class, whose ascendancy was originally founded on wealth alone, tended to transform itself into a politically privileged patriciate, capable for that reason of modifying to its own advantage the conditions of material life. On the other hand, in those places where, about 1300 or later, the lower class was able to assure itself even a modest participation in the management of public affairs, it also exercised an influence on economic life by striving for regulation, with the object no longer of higher productivity but of a socially more equitable distribution of existing sources of wealth. This question, however, will be the subject of later chapters.[1]

[1] The first draft of this chapter was finished in 1940. The text was revised in 1953 and retouched in 1956. The author has not thought it necessary, however—due regard being paid to the difference of viewpoint—to modify the structure of the chapter following the appearance in the meantime of important works such as E. Ennen's book, *Frühgeschichte der europäischen Stadt* (Bonn, 1953). Moreover, the appearance of the collective *Studien zu den Anfängen des europäischen Städtewesens* (Lindau–Constance, 1958) has necessitated several adjustments of detail.

CHAPTER II
The Organization of Trade[1]

I. *A General Picture*

From the point of view of business organization, the Middle Ages present no uniform picture either in time or in space. During the so-called Dark Ages, the manorial economy was dominant and most landed estates were relatively self-sufficient. Exchange, at any rate, was reduced to a minimum, and trade, while it did not disappear altogether, fell to a low ebb. What little survived was carried on by groups of travelling merchants who catered for the rich by selling them luxuries or who exploited the poor by charging high prices for necessities in times of famine or distress. A real revival did not occur until the eleventh century with the cessation of the Norman invasions and the decline of feudal anarchy. In Italy urban life regained vigour; in Flanders it sprang up anew. From these two centres, the movement spread and gained momentum. The Crusades gave it further impetus. Latin merchant colonies were established all over the Levant. Soon the Venetians, the Genoese and the Pisans controlled the foreign trade of the Byzantine Empire. Methods of business organization made steady progress, but the merchants continued to be peregrinators, moving constantly about in unending pursuit of profit. They and their servants still accompanied their goods either by land or by sea. In the twelfth and thirteenth centuries, the travelling trade of western Europe gravitated to the fairs of Champagne, and their rhythm regulated the coming and going of the merchant caravans from Italy, Flanders, Germany and all corners of France.

The Italians played an important part, but as yet they did not dominate, although they were spreading their tentacles and slowly choking off their rivals. Flemish and English merchants still went as far as Genoa to fetch spices or silks and to sell their cloth. As early as the thirteenth century, the enterprising Italians, by-passing Flanders, were penetrating into England as papal bankers, but the transfer problem forced them into the wool trade, since the exportation of specie was forbidden and English wool was in great demand on the continent. Paris proved to be another attraction, and the Italian companies began to establish permanent agencies in the French capital, so favourably situated close to Champagne. This new development was only the spearhead of far greater changes which transformed the entire fabric of medieval trade.

Instead of travelling to and from the fairs, the Italian merchants, es-

[1] The writer wishes to express his appreciation to the Social Science Research Council for a grant that enabled him to collect material for part of this chapter.

pecially those of the inland cities, Siena and Florence, began to direct their
affairs from the counting-house and to secure permanent representation
abroad by means of partners, factors or correspondents. The one-time
traveller gradually turned into a business administrator, who spent most
of his time behind a desk reading reports and giving instructions. How to
get satisfactory representation in foreign parts was perhaps the major
problem of this sedentary type of merchant, and success or failure often
depended on the selection of efficient and honest representatives. Since
the merchant no longer went abroad himself, he had to delegate power to
someone he could trust and who would attend to his business.

The rise of this new system of business organization based on correspondence and representation abroad is intimately connected with the
rapid decline of the fairs of Champagne after 1300. There was no longer
any need for the Italian merchants to visit the fairs after their companies
had established permanent branches in Paris, London and Bruges. As
initiators of the new system, the Italians reaped the greatest benefits from
its success. During the fourteenth and fifteenth centuries, they dominated
trade and banking in the entire area from Constantinople and Alexandria
in the east to Bruges and London in the west. To a large extent, this
supremacy rested on superior business organization, since the military
power of the Italian republics did not extend beyond the Alps. In the
Levant, however, Genoa, Pisa and Venice maintained powerful fleets to
protect their colonies as well as their trading interests. The only competitors who more or less succeeded in holding their own were the
Catalans, who, at an early date, had adopted Italian business methods.
The Flemish carrying trade was completely eliminated. In England,
however, the Italians did not succeed in rooting out the native merchants,
but it is true that the English merchants did not yet seriously challenge
Italian supremacy. They confined their activities to the intercourse with
the Low Countries, Scandinavia, Germany, northern France and Gascony. The Italians also tried to gain a foothold in the Baltic, but they
failed. In the middle of the fifteenth century, several Florentines, among
others a Francesco Rucellai and a Gherardo Bueri, were doing business in
Lübeck. Apparently they had to struggle against overwhelming odds and
barely succeeded in eking out a living; the Italian colony in Lübeck failed
to grow. Probably Italian business methods, although superior, afforded
no advantages in the Baltic region, where they did not fit in with local
customs. Moreover, the Hanseatic League, one may be sure, was on the
alert and stood ready to defend its monopoly by economic and political
means against any serious encroachment.

Throughout the later Middle Ages, the Hanseatic cities, under the
guidance of Lübeck, controlled the Baltic trade as the Italians dominated
in the Mediterranean. Any Scandinavian competition had long been

crushed, and most cities, including Stockholm, were German settlements. Business methods in the Baltic were relatively backward as compared with those of the Italians, but they met the needs of a different environment where operations were on a smaller scale, where commodities were not high-priced and where merchants still needed to travel a great deal more than did the heads of Florentine banking-houses.

It is now an accepted view that the Black Death (1348) marked the end of a long period of demographic and economic expansion and the beginning of a downward secular trend characterized by the closing of markets, the recurrence of wars and epidemics and the contraction of the volume of trade. Without challenging this view, it may be pointed out that no such setback is noticeable with respect to the improvement of business techniques. On the contrary, the fourteenth century, especially, is one of continuous progress, innovation and experimentation. The draft form of the bill of exchange, for example, although known before 1350, did not come into general use until after that date. The same applies to marine insurance. Mercantile book-keeping, too, did not reach full maturity until 1400, as is clear if we compare, for example, the account-books of the Peruzzi company (failed in 1343) with those of Francesco Datini (1410).[1] Another innovation introduced after 1375 is the combination of partnerships similar to the modern holding company. The best example of this is the Medici banking-house founded in 1397. It is true that the foundations of all these new commercial institutions were laid in the twelfth and thirteenth centuries. Nevertheless, they did not fully develop until later. Perhaps it could be argued that the secular decline which set in with the Black Death, by sharpening competition and reducing profit-margins, spurred the merchants to improve methods, increase efficiency and reduce costs, with the result that only the fittest were able to survive.[2] Perhaps it is significant that no firm, not even the Medici bank, ever attained the size of the famous Peruzzi and Bardi companies, which both failed shortly before the Black Death.

In one respect, medieval trade differed totally from modern trade. Today most goods are sold before they are shipped. This is especially true of heavy equipment and machinery. Medieval trade, however, with few exceptions involved venturing. An assortment of goods was shipped to a distant place in the expectation that it would be sold at a remunerative price and that the merchant would be able to make his returns in other commodities demanded at home. The same principle applies to the earlier as well as to the later period. It really does not make much difference whether goods are entrusted to a travelling merchant or sent on consignment to a correspondent who has the burden of finding a market for them. Each transaction, therefore, involved a speculative element and,

[1] For a biographical sketch, see *Camb. Econ. Hist.* II, 337 f.   [2] *Ibid.* 310 and 335.

in a certain way, was an adventure. It is with good reason that the exporters of English cloth called themselves the Merchant Adventurers, since they bought cloth in the hope of finding customers at the marts of Brabant. As late as the sixteenth and seventeenth centuries, mercantilist writers insist on this venturing aspect of foreign trade, although some point out that the Merchant Adventurers do not run great risks, that the distance to the marts in the Low Countries is short, and that their trade is well established. Nevertheless, it sometimes happened that the English expected big sales, but that the continental buyers failed to appear. We have mentioned that there are exceptions to venturing. Most of them concern luxury articles, such as tapestries, paintings and silks with armorial bearings, which were made to order according to the specifications of foreign customers. Thus the Medici branch in Bruges had tapestries of prescribed dimensions and on requested subjects made for Italian princes.

Venturing also affected the way of thinking of medieval merchants. It largely explains the prevalence of venture accounting. As a result, it was a widespread custom to open a separate account for each shipment. By this method, it was possible to determine which ventures yielded a profit and which resulted in a loss. Undoubtedly, the medieval merchant was keenly interested in this type of information. Moreover, in order to divide risks, medieval merchants resorted to an infinite number of combinations, and frequently participated in joint ventures with other merchants. Thus the Medici of Bruges, in 1441, had for sale three different lots of pepper: one they were selling for their own account, another lot was being sold in joint account with the Medici of Venice and a third was simply handled on a commission basis for an outsider. This may be considered as a typical situation, in no way limited to Florentine firms. The account-books of the Venetian Andrea Barbarigo (1418–49) contain other examples of the same sort. It is safe to assert that this way of doing business was fairly general.

The explanation lies, of course, in the desire to split risks, and medieval business was beset with all sorts of hazards. The magnitude of the risks is perhaps another outstanding feature. Shipwrecks were frequent, but disaster at sea was not the only peril: piracy was an even greater threat. Even on land, roads were often insecure because of warfare or robbery. The slowness of communications favoured the spread of false rumours, which were sometimes deliberately planted by unscrupulous speculators in order to drive prices up or down. Drastic price fluctuations were likely to upset the most careful forecasts, since a market, lacking supplies, might be glutted the next moment by the unexpected arrival of a cargo or the sudden curtailment of the demand. Embargoes and reprisals were another source of uncertainty and frequently led to spoilage through lack of care and to plunder through lack of supervision. Credit risks created another serious problem, because recalcitrant debtors often took advantage of legal technicalities and conflicting jurisdictions to evade their obligations or to delay the course of justice. Besides, judges were often hostile to foreign claimants and lenient with local debtors, even when these were patently lacking in good faith. As a rule, trade privileges contained provisions promising prompt and impartial justice, but whether they were always carried out is another matter. Much might depend on the political mood of the moment. Conditions varied from one country to another. Flemish courts, for example, enjoyed among the Italians an enviable reputation for impartiality. As a matter of fact, the Bruges *échevins* or aldermen went so far as to consult alien merchants on points of law or merchant custom, namely in difficult cases concerning bills of exchange.

Against these hazards, the medieval merchant protected himself in various ways, but chiefly by dividing the risk or sharing it with others. Diversification was, therefore, the rule rather than the exception. As the account-books clearly show, merchants rarely specialized in one line of business; they dealt in all kinds of commodities and tried to take advantage of all profit opportunities that might present themselves. Even banking was not a special field. Without a single known exception, the great Italian companies combined international banking and foreign trade. Merchants usually sold wholesale. Although they did not disdain occasionally to retail their wares, they were often barred from the retail trade by the privileges of the local gilds. Infringements of these privileges gave rise to numerous conflicts. In Bruges, there were instances of 'Lombards' being fined for selling silk by the ell. In London, too, violation of the rule was a perennial source of grievance, aroused steady complaints from the mercers and other gilds, and made the Italians unpopular in the city.

II. *The Travelling Trade before 1300*

1

Of the organization of trade before the twelfth century, not much, if anything, is known. Extant sources do not contain much information on this particular aspect of economic life.

Merchants, in any case, had no assigned place in the pattern of feudal society, and their activities, under the influence of Church doctrine, were regarded with distrust as something tainted with the stigma of usury or wickedness. Did not the Canon Law, from early times, declare that it was difficult to distinguish honest from ill-gotten gain and that it was nearly impossible to avoid sin in the course of buying and selling?[1] Moreover, trading was forbidden to clerics because being constantly on the road was incompatible with requirements of residence.[2] The implication is clearly that merchants were always on the move.

In order to protect themselves against high risks, they formed bands and 'fraternities' which, in northern Europe, were called merchant gilds. Such a gild existed apparently in the tenth century among the merchants of Tiel, a town near the mouth of the Rhine, at that time presumably a Frisian settlement. The monk Alpert, who reports on their activities, considers them as wicked and lawless men, and relates, what is more significant for us, that they pooled their resources, shared their profits and spent part of their gains in licentious feasts. Unfortunately, he does not go into more detail about the operation of this profit-sharing scheme.

From the statutes of another gild, the *frairie* or brotherhood of Valenciennes, portions of which probably date back to the tenth century, we also learn that the members did not stay at home but were constantly exposed to perils 'on sea, water, and land'. They probably travelled together in armed caravans, since an article of the statutes fines the member who appears in the ranks without armour and bow. Once a caravan has left town, the statutes provide, no one is allowed to leave but all are to stay together and to give each other aid and assistance in case of emergency. If anyone dies on a journey, his companions are under obligation to carry the corpse for at least three nights and to bury it, if possible, according to the wishes of the deceased.

An excellent picture of the venturesome career of a merchant in those early days is afforded by the life of St Godric of Finchale (1080?-1170).[3] He started as a beachcomber, earning his first pennies by selling jetsam. With this money he set out as a pedlar roaming the countryside and then going from market to market. Thus he met and joined a company of merchants and with them visited all the shores of the North Sea. Using his earnings to expand his business, he bought his own ship and became

[1] *Decretum Gratiani*: c. *Qualitas lucri*, Dist. 5, c. 2, *De poenitentia*. This canon is an epistle of Pope Leo the Great (440-61) to the bishop of Narbonne (J. P. Mansi, *Sacrorum Conciliorum . . . collectio*, VI [Florence, 1761], col. 404). It is quoted in all the earlier collections of canons, including those of Dionysius Exiguus (sixth century), Regino of Prüm (906-13), Burchard of Worms (1008-12), and Ivo of Chartres (†1115), as well as in the *Polycarpus* of Cardinal Gregorius of S. Crisogono, compiled between 1101 and 1120. Through these collections, the canon *Qualitas lucri* found its way into the *Decretum* of Gratian, composed about 1140 and destined to become the standard compilation until the publication of the new code of Canon Law in 1917.

[2] Franz Schaub, *Der Kampf gegen den Zinswucher, ungerechten Preis und unlautern Handel im Mittelalter: Von Karl dem Grossen bis Papst Alexander III* (Freiburg, 1905), 109.

[3] See *Camb. Econ. Hist.* II, 239. The story has been told briefly by Pirenne, but a more detailed study is that of Walther Vogel, 'Ein seefahrender Kaufmann um 1100', *Hansische Geschichtsblätter*, XVIII (1912), 239-48.

his own captain. Favoured by good luck, he prospered and acquired shares in other vessels. At this point, he probably settled in a port and let others do the travelling and expose their persons to the fortunes of the sea. Late in life, he was touched by grace and gave up the pursuit of wealth in order to become a saintly hermit whose *vita* a pious biographer thought well worth telling for the edification of less devout men.

Details of business organization are not given, but we gather from the story that the ownership of ships was divided into shares and that merchants were often shipowners and navigators as well, a situation duplicated in contemporary Mediterranean trade. In order to succeed, a travelling merchant had to possess a great deal of physical endurance and be ready to face many hardships. Although conditions were primitive, he needed more than brawn: moral stamina and some intellectual baggage were indispensable prerequisites to success. A good idea of the knowledge and the character indispensable for a successful business career is given in the *King's Mirror*, a Scandinavian treatise on education, probably written in the early part of the thirteenth century. The date is rather late, but the author's bits of advice are so precious that they constitute a *vade mecum* for any enterprising youth.

The unknown author of the *King's Mirror* starts out by stressing the obvious fact that a merchant needs a good dose of bravery and must expect to encounter perils at sea and in heathen lands. While he should be polite and agreeable, he should also be wary and not buy any goods without first checking their quality and condition. When abroad, he should live well and go to the best inns, but not indulge in extravagance. It is also advisable to keep away from drink, harlots, brawls and dice. A knowledge of foreign languages, especially French and Latin, might be handy, and he should not neglect the study of law and the observation of local customs. Some notion of arithmetic and astronomy the author of the *King's Mirror* considers as fundamental, since a merchant must know how to figure and to read the skies when navigating. It is desirable to sell quickly, at reasonable prices, for a quick turnover is a stimulus to trade. If the merchant owns a ship, he should have it tarred every autumn, keep the tackle and apparel well in order, sail in the spring, and be sure to return by the end of the summer. Shares should be bought in good ships only or in none at all. If successful, he might invest his earnings in partnerships, but he should be extremely careful in selecting his associates. This policy will eventually enable him to discontinue his own journeys and instead finance the business ventures of younger men. As profits continue to pile up, they should not all be reinvested in business. It would be wiser to devote the major part to the acquisition of land. Land being the safest form of investment, it alone will provide security for him and his descendants.

Although safety along the roads greatly increased in the course of time, the merchants from the Flemish towns, visiting the fairs of Champagne, still used to travel together in armed caravans as late as the end of the thirteenth century. The caravan would set out on a given date under the command of a 'mayor', preceded by a standard-bearer, armed servants and crossbowmen flanking the carts and wagons carrying the precious cloth. In 1285, about twenty-five merchants of Douai journeying together had with them thirty-six attendants, all armed, in case of need. It is true that such a military display had become more traditional than necessary. Single merchants—or were they professional wagoners?— were already going to the French fairs leading a train of four or five carts with several servants to take care of the teams.

The organization of the fairs of Champagne is, however, a separate subject. On the whole, the documentation regarding early medieval trade in northern Europe is scanty and gives us only fleeting glimpses of the conduct of business. To gain more insight, we have to turn south, to the magnificent series of the Genoese notaries which starts in 1156 with the published cartulary of Giovanni Scriba or John the Scribe. Several thousand contracts of later notaries have also been published, including those of Oberto Scriba de Mercato (1186–90), Guglielmo Cassinese (1190–2), Bonvillano (1198), Giovanni di Guiberto (1200–11), and Lanfranco (1202–26). This unique source material is complemented by a series of Venetian acts, which are less numerous but start even earlier; the first date is 1021 and the last 1261. There are also available the acts of Pietro Scardon (1271) and Benvenuto di Brixano (1301–2), Venetian notaries in Crete. Some studies based on this superabundant material have already appeared, but much remains to be explored.

From these Genoese and Venetian records, it appears that the two most typical contracts in overseas trade were the *commenda* and the *societas maris*—they were called *collegantia* in Venice, but the name has little, if any, importance.[1] Both contracts were partnership agreements, concluded not for a period of years, but for a single venture or voyage, usually a round trip to the Levant, Africa, Spain or even Provence. There were also *commenda* contracts *per terram*, that is, relating to distant trade overland, or even to local undertakings, but these were relatively few.

The *commenda* and the *societas maris* both involved co-operation between a travelling partner, called *tractator* or *procertans*, and an investing partner who stayed on land and was called *stans*. In the case of the *commenda* the venture was financed entirely by the *stans*; the travelling partner did not supply any capital, but he took the risk of embarking upon a dangerous sea voyage and had to endure all the discomforts that went with it. As a reward for his labours and his hardships, he usually received

[1] On the origins of the *commenda*, see *Camb. Econ. Hist.* II, 267.

E

only one-fourth of the profits; and the investing partner, who ran only the risk of losing his money, received the remaining three-fourths. This arrangement may seem unfair, but in the twelfth and thirteenth centuries life was cheap and capital scarce.

In the *societas maris*, profits were shared equally by the two partners, but the *tractator* supplied one-third of the capital and the *stans*, two-thirds. Essentially, the two contracts were the same, since in both cases, one-fourth of the profits went to the *tractator* for his labour and three-fourths to the investors of capital. In the *societas*, however, the *tractator* received an additional fourth, or one-half the profits in all, because he had supplied one-third of 'the capital. The only difference is really that the Genoese notaries called one contract a *commenda* and the other a *societas maris*.

Among Italian scholars, there has raged a fierce controversy about the legal character of the *commenda*: some argue that it is a kind of loan and others that it is a partnership, but all the medieval jurists, canonists as well as civilians, regard the *commenda* as a licit partnership agreement and not as a loan subject to the usury prohibition. The practical result was that the lawfulness of the *commenda* was never questioned by either jurists or theologians; in the Middle Ages, as everyone agrees, it was considered a partnership. Moreover, legal writers tend to exaggerate the importance of their categories and they tend to overlook the fact that, in economics, partnership agreements and loans are basically alternative and interchangeable forms of investment.

There are different types of *commenda*. In some cases, the *tractator* was left free to make his returns as he saw fit or deemed most profitable. In others, he was bound to bring back certain specified commodities. It would be a mistake to consider the *stans* as a sort of sleeping partner, who was only interested in getting a return on a speculative investment. This was certainly true of the numerous cases in which the investing partners were widows and orphans, priests and nuns, public officials and notaries, artisans or other persons without business experience. However, there were other cases in which the *stans* was an older merchant who no longer went overseas, but who was still actively engaged in business and sometimes undertook the sale of the goods brought back by his partner. It also happened that an experienced *stans* acted as adviser to relatives or other persons and helped them with their investment. Without more information than the abstracts of notarial contracts give, it is dangerous to make any dogmatic statements: real situations do not always fit into neat classifications.

In Genoa, it was also common for a merchant starting out on a trip to conclude a number of *commenda* and *societas* contracts with several persons in all walks of life. In other instances, he dealt with only a single *stans*. Examples of reciprocal *commendae* are not rare: a merchant starting out for the Levant might entrust goods in *commenda* to another about to leave for Champagne and vice versa. It even happened that a travelling merchant concluded a *commenda* with another sailing on the same ship and bound for the same destination. Usually travelling charges were deducted from gross profits and only net profits were distributed, but it also occurred, especially in the case of a reciprocal *commenda*, that the contract provided that no account should be taken of expenses. There are not, consequently, two opposed or antagonistic groups of investing and travelling partners, or of exploiters and exploited. In a great many cases, the *tractatores* were ambitious young men who were willing to take heavy risks in order to accumulate sufficient capital to join eventually the ranks of the *stantes*.

How the *commenda* favoured the rise of capable young men is illustrated by the story of Ansaldo Baialardo.[1] When he started on his first trip, in 1156, he was still a minor, since he had to be emancipated by his father in order to enter into a *commenda* agreement with an important merchant, Ingo da Volta. Apparently, Ansaldo received from the latter an amount of £205 4s. 1d. Genoese currency, for a coastal voyage to Provence, Montpellier or Catalonia. At the termination of this venture, profits amounting to 74 Genoese pounds were divided as usual: three-fourths or £55 10s. to the *stans* (Ingo da Volta) and one-fourth or £18 10s. to the *tractator* (Ansaldo Baialardo). This was a return of more than 30% on invested capital. Such a highly satisfactory result probably induced Ingo da Volta to entrust another *commenda* to Ansaldo by reinvesting his initial capital plus the major part of the profits or £254 14s. 1d. Genoese in all. In addition, Ansaldo invested £18 10s. Genoese, or the earnings of his previous trip. This sum, however, remained outside the *commenda* agreement and Ansaldo was consequently entitled to the full profit on his own investment. This second voyage was exceptionally profitable and yielded a total return of £244 15s. 11d. Genoese, of which £17 9s. 11d. represented the earnings made privately by Ansaldo. The remainder, or £227 6s. Genoese, was then divided according to customary proportion: £170 9s. 6d. to the *stans* and £56 16s. 6d. to the *tractator*.

Because Ansaldo managed his affairs so well, Ingo da Volta continued to give him financial support, but this time for a voyage to Syria, Palestine and Egypt. Since Ansaldo had now accumulated some capital, the two parties, on 3 August 1158, concluded a *societas maris*, in which Ingo da Volta supplied £128 17s. 4d. and Ansaldo half this amount, or £64 8s. 8d. Genoese. Furthermore, Ingo da Volta put up an additional £284 9s. 8d. Genoese under the terms of a *commenda* agreement which entitled him, as usual, to three-fourths of the profit. The remaining fourth,

[1] Cf. *Camb. Econ. Hist.* II, 306.

instead of going to Ansaldo personally, was to be assigned to the *societas maris*. By virtue of this arrangement, seven-eighths of the profits of the *commenda* went to Ingo da Volta and only one-eighth to Ansaldo. According to these data, the total invested in the venture, both *societas* and *commenda* combined, amounted approximately to 478 Genoese pounds.

This third venture proved to be profitable, but not quite so profitable as the second. The sale of the goods brought back by Ansaldo produced 760 Genoese pounds, so that there was a total profit of 282 Genoese pounds. This amount was divided between the *commenda* and the *societas maris* in proportion to the capital invested in each, so that £168 was allocated to the first and £114 to the second. The partners received, consequently, the following amounts:

Ingo da Volta
$\frac{7}{8}$ of the *commenda* profits   147 Genoese pounds
$\frac{1}{2}$ of the *societas* profits   57
————
204

Ansaldo Baialardo
$\frac{1}{8}$ of the *commenda* profits   21
$\frac{1}{2}$ of the *societas* profits   57
————
78

In about three years, Ansaldo Baialardo, who had started with nothing, had accumulated a capital of 142 Genoese pounds (£64, his investment, plus £78, his profit on the last venture). On the other hand, Ingo da Volta had nearly trebled his capital in the same period.

This unique information about the actual operation of twelfth-century partnerships is taken from data scribbled on three small scraps of paper inserted in the cartulary of John the Scribe. They are regarded as the earliest examples of medieval mercantile accounting. Although crude, they prove that partnership arrangements made it indispensable for the merchants to keep records, not only about accounts payable and receivable, but also about any elements that would enable them to determine profit or loss.

In Venice, Pisa, Amalfi, Marseilles and the entire Mediterranean area, the *commenda* and the *societas maris*, although known under different names, were no less popular than in Genoa. As a matter of fact, the earliest example of a *societas*, or a *collegantia*, as it was called in Venice, is a contract dated August 1073, according to which a *tractator* or *procertans* binds himself to a *stans* named Sevasto Orefice to take his cargo on a voyage (*in taxegio*) to Thebes in Greece and there to make the best possible returns (*in quo melius potuero*). Profits are to be divided equally between the partners, without fraud or evil intent. If the venture, because of disaster at sea or enemy action, results in a total loss, neither partner will have any claim on the other. If any of the invested capital is recovered, each will participate in it in proportion to his investment. Consequently, it is plain that profits were shared half and half, but that losses were borne two-thirds by the *stans* and one-third by the *procertans*.

One of the great advantages of the *commenda* and the *societas maris* was that the investors assumed only limited liability: they could lose their initial investment, but no more, whereas, in the case of the *compagnia*, or ordinary partnership, the partners were held liable to the extent of all their property. Another advantage was that any investor could easily reduce risks by placing his money in several *commendae* instead of staking it all on a single venture. Still another feature of the *commenda* and the *societas maris* was that they lent themselves to any number of combinations and were usually dissolved at the completion of each voyage. The resulting flexibility explains why the two contracts in question were admirably suited to the conditions prevailing in the twelfth and thirteenth centuries, especially in overseas trade. They persisted even in the later period, and disappeared only gradually as more elaborate forms of business organization gained ground. The *commenda* is still discussed by legal writers as late as the seventeenth and eighteenth centuries, though this may be an indication of conservatism on the part of the jurists rather than of extensive use of the contract.

Next to the *commenda* and the *societas maris*, the sea loan was frequently used to finance overseas ventures. It differed from a straight loan in that repayment was contingent upon safe arrival of a ship (*sana eunte nave*) or successful completion of a voyage. The risk of loss through the fortunes of the sea or the action of men-of-war was thus shifted from the borrower to the lender. Prior to the days of premium insurance, the sea loan performed, to a certain extent, the same function of protecting the merchant against loss through shipwreck or piracy. At any rate, in case of misfortune, he was relieved from any further liability which might otherwise have thrown him into bankruptcy. The only trouble with the sea loan was that, in order to get protection, the merchant had to borrow at high rates whether or not he needed additional funds. In the twelfth century, charges of 40 or 50% were not uncommon for voyages from Italy or Constantinople to Alexandria or Syria. Thus Romano Mairano, a Venetian merchant residing in Constantinople, borrowed, in 1167, 88 perpers and promised to repay 129 perpers, both principal and interest (*inter caput et prode*), twenty days after the safe return of his ship from a voyage to Egypt. This is an increase of more than 45% which, of course, does not represent pure interest only, but also includes a heavy premium for risk. Nevertheless, such high charges absorbed most of the merchant's trading profit.

What distinguishes the sea loan from the *commenda* is that the investor assumes the sea risk (*ad risicum et fortunam Dei, maris et gentium*), but does not enter into partnership with the borrower and share with him the business risk. If the ship or the cargo arrives safely at destination, the debt is due in its entirety, regardless of the debtor's success or failure in earning enough to cover the charges on the loan.

There are at least three different types of sea loans. In English they bear different names, but not in French or Italian, which has been a source of confusion. All three types appear in the Genoese notarial instruments from an early date. The first is the ordinary sea loan or *foenus nauticum*, which was unsecured save for a general lien on the debtor's property. One example among many is a contract concluded on 5 September 1155, in which the debtors pledge all their property (*bona pignori*) in security of a sea loan at the rate of 25% granted for a round-trip voyage from Genoa to Tunis. This type may be older than the other two. It occurs frequently in the cartulary of John the Scribe, but it soon gives way to another variety called in England the *respondentia*. Upon such a sea loan, principal and increment must be paid, even though the ship itself perishes, provided the cargo be safe. An example is found in a contract of 17 August 1190, enacted by the Genoese notary Oberto Scriba de Mercato. According to its provisions, a borrower who has received a loan of £10, Genoese currency, obliges himself to repay a like amount plus ten measures of barley, if a certain vessel or the major part of its cargo (*vel maiori parte rerum navis*) returns safely from a voyage to Sardinia. The appearance of this new clause shows that the drafting of contracts was gradually improved by inserting safeguards which prevented debtors from seizing upon any pretext to evade their obligations.

The third type of sea loan is the bottomry loan. It is usually made in order to equip a ship or to pay for emergency repairs in a foreign port and is secured by the hull, tackle and apparel. Sometimes the lender is also given a lien on the freight at the termination of a voyage. In Genoa, bottomry loans could also be secured by part of a ship, as in a contract of 6 April 1213, according to which a borrower offered as security all his property (*omnia bona mea*), but especially four *loca* or shares in a company operating a vessel fully manned and rigged. In addition, he pledged the expected income from freight which would be allotted to his four shares. As usual, fulfilment of the contract depended upon the fortunate outcome of a sea voyage. Although the contract relates only to a short trip from Genoa to Sardinia and return, the rate was presumably as high as 30%, since the debtor, who promised to repay £26, Genoese currency,

THE CAMBIUM MARITIMUM

had apparently not received more than £20. The contract, it is true, does not specify the amount actually borrowed, but the notary, in his register, first wrote it down and then crossed it out, substituting the vague expression *tantum de tuis denariis*. Why? Perhaps because the borrower was a cleric. Another and similar contract, bearing the same date, involving the same lender, and relating to the same ship, states openly how much was borrowed by a layman, owner of eighteen *loca* or shares, instead of four. At any rate, our example proves first that ownership of shares in merchant vessels was widely diffused and was not confined to classes closely connected with shipping or mercantile interests. Second, it seems to indicate that the sea loan was considered as a dubious contract even before the promulgation of the decretal *Naviganti*.

Although the sea loan had been used since Antiquity, the Genoese notarial records give the impression that after 1250 it suddenly lost its popularity in favour of another contract, the *cambium maritimum*. This decline is undoubtedly due to the impact of the decretal *Naviganti*, by which Pope Gregory IX, in 1236, formally condemned the sea loan and similar contracts as usurious, even though the lender assumed a risk not present in a straight loan.[1] It would certainly be a mistake to believe that the usury prohibition had no repercussion on business practices. As a matter of fact, it influenced greatly the development of banking because the theologians, while frowning upon discount, did not object to *cambium* or exchange. The decline of the sea loan is another instance of the same sort. Since any form of loan aroused the suspicion of the ecclesiastical authorities, the merchant found it preferable to shift from the sea loan to the *cambium maritimum*.

The difference between these two contracts was that the *cambium maritimum* involved an advance of funds repayable in another, instead of in the same, currency. In both cases, of course, the debtor was relieved from any obligation if the ship or the goods failed to reach their destination. In the *cambium maritimum*, however, the lender's gain, instead of being expressed in a percentage of the principal, was cleverly concealed in the rate of exchange. Incontrovertible evidence is found in a contract, dated 19 July 1157, and enacted by the Genoese notary, John the Scribe, according to which a merchant going to Constantinople acknowledged the receipt of £100, Genoese currency, and promised to repay the equivalent of this amount at the rate of three perpers per pound if a certain vessel safely made port. However, should this repayment not take place in Constantinople, then the debtor was bound to pay in Genoa 300 perpers, at 9s. 6d. Genoese for each perper, one month after the safe return of his ship from the Levant. In other words, the debtor, who had borrowed 100 Genoese pounds before sailing for Constantinople, incurred the

[1] *Decretals*, in X, v, 19, 19. The authenticity of *Naviganti* is beyond question.

obligation to give his creditor either 300 perpers at destination or £142 10s. Genoese upon completion of the round trip. To explain the gist of the agreement in another way, the lender, who had lent 300 perpers at 6s. 8d. Genoese each, expected to be repaid at the rate of 9s. 6d. Genoese and to gain the difference, viz. 2s. 10d. Genoese on each perper, in case of successful completion of the voyage. The figures show a profit of exactly 42·5%. This rate may seem high but, as stated before, it was normal at that time for a long voyage to the Levant. On the much shorter trip from Genoa to Sicily, a return of 25% was not exceptional. As the presence of this and similar contracts in the cartulary of John the Scribe proves, the *cambium maritimum* was known long before the promulgation of the decretal *Naviganti* and, hence, was not invented because of it and for the sole purpose of evading the ban against usury.

In the thirteenth century, agreements become more precise and elaborate. In general, repayment is secured by pledging the goods bought with the proceeds of the loan and registering them under the creditor's name in the ship's cartulary. As a rule, contracts also stipulate that the loan will be repayable upon safe arrival of a certain ship or most of its cargo (*sana tamen eunte dicta nave vel maiore parte rerum*). This clause offered better protection to the creditor, since it occasionally happened that a ship ran aground on entering a harbour, but that the cargo was salvaged before the hull was broken up by the pounding waves. The loss of the ship, then, could not be used by the owners of the cargo as a pretext to repudiate their debts. After 1250, the Genoese notaries, when drafting contracts relating to *cambium maritimum*, took the precaution of stating explicitly that the agreement was concluded *nomine venditionis* or *nomine cambii*, no doubt for fear that otherwise it might be invalidated in court as a usurious loan.

Besides the *cambium maritimum*, there existed also a contract called *cambium quasi nauticum* by modern jurists. For example, according to an act of 17 December 1215, a merchant borrowed in Genoa an unspecified sum in local currency and pledged as security certain goods which he was sending to Champagne. Repayment in money of Provins was to take place at the forthcoming fair of Lagny, with the restriction that the goods travelled at the creditor's risk. In other words, the debt would be cancelled if they were stolen or, for some other reason, failed to arrive. Perhaps fulfilment of the contract was made dependent upon this contingency because the goods were entrusted to a third party—possibly chosen by the creditor—instead of being accompanied by their owner as was usually the case.

Premium insurance did not develop prior to 1300, but merchants in the thirteenth century were searching for a solution of the risk problem and were experimenting with different types of contracts that would offer protection. The role of the sea loan has already been mentioned in this connection. Another type of contract was the so-called insurance loan by which a shipowner made an advance to a shipper with the understanding that it was due, together with freight charges, only upon arrival of the shipment at destination. Complete coverage was not achieved, since such advances rarely exceeded 25 or 30% of the cargo's value.

The earliest known examples of insurance loans date from 1287 and are found in deeds drafted by a notary in Palermo. Later, this form of contract is also encountered in Pisa (1317). Its rather late appearance may be explained by the fact that insurance loans were usually granted to merchants remaining ashore instead of travelling aboard the same ship with their merchandise, as had been the common practice hitherto.

Fictitious sales were also used for shifting risks. An example is afforded by a curious and involved contract entered into by Palaeologus Zaccaria, in his own name and that of his father, Benedetto, the famous Genoese admiral, colonizer and owner of the alum mines at Phocea, near Smyrna.[1] According to this contract, concluded on 29 October 1298, Palaeologus sold for £3,000, Genoese currency, 650 cantars of alum, which he had in Aigues-Mortes ready to be shipped to Bruges in his own galley. The seller, however, retained the option to repurchase this shipment in Bruges for 3,360 *li. tur.*, which he did not need to disburse but could keep as a loan until the galley got back to Genoa, by offering as a guarantee the return cargo bought with the proceeds from the alum. The sea risk was assumed by the lenders who, upon safe arrival of the galley in Genoa, were entitled to 13s. 5d. Genoese for every sou tournois or 3,780 Genoese pounds. However, a modifying clause limited the duration of the contract to 1 November 1299, and released the lenders from any further commitments after this date. In other words, the debt was due not later than 1 November 1299, even if the galley were still under sail. To put the matter more succinctly, Palaeologus borrowed 3,000 Genoese pounds and promised to repay £3,780 within a year, or sooner, upon the safe return of his galley from a round trip to Bruges. The charges on the loan were, consequently, 26%, which not only represent interest, but include a premium for risk. If this figure is at all representative, the rate of interest must have dropped considerably by the end of the thirteenth century.

This agreement is a curious mixture of two different contracts. Why did Palaeologus Zaccaria, in order to raise money, resort first to a fictitious sale and then to a *cambium maritimum*? It looks as if he sought to protect himself not only against the perils of the sea but also against a drop in the price of alum. The clumsiness of the methods used to achieve this purpose is due in part to the rigidity of the formulas used by the notaries and in part to the necessity of circumventing the usury prohibition

[1] Cf. *Camb. Econ. Hist.* II, 336.

by adopting a legal form acceptable to the theologians. The medieval mind was legalistic, and the Doctors—theologians as well as canonists and civilians—accorded an exaggerated importance to the legal mould in which contracts were cast.

In order to divide risks—always the same problem—the ownership of ships was commonly divided into shares called *partes* or *loca navis* in Genoa and *carati* or *sortes* in Venice. It even happened that vessels were owned by one group and operated by another. Membership in one, however, was compatible with membership in the other. There has been a great deal of discussion about the meaning of the expression *loca navis*, but it seems that it referred to shares in a company operating rather than owning a ship. According to a plausible hypothesis, a *locus* represented a certain capacity and, hence, the number of *loca* bore some relation to the tonnage of a vessel and the size of its crew. Documentary evidence shows that, in certain cases at least, there were as many shares as there were mariners. Apparently, ships could be operated jointly by the entire group of owners or of charterers, or separately by each of the shareholders. In the first case, a manager acting for the whole group would be in charge of hiring a crew and of finding a cargo and would be responsible for operating the ship in the common interest of all concerned. In the latter case, each owner of a share or *locus* had to serve as a mariner himself or else hire someone at his own expense to take his place. On the other hand, he could dispose freely of his allotment of cargo space, either by loading it himself or by letting it to a merchant. Of course, some common expenses were unavoidable. For one thing, the operators had to select a master to command the ship and had to pay his wages from the common purse. Neither statutes nor notarial contracts throw much light on the inner structure of medieval shipping. Moreover, historians up to now have been more interested in legal than in business procedure. If only some ship's accounts were available, their study would quickly solve all the puzzling problems which have stirred up so much discussion.

At any rate, the system of *loca* or shares, so pervasive in Mediterranean shipping, made it possible to experiment with the management of joint business ventures, at first on a small, and later on a larger, scale. This experimentation has an important bearing on future economic development. Did not the first joint stock companies arise in overseas trade? It is true that they were set up by the Dutch and the English, but their promoters were certainly familiar with Italian precedents in the financing and management of collective colonial enterprises, such as the *maone* of Chios and Ceuta. Was not a Genoese Pallavicini among the shareholders of the Virginia Company; and did not Thomas Mun reside for many years in Leghorn and Pisa before he returned to London and became one of the first directors of the East India Company? Moreover, let us not overlook the fact that, even in the East India trade, a permanent company was not created at the beginning. The first voyages were each separate ventures, much like the temporary partnerships in the pioneering days of Genoese and Venetian shipping.

2

It is clear that in medieval times 'the major direction of a voyage was in the hands of the merchants, not of the shipowners, one of the characteristic differences between medieval and modern shipping'.[1] Contracts usually provided that the merchants taking passage on a certain vessel had the right to appoint a committee to inspect the ship before sailing and report on its seaworthiness and the state of its equipment. During the trip, they were lodged in the best quarters: the stern cabin under the captain's. As pilgrims usually were noisy and troublesome, none could be embarked without the merchants' consent. According to the sea laws, the master also had to take a vote among the merchants on board in order to change itinerary or to decide upon ports of call. Their agreement was even required when the safety of the ship made it necessary to jettison some of the cargo, although the captain could override their opposition in case of extreme peril, after consulting his mate and three mariners.

Next to the captain, the scribe was the most important member of the crew. By the thirteenth century, the management of a galley or a large merchant vessel required so much paper work and book-keeping that regulations in Barcelona and Venice prescribed the employment of two scribes, but in Genoa one was regarded as sufficient. The scribe was sworn to his office and his records had the same value as notarial deeds. One of his main duties was to keep the ship's cartulary in which the cargo aboard was listed, item by item, as in the modern manifest. The merchants were even required to declare to him the money which they carried in their belts or concealed in their bales. The scribe also tallied and recorded the goods loaded or unloaded, kept the roll of the crew, computed freight charges: in short, he did all the clerical work and was an indispensable business auxiliary.

Pirates and corsairs being a perennial menace, medieval vessels sought protection by navigating in convoy or in company. The Italian republics tried to increase security along the sea lanes by concluding treaties of amity and commerce with the powers bordering on the Mediterranean. This was only the first step. Usually, it was accompanied or followed by attempts to secure trading privileges, if possible on more favourable terms than those granted to rival cities. In the Middle Ages, protectionism

[1] E. H. Byrne, *Genoese Shipping in the Twelfth and Thirteenth Centuries* (Cambridge, Mass., 1930), 36.

was not yet born; the aim of commercial policy was to get preferential treatment and to strive for control of the carrying trade.

With this purpose in mind, the Italian maritime cities, especially Genoa, Pisa and Venice, put their sea-power at the disposal of the crusaders; in exchange for this aid, they secured valuable trading privileges and obtained permission to establish 'colonies' in the ports of Palestine and Syria. In some cases, the grants included only a few houses or a street (*ruga*), but sometimes they extended to an entire quarter of a town. Like the concessions in the Orient and the capitulations in the Ottoman Empire of more recent days, the Italian colonies in the Levant enjoyed extraterritorial rights. They were administered by officials sent by the mother city, called at first viscounts and later consuls, whose functions were, of course, much more extensive than those of consular officers today. The medieval colonial consuls were invested with both administrative and judicial powers and had the right to decide any disputes involving only their own countrymen. In certain cases, they even had criminal jurisdiction and authority over life and limb. As a rule, the agreements entrusted the consuls with the custody of any property left by deceased nationals. Grants usually allowed a colony the right to have landing place, mill, bakery, warehouse, baths and church of its own. Besides a floating population of travelling merchants, the Italian colonies had a core of permanent residents made up of officials, artisans, brokers, shopkeepers, and local tradesmen. Not all the settlers were Latins: the security enjoyed in the foreign concessions also attracted Levantine Jews, Greeks and Syrians.

In Moslem lands, for example in Tunis or Alexandria, conditions were different and less favourable. The concession usually reduced itself to a compound or walled enclosure, called *fondaco* in Italian and *funduk* in Arabic. It ordinarily contained lodging quarters, a warehouse, a bake-oven, a bath-house, a chapel, and a graveyard. The gates were closed each evening, and residents were locked in for the night. These precautions were no doubt vexatious but they afforded some protection in a hostile environment where religious fanaticism could touch off a riot at any time. In Tunis, customs duties were carefully regulated by treaty. Dealings with native merchants could take place either within or without the customs-house. In the first case, the administrators of the customs assumed all responsibility for the execution of the deal. In Alexandria, conditions were much the same. Genoese, Pisans, Venetians, Catalans, Provençals, French and Ragusans had separate establishments. As in Tunis, the customs officers guaranteed payment for any sale concluded through a dragoman or licensed broker. The treaties generally contained detailed provisions concerning the rates of import duties and also stipulated that the consul could present any grievances directly to the sultan, either in writing or by word of mouth. To leave nothing to chance, it was even agreed that the western consuls in Alexandria should be granted ten audiences a year. The detailed provisions of the treaties definitely give the impression that business relations were carefully regulated in order to forestall as far as possible any causes of conflict or friction that might enrage the despotic Egyptian sultans and have dire consequences for any westerners on whom they could lay their hands.

In the early Middle Ages, Amalfi and Venice were subject, at least nominally, to the Greek emperor and, hence, the merchants hailing from these two Italian ports needed no special privileges to ply their trade in Constantinople or in any part of the Byzantine Empire. This advantage was lost after Venice, around 950, had gained its independence and after Amalfi, in 1076, had been conquered by Robert Guiscard, the Norman king of Sicily. However, this ruler's invasion of Albania caused the Greek emperor, Alexius Comnenus, to seek the support of the Venetians and to issue in their favour the Golden Bull of 1082, by which they were granted complete exemption from customs duties, or κομμέρκιον, and permission to have their own quarter and landing steps in the capital. The grant of 1082 was renewed in 1147 and extended to the islands of Crete and Cyprus. The Pisans did not receive similar privileges until 1111, and the Genoese until 1155; but the concessions which they wrung from the Greek emperors were less favourable than those granted to the Venetians and involved only a reduction of duties from 10 to 4% instead of complete exemption. In any case, the excessive privileges granted to the Latins, especially the Venetians, put them in a strong competitive position and enabled them to capture the Greek carrying trade and to exploit economically the Byzantine Empire.[1] Their overbearing attitude and monopolistic practices were bound to create resentment among the Greeks and to invite a hostile reaction.

The emperors, too, realized the dangers resulting from economic infiltration and alien political interference. After 1147, Manuel Comnenus gradually changed from an open-door policy to one of xenophobia. To begin with, he issued a decree which required all permanent Venetian residents to take an oath of allegiance and to become denizens, or βουργέσιοι, obviously a term borrowed from the occidental languages. On 12 March 1171, the emperor ordered the arrest of all the Venetians in Constantinople; many were killed in the fray and only those escaped who took to the ship of their countryman Romano Mairano, putting out to sea and outsailing a Greek fleet launched in pursuit. Although peace was restored in 1175, this incident started a chain of events which culminated in the Fourth Crusade and the establishment of the Latin Empire (1204), a Venetian protectorate. It ended in 1261, but the Greek restoration resulted only in replacing the Venetians by the Genoese, who now

---

[1] See *Camb. Econ. Hist.* II, 99, 311.

also obtained complete exemption from customs duties. Soon the Greek emperors adopted the policy of pitting these two rivals against each other. To no avail: it did not prevent them from reaching a *modus vivendi* at the expense of the Greeks and from dividing the Aegean into spheres of influence. The Venetians kept Candia and Negropont, which they had possessed since 1204; but the Genoese Manuele and Benedetto Zaccaria managed, in 1264, to acquire in fee the alum mines of Phocea and, in 1304, to take possession of Chios. In 1329 the Greeks regained control of this island, but not for long. They lost it again in 1346, and this time irretrievably, to a fleet sent out by Genoa to reconquer its outposts in the Aegean. With all its major resources and its strategic points in foreign hands, the Greek Empire was undoubtedly weakened to the extent that it was unable to resist the Turkish onslaught. It is not surprising that Byzantium succumbed; rather it is a wonder that it lasted so long.

At first, all the Latin quarters in Constantinople were located in the city itself along the shores of the Golden Horn, each with its own landing steps. It was only in 1267 that Michael Palaeologus thought it advisable to transfer the seat of the Genoese colony to Pera, or Galata, on the other side of the Golden Horn. For one thing, this transfer eliminated the possibility of riotous fights between Latins from neighbouring quarters. Second, it put an end to the uncomfortable presence of a large body of foreigners within the walls and in the immediate vicinity of the imperial palace.

After 1267, the Genoese colony was headed by an official called *podestà*; the Venetian, by a *bailus*; and the Pisan, by a consul. These officials were not elected by the local residents, but appointed by the home governments. Like the consuls in Syria and Palestine, they were at the same time governors, judges and diplomatic agents. It was their duty to iron out any difficulties that might arise between their nationals and the Greek authorities. Their powers, however, did not extend to treaty making, and any important negotiations were conducted by special diplomatic missions. The Genoese *podestà* held court in Pera and was assisted in his duties by a staff of clerks, sergeants and notaries. According to the regulation of 1304, he was bound in certain cases to consult either a large council of twenty-four or a small council of six. It is even said that he could not dismiss a dragoman without their approval. One of the most important branches of the administration was the *officium mercantiae*, or commercial bureau, which had the difficult task of co-operating with the Greek customs in the detection of frauds. The purpose was to prevent goods from being falsely entered as Genoese property in order to pass them duty free. Merchants who defrauded the customs in this way exposed themselves to severe penalties inflicted by both the Greek and the Genoese authorities. The jurisdiction of the *podestà* in Pera extended beyond the local colony to all the Genoese establishments in the Byzantine Empire, and even to those in Trebizond and the Crimea. Save that the officials bore different titles, the colonial organization of the Venetians and the Pisans was much the same as that of the Genoese.

Perhaps a word needs to be said about the Genoese colonies of Caffa in the Crimea and Tana at the mouth of the Don. They were the great slave markets of the Middle Ages, a trade in which the Christian merchants played a conspicuous part. The Genoese colony of Caffa was not founded until 1266, or thereabouts, after the treaty of Nymphaeum (1261) had given the Genoese free access to the Bosphorus and the Black Sea. The organization was much the same as that of the other colonies. In the regions around the Black Sea, conditions were still primitive and coin was only in the process of being introduced. Even in Tana, ingots of silver, called *sommi*, were the principal means of payment, and farther east trade was still based on the barter of cloth and linen against fish, caviare or slaves.

Books on economic history written fifty years ago were concerned only with commercial treaties, trade privileges and colonial establishments, but paid little or no attention to business organization itself. This is a one-sided approach. However, it should not be overlooked that these agreements and institutions provided a setting which made possible the orderly conduct of business and afforded some protection against molestation, seizure or arrest. It is not surprising that the Italian maritime cities considered any serious violation of the existing treaties as a *casus belli* and did not hesitate to use force if they failed to obtain prompt redress. The role of the colonies is important in yet another respect: they were usually outposts where the Italians, or at least the merchants of southern Europe, came into contact with another world from which they were debarred by religious, political, linguistic and other obstacles. Thus, Alexandria, for example, was the place where they met the Arabs who brought spices all the way from India. The settlements in Syria performed the same function. Tunis was the terminal of the caravans which brought the gold from mysterious Palola across the Sahara. As for Caffa and Tana, they were the two points where the Italians traded with the Russians and bought Chinese silk from Mongolian camel-drivers. Although Pegolotti asserts that the road to China across the endless steppes of Asia was perfectly safe by day and by night, the number of those who took him at his word must have been exceedingly small, and most Italians undoubtedly preferred to transact their business in Caffa or Tana rather than to imitate Marco Polo and run undue risks. In their colonies the Italian merchants found all they needed in order to deal with strangers: resident friends to give them advice about local customs, interpreters and brokers to make contacts, notaries to draft deeds and trustworthy judges to settle disputes. Why should they have ventured outside? Clearly it was preferable not to take any chances and to deal in an organized market, and that is exactly what most of them did.

Unlike the other colonies or establishments, Constantinople was not an outpost on the fringe of the Mediterranean basin, but a trading and distribution centre located at the most strategic point of the Greek Empire. Instead of being just a port of call, it was a base of operations for many Italian travelling merchants of the twelfth and thirteenth centuries. Since the Greek carrying trade had fallen under their control, they had their headquarters, not in Italy, but in Constantinople, and from there they organized trips either inland (into the Balkans or Asia Minor) or overseas (to the Black Sea, the islands in the Aegean or even the northern coast of Africa).

An excellent example is furnished by the career of Romano Mairano, on whose ship, as we have seen, a number of Venetians made good their escape when their colony, in 1171, was suddenly assaulted by the Greeks. From 1155 to 1169, Mairano seems to have resided continuously in Constantinople, where he owned a house and from where at first he made short trips to Smyrna and to the ports of Macedonia and Thessaly. As these ventures were apparently successful, Mairano used his profits to develop the scope of his business and, after 1162, to extend his travels to Acre and Alexandria. The records show that, in 1167, he organized a voyage from Constantinople to Citro (near Salonika) and Alexandria with two ships of his own, sailing one himself as *nauclerius* or master and entrusting the command of the other to a Venetian, Bartolomeo Zulian. This venture was financed in part by eight sea loans amounting to nearly 900 perpers (July 1167). Judging by their names, the lenders, with one exception, were Italians rather than Greeks. It also appears from the records that at least four of them, who had advanced a total of 488 perpers, made the same voyage and were repaid principal and interest (*caput et prode*) upon arrival in Alexandria (November 1167). The others did not receive their due until February and March 1168, after successful completion of the round trip.

Apparently, Mairano was a merchant as well as a shipowner and had an interest in the cargo loaded on his two ships. While in Alexandria, he entered into a *collegantia* contract with one Domenico Giacobbe, according to which he invested two *sortes*, worth 18 perpers and 7 albos, of the ship commanded by Bartolomeo Zulian, and his partner only one *sors*, worth half this amount or 9 perpers and 3·5 albos. Domenico Giacobbe was apparently travelling on the same ship, since he was expected to trade with these three *sortes* in Almiro (near Volo, Thessaly) and to render accounts to Mairano fifteen days after its arrival in Constantinople. As usual, profits were to be divided equally between the two partners, but losses were to be shared proportionately to investment. From the context it appears that the word *sors* refers to cargo or, more precisely, to the cargo stowed in a definite amount of space. According to the surviving records, Romano Mairano was partial to the sea loan, but he did not resort exclusively to this method of finance. Besides the *collegantia*, he also used the *cambium maritimum*. In February 1167, for instance, he borrowed 100 Byzantine perpers in Constantinople and promised to repay 134 Saracen perpers at Acre.

In 1169, after several years of absence, Romano Mairano returned to Venice and took advantage of this opportunity to conclude with the patriarch of Grado an agreement by which he was to farm all the patriarch's revenues in Constantinople for an annuity of £500, Veronese currency. The contract was to last six years, but was voided after a few months, since the Venetians, on 12 March 1171, were either massacred or driven from Constantinople. As we have seen, Mairano managed to escape with his ship and even to save the lives of many of his countrymen. Nevertheless, he lost heavily and it took him years to recover from this blow, if he ever did.

Back in Venice, Mairano did not lose heart, for he was soon busy organizing new ventures. In 1173, he went on his own ship to Alexandria with a cargo of timber and brought back pepper and alum. At that time, his principal financial backer was the son of the Venetian doge. In 1177, Mairano undertook the organization of a trip from Venice to Alexandria and thence to Bougie and Ceuta, but this venture proved a failure and was not repeated. From 1179 onward, he resumed his voyages to Syria, Palestine and Egypt. In 1184, he built a new ship. During this period, he raised needed capital by means of a new type of contract which involved an advance of funds in Venice and the delivery of so many cantars of alum or centers of pepper upon termination of a voyage to the Levant. As usual, the goods travelled at the risk of the buyer. Although the Venetians, after the events of 1171, had re-established commercial relations with the Byzantine Empire, Mairano did not reappear in Constantinople until 1189 or 1190. Not until then do we find several contracts which show him in Tyre (Syria) taking up money on the eve of a trip to Abydos (Dardanelles) and Constantinople. Although by now sixty years old, he was still commanding his own ship, but he was about to retire from active leadership. After 1192, he apparently remained ashore and placed his son Giovanni in command of his ventures. In May 1200 this son was still managing his father's business affairs, since a contract of this date mentions him as settling the accounts of a *collegantia* relating to a trip from Venice to Alexandria.

Romano Mairano was still alive in November 1201, but he seems to have been living in straitened circumstances, since a cousin had to lend him £50, Venetian currency, *pro amore*, without interest. Did his luck

F

run out at last? Did one of his ventures end in a disaster involving his son? In any case, Romano Mairano must have died soon after 1201, without heirs other than a daughter who was a nun. Her convent inherited all of his property, including a bundle of business papers which tell the story of his career.

3

The twelfth and thirteenth centuries witnessed not only a great expansion of trade and industry, but also saw the development of banking. It seems likely from a number of references that this development had its roots in Byzantine and even in Roman and Greek precedents. The trouble is that the incidental mentions give little indication as to the nature of the banking business to which they refer. According to the Book of the Prefect, which dates from the tenth century, bankers of Constantinople were certainly engaged in money-changing; unfortunately, the text alludes only vaguely to their other activities.

The first documents to lift the veil are the Genoese notarial records of the twelfth century. According to this source, the designation *bancherius* was reserved exclusively for money-changers—undoubtedly because they conducted their business seated behind a table (*tabula*) or bank (*bancum*). By 1200—as the Genoese notaries reveal—these so-called bankers no longer confined themselves to money-changing, but had already invaded the field of banking proper. They are shown forming partnerships, accepting time and demand deposits, extending credit to customers and even participating directly in business ventures beyond the seas. The most useful details, however, are given in a series of sworn statements collected in 1200 by the Genoese notary, Guglielmo Cassinese, in connection with a lawsuit. They prove first of all that it was common among merchants to have bank accounts and to make payments by book transfer rather than in specie. Not infrequently, the bankers granted credit to customers by allowing them to overdraw their accounts. Finally, arrangements between banks made it possible to transfer funds even when the debtor and the creditor had accounts with different money-changers. The exact procedure followed in such settlements is not clear from the records. At any rate, cheques were not in use, but transfer orders were given by word of mouth and written down by the banker under the dictation of the customer, so to speak. The Bank of Venice remained faithful to this way of doing business until its dissolution on the eve of the nineteenth century, and its regulations strictly forbade book-keepers from entering any transfers in their journals unless the order came from the lips of the depositor or his lawful attorney.

The notarial records show that the Genoese money-changers, or bankers, occasionally made advances against promises payable abroad, but this type of activity remained the exception rather than the rule. During the thirteenth century, not only in Genoa, but also in Marseilles, exchange dealings with the fairs of Champagne were mainly in the hands of Sienese and Placentine mercantile companies. In these transactions they made use of an instrument, called *instrumentum ex causa cambii*, by which a borrower having received an advance in local currency promised repayment in another currency and in another place. By definition, such a *cambium* contract necessarily involved a credit and an exchange transaction. The *instrumentum ex causa cambii* is undoubtedly the prototype of the bill of exchange which, as the name indicates, served originally to implement a *cambium* contract. According to circumstances, the mercantile and banking companies were at one time takers, or sellers of foreign exchange, and at another, deliverers, or buyers who made advances on the spot in order to acquire balances abroad.

The ordinary *cambium* contract differed from the *cambium maritimum* in that repayment of the debt was unconditional (*salvos in terra*) and ceased to depend upon the safe arrival of a vessel or the major part of its cargo. Among many others, a good example of a *cambium* is furnished by a contract, dated 26 March 1253, according to which Roffredo Bramanzoni, the Genoese representative of the Sienese Bonsignori firm, recognizes that a Flemish merchant from Dixmude has given him £390 in Genoese currency, and binds himself and his partners to furnish in London 100 marks of 13s. 4d. sterling each not later than fifteen days after Easter, or on 5 May 1253. According to these figures, the pound sterling was rated at £5 17s. 0d., Genoese currency. Since the Bonsignori company was a powerful banking-house, it is likely that the main purpose of the contract was to transfer funds from Genoa to London or perhaps from Genoa to Flanders by way of London. In any case, this is an instance of a banking-house selling what may be considered the equivalent of a draft on its branch in London.

Prior to 1200, we already meet in the Genoese notarial records unquestionable examples of dry exchange, a spurious exchange contract designed to conceal a loan at interest. Thus, in a contract dated 9 April 1188, two Frenchmen acknowledged having received from the banker Beltrame Bertaldo an unspecified sum of Genoese currency and promised to pay £4 in French currency at the forthcoming May fair of Provins, with the proviso that if the debt were not repaid in Champagne it would be due in Genoa upon the return of the merchants who went in caravan to the said fair.[1] In the latter case, the four pounds in deniers of Provins were to be converted into Genoese currency at the rate of 16d.

[1] An English translation of this contract is available in Robert S. Lopez and Irving W. Raymond (eds), *Medieval Trade in the Mediterranean World* (Records of Civilization Series, No. 52, New York: Columbia University Press, 1955), 166.

Genoese per sou. In other words, the amount due would be £5 6s. 8d. Genoese. It may be taken for granted that, from the outset, the contracting parties had every intention of taking advantage of the proviso and of repaying the loan in Genoa instead of in Champagne. Besides, speculative risks were completely eliminated by determining in advance the rate of exchange, so that the contract reduces itself to a straight loan calling for the final payment of £5 6s. 8d. Genoese.

During the thirteenth century, the fairs of Champagne were the great international money market and clearing centre as well as the great mart for commodities of all kinds. Exchange-rates were always quoted on the basis of one sou or twelve deniers of Provins (which were the same as the deniers tournois) and in a variable amount of foreign currency. This method of quotation was used both at the fairs and in Genoa or any other Italian centre in regular relations with the Champagne fairs, just as today the exchange is quoted both in London and on the continent on the basis of the pound sterling. A rise of the rate was favourable to the fairs and unfavourable to the other places, and the opposite applied to a falling exchange. In accordance with medieval practice, interest, as a rule, was included in the price of foreign currency.

In comparison with the enormous quantity of notarial records still extant in Genoa, the source material relating to the other Mediterranean ports is much less abundant. In Venice, only a few hundred notarial contracts seem to have escaped destruction, although the oldest of them go farther back than those of Genoa. For Marseilles, the surviving records are not numerous; they include the register of the notary Giraud Amalric (1248) and a series of contracts relating to two prominent merchants, Etienne Manduel and his son Jean, executed in 1264 for plotting against the count of Provence. Other notarial contracts are extant for Amalfi, Barcelona, Caffa, Lucca, Palermo, Pera, Pisa, Ragusa and Zara. The Pisan archives, one of the most important, remain largely unexplored, and the same applies to Barcelona. At any rate, the available source material shows plainly that business practices were nearly the same throughout the Mediterranean area.

Despite the fact that merchants had ceased long ago to be illiterate, the notary played a cardinal role; he was requested not only to draw up deeds and testaments, but also to prepare all types of business contracts. His busiest days were on the approach of sailing dates. Thus the Marseilles notary Giraud Amalric drafted no less than fifty-seven contracts on a single day, 30 March 1248. Fifty of them were *commenda* agreements: thirty relating to the vessel *Saint-Esprit*, bound for Syria, and eleven to the *Saint-Gilles*, sailing for Sicily. There were also two *societas* contracts, both in connection with the impending departure of the *Saint-Esprit*. The next day, 31 March, Amalric was a little less rushed, but he still enacted forty contracts, including seventeen *commendae* for the *Saint-Esprit*, which actually weighed anchor the next day, and ten for the *Saint-Gilles*, which also was expected to leave port at any time.

Although notarial fees were low, it was inconvenient and time-consuming to approach a notary for every business transaction of any importance. This inconvenience was felt more and more as the volume of business grew, and as the *ius mercatorum* gradually recognized the validity of informal instruments. Yet it is not easy to change accepted ways of doing business, and the Mediterranean seaports, in particular, were conservative in their methods. It was only gradually that the notary was dispensed with save when his services were absolutely required to give legal validity to a contract, as with powers of attorney or protests of bills of exchange. In Genoa, even as late as the fifteenth century, insurance contracts continued to require the intervention of a notary, although it was no longer the custom in Pisa and Florence, where the brokers made out insurance policies and circulated them among prospective underwriters until they had collected enough subscriptions to cover the risk. Genoa, too, was much slower than Florence in replacing the notarial *instrumentum ex causa cambii* by the informal bill of exchange.

Conditions in the twelfth and thirteenth centuries were such that the merchant usually accompanied his own goods, whether on sea or on land. In this respect, practice began to change around 1250. Nevertheless, as late as 1287, a contract states explicitly that a merchant of Palermo, who has received a *commenda* invested in a cargo of salt pork, expects to sell it in Genoa and, for this purpose, intends to go there in person (*personaliter*) and to travel on the same ship as the goods entrusted to his care. In the case of sea loans, it is by no means exceptional for the borrower to declare that he is ready to go (*paratus est ire*) on a certain trip and to repay the loan if the ship carrying him and his goods safely reaches port.

As a rule, each voyage was considered as a separate venture. Although terminal partnerships extending over several years were not unknown, such agreements were rare in overseas trade, but more frequent in local retailing and manufacturing. Sometimes one of the partners supplied all the capital and the other only his labour, as in the case of a partnership, concluded in Genoa on 6 July 1156, between an entrepreneur named Bernardo Porcello and a capitalist named Pevere Lanfranco, who invested 50 Genoese pounds and, in addition, put at the other's disposal a place to carry on the business. According to the provisions of the contract, the agreement was to last five years and profits were to be divided in the proportion of one-third to the managing and two-thirds to the investing partner. Unfortunately, the contract does not disclose the nature of the business.

Similar provisions are also found in a Venetian partnership contract of

1160. According to its provisions, an investor, Pietro Memo, went into partnership with Enrico Serzi and entrusted him with £300, Veronese currency, to start a business. It was understood that profits would be divided equally and that the managing partner would use the investor's own premises as his base of operations and not do business outside Venice except that he was allowed to visit the regional fairs of Ferrara.

Despite the prevalence of the *commenda* and the *societas maris*, terminal partnerships also occurred in foreign trade and perhaps have been unduly neglected by historians. There are quite a few examples among the surviving Venetian contracts of the twelfth century. In one case, the partnership was composed of an uncle and his nephew, the first residing in Constantinople and the second in Thebes (Greece). They were to trade together by shipping goods to each other. All profits were to be shared equally and the partnership was extensible from year to year by way of tacit agreement. Apparently, it had lasted for some time until it was terminated abruptly in 1171 by the expulsion of the Venetians from Constantinople and the Byzantine Empire. Because of the losses suffered in this catastrophe, a final settlement between the two partners was still pending in 1179.

After 1300, terminal partnerships became more and more common, even in the seaports. This does not mean that temporary arrangements disappeared entirely. Since they fitted in so well with the venturesome character of medieval trade, they continued to prosper, but within a framework of more permanent and steady relationships.

III. *Italian Hegemony in the Fourteenth and Fifteenth Centuries*

In establishing continuous business connections, the inland cities (Piacenza, Lucca, Siena and, later, Florence) rather than the coastal cities (Genoa, Pisa and Venice) took the lead. This development started early in the thirteenth century, when the Placentine and Sienese companies, instead of having roving representatives, began to maintain more or less permanent factors in Genoa, Marseilles, Bruges, Paris and even in distant England. Thus Roffredo Bramanzoni, already mentioned in connection with the sale of a draft on London, seems to have resided in Genoa around 1250 as the agent of the powerful Bonsignori company, in which he was also one of the partners. Whenever he assumes any obligation, he carefully states that he contracts in his own name and in those of his partners (*nomine meo et sociorum meorum*). The company was already emerging as a separate legal entity. But the Sienese company of the Bonsignori was not the only one to have resident representatives; the Placentine bankers were following the same policy and the notarial records reveal that their agents dealt actively in exchange with the fairs of Champagne. What applies to Genoa applies also to Marseilles: there, too, the local representatives of the Placentine banking companies, especially one Otto Anguissola, were the main exchange dealers. Of course, they did not confine their activity to exchange business but also controlled the importation of cloth from Champagne and even invested in overseas ventures. As earlier, diversification remained the rule. The decline of the travelling trade did not lead to greater specialization: on the contrary, the new Italian companies made it their policy to branch out in order to spread risks over a larger area.

In England, the presence of Italians representing banking-houses is recorded as early as 1220. Although law and custom did not allow alien merchants to dwell in the realm, the Sienese and the Florentines secured from Henry III permission to stay for three years at a time. Matthew Paris in his Chronicle (1235–59) is shocked by the thought that they abide in London like respectable citizens. Being 'Cahorsins' and manifest usurers, they ought to be expelled, but far from it, they enjoy instead the protection of the Court of Rome and call themselves the Pope's exchangers. Matthew Paris gives 1229 as the date of their first appearance, although the evidence shows that from 1224 onward safe-conducts and export licences were issued to Florentines. Whatever the exact date, it is certain that, prior to 1250, the Italians had gained a firm foothold in England.

In Flanders, they did not settle until close to 1300, or even later. As late as 1322, a privilege granted to the Venetians gave them only forty days to sell their wares, which suggests that they did not yet have permanent establishments. It is true that the Venetians, like the Genoese, were conservative and did not readily adopt the new forms of business organization introduced by the Tuscans and the Lombards. In any case, later privileges no longer put any restriction on residence. Moreover, other records show that the Italians, unlike the Hansards, did not constantly come and go, but sometimes stayed in Bruges for several consecutive years. In the fifteenth century, Tommaso Portinari, the local manager of the Medici bank, lived in Flanders for more than four decades almost without interruption, save for occasional trips to Italy.

By the close of the thirteenth century, the Italian mercantile and banking companies, instead of sending special delegates to each of the Champagne fairs, were opening branch offices in nearby Paris. In 1292, the Parisian roll of the *taille* lists more than twenty companies, including the Bonsignori and the Salimbene of Siena; the Burrini, the Guadagnabene and the Scotti of Piacenza; the Francesi, the Scali and the Frescobaldi of Florence; the Ammannati of Pistoia, and a dozen firms of lesser importance. Moreover, the Italians were among the most heavily taxed. The highest quota of all was paid by Gandolfo degli Arcelli (Gandoufle d'Arcelles), representing the Burrini company of Piacenza, who may very likely have been the richest man in Paris in the time of Philip the Fair. The Lombards as a group paid more than 10% of the total tax, although they were only a little more than 1% of the total number of taxpayers. Consequently, their average quota was ten times as high as that of the native burgesses of Paris. Among the latter, only a handful of rich money-changers and *drapiers*, or clothiers, paid a larger assessment than the smaller Italian companies.

As for Gandolfo degli Arcelli, there is no doubt that he resided habitually in Paris where he died in 1300 and was buried in the church of St Merri. Apparently he was, or became, the principal partner of the Burrini company of Piacenza. Its activity embraced not only trade and exchange, but also money-lending to persons in all stations of life from feudal lords and prelates to a poor shepherd. True to form, Gandolfo provided in his will for the restitution of his usurious gains. Endowed with unusual business ability, he proved to be irreplaceable, and his company declined rapidly after his death.

The fact that by 1300 the Italian mercantile and banking companies maintained branch offices in Paris, Bruges and London is symptomatic of a new trend which was bound to spell the doom of the caravan trade revolving around the fairs of Champagne. Because of the nearness of Paris, fairs could easily be visited by the partners or factors residing in the French capital, and there was no longer any need to send someone with the regular caravans. Moreover, now that the roads were better policed, it ceased to be necessary for the merchants or their servants to accompany their own goods, which could henceforth be entrusted to companies of *vetturali*, or wagoners, as they were called, even if they did not use wagons but actually drove trains of pack animals. About their role in medieval trade little is known, but occasional glimpses in stray documents leave no doubt about its importance.

An inter-local federation of Tuscan *vetturali* is already mentioned in a Pisan document of 1219. There is also a contract of 1200 between a carrier and several Placentine merchants concerning the safe transportation of persons and goods from Genoa to Bobbio, a small town on the route to Piacenza. These documents show that *vetturali* were operating between Italian cities, but not that they were engaged in the long-distance or transalpine carriage of goods. In this connection, they do not appear in the notarial records of Genoa and Marseilles until 1250 or thereabouts. This was not a very recent development, however, since their services were already used extensively by Italian and other merchants.

In Marseilles, most of the wagoners hailed from Dauphiné and carried goods by pack animals or carts to and from the fairs of Champagne. In a

typical contract, dated 12 July 1248, a wagoner (*vetturarius*) acknow-
ledges that he has received two bales of pepper from Rinaldo Bracciaforte and Raniero Malano, merchants of Piacenza, and undertakes to deliver them to partners in Troyes for the price of £7, currency of Vienne.
It is further agreed that the said bales will be carried thither by pack animals (and not on carts) and that the wagoner will take good care of the
goods as carriers are wont to do for merchants (*et omnia vobis attendere et
complere que vetturarii tenentur mercatoribus attendere et complere*). In another
contract of the same year, a wagoner promises not to untie and open any
bales save in an emergency. Similar provisions are found in the Genoese
contracts. Sometimes it was explicitly stipulated whether the goods were
to be sent to Champagne by way of Provence or through the valley of
Maurienne (*per caminum seu stratam Moriene*), that is, over the Mont Cenis
pass. Carriers were also operating trains of pack mules between Genoa
and Rome and between Genoa and Florence. Among their best customers were the Placentine and Sienese merchant-bankers. One of them,
Giovanni Pagano, called in a notary, the Placentine consul and several
merchants to witness the fact that two bales of cloth brought by carrier
from France did not contain the requisite number of pieces. These details, however, are adduced only as evidence. The important point to
stress here is that the use of wagoners and carriers relieved the merchants
from the need of organizing transport. So they were free to turn their
attention to other tasks.

There is still another factor which favoured the rise of the Italian companies with branches abroad: the steady progress in business management. This is often overlooked, but is not therefore of lesser importance.
Merchants had to learn how to do business by correspondence rather
than by personal contact. As paper work increased, it tied them more and
more to the counting-house. This development is very difficult to trace,
but business letters give some indication. A few—very few—from the
end of the thirteenth century have survived. They are models of business-
like procedure, matter-of-fact and to the point, without any of the verbi-
age so characteristic of the notarial contracts. Take, for example, the
letter written on 24 March 1291, by the Cerchi company in Florence to
their agents in England. After the customary greetings, the principals in
Florence mention the letters received from London, then deal with shipments of wool and cloth, and go on to discuss the prospects of an abundant spring clip in England and Scotland. After that comes a long paragraph concerning the promotion of a suit or petition which the Cister-
cian monastery of Kirkstead (Lincolnshire) wanted to introduce in the
Court of Rome. The letter ends by giving instructions regarding the payment of a draft of £1 4s. 8d. sterling and by quoting the rates of exchange
for the forthcoming fairs of Bar-sur-Aube and Provins. The same pattern,

more or less, was followed in commercial correspondence throughout the fourteenth and fifteenth centuries.

Another clue to the advance in business management is furnished by the high level of technical efficiency achieved in book-keeping. Surviving fragments of account-books show that, by 1300, considerable progress had been made in agency accounting. Merchants kept detailed records not only of amounts owing and owed, but also of cash transactions and operating results. Judging from the extant fragments, the records of the great mercantile and banking companies were certainly adequate to permit an orderly conduct of business.

By eliminating a good deal of wasteful travelling, the new organization introduced by the Placentine and Tuscan companies was certainly more efficient than the old. It permitted the merchant to conduct his business from his desk without leaving the counting-house. Representation in foreign parts was provided by partners, factors (employees) or simple correspondents. This novel method of doing business gave rise to a new type of merchant whom Professor N. S. B. Gras has called 'the sedentary merchant'; and it was especially well adapted to the needs of overland trade as population in western Europe grew, markets expanded and security increased. No wonder that the Placentine and Sienese companies reaped great benefits from their innovation; they well-nigh dominated the trade across the Alps—at least the Genoese records of the thirteenth century definitely give this impression. Superior business organization may well explain why a city like Siena, with an unfavourable geographic location, succeeded for more than half a century in playing a major role as a commercial and banking centre.

The change from the old to the new system was certainly very gradual. In the overseas trade, where risks were greater, the old system of temporary partnerships lingered on. It had not entirely disappeared by 1600, and the first joint-stock companies in the colonial trade were formed for a single venture and dissolved after its completion. Even today, something of the old system remains: in shipping, the voyage account is still the basic unit for profit or loss computations. But even in the overland trade, the new form of business organization, despite its advantages, did not easily gain the upper hand. In 1306, the Alberti company of Florence still had several factors who were travelling back and forth between Italy and Champagne to fetch Flemish cloth. When the books were closed on 1 January 1307, three of them, it is stated, were on the road (*sul kammino*), bringing cloth to Florence. Later on, it seems that the company no longer sent factors to the fairs, but had permanent representatives in Flanders and Brabant. The trend of the times was too powerful to resist; one had to follow it or lose the race to more adaptable competitors.

For lack of documents, not much is known about the internal organization and the financial structure of the great Placentine and Sienese companies of the thirteenth century. These companies were, of course, partnerships, but the word 'company' is correctly applied to them, since it is constantly used in contemporary sources and business documents. Originally, the companies were family partnerships. Even after admitting outsiders as partners, the nucleus was still formed by the founding family, which, without exception, gave its name to the company. Thus the Sienese company of the Bonsignori, which failed in 1298, had twenty-three partners, four of whom were sons of the founder, Orlando Bonsignori, one a nephew of Orlando and eighteen outsiders. The outsiders usually accepted the leadership of the family group, but in this case disagreement among the partners about policy seems to have been a major factor in bringing about the downfall of the entire concern. Although the matter has been debated, it seems that partners, in the thirteenth century, assumed joint and unlimited liability. It was not until 1408 that a Florentine statute allowed the creation of *società in accomandita*, or limited partnerships, in which dormant partners were liable only to the extent of their investment.

Since the Italian mercantile and banking companies had branches or correspondents in all the principal centres of western Europe, their names occur frequently in English as well as continental sources. It may, therefore, be useful to include a reference list, however incomplete, of the major companies and merchant dynasties active in the later Middle Ages:

ASTI: Alfieri, Asinari, da Saliceto, Garetti, Leopardi, Malabaila, Pelleta, Roveri, Scarampi, Solari, Toma.

FLORENCE: Acciaiuoli, Alberti, Albizzi, Altoviti, Antella, Ardinghelli, Bardi, Baroncelli, Bondelmonti, Cambi, Canigiani, Capponi, Cavalcanti, Cerchi, Da Rabatta, Del Bene, Falconieri, Francesi, Frescobaldi, Gianfigliazzi, Guadagni, Gualterotti (Bardi), Guicciardini, Mannini, Mazzi, Medici, Orlandini, Pazzi, Peruzzi, Pigli, Portinari, Pulci, Rimbertini, Rucellai, Scali, Spini, Strozzi, Tornabuoni (Tornaquinci).

GENOA: Adorno, Balbi, Calvi, Cattaneo, Centurioni, Dalla Volta, Di Negro, Doria, Embriaci, Fieschi, Gentili, Giustiniani, Grillo, Grimaldi, Imperiali, Lercari, Lomellini, Mallone, Malocelli, Pallavicini, Pessagno, Piccamiglio, Spinola, Squarzafico, Usodimare, Vento, Zaccaria.

LUCCA: Arnolfini, Balbani, Barca, Bonvisi, Burlamacchi, Calcinelli, Cenami, Dal Portico, Forteguerra, Guidiccioni, Guinigi, Interminelli, Moriconi, Onesti, Rapondi, Ricciardi, Schiatta, Spada, Spiafame, Trenta, Vinciguerra.

MILAN: Amiconi, Borromei, Castagniuoli, Da Casale, Da Fagnano, Del Maino, Della Cavalleria, Dugnano, Serrainerio, Vitelli.

PIACENZA: Andito, Anguissola, Arcelli, Bagarotti, Baiamonte, Bracciaforte, Burrini, Capponi, Cavessoli, Guadagnabene, Leccacorvo, Negroboni, Pagano, Quattrocchi, Rustigaccio, Scotti, Speroni.

PISA: Agliata, Aiutamicristo, Assopardi, Baccone, Buonconti, Buzzacarini

(Sismondi), Carletti, Cinquina, Del Bagno, Dell'Agnello, Delle Brache, Del Mosca, Duodi, Falcone, Gaetani, Gambacorta, Gatti, Griffi, Gualandi, Laggii, Lanfranchi, Martelli, Murcii, Orlandi, Papa, Pedone, Roncioni, Sampanti, Scacieri, Sciancati, Sciorta, Seccamerenda, Sismondi, Vernagallo.[1]

PISTOIA: Ammannati, Cancellari, Chiarenti, Dondori, Fortebraccio, Panciatichi, Partini, Simiglianti.

PRATO: Datini (Francesco di Marco).

SIENA: Bonsignori, Cacciaconti, Fini, Folcacchieri, Gallerani, Maffei, Malavolti, Marescotti, Piccolomini, Salimbene, Sansedoni, Scotti, Squarcialupi, Tolomei, Ugolini, Vincenti.

VENICE: Badoer, Baldo, Barbarigo, Bembo, Bragadin, Capello, Contarini, Dandolo, Garzoni, Lippomani, Loredan, Molin, Morosini, Pisani, Priuli, Soranzo, Ziani, Zorzi.

Owing to the chance preservation of documents, and to the studies of Professor Armando Sapori, we are much better informed about the structure of the Florentine companies, especially the Peruzzi, than about those of Siena or Piacenza. Next to the Bardi, the Peruzzi company was the largest in Florence. It had a continuous existence from 1275, or thereabouts, to 1343, when it failed because of frozen credits to the kings of England and Naples. Between those dates the articles of association were renewed several times, namely in 1300, 1308, 1310, 1312, 1324, 1331 and 1335. In the interval between two renewals, no new partners were admitted and none were allowed to withdraw. At each renewal, the books of the old partnership were closed and a general financial statement, or *saldamento generale*, was drawn up. The partners then proceeded to a division of profits. Usually this division was not final but subject to later adjustments, because the balance was apt to include a great many contingent claims and other items which remained in abeyance. The final liquidation often took several years, as is evident from the account-books that are extant.

In 1310, the *corpo*, or capital, of the Peruzzi company reached a peak of £149,000 *affiorino* or about $400,000 at the present official valuation of $35 per ounce. This is a tremendous amount if one considers that the purchasing power of gold in the Middle Ages was many times what it is today. The share of the Peruzzi family in this total amounted to £79,000 *affiorino* and that of the outsiders to £70,000 *affiorino*. It was only in the settlement of 1331 that the latter acquired control of the majority of the capital by owning £52,500 *affiorino* out of a total of £90,000. The reduction of the capital at the time of the renewal of 1312 was not due to losses, but to the fact that several partners withdrew and were not replaced by newcomers. In 1324, the capital fell to a low point of £60,000 *affiorino*, but there is no evidence that the company, as a result, curtailed

[1] This list for Pisa I owe to the generosity of David Herlihy who is preparing a study of merchants and trade based on the Pisan notarial cartularies and other sources.

its activities. It was only in 1331, when the first cracks in the structure began to appear, that the capital was increased from £60,000 *affiorino* to £90,000 *affiorino*, probably in order to infuse new blood into a decaying body; but to no avail, as we know, since the company collapsed in 1343.

An interesting detail: one of the partners was 'Messer Domeneddio', or the Lord God. In 1310, He was allotted £2,000 *affiorino* for His share in the capital, without any corresponding investment, of course. Messer Domeneddio received His regular quota of the profits which was set aside and distributed in alms to the poor. When the company failed, this account showed a credit balance. In the name of the poor, the Capitani di Orsammichele, a religious fraternity, not only laid claim to this balance but contended that it should be treated as a preferred creditor with first priority. This claim was actually granted and the fraternity managed to get hold of some choice pieces of property to the detriment of the other creditors.

The *corpo*, or capital, of the Peruzzi company did not represent total investment. In addition to their shares, partners were encouraged to invest additional funds, *sopraccorpo* or *fuori del corpo*, that is beyond the capital. On such additional investment they received interest at the rate of 8%, prior to any distribution of profits. The company also accepted time deposits from other investors on similar terms.

In the Peruzzi company, profits were divided among the partners proportionately to capital investment. It would be a mistake, however, to assume that this procedure was typical and observed by all companies. In the case of the Alberti company during the early years of its existence, *corpo* and *sopraccorpo* were not segregated; they did not exist as separate accounts and there was no stated limit to the capital. From 4 September 1304 to 1 January 1323, each partner first received 8% on his total equity or investment. The remaining profits, if any, were then divided among the partners according to a pre-established quota system. From 1304 to 1307, for example, the partners—three brothers—divided these net profits equally, that is, to each one-third. In 1310, each of the three brothers received only three-tenths, and one-tenth went to the son of one who had been admitted as a partner. This system remained in force until 1315, when the quotas were changed again to take care of more sons brought into the family business. It was only in 1323 that the Alberti company completely changed its system of distributing profits and adopted one similar to that of the Peruzzi. A *corpo* of £25,000 *affiorino* was set up and each partner was assigned part of this amount and was expected to keep it in the company. On any additional funds furnished by a partner, the company paid 8% interest. If, on the other hand, a partner failed to supply his full share of the *corpo*, he was charged 8% on any deficiency. The remainder of the profits was then divided by the partners in proportion to their shares of the *corpo*. There is little doubt that this system was adopted by the Alberti company in order to discourage one of its partners from drawing out most of his equity.

Consequently, there existed no hard-and-fast rule determining the distribution of profits in the Florentine companies. Everything depended on the agreements made by the partners and incorporated in the articles of association. In the Datini partnerships of the fifteenth century, the division of profits was seldom proportionate to investment; the managing partner, who invested little, usually received a more than proportionate share of the earnings in reward for his services. It is true that the structure of the Datini firm and the Medici banking-house, with a separate partnership for each one of the branches, differed greatly from that of the earlier companies.

The Peruzzi company—and the same is true of the Bardi and the other companies prior to 1350—was *one legal entity* only: it comprised the headquarters in Florence and the branches outside the city, those in Italy as well as beyond the Alps. In theory, all the partners residing in Florence had a voice in the management, but in practice the business was run by one of them who inspired confidence and assumed the same function as the president of a modern corporation. Several of the branches were administered by factors who were generally provided with a power of attorney. Incidentally, the word 'factor' had a different meaning in the Middle Ages from that which it has today; it did not designate a commission merchant, but always referred to a salaried employee doing clerical work for a trading company, a banking-house or a merchant. Branch managers, being employees, received a salary and occasionally a bonus, if the company had been pleased with their services, but never a share in the profits. It also happened that a partner was sent abroad to take charge of one of the branches. In such a case he received a salary for his services as a factor besides his share in the profits, to which he was entitled as a partner.

This form of organization was rather rigid and its weaknesses showed up when the big three, the Acciaiuoli, the Bardi and the Peruzzi companies, all failed shortly before the Black Death. After the crash, the Florentine merchants seem to have evolved a new form of organization which appeared to them to be more flexible and to offer greater protection from entanglements so that the fall of one branch would not involve the whole concern. Perhaps this expectation was a delusion. This new set-up occurs already in the Datini firm, which was a combination of autonomous partnerships, one for each branch office, but all controlled by one man who kept the reins firmly in his hands and did not allow the branch managers any deviation from his instructions. Francesco Datini (†1410) judged others only by their performance and knew how to pick out reliable and devoted assistants, although he made practically no use of relatives at a time when the cult of the family was still great. The same form of organization was no doubt adopted by most Florentine firms after 1350, but it is encountered in its purest form in the greatest of them all: the Medici bank.

This famous banking-house was founded in 1397 when Giovanni di Bicci de' Medici, who had managed for a time the Rome branch of a partnership founded by a distant cousin, Vieri di Cambio de' Medici, established a rival firm in association with members of the Bardi family. At first, it had only two offices, one in Florence and the other in Rome. During the lifetime of Giovanni, branches were opened in Naples (1400) and in Venice (1401), but the former was discontinued in 1426, perhaps because it was not successful. In the same year, a branch was created in Geneva, the fairs of which had acquired international importance. In the beginning, this branch was financed by an *accomanda* which was only transformed in 1437 or 1439 into an unlimited partnership, the Medici assuming henceforth full responsibility. The great period of expansion of the Medici bank came, however, only after the death of Giovanni di Bicci (1429), under the administration of his son, Cosimo. Successively branches were established in Bruges (1439), Pisa (1442), London (1446), Avignon (1446) and Milan (1451 or 1453). In 1433, the Medici, as papal bankers, opened a temporary office in Basle to handle the financial business of the Church Council which was then in session. About 1464, the Geneva branch was transferred to Lyons where the new fairs created by Louis XI were such a tremendous success that the older fairs ceased to attract any trade.

In marked contrast to the Peruzzi company the Medici firm was not one unit, but was made up of several partnerships which were separate legal entities, all under the control of the same family. Its structure resembled more or less that of the modern holding company with the important difference that it was, of course, a combination of partnerships rather than of corporations.

At the summit of its prosperity, the entire complex included the 'bank' in Florence, the branches 'outside the city', that is, in Italy and abroad, and three manufacturing establishments within the walls: two woollen 'shops' and one silk 'shop'. Of course, these 'shops' (*botteghe*) were not factories or even workshops in the modern sense, but establishments which put out the materials to be worked up at home by a succession of craftsmen. In Florence, in the woollen industry, only a few operations, such as beating the wool, carding and combing, were performed in the *bottega* itself; all the others, including spinning, weaving, dyeing and finishing, were done outside. This method of production, known as the putting-out system, gave rise to a very complicated organization which can best be studied from the account-books of another and much less famous branch of the family, since no industrial records of the historic Medici have survived.[1] The same is not true of the other records relating to their banking business. Fragments of the correspondence and the account-books are still extant and have been used by historians. Recently, a systematic search of the Florentine archives brought to light a crop of new documents, including partnership agreements, balance sheets, correspondence and, most important of all, three *libri segreti*, or secret account-books, covering the period from 1397 to 1450 without any break. In the Florentine companies, the *libri segreti* were the key books which contained vital information relating to the composition of capital and the allocation of profits, not only of the main office but also of the branches. Although this new material still requires further study, we are now much better informed than we were only a few years ago about the internal organization of the Medici bank.

According to data for the year 1335, only the major branches of the Peruzzi company (Avignon, Bruges, London, Naples, Palermo and Paris) were managed by partners; the others were administered by factors who were salaried employees. In the case of the Medici bank, branch managers were as a rule junior partners who, instead of receiving a salary, were remunerated by means of a share in the profits. It does not follow that these managing partners were on the same footing as the *maggiori* or senior partners belonging to the Medici family. Quite the opposite. The Medici records make it clear that these two categories did not have equal rights and that the managing or junior partners were definitely placed in a subordinate position. In all important matters of business policy the *maggiori* or senior partners had the final say. If a junior partner failed to follow instructions, it was always possible to get rid of him by terminating prematurely the partnership agreement, and all the surviving articles of association granted this right to the *maggiori*. A junior partner also was not permitted to leave his post and was expected to report to the *maggiori* on all the acts of his management. In other words, it is clear that the *maggiori* were masters and the managing partners only servants. An analysis of a Medici partnership agreement will further illustrate this point.

For this purpose, let us take the articles drawn up in Bruges on 25 March 1454, and relating to the London branch.[2] According to the pre-

<hr>

[1] For the business organization of the Florentine woollen industry in the fourteenth to sixteenth centuries, see the studies, based on the account- and letter-books of the Medici-Tornaquinci, in Florence Edler, *Glossary of Mediaeval Terms of Business, Italian Series, 1200–1600* (Cambridge, Mass., 1934), Appendices, and the essay of Raymond de Roover, 'A Florentine Firm of Cloth Manufacturers: Management and Organization of a Sixteenth Century Business', *Speculum*, XVI (1941), 3–33.

[2] An earlier contract, dated 31 May 1446, is discussed by Lewis Einstein, *The Italian Renaissance in England; Studies* (New York, 1902), 242–5.

amble, the partners were to be: the two sons of Cosimo and their first cousin, Pierfrancesco de' Medici, Giovanni d'Amerigo Benci (the general manager of the bank), Gerozzo di Jacopo de' Pigli (a former manager of the London branch) and Simone d'Antonio Nori (the new manager). Next it was stated that the purpose of the contract was to form a 'company in order to deal in merchandise and in exchange' in the city of London. In this context, 'exchange' is synonymous with banking which, at that time, consisted chiefly in the negotiation of bills of exchange. Consequently, the new partnership was intended to combine trade with banking, a common practice, since the Italian companies carried on diversified activities. It was also provided that the agreement would last four years ending on 24 March 1458. According to article 1, the partnership was to be styled 'Piero di Cosimo de' Medici e Gerozzo de' Pigli e Compagni di Londra'. The capital of £1,000 sterling was to be supplied entirely by the senior partners (Medici, Benci and Pigli). Simone Nori was not expected to invest any money, but he was to give his services and to attend to the management of the company's affairs (article 2). Although he had no money invested, Nori was entitled to one-eighth of the profits or 2s. 6d. in the pound, and the other partners to seven-eighths or 17s. 6d. in the pound (article 4). During the duration of the agreement, no partner was permitted to withdraw either his capital or his share in the profits, except that Nori was given an annual allowance of £15 sterling to cover his expenses.

The succeeding articles make it abundantly clear that all the burdens of management rested on the shoulders of Nori and that he was strictly accountable to his co-partners. Under the threat of a penalty of 100 nobles, he was not allowed to grant credit except to merchants or artificers (article 6); neither was he free to stand surety for others except with special permission of his partners (article 7). In addition, the agreement forbade him to do business for himself (article 8), to gamble and to keep women at his quarters (article 9), to underwrite insurance (article 17), to accept gifts worth more than one pound (article 18), or to leave England without express authorization (article 14). At the end of each year, on 24 March, he was expected to close the books and to strike the balance which was to be sent to headquarters in Italy. At the termination of the agreement, he promised to come to Florence in order to report in person concerning his management (article 10). He had no power to hire factors or even office boys (article 12). As a matter of fact, the Medici followed a constant policy of doing this themselves. Nori was not supposed to invest in wool, lead or tin—the products of England—more than £300 at any one time (article 15) and he was placed under strict obligation to insure all shipments sent to Italy by sea (article 16).

While the partnership agreement thus placed all kinds of restrictions

G

upon the freedom of the junior or managing partner, the *maggiori* were not limited by any such disabilities; not only did the provisions preserve their entire liberty of action, but they also gave them the means of exercising and retaining control. After the liquidation of the partnership, the *maggiori* were to have the custody of all books, papers and other records, although Simone Nori would have access to them whenever he needed it. More important still, the Medici kept the exclusive right to the use of the style and the mark of the partnership and remained in possession of its place of business or *fondaco*. Finally, it was explicitly stipulated that they could terminate the partnership at any time without Nori's raising any objection. In other words, it is plain that ultimate authority was vested in the senior partners and that the junior partner was expected to manage the London branch within the framework of their instructions.

Since the Medici were so involved in politics, they could not devote all their time and their attention to the management of their business interests. Of necessity, they had to delegate power and to rely for assistance on advisers. According to the records, their principal administrator was called *ministro*, and it is likely that he performed about the same functions as those of the general manager in modern corporations or joint-stock companies. His main task was to supervise the branch managers, to read their reports, to give them instructions, to examine the yearly balance sheets sent to headquarters by the branches and bring all matters of importance to the attention of whichever Medici was the head of the firm. It was also the duty of the *ministro* to prepare written instructions for managers who left Florence for their new posts and to interview those who came to Florence to report or to negotiate the renewal of partnership agreements.

From 1397 to 1433, the general managers were successively two brothers, Benedetto and Ilarione di Lipaccio de' Bardi. They were followed by Giovanni d'Amerigo Benci (1435–55), a very able man who had been trained in the Rome and Geneva branches. After him came Francesco di Baldovino Inghirami (1455–70) and then Francesco di Tommaso Sassetti (1470–90). The latter, also, had received his training in Geneva. His record as a factor and as a branch manager was so impressive that he was recalled to Florence in 1458 to help Francesco Inghirami whom he succeeded after the death of Piero di Cosimo de' Medici. Under the administration of Lorenzo the Magnificent, who had little aptitude for business, Sassetti became all-powerful, and nothing was done without or against his advice. In the course of the years, he became less adaptable and failed to keep a strong hand over the branch managers. Among other errors, he did not detect in time the frauds of Lionetto de' Rossi, the manager of the Lyons branch, or restrain Tommaso Portinari, the manager of the branch in Bruges, from lending excessive amounts to Charles the Bold. Sassetti's laxity and faulty judgment were certainly a major cause of the downfall of the once powerful bank which was virtually bankrupt when, in 1494, the Medici rule was overthrown in Florence. A noteworthy fact is that Sassetti did not become a partner of the 'bank' in Florence until 1482. As general manager, he was rewarded for his services by being kept as a senior partner in the Avignon and Lyons branches. Sassetti's successor was Giovambattista di Marco Bracci (1490–4), who tried in vain to repair the damage during the short lease on life remaining to the Medici bank. One should not forget, however, that the bank lasted nearly a century, from 1397 to 1494, a long time for a business firm.

In 1420, the capital of the Medici bank amounted to 24,000 gold florins, of which 16,000 florins were supplied by the Medici and 8,000 florins by Ilarione de' Bardi, their partner and general manager. This capital was invested as follows: 10,500 florins in the bank in Florence; 6,000 florins in the branch in Rome; and 7,500 florins in that in Venice. Subsequently the capital was increased from 24,000 to 32,000 florins. By 24 March 1451 (N.S.), when the last of the three extant *libri segreti* was closed and balanced, the capital of the Medici bank had reached 72,000 florins, of which 54,000 represented the quota of Cosimo de' Medici and the remaining 18,000 florins that of his *ministro*, Giovanni d'Amerigo Benci. To this amount must be added a sum of 3,083 florins *di suggello* and 24s. 10d. *affiorino* due to the heirs of Antonio di Messer Francesco Salutati, a partner who died in 1443. Table I indicates how this amount was allocated. The reader will notice that the Rome branch, managed by Robert Martelli, is not listed. This is not an oversight, for no capital was assigned to this branch after the mid-1420's because the papal court was a source of funds. According to modern notions, it seems strange that a bank should have no capital. However, there is no mistake, since the Pazzi followed the same practice; like the Medici, they state explicitly in their *catasto* or tax reports, from 1427 onward, that their branch in Rome, because it needs no capital, does not have any. It should be emphasized that the amount of 75,083 florins does not represent total capital investment, but only the share of the Medici bank, properly speaking, in the capital of the various subsidiaries. Consequently, this figure does not include the amounts invested by other partners. If these are taken into consideration, the total capital investment amounted to nearly 88,300 florins, Florentine currency, or about $353,200 in gold at the present price of $35 an ounce. This figure of 88,300 florins is based on the data found in the *libro segreto* and in partnership agreements; it may be considered accurate, but it is not a balance-sheet total like the sum of 75,083 florins mentioned above.

Capital investment represented only a fraction of the funds with which

Table I. Allocation of the Capital of the Medici Bank to Different Branches on 24 March 1451 according to the 'Libro Segreto No. 3'

Office or Branch	Manager	Share of the Medici Bank		Total Capital Investment	
		Local Currency	Florins* (F. s. d.)	Local Currency	Florins* (F. s. d.)
Florence	Giovanni Benci		12,952 1 10		12,952 1 10
Silk Shop	Berlinghiero di Francesco Berlinghieri and Jacopo Tanagli		4,800 0 0		7,200 0 0
Same	Same		7,824 16 2†		7,824 16 2†
Wool Shop I	Antonio di Taddeo		2,500 0 0		4,000 0 0
Wool Shop II	Andrea Giuntini		3,500 0 0		6,000 0 0
Avignon	Giovanni Zampini	14,000 fiorini di camera or papal florins	8,400 0 0	16,000 papal florins	9,600 0 0
Bruges	Angelo Tani	£2,160 groat	10,800 0 0	£2,700 groat	13,500 0 0
Geneva	Francesco Sassetti	10,500 écus of 64 to the marc	11,807 6 10	12,000 écus of 64 to the marc	13,493 0 0
London	Simone Nori	£800 sterling	4,800 0 0	£1,000 sterling	6,000 0 0
Venice	Alessandro Martelli	£700 groat or 7,000 ducats	7,700 0 0	7,000 ducats	7,700 0 0
Total			75,083 24 10		88,269 18 0

SOURCE: Florence, State Archives, Mediceo avanti il Principato, Filza 153.
* These florins are fiorini di suggello divided into 29 soldi affiorino, each subdivided into 12 deniers.
† Undivided profits.

the Medici bank operated. Like other merchant-bankers, they accepted time deposits, or *depositi a discrezione*, on which they promised to pay, if earned, a return of 8, 10 or even 12%. Although the banker assumed no legal obligation to pay interest, he was under pressure to do so if he wanted to keep his customers. In answer to the upholders of the usury doctrine, the bankers argued that a return payable at their discretion was a free gift and that nothing prevented them from making presents. Nevertheless, the more rigorous theologians, including San Antonino (1389–1459), archbishop of Florence, condemned deposits *a discrezione* as 'palliate' usury. Despite this attitude of some of the leading 'Doctors', the pope himself, not to mention several cardinals, had money on deposit with the Medici; the balance sheet of the Rome branch, dated 12 July 1427, includes an item of nearly 1,200 florins standing to the credit of Martin V personally. According to the same balance sheet, Henry Beaufort, cardinal of Winchester, had a credit of 4,000 florins, and the papal treasury or *camera apostolica*, far from being in debt, had almost 24,500 florins of idle money on deposit with the Medici. It is not surprising that the Rome branch had been in a position to advance about 30,000 florins of working capital to the head office in Florence and about 13,000 florins to the Medici subsidiary in Venice. Rome, indeed, was the principal source of funds.

Capital investment is only one method for gauging the size of a business concern. The number of employees is another yardstick. What was the size of the staff employed by the Italian banking and trading companies? No figures are available for the Bardi company, apparently the largest of the big three which crashed around 1345. In 1336, the Peruzzi company, the second largest, probably employed between eighty-five and ninety-five factors. The Acciaiuoli company, the smallest of the three, had, in 1341, sixteen branches with a total of forty-two factors, not including the home office in Florence where there were eleven partners and an unknown number of employees (Table II). The plausibility of these figures is confirmed by a reliable estimate concerning the personnel of the Medici bank. At the time of Piero di Cosimo's death (1469), it included close to sixty persons of whom fifty were factors and ten, managers and partners (Table II). In an epoch when large corporations have thousands of employees, these figures may not be impressive, but the Medici bank was a giant for its time. In Lucca, during the last quarter of the fourteenth century, all firms were required by law to register their marks and to list their partners and factors. According to the business register for 1372, the largest company in Lucca was that of the Guinigi: it had five branches—Bruges, Genoa, Naples, Pisa and Venice—and the staff, including both partners and factors, numbered nineteen persons, seven of whom were members of the family. Only eleven Lucchese

Table II. *Size of Three Major Florentine Companies*

Office or Branch	Peruzzi 1336 Size of Staff	Acciaiuoli 1341 Size of Staff	Medici 1469 Size of Staff
Florence	11	11	12
Avignon	5	3	5
Barletta	5	4	No branch
Bologna	No record	1	No branch
Bruges	4	2	8
Castello di Castro (Sardinia)	1	No record	No branch
Chiarenza (Greece)	No record	2	No branch
Cyprus	4	3	No branch
Genoa	1	6	No branch
London	7	2	4
Lyons	No branch	No branch	8
Majorca	2	No record	No branch
Milan	1	No branch	8
Naples	8	5	No record
Paris	3	1	No branch
Pisa	7	2	No record
Ravenna	No record	1	No branch
Rhodes	3	3	No branch
Rome	No record	2	8
Sicily	7	3	No branch
Tunis	3	2	No branch
Venice	3	No branch	7
Unidentified	13		
Total	88	53	60

SOURCES: *Peruzzi*, Armando Sapori, *Studi di storia economica*, 3rd ed. (Florence, 1955), 717–29. *Acciaiuoli*, Jean Alexandre Buchon, *Nouvelles recherches historiques sur la principauté française de Morée et ses hautes baronnies à la suite de la quatrième croisade* (Paris, 1843), I, i, 46 n. *Medici*, Florence, State Archives, Mediceo avanti il Principato.

firms employed more than six persons. In 1371, the register lists eighty-nine firms and 186 factors or an average of a little more than two factors per firm. Thirty merchants declared they had neither partners nor factors. The figures for 1372 are slightly different, but do not alter the general picture. If Lucca is at all typical, one may safely conclude that individual merchants and small firms predominated and that 'large' companies employing ten factors or more were the exception. After 1350 no medieval firm, with the lone exception of the Medici bank, even remotely approached the size of the big three, the Bardi, the Peruzzi and the Acciaiuoli companies, which the Florentine chronicler, Giovanni Villani, called 'the pillars of Christendom'. Perhaps it is not devoid of significance that only one company attained comparable size during the period of stagnation, and even contraction, which extended from the Black Death to the Great Discoveries.

Seldom were more than eight factors employed in any one branch. In 1469, the Bruges branch of the Medici bank had a staff of eight persons: the branch manager (Tommaso Portinari), the assistant manager (Antonio di Bernardo de' Medici, a distant relative of the *maggiori*), four factors and two *garzoni* or office boys. Of the four factors, one (Adoardo Canigiani) was the book-keeper; another (Carlo Cavalcanti), who spoke fluent French, had the more pleasant duty of selling silks and velvets to the court of Burgundy; the third (Cristofano Spini) took care of the purchases of cloth and wool and the fourth (Tommaso Guidetti) was probably the cashier. In the fifteenth century, London was less important than Bruges. It is, therefore, not surprising that the Medici branch in London employed fewer people than the one in Bruges. When Gerozzo de' Pigli was sent to London in 1446 to take charge of the Medici branch, he had only three factors to assist him: (1) Angelo Tani, later transferred to Bruges, who was good at correspondence and could replace the manager when absent; (2) Gherardo Canigiani, who was best suited for the job of book-keeper, and (3) Alessandro Rinuccini, who was fit for the task of cashier and for running errands, since he knew English. Only Gerozzo de' Pigli, the branch manager, and Angelo Tani, the assistant manager, had the power to commit the London branch and to draw or accept bills of exchange. This information is so precise and detailed that it settles the problem of the size and the organization of the branches which the great Italian banking and trading companies had established abroad.

From a practical point of view, the legal structure of the companies made little difference, and it did not matter much whether the branch managers were partners or simple factors. Because of the slowness of communications it was necessary to give them a great deal of freedom. Business decisions could not be postponed two or three months in order to consult headquarters. As a matter of fact, the control of agents in distant places remained one of the knotty problems of mercantile capitalism until the end of the eighteenth century. In the case of the Medici bank, one of the main causes of its downfall was probably Sassetti's failure to take drastic measures while there was still time and to replace branch managers, like the Portinari brothers, who were steering a dangerous course and involving the firm in risky enterprises. Francesco Datini, on the contrary, was not so lenient and did not hesitate to pen angry notes in his own hand whenever branch managers bought bills from doubtful takers or, in any other way, exposed the firm to losses. The keynote of Datini's policy apparently was: it is better to turn down business than to run undue risks. He steadfastly refused to become involved in loans to princes which so often caused the ruin of the medieval banking-houses. Co-ordination seems to have been another serious problem. Sassetti also failed to solve this, and the correspondence of the Medici bank under the administration of Lorenzo the Magnificent is filled with the recriminations of the branch managers against each other. Rome and Bruges were at odds over the alum monopoly, and Rome complained to headquarters —apparently with good reason—because Lyons was draining away working capital by drawing bills without making equivalent remittances.

In spite of such difficulties, the companies with permanent branches abroad had a slight advantage over independent merchants, because they possessed at least some authority over their managers in foreign parts. Independent merchants, unfortunately, were entirely at the mercy of the correspondents to whom they sent goods on consignment. Usually there was no remedy against agents who were ill-chosen and proved to be either inefficient or dishonest. The Venetian merchant, Guglielmo Querini (1400-68), was especially unlucky in this respect. A voluminous bundle of his letters is still preserved in the Venetian archives. Although well informed because of his many connections in the political world, he was unsuccessful as a merchant. One of his main shortcomings was presumably that he dealt with agents whom he did not know very well and who either cheated him or mismanaged his affairs. After losing most of his business capital—fortunately he also owned landed property—he had the wisdom to retrench and spent twelve years in futile and obstinate attempts to collect outstanding claims in Flanders, in England and in the Levant. In only one instance did he succeed, but it was near home and not in distant lands. An unfaithful agent in Ravenna was forced to disgorge what Querini claimed as his due. Even so, to win his suit, Querini had to marshal all the political influence at his disposal. The problem of securing satisfactory representation in foreign parts is also well illustrated by the career of another Venetian merchant, Andrea Barbarigo (fl. 1418-49). He was more cautious and more successful than Querini, but he, too, had his share of troubles with unreliable correspondents. His agent in Syria, Alberto Doceto, failed to give him satisfactory service by overcharging him on the price of cotton and discriminating against him in favour of other principals. In Spain, Barbarigo used as his commission agent Bertuccio Zorzi, the son-in-law of banker Francesco Balbi. As Barbarigo was one of Balbi's protégés, it is not surprising that he received better treatment from Zorzi, not only with regard to price, but also with respect to cargo space, quality and other matters. In dealing with London and Bruges, Barbarigo took advantage of his connection with the Cappello brothers, whose sister he married. Since family ties were so strong, he got satisfactory service and his agents let him share in several profitable deals. Medieval business letters give the impression that principals were often disappointed because their agents sold their consignments for less than they had expected to get or paid too high a price for local commodities. Whether the agents were always to blame is another matter.

The role of commission agent was not without risks, and Francesco Datini repeatedly cautioned his branch managers against opening accounts for new principals who were not of good repute. The danger came from merchants who, being short of funds, drew on their agents in anticipation of the sale of their goods and thus forced them to make advances. An even more dangerous course was frequently followed by principals who drew on their correspondents and expected them to pay the drafts by means of redrafts. This practice was widespread because of the peculiarities of medieval banking, which rested on exchange and not on discounting. Despite Datini's warnings, the Barcelona branch, in 1400, lost two years' profits because it was held responsible for the payment of a bill of exchange drawn on Guglielmo Barberi, a principal in Bruges, who had financed himself by selling drafts on his agents and telling them to redraw. The game went on until Barberi became insolvent and the redrafts on Bruges were returned with protest.

The conduct of medieval business certainly presupposed a fairly high degree of education. In any case, the surviving business records prove conclusively that, contrary to the thesis of Werner Sombart, the merchants were far from illiterate and knew how to write letters, how to make difficult computations and how to keep books. Some of them were even the authors of chronicles and diaries, which, in the words of Professor A. Sapori, 'achieve the dignity of history'.

Where did the merchants acquire their training? The fundamentals, in grammar school; and professional knowledge, in the counting-house by being apprenticed to a merchant, a clothier or a silk manufacturer. It is certainly untrue, as Sombart contends, that economic rationalism was non-existent, in that there was no planning, no intelligent direction and no adequate accounting control. It has also been said by certain writers that medieval merchants did not know how to figure and that they made countless errors, not only in complicated operations but even in simple additions or subtractions. Yet very many medieval account-books and a great number of computations, such as conversions of sums of money from one currency into another, have shown that medieval merchants, while they were not mathematicians, were experts in commercial arithmetic. As a rule, errors were few or negligible. Medieval businessmen did not ignore the rule of three and were remarkable in discovering short cuts to simplify complicated calculations. Refunds granted for the payment of a debt before maturity were not reckoned according to the current method of commercial discount, but according to the more refined and accurate procedure of true discount. An indispensable preparation for a business career was to learn 'the lines', that is, the use of the abacus. This device was the calculating machine of the Middle Ages and was found in every counting-room. Originally a counter (Fr. *comptoir*) was a table used for the abacus. Counting-house, in the meaning of business office, has the same derivation.

A typical Florentine counting-house—according to an inventory of the Alberti company (1348)—contained several desks (*deschi*), sometimes provided with compartments for books, large tables for displaying and measuring cloth, shelves along the walls, a large case (*armario*) with pigeon-holes for classifying mail, a strong-box for keeping cash, a couch for napping, a heavy steelyard, inkwells of brass and copper and miscellaneous other fixtures. The precious *libri segreti* were kept in a locked chest at the home of one of the partners and not in the counting-room or *fondaco*.

According to the Medici records, there were two sorts of business letters: private letters (*lettere private*) and ordinary letters (*lettere di compagnia*). The first were private messages directed to the *maggiori* themselves by the branch managers. The tone is that of a subordinate writing to his superior, which confirms what has been said about the inferior position of the junior partners. The private letters deal either with social events—congratulations for births and marriages, condolences, etc.—or with important matters relating to the conduct of the business and requiring the approval of the *maggiori*. The instructions handed to the branch managers when they left Florence belong to the same category as the private letters and also deal with overall policy instead of with specific transactions. Usually such instructions are carefully mapped out and prescribe a definite line of conduct which the branch manager is expected to follow.

In contrast to the *lettere private*, the *lettere di compagnia* dealt only with routine matters. Usually, they begin with information for the bookkeeper about drafts and remittances. Sometimes they contain comments about the state of the market or the course of political events, since these might affect business decisions. It is evident from check marks in the margin of extant copies that the *lettere di compagnia* circulated within the counting-house so that each employee would take note of the items requiring his attention. The *lettere di compagnia* invariably end by giving the rates of exchange prevailing on the date or the eve of their dispatch. Thus a letter sent from London to Florence on 4 October 1453 reports in the last sentence: *Per costì 36 2/3, Vinegia 40 2/3, Bruggia 19 2/3 in 3/4, Genova 22 3/4*. This statement means that the foreign exchanges were quoted in Lombard Street as follows: Florence 36 2/3*d*. [sterling] per florin *di suggello*, Venice 40 2/3*d*. [sterling] per ducat, Bruges from 19 2/3*d*. to 19 3/4*d*. [sterling] per écu of 24 Flemish groats, and Genoa 22 3/4*d*.

[sterling] per florin of 25s., Genoese currency. Collections of medieval business letters contain invaluable statistical data about exchange fluctuations, but this material has been entirely neglected up to now.

Until lately, it was thought that double-entry book-keeping was not much older than 1340, because this was the date of the earliest known example which is found in the ledgers of the Genoese *massari* or municipal treasurers. As a result of recent research, it appears probable that double entry is much older than was commonly assumed and may have originated in Tuscany rather than in Genoa or Lombardy. It now seems that double-entry book-keeping makes its first appearance in an account-book for the years 1296–1305 kept by Rinieri Fini, the agent of a Florentine banking-house at the fairs of Champagne, and in a similar manuscript (1299–1300) once belonging to the Farolfi company, a concern of Tuscan merchants operating in Languedoc and Provence with headquarters in Nîmes and a branch office in Salon. It is true that these two account-books contain accounts not only for receivables and payables, but also for operating results, and that each entry has a cross-reference to the corresponding debit or credit, as the case may be. Still, evidence based on small fragments can never be conclusive.

These thirteenth-century account-books are still in 'paragraph' form: after an initial debit entry in the case of receivables or an initial credit entry in the case of payables, enough space was left blank to add two or three entries and to indicate how the settlement was effected. As yet, there were no accounts current and each transaction was considered separately. It was only gradually that all items concerning the same person were grouped together so as to form a running account. The next step in this direction was accomplished by relegating all debits to the front half and all credits to the rear half of the ledger. This form is encountered in the Peruzzi ledgers (1335–43), while the slightly earlier Alberti account-books (1304–32) are still in paragraph form. The new arrangement is also found in cash books, such as the *libro dell'entrata e dell'uscita* ('book of income and outgo') of an unidentified Sienese company (1277–88). Instead of using two columns, the receipts are recorded in the front section of the cash book and the expenditures in the rear. This method of presentation made it somewhat awkward to strike the balance and to close an account, because debit and credit were in different sections of the ledger; and it was necessary to transfer the smaller total of the two to the other section and deduct it from the larger in order to obtain the balance that was either due by, or owed to, a correspondent. A more satisfactory form was eventually devised by placing the debit next to the credit either on opposite pages or in two columns on the same page. In all likelihood, this arrangement originated in northern Italy and spread from there to other trading centres. By 1366 we find it adopted by

Bruges money-changers. Among specialists, it is known as the bilateral or 'tabular' form. In Tuscany, books in which the debit faced the credit were said to be kept *alla veneziana* or according to the Venetian manner.

The adoption of the bilateral form does not necessarily mean that books are in double entry. As a matter of fact, form has little importance, but there is no double entry unless certain rules are strictly observed. First of all, it is necessary that each transaction be recorded twice, once on the debit and once on the credit side (or section), so that the books will balance if correctly kept. Second, there must be a complete set of accounts, real as well as nominal, including expense and equity accounts. Third, the records must lead up to a comprehensive financial statement or balance, which shows the assets and liabilities and enables the merchant to ascertain his profit and loss. These requirements seem to have been fulfilled in the case of the Genoese records of the *massari* or municipal stewards (1340), but it is extremely doubtful whether the contemporaneous Peruzzi account-books (1335–43) meet the test. As for the Alberti (1304–32), ten financial statements covering this period are still extant. Their arrangement shows definitely that books were not kept according to the canons of double entry.

As stated above, the branches of the Medici bank were expected to send each year a copy of the balance sheet to headquarters in Florence. There is no doubt that this provision was carried out. In any case, the assertion that 'the striking of balances was performed primarily for narrow book-keeping purposes' conflicts with easily ascertainable evidence. Check marks on extant Medici balance sheets show that they were scrutinized for ageing accounts and uncollectable claims, a perennial threat to the solvency of the medieval banking and mercantile companies. Balance sheets were also used for taxation purposes. In Florence, the law required taxpayers to attach the balance sheets of their firms to the *portate*, or returns, filed in connection with the *catasto* or income tax. For the *catasto* of 1427, numerous balances and financial statements are still extant in the Florentine archives; they range all the way from brief statements submitted by master artisans, including such artists as Michelozzo Michelozzi and Donatello (Donato di Nicolò di Betto de' Bardi), to booklets of several pages in which are listed item by item the assets and liabilities of the great banking-houses, such as the Medici, the Pazzi, the Strozzi, the Tornabuoni and others. Balances were also attached to the returns for the *catasto* in 1433, 1451[1] and 1458. Later on, the law was changed and this practice, which had aroused a great deal of opposition from the mercantile interests, was discontinued.

[1] Florence, State Archives: Archivio delle Riformagioni, Carte della Classe VIII, No. 35: Registro dei traffichi, 1451.

According to their *libri segreti*, the Medici followed a standard practice of setting up reserves for bad debts and accrued salaries before proceeding to a distribution of profits. No doubt the same policy was followed by other firms. Around 1400, the Datini branch in Barcelona set aside a provision to take care of unpaid taxes. Depreciation on equipment (*masserizie*) appears as early as 1324. It did not, however, develop into current practice, since investment in machinery was negligible prior to the Industrial Revolution. In the Farolfi accounts (1299–1300), there is an example of prepaid rent which is correctly handled as a deferred expense. Because of the prevalence of venture accounting, inventory valuation did not have in the Middle Ages the importance that it has today. Usually a separate account was opened for each lot of merchandise and the book-keeper waited until everything was sold before transferring the balance to profit and loss. This practice should cause no surprise, since venturing did not pass away with the travelling trade, but persisted throughout the fourteenth and fifteenth centuries, albeit in a somewhat modified form.

The origins of cost accounting can be traced back to the end of the fourteenth century. A fine example of job accounting was discovered in the *memoriale* or memorandum book (1395–8) of a Pratese cloth-manufacturing establishment founded and controlled by Francesco Datini.[1] In it an attempt is made to determine the cost of production as accurately as possible by allocating to each piece of cloth its share of overhead and indirect costs. It does not follow, however, that these refinements were integrated into a fully developed system of double entry. In Florence, especially, progress along this line was hampered by the complexities of a monetary system based on parallel standards of gold and silver with no fixed exchange ratio between the two. The merchants and bankers reckoned only in gold; the *lanaiuoli* or clothiers used both standards simultaneously: gold in buying wool and selling cloth and silver in paying wages, a custom which greatly complicated their problems in times of monetary instability.

Double-entry book-keeping was undoubtedly an Italian invention. Its diffusion in other European countries did not take place until the sixteenth century, and was greatly promoted by the publication of Luca Pacioli's treatise (1494) and of later manuals in Italian as well as in other languages. These manuals, one should not forget, are text-books for beginners and, hence, do not give a fair picture of the more advanced practices actually achieved in the counting-house. In the opinion of experts, the greatest progress in book-keeping was accomplished during the period from 1250 to 1500. From then on, accounting made little headway

---

[1] Federigo Melis, 'La formazione dei costi nell'industria laniera alla fine del Trecento', offprint from the journal, *Economia e Storia*, 1954., fasc. I–II (June–Dec.).

until the growth of large-scale enterprise in the nineteenth century brought to the fore new problems and new solutions.

According to Werner Sombart, the introduction of double-entry book-keeping marks the beginning of 'capitalist enterprise' and the triumph of the profit motive as the guiding principle of economic activity. If Sombart's criterion were accepted, capitalism would date back to the thirteenth century, or much earlier than he himself would have been willing to admit.

The great variety of weights and measures and the complexities of medieval monetary systems led, in the fourteenth century, to the compilation of the first merchant manuals. There was little need for such guides as long as trade was concentrated at the fairs of Champagne, since their regulations were well known and generally observed. This situation was greatly altered as the fairs declined and as their place was taken by several focal points, such as Paris, Bruges and London. As a result, it became more difficult for the merchant to keep track of the customs of the different places of traffic without a manual to give him secure and up-to-date information. Soon such a manual became an indispensable fixture in any self-respecting counting-house.

The most famous of the medieval merchant manuals is that compiled around 1342 by Francesco di Balduccio Pegolotti, one of the most able factors in the service of the Bardi company. The text is now available in an excellent modern edition with an introduction in English. There are also recent editions of an anonymous Venetian tariff, also of the fourteenth century, and of the manual attributed to Lorenzo Chiarini, first printed in 1481. The *Pratica della mercatura* (1442) of Giovanni di Antonio da Uzzano exists only in an eighteenth-century edition. Besides the manuals extant in print, there are numerous manuscript copies still preserved in the Italian libraries and archives. After the invention of printing, booksellers took advantage of the steady demand for merchant manuals, and the genre continued to flourish throughout the sixteenth, seventeenth and eighteenth centuries. Giovanni Domenico Peri's *Il negotiante* (1638), Lewes Roberts' *The Merchants Mappe of Commerce* (1638), Jacques Savary's *Le parfait négociant* (1675), Jacques Le Moine de l'Espine's *De Koophandel van Amsterdam* (1694), Samuel Ricard's *Traité général du commerce* (1700) and even Malachy Postlethwayt's *Universal Dictionary of Commerce* (1751) are prominent examples of this type of useful literature. Some of these books were so popular that they ran into several editions.

What are the contents of the medieval merchant manuals? They chiefly contain practical information about the usages and customs, the weights and measures, the coinage and the monetary systems of the different places of traffic. The manuals also give data about brokerage fees, usances of bills of exchange, exchange quotations, mint regulations, postal service, couriers and the qualities of merchantable commodities. The information given in the merchant manuals is purely factual and descriptive and one should not expect to find in them anything that even remotely approaches economic analysis. However, Giovanni da Uzzano observes that the money market was subject to seasonal fluctuations and indicates when money in different places was likely to be tight or easy. He advises arbitragists never to draw on a place when money is scarce or to remit to a place when it is abundant.

According to the merchant manuals, traffic was concentrated in certain places, or trading and banking centres. In the fifteenth century, those places were Barletta, Bologna, Florence, Genoa, Lucca, Milan, Naples, Palermo, Pisa, Rome, Siena and Venice in Italy; Barcelona and Valencia in Spain; Avignon, Montpellier and Paris in France; Bruges in Flanders; and London in England. Paris declined rapidly after 1410 and its place was taken by the fairs of Geneva and later those of Lyons. Until its capture by the Turks in 1453, Constantinople was a banking place for the Genoese and the Venetians. The Court of Rome was ambulatory and followed the pope in his travels. Because of the needs of the papal treasury, the pope had the reputation of creating monetary stringency whereever he went.

One of the main characteristics of a *piazza*, or trading and banking centre, was the existence of an organized money market. In the Middle Ages, such a market rested on the negotiation of bills of exchange. On nearly all *piazze*, the Italian merchant-bankers were the principal exchange-dealers. In the Middle Ages, a bill of exchange, as the name clearly implies, was mainly used to implement a *cambium* or exchange contract. With few exceptions, such a contract involved an advance of funds in one place and its repayment in another place and in another currency. Because of the slowness of communications, there necessarily elapsed a period of time between the conclusion of the contract in one place and its fulfilment in another. Consequently, the *cambium* contract rested on an exchange and a credit transaction. The two were inseparably linked together, even in the case of sight drafts. It further follows that medieval bills of exchange were at the same time credit and transfer instruments. Instead of being discounted, they were bought and sold at a price determined by the rate of exchange. The merchant manuals explain how foreign exchanges were quoted in different places. Unless otherwise specified, bills of exchange were payable at usance. In London, the usance on bills varied according to destination from one to three months.

Table III indicates how, during the fifteenth century, the exchanges were quoted in London. In the Middle Ages, Lombard Street was a satellite of the Bruges *bourse* and only the Italian residents dealt extensively in

Table III. *Exchange Quotations in Lombard Street during the Fifteenth Century*

Place of Payment	Exchange Quoted	High	Low	Usance
Bruges	In so many deniers sterling per écu of 24 groats, Flemish currency	22	18	30 days from date
Florence	In so many deniers sterling per florin *di suggello* (after 1471, per *fiorino largo* or large florin)	43	38	90 days from date
Genoa	In so many deniers sterling per florin of 25s., Genoese currency	26	20	90 days from date
Venice	In so many deniers sterling per Venetian ducat of 24 *grossi*	46	38	90 days from date

SOURCE: *El libro di mercatantie et usanze de' paesi*, Franco Borlandi ed., Turin, 1936.

exchange with Genoa, Florence or Venice. As for the English merchants, they were ordinarily takers who used the money market mainly to raise funds by selling bills payable across the Channel in Bruges or Calais. At first, the exchange, contrary to the practice prevailing today, was quoted in sterling and based on the écu, the florin or the ducat. Under these circumstances, a low exchange was favourable to England and a high rate unfavourable. It was only towards the end of the fifteenth century that the English merchants reversed this practice and began to quote the exchange in shillings and deniers groat, Flemish currency, on the basis of the noble of 6s. 8d. st. or one-third of a pound sterling. This is the method followed in the Cely papers, a collection of business letters stemming from a firm of wool merchants.

To be sure, interest was concealed in the rate of exchange, but its presence did not greatly alter the speculative character of exchange dealings. Whoever chose to operate in the money market, whether borrower or lender, had to follow the rules of the game and to run the risk of adverse exchange fluctuations. In this regard, the account-books of the Italian merchant-bankers and the treatises of the moralists give such decisive and concordant evidence that there remains no room for any doubt. The speculative element, in the eyes of the churchmen, justified exchange transactions unless they were obviously misused to conceal a loan at usury.

Whereas international banking was closely tied to foreign exchange, local banking continued the traditions established by the Genoese *bancherii* of the twelfth century and remained an activity closely connected with money-changing. In many centres, including Barcelona, Bruges, Pisa and Venice, the offices of the money-changers had become local transfer and deposit banks which operated on a fractional reserve ratio and extended credit to their customers by means of overdrafts. As earlier in Genoa, transfer orders were usually given by word of mouth, but written assignments were occasionally accepted when a depositor was prevented from going in person to the bank. Since deposits were only partly covered by cash on hand, there can be no doubt that the money-changers created fiduciary money by their lending and investing activities and that this creation of credit had inflationary effects. The volume of bank-money in the major trading centres was far from negligible. In 1369, total deposits of the Bruges money-changer Collard de Marke exceeded £5,500 groat, Flemish, equivalent in bullion to $154,000. This figure is impressive if one remembers that the purchasing power of money was much larger than it is today, that Collard de Marke was only one of fifteen money-changers, and that the city of Bruges had less than 50,000 inhabitants. One great weakness of medieval deposit banks was the prevailing practice of making direct investments in business ventures, undoubtedly the cause of many failures. The money-changers were also accused of driving towards debasement either by uttering current coins above the proclamation rates or by sending bullion to foreign mints. In order to curb these abuses, the city of Barcelona established in 1401 a municipal bank, the prototype of the public banks which became so popular after 1550. In Genoa, a similar institution, the Bank of St George, was chartered in 1408 in the hope that it would be able to stem the steady rise of the gold florin. As this attempt proved a failure, the bank was dissolved in 1444 and not revived until 1586. According to the first balance sheet (1409), total liabilities, chiefly deposits, exceeded 50,000 florins or more than $200,000 at the present valuation of $35 per ounce.

In the fifteenth century, the malpractice of the money-changers and the numerous bank failures caused the public authorities to adopt an increasingly hostile policy. In the Low Countries the dukes of Burgundy, eager to preserve the stability of their currency, practically abolished banking in their dominion by forbidding the money-changers to accept deposits and to make payments by book-transfer for the merchants. In Venice, a series of bankruptcies at the end of the fifteenth century brought the private banks into disrepute and eventually led to their elimination.

To the sedentary merchant of the Middle Ages, news about market conditions and business prospects in other places was of vital importance. He depended on such information to make his decisions and his forecasts. Of course, it was to his advantage not to send any goods to a place where they were likely to be a glut on the market. On the other hand, he was on the lookout to benefit from any increase in the demand. One can understand, for example, the disappointment of a Lucchese silk merchant whose Barcelona correspondents notified him too late about a prospective

H

wedding at the Court of Aragon. According to the merchant manuals, the money market, in particular, was sensitive to reports from abroad and the exchange-rates responded quickly to the trends prevailing elsewhere. The importance of news was so great that unscrupulous speculators sometimes reaped large profits by spreading false rumours or withholding intelligence received by special messengers.

In these circumstances, an efficient organization of the mails was an imperative necessity. In the absence of any public service, the merchants were forced to take matters into their own hands. Already in 1181, a treaty between Lucca and Pisa provided for the free passage through Lucchese territory of the Pisan couriers travelling over the *via francigena* and carrying the *scarsella* of the fairs of Champagne. More than a century later, the existence of a similar service is mentioned by Pegolotti, who even states that the arrival of the *scarsella* regulates the maturity of the bills of exchange issued at the fairs and payable in Genoa. Giovanni da Uzzano in his manual (1442) gives the impression that the *piazze*, or principal trading centres, were all connected by a network of regular mails. This information is confirmed by the Datini and other business letters which mention the *scarsella* so frequently that it must be considered as a well-established institution. At first, the word *scarsella* applied only to the mailbag, but this meaning was soon extended to the private mail service organized by the merchant communities in the chief trading centres of western Europe.

The only document which sheds any light on the organization of the *scarsella* is a Florentine statute of 1357. It reveals that the *scarsella* of Avignon was organized under the auspices of the *mercanzia*, or merchant gild, by a group of merchants having correspondents at the papal court. This group elected bi-monthly two masters of the *scarsella* whose duty it was to hire the *fanti* or couriers and to collect and distribute the mail. The service was limited to members, and it is not clear whether postal charges were collected by the couriers or by the masters of the *scarsella*. The letters were apparently carried in a sealed pouch which was opened only at destination. When, in 1382, the *scarsella* of Bruges was diverted from its usual route to one crossing Milanese territory, the Lucchese Republic asked the duke of Milan to let it pass without breaking any seals or inspecting any bags.

According to the Datini letters, the *scarsella* of the Catalans left Bruges for Barcelona twice a month, and probably carried also the mail for Paris and Montpellier. Although Uzzano's manual states that the trip was made in nineteen or twenty days, in fact it usually took from twenty-two to twenty-four days. Despite the numerous references in business records, there is almost nothing on the *scarsella* save one inadequate article. Historians dealing with the history of the postal service have devoted all their attention to the courier service of the princes, but the mail services of the merchant communities might better repay detailed study.

This is not the place to discuss the polemics that have raged about the origins of premium insurance. In the present state of research, the first unquestionable examples are found in some Palermo notarial contracts dating from 1350 and relating to shipments of grain from Sicily to Tunis. In one case, the underwriter receives a premium of 18% and assumes explicitly all risks arising from an act of God, from men-of-war or from the perils of the sea. Among the Palermo contracts, there is also one covering not the cargo but the ship itself with all its tackle and apparel. The premium is 14% for a voyage from Palermo to Tunis with two or three calls at other Sicilian ports; no deviations are allowed except in an emergency.

Since Palermo was a secondary centre, and since some of the underwriters were Genoese, it may safely be assumed that premium insurance was known prior to 1350 in Genoa, Pisa and perhaps Venice. In Genoa, however, insurance contracts continued to be disguised under the form of a *mutuum*, or gratuitous loan, and later of an *emptio venditio*, or sales contract. This practice may be due to the influence of the decretal *Naviganti* condemning the sea loan, although the moralists from the start were disposed to consider insurance as a contract made valid by the risk involved. Whereas, in Genoa, insurance contracts were entrusted to notaries, a different practice prevailed in Pisa and Florence where policies were drafted by brokers and circulated by them among prospective insurers until the risk had been completely underwritten.

Premiums varied a great deal according to circumstances and seasons, but they were as a rule much lower on galleys than on round ships. In 1454, the rate was only 3% on a cargo shipped from Sandwich to Venice on board the Venetian galleys. In the same year, the premium charged on a shipment from Venice to Sluys, the seaport of Bruges, by an ordinary nef was as high as 11%. Some merchants even considered the Venetian galleys so safe that they deemed it unnecessary to take out insurance, but limited their risk by not 'adventuring' more than a certain sum in a single bottom. Large shipments were divided as much as possible among several galleys. Since medieval merchants were used to assuming risks, shipments were rarely insured for more than half their value or even less.

Despite high premiums charged by underwriters, the insurance business was not especially profitable. According to his records, Bernardo Cambi, a Florentine underwriter of the fifteenth century, paid out more in claims than he received in premiums. Presumably the business was highly competitive. Another trouble was that insurance lent itself easily to fraud. Ships were sometimes deliberately shipwrecked in order to claim insurance for goods that were not even on board. It also happened that shippers rushed to take out insurance after they had received secret intelligence of a disaster. Such frauds still gave rise to complaints in the sixteenth century. It is only much later that their perpetration was made more difficult by the organization of Lloyd's.

Although uncommon, overland insurance was not unknown in the fifteenth century. On the other hand, the lack of statistics did not permit the establishment of life insurance on a secure basis. It was still undistinguishable from pure wagers.

A significant development in the matter of insurance was the building up of uniform customs and rules of law. This situation was undoubtedly favoured by the diffusion of Italian business methods and practices all through the Levant and western Europe. Even the Bruges court often consulted leading Italian residents regarding the law merchant before deciding cases involving insurance, bills of exchange or other matters. Codification of the prevailing rules did not start until 1484 when the Barcelona customs on marine insurance were framed into a statute, printed in 1494 together with the *Libro del Consolat del Mar*, a collection of sea laws. This publication exerted great influence on similar legislation.

In the field of merchant shipping, the most spectacular development of the fourteenth and fifteenth centuries was the creation of regular lines of galleys from Genoa and Venice to the Levant and to the West. In Venice at least, these galleys were state-owned, but they were chartered to private individuals who operated them at their own risk. The Senate, however, accepted bids only from Venetian nobles with experience in shipping affairs and sufficient financial backing. After approval of his appointment by the Senate, the master or *patronus* received permission to set up his bench (*ponere banchum*) in the Square of St Mark's in order to enrol his crew. He usually began by hiring a *nauclerius* or mate who was trained in navigation. Then came the second mate, the scrivan, the barbersurgeon, the chaplain, the bombardiers, the archers, the carpenters, the cooks, the trumpeters, the helmsmen, the sailors and, finally, the crowd of oarsmen, who, in Venice, were free men and not galley slaves. It is true that these wretches belonged to the scum of society and were chiefly recruited among the Dalmatians and Albanians who flocked to Venice in quest of a pittance. A large merchant galley carried a crew of 300 men. As cargo space was consequently rather limited, the galleys were not suited for the transportation of bulky goods of low value, but carried spices, silks, wool, cloth and other luxury products that could bear high freight charges.

Although the *patronus*, on board his galley, was master after God, he was accountable to the Senate and subordinate to the authority of the captain, a government appointee, who was in command of the entire fleet or *muda*. The galleys were expected to navigate in company and to lend each other support, if attacked. Freight rates and wages were strictly regulated, and the *patronus* who failed to comply could get himself into serious trouble.

In good years, Venice sent out several fleets: twelve galleys, in two fleets, to Syria and Alexandria, four to Constantinople, four or five to Flanders and England and two or three to Barbary. The Flanders galleys usually went straight to Sluys or Zeeland and called at Southampton on the homebound voyage. In the fifteenth century, Florence, after conquering Pisa in 1406, entered into competition with Venice and Genoa and sent galleys to Flanders and the Levant (1422–78). Documents of this period likewise mention the Ferrandine galleys of Naples, the Catalan galleys of Barcelona and the French galleys of Narbonne. For a short while there were also the two Burgundian galleys which flew the St Andrew's cross raguly of Burgundy, but were operated by the Medici with Florentine crews. Even Edward IV, in order to promote distant trade, equipped a ship, not a galley, which made trips to Porto Pisano and is called in medieval records 'The nef of the King of England'. This was the first dent in Italy's dominant position in the Mediterranean trade.

Although the Italian merchants resided in London, Southampton—the *Antona* of Italian and Spanish records—was the favourite port of call for the galley fleets. Their regular visits brought animation to the town and gave it a cosmopolitan atmosphere quite exceptional in medieval England. Since Southampton's prosperity depended upon the presence of the Italians, they were welcomed by the townspeople; and anti-alien feeling, despite occasional brawls caused by the turbulent crews of the galleys, was far less virulent than in the city of London, where it was nurtured by the rivalry of the Staplers, the mercers and the grocers. With the passing of the galley fleets early in the sixteenth century, Southampton, too, declined as an outport of London, to regain its prosperity only in the nineteenth century by becoming the terminus of the great transatlantic liners.

The Italian colonies in the Levant have already been mentioned. They were firmly established before 1300. Since their organization changed little during the fourteenth and fifteenth centuries, there is no need to return to the same subject. In Bruges and London, however, Italian colonies were not founded until after 1300 and they never attained either the size or the autonomy of the settlements in the Levant. These colonies in the north were also placed under the authority of a consul whose duty it was to settle any disputes between his nationals, to protect them against any arbitrary acts of the local authorities and to guard against any violation of the existing trade privileges. The consuls were either elected by the local residents (as in the case of the Lucchese) or appointed by the home government (as in the case of the Florentines and the Venetians). Like the gilds, the colonies participated in social and religious activities at which attendance was compulsory for the members. To defray expenses, a tax called *consolaggio* was levied on all exchange and commodity transactions. In London, toward the end of the fifteenth century, the Florentines were taxed at the rate of one-twelfth of a penny per pound sterling on exchange, a penny half-penny per pound on merchandise and one-eighth per cent on insurance. In addition, each galley calling at Southampton was supposed to contribute a lump sum of £10 sterling —chargeable to general average. On the galleys the cargo, in addition to paying freight charges, was assessable for ordinary and extraordinary average.

Both in Bruges and in London, the Italian colony was divided into several 'nations', each headed by its own consul. Nevertheless, they sometimes presented a united front when common interests were at stake. So, after the anti-alien riot of 1457, all four Italian 'nations' in London got together and signed an agreement by which they threatened to boycott the city and to remove their residence to Winchester. The threat was not carried out, but if it had been it might have caused a serious slump. One should not forget that the Italians controlled the money market and that English merchants depended upon them for credit accommodation.

The official register of the consulate reveals that, in 1377, there were in Bruges about forty-six Lucchese residents, not counting women and children. In the next century, this number dropped to twelve, no doubt because of the decline of the Lucchese silk industry. According to the chronicle of N. Despars, in 1468 about 175 Italian merchants walked in a parade at the celebration of the marriage of Charles the Bold and Margaret of York, sister of Edward IV. This number comprised 103 Genoese and Milanese, 40 Venetians, 12 Lucchese and 22 Florentines; these figures are plausible and probably not far from the truth.

The Italian colony in London was smaller than the one in Bruges. It is doubtful if it ever exceeded 100 members. Apart from size, an important difference is that the Italians were welcomed in Bruges, but that they were hated in London. The explanation is no doubt that, in Flanders, they did not compete with the natives, since the Flemish carrying trade had been eliminated long ago. In London, on the contrary, the Italians were in keen competition with the English merchants, for each of the two rival groups sought to exclude the other from the wool and the spice trades. Moreover, pamphleteers accused the 'Lombards' of pursuing the destruction of the realm by carrying out England's valuable wool in exchange for apes, trinkets, sweet wines, velvets and other superfluities. Finally, the English traders resented being dependent upon Italian capital and viewed the exchange business—which they did not understand—with profound suspicion. This attitude found its expression in legislation, such as the Statutes of Employment or the hosting law of 1439. Hostility against aliens in general and exchange-dealers and bankers in particular still pervades the writings of the mercantilists in the sixteenth century. It would be a mistake to overlook the fact that the prejudices of these early economists had their roots in the past.

This description probably gives a distorted picture of business organization in the Middle Ages by stressing the optimum, and neglecting the fact that it was not typical and that it was achieved only in a few major centres. The trouble is that the organization of local trade has yet to be studied. None the less, a recent work on Toulouse makes it possible to put the picture into better focus.

Toulouse, in the fourteenth and fifteenth centuries, was a secondary centre which revolved in the orbit of Barcelona and Montpellier. Besides, the town had connections with Bordeaux to the west and with Paris to the north. Early in the fifteenth century Toulouse was also in relations with the distant fairs of Geneva which, during the troubled reign of Charles VI, had supplanted Paris and risen to the rank of an international market for commodities and a clearing centre for bills of exchange on all places.

In Toulouse, there were no branches of the great Italian companies, although an occasional Italian makes a fleeting appearance in the records. The only ones who left any traces were the Florentines Otto Castellani, who was for some time collector of the king's revenue, and his partner, Jacopo Medici, who engaged in money-changing. The latter is possibly the same as Jacopo di Bernardo d'Alamanno de' Medici, a distant cousin of the historic Medici, who was living in Florence in 1498 when he was chosen *gonfaloniere*. By various and sundry means, including magic spells, this Castellani is said to have caused the downfall of Jacques Cœur in order to succeed him as *argentier* or minister of finance. Castellani himself came to a bad end and died in prison where he was held on charges of sorcery and fraud. His partner, Jacopo Medici, in 1459, obtained a pardon for murder, perjury, usury and other crimes committed at the instigation of Castellani.

For the most part, the trade of Toulouse was in the hands of local merchants who were no more specialized than the Italian companies, but who took advantage of any bargain offering profit opportunities. One of the main articles in which they dealt was fine cloth from Flanders, Brabant, Normandy and England. It was worn by the upper classes in preference to the cruder product of the local industry. English cloth was imported by way of Bordeaux and brought to Toulouse by merchants from Béarn, who exchanged it for woad grown abundantly in the Garonne valley. Among the Flemish woollens, those of Courtrai and Wervicq were the most popular, but the demand fell drastically after 1400, while the English textiles gained ground. On the other hand, Norman cloth, especially that of Montivilliers and Rouen, retained a steady market throughout the period from 1350 to 1450. To fetch these luxury goods, the merchants of Toulouse maintained factors in Paris or sometimes went themselves on trips to Flanders or Normandy. Italian silks and merceries were chiefly bought at the fairs of Pézenas and Montagnac, near Montpellier. The Toulouse merchants either visited the fairs themselves or sent their factors. Apparently, the fairs of Pézenas and Montagnac played in southern France the same role of regional distribution centres as the fairs of Antwerp and Bergen-op-Zoom in the Low Countries. They attracted the merchants from the hinterland who came there to sell their native commodities and to buy supplies of spices and other exotic products. According to an Italian manual, extant only in manuscript form, Toulouse exported cheap local woollens and found an outlet for them at the fairs of Pézenas and Montagnac, while importing at the same time the fine and high-priced cloth mentioned above.

Not only was diversification the rule, but there existed no clear distinction between wholesalers and retailers. The Toulouse drapers sold by the ell as well as by the piece. According to the inventory of a deceased mercer, his shop contained a wide assortment of goods: Italian silks, brocades and velvets; Dutch linens and other fabrics; a variety of liturgical vestments (copes and chasubles), all ready-made; seat and bed covers; caps, purses, decorated belts, mirrors, rosaries and trinkets of all sorts.

The book-keeping of the Toulouse merchants did not reach a high level, but was probably adequate for their purpose. Double entry was entirely unknown, but records were more or less systematically kept. If the account-books of the Brothers Bonis in Montauban (1345–65) are at all representative, the merchants of southern France used a ledger for receivables and payables as well as other books. The only surviving fragment of mercantile book-keeping in Toulouse is represented by four folios which show that the mercer Jean Lapeyre (†1442) kept some kind of perpetual inventory of his stock of textile wares.

Because of the chronic shortage of currency, barter arrangements were common and credit was ubiquitous. The money-changers accepted deposits, but it does not seem that payments were frequently made by transfer in bank. There was no organized money market in Toulouse, and bills of exchange were used only to a limited extent. The money-changers did, however, sell drafts payable at the neighbouring fairs of Pézenas and Montagnac and even made arrangements for the transfer of funds to Rome or Avignon.

Since the Toulouse merchants did not operate with correspondents in other places, they were still forced to travel a great deal or to send out their factors. Usually they had ceased to accompany their own goods and instead used the services of wagoners or mule-drivers who were chiefly Basques.

A few merchants, favoured either by good luck or by superior business ability, founded unglamorous dynasties of country squires, such as the Ysalguier. On the whole, the picture is far from rosy. Trade was repeatedly disturbed by wars, epidemics and dearths. In 1442, a fire destroyed half the town. The whole century from 1350 to 1450 was one of stagnation, if not of economic decline.

IV. *The Organization of the Hanseatic and English Trade*

The Mediterranean and the Baltic trades during the Middle Ages had hardly anything in common, save for one striking analogy: both were dominated by the merchants of a single nation, the Italians in one case and the Germans in the other. The grip of the Hanseatic League on the Baltic trade was even tighter than the control of the Italian cities over the Mediterranean area. Moreover, the Italian city-states were sometimes deadly rivals, whereas the Hanseatic towns were united in one powerful league.

In the Mediterranean, Italian sea-power was far from negligible and was actually used to back up economic demands or to defend existing privileges. Beyond the Straits of Gibraltar, however, the Italian republics no longer had any power, and their economic hegemony rested exclusively on superior business organization. They had to maintain themselves by peaceful means and could not, as did the Hanseatic League on several occasions, resort to boycott, blockade or privateering. Thus the Hanseatic cities, in 1358, ordered their merchants to withdraw from Bruges and not to trade with Flanders until they had obtained a satisfactory settlement of their grievances. Trade relations were again broken off between 1436 and 1438. This rupture was followed by a blockade of Holland (1438–41), which proved to be a boomerang and harmed the Wendish towns more than it did their enemies. In a clash with England from 1469 to 1474, the Hanseatic League engaged successfully in naval warfare. It is during this campaign that a Danzig privateer captured one of the Burgundian galleys which had on board Memling's *Last Judgment*, painted for Angelo Tani, the Bruges manager of the Medici bank. At any rate, the League obtained from Edward IV the restoration of its old privileges and succeeded in halting for many years the penetration of the English merchants into the Baltic. As these cases show, the consistent policy of the League, and especially of Lübeck and the Wendish towns, was to preserve its control over the Baltic trade against any intruders. In the absence of superior business techniques, this monopoly was maintained by force if necessary.

A characteristic of the Mediterranean area was the great number of focal points from which trade radiated in all directions, but the Baltic region presented quite a different picture. Hanseatic trade extended along a single axis with its centre in Lübeck and two arms: one stretching out west to Bruges and London and the other, east to Riga and far-away Novgorod. Only one important off-shoot branched off to Bergen in Norway. This situation was not without a considerable repercussion upon business organization. It enabled the Hanseatic merchants to get along with less elaborate machinery than the Italians. In general, conditions were more primitive in northern than in southern and western Europe. Urban life was not as well developed: even the largest towns, like Cologne for example, had barely 40,000 inhabitants, whereas several Italian cities, including Genoa, Florence, and Venice, had more than 50,000. In the north, too, the value of trade was small in comparison with the south, and the principal products of the area, with the possible exception of furs, were relatively low-priced and bulky commodities. These factors explain to a large extent the great structural difference between Hanseatic and Italian trade. It is not surprising that business methods were less advanced in the Baltic region and still forced the merchant or his factors to be constantly on the road.

Large companies with many branches, such as those of the Bardi or the Medici, were entirely unknown in Hanseatic territory. The individual merchant trading on his own was still in the centre of the stage. To be sure, partnerships did exist, but they were more or less temporary associations in which two or three merchants joined forces for a specific and limited purpose. Some of these contracts were occasional partnerships formed for a single venture only, but others were of longer duration and might even continue year after year. All these contracts had the common feature of being well suited to the persistently colonial character of the Hanseatic trade.

Prior to 1300, the expansion of German commerce along the Baltic coast was an important aspect of the great movement which led the Germans to colonize the Slavic lands beyond the Elbe. In the fourteenth and fifteenth centuries, such towns as Riga, Dorpat or Stockholm were still German settlements ruled by merchant families which maintained close connections with their ancestral homeland.

Among the occasional partnerships the most typical were the *Sendeve* and the *Wederlegginge* or *societas vera*. The former had some similarity with the *commenda*, but was not quite the same. Perhaps it came closer to being an agency contract, since it involved the purchase or the sale of a stock of goods by a servant (*Knecht* or *Diener*), a fellow-merchant, or an innkeeper, according to the instructions of a principal who assumed all the risks of the venture. It made no difference whether the agent travelled along with the goods or whether they were shipped without being accompanied. The agent was apparently entitled to a commission or a fixed remuneration, but it does not seem that he shared in either the profit or the loss. In the fifteenth century, it happened frequently that an agent was commissioned by several principals. The *Wederlegginge* (High German *Widerlegung*), like the *Sendeve*, was a contract limited to a single venture. Usually, it involved two partners: one who supplied the funds and the other who conducted the business and usually went on a trip abroad. However, there are examples of both investing money in equal or unequal amounts. The managing partner usually dealt in his own name without revealing the name of his associate. With regard to the division of profits, there existed, apparently, no fixed rules such as there were in Genoa. The law of Lübeck, in the sixteenth century, stipulates that managing partners with no investment are to share in the profit only and not in the loss. But they are not entitled to any reward for their trouble. This rule may have been a late innovation. In southern Germany, the *Wederlegginge* was also known, but under the name of *Fürlegung*.

By far the most typical institution of the Hanseatic trade was neither the *Sendeve* nor the *Wederlegginge*, but the so-called *gegenseitige Ferngesellschaft*, or mutual agency partnership. It was usually an informal arrangement whereby a partner in one place and a partner in a different place, let us say one in Lübeck and the other in Riga, agreed to act as each other's agents and to sell reciprocal consignments at a common profit. Such an arrangement was not necessarily temporary, but could last for years on end. It was well adapted to the needs of the Hanseatic trade which, as already mentioned, moved along a single axis. Such a *Ferngesellschaft* had neither its own capital nor its own style. The agreement remained concealed to outsiders, since each partner acted in his own name. As there was no central book-keeping, each kept his records according to his own system, a practice which led to many disputes when accounts failed to agree. Neither partner had any authority over the other and distance prevented frequent consultation. There were no means of control, and the arrangement rested to a large extent, if not exclusively, on confidence and business integrity. These drawbacks were so serious that they became a frequent source of litigation, especially since the Hanseatic merchants had the bad habit of letting years go by without settling accounts. With their rudimentary methods of book-keeping, discrepancies and errors were bound to occur and lead to all sorts of difficulties. In one late instance (1507–23), involving a merchant residing in Reval and another in Lübeck, no settlement was made for sixteen years.

Representation abroad could also be secured by sending factors or by using commission agents. Reciprocal agency without profit-sharing, as in the case of the *Ferngesellschaft*, was also common. Some merchants used *Lieger* or resident factors. The most prominent of these was the *Lieger* or permanent representative of the Teutonic Order in Bruges. Those who had no satisfactory connections in other places had to go abroad themselves, since it was not customary to place orders by correspondence or to buy goods without previous inspection.

How prevalent travelling still was is revealed by the widespread use of such expressions as *Bergenfahrer*, *Flandernfahrer* or *Englandfahrer*, which designated merchants trading with Bergen, Flanders or England. Since *Fahrer* in German means 'traveller', it is clear that these merchants were so called because they were constantly journeying to these places.

Historians of the Hanse insist a great deal on the fact that, during the fourteenth and fifteenth centuries, Hanseatic trade tended to become more sedentary because of the growth of business by correspondence (*Schriftlichkeit*), so that merchants were enabled to direct their affairs from the counting-room (*Scrivekamere*). Such a trend undoubtedly existed but it was carried much farther by the Italians.

In order to illustrate this point, let us take the situation in Bruges, which lends itself admirably to comparison, since both the Italians and the Hansards, or Easterlings, had establishments there. Since the Italian companies had permanent branches, their branch managers and their factors were also permanent residents. If they were married, they lived in Bruges with wife and children. For example, Tommaso Portinari, the local manager of the Medici bank, resided in Flanders for more than half a century from the time that he came there as a young office boy (1439) until he withdrew from business in 1496. In 1470, at the age of forty-one, he brought his young wife to Bruges, where he reared his family. Certainly, Portinari visited Italy from time to time for conferences with the *maggiori* or senior partners and for vacations with relatives and friends; but while retaining a great attachment to the country of his birth, he became thoroughly assimilated into the Flemish environment. He was a member of the council of the duke of Burgundy. He certainly knew French and perhaps even a smattering of Flemish. Of course, the Medici employees and the other Italians did not stay in Bruges without ever passing through the city gates: they rode on business to Calais, made trips to the anchorages in Zeeland and visited regularly the marts of Antwerp and Bergen-op-Zoom. These short trips in the neighbourhood, however, did not alter the fact that most of the Italian merchants were permanent residents. The same was true in London: that is why the hosting law of 1439 was a piece of reactionary legislation that was bound to end, as it did, in a complete fiasco.

The situation of the Hanseatic merchants in this respect was quite different: they were not permanent residents. The records, Flemish as well as German, show clearly that they were constantly coming and going, riding back and forth between Bruges and their home towns.

In contrast to the Italians, most Hanseatic merchants stayed at the inns or hostels and, in transacting their business, relied a great deal on their hosts, who often also acted as their brokers. Confidence in the broker-innkeeper was so great that the Hansards entrusted him with their money instead of placing it on deposit with one of the money-changers. Thus the Hanseatic League created a stir because the city of Bruges, which was bound by treaty to guarantee bank deposits, refused to make good any losses suffered by German merchants because of absconding or bankrupt innkeepers. Seldom did the Easterlings live in Bruges with wife and children but there are exceptions, such as Hildebrand Veckinchusen (†1426), who rented a large house which he occupied with his family from 1402 to 1417. As his business was not prospering, he sent his wife and children back to Lübeck where the cost of living was much lower than in Flanders. The case of Hildebrand Veckinchusen is exceptional in other respects. He tried to establish business connections with Italy as well as with the Baltic. Unfortunately, his plans went awry, probably because he had to rely too much on agents over whom he had no control. The more rudimentary forms of business organization did not permit the German merchant to delegate power without giving up control. In all likelihood, Veckinchusen failed because he miscalculated risks, engaged in speculative ventures with borrowed funds and overreached himself by undertaking too many projects at once. Even while residing in Bruges, he was constantly called abroad and forced to neglect one thing in order to take care of another. As Veckinchusen's example shows, the methods prevailing among the Hanseatic merchants not only entailed a great deal of travelling back and forth, but put strict limitations on the size of the firm.

Of the backwardness of Hanseatic techniques, the state of the book-keeping is as good an example as any. Double-entry book-keeping, an Italian invention, was not adopted by the Hanseatic merchants until the sixteenth century. Prior to 1500, their system of book-keeping left much to be desired. Payments due and owed were recorded in the way still used by small shopkeepers: there were no real accounts, but debit or credit items were simply crossed out when paid. Occasionally, some space was left blank to take care of instalment payments. Because of the prevalence of agency and *Ferngesellschaften*, it was also necessary to keep record of any amounts collected or paid for principals or partners. This was done in a haphazard manner by opening a separate account for each lot of merchandise and recording receipts from sales on the one hand and charges on the other. Between the two sets of records, that is, the mer-

chandise accounts and the personal accounts, there was little co-ordination, if any, with the result that the books gave no comprehensive view
of the financial state of the business without going to the considerable
trouble of taking an inventory. There were also no automatic checks
which facilitated the detection of any errors or omissions. As long as the
business was small, this system was more or less adequate and fulfilled its
purpose, but it broke down when the structure became complicated. In
the opinion of an expert, the late Gunnar Mickwitz, inefficient book-
keeping, with the resulting confusion, may well have been a contributing factor to the downfall of Hildebrand Veckinchusen.

Insurance is another technique which, although known to the Italians
prior to 1400, was not adopted by the Hanseatic merchants until the sixteenth century. The first known example is an insurance policy of 1531
relating to a shipment from Lübeck to Arnemuiden in Zeeland. It gives
the names of forty-four underwriters, but the overwhelming majority
are southerners with only one Flemish name and one south German house
(the Welsers). Not a single north German name appears on the list. Risks
were reduced by using small ships and by dividing shipments among
several bottoms. Although the Hanseatic cogs were seaworthy, the inner
route from Hamburg to Bruges was preferred to the outer route, especially during the bad season. This inner route went almost entirely
through protected waters: it followed the coast of the North Sea behind
the Frisian Islands, then entered the Zuider Zee and reached Bruges
through the waterways of Holland and Zeeland.

East of the Rhine, there were no banking centres and no organized
money markets. One should not exaggerate and jump to the conclusion
that no use was made of credit instruments, but there were no regular
dealers in commercial paper, like the Italian merchant-bankers, a situation which seriously hampered the international transfer of funds. The
formalized version of the bill of exchange was unknown, but it was replaced by informal bills obligatory and mandates to pay which nearly
fulfilled the same purpose. *Overkopen*, or payment by assignment, was
fairly common, but settlements in commodities were also quite common. Despite the scarcity of currency, Hanseatic merchants were compelled, oftener than their Italian counterparts, to settle debts abroad by
shipment of specie, the least efficient method of transferring funds.
There are several instances in the account-book of Vicko van Geldersen
(1367–92), a Hamburg draper, who used his servants and friends to send
gold and silver coins to Bruges in order to buy Flemish cloth. In other
cases, the account-book shows him buying assignments on funds placed
on deposit with money-changers or innkeepers. Another illustration of
the difficulties connected with the transfer of funds is afforded by the
troubles of the papal treasury in Poland. In order to send funds to

Avignon, the papal delegates in Cracow used the services of travelling merchants who frequented Bruges, and invested in commodities the funds to be transferred. It normally took a year to remit money from Cracow to Bruges. From there to Avignon, the Italian merchant-bankers made the transfer by remittance in a few days. In general, Hanseatic business methods were backward as compared with those of the Italians. Prior to 1500, there was a lag of at least a century between the two. It is only in the sixteenth century that the Hanseatic merchants begin to improve their practices and to bring them up to the same level.

From an early date, the name 'hanse' was given to associations of travelling merchants frequenting a foreign country. Thus the Flemish 'hanse' of London was an association of merchants hailing from different Flemish towns and making regular trips to England. Members paid dues which were also called *hansa*. The purpose of such associations was, of course, to provide collective protection in foreign lands, to secure trade privileges, if possible, and to watch over the strict observance of those already in effect.

Originally, the German 'hanse' was an organization of the same type, which grouped together the German merchants frequenting Visby on the island of Gotland (*teutonici Gotlandiam frequentantes*). Similar associations were later founded in London, Bruges and Novgorod. In the beginning the Hanseatic League was, therefore, not a league of cities. It gradually grew out of merchant corporations and it never became a political federation, but always remained a loose alliance of German towns for the defence of common economic interests and exclusive privileges. The expression 'German hanse' itself was not used until 1358, when the delegates of the German towns assembled in Lübeck to adopt a common policy in response to alleged violation of the privileges enjoyed by the German merchants trading in Flanders. In later years, those reunions were held regularly, and the Hanseatic League was thus transformed from a merchant gild into a confederation of towns.

In the fourteenth and fifteenth centuries, the four major establishments (*Kontore*) were St Peter's Court (Peterhof) in Novgorod, the 'Bridge' (Brücke) in Bergen, the Steelyard (Stahlhof) in London and the 'German Merchant' in Bruges. There were also smaller outposts: Stockholm, Visby and Hull. The German towns in the dominions of the Teutonic Order, such as Danzig, Dorpat, Königsberg, Reval and Riga, were actually members of the League and not outside trading posts. Most north German and Westphalian towns belonged to the League, and so did Cologne. It also included Dutch towns east of the Zuider Zee, such as Deventer, Groningen, Kampen and Zwolle.

Among the four major establishments, the one in Novgorod was perhaps the most precarious because it was located in a totally alien environment among a sometimes hostile population. In this respect, the situation somewhat resembled that of the Italian *fondachi* in Egypt or Tunis. Like them, the St Peter's Court, established before 1200, was also surrounded by a wall, a useful precaution against any surprise attack by a riotous Russian mob. Within the walls there was a church of the Latin rite, with vaults used as warehouses, living quarters for the merchants and the customary bath-house. When the vaults were filled, the merchants piled up their goods in the church itself so that it was necessary to pass a regulation forbidding the storing of anything on the high altar. Each night the gate was closed and no Russian was allowed to remain inside.

No German merchant resided permanently in Novgorod. The Russian traders arrived with two caravans, one in summer and the other in winter, and departed together after a few weeks' stay. Between caravans, the Court was nearly empty and left to the care of the porter. In the fifteenth century, fewer and fewer merchants made the seasonal trip to Novgorod, preferring to send their factors. To facilitate business with the Russians, the Court provided an interpreter. Most exchange was on a barter basis, although the goods may have been priced. Sad experience had taught the Germans that it was dangerous to extend any credit to the Russians. The general impression is that conditions in Novgorod were rather primitive and that business was conducted according to a certain ritual from which it was not advisable to deviate in the least.

In Bergen, conditions were less strained than in Novgorod. Nevertheless, there also the German merchants lived in a special quarter called Deutsche Brücke, but it was not a fortified enclosure that could, if necessary, withstand a regular siege. This quarter formed a unit with its own wharf, warehouses and lodgings.

After 1388, the German colony in Bergen was ruled by aldermen assisted by a council. They had jurisdiction in civil matters, not only over the merchants but also over the German resident craftsmen. Criminal cases, however, were reserved for the Norwegian authorities. Women were not tolerated on the Brücke, but this rule eliminated one problem only to create another, since it encouraged gambling, drinking and rough play, and it was difficult to maintain discipline among unruly bachelors.

The trade with Bergen was almost exclusively in the hands of the Wendish towns: Lübeck, Wismar and Rostock. Stockfish was the principal article of trade, like herring at Scania. In the course of time, the Brücke of Bergen became more and more a training school for young apprentices who were sent there by their masters to gain practical experience. In the sixteenth century, factors formed the majority of the colony, but this trend was already in evidence earlier, as the Hanseatic merchants gradually learned how to delegate power and how to conduct business from a distance.

For the Hanse, London, although not yet a world metropolis, was far more important than the fish market on the shore of Bergenfjord. Most probably the merchants of Cologne were the first Germans to trade with England. Their presence is already recorded in the early Middle Ages. At any rate, they formed a gild, since a privilege issued by Henry III in 1260 mentions a *gildehalle* possessed by the 'merchants of Almain'. It was not without difficulty that the merchants from Lübeck and other towns gained admittance to this already established fraternity. It even seems that, early in the fourteenth century, there existed, for a while, two separate organizations.

In London, the Hansards had their headquarters in the Steelyard, a compound bordering on the Thames and including a wharf, a mess hall, storehouses and living quarters. In it the Hansards lived an almost collegiate life under the control of their own alderman and a committee of twelve. The members of this committee were elected by the residents; one-third by each of the following sectors: (1) the Rhinelanders including the merchants of Dinant in present-day Belgium, (2) the merchants from the Westphalian, Saxon and Wendish towns, (3) the Prussians and the German Balts. As elsewhere, the German colony was subject to the jurisdiction of the aldermen in civil and commercial matters. In addition to the German aldermen, the members of the Steelyard were required to appoint an alderman of London as an assessor. His functions were to sit in, as a judge, on certain cases and to act as a go-between in any negotiations or dealings with the authorities of the city. According to tradition, the guard of Bishopsgate, giving access to London Bridge, was entrusted to the merchants of the Steelyard; it was at the same time a burden and a privilege, but the Hansards valued it enough to have their right confirmed at the Peace of Utrecht (1474).

Like the Italians, the Germans were envied by the merchants of the city, and the friction grew worse during the late fourteenth and fifteenth centuries as the English tried to penetrate into the Baltic and to wrest control of this trade from the Hanseatic League. One justified source of complaint was that the Hansards, by virtue of antiquated privileges, paid lower customs duties than either the Englishmen themselves or other aliens. However great the pressure put on the English government to repeal the privileges of the Hanse, they were not definitely lost until the reign of Elizabeth I, after a temporary suspension from 1468 to 1474 during the war between England and the Wendish and Prussian towns.

In contrast to the conditions existing in Novgorod, Bergen and London, the Hanseatic merchants in Bruges were not confined to certain quarters but lived in town. The Hansa House, a magnificent structure

I

with a lofty tower and lovely gothic windows, which was not erected until 1470 upon property donated by the town, was not a residence hall, but a club which also contained cellars for the storage of goods, and offices for the aldermen. When later the Hansa House in Antwerp was built to accommodate guests, it proved difficult to rent all the chambers, as most of the merchants preferred to stay in town instead of being put up in barracks.

In Bruges, the Hanseatic merchants felt more at home than in any other foreign country. For one thing, they did not need an interpreter in order to converse with the natives. In the Middle Ages, Low German was much closer to Flemish than it is today owing to the influence of High German, which has become the literary language and is taught in the schools. In Bruges, also, there was not the same antagonism as in London. Merchant strangers were welcomed by the municipal government and the townspeople. Since the Flemish carrying trade had died long ago, they knew very well that they depended upon the foreigners to bring prosperity, and upon the Hanse especially for imports of Prussian and Polish grain. It is true that there were some incidents and occasional outbursts, but there was nothing like the chronic hostility which poisoned the atmosphere of London.

The Hanseatic colony in Bruges was administered by a board of six aldermen or elders, two for each of the three sectors, the Rhenish, the Westphalian-Wendish and the Prussian-Baltic. After 1472 the number of aldermen was reduced from six to three with an advisory committee of twelve. The task of the aldermen was threefold: (1) to watch over the preservation of the all-important trade privileges, (2) to enforce the staple rules and (3) to judge any suits brought by one Hanseatic merchant against another. In Bruges, as in other cities, these cases were outside the jurisdiction of the local courts. The staple included wool, wax, furs, copper, grain and a few other products which, according to treaty, could not be brought to the Swyn in Hanseatic ships without being unloaded and offered for sale in Bruges. Besides *stapelgud*, or staple goods, there were other goods called *ventegud* to which the staple regulations did not apply. Such goods were allowed to pass in transit without any interference. These staple agreements gave Bruges a considerable advantage over neighbouring rival towns, in particular, Antwerp. Of course, the staple rules did not apply to goods shipped directly to England or Scotland without touching the Swyn.

As previously mentioned, the Hanseatic merchants in Bruges transacted most of their business through the innkeepers who also acted as brokers. According to the historian Rudolf Häpke, the Flemish 'hosteler' was the most important personage whom a merchant was likely to encounter on a trip to Bruges. Not only did the 'hosteler' provide lodging, but he rented his cellar to store the merchant's goods and was usually privy to all contracts. If necessary, he stood surety for his guests or collected their outstanding claims after they had left town. His integrity was of the greatest importance in taking advantage of the best obtainable price. The Italians, of course, also used the services of the brokers, but probably not to the same extent as the German merchants. In Bruges, the broker-innkeepers belonged to the upper strata of society immediately below the *poorterij* or the rich rentiers who did not belong to any craft.

The only region which escaped either Italian or Hanseatic control was southern Germany. International trade in this area was geared mainly to Venice and Milan, although, after 1420, the fairs of Geneva emerged as an important connection with other parts of Europe.

One of the main characteristics of the south German trade is the existence of some very large companies, such as the Great Company of Ravensburg (*Grosse Ravensburger Gesellschaft*), which lasted for 150 years (1380–1530) and is said to have equalled in size the major Italian companies. These large business units were exceptions, however, and it is doubtful whether their organization excelled that of the Italians. One of the difficulties is that no articles of association for any of these south German companies have survived. In any case, the Great Company of Ravensburg had, in 1497, thirty-eight partners. Of course, they did not all have an equal voice in the management. Most probably the real power was vested in a small committee of three, one of whom was the treasurer and chief accountant. General financial statements were not drawn up every year, but at irregular intervals. Sometimes three, four or more years were allowed to elapse before the books were closed and profits were determined. Certainly, double-entry book-keeping was not in use, since it was still unknown to the Fuggers in the sixteenth century. Accounts were more systematically kept, however, than was customary in northern Germany. The Great Company of Ravensburg was not any more specialized than the Italian or Hanseatic firms. As everywhere in the Middle Ages, diversification was the rule. Personnel was a major problem, and the correspondence suggests that the behaviour of factors and apprentices gave plenty of worry to the leaders of the Ravensburg company.

This general picture finds confirmation in the recently published account-book (1383–1407) of Matthäus and Wilhelm Runtinger, a Regensburg partnership. Its connections extended from Venice, Austria and Bohemia in the east to Frankfurt-on-Main and the Low Countries in the west. The partnership's activities were, as usual, very diversified. From a technical point of view, its book-keeping is on a relatively high level, but does not meet the canons of double entry.

In order to maintain their control of the overseas trade, the Venetians subjected the south German merchants who visited Venice to strict supervision. They could not stay where they wished, but were forced to take a room at the *Fondaco dei Tedeschi*, a special hostelry maintained by the Venetian Republic and managed by a superintendent accountable to the Senate. The visitors were allowed to import only the products of their own region—and not any English or Flemish cloth, for example—and to purchase spices and luxuries brought by the Venetians from overseas. To prevent any evasion of the regulations, all business had to be transacted through sworn brokers and interpreters. This draconian system was not without compensation for the Germans, since no Venetian was allowed to compete with them in their own territory. In other words the trade between Venice and south Germany was entirely in German hands, and any infringement of this monopoly was severely punished.

On the organization of English trade, a number of studies, among others those of E. M. Carus-Wilson, M. M. Postan, Eileen Power, L. F. Salzman and George Unwin, are available and easily accessible in any college or university library of the English-speaking world. Since it is impossible to do full justice to the subject in a few paragraphs, the ensuing remarks are merely intended to emphasize for purposes of comparison certain peculiar aspects of the English trade.

Since no account-books have survived for this period, with the exception of the memorandum book of Gilbert Maghfeld, one must rely for information concerning the internal organization of the English firm on the Cely and Stonor business correspondence and on casual references in official documents and court records. There were some substantial English merchants doing a large volume of business, but they operated with only a few factors and apprentices.

Partnerships were fairly common, but there existed no firms with a network of branches even remotely comparable to the great Florentine companies. English merchants frequently 'committed' goods to servants, factors or other merchants to be sold either on a commission basis or according to a profit-sharing scheme. It also happened that investors 'entrusted' money to someone 'to merchandise therewith' and to give them 'a parte of the encrece'. Such a contract, of course, resembled the Italian *deposito a discrezione* and the difference between it and a loan was sometimes hard to draw. English merchants concluded occasional partnerships in which they bought 'certain merchandize' in common. These arrangements, consequently, applied to a single venture, but they were frequently renewed: no sooner was one liquidated than the same partners embarked on another. In England, there also existed partnerships of a more permanent nature in which the partners operated together 'on joint stock'. The Cely brothers after their father's death formed such a partnership. As elsewhere in Europe, vessels were often owned by several shareholders, but chartered to one master who assumed command and respon-sibility for actual operation.

In contrast to Italy, where the civilians developed a body of doctrine designed to differentiate between the partnership and other forms of con-tract, clear legal and terminological distinctions failed to emerge in England, probably because of the pragmatic character of English law. In most cases, the only remedies available at common law were the action of debt and the action of account, by which a creditor could sue a deb-tor for not rendering account of the money or the goods entrusted to the latter's care. With reference to mutual partnerships, the English law did, however, recognize at an early date that merchants trading together were jointly and severally liable for common debts.

In the fifteenth century, the English may have known about marine insurance, but they found no need to insure on short cross-Channel trips. Double-entry book-keeping was probably introduced prior to 1543, the date of Hugh Oldcastle's text-book, the first on the art of book-keeping after the Italian manner; but it is doubtful whether the English had made any effort before 1500 to master this art, although it was assiduously prac-tised in the counting-houses of Lombard Street. Around 1450, the English merchants were beginning to make extensive use of the bill of exchange, whether in the form of a draft or a promise to pay; but they still preferred bonds or obligations and more informal bills of debt which, beyond the seas, circulated from hand to hand without formality. In England itself, the position of the bearer was still uncertain at com-mon law, although the mercantile courts were more willing to provide a remedy. The Italian merchant-bankers adapted themselves to English practice, and the ledger of the firm Filippo Borromeo & Co. in London (1436-9) shows that they made advances on bills obligatory payable to a certain person 'or the bearer thereof', which was contrary to Italian usage.

The English trade owes its originality less to the retarded adoption of Italian business procedures than to a set of unique institutions, which pro-tected it very effectively against the inroads of foreign competition. This was especially true of the export trade, which was to a large extent con-trolled by native merchants, whereas the Italians seem to have retained their hold on the importation of spices, merceries and other products. Their control was, however, by no means absolute, and the London mercers and grocers frequented Bruges in order to replenish their stocks. Nevertheless, by and large, the export and the import trades were in different hands. This situation still prevailed in the sixteenth century, with the result that, in the money market, the English merchants were usually takers or sellers of bills in Lombard Street, but deliverers or buy-ers of bills in the Low Countries, where, after collecting the proceeds of their exports, they had funds to transmit to London. The Cely papers (1475–88) give evidence to the same effect: they are full of complaints about the harm done to the Staplers, or wool exporters, by the rise of the English noble. This was quite natural; since they had money coming to them on the continent, the rising exchange was disadvantageous to them because they received less in English currency for the same amount of Flemish money.

Besides the divorce of import and export trade, an important characteristic of English commerce during the fourteenth and fifteenth centuries was that it was confined to the Channel and the Bay of Biscay. Consequently, only short distances were involved. Although one of the two trading companies called itself the Merchant Adventurers, the adventure, if any, was not very great. Moreover, the current of trade followed well-known channels, so that an experienced merchant did not run undue risks.

Another distinctive feature of English trade was that it was strictly regulated by the trading companies. Although each member traded on his own, he had to comply with the regulations which tended to lessen considerably the degree of competition by price-fixing, quotas and allotment of shipping space. In the fifteenth century, the trading companies were two: the Fellowship of the Staple and the Merchant Adventurers. They specialized respectively in the exportation of wool and of cloth, the two principal articles of export. As the exports of wool were steadily falling and those of manufactured cloths steadily rising, the Merchant Adventurers were inevitably gaining ground to the detriment of the Company of the Staple.

To complete the sketch, it should be added that, for fiscal and political reasons, the trading companies received the strong support of the English government. Home staples for wool tended to cut out the English from the carrying trade, but staples abroad had the opposite effect of eliminating the foreigner and of placing the carrying trade under the exclusive control of the Staple Company.

Although the means were different, the English government in its economic policy pursued more or less the same objective as the Italian republics or the Hanseatic League. In the Middle Ages, the aim was always to gain control of the carrying trade and to secure and retain a privileged position. According to circumstances, this aim was achieved by superior business organization, by force or by a combination of both.

CHAPTER III
Markets and Fairs

I. *Early Fairs and Markets*

It is no longer possible nowadays to take the view that the Germanic invasions put an end to the commercial life which still characterized the last centuries of the Roman Empire. The new states which arose on all sides upon the ruins of Romania were still the scene of relatively intensive trading operations. Foreigners as well as natives took part in this economic activity. Among the former the Syrians especially attract attention. They were already to be found everywhere during the Imperial period: from Egypt to the Danube, from Spain to England. M. P. Charlesworth, among others, has fully demonstrated this point. In the fifth century Salvianus speaks of the *negociatorum et Syricorum omnium turbas quae majorem ferme civitatum universarum partem occupant*. These 'Syrians' are, however, at least in part, Greeks, and in their ranks should no doubt be included those Greek merchants of Orléans mentioned by Gregory of Tours who received a visiting Merovingian sovereign to their town with songs.

In the Midi towns especially the population was a cosmopolitan one. At Narbonne, in 589, it comprised Goths, Romans, Jews, Greeks and Syrians; certainly these three last groups lived primarily by trade. The Jews, who were numerous throughout Gaul and in Spain, were frequently forbidden to possess and to traffic in Christian slaves, a fact which is proof that they did play an important role in this trade.

Port organization continued to follow the Roman pattern, witness the *catabolus* or *cataplus* of Marseilles found in Gregory of Tours and in a document of Clovis III dated 692. Further evidence is to be found in the *thelonearii* who welcomed to Visigothic Spain the *transmarini negociatores*. There existed, however, between the institution of the *cataplus* and the markets and fairs a connection which, so far as I am aware, has not yet been noticed. Does not Sidonius Apollinaris speak of a merchant who *catapli . . . nundinas adit*, and does not a Spanish council in 693 make provisions for a Jew who *at catablum pro quibuslibet negotiis peragendis accedat*? If these items are taken together, the logical deduction is that there existed markets or even fairs (*nundinae*) in the principal ports of Merovingian Gaul and Visigothic Spain. Trade there must have been subjected to a fairly strict control on the part of the royal agents who superintended the customs store-rooms, which were a kind of bonded warehouse, somewhat analogous to the Byzantine ἀποθήκη τῶν βασιλικῶν κομμερκίων. In the markets of the maritime towns trade was most probably undertaken both by foreign and by native merchants, the former assuming primarily the function of importers. In conjunction with the native merchants they then distributed the goods among the towns of the interior. Some of these latter certainly possessed markets. In Provence the *curator civitatis* and the *defensor civitatis* were responsible for the supervision of the market. Further north, however, it is possible that transactions took place rather in the shops of the trading quarters. We know through Gregory of Tours that such a quarter existed in Merovingian Paris. As for the fairs, these existed at Rodez and in other southern towns from the middle of the seventh century onwards. That at St Denis near Paris seems to date from *c.* 635.

Mentions of both markets and fairs are, however, rare. In Spain none are explicit in the Visigothic period. It would be rash nevertheless to deduce therefrom that the various fairs and markets indicated in the texts were lacking in importance. That is certainly not true in the case of the St Denis fair, instituted by Dagobert I. It was this king who, in 634 or 635, gave up the tolls and revenues of all kinds accruing from this fair and ceded them to the Basilica of St Denis, thus providing the oldest known example of such a favour. A judgment of Childebert III in 709 attests the 'international' importance of the fair. It mentions *illo teleneu, quicquid de omnes neguciantes aut Saxonis vel quascumquelibet nacionis ad ipsa sancta fistivetate domni Dionisii ad illo marcado advenientes*. The shortage of information about the goods sold at this time does not mean that the fair was not already at this period a notable source of revenue for the abbey.

The *portus* found in Merovingian texts must also have been the scene of commercial transactions, if one is to judge by the official document of Sigbert III dated 652, according to which *negotiantium commertia* are obviously being practised there. The reference here is to Champtoceaux on the Loire and to Port-St Père on the Tenu, a left tributary of this river not far from its mouth. Tolls in these places are granted to the abbey of Stavelot-Malmédy, as well as authority over their inhabitants and defenders.

In the Carolingian period markets are very numerous. They existed in each *civitas*, in many townships and on the domains of many abbeys. As for fairs, scarcely any others than those of St Denis are known.

Alongside the fair dating from the Merovingian period, a St Mathias fair, held in February, begins to emerge at this time at St Denis: it is certainly not earlier than 775. However, the old fair—which, we know, was held in October—must have been the more prosperous. A document of Pepin the Short dated 753 speaks of foreigners visiting there *ad negociandum vel necocia plurima exercendum et vina comparandum*. In 814 Louis the Pious granted exemption from the tolls to all wagons, ships and other vehicles bringing to the fair wine, honey and various other kinds of mer-

chandise. Some information is therefore available as to what was sold at
St Denis. Moreover, we learn, too, that under Louis the Pious permanent
local trade was not suspended during the fairs, contrary to what is often
to be observed at later periods. What is more, merchants visiting the fair
could undertake business outside the field in which the fair was held.
L. Levillain, to whom we owe a penetrating study of economic activity
at St Denis, was of the opinion that the October fair, by reason of the season of the year in which it was held, was primarily a market for wine and
honey intended for the regions lying further to the north which had no
vineyards and apiculture. He thought, too, that Anglo-Saxon and Frisian
wools and cloths were probably sold there, but that is not proved by the
texts. All we know with certainty is that St Denis was a great annual market for agricultural produce.

Under the Carolingians, many markets, and the dues thereto attaching, were granted to the Church. Thus, by a document of 869, Charles
the Bald assigned to the monastery of St Bénigne at Dijon *burgum quoque,
mercatum et districtum*. At Noyon, in 901, mention is even made of an annual market belonging to the bishop. The same applies to Italy as to
France. In 869 Arnold of Carinthia granted to the monastery of St Sixtus
at Piacenza jurisdiction over the market. This situation continued in the
tenth century as is shown, for example, by an act of Otto I in favour of the
cathedral of Asti. These markets were, until the tenth century, weekly
and not daily markets. Fairs were rare and no doubt of short duration.
One example has been found at Noyon; and another, and older one, at
Flavigny, may be quoted from a document of Lothair dated 841 in which
is mentioned a *forum venalium rerum tam anniversarium quamque hebdoma-
darium*. Consequently there was at Flavigny both a weekly market and
an annual market, and therefore a fair. One may ask whether this document does not provide the key to what was, in fact, the character of the
majority of these Carolingian 'fairs', that is to say, simply rather more
important markets coinciding with the festival of the local saint (*anniversarium*). If by this time at St Denis—the only fair of importance whose
activity is to some extent known—trade in agricultural products is visibly
predominant, why should not the same be true of the few annual
markets, undoubtedly of far less importance, encountered in the texts?

It is indeed true that in the Carolingian period there were places in
which major trade operations were carried on. For example, those frontier markets indispensable for transactions with neighbouring countries
which are mentioned in the capitulary of Thionville dated 805: Bardowiek, Schesel near to Celle, Magdeburg, Erfurt, Halazstadt near Bam-
berg, Forchheim, Pfreimt, Ratisbon and Lorch. But none the less Carolingian Germany did not possess, in addition to these commercial centres
which were primarily dependent on the trade with the Slav and Avar

regions, more than six internal markets, of which only two (Korvey and Herfort) were located in the north of the country. The places known with some certainty to have regularly sheltered a merchant population are generally—at least in north-western Europe—ports and not places located in the interior. This is the case at Quentowic and Duurstede, as well as at Birten, Hamburg, Birka and Bremen.

There were, however, regions which were an exception to this rule, in particular the valleys of the Rhine, Meuse and Scheldt, which were stimulated by the trading activities of the Frisians and, less directly, of the Scandinavians. In the course of the ninth century there grew up commercial centres known as *portus* or *vicus*. This is the case at Mainz, Worms, Maastricht, Namur, Valenciennes, Tournai and Ghent. These centres, however, were generally ruined by the Norse invasions. Everything had therefore to be started afresh in the tenth century, a period distinguished by a general resumption of trade.

In northern Germany alone, so little favoured under the Carolingians, twenty-nine markets are known in the Ottonian period. In those regions where, in the previous century, *portus* had grown up, the latter took on a new lease of life. At Ghent, for example, a second *portus* was established on both banks of the Lys, at the foot of the comital *castrum*. By 1000 this *portus* was already the centre of an important trade. The existence of a St Bavon's fair (1 October) is attested there from 1013 and it is likely that it dated from much earlier. The original market lay directly in front of the bridge which was the exit from the count's *castrum*. Starting from the market, a main street ran right across the *portus*, which was bounded by the Lys and the Scheldt. This street threw off alleys, at the end of which new markets successively appeared, the Friday market and the grain market. This development, which is earlier than the twelfth century, already reveals the existence of what is, in fact, a real urban market organization.

It is obvious that the old *portus*—even in regions as developed as the valley of the Scheldt—did not all afford the possibility of a development of a system of urban markets. Thus the *portus* of Eename disappeared by the middle of the eleventh century. This very fact has allowed an archaeological investigation to be made. It is known that at the end of the tenth century or at the beginning of the eleventh a *navigium*—no doubt a wharf—existed there, as well as a market where tolls were levied. The centre must have been a fairly large one for as many churches are found at Eename as at Ghent, but between 1044 and 1063 the *portus* was destroyed, and it was Oudenaarde which then took over the role of commercial centre for the region.

We have already seen that at Ghent the oldest market was set up near the pre-urban nucleus, the comital *castrum*. Similar cases are to be found elsewhere. The market or *forum* is the essential element of the *portus, bur-*

gus or *suburbium* which grew up beside the primitive nucleus. At Cologne, for example, the market of the *Rheinvorstadt*, set up in the tenth century, was situated in front of one of the approaches to the fortified *civitas*. This *Alter Markt* originally formed with the *Heumarkt*, a haymarket, a single large market place. At Basle and at Bonn similar situations existed at the same period, and the same applies to Namur, from the tenth century onwards, to Liège, Bruges, Douai, Ypres at the same period, to Brussels, Louvain, Antwerp in the following century. The same phenomenon is found at Middelburg in Zeeland before the end of the eleventh century, at Utrecht from the tenth century. At Paris, in the tenth century, the merchant quarter lay on the right bank of the Seine, and backed on to the Ile de la Cité, the walled episcopal *civitas*. It is there, too, that the oldest market was located. In Champagne, at Troyes, one of the centres of the celebrated fairs, the site of the oldest market was not far from one of the gates of the *civitas*. At Provins, the old market was less than 100 metres from the entrance to the count's castle.

There are also cases where the market developed further away from the primitive nucleus. At Dijon, in the eleventh century, two *burgi* grew up, one around the fortified abbey of St Bénigne, the other to the north of the *castrum*. The market of this second *burgus* lay in the twelfth century near to one of the gates of the *castrum*, but it shifted later towards the outskirts. At Étampes, along the Paris–Orléans highway, Louis VI founded, in 1123, a *forum novum* half-way between the royal *castrum* and an old domanial village.

It is not only between the Loire and the Rhine, the classical region for towns owing their birth to trade, that origins similar to those just described can be postulated for the town markets. In Spain, at León, there existed in the tenth century a *suburbium* outside the town wall, and it was there that the market enjoying royal protection (*mercato de rege*) was located. By the beginning of the eleventh century permanent shops already existed on this market site. Yet the market itself was a weekly one, held on Wednesdays. The main sales were of agricultural produce, but tools and utensils of all kinds were also sold. So far the parallel with the situations found in the northern regions is complete. The analogy is less complete, however, if one examines the provenance of the articles sold in the León market. Meat came from the neighbouring township of Macellarios, where there was a large number of butchers, a fact to which it owes its name. The inhabitants of Grullarios sent cranes, a delicacy much in demand at this period; those of Tornarios sold dishes and earthenware jars; those of Rotarios wheels for agricultural transport. The inhabitants of Sejambre were nearly all cartwrights; those of Arbolio made waterskins and those of Toletanos worked in leather. All these craftsmen fed the urban market. The outlet for the market must, moreover, have been more or less adequate. In fact, the León market not only attracted the town inhabitants, but must also have found a clientele among the numerous small monasteries of the neighbourhood and even, for certain articles, among the inhabitants of the rural estates. Yet this market was not an exclusively local, or even regional, one. From the borders of Portugal came Toro wine and Zamora oil. Salt from the Castilian salt-pans and Asturian cider also found their way there. There were, in addition, several shops *intra muros* and it does seem that in those shops were sold especially rich fabrics imported from Byzantium and—in greater quantity obviously—from Moslem Spain.

A similar situation, though less well defined and at a somewhat later date, can be seen in other towns of the Iberian peninsula, both in the different Spanish kingdoms and in Portugal. The same may also be true of the French Midi, but in both cases information is at present lacking. By and large, the same causes—that is to say, the resumption of long-distance trade—must have produced the same results everywhere. The only differences are those of time and degree.

The urban markets evidently changed their character at the same time as the towns they had helped to create. As a result of recent research even the details of the topographical development can be traced in some cases. An extremely careful and ingenious study has been devoted to the market of one particularly important commercial town, Lübeck. Its author, F. Rörig, has examined the difficult question of privately owned land lying within the market boundaries. By studying the *Oberstadtbücher*, in which property transfers were recorded in chronological order, he has shown that Rietschel's theory that the market is normally situated on ground belonging to the seignorial landlord is not confirmed in the case of Lübeck. Originally the built-up land was in the hands of the oldest patrician families, from whose ranks the town council sprang, either as private property or, less commonly, as collective property. It was the latter which later, about 1200, constituted the first municipal lands.

The well-known theory of the *Marktzwang*, formerly developed by Keutgen, and according to which there existed in the medieval towns a general obligation to sell in the market, can scarcely be applicable to any but the oldest towns, for, in the case of twelfth-century foundations like Lübeck, no such obligation is confirmed. In these towns only the bakers and the butchers were expressly required to sell in the market.

Originally intended for the sale, and, in some measure, for the production, of goods, the market at Lübeck gradually changed its character by reason of the fact that the shops there began to be used also as residences. The exceedingly large number of inhabitants burst the bounds of the old organization about 1300.

It would obviously be erroneous to imagine that the outlines of market development observable in an important town like Lübeck are applicable *in toto* to the market of any other town in west and central or southern Europe. In certain parts of Spain there were markets which were held only fortnightly or even monthly. It is quite certain that small markets of this type had but few characteristics in common with the one just discussed. Nevertheless, generally speaking, the evolution towards permanent trade occurred at an early date in Spain. Already in 1117 the *fuero* of Ucles mentions a daily market. The Arabic name of *azogue* given to similar markets proves Moslem influence here. At Guimarães in Portugal there was even a royal *azogue* and another for the town. In the Iberian peninsula also the existence of specialized markets is attested, such as the *fangas* of Portugal where cereals especially were sold. Yet in spite of these evident signs of the development of market activity in these regions, it is certain that it was practically only in the maritime regions of Catalonia and the eastern seaboard that in Spain the town markets had evolved as far as those of north-western Europe or Italy. It must not be forgotten, however, that studies of these countries, and even of the Midi of France and Italy, are far less numerous and far less extensive than those devoted to the markets of the northern countries. There is no doubt that many peculiarities would largely be reduced to analogies by more detailed research.

While the first town markets were developing, the fairs, too, were multiplying everywhere. At St Denis, near Paris—which already had fairs in the Merovingian and Carolingian periods—a new fair emerged in the eleventh century as a result of the resumption of trade. This was the Lendit fair held in June, although the St Denis fair itself opened on 9 October.

The name Lendit derives from the custom of announcing (*indicere*) the institution of a religious festival. The word *indictum* (*endit*) serves to designate the festival itself. The institution of an *endit* had as a corollary the institution of a market, also called *indictum*. Soon the term *Lendit* indicated alternatively the whole plain of St Denis or the part reserved for the fair. Before the eleventh century there is no mention of this fair, a fact which, like the date at which it was held, proves that it is quite distinct from the commercial assemblies of earlier times. Towards the middle of the eleventh century the abbey of St Denis obtained royal authorization to establish in the township of St Denis a fair beginning on the second Wednesday in June and lasting until St John's Eve. A second fair was instituted by Louis VI between 1109 and 1112 in the plain of St Denis, but it lasted only for three days. This was the outer *Lendit*, granted to the abbey in 1124. The two Lendit fairs co-existed until 1213, and, at this time, were of the same duration. After 1213 the two fairs gradually merged into a single fair, the 'Lendit of the plain of St Denis'.

From the eleventh century, too, dates our first really detailed information about the Flanders fairs. In this region, destined to be the scene of intensive commercial and industrial activity, the oldest fairs are those of St Omer, Douai and Ghent. That of Torhout is mentioned from 1084 onwards and those of Ypres and Lille from 1127. Messines, too, quickly became the site of a fair of some importance. Lille, Messines, Ypres and Torhout, all lying to the west of the Scheldt, formed a kind of commercial axis pointing towards Bruges. The places where fairs were established were generally the seats of fairly important ecclesiastical institutions and sometimes of a comital *castrum*.

The case of Messines has been closely studied and deserves a brief consideration. The fair held in this place was older than the abbey. In 1159 an extension of four days brought its total duration to nineteen days. The fair was then held on the *forum* or market of the community and was also located in the cemetery. The development of this market during the second half of the twelfth century can be tentatively traced. Houses and shops (*stalli*) appeared. In the thirteenth century a second and more extensive *forum* was set up outside the walls. The cemetery at this time no longer served as a market. The old *forum* specialized and was henceforth reserved for wool. The *hospicium* and the *domus canonicorum* were used as a warehouse and hostelry for the merchants.

At Messines, some towns apparently paid the tolls and market and stallage dues at lower rates. These towns were Furnes, Dixmunde, Aardenburg, Oostburg, Oudenburg, Gravelines, Ypres, Ghent and Oudenaarde, all of them Flemish localities with which obviously the most frequent connections existed. No doubt their merchants came primarily to Messines to buy wool. Wool, in fact, seems to have been the most common merchandise at Messines. This traffic, however, did not give rise to a cloth trade of any importance at Messines. The place remained a small abbey town and, although it had a certain permanent trade and industry, no mention is found abroad of Messines cloth or even of Messines merchants. Moreover, it did not have a covered market until 1445 at a time long after the decline of the fair had set in.

II. *The Fairs of Champagne and Flanders*

A fair like that of Messines, considered by itself, is not of very great international importance when compared with the cycles of associated fairs which grew up from the twelfth century onwards in certain regions, notably in Flanders and above all in Champagne. It is hardly necessary to repeat that these associated fairs were the centres of what has been called the 'world' economy of the Middle Ages.

Continuous information about the Champagne fairs is available from

1114 onwards, although these fairs themselves are considerably older. It is, however, in the thirteenth century that these commercial assemblies assumed their classical and characteristic aspect. The six fairs which formed the now traditional cycle were held in four towns of the counties of Champagne and Brie. Two were held at Troyes, the summer fair at Troyes itself and the winter fair in the suburb of *Troieces*, the *Tresetto* of the Italians. Two others were held at Provins in Brie, the May fair in the upper town, the autumn fair in the lower town. One took place at Lagny, not far from Paris, another at Bar-sur-Aube. They attracted visitors from all parts. All the regions of France sent their merchants there, as did northern and central Italy, Flanders, Hainault, Brabant, Spain, England, Germany, Switzerland and Savoy. Goods were of the utmost variety: cloths and woollens from Flanders and northern France; silks imported from Lucca; leather from Spain, Pisa, Africa and Provence; furs from Germany; linens from Champagne and Germany. It was the Italians above all who imported what are called *avoirs-de-poids*: spices, wax, sugar, alum, lacquer, dye-woods. There are also several mentions of cotton; also of grain, wines and horses, used in large numbers for transport.

The trade which surpassed all others, however, was the cloth trade. A commercial organization like the 'hanse' of the seventeen towns, uniting cloth-producing towns of the Low Countries and northern France, could not sell its cloth except at the Champagne fairs. This region, however, was itself a cloth-producer and Provins was an important cloth centre in the thirteenth century.

The lords of the fairs were at first the counts of Champagne, and later the kings of France. They derived considerable revenues from the fairs: taxes on the residences and stalls of the merchants, entry and exit tolls, levies on sales and purchases, dues upon weights and measures, justice and safe-conduct charges upon the Italians and Jews. The chief officers attached to the fairs were the wardens of the fair who were responsible for order and justice and controlled the fair seal, at least until 1318 when a chancellor or keeper of the fair seal was appointed. Under them were the wardens' lieutenants or clerks, together with sergeants-at-arms to maintain order. It should not be forgotten that, conjointly with the special jurisdiction set up for the fairs, the town magistrature and the local ecclesiastical dignitaries also exercised a certain authority over the merchants and their transactions. The court of the fair wardens was, however, a tribunal of capital importance as can be seen especially by the number of sergeants it employed. In 1317 there were no less than 140, although the Châtelet of Paris, about this time, had no more than 150. There were sixty notaries at the Châtelet and forty at the fairs.

If we had the notarial deeds, we should have at our disposal a documentation so rich and accurate that it would leave nothing to be desired.

The numerous acts and notarial registers lodged in the archives of southern Europe can help in some measure to fill this lacuna, but they offer only a somewhat unilateral documentation and one necessarily limited as to area. They give, however, an idea of the nature of the notarial documents drawn up at the fairs, for a proportion of the notaries operating there came in fact from the Midi in the company of the businessmen, and above all of the Italians.

The notaries worked under the orders of the lieutenants of the fair wardens. Soon the minutes recorded in their registers served as enrolments of deeds, the deed given to the parties being no longer anything more than a copy. It is certain therefore that there existed at the Champagne fairs a real records department. At first sight it is perhaps surprising that these records have disappeared, since the fairs continued up to the French Revolution. It is true that economically—and this had been the case for a long time—they no longer had any importance. The administration had been simplified in the course of time and it is this no doubt that explains the disappearance of their archives.

A meagre fragment has recently been found: a leaf from a register of the Troyes summer fair of 1296. Drawn up by an Italian notary, it contains fifteen deeds mentioning merchants from Piacenza, Genoa, Milan, Asti, Como, Savona, Florence, as well as from Montpellier, Narbonne, Avignon, Carpentras and St Flour. These deeds are concerned with exchange transactions as well as with sales of cloths and horses. Seven of the fifteen are letters by which a carrier undertakes to convey to their destination within a prescribed time consignments of merchandise. Similar way-bills for the passage from Marseilles to the Champagne fairs were already known through the famous notes of Amalric, edited by L. Blanchard. The carriers sometimes dispatched several convoys at once. These had to follow the 'direct king's road' in order to enjoy the fair safe-conduct. For the Troyes–Montpellier journey 23 days were allowed at a rate of 32 kilometres per day. Via the Alps, as far as Alba, a convoy would take 30 days at a rate of 24 kilometres per day. This is a speed comparable to that of modern European transport before the advent of the railways.

Italian merchants were particularly numerous at the Champagne fairs. As early as 1209 Philip Augustus promised all merchants, and particularly the Italians, who visited the fairs of the countess of Champagne, a safe-conduct and three months' grace to leave the country if at any time he withdrew his protection. In 1222 the count of Champagne took the Sienese under his protection and allowed them to undertake banking transactions, except for loans at weekly interest. In 1245 he exempted the Roman, Tuscan, Lombard and Provençal merchants from the jurisdiction of the fair wardens and granted them the right of their own justice.

This privilege was confirmed by Philip the Fair in 1294 and 1295. The *universitas* of the Italians dates from 1278. It was under the jurisdiction of a *capitaneus* or *rector*. In 1294 Lanzalotto Cucherla of Piacenza, *capitaneus et rector universitatis mercatorum Italiae nundinas Campaniae ac regnum Franciae frequentantium*, and an assembly of merchants from Florence, Genoa, Rome, Urbino, Pistoia, Parma, Como, Piacenza, Milan, Venice, Asti and Alba held at Lagny approved an agreement signed between the delegates of many other Italian towns and the count of Salins. This agreement dealt with the routes to be followed, the passage and the tolls between Geneva and Troyes.

These documents are in themselves sufficient to prove the extent of the commercial relations existing between the Champagne fairs and Italy, but unlimited additional evidence is to be found in the notarial acts of the latter country itself. Italians, in fact, conclude a great number of agreements in connection with Champagne, especially acts of *commenda* and deeds of partnership involving a number of participants. An impressive series of acts is available for Genoa which, from about 1250 onwards, had become a kind of financial ante-room to the fairs, where merchants from Lucca, Siena, Piacenza, Parma, Milan, Florence awaited those from Bologna and Pistoia. There these merchants could raise the necessary capital through bills of exchange and credit purchases. In 1304 Genoese merchants alone were granted loans for at least 13,537 Genoese lire, and yet the fairs at this time were already on the decline.

Another effective method of ascertaining the activity of the Champagne fairs—and one which has not yet been sufficiently utilized—would be through a study, in the greatest detail, of the most important tolls levied on the crossings leading to the fairs. The most important for such a study would be Villeneuve near to Chillon on the Lake of Geneva for the road to Italy, and Bapaume in Artois for the Flanders traffic.

The latter was extremely important. It was in fact through the Champagne fairs in the thirteenth century—before the development of sea traffic between the North Sea and the Mediterranean—that the greater part of the output of the most important industry of the time, the Flemish cloth trade, flowed. It may even be said that the recession in this cloth trade in the fourteenth century, together with more general causes due to the combination of economic and political circumstances, was one of the main reasons for the final commercial decline of the Champagne fairs.

The picture here drawn of the Champagne fairs reflects the somewhat static general view which has prevailed until recently. Recent research, however, allows the evolution of the Champagne fairs to be set within that of the economy of western Europe, a fundamental approach which had hitherto been far too neglected. It has been generally thought

K

possible to utilize, even for the twelfth century, information supplied by documents such as the *Coutumes, style et usages* which go back only to the end of the fourteenth century, a period at which the fairs no longer have any real economic importance. Even the *Privilèges et coutumes des foires*, much shorter, but dating from the end of the thirteenth century, are of no use for the period of origins.

If one follows R. H. Bautier in the study of the oldest documents, one sees that at the time of the appearance of the fairs of Troyes, Provins, Bar-sur-Aube and Lagny, other Champagne towns also had fairs which did not enjoy the same success. Contrary to some opinions, it was not the road system which determined the localization of the fairs which did 'succeed'. Even the fact that some fair towns had cloth factories was not a determining factor, since these industries were too recent or, alternatively, had remained of secondary importance. On the other hand, although it is the meeting in Champagne of Flemish and Italian merchants which ensured the success of the fairs, it should be noted also that the cloth trade of Flanders and of northern France was, in Italy, and particularly in Genoa, in the hands of merchants from northern Europe until about the end of the twelfth century. At Milan the first mention of merchants going to the fairs to acquire cloths and wool is in 1172. Genoa obtained in 1190 a privilege from Duke Hugh III of Burgundy allowing its merchants to go to the fairs under the same conditions as the merchants of Asti. The Burgundian toll-houses by which they passed were located at Chalon-sur-Saône, Châtillon, Chagny and Dijon.

In fact, the Champagne fairs existed before the arrival of the Italian merchants, but were at that time purely local or regional markets. *Nundinae* at Troyes are even mentioned by Sidonius Apollinaris. At the beginning of the twelfth century the Champagne fairs were still agricultural markets. In 1114, the oldest document relating to the fair of Bar-sur-Aube mentions only horses and other animals.

The growing importance of these markets in the twelfth century was no doubt due to the growth of the regional population whose needs were thus increased. It was in 1137 that, for the first time, it is recorded at Provins that the *homines de Arras et de Flandria* could lodge outside the fair limits, which had now become too confined. From 1148 money-changers from Vézelay are mentioned, in 1164 cloth manufacturers from Hesdin and merchants from Eu. In 1175 mercers selling at the Provins fairs included men from Rheims, Paris, Rouen, Étampes and Limoges.

It was the institution of a regular cycle which ensured the predominance of the fairs of Troyes, Provins, Lagny and Bar-sur-Aube. From 1191 this system was in operation, as is attested by the acts of the Genoese notary, Guglielmo Cassinese (1190–2), studied by R. L. Reynolds. The choice of fairs participating in the cycle seems to have been made by the count of Champagne. He interested the ecclesiastical institutions, the sole possessors of large-scale capital in Champagne, in the fairs, and they in return began the construction of lodging quarters for the merchants.

The safe-conduct system and the fair wardens, both comital institutions, likewise contributed to the development of the fairs. From the middle of the twelfth century onwards the safe-conduct is not without effect outside the county itself. In 1209, as we have seen, the king of France added his own royal safe-conduct. The wardens are attested from 1174 but more than a century was to elapse before they acquired the higher jurisdiction which characterized them at the end of the thirteenth century. It is only in 1247 that mention is made of the official seal, the *sigillum nundinarum Campanie*. It is not until after 1260 that contracts bearing the wardens' seal occur in quantity, and it is about the same time that the notarial contracts drawn up at the fair by the Italian notaries increase in number. The latter, in fact, in order to be operative in France, had to be inscribed on the registers of the fairs under the wardens' jurisdiction. There is thus a connection between the two facts.

During the first half of the thirteenth century the wardens of the fairs only entertained suits arising from the market regulations and from infringements of those regulations. Up to then, the role of the count and of the ecclesiastical jurisdictions was the more important. In 1260, however, the wardens themselves pronounced sentence of exclusion from the fairs and this exclusion extended to the compatriots of the defaulters if the judicial authorities of their own town or seigniory did not compel them to fulfil their obligations.

The surviving series of wardens' letters is a priceless source of information. They are really continuous from 1274 onwards. The wardens thereafter claim a jurisdiction allowing them to ensure everywhere the execution of agreements concluded at the fair. No doubt the fact that the king of France controlled Champagne from now on was not without relevance to this innovation.

About the same time the merchant communities organized themselves. By the middle of the thirteenth century the Italians had already set up permanent consulates. That of the Sienese, mentioned in 1246, is the oldest. The consuls exercised their authority over their fellow-citizens attending the fair, but they represented also the government of their city *vis-à-vis* foreign rulers and justices. They presided over the assemblies of merchants from their town who took part in the fairs, adjudicated on their differences and represented their interests at law before count or king, at the Parlement or at the fair court. In the second half of the thirteenth century the following Italian towns were represented by consuls: Alba, Asti, Bologna, Como, Florence, Genoa, Lucca, Milan, Orvieto, Parma, Pistoia, Piacenza, Rome, Siena and Venice. These consuls generally exercised their jurisdiction also throughout the remainder of the king-dom of France. On the other hand, a consul of the cordwain merchants of Lérida seems to have had a somewhat different character, although the diploma of 1259 emanating from James I of Aragon, which mentions him, alludes also to the Barcelona and Montpellier consuls, who no doubt resembled more closely those of the Italian towns.

The 'hanse' of the seventeen towns which associated the towns of Flanders, Champagne, Picardy, Hainault and Ponthieu selling cloths at fairs appears about 1230. It was not, in fact, a 'hanse' in the proper sense, although this name is given to it by historians. It held meetings but did not admit either a head or elections. In short, it is simply an organization encouraging a certain solidarity among towns having a cloth industry of a corporative character; it is an organization which continued, after the decline of the fairs, down to the seventeenth century.

Besides the Italian *universitas*, already mentioned, there was another for the Provençaux. The Italian captains (*capitanei*) regularly assembled the Italian consuls and merchants. Occasionally there were two captains, one for Champagne, the other for Beaucaire and Nîmes. In 1281 the *universitas* of Nîmes comprised, besides the captain, a chamberlain or treasurer, a juror and an usher. The election of the captain seems to have been made annually. Any dissension among the consuls of the towns seems to have been settled by majority vote.

Unlike the Italian *capitanei*, those of the Provençaux and Languedocians were not elected by the consuls of the cities but chosen by the Council of Montpellier from among the notables of that town. In 1290 the captain and consul of Montpellier exercised his jurisdiction over the merchants of Narbonne, Figeac, Aurillac, St Flour, Combes, St Tibéri, St Guilhem-du-Désert, Béziers and Sommières in addition to those of his own town.

The character of the fairs changed between the twelfth and fourteenth centuries. At the end of the twelfth century and during the first half of the thirteenth, the Champagne fairs were indeed the centre of the inter-national commercial activity of the western world. It was there that the Italians acquired the northern cloths, the essential industrial product of the Middle Ages, for subsequent distribution throughout the whole Mediterranean world. This trade stimulated an extensive movement of foreign exchange between the fairs and their distant outlets. It is this fact which explains why, from the middle of the thirteenth century onwards, money-changing begins to take precedence over trade.

By 1262 the letters of the Tolomei of Siena provide evidence of this transformation which has usually been held to be a later development. The Tolomei in France obtained at the fairs the necessary funds for their purchases of cloth by means of advances, loans, exchanges made by their Italian head office. For purchases at a fair the agent went north at the time of the preceding fair and the Tolomei funds he employed were considered as an advance, his account being debited with the interest on this sum from one fair to another. The Del Bene of Florence in 1320, or, even earlier, the Sienese in 1294, operated a similar system but with the major difference that the cloths were no longer dispatched from the fairs, but from Paris. In any case, from this time onwards the fairs began to lose much of their truly commercial importance, although it was at this precise moment that the German merchants began to take an increasing part in them. The chief function of the fairs now became the regulation of the capital market. Currency and bill quotations at the fairs, which quickly became known outside through the fair couriers, became a factor in international speculation. In fact, the financial system of the Lyons fairs in the fifteenth century, the Besançon fairs in the sixteenth and those of Piacenza up to the seventeenth, was already heralded in Champagne by the end of the thirteenth century.

There is no agreement yet upon the date at which the decline of the fairs is properly to be placed nor upon the causes of that decline. If, however, the fairs are considered from the point of view of their commercial character, it seems that a recession set in from about 1260; but as financial markets they still enjoyed a considerable boom and this prosperity continued until about 1320. After this date, their decline was pronounced and the last important group of Italians, that of Piacenza, disappeared in 1350. This group, however, was composed of financiers. The Venetians, on the other hand, were authorized in 1351 to trade within the kingdom without going through the Champagne fairs. Thereafter one finds only attempts at reform and plans to re-establish the ancient splendour or to revive the traditional trade routes.

Contrary to a commonly expressed opinion, it was not apparently the localization of large-scale trade in the towns which caused the decay of the Champagne fairs; otherwise, it would be difficult to understand how, later, fairs such as those of Geneva, Lyons, Antwerp, Frankfurt and others could have played such an important role. It is true, they were held in regions which developed later. Taxation, too, has been blamed, but close examination shows it to have been fairly light. The temporary importance of Nîmes, and the more permanent importance first of Chalon-sur-Saône and subsequently of Lyons, are results rather than causes. There is no doubt that the wars of Philip the Fair and his sons impeded trade considerably, but they are not to be viewed as the essential cause of the abandonment of the Champagne fairs. These fairs were no longer the turntable for trade between north and south which they had been seventy-five years earlier. The competition of the sea routes began to be felt especially from about 1320 onwards. R. H. Bautier sees two prime reasons for the recession of the fairs: first, the industrialization of Italy, and secondly, the change in the precious-metal market. The cloth trades of Milan and Florence now competed with that of Flanders. In the latter region the traditional urban cloth trade lost ground to the rural cloth trade which produced textiles more suitable for ordinary use. Concurrently with the fairs the Italian companies, whose prosperity depended upon the traditional cloth trade north of the mountains, likewise declined. This happened in the case of the *arte di calimala* at Florence, and many firms at Lucca, Siena, Pistoia and Piacenza similarly disappeared.

The end of the thirteenth century also saw the substitution of gold for silver in international large-scale trade. The fluctuations in the relative values of the precious metals disorganized the companies which controlled the money-changing business at the fairs. The new companies which followed in their wake and which were adapted to current conditions established themselves at Paris and not at the fairs.

In Flanders in the thirteenth century the fairs likewise adopted a method of organization which became classic. Each of the great Flemish fairs comprised at this time about fifteen assembly days, three 'display' days, eight dispersal days and four payment days. The first Ypres fair was held from 28 February to 29 March; from 23 April to 22 May that of Bruges; from 19 May to 26 May the second Ypres fair; from 24 June to 24 July that of Torhout; from 15 August to 14 September that of Lille; and from 1 October to 1 November that of Messines. Hence, a cycle of six fairs as in Champagne. Besides these main fairs there existed others less important, such as that of St Omer, which adopted in 1269 the customs of the Torhout fair. The annual fair granted to Bruges by Baldwin of Constantinople on 14 August 1200 was likewise governed by the customs of Torhout; hence it is evident that the customs of this very ancient fair served in some measure as a basis for others. At Bruges, the fair seems to have been important even before the increase in the permanent international trade, which occurred there from the second half of the thirteenth century onwards. As a result of the broadening of economic activity, many foreign merchants were already making payments at the fair, but in the fourteenth century, when permanent trade had long been prevalent, certain features still persisted which evidently dated back to the origins and attested the somewhat archaic character of the fairs. Thus the beginning of the display of the cloths coincided with the Ommegang or Festival of the Holy Blood.

At the end of the fifteenth century the attraction of the Bruges fair suffered a considerable setback which coincided with that experienced by the permanent trade of the town. But, at a time when its international importance had decreased, the town made every effort to obtain the concession of a second fair, to be held in January. This fair was granted in 1509. Apparently the principal merchandise sold there was Spanish wool and the textiles produced by the new Flemish cloth industry which used these raw materials. Thus the Bruges fairs seem important primarily at a time when permanent trade of an international nature did not yet predominate; and they seem to recover when the latter's importance had vanished.

In addition to Bruges, most of the Flemish fairs seem to have assumed a character which was regional rather than international, with the exception of the Ypres fair which was very important for payments. It was at Ypres during the days for the display of the cloths that, in the thirteenth century, wool bought from the English merchants at the Torhout and Lille fairs was paid for. As late as the first half of the sixteenth century the commercial gatherings at Ypres still retained some prosperity. As for Lille, we know that merchants from Ghent, Bruges, Ypres and St Omer already enjoyed special privileges there in the twelfth century; but, as elsewhere, it was naturally to the foreign merchants primarily that the fair looked for its prosperity. In the second half of the fourteenth century the kings of France still granted their safe-conducts for journeys to the Lille fairs, although the latter were already on the down-grade.

Statutes for foreign merchants visiting the Flanders fairs had been drawn up by Countess Margaret by 1252. They were exempt from trial by combat and from reprisals. Only their personal goods could be confiscated. Imprisonment for debt existed only for the principal debtor or his guarantor. A case in which a merchant was a party had to be judged within a week.

Exemption from the law of escheat was normal for foreign merchants in the medieval fairs. It is found in Champagne for the Italians in 1294 and similar indications are available for the later fairs, for example, Chalon-sur-Saône, 1465; Lyons, 1463. In Flanders it is known that the Genoese and the Castilians were exempt from this law as well as from that governing shipwrecked property. As a general rule, the privileges granted to foreign merchants, and especially to the English and the Scots, increased in Flanders in the fourteenth and fifteenth centuries, a period when trade in Flanders had passed almost entirely under foreign control. These privileges, however, are not exclusively connected with the fairs.

At the Flemish fairs the installation of the merchants had to be completed by the evening of the day preceding the opening of the fair. The fair was announced by heralds in the town and in the neighbouring districts. Whereas cloth merchants had seats in the cloth-hall, the small traders drew lots for their places. Groupings were ultimately made, however, according to the class of goods sold, whereas in Champagne grouping by nationality was essential. This feature emphasizes the more 'international' or 'world' character of the Champagne trade.

In Flanders, what was in fact a monopoly was assured for fair sales. All trade outside the fair boundary was forbidden in the town and the halls in other towns were obliged to close. At the Champagne fairs, on the other hand, the display period was split up and goods were put on sale in turn: first cloths, then 'cordwains', then goods sold by weight. For cloths and cordwains, the sale came to an end at a cry of *hare* from the fair sergeants. In Flanders, *hare* was called only for cloths. In both regions the merchant himself looked after his merchandise or was represented by a partner or by an authorized agent under appropriate contract to the merchant.

At the Flemish fairs the products sold were obviously very similar to those which could be bought in Champagne. A considerable quantity of cloth, the staple product of the country, was handled. The merchants and the industrial entrepreneurs bought English wool as well as dyestuffs and other materials necessary in cloth manufacture, such as alum, Brazil-wood, chalk, Spanish green, vermilion, cumin, madder, woad or pastel. There were also many *avoirs-de-poids* of southern origin which came via Champagne in the thirteenth century and by sea in the fourteenth: for example, spices such as pepper, ginger, cinnamon, nutmeg, cloves; pharmaceutical products such as aloes, senna, galipot, alkanet root, henna; perfumes, essences, fats and wax. As regards raw materials, iron and steel came from Spain; lead, tin, copper from England, Bohemia and Poland; precious metals from these two latter countries as well as from Hungary. Wines were imported in great quantity, particularly from the Rhine, Poitou, Gironde and Champagne vineyards.

In all the fairs trade in precious metals and money-changing, as well as credit and banking operations, were restricted to specialists. These specialists were the 'Lombards' and the money-changers who were found everywhere. The first were generally not merely financiers, but also merchants. The money-changers, on the other hand, performed a public office. The former were Italians, the latter local men.

The role of the money-changers at the fairs was important because they had a monopoly of the exchange business. At Bruges exchange broker-age was actually forbidden. No one could act as intermediary between the individual and the money-changers. Moreover, it seems that it was the money-changers permanently established in the towns who under-took the office of money-changers at the fairs. At Torhout, where the permanent trade was evidently not as important as in Bruges, this did not happen. Some twenty-eight money-changers are known for this fair in the thirteenth century. Up to about 1280 they came from Arras, after-wards from Lille.

Much less is known about the exercise of justice at the Flemish fairs than at those of Champagne. In Flanders it was entrusted to bailiffs, to fair *mestres*, and to *eschevins de la fieste* who are probably the same as the magistrates of the fair towns. The procedure in their courts was usually summary. The debtor had no recourse to an adjournment. Deeds of agreement often contained a waiver of legal process likely to slow up the course of the proceedings.

In all the medieval fairs, in Champagne, Flanders, and elsewhere, recourse was sometimes had to collective reprisals against merchants coming from a prescribed region, if satisfaction could not be obtained from foreign courts. In this event exclusion from the fair was a particularly rigorous form of reprisal, involving as it did an interdiction upon all the nationals within the jurisdiction of the courts which had refused to accede to requests from the fair courts.

The Flemish fairs played an important role as places and times of payment. Those of Ypres gave rise to the compilation of important series— more than 7,000 specimens—of registered obligations (*lettres de foire*) of which the oldest examples, destroyed in 1914, dated back to the middle of the thirteenth century. These letters constituted promises of payment falling due at the next fair. They were payable at one of the six Flemish fairs or at one of the Champagne fairs. Occasionally the letter did not specify the fair place itself, but only indicated the time. The settlement could be made in cash but also by the delivery of merchandise or by the performance of services. Letters were transferable to third parties. From the end of the thirteenth century they suffered competition from the letters of exchange which, like so many other improvements in the commercial system, were an introduction from Italy.

III. *The Fairs of Chalon, Geneva and Lyons*

We have described in very general terms the character of the fairs of the two great regions where there grew up, during the period when merchants still travelled as a rule with their goods, the two cycles of associated fairs which exercised the greatest influence upon the European economy before the beginning of the fourteenth century. It was at the latter time that these two complementary cycles declined as a consequence of a combination of political and economic phenomena. Among these one of the most important is the fact that urban life had now developed sufficiently in the north of France and in the Low Countries for permanent trade to meet all needs. From Bruges—the principal nodal point for the long-distance trade of the whole of north-west Europe—any kind of merchandise could be brought without interruption to all the towns in the north-west area. Merchandise could also be sent there for distribution in all directions. All this, of course, in times of peace.

As we have already said, it has also been held that the merchant's mode of life had changed to the extent that he now preferred sedentary trade. That is true, however, only for the merchants of certain countries, such as those of Flanders who, however, had journeyed far afield until about the middle of the second half of the thirteenth century. The Italians, on the other hand, always travelled the trade routes and many others did the same. They still frequented the fairs. But these fairs—at least the large fairs of international importance—were no longer located on the axis joining Italy and Flanders via Champagne. From now on they developed to the east, in regions where urban life, and consequently regular trade, was not yet so highly developed as in the north-west of the continent. The fairs shifted from west to east because they depended more and more on the economic contrast existing between those regions which had become industrialized and those which had not, but which could purchase the industrial products of the former by providing them through the fairs with their own natural produce.

The fairs located to the east of the Champagne–Flanders line did not of course appear by magic. They did not suddenly replace those of Troyes, Provins, Ypres or Lille which continued to exist, but with less splendour than formerly. Moreover, the later fairs had already existed at an earlier date but were to attain full vigour primarily during the later centuries of the Middle Ages.

Some fairs clearly show the transition. A good example is that of Chalon-sur-Saône. Chalon is of some commercial importance from the time of the eleventh-century commercial renaissance. The town had a Jewish colony trading in luxury goods and precious metals. The earliest mention of its fairs is at the end of the twelfth century. Thereafter they began to appear in the background of the Champagne fairs and gradually succeeded in establishing themselves on the flank of the great north-south trade axis. The first period of real prosperity dates from c. 1280. It was at this time that the fairs became ducal and had thenceforward, like those of Champagne, the backing of a well-organized territorial authority.

The cloth-halls are mentioned from 1244. They lay outside the boundaries of the old town and nestled against and within the second town wall which ran along a branch of the Saône. During a first period of prosperity, merchants from Arras, Troyes, Provins and Paris took their place alongside those of Rheims, Ypres, Ghent, Douai, Tournay and Valenciennes. Chalon had contacts as well with the textile centres of Beauvais, Étampes, Chartres, Huy, Namur, Chimay, Avesnes, Aubenton, St Quentin, Rouen, Abbeville, Lille and Malines. In the fourteenth century Dinant and St Omer were added to the list; in addition, more Norman (Louviers, Bernay, St Lo, Torigny) and Brabant (Brussels, Louvain, Diest, Lierre) cloths were imported. From Chalon cloths coming from these regions reached the papal court at Avignon.

From the south in the thirteenth century there came silk merchants from Lucca, Bologna and Marseilles, and a little later, traders from Milan, Genoa, Turin, Asti and Pignerol in Piedmont. The neighbouring regions were, of course, represented: west Switzerland up to and including the Vaudois, Savoy, Bresse, the Lyonnais, Dauphiné, and, further still, Provence, the Vivarais and Languedoc. To the west, the attraction of Chalon was felt as far as Auvergne, the Bourbonnais and Berry. There is no trace of the English or Spaniards and scarcely any of merchants from western France either, despite the business connections with the cloth centres of Normandy. On the other hand, Rhinelanders are found there in the fourteenth century. As we have already observed in regard to the cloth-hall, many fabrics from the Low Countries were sold at Chalon. The Italians brought silks and spices, and there is frequent mention of leather and haberdashery articles from Paris.

Despite the diversity and extent of the commercial transactions which took place at Chalon, the fairs of this town were certainly far less important than the groups of fairs in Champagne or Flanders. The Frankfurt fairs, to which we shall return in some detail, also seem to have been more thriving. On the other hand, Chalon was apparently more important than fairs like those of Nördlingen in Swabia and of Zurzach in Switzerland.

Relations with Flanders and Brabant were particularly highly developed, although in 1384 Flanders was the most distant region to be invited to the fairs. There were Flemings at Chalon from the middle of the thirteenth century onwards. The town's fairs are frequently mentioned in Ypres documents of the thirteenth as well as the fourteenth century. Even a place of secondary importance like Grammont is represented by its merchants from the middle of the fourteenth century. Whereas merchants from Malines are reported as early as 1280, the Brussels merchants only appear in the second half of the fourteenth century, and the same applies to those from Louvain. This picture agrees closely with what is known from other sources of the comparative chronology of the commercial evolution of Flanders and Brabant. In 1443 Philip the Good is still urging merchants from the Low Countries bound for Geneva to visit Chalon also, an obvious proof that the fairs of the latter town were already on the down-grade. The export of Burgundy wines, which developed about this time, failed to remedy the situation. It should be noted, however, that nothing is known of the export of these wines via Chalon.

In the fourteenth century, the southern successor of the Champagne fairs was the Geneva fair which reached its apogee in the fifteenth century. At this time there were four fairs per year at Geneva, at Epiphany, Easter, August and All Saints' Day. These commercial gatherings were frequented by merchants from the whole of France, from the Netherlands, the Rhineland, northern and central Italy, as well as from Spain. A curious feature is that the Swiss themselves went there less than to Frankfurt. Only Freiburg and Berne are an exception to this general rule. The Geneva fairs were more important for Freiburg than the later ones of Zurzach and the more distant ones of Frankfurt. The first relations of the town with Geneva date from the first half of the fourteenth century. When Louis XI favoured Lyons to the detriment of Geneva, the Freiburg merchants remained faithful to the latter town. It was only when the Reformation came to Geneva that relations between its fairs and Freiburg—itself in decline—came to an end. In the case of Berne, too, commercial connections with Geneva date from the first half of the fourteenth century. In Geneva the Bernese sold primarily leather and agricultural produce. Unlike the Freiburg merchants, they frequented Lyons after the decay of the Geneva fairs.

F. Borel, who has made a detailed study of the internal history of the Geneva fairs, ends his survey in 1500, although these commercial gatherings did in fact continue for two or three decades longer. An examination of various accounts not known to this historian reveals that at the end of the fifteenth century business at Geneva had a tendency to spread over the whole year, a fact which obviously indicates a diminution in the importance of the fairs. Already in 1489 the seasons at which the Geneva fairs were held no longer corresponded to the traditional dates indicated by the usual names, a situation which resulted from the fact that Louis XI had fixed the Lyons fairs precisely at the date of the old Geneva fairs in order to turn the latter's decline to the profit of the fairs of the French town. The Geneva authorities thereupon put back their own fairs while still retaining their old names.

As elsewhere, spices and produce deriving from the Mediterranean and the colonies of the Levant played their part in the Geneva trade. The Germans, above all the Swabians, brought, in addition, metals, wax and feathers. Cloths from the Low Countries were less frequently sold at Geneva than in the fairs studied above, a circumstance explained by the recession of the Flemish cloth industry in the fifteenth century, and, to some extent, also of the Brabant industry, which, however, occurred later. There are still many points to be cleared up, however, in the overall picture of the purely commercial history of the Geneva fairs—as of many others—and this is due above all to the fact that until recently it was thought that the history of the fairs could be treated by an investigation more or less limited to the local documentation of the fair towns, whereas it is now becoming more and more obvious that a study of foreign archives—and particularly of notarial documents and account-books—is not only indispensable but must also be undertaken over as wide a radius as possible.

We have already alluded to the rivalry, above all a political rivalry, existing between Geneva and Lyons at the end of the fifteenth century. The part played by the royal authority in this quarrel is a sign of the times and a proof of the characteristic interventionism of the nascent mercantilism peculiar to the centralized state. Whereas all the preceding fairs—even if the territorial authority controlled and protected them very efficiently—were in large measure the spontaneous result of economic circumstances, the Lyons fairs are essentially a royal creation.

In 1420 the Dauphin Charles, later Charles VII, established the Lyons fairs by granting them privileges formerly enjoyed by the Champagne fairs. The Lyons magistrature immediately decided that the spring fair would be held on the right bank of the Saône, that is, on the French side, whereas the autumn fair would take place on the left bank in imperial territory.

The proximity of Geneva, later a cause of rivalry, at first facilitated the trade of Lyons by attracting thither merchants already accustomed to visiting the Geneva fairs. Other early connections are indicated in the texts. Thus, in 1454 the Lyons magistrates asked that the central authority, when fixing the dates of the fairs, should avoid clashes with the Lendit fair of St Denis and the fairs of Languedoc.

As we have already seen, the prosperity of Lyons really dates from Louis XI. This king, in fact, re-established the fairs of the town in 1463. The *bailli* of Macon, who was the seneschal of Lyons, was then named warden of the fairs with competence in trade matters. Rivalry with Geneva thereafter became systematic. In this same year of 1463 the Lyonese had a royal prohibition against attendance at Geneva published as far afield as Flanders and Picardy. The Genevese replied by holding up the Germans, Lombards and Florentines passing through their territory on the way to Lyons. The Lyonese on their side paid guards to control the Dauphiné roads. In 1467 the quarrel was temporarily dropped. Agreements signed with Geneva, and at the same time with Berne and Savoy, allowed German merchants to travel freely to Lyons. About the same time, however, and in France itself, the merchants of Paris, Tours, Orléans and Montpellier campaigned against the new fairs.

Nevertheless, the town prospered. Under Louis XI the spice trade found an important market at its fairs. Lyons superseded Aigues Mortes and Narbonne, formerly ports of call for Italian galleys but now silted up. This development was no doubt due to the city's advantageous position. In 1484, the Lyonese themselves declared that all the important fairs lay in the marcher regions and that those lying far from the frontiers—like the Lendit fair of St Denis—attracted few foreigners.

This year 1484 did not come to an end without bringing new anxieties for the Lyonese. The king, in fact, transferred the Lyons fairs to Bourges

and a bitter struggle for the possession of these trade gatherings broke out
between the two towns. A surprising thing is that one of the decadent
sites of the Champagne fairs, the town of Troyes, also tried to profit from
the quarrel with, of course, no success. Major trade had long since, and
for good and all, moved away from Champagne.

Finally, in 1487, partly at the request of the German merchants, the
Lyons fairs were re-established and, from 1494 onwards, there were four
commercial gatherings per year. They reached their peak in the sixteenth
century, primarily as a result of the spice trade and the silk industry. In
the fifteenth century, Lyons, at least from the commercial point of view,
was already *the* silk town. If under Louis XI the cloth trade still played
an important role, it was nevertheless a medieval feature. The future lay
elsewhere and Lyons fully recognized the fact. Geneva had lost its importance and Antwerp was only beginning to develop. For several decades Lyons was to be the main European fair centre.

IV. *Fairs of Germany, Scandinavia and Brabant*

Still further to the east than the fairs of the Saône–Rhône–Lake Geneva
axis developed the German fairs, among which the fairs of Frankfurt-on-
Main replaced those of Champagne in the fourteenth century. Their
origin is, of course, much older. It was only when the Rhine and Main
regions had a production surplus, however, and when, in consequence,
they had new requirements, that the Frankfurt fairs could develop. It is
possible that *c.* 1150 they were held round about 15 August, but it is only
in 1227 that they are explicitly mentioned in a charter of Henry of Swabia,
in which allusion is also made to fairs at Wurzburg and Donauwörth. In
1240 the Frankfurt fairs received their first imperial licence. When the
towns of southern Germany began to trade with Venice, when the increasing colonization of the Slav countries had emphasized the prosperity of the Hanse towns, Frankfurt could occupy an intermediary
position between north and south, west and east.

That did not happen before the fourteenth century. Up to this time
agricultural products are by far the most numerous at the Frankfurt fairs,
although Alsace wines brought by the Strasbourg lightermen were already on sale there. Moreover, up to 1330, there was only a single fair—
the autumn one. In this year appeared the new Lenten fair, which lasted
fifteen days and which, from *c.* 1340, became an important market for
foreign cloths. There existed also at this time two fairs in the neighbouring town of Friedberg which formed a cycle with the Frankfurt fairs. In
addition to agricultural produce and both sea and fresh-water fish, spices,
iron, lead, tin, glassware, wool and linen were now on sale; also, as we
have just seen, wine and cloths.

The first period of prosperity extended from 1330 to 1400. One of the essential characteristics of these fairs is that they were in great measure devoted to craft products, a fact which proves that these regions were at a less advanced stage of economic organization than the western part of continental Europe. Gilds, and especially those of the weavers, journeyed to the fair as a group. To Frankfurt came weavers from Schwalbach, Königstein, Weilnau, Cronberg, Oberussel, Usingen, Limburg, Montabaur, Friedberg, Butzbach, Marburg, Giessen, Nastätten, Grünberg, Alsfeld, Windecken, Gelnhausen, Fulda, Seligenstadt, Mainz, Spires, Worms, Oppenheim, Bingen, Oberwesel, Andernach, Cologne, Düren, Aachen, Trier, Luxembourg and Metz. These craftsmen lodged together and made their purchases collectively. Frankfurt itself had an export cloth trade. Later there came, too, fustian producers from Nördlingen and Ulm. This commodity was also brought from Münster and Osnabrück, as well as from St Gall and Constance.

In these latter cases it was evidently a question of a major trade similar to that operating further to the west. At Frankfurt were also sold, however, cloths from Louvain, Malines, Maastricht, Brussels and St Trond. Nuremberg sent arms, Lübeck herring, Breslau dye-products, while Italy sent glassware and silk. Between 1383 and 1407 the merchants William and Mathew Runtinger from Ratisbon sold at Frankfurt products purchased at Venice, Bologna and Lucca and bought there Brabant cloths which they sent to Vienna and Italy. At this date the western and Italian trading system was fully operative at Frankfurt.

The Rhenish and Alsatian wine trades had developed considerably by this time; Hungarian horses, too, were sold in quantity for transport. The whole Rhineland from the St Gotthard to the North Sea now had close connections with Frankfurt, and the same is true of the Meuse and Moselle valleys. Further afield, the limits of the zone from which merchants came to Frankfurt are marked by Lübeck, Poznan, Cracow, Lemberg, Brno, Ofen or Buda in Hungary, Innsbrück, Berne, Freiburg, Montbéliard, Besançon, Épinal, Metz, Ypres and Bruges. The goods themselves, however, evidently went still further afield and flowed, moreover, in all directions. No less frequently they came from still more distant regions; for example, Italian and Oriental products, English cloths, Scandinavian herring, Russian furs.

In the fifteenth century a relative decline set in from which Frankfurt would not fully recover until the second half of the sixteenth century. This decline was due to a recession in the German, Flemish and Brabant cloth trades in face of competition from England, to the growing insecurity of the highways as a result of the activities of robber-knights consequent upon the internal break-up of the Empire. The last characteristic features of the old craft fair disappeared. Only the great capitalist merchants succeeded in keeping up some activity which would ensure continuity into the following century.

Less important fairs were held at Nördlingen at the junction where the Frankfurt–Augsburg road crossed that from Nuremberg towards Lake Constance. The earliest mention dates from 1219, but the period of prosperity began in the fifteenth century and corresponded, therefore, to the relative decline of the Frankfurt fairs. In 1434 the Nördlingen fair lasted for the fifteen days following the first Saturday after Whitsuntide. Nevertheless, it is only in 1521 that a second fair, of the same duration, appears. To this fair came especially German merchants from the whole of the central zone, ranging from the Rhinelanders of Aachen and Cologne, through the traders from Leipzig, to the Silesians from Breslau. There were also Swiss from St Gall, Berne and Geneva; more rarely, merchants from Scotland, Milan and, among those from the Low Countries, from Antwerp, Malines and Tournai. The fair registers for the period 1451 to 1476 have been preserved. They mention foreign merchants who rented booths from the town or who operated in the *Messhäuser*. On the other hand, no account is available of the places of sale located in private houses.

The small Swiss fair of Zurzach was also linked with the group of German fairs. Some stress may be laid on this fair because it was a good representative of the secondary fairs and one about which considerable information is available.

Zurzach lies on the Rhine to the west of Schaffhausen near to the junction of the Aar. Its situation was a particularly good one from the point of view of inland navigation. The town was a place of pilgrimage, a fact which gave rise to a regional market held on 1 September. In the fourteenth century, at the time of the development of the fairs of Upper Germany, commercial activity increased. Reference is already made at this time to a *Verenamesse*, from the name of the saint whose cult had originated the pilgrimage. Up to 1408, however, these commercial gatherings only lasted one day. From this date onwards they continually expanded. The Zurzach fair was much frequented by the inhabitants of the small neighbouring towns, some of which at this time were part deserted, but visitors also came from further afield. Freiburg cloths were sold at Zurzach as well as at Geneva, Lyons, Frankfurt or Nördlingen. The Bernese, too, were frequent visitors. Many transactions involved leather goods and proportionately as many payments were made at Zurzach as at the large fairs. Furthermore, the south German merchants, whose new financial technique turned the most important of them in the sixteenth century into magnates of financial capitalism, also visited Zurzach either from Nuremberg with metals or from the textile district of Swabia with linens and fustians. Along the middle Rhine, relations existed with Basle and, to a lesser extent, with Strasbourg. Sometimes Venetians on the way to the Low Countries also stopped there.

Booths were set up in the streets as well as in the cemetery, in spite of the opposition of the bishop of Constance. All the houses served as warehouses or hostelries, and necessarily so because of the great influx of visitors from the neighbouring towns. But in spite of the somewhat regional character of the Zurzach fair, exotic products, such as spices and fruits from the Midi, were sold there as elsewhere. Flemish and Brabant cloths were naturally also represented and direct transport was even organized from Flanders and Brabant. This prosperity was maintained up to the middle of the sixteenth century.

The two fairs of Linz in Upper Austria assumed a similar character. Merchants came from Austria, Bavaria, Swabia, Franconia and Bohemia, more rarely from Saxony, Poland, Hungary or Italy. Cheap cloths from Franconia, Bavaria and Bohemia were sold there, as well as linens and fustians from Swabia. Oriental products came from Venice via Salzburg, and metal goods from Nuremberg. These fairs are known to us above all in the fifteenth century.

At Bolzano, on the Brenner, fairs existed from the beginning of the thirteenth century and are explained by the town's position. In the fifteenth century, when trade between Germany and Italy expanded, there were as many as three annual fairs at which the Venetians were particularly numerous.

Leipzig became, in the fifteenth century, the fair for the eastern part of Germany. This fair, however, was oriented towards eastern Europe. Poland and Russia sent furs there but it was also via Leipzig that cloths from the Low Countries passed on their way to the Slav countries. After the invention of printing Leipzig almost immediately added a book fair. About this time three annual fairs were held at which merchants from the Rhineland as well as from Russia took part.

These German fairs never developed a jurisdiction of their own but were, in general, greatly influenced by the institutions which had come into being in the fairs of western Europe. It is typical that in Germany, too, a progressive shifting of the fairs towards the east is to be observed, and this is undoubtedly a continuation of the evolution described above. Fairs originated here, as elsewhere, from the contact between more industrialized zones and zones having raw materials or producing unfinished goods. As industry and town life spread towards the east of Europe so did the limit of the fairs' zones keep pace with the movement.

The fairs of Deventer in the eastern part of the Netherlands were in some measure German fairs, since, from the fourteenth century onwards, they assumed a great importance for the whole of north Germany as far

L

as the Elbe, as well as for the Rhineland and Hesse. They were not, however, the oldest of the fairs which sprang up within the territory of the present kingdom of the Low Countries. In the twelfth century fairs already existed at Utrecht and others, apparently less important, are referred to in the following century at Vlaardingen, Delft, Voorschoten and Valkenburg. In the fourteenth, fifteenth and sixteenth centuries fair licences were granted to many Holland and Zeeland towns. Nearly all of them had only a very limited radius; often their function was merely to supply the citizens and even the peasants of the neighbourhood with such goods as needed to be bought but once a year.

As for Deventer, it is significant that at the end of the thirteenth century, when the fairs began to assume a certain importance, the active foreign trade of the town declined. Its merchants had previously been reported in Germany and in the northern countries. From now on, this role was taken over by Kampen merchants, while the Deventer fairs came to be a meeting-place for traders from elsewhere.

The brightest moment in their history came in the middle of the fifteenth century, but as early as the fourteenth century Holland merchants were already selling cloths and dairy produce at Deventer, while buying at the same time from the German merchants wood, wine and metal goods. The town was favourably located on the Yssel and was moreover subjected to a lord, the bishop of Utrecht, too far away to be troublesome. There were five fairs a year, of which four lasted fifteen days each, and the fifth, three weeks. It is true that the existence of five fairs in one and the same town is not necessarily a proof of their importance, because at Gorinchem, in the county of Holland, there were as many as six: four lasted fifteen days each, one of them being a cattle market; another lasting six days was a cloth fair and there was yet another one of four days for horses. The mere fact that there were two fairs for the sale of animals coming certainly from the neighbourhood, and that the fair for cloths, an international merchandise if ever there was one, only lasted six days, is sufficient proof that these were limited and secondary fairs.

There were also fairs in other towns of the Yssel region, in particular at Zwolle, Zutphen and Arnhem. These latter fairs, which were fairly prosperous in the fourteenth century, were eclipsed by Deventer in the fifteenth century. At Zwolle there were five fairs of unknown duration. One of them in the sixteenth century was a cattle fair which even attracted merchants from beyond the Elbe. Zutphen, in the duchy of Gelderland, had four fairs, of which two were established by the duke of Gelderland in competition with Deventer, which, as we have said, belonged to the bishop of Utrecht, as did Zwolle. In some places of secondary importance the institution of the fairs went back to a very early period. Thus at Oldenzaal, a dependency of the bishop of Utrecht, an imperial charter of 1049 established an annual fair lasting five days, but there is no proof that it ever served a very wide area.

It should be noted that all the Dutch fairs developed in the east or in the centre of the country and therefore relatively far from the sea. Sea trade, on the other hand, took on a permanent character. When, in the sixteenth century, the Dutch mercantile marine acquired great international importance, the Deventer fairs declined.

These fairs had been protected by an imperial safe-conduct covering the whole Empire, and the territorial princes of the neighbourhood also granted them. In Holland there was no special fair jurisdiction, and from this point of view the position was therefore the same as in Germany. It was the ordinary tribunal of the town magistrates which settled actions in which foreign merchants were involved, but the procedure of the court was more expeditious. The Deventer fairs were also centres for payments. These were made in cash as well as on credit, but without recorded letters of obligation. The money-changers who accepted deposits played an essential part.

One region which has not so far been considered is Scandinavia.

The Scandinavian towns had generally grown up about a weekly market protected by a special peace. Once or twice a year some of these markets assumed larger proportions and attracted professional merchants who were frequently foreigners. The latter brought in products from distant regions and exported some of the local produce. Alongside the town markets there existed also rural markets, frequently connected with monasteries or with places where the assemblies of freemen (*thing*) were held. The towns opposed these markets on a number of occasions but never succeeded in ousting them completely.

Only the Scania fairs assumed any degree of international importance. The other Scandinavian markets lost much of their importance because of the predominance, from the twelfth century onwards, and especially from the thirteenth century, of the permanent colonies of German merchants, such as those of Visby in the island of Gotland, as well as those of Stockholm and Bergen.

The Scania fair was based upon the herring fishing in the Sound, which expanded above all from the thirteenth century onwards. The herring shoals were there so dense that at certain times the vessels, if we may believe Saxo Grammaticus, were unable to move forward. Foreign merchants came in great numbers and *nundinae piscationis* soon appeared there. It was these merchants too, and above all those of Lübeck, who financed the organization of the fisheries. Having provided the capital, they ensured the distribution of the herring and provided the Lüneburg salt which made the Sound herring the supreme Lenten dish in northern Europe. As a result the fairs were controlled by the Hanseatic League but, on the other hand, the Dutch and English themselves began to visit the Sound in the middle of the thirteenth century to take part in the fishing and trade. The Dutch in particular brought linens and food products. They visited the Baltic ports and often returned home via Norway.

The king of Denmark soon drew up statutes governing the peace which was to reign at the Scania fair during the fishing, that is, from 15 August to 1 November. This peace extended to the whole area where the nets were put out to dry, and at sea to the area where they were spread. From this arose a royal code of laws or *môtbôk*, proclaimed each year at the opening of the fair and mentioned for the first time in 1352. Danish and Low German versions of this code exist. There were also special statutes at Dragör for the island of Seeland, communal statutes at Malmö and ordinances at Lübeck, all relating to the same subject.

The Scania fair was located in the sandy peninsula of Skanör which separates the Sound from the Baltic. Two small towns grew up there around the royal castles, first Skanör, then Falsterbo which became the more important centre from the end of the fourteenth century. Dragör developed on the coast of the Danish island facing the Skanör peninsula while Malmö prospered in Scania. From the thirteenth century all the Baltic towns from Kiel and Lübeck to Riga sent their merchants and their fishers into Scania, and the same was true of the German North Sea towns and the Dutch towns on the Zuider Zee. These men acquired landed properties, called *fed* in Danish and *vitten* in Low German, with permanent booths under their own jurisdiction. Some of these properties were collective, like that of Danzig, which served the six towns of the Teutonic Order. The *fed* of Amsterdam served the towns of northern Holland.

The Scania fairs were gradually dominated by the Hanse merchants. The Danish and English merchants were progressively eliminated. The same was true of the Scots and, later, the Flemings, the northern French, the Dutch and the Zeelanders. In the fifteenth century this monopolist policy led to a decline which resulted in final disaster in the following century.

The Scania fair was primarily, but not exclusively, a herring fair. In the fourteenth century the fishing itself was done almost entirely by Danish peasants and townsmen, but the latter were excluded from the sale at the fair. The herring-barrels, together with the salt, were brought by the foreign merchants, except when they brought coopers who worked in the *fed*. The place of origin of the herring was indicated on the barrels.

In 1368 some 34,000 barrels of herring were acquired and resold by the Lübeck merchants. The other German Baltic towns came into the reckoning to the tune of some 62,000 barrels and a large consignment was dispatched to western Europe. In 1398–1400 these figures apparently almost doubled, Lübeck alone taking some 80,000 to 90,000 barrels on its own account. As the Hanseatic supremacy became established, so did the importation of various products, and in particular of textiles, by foreign merchants decrease.

The fair came within the jurisdiction of the Danish king. Dues were levied in the king's name and the peace ruling there was the royal peace, contraventions of which were punished by fines and even, in the case of fraud or embezzlement of funds, by death. Such at least was the situation before the Hanseatic supremacy. Later the king contented himself in the main with levying taxes and tolls. The *fed* finally obtained a kind of extra-territoriality. They were administered by a bailiff responsible to the town to which they belonged. This bailiff enforced the law of his town, but gradually Lübeck law superseded all other laws.

Carrying was reserved on the whole to the Danes and was strictly controlled by the *môtbôk*. The same was true for the supervision of the fishing and also for the guarantee covering place of origin and quality. Within the *fed*, the herring market was separate from that reserved for other business; transactions could not be carried out elsewhere. Trade deals were apparently settled in cash. At the outset settlements could only be effected in Danish currency, the value of which was often changed by the king, sometimes even in mid-fair; but in the fifteenth century the use of Hanseatic silver money and of west European gold coinage was general.

The decline of the Hanseatic League in the Baltic region and the triumph of the Reformation which did away with the Lent fast in a great part of northern Europe heralded, *c.* 1545, the end of the great Scania fairs. Moreover, herring fishing in the North Sea was steadily increasing. Lübeck and several other Hanseatic towns, however, still kept up some activity in the much curtailed fairs until about the end of the seventeenth century.

It would be wrong to believe that, after the decline of the Champagne fairs, the whole movement of the fairs was a slow and steady shift towards the less developed regions of the east. The economic phenomenon of the fairs was too old and too firmly rooted in the pattern of trade, too profitable also for town, territorial and national governments, for this to happen. Hence, what may be called a low tide begins to recede and give rise to new fairs, sometimes far to the rear of the line of those fairs which had grown up gradually and always further towards the centre of the continent. In fact, Lyons is already one example which has the future on its side. The same applies to the Brabant fairs, Malines and the group Antwerp–Bergen-op-Zoom.

Malines came into existence only in 1409 under John the Fearless who set up two annual free markets each of eight days, one after Ascension

Day, the other after the festival of Saints Cosmas and Damian, at the end of September. These fairs, however, were never as important as those of Antwerp.

The two Antwerp fairs apparently date from the end of the first quarter of the fifteenth century. One was held at Whitsuntide, the other on 1 October, St Bavon's Day. They soon formed a cycle with those of Bergen-op-Zoom where the first fair took place at Easter and the second on St Martin's Day (11 November). These latter fairs date from the middle of the fourteenth century. The late origin of these four commercial gatherings is explained by the relative slowness of the economic development of the Duchy of Brabant in comparison with neighbouring Flanders. At the end of the fourteenth century the trade in leather and hides was intensive enough at Antwerp to attract the English and Hanseatic merchants. From the beginning of the fifteenth century, the Hanseatic colony at Bruges began to make the journey twice a year to Antwerp and to Bergen-op-Zoom.

At the very end of the fourteenth century the English started to bring over vast quantities of cloth to the Brabant fairs at Antwerp and Bergen via the intermediary Zeeland port of Middelburg. In the course of the fifteenth century these cloths were increasingly bought by the Cologne merchants who carried them into central Germany and disposed of them at the Frankfurt fairs, where the cloth trade was now the chief activity. The Germans themselves brought the products of their smelting industry as well as spices obtained from Italy or fustians from Augsburg and Ulm. Bruges suffered increasingly from this competition. Biscayans from Bruges visited the Antwerp fairs from the middle of the fifteenth century onwards. At the end of the fifteenth century the Italian trade also switched from Bruges to Antwerp. The Portuguese royal agent was there in 1498. The Antwerp fairs could only gain from this transference of activity which, in conjunction with the enormous transformations in the world situation resulting from the great discoveries and from colonization, were to ensure for the Scheldt metropolis the truly unique position it was to occupy at the beginning of modern times.

V. *The Smaller Fairs and the End of the Middle Ages*

Nearly all the fairs so far discussed assumed to a greater or less degree a real importance in the inter-European, and often even in the intercontinental, trading activities of the medieval world. Nevertheless, the economic atmosphere which had engendered the fairs had so profoundly permeated commercial life that the fair became something of a necessity for almost every stage of inter-regional exchange, with the result that, in the majority of western and central European countries, the later Middle Ages were in this respect characterized by what can only be described as a rash of annual and biennial commercial gatherings. A great many of these gatherings were certainly of secondary importance only; but just as any summary of the great fairs' movement expressed only in terms of the Champagne and Flanders fairs would imply a lack of historical perspective, so, too, a false appraisement of the phenomenon represented by the medieval fair in general would result from a failure to stress the multiplicity of these small fairs.

Thus the Champagne fairs themselves were far more numerous than has been generally believed. Besides the great international fairs of Troyes, Provins, Lagny and Bar-sur-Aube, there were small fairs at Bar-sur-Seine, Châlons-sur-Marne, Château-Thierry, Nogent, Rheims, Vitry, Tonnerre, Sézanne, St Florentin, La Ferté Gaucher, Ervy, Mérysur-Seine and Ramerupt. In the old royal demesne, in addition to St Denis there were two fairs at St Germain-des-Prés, the second of which was established by Louis XI as late as 1482. Others were held at Paris—the St Lawrence and St Lazarus fairs—at Orléans, Puiseaux, Morigny, Étampes, Liancourt, Dreux, Mantes, Montlhéry, Melun, St Quentin and Beauvais. Some resulted from the resumption of long-distance trade; others were later, like the St Quentin fair, established by Philip the Fair, or the Beauvais fair, which dated from 1360.

Some of these fairs were purely regional, while others participated more or less directly in major trade. This happened, for example, in the case of the Calais, Boulogne and Abbeville fairs, which were busy stagepoints for the English trade, and the same is true for those of Rouen—the Purification and the 'Pardon' fairs—which were to play a leading role in the fifteenth century. Other Norman fairs, such as those of Caen, Avranches, Carentan and Cherbourg, were less important. In Brittany, there were fairs at St Malo, Rennes, Tréguier and Quimperlé. In Anjou, besides the old Lande-aux-Nonnains fair, Angers had no less than three others. In Touraine, Chinon and Tours were important, Tours itself having a markedly international character in the fifteenth century. More to the south, Nevers, Aurillac, Poitiers and Angoulême came into existence at different periods. The Bordeaux fairs were established by Edward III but only reached their full peak of development in the sixteenth century. Languedoc had a considerable number of fairs, of which that of Nîmes, on the wane by the fourteenth century, was the oldest. Not a great deal is yet known about the much-frequented Beaucaire fair, but it apparently attained its maximum prosperity primarily in the sixteenth century. Second-class fairs included those of Montpellier, Narbonne, Montolieu, Aigues-Mortes, Carcassonne and Toulouse.

Similarly, the Italian fairs must not be viewed as being very important for long-distance trade. The real Italian fairs are those of Flanders and, in particular, of Champagne. Yet there were fairs in the peninsula itself, for example, at Vercelli, Piacenza, Borgo San Domino, Pavia, Milan, Bologna, Ferrara, etc. The latter were visited fairly frequently by French and German merchants at the end of the Middle Ages. Lombardy even had at this time a cycle of eight associated fairs which extended over a great part of the year. These Italian fairs, however, never had a great international importance. Even in a commercial metropolis like Venice the annual fair did not assume any great international significance.

There were weekly markets at Venice on the Campo San Polo and the Piazza San Marco. The fair was held round about Ascension Day; it was initially of eight days' duration, and subsequently, from the fourteenth century onwards, of fifteen. It was also located on the Piazza San Marco. The main visitors were merchants belonging to the Venetian *arti* and the Murano glassmakers. It was these gilds which put up their members' stalls in the square and beneath the galleries of the procurators' palaces. The attendance of the members of a certain number of gilds was compulsory. This obligation was even resented as a useless burden by some of them, like the haberdashers who preferred to sell in their regular shops. There were, however, some twenty places reserved for foreign linen merchants, but these 'foreigners' were simply non-residents of northern Italy. Moreover, the control of these fairs was vested in those procurators of St Mark who were in charge of the religious festivals, which emphasizes the fact that the character of the fairs was civic and cultural rather than economic in the regional or international sense.

At Venice, in fact, trade was open to foreigners all the year round, and this explains the local character of the fairs. Trading took place in the Rialto market every day of the week, and it was there that the *banchi di scripta*, where all the merchants had their current accounts, were located. It was there, too, that credit was to be had at the *Camera degli Imprestiti*. Throughout this quarter, the shops at any given moment were full of all the various kinds of merchandise which formed the basis of international trade. It was not a *bourse* because goods were bought in the market itself and no forward contracts were concluded; it was rather a permanent international market which did away with the need for a fair.

In Spain, there were fairs at Valladolid, Sahagun—lasting three weeks and held about Whitsuntide—Cuenca, Cáceres, Seville, Alcaraz, Córdoba, Badajoz, Merida, Segovia, etc. Before the fifteenth century, the most famous were those of Brihuega, Alcalá de Henares, Burgos, Santiago de Compostella, Palencia, Toledo and Madrid. From the fifteenth century onwards, the best-known were those of Medina del Campo, which, together with the Villalón and Medina de Rio Seco fairs, played a world-wide role in the sixteenth century.

In Portugal, fairs were very numerous; but the rather limited importance of the majority of them is proved by the fact that, up to the end of the fourteenth century, they could make do with the restricted area reserved for them in the small urban markets in the interior of the country.

These examples could naturally be multiplied in the other regions of western and central continental Europe; and again, outside the geographical limits prescribed for this chapter, mention might be made of the whole group of English fairs. Even without these, however, the foregoing examples are sufficient to prove the quasi-universal phenomenon represented by the fairs. The additional observation may be made that the medieval fair is also to be seen within the perspective of historical continuity; nor should it be forgotten that many fairs originating in the Middle Ages continued throughout the whole *ancien régime*, often after an official revival at the end of the medieval period.

In conclusion, a word must be said about the connections existing between the fairs and the development of the towns. The latter did not owe their genesis to the fairs, but the repeated and prolonged residence of numerous merchants brought wealth to them. In individual cases, and from the topographical point of view, the fair grounds could weld together the various component elements of the urban centres in question. This happened *inter alia* in a secondary town like Autun, where the Champ St Ladre, the setting of the September fair, lay between the two old nuclei, the castle and the Marchaux. In Champagne, on the other hand, revenues derived from the fairs by the counts strengthened their position *vis-à-vis* the municipal administrations of the fair towns whose emancipation was thus impeded.

It is, therefore, no exaggeration to conclude by saying that the fairs were as important for medieval long-distance trade as were, for example, first, the development of navigation in the Mediterranean and North Sea, and, subsequently, the sea-route link between these two major areas. If one ignores the phenomenon of the fairs—and of the markets which brought them into existence—the trade economy of the Middle Ages is incomprehensible.

PART II
POLICIES

CHAPTER IV
The Economic Policies of Towns

I. *Introductory*

Is it proper to speak of the economic policies of medieval towns? The answer must depend on the definition. If this is overexacting, if we demand both explicit statements by medieval townsmen of their aims and methods, and proof that these were then applied in practice, we strike at the roots of the whole subject; study would then be restricted to such rare congruences as that between the industrial protectionism advocated by Lippo Brandolini in his *De comparatione reipublicae* and the policy of fifteenth-century Florence. A more liberal and more realistic attitude will allow far greater scope. There is abundant evidence in the preambles to municipal statutes, in the reports of chroniclers, in the arguments used by interested bodies in economic disputes, that principles informed practice. Sometimes the aims and ideas made public were those which really gave coherence to economic activity, sometimes they were a dishonest façade hiding a shabby structure of selfishness and opportunism. Yet the most disingenuous statements of policy have their value; they argue a need to indulge popular belief that certain patterns and principles of economic behaviour were good and useful.

It is reasonable to use another type of evidence—indirect evidence. This consists of the elements of regularity and consistency in urban economic practice. Where there are such regular trends the policy of a town may be considered as less or more 'conscious', but policy it is so long as the regularities are genuine and can be referred to probable motives. Medieval townsfolk did not always expound the aims and ideas which underlay their activities—they did not trouble, they would not, they could not; when they did their words may have been lost. Common sense suggests that hidden motives may properly be deduced from known practice.

By either criterion medieval towns had economic policies. This is only to be expected, for the size and nature of these communities made the appearance of distinctive and consciously held attitudes to economic affairs in the highest degree probable. Medieval townsfolk could hardly cheat themselves or be cheated by others about the importance of economic matters, for their livelihood depended on the preservation of a particular economic situation. Furthermore the connection between cause and effect was rapidly and directly visible in the constricted milieu of the town; the population could not easily be hoodwinked by the interested or rendered purblind by its own apathy in a close and intense community where each knew his neighbour's business and how it affected his own. Again, the sharp contrast between town and country, between burgesses and other groups and authorities, sharpened the focus of economic and political thinking; conflict and antagonism chiselled out clean-cut policies.

Yet scepticism as to the existence of medieval town policies is perhaps less dangerous than blind faith in their strength, consistency and easy intelligibility. These policies underwent major changes as environment and internal constitution varied, and they were disturbed in a minor way by acts of expediency and considerations of day-to-day convenience. 'Regrators' who kept small shopkeepers or the housewife at her door supplied with fresh pies and pastries were legalized as a sensible amenity in a town which otherwise hated middlemen, and one does not have to search far to see why at Douai the sale of coffins or manure was not forced into the market place, as were many other kinds of business, but allowed at the workshop or shed. But there are more serious difficulties of interpretation, a severe case being the problem of distinguishing between economic *measures* and economic *policies*. A given measure had no more a *necessary* connection with a given policy than have many symptoms with a specific disease; for example, insistence on low selling prices for craft products might betoken either a policy of defending consumers or a policy to benefit merchants who wished to sell such goods abroad. There is the further danger of anachronistic interpretation, of generalization from the period of fullest documentation to the rest of the Middle Ages, so that the history of policy loses all its dynamic qualities and the peculiarities of two centuries are made the general truths of five. Finally, it must be remembered that actual policy, in an age of extreme legal formalism and interlocking institutions, was not always as sharp, rigid and uncompromising as the evidence suggests. It was modified by the give and take of practical administration, by an infinite capacity for evasion and by friction between overlapping authorities.

II. *The Permanent Elements*

Nevertheless there are some fixed points. Beneath all the changes and complexities of town policy in the Middle Ages can be seen the operation of certain principles whose basic and permanent character was assured because they were rooted in the very nature of medieval towns.

There is no need to stress the most important consequence of the position occupied by towns in medieval society—a peculiarly intimate and vital dependence on the existence of trade and on the control of its conditions. The merchants, often an important section of the town population, made a living by trade; another large group, the artisans, needed to trade to procure their raw materials and to dispose of their finished products. Other citizens drew wealth from trade in less direct fashion: as sleeping partners they financed those directly engaged in trade and industry and took a large return on their capital; as property owners they won a comfortable living from rents whose high level depended on competition for living and working space among merchants and craftsmen. Finally the town as a whole relied on trade, not only for that large proportion of its corporate income which came from tolls and other commercial levies, but for the very necessities of life.

Two major aspects of medieval town policy can be ascribed directly to these facts. Because prosperity, or livelihood itself, was so closely linked to the volume of trade handled by a town and to the terms on which it was conducted, increase in this volume and bettering of these terms were fundamental aims of the burgesses. In practice these aims were only moulded into definite policy when thwarted by two types of adverse circumstance. There were in the first place all those conditions inimical to trade development in general. Prominent in this class were those aspects of feudal organization which obstructed commercial expansion and engendered 'anti-feudal' elements in town policy, difficulties not of human making, such as physical obstacles, and the inadequacy of trading organizations and credit facilities to the task in hand. These difficulties were more prominent in the earlier Middle Ages; later the main threat came from a different quarter. The removal of former obstacles and the rapid expansion of trade led to conditions where the chief menace to towns lay in the number and strength of competitors, and this situation caused the adoption of distinctive tactics.

It was a natural desire of merchants and craftsmen to maintain and increase the volume of their trade and to see that this trade was conducted on favourable terms. This is a more general statement of the issue than that often given. Schmoller, for example, claims that 'the soul of that [town] policy is the putting of fellow-citizens at an advantage, and of competitors from outside at a disadvantage';[1] but such emphasis on the competitive and monopolistic aspects does not truly reflect the conditions in all towns at all times, and if the basic interests which underlay such an attitude were always present they could still take very different forms. It must be admitted however that if these aims did not always lead to bitter competition and struggle for monopoly they were at least self-centred and, it would be fair to say, selfish. All was intended for the profit of the policy makers; a just and responsible attitude to outside interests usually depended on the exercise of superior pressure or on the promptings of self-interest.

A distinction should be made at this point. There were two main ways

[1] Translated in A. P. Usher, *An Introduction to the Industrial History of England* (London, 1921), 134–5.

of profiting from trade which, with more convenience than propriety, may be distinguished as exploitation *of* trade and exploitation *by* trade. Exploitation *of* trade involved profiting from imposts on traders or the processes of trade; in such cases money was made by tolls, market dues, taxation of the wealth of merchants and shopkeepers and like methods. Exploitation *by* trade implied actual commercial activity, and its profits came from taking advantage of differences between buying (or production) price and selling price; money was made by buying cheap and selling dear. In both cases those in a position to profit would favour vigorous and expanding trade, but beyond this point there would be little similarity of policy. Those employing the first method would not be unduly worried as to whether trade was in the hands of natives or foreigners, nor would they be directly interested in the terms of trade unless it were to show a natural consumers' preference for low prices.

It is tempting to assume that there was a simple change from the first kind of interest in trade control to the second, a change which took place when feudal lords were replaced by merchant patricians as city rulers. Certainly exploitation *of* trade was more typical of the feudal lords who controlled towns and encouraged their growth, and the policy of these lords was in large part moulded by this interest. On the other hand it is impossible to make a simple equation between the period of town independence and a policy run for and by 'mere merchants'. Even when the interests of merchants were dominant the town retained a public and fiscal interest in trade side by side with a growing private and mercantile interest. Revenues for a community as well as profits for individuals had to come from the commerce of a town and the different ends could lead to different measures. Moreover, the interests of consumers always had some effect in countering the strokes of patrician policy when these threatened to bring trade monopoly and high prices. Finally there is reason to doubt even the basic idea that the leading men of medieval towns were always ambitious full-time merchants, men impelled to turn the organization and terms of trade to the advantage of their private business. Some patricians had a closer affinity with the 'feudal' than with the merchants' way of life, and derived wealth from fiscal and political control of the town and from the power given by land and social standing. Such men were not rare amongst the earliest leaders of town life and could play a large, even dominating, role in the civic oligarchies of the later Middle Ages.

Two types of evidence illustrate this point apart from patrician histories themselves. The chief object of hatred in the internal struggles of the thirteenth and fourteenth centuries was not always a patriciate which used its power to turn the terms of trade to its advantage and against consumers and producers, and which forced low wages on those who supplied goods for their trade; it was sometimes a patriciate which exploited directly by means of political power and the taxation system; it was a tyranny of administrative authority rather than of the power of mercantile capital. Sometimes indeed, as in fourteenth-century Augsburg, the opposition seems to have been led by just those groups which did wish to use town machinery for the purposes of trading advantage in the strict sense. Secondly, some towns derived wealth from trade in a manner which suggests the feudal lord rather than the merchant; such, for example, were some of the towns controlling the Italian entrances to Alpine passes, towns like Vercelli, Novara, Como and Treviso, which by and large did not exploit their favourable position to become great middlemen in the active sense, but rather to exact tolls from merchants passing along these routes.

The special position of town-dwellers in medieval society involved another form of dependence, their dependence as consumers. It was a chief concern of the towns to obtain consumer goods of adequate quantity and quality for the general population, and raw materials for craft workers. This concern was the source of other elements in town policy. Consumer defence, however, involved issues beyond that of ensuring supplies from outside; it implied internal regulation and adjustment of claims between conflicting groups within the town itself, for the special interests of the few easily ran counter to the consumer interests of the many. It also gave scope to considerations less 'economic' in nature, to social and ethical principles, to ideals of commonweal, to church teaching on fair price and neighbourly dealing; for however amoral might be the treatment of 'foreigners', within the town there was a strong sense of community. There was constant insistence that economic laws should be 'for the public good', for 'the good and profit of the whole community', and that every economic act and relationship should be 'good, loyal and true'. These ideals exerted a constant and powerful influence on town policy despite the frequent control of legislative machinery by sectional interests.

In brief, both livelihood and life depended, directly or indirectly, to a greater degree or a lesser, on a suitable trading situation. These two aspects of dependence, as they issued in policy, may be treated as the defence of trading interests and the defence of the consumer.

(1) THE DEFENCE OF TRADING INTERESTS

For 'mere merchant' and for trading craftsman—and one or both often directed town policy—there was one main way to satisfy need and ambition and this was to increase the amount of trade available to

M

themselves, and to ensure that in this trade they bought as cheaply and sold as dearly as possible. They tried to increase profits both by forcing the terms of trade in their favour and by ensuring that as much business as possible came their way.

At first the creation of a favourable trading position was not necessarily a matter for conscious policy, nor indeed for any effort on the part of the town. With poor communications, absence of competition and limited output of many necessary and desirable goods, general conditions themselves ensured a large 'natural' disparity between buying and selling price. Satisfactory profits could be expected without elaborate human interference. The growth and spread of production, the development of routes, the improvement of marketing facilities and the increase in the number and efficiency of competitors altered this situation. It became necessary to maintain the profitability of trade by artificial control and to protect or increase a town's share in trade by a conscious policy.

The most important single aim was to give the town population a favoured position as middlemen, to guarantee that they enjoyed as nearly as possible a monopoly in the handling of trade between one area and another. It might seem proper, has indeed seemed proper to some, to adopt the term 'staple policy' to describe this aim. Such usage is misleading. Apart from the fact that the English staple system differed essentially in both form and purpose from the typical continental staple system, even the continental *Stapelrecht* did much more, and much less, than ensure a middleman monopoly to a group of merchants. This staple system involved the power to make merchants pass through a given town where they could be taxed, where their goods could be forced to a sale on the local market, and where their further progress could be stopped or made conditional on terms imposed by the local traders. Clearly such an arrangement could serve various policies, not merely that of entrepreneurial monopoly, and in particular it could be and was an instrument for ensuring abundant, cheap supplies of necessities in a town, in other words was a part of a 'provisionist' or consumer-defence policy. On the other hand, the drive for a privileged position as middlemen led towns far beyond the confines of any system which can reasonably be called a staple system. No 'staple' was involved in those highly important struggles conducted by burgess groups to oust other merchants from foreign markets, or to exclude them from trade routes which might pass nowhere near the home town.

It remains true however that *one* great method by which a town might build up a trade monopoly was by diverting and concentrating trade into its own market square. An obvious element in such a policy was the insistence by towns situated on some trade route that merchants should not by-pass them. Poland, which handled a considerable amount of transit trade but boasted relatively few important trackways, saw an intense development of the *przymus drogowy*, the duty to follow a staple route. A main line of traffic through Poland in the later Middle Ages was that running north and south from Danzig, through Thorn, Piotrkow and Cracow, to Nowy Sacz and Hungary. Danzig, Thorn and Cracow fought bitterly to force merchants to keep to their part of the road and to by-pass those stages controlled by their rivals. Cracow, for example, won a position as the staple for all trade between Hungary and the north in return for submission to Ladislas Lokietek in 1306, and so countered Thorn's attempt to develop trade with Hungary; at the same time it leagued with Danzig to develop a westerly route through Bydgoszcz and up the Brda river which would defeat the staple rights of Thorn in the northerly section of the highway. The story is the same in almost any part of Europe. Genoa tried to build up a position as compulsory port for all sea traffic of the south French and north-west Italian coastal areas; the bricks it used were such one-sided agreements as the 1153 treaty with Savona by which all Savona ships bound for Sardinia and Barcelona had to set sail from Genoa, unload at Genoa on their return and carry a proportion of Genoese merchants. Across the peninsula Ravenna was forced to conduct virtually all her overseas trade and even most of her north Italian trade through Venice. In England, fifteenth-century Southampton buttressed a trade concentration of huge dimensions with special privileges from the Crown. In Brabant a major public utility, the Brussels–Antwerp canal, projected by the Brussels council, was obstructed until 1531 by the fierce opposition of Malines and Vilvoorde which would have been by-passed by this waterway.

Some of the most notorious examples come from Germany. Mere concentration of trade at some town on a natural route was not enough; there was a large-scale diversion of trade. The line taken by foreign merchants could be the longest distance between two points as long as that line passed through one's own town. So Küstrin skippers wanting to trade a cargo at some Baltic port had first to navigate up the Oder to Frankfurt, disembark their goods, pay dues, load their vessel again and then sail down-river to the sea. Hamburg similarly forced river shipping to call at its wharves though the ultimate destination might be in the opposite direction, and goods under shipment from one town on the Elbe to another were forced to leave the river and make a long and costly diversion in wagons to Lüneburg.

Another method of achieving the same end of trade concentration and monopoly was the frank exclusion of adjacent towns or merchant groups from certain branches of trade which were thereby automatically forced into one's own city. This method found its fullest expression in the treatment by towns of the areas under their direct control, where all competing merchants and trade could be suppressed; but the principle was applied more widely than this, as can be seen in the case of such successful towns as Genoa and Venice. Genoa forced Narbonne in 1166 to give up the transport of all pilgrims embarking at any port from Montpellier to Nice; Venice in like manner insisted that Ravenna should withdraw from the pilgrim business in 1234 and enforced the same prohibition on Ancona in 1264.

The concentration of trade at the home town, the forced diversion of traffic to one's own market square or quayside, was by no means the end of the matter. A town was not merely a point at which trade was concentrated, it was a point at which trade was arrested. The free carriage of the goods so assiduously channelled to one point was now interrupted in the interests of local monopoly. The native merchants hastened to make themselves the unavoidable link in the chain of trade which passed through their city. Sometimes it was decreed that stranger merchants could not enter the territory of a town, or else foreigners would be allowed to bring their goods as far as a given city but not to trade beyond it; on other occasions direct trade between one outsider and another would be prevented, or there would be a rule that all goods brought into a town had to be put up for sale. In all such cases the general upshot was to guarantee or at least to favour the monopoly of transit trade by the local merchants.

Examples come from every corner of the continent. Compulsory sale of incoming goods and the interposition of native merchants between foreigners who wished to do business together were commonly secured by civic ban in towns everywhere. More surprising, perhaps, is the great number of cases where a town successfully refused through-passage to alien traders. In Italy, Bologna was able (in 1116) to persuade Henry V to prohibit Tuscan merchants from passing through Bolognese territory more than twice a year, though Bologna was a virtually unavoidable transit centre for much of Tuscan trade. Genoa, in return for help against a rebellious Montpellier, was able to prevent sailors of that town carrying on any sea-trade further east than Genoa itself. Early in the thirteenth century Viennese law prevented south German merchants from going through to Hungary for trade; they were stopped at the city and there had to dispose of their goods which were carried further east by Viennese merchants only. The system was peculiarly complete at Cologne after 1259, when that city became an enforced terminus for merchants from each and every direction, and in the case of such Baltic towns as Danzig and Riga which built up a position as sole intermediaries between the east European hinterland and the traders who sailed the Baltic.

The pursuance of 'staple' policies in the interests of trade concentration and monopoly was but one facet of a much wider struggle for the control of markets and routes. True it was a common and natural feature because the home town was an obvious base and centre for monopolistic practices, and it became peculiarly important in the later Middle Ages when competition made towns fall back on the defence of the one sector of trade directly under their own control—trade passing through their territory. But it fell far short of being the only way in which towns realized their ambitions.

A desire to maintain old and to open up new markets, to secure a firm hold on the carrying trade between one region and another, was so obviously a major strand of town policy that it needs little comment. A great part of the external history of the more important medieval cities can be written around their conflicts one with another to secure control of a trade route, to dominate the source of a vital commodity and to monopolize access to a great market. Such contests are to be found in all regions and at all times. Even in Carolingian days Venice opposed the Lombards in her quest for expanding commercial opportunities, and by the eleventh century, in the south of Europe at least, competitive warfare was becoming endemic, with Milan set against Pavia on land or Genoa against Pisa at sea. It was not long before there emerged some of those great and general patterns of conflict which coloured so much of medieval history. There was a major struggle between Genoa and Venice for control in the east Mediterranean and Black Sea regions, which opened in 1177 when Genoa negotiated a treaty of commercial privilege with the sultan of Egypt and broke into what had hitherto been a virtual monopoly trade for Venice. In the western Mediterranean there was a running fight between Genoa and Pisa for mastery of the trade of the south French and east Spanish coast areas, a fight which began as soon as the two cities had conquered Sardinia as allies in 1016 and did not end until, in 1284, Genoa built a mole across the outlet of the Arno and choked her rival's port with silt. Each major struggle embraced a variety of minor collisions: acts of piracy and retaliation, trade embargoes and contentious diplomacy, isolated wars in specific areas for specific aims. The whole Mediterranean was embroiled: Pisan war-vessels menaced Genoese merchantmen in the very roadstead of Barcelona, Genoese seamen drew knives on Pisans in the streets of Constantinople; and all the smaller towns were swung into diplomatic and commercial orbits determined by the pull of the greater cities. The wars of the Titans were themselves fought out amidst the more trifling but no less bitter squabbles of second- and third-rate towns, each avid for the scraps of trade which escaped the appetites of the great.

The motive force behind these conflicts is obvious enough; there is no cause therefore to pursue their detailed history, which would indeed be little short of a complete history of Mediterranean affairs. It only remains to stress the universality of such struggles in time and space. The northern seas were ranged by crews as toughly ambitious as any in the south. Landsmen, too, fought for the same cause and with similar weapons; in 1168 for instance, Milan, heading the Lombard League, struck hard at Genoa and Pavia by founding Alessandria as a southern stronghold which blocked the road between the two, menaced the whole economic position of Pavia and seriously fettered the northward flow of Genoese traffic. Nor did struggles develop solely between one town and another. The League of the Rhine defended its trade in military action against the local nobility, the Hanseatic League went to war with the king of Denmark, Venice attacked the Empire, while the favourable position established by Jewish communities in Carolingian times was assailed by one city after another ever after Venice, in the early tenth century, prevented Jews from using Venetian ships and negotiated vainly with the archbishop of Mainz to prevent their trading in metals, cloth and spices in his province.

One interesting consequence of the continuous strife to control routes and markets and deny them to others was the formation of 'chequerboard' groupings of the towns, especially where state authority or the need to unite against some common difficulty did not check the competitive struggle. The jealous cities tended to find their worst enemies in their nearest neighbours or those who controlled routes they had to use, and their natural allies in cities which suffered equally from the presence of some intermediate town. In the twelfth century for instance there was a certain stability in a situation which bound together Catalans, Genoese and Lucchese against the Provençal cities, Pisa and Venice. 'Side-chains' linked on to such groups; there was throughout much of the century an alliance of Pisa with Florence because the latter town was coming into conflict with Pisa's enemies, Lucca and Siena. In the early twelfth century struggles on land led to an equally natural *entente* between Pavia and Lodi, Piacenza, Reggio, Novara and Asti, against Milan at the head of a group containing Parma, Modena, Cremona, Tortona and Brescia.

A wholly successful policy meant complete monopoly of the trade in some commodity, unchallenged command over some vital route or sole access to some market, together with freedom from fiscal and other interference in the trade so monopolized. Such success was not rare among 'staple' towns, either those which were compulsory stages on a given route or those which received the sole right of handling some one commodity like grain, wine or salt. It is also to be found in situations where there was no question of the favoured town being a staple. Genoa made a treaty in 1109 with St Gilles by which Genoese, and Genoese alone, could conduct sea-trade with St Gilles and this trade was made customsfree. In 1167 the Genoese made a more comprehensive agreement with Aragon which guaranteed them full freedom of trade and exemption from taxes in all ports from Tortosa to Nice; at the same time Pisans were explicitly excluded from trade in this area, and as the Pisans were in fact the only serious competitors of the Genoese the latter won by this treaty a virtually watertight monopoly. Even where absolute monopoly was not within reach it was possible to win 'most favoured nation' treatment, especially in the matter of customs, and even, like Germans in England and Venetians in Byzantium, to gain terms more favourable than those allowed to native merchants themselves. Below such triumphs was every grade of partial success in attaching advantage to oneself and denying it to others.

If staple policies were merely one branch of a more general struggle for monopoly and privilege, this in turn was only part of all the activity based on a policy of increasing trade and the profits of trade. Competitive features were commonly dominant, but they were engendered by the circumstances in which the policy worked itself out and were not co-terminous with the policy itself. This fact can be obscured because circumstances so often did compel competitive methods; indeed opportunities for non-competitive expansion were rapidly reduced by the very success of a process which aroused emulation in each area penetrated and tempted rivals from outside. A false impression is also encouraged by the partial nature of the evidence: war 'made news' for the medieval chronicler when peaceful trading did not, conflict filled the official archives with records of treaties between powers and lawsuits between individuals, while unopposed and unregulated trade might leave little trace; also the earliest centuries and the more backward regions, the most suited to non-competitive expansion, are those for which there is the least documentary material.

However there is abundant evidence that towns laboured as strenuously to open up new markets as they did to oust rivals from the old, and fought as hard against the obstacles set by geography or moral scruple, by technical inadequacy or deficient organization, as they did against commercial opponents. In the early thirteenth century Venice exploited her success in the Fourth Crusade by sending agents into the mountains of Armenia, across the steppes of north Syria, and to Mongol princes inland from the Black Sea ports. Later in the century the individual courage which opened routes across sea and desert to Persia, India and China was quickly reinforced by the corporate action of the great Italian cities. Current indignation against the immorality of trade with the infidel was set aside time after time by towns anxious to open up rich markets to the south and east of Christian Europe and to establish contact with the caravans coming from the Orient; the failure of Leo Marsicanus, who fulminated in vain against the un-Christian traffic of Amalfi and Salerno in the ninth century, was never properly avenged in later times despite ephemeral and partial victories won by the efforts of popes, kings and friars.

Once set on foot, policies of expansion fed on themselves; each extension of a town's trade involved further extensions, quite apart from the growing ambitions of the townsfolk. When Genoa between 1097 and 1109 established *fondachi* at Antioch, Jerusalem, Acre and Tripoli she was soon forced to secure her communications by trying to build up her position at Syracuse and Messina and in Crete; from the middle of the twelfth century she established herself at Bougie, Ceuta, Tripoli and Tunis on the north African coast, partly to open up fresh markets, partly no doubt to secure the flank of her route to Syria. Perhaps, too, the rapidity and forcefulness of Genoese penetration to the north and west in this period should be seen as part of the same pattern, resting not merely on growing wealth and determination but on the sheer need to trade in areas whose imports and exports were the necessary complement to her recently established Moslem trade.

The policy of extending markets was, of course, anything but simple as it issued in action and it showed infinite variety as it adapted itself to detailed circumstance. Beside straightforward expansion there were all the efforts to open up alternative routes when an old road was closed, the attempts to prevent old markets from being disturbed, the schemes to compensate for the loss of one outlet by the acquisition of another. Apart from any positive advantages which might accrue, Venice, for example, had an obvious negative motive in arranging that the Fourth Crusade should attack Constantinople; one of her greatest single interests, the Egyptian trade, would have been seriously interrupted had the expedition gone to the Nile. This Egyptian connection in turn grew rapidly in importance after the treaty of 1262, negotiated by Venice immediately following her loss of a monopoly market in the Byzantine Empire in 1261, as it had also grown when the Third Crusade had failed to recover the Holy Land. The need to compensate for lost outlets similarly forced Genoa to reconsider her position after Alessandria appeared in 1168 to block her northern route; she straightway attempted a much more thorough-going use of the south French ports, and showed herself willing to adopt a less cavalier attitude than formerly to Narbonne and Montpellier whose friendship was now of vital importance.

There is an intimate connection between the above methods, intended to secure optimum trading conditions, and the whole corpus of town legislation which regulated the activities of foreign merchants; in fact, as has already become apparent, there was much overlapping between the two, as some control of foreign traders was inevitable in the pursuit of trade advantage. However the treatment of foreigners inside a given town deserves separate attention, for it did not wholly coincide with the fight for trade privilege, and when it did fall in this category it showed certain special features. As with the staple policies mentioned above, many of the restrictions imposed on outside merchants can be attributed to a variety of distinct motives, not to one alone. Enforced resort of aliens to a given market and compulsory disposal of goods at that market were methods of increasing the revenue of a town and, a more common motive, of ensuring abundant and cheap supplies to local consumers; again, many of the acts which forbade the import of finished goods and export of raw materials by aliens must be ascribed to a wish to protect local industry. There are other features of the treatment accorded to outsiders which suggest that it was not always based on the desire for trade preference. A great deal of this legislation in earlier days, in English boroughs for example, seems to have owed much to the principle that foreigners should pay, through tolls and the like, for the personal protection and trading advantages which they shared with the citizens but which the latter had paid for with their taxes. Why should a man who was not 'in scot and lot' with the townsmen enjoy the same customs exemptions, a free site for his stalls, the protection of town guards and walls, free of charge? If he shared the civic burdens he would be allowed to enjoy these privileges like any resident native, if not he must be 'discriminated against' by market dues and other means.

While some of the regulations affecting alien traders were not meant to give the townsfolk a preferential position in trade, those which were so intended often gave a special twist to this policy. This was the case with those laws which restricted the actual operations of strangers within the town walls, and especially those which denied them access to retail trade. As Heckscher points out, 'the regulations were obviously intended to limit not only the competition of foreign merchants with the native in intermediary trade, but also their buying and selling *in the city itself*'.[1] In the first case foreigners alone paid for the advantage gained by local merchants, in the second the monopoly was paid for, in part at least, by consumers and producers within the town; the terms of trade were not only turned against outside producers, consumers and distributors in the interests of the town as a whole, but were set against consumers and producers in the town itself in the interests of a privileged section. This feature is important and accounts for the way in which the attitude to foreigners could vary significantly with shifts of political power in towns from one economic group to another; but it must not be exaggerated. In the first place only one special section of *Fremdenrecht* is involved, for the rest served the general interests of the townsfolk; in the second, it is hardly fair to discriminate so sharply between the effects of restricting alien traders

[1] Eli F. Heckscher, *Mercantilism*; transl. Mendel Shapiro (London, 1934), II, 75.

within the town and those of excluding them from markets outside. The merchants of a given city could exploit their neighbours just as truly when they controlled a distant source of vital consumer goods or monopolized distant markets for the town's manufactures as when they engrossed distribution inside the town. The internal struggles of the thirteenth and fourteenth centuries show contemporary awareness of this fact.

With proper qualifications, however, it remains true that a great part of the regulation of alien merchants falls within the scope of this section; it aimed at keeping as much internal trade as might be in the hands of the citizens, while business which had to be left to foreigners was controlled as strictly as possible and so managed that natives would share in it and profit from it.

The chief methods used were similar in all parts of the continent. When circumstances allowed, the foreigner might be forbidden certain kinds of transaction altogether; for instance it was commonly decreed, as in the regulations of many Gilds Merchant in England or in the 1221 municipal laws of Vienna, that one stranger merchant should not deal with another but must trade with citizens alone. In some towns this was narrowed even further to compulsory use of the strictly regulated brokers, sworn civic officials like the *makelaeren* of Flanders. Equally common was the closing of retail trade in a town to the outsider; this is another feature which is well represented in the laws of English Gilds Merchant. The more vital a branch of trade, the more insistence was laid on such clauses, and the twelfth-century charters granted to several English towns made special provision that retail sales of cloth should be confined to burgesses.

It was possible for aliens to circumvent these laws and a common way of doing this was by entering into partnership, formal or informal, with a denizen. As a result towns were forced to attack such arrangements; the 1260 regulations of the Leicester Gild Merchant laid it down that no gildsman could sell the goods of a non-gildsman unless he had first genuinely bought them; at Guines in north-east France the statutes expressly denounced all associations of foreigners with citizens intended to evade the law which said the former could not sell wine retail; and Hanseatic towns banned 'mixed' partnerships and debarred their citizens from providing freights for alien ships. Here again the main emphasis was often on those branches of business most important to the town; at Douai for instance 'non-co-operation' between townsman and outsider was prescribed in the case of the cloth and wheat trades which were the main pillars of Douai's economy.

Where they were not barred from trading, strangers were often subject to various limitations and disabilities, over and above the obvious one of discriminatory taxation. Laws which forced aliens to wait until all the burgesses had made their purchases before they themselves bought on the market were quite common, and were of advantage not only to the local consumer but also to the local merchant. There were limits on the time a foreign trader could stay in a town, sufficient to enable him to do his necessary business but giving him no opportunity to entrench himself in local trade; forty days was a common period, being the time allowed to foreigners by the 1188 charter of Bristol and to merchants from Germany, Lorraine, Denmark and Norway by the early twelfth-century laws of London. Guines, a petty market town, had typically petty regulations. When Guines held a fair, citizens could put up two stalls but foreigners only one, and in the case of cloth the outside merchant was restricted as to the length of his pieces and could bring in only what he could carry under his arm. He was denied the use of a stall altogether. At the great Saturday market of Paris, drapers coming in from the northeastern towns were allotted a special chamber in the Place des Métiers, kept strictly to the times of opening and closing of the market as told by the bell and had to retire as soon as the market closed. Some degree of segregation of foreigners was also a frequent practice; in 1463 the London council ordered all foreign shopkeepers into the Blancheappleton district near Mark Lane, while it was common both in England and on the continent for the stalls of aliens to be forced into a separate annexe of the town market or even to be organized into markets distinct in time and place from those of citizens, as was the case at Douai in the fourteenth and fifteenth centuries. Presumably however such measures owed as much to the authorities' desire to avoid hard words and hard blows as to their wish to reduce competition.

Strict regulation was often combined with strict supervision. A notable example of this was the working of the hosting system, which forced the alien merchant to lodge with a burgess of the town in which he was staying and enjoined him to report all his dealings to his host, or to conduct all his business through the latter. In England for instance it was pressure from towns like London, York, Chester and Coventry which forced a reluctant government to pass hosting statutes. By the Act of 1439 all alien traders coming to an English port had to register at the mayor's court where they were allocated hosts with whom they had to stay during their visit. Each merchant had to inform his host of all business done by him and the host in turn had to send a biannual report to the Exchequer. This Act was but the culmination of numerous petitions by the Londoners, and the London policy itself but an extension and strengthening of a practice known much earlier in various towns like Ipswich, which in 1291 had insisted on having full burgesses as hosts to aliens. A similar end was achieved by different means with the famous Fondaco dei

Tedeschi, the compulsory residence, storage place and centre of business for German merchants in Venice, run entirely by Venetian officials.

(2) THE DEFENCE OF THE CONSUMER

The second great purpose underlying the policy of a medieval town was the defence of its interests as a community of consumers. The town authorities had three main objectives here: they had to make sure that adequate supplies of reasonably priced goods reached the town, they had to guarantee that goods were properly distributed within the town, and they had to safeguard the quality of goods so distributed. These aims gave rise to a body of measures which was probably better developed and more permanent than any other element in town policy and can indeed be traced to the period before there was a truly urban policy at all, when towns were still growing up under their feudal lords. There were, of course, variations in the strength of the policy and the methods it used in response to changes in environment, but the essentials remained firm and they did so because consumer needs were inevitably of basic importance. They were the one great interest which united all sections of the population.

The main categories of goods involved in such policies are obvious enough. First and foremost came foodstuffs and above all bread grains. Then there were materials important for various domestic and industrial uses: wood for fires, for building and for furnishing; leather, stone and metals needed by a multitude of crafts, and all the materials needed by the textile industry—wool, flax, alum, fuller's earth, teasels, dyestuffs, unfinished cloth and the rest. Finally there were arms.

Why were special efforts and a conscious policy needed in order to obtain these various goods? The essential reason was, of course, the very nature of the medieval town, which combined a relatively large population and a commodity-consuming economy with direct control of an area which rarely provided enough food and raw materials. This inadequacy increased with the growth of a town's population and the intensification of its industrial development, and was exaggerated when a town was situated in a region naturally infertile or one which, like the wine and woad regions of Gascony, was given over to highly specialized production. A keener edge was given to these problems of supply by political and military considerations, by the fact that the medieval town was in varying degrees an independent unit which had to fend for itself and was encompassed by coldness or positive hostility, and by the fact that towns had to ensure provisions and safeguard supply routes, not in a context of peaceful and open trade, but under the threat of competition for these supplies and the purposeful closure of these routes by its foes.

Heckscher draws a fundamental distinction between policies in which a 'hunger for goods' issues directly in the encouraging of imports and the discouraging of exports, and those more sophisticated attitudes where consumer goods are guaranteed by favouring exports so that the home production thereby stimulated will itself ensure adequate supplies.[1] He argues that the first kind of policy was typical of the Middle Ages, not because of a scarcity of goods or uncertainty in obtaining them, but because under the conditions of a 'natural economy' economic facts are seen simply and directly; so a 'naïve', 'ingenuous' belief that goods are useful and that their abundance should be encouraged in the most obvious and direct way is not obscured by the 'veil of money'. The 'provisionist' measures of medieval towns, hindering exports and favouring imports, cannot be explained in this manner. The fact is that medieval towns *were* peculiarly vulnerable in a way in which whole nations were not and no amount of encouragement to home production by allowing exports would have resulted in urban territory producing enough wheat, wool or leather to keep the population supplied; also there were many goods vital to towns which were not home-produced at all. Secondly, towns did not typically show an indiscriminate 'hunger for goods'; they took strong measures to assure a steady inflow of foodstuffs and necessary raw materials, but they did not lightly restrict the export or encourage the import of goods outside these categories. When they did so there were usually special reasons. Sometimes the favoured imports must be accounted raw materials despite appearances, like the woven cloth that came in for dyeing and finishing; or were arms, which enjoyed a privileged position. Sometimes the export of finished goods was forbidden, but only to alien merchants who were kept out of a branch of trade reserved to natives, while similarly the import of manufactured goods might be allowed after pressure from local trading interests which saw in this an opportunity for high profits. Sometimes apparent discrimination against finished goods was merely normal fiscal practice, charging a higher duty on valuable (finished) goods than on less valuable (unfinished) articles, so that there is nothing 'very peculiar'[2] in the fact that a load of pig iron leaving Bergamo paid six shillings duty while manufactured iron paid eight shillings. Finally, though medieval conditions may have allowed townsmen to see economic facts 'clearly and simply', there were not 'conditions of natural economy' in the twelfth to the fourteenth centuries; the significance of this period is not that it allowed *naïveté* but that it was the period when towns had developed sufficiently to have policies of their own and to be placed in a vulnerable economic and political position.

---

[1] Heckscher, *Mercantilism*, II, 103.   [2] *Ibid.* 89.

The first task facing the town was to bring the goods to its market. Much depended here on the pressure that could be brought to bear on the supply areas, and this suggests an immediate distinction between the environs of a town and more distant territories. In the former the aims of the town could be realized with little opposition; all the produce could be forced into the town market and the most drastic measures taken against the diversion of this traffic or its seizure by monopolists. Further afield there was greater variety in the methods used and success won by various towns. Strong towns dealing with the weak could use a thoroughgoing and compulsory staple system to achieve their ends, and could turn supply regions into private reserves. Thirteenth-century Venice demonstrates the use of such overriding power; a treaty of 1234 made her the only city at which Ravenna merchants could sell corn and salt, and a 1236 settlement barred to Ragusa all trade in the northern Adriatic except for the carriage of foodstuffs to Venice; at the same time Venice claimed a monopoly of the export of corn in the lower Po valley and the Mark of Treviso, and a virtual monopoly further south, as when in 1273 Bologna was forbidden to purchase more than 20,000 *corbes* of wheat annually in Romaniola or the Mark of Ancona without Venetian permission. Of course, such agreements, even when one-sided, were not always so drastic. In 1230 Milan contented herself with obtaining from Novara the right to buy corn in the latter's territory and permission to import foodstuffs through this territory without paying tolls.

Where the coveted goods could not be forced into the local market by a staple system or otherwise they had to be attracted there. Foreigners who brought necessities to a town were always spared much of the usual xenophobia. In London, for example, the cloth-workers, the poorer classes and the *rentiers* were all reasonably well disposed towards Hanseatic merchants who brought in cheap and indispensable goods, and it needed little to make such attitudes generally effective. Middlemen, even foreign middlemen, might be tolerated, and strangers allowed into the retail trade itself, when local traders could not satisfy the market; such arrangements were incorporated in the 1286 charter of Bakewell for instance, while it was common practice in English towns with a Gild Merchant for non-members of the gild to be allowed to buy and sell foodstuffs quite freely. The more vital the need the greater the pressure on normal behaviour, and a corn shortage in Bordeaux and neighbouring towns could force a welcome to foreign merchants bringing supplies from interior regions which were at war with English Gascony.

Besides removing prohibitions towns had to offer positive inducements if they meant to attract the required goods. Much of this encouragement would be of a general nature, indistinguishable from the measures taken to improve trade as a whole. Under this head can be included provision of frequent and well-regulated markets and fairs, special guarantees for the security of traders on the roads and their safe lodging in the town and an efficient legal and financial system at the disposal of visiting merchants. The town busied itself with everyone who disturbed good trade, from importunate porters at thirteenth-century Douai to the king's officials whose frequent levies frightened so many country vendors from bringing provisions to Oxford market in the fourteenth century. More specific in purpose were toll concessions which differentiated between various goods or between the same articles when imported and exported. Complete or partial freedom from tolls was allowed to corn imports in many Italian cities from the twelfth and thirteenth centuries onwards, and in fifteenth-century Bordeaux grain was the only commodity imported duty free. Nor were foodstuffs alone involved; in the 1303 tariff of Berwick, alum, dyeing wood, coal, onions, and wax only paid customs on export, while a century earlier Cologne charged merchants of Dinant on industrial raw materials they bought in Cologne but let them sell the same quit of all charges. Such freedom was sometimes the subject of reciprocity treaties between towns. Modena made arrangements with Ferrara about 1200 and with Bologna in 1229 by which the contracting parties agreed to allow free export of products from areas under their control one to the other, and mutual right of access to their food markets.

The most attractive trading conditions did not always ensure a sufficient supply of vital materials and the town authorities might fall back on more drastic measures. They could institute a system of 'tied imports' under which a certain proportion of, say, wheat had to be included with every general freight imported into the town, or they could simply force private traders to bring in whatever the town needed during a period of emergency. At other times towns engaged in corporate trading, using communal ships and large capital sums provided by taxation or public loans to satisfy urgent requirements. This was most commonly the case with the town's food supply, where civic trading sometimes became a regular and recognized practice, but the principle was more widely applied. At Siena large purchases of wool for the Arte della Lana were made in the city's name by officials specially appointed by the government.

Vital goods had not only to be brought into a town, they had to be kept there. The most obvious way of doing this was to prohibit export. Permanent and complete restriction of certain exports did occur in the staple towns of Germany and Poland and at Florence, for example, but partial or temporary prohibition was more common. Often a town would content itself with burdening exports with heavy duties, resorting to total prohibition only when faced with patent scarcity; in other cases it was thought enough to stop exports by aliens, as in the twelfth-century charter to Wells, which forbade non-burgesses to buy untanned leather; in others again exports automatically became illegal when prices rose above a fixed ceiling. This was so in the 1230 treaty which Ferrara signed with Venice, agreeing to Venetian exports of corn, fish and vegetables from Ferrarese territory as long as their prices remained below a given level. Similar ends were served by various regulations which, without barring exports, made such business conditional on the satiety of the local market. This was done by ordering that all goods should be offered for sale to the burgesses and to burgesses only, and should remain on the market for a stipulated period. Such rules had a wide distribution, though again they are best seen in those continental towns with a well-developed *Stapelrecht*. The delay imposed on foreign traders might be as long as a fortnight in some east German and Polish towns though departure was more usually allowed on the third day.

By favouring imports and discouraging exports the towns were able to guarantee a sufficiency, even an abundance, of consumer goods under normal conditions and this abundance was itself one of the main guarantees of cheapness. Yet cheapness could not be assured without a fight on another front, a fight against middlemen in general and monopolists in particular. Towns were generally mistrustful of entrepreneurs whose functions, though often necessary, involved an increase in the price paid by the consumer; they were actively hostile to private and corporate monopolies which made high selling prices a matter of conscious policy.

The gilds were the most obvious vehicles for monopoly practices and great efforts were made to prevent such abuse. When gildsmen made up the ruling group in a town, and still more when the gild-system itself was an integral part of government, outright attack was often difficult. Even so a great deal was achieved; in particular the town authorities were able to win general support when crushing monopolies in the food trades. Fifteenth-century Brussels, where the gilds finally won a share in town government and exploited their newly won power to push craft exclusivism to the limit, is an apt example. There the last callings to gain the right of enforcing compulsory membership of their gilds were those devoted to feeding the population, and even when compulsory membership was introduced loopholes were left if public interest so dictated. For example, ungilded innkeepers and countrymen were authorized to sell their goods in the town. The butchers provide a noteworthy case: they formed one of the most powerful gilds in Brussels, yet their claims for complete monopoly were rejected; private individuals were allowed to slaughter sheep for their own consumption, and when, after a dispute between Brussels and Vilvoorde, the former won the right to pasture 300 sheep on Vilvoorde plain, the authorities gave the butchers a stint of fifty sheep, the other 250 being given in tens to burgesses who registered with the city finance department and promised to slaughter only for family use.

The gilds lent themselves to monopoly practices, but these corporations were not the only offenders; private individuals and companies were also guilty of cornering supplies, either before they reached the town or inside the town itself. Against such forestallers and engrossers the towns waged constant warfare. The municipal records are full of charges against men who met the countrymen's wagons or the fishermen's boats and bought up the town's supplies, and the city regulations are equally full of injunctions against butchers storing more meat in their cellars than was needed for current trade, bakers hoarding more flour than was needed for their ovens and householders buying more grain than was needed by their households. Sometimes the actual amount which could be bought by any one person or partnership was fixed, as in the 1268 ban by the *échevins* of Douai which fixed one *muid* of wheat as the maximum to be purchased on any given day. Such regulations could be evaded without much difficulty and more elaborate precautions had to be taken. In 1392 the Douai government ordered that all members of a company trading in wheat should do business as a group and not split up to carry out several deals whose total would exceed the statutory maximum.

The authorities often felt the need to interfere in a way which left less scope for evasion and was more certain in its effect; they then resorted to price-fixing. Sometimes this was left to the discretion of an official who set a price on various goods as he passed through the market inspecting and testing at the various stalls; more commonly it was done by decree, by assizes which covered a whole class of goods, carefully relating price to quantity and quality. Bread and wine were the most common objects of price control, but the list was often longer. Douai, for instance, had assizes covering wood and peat, hay and lime, beer and coffins; here the price was a maximum price in every case except that of bread where a lower as well as an upper limit was set, presumably in the belief that an excessively cheap loaf would be of poor quality. The control of bread prices was in fact a matter for much thought and elaborate legislation as befitted its key position in consumer defence. Detailed calculations concerning the costs of different grains and the sizes of loaves, the proportion of various flours and the expenses of production were pondered by the city fathers before a tariff was issued. A device which one may suppose to have been practically convenient and psychologically sound from the consumers' point of view, and one which eased the problems of administration, was the production of a 'standard loaf' which did not vary in price but instead changed in quality and size as flour became dearer or cheaper. The 'standard loaf' had a great vogue and was known in both

N

France and Germany as early as the twelfth century. Augsburg, for example, made monthly 'test-loaves' of constant value but varying weight which became the temporary standard for the town bakers.

The day-to-day control of prices, weights and measures had to be supplemented when there were special circumstances. Natural disasters could breed sudden demands and great opportunities for profiteers, and then an alert council would act promptly, as promptly as did London in forbidding any increase in the prices charged by the carpenters, masons, tilers and others who were needed everywhere to repair the citizens' houses after the great storm of 1362. Sometimes 'emergencies' could be anticipated and appropriate steps taken. There is a great variety of such precautionary legislation. A 1455 agreement between the bakers of Oxford, the Oxford authorities and Oseney monastery (which owned the only mills at which Oxford men were allowed to grind their corn) provided that, when breakdown of one of these mills threatened a bread shortage, then the bakers were to be free to have their corn ground elsewhere on payment of the 'gristpenny'. At York, when a huge crowd was expected for some official function or church festival, the normal restrictions went by the board and country dealers were allowed to come inside the walls and sell food free of tolls. Sometimes it was not dearness but an actual bottleneck in supply which worried the magistrates when the town was unusually full and busy. There is an interesting example of this at Guines where, as in many other small towns, the harvest was of great importance. Here an urgent concern during the harvest weeks was to make sure that enough bread was turned out at a time when normal economic life was upset and the town crowded with workers, and so the ordinary rules which called for careful weighing and measuring were set aside and the bakers allowed to bake as fast as they could without being sticklers in matters of quality. Finally it may be remembered that there was a special problem which faced most towns not merely as an emergency but as a permanent burden, the problem of the poor. Special provision had to be made for the less fortunate as a matter of moral duty and for reasons of political expediency, and such provision normally covered all the vital items in the family budget. The officials of Bristol were specially charged to see that sufficient supplies of cheap small wood were kept in side streets near the town wharves to make up halfpenny and penny bundles for the poor, and to ensure that brewers made cheap small beer as well as the better drinks for well-to-do customers. Of course bread and meat received the most attention; wheat was often subsidized, bought in bulk by the town and sold below cost price to the more needy inhabitants in time of shortage. Occasionally the local authorities even forced butchers and bakers to furnish buyers with credit, as happened at Guines in the fifteenth century.

Towns were as deeply concerned with the quality of goods as with their abundance and cheapness, and, though this interest sometimes sprang from a desire to protect the town's good name in the export market, it was more often rooted in a desire to protect local consumers. Such protection could be achieved by official interposition at three stages: the town could control the quality of imported goods, denying admission to spoiled grain or high meat; it could exercise a thorough control over all sales inside the town, confiscating or destroying all commodities which the regular and careful inspections showed were not 'good and loyal'; and it could control the actual course of local production either directly or through the medium of gild organization. Examples which testify to both the thoroughness and generality of such methods are perhaps too familiar to need repetition here, nor is there need to stress the strictness of the penalties incurred by those who broke the law—loss of goods, exclusion from a craft, banishment from the town and exposure to public shame—punishments whose harshness measured equally the strength of town feeling and the ease with which private operators or organized interests could betray the town's intent.

III. *The Elements of Variety and Change*

To defend a commonweal of consumers, to secure plenty of trade on good conditions, these were permanent aims of town policy. They were the basis for whatever similarity can be found between town policies at different times and in different areas. But policies are not made by aims alone, they are moulded by all the particularities of internal and external environment. It is only reasonable to expect, and a cursory glance at the evidence proves, that there was great variety and great change in the policies adopted by medieval towns over a period of many centuries and throughout the major part of a continent. Nothing short of a collection of individual town histories could do justice to the complexity and dynamic nature of the subject; the most that can be attempted here is a description of the chief types and phases of policy. The whole range of accident and individual peculiarity must be left aside. The storms which blocked the roadstead of one port while they scoured out the approaches to another, the partisan warfare with no clear economic basis which rent the social fabric of some cities, the fickle changes of international boundaries which decided the economic fate of many towns—all these and other 'accidents' had great effects on urban policy but must be ignored here.

There were two fundamental reasons why town policies varied. In the first place towns were of different types and had different functions in society. Various classifications are possible—and useful—but the overriding distinction must be between two main groups of towns, between those with predominantly local interests and those which depended on trade with distant markets. On the one hand were petty market centres (some of them would scarcely deserve the name of village today) whose inhabitants were rarely concerned with what went on beyond ten or fifteen miles from their walls; on the other hand were cities whose interests ranged from the regional to the intercontinental, which carried the bulk of Europe's long-distance trade, were subject to constant pressure to seek far-off outlets for their industrial production and numbered in their ranks such mammoths as Florence whose annual outlay in trade and banking would have bought up a dozen quite important towns.

The second basic reason for variation is to be found in differences of environment and two such differences stand out above all others. There were contrasts in *political* environment and especially between towns which won complete, or near-complete, autonomy and those which could not give free expression to their interests but were cramped by the control of superior authority. The most obvious examples of this latter class were towns in strong monarchical states and those which never won great success in the struggle against their feudal lord.

There were variations also in the *economic* conditions within which towns had to operate and the most significant and general change here was that caused by the evolution of the European economy as a whole. Broadly speaking that economy passed from a 'pioneer' stage, from an era of boundless opportunities, of imperfect techniques, of calls to 'adventure', to an age where opportunities were less obvious, techniques were improved, competition became intense and there were marked clashes of interest both between and within towns. Finally, in the later Middle Ages, came a period when, often against a background of grave economic difficulties, towns adapted themselves in two main ways: either they came to the top as one of the great metropolitan centres monopolizing the 'great' industry and trade of the time or, having lost in the race, fell back on a stiff-necked defence of their interests in their immediate locality.

The remainder of this essay will be concerned with the interplay between these various factors. For convenience, and in order to emphasize that town policies were not static, the treatment will be chronological. The convenience has its limitations. Apart from the fact that the periods chosen are necessarily rather arbitrary, two considerations must be kept in mind. Differences in town policy due to differences in town function cut clean across those caused by changes in the overall economic background; above all the contrast between those towns with local interests and those operating on a vast scale held firm throughout the various periods. Secondly, these 'periods' cannot be tied too closely to actual centuries: a marked lack of synchronism existed between various areas. The towns engaged in Mediterranean trade reached a stage of competitive struggle, of saturation of opportunities, in the late twelfth century which was not equalled over much of northern Europe until the fourteenth century; while even within a single region some towns far outpaced others in their social and economic evolution and had to face various economic problems generations before these were posed to their more tardy neighbours.

(1) THE EARLY PERIOD: 'FREEDOM' AND FISCAL POLICIES

The evidence of the fourteenth and fifteenth centuries makes it quite clear that most town economies of that period were highly regulated economies and that this intense regulation normally issued from certain common features of late medieval policy. The external policy of most towns was the reflection of a struggle for prosperity, even for survival, in a competitive world which bred 'exclusivism', 'selfish protectionism', 'a competitive spirit', 'monopoly practices' and 'xenophobia', to use the phrases which recur in almost any description of the period. The internal policy of towns also led to a high degree of regulation which secured the control of the majority by an oligarchical minority or maintained a nice and precarious balance between a variety of craft gilds.

Now, though towns were always especially dependent on the maintenance of favourable trading conditions, it is hard to see that this necessarily meant action of late medieval type, that it involved such intensive and detailed control, such hostility to 'foreigners', such multiplication of monopolies. Looking at the position inside the towns, it does not seem inevitable that there should always have been such elaboration of measures to defend an oligarchy nor—when oligarchy was absent—such effort and artifice to avoid it and secure to each subordinate group its own rightful place. Suspicion grows that the particularities of the fourteenth and fifteenth centuries are due to particularities of the contemporary background, and that earlier centuries may have allowed greater freedom and encouraged more liberal attitudes. Indeed there does seem to be *some* evidence that there was a more liberal disposition, a greater freedom of temper in economic affairs among townsfolk before the thirteenth century and that such freedom was no less real because it was relative, no less telling because it was manifest as a disposition rather than as a coherent and whole-hearted policy. This hypothesis of a period of greater 'freedom' will be used as a starting-point.

Perhaps the most useful sense of 'freedom' in urban policy, and the criterion which will be most used here, is tolerance towards strangers, towards merchants and craftsmen from outside the town, as opposed to local exclusivism and local monopoly which feared and repulsed these strangers and could only be broken by pressing necessity. Linked with this might be similar liberality within the town itself: the policy-making elements would allow comparative freedom in various spheres, with no oppression of craft producers for example, and no marked restriction of entry into trading and industrial associations. In the background will be the more general sense of freedom as absence of regulation, absence of that meticulous regimentation of economic life so pronounced in the later Middle Ages.

If the reality of this period of greater freedom is accepted for the moment, the question arises as to what conditions might have made it possible. It has been suggested that in the earlier Middle Ages 'deliberate encroachment on economic activity was impossible simply because there was no institution powerful enough to identify [itself] with such a policy'.[1] This explanation may be true of states but seems ill-fitted to the problem of towns. It is hardly an exaggeration to say that the right and ability to control important economic matters was of the very stuff of which towns were made, while from the practical point of view there was many a city which tightened its control of economic affairs without any noteworthy change in its powers. Further, when towns *did* strive for more power, it was often as a direct result of an ambition or need to intensify economic regulation or pursue a more competitive policy.

The real reasons are to be found in general social and economic conditions, and especially in certain circumstances which were external and common to most towns. Economically speaking, early medieval society was 'unsaturated': it could use and absorb, without great difficulty, more traders and capital, more goods and services, than were actually 'in circulation'; it had large untapped resources, an expanding territory, a growing population, a rising overall consuming power and so there were great opportunities for the expansion of trade, finance and industrial production. More ships, more pack-horses, more looms could find employment without overcrowding or need for hard competitive struggle. Clearly it would be dangerous to rely on less than an exhaustive list of examples to illustrate what must essentially be a general problem, but it may be noted how Aardenburg, small and very near to Bruges, still managed to achieve prosperity before 1280, yet after that date had to begin a desperate fight with her neighbour for mere livelihood.

To talk of lack of saturation is to say too little. It was not merely a question of the overall quantity of traders and goods in relation to need; equally vital was the unevenness of distribution of these goods and services. If there was greater freedom in the earlier Middle Ages it did not spring merely from the abundance of good markets open to all, but

[1] Heckscher, *Mercantilism*, II, 56.

derived also from the fact that merchants, capital, technical knowledge and productive capacity were concentrated in some areas while others lacked and needed them. Such inequalities encouraged more freedom of economic intercourse than was feasible when each region had gone much further towards economic self-sufficiency.

In the simpler cases a relatively backward area would need, or at least would be unable to resist, penetration by foreigners from a more highly developed region, as happened between the Baltic hinterland and the north German cities where a more or less colonial relationship was established. Sometimes conditions were more complex: a town might need to draw on outside resources and at the same time be able to invest in less-advanced economies. Until the early thirteenth century Genoa relied on the merchants of the 'hanse' of the seventeen towns for the importation of most of the cloth which she shipped through the Mediterranean. In the middle decades of that century she was able to go far towards dispensing with these merchants and bought her cloth at the Champagne fairs. Yet in order to do this the Genoese buyers had to lean heavily on capital advances from the merchants of Asti, Milan, Piacenza and other north Italian towns. It is typical that, when the replacement of northern merchants was getting under way early in the thirteenth century, two of the richest Genoese bankers and clothiers, Bertramis Bertaldus and Manfredus de Serra, acted in very close association with an important Asti trading family which had strong interests in textile dealings at the Champagne fairs. Tolerance towards, even encouragement of, foreigners remained characteristic of Genoa throughout the thirteenth century and had not disappeared in the early fourteenth century. Foreigners were allowed to do business under conditions of remarkable freedom, and even the brokers' profession included members from Florence, Lucca, Piacenza and other Italian towns, not to speak of Provençaux, Frenchmen and Germans; indeed Genoa at this time must have owed an appreciable part of her wealth to the activities and the capital of foreigners. On the other hand, just when Genoa was drawing so heavily on the resources of others, her own were being committed in less advanced regions; up to the sixties of the thirteenth century Genoa stood in a dominant economic relationship to a city like Barcelona which she provided with capital, technical knowledge and shipping, and by the 1153 treaty with Lucca she dominated traffic between that city and the French fairs.

These conditions would have a strong influence on town policy. For merchant capitalist and for craftsman producer—and one or both would usually be influential in town policy—there would be no great difficulty about the *terms* of trade: profit-margins would not be dangerously narrow. When distributive machinery had by no means caught up with the potential market, when competition was barely felt, when the output of many desirable and necessary goods was not as great as latent demand, when there were new areas and new commodities to be exploited, satisfactory profits could be expected without elaborate human interference or measures to exclude the other fellow. The need to recruit artisans and traders, the need to concentrate capital, the need to open up markets in the face of political and physical obstacles, all these remained; but all these were just the circumstances likely to push in the direction of 'freedom' and mutual understanding within the towns and between the towns.

These conditions did not coincide with any definite period of time: in Italy, for example, they were threatened at many points by the twelfth century at the latest; but taking the west as a whole it will be assumed that the period lasts until the thirteenth century. Did this period in fact show greater liberality in town behaviour than later centuries?

An inferential argument is that, if trade and production were always as regulated and restricted as they were in the later Middle Ages, if admissions to citizenship and to craft membership were always so limited, if towns were always so antagonistic and competitive one with another, it is difficult to understand how towns or the economic activities for which they were responsible could possibly have increased as they did. How could populations have grown if all attractive callings were barred to newcomers? How did the size and number of craft associations increase so rapidly if there was restricted recruitment? How was the early growth in membership, influence and vigour of trading bodies sustained if exclusivism was the order of the day? And how, in times and areas where few or no towns had really large resources, did they solve the problems of concentrating money, knowledge or equipment for the rapid exploitation of new opportunities without accepting help from outside? There are of course many individual instances of freedom of recruitment and of mutual aid between towns to be found in the Middle Ages. The point here is that it seems a fair inference that such cases *must* have been quantitatively much more important in the earlier centuries to make sense of economic and social trends then apparent.

A second argument notes the disproportion in the amount of surviving evidence about town organization in the last two medieval centuries as compared with earlier periods. There is a notable and widespread increase in the bulk of town records, especially from the late thirteenth century onwards, and a large proportion of this increase is accounted for by the appearance of regulations, bans and injunctions directly or indirectly affecting economic life. Occasionally the beginnings of a flood of material around 1300 can be traced to a local accident—a fire in the Barcelona archives in the 1290's for example—but such accidents cannot begin to explain so general a fact.

It seems that here is a crude means for estimating the degree of 'regulation' obtaining in urban economies at different periods; *prima facie* the twelfth century was a time of freer, less hampering policies than was the fourteenth century. Allowing for the quantitative crudity of the judgment, is there any objection to it on principle? It is not a question of the number of documents increasing *pari passu* with the number of towns, for the phenomenon can be noted in many individual towns. Perhaps there was a 'clerical revolution' and the written rather than the spoken or 'cried' word came into its own? Perhaps it was a question of the accidents of survival? Yet these accidents did not make the same, often very striking, differentiation for all other classes of medieval material, and the impression grows that there was a great deal of writing down because there was a great deal to be written down in the way of town and gild regulations, that town needs stimulated the greater use of documents in the public sphere just as company needs did in the private. In any case the matter is beyond dispute in many cases; of the mass of fourteenth-century and fifteenth-century legislation, a great part is explicitly new, new in its detailed provisions and very often new in that it represents interference in fields hitherto untouched by civic authority.

The argument from silence is valuable because silence presupposes a town policy which did not multiply occasions for litigious strife and did not foster the growth of controls. But the mind hankers for more positive evidence and here other difficulties arise: the subject is so complicated when looked at in detail, so large when looked at in the round, that general decisions about trends are bound to have a strongly subjective element. Allowing for this the evidence does suggest an overall change from policies where the attitude to strangers was more tolerant to those where it was less tolerant, from situations more free from competitive and monopolistic features to those which were less free. The growth of a firm system of *Fremdenrecht* in the towns of central Germany seems to date from about the middle of the thirteenth century, illegal contraventions of toll exemptions granted to other towns seem a common weakness in fourteenth- and fifteenth-century English towns but much more rare before this period, Venice began to feel her way towards a 'staple' policy in the early thirteenth century and had matured such a policy by 1300. Again and again occur these cases which point to an increase in competitive spirit, in mutual hostility and in conscious desire for monopoly, often dating from the later thirteenth century or thereabouts.

Town leagues and associations afford some interesting evidence. Concerted action by towns has a bad reputation; it is most likely to suggest the Hanseatic League of the later Middle Ages, an oligopoly precariously maintained and showing an inherent tendency to break down because the forces of exclusion and monopoly which underlay it acted as strongly between member towns as between them and the outside world. Or it might suggest the thirteenth-century form of the two great 'hanses' of the Low Countries, when illiberal tendencies were well to the fore. Even so, the exclusivism shown by these 'hanses' was a group or class matter, with merchant patricians set against the rest; there was still co-operation between towns. It was not until the fourteenth century that three towns came to have a virtual monopoly of the most important branches of trade and attempts were made by one town to dominate all the others. This was managed more than once by Bruges, and, a little later, by Ghent.

Co-operation between towns is not restricted to the later Middle Ages. What is more, though town associations of this period are characteristically attempts at group monopoly or compulsory groupings under a powerful leader or alliances natural to competitive warfare, the earlier associations have contrasting features. They approximate to free confederations, giving mutual satisfaction and working in a context where there were adequate markets, and so little used as leagues designed to give *competitive* strength. Strength was an immediate purpose of early leagues but it was applied to different ends. Individual towns were often hampered by lack of capital or by an imperfect economic organization, they suffered because they could not muster the force needed to suppress feudal anarchy or to put pressure on political authorities. Town leagues then represented a gathering up of strength which made possible or easier the penetration of markets and their peaceful organization.

A somewhat specialized form of such co-operation is to be found among merchants of different towns when settled abroad; need for the strength born of union was here of such importance that it was often sought even when the home towns had for long been engaged in trade warfare. So in 1278 Folcio Cacia of Perugia, as *capitaneus universitatis mercatorum lombardorum et tuscorum* and on behalf of the 'consuls of the merchants' of Venice, Genoa, Rome, Lucca, Piacenza, Florence, Siena, Milan, Asti, Bologna and Pistoia, obtained trading privileges for all these towns from Philip III of France. Similarly Catalan and Provençal towns combined forces to establish *fonduks* in Syria in the twelfth century at a time when greater cities were able to provide their own organization.

The town leagues of Europe are more pertinent as evidence. Leagues like the 'hanse' of London or the 'hanse' of the seventeen towns started when merchants in various towns were interested in developing markets too big for any of them singly; how useful association could be is shown by the experience of northern merchants selling cloth at Genoa in the thirteenth century. Easily the most successful were those grouped in the 'hanse' of the seventeen towns, but this was not because of any monopoly; merchants from other towns were *not* excluded from the trade.

Presumably the beginnings of such leagues were associations like that between the merchants of Gravelines and the men of the territory of Bourbourg, which association in turn joined itself to the Gild Merchant of St Omer. The reasons for this grouping cannot be given with certainty, but the view that affiliation was necessary to the weaker group because St Omer would otherwise have beaten all competition seems to overlook the fact that St Omer was *not* exclusive, *was* willing to associate, although by the very terms of this argument she should have had the strength to adopt an intransigent attitude.

The associations which preceded the fully formed Hanseatic League are equally instructive. They offered advantages to merchants interested in adventurous expansion and concerned with thrusting into new markets rather than with keeping their grip on old; but the additional problem of overcoming physical insecurity was of major importance. The 1259 agreement establishing a league between Lübeck, Rostock and Wismar declared that 'everyone who robs traders in churches or cemeteries, on water or on land, is to be outlawed and punished by all towns and merchants. Wherever such robbers go with their loot, the town or territory receiving them is to be held equally guilty and proscribed by all towns and merchants.' Similar motives prompted the formation of other thirteenth-century German leagues; they were sometimes due almost entirely to the failure of authority to ensure physical security and preserve fiscal decencies; they were reactions to the *furiosa Teutonicorum insania* of the thirteenth-century Rhenish tolls, to the irresponsible armies which made the long land-ways a perilous nightmare, to the nobles who as amateurs or professionals plundered the merchant convoys. The preamble to the declaration made by the League of the Rhine in 1254 is explicit enough: 'As many of our citizens have been utterly ruined by the violence and injuries inflicted on them in the country and on the roads for a long time past, and their ruin has involved the ruin of others . . . it is high time to find some way of avoiding such violence and of re-establishing peace and justice throughout all our territories. With this object we have together engaged ourselves by oath to observe a general peace for ten years.' In these cases we have in fact typical Leagues of Peace—the League of the Rhine included archbishops, bishops and many counts and other nobles; indeed most early urban associations, especially in Germany, seem to have been varying blends of peace leagues and 'development and exploration' companies. The drive for mercantile monopoly and the urge for competitive strength are much less in evidence; it is only the readiness with which the organization could be switched from one goal to another when circumstances changed which encourages a different impression.

Some of the apparent and real objections to this conception of a more liberal period must now be examined. First, a distinction made earlier may be revived, the distinction between two methods of profiting from trade: there was the 'fiscal' method of taxing traders and the processes of trade; there was the 'mercantile' method of actual commercial activity. The pursuit of wealth by either of these means could result in measures or policies which in some respects were identical. This identity is based mainly on the fact that increasing the amount of trade actually taking place in a town and ensuring control of this trade by a single public authority could serve either set of interests. A ready proof is afforded by the activities of some feudal lords of towns who did not engage directly in trade and whose policy was therefore one of fiscal gain tempered by some consideration for the town's well-being. From Carolingian times onwards there were examples of lords forcing merchants to use routes which brought them into the town concerned so that they could be subjected to tolls. There are cases where feudal lords acted as vigorously as any town council in the fight to eliminate competing markets within as wide a radius as possible; moreover, seignorial suppression of all private jurisdictions within the town which claimed authority and financial rights in matters of trade set many precedents for burgess authorities.

What are the implications of these facts? In the first place, the similarity of the response to fiscal or mercantile motives can make it very difficult to determine which were operating in a particular case. This is especially true of the earlier period when the evidence which would allow discrimination is generally absent. Yet the very difficulty is a useful warning: there can be no jumping to conclusions, no unhesitating assumption that all measures of the type mentioned are to be interpreted as reflecting the interests of pushing traders. In the absence of those facts which would make a decision possible, interpretation must be based on probabilities and on one's view of such matters as the social structure of early towns. Even if it is believed that the 'pushing traders' were the policy makers in early towns there is a danger of over-emphasizing the role played by individual motives and underrating that of collective needs. Towns *contained* merchants, craftsmen, rentiers, but they *were* 'communities', 'polities', and as such suffered from severe revenue problems which had to be met by appropriate fiscal measures.

The mere fact that many measures should be ascribed to fiscal motives rather than to a search for trading advantage does nothing by itself to strengthen belief in a liberal epoch. It does alter our conception of the mode of illiberality involved and it may alter our moral judgments. Filling the city chest at the expense of others is perhaps more venial than the filling of private coffers. The shift of attention to the fiscal sphere also makes it easier to see a further point; some measures which came to operate unfairly and restrictively had a more agreeable infancy as fair and convenient financial methods. Many fiscal measures were not conceived so as to give an advantage to the townsmen, but were based on justice, necessity or historical precedent.

Pertinent examples are provided by the territorial monopolies enjoyed by some early English towns. Some of these must be accepted at their face value; they are clear examples of monopolies operated by the town in defence of local trade and industry and at the expense of outsiders. In particular the regional monopolies enjoyed by textile workers, by the weavers and dyers of Lincoln and Leicester for instance, seem to belong to this category. Other cases are not so simple. The restriction of all the trade of an area to a single town had a long history in England. It was a fixed policy with Edward the Elder and with Athelstan to confine trade to borough 'ports' as far as possible, and though this policy broke down the idea constantly asserted itself with later kings. Henry I's charter to Cambridge provided that no boat was to be loaded or unloaded anywhere in Cambridgeshire save at the hithe of Cambridge itself and that no toll should be taken anywhere in the county except at Cambridge; this charter came two, even three generations before Cambridge gained the farm of its town revenues by the charter of Henry II and even longer before a Gild Merchant was authorized in 1201. There was a similar concentration of Lincolnshire trade at Lincoln.

A royal policy which favoured trade concentration in certain towns probably owed a great deal to the fiscal advantages which accrued; toll collection was easier and cheaper and leakage far less likely. The policy owed something also to the Crown's wish to strengthen the towns concerned; this motive was dominant in Edward I's order that all trade in north Wales except petty traffic in foodstuffs must be transacted in Conway, Beaumaris and four other towns. Whatever the royal purpose it was only to be expected that a town which was beginning to take over the management of its own destiny should consider it had a kind of natural right to continue this kind of monopoly.

Looked at in this way a striving for monopoly still remains but it has a less aggressively mercantile character; it suggests that a more conservative desire to preserve the proper and historical order of things was also present in some degree. But circumstances may have obtained which will force a more drastic change in our appraisal of urban motives. Communities like Cambridge or Lincoln, in their advance towards independence, acquired the farm of their town, and when they farmed the town's revenues they paid annually to the exchequer *a firma burgi*, a lump sum equal or more than equal to the Crown's yearly income from the borough up to date. Now imposts on trade were one great source of such revenue, one of the greatest in fact; in eleventh- and twelfth-century

English towns, tolls were the largest contributors to royal revenue or second only to money rents from tenements. When a town enjoyed a monopoly of trade in an area before the period of *firma burgi* it is obvious that this would have had an important effect on the size of the borough revenues, and if the town was made responsible for these revenues then it had a clear claim to preserve those conditions in which alone a similar income could properly be expected. In such cases the claim for monopoly rests as much on fiscal equity and fiscal necessity as on any other motive. This consideration gains weight when it is remembered that, in the twelfth century at any rate, little margin for profit seems to have been allowed to the town; royal income from towns was generally raised, often steeply raised, after the Conquest, and when this income was farmed to the inhabitants the assessment might be even higher. Lincoln's burden was more than tripled from £30 in 1066 to £100 in 1086, but the amount of the farm was £140 in 1130 and later in the century reached £180.

A town had an automatic right to those privileges which were integral to the original assessment of its burdens; that this principle should be accepted was only natural and fair; that the Crown should acknowledge it is also natural, for after all it was royal revenue which was at stake in the last resort. So the charters of Henry I and Henry II to Lincoln affirm that all *mercatores forinseci* of Lincolnshire should trade at Lincoln alone 'so that my reeves of Lincoln may not lose my royal customs'.[1] Indeed, the idea of relationship between a town's collection of tolls and its payment of farm to the king was still very much alive in the fifteenth century. At least it was an extremely handy argument when a town wished to appeal to the Crown about loss of toll revenue, as did Oxford in its representations to the Council about 1429.

There is no sharp dividing-line between the above argument and the idea that many measures which appear monopolistic and discriminating were merely insistence on payment for services rendered, for the use of markets, the enjoyment of various trading privileges and so on. These and related topics can perhaps best be studied through the medium of a subject which at first sight seems to create grave difficulties for the general argument, namely, the role of the English Gild Merchant. The importance of this question for our theme will perhaps excuse a digression with rather insular emphasis, for no objection to our interim hypothesis seems as telling as the existence of these gilds. That the Gild Merchant was based on a monopoly is true. But is it true that the gild was an instrument of the monopolistic and exclusive *policy* of all or part of the townsfolk? In particular, can it be viewed as the means by which local traders eliminated

---

[1] The idea is well illustrated in J. W. F. Hill, *Medieval Lincoln* (Cambridge, 1948), 185.

as much competition as possible? This is an opinion commonly held; as one great authority says, the Gilds Merchant *affectaient toujours, on le sait, un caractère local, particulariste et profondément xenophobe* (Pirenne).

The original situation seems to have been as follows. The right to a Gild Merchant was a right granted to a town community, not to any particular group of townsfolk, and it was a right not to a specific kind of association but to a particular method and purpose of associating. The essence of the situation was that all bodies and individuals with an interest in the trade of the town in any of its aspects should 'geld' together—should submit to mutual taxation. Those interested might well include the community acting as a whole and might equally well include outsiders. The money so raised would replace the earlier day-by-day tolls on all individuals and organizations which chanced to be trading on any occasion; if, as was often the case, the town farmed the revenue it owed the king, the gild dues could be 'put against' that part of the bill which corresponded to the Crown's earlier toll revenue. Any other gild income would probably be thought best used if applied to festivities, to the improvement of trading facilities or, occasionally, to the general well-being of the town.

Looked at from the inside the purpose was as follows. The town needed the money which came from taxes on trade; it needed it either to meet a specific outside obligation (payment to the lord) or to meet internal needs. For those who regularly traded in the town, and this would include most natives and many outsiders, the Gild Merchant system had definite advantages. It was convenient financially, as a lump sum replaced a host of petty payments; it worked fairly equitably, for there are traces of an original principle that dues should be roughly proportionate to the amount of business that a man was likely to transact; and, finally, trading interests obtained both the organization and funds with which to further all aims concerned with the commercial well-being of the town. Looked at from the outside the arrangement would seem equally defensible. The town had something between a regular department and an organized 'aspect' of its community life which would deal competently with a vital sector of affairs. There was a rough and ready justice to individuals from a fiscal point of view, for those who benefited paid for the benefits. This was of particular concern to a town enjoying *firma burgi*, for it had to meet obligations which included the trade taxes payable to the king. The Gild Merchant could act as an arrangement by which those who used to pay, and properly paid, these dues would continue to do so; the alternative would have been to spread this burden over the population at large whether they traded or not.

The monopoly aspect of the Gild Merchant now takes on a different appearance. If the gild was a 'gelding together' of those who thereby made themselves quit of tolls, it was only proper that those who were not associated thus should not enjoy exemption; if gild money provided trading facilities and privileges, these could properly be denied to non-members; if, in those cases where a town farmed its revenues, the gild was used as a means of providing some of these, then the association had a right to control the activities which furnished the money and it had a right to enjoy any advantage or monopoly implicit in the original assessment of the revenues. In other words, Gild Merchant monopoly is in part explicable as insistence that only those who pay for a privilege can enjoy it, and in part as the consequence of farming, for farmers must be allowed complete command over whatever business is involved. The trouble was that this situation was very unstable. The nature of the Gild Merchant was such that it made a perfect instrument for different motives: it could so easily be adapted to promote the interests of one town or one class against others. Indeed the very way the Gild Merchant monopoly worked must have suggested such use even when there were no strong environmental factors encouraging a change. It is the ease and rapidity with which the policy underlying this institution altered in the thirteenth century that lends colour to the usual interpretation of this policy.

Some of these ideas must now be substantiated; and first that the Gild Merchant was not a gild of merchants. All the evidence suggests that it was an association of those with trading interests rather than a group to advance the interests of 'mere' traders. In England it was usually the *gilda mercatoria*, and if not that, then the *gilda mercanda, gilda mercatorialis, gilda mercalis, gilda mercatrix* or simply the *gilda* or *hansa*; it was not typically the *gilda mercatorum*.[1] Among its members appeared those who were neither pure merchants nor craftsmen-traders, and *a fortiori* the latter were usually admitted freely in the twelfth and early thirteenth centuries and probably made up the bulk of membership in most cases. The Leicester and Shrewsbury gild rolls dating from the beginning of the thirteenth century show coopers, carters, miners, carpenters and masons by the side of butchers and bakers, dyers, mercers and merchants. The privilege of Gild Merchant was of course given to the community as a whole in the first place. This is clear enough in those English borough charters which include the privilege and there is the instructive example of Ipswich to show how a town population set about exercising their right in this spirit.[2] When this spirit was perverted in later days there was always a strong likelihood of protest and an appeal to the original conception. This can be seen in the fulminations of 'popular' parties against civic oligarchy in the fourteenth century or in the 1330 *quo warranto* proceedings against

---

[1] In any case a *mercator* was not a 'mere' merchant.

[2] Charles Gross, *The Gild Merchant* (London, 1890), II, 115–23.

towns like Derby and Bedford.[1] These considerations, joined to the fact that Gild Merchant functions deeply concerned the town in one of the most vital sectors of its activity, explain how the gild could be regarded as 'an organization of the whole community for the control of trade by the common consent of the people'[2] or, more formally, as 'the department of town administration whose duty was to maintain and regulate the trade monopoly'.[3] The situation has been well put in connection with Cambridge: 'it seems . . . to be extremely doubtful whether at Cambridge—and the same might be said of some other towns of equal rank—any Gild Merchant took definite shape and stood apart from the general body of burgesses. Apparently the freedom from toll which King John conceded was conceived to belong to every burgess of Cambridge merely because he was a burgess. In other words, no trace seems as yet to have been found in later documents of any smaller body organized as a gild of merchants which was treated as having an exclusive right to that liberty which had been obtained from the king.'[4]

More vital for the argument is evidence that gild membership was open to non-burgesses and indeed to people not resident in the town at all. Pembroke's twelfth-century charter said that burgesses could allow all merchants of the county of Pembroke into their Merchant Gild; the 1157 charter to Lincoln speaks of 'the merchant gild of the men of the city and of other merchants of the county' which had already existed in this form for a long time; citizens of Hereford could receive Frenchmen, Welshmen, Scots and anybody else into their gild so long as they were true subjects of the king and were in scot and lot with the citizens. There were over fifty *forinseci* in the Shrewsbury gild at the beginning of the thirteenth century and 234 in 1249; between one-third and one-half of Barnstaple gild membership at the beginning of the fourteenth century seems to have been made up of 'foreigns'; and in 1281 Leicester allowed all worthy tenants of the nearby fee of the bishop of Lincoln to enter their Gild Merchant so long as they submitted to being in scot and lot in all things concerning the gild.

It is generally clear that the decisive condition of entry was originally a willingness to submit to mutual taxation, to be in scot and lot or to 'geld' with other members. What did this gild payment represent? It was by and large an equivalent for toll payments, it was analogous to a collective farming of these dues, which made members quit of individual

---

[1] Gross, *Gild Merchant*, II, 17–18 (Bedford) and 51–3 (Derby).
[2] Mrs J. R. Green, *Town Life in the Fifteenth Century* (London and New York, 1894), II, 193.
[3] Gross, *Gild Merchant*, I, 43.
[4] F. W. Maitland and Mary Bateson (eds), *The Charters of the Borough of Cambridge* (Cambridge, 1901), xv–xvi.

O

and piecemeal exactions. When King John's charter to Gloucester was confirmed in 1328 gild dues were in fact lumped together with other imposts on trade: Gloucester gildsmen were to be free from all *muragio, passagio, gildagio et gilda mercatorum* and all other customs throughout the kingdom. When a 'toll-farm' was so constituted in a royal town its identity would be lost in the *firma burgi*, though we do hear, at Winchester for example, of gild fees being handed over to the civic authorities, and it was a generally accepted principle that the gildsman *reddere debet simul cum burgensibus talliagia et defectus burgi adimplere*. This merger of gild payments with farm payments explains why there is mention of Gilds Merchant reimbursing the lord in mesne boroughs only, at Leicester, Lewes and Reading for instance, and why in royal towns there was so close a relationship or even identity between burgess status and gild membership, between gild fees and urban taxes.

Where a town was under a mesne lord and when gildsmen did not lose fiscally if outsiders were quit of toll, there could be very significant happenings. At Totnes for example the inhabitants claimed to have *quandam libertatem inter se que dicitur Gilda marcatoria, per quam possint mercatores extraneos facere liberos, ne solvant Theoloneum de rebus seu mercandisis suis emptis et venditis, prout dicti burgenses quieti sunt et liberi; et hoc utuntur et usi sunt a tempore quo non extat memoria*;[1] they fought their lord, William de la Zouche, for this right which he opposed as robbing him of his revenues. There was rioting, a judicial inquiry, and the town had to make arrangements more financially favourable to its lord. At Barnstaple, on the contrary, victory went to the townsfolk in their fight with John Cornwall over the right to admit merchants and victuallers visiting the town. Such cases are strongly reminiscent of some continental examples, such as the 1199 decree of Baldwin of Constantinople which forbade men of Ghent to allow into their gild anyone not resident in the city or in the count's castle.

One important qualification must be made. Gilds Merchant typically excluded non-members from any share in certain types of trade—all the retail trade of a town or the retail trade in finished and dyed cloths or, occasionally, trade in such primary products as skins. Such exclusion is distinctive because it was total; there was no way round it by paying tolls. Because this was so it suggests that something more was involved than financial justice or convenience: there was real monopoly. Two motives could be involved: the desire to confine some functions to a certain *place* and the wish to restrict them to certain *people*.

The first, which is a basic and crucial motive of policy, will be dealt with later; what of the second desire? If gildsmen tried to restrict some trade to certain people they must have wished to exclude other groups.

[1] Gross, *Gild Merchant*, II, 236.

Who were these? There were two principal candidates, 'foreigns' and local craftsmen; yet both were admitted to Gilds Merchant as has been seen, and to the extent that admission of non-residents, non-citizens and craftsmen was allowed, to that degree exclusion of persons disappeared and only restriction to a prescribed place remained. But there were *some* early attempts to deny burgess-ship or membership of the Gild Merchant to certain craftsmen and especially to weavers, fullers and dyers.

This policy seems to have shown itself earlier than any firm movement to exclude outside merchants. In the time of King John, for example, Lincoln aldermen declared that their fullers and dyers *non habent legem vel communiam cum liberis civibus*; and in the early thirteenth century similar exclusivism was apparent in many of the English towns in which there was a significant concentration of textile workers. The conclusion must be that, in the most paying branches of local trade, a tendency to exclude some sections of the population developed very early. However tolerant the bigger traders and landholders of the town might be towards outsiders, they took steps to keep some craftsmen out of the more lucrative business. This development should not be exaggerated; though signs of such exclusivism can be traced to the twelfth century it was undoubtedly in the thirteenth that the policy grew strong and dominant. But there is certainly a suggestion, here as elsewhere, that 'illiberal' policies first developed at home, that early oligarchs found various motives for co-operating with outsiders, but soon found cause and means for putting pressure on less fortunate classes in their own towns.

Despite this, the internal policies of early towns, like their external policies, did show some contrast with later conditions. Three suggestions can be made. Firstly, that early internal policy was often more liberal in the sense of not expressing so tight and extended a control by one class interest over others; secondly, that when it was a class policy the form of exploitation was not necessarily commercial or industrial, was not the form proper to an oligarchy of merchants, but was fiscal exploitation; thirdly, that internal policy, like external, was responsible for less 'regulation' of activities than was common later.

The basis of the first suggestion is the fact that there were smaller social and economic differences between the inhabitants of early towns than between their successors; opinion was more homogeneous if not more democratic. There is no room here for details and perhaps no need, as it is generally conceded that class distinctions, political cleavage and oligarchical imposition of minority policies became more prominent in the thirteenth century, though there were naturally important exceptions and wide variations in timing. The overriding of consumers' interests by great merchants, the oppression of craft workers by entrepreneurs, the harrowing of housewives by wholesale victuallers, all these may have been present; but by and large they were less severe, they had rather less social foundation and disposed of less political machinery.

As in the case of external policy the argument *ex silentio* can be added to the inferential argument. A rough index of the degree to which town policy was a minority policy is given by the extent to which the majority complained. Though the twelfth century was not free from such complaints there is a marked increase in their number and in the bitterness with which they were expressed during the thirteenth century. In many regions the growing vehemence of the record of protests, strikes, riots and insurrections is so patent during the later thirteenth century and after, that a relatively greater popular satisfaction before this time seems an inescapable conclusion. What is actually known of internal policies during the eleventh, twelfth and thirteenth centuries does not allow an exact and detailed estimate, but it certainly does not contradict the idea that town policy became more remote from the general will as time passed. Town law and, even more important, town 'case law', do give this impression on balance. Even when special interests won control at an early date there is no presumption that this represented the original situation. The merchants of the 'hanse' of London were acting restrictively towards craftsmen in their constituent towns by the end of the twelfth century, yet we cannot assume the absence of a still earlier and more 'liberal' epoch.

It is quite clear however that there *are* features in many towns which prove a class policy before 1250, a policy serving a dominant minority at the expense of others. It is an easy step from this truth to belief in policies serving the domination of mercantile capital; an easy but often a false step. Though control of town policy was often the means by which merchant capital arranged conditions to its own advantage, a more direct use of political power is at least as common and often dominates the scene. The economic aspect of this direct abuse of power may be called fiscal or financial exploitation; it was simply a means by which the favoured few put money into their own pockets at the expense of the many and this by manipulating the ordinary financial machinery of the town. The principal ways of doing this were frank malversation of public funds and unfair distribution of taxes; the sale of justice may be included under the same head.

A great deal of the popular resentment in towns seems to have been generated by such policies of fiscal exploitation, and as we move back in time they become relatively more important as causes of unrest. This is in great part connected with the circumstance that the earliest ruling groups in towns were not typically groups of mercantile capitalists but only gradually became *transformed* into such. When William Fitz Osbert led agitation in London in 1195–6 the burden of his accusations was that the city fathers defrauded the king of his revenues and at the same time thrust the main burden of taxation onto the poor. Some ten years later King John, upbraiding the city barons, told the same tale: there had been complaints that those who were in power were partial in administering justice, unfair in their way of assessing and levying tallages and dishonest in keeping sums raised by taxation to themselves. In contemporary Italy there were striking similarities. There the commons of many towns pressed for a policy of proportionate taxation to replace a system which exempted the magnates and imposed a uniform poll-tax on the rest; this was a system based ultimately on feudal privilege. In late twelfth- and early thirteenth-century Italy taxation was the prime economic issue in most conflicts over internal policy. At Milan, Pisa, Siena, Perugia, Lucca and other towns the *popolani* made the same demand of the *magnati*—a proportional tax on wealth in place of a fixed tax per head.

Such observations can have interesting consequences for the study of early class structure, but what matters here is the evidence that even when oppression did exist it was not necessarily a result of moulding town policy to further commercial and industrial exploitation.

There was then greater freedom in the early Middle Ages in the sense that there was nothing like the detailed yet comprehensive regulation of the town economy so characteristic of later history. This is true when all allowances are made for the fact that earlier towns were smaller and their problems intrinsically less complicated. It is true also of both the internal and external aspects of policy. Secondly, there was a large measure of freedom from the restrictions, aggressive and defensive, proper to merchants and craftsmen who find themselves in a highly competitive situation. Xenophobia, for example, and the laws which give it substance, were not so much in evidence. It is also true that there was at least relatively more economic freedom for the weaker groups in town society. Where town policy did reflect the exploitation of the many weak by the few strong this was commonly by what has been called 'fiscal' exploitation. Mercantile capital was not so obviously a separate and dominant interest, and there was far less legislation to exclude the non-capitalist trader from power and profit or to subordinate craft workers to great merchants, than was common at a later time.

One last but important observation must be made. There was one sense in which town policy always *had* to be monopolistic. Unless certain economic functions, trading principally, industrial production to some extent, had been concentrated at certain places towns would hardly have appeared. Such concentration was not so much an original *purpose* of the townsfolk as the *cause* which brought them together as members of a town. Towns became distinctive economic and social units just when and because certain places were set apart and defended by laws or privileges making them market and production centres and denying some or all such rights to the countryside around. In origin and essence the early towns depended on such segregation of economic functions and so, in a definite though particular sense, on the existence of monopoly. They *were* because other places were not, they *had* because other places had not. They grew when and where lords restricted trade to a centre, granted special protection or privileges to those who settled or did their business at a defined place, gave a legal market to some locality and so denied some economic activities to everywhere else. The monopoly belonged originally to a certain place rather than to certain people, but of course it easily and normally came to embrace the latter.

This was the basic position the town could not give up without ceasing to be a town. Non-residents might be allowed to import—but they imported to the town's market; they might have permission to export— they exported from the town's market; they might even, by 'gelding' with the inhabitants, participate in retail trade—at the legal market place and time. *The* trade of a place, that is its internal retail trade, was strictly reserved to those who had joined the trading community of that place. What was always intolerable was that the vital functions of the town should leak and diffuse over the countryside. Of course, it was natural for a monopoly of trade at a place to become a monopoly of those who lived at that place and finally a control of all trade by the richer merchants among local inhabitants. Once the operation of the original monopoly was entrusted to any association made up wholly or primarily of residents this evolution was almost bound to begin.

(2) THE THIRTEENTH CENTURY: SATURATION AND EXPLOITATION

There came a time when whatever 'freedom' characterized early town policy faded, when tolerance towards outsiders diminished and economic exploitation within towns intensified. 'Time' is a poor word, for this was no datable event but a trend manifest in town policies at periods which varied with every individual circumstance. If a time must be specified then the thirteenth century seems as convenient as any. This was a critical era in many cases, and in particular saw a rapid change of temper in the internal policies of many towns.

There seem to be two main reasons for change. The most important reason inside towns was the consolidation of patrician oligarchies and a significant increase in the extent to which their power depended on the control of trade, industry and finance. Outside the towns the vital circumstances were those which can be interpreted together as indicating 'saturation' of the European economy.

The rule of oligarchies is a well-attested feature of the thirteenth century. Restricted groups of 'patricians', generally including a strong representation of merchant capitalists, made themselves masters of the town government. These patricians dominated towns socially and politically and had the power to direct urban policy on the course best suiting their private interests. Not uncommonly this development went to extremes and there was actual identification or fusion of a professional association of merchants with the town council: an exclusive trading gild became indistinguishable from the town government. Even after the notorious XXXIX were removed from power at Ghent in 1275 by the Countess Marguerite, the office of *échevin* was restricted to members of the gild; and a similar rule was common in other Flemish towns, whether large like Bruges or small like Aardenburg. In England many Gilds Merchant acted as the governing bodies of their towns and at the same time made entry more difficult for all save important merchants. Even when outward form did not so readily betray the inner fact, the preponderance of men of (relatively) big business and members of the more notable trading companies was generally well developed in political affairs.

Such oligarchies held all the trump cards; they combined political and economic power, public and private authority, legal rights with illicit influence; they were masters in the gild-hall and the market, the finance committee and the workshop. They were tempted as rulers to exploit the community through the normal fiscal machinery, they were tempted as businessmen to further private interests by appropriate laws and policy, and they were more easily led to both courses as outside pressures made themselves felt.

These external pressures resulted from growing saturation of the European economy. This saturation is here regarded, not as a crisis, but as a gradual change in the balance between the goods society could produce and distribute and those it could consume, a change which *culminated* in a crisis.[1] The earlier gap between supply and potential demand was lessened, and in many ways it was the very power, efficiency and success of merchants and mercantile capital in industry, the victories of the 'commercial revolution', which bred these difficulties. An ancillary process which had similar effects was the tendency for productive and commercial capacity to be more evenly spread; though local specialization was often fostered and though international trade intensified, economic change in the twelfth and thirteenth centuries often lessened the dependence of major regions upon a few small and highly developed areas.

Several elements went to produce this situation. The distributive needs of society were satisfied by a merchant class which steadily increased its numbers and improved the quality of its organization. From the point of

[1] Cf. *Camb. Econ. Hist.* II, 338, n. 1.

view of individual merchants this would involve a diminution of opportunities in general and a shrinkage of profits because of increased competition. Improvements in all aspects of the supply-system, joined to a greater availability of goods, would cut the large easy profits which made fortunes when distribution methods were primitive, production was inadequate to demand and traders could find non-competitive markets. Many regions, which had been easy markets for finished products and cheap producers of raw materials, changed their role. They became centres of political power able to resist gross exploitation; they became centres of economic power and accumulated the capital, equipment and knowledge to compete with those under whose tutelage they had developed. The whole process of industrial and commercial expansion working through the inducements of easy opportunity and ready profit was now challenged and this had important consequences for the temper and motives of townspeople, and merchants especially.

Speaking generally the response of merchants was an attempt to keep the old profit opportunities, and since these no longer occurred naturally they had to be produced artificially. Now, merchants were strengthening their control over towns at just this time and this fact gave them special opportunities for maintaining and creating disparities between buying and selling price. Indeed the very consolidation of town oligarchies may owe at least as much to the new economic pressures as to 'natural' social evolution. There were at least three important ways of guaranteeing large profit-margins: restricting the numbers sharing in the more important branches of trade, tolerating a rise in the price of consumer goods which merchants imported into the town, and forcing down the price of manufactured goods which merchants exported by depressing the condition of craft workers. Because merchants were so often masters of the towns, these methods became parts of town policy and were fused, too, with the fiscal exploitation common to any ruling group.

It is important to mark that this was not, for towns as a whole, a period of economic decline or recession. Overall decline, where it does occur, belongs typically to the fourteenth century; the late thirteenth century and the beginning of the fourteenth were a period of maximum prosperity and power for many towns, even when they were producing grave internal unrest with their new policies. It was the absolute loss of business found in some towns of the later Middle Ages which produced the more drastic changes. Economic contraction was met by contraction of outlook; there was more concentration on the immediate locality, more jealousy of neighbouring towns, and often this was matched by a corresponding change in the type of man who made town policy. The ealier period, by contrast, showed much more continuity with the past. Towns were submitted to gradual pressure rather than the threat of ruin;

policy was not transformed at the hands of a new type of ruler acting within the context of novel aims and possibilities, it was adapted by the old rulers who thought and acted along the old lines but had to devise means of shifting the pressure onto others. Far indeed from being coincident with the period of crisis, the time when merchant patricians intensified exploitation and provoked social and economic unrest must be accounted an important cause of this crisis.

This idea of a period of saturation must not be bound too closely to given dates, for it was something of gradual growth and variable duration; nor can it be taken as more than a reasonable hypothesis in the absence of elaborate and tabulated data. It does, however, square well with a large number of known facts and with economic and historical probabilities. The development of town policies at this time can be seen against its background. There are no policy features which were completely absent before, none which cannot be found later; but taken together they have a coherence and emphasis which are characteristic of the period. The emphasis is on the use of town policy to advance the interests of mercantile capitalists at the expense of other inhabitants. We can assume that the very large class of small towns, those where the biggest 'capitalist' cut a pretty sorry figure, were a partial exception; there simply is not enough evidence before the fourteenth century to say anything with certainty. Even so it is not unlikely that petty country towns had a fair sprinkling of that type of general wholesale and retail merchant who supplied his own locality and country traders too, and who has been described by Fanfani from late fourteenth-century Tuscany.[1]

Typical elements of such policies have already been mentioned. They were the limitation of entry into the most profitable departments of trade, the enfeebling of consumer defence, the subordination of craft production and producers to the great merchants and the intensification of fiscal exploitation. The choice and the division are somewhat arbitrary; in fact the way in which these elements overlap and become indistinguishable is itself evidence of how they stem from a coherent set of interests and express a single policy.

There is little need to say more about the question of exclusion from trade. Given the abundant evidence that trading associations acted restrictively, especially with regard to craftsmen, it only remains to show that there was a connection between the policy of these associations and that of the towns. This was true in very many cases. It is easy to point to town after town where a single major trade gild either *was* the government or had in law or in practice the monopoly of office. There are plenty of other cases where a small group of such gilds enjoyed the same powers. The same principle held even when the monopolizing gild worked on a

[1] Amintore Fanfani, *Un mercante del Trecento* (Milan, 1935).

supra-urban basis. By the thirteenth century it was impossible to join the London 'hanse' directly; admission was granted only to those who had first been enrolled in the gilds of constituent towns, and these erected stiff obstacles to the recruitment of craftsmen. The constituent gilds in turn acted through the town governments, from which in fact they cannot readily be separated. It lay with the town council to decide whether a craftsman, who must already have renounced his calling for a year, should be admitted to the 'hanse' for the sum of one mark of gold or whether he should pay even more. Clearly the town government as such could block admission at will. These gilds and hanses, notable mainly in north France, the Low Countries and the Rhineland at this time, are significant. In their thirteenth-century form they represent combinations for the mutual defence and restriction of long-distance trade and for common control over restive craft workers, but are still combinations *between* towns and to defend far-flung interests and do not show the narrow concentration on the immediate locality which was so common a feature in many later towns.

Betrayal of the interests of the ordinary consumer was often a consequence of the domination of towns by their more important traders. When merchants had the power the course was more likely to be set towards high profits for themselves than towards low prices for the man in the street; the community suffered accordingly, especially if monopolies were tolerated in the food and drink trades. Of course there could be no question of making it official town policy to allow monopolies and high prices: the established principle was that goods should be cheap and plentiful. Yet effective policy, the policy followed in practice, could diverge from accepted standards. Just how wide the divergence might be depended on an extremely complicated balance of forces within any one town. When a town had highly developed export industries the merchants who dealt in its products would fight for cheap consumer goods to keep living costs down for the producers. Where a town was particularly sensitive to social unrest for political reasons, then it would take care never to flout the consumers too boldly. There were many more such motives, last but certainly not least being genuine concern for the consumer. London, for example, shows a bewildering variety of purposes, so that confusing cross-currents are more often apparent than a uniform stream of policy. Even so some victualling groups like the fishmongers were particularly successful in advancing their interests against the commonweal between the late thirteenth and late fourteenth centuries because their gilds enjoyed so much political and social influence.

It is sometimes difficult to decide whether monopolies in foodstuffs and other goods existed as illegal private enterprise merely, or as a normal practice countenanced and encouraged by town authorities. A high proportion certainly fell within this latter category even when the documents are not specific on the point. There were many complaints and appeals concerning engrossers and forestallers which did not lay the charge of condonation at the door of the city rulers by name; yet such complaints were commonly framed as being on behalf of 'the commons' and against 'the rich' and these social divisions were certainly understood as political ones too. This comes out clearly when the townsfolk, realizing the identity of rich forestaller and city councillor, appealed to superior authority; so in 1304 the 'poor men' of Norwich persuaded the Crown to investigate how the rich bought up food and other goods before they reached market despite all the laws against forestalling.

The weakening of consumer defence can be seen in other features of town policy. Taxation methods, for instance, though they benefited patricians in more than one way, are evidence on this especial point. Particularly resented by the general population of towns were the sales taxes on consumer goods, the 'evil customs' which fell on foodstuffs and other articles of day-to-day consumption and were one of the principal sources of current revenue. The burden of this form of taxation weighed more and more heavily on the poorer classes as the thirteenth century progressed and became extremely grave by the end of that century in some towns; food prices at Florence, for example, were very high at the beginning of the fourteenth century and this was a major cause of the social strife which mounted to the crisis of 1378-9. Much of the rise in prices was not attributable to taxation and was due in fact to circumstances beyond the control of any city government; but those who suffered were not finical about economic truths and properly resented any policy which made things worse.

In the larger industrial towns, where the craftsmen made goods for a wide market, they became increasingly dependent upon the merchants who supplied their raw materials and disposed of their finished goods. These merchants, whose control over production grew with the spread of the putting-out system, turned to a policy of direct depression of producers and in this way tried to guarantee cheap and abundant production and maximum profits in the goods with which they traded. The more a town depended on industrial production for wide markets the more it was likely to show a policy framed in the interest of 'putting-out capital'; as a result such types of policy are not related to the overall size or commercial importance of towns but to the proportionate significance of export industries. So, for example, the policy of London in the late thirteenth century does not seem any more favourable to putting-out capital than does that of Leicester at the same time.

The policy of merchants with a stake in production is being treated as *town* policy; once again justification lies in the fact that class policy *was* town policy when these merchants dominated the policy-making organs. In towns with large export industries this was very generally the case. To take but one example: from the middle of the thirteenth century the *échevins* of Douai were responsible for nearly all the bans concerning the textile industry of the town and the identity of these magistrates with capitalist interests was reflected in the way in which the bans became more openly favourable to putting-out capital in the third quarter of the century. A climax came in 1275 when laws were promulgated which so outraged the working masters of the textile crafts that they protested to the Countess Marguerite. She ordered the withdrawal of the offending laws in 1276; slowly and reluctantly the *échevins* obeyed, only to rush the bans back into operation in 1280. There were strikes and riots, but merchant interests had all the town authority behind them and the strike leaders were banished or executed with disgusting barbarity.

Entrepreneurs used various methods to subordinate producers. The exclusion of craftsmen from the major trading gilds has already been mentioned in another context; here it is only necessary to stress its unusual importance where there was appreciable industrial development. The more important master craftsmen, especially those who were capitalist employers themselves in a small way, were the most serious challengers of a professional traders' monopoly, and, even more important, the very ability of merchant capitalists to put pressure on producers depended in the last resort on their controlling the import of raw materials and export of finished goods. The trading monopoly was the real guarantee of the dependence of producers. This was clearly perceived by both sides in Flemish textile towns at the beginning of the fourteenth century. One thing which bound together all grades of craftsmen was the demand that old policies should be reversed so that all could buy and sell freely.

There is no need to describe all the ways in which towns acted to keep craftsmen 'in their place'. Wages, hours and conditions of work, prices, all were subject to town regulation, as were less obvious but equally important considerations; for example, it was ordered at Liège in the middle of the thirteenth century that, whenever the town wardens and the merchants felt that there was a labour shortage in the cloth industry, working masters should be forced to take apprentices in such number 'that the work of the town shall be done'. Here only one feature need be mentioned, for it was crucial, namely the 'anti-combination laws'.

Gilds of craftsmen could raise wages or prices directly or raise them indirectly by restricting production or the numbers of producers. This creates a difficulty, for such activities would not only antagonize merchant entrepreneurs wanting a cheap and abundant flow of saleable articles: they could also threaten the ordinary town consumer. Thus opposition to the formation of artisan gilds could spring from more than one motive. In early times and in towns where production was destined for a local market there is always the possibility, sometimes a probability, that defence of the consumer was the prime consideration; so the various twelfth-century cases, where towns acted like Rouen in prohibiting craft fraternities, must be ignored in the present context. In the late thirteenth and early fourteenth centuries, and in towns where there was large-scale industrial production, generally of textiles, all the evidence points the other way. In such cases it is clear that it was the aims of merchant capital that governed policy; the interests of the consumer were brought in because they marched so conveniently with the designs of the merchants, because they helped to strengthen the argument and confirm the policy.

In the important industrial towns of thirteenth- and fourteenth-century Europe attacks on craft gilds were a very common feature. Such gilds were prohibited at Dinant in 1255, at Tournai in 1280 and at Brussels in 1290; Ghent had practically no craft-gild organization before 1302; in the towns of Brabant craft fraternities were not officially recognized until after the middle of the fourteenth century. Where producers and traders were joined in one gild the same principle applied; control of the gild belonged to the trading element and separate combination was forbidden to the industrial section. A 1324 statute of Florence condemned out of hand all associations not sanctioned by civic authority and then went on to ban specifically the assembly or combination of the members of any gild, and especially the workmen of the Arte della Lana, without the consent of the Consul of the Gilds. Where advisable the patriciate tried to secure state backing for such policies. So, in 1301, the duke of Brabant granted a privilege to Malines whose provisions stated that there was to be no gild or fraternity in the town save only the St Loys merchant gild and the Wollewerk, the drapers' gild in the hands of textile merchants. It was the same duke who promised the rulers of Antwerp never to allow gild status to any craft.

It was not always convenient to ban formal gilds or feasible to prevent informal association; but even when craft gilds were tolerated it was possible to draw their teeth by barring strike action or the use of any other effective weapon. Many towns struck a shrewd blow by preventing artisans from accumulating fighting funds; in these towns the patricians saw to it that the weekly fees the craftsmen raised among themselves were paid over to town magistrates instead of into a gild chest. The magistrates of Bruges made arrangements of this kind in 1280, Ghent did the same and the idea spread quickly to Brabant where Louvain imitated the policy in 1290 and Antwerp in 1291. Such measures were commonly accompanied by laws which prevented craftsmen from forcing fellow-workers to pay 'union' fees.

The last aspect of town policy to claim attention during this period has already been referred to as fiscal exploitation; that is, use of the public revenue system to benefit a minority *directly* rather than as an instrument in some other policy. Fiscal exploitation had no essential connection with merchant capitalist interests though eagerness to exploit in this way might grow with the difficulties of making good trading profits in saturation conditions. It was the very independence of this factor from any particular kind of ruling class which makes it important, for it could operate in any town where there was an oligarchy of any type. A second point: fiscal exploitation was not new in the thirteenth century but it did increase in intensity, especially after about 1250. So severe and widespread was this development that it is true to say that harsh and improper fiscal policies were the most prominent—perhaps easily the greatest—single cause of urban troubles in the late thirteenth and early fourteenth centuries, taking western Europe as a whole.

Specialized forms of oppression waited upon specialized circumstances but fiscal tyranny depended on the mere fact of oligarchy and not on its form; thus it was almost universal. In English towns of the late thirteenth century and the beginning of the fourteenth there was a striking uniformity in the complaints against unjust assessment of tallages, levying of illegal taxes, squandering or embezzlement of public funds, the sale of justice and so on. At Leicester, Lincoln, Oxford, Lynn, Norwich and Ipswich there were the same charges that tallages were imposed without the consent of the community and charged on the lower classes alone, that the patriciate turned public funds to their own purposes and that no accounts were published. Often these grievances were the whole burden of complaint; at the least they were as prominent as anger at policies concerned with trade and industry proper. It was the same on the continent. Fiscal policy was not invariably the main bone of contention. It could be overshadowed by other problems as it was in some of the more important textile towns; but even there it was a major issue. Elsewhere it could dominate the scene; there were whole large groups of towns like those of south-western France, towns not of international importance in either trade or manufacturing, where the fiscal problem lay at the root of civic discord. Of how many towns must we say, as did Espinas of Douai: 'it was the fiscal question which not only opened and closed the revolution [of 1296 to 1311] but never ceased to dominate it', that the 'Democratic Revolution' was a revolt against 'fiscal tyranny'?

(3) THE LATE MIDDLE AGES: CRISIS AND RESPONSE

The period just examined was one in which town policies underwent some marked and characteristic changes; these were attributed to the consolidation and abuse of power by an oligarchy and to the development of 'saturation' conditions in the thirteenth century, or, in precocious regions, during the twelfth. However, this period, and the economic policies which marked it, were not distinguished by any overall contraction of trade or industrial production, any weakening of urban strength or any major change in the kind of interests directing town policy.

In the fourteenth and fifteenth centuries the situation was different, though the difference did not always appear suddenly. There came for many towns a period of genuine crisis, a time when they had to fight bitterly for their share in a stable or diminishing amount of trade and production, when they often declined in population, prestige and economic power, and when control of their destinies was either taken right out of the hands of the townsfolk to be placed in those of a prince or else was retained by townsmen of narrower ambitions.

It is hard to assign responsibility for the economic embarrassment of towns at this period and this is especially true where liability rests with general economic conditions whose nature is contested and whose origins are imperfectly understood. So close is the connection between economic circumstances and policy, however, that the problem cannot be shirked entirely and a few features of the fourteenth- and fifteenth-century background which are vital to the questions in hand will have to be isolated rather arbitrarily from the extremely complicated scene.

At first there was a continuation of old processes; the changes making for saturation persisted and were intensified and brought with them corresponding policy changes. These policy responses could in turn cause a deterioration of conditions. Strikes and riots, loss of labour time and of incentives, weakened the economic position of towns where a majority was exploited, while trade and production were clogged by a growing body of restrictive and monopolistic practices.

Causes external to the towns were also at work. The fall in the rate of population increase in some areas, followed by the devastating epidemics of bubonic plague; the deterioration of conditions in the eastern trade with the loss of the crusading states, the end of the 'open century' and the beginnings of Turkish expansion; the wars of England, Flanders and France involving a vital sector of the western economy; the growth of state power which attacked towns and their privileges; possibly too a deterioration of climate in temperate Europe—these and many other factors had their effect. Finally many troubles, before the Black Death at least, may have been prepared by deeper causes. In particular there was the intensifying pressure of a swollen population on readily available natural resources. As the best land was taken up, as the Mediterranean pastures were overstocked, as the finest and most accessible stands of timber were felled, the rivers overfished, the more easily reached ores exhausted, there was a grave danger that Latin society would become genuinely poorer in the basic sense that more man-hours would have to go into the production of a given unit commodity. Without adequate technical advance and social readjustment or the discovery of fresh resources to offset these effects, this should have meant dearer and relatively scarcer goods and diminished *per capita* purchasing power. The effects of this would be exaggerated when the groups with power did not reduce their demands, but often increased them and intensified exploitation.

Yet not for towns as a whole and still less for the 'European economy' is a simple picture of decline sufficient or wholly accurate. Nor is this inadequacy due only to the fact that eastern Europe weathered the fourteenth century quite well—it was an 'unsaturated' region—while southern Europe showed, to say the least, remarkable powers of recuperation. In the fourteenth and fifteenth centuries, as in earlier periods, we have to take account of the *redistribution* of wealth and economic activity. There was redistribution in the simple, quantitative sense that business and wealth passed from some areas and some people to others and, in the more vital 'qualitative' sense, that new forms of economic activity replaced the old. There are no good grounds for believing that the growth of new business always provided compensation for the decline of the old during most of this period; yet clearly we have more on our hands than a simple downward swing of the economic curve.

Important evidence of redistribution is to be found in the agrarian history of the period, but as this has only indirect concern with the theme it must be ignored here. There were, however, many processes of redistribution in which towns were intimately and directly involved and these must be illustrated as they are the key to many changes in policy. For convenience the processes may be divided into two groups: those where redistribution meant a loss to towns in general and those where some towns gained at the expense of others. In the first category an obvious example is the development of rural industry where such industry grew at the expense of town production. Another change which weakened towns as corporate economic units (though not necessarily as active economic centres) was the increasing tendency for some individuals and groups to operate at a 'national' level, to transcend the petty restrictions and limited opportunities of the town association by pressing for a 'national' policy, associating themselves with princes and courts and picking up contracts and supply jobs with sovereigns.

On the other hand some towns clearly lost ground because others gained. This was the case when, in the early fifteenth century, the Scanian herrings were over-fished and attention was switched to those which made the swim between East Anglia and Holland. Sometimes a diversion of traffic routes was the cause: Cologne gained much that Flemish towns lost when English trade to the Rhineland made it the transit centre of choice. Similarly industry could shift from town to town as well as from town to country. The old centres of cloth production in Flanders and north-east France were badly hit during the fourteenth century when the towns of Brabant, Hainault and Champagne still did good business with their inferior but cheaper goods, while it was in the fifteenth century that the woollen cloth manufacturers of Holland, and especially Leiden, got under way and south German fustians became important.

Still more fundamental processes were at work, for in most regions there seems to have been a trend causing a very small number of towns to achieve striking superiority over a host of insignificant competitors; a very few great 'metropolitan' centres overshadowed numerous petty towns with which they were sharply contrasted. In England, London, Southampton and Bristol, in Flanders the 'big three' of Ghent, Ypres and Bruges until they were broken by the counts, in northern Germany the tiny group dominating the Hanseatic League, all showed this tendency; while in Italy a few cities made themselves masters of extensive territories in which they crushed most of the life out of lesser towns. This development must be explained as the natural outcome of conditions of intense competition; it is the situation produced when big fish have swallowed most of those not quite so big and a near-oligopoly has resulted. Technically it was based on changes in the organization of trade which made feasible its effective control by fewer people from a smaller number of centres.

These observations on the fourteenth- and fifteenth-century background certainly do not suggest that there should be anything very simple or uniform about late medieval policies; clearly it will not do to try to describe them all as stereotyped reactions to a period of decline. On the other hand conditions of adversity were sufficiently general and widespread to cause a hardening of attitude and a similarity of attitude in many cases; there was enough difficulty and hardship to encourage intense economic regulation, a deep antagonism to all 'outsiders', a contraction of the sphere of interest and a defensive approach to affairs in very many towns. Even so the great variety in conditions was bound to leave its mark in a variety of policies and this effect was exaggerated by other facts. Town policy was strongly influenced, for example, by the degree to which central authority was able to check the 'natural impulses' of citizens; English, French and Flemish towns clearly could not carry particularist policies to extremes, whereas there was little check on many German cities and virtually none on some of those in Italy. Another important cause of variation was lack of synchronism in town development. The amount and stages of growth shown by towns were always a source of contrast; small new towns and large mature towns always differed in

P

nature and hence in policy, but these differences were increased in the later Middle Ages as were the allied functional differences between towns. In the fourteenth and fifteenth centuries the range in age and type between minuscule market centres and ancient cities, elaborately differentiated to serve special needs in society, was greater than ever before.

This last point leads straight to the question of the internal constitution of towns in this period, for the social structure, the balance of forces, the political constitution inside towns, were naturally connected with their type of function. It is possible to make some general statements about the majority of late medieval towns in this connection. It was common in each town for the members of most callings to be joined in an association, a gild. These gilds were an intimate and vital part of town life: not only was it necessary to belong to one of these gilds to follow an occupation but membership was typically necessary to obtain citizenship itself. Moreover, the actual government of towns leaned heavily on gild organization. Sometimes gilds had rights of supervision within their appropriate calling but were subject to overall control by the municipal authorities, and sometimes the town government itself was made up of the elected representatives of gilds or groups of gilds. Even in the former case the town was generally ruled by men who were gildsmen, and owed loyalty to their associations and the ideas which these represented.

Here was a change, great or small according to circumstances, from an earlier state where power had most typically belonged to a combination of rentiers, landowners and professional merchants, where the only gilds were characteristically the gilds of the more important traders and where craft associations had been opposed or stringently controlled.[1] This change corresponded with a shift in outlook, interest and policy. In the first place, it could mark some kind of an approach to a balance of power between the varied economic interests within towns. To the degree that all crafts had control over their private concerns and some voice in the general government of their city, to that extent there was an abandoning of narrow social and economic oligarchy; government was more broadly based, there was a fairer representation of sectional interests. This change was accompanied by no greater liberality of outlook, no loosening of economic controls, but rather the reverse: rule by and through a group of jealous gilds was government which was *founded* on the principle and practice of regulation and had all the means at its disposal for an intense, detailed and effective control of economic affairs. Another consequence was that the interests of producers were often

[1] The English convention is unfortunate in this matter and it confuses many issues by using the word 'gild' too widely. It is a pity that 'gild' cannot be confined to those associations in which mercantile interests were dominant and 'craft' or 'mystery' (the medieval words) used for those in which producers were most important.

better represented and less weight was given to the great distributive or mercantile interests; one effect was that industrial protectionism of a kind which might even *harm* traders became a feature of some town policies. There was also a tendency for the ambitions and activity of towns to become more circumscribed and more sharply defined; there was an emphasis, a defensive emphasis, on the local region and on the closely regulated staple.

Fundamental was the existence of monopoly. Monopolistic corporations—the town itself or the constituent gilds—were the instruments of action, monopolistic privileges were the ends of action. If there was some kind of balance within cities then it was a balance between monopolies, if there was intense regulation it was implemented by monopolistic bodies, if ambition was narrow and more local, it was revealed as a desire for monopoly in a specific region or a particular branch of trade.

There is no need to detail the various forms taken by the drive for monopoly as these were discussed above. It is enough to remark that it was in the fourteenth and fifteenth centuries that the pattern of exclusion and privilege was fully developed and became the normal framework for all business within and between towns. Classical *Fremdenrecht* or classical *Stapelrecht*, both are known from the bans of the late medieval towns of Germany; the great staple struggles between Polish towns belong to the fourteenth and fifteenth centuries; it was during the same period that Dordrecht and Bruges won the staple of all goods passing along their rivers, that Passau acquired its staple of wine, Malines of fish and salt, Bruges of wool, Ghent of grain. What was won by the powerful was denied to the weak; the great towns of Flanders and Italy crushed their small neighbours, a few great Hanseatic cities were virtual lords and chief beneficiaries of the League, a revolution in Brussels forced the duke of Brabant to suppress the newly granted gild at Merchtem. The pressure felt by the weak was passed on to those still weaker. Oxford, which in 1368 was having trouble with London because that city had circumvented its charter of customs exemption and was demanding 'the custom known as yssue', had itself denied their due privileges to the men of New Sarum and had only been forced to respect them by a royal writ of 1321.

The development of the policy of protecting local industry was an even more striking feature of late medieval times. Sometimes it was based on the need of towns to fall back on their own resources when they could no longer find an easy profit in trading other people's goods; sometimes it was due to the greater relative power of the producing interests themselves within towns; most commonly it was a combination of both factors. Perhaps the best illustration is given by fourteenth-century Flanders where, after 1302 and the (not always final) removal of old patriciates, there was a rapid increase of such protection. Only a few weeks after Courtrai the import of cloth woven outside the city was prohibited at Ghent and in 1359 Bruges insisted that Hanseatic traders should not bring English cloth up the Zwyn. Soon such laws became so general that all types of foreign cloth were denied a sale in the major Flemish cities.

Such policies were readily established when control of the town fell to the producers in the actual industries concerned, after ousting the merchants of the old oligarchies who had preferred trading in foreign goods to protecting local products. But there was also a gradual change to industrial protection in many towns where this governmental change did not take place. At Leiden, for example, it was only in the fifteenth century that the cloth industry became considerable, at a time when mercantile interests had great power. It was in 1449 and 1468 that the council of Leiden, wishing to help local cloth-producers, tried to stop Leiden merchants buying more wool from English staplers than could be made up on the town looms, the fear being that any additional wool would be carried farther to supply competitors.

A clearer example is given by Florence. In the fourteenth century most of the economic life of the city, and in particular its great woollen trade and industry, was strictly controlled by great merchant capitalists. These held firm sway over craftsmen: they held power in the city council, they suppressed or severely controlled all attempts at craft association, they weakened the bargaining power of the workers by making great use of rural weavers and immigrant German labour. The 'commons' made several attempts to improve their position, mainly by political action, attempts which had their climax in the revolts of 1379 to 1382. In the latter year the great gilds of capitalists recovered their position and within little over a decade were able to wipe out all the advances made by the textile workers, including their right of combination. If the weavers, fullers and others had won power, had established craft gilds with a large say in government policy, measures to protect their industry against all outside competition could have been predicted quite confidently. They failed, and yet just this policy was followed by the patricians themselves. Outside trading conditions weakened the position of those who dealt in foreign cloths, more power accrued to those who controlled home production through the putting-out system and policy became increasingly one of local defence and industrial protection. Already in 1393 a virtually prohibitive duty had been placed on all cloth not made in Florence, with the exception of a light cloth which Florentines did not produce and the Flemish and Brabantine products in whose importation the still powerful traders of the Arte di Calimala were engaged. In the early fifteenth century this was followed by law after law designed to prevent manufacturing secrets being lost to foreigners and prohibiting the export of alum, dyestuffs, wool pickings or modern iron looms; finally in 1458 a decree was passed which flatly prohibited the sale of any foreign-made cloth in the city.

Towns were concerned not only to prevent the entry of competing goods from a distance but also to eliminate production in nearby small towns and villages. Here again fourteenth-century Flanders provides a classic example. From the beginning of this century Ghent, Ypres and Bruges prohibited textile production outside their walls, suppressed the looms in small towns like Poperinghe and Termonde and sent search-parties into all the villages within a radius of five leagues. In other regions towns were not as successful as were the great cities of Flanders, partly because they did not win the same rights of control outside their walls, partly because working masters were not able to eliminate the power of trading interests which found profit in rural industry. Even so there are many signs that the same aims held and received town backing. This is so in English towns. For example, the craft ordinances of four-teenth-century Bristol fullers, which had civic assent, declared that no one was to have unfulled cloth taken outside the town to be fulled; the cloth makers of Winchester at the beginning of the fifteenth century were not allowed to employ fullers or weavers outside the city walls; and the same rule applied at Norwich and other textile towns. The policy never won anything like complete success, however, and the complaint of Northampton in 1464, that work was being put out to craftsmen be-yond the boundaries of the town, is repeated in one town after another.

Inside the towns policy was in most cases determined by the existence of gilds as the normal means of economic organization and quite often as a major feature of the political machinery. Internal policy was thus closely linked to the nature and interests of gilds and in a sense was gild policy raised to an urban level. Such gild policies are dealt with elsewhere in this volume; here it is only necessary to summarize such general fea-tures as affected town policy as a whole. Monopoly and restriction were again characteristic; all branches of production and distribution were monopolized by the appropriate gilds and the main concern of these was corporate defence of the interests and standards of existing members. A very common weapon was restriction of the right of entry, and admission to gilds tended to become progressively more difficult; more rarely gilds resorted to limitation of output in order to keep prices suitably high; and of course each gild supported, in the external policy of a town, those measures which promised elimination of outside competition in its particular field. With their strong sense of corporate defence the gilds combined a desire for a rough equality among their members. This desire was rooted in a feeling of brotherhood, in the belief that only equal shares would guarantee work for all and in the fear that the over-successful gildsmen could bring others into economic subjection. Tight control of individual enterprise was often engineered to avoid these dangers and to secure fair employment to all members, and this led to much legislation limiting the number of apprentices a master might keep, the hours he might work and the tools he could use, and forcing him to share his purchases of raw materials with gild brethren. These various attitudes all worked their way into town policy. Each town was a commonwealth of corporate monopolies, and its policy was one of intense regulation of all activity by or through these monopolies and in defence of their interests individually and collectively.

Yet town policy could not be simply the sum of all gild policies, and this for two main reasons. In the first place the town as a town had some interests which transcended those of the subordinate bodies; in particular it had to defend the consumer interest of the population as a whole. So town councils were always under pressure to prevent such use of gild monopolies as might threaten the well-being of inhabitants and not just harm outsiders. Secondly, the interests of different gilds, even of different elements within gilds, often conflicted, and then the final arbiter had to be the town government. Generally speaking such conflicts were at a minimum when production was on a handicraft basis, trade was local and no particular industry or trade was much more important than the others. This was the situation prevailing in most of the less important medieval towns and in such cases it was relatively easy for the town authorities to keep a fair balance within and between the various occupations and between their interests and those of the whole town. This balance was increasingly hard to maintain when one or more branches of trade or industry were highly developed to serve a wide market, overshadowed other callings in importance and involved much deployment of mercantile capital. For example, in those industrial occupations into which capitalism had penetrated by means of the putting-out system there was conflict between the trading masters and the actual producers, conflict which might take the form of a struggle between gilds, a struggle inside a single gild or a struggle between the capitalists grouped in a fraternity and ungilded workers. Similarly there were occasions for conflict between one great industry and another, between great industrial and great trading interests and between any of these and the general advantage of the town. In such cases it was difficult to achieve the harmony of purpose possible in minor towns which had only to regulate the affairs of local shopkeepers and small master craftsmen. Town policy was then the resultant of shifting forces, ultimately dependent on the distribution of real economic power in the town, but complicated by numerous facts such as the interference of outside authority or the delay with which political events expressed the economic situation.

Towns with exceptionally developed trade or industry had some exceptional features of policy, as might be expected, but a great number of towns shared to a large degree in the characteristics mentioned above. Their policies were typically monopolistic, xenophobic and exclusive; they reflected not the interests of a clique of great merchants but a compromise between different occupations, with craftsmen and smaller traders often well represented; they were rather narrow and local, they were intensely regulatory and the power of craft gilds often meant that the safeguarding of producers became very important. Perhaps the clearest examples of such a situation and such policies, and more especially of the victory of working masters and shopkeepers over old-style patricians, came from towns which experienced a classical *Zunftrevolution* of the central German, Zürich or Liège type. In such cases the moulding of town policy clearly fell to a larger and humbler section of the community, to men interested in producing for and trading in a more circumscribed area. What remained of big business was removed from the hands of patricians and devolved to individual gilds which received near autonomy in their internal affairs. The policy of these towns involved the elimination of rural industry in favour of masters within the walls, a sharp fight to preserve the environs of the town as a strictly private source of raw materials and selling area for town-produced goods, a jealous antagonism of foreign merchants who wished to break into the trade of this sacrosanct area or to introduce foreign manufactures. It entailed enmity to any large-scale merchant capitalists who might reproduce the patrician rule of earlier days, might interpose between the craftsmen and their raw materials or their markets, might abuse their position to monopolize and force up prices in the food trades, might be tempted to deal in foreign goods or rural manufactures because they allowed a greater profit-margin.

Such policies are well known from towns which had been of some importance in the earlier Middle Ages and which had to overthrow patrician rule and establish a 'gild government' of some complexity to accommodate the interests of a diversity of crafts; but the essentials are reproduced in various centres at the very margin of urban existence, towns which had never known a real patriciate, which contained one or two tailors, one or two butchers, a small group of weavers and so on, and were still deeply committed to agriculture. Guines in the fifteenth century may be taken as typical of a very large class. It had just a little in the way of cloth production and this the town authorities jealously guarded; they restricted the activities of small working masters and of drapers indifferently in their anxiety to see that this business was not lost to the town. Drapers were forbidden to have their weaving and fulling done outside the town or to export cloths which had not been made in it and inspected and sealed by the local authorities, while weavers, fullers and shearers were forbidden to go to work outside the town as long as they could find work within it. Restrictions on foreign merchants give clear evidence of the mentality of the townsfolk and are a salutary reminder of the humble level at which such grand forces as 'protectionist policy' or 'restriction of foreign imports' might operate; for strangers importing cloth were not allowed to have a stall in the market place but could deal only in what they could carry in under their arms.

Distrust of the foreigner and distrust of monopolizing middlemen appear in many other rulings of fifteenth-century Guines law. To prevent collusion and monopoly it was decreed that only two companions should act jointly in the sale of any goods; to prevent undue dominance by any individual it was laid down that no trader of the town could have more than two stalls—one for himself and one for his *amy*—at the August fair; a stranger could only have one. Strangers, moreover, could only sell wine wholesale, and local innkeepers were forbidden to make a company with foreign wine merchants. In the supply of everyday essentials, restrictions were even more severe. Take the case of fish: here *any* association was forbidden; each fishmonger had to act alone and the purchase of fish for resale was totally prohibited.

In so small a town there were special features, notably those connected with the importance of agriculture in the town's economy. Several special modifications of law applied to the period between 22 July and 29 August when the 'Ban of August' was in effect, for this was harvest time. It was forbidden to put out *any* textile work during this period, presumably in order to ensure that there was enough labour for harvesting, although the regular textile workers, their wives and genuine dependants were allowed to carry on with their ordinary work.

The case of Guines is a reminder that in many towns where a craft could mean less men than needed two hands for their counting, and where the merchant capitalist was most nearly represented by a prosperous 'village' tradesman, there was no need for the overthrow of a patriciate or the establishment of craft rule to ensure a thoroughly *petit bourgeois* policy. On the other hand great economic centres like Barcelona, London and Florence could allow an important place to gilds in both government and economic regulation without this altering the fact that they were ruled by great traders who were quite clearly distinguished from the rest of the population. In other words, there is no necessary or exact correlation between town constitution and town policy. This is made even clearer when it is remembered that in towns which had a 'democratic' revolution or *Zunftrevolution* overthrowing an old patriciate and founding government by an association of gilds there was by no means a uniform outcome as far as town interests and policy were concerned. Furthermore not all 'gild' revolutions were craft revolutions in the classic sense, movements by which a patriciate of merchant capitalists and *rentiers* were overthrown or forced to share power with a class of independent master craftsmen and small shopkeepers organized into craft gilds. The men opposed to the old patriciate might be rich traders debarred from civic office and privilege, large-scale producers with extensive interests in trade, petty artisan-shopkeepers interested in the local market, wage-earners in the great export industries, or any combination of these. The result of a successful movement by such people might vary in corresponding fashion, being the establishment of a new patriciate almost indistinguishable from the old, the rule of the petty trading and craft interests, control by the masters of a dominant industry or some constitution embodying a compromise between the various interests.

One critical factor was the extent to which a great industry (generally the textile industry), built up to meet a large export trade, had passed beyond the stage of handicraft organization and had fallen under the control of mercantile capital. When such a state of affairs existed a simple change from conditions of patrician dominance to rule by small-scale independent workers was impossible, though this might be the ideal inspiring many of the discontented. A great industry was dependent on large-scale market contacts and so could not dispense with merchant capital organization; it involved the dominance of one economic activity over all the others in the town and made likely the sacrifice of these latter; it caused differentiation within the ranks of producers themselves and so made possible complex internal struggles even when patrician control was removed.

Until textile production had fallen drastically some machinery for the export of finished goods and the import of raw materials to and from distant areas had to be retained. Concentration on a local market was not enough, though the fight for this market was, of course, fiercely pressed. In Flanders the great city trading gilds and the London 'hanse' were suppressed, and at Bruges, for example, the right of entry into every trade and craft was thrown open to all citizens within three weeks of Courtrai; but this did not mean the sudden supersession of trading in the grand manner by trading on a petty scale. Industry itself had thrown up masters anxious to gain profit from the sale of the work of their apprentices and journeymen, anxious to increase their profit-margin by buying their raw materials more directly and so more cheaply. Such men were eager to oust the patricians only in order to replace them. Nor, when the old patrician families lost their monopoly of political power and their exclusive trading privileges, were they necessarily beaten as individuals; many regrouped themselves into the forms appropriate to new conditions—associating themselves with the policies of Jacques van Arte-velde, for instance. Finally, in so far as there seemed to be a weakening of the hold of mercantile capital on the textile industry, this was largely due to the tendency, marked at just this time, for foreigners (especially Italians and Hanseatics) to take over many of the purely distributive and financial functions connected with the industry, and not to any absence of these functions.

Further, although gild control and gild monopoly became an integral part of government and economic life in great industrial centres, four-teenth-century conditions did not allow for any of that rough equality, that nice balancing of interests between the various crafts, characteristic of towns of less specialized type. The very men who led the revolt against the patriciate, the more important masters in textile production, wished to retain and develop a position as employers, to subordinate the workers in their own industry and even to sacrifice the interests of the town as a whole when these conflicted with their own. So the weavers of Flanders tried to reduce the fullers to subjection, just as the Wollen Amt of Cologne suppressed the weavers whose help they had so recently sought in the *coup* against the patricians.

Finally, it must be noted that, while economic tyranny over the sur-rounding countryside was a very marked feature in the major Flemish towns in the fourteenth century, their policy was far removed from the mere parochialism of small craft workers. Nothing is more instructive in this regard than the period between 1338 and 1345. The stoppage of the export of English wool meant that after 1336 the masters of the textile in-dustry at Ghent, Ypres and Bruges were faced with a mounting crisis—by a desperate shortage of material and a multitude of unemployed, starving, angry workers. Mainly under the guidance of Jacques van Artevelde, they pursued a course of action remarkable alike for its bold-ness of scale and for the close co-operation between the three cities which it involved. To co-ordinate policy they held *parlements* where their dele-gates made decisions binding on all; acting in union they made an alli-ance with England in 1339, forced Louis of Nevers to fly to France and later recognized Edward III as king of that country; after the alliance was made they had to go still further and create a regular common executive which they did by electing the Lombard Simon de Mirabello as regent. Their co-operation was extended to other branches of policy; all three cities, for instance, gave mutual support in the drive to subordinate minor towns and villages; their troops co-operated in this task and when dis-putes arose between one of them and a small neighbour during the ab-sence of the count, it fell to the other two to arbitrate, which they always did with a judgment which favoured their mutual interests.

A still more drastic example of the danger of equating every revolt by 'gilds' against a patriciate with the establishment of a regime and policy suited to men of narrow, local interests is the case of Augsburg. Like some other south German towns Augsburg was not declining in the later Middle Ages but was the centre of a vigorous trade and industry controlled by capitalist entrepreneurs. The Augsburg patriciate at this time did not contain the most important traders of the town, but was a group concerned above all with increasing revenue from land rents and fiscal exploitation and with the advancement of its social ambitions. In 1368 the gilds of Augsburg forced the patriciate to share its power with them; two groups virtually monopolized the advantages won by this revolution and these were the great traders united in the Merchants' Gild and the merchant capitalists who had control in the Weavers' Gild: Hans Fugger's sons were members of both. Here the 'anti-patrician revolt' was a victory for the great wholesalers; it was not a 'craft revolution' nor a 'democratic revolution' but essentially homomorphic with the phase which saw the emergence of a mercantile patriciate—and was typically reached much earlier—in other towns.

Augsburg serves as a reminder of the importance of the redistribution of economic activity in the later Middle Ages. There was a whole group of such towns which were able to make opportunities of the difficulties of others, expanded their trade, supported a vigorous merchant patriciate and even saw merchant capitalist rule appear where hitherto it had been absent. Many towns in Brabant, for example, started their growth late and engaged so successfully in textile production and general trade during the fourteenth century—to an appreciable extent at the expense of the declining Flemish cities—that the 'democratic' movement made no headway, and indeed hardly revealed itself before the fifteenth century. The patriciates of the Brabant towns were strong and active during much of the fourteenth century; though temporarily overthrown soon after 1302 by risings inspired by those in Flanders, they soon recovered their position. In Brussels the patricians were displaced in 1303 but re-established themselves within three years and from then on ruled unchallenged until 1421 when they were forced to share their power with the craft gilds, organized into nine 'nations'. Even then patrician influence was not thoroughly eliminated until the end of the fifteenth century.

At Dortmund there were even more unusual conditions. The growth of trading opportunities during the fourteenth century, a by-product of Hanseatic activity, made possible the supersession of the existing government by a council made up of the members elected by six craft gilds and a gild of (mainly landowning) patricians. In 1332 this earlier, more 'democratic' regime was upset in favour of virtual control by select patrician families. This situation lasted until the opportunities in long-distance trade contracted once more in the later fourteenth century, and in 1399 the old constitution, established when the city won its independence in 1260, was restored. The butchers and bakers, smiths and dairymen, tanners, cobblers and shopkeepers once more came into their own.

So far late medieval changes in the nature and policy of towns have been seen against the background of successful 'craft revolutions'. Typically these revolutions led to a victory for the *petits bourgeois* and their policy, though such changes were not needed, of course, to secure similar policies in some very small towns, and elsewhere the story was complicated by the survival of a major industry or by differences in timing. Cases where a 'gild revolution' meant victory for great merchant capitalists, as at Augsburg where the changes were closely analogous to the victory of the great trading gilds over the *grandi* in thirteenth-century Florence, are seen to belong to quite a different order of events. Their spurious claim for inclusion is based on the ambiguity of the word 'gild' in our language.

There were however large areas of Europe where craft revolutions were quite absent or rare and weak. In many towns of these regions a relatively small, closed group of traders, often lineal descendants of an earlier patriciate, controlled civic policy; there was no effective 'democratic' movement and mercantile capital retained its primacy. Of course 'capitalists' were sometimes quite humble figures, the leading drapers, butchers and mercers of some town of a few thousand souls, yet they merited the title because of their economic relationship to the more humble 'commons'.

Many towns in England fall into this class; so do many in north France (Rheims, Rouen and Verdun for example) and some southern towns such as Montpellier and Nîmes. The group includes most towns in what is now Holland and those of Hainault, excepting Utrecht, Valenciennes and Maubeuge. Further additions come from the towns east of the Elbe where the patriciate maintained its supremacy at the price of falling under the influence of local margraves, and Castilian towns where the old oligarchies remained in power and linked themselves with the minor nobility. The Italian cities where a 'democratic revolution' failed or was not attempted would also qualify for admission were their situation not so distinctive on other counts.

A few preliminary remarks are necessary on this 'group' of towns. In the first place it excludes a quite appreciable class of very small centres (Guines or Totnes for example) which, though they had no craft revolution, had no real oligarchy either because they lacked the wealth and social differentiation on which such could be based. Secondly, the towns mentioned range from those where the oligarchy was an old-established group which became increasingly restrictive and locally minded, as was often the case in England, to those, like many Dutch towns, where the patriciate was of late growth and showed vigour and an expansionist outlook right through the fifteenth century. Finally, mere absence of a 'democratic revolution', like its presence, is an artificial basis for division though a useful first step in analysis. The fact that such upheavals were avoided gives no direct information about the real nature of the controlling forces in a town or the policy implemented and does not even preclude a considerable role for gilds.

The most characteristic members of this group where oligarchical control and policy persisted and developed in the later Middle Ages are the English and French towns. In these there were several typical features. There was generally a division between the bigger merchants (including those trading in local manufactures) and the craftsmen and small retail traders who made up the commons. The more important traders were either grouped in one or a few trading associations or found as a controlling element in gilds which included producers; the artisans and small shopkeepers were often formed into gilds too, though this development was still being opposed by some merchant oligarchies. The government of these towns was controlled by the more important traders, the constitutional means for doing this varying from place to place.

In towns where an oligarchy of this kind was maintained town policy was largely the policy of a limited group of traders. In many cases it aimed at restricting wholesale trade to the few. Occasionally in England the Gild Merchant survived as an exclusive body, though more commonly it was a dominant gild of mercers or a combination of one or two such wholesaling gilds which monopolized government and excluded 'men of manual art' from their privileges. Such exclusion was marked at York, Newcastle, Hull, Bristol, Chester, Yarmouth and many other towns. Not only so, but the oligarchy often carried on a fight against the craft gilds themselves. The growth of these gilds was not checked entirely but it was often hampered and so were the policies which it would have favoured. Town authority was always supreme over the craft gilds and did much to prevent craftsmen from fixing minimum prices for their goods, restricting their output or making fresh recruitment to the ranks of producers as difficult and limited as it was in towns where the gilds had more power. There was similarly a restriction on those gild rights—rights of search, justice and so on—which flourished where gilds had a greater measure of self-rule.

Coventry is an example. The middle of the fourteenth century saw here the appearance of various wholesaling associations: the Gild of St Mary established in 1340 by traders in wool, cloth and general goods, the Gild of St John the Baptist founded in 1342 and that of St Catherine dating from 1343. These three combined forces in 1364 to 1369, and in 1392 coalesced in turn with the powerful Trinity Gild whose name was taken by the new, enlarged body. This process of fusion brought all the important traders of Coventry into one almost irresistible body—all, that is, except those in the prior's section of the town. These were grouped in the Gild of Corpus Christi, but the mutual interests of the Trinity Gild and the Corpus Christi Gild soon caused them to co-operate and share power in the town; in fact they were the effective government. Virtually all town offices were held by mercers, drapers and the like, while craftsmen were denied not only office but sometimes gild organization itself. In 1407 the trading gilds secured a charter prohibiting the formation of any association outside their own, a charter which was confirmed in 1414 and was aimed primarily against fullers and tailors who had tried to secure some independence from control by the wholesalers in establishing their own gilds. The struggle went on, the main blows being struck by the dyers, who led opposition by fullers, weavers and small dealers in finished cloth. The dyers continually combined though such action was illegal. The oligarchs complained to Parliament in 1415, bolstering up their case with charges that the dyers had used a fraternity to raise dyeing prices and had caused the price of wool to go up 50% in a year; they broke a gild of fullers and dyers which was licensed in 1438; they had the statutes and oaths of dyers and other craftsmen declared void by a decree of 1475. The main worry of the drapers and others was that their wholesale monopoly would be broken and that gild organizations would raise the prices for goods in which they traded or restrict supplies in the interests of producers; dyers were not allowed to have cloth made for sale and they were not allowed to dye any cloth other than that provided by local drapers, but these drapers were free themselves to engage in the work of dyeing.

The policy of reserving wholesale trade to a minority and subordinating or even suppressing craft gilds, which represented other interests than those dominant in the gild-hall, commonly went hand in hand with another feature—with failure to take action against rich victuallers. Richer merchants in the food trades often shared power with the wholesalers in other goods and, despite the universal existence of laws devised to protect the common consumer, were able to disregard the various assizes and circumvent the elaborate systems of inspection. Where a show was made of pursuing a popular policy and fines were imposed on the bakers of short-weight bread or sellers of tainted meat, these fines might end the business of a small dealer but were mere pin-pricks to the rich, mere licensing fees for dishonesty. It was at Coventry again that the fifteenth-century records tell of constant rioting against light loaves and against the false measures used in selling corn.

It can be seen that the distinction between towns which were 'oligarchical' and those which were more 'democratic', in the sense of giving a large range of monopolistic craft gilds a voice in town government, did have some meaning in the field of internal policy. It did mean a narrower or broader distribution of the right to trade, it did mean weaker or stronger defence of the interests of craft producers, it did mean less or more effective care for the general run of consumers. But the distinction is far from being clear cut; under a 'democratic' regime the share in power enjoyed by various gilds could vary enormously and gilds themselves could be under the control of trading minorities to a greater or lesser degree. Conversely the oligarchies could be forced to make concessions to the more important craft gilds, especially when these were throwing up their own trading elements, and could be under strong pressure from outside authority to lessen their pressure on the commons. There was in fact a continuous gradation from one extreme to the other.

In external policy the distinction between 'oligarchic' and 'democratic' towns is of little value; excluding a minority of unusually large cities, most towns in England for example were as locally minded as any others. Their oligarchical rulers, their 'great merchants', were mainly concerned with keeping their rights in a limited area. Their policies were restricted and defensive. They were drapers, victuallers and general dealers to their town and part of their county; they were engrossed with the problem of holding on to their position there and sacrificed wider ambitions to the security and familiarity of their home ground. Characteristically they opposed the development of rural industry just as keenly as would the weavers they kept under control within the walls, had these had a say in the matter. They preferred, in a world where they did not see large opportunities, to keep the conditions of an adequate livelihood rather than venture into speculative development. The more adventurous did try new ways but they did so increasingly outside the framework of the old country towns.

A few of the ways in which town policies differed from and resembled each other have now been mentioned, but one of the most useful indices of policy needs further treatment, namely the way in which towns behaved towards foreign traders. The main aspects of this branch of policy have already been suggested. Nearly every town was concerned to keep as much trade as possible to itself and, where outside merchants had to be tolerated, every effort was made to see that their operations were rigidly controlled and that they made as much profit as possible for natives and as little as possible for themselves. To implement such policy towns had developed measures which were basically the same all over the continent.

The toll system of the town was used to discriminate against strangers, in the simplest and most universal form by imposing taxes on strangers from which citizens were wholly or partially exempt; foreigners were generally forbidden to engage in retail trade in a town, this being a privilege of citizenship; direct trade between strangers was generally prohibited; and finally, efforts were commonly made to establish an absolute monopoly for the town in a commodity or commodities, in a specific area or along a specified route.

The universality of such action was based on the fact that it was rooted in the very nature of towns and served such a variety of special ends. It was far from being a novelty in the late Middle Ages. What was characteristic then was the multiplication, elaboration and rigidity of these measures, the great development of specific monopolies and the defensive and local nature of these policies. All the more significant therefore are those cases where some freedom was allowed to foreigners and monopolies were attacked.

Many vehement pleas for greater freedom for outsiders and for the removal of monopolies can be more or less discounted. They came from towns which showed scant willingness to liberalize their own policies but attacked the monopolistic practices and legislation of *other* towns, especially of those which lay across a trade route or engaged in traffic vital to themselves. So Danzig attacked the staple policies of Thorn and Cracow which bestrode the routes from the Baltic to central and southeast Europe; so Bristol merchants, who carried on a lively trade with Hanseatic merchants in London, protested in the King's Council against the proposal that Hanseatic traders should be banished from London, saying that the London merchants would be their only intermediaries in the continental trade and would make such terms as would utterly ruin the men of Bristol.

Sometimes, however, there was a more genuinely liberal attitude. This was especially the case where weak towns were faced with competition from those which were much more powerful and were entrenched behind a barrier of privilege. Sometimes more tolerant behaviour towards foreign merchants was adopted by a small town as a positive means towards gaining advantage in a fight with a neighbour. Aardenburg prospered in the period 1240 to 1280 despite its closeness to Bruges; but with the late thirteenth century came harsher times and a growing threat from the competition of the larger town. Aardenburg was able to win through, for a time at least, by taking advantage of Bruges's policy of intensifying restrictions on strangers; it set out to attract foreign trade by offering greater freedom to these outside merchants than they could find within its adversary's walls. In 1280 it obtained from Guy de Dampierre the right to grant privileges to Germans and to

Spaniards and this policy was furthered by other measures in 1283 and 1307.

A more negative attitude was shown by weak towns willing to adopt freer policies mainly because they had little to gain from exercising monopolies themselves (or little hope of doing so) and much to fear from the monopolies of the greater cities. Such towns often attacked urban monopoly. Small inland towns in England were opposed equally to the creation of staple towns abroad and at home; they wished their merchants to attend all markets freely. When disaster overcame Charles the Bold in 1477 and the major Flemish cities tried to recover the privileges they had enjoyed in the fourteenth century, the smaller towns allied with the villages and with 'free-trade' Antwerp to thwart this move. Nearby in Brabant the minor towns were willing, in the later Middle Ages, to support a count who fought against urban monopoly and privileges because they lost more from the special rights of the large towns than they gained from their own.

There was another kind of situation where liberality to 'foreigners' was obviously demanded, the case of towns which had great interests in mutual trade. In such cases it was ridiculous for each to levy tolls on the burgesses of the other and it was common, as well as common sense, for a mutual abolition or reduction of these tolls to be arranged. Such agreements were not uncommon before the fourteenth century, but they are a typical feature of the later Middle Ages, a natural corrective to the stupid burdens that even towns existing in mutual dependence could place on each other. Reciprocal toll concessions were arranged between Dinant and Cologne, for example, in 1277; but it was in the mid-fourteenth century that these two towns really took up the policy, when Dinant needed to expand outlets for its manufactures and Cologne was beginning to lose its late thirteenth-century position as chief among such markets. In England also thirteenth-century cases are known but it was in the fourteenth and fifteenth centuries that such concessions became increasingly common, between Salisbury and Southampton, Cambridge and Northampton, Coventry and Nottingham, Lincoln and Coventry and many others.

In the foregoing cases a more liberal attitude towards foreigners was dictated by the relationships of towns with one another; the principle was that one town would drop a certain right or advantage if others gave at least as much in return. Rather different was the situation in those towns whose main function was to act as great centres of trade. Distributive centres of international importance depended on the coming and going of merchants native to towns all over the continent; they simply could not afford to apply the whole range of xenophobic legislation common in minor towns, for to have done so would have undercut their

Q

whole position, would have made their chief activity impossible. It followed that in a small number of great trading cities the law was different at a few vital points from what was customary in humbler towns. Perhaps the most striking illustration of this was the relaxation of the provision that stranger could not deal with stranger. Such dealings were allowed in fourteenth-century London, in fourteenth-century Genoa, in fourteenth-century Bruges. Sometimes, it is true, the policy was found distasteful: at Bruges there were various attempts at reversing it from the late thirteenth century onwards and one such, in 1307, succeeded. The obvious result was to drive foreigners to do their business in more liberal Aardenburg, so freedom was restored in 1309. It was generally compulsory for this trade between foreigners to be done through brokers but even these brokers might be aliens. This was true of Genoa in the fourteenth century as in the thirteenth century, and was also the case in London. In the latter city the position of foreign brokers was, it is true, always under challenge; the Londoners were suspicious and periodically had the alien brokers investigated or disqualified. However, as typical a reflection of their general position as any is the law of 1373 which stipulated that strangers should be allowed to act as brokers if they paid a 40s. fine and produced two or three sureties among citizens; there were aliens, mainly Lombards, among the brokers sworn in that year.

It is clear that policies granting greater freedom to strangers were generally forced on towns by external or internal circumstances; they were applied grudgingly and piecemeal and were not usually seen as a desirable course of action which a town should adopt positively and purposefully. There were a few cases where this was not true, though even in these there was often a strong element of outside pressure. Aardenburg was a case in point, but its efforts did not last long. Rather different is the case of Winchester. Winchester, in the difficult years of the mid-fifteenth century, was losing business and population and it was this that forced it to experiment along lines already suggested by Salisbury and Coventry. True, the depression in the town was a form of pressure but the response to this might equally well have been an intensification of restrictions and not the course actually adopted. The purpose of the Winchester councillors is clearly set out in the preamble to their law of 1430 which described it as devised *pro communi utilitate et publico incremento dicte Civitatis et ad faciendum tam extraneos quam propinquos homines et mercatores ad dictam Civitatem convenire et ibidem avidius inhabitare et eandem Civitatem gracia divina mediante accrestere et meliorare in futurum*. The main purpose of this law was that *omnes mercatores tam extranei quam indigine [sic] extra Gyldam mercatoriam, cuiuscumque status, artis vel operis fuerint, exceptis carnificibus et piscatoribus extraneis pro stallagiis et tabulis suis, erunt quieti et liberi infra dictam Civitatem et libertatem eiusdem ad emendum et vendendum, scindendum, operandum, faciendum, exercendum et usitandum omnes mercandisas, mercimonia et artes suas* [etc.] . . . *pari forma sicut homines et mercatores sunt infra villam de Covyngtr' et Civitatem Nove Sarum.*[1] This policy did not last long; by the time of the regulations of 1471 and 1488 it was dead.

A rarer case, an example of a city which based its outlook and founded its prosperity on the principle of giving, if not the wholesale freedom sometimes claimed, at least far more liberal conditions than most, was Antwerp. Antwerp grew to importance when old towns were piling up their economic defences and becoming increasingly restrictive, and it turned this situation to its own advantage by attracting the foreign traders who were hampered and antagonized by these developments. Certainly, Antwerp had some outside advantages; it received powerful support from the dukes of Brabant and Burgundy, and storms scoured and enlarged its port at a time when silt was choking the way to the sea for its chief competitor. Yet its main advantage lay in the 'newness' of the town and population, in the freshness of approach to economic problems this made possible. A policy of encouraging alien traders was well established in the fourteenth century. As early as 1315 Portuguese merchants were granted the right to import and sell their wines without paying higher tolls than did natives; in the same year Duke John II granted a charter to merchants from Genoa, Florence and the Empire who should settle in the city; and in 1324 came the famous invitation of the city authorities to the captains of galleys anchored at Sluys to go and trade at Antwerp. During the rest of the Middle Ages the city worked with the prince to further the same policy. Sometimes it was a question of giving privileges to an alien group: Louis de Mâle freed Spanish merchants in 1357 from all new taxes on goods they landed or sold at Antwerp and over a century later, in 1468, Charles the Bold granted privileges to the Genoese in the city. Sometimes outside monopolies had to be abolished, as when Malines was deprived of its staple rights in salt, fish and oats in 1411. Two annual fairs, each of three weeks' duration, were granted by the Emperor Sigismund in 1415 and at once became a major attraction for foreigners and a vital blow to Bruges's staple rights. Even the right of money-changing was granted to all citizens so that there was no clogging of machinery by restriction to official exchanges.

Such policies were uncommon in late medieval times. The great majority of towns shared policies of a monopolistic and defensive character, relied on privileges and restrictions, and though the particular functions which were monopolized and the particular interests which were defended varied with the economic and social structure

[1] Gross, *Gild Merchant*, II, 261.

of each town, such differences did not override their common nature.

A fundamental consequence of later urban policies was that towns were no longer in the van of economic progress. For the first time they failed as vehicles for improvement and expansion in trade and industry. Like Mesozoic reptiles they speeded their decline by the very weight of their defences and by the entrenched specialization of their structure. They lost in vigour and adaptability and speed of response. They could not seize the new opportunities nor contain or attract the men who wished to use them. The very success of their protective mechanisms aggravated the economic difficulties with which they were meant to cope and raised up a host of enemies and detractors within and without their walls. Kings and princes who wished to establish uniform state control unchecked by urban immunities, peasants and the inhabitants of smaller towns who had suffered under the political and economic hegemony of proud cities, great go-ahead merchants and contractors who wished to develop rural industry, to buy for court and army on a free and cheap market or to trade on a large scale without the checks and expense created by urban monopoly, small men within the towns who resented privileges from which they were excluded or burdens which pressed too heavily upon them—all these opposed the policy of the towns. This happened at a time when towns were loth to give each other mutual support. When Bruges revolted in 1436–8 to recover its old privileges it found itself opposed not only by the duke but by the peasantry, the minor towns and by some groups within its own walls. Yet it received no help from any other Flemish city and neither did Ghent when it found itself in a similar position in 1449–53.

The position of the towns was seriously weakened by the operation of those forces for which their policy could find no place. The textile industry developed in the countryside at the expense of the jealous town crafts; great traders either individually or in corporations operated on a scale which transcended and flouted the localism of town regulations; even artisans and petty traders settled outside the limits of city jurisdiction to work with greater freedom and greater profit, and were encouraged to do so by ambitious elements within the towns. Politically also this was a period of reverse; towns often lost the ability to decide their own policy. In Flanders and north France the direction of many was taken over by king or duke; in Italy princes emerged in several cities which became petty states rather than towns controlling a surrounding area; in England, where the strength of the Crown had always braked urban extremism, there was a growth of state legislation which intermeddled with urban affairs and policies; and in various parts of Germany towns fell under the influence of the local nobility. With the exception of a few expanding, and generally newer, centres which followed less rigid and restrictive policies, and a few more which traded on an exceptionally large scale, most towns ossified as market centres and producers for a limited region, limited their methods to the needs of that market and their ambitions to its confines and accepted a progressive loss of their power to regulate their external and even their internal affairs.

CHAPTER V
The Gilds

I. *The Problems of Gild History*

The occupational gilds of the west are one of the best-known forms of medieval association, familiar both on account of their long post-medieval career, and because they had early lent themselves to the ordering of economic and political life in urban society. Their traditions of corporate charity and piety further attest that they were once genuine communities within the larger community, with a social and religious character transcending mere economic interest and struggle for power. The economic historian has to study every aspect of the gilds, but always with an eye to the central problem of their influence on the economy. Did the various means by which they sought to secure their members' interests, as these were conceived at the time, retard or stimulate economic growth? Did gilds hinder or promote the flow of trade? Did they try to expand the market for manufactured goods? Had they any general policies regarding innovation? Did they affect at all the amount of saving or the direction of investment?

If we plot our earliest information as to the organization of gilds on a map, dating their appearance in each local industry, we immediately narrow the scope of these inquiries in two ways. In the first place, it becomes apparent that, so far as artisans were concerned, the craft gilds were of little account before the thirteenth century. In the great economic expansion of the eleventh and twelfth centuries, artisan gilds were too few and too scattered to have exercised any effective influence either as help or as hindrance. It was not until the latter part of the thirteenth century, when the expansion was slowing down, that they became at all widespread. They multiplied most rapidly in the fourteenth and fifteenth centuries, often in circumstances of population decline, trade recession and fiscal crisis. In the second place, certain types of town were clearly more favourable to a gild movement than others. Among the least favourable were the greater seaport towns given over predominantly to commerce, and the textile towns, given over to manufacturing for export. Nor is there much evidence of gilds being important in the little towns with a population of barely a thousand or two, which made up the vast majority of medieval urban centres. Their best field of action was in towns of middling size, with a population of up to about 10,000, or, in Italy, of up to 20,000 or 30,000, towns that were not dominated by a single interest, but lived mainly by industry for local consumption, with some admixture of trade. This environment offered more scope for specialized skill than did the little rustic towns. At the same time, demand remained more stable than in ports and manufacturing centres dependent on markets and sources of supply that were under foreign political control and far distant. Skilled craftsmen had more chance to get ahead and to reach for political influence alongside merchants and other men with local power.

The decision to form a gild did not fundamentally alter the economic organization of a trade. Urban trades were always on an individual or a family basis, with perhaps some employment by merchants. Formal association among the individual masters did, however, enlarge the possibilities of promoting common interests through joint action. Discussion of trade difficulties could now lead to definite and continuous policies. It could lead to improved relations with the public authorities and to negotiation for special privileges. At this point, if not before, gilds encountered chronic suspicion of their policies as tending to raise retail prices. The suspicion, strongest in the commercial and manufacturing towns, and strong wherever aristocratic, ecclesiastical or professional groups carried political weight, was an ever-present potential check to the extension of the gild movement. Consumers probably over-estimated the economic powers of gilds, giving them an unfair share of blame for upward price trends. Even when they had the support of public authority, their power to raise prices through cartel agreements or suppression of local competitors was limited by conditions that were beyond their control. The influence of any particular gild has to be considered in the light of the regional conditions of supply and demand that would have affected its line of trade. In the circumstances of urban trade recession in which many of the fourteenth- and fifteenth-century gilds were organized, they could have done little to promote their members' interests save through political schemes for drawing business to themselves to the detriment of neighbouring small towns and villages. The end of ambition, in the more hard-pressed localities, was simply to keep one's town alive. Fiscal problems complicated the situation, entailing a desire on the part of town authorities to shelter those small gild masters who typically formed the bulk of the tax-paying population.

In the logical extreme this set of conditions could tend to a static collectivism, militantly *kapitalfeindlich*. Yet it would be an error to identify medieval gilds solely with so desperate a conservatism. Their policies could move also in opposite directions, open to innovation and favouring the masters who had capital.

It was not only through deliberate policies of promoting sectional interest that gilds were of significance in medieval economic development. Their organization was important also in bringing more formal deliberation to bear on the shaping of the law and custom and on the administrative procedures through which orderly relations were maintained among buyers and sellers. Finally, their non-economic activities were of economic consequence. Their religious, benevolent and convivial customs, and their political activities, involving very considerable collective expenditures, markedly affected their members' individual habits of saving and consumption. Gilds thus indirectly influenced the local structure of demand.

II. *The Development of Gild Organization*

Although the economic influence of gilds was far from being solely a matter of their legal powers, at every turn it depended in part on how much freedom of corporate action they enjoyed. Internally, what sanctions could be applied against recalcitrant members? Externally, in what ways did juridical personality come to be recognized? What was the relation between gild officers and town governments or higher authority? These points are still in need of further monographic treatment, so that an introductory sketch can at present do little more than outline the development of gild relationships with governmental authority. From the point of view taken here, that of an interest primarily in gild influence on medieval economy after 1200, the critical period in definition of these relationships was the thirteenth century. Town governments were then making increasingly systematic use of gilds in general administrative work, treating their officers as quasi-public officials. It became the custom to demand that their current regulations be reduced to writing in a common form and be kept ready for inspection. This process of codification was thereafter continuous. The regulations normally defined what degree of autonomy each group possessed in respect of election of officers and in the collection and disposition of entrance fees and fines, and laid down a mixture of general principles and detail as to technical and ethical rules. Major revisions involving principle required approval by higher authority. The public interest arose partly out of concern with public order.

The codified regulations, in Italy usually dignified by the name of statutes, make up our best-known source of information as to the nature and activities of gilds. Like all historical sources giving only the letter of the law, they are in two ways deficient. They are a façade, concealing often more than they reveal. They do not show us how gild institutions actually worked, nor how they had arisen. Only as revisions were entered do they indicate any of the points at which administrative friction occurred. They are much more useful when they can be supplemented by the other records that gilds were keeping, from the thirteenth century. Minutes of deliberations and records of elections, accounts and membership lists, leave no doubt as to what was routine business and what was matter for debate. From the fourteenth and fifteenth centuries they have survived in surprising quantity, but they seldom find their way into print.

All of these sources disappoint us when we try to date the foundation of the gild in question or to discover the customs of the trade before the period of codification. Statutes may claim to state ancient custom, but there is a fair presumption that the transition from oral to written rules forced a clear and hence a novel definition of many customs that had previously been left ambiguous. The rule that a fuller's servant in Paris should possess exactly twelve articles of clothing when hired may seem to have the ring of oral folk custom, yet may at least equally well have been the result of recent decision. Falling back on miscellaneous fragmentary evidence, a century of historical research has failed to pin-point with certainty the date and circumstances of the first steps taken in formal organization of the individual urban crafts. This failure must be due in part to loss of records, but it is due also to the fact that settled continuity of gild life depended on the assumption of responsibility within a permanent administrative context, or on a grant of privilege, or on the accumulation of corporately owned property. Without public responsibility, privilege or property, the corporate bond was apt to be weak and discontinuous. In good times, it could dissolve in members' indifference to holding together. In bad times, petty friction could break it up. Preambles to the later medieval gild statutes sometimes allude to recent quarrelling or to a lapse of organization through apathy as having necessitated a fresh start.

A survey of pre-thirteenth-century gild relationships with governmental authority starts logically with Italy, for Italy offers the oldest evidence and the greatest variety of experience. Four long-debated theories, each of them with some validity, have been applied to the interpretation of the evidence. One of these, seeking to trace a connection between the older medieval gilds and the collegial movement of ancient Rome, assumes the survival of a tradition subordinating private associations to the public interest under public authority. The Roman trade gilds or colleges, whatever their origin, had undoubtedly been drawn into the imperial system of administration. In the fourth century, as a fiscal expedient and as a means of assuring the continuance of essential urban trades and services that were becoming unprofitable, official policy had aimed to extend the colleges into hitherto unorganized occupations. All occupations were to be endowed with hereditary right and collegiate monopoly, under the check of public price controls and taxation. This plan was an administrator's dream, a blue-print. It was never systematically imposed on outlying provinces, and there is no way of knowing how far it materialized in Italy. New research into the trades of transport, building and smith's work, which are known to have been among the most widely organized trades in Roman towns long before the fourth century, may still disclose direct institutional continuities. Yet even supposing that the formal relations of a few gilds with public authority could be shown to have persisted unbroken and unaltered, it is difficult to conceive that actual working relations would not have varied significantly, that early medieval experience did not pass on also the memory of crises brought about by abuse of authority on the one hand or of monopoly power on the other. One of the few extant pieces of evidence of gild life in the sixth century, Pope Gregory I's letter to the bishop of Naples advising him to warn the count of Naples not to interfere with the town soap-makers, indicates that the latter were shrewd politicians, skilfully playing the ecclesiastical power against the civil power in the interests of independence. A sworn body (*corpus pactum*), with a set of rules that they themselves revised periodically by unanimous vote, and charging a fee to new entrants to the trade, they had fallen out with the count of Naples over taxation and other matters that the pope's letter does not specify.

A second theory would modify the first by admitting that political decay, in the south, and the Lombard conquest, in the north, must have broken the continuity of gild organization, but it insists that in Lombardy gilds were sooner or later reconstituted under governmental authority. The theory has been carefully tested only for the moneyers. Their gilds were a unique type, charged with the highest possible degree of public responsibility, for in the issue of coinage they were the direct instruments of public policy in the exercise of a sovereign power. They are known to have been affected by the fourth-century reforms, which tightened their collective responsibility and their internal discipline and redefined their privileges. The form of organization then set persisted thereafter on Byzantine territory with little change. In northern Italy the Lombards disrupted it altogether by closing the official mints for seventy-five years. When monetary sovereignty was finally resumed, in 643, it was exercised through gilds reconstituted, as Lopez has shown, on a system similar to that of contemporary Byzantium, and possibly manned with craftsmen who had worked in the Byzantine Empire. Through the gild privileges, which included opportunity of profit through money-lending, moneyers for the next 500 years ranked among the wealthier and more influential townsmen.

Other gilds that may have existed at the time of the Lombard conquest were less liable to long suspension, but more liable to some change of constitution. The Lombard kings, and the emperors after them, favoured gild organization if it could be a means of levying contributions in money, kind or service from the members in return for a formal grant of monopoly. Few details are known except for Pavia, and there only through an early eleventh-century protest against change in the customs described. The privileges that were claimed took such forms as the monopoly of soap-making, the maintenance of twelve key positions in the leather industry with the high sale value of four pounds, and the limitation of fishing vessels to a fleet of sixty. In return for the privileges payments were owed in appropriate products or services. The fishermen, for example, provided a fixed quantity of fish annually and on the occasion of royal visits to Pavia were under obligation to co-operate with the boatmen in outfitting a certain number of vessels for official use. These four groups and an indeterminate number of other gilds were, like the moneyers, under the jurisdiction of the chamber. It is therefore possible that like the moneyers they had been reconstituted by governmental authority after some interval of suspension and that in many particulars, apart from the requirement of payments in kind, they continued a Roman tradition. The fishing gild was still in existence in 1179, when its members gave way in recognizing certain monastic fishing rights. By this time the plan of granting economic privilege in return for payment in kind or service was inappropriately rigid and must have appeared increasingly anomalous and archaic.

A third theory points to the illicit institution of the oath taken to secure combinations for economic advantage as an antecedent to official gild organization and as significant of chronic potential conflict between gilds and public authority. The institution was well known in the late Roman world; the jurists of the fifth and sixth centuries believed it to be widespread. From the early twelfth century it was sporadically prohibited in town law, most frequently with reference to the building and victualling trades, and it was prohibited also in a number of codified gild statutes in the next two centuries. Any *conjuratio* binding the members of a trade group to hold a privately fixed line of price or wage demands was clearly regarded as conspiracy against the public interest. Other terms used for such an oath or for conspiratorial meetings to fix price and wage demands were *coadunatio, camorra, lega, rassa, asseptum*. The twelfth-century evidence is insufficient to show whether private price and wage agreements had enough binding force to give rise, of themselves, to new gilds, or whether they were merely a product of passing crises. The private oath, as used for this purpose, was nevertheless of immense importance as a test of strength for the authorities of the newly organizing communes. It goaded them into developing the counter-institution of the public oath binding the members of a trade not to enter into conspiratorial agreements. Usually this was administered to gild officers, but the evidence is again insufficient to show whether it was ever the means of bringing formal gild organization into existence. Nor does the evidence show whether the public oath was a mere adaptation of the oath traditionally administered to the officers of moneyers' gilds or of other gilds carrying a Roman tradition, or whether it was a result of renewed interest in Roman law. In any event, it was a statesmanlike move, for it formally charged the gilds with the public interest. One of the earliest twelfth-century experiments on record was in Pistoia, where smiths and victuallers had been accused of over-pricing by agreement. A number of gild officers (*rectores artium*) were then sworn to the maintenance of a free market. Once put in this position, it was difficult for them to object to it without loss of face. Nor could they well object when the demand came for codification of statutes. The entire code of the millers of Piacenza, a long and impressively systematic constitution first recorded in 1266, was cast in the form of an oath exacted of the officers.

A fourth theory, without attempting to deny the survival of more ancient gilds and their possible indirect influence on the formal relationships of new gilds with the new communes, insists that in any period a gild movement can be understood only in terms of the forces, political, economic and social, of that period. On this view there is a danger of over-emphasizing the importance of survivals. Even the institution of the public oath is open to misinterpretation if it is isolated from the political background. It is a mistake to think of twelfth- or thirteenth-century artisan gilds either as defying an established government or as subjected to its authority, since they were themselves one of the principal organizing forces through which a new type of government was taking shape, and bore as great public responsibilities as any other kind of group on the scene. By the end of the twelfth century one finds them, in Milan, organized in a federal league (*credenza*) that bore a share of administrative work and of defence. Several, in Bologna, contributed as much to defence as the older military societies of the city. In early thirteenth-century Siena the heads of artisan gilds appear alongside the merchant consuls and other officials as parties to treaty-making with other towns.

Leading artisans must certainly often have had a share, under merchant leadership, in the shaping of Italian systems of economic administration. When these were based on gild organization they could be extraordinarily complex, presenting the aspect of a commune for economic affairs paralleling the organization of the political commune. Unified control at the top was a necessity if only by reason of the frequency of war or threat of war, and because of the need of consistency in the development of commercial law. It was equally unavoidable that the men at the top should be men with an experience of commercial and financial affairs that only merchants could command. Artisans had to accept this situation. They did so with a good grace provided that they had a reasonably fair chance to defend their interests by political means against those of merchants who might be in a position to raise the prices of raw materials by agreement, or to depress wages and piece-rates. As regards local trade and industry the general lines of economic policy were not altered by constitutional changes giving artisan gilds more political representation and influence. The standard policy remained one of trying to moderate any marked increase in price, preferably by promoting increase in supply. The greater conflicts of interest occurred in the export industries. It was here that artisan revolts were engendered, and artisan political advances brought important changes of policy.

An increase in artisan political power was won always at a certain cost. Gilds then became primarily political associations, and heavier miscellaneous responsibilities were thrown on their officers' shoulders. The political gild would become the basic unit through which the citizen population was organized for public assemblies and for military duty. For political convenience the number of gilds would be frozen, forcing allied trades to federate and sometimes bringing together trades that were quite unrelated economically. There might have to be swarms of subordinate gild officers engaged in police work and military organization. Under the constitution that was drawn up in Perugia in 1342 the head officer of each gild was required to have a number of local assistants in each quarter of the city. For the shoemakers there were to be fifty local *rectores*. Whenever the ruling committee of lord priors ordered alarm bells to be rung, all gildsmen were to drop their work and fall into military formation behind their officers in a designated place of assembly. Once a well-disciplined gild organization was set up it was liable to continue to be used for disciplinary purposes by a new ruling group. A change of constitution in Pistoia in 1284, which reduced the political status of gild officers, obliged them to administer to all gild members an oath of loyalty to the Church and to the city captain.

In the great ports conditions were altogether different. Industry, subject to heavy competition from imports, was a marginal interest. The more successful of the Genoese craftsmen and retailers, the men who might have become leaders in a gild movement, were more excited by maritime investment, in which anyone could lay out small shares, than by the idea of starting a political struggle in which the odds were hopelessly against them. Organization was feeble and late, and leaned on public authority for support. Venetian gilds were more numerous and of much earlier origin, but they were kept under firm governmental control without any chance of political power.

All recorded activity of Italian gilds shows them sharing, or striving to share, in the formal dignity of public life. There are traces of an early recourse to patronage relations, a device in the reaching for status that is reminiscent of the late Roman colleges. Vaccari notes that the old regime of gild privilege in tenth-century Pavia had been protected by the landed knightly class there whose members had profited by the growth of urban demand for agricultural products. The market-gardeners of Rome in 1030 recorded the election of *il magnifico Amato*, who presumably had some pretensions to nobility, as their prior. A century later the shoe-makers of Ferrara were electing a certain Marquis di Mayardo as their *maior*, agreeing to pay him for his services. He was not one of their own number, but lived out in the country. Early thirteenth-century heads of several Sienese artisan gilds were referred to in official civic documents as *domini*. Once they were recognized by the commune, gild officers shared in the dignity of magistral office. They might carry a rod, as a symbol of authority, and were frequently designated, from this, as mace-bearers (*massarii*). The gilds themselves were often described simply by the con-temporary generic terms for societies—as *paratici*, or *corpi d'arte*—but in some places Roman tradition was revived by the venerable terms *collegium, ministerium, officium.*

The impression of dignity is borne out further by the minutes of gild meetings, which were conducted with a formal ceremony identical with the procedure of meetings of the higher councils of the commune. De-bate and the procedure of voting, by black and white beans, were the same. The more detailed minutes show another aspect of gild affairs on which constitutional rules are uninformative, that is, the extent to which most business was left in the hands of the officers. At meetings, resolu-tions were ordinarily introduced by one of the officers, and it was they who led discussion and brought it to a close by calling for a vote or division (*partito*). Eloquence was admired. The word 'harangue' recurs constantly, members being exhorted to cast their votes according as the *harengatores* had pleased them or not. Clearly the gilds generated a distinct group of administrators who cultivated political skill.

The officers were the better able to conduct themselves with dignity because their power, while it was supported and defined by the com-mune's recognition, had an independent source in the gild's solidarity. The men of every recognized artisan gild were aware of themselves as organized in at least two different ways simultaneously. They were an organ of the commune and they were a private group concerned with technical and trade interests. In most cases they were organized in still a third way, as a fraternity under the auspices of patron saints. The religious and fraternal sanction was the source of their deepest solidarity. In their capacity as fraternities the gilds accumulated special reserve funds, dis-tributed relief to members in distress, bought property, endowed hos-pitals, and made regular contributions to religious houses and other charities. As fraternities they honoured the dead, covering the burial costs of poor members, and requiring members to attend funeral services. The patron saints were honoured at their festivals, and it became a custom to pay on these occasions for sermons from popular preachers. In their capacity as fraternity brothers or fellows (*socii*), members could be called on to aid each other by any legal means or in emergency even according to the justice of the feud. The smiths of Bologna, with the help of an allied *societas*, in 1316 avenged the murder of one of their men by tearing down the houses of a noble family that was held responsible. Such clan-like solidarity may have drawn on sentiment nourished by inter-marriage within the gild, but it far transcended actual family ties. Al-though the gilds were tender of blood relationships to the extent of lowering or eliminating entrance fees for the sons of masters, they were wary of family influence as a potentially disruptive force. One does not often find men of the same surname listed as in office together. It was probably a deliberate policy to oblige different family groupings to co-operate in carrying the responsibility of gild affairs.

Internal discipline was sustained partly by help of the institution of the informer. One does not have to look far for the origin of this institution. It was familiar in rural parishes, where it was encouraged if not actually introduced by the Church as a means of control over moral conduct. Again, as with family influence, the gilds were wary of disruptive force. Members were urged to inform the officers of breach of rules, but only in the case of specified regulations that were held to be particularly import-ant. Even so, the institution enhanced the personal power of the officers. At their judgment, fines could be imposed on the strength of a single in-former's sworn word, taken secretly, without record of the name, often with the prospect of the informer having a share in the fine.

Besides skilled leadership, solidarity and internal discipline, the gilds required security in the handling and disposition of funds. Their needs in this regard, along with those of other lay societies, pushed on develop-ment of the concept of juridical corporate personality. The exact stages of this development are difficult to discern. Description of a gild as a *com-munitas*, *societas* or *universitas* attests only public recognition of a group that appeared to be holding together continuously under responsible officers. In the twelfth century property was commonly held not in the name of the gild, but in the names listed of a part of the membership. By the fourteenth and fifteenth centuries two members, or the chief officers, would hold it in trust in the name of the gild. The fifteenth-century gild of smiths at Reggio, which had been accumulating small pieces of pro-perty over a long period, had them held by its officers *ad usum, com-modum et utilitatem dicti universitatis*. Disbursements and the collection of money owing to a gild were handled by officers appointed to represent it legally as *syndici*. There remained the problem of misuse of funds by officers. The smiths of Modena required officers to give security for all funds in their charge and insisted that any expenditures that were not a matter of routine be authorized by a full meeting of the gild. Annual accounting to the membership was a universal custom. Most gilds cover-ed personal expenses that their officers incurred on common business, and some paid a regular small salary for the purpose. The fifteenth-century tailors of Reggio allowed their *podestà* three pounds a year and their mace-bearer and consul each two pounds.

The subjection of Italian communes to great lordships (the signory) marked a change in gild history. The immediate source of the authority that ratified gild statutes was now the lord. This might appear a merely formal change, but in most towns it operated so as to increase the political weight of artisans and reduce that of merchants. In export industry wage demands had a quicker hearing. In local industry artisan gilds had more legal support than before, for what it was worth, in their efforts to assert authority over country workers.

How far Italian example affected the development of gild systems in other countries is an open question. Where the influence of Italian culture was strong, as in the western Mediterranean, there was undoubtedly some communication of stimulus. To the north, lag in industrial de-velopment, or in economic development generally, delayed the move-ment. In no country did it ever become quite so prominent as in Italy, because in no other country were there so many considerable inland towns. In coastal areas merchant rule, or merchant coalition with terri-torial lords, kept artisan gilds down. They therefore seldom played more than a subordinate administrative role. The main variations in the situa-tion arose from the presence of royal power, which could upset the sym-metry of a well-controlled gild-system by permitting negotiation for special privilege.

In the Spanish peninsula it was the presence of royal power that lent gild history its chief local peculiarities. Many gilds here took shelter from town controls under the Church and under monarchical protection, applying for charters to conduct fraternities. As a bid for autonomy the move was a failure, for it hastened the appearance of national controls. The fact that gilds had appealed to royal power but had been licensed in the main only for religious and fraternal practices left the way open for the issue of royal codes of industrial regulation. Thereafter gild freedom depended on such good relations as could be established with royal officials.

In the south of France there was at first more inclination to remain con-tent with checks resembling those of Italian urban administration. The design of communal control was firmest in Marseilles, where by the middle of the thirteenth century there were a hundred gilds under sys-tematic regulation with the aim of ensuring a satisfactory supply of goods and services at prices regarded as reasonable.

To move from Marseilles to central or northern France was to enter a different world, a world where throughout the age of medieval expansion it remained possible to think of urban industry, like agriculture, chiefly as one of the means of maintaining the apparatus of royal or feudal power. The trades of Beauvais had to support more than a dozen wardens and sergeants whose sole function was to collect revenue for the bishop and for members of the nobility who had been enfeoffed by him with rights to tolls and to a miscellany of other customary charges. Some of the collections were in kind, as festival bread from the bakers and dice for gaming from the petty retailers known as mercers, serving frankly no aim but to keep members of the bishop's entourage happy; and there could be reciprocal social arrangements. The fullers were entitled to a cheese dinner every spring or summer, on a table laid with a cloth, from officials of the fief to which their licence fees belonged. Simple technical matters were by custom handled in the same personal manner. Tanners, for example, were entitled to soak skins at certain stakes in the river provided each man presented each new bishop of Beauvais with a dog. Customs of this kind did not call for any formal organization of the trade, nor did taxation, nor enfeoffment, as such. When gilds emerged in this kind of regime, as they did in the twelfth and thirteenth centuries in Paris and at least half a dozen provincial cities, authorized by the royal power or by local lords, it was to serve various special purposes. In one form they resembled those of tenth-century Pavia in being collectively responsible for providing the lord with certain services. The *communitas* of smiths in Amiens was still in 1301 under legal obligation to make keys for the bishop's great hall, and gear for his tents when he should be summoned to war. Arrangements of this kind served the double purpose of binding the men to the lord and of reducing the latter's dependence on the market. The idea of spreading obligations over the whole of a trade within a lord's urban jurisdiction, instead of simply recruiting a few special servants, as was done among unfree tenants on a country estate and continued to be the practice in episcopal cities in the Rhineland and in southern Germany generally, was an innovation that in France should possibly be credited to royal officials in Paris as early as the eleventh century. It is unlikely that lords saw any further reasons for authorizing gilds except as an improved means of handling trade disputes and keeping artisans under control.

Legal precedents that were set in early instances of organization had a continuing influence on later phases of the development of French gilds and their policies. The questions arose, who was to head an artisan group, and what powers were to be delegated to him? Seignorial and official preference was for an appointed *magister*, and the right to elect officers freely became a matter of special concession that was never to be quite

R

secure. Judicial powers were delegated with the reservation that they be exercised according to approved custom. Otherwise only fiscal power was delegated, as in the right to collect licence fees from all who practised the trade, both on their first taking it up and annually. This form of taxation stemmed from seignorial power to confer the right to practise a trade in a given area. The limitations of gild power in regard to the right to restrict entry to its trade were never defined. Vagueness on this point may well have been increased by the fact that some gilds, for example the bakers of Pontoise, in their royal charter of 1162, and the butchers of Beauvais, in the bishop's custumal, had legal recognition simply as groups of individuals who, with their heirs, were in possession of certain rights. Indeed, this view of a gild as a self-perpetuating group of privileged families is the clearest conception that emerges.

French royal power, for its own fiscal and political purposes, later evolved the conception of a gild as a group that by royal favour could become a sworn community with full power to elect its officers. From about the middle of the fourteenth century, when gilds began to multiply in the provinces, many were induced to take out royal charters. The effect of these was to weaken local authority without ensuring gild independence. Provincial artisans continued to apply for them, and to pay for their renewal at the beginning of each new reign, partly because they could be drawn up to include the same kind of technical rules as prevailed at Paris, and could thus probably provide an excuse for trying to charge Parisian prices. In economic policy the royal power gave no clear lead. Attacks on the gilds in price ordinances of 1307 and 1351 were nullified by the type of charter that was subsequently issued. In Paris, where a system of splintering trades into small gilds had been adroitly and widely extended in the 1250's, ostensibly as a police measure, they fell foul of authority only when they engaged in political activity.

In Germany and central Europe the medieval gild movement is best known for its political record. Its successes, from this point of view, were concentrated in the older towns and cities of the central and southern Rhineland. Elsewhere it was checked by merchant rule, as in the Hanse, or by reactionary alliances between merchant patricians and territorial lords. The political record, however, does not tell the whole story. On the one hand, democratic victories did less for gild autonomy in economic affairs than might have been supposed. Well into the fourteenth century the victualling trades in several of the older centres remained under the jurisdiction of permanent officials of the town lords, and in some instances gilds in these and other trades were continuing into the next century to apply to the lords' officials for formal appointment of their heads. On the other hand, patrician ascendancy nowhere entirely suppressed artisan organization as a social movement. In Cologne, where artisan leaders had played the ecclesiastical power against the ruling merchants, and also in Bremen, over a dozen gilds had been built into the administrative system by the thirteenth century, and the number grew. All regions, especially in the latter half of the fifteenth century, saw the emergence of new gilds. These might be small and of no political importance, but they regularly had some administrative responsibilities.

A few of the older gilds had large exclusive rights. At Worms, the most obdurate of the old strongholds of administration by lords' officials, the bishop in 1106 paradoxically set a precedent for gild monopoly by endowing twenty-three men and their heirs with certain fishing rights. In Brunswick ducal and civic charters of the thirteenth century conveyed a 'grace', implying exclusive trade jurisdiction, to gilds of drapers, leather-workers and smiths. The type of gild that was spreading in the fifteenth century had no such sweeping privileges. To the extent that the right of restricting entry to a trade existed, it was sanctioned only as a means of screening out morally and politically undesirable people. Free birth was a normal condition of entry. Local prejudice allowed several of the Lüneburg gilds to exclude men of Wendish birth. Preambles to gild statutes were so framed as to give a reassuring impression of solid citizen responsibility.

Politically, the gilds nowhere played a more spectacular and militant role than in the Low Countries, under the leadership of the textile workers in export industry. The merchant control that they fought here had met the first signs of unrest, in the late thirteenth century, by a system that far exceeded any feudal bishop's schemes of authoritarian order. As demonstrated in the *keures* that were issued in St Omer, it called for the enforcement of rules in each line of trade by men who, like non-commissioned officers conscripted to serve in an industrial army, were appointed by civic magistrates and were responsible solely to them. The political movement that broke through merchant rule modified the system to allow of election of officers from below and some degree of autonomy in legislation. Yet a high degree of civic regulation continued to characterize the textile industries, even in the new centres that entered export trade in the fifteenth century.

Least use was made of gilds in the northern countries. In the Scandinavian peninsula the fostering and supervision of town life was a major strategy of the royal power. A royal code of industrial regulation in 1282 deprived gilds of any economic function. Privilege went only to immigrant Germans.

England, again, long offered poor soil for continental types of gild system because of the small size of her towns and the thoroughness of royal organization of justice. Presentment for breach of any alleged custom in craft processes or retail trade could be made in courts leet. For these reasons the royal charter issued to Norwich in 1256 banned gilds as detrimental to the royal interest. Scattered gilds of weavers and fullers in twelfth-century royal boroughs had been heavily mulcted, presumably for holding courts. In the case of the London weavers the right to hold a court was granted as a special privilege. A gild of smiths in Canterbury[1] at the end of that century appears to have escaped the royal attention, possibly being protected by the influential body of local moneyers. At Bury St Edmunds, in the same century, a gild of bakers was set up under hereditary aldermanship responsible to the sacrist of the monastery, but evidence that this 'ministerial' type of organization was extended to other trades or was copied in other monastic boroughs is lacking. Gilds spread in the provinces, only after artisans and retailers in London had given a lead, in the latter part of the thirteenth century. For the settled operation of provincial gilds in administrative systems one has to look to the fifteenth century. In return for organizing citizen militia, and for producing communal pageantry and plays at the festival of Corpus Christi and on other civic occasions they were then allowed to levy dues on the whole of their trade. Legally, no one could practise any trade in Coventry without paying dues to one of the gilds, and country tanners and barkers visiting York to buy or sell had to contribute to the leather gilds on the grounds that it was unfair to expect the latter to bear the whole expense of their pageant. At the same time that they enjoyed these powers, all gilds were subject to watchful and fussy control by town magistrates. Submission was not always ready. There were bakers' strikes. Coventry dyers, after being ordered to accept more competition, were accused of hiring Welsh and Irish murderers to ambush their competitors. Shoemakers at York, angered at standards set for them by the cordwainers in 1490, a year of high costs, were rumoured to be preparing to spend 'large money' in recruiting several hundred outsiders for a riot, and to be looking for a skilled agitator, 'a furiouse man', to captain them. In any gild-system, such stresses and strains were recurrent.

The close of the Middle Ages, then, saw the gild movement infiltrating urban administration in all parts of western Europe. Their many-sidedness shows that the gilds were able to command the loyalty and energies of the artisan élite as no other form of association could. This made them both useful and dangerous. Their high development of corporate responsibility made it seem natural to load upon them duties of defence and police and the arrangement of the ceremony that was so vital to medieval civic life, as well as the duties of oversight of their trades. The very same corporate sense caused them to bring conflicts of interest into

---

[1] My reference to this hitherto unnoticed gild is owing to the courtesy of W. Urry, Archivist of the town and cathedral of Canterbury, who has in preparation a work on the early history of Canterbury.

the open with a vigour that often threatened public order. Both because they were useful and because they were dangerous, it was essential, in every type of town in which they appeared, whatever the ruling group, to subordinate them to the authority of the town's chief magistrates.

Royal and imperial power, merchant groups and other landed townsmen were ambivalent towards the artisan gilds, uniting only to check their bids for political power. Royal power was often willing to encourage them a little, as a source of revenue and as a means of dividing a town the better to advance its own influence. Merchants were ambivalent towards them because they had their own gilds, some of which were closely associated with subordinate artisan gilds. The merits of each gild were, from the point of view of the public welfare, equally debatable. Responsible magistrates and magnates had always to face the question, how would they replace the administrative services that gilds could be made to undertake? For all these reasons opposition to the gilds, though endemic, was confused, much weaker than its fulminations sound. Frederick II's ban on gild organization throughout the Empire, issued in 1219, and followed by bans applying to a number of separate German towns and cities, was nowhere successful in suppressing the movement. It was futile for authoritarian reactionaries to advocate turning the administrative clock back. To consider only the problem of maintaining orderly relations, and confidence among buyers and sellers, in retail trade, the old systems had amounted to little but the policing of market places and receiving of complaints proffered there for a quick hearing. These continued to serve well enough, in all countries, in little seignorial towns where selling was not dispersed in shops and where no crafts were carried on for export trade. The sleepier little towns could everywhere dispense with gilds. Gilds could be dispensed with also in many crafts in the larger inland cities and in seaports where a brisk import trade made for competition. It was in market conditions intermediate between these that they arose, meeting a variety of specific needs. If they were abolished here, the needs still had to be met. An attempt at abolition in Vienna in 1276, pushed on the grounds that gilds were the cause of decline in immigration to the city, lasted only half a year. A town that tried to abolish gilds permanently would have had to expand its permanent administrative staff. Paid inspectors would have had to substitute for gild officers in handling problems of dishonesty, and in aiding craftsmen to maintain supply in seasons of scarcity. Few towns were prepared to go to this length except to victual themselves under continuous pressure of rising prices. Much anti-gild sentiment, therefore, persisted as a chronic ineffectual grumbling that made gilds the butt of general discontent over the cost of living.

III. *Gild Economic Power in Local Trade and Industry*

Did the gilds, then, as medieval writers hostile to them alleged, exercise upward pressure on prices? One cannot take direct testimony on this point at its face value. Beaumanoir's opinions are acid with the disdain of a professional jurist and administrator for men of the people who lacked training in considering the public interest. Alain Chartier was a rigid moralist, content to blame the hardships of the poor on the sin of avarice in others. The same narrowness vitiates literature such as *The Reformation of King Sigismund*. Nor can the indirect testimony of the precautions for price control written into civic regulations fairly be interpreted as evidence of gild action to enhance or maintain prices. For example, in regard to lime, introduction of price control might signify only that increased demand created by improvement in standards of housing or by the extension of a town had not yet been followed by an increase in supply. As regards bread, price control came through recognition of the inherently erratic nature of supply and was in no way a response to gild organization. Records of dispute between gilds and town authorities show efforts to be objective, both sides appealing to costs and prices. But the figures that they produced are usually from years of crisis and are too fragmentary and contradictory to sustain any conclusion. Local price history is not yet far enough advanced for us to be able to compare and analyse the course of prices over any length of time under a gild regime with the course of prices under conditions similar save for absence of gilds. Scarcely any medieval craftsmen's accounts have survived, so that our data as to their working costs are very deficient.

The question can be treated only by reference to the degree of competition that existed in different trades. In general, gild power to affect prices must have depended on local conditions of supply and demand and on the interest that town authorities took in the maintenance of competitive conditions. No medieval gilds had an absolutely watertight control over supply, and none were entirely sheltered from retail competition. Villagers from the surrounding countryside might provide an appreciable proportion of the processed foods and the rougher small manufactured goods that a town needed. Custom restricted them to selling in open market places under public supervision, or else to peddling, but did not ordinarily limit their share of a trade. If a gild used political influence to make restrictions over-harassing, astute villagers were likely to find ways of acting in collusion with other competitors of the gild within the town. Gilds had to face resident competitors of two classes. First there were the townsmen of inferior legal and political status, *forin-*

seci and aliens. In the later Middle Ages these were often forbidden to keep shop in any area of the town that was under the central municipal jurisdiction, but in areas of special jurisdiction, which existed in every medieval town, they were normally free to sell as they pleased. The second class of competitors, a potentially more formidable one, that a gild had to consider was to be found among members of other citizen gilds. These might openly employ villagers, *forinseci* or aliens, in another trade, or encourage their wives to do so, and, as important merchants, they might at any time introduce competitive products from other towns. The town government was arbiter of all disputes, sometimes supporting a gild, sometimes promoting competition. With so many variables to be taken into account, no single generalization about a hypothetically average outcome is of service. It is more helpful to distinguish points along a scale of conditions favourable to gild power. Gilds can then be roughly classified according to the relative positions that they most typically occupied, along this scale, in different industries.

At the top of the scale a gild would approximate to 'monopsony' power in buying and monopoly power in selling. To enjoy these continuously over any long period would of course call for remarkably close solidarity, with sharp sanctions against breaking the line in price and output agreements. Sources of supply would preferably be few, demand for the product fairly inelastic at high price ranges, and substitutes difficult to devise. It would nevertheless be desirable to keep the public authorities friendly or neutral. Conditions at the mid-point of the scale would approximate to those of perfect competition in that gilds would have no power to affect prices. Either through sheer abundance, or through special action by the public authorities, supplies of raw material would be equally available to gild members and to outsiders. Given legal enforcement of reasonably free entry to the trade and to the gild, it would not actually be necessary to have resident competitors outside it. Fear that new competition might be introduced could conceivably serve as a deterrent to output agreements designed to raise prices. Intermediate positions, both above and below the mid-point of the scale, would represent conditions of imperfect competition among rival groups. At the bottom of the scale a gild would be losing business to more efficient competitors. It could survive, and rise in the scale again, only by amalgamating with some other group and adopting its policies.

This theoretical scheme will account for the essential features of medieval gild economy and its general trends. In local trade and industry the only gilds able to dig themselves into a steadily secure position near the top of the scale of power were those working in the precious metals. Butchers fought hard to reach the top and not infrequently came very near it. Leather gilds, and some of those working in base metals, might rank next in economic power, but except in very high-quality products they had a harder fight to maintain their position and by the end of the Middle Ages were apt to be sliding down. In foodstuffs other than meat, in textiles, wax and tallow, and in wood, trade conditions were more constantly competitive. Gilds producing for the local market were kept close to the middle of the scale of power. Gild fortunes were least stable in highly specialized branches of trades that might for a time command quality custom but later proved vulnerable to competition from new processes and new substitutes.

From the point of view of artisan history the goldsmiths' gilds, at the top of the scale, present fewest problems. In the larger cities many members were wholesale merchants with an interest in high mint offices, finance and general trade. Commanding both capital and political influence, they were able to keep the artisans in a subordinate position within the gild. In London the leading goldsmiths were all of them merchants and in the fourteenth and fifteenth centuries it was their policy to keep the artisans working for them at piece-rates set by gild committees. A number of these artisans were immigrant Germans. In smaller places the situation was simpler. The artisans were in control and, with a clientele that was tolerant of a good profit-margin, were freer than most of their fellows to practise some degree of restriction. The account-book of a goldsmith in fifteenth-century Constance shows the proceeds of one small workshop becoming the base of considerable investment in land and rents.

Butchers' gilds universally gained a reputation for seeking power through cartel buying. They were led to this by scarcity of supply that was rooted in the high costs of fattening stock. The nature of demand favoured them, fresh meat, notably in France and Italy, being a prestige item of diet. Poultry and rabbit were not highly esteemed and were usually left to lesser victualling gilds. Another circumstance that butchers were able to turn in their favour was the desirability, for reasons of sanitation, of closely delimiting the sites that were used for slaughter and for retail selling. In many French towns they contrived to acquire hereditary leasehold title, as a group of families, to the market sites. At Senlis this occurred as early as 1193. Policy would then keep the number of stalls down. Often the chief members of the gild would specialize in buying and fattening animals. Some would retire from the trade altogether, living by letting out their stalls to subordinate working butchers who were not admitted to the gild. Where an extreme concentration of high-quality trade became possible, as at the *Grande Boucherie* in Paris, the returns enabled an entire gild to move into the *rentier* class. This gild consisted, when in 1260 it acquired a perpetual lease of the twenty-five stalls in the market, of twenty families. A century later, through deaths and the exclusion of new entrants, it had shrunk to six families, all of them wealthy and influential and having no direct connection with the trade.

The opportunities of the trade fostered a strong gild solidarity, measurable in an unusually high rate of intermarriage and occupational heredity. Social solidarity had probably always been strong among localized groups of butchers. The country practice of carrying on all the work of the craft in or beside the family dwelling long persisted in the towns, creating a nuisance problem that set the group apart. Butchers may have been feared, too, because of the slaughterers' weapons. In France group solidarity clearly contributed to the formation of gilds of an exclusive type.

Yet by the fourteenth century even the French gilds were on the defensive, seeking royal charters and developing what may properly be called a public-relations policy. Critics contended that they overdid their pressure on country sellers, with the result that supplies were withheld and urban prices forced up. Local authorities did not hesitate to challenge points in the late medieval royal charters. Some of these, dating from times of disturbance when displacement of population through war or epidemic had unsettled local custom in the organization of trade, may represent not existing fact so much as the aspirations of an old gild in decline, or of a newly organized group, to beat out competitors by political means, through buying the favour of royal officials. Meanwhile, experience of breakdown in economic administration had been a stimulus to citizen thinking on public policy. That it gave rise to desire for absolute freedom of craft enterprise, without any authoritative supervision of standards, is hardly conceivable, but it did strengthen criticism of the system of administration through privileged bodies. The point on which the butchers' gilds were most challenged was their policy of extreme family exclusiveness. In defending this, they may be said to have tacitly given evidence against themselves, for none of them attempted to argue that their policies made for plenty or for cheapness. The *anciens Bouchers* of Angers, in 1388, took their stand on sheer traditional right, simply claiming *saisine et possession, seulz et pour le tout*, of the retail trade. Other groups took a pragmatic stand on the grounds of their service to the public in handling nothing but good-quality stock. New men would not be expert, they would make *de folz achatz*. At Arras the town authorities nevertheless brushed aside the gild rule that none should be admitted save sons of members or men married to the legitimate daughters of members. The old guard countered in 1407 with the charge that the new entrants had sold meat carrying the infection of leprosy. In an age that was becoming more conscious of the dangers of bad food an accusation of this kind may have been good strategy. It was a trick of the men selling in the *Grande Boucherie* in Paris, when any of their number was convicted of passing off a bad piece of meat, to order him to move out and join the competing group of butchers whose stalls were on the *Petit Pont*. In new charters the butchers everywhere made great play of their concern for public health, and of the fact that they did not permit the sale of animals raised by barbers or by other professional blood-letters.

Where supplies long continued to be short and where the political situation also was unfavourable, the butchers' best efforts to build good public relations failed. Erfurt in 1264 suppressed organization among both butchers and bakers. The Italian cities adopted a unique combination of public control of trade in livestock with open competition in the retailing of meat. They obliged country producers to send in livestock for sale in supervised markets, and threw the retail trade open to innkeepers. The old butchers' gilds were not necessarily suppressed, but they lost all independence.

Short of adopting the drastic Italian policies, it was extremely difficult to curtail the power of a butchers' gild whose members had once moved into large-scale buying and had established a cartel policy throughout a region. Police surveillance of gild meetings, as was enjoined on the *bailli* at Bourges in 1359 with the aim of preventing *machinatio*, would have been useless. Abolition of the formal privileges of the gild at Chartres, in the war-time political crisis of 1416, brought no change in the members' buying practices. It is likely that many of the leading butchers in France and England had political protection because of their usefulness to the monarchies in the victualling of armies. The French monarchy occasionally ordered the admission of a few new members to gilds that were complained of as being too exclusive, but it gave no consistent support to the policy of enforcing competition. The most spirited example of the enforcement of competition is to be seen in early fifteenth-century Coventry, where restrictive agreements were banned, and, over the passionate protests of the gild, country butchers were given an open invitation to settle in the town.

Most towns were content to rely on futile reiteration of a ban on forestalling, that is, on the buying of animals before they were brought into the town market, and on retail price controls. Periodically revised schedules set maximum prices to the consumer either by the pound or by the cut. If these did not cover costs, gild officers could enter a protest and have the schedule modified. The defect of the system was in leaving the fundamental problem of supply untouched. The controls could, however, moderate the sudden upturns of retail price that came with rumours of abnormal scarcity, and it was for this reason that they were considered a sound and reassuring item of public policy.

A far greater embarrassment, for butchers' gilds, was created by a situation of increasing plenty. Where the gilds were strongest, in France, they gave small encouragement to producers to expand supply. Yet butchers' prices were not the only influence affecting production. Cessation of war-time discouragements led to improvements in the feeding of French stock, and in England the late fifteenth-century boom in wool produc-tion inevitably increased mutton supply. Some of the gild manœuvring for privilege may represent efforts to keep new competitors from ex-panding the meat trade at lower prices. Where limitation of numbers in the trade had legal sanction it could be supplemented by privately imposed restrictions on a quota basis, although sooner or later a fixed-quota policy was liable to provoke attack through the courts. Twenty-two butchers of Sens were in 1529 convicted on a charge of monopoly on these grounds.

The land of greatest plenty, where tables were most heavily loaded with meat, was fifteenth-century Germany. In Frankfurt-on-Oder it has been estimated that consumption ran up to 250 pounds per person annually. The heavy urban demand was responsible for stimulating cattle production on the north-easterly plains, and also pork production, on a small-scale basis, in the neighbourhood of towns. Skill in preserva-tion built up town sausage industries. These forces of expansion were so vigorous and popular that the gilds cannot be detected attempting to re-strain them, and reasonably competitive pricing ensued without the need of special political intervention. This was partly because the changes in-duced a great deal of new specialization. The gilds kept themselves occu-pied with administrative problems created by the new division of labour, and in trying, with the aid of town authorities, to keep slaughtering and food-preservation an urban industry. The ambitions of old-guard cliques, which in France went into restrictive practices, were satisfied in German towns by administrative responsibilities and by opportunities, shared with general merchants, of building up export business in locally preserved products. Typically, as for example at Dortmund, the old gild lived on as a limited group favouring the admission of sons of masters and of sons-in-law, setting standards of moral character for other new entrants, and keeping the higher-quality trade in fresh meat in its own hands. The less profitable lines of work and trade were left to outside or subordinate groups.

The fortunes of leather gilds using local supply closely paralleled those of butchers' gilds. The tanners of fourteenth-century Troyes had the reputation of having risen, through their 'monopsony' power in cartel buying, into the richest circles of the town. In many places they came to an agreement with the butchers' gilds on the price of skins and hides. At Chartres in 1265 tanners and butchers deadlocked their trade in a dis-agreement that was broken only by action of the public authorities. Until 1484 periodical price-fixing by conference between officers of the two gilds continued to have legal sanction. The nature of demand, leather lending itself superlatively to personal display, made it possible to play for high prices on fine finished work. The poor had substitutes for leather-work, using cloth bags, the cord girdles that the Franciscans copied, wooden shoes and their own bare feet.

Collective ownership of trade equipment and markets gave tanners' gilds a long lead over competing groups. In fourteenth-century Siena the gild that tanned and worked up cowhides leased the use of common vats to members for a charge of seven pounds, but charged outsiders fifty pounds. Liège records indicate that the strong local gild came into formal existence through recognition of its juridical personality in the possession of mills for mechanical crushing of bark. The arrangement allowed in-dividual members an hereditary right to share in the ownership. In 1347 this same gild was granted a perpetual lease of the leather market-hall in return for paying off a part of the city's war debt.

But the fourteenth century brought many tanners' gilds down. War-time emergencies and spurts of inflation forced new competition on the trade through experimentation with substitute materials and time-saving methods of production. Probably new levels of demand were tapped. Where tanners were organized together with the finishing trades in a single gild, they tried to enforce strict specialization within it. Charters obtained at Brunswick, Leipzig and Chartres provided for this. At Sens, where specialist regulation broke down completely *en voulant chascun son fait a sa voulente*, twenty tanners in 1375 bought a royal charter authorizing them to restore it in a fashion that they themselves had planned. The tanning trade in England, under what leadership is not known, repeatedly formed a political lobby to seek domestic protection against competition from other leather-workers. In 1395 the trade was successful in obtaining legislation that prohibited tanning by cord-wainers and shoemakers, but this was twice rescinded, and when in 1423 it was finally confirmed, parliament erected no machinery for enforce-ment. Town governments, to whom tanners appealed locally, were in-clined to compromise on the letter of the law, trying simply to keep the various gilds co-operating in the inspection of tanned leather. For the parliamentary policy of compulsory specialization they substituted a practical policy of open competition subject only to the meeting of cer-tain minimum standards of quality.

Situations of increasing plenty also affected tanners' gilds adversely. The change in fifteenth-century German conditions worked greatly to the advantage of shoemakers. Now able to buy raw hides and skins for themselves, they insisted on getting them tanned as cheaply as possible. The Lüneburg tanners stated in 1450 that they had once been a gild of rich men and were now poor. The shoemakers at Riga, in 1488, took over the town tannery.

The gilds that appeared in the top-quality branches of the leather trades, those using the fine calf leather known from its Spanish origin as cordwain, had certain advantages that tanners and other groups using local supply lacked. The same was true of skinners and furriers using imports from the forests of eastern Europe. These trades all offered opportunity to men of mercantile ability. The strong gilds were directed by men who, without necessarily abandoning supervision of a workshop of their own, tended to specialize in supplying material to the poorer artisans and often in selling the latter's products. Gild organization improved the position of these entrepreneurs in several ways. It facilitated cartel agreement on prices to be offered for imported material and for labour or piece-work. When several groups of artisans could be drawn into a single gild, the combination of administrative and economic power over them tightened control of output and gave promise of a potential upward pressure on prices to be charged the consumer. The skinners of London were in a position to run their gild in regard to artisan work in much the same way as the goldsmiths ran theirs. Cordwainers and girdlers, although operating with less capital, in many places tended towards similar policies. In the saddle craft, which gave employment to workers in wood and metal as well as in leather, the saddlers controlled output through the circumstance that the finished product was assembled in their workshops. It was therefore a matter of little or no concern to them how the subordinate workers might be organized. Separate gild organization, it was true, could give the piece-workers an engine of political protest and agitation. Yet under any regime saddlers carried more political weight than their dependent workers.

The regime in Paris, which was calculated to prevent concentrations of gild power in the great luxury crafts of the capital, may actually have favoured the throwing of administrative power to the mercantile elements in the leather trades. Under the thirteenth-century code of regulation these were divided into over a dozen different groups, none of them having any official right to restrict entrance. Yet those in which one would expect to find mercantile elements or entrepreneurs—the cordwainers, saddlers, belt-makers, glovers and pursers—were distinguished by private fraternities, and the statutes for which they obtained approval embodied restrictions on night work and on the numbers of apprentices. The inflationary crisis of 1351 produced a royal decree abolishing these restrictions, but only for a separate group that made shoes. In hope of bringing prices down by directing more attention to increasing the supply of good cordwain, the decree called in addition for clear-cut specialization between the occupations of craftsman and merchant. Logical enough as a temporary measure, the policy would have given the merchants still more political support.

All types of French leather gilds, however, applied for the formal support of royal charters. In these they constantly asseverated their devotion to high standards of craftsmanship through strict specialization. If their charters were enforceable, they may in the fifteenth century have improved their position. Villagers who came to sell leather or shoes in Amiens, for example, were liable to be harassed by officials of the shoemakers and the cordwainers, who had legal authority to inspect their packs and to collect heavy fines if they judged the work to be below gild standards. By 1408 even country pedlars who came to cry a sack of *solers viez* about the streets were supposed to buy a licence. The exaction of expensive masterpieces as a condition of entrance to a leather gild came into vogue, serving to keep down the number of new entrants and also, as a matter of public-relations policy, to proclaim a reputation for skill that was not necessarily borne out by daily workshop performance.

In base metal work for local trade gild organization could have achieved little power over prices save in heavy casting, which called for skill and capital above the average, and in lines in which demand could be differentiated. Medieval uses of metal were so few that the latter were virtually limited to the arms trade. Otherwise demand sought only dead utilitarian quality. On the side of supply, town smiths were often at the disadvantage of being dependent on general wholesale merchants, men outside their gilds. Cartel buying of metal seems to have occurred only in times of peak prices and as a means of combating price conspiracy among merchants. Country competition was ubiquitous, and merchants also instigated competitive manufacture of light wares within the towns. The principal economic benefit that town smiths derived from organizing was economy through cartel buying of fuel, a cost item on which rural smiths had probably a distinct advantage. The saving achieved was maximized by the grouping of different kinds of specialist workers in large federal gilds, the sub-gilds each setting their own technical standards and agreeing not to trespass on each other's work in heavy casting or in other highly skilled lines. In good times these gilds were not ordinarily exclusive. The normal policy, set possibly under some pressure from town governments, was to accept immigrant applicants for membership as they appeared.

The evidence from gild records has chiefly to do with efforts to surmount the trade difficulties of the later Middle Ages. To begin with England, the difficulties of town smiths here stemmed from the sharp mid-fourteenth-century rise in labour costs, particularly as this affected smelting, in the neighbourhood of iron-mines. Parliamentary petitioners reckoned in 1354 that the price of bar iron had risen to four times its level of six years before. Subsequent attempts at price-fixing would have tended simply to diminish town supplies to the advantage of country smiths. Town smiths lost country business, and country-made products everywhere came onto town markets through the agency of the same merchants who provided the town artisans with iron and with imported steel. In London the ironmongers formed a merchant gild with far more political influence than smiths could muster. The latter could not feasibly even propose protection. They could not even retain enough spirit to organize federally. The strongest group among them, as one would expect, was that of the founders, who produced the heavier work. An action for price conspiracy was brought against them in 1504 in the Court of Star Chamber. The evidence adduced, however, was so confused that it points to only very clumsy and inefficient attempts at agreement. The pewterers were just strong enough to enlist the help of the mayor and aldermen in breaking a mid-fifteenth-century merchant corner in tin.

Other difficulties of the light metal-ware gilds in fifteenth-century London were opposite in cause from the high labour-cost problems of the previous century. They stemmed instead from the abundance of labour in the capital. Petty entrepreneurs in the gilds seized on the opportunity of putting out miscellaneous kinds of work—pins, wire and spurs —to be worked up by unenfranchised labour. Official gild policy tried to check this by appeal to the principle of specialization, of proper craft training. The spurriers invited this competition by working too slowly to keep up with the smiths who did the preliminary rough forging for them. In a bill of complaint addressed to the mayor in 1421 the gild asked for power to compel the smiths to deposit the half-finished work in a central depot that would be accessible only to the gild members. The bill gives an interesting description of the competing labour, slum 'chamberers', not householders, some of them women: '... they dwell in holks and hyrnes in hie sollers that they [sic] wardens may not see theym, and gothe oute of the Cittey to fayres and mayrketts and in to lords Innes and in to other privye places and sels such fals work in greate disceite hynderynge of all the comyn people and in greate dysclaunderynge of all the crafte'. Merchant magistrates who received appeals of this kind were not inclined to take action unless a gild could prove that tax-paying householders and servants in its membership were being driven out of business. In that event it was a London policy to grant the gildsmen a legal priority in piece-work.

In France, metal gilds were so widely dispersed that the country industry does not appear to have gained on them as it did in fourteenth-century England. Competition was felt, however, from the import of German iron for industrial use. In 1382 the Rouen wire-makers appealed to the king for protection and for authority to enforce common regulations throughout Normandy. Records of the attempts to enforce the

regional controls bring to light the existence of little pockets of hereditary right. At Bellencombie, for example, the gildsmen were entrepreneurs putting work out to their servants. In 1416 they were trying to
prevent independently minded workers who had migrated to the neighbourhood of lower-cost ore diggings from evading their regulations.
Normally one would assume that complaints emanating from local
quarrels of this kind would exaggerate the issues, especially in painting a
picture of prior harmony or stability. Yet a statement by the Norman
smiths in 1406 that their craft was peculiar (*estrange*) in that their servants
knew no other (*les gens qui en ouvrent ne sauroient vivre d'autre mestier*) is
arresting. Intended to prove that hereditary privilege was essential to
them, it implies that production was customarily so restricted that serious
cut-backs, driving workers to try their hand at other skills, were unknown. If men in other crafts were more versatile, it was certainly in part
because of irregular slack periods arising from over-production. How
long Norman gild organization under the direction of small-town entrepreneurs had been able to maintain such stability is not clear.

Among the more specialized French metal gilds the armourers had
probably most influence to back them. The Paris *heaumiers* in 1418 won
exemption from taxation on the claim, airily asserted, that they made a
profit only in war time. Since knightly customers often broke their
wares in testing them before purchase, on the whole they made no profit
at all, they said, or *tres po de chose*. Gilds specializing in the manufacture
of light metal wares experienced some strain in this century from the
heightened flow of trade through the hands of mercers and other general
dealers. These men sought the cheapest sources of supply, regardless of
gild reputation. Petty entrepreneurs put material out to be worked up
under the same conditions as existed in the London slum tenements.
Gilds constantly complained that these practices were contrary to the
public interest, in producing goods of poor quality. They seem to have
hesitated to exercise rights of inspection, however, save in a search for
second-hand goods refurbished for sale as new. Their position was therefore very weak, for live-wire competitors could then legally evade inspection by representing new goods as second-hand. At Amiens makers
of bread-boxes and other small chests that they fitted with cheap locks
foiled the locksmiths by simply putting a piece of bread in a box, taking
it out, and selling the box as second-hand.

The German town gilds, so long as they could keep heavy work under
their control, were at first indifferent to competition in light wares.
Goslar gild statutes of the year 1320 envisage no exclusive rights for
members, even against country smiths, in the latter. The statutes list over
fifty articles according as they were reserved for gild manufacture or not.
Anyone, in or out of the gild, was free to make nails, hooks and hasps,

locks and keys, cooking-grills, curry-combs, hatchets, hay-forks, the spokes and tyres of wheels, and small hammers valued up to a shilling. Only gildsmen were to forge mining-picks, harrows, weighing-scales, helms for boats, window-grills, scythes, shovels, and other heavy tools. A century later, country competition was being taken more seriously. The Hildesheim gild tried to have country smiths excluded from selling any-thing at all in the town, and was successful in having them relegated to the periodic 'free' markets. The next step was to build regional alliances among town gilds. Goslar and Hildesheim joined with over twenty other towns, including Brunswick and Magdeburg and smaller places, in gild agreements that were mainly designed to keep down labour costs. The agreements were incidentally a means of tightening lax organization in the smaller towns. Wherever possible the German gilds went on to extend policies of alliance to country smiths. Agreements dealt with labour policy and with seasonal restriction of output through the observance of equivalent holiday periods. In some districts of Ger-many, and in Switzerland, country smiths were already organizing on their own account, under the authority of territorial lords.

One would expect to find smiths' gilds in a fairly favourable position in Italy, because of the heavy concentration of artisan population in the towns and because the gilds had legal authority over the whole of a com-mune's territory. On the other hand, constant involvement in the arms trade must have made it difficult to exercise any calculated control over output. Fortunately, Italian records are full enough to penetrate the façade of legal regulation. A long series of documents preserved at Modena illustrates, dramatically and statistically, the actual problems that officers of the local smiths' gilds had to confront. Membership records beginning in 1306 show a total enrolment of about 300 masters and *discipuli*, representing 92% of the smiths in the city and its territory. Most of them lived in the city, specializing in heavy foundry work or in swords or knives for general export. From the point of view of gild power the figures suggest a satisfactory enough situation, but the margin between the supply price of metal and the wholesale selling price of knives was not allowing a satisfactory profit. Over the next few decades the industry was steadily on the decline, until by the middle of the cen-tury the gild had little to rely on securely but local trade. Labour was fluid and membership fell, but the adjustment was far from smooth. The majority of the hundred or so masters left in the 1350's were small men determined to use their voting power in the gild to fight for survival and to prevent the concentration of the industry in the hands of the larger men. By a vote of 64 to 3, a two-thirds quorum upheld the liberality of licensing entry to the trade that had endured for at least a century. There was no regulation of apprenticeship, and anyone known to have had

S

training could set up a workshop on payment of a small fee to the gild. The officers then turned to the use of individual trade-marks as a means of control over output. A rule that had not hitherto been enforced required all masters to stamp their work with an individual mark registered, for a fee, with the gild. Many of the town masters either had no mark or refused to pay for registering it. A conflict was precipitated that nearly wrecked the gild. Threatened with ruinous fines and with confiscation of their wares, the rebels appealed to the city captain for justice. The party standing for restriction won a legal victory, a civil lawyer appointed to arbitrate in the dispute in 1366 deciding that marks were for the common good; but for a century thereafter the gild's authority was in practice very feeble. Its economic power must have been negligible.

Already in 1362 a group of smiths from Bologna was settling in the city and suburbs, competing for local trade in defiance of gild rules. The officers spent £10 to induce them to join, without effect. By the 1420's membership in Modena city had fallen to about sixty working smiths, masters and servants, with a few merchants and fifteen other Modena citizens, who were not connected with the trade but used the gild as a club. Since the 1370's it had leased a house as headquarters. In 1438 the gild's weakness appeared in the pathetic misfiring of action taken against a merchant from Mantua, presumably for breaking gild prices in some direction. The man had so much influence at the Este court that he had to be invited to settle in Modena. In the same year it was reported that itinerant smiths, strangers, were travelling about Modena territory, selling and working at their will without regard for the gild's traditional holidays. After a vote of 37 to 4 for taking action against them a statute was entered on the gild books claiming a monopoly in the sale of all new work in iron and copper, outsiders selling to be fined £10. The town crier was hired to proclaim the statute but that it banished the pedlars seems doubtful, for the saddlers' gild took five years to acknowledge its legality.

The internal discipline of the Modena smiths' gild must have remained low until the sixteenth century, when it began absorbing outside groups as *obedientes*. The ultimate sanction of gild rules was always expulsion, carrying exclusion from benefits and social ostracism. This could have been no great penalty for fifteenth-century members. In 1450, although total membership was now rising, the proportion of the town smiths choosing not to join was high, 23%, much higher than in 1306. The sole economic advantages in belonging consisted in intermittent opportunities of sharing in large purchases of good-quality fuel and in the chance of an occasional bread dole in hard times.

An unusually large country membership was listed in 1450: 41 men in 23 different villages and *borghi*, making up 29% of the gild's total roll of 140. This may not have included all the smiths in the territory, for in 1339 names had been counted from 38 localities. In any event, the country smiths were enrolled only sporadically. They could have derived little benefit from belonging and the gild's touch with them was tenuous.

In the remaining industries to be considered, conditions on the whole set more clear-cut bounds to gild opportunities of economic power. Restrictive policies in textile industries primarily concerned export trade, and will be viewed under that heading.

In wood-working, almost the only strong medieval gilds were those of coopers, or barrel-makers. In any town where goods were shipped by water their services were so important that, when a gild appeared, it readily obtained a monopoly for its members in return for guaranteeing sound workmanship. In London the gild could prosecute even a merchant for infringing the monopoly. Prices varied with costs, and were affected by competition only remotely, according as merchants might be aware of trade rivals in neighbouring towns being able to order barrels more cheaply. There is evidence that coopers sometimes planned to push prices up by slowing production, trying to hide their policy behind the need of special kinds of wood supply and long seasoning. Their merchant customers would then bring prices down by threatening to take over the industry themselves. In fifteenth-century Lüneburg the gild repeatedly overdid the cut-backs that must have been necessitated by decline of the local salt trade. What broke up each restrictive agreement here was incipient competition among the members. By 1479 the men habitually stopped work at noon every day. At this point the town council ordered a lowering of prices, under threat of organizing competitive production through the merchants of the town. The gild protested at length that there was not enough wood, that merchants could not fairly be allowed to trench on scarce supply. Lüneburg's general prospects were at the time so discouraging that nothing was done, and in 1490 the town council legalized the afternoon lay-off. At Dunkirk, in 1515, when the gild raised prices, the merchants had enough enterprise to make their own barrels with hired labour. The gild, counting on the town lord's reluctance to lose tax-paying citizens, tried to stop them by threatening secession. All forty-six of its members, it professed, were faced with ruin; without protection they would have to abandon the town (*aller refuger ailleurs*). But the lord would concede only that they might collect gild entry fees from the competitors.

It was in respect of the basic victualling trades that the public authorities were most responsive to anti-gild sentiment. The conditions of medieval food-supply made for perennial anxious suspicion of fraud in every branch of the trade. Given the low crop yields of the age, and the poor storage and transport facilities, harvest variations necessarily brought violent fluctuations of price, fluctuations frequently of several hundred per cent from one season to another. In the bad years the towns were the worse off because any efforts to hold prices down led country producers to withhold supply. At the same time country labourers tended to flock into the towns to beg. Dealers and retailers alike then became objects of hatred, everyone suspecting them of being in collusion to drive prices ever higher. As a London chronicler wrote, of the scarcity of 1438, 'that made Bakers lordes, but I pray God lette us never see that Day no more if hit be his will'. A ban on speculative dealing was felt to be morally expedient, and the universal institution of open markets, where there could be periodic official proclamation of just and legal prices, helped to allay the effects of false rumours of scarcity. The autonomy of gilds was severely restricted, and any long-continued upward price trends would lead public officials to take over their functions.

The degree of monopoly power that butchers obtained was quite exceptional. Where their gilds remained strong, it was partly because their ability to tap the remoter regional channels of supply was recognized, after all, to be a service. The only other victuallers who approached their position were the great wholesale importers of fish, who controlled retail distribution through subordinate gilds, and through street vendors. But since fish was the food of the poor, price combination was politically too dangerous ever to last long. In fresh fish, as opposed to the dried and salted imports, there were usually too many separate sources of supply for any one group to have a monopoly. What the retailing gilds aimed at was to control the best market locations and the better quality fish, and to assert a priority in buying from wholesalers when supply was short. The smaller French towns checked them in the fourteenth century by diverting wholesale shipments through the hands of a public broker who was responsible for fair division of supply, at a fixed rate of commission, among all the local retailers. In Paris and the other larger towns the gilds were made to appoint brokers with this function. There were many little gilds in France and Germany with a monopoly of fishing certain local waters, but these were probably more often merely pleasant social institutions, intended to assure members of a family supply, than means to market power.

In the northern countries there were possibilities of monopoly power in the wine trade, but only for the great importing gilds. For numerous police considerations taverners and innkeepers were not normally allowed to organize in any country. Covert price combination was checked by the regular setting of maximum retail prices for wine, so that consumers were free to have anyone prosecuted for overcharging.

Bakers' gilds occupied a very curious and difficult position. So few medieval town houses were equipped with ovens that even the well-to-do, although they usually had their own grain supply from country estates and a servant who could mix dough, had to send it out to be baked, and the poor were absolutely dependent on bought bread. If only from suspicion of enhancing prices through limiting oven construction (a scheme that appears to have succeeded in thirteenth-century Pontoise, under an indiscreetly generous royal charter granted in 1162, and was said to have been attempted in late fifteenth-century Cologne) gild affairs would have been liable to periodic investigation. But from fear also that they would exploit and enrage the public in time of scarcity, bakers were subjected to an ingenious system of control, or assize, that tied the price of bread to the price of grain. The system is outlined in Carolingian legislation, and its first adoption in urban administration cannot be dated. In theory it made the baker a public servant operating under rates of return fixed by the community, but in practice, owing to inefficiencies and laxity, it worked very unevenly.

It was a regular defect of the system that it could not take precise account of the top-quality trade, in which the better bakers probably made their chief bread profits. The weight of a loaf of standard price was supposed to vary inversely with the price of grain, an allowance being made for bakers' costs, but the tables that were calculated could not cover all fancy types of loaf. Bread had to be very fine to please foreign merchants and other travellers, said the bakers of Harfleur in 1388, and the lightness and whiteness of Parisian bread were already boasted. Inspection of the weight and pricing of loaves was carried out by town officials in a random fashion, with enough infliction of fines to yield a revenue that was in effect a tax on the trade, but a tax without a fixed basis. In Italy imposition of the fines was sometimes farmed out, like any other tax. A corollary defect of the system was its invitation to corruption. It was alleged at Piacenza in 1190 that bakers made bread for sale of any weight they chose, bribing the officials to let them alone, and incidents of the kind can often be uncovered. The *bailli* of Rouen had apparently not been enforcing the regulations at all before 1406, when public indignation over high prices forced him to act. He ordered a trial baking of the flour from a quarter of wheat, which was the means of estimating costs. This particular trial proved nothing, since the bakers in charge burned the bread, and it was only more urgent *plaintes et clameurs*, two years later, that brought controls into operation.

It was a third defect of the system that when, in years of scarcity, controls had to be applied strictly, there was apt to be a lag in the adjustment of allowances for costs. In consequence the bakers might for a time be expected to take a loss. In England they had genuine grounds for grievance because the allowance was based in part on monetary estimates fixed by the central government in the thirteenth century and not revised after 1303 except through local agitation. Coventry bakers won a slight increase in 1484, but only after staging a secession from the town. At one point in fifteenth-century Dijon, however, protest was temporarily silenced by a warning that a group of merchants was prepared to take over the industry on the basis of cost estimates that the gild had rejected.

The power of bakers' gilds to enhance prices was probably limited to the fancy trade, which in turn was likely to be limited to seasons of plenty. In Paris, when grain was short, the use of the finer grade of white flour was forbidden. The gilds could also exercise some degree of 'monopsony' power in buying, either through publicly accorded privilege in a grain or meal market, or on their own initiative through negotiation with millers. The latter were seldom if ever so strongly organized as the bakers. On the other hand, the bakers' gilds were exposed to a good deal of competition from groups of suburban and country bakers. Town governments in Italy and elsewhere, to the gilds' indignation, often exempted these competitors from fines as a matter of policy. Suburban Paris bakers who, according to their spokesmen, had served the mass of the city's population in the *Halles* from time out of mind unmolested, *pour tel pris come ils en pevent avoir*, in 1372 accused the gild of bribing the provost's market officials to harass them. At York in 1482 the gild alleged that country bread was made with chalk, badly leavened and underweight. The further allegation that, because it was not inspected, competitors were able to set up in business in the town without joining the gild, evading inspection by calling their product country bread, sounds plausible.

In other victualling trades the gilds were much weaker, with less autonomy and, often, more competition. Gardeners, fruiterers and others experimented hopefully with price combination but could never control all sources of supply. Chandlers, cheesemongers and import merchants competed with them, and street vendors abounded.

Gilds had small scope in the building trades, chiefly because municipalities, being substantial property owners, were prepared to use coercion to keep down costs of construction and maintenance. Organization among tilers, lime-burners and paviours was often suppressed, and the holding of 'parliaments' forbidden. Up to 1397 carpenters and masons in Cologne were permitted to form only fraternities, with the injunction that they were not to harass strangers seeking work. English evidence suggests that building gilds would in any event have tended to be weakened by conflicts of interest between contractors and labourers. The London masons' gild in the fifteenth century was a loose and half-hearted organization controlled by the contractors.

The conditions of the transport services, for which municipalities, again, and merchants provided the heaviest demand, were also unfavourable to gild organization, yet allowed some curious exceptions. The unloading of wine-ships was one of the little pockets of privilege that survived in Paris in the guise of an *office*, as opposed to that of *metier*. Membership was limited, and patronage was in the hands of the merchants' provost. The salt-carriers of Riga won the same degree of autonomy as other gilds at the cost of undertaking to serve as the town fire brigade. The wine-carters of Rouen had recognition as a gild, and were so sure of their position that in 1409 they lodged complaint against an outsider who was giving better service to merchants at half the gild rates. The town council merely commended the competitor.

To sum up this survey, then, in any medieval town, at any given time, the various gilds would have been strung out along the scale of economic power, with most of them bunched in positions in which they could have exercised little or no influence on selling-prices in local trade. It may be true that all at times sought to raise prices, especially in their better-class trade, or at least to maintain them against downward pressure. Barbers in fourteenth-century Italy would set a minimum price for a shave. But direct evidence of price policies in a local industry, or of their success, is rare. Contemporary charges of price conspiracy will be found to cluster in years of inflation of money supply or of abnormal scarcity of goods, when it would have been difficult to prove a case against a gild. The historian has therefore to fall back on evidence that points to restrictive policies, and this is seldom conclusive. For example, the raising of gild entry fees would seem to be obviously restrictive, yet in times of prosperity it may not have been so, even in intent. When the Amiens *tonneliers* raised their entry fee from 10s. to 40s., in 1488, they were increasing their numbers and expanding production in response to new demand from the local wine industry. Moreover, they had let the fee stand at the lower level for 200 years. Fifteenth-century gild objections to the competition of *forinseci* and aliens were certainly restrictive in intent, but it is well to recall that they were occasioned partly by inequities of taxation. Many of them come from years when towns were beginning to grow again after long stagnation or decline of population. Under north European systems of urban administration, if new immigrants were ineligible for citizenship or were loth to take it up, then the burden of taxation, and the expenses of defence and police work, could fall with new and disproportionate severity on citizen gildsmen. It was on this score that the London common council of 1474–5 sympathized with the haberdashers and hurers. Outside competition in their trade of cap-making, it was said, had brought their numbers down to 'right fewe', and had filled tenements formerly occupied by tax-paying citizens with non-taxpayers.

The key restrictive policies were those that bore on the supply of skill. From the thirteenth century on, opponents of the gilds accused them of abusing the power of regulating apprenticeship. In so doing, artisans would only have been following the example of the great merchant gilds, than whom, at least in German and English towns, no groups were more shrewdly restrictive. There is no doubt that artisan gilds favourably placed, such as goldsmiths, saddlers, butchers and the like, developed carefully calculated policies in regard to admission through apprenticeship. In many other gild trades, too, a ban on the enticing away of another man's apprentices, and the fact that there was a market for the unserved years of apprentices' terms, attest to labour scarcity. But a number of other circumstances, besides gild organization, helped to produce this result. Medieval artisan apprenticeship was a product, not of gild monopoly, but of the family workshop. It was the simplest means by which small masters could find cheap help to supplement that of the family circle. Yet it had certain inconveniences. Under medieval conditions of life expectancy, the death rate among young apprentices was very high. Scarcity could often have been due to a neighbourhood epidemic. Moreover, boys sent far from their home were apt to be restless. Fifteenth-century London evidence shows that in merchant gilds, in which boys were apprenticed at the age of twelve or fourteen, barely half of them completed a seven-year term of service. The rest either died or dropped out in discouragement, some of them running away. Artisans, who bound apprentices younger, must also have lost many by death, and in Paris as well as in London there is evidence of the problem of the runaway. In many trades labour supply was supplemented by the hiring of servants who had not necessarily served an apprenticeship, but even so, the majority of artisans, in or out of gilds, seem not to have kept more than two helpers besides their wife and their own young children.

Gild rules had ordinarily not much effect on this situation. When they imposed limitation it was usually with a cautious eye to braking what the older masters considered too rash an expansion, and the limitation was often modified on a sliding scale according to a master's status in the gild. Even so, the richer men tended, especially if there was any regional export market to be developed, to exceed the number of employees officially allowed them.

The conclusion that most gild organization had little influence on selling-prices in local trade does not exclude the possibility of some slight increment through collective bidding for customers' goodwill. Most gilds forbade their members to sink to street peddling, because of its low repute. The essence of their public relations policy was a plea for solidarity among people of good repute. Men were admitted to gild mastership only after some inquiry into character, on the assumption that they could thereafter be trusted to do reliable work. There was no claim that all gild work would be of first-class quality, but only that if you bought from a gild member his goods would meet reasonable expectations. The term used to convey this idea was 'loyal'. A gild of locksmiths would make only loyal keys, and gild pastry-cooks in Paris would use only loyal eggs.

IV. *Gild Influence in Export Industry*

The same circumstances that varied and limited gild economic power in local urban trade applied also in much of the regional export trade that medieval towns conducted in miscellaneous manufactures. In France and England and in western Germany it was a continuing custom for town artisans, both in and out of gilds, occasionally to accumulate a stock and take it to country fairs to sell. Some gildsmen specialized as merchants, constantly visiting fairs. Conservative gild opinion nevertheless looked askance on the custom, for the wide-open competition at fairs pulled prices down, and the barring of gild jurisdiction made it difficult to build up any special goodwill for gild trade. Gild jurisdiction over standards of goods exposed at fairs held ordinarily only for goldsmithing. All that most gilds could do towards control of this haphazard flow of exports was to insist that their members' goods be inspected before leaving the town. There was difficulty in enforcing the rule, and it was impossible to check all merchants' shipments or the trade that filtered out in pedlars' packs. Several of the London metal and leather gilds paid to have their rights of search extended to fairs by royal charter, and in the fifteenth century London merchant gilds led a movement to ban all citizen gilds from selling at fairs at all.

A certain fringe of miscellaneous urban export trade entered the great *Fernhandel* routes by way of special orders placed with individual artisans by visiting foreign merchants who were in a position to vary their return cargoes. These orders may often have escaped any special gild surveillance, and would have been subject to gild influence on pricing only in the better lines of metal- and leather-work. Textiles, if they were in export demand, came under firm control either by merchants or by gilds.

The unique problems of gild influence on manufacturing for export were peculiar to the great textile and metal industries, which tapped continent-wide markets for their raw materials, and for which export demand regularly exceeded any local demand. The structure of these industries could differ widely from that of typical small local industries, and they offered a correspondingly diverse field for gild action. In place of casual selling by semi-migratory artisans, export outlets were controlled by wholesale merchants. These men's relations with the artisan were of two general types. Either they contracted to take the output of groups of independent producers, or, playing the role of entrepreneur, they organized production themselves on the putting-out system. The latter was characteristic of fine textiles, in which the elaborate division of labour called for a co-ordinating figure, and it could occur also in metals, as in the Norman wire industry. The independent producer was more common in the metal trades, in which there was less division of labour, and could be found also in the coarser textiles.

Under the putting-out system several different kinds of gilds emerged. The merchant entrepreneurs, who were organizing export from at least the twelfth century, were slow to form special industrial gilds. Their social position and their relations as wholesale merchants brought them ample support from town authorities in shaping technical standards and in trying to keep down labour costs. Many of the gilds that came to be formed around the entrepreneurial interest consisted of a socially inferior type of entrepreneur, of men who rose within the industry and who retained personal charge of some one process in it. Only later, usually after a period of repression, were gilds permitted among the dependent piece-workers. The clash of interests between these and the entrepreneurs on the score of labour costs was confused by a tendency for petty entre-preneurship and petty trade to emerge in every branch of an industry. There existed, in effect, mixed gilds. There were mixed gilds also among the independent artisans, merchants agreeing to be tied by membership to the gilds with which they contracted.

The net economic influence of medieval gilds on the growth of long-distance trade at the level of manufacturing depends on the answer to two questions. The first refers to phases of expansion of trade. Did the gilds contribute to efficient use of resources at such times? The second concerns the problems of adjustment that arose in phases of contraction of trade, in particular when an industrial centre suffered a loss of com-petitive power. This question has been often discussed as though nothing were at issue but a rise in labour costs forced upon an industry as a result of political agitation by artisan gilds. Yet the disadvantage of a rise in labour costs is a matter of historical contingency, dependent on the general movement of all costs in all the competing centres, and the long-run survival of any export industry depends on ingenuity in compensat-ing for loss of advantage at one point by economical innovation in other directions. The record of the gilds in these respects is in many directions still obscure.

In one important particular, that of promoting the standardization of products on which export trade had to build, gilds of all types may be credited with constructive policies. True, they did not introduce the principle. It was a matter of economic necessity, and sanctioned by a sense of moral duty to the community. Merchants were obliged to reject cloth that was not of standard gauge and uniform finish as fit only for local sale. At Chartres, lest the reputation of the town be endangered, defective cloth was assigned to be cut up for sale to the poorer local tailors. At Beauvais there is an instance, in 1309, of the public authorities invoking penitential sanctions against a careless worker. At Eu, in Normandy, two of the town's principal merchants were expelled from the council of magistrates for handling sub-standard cloth and were declared for ever ineligible for re-election. The objective of building up a special demand for the products of one's town, symbolized by the use of town seals as trade-marks, was well understood.

To combine the requisite standardization of skill with flexible control over output and alertness in retaining cost advantages over competing centres was difficult in the extreme. The easiest course was to try to create a special upper-class demand that would be fairly inelastic and to maintain constant restrictive powers over output. In the case of goods for which there was a wider and more elastic demand this policy was not feasible. The mercantile interest then inclined towards drawing labour in freely while business was good, forcing masters to train it as fast as possible, and letting wage-workers and the smaller masters look for some other occupation when business was poor; but any well-developed gild-system would mobilize resistance to this on the score of security. Even gilds of artisan entrepreneurs preferred to modify it by a modicum of mutual aid that would help as large a group as possible to tide over bad times.

The metal trades offer many examples of gilds relying on restrictive policies, although, as the story of friction among the smiths of Modena has shown, to apply restriction after any prolonged boom in the arms trade was not easy. The most successful of the metal gilds were those making copper vessels, at Dinant and at Bouvignes. The location of the industry here can be accounted for only by the proximity of good clay for moulds, the copper coming, at first, from Goslar. The Dinant gild was formed by artisans who in 1265 won the right to control the conditions under which they worked for the merchant entrepreneurs. Despite crises that broke the connection with Goslar, the manufacture continued to prosper for over a century. There was a switch to English copper, and new markets were found in northern France and in England. Decline came only with a loss of markets towards the end of the fourteenth century from which the gild industries never fully recovered. Dinant merchants remaining in the business joined the gild, and there was probably restriction of output along the same lines that were adopted in Bouvignes. The Bouvignes gild, which had a legal monopoly of all the clay diggings in the county of Namur, acquired in 1375 the right to limit annual output per man and to hold workshop staffs down to seven men per master. On the basis of an eight-man force, annual output could be 8,000 pounds of small wares or 5,000 pounds in cauldrons. The extent of putting out to smaller masters was controlled, and all production plans were to be submitted to gild officers for approval half a year in advance. Few apprentices were taken, and admission to mastership was reserved for men born in Bouvignes or marrying daughters of masters. There must have been some revival of trade in the 1440's, for apprenticeship rules were then relaxed. But since admission to mastership was made no easier, apprentices from outside Bouvignes took to returning home to set up in competitive business. The Bouvignes gild absorbed a group at Namur, the chief competitive centre in that county, in a price cartel. It had the satisfaction of seeing the Dinant gild temporarily put out of business by the military sack of the city in 1466, but only to find that dispersal of Dinant workers gave a permanent stimulus to village industry.

If political circumstances had favoured a wider regional alliance, these copper gilds might have held their own a little longer. But by the end of the fifteenth century a long-run rise in fuel costs was in many places reducing urban metal trades to work in small wares. Gild organization could not have altered the situation and was certainly not responsible for it.

A similar trend towards rural dispersal, consequent on increased use of water power in heavier production, was to weaken the gilds that were concerned with export in the German iron and steel trades. These gilds had helped to concentrate industry in the towns and had served the interests of merchants and of artisans harmoniously in standardizing export quality, but they could not retain control of new expansion into larger-scale production. The smaller members were interested in gild acquisition of new facilities if there could be collective use of them, but it was seldom possible to exploit water power to fullest advantage in the immediate neighbourhood of towns. Capital came to be applied more by individuals choosing dispersed sites. Being able to contact merchants for export sale independently, these men had no economic need of gild membership. But the whole movement was extremely slow. At Siegen, in Nassau, the merchants (*Reidemeisters*) still belonged to the steel-smiths' gild at the close of the fifteenth century and could be appealed to for help in disciplining recalcitrant artisan members. It was not until the end of the sixteenth century that there is evidence of any conflict between the gild and a body of outside *Reidemeisters* dealing with country producers. But the town *Reidemeisters* were still among the richest of the burghers, and the separate gild of *Kleinschmieder* was the second richest gild in the town. This typifies the general trend, expansion in high-quality small wares in specialized workshops continuing under gild auspices. In small centres gilds without merchant members were on occasion conducted somewhat like Russian 'artels', negotiating for sale of the collective output to outside merchants.

Gild influence on the development and maintenance of export power in the textile industry was very mixed. The fact that cloth could be made at home, and that local peasant-made cloth was almost universally available, made export trade peculiarly dependent on upper-class demand and hence on superior skill. Gilds of any type could only too readily decide to rest on a special limited market and they were pushed into making changes only as international competition became disturbing. Once they had learned that rapid expansion was risky, artisans who lacked capital and had no other skilled trade to fall back upon favoured extreme caution, using gild regulation of quality as a means of restricting output. Lopez has shown how it was actually the collapse, after a brief boom, of cloth export from mid-thirteenth-century Genoa that led to firm establishment there of gild authority over weaving. Merchants were ready enough to deal with artisan gilds if business was steady or expanding slowly, but if they became impatient to expand faster they would be inclined to break through earlier gild regulation, bringing the industry under entrepreneurial control. This occurred in thirteenth-century Aragon, where merchants in the course of widening their markets were enabled to draw in more capital from trade and from landed nobles. The reaching out from a small regional export into international markets often entailed the need for further improvement of quality, a step that artisan gilds might be slow to take without sharp pressure. England offers prime examples of obstinacy in this regard. The London weavers' gild, discouraged by fall in demand for its old-fashioned product, took to impounding looms at the death of members. Between 1290 and 1321 the number in operation was reduced from approximately 300 to 80. The surviving members hoped then to shelter under a renewal of the gild's ancient royal charter of monopoly. But in actually destroying looms they had aroused indignation and probably gave a stimulus to new competition. Merchants were advised by the city authorities to ignore the charter. Consequently they hastened to employ the cheaper and more adaptable labour that was arriving from France and from Flanders.

Export power was frequently developed through the initiative of entrepreneurs of the type of the *granz mestres* who controlled the woollen industry of Paris. They may be classed as artisan entrepreneurs in that membership in their gild was based on purchase from the king of an industrial right, the right to weave and to dye, and because they supervised work in their own households. According to mid-thirteenth-century regulations that were registered as approved, they limited their capacity by agreement to nine looms for a master in business with a brother and a nephew plus three more for each unmarried son. Some of their weaving was probably done by 'valets', for wages, and the rest was put out to *menuz mestres*. A family firm keeping a dozen looms in operation would have had business equivalent to that of the middling *lanioli* in fourteenth-century Florence, providing employment, in all, including spinners, to about forty people. The Paris gild had corporate ownership of two dye-houses, but these were not adequate to handle their whole output.

Entrepreneurs of this type carried corporate action to its furthest limits in Italy. The woollen gild in Florence achieved probably the maximum labour-saving use of water power that could have been found in any medieval textile centre, along with supreme efficiency in standardizing quality at a high level. No two of the Italian woollen gilds were identical in their structure, but nearly all acted to some extent as production and sales cartels.

This raising of productive power through investment and through convenient arrangement of technical facilities, including transport services, was a contribution of very definite economic value. The Italians believed gild organization in an industry with a complex division of labour to be of service also as a clearing-house in internal business relationships. Fifteenth-century Visconti policy, in seeking to make Milan the chief Italian centre of silk manufacture, did not use gild organization in the first instance because it was necessary to lure firms from other cities by promise of special personal privileges. Once men had been attracted to set up in the business in Milan, privileges were extended on a gild basis and a gild court was authorized with jurisdiction over small debts.

The final and most searching test of the value of gilds for export power in textiles came with phases of trade recession, and especially in regions such as Flanders and northern France in the late thirteenth century, that were being caught after long prosperity in unfavourable market conjunctures. The record of the Flemish artisan gilds is stormy and miserable because they emerged only as a means of resisting the entrepreneurs' efforts in these circumstances to lower their labour costs. Gildsmen may have contributed to a solution of the hard technical problems that were involved in turning to the use of cheaper types of wool. But gild organization cannot be credited with solving the economic problems of the industry, which ultimately shifted to smaller centres. By then, much of the old gild membership had emigrated to other countries. The depleted gilds survived, clinging to a residual business, chiefly local.

The woollen industries of France having been less highly developed, crises were felt less acutely. French textile gilds settled into policies of constant cautious restriction, the wisdom of which is difficult to assess without quantitative data. In Paris, for example, the provost as early as 1270 placed on record his displeasure with the *granz mestres* for the fact that royal customs revenue on their trade had ceased to grow, and for the closing of their gild mastership to all but their sons. Minor gilds of the artisans on piece-work, too, were trying to close their ranks. Through the provost's intervention collective bargaining was instituted, and weavers' rates were fixed by a contract that allowed no provision for change. There was a ban on truck, the employers' device for lowering rates. By 1287 the industry must have been in genuine trouble, for it was alleged that half the valets seeking work often went unemployed. In the next decade fullers' rates were said to have been depressed by a third to a half through payment in truck. The gild did not embody immediate strong resistance to the cut, for masters at first simply passed it on to their *menuz ouvriers*. Finally the dyers' gild was obliged to bring its rates down to the level of country dyers.

This last move illustrates a constructive arrangement that many late medieval gilds containing small or large entrepreneurs among their members attempted. There was some resort, when an industry needed to stiffen its competitive power, to country workers. Through country spinning, dyeing and mill fulling a fairly stable symbiosis between urban and rural industry could be effected. Thirteenth-century Winchester and fifteenth-century York and London offer examples.

In the cotton and linen industries that were developing export power in southern Germany and Switzerland in the fifteenth century the attempts of town artisan gilds to bring political pressure to bear against village competition aroused retaliatory organization among the village workers. Merchant entrepreneurs, who were here outside gild ranks, then simply played town labour against country labour to the end of keeping production costs as low as possible. Gild organization may be said to have co-operated involuntarily.

V. *Gild Influence on Investment and Innovation*

Comparison of the role of gilds in relation to local trade and to export markets sets in clear relief the range of economic effort that they represented. The great majority of gild members working for local markets were at any given time, in respect of workshop output, very near the bottom of the scale of artisan productivity for their day. Gildsmen in export industry, on the other hand, could reach the peak of productivity for their day. They could enlarge workshop staffs up to the limits of convenient personal supervision and they could have the use of gild mills and other equipment at low cost. By these means and by putting materials out on contract with small masters and women workers they were enabled both to increase quantitative output of small wares and to raise efficiency through the integration of related processes. At both extremes gild organization helped, through cartel action in buying and selling and through collective effort in creating goodwill among consumers, to widen profit-margins. This fact gives point to the question that in one form or another has teased all gild historians: why did the medieval gilds not give a greater stimulus to economic life? Why did they not go further in promoting either collective or individual investment? Is the timidity so often observable in their policies best explained by emphasis on external conditions making for sluggish demand and high risk, or by the social relationships that were set up within a gild, or by beliefs and principles that detracted from imaginative innovation?

The problem of whether or not to enlarge productive power was often before medieval gild and town assemblies. French and Italian textile men were familiar with the possibilities of water power applied to fulling from the twelfth century. Many French textile gilds for long took the line that it was suitable only for rough work, and they were slow both in trying cheap coarse production and in adapting mills to finer work. Sluggish market prospects may well have justified their stand. Royal officials who in 1379 were trying to make Rouen accept cloth-workers displaced by the wars used the argument that a larger trading and industrial population would itself help to generate trade (*car plus a en un lieu, Ville et pais, de bons ouvriers et marchandises . . . plus est chose proffitable*). Both town and gild authorities were sceptical and grudging. Near the end of the next century the gilds here were suffering from the competition of mills in the neighbourhood. In 1494, at a time when 500 artisans were said to lack work, a town assembly met to discuss what should be done. No plans were ready for opening up new markets, which would have been requisite if more mills were to be constructed. One speaker, who perhaps had a touch of the revolutionary egalitarianism that had flared up two centuries before among Flemish artisans in distress, urged flatly that mills should be open to all, or else be destroyed.

The idea of equality in gild circles referred to independence, not to absolute equality of income. Equality of income was never a rule of practice except among gild brokers, who were in effect public functionaries. Coal and wine brokers in Arras made a practice of dividing their takings evenly, and fish brokers in Amiens petitioned in 1440 for equal turns in selling, *ad fin de equalité estre gardee entre lesditz grossiers et que chacun puist vivre*. The brewers of Eu in 1483 used the same language in regard to fair rationing of grain in time of scarcity, when they too would properly consider themselves public functionaries. All other types of gild took for granted a certain spread in the scale of operations. In local trade the top masters in a gild might have at least five times the amount of workshop help that the poorer men could keep, and would increase their income by auxiliary trade in the materials of the craft and by occasional deals in the staple commodities of the region. Export business widened the spread. The labour force of fifteenth-century London pewterers ranged from a merchant's staff of eighteen to a master working alone.

The output of the Florentine *lanioli* in 1382 is estimated to have run from 21 pieces in the year to 210.

It was possible for a gild to be consciously conservative in its policies from attachment to the democratic equality of independence. Lejeune has shown how the small drapers of sixteenth-century Liège voted against improved looms, for fear that expenditure on these, giving a cumulative advantage to the richer men, would cost them their independence. They far preferred independence in a small slow-moving business to the prospect of working under the direction of great merchant entrepreneurs in a thriving export trade. The same determination pervaded the gilds in local catering in Liège at this time.

A similar temper may have obstructed investment and innovation in small medieval towns, but evidence of comparable episodes is rare. There seems not to be any exact medieval parallel to the stubborn conservatism of small artisan gilds in the sixteenth century, a period when they had greatly multiplied in skilled trades and could reinforce each other's influence. Much urban mill construction was undertaken by landlord interests during early phases of town growth, before gilds were well established. The bishop of Beauvais had financed the construction of fulling-mills before the end of the twelfth century, and had arranged other ecclesiastical help for the tanners in construction of a bark mill. In exporting gilds, later, if artisans had at any time been obstructive, they could have been quickly deprived of voting power by separate organization. The provost of Paris had authorized separation of the small master-weavers in the middle thirteenth century. The proposal of the Erfurt makers of wooden shoes, at the close of the fifteenth century, to limit membership in their gild to men who could stock 600 pairs of shoes, is an instance of the same kind of situation. The chief Rhineland gilds in the industry had long had a price cartel and had been trying to force their regulations on village workers.

Gild action could on occasion delay innovation that was being introduced under cover of the integration of two trades, either through a partnership or in a single master's shop. Disputes among fifteenth-century smiths in Coventry led to intervention by the town authorities ordering that several experiments in enlarging workshops be abandoned. Entrepreneurial gild statutes sometimes banned partnerships with men in the subordinate trades. The code drawn up for the Sienese woollen industry in 1298 forbade wool masters to set up in partnership with fullers or carders, a practice that had perhaps aroused jealousy through success in enlarging capital. Prohibition, it was said, would check quarrelling and would keep things more even (*communali*) as between the small men and the *grandi*. The Milanese silk gild had a similar rule, yet notarial records show large partnerships uniting its merchants and weavers.

T

The ban on mixed partnerships and on the union of two trades in one business arose out of the desire of town officials for the appearance of simplicity and order in their systems of administration. It gives a theoretical picture that was in fact quite generally at odds with the realities of medieval economic life. In certain directions it had moral point, as in the common prohibition of partnership between doctors and apothecaries. But in trade and industry the regulations were not normally enforced, and could be legally evaded by taking out membership in two gilds. Town authorities were more conservative in the matter than the gilds. In the baking trade, for example, statutes of the north Italian town of Sarzan in 1269 empowered the *podestà* to dissolve any partnership linking the occupations of mixing dough and operating ovens. Bakers' gilds, on the contrary, promoted integration of trade processes and in France and Germany permitted members to form partnerships with millers. The bakers' gild at Hildesheim was in 1366 drawing up agreements with the bakers of several other towns on labour policy in mills.

Small artisans could be very receptive to new techniques provided that these would serve the interests of the trade without threatening anyone's independence. In metal gilds serving war demand, in the art industries and in fashion trades there is a long record of medieval innovation, and artisans often shocked conservative opinion. The *podestà* of Parma was in 1266 empowered to fine shoemakers 25 pounds if they introduced any more new fashions, and town authorities in Coventry later objected to trade changes in the names of dye colours. In the Parisian fashion trades competence was held to depend not on traditional training so much as on familiarity with the latest styles. As the doublet-makers expressed the case for exclusion of another group, in 1358, it was essential to know what was *en cours . . . selon la mutation des temps*. Bristol tailors, however, resented the sale by outsiders of caps and hose cut ready for sewing, a fourteenth-century innovation which could have lent itself to large-scale production by entrepreneurs.

The caution with which gild artisans viewed radical innovation in methods of production is reflected in their policies regarding competition. Within the membership of independent gilds it had some play, enough to allow of the exercise of individual initiative in trying out new sources or types of supply, or small changes in techniques, but not enough to run far in price competition. The secret of economies or improvements effected by individuals would if possible be passed on and would become gild property. Gild officers were not entrusted with the responsibility of supply as a regular duty except in the event of marked upward price trends or when it was necessary to travel in search of rare materials not offered by local merchants, such as ivory for knife-handles or industrial crystal. Otherwise bulk purchase was resorted to only in the face of abnormal scarcity or collusion by merchants. The Modena smiths bought fuel together only intermittently, much preferring to rely on personal judgment and initiative. Competitive bidding was normally kept in check by agreements sanctioned by fine and also by the right of sharing in another member's purchase at the original price. An extension of a neighbourly citizen obligation that was written into some of the northern town custumals, this right of sharing helped to safeguard the poorer masters, who could buy only in very small lots. They had, however, to be able to pay the market price, and fraternal obligation did not entirely eliminate commission charges on sharing.

There had to be some degree of tolerance of price competition in selling, given the existence of competition from outside the gild, but there were perennial efforts to prevent its disguise through sales on credit and through variations in measure and quality. The limits of tolerance must have been well under 25%, for three weavers in fifteenth-century Erfurt who sold coverlets one-fourth as wide again as those the gild had standardized, and sold them at the gild price, were able to remain in business only by buying protection from the archbishop. There was often tension within a gild between the richer and poorer masters and between the older and the younger over open price competition. London fullers deplored the folly of young men who borrowed a stock of wares from members of other gilds 'at grete and excessive prices . . . and serve it oute ayen in the Craft of fullyng at so lowe price that thei in no wise can lyve thereuppon, but daily fall into grete Daunger Penurye Imprisonment and beggery'. Their statement was offered in 1488 in support of a rule by which they had instituted a property qualification for mastership.

Competition was further limited by regulation of hours of work. This would have favoured the larger men, who could hire extra help at need, as against the poor, who could get ahead only by working overtime. The hours set were about twelve during winter days and up to fifteen or sixteen in summer, yet the poor would still try to exceed them. Feeling on the question, and enforcement, was perhaps not strong except in noisy work disturbing the neighbourhood's sleep. Siena locksmiths denounced the avarice of those who rose to work too early, and Labal describes a riot in the Rue des Forges, Dijon, in which a cutler was stabbed for working too late.

The most severe limitations were on competition for labour. The only settled principle in gild relations with hired labour was to present a solid front on money wages. Some gilds admitted servants to fraternity sick benefits, but this was not a generally admitted charge. Some gilds preferred contracts to run from one to three years, with money payments withheld until the end of the year if the servant lived in the master's household. This kind of arrangement rarely endured through the labour shortages of the fourteenth century and was in any case inconvenient when trade fluctuated. In the larger towns contracts in most gild trades came to be shorter and could be weekly, and many servants, whatever their contract, lived out, often marrying before the gild admitted them to mastership. Besides forming their own fraternities to embarrass the gilds by agitation for wage increases, servants of this type engaged in fringe competition in trade in small wares, through their wife's agency and in their own spare time. Rouen card-makers and Coventry cappers decided to permit second-hand trading by servants.

The system of regulating the numbers of servants and apprentices to be employed favoured the larger men. Officers and ex-officers of the gild were allowed more than other masters and could go beyond the stipulated numbers without fear of legal penalty. If labour was abnormally scarce, however, it had to be rationed a little more fairly. Otherwise competition in wage offers threatened.

Finally, in view of their police responsibilities, gilds had to require a certain orderliness in retail selling. In so doing they controlled and developed advertising. They could not interfere with the use of individual marks, which were a property right, and the oldest and most discreet means of building up special demand through a personal clientele. Nor did they diminish any of the vocal entertainment and display that enlivened streets and market places, and which had a very individual character. Writing of Paris as he had known it in his student days in the 1380's, Guillebert of Metz recalled the shops of several craftsmen which had fascinated him, in particular a potter's shop where nightingales sang through the winter. But there were other features of retail selling that called for restraint. The detail of gild regulations implies that small masters and apprentices were given to aggressive rivalry, contending over customers as though they were prizes of war. In trying to check this, the gilds went on to develop a subtle collective form of advertising by enjoining neatness of dress in all public appearances. Riga shoemakers advertised their handiwork by agreement never to cross the gutters at their doors barefoot. In Paris there had been an advertising gild from the eleventh century, a group of wine-criers, who offered passers-by samples of the wines of taverners.

In gilds that were not independent, whose members worked for the entrepreneurs in the trade, there was less room for initiative because the decision how much to produce was not their own. In entrepreneurial gilds, on the other hand, there was usually more room for individual initiative than in independent artisan gilds. But freedom to introduce innovations was broadly speaking in inverse ratio to the degree of cartelization, which, carried to an extreme, led to rigid administrative arrangements. In the most highly cartelized of the Italian gilds there was, theoretically, no internal competition whatever, for members' books could be opened to inspection, and the main supplies were channelled through gild officers or agents. Whereas the chief reaction of the Florentine woollen gild to mid-fourteenth-century labour shortage was to ration labour equally among the masters, at twelve servants per *laniolo*, the less highly cartelized industries in Milan and the silk industries responded to the same situation by experimenting with more labour-saving mechanization. The highly cartelized gild was itself, of course, an impressive innovation and one that was instrumental in bringing about new productive investment. But it tended to remain on a plateau in this regard, and not to advance.

Direct investment by the gilds in capital equipment was on the whole slight. In phases of population growth there was sufficient investment by landlord interests to provide most of the dye-houses, the butchers' scalding-houses, the tanneries and the mills that gilds operated collectively. Town authorities assisted. In phases of population decline and war-time disturbance there was naturally no question of enlarging this kind of equipment. Gild corporate saving was directed primarily to social purposes and to ensuring the continuity of organization. It was evoked in order to acquire town house-property for use as club and office headquarters or as hospitals and almshouses or simply for renting out as a safe source of income. Italian gilds, like prudent citizens, diversified their investment in real property by buying plots of meadow-land and woodland nearby. Some smiths' gilds offered business loans to members, but liquid funds were not ordinarily adequate for more than small benefit payments to the sick and the destitute.

The value of medieval types of gild in stimulating new investment and innovation has to be judged on their record in directions in which these could have been justified to contemporaries by evidence of new demand. New demand in the later Middle Ages took four chief forms. Upper-class demand was always ready to absorb new styles of art product and textile for display in furnishing or apparel. The warring monarchies and territorial lords were intermittently in the market for equipment for troops. When groups lower in the social structure were increasing their money income their demand was in the first instance for foodstuffs, and secondarily for cheaper textiles and other consumer goods.

Urban gilds were adapted to hold the lead only in the first of these forms of business. The need here was to foster skill by divorcing labour from agriculture and to draw constantly on mercantile capital. Yet the lead remained secure only in art industries, in precious metals, embroidery, silk, velvet and the very finest woollens, and in fashion novelties calling for dyed leather. Otherwise gild industry was vulnerable to competition from lower cost manufacture in the areas where its raw materials originated. The capital and enterprise that were generated in the English woollen trade thus gradually induced sufficient concentration of skill in rural areas, with the aid of water power but without the aid of gilds, to undercut urban industry.

The business of equipping troops far outran the capacity of armourers' gilds, calling for large-scale supply of light protective clothing, of leather for boots and harness, of canvas for tents and of gunpowder and ammunition. Hazardous and intermittent, this form of business fell into the hands of a type of entrepreneur who normally made a livelihood, without gild affiliation, in the service of nobles and princes, negotiating contracts through personal influence and sub-contracting with other merchants, with gild artisans or with country workers as they could best conjure up supply in a hurry. It was this type of man who plunged, largely on the basis of army contracts, into development of the new chemical and armament industries of the Low Countries.

Trade in foodstuffs, on the contrary, was everybody's business. Public policy, preferring to rely on competition from numerous small local suppliers, to some extent hampered gild initiative in tapping supply further afield and hence made it difficult to attract or to build up capital. When in emergency it became necessary to go further afield it became necessary to draft capital for the purpose. The much-criticized butchers' gilds deserve credit for extending town lines of supply and, in Germany, for innovations in processing. Gild organization among bakers, too, was more far-sighted than town authorities in extending connections with country millers and promoting trade in flour. The gilds also developed the innovation of utilizing for horse feed the coarse meal that town consumers rejected to make bread.

Where gild performance appears to have been weak was in exploiting demand for cheaper consumers' goods. So far as country demand was concerned, the primitive institution of the itinerant artisan and pack pedlar survived in many regions with little change. German shoemakers' gilds were early sending their young servants on a year's touring work, and Erfurt smiths were still in the fifteenth century going on occasional tour through neighbouring villages. The country fair remained a place for work as well as for distribution of town-made goods. Gild organization grew up among French country distributors, culminating in disciplined regional and national organization under the *roi des merciers*, but rather as a form of social organization for mutual aid among men on the move than as any step towards opening larger markets. Whether population was dense or thin, the needs of stay-at-home peasants were small and could be met most economically by their own spare-time handicraft. Their wants were stimulated as they came into the towns.

In regions of denser population, and especially where small towns were thickly planted, as in western Germany, there was accordingly more gild effort to produce the coarser consumers' goods. Ready-made clothing that found its way into general merchants' stocks in country towns may have originated in gild tailors' workshops. German workers developed export power in cheap mill-fulled caps made of mixed wool and cotton-waste for town working-class wear. London gild cappers at first resisted the competition with their own foot-fulled pure woollen product, but they later imitated the German innovation. Rhineland gild development of larger-scale dealing in wooden shoes, which encroached on village industry, has been mentioned. Larger-scale production, either of these coarser goods or of the mirrors and odds and ends of haberdashery with which many gilds competed in trying to build up in customers a taste for elegance, was probably still far from justified. Turnover even in cheaper metal goods was slow. Entrepreneurs making new applications of water power in metal industries were faced with a long, slow fight to achieve enough economy to reduce appreciably the universal competition of wooden articles.

There is no denying that medieval types of gild organization were poorly adapted to rapid expansion of investment. The social relationships that they embodied could strengthen explicit devotion to small artisan independence as preferable to a more energetic pursuit of profit. Stiffening cartel agreements by social as well as economic sanctions, they tended often to extreme caution among entrepreneurs as well as among the small artisans. Yet external conditions, between the late thirteenth and the late fifteenth centuries, usually dictated caution. In the urban environment in which the gilds were rooted, entrepreneurs who stood outside their ranks made no better showing. Both in and out of gilds, individuals who could raise any capital diversified their interests in general dealing and sought security through buying land. With extractive industries and trade in raw products everywhere dominating the distribution of income and rural industry a constant potential competitor, urban manufacturing gilds, although their appearance probably more often encouraged investment than not, had no great leeway for influence. Within the limited sphere of handicraft, however, and possibly in elementary applications of water power and wind power, they gave a lead to innovation.

VI. *Conclusions*

Regional research, as it builds up more accurate surveys of trends in medieval population, prices, income and investment, should before long be able to assess the net influence of gild organization on medieval economic growth much more exactly. Meanwhile it is clear that several of the theses in the field have been too extreme. In erecting the equality of

producers into a principle of gild policy, and neglecting the omnipre-
sence of small-scale putting-out, von Below overstressed gild conservatism. Mickwitz, ably demonstrating the universality of cartel policies,
exaggerated their effectiveness. In his view, initial gild success in enhancing prices by agreement was the cause of mass rural migration to the
towns, with consequent over-production and a need for restriction
through exclusive gild policies. There were in fact so many other causes
for migration to the towns and for the accompanying rise in prices that
the thesis cannot be proven. Again, the judgment of the physiocrats and
the early liberal economists on the gilds of the eighteenth century as
standing for purely obstructive monopoly has sometimes been pushed
backwards without justification into the Middle Ages. Gild monopoly
power was then in general far too weak to be made to account for any
features of backwardness in the economy. Medieval labour was so
mobile that if gilds overdid restriction of admission to mastership, servants and apprentices disappointed of advancement would leave to set up
in competitive business in suburbs or villages.

Some of the more significant aspects of gild influence were less the
planned result of policy than unplanned side-effects of organization. For
example, the existence of gilds eased the mobility of skilled labour. A
certificate of service in a gild became the best possible passport to employment in another town. Communication between the journeymen's
gilds of south-western Germany, in the fifteenth century, distributed
labour efficiently where it was most needed. These journeymen societies
were a quite unplanned offshoot of the parent gilds, and in respect of
wage demands an embarrassing one.

Again, in most lines of consumer goods the mere existence of gild
society went far to stimulate demand. Participating in the political and religious ceremonial of the towns, leading gildsmen had a double opportunity and incentive to demonstrate social importance, through expenditure of the collective funds of their gilds in symbolic display and in feasting and through expenditure on their personal clothing, on the dress of
members of their family, and on their household furnishing. Sumptuary
legislation sought in vain to hold this game of conspicuous consumption
in check. It was not dependent on gilds, but they contributed much to
the zest with which it spread downward in the social scale, obliterating
outward signs of rank.

CHAPTER VI

The Economic Policies of Governments

I. *Introduction*

Writing in the year 1805, David Macpherson summed up his reflections on the economic legislation of later medieval England in the following words: 'From the perusal . . . of most . . . ancient statutes relating to commerce, manufactures, fisheries and navigation, it is evident that the legislators knew nothing of the affairs which they undertook to regulate, and also that most of their ordinances, either from want of precision, or from ordering what was impossible to be obeyed, . . . must have been inefficient. No judicious commercial regulations could be drawn up by ecclesiastical or military men (the only classes who possessed any authority or influence) who despised trade and consequently could know nothing of it.'[1]

This judgment upon the incapacity of medieval governments to deal with economic problems still has a certain validity. The 'inefficiency' and lack of grasp which Macpherson stigmatizes are not, perhaps, peculiar to the actions of medieval governments in the economic field alone; but they are as characteristic of that field as any other. It is, however, of greater significance that the very concepts of government responsibility in economic matters, either of our own day or even of Macpherson's, are anachronistic when applied to the Middle Ages. Even in most of the 'under-developed' parts of the modern world, it can be regarded as proper or obligatory for the central authority, apart from maintaining law and order and conducting national defence, to sustain expenditures yielding indiscriminate benefits, to issue money, to provide minimum health and education services, to aid the victims of catastrophes, and so forth.[2] In medieval times, on the other hand, in so far as such matters fell within the province of authority at all, they were very often the responsibility of a network of small-scale and more or less autonomous local authorities. These authorities, moreover, were often not only local but private—in the sense that the performance by them of governmental functions was indissolubly connected with profit for the individual or group invested with power.

The distribution of authority, then, is one of the facts which make government economic policies in the modern sense hard to discern in the Middle Ages. Apart from that, however, much of the content of modern economic policies is alien to medieval ideas about the functions of public

[1] *Annals of Commerce*, I, 557.
[2] P. T. Bauer and B. S. Yamey, *The Economics of Under-developed Countries*, 163 ff.

authorities. John of Salisbury, for instance, had quite a sophisticated notion of a kingdom as an ordered community composed of mutually interdependent social groups. On the other hand, he attributed to its ruler quite a limited and in many ways a negative role. It was his task, certainly, to preserve the social harmonies; and so he was equipped with coercive powers to safeguard peace and justice and established rights. Behind this, however, lies a very static notion of the scope of the public authority, and he can conclude that the king's office 'deals with the punishment of criminals, and seems to resemble that of the executioner'.[1] This was a somewhat narrow basis for the development of positive government action in the field of economic affairs.

Dispersal of authority, then, and current assumptions about the powers with which rulers were endowed, make many of our present-day conceptions about government economic policies inapplicable to medieval circumstances. That is not to say, however, that there were no such things as government economic policies in the Middle Ages: it means, rather, that their scope, character and objectives have to be defined in relation to the nature of medieval government and its circumstances. It must be accepted that government operated at a number of levels, and that account must be taken, for example, of the policies pursued in Italian communes and feudal principalities. It must be remembered that every medieval government had to grapple with one basic economic problem: that of its own maintenance. Fiscal policies, however elementary and hand-to-mouth, play a continuous part in the history of government. Further, even government acts which fell within the limited range accepted by medieval assumptions might well have consequences (whether or not they were foreseen) in the economic field. The maintenance of peace and order was not a matter of indifference to the merchant or the cultivator, for even today 'commerce cannot flourish unless it is given the shelter of a *pax*'.[2] What is true of commerce is no less true of other economic activities.

Fiscal policies and the economic consequences of policies aimed at public order, however, are merely the groundwork in the history of medieval economic policies. It is no less to be borne in mind that it is no longer possible to treat the Middle Ages as a single epoch. Large changes took place in the capacities and institutional equipment, and even in the very nature, of government during these centuries; and with these changes went a corresponding transformation of the scope and effectiveness of government intervention in economic affairs. There were also equally far-reaching changes in the economic environment, which altered and diversified the problems and opportunities of governments—

[1] *Policratus*, ed. C. J. C. Webb, bk IV, chap. 3.
[2] W. K. Hancock, *Survey of Commonwealth Affairs*, II (2), 162.

directly in so far as they affected the fiscal situation, and indirectly by creating new social interests and tensions which forced themselves on the attention of rulers. The problem presented by the economic policies of medieval governments, therefore, has multiple aspects governed both by institutional and by economic change. These two strands may for convenience be separately followed, though in practice they were inextricably intertwined.

Looking at the problem from the angle of government, it is proper to begin (both chronologically and to point the contrast with more modern times) with the extreme dispersal of power during much of the Middle Ages. It is perhaps convenient to describe this dispersal of power by the term 'feudal disintegration', although feudalism in the strict sense was one only of the forms of organization which took root in medieval Europe and consecrated disintegration. Whatever label we apply to the facts, however, it remains true that, particularly during the early Middle Ages and for some purposes and in some places throughout the Middle Ages, the effective political unit tended to be small (the seigneurie, the town, the provincial grouping under non-feudal aristocratic leadership found in Frisia and Scandinavia). Furthermore, governmental powers, once acquired by such 'infra-state' authorities, tended to persist even when they had been embodied into some larger grouping. Finally, the spread of feudal institutions from the Carolingian west to much of the rest of Europe helped to give a private patrimonial character to this dispersal of power as well as providing it with a juridical validity.

There were times, like the tenth century in Gaul, when this process of disintegration went so far that it is hardly appropriate to think of the economic acts of 'rulers' in any 'public' sense at all. However that may be (and there is a sense in which every feudal lord was a public authority), it is another matter when we come to consider the secular trend from the eleventh century onwards for the reconstitution of organized political communities and recognized public authorities. Such communities and such authorities were not necessarily on a large scale: an enlargement of the scope of governmental action is as significant as an expansion of its range. From this point of view the governments of the Italian communes in the twelfth and thirteenth centuries display a capacity for concerted 'public' action as notably as the government of Flanders under Philip of Alsace, or of France and England under the Capetians and Angevins. It is for this reason that the history of government economic policies in the Middle Ages has to take account of government at various levels, including the governments of 'states' which, by modern criteria, hardly merit that description.

At the same time, one of the features of Europe from the eleventh century onwards was a tendency for disintegration to give way to the internal unification of political communities. This tendency did not always go very far, for formidable obstacles stood in its way. Some were rooted in the social milieu: the sparseness of settlement, the barriers to communication, the immobility of whole sections of the population. Others, again, were represented by the lien established on governmental powers by the beneficiaries of earlier phases of disintegration. In consequence, where enlarged political communities were created, they were not an outcome of 'natural' causes: they were the result of artifice, and were composed of unstable elements which, even after medieval times, were liable to fall apart and to be re-combined in new ways. The trend towards unification, nevertheless, was a feature of the times; and its corollary was the acquisition by the ruling power (the king or the prince) of superiority over those other interests (the territorial nobility and the towns in particular) which previously had shared in the exercise of regalian rights. Much progress had been made in this direction by the end of the Middle Ages in France, England and the Iberian peninsula; there were signs of equilibrium even in such deeply fragmented lands as Italy and Germany; and some foundations had been laid for stable kingdoms in the countries which look out on the Baltic.

One condition of this political development was an increase in the control which the ruler was able to exercise over military force—a governmental power which, like every other, was widely dispersed in the earlier Middle Ages. The achievement of government monopoly in the control of force had to wait until the paid, professional army had made its appearance as part of the normal equipment of the state; and that, as a general phenomenon, post-dated the Middle Ages. On the other hand, some progress was being made in this direction (particularly in the fifteenth century) despite the fact that military control, even in the relatively advanced states, was still shared to varying degrees with the nobility. Indeed, military expenditure was one incentive for another political development with a more direct economic significance—the creation of a revenue system adequate (within limits) to sustain the public authority. Over the long term, this involved two sets of changes. The first had been the conversion of revenues in kind into cash revenues, which was indispensable for the effective management of public funds and for a flexible exercise of power. The second was the acquisition of the right, to satisfy the requirements of government, of putting under contribution the major sources of wealth in a community. The right to tax was seldom quite unfettered, but by the end of the fifteenth century most European governments had added an 'extraordinary' element to their traditional resources, and one which commonly completely overshadowed the latter. This achievement was at once cause and consequence of the concentration of political authority.

A further aspect of concentration was the development of administrative institutions. It is certainly true that, even in the succeeding mercantilist epoch, paucity of administrative resources often nullified the attempts of governments effectively to exercise their theoretical powers. On the other hand, these resources were different in kind from those at the disposal of rulers at the low point of 'feudal disintegration'. When government was scarcely distinguishable from estate-management, the small, itinerant *familia* of the ruler and his partially autonomous local officials were ill-endowed with strictly 'public' powers and with the capacity to exercise those they possessed. Men of unusual capacity—Charlemagne, Otto I, William of Normandy—might do wonders with this recalcitrant material; but continuity and large enterprises could hardly be normal features of government action. By contrast, the Sicily of Frederick II, the England of the Angevins and the France of Philip the Fair exemplify the growth of a professional government service and of an administrative machine capable of transacting at least some parts of the business of government as a matter of routine. Government was still elementary in its structure by modern standards, but it had developed rapidly by medieval standards. This was a prerequisite for an effective exercise of public power, and for that measure of consistency in government acts that was necessary to give to them the character of a policy.

Some reflection of all this is to be seen even in the realm of political ideas. Compared with John of Salisbury, St Thomas Aquinas had a far more positive and comprehensive conception of the functions of government. These functions, moreover, extended in his view into the economic field. It was the duty of a ruler to ensure that the community was supplied with what was necessary for its sustenance and had a proper equipment of crafts and professions.[1] These injunctions may not coincide with those which modern notions would impose upon governments as the most important of their economic obligations; but they constitute the principles upon which a government economic policy relevant to medieval circumstances might be based. From this time forward, there was increasing insistence that it was a ruler's duty to pursue what Oresme called *publica utilitas* and the ordinances of France *la chose publique*. Such notions included within the sphere of government action at least certain matters involving the economic interest of the community at large or of the state power as such. It was a relatively advanced conception of the role of government, which was doubtless rarer in action than in theory and rarer still in consistent application. The fact remains, however, that an economic sector had been added to the accepted practice of statecraft by the later Middle Ages.

At the same time, this was an outcome of economic as well as of political

[1] *De Regimine Principum*, I, chap. 15.

developments. The very character of government was strongly influenced by the material environment in which it acted. The tendency towards political disintegration, which proved so difficult to reverse during the Middle Ages, was not due merely to a failure of power or institutions; it also corresponded to certain basic features of economy and society. There was a subsistence core to much of the life of the Middle Ages. Society was largely constituted of relatively small groups, which were mainly self-supplying in character or at the most satisfied their needs by means of short-range exchanges. Furthermore, there were long periods when a good deal of Europe was sparsely peopled, so that communities might be physically separated by tracts of unsettled 'waste'. The Norwegian valleys are perhaps extreme examples of this phenomenon of separation, but to a lesser degree it had characterized much of the heart of western Europe before the great colonizing movements of the eleventh and twelfth centuries. Basic economic interests, therefore, tended to be local or at best provincial; and economic policies were likely to emanate from authorities at this same lowly level. The growth of long-range trade and the appearance of economic specialization never completely destroyed these features of medieval economic life: self-supply and local provision continued to absorb the activities of the majority of medieval men. This may help to explain the persistence of political disunity in medieval Italy and Germany, the formidable obstacles to state-building in Iberian and northern Europe and the tendency for even the relatively advanced political structures in France and England to disintegrate under stress.

Of more direct relevance, however, is the extent to which these features of medieval society conferred an extraordinary longevity upon purely local economic policies. Despite all the work of state-building in medieval times and the creation of an economy superficially 'European', a great deal of economic regulation even at the end of the Middle Ages was still the province of small-scale or relatively autonomous 'infra-state' authorities. This applies particularly, of course, to regulation designed to safeguard supplies of the basic necessities of life. At a time when most food-supplies were locally grown, and when local crop failures meant famine, epidemics and mortality, a 'provision policy' was the most vital of all economic policies and local considerations were apt to be the most weighty of all determinants in framing it. Even the rivalries between the great Italian cities have some of their longest roots in the struggle for control over those rural hinterlands which provided their daily bread.[1] This localization of a basic sector of economic policy was one among the obstacles to political unification, and to the emergence of 'national' economic policies where political unification had made sub-

---

[1] See H. C. Peyer, *Zur Getreidepolitik oberitalienischer Städte im 13. Jahrhundert*.

stantial progress. Princes themselves might be persuaded to give high priority in framing their economic actions to the purely local interests of their capital cities. There are times when the economic policy of the government of France has the appearance of being little more than a local policy of provision for Paris.

On the other hand, particularly from the eleventh century onwards, unifying forces were at work in the economic as well as the political sphere. Internal colonization, particularly in western and central Europe, was filling empty spaces and eating into the physical barriers between communities. At the same time active external colonization was bringing new areas, especially in the north-east and the Iberian peninsula, into the European economic system—an expansion which, in Spain for instance at quite an early date, owed a good deal to royal sponsorship, though for reasons which were probably military rather than economic.[1] Finally, the growth of both long-range and short-range commerce similarly broke down barriers and enlarged horizons. This made possible a greater degree of economic specialization as between towns and countryside and also between regions, as merchants linked the Near East and Mediterranean via the fairs of Champagne with the industrial Netherlands and the primary producing areas of the North Sea and Baltic.

One consequence of this complex process of economic growth was a rapid accumulation of new wealth which enlarged the range of fiscal opportunities open to governments. To the extent that rulers succeeded in grasping that opportunity, the economic expansion of the high Middle Ages underlay the contemporaneous concentration of political authority. At the same time, it became more and more difficult to attribute to the social structure the immobility which seems to be assumed by John of Salisbury. Economic expansion created new social interests—urban, commercial, industrial; and corresponding tensions within the existing fabric of society. The art of government had to be enlarged in the effort to come to terms with these new forces. In some instances, particularly in the Italian communes, new political communities arose in which the trading classes exercised a substantially autonomous control. More commonly, perhaps, the new interests were integrated into the political and juridical structure through the medium of privilege and franchise—a process facilitated by the fact that the creators of new wealth were in a position to buy favour by satisfying the pressing financial needs of governments.

This intrusion of new economic interests to a greater or lesser degree into the political structure diversified the influences to which governments were subjected and helped to generate a more positive attitude to economic affairs. The forces working in this direction, moreover, did not

[1] L. G. de Valdeavellano, *Historia de España de los orígenes a la baja Edad Media*, 471–8.

cease to operate when (except perhaps on the north-eastern frontier of the European economy) expansion was succeeded in the later Middle Ages by stagnation or contraction. Indeed, the very facts of political and economic crisis sometimes seemed to sharpen and accentuate them.

One illustration of this fact is provided by the economic preoccupa-tions of governments themselves. Everywhere in the later Middle Ages, from *dolorosa Dacia* to the Iberian peninsula, Europe was afflicted by dynastic conflicts which often revealed the insecure foundations of mon-archical or princely authority. Yet these same conflicts called for attempts to buttress and enlarge the powers of central governments, often threa-tened from both within and without. Thus, the later Middle Ages wit-nessed continuous attempts to develop still further the methods by which governments could exploit the economic resources of their territories. Direct and indirect taxes are not the only manifestation of this endeavour. Claims with an ultimate origin in domanial rights (like that to a mono-poly control of mining, particularly of the precious metals) began to be generalized. A desire to maintain stocks of mobilizable wealth available for government exploitation easily gave rise to measures of exchange control or a concern about the balance of trade. Thus revenue preoccupa-tions, and the power preoccupations of which they were a manifestation, gave governments a specific interest in an expanding range of economic activities. In short, the elements of a *political* pre-mercantilism were be-ing assembled, even if they were not integrated into a coherent system of ideas.

Economic forces abetted these political tendencies. The integration of the European economy was from some points of view strengthened rather than weakened during the later Middle Ages. The check to the agrarian expansion of the west after the mid-thirteenth century helped to create a compensating long-range trade in primary commodities, especi-ally from the Baltic. The increasing demand for English wool on the part of English cloth-workers turned both Flemings and Italians to the merino flocks of Spain. If the fairs of Champagne declined, the galleys of Venice and Genoa found their way to Bruges and Antwerp and London. In such ways, among others, the forces which had been creating a 'European' economy were prolonged into the later Middle Ages. On the other hand, economic regression set every group seeking to salvage what it could from the wreckage of fortunes; and public catastrophes seemed to multi-ply, adding to the prayers in common use that which asked, *A fame, bello et peste, libera nos, Domine*. The tensions between classes, and between the demands of localities or particular interests and *la chose publique*, were in-tensified—a situation which made new calls on the prince or monarch as arbiter between diverging interests. This was a factor making for an enlargement of the governmental power in general as well as in the economic and social field in particular. At the same time, endeavours to safeguard established interests, whether in the face of contracting markets or new competitors, created a demand for the intervention of the public authorities. 'Protection' was called for by the old industrial towns of Italy against developing newer centres, by the Flemish cloth towns against English competition, by the English merchants against the privileged Hansards and Italians. Restrictive policies required governmental sanction and enforcement, and in some places had developed into a protective commercial and industrial code by the end of the Middle Ages. In so far as this was so, elements of an *economic* pre-mercantilism had, by that time, been conjoined with those elements of political pre-mercantilism which owed their origin to reasons of state.

Associated with these changes is another which is not without its importance in the history of economic policy: the undermining of the unique influence of the landowning nobility in medieval political life. The curtailment of its wide political powers was a condition of bourgeois emancipation and the rebuilding of political communities on broader foundations. No less effective (except in the new grainlands of eastern Europe) was the crisis in noble fortunes, already evident in France before the end of the twelfth century, which was made permanent by the stabilization of *rentier* incomes at a time when the general trend was for the value of money to fall. The nobility more and more lost control over the expanding sources of wealth (again with certain exceptions, including the magnates of the Swedish mining area of Dalecarlia); and if they sometimes found compensation in the profits of political gangsterdom, large gains from this source were naturally for the few. These facts help to explain the tendency for the nobility to become subject to princely rule, and to accept the expansion of central authority in return for pensionerdom and the empty glory of playing their part in court ritual.

The political fortunes of the nobility were not unconnected with the major shifts of emphasis in the history of economic policy. The noble household of the earlier Middle Ages was a centre of consumption and of a great estate which could be adapted to the production of surpluses at least of the primary commodities. It was in part the nobility behind the throne who were responsible for a certain 'liberalism' in the early economic attitudes of rulers; for they created an atmosphere in which the merchant, from wherever he came, was a welcome customer and still more a welcome purveyor of those things which added variety to consumption and pomp to power. By contrast, the symptoms of 'economic nationalism' or of 'protectionism' apparent in the later Middle Ages are evidence of the fact that bourgeois interests (along with princely interests) had gained in effectiveness at the expense of those of the nobility. Individual bourgeois families might allow no more than a few generations

U

to elapse before seeking in land or title a position which opportunities for accumulating wealth could not alone confer. On the other hand, merchants, financiers and entrepreneurs had become a permanent part of the social structure, had acquired some of the instruments for exercising influence over government policy and opinion, and in some places had obtained a hold over the instruments of government themselves.

Writing in general terms about the emergence of economic policies in medieval Europe inevitably conceals one of the most important features of this process. Despite all the unifying forces at work, economic and political developments were most uneven and varied widely from region to region. Not only were the main trends differently manifested in different places, but the chronology of their manifestation displays a similar diversity. These variations in rhythm, as well as in the completeness with which general developments were worked out in the different regions, are the province of the detailed studies which follow.

II. *France and England*

(I) INTRODUCTORY

The nature and the scope of government action in relation to economic affairs are, generally speaking, problems of medieval history which still await detailed investigation. An attempt to clear the ground for such an investigation within the territorial limits roughly defined by the modern frontiers of France and England demands, first, that some brief notice should be taken of the broad political and economic context within which government economic action took place in the two countries. These modern states were being created in medieval times, but the work of creation was long and uneven. The retreat of Rome and the barbarian invasions left Britain much more deeply fragmented and with a far smaller direct legacy from the Roman order than Gaul; yet England achieved a measure of unity at a time when the dispersal of authority across the Channel was reaching its extreme point. The work of unification of the West-Saxon, Anglo-Danish and Anglo-Norman kings, moreover, proved substantially enduring: thenceforward there was no authority comparable to that of the Crown. In France, on the other hand, the legacies of Rome and of barbarian kingship were dissipated in the ninth and tenth centuries, and the reconstitution of authority was in the first instance as much the work of great feudatories (the prime beneficiaries of the dispersal of power) as of the monarchy. For many generations, therefore, 'regalian powers' (including powers of economic direction) were shared in varying proportions between the Crown and the great provincial magnates. There were also substantial areas of

French territory which were for long periods appendages to foreign kingdoms: Normandy and Gascony to England, Provence to the Empire or the Angevin kingdom of Naples. Medieval France comprehended a number of 'states' of which the kingdom was only one, each pursuing policies to a greater or lesser degree independent though not necessarily dissimilar.

There are economic as well as political contrasts between the two countries. England lay at the end of the medieval trade routes and could for the most part show a single face to the Continent—to the ports of the Low Countries, the Baltic and western France which linked it with a wider world beyond. Furthermore, the primacy first of wool and later of cloth in English overseas commerce led to the emergence of native commercial interests with a range of activities national in scope, and important enough to solicit and attract government intervention to their own advantage or to the financial or diplomatic advantage of the Crown. Something like a 'national' economic policy could develop from these dealings with the wool trade and the cloth trade. By contrast French commerce in the Middle Ages was not dominated by any single commodity, not even by wine; and France was essentially a country of transit, lying between the great industrial and trading regions of the Low Countries and northern Italy. To extract a profit from this position of intermediacy became one of the objects of the 'states' of France; on the other hand it provided less stimulus to the growth of long-range commerce in native hands and helped to militate against the economic integration of the country. The Midi was subject to the pull of the commercial powers of the Mediterranean, while western and northern France looked to England and Flanders and Brabant for economic contacts. These circumstances abetted political factors making for disunity and did nothing to counteract the external dynastic attachments of provinces like Gascony or Provence. They help to explain why the history of economic policies in the two countries is a history of contrasts as much as of similarities.

(2) THE EARLY MIDDLE AGES

It is perhaps paradoxical that the foundations of the medieval order were laid at a time when the Roman emperors intervened most comprehensively in economic affairs. Economic regulation was part of the policy of Diocletian and his successors for the salvation of the Empire. The exchange and movement of goods were rigidly controlled. Men were regimented into and tied to their offices and occupations to assure the supplies the army and the bureaucracy required. Diocletian attempted to fix prices and wages, which had soared mainly in consequence of debasements, in order to ensure adequate pay to the soldier and goods and services at reasonable prices to the government. The system of direct taxation was recast; forced labour was exacted for public works; and the government took over much of the transport system and became an entrepreneur on a large scale, especially in the manufacture of textiles and armaments. Everywhere the free enterprise of the early Empire gave way to compulsion and control in the attempt to avert the disintegration of the Roman political order and to sustain a state of siege envisaged as enduring to all eternity.

The attempt to achieve salvation through centralization failed in the long run. It failed to check the economic retrogression already evident in the third century, and economic retrogression made its contribution to the break-up of the Empire. Moreover, as the Roman provinces were occupied by the barbarians, the large-scale enterprise maintained by the imperial government collapsed and the system of economic controls disappeared save for fragments of them which were annexed by the rulers and the seignorial authorities of the successor states. The barbarian occupation also introduced a long period of political fragmentation and instability. England and Gaul in the early Middle Ages seldom enjoyed effective or enduring political unity; and the institutional framework of the Empire, if it survived at all, survived in an attenuated form. This decay of imperial institutions led also to the decay of those economic policies in which the rulers of the later Empire had sought a remedy for some of the maladies of Rome.

The successor states of the western Empire, therefore, emerged with a less sophisticated economy and with rulers who had entered only very imperfectly into the imperial heritage. The range of economic activities calling for intervention was curtailed at the same time as the capacity of governments to intervene was reduced. In consequence the legislation of the Dark Ages, though far from small in quantity, hardly touched the field of private right and economic enterprise. This characteristic of the times was reinforced by the decay of the Roman system of government finance, support of which had been a primary object of many of the measures of economic control under the later emperors. In Britain it disappeared altogether, and even in Gaul it soon ceased to be the basis of government. The Roman direct tax, the *census*, survived for a time in the Visigothic and Frankish kingdoms, but Charlemagne's very limited attempt to reassert his right to it was already anachronistic. Where it survived it did so as one of the elements of customary rent, dispersed between kings and the lords of land. Much the same happened to the *munera*, which underlie some of the *corvées* of the Middle Ages; and to tolls and other charges on trade, which were already being multiplied in Merovingian times both by kings and by other lords to an extent which gave rise to concern. The public charges of the Roman state, therefore, withered away or passed in an attenuated form into the domain of private right in that dispersal of 'regalian' powers which is characteristic of the early Middle Ages.

This fact in itself, of course, made necessary the search for alternative financial bases for government. In the emergencies of Viking invasion in ninth-century France and tenth-century England there were attempts to re-institute general land taxes. They left little mark upon the fiscal history of France, but in England they bore fruit in the *danegeld* or *heregeld* which was levied as an occasional impost down to 1162. The early Carolingians, again, expected to receive annual *dona* from their great subjects, and later rulers might persuade their feudal vassals to concede them gracious aids. None of these things, however, constituted the basic resources of governments, the character of which is adequately enough summarized in Abbot Suger's description of the revenues of Louis VII of France. These derived from the profits of justice, feudal incidents, the produce of the royal domain and tallages upon the inhabitants of the domain (*causas et placita vestra, tallias et feodorum relevationes, victualia etiam*). Henry I's English revenues in 1130 (leaving aside the tenth of them which came from the *danegeld*) were strictly comparable. About half came from the county farms, i.e. mainly from the royal domain and the local courts. The balance came from the profits of royal justice, reliefs and other feudal incidents, fines for privileges, the issues of vacant abbeys and bishoprics, and more or less arbitrary imposts on the domain. Normal revenues, in brief, were derived from lordship over a territorial domain, from feudal suzerainty and from the profits of administration in general and of justice in particular.

There is nothing distinctively royal about these revenues. The resources of the dukes of Normandy or the counts of Champagne in the twelfth century differed in no important respect from those of the king of France. This was due, in the first place, to an extensive devolution of regalian rights (tolls, church patronage, administrative powers), particularly to the greater feudatories. This might not be quite so marked in England as in France, but even there many franchises impaired the king's hold at least upon the lower ranges of administration. But it was also an outcome of the fact that economic circumstances in the early Middle Ages made it necessary to root all authority in land. This aspect of early medieval government already had a long history behind it by the time it emerged into the comparative daylight of the twelfth century. Some land was doubtless appropriated to royal use as the barbarian kings established themselves in their new territories. In addition, in Anglo-Saxon England, all free landholders may originally have been under an obligation to provide hospitality for the king and his servants. This obligation was eventually formalized into the duty of contributing to the king's *feorm* (i.e. to provide provender for the king to an amount roughly determined by the extent of a man's property). The right to *feorm*, however, was continually being abandoned by kings to reward followers and endow churches; and in the eleventh century Cnut ordered his reeves to provide for him from his own property only 'so that no man need give me anything to *feorm fultume* unless he himself is willing to do so'. In other words, the produce of land available to the king was gradually narrowed to that from the royal domain, which was managed like any other great estate.

The resources of the early Capetian kings of France were even more restricted than those of contemporary English rulers. A great part of the Carolingian fisc, together with many of the administrative powers exercised by the functionaries of the Carolingian Crown, passed into the hands of provincial magnates during the ninth and tenth centuries. Hugh Capet's domain was less extensive than that of Raoul of Burgundy;[1] and the effective authority of Hugh and his successors hardly extended beyond its boundaries. Their government not only depended upon the exploitation of their domain; it was scarcely distinguishable from it.

A corollary of this narrowing of fiscal horizons, both in kingdoms and in the great feudal principalities, was that an important objective of rulers came to be the enlargement of the extent and yield of their domains. Territorial aggrandizement on the part of princes, at the expense of their neighbours and their own vassals, was a road to power and one cause of the political instability of the times. The same end might be achieved more peacefully. 'The king farmed his land as dearly as he might', a chronicler wrote of William the Conqueror; and the rise in the value of many royal manors recorded in Domesday Book tells the same story. William may have achieved this result merely by turning the screw upon the peasantry; but the same purpose could be served by efficiency in managing the royal estates and support for agricultural improvement. Louis VI sought to ensure that no serf escaped him, and to further and profit from the colonizing movement of his day. Earlier, Charlemagne showed concern in several of his capitularies for the efficient management of his domain, even though the most famous (the *capitulare de villis*) probably had mainly a local significance. He also put himself behind the reclamation and repopulation of devastated areas in the south-west, though valorization of the fisc was only one of the reasons for this. Much of the reclaimed land in fact was granted away as a special form of allodial property, a bait for settlers who would form a local militia to meet the first shock of future Moslem invasions.[2] Estate-management, however, had become part of the work of government; and rulers were playing their part with other *potentes* in extending and consolidating territorial

[1] F. Lot, *Études sur le règne de Hugues Capet*, 187.
[2] A. Dupont, *Les cités de la Narbonnaise première*, 327 ff.

lordship as the almost universal principle of organization in western society.

Here again, however, rulers had ceased to play a distinctive role, if only because the counterpart of these changes in government finance was what has been called the 'feudal disintegration of the state'. For this there were many causes. The long siege of Europe and the internal instability of kingdoms compelled men to seek the protection of local *potentes*; and the deterioration of communications isolated localities and prejudiced the effectiveness of distant central authorities. But to these circumstances must be added the necessities of rulers whose financial resources were exiguous and who lived in a society in which almost all wealth came from agriculture. They had to pay in land or the issues of land for political support, military and administrative service and the salvation of their souls. Bede speaks quite explicitly of the royal estates in Northumbria as a fund for purchasing service, and particularly military service; and the surviving Saxon land-books are a memorial to the manner in which the Old English kings dispersed crown lands and rights to *feorm* to noblemen and churches. These grants, moreover, seem normally to have been permanent: *ita ut in proprio possideat perpetualiter* is the phrase used in 778 in a diploma of King Cynewulf. Thus the monarchy must have tended to grow progressively poorer save where its land-fund was recouped by conquest. Such accessions of land to the fisc were doubtless by-products of the assertion of Mercian or West-Saxon supremacy over the rest of England, and of Cnut's or William's conquest. It is probably no accident that these were periods of strong government, for land to dispose of was a condition of successful ruling.

In Gaul, too, the Merovingian kings used their domain as a fund from which permanent grants were made to secure service and support, and in the process they narrowed the basis upon which their authority rested. The early Carolingians seem to have been aware of this dilemma and to have sought to avoid it. Charles Martel seized church lands to reward his followers, and Charlemagne tried to achieve the same end by fostering feudal relationships. He expanded the ranks of his vassals, both to enlarge the military force at his disposal and to bind state functionaries more firmly to him. By encouraging men to become vassals of lords and lords to become vassals of the Crown, he sought to mobilize the wealth and influence of the magnates in the military service of the Crown, and for the maintenance of political discipline. The rewards he could offer to those who did become his vassals were comital or other offices and territorial fiefs—conceded not in perpetuity, however, but for the duration of life or of the contract of vassalage. In this way he may have hoped to strengthen his authority and satisfy his military and administrative needs, while at the same time providing for a constant renewal of the territorial basis of his government as fiefs fell in. The outcome was very different. As early as the reign of Louis the Pious it was proving impossible to insist upon the temporary character of the fief, and there was even a reversion to grants in perpetuity from the imperial domain. As the Empire broke down the *potentes* swallowed up the Carolingian fisc, asserted control over the lesser vassals of the Crown and parcelled out amongst themselves as hereditary benefices the offices which had belonged to Carolingian functionaries.[1] The new principalities which emerged were themselves subject to the same forces of disintegration. Their lords, too, were compelled to concede territorial and administrative rights to their vassals, and the workings of the patrimonial principle (seemingly an innate feature of agrarian societies) perpetuated this dismemberment of authority. The habits of mind and many of the institutions which arose at this time in France were transplanted to England in 1066. They produced a disintegration of the state much less extreme than across the Channel, but the difference was one of degree and not of kind.

Thus as parents, midwives or helpless spectators the rulers of the Dark Ages presided over a political and economic revolution. Powers of economic direction (amongst other powers) were fused with the managerial powers of great landowners. By the tenth century there was not one 'state' within the confines of Gaul, but many. The Norman duke who conquered England, for example, was at home the lord of wide agricultural domains. He was the lord of towns and could regulate their economic affairs. He had the right to levy tolls, to authorize markets and fairs, to control communications and to strike money, which made his authority one that the trader had to reckon with. In England no subject possessed quite such autonomous powers, but some rights of economic direction (over land, markets, even towns) were devolved upon feudatories, just as they were upon lesser lords within the French principalities. The authority of the 'state' was not only divided; it was parcelled out at different levels of power. Economic direction did not disappear, but it ceased to proceed from any single centre. It is to be found in the practice of estates and seigneuries, which created in the long run the economic institutions of the high Middle Ages. In creating them, however, public authorities had in great measure ceased to act in a public way: they are hardly distinguishable from the network of private authorities to which the feudal order gave birth.

For much of the early Middle Ages, therefore, economic direction is absent or confined to the financial exploitation of such powers of economic direction as rulers might possess. Only in periods when some attempt is made to reknit the fabric of political society are tentatives at 'state' economic intervention in anything like the proper sense to be discerned.

[1] J. Dhondt, *Études sur la naissance des principautés territoriales en France*, 6 ff., 231 ff.

Charlemagne's activity in this direction is a case in point. He was active in the establishment of markets, though his willingness to concede rights in them to subjects suggests that some of the initiative came from below. He tried to check the multiplication of tolls, to improve roads and to standardize weights and measures. Famine or inflation led him to control the prices of essential foodstuffs and forbid their export. To prevent fraud and the disposal of stolen goods, he prohibited trade by night and in the absence of witnesses. All this (and also perhaps his currency reforms) suggests a deliberate effort to revive internal trade after the troubles of late Merovingian times, as well as a concern for fair-dealing and social justice inspired no doubt by his ecclesiastical advisers. Their influence is also to be seen in the decrees forbidding the sale of slaves to the infidel and in the gradual acceptance in the capitularies of the illegality of usury.

Overseas trade too came under Charlemagne's attention. He seems to have been anxious to maintain the commercial relations between Gaul and England. A quarrel with Offa of Mercia in 790, fomented by the Devil according to Alcuin, caused the passage of ships on both sides to be forbidden to merchants; but by 796 the incident had been closed by an agreement between the two rulers. They promised protection and support to each other's merchants 'according to the ancient custom of trading', and Offa agreed to supervise the quality of English exports to Gaul. Commercial advantage was thus secured as well as the political advantage of good relations between countries discerning in the sack of Lindisfarne the first harbingers of the viking menace. In the Mediterranean, too, Charlemagne made some attempt to minimize the effect of Moslem piracy upon the ports of the south; economic relations with the Islamic world may have been a by-product of his diplomatic contacts with Baghdad and Spain and the establishment of the March of Barcelona; and his Italian policy secured access to the termini of Byzantine commerce, now in Italy rather than on the Provençal coast. This forms the background to something of a revival in the inflow of spices and oriental fabrics—the silks with which Charlemagne, despite his distaste for 'oriental luxury', flattered Offa of Mercia; which Louis the Pious bestowed upon the dignitaries of his court; and which were coveted so much by Carolingian princesses and the Carolingian nobility.

These policies petered out in the shipwreck of the Carolingian state, and by the tenth century it is perhaps anachronistic to attribute political or economic aims of any sort to the 'states' of Gaul.[1] England was more fortunate, despite much interruption of continuity by the viking invasions. A well-organized and united kingdom was established in the tenth and eleventh centuries, and its range of activity extended into the

[1] E. Lestocquoy, 'The Tenth Century', *Econ. Hist. Rev.* 1947.

economic field. Internal trade was brought under a measure of control by confining it to recognized town markets. The main purpose was probably to inhibit cattle stealing and the evasion of market dues; but a degree of political order is implied, in itself favourable to settled trade. Attempts were made to establish standard weights and measures. Minting was brought more or less under royal control, and an increase in the number of mints was no doubt a necessary provision for a reviving economy at a time when localism was still too strong to make centralized minting feasible. Overseas trade, too, attracted a measure of kingly patronage. Under Aethelred II the merchants of the emperor enjoyed in England the same rights as native traders; commercial clauses were inserted in the treaty with Olaf Tryggvason in 991; and Cnut diversified a pilgrimage to Rome by securing easier conditions for his subjects trading to northern Italy. The Confessor's grant of Warmsacre to St Peter's of Ghent may also have been designed to further trade by giving to the men of that city wharfage facilities in London similar to those the men of Rouen had secured at Dowgate.

These instances may amount in aggregate to very little; they lacked continuity and the motives which inspired them were very mixed. Frequently the inspiration came, not from economic calculation, but from ecclesiastical influence upon rulers, or a will to order, or a sense of political advantage. In so far as economic ends were envisaged for these measures, only two seem to have any great importance. The first is closely connected with the character of the ruling circles in early medieval 'states'. Kings and princes were dependent in some degree upon the concurrence in their acts of the lay and ecclesiastic landowners of their dominions. It was precisely this class, together with kings and their functionaries (often drawn from or climbing into the class of great landowners), who disposed of the wealth required to make them great consumers of both luxuries and necessities. The organization of lordship, as the condition for securing wealth and the necessities of life, would therefore find backing at court; and the predominance of a 'consumer interest' there (even an interest prone to 'conspicuous consumption') does much to explain government attitudes to trade and the trader. To multiply facilities for internal trade was a convenience for provisioning royal and noble households as well as for disposing of domanial surpluses. To protect the foreign trader or the Jewish colony was a condition for securing the silks, wines, spices and other desirable things which great domains could not supply. The other motive is more straightforward. Powers of economic direction could yield considerable profit. Fairs and markets were sources of revenue, and so was overseas trade. Charlemagne had an agent levying *tributa atque vectigalia* upon the English trade passing through Quentovic; and the control points for the transalpine trade and the trade with the

Slavs may have been points where duties were collected as well as search-points to check the export of arms. It was the same across the Channel. Tolls were being levied upon ships in the port of London as early as the eighth century, and the records of Aethelred II's interest in the trade there characteristically are mainly financial records.

This background no doubt explains the limited scope of government economic intervention even under Charlemagne, that 'grand policier', just as political vicissitudes explain its lack of continuity. The fact, more-over, that powers of economic regulation could be used to produce revenue helps to explain why such powers were so frequently delegated and usurped, and exploited in ways detrimental to economic prosperity —as tolls were, for example, to impose barriers against trade, which in-tensified the localism and economic stagnation of the times. The feudal order, furthermore, gave birth to a military nobility whose industry *par excellence* was warfare. The very prospect of the campaigning season brought joy to the heart of Bertrand de Born, but he is no less explicit about some of its economic consequences. 'And the times will be good times... Packhorses will no longer pass along the roads by day in all se-curity, nor townsmen without fear, nor the merchant who takes his journey towards France.' It was not only love of fighting that attracted a man like Bertrand: warfare also meant that the barons would be willing to buy his services and offer him the opportunity to indulge that 'simple pleasure in pillaging' which characterized so many of his class. Merchants coming to France in 1074 found even King Philip I a 'rapacious wolf' of this sort, for he robbed them of much money and earned the denunciation of Gregory VII for it. Economic intervention on the part of the powers of the early Middle Ages might fall lower than domanial exploitation; it might degenerate into plunder.

(3) THE TWELFTH AND THIRTEENTH CENTURIES

A. *Administrative Progress and Urban Liberties*

The period from the eleventh to the early fourteenth century is one of rapid change, a period of expansion both in the internal economies of the west and in their external commercial contacts. New sources of wealth were put at the disposal of governments and subjects, and new economic problems were forced upon the attention of rulers. It was also a period of political reconstruction. The tendency for power to be endlessly sub-divided was halted and then reversed. In this work the great provincial magnates of France were as prominent originally as the ruling houses of France and England. Their acts at first were often characterized by that sort of force and fraud in the use of which Fulk Nerra of Anjou was such a master, but eventually a more regular and elaborate organization of government became necessary. This point was being reached in eleventh-century Anjou and Aquitaine just as much as in the contemporary kingdoms of France and England. The progress of administrative capacity, involving the increased importance of bureaucratic elements in government, is of great significance. It gave a new effectiveness to central authorities and a greater continuity of administration,[1] and was one precondition for the transformation of mere acts of economic intervention into economic policies. The Crown was the ultimate beneficiary, even in France. Political reconstruction often started at the provincial level, and at the beginning of the fourteenth century there were still provinces of France which formed no part of the kingdom. Nevertheless, in France as in England, the tendency was for the royal authority to outstrip all others and to supplant some at least of the infra-state authorities born in the age of feudal disintegration.

If centralization was the long-term trend of these centuries, at first a contradictory trend was very much in evidence. Rulers continued to divest themselves of regulative powers in the form of the 'franchises' they bestowed on the nobility and the churches, and they also began to do so for the benefit of towns. The use made by townsmen of their privileges is treated elsewhere; here it is only apposite to say something of the reasons prompting rulers to multiply in this way the number of infra-state agencies amongst which powers of economic direction were partitioned. In many cases, of course, townsmen owed their freedoms largely to their own efforts. The communes of the north and centre of France were sometimes won by successful conspiracy or even revolt, and the consulates of the Midi generally acquired their privileges by a steady usurpation at the expense of their lords. Only some towns, however, became communes or consulates; but most urban centres of any importance, and some of very little, acquired some degree of privilege. The reasons were often political. The kings of France, as chary at first as Henry II of England of granting privileges to the towns of their domain, were generous when it was a matter of Auxerre or Dijon: there the opportunity was taken to make the royal authority felt in the lands of the feudatories. During the struggle for Normandy and the adjacent provinces, too, the Angevins were willing to make concessions to urban aspirations, and Philip Augustus to confirm these concessions afterwards. The towns seem to have been reckoned an important enough interest in these disputed territories to make such proceedings necessary for their defence and conquest. The policy of founding *bastides* adopted by Edward I and Alphonse of Poitiers in the south-west of France seems likewise to have been governed by political and administrative considerations. The *bastides* were ad-

[1] Cf. R. W. Southern, *The Making of the Middle Ages*, 89.

ministrative centres, the strong-points of the seignorial authority of the ruler, defining his lordship in frontier areas which previously had been a kind of no-man's-land.[1]

At the same time the *bastides* soon became something more. In 1306–7 they provided half the revenues Edward I drew from the *bailliage* of Périgord and three-quarters of his revenues in Agenais. They developed into centres of new population, of a more vigorous economic life, of settlement and reclamation. From this point of view they fitted into the policies rulers were adopting for a more rigorous exploitation of their domains. The direct economic value of urban development had not escaped notice elsewhere. Towns were granted freedoms, towns were even founded (not always very wisely) because some lords realized that free boroughs could be appreciating assets by comparison with rural manors. Even where such providence was absent urban communities were recognized as assets which could be capitalized by conceding liberties for cash down. The count of Ponthieu in 1184 did not mince words. His grandfather, because of the injuries suffered by the men of Abbeville, *eisdem communiam vendidisset*; and in like manner the grant or confirmation of urban liberties in England leaves a train of fines upon the Pipe Rolls. At the same time these English charters, and the Norman charters of Richard and John, the charters of Philip Augustus, of Henry the Liberal of Champagne and of the thirteenth-century dukes of Burgundy contained provisions designed to rationalize the financial exploitation of the towns. Privileged communities had to pay a farm or *census*; and there was some advantage in substituting a fixed round sum, for payment of which the burgesses were collectively liable, for many miscellaneous dues and charges which were difficult to collect. Privilege seldom extinguished and sometimes increased the financial obligations of towns to their lords.

At this point, however, devolution of economic direction was reaching its limit. The legislative powers of the Crown were expanding, particularly in England; royal suzerainty was extending over the feudal provinces; royal justice was advancing at the expense of competing jurisdictions. The towns felt the effects of this progress of the central authority. In England their liberties were scrutinized as closely as those of the nobility, and were withdrawn if they were abused (as those of Winchester were in 1274, or London's for thirteen years on end by Edward I). Government policy began to invade the province of urban regulation, reducing town governments to an executive role on the king's behalf. In France social conflicts, arising out of financial inefficiency and corruption and the grip of oligarchies upon town governments, provoked increasing interference in urban affairs. Raymond Berengar V and Charles of Anjou in Provence, Alphonse of Poitiers in the county of Toulouse and Duke

[1] J. P. Trabut-Cussac, 'Bastides ou forteresses?', *Moyen Age*, LX (1954), 81 ff.

Robert II in Burgundy all pursued policies designed to subject the towns to political control. St Louis and his successors pursued a similar policy. Royal officials interfered more regularly in the internal affairs of the towns; the king's courts made their influence felt there as elsewhere; and in 1256 the financial affairs of the towns of the domain and Normandy were subjected to regular scrutiny by 'king's men'. As the royal power spread across the face of France the king came to be regarded as the *chef des villes*, and his authority was brought to bear even upon their internal organization. In Paris the system of corporations was being deliberately extended as early as the reign of Philip Augustus. Towards the end of St Louis's reign the king's *prévôt* was responsible for drawing up the *Livre des Métiers*, which was designed to fix not only the technical rules of trade and industry but also the judicial, fiscal and military responsibilities of the crafts to the Crown. These groups, in fact, were becoming administrative organs, and their officers agents of the king as well as of their communities. In the late thirteenth century, similarly, the king's *viguier* is found disputing control over the crafts of Toulouse with the *capitouls*, particularly in the matter of promulgating gild statutes. In short, the communal phase was ending and the towns were on their way to becoming *choses du roi*. The disintegration of the state was beginning to be reversed.

B. *Government Finance*

The prominence of financial considerations in the dealings of rulers with towns is symptomatic of one of the most urgent problems with which rulers were faced. Rising prices, administrative expansion and the decay of unpaid services occasioned a steady rise in normal expenditure; extraordinary expenditure rose more steeply still with the entry of Capetians and Angevins into large-scale European politics. The nature of this financial problem can be deduced from 'the first budget of the French monarchy' dating from 1202–3, a year of war calling for every effort to raise money. The first constituent of the revenue of the king of France in that year consisted of the payments of the *prévôts* and *baillis*, amounting to about 60,000 *li. par.* after certain fixed local charges were met. This sum was derived from the issues of the royal forests and agricultural domains, a variety of seignorial rights, and the profits of justice, markets, ecclesiastical patronage, etc. In addition, the king received certain extraordinary payments directly related to the emergency of war—payments from non-nobles and vavassors for the commutation of military service, a *taille* levied on the domain and contributions exacted from towns, churches and Jews in the domain—amounting in all to about 63,000 *li. par.* The English revenues of King John two years later were in the region of

£20,000,[1] derived in the main from the farms of shires and boroughs, the proceeds of feudal escheats and incidents, the issues of ecclesiastical estates in hand during vacancies and the profits of royal justice. On that occasion, however, the total also included part of the proceeds of a scutage and of fines for the commutation of military service and of a tallage levied on the domain and the Jews, which in aggregate produced in this and the following year a sum of about £6,900. King John also succeeded in imposing duties on trade in 1202 and levying general taxes on movables in 1203 and 1207, the last yielding the astonishing amount of £57,000. The customs were soon abandoned, however, and like the taxes on movables represented merely the first harbingers of the fiscal system of the future.

At the beginning of the thirteenth century, then, a high proportion of revenue was still derived from the traditional sources. Extraordinary supplies were almost impossible to procure in peacetime and not easily available even in war; and their individual sources were, for the most part, modestly productive. For this reason rulers, faced with a constant tendency for expenditure to outrun receipts, turned first to an attempt to augment their normal revenues. The thirteenth-century dukes of Burgundy, for example, steadily enlarged their domains by purchases, exchanges and escheats. They sought to consolidate their property for more efficient management, and to exploit the iron-mines on it. They simplified and r tionalized the rents paid by rural communities and made the grant of r ban liberties dependent upon the payment of an annual *census* to the duke. They developed their fairs at Chaumont, Autun and particularly Chalon to compete with the fairs of other lords. They augmented the profit they derived from justice, *tailles* and feudal aids, and drove out the money of all competitors save the king. One condition of the success of these efforts to maximize normal revenues was the steady improvement in the financial administration of the duchy.

The policies of the dukes of Burgundy were also those of the kings of France. The acquisition in the thirteenth century of Normandy, Languedoc and the domains of Alphonse of Poitiers and of the counts of Champagne represented a spectacular expansion of the royal domain. St Louis and his successors made the most of this opportunity. The resources of the domain were augmented by purchase, exchange, forfeitures, escheats and *pariages*, and better administration led to a steady rise of revenue (in the *bailliage* of Rouen alone the issues of the domain increased from 15,000 *li.* to 18,000 *li.* between 1238 and 1260). The English kings received no such accretion of domanial resources (though Edward I, at least, was a great dealer in land); but they were no less concerned to valorize what they had. Henry III's reforms at the exchequer in the 1230's

[1] *Pipe Roll*, 7 John, xxv–xxvi.

were typical of their proceedings. The financial resources of the Crown were thoroughly surveyed—feudal obligations which could be turned into money, the royal domain, the sources from which the sheriffs drew revenue in the shires. New farms were set for royal manors, and the outworn services of serjeanty tenures were converted into money rents. Searching inquiries were instituted to determine by what warrant men held royal properties or regalian rights, so that the king might recover anything which had been filched from him. This policy, like the augmentation of the domanial revenues of the French kings, inevitably affronted some vested interests; and in time of need it was easy for kings to fall into the temptation to press their advantages too hard—to exploit justice for its financial yield, levy excessive feudal incidents, etc. The attempt to maximize normal revenues, therefore, aroused opposition which had to be mollified by concessions like the Great Charter of England or the charters won by the Leagues of early fourteenth-century France.

By the early fourteenth century, moreover, normal revenues were quite inadequate, at least in times of war. The age of Edward I and Philip the Fair saw 'extraordinary' levies become more frequent, more general in their incidence and more indispensable. In England under Edward I taxation of the Church provided some £200,000 towards the king's needs. General parliamentary taxes on movables yielded a further £500,000, and a national customs-system was established. In 1275 export duties were imposed on wool, wool-fells and hides; the rates were augmented for a time in 1294–7, and in 1303 additional export and import duties were negotiated with the alien merchants trading to England. The average yield of the custom of 1275 for the years 1275–94 and 1299–1304 was about £10,000 yearly,[1] and revenue from taxes on trade must have been higher in 1294–7 and in the last years of the reign after the new charges imposed on alien commerce had come into operation. In all Edward I raised £1,000,000 or more in the course of his reign by direct and indirect taxation.

Philip the Fair of France had no less need of taxes.[2] Like Edward, he laid the clergy under frequent contribution. On the other hand, he encountered more formidable obstacles in his attempts to establish general direct taxation, and the resultant story is one of empiricism and improvisation. Many experiments were tried, including taxes on income from property or chattels, hearth taxes, the commutation of military obligations imposed *ad hoc* on the different classes and communities, and feudal aids extended to include rear vassals. Some of these levies yielded notable

[1] Extracts from the Pipe Rolls giving the yield of the customs for these years have been kindly communicated to me by Dr E. B. Fryde.
[2] See particularly the summary of research in this field in F. Lot and R. Fawtier, *Histoire des institutions françaises au moyen âge*, II, 225 ff.

sums: the subsidy of 1295 possibly 350,000 to 360,000 *li. par.* and that of 1304 700,000 *li. tur.* or more, though in a depreciated currency. At the same time, they became progressively more difficult to raise. The king was compelled to accept in their place special compositions with individual towns and communities; and as early as 1295 had to buy the acquiescence of the nobility by conceding to them a share of the taxes levied in their domains. Direct taxation, therefore, had to be supplemented by other methods of raising revenue. A tax on sales was imposed in 1291; but it provoked a riot in Rouen, towns and provinces bought exemption from it, and it was abandoned in 1295 (though similar charges were imposed in 1296, 1314 and under Charles IV). The Jews were tallaged time and time again, 44,000 *li. tur.* being taken from them in the years 1298–1301 alone; and eventually they were expelled for a time and their property seized in 1306. Italian merchant-financiers were compelled to buy from the king immunity from spoliation, receipts from this source amounting to 221,000 *li. tur.* in 1291–2 and 65,000 *li. tur.* in 1295. Forced loans were raised and not always repaid. Manipulation of the currency on a massive scale was perhaps the most important financial expedient of all: 1,200,000 *li.* was procured by this means in 1298–9, about two-thirds of the total receipts of the treasury. Foreign trade, finally, was put under contribution, though for a long time in an arbitrary and unsystematic manner. The prohibition of exports (particularly of wool and foodstuffs) enabled Philip IV and his successors to sell export licences. In 1321 the *Chambre des Comptes* was empowered to sell these licences according to a regular tariff (*droits de haute passage*), and in 1324 certain goods were removed from the prohibited list on condition that fixed export duties were paid on them (*droits de rêve*). In the absence of a staple export like England's wool it is perhaps natural that French export duties should have come into existence in this scrambling way, and that revenue from the sale of export licences was fairly modest (55,000 *li.* in 1322–3, or about 5% of the receipts of the treasury in those years).

In this generation, then, royal revenues rose sharply. In England a national system of direct and indirect taxation was becoming established, and even in France substantial sums were raised over and above the traditional revenues of the Crown. Yet both Edward I and Philip the Fair were in continual financial difficulties. The needs of governments, in short, were still tending to outrun the capacity to satisfy them. By the standards of the time, however, Edward's and Philip's financial demands had been onerous. They must have done something to divert capital from productive investment. Prior Henry of Eastry of Christchurch, Canterbury, disbursed one-third of the expenditure of his house in the form of papal and royal taxes, as much as he ploughed back into its estates. The fall in the yield of Edward I's parliamentary taxes in his later years, too, may point to an increasing shortage of cash in the hands of taxpayers as well as to successful evasion; and the falling value of land and rent in Normandy at the end of the thirteenth century was possibly due to the heavy taxation of Philip the Fair. Thus the slowing down of the rate of economic expansion was probably partly due to fiscal causes. The reserves accumulated during the years of prosperity were being dissipated to fulfil the ambitions of the warring nations.

C. Governments and Economic Affairs

The financial stresses of these times, and the consequent efforts of rulers to augment inadequate revenues, are perhaps the most important single explanation of increased government intervention in economic affairs. The domanial resources of rulers included rights of economic regulation which could be exploited and extended, both within the established circumscription of a ruler's authority and at the expense of subordinate authorities. The conquest of such powers, because they were profitable, is part of the history of the consolidation of political authority in this period. There were other reasons, of course, for the economic policies which governments adopted: strategic reasons, for instance, or the attempt to solve the problems posed by a period of rapid social and economic change. Such policies, however, were normally enforced by means of financial penalties or sanctions which easily acquired in the circumstances an importance transcending the original objectives in view. Fiscal advantage not only dictated policy, but diverted it from its primary channels.

One instance is furnished by the dealings of governments with the agrarian problems of the times. Very real problems arose in this field. The fall in the value of money in the thirteenth century, combined with the fixing of many tenant payments, led to a fall in the real incomes of landlords. This tendency was aggravated by the weakening of their control over their tenants. Holdings were more and more regarded with a proprietary air. They were broken up to suit the convenience of family settlements, and bought or sold according to the advantage or necessity of the tenant. This undermining of lordship by tenant right was particularly serious in view of the decline in the purchasing power of the incomes of landlords. It prejudiced their power to revise contracts with their tenants, and their capacity to maximize (or even to exact) periodical windfalls in the form of feudal incidents, tallages, *mainmortes*, etc.

The attention of governments was called to these problems by the domanial interests of rulers, the manifest grievances of the politically influential nobility and the fact that the dissolution of the feudal territorial order destroyed the groundwork of political obligation. The dynastic ambition of great families and the concern of rulers for the services due to them led to some attempts to check the dissolution of fiefs. Primogenitary succession to feudal tenements came to be the rule in England and for principalities and baronies in France, and attempts were also made to impose it on their vassals by the rulers of Normandy, Brittany and Champagne. The line of least resistance, however, was to drift with the tide of tenant freedom, particularly where lords could exact a charge for their indulgence. In England the Statute *De donis condicionalibus* of 1285 allowed portions of fiefs to be detached for the purpose of family settlements. In the French royal domain the partibility of fiefs was conceded by Philip Augustus in 1210 providing the parceners held directly of the chief lord, thus saving feudal control and the incidents accruing from it; and a similar concession was made by the count of Champagne in 1224. The alienability of fiefs and of peasant holdings, particularly as servile obligations were commuted, came to be very generally allowed subject to the purchase of the lord's licence. Government policies for the most part were limited to attempts to revive seignorial control over tenants as a precondition for exacting seignorial dues. The English Statute of Mortmain gave lords power to control gifts made by their tenants to churches, and the Statute *Quia emptores* halted the attenuation of lordship through the medium of subinfeudation. Similar results were achieved by the inquiries into alienations in mortmain carried out by the counts of Champagne in 1222, 1250 and 1263-5, and by Charles of Anjou's prohibition of alienations of fiefs to churches and non-nobles in Provence in 1289. This last measure followed closely the royal ordinance of 1275 in France which had the effect, not so much of preventing such alienations, as of establishing the right of the king to license them and to exact payment for so doing. In short, if there was competition between kings and lesser lords to control the trends of the times, both government and seignorial interests were commonly satisfied when methods had been devised of extracting a profit from the changes transforming rural society.

Industry, too, attracted only limited attention. The English kings might establish forges in their forests, rationalize the exploitation of the lead- and tin-mines of Derbyshire and Cornwall, or concede to gilds of weavers local monopolies of manufacture in return for an annual farm. These were methods of raising revenue and of exploiting the resources of their domain. Only the textile industry attracted more general attention. The first great measure of government control of the English cloth industry was the Assize of Cloth of 1197, which confined the manufacture of dyed cloth to the towns and laid down comprehensive regulations for its size and quality. The initiative in procuring this legislation may have come from urban entrepreneurs and cloth merchants, but it suffered a fate characteristic of the times. As early as 1202 payments were made in every shire where cloth was manufactured for exemption from the assize. For the time being it was used for the most part to control the standard of cloth imported into the country (though again importers might buy exemption, as the Flemish did in 1270). The policy of 1197 was diverted to some extent by consumer interests and to a much greater extent by fiscal exigencies. The prohibition of wool exports from France by Philip the Bold in 1277 is another matter. It seems to have been deliberately designed to assure raw materials to the cloth industry of the Midi. But this policy, too, was soon sacrificed to financial expediency by Philip the Fair. In 1305, for example, he reiterated the prohibition upon the export of wool and secured in return the concession of a tax on manufactured cloth from the cloth-workers of Carcassonne; yet at the same time he readily sold licences to export wool despite the prohibition. A similar embargo on wool exports from the Midi in 1318 (extended to the rest of France in 1321 at the instance of the bourgeoisie of the towns) had precisely similar results. The prohibition of exports was simply a method of establishing export duties. A policy of industrial protection was not yet a platform of government policy.

It is, then, only in the commercial field that government regulation played an important role at this time. In this regard the situation was being transformed by the rise of great industrial areas in the Low Countries and Italy and by the revival of long-range commerce. Yet industrial enterprise and the long-distance trader had to operate in an economic environment which had emerged deeply fragmented from the early Middle Ages. Both France and England were full of lords who were toll-takers, and their ranks were joined by the towns as they acquired rights of self-government. Communications were a local responsibility all too apt to be neglected. A chaos of local measures and local currencies was an inhibition to all but local exchanges. Disorder was still endemic enough to make life hazardous for the trader: even in much-governed thirteenth-century England the burgesses of Colchester had to seek the king's aid against the men of Winchelsea and Rye, the men of Yarmouth against damage to their fair by the men of the Cinque Ports, and the 'barons of London', going to Winchester fair, against the earl of Salisbury. The new towns, too, were parochial in their attitudes. The London customs of the first half of the twelfth century embodied the principle that local trade should be the preserve of local men, a principle which appears soon afterwards in the charters of other towns; and the 'hanses' of Paris and Rouen fought bitterly for predominance in the water traffic on the Seine. This narrowness of urban attitudes was partly inspired by a concern to safeguard their provisioning arrangements in case of dearth, something never far away in consequence of the low yield of medieval agriculture. Its catastrophic character, however, was aggravated by the barriers to communications and trade, including the defensive policies of the towns themselves. A local shortage, therefore, because of the difficulties in the way of securing supplies from a distance, might mean starvation for some and the spread of epidemics amongst an undernourished population. This was what happened in England in 1257-8 when a single poor harvest sent the prices of corn soaring in London (according to Matthew Paris) to a level four, or even six, times that of the preceding years. Many poor people died both of hunger and of pestilence, and even the rich could hardly escape death. The perennial problem of famine was one which faced governments in these centuries, as well as the problem of adjustment to the new economic circumstances of the time.

To one degree or another governments played their part in this process of adjustment. The Angevin rulers of England, indeed, made some sort of effort to weld their scattered dominions into a single trading area. Gascon merchants, those indispensable purveyors of wine, had special privileges in England. Welsh traders were welcomed in time of peace and Irish corn and victuals were normally given free entry. New customs were abolished which might have hampered trade between England and the Channel Isles. As for internal tolls, if burgesses cherished their own as an important source of borough revenues, kings showed sympathy for their desire for exemption from everyone else's. The men of Dover had freedom of toll throughout England in 1086 and the men of Bury St Edmunds in 1102-3. Similar freedom throughout the Angevin Empire was secured by Wallingford in 1156 and by a number of other towns (including London, Winchester, Newcastle, Bristol, Southampton and York) before the end of the twelfth century. The licensing of new tolls became a regalian right, sparingly exercised except for short periods and specific purposes (road- or bridge-building, walling towns, improving quays, etc.). Unauthorized imposts were quickly put down and 'outrageous' tolls prohibited by statute in 1275. In France the situation was more difficult. St Louis in 1256 forbade his officials to clog trade with prohibitions save for urgent causes; and it was ordained from time to time that new tolls should be put down and old ones used only for the maintenance of communications. But when almost every lord enjoyed some measure of 'toll autonomy' there were bound to be some tolls administered purely for their financial yield and created in restraint of trade.

Meanwhile other measures were stimulating the flow of commodities. The reform of currencies in the thirteenth century and, in France, the circulation of the 'good money of St Louis' in the baronies perhaps did something to this end. The English kings endeavoured to exercise some degree of supervision over the maintenance of roads and bridges and to keep waterways free for navigation. Both French and English rulers

were prodigal of licences establishing fairs and markets, though the initiative came generally from lords and towns desirous of augmenting
their revenues. It was doubtless in pursuit of such financial returns that
the kings of France developed the *Halles* of Paris as the markets of the
capital, though their achievements in this respect were far less spectacular
than those of the counts of Champagne. The Champagne fairs, still local
agricultural markets at the beginning of the twelfth century, were the
meeting point for the merchants of Flanders and Italy as well as all France
by the end of it. This was due in part to the positive policy of the counts.
They established the cycle of the fairs and covered with their protection
all merchants coming there. They gradually extended the radius of this
protection by agreements with neighbouring lords, and a seal was set on
this process in 1209 when Philip Augustus placed under royal safe-conduct all merchants going to the fairs. Comital *custodes* took charge of the
internal order and organization of the fairs, the complement to the protection offered by the counts to merchants in their coming and their
going.

At the same time, policies towards trade were not governed by an un-
diluted spirit of *laissez-faire*. The interest of kings and lords and towns
would not have been served thereby: the kings of France not only established the *Halles* of Paris, but made them the compulsory markets of the
capital. The king's profit from them depended on that degree of compulsion. Dearth, or the fear of dearth, tended to make the trade in victuals a trade controlled by authorities at every level. By the thirteenth century the rulers of kingdoms were beginning to take their hand in this
control. In France the export of grain was forbidden on a national or
regional level in 1270, 1274, 1277 and 1302. In England the attempt to
regulate the food trade was even more continuous, and included the laying down by the central authority of the prices and standards of quality of
the prime necessities of life by the assizes of bread and ale and wine.
Governments on the whole were concerned to foster commerce in their
lands, but they were not prepared to do so unconditionally.

Fostering commerce, however, as often as not meant attracting foreign traders, whose need for protection was even greater than that of
denizens. It is for this reason that the kings of England are found offering
safe-conducts, not only to individuals and merchants of particular cities,
but to whole 'nations' of merchants—Flemish (1204), Norwegian (1217),
French and Florentine (1234), Brabançon (1235), Swedish (1237), Portuguese (1308). Foreign traders came to enjoy special trading privileges
which, built up by piecemeal negotiation, were generalized by the *Carta
Mercatoria* of 1303. By this charter all alien merchants in England were
taken into the king's protection, freed from certain local charges, permitted to sell wholesale to whom they would and mercery by retail, and

promised speedy justice in pleas to which they were parties. Some aliens
had even greater privileges. As early as the mid-twelfth century the merchants of St Omer had their own *hospicium* in London and freedom of
access to markets and fairs, rights which the Danes and Norwegians
may have enjoyed even earlier. Eventually two groups of traders emerged with very special franchises: the Lombards and the Hansards. The latter succeeded to privileges first acquired by the citizens of Cologne who
were taken into Henry II's protection in 1175, had a gild-hall in London
by 1194 and the right of free access to all markets and fairs. Early in the
reign of Edward I the Londoners were coerced into recognizing that
these privileges belonged to all the German merchants who had come
together into a single 'hanse' at that time; and this association also won
the right to have its own 'mayor' who was empowered to hold a court
for pleas of debt, covenant and contract arising between members of the
'hanse'.

The kings of France made similar concessions to the merchants of
Flanders and Lombardy, the main groups of traders who met at the fairs
of Champagne. As early as 1193 Philip Augustus took into his protection
the men of Ypres, and Flemish merchants were the main beneficiaries of
the safe-conduct he extended to merchants frequenting the Champagne
fairs. By the end of the thirteenth century the Italians had also established
a privileged position. Philip III allowed them to settle at Nîmes with the
same protection as he gave to his bourgeoisie of Paris; they were not to
be impleaded outside the town, were exempt from guard duties, *tailles*
and *chevauchées*, and were allowed to form their own association under
their own 'rector'. Philip the Fair from time to time confirmed these
privileges; and Louis X proclaimed his intention of attracting the Lombards to his realm and permitted them to be domiciled in Paris, St Omer
and La Rochelle as well as Nîmes.

One problem which bulked large in negotiations with foreign traders
was the difficult one of trading debts. It was a common practice, where a
merchant failed to meet his obligations, for his creditors to seize upon the
goods of his co-townsmen or co-nationals. Conversely, merchants also
sometimes had difficulty in securing payments due to them. Thus, in the
first place, merchants were continuously seeking to avoid liability for
debts for which they were not principals or pledges. A privilege to
this effect was widely conceded to English townsmen in the twelfth
century and extended to all English merchants by statute in 1275.
Italian, Flemish and Hanseatic merchants obtained a similar privilege
both in England and France, and the English monarchy did its best to
make the licensing of commercial reprisals a regalian power to be used
only in the last resort. Again, something was done to assist merchants in
collecting debts due to them. Philip the Fair helped the Lombards in this

respect; from John's reign the machinery of the English exchequer could be used by merchants to levy business debts; and in 1283 and 1285 Edward I made provision for the enrolment of such debts and rapid processes to satisfy creditors, measures which seem to have the foreign trader particularly in mind.

There were many reasons for this benevolence to alien merchants. It might be directly profitable. The first general licence for Flemish merchants to trade in England cost them 400 marks; royal protection to foreign traders in 1204, 1266 and 1303 was given in return for charges on their trade; and in 1245 Henry III told the Italians and Cahorsins that if they wished to carry on trade and usury in his lands they must make him a large gift or loan. The dealings of Philip III and Philip IV with the Italians in France were of like sort and the *financia Italicorum* became a regular receipt of the royal treasury. At the same time foreigners (and Italians in particular) were valued as financiers, financial agents, minters, even as diplomats: it was, for example, as financial officers of the English Crown that merchants of Genoa and Florence first came to Bordeaux. Yet these financial and political arguments in themselves are perhaps insufficient to explain the deliberation with which the alien merchant was protected in face of the hostility of native townsmen. When the Londoners in 1290 demanded the expulsion of foreign traders, Edward I replied roundly *rex intendit quod mercatores extranei sunt ydonei et utiles magnatibus*. This view he upheld against the Londoners on other occasions; and the English magnates themselves expressed their sense of the utility of the foreign trader in their petition of 1258 and in the Great Charter of 1215. The kings and magnates of France seem to have been in substantial agreement with them, particularly where the merchants of Lombardy were concerned.

No doubt the nobility were moved by the financial services which stranger merchants rendered them and by the profit accruing from their presence at markets and fairs. At the same time, this confluence of royal and noble sentiment provides the link between the policies of the time towards internal and overseas trade. Royal and noble households were still to a large extent peripatetic and were very large centres of consumption. An internal policy designed to increase the available supply of goods of reasonable price and quality was clearly to the interest of both; it was no less in their interest to smooth the path of the foreign importer. England relied for the most part on Gascons to bring wine, Flemish to bring high-grade cloth, Hansards to bring furs and wax, and Italians to bring the silks and spices of the Mediterranean and Levantine lands. For this reason they were 'useful to the magnates' and indispensable purveyors to the courts of kings; and policies contravening the narrow interest of town traders and craftsmen commanded the assent of the dominant political classes. But these policies came to serve other purposes. Italy, Flanders and even the Midi required English wool and Flanders the agricultural surpluses of northern France: thus the long-range commerce which kings and princes helped to foster was also useful to the magnates in providing an outlet for the produce of their estates. Not until the end of the thirteenth century was this confluence of interests reaching something of a term. Restraints on wool exports from the Languedoc after 1277 to satisfy the clothing interest provoked opposition from the countryside, as did the embargo on the export of foodstuffs against which 'various religious, nobles and others' petitioned Charles IV in 1324. Government policy was beginning to fall out of line with the desire of the agricultural classes that all should have access to their supplies. Export taxes worked in the same direction; for, as the English landowners pointed out during the crisis over the *maltote* on wool in 1297, they tended to depress producer prices. The growing importance of industrial interests in the primary producing areas was combining with government financial measures to undermine the identity of royal and landlord interests which had inspired the commercial policies of the twelfth and thirteenth centuries.

D. *War and Economic Policy*

Export taxes, however, were primarily war taxes in the first instance, and must be considered in relation with other effects of war upon economic policies. Any military campaign, of course, involved economic measures. It had to be financed. In the absence of regular navies trading vessels were seized to transport troops and supplies. The supplies themselves had to be requisitioned. Such 'prises' were amongst the rights of the Crown the English barons desired to regulate in 1215, and in 1297 the archbishop of Canterbury threatened to excommunicate the royal ministers responsible for purveying goods for the king's needs. It is also probably no accident that promises by St Louis to redress grievances about prises in 1254 and 1256 followed close upon his first crusade. But requisitioning did not exhaust the economic consequences of war. Even the relatively minor Welsh campaigns of Henry III were prefaced by orders closing the markets of the marcher counties to compel merchants to bring their goods to the king's camp, concentrating boats on the Severn for transport and prohibiting trade with the enemy. The export of foodstuffs might be forbidden to conserve supplies and keep down home prices: Edward I took this step during the Scottish campaign of 1307 and Philip the Fair in 1302, 1304, 1305 and 1314. Trade might only be permitted under royal licence, in order that enemy countries could be denied essential supplies. At the same time, the interruption of normal trading often helped to exacerbate the difficulties of provisioning the great consuming centres, with the consequent danger of an outbreak of civil disorder. In 1304, for example, Philip the Fair was compelled for this reason to ordain that all surplus grain in the Paris region should be brought to the city markets for sale at fixed prices. Fixing prices merely dried up supplies, however, so instead anyone was allowed to pursue the mystery of baking in the city, grain was to be sold only on the open market at reasonable prices, and everyone was urged to bring victuals of all sorts for sale in Paris. In 1307, to keep down prices and increase the supply of goods, an ordinance fixed wages and the conditions of trade in the capital and set aside gild statutes restricting the number of apprentices and forbidding night work. These were emergency and transitory measures, but they marked a significant extension of the range of government intervention.

Measures of economic warfare also began to play a larger part in diplomatic history. One focus of these measures was the Low Countries. This great industrial area depended on England for wool, on both France and England for markets and for supplies of grain and other foodstuffs, and on France for transit facilities for its south-bound commerce. It was vulnerable to economic pressure and strategically important in any conflict between France and England, while the riches of Flanders made the French kings anxious to give reality to their claims to feudal superiority over the county. Thus in 1173–4 Henry II included economic retaliation amongst the measures he took to punish the count of Flanders for supporting his son's rebellion. Richard and John forced Flanders into their coalition of the princes of Germany and the Low Countries, directed against Philip Augustus, by confiscating the goods of Flemish merchants in England and forbidding the export of grain and wool to Flanders. Edward I used similar methods to build up his system of alliances against France in 1294. The men of Holland, Brabant and Germany were rewarded for their adherence by the grant of commercial privileges in England, and Flemish loyalty to the French connection was answered by the withdrawal of the English king's protection from the merchants of Flanders. When Flanders renounced her French alliance in 1297 and recovered the right to trade in England her merchants were promptly arrested in the fairs of France. The Flemish, however, were soon deserted by Edward when he composed his differences with France: in 1303 he excluded them from trade in England in return for a promise by Philip the Fair to ban Franco-Scottish trade. Flanders was left alone to face the full weight both of military and economic action on the part of France. Flemish merchants were denied transit facilities and access to French markets, and agreements with Hainault, Brabant and Cologne were aimed at preventing the merchants of these places being used by the

Flemish as intermediaries. Economic warfare had become an indispensable adjunct of the more conventional arms.

Economic aims, of course, were here subordinated to military or diplomatic ends. Measures of economic warfare form part of an assemblage of governmental acts which harnessed economic enterprise to political expediency, cast it into new moulds, and sought to extract from it revenue and political advantage. Edward I's dealings with the wool trade are typical. He greatly increased the taxation of that trade with his *maltote* of 1294–7. In addition, in order to facilitate his financial manipulation of the trade and the realization of his diplomatic ends, he diverted most of the wool exports to specified ports in Holland and later in Brabant. The establishment of a system of export licences in France also made it desirable to drive trade into channels which were convenient to the financial administration. Less regular methods than customs duties and charges for trading licences were used, particularly in France, to secure contributions from traders to financial needs aggravated by war. The 'sudden riches' of the Italians proved especially tempting to rulers. Their banking and money-lending operations made them vulnerable to charges of the sin of usury; and attacks on usurers were a popular political gesture, the efficacy of which had been proved time and time again by the measures taken against the Jews. It was this pretext which was used by Philip III when he arrested the goods of the Lombards in 1277. He was then in a position to exact a substantial payment from the Italian community before he restored its property. Similar operations were carried out by Philip the Fair on a number of occasions, to say nothing of the dukes and counts of Burgundy and others. The regular annual payments made by the Italians for their privileges in France were supplemented by periodic ransoms.

Thus, especially in the war years at the end of the thirteenth century, the pattern of commercial relationships was being wrested to fit changing diplomatic and military situations. Raids on commercial capital, like those of the French rulers upon Italian resources, undermined confidence. Taxation began to have a noticeable effect on economic life: the English barons in 1297 were able to point to the effect of export taxes on producer prices for wool, and in 1309 parliament expressed its conviction that the import taxes paid by alien merchants raised the cost of living. Currency manipulation, too, especially by Philip the Fair as one method of raising money for his wars, was yet another disturbing factor. Apart from raising the cost of living and devaluing fixed incomes at home, it had its international effects. Pope Boniface VIII was probably right in arguing in 1296 that it precluded merchants from the customary ways of trade; certainly it devalued the debts due to Florentine merchant-bankers in France (it was not for nothing that Dante denounced Philip as a false moneyer) and forced the count of Flanders to debase the currency of his county. Monetary disequilibria between nations were aggravated and more stringent exchange control became the order of the day to safeguard internal supplies of currency and bullion. The transfer of balances on which international trade depended became correspondingly more difficult. Some place must be allowed to all of this amongst the assemblage of causes of the contraction of economic activity during the later Middle Ages; and some check was imposed upon the tendency of western Europe to become more of a commercial unit and a single field of operations for international business firms. The interruption of normal trade, raids on their capital and the heavy demand of governments for loans which were not always fully and seldom promptly repaid caused exceptional difficulties precisely to these international firms: the ruin of the Riccardi, for instance, was very largely due to the Anglo-French war which began in 1294. Nor was it easy for such firms to retain their interest and their assets in both of two warring countries, however essential that might be for their prosperity. Political factors were coming to dominate economic development much more positively than in the past.

(4) THE LATER MIDDLE AGES

A. *The Economic Background and Government Finance*

Government economic measures during the later Middle Ages were conditioned by two sets of influences. Displacements in the pattern of communications and the centres of economic activity caused local and temporary crises which broadened into something like a general crisis of the medieval economy. The fall in population called for regulation of the conditions of labour. Changes in the direction of commerce and the location of industry combined with monetary fluctuations and the contraction of markets to provoke demands for commercial regulation, import control and industrial protection. Everywhere political backing was sought for monopolistic privilege which would assure to the beneficiaries a disproportionate share of the reduced economic cake. Governments, moreover, were more sensitive to such demands when the growth of representative institutions strengthened the hands of subjects in bargaining with their rulers. But if subjects called for some of the tunes, reasons of state continued to be no less effective. The financial needs of governments expanded, particularly during the fairly prolonged periods of warfare. In terms of the resources available, war was still costly enough for financial considerations to dominate very many of the acts of governments.

The thirteenth-century transformation of royal budgets therefore, became permanent. Traditional revenues were increasingly overshadowed by 'extraordinary' levies, though subjects refused fully to accept that fact. Richard II's parliaments more than once demanded that he should 'live of his own', and Henry IV won some support in 1399 by pretending he would tax neither clergy nor laity. In France, too, the *ordonnance Cabochienne* and the Estates in 1484 clung to the notion that taxation was 'extraordinary'; and Charles VIII was credited with the intention of living from his domain, though in fact his chancellor in 1484 committed him to no such impossible course. Such sentiments had been outstripped by the facts. The receipts of the English exchequer in 1374–5, for example, totalled £112,000 of which only £22,000 came from the hereditary revenues of the Crown; £82,000 came from direct and indirect taxes and the balance from borrowing.[1] In the early years of Henry VI, again, the customs alone accounted for over £30,000 out of an annual revenue averaging £57,000. Taxation, in short, had become indispensable.

Direct taxes in England, it is true, could not be levied as a matter of course. The normal taxes were the lay subsidy (of the type established by Edward I) granted by parliament and the clerical subsidy granted by the convocations of the two provinces of the English Church. The lay subsidy, moreover, had been stabilized in amount in 1334, though the king could and did in case of grave necessity secure the grant of more than one 'tenth and fifteenth'. Stabilization did, however, make it more difficult to keep taxation abreast of changes in the distribution of wealth, and rebates had to be made from time to time to depressed areas. In addition, the lay subsidy had to be extracted on each occasion from an unwilling parliament. Alternative experiments in direct taxation (the poll-taxes of 1377, 1379 and 1381 and the taxes on incomes from land in the fifteenth century) also required parliamentary sanction; and in the end it was from the taxation of trade that the English Crown acquired the most substantial regular addition to its revenues. The customs established by Edward I were augmented by an export duty on cloth in 1347 and, about the same time, by tunnage on wine imports and poundage on the import and export of general merchandise. The wool export tax, however, remained the pre-eminent indirect tax. The duty of 6s. 8d. per sack established in 1275 was progressively raised from the 1330's, and eventually settled down at 33s. 4d. for native and 66s. 8d. for foreign merchants. This custom, together with tunnage and poundage and the cloth duty, was eventually granted for life to Henry V, to Henry VI after 1453, and to Edward IV. Thus, although parliament in the fourteenth century established the same theoretical control over the customs as it did over direct taxes, the former in fact more and more became part of the 'normal'

[1] Calculated from the Receipt Roll by Dr G. A. Holmes and kindly put at my disposal.

revenues of the Crown. Yielding £30,000 or more yearly in the early years of Henry VI, £25,000 even in the depression of the 1460's and £35,000 in the 1470's, the customs were the very basis of late medieval government finance.[1] On the other hand, the importance in the customs revenue of taxation of the wool trade (in full decline from the late fourteenth century), combined with the antiquated assessment of the lay subsidy, made English Crown revenues increasingly out of touch with economic realities. This may help to explain the apparently archaic tendency at the very end of the Middle Ages for Edward IV, Richard III and Henry VII to revert to a much greater dependence upon the issues of the swollen royal estates (from which Richard extracted a gross income of £35,000 and a net income of £25,000 yearly).[2]

There were certain direct economic consequences of this development of Crown revenues. Firstly, from the middle of the fourteenth century, the wool customs were far heavier than the duties on exported cloth. The English cloth industry was, therefore, doubly protected: cloth could be exported at charges which were extremely light compared with those on the raw materials of the rival industry across the Channel, while the heavy export duty on wool helped to depress the price paid by the English manufacturer for his raw materials. This need not be accounted deliberate policy. In the early years of the Hundred Years War wool was both the major export and the traditional object of taxation: thereafter the pattern simply persisted till the goose was killed that had laid the golden egg. The protection afforded to the cloth industry was an accident of fiscal policy. Secondly, Edward I had already imposed heavier charges on alien than on native merchants in 1303. In the later Middle Ages this disparity was increased and probably helped native traders to secure a growing share of English trade. That this was a primary intention is more doubtful, for the pattern of the customs-system is at least as likely to have been determined by the vulnerability of the foreign trader to financial exactions. On the other hand, the pressure of English interests as time went on certainly gave encouragement to the imposition of discriminatory taxes on alien merchants.

Changes in French government finance in this period were both similar and dissimilar to those taking place in England. War and civil war brought the domain of the French Crown, in the phrase of the Ordinance of Saumur of 1445, *en ruine et comme en non-valoir*. In 1460 the 'extraordinary' exceeded the hereditary revenues of the Crown by thirty-three times, and by forty-five times at the death of Louis XI. In the earlier part of the Hundred Years War desperate improvisation had continued

[1] F. Dietz, *English Government Finance (1485–1558)*, 12–13, 25.
[2] B. P. Wolffe, 'The Management of the English Royal Estates under the Yorkist Kings', *Eng. Hist. Rev.* LXXI, 1–27.

to be the hall-mark of French government finance, as it had been in the days of Philip the Fair. The outlines of the French financial system of the future, however, were firmly drawn by Charles V. By about 1370 he had established his right to receive the *taille* (a direct tax payable by non-nobles in the north and centre and on non-noble property in the south), the *aides* (internal sales taxes) and the *gabelle* (the proceeds of the royal monopoly of the salt trade). Though overturned at his death, Charles V's system was substantially restored by 1388, continued to underlie the shifts and expedients of the troubled times in the early fifteenth century, and was re-erected by Charles VII. Under Charles VII, too, the *taille* and the *aides* largely ceased to be extraordinary taxes in the strict sense. They were levied, at least from 1451, solely on the royal authority and at rates determined by royal authority. Towards the end of Charles's reign the *taille* produced an annual yield of about 1,200,000 *li.* or about two-thirds of his revenue; under Louis XI its yield was as high as 4,600,000 *li.* in 1481 and 3,900,000 *li.* in 1483, accounting for as much as 85% of the total revenue.

There is, therefore, a considerable divergence between the financial histories of France and England in the later Middle Ages. In the first place, taxes on foreign trade, so important to the English kings, were comparatively unimportant in France. Such taxes existed: the *imposition foraine* was added in 1369 to the export duties established earlier in the fourteenth century, and Louis XI imposed a few import duties. But in 1523 all of these together produced only 15,000 *li.* as compared with the 1,000,000 *li.* from charges on internal trade (the *aides* and the *gabelle*).[1] The export duties, too, were partly charges on internal trade, being levied on goods passing from the north into the Midi and thus combining with other tolls (in Colbert's words) to 'divide the kingdom into two parts'. All this, no doubt, reflects the French lack of a staple export commodity and the comparative importance in the economy of internal and transit trade. Secondly, indirect taxes were of far less importance than direct taxes to the French Crown. This was due in part to the failure of France to secure a major independent stake in the grand commerce of the day; but it was also due to the fact that national and provincial representative institutions failed to obtain the control over the *taille* which the English parliament exercised over the lay subsidy. This in turn may have been partly due to the fact that the clergy and the nobility, the most influential classes politically, from an early date secured exemption from the *taille*, and that in the late fourteenth and early fifteenth centuries some of the greater feudatories acquired a vested interest in it by reason of the share of the *taille* they were permitted to collect in their lands and the pensions they exacted from the Crown. The *taille*, therefore, was a

[1] R. Doucet, *Institutions de la France au XVIe siècle*, II, 556 ff.

tax falling upon the ordinary townsman and above all upon the peasant.[1] The only economic argument which can be advanced to justify this discrimination was that the long-term trend for the value of money to fall reduced the burden of peasant rents and increased the market value of peasant produce. So it is that Alain Chartier could write of the peasantry in 1422 that 'their purse is like the cistern which has gathered and is gathering the water from the gutters of all the wealth in the kingdom'. The financial policy of the Crown was designed to take advantage of this redistribution of wealth in favour of a class particularly vulnerable to exploitation by siphoning it off through the *taille*.

The rise of more or less regular taxation does not, of course, exhaust the multiplication of financial burdens. Currency manipulation, though its incidence may have been exaggerated, continued to be a regular expedient of the kings of France and was pursued to extreme lengths in 1336–43, 1349–60 and 1415–30. Borrowing, sometimes under some degree of compulsion, from churches, towns, trading companies and individuals was necessary in peace and vital in war; and there was nothing unusual in the order Louis XI gave to his treasurer to 'find money in the magic box', the purses of his citizens of Paris. Requisitioning of goods, particularly of military supplies, was a constant grievance. This was the sort of irregular levy for which no allowance could be made in private budgets, and payment (if made at all) was apt to be in government paper which had to be discounted at a loss. It is hardly surprising that in 1338 the clergy were called on to soothe the people in face of the demands of Edward III's purveyors or that in 1351 the Commons sought to subject their activities to parliamentary control.

The total effect of government financial measures upon the economy of the later Middle Ages cannot be accurately determined. Government purchases must have stimulated some branches of industry and a crop of war profiteers (contractors, financiers and mercenary captains) invested some of their gains, particularly in landed property. On the other hand, a good deal of capital was diverted to non-productive uses through the medium of taxation and borrowing. Currency manipulation and the treatment of government creditors at times threatened the basis of all credit and international trade. The bankruptcy of the Bardi and Peruzzi in the 1340's, like that of the Riccardi half a century earlier, is merely a particularly striking instance of the effect of war on international trade and finance. As for the ordinary man, there is the first-hand comment of a fourteenth-century English rhymer: 'Now the fifteenth runs in England year after year . . . the common folk must sell their cows, their utensils, even their clothing. . . Still more hard on simple folk is the wool col-

[1] Exemption from *taille* was also accorded to many towns, especially by Louis XI; see p. 490.

lection; commonly it makes them sell their possessions... At market the buyers are so few that in fact a man can do no business... because so many are destitute.' This may not be a true picture all the time, but it is not complete exaggeration any more than the comments upon the misery of the French peasant in the reign of Louis XI. Raids on the margins of small men, as the peasantry took over from their lords almost the whole work of agricultural production, contributed to the running down of agricultural investment; and they also aggravated the stresses to which the late medieval polity was subjected. The English peasants' revolt of 1381 followed directly upon an attempt to levy a poll-tax; while in 1380–2 the men of Rouen rose against the attempt to re-impose the *taille* and taxes on liquor and cloth, and the Parisians against the attempt to re-establish the sales taxes abolished at the death of Charles V. The fact that the increase in centralized authority displayed itself so often as an authority to tax the small man is one explanation of the *jacqueries* and urban revolts which bulk larger in political history.

B. *Wages, Agriculture and Industry*

In the meantime other economic problems were forcing themselves into the forefront of politics. One of them was the labour problem created by the Black Death and succeeding pestilences. Heavy mortality led to a dearth of labour and demands for higher wages; dearth of labour and higher wages made ordinary consumer goods scarce and dear. Thus concern on the part of employers coincided with concern on the part of governments, the traditional defenders of consumer interests. In England the series of labour laws beginning in 1349 gave primacy to the problem in the countryside. These laws fixed maximum wages, first at pre-1349 rates and later according to the current price of wheat; compelled labourers to observe their contracts; and restricted the mobility of labour in the interests of agriculture. In 1376, for example, the export of Cotswold yarn was forbidden partly because the spinning industry drew labour from the harvest field. In 1388 anyone who had served in husbandry up to the age of twelve had to continue to do so, and in the fifteenth century men with less than 20s. a year in land were debarred from apprenticing their sons to a craft because of the 'great dearness of labourers and other servants in husbandry'. Similarly, legislation directed against beggars and vagabonds was designed to mobilize all possible sources of labour. Labour legislation, however, was not only concerned with rural labour. The ordinance of 1349 also stabilized the rewards of a long list of craftsmen and artificers; and a statute of 1416 laid down 'certain wages... for bailiffs and other servants of husbandry, and likewise for other servants and labourers as well within cities and boroughs as elsewhere throughout

W

the realm'. In both town and country these laws were only partially successful: employers themselves, competing with each other for labour,
more than once sought statutory indemnity for having broken them.
Wage-levels certainly rose in the century after 1349, though it is likely
that the labour laws kept the rise within bounds which the economy
could stand.

The French ordinances dealing with the labour problem differ
markedly from the English statutes. There were general edicts dealing
with wage-levels; but either they arose (like those of 1330, 1332, etc.)
out of the chaos introduced into wage contracts by currency changes, or
like that of 1351 they were attempts to grapple with a specific catastrophe (in this case the aftermath of the Black Death). There is nothing
comparable to the consistent and continuous English legislation. This
may have been due in part to the fact that manorial exploitation decayed
earlier and more completely in France, and that the government was
under less pressure from the landed classes to regulate wages and conditions of labour (save occasionally for the vineyards). More important,
however, wages seem to have risen less sharply in France and therefore
attracted far less government attention. It was not that France escaped a
reduction of population by plague, but that disruption due to war, restrictive town and craft by-laws and other circumstances which have yet
to be established kept the level of production low enough to prevent any
very marked upward trend in wages over the long term.[1]

Thus, even in 1351, wage regulations were a secondary matter. The
basic concern of the great ordinance of that year was the cost of living in
the capital. The control of wages and the rates of profit of middlemen
were merely a small part of a code which annulled the rules of the Parisian corporations which, in the words of the Dauphin Charles, served the
interests of the persons engaged in each trade rather than the common
good. Masters were allowed to take more apprentices and the period of
apprenticeship was lowered, the victualling trades were put under closer
supervision, barriers to the entry of new masters were lowered, 'foreign'
traders were allowed to do business freely in the city. In short, high
prices were attacked by attempts to increase production and supply.
Moreover, the ordinance was a measure to deal with a specific emergency
and soon passed into the limbo of forgotten things. Its main significance,
perhaps, is in demonstrating the increasing detail of royal control over
the towns and the crafts within the towns.

Royal policy towards the towns and crafts of France, however, cannot
for this reason be dismissed as one hostile to bourgeois interests: on the
contrary, it culminated in the 'tacit alliance of the monarchy and the

[1] E. Perroy, 'Wage Labour in France in the Later Middle Ages', *Econ. Hist. Rev.*
1955, 232 ff.

masters' of Louis XI's reign. Both sides derived advantage from this marriage of convenience. The king found administrative instruments in the governments of towns and crafts, and won the political support of those classes with an interest in imposing discipline upon the forces of discontent within the towns. In return the *haute bourgeoisie* was confirmed in its control over cities and corporations, and secured royal backing for town customs and craft regulations safeguarding its interests. It could turn to the king for support against a disorderly nobility, as the citizens of Puy did to Louis XI against the vicomte de Polignac; or against the lords of the towns, Louis again aiding Lyons and Beauvais against their bishops and Rodez and Figeac against the count of Armagnac. This royal protection was not to be despised in a land so often threatened by foreign invasion and civil disorder.[1] The price which had to be paid was the subordination of the craft corporations to town governments and of both to the central authority. The towns, both in the domain and the lands of the nobility, were integrated into the system of royal administration—one aspect of the internal conquest of power by the monarchy. It was the same with the corporations. They served to assess and collect taxes, to raise troops, to police the towns, and as the agencies for executing royal economic policies. They had to seek royal confirmation for their statutes, which permitted the Crown to buttress its alliance with the *haute bourgeoisie* by sanctioning rules in their interest. At the same time the Crown had achieved a position which enabled it to intervene with larger objectives in view at times of emergency like those which followed the Black Death, or of reconstruction like those following the major campaigns of the Hundred Years War. The ordinance of 1351, Charles VI's suspension of restrictive rules about apprenticeship and the employment of 'foreign' workers at Rouen, and the sanction given by Louis XI to night work at Troyes are examples of the way in which the power of the Crown over town and corporation could be used to set aside particular interests for that of *la chose publique*.

Town interests in great measure also dominated the regulation of the grain trade in later medieval France. Production of grain was clearly affected by the demographic crisis and also by the ravages of war: it was at the height of the English domination round 1420 that the bodies of children dead from cold and starvation could be seen upon the dunghills of Paris. But these difficulties merely aggravated the periodic problem of famine which was still taxing all the ingenuity of Colbert in 1662; and famine brought in its wake pestilence, civil disorder and the exacerbation of class hatred. There was no exaggeration in the remark of a bourgeois of Puy-en-Velay in 1529 that 'when God afflicts his people with famine the

[1] R. Gandilhon, *Politique économique de Louis XI*, especially p. 166; H. Sée, *Louis XI et les villes*, 8–10, 165–7, 248 ff.

government of communes is very difficult'. The barriers to inter-regional communication continued to make local dearth the consequence even of a single bad harvest in any given locality; while dearth or even fear of dearth immediately gave rise to a demand for strict control over the movement of grain between districts, thus tending to perpetuate inter-regional barriers. Grain policy, therefore, took only a limited account of the interests of agricultural producers and was for the most part a local or regional matter. Only in the reign of Louis XI did something more like a national grain policy begin to be superimposed upon local regulation. This policy was still in the main unfriendly to freedom of export abroad; on the other hand, in 1482 Louis attempted to establish free circulation of grain within the country in order to relieve the famine conditions prevailing in many parts. At the same time the restraints on exports abroad were only partly designed to safeguard domestic supplies and keep down home prices; for they were also designed to apply economic pressure to the Burgundian provinces in the Low Countries. The complaints of the landed interests in the Assembly of Notables in 1470 failed in any way to prevail against these reasons of state.

Grain policy in England, like labour policy, treated the landed interests far less cavalierly. In the fourteenth century both government policy and public sentiment, as reflected by petitions in parliament, favoured export restrictions in view of high prices and scarcity at home. By the end of the century, however, grain production seems normally to have been adequate for domestic needs, and Acts of 1394 and 1426 allowed grain to be freely exported. Further statutes of 1437 and 1442, made permanent in 1445, repeated this concession provided nothing was exported to enemy countries and domestic prices did not rise above specified levels. The grain trade, therefore, was exempted from control save for political reasons and during years of scarcity. In 1463 an Act more definitely protective of occupiers in husbandry forbade the import of grain until domestic prices had passed a specified point. The grower could thus expect something like a minimum price, and the Act is a further indication that supply could normally be expected to satisfy or even exceed the needs of the home market.

If agriculture, in these ways, was falling within the province of government regulation, so too was industry. In England in the later Middle Ages the major economic change was the growth of the cloth industry and the export trade in cloth. Since 1197 the English government had professed concern for the standard of cloth coming onto the English market, and as late as 1328 the Statute of Northampton ordered royal officials, the ulnagers, to measure imported cloths to determine whether or not they conformed to the assize. In 1315, however, English merchants were demanding that the ulnagers should search out defects in the products of the native worsted industry; and more and more the inspection of native fabrics (together with the collection of penalties for cloths below standard and of the subsidy on cloths for sale) became the most important task of these officials. The fact that the cloth industry of the later Middle Ages was increasingly a scattered rural industry, in which the gilds played little part, no doubt made this government inspectorate of particular value to the export merchants.

These measures were far from being the end of state intervention. In 1326 the Londoners obtained a ban on the export of teasels and fuller's earth to the Low Countries, and the reign of Edward III was fertile in expedients which stimulated the growth of the English textile industry. The export of wool to and import of cloth from Flanders were forbidden, foreign cloth-workers were welcomed in England, and heavy export taxes were levied on wool. Edward was mainly concerned by these measures to apply pressure to Flanders for diplomatic ends or to raise revenue, but they helped the expansion of the industry none the less and helped to create an interest (both manufacturing and mercantile) which could claim more deliberate support. As early as 1377 export of unfinished cloth was forbidden; and under Henry VI regulations compelling alien merchants to pay cash for what they bought were relaxed for their cloth purchases, and men were forbidden to buy yarn unless they intended to make cloth from it. Public policy, however, was outstripped by private sentiment. It was one of the counts against the Lancastrian kings that they permitted wool to be exported and Edward IV was soon pushed into measures protecting the cloth industry. A statute of 1463 was prefaced by a declaration to which the king could expect a favourable response. 'The chief and principal commodity of the realm of England consisteth in the wools growing in the said realm', and it was intended that 'sufficient plenty of the said wools may continually abide and remain within the said realm as may competently and reasonably serve for the occupation of clothmakers'. In the next few years restraints were imposed on the export of wool, yarn and unfinished cloth, and advance purchase of the wool clip by export merchants was forbidden.

These measures were neither without precedent nor long-lived, though they were inspired by genuine competition with the Low Countries. For some time English manufacturers had been seeking to divert to their own use the wool upon which the Flemish industry depended, and the textile industry across the Channel had been meeting competition from English cloth, much of which was marketed in such entrepôts as Antwerp and Bergen-op-Zoom. Thus the English clothing interests were inclined to demand restraint on the export of wool and the Low Countries a ban on the import of English cloth, demands to which their rulers from time to time acceded in the course of the fifteenth century. At the same time, since an embargo on one side was commonly answered by a counter-embargo from the other, the result was generally stalemate: for the Low Countries could not for long dispense with English wool or England with the markets of the Low Countries. The dispute of the 1460's followed the familiar pattern, and there were also diplomatic reasons for ending such a situation. Neither Edward IV nor the duke of Burgundy could afford to sacrifice their alliance against Louis XI to satisfy the clothiers of their respective lands. The restrictive measures on both sides were soon considerably relaxed, even though Bruges remained intransigent about the admission of English cloth.

In this instance a protectionist policy was procured by the exercise of pressure on the government by the industry and the exporters, but it was soon modified because it had undesirable economic consequences and came into conflict with diplomatic expediency. None the less the English kings were now expected to foster the clothing industry, and even a poet adjured Edward IV to

> Restrayne strayttly the wool,
> That the comyns of thys land may wyrke at the fulle.

One consequence was that diplomacy itself in the later fifteenth century became more and more concerned with economic matters. In the meanf time other industrial groups were demanding protection. The import osilk was banned in 1463 and 1484 at the instance of the 'king's woeful men and women of the whole craft of silk-work' in London; and in the same years statutes directed against the Flemish and Italians respectively prohibited the import of divers goods—caps and cloth, lace and silk, dice and tennis balls, chafing dishes and sacring bells, painted images and holy-water stoups. These Acts were neither permanent nor effective, but at least they show that there were now many voices asking for protection and that in favourable circumstances their demands could be translated into government policy. This was due in part to the fact that such voices could make themselves heard in parliament.

French industrial policy in the later Middle Ages was less protectionist and less dominated by the interests of a single industry. The clothing trades, even in Languedoc, failed to secure more than intermittent support for their policy of restraint upon the export of wool, dyestuffs, etc.; and for the most part government policy was directed to maintaining standards of manufacture through town and craft regulation. Wider objectives make their appearance only in the fifteenth century. The government played some part in the work of reconstruction which was necessary after the Hundred Years War. Louis XI established *l'art de la draperie* at Montpellier to remedy the decayed state of the town and exempted the cloth industry in Poitiers from taxation, 'because by no other means can it people and fortify itself'. The establishment of the silk industry at Lyons and Tours also owed much to his deliberate policy. His motives in this were not unmixed. It was partly an act of economic warfare directed against the Venetians, though Louis also professed a desire to check the drain of bullion abroad (estimated by him to amount to half a million crowns of gold yearly). The armament industry attracted even more attention. Louis reorganized the machinery for supplying the armed forces, imported prototypes of improved equipment (particularly artillery) and set native manufacturers to work reproducing them, and made the manufacture of saltpetre a veritable state industry. Foreign technicians were welcomed in France—silk-workers, miners, Dinant coppersmiths, German glass-workers, even printers, whose value Louis recognized for the production of government propaganda. Parts of the mining industry were more or less 'nationalized', particularly mining for precious metals. Some sectors of industry were becoming very much the concern of the state.

Late medieval policies safeguarding home producers are hardly patient of any single explanation. Some were bought by hard cash or won by effective political pressure applied by the interests concerned: the measures favouring agriculture in England, for instance, or the cloth industry both in England and Languedoc. Policies of this sort, however, were all too apt to be quietly shelved when they interfered with the grand strategic interests of governments or were countered by the effective representation of contrary views. Policies deriving more narrowly from government initiative were more often designed to further the power of the central authority, and were most prominent in France where that power had still in some respects to be created. Royal control over towns and corporations broadened the base of the king's authority. The creation of state industries or state-controlled industries was a method of securing revenue or military supply, or of safeguarding within the kingdom stocks of wealth needed to satisfy the mounting demands of the Crown. Only the need for reconstruction in a country devastated and disorganized by war seems to have prompted more disinterested attempts to stimulate economic activity. In other respects and at other times the primary concern of government seems to have been the protection of the interest of the consumer, with his call for an adequate supply of low-price goods of reasonable quality. This policy reflected the common interest of courts, the landed nobility and the patriciates of towns. Its persistence in medieval economic history is perhaps due in the last resort to the fact that these classes, in kingdoms and local communities, were the rulers of the land.

C. *The Home Market and the Foreign Trader*

Side by side, therefore, with incipient manifestations of a policy of power, the old policies of plenty persisted through the later Middle Ages. Markets were controlled in the interest of the buyer and of public order, always likely to break down when provisioning arrangements collapsed. Attempts were made, for instance, to check the tendency for prices to rise owing to wartime difficulties, dislocation due to plague and tampering with the coinage. The English labour laws empowered the justices to fix local tariffs for victuals, the prices of poultry and candles were fixed by statute, and constant attention was given to wine prices, which rose rapidly when Gascon supplies were interrupted by war. In France the Crown was continuously concerned about prices in the capital and currency changes evoked pious adjurations to merchants and craftsmen to charge only 'just, lawful and reasonable prices'. In Brittany, too, in 1425, the *juges ordinaires* were ordered to fix prices for foodstuffs, and prelates, barons and others to see that their men obeyed them. The quality of goods brought to market aroused a similar concern. A network of royal wine-gaugers in England enforced regulations for the quality of wines, and a like preoccupation may explain the powers of search conferred by Edward III on the London skinners and girdlers or by Charles VI on the drapers of Rouen. The old battle for standard weights and measures also pursued its unsuccessful course, with Philip V's efforts in this direction in France and the monotonous series of English statutes which even prescribed the capacity of barrels for eels and butts for salmon.

It was, however, the problem of food-supply which remained the overriding preoccupation of subjects and governments. It dominated the grain policies of the later Middle Ages, cancelling the liberalism of English governments in years of dearth and winning royal backing for the provisioning policies of the French towns, particularly in the famine years of the early fourteenth century, the 1340's, the early 1430's and the early 1480's. Ordinances commanded growers to deliver foodstuffs to the town markets and forbade middleman-dealings in victuals. Royal officers backed up the town authorities, as at Toulouse in 1375, in requisitioning grain and forbidding the export of local stocks. The duke of Brittany, likewise, in 1425, prohibited the export of foodstuffs and forbade victuallers to 'make monopoly and congregation together' to exploit shortages and raise prices 'to the fraud, deception, damage and prejudice of all the common good'. English legislation generalized urban rules directed against forestalling and regrating essential foodstuffs, and displayed considerable suspicion of the victualling trades. Edward III at one stage empowered everyone, and not merely members of those trades, to retail foodstuffs in London and Richard II excluded victuallers for a time from municipal office. Government policies were not always consistent. Yarmouth sometimes secured official backing for its monopoly of the east-coast herring trade, and Charles V granted a monopoly of brewing in Paris to twenty-two men in return for a tax on the ale they made. The policy of provision, however, was still the dominant one. Men landing fish in England were exempted from the laws forbidding the export of bullion, and licences were granted to Dutch fish importers even during periods of Anglo-Burgundian war. In time of dearth the government facilitated the import of Baltic wheat to supply London, though leaving the 'bulk-buying' arrangements to the city authorities. French kings were equally concerned for the provisioning of Paris. Charles VI forbade forestalling in 1402, while Charles VII reorganized the Parisian markets in 1454 and every effort was made to protect traders from molestation on their way to the capital. In the mid-fifteenth century the first breaches were also made in the monopolistic rights of the *marchands de l'eau*, when the men of Rouen were partially exempted from the obligation of assuming *compagnie française*.

Closely related to these policies were measures designed to ease the flow of internal commerce, particularly in France (where so much remained to be done to achieve economic unity) during the periods of economic reconstruction under Charles V, Charles VII and Louis XI. New markets and fairs were authorized and old ones restored. Attempts were made to improve communications and to cut out some part of the jungle of tolls which grew even more luxuriant in years of war: the abolition of tolls, said Charles V, was 'for the good and utility of his people and in order that trade may be re-established as well by land as by water'. The results were not always spectacular or the motives entirely disinterested. The tolls remained for Colbert and his successors to tackle. Local communities might pay for the establishment of fairs and markets, or fairs might be designed as weapons of economic warfare. Charles VII, in re-establishing the Parisian markets, thought primarily of the 'diminution of his domain' when they had been in abeyance. None the less the traditional policy of provision was that which appealed most readily to rulers—a policy designed to further internal exchanges and to cheapen and diversify the range of goods within their realms, even goods brought by alien merchants. It was this which brought that policy, particularly in England, into the arena of controversy.

Stranger merchants continued to claim government patronage on two grounds. On the one hand, as the Italians in London asserted in 1423, 'the multitude of merchants alien there buying of the merchandise within the realm increaseth the value of English merchandise within the realm to the great advantage of the commons of the said realm'. It was probably this argument which led to Edward I's defence of the utility of the foreign trader being echoed in the Ordinance of the Staple in 1353 and by the Commons in parliament in 1354. The other side of the foreigner's case was put by Charles V of France in 1369 when granting privileges to the Italians at Harfleur 'for the good and increase of that town ... and for the multiplication of goods, commodities and merchandise'. Charles VI, too, declared that the Hansards brought to Harfleur 'many and divers commodities for the common good of our whole kingdom', and he spoke in like manner of the men of Kampen who acted as intermediaries between France and the great international mart at Bruges.

It was as an importer that the alien merchant first became a figure of controversy. The stage was set in England by a statute of 1335. Townsmen, it stated, compelled foreign merchants to deal only through themselves as intermediaries, so that goods were sold dearer than they ought to be; in future foreigners were to have complete freedom of buying and selling, including selling by retail if they so wished. The legislation was repeated in 1351, 1353, 1378, 1388, 1399 and 1435. Yet this very reiteration indicates the difficulty of enforcing such a law. This is perhaps hardly surprising, for it included the concession of rights of retail trading which the burgesses of Southampton denied to the men of Winchester and Salisbury or the citizens of Norwich to all strangers to their franchise; and kings themselves continually granted town charters incompatible with the statutes for foreign traders. The Londoners in particular waged a bitter struggle against alien competition. They secured exemption in 1337 from the statute of 1335, and in 1371 a smith's servant was put in the pillory with a whetstone round his neck merely for spreading a rumour that the Italians were to be allowed to trade as freely as denizens. Rooted in this urban xenophobia, opposition to government liberalism gained ground. Every possible charge was levied against the foreigner: he took bullion out of the realm, formed rings to rig prices, spied for the king's enemies. His privileges were steadily whittled away and in the fifteenth century there was a stream of legislation to curb his activities. His stay in the country was limited, his freedom of action circumscribed, he was compelled to live with an English 'host' who would supervise all his dealings.

By that time, however, English overseas merchants had joined forces with English townsmen and urban xenophobia was broadening into economic nationalism. In the late fourteenth century the attempts of English cloth exporters to penetrate the Baltic met with small welcome in the Hanse towns. In these circumstances the privileges of the Hansards in England (which included duties on cloth lower even than those paid by denizens) seemed grossly unjustified, and the English traders demanded either reciprocity in the Baltic or the curtailment of Hanseatic privileges in England. From time to time in the following century the government was prevailed upon to take action against the Hansards, but in the long run their privileges were confirmed by Edward IV and Englishmen were more or less shut out of the Baltic. Meanwhile the Italians became the centre of a similar controversy. Though the Venetians brought presents for Henry IV for his friendship towards the Signory, it amazed John Gower that they could live in England as freely and as cherished as though they were born and bred there. Even in Southampton the Italians were excluded from retail trade and crafts competing with those in which burgesses were engaged. The Londoners were far less tolerant and were quick to turn against them bullionist notions which were coming into common currency. Their banking and exchange operations were said to lead to an export of gold and silver, and the character of their trade to a constant drain of bullion, for all they brought into the land were:

> ... Things of complacence ...
> Apes and japes and marmusets tayled,
> Nifles, trifles that little have avayled,
> And things with which they fetely blere our eye.

Such onslaughts, of course, masked more specific grievances. Craftsmen faced competition from Italian imports. Grocers wished to buy spices on more favourable terms. The Staplers had no liking for the Italian exemption from seeking the Calais staple, particularly as they bought wool for cash rather than on credit and so found it easier to buy than Englishmen did, as the Celys noticed in 1480. The Italians, too, blocked tentative English attempts to penetrate the Mediterranean in the early fifteenth century, and their competition with British shippers in the coastal trade to Brittany, Gascony and the Iberian peninsula was a matter of parliamentary complaint in 1439. A formidable anti-Italian sentiment was generated to which the later Lancastrians and Yorkists capitulated. An embargo was imposed on many of their imports in 1484 to protect native crafts, and special taxes were laid upon the Italians. Edward IV's hostility to the Genoese forced them to transfer the northern centre of their trade to Antwerp. The statute of 1463 forbidding aliens to export wool was a severe blow to the Florentines, who had ceased to come to England by 1478 and were forced to throw open the port of Pisa to obtain the wool their industry needed. English merchants began making yearly voyages to Italy and by 1485 they had a regular organization at Pisa. The Venetian galleys still came to England, but government support had been mobilized by the native interests to reduce the share of the trade between England and the Mediterranean in Italian hands and to lay the foundations for the future expansion of English trade in that sea.

There were fewer breaches with traditional policies in France. In 1463, Louis XI set about reknitting commercial ties with the Hanseatic League.

The fact that the Hansards had ceased to frequent the ports of France, he said, was contrary to *la chose publique* and detrimental to *le fait de la marchandise* in his land. Therefore he restored their ancient privileges, took them under his special protection, allowed them complete freedom of trade (including trade in English goods) and made his will known by publishing the treaty in La Rochelle, Rouen, Harfleur and Dieppe. In like manner he renewed the privileges of Spanish merchants in 1470 and welcomed foreign merchants to Bordeaux, so that after 1475 even the English were allowed to go 'chasing about all the country' round to buy their wines. After the annexation of Provence, Louis announced his intention of making Marseilles a port 'to which . . . we intend to make flow more than ever all stranger nations'. To some extent, no doubt, these policies were designed to strike at the economic resources of the Burgundian dominion and to be steps towards freeing France from the economic tutelage of Geneva, Bruges and Antwerp. On the other hand, they also fitted into the accustomed pattern of things which, as Louis told the Hansards, had existed 'far into the past in the times of our predecessors, kings of France'. In the eyes of Louis XI the trade of aliens as much as of denizens contributed to *la chose publique*.

Of course there were cross-currents. The French townsman was no more patient than the English of too much freedom for the foreigner. Even in the fairs of Rouen, deliberately created to draw traders from abroad, aliens were denied the right to engage in retail trade. But genuine commercial nationalism is little in evidence. Economic reconstruction after the Hundred Years War seems to have been regarded as demanding first and foremost the return of foreign traders whom war had kept away. One example was the attempt to set up international fairs in the later fifteenth century at Caen (later Rouen) and Lyons to compete with the fairs in the Low Countries and at Geneva. It was a concomitant of this policy that the English should be given a privileged position at Caen and Rouen and that the Lombards should enjoy similar favour at Lyons. The only major exception to this attitude was the support given by Charles VII and Louis XI to Jacques Cœur and his followers in their efforts to wrest from the Italians the Mediterranean spice trade. This support, however, was not continuously given and was frequently qualified in order to maintain the fairs of Lyons as the termini of the Italian spice trade across the Alps. In the end, moreover, the whole scheme was abandoned, a course all the easier for Louis XI since genuine commercial nationalism had only been to the slightest extent the basis of his policy.

D. *The Balance of Trade and the Organization of Commerce*

In the later Middle Ages, therefore, French trade policy departed little from tradition. This was doubtless an outcome of the importance of the transit trade in the French economy, the substantial financial stake of the Crown, the lords and the towns in that trade as owners of fairs and markets, and the lack of a highly organized native interest engaged in the grand commerce of the day. In England, on the other hand, trading interests were coherent and strong enough to leave a much firmer imprint on government policy. In both countries, however, alien merchants were beginning to find their utility measured by a new criterion. It came to be a serious charge against the Italians in London and Southampton, in Lyons and Aigues-Mortes, even against the Spaniards whom Louis XI accused (as the Londoners accused the Italians) of bringing unnecessary luxuries into the realm, that they took treasure out of the land. This criticism arose out of the monetary problems of the later Middle Ages, which call for some measure of attention here in view of the influence they exercised upon commercial policy. The tendency of national currency to leak out and be replaced by inferior foreign coins, combined with the frequent complaint that there was a shortage of money current for day-to-day needs, led to a much closer government control of overseas payments. The export of bullion and coined money from England and France was forbidden with monotonous regularity. Richard II of England forbade anyone save nobles, merchants and the king's soldiers to go abroad, and the pilgrim traffic was rigorously controlled as a possible source of leakage. In 1419 parliament decreed that supplies for the army in France should be bought in England and that its pay should be raised by exporting wool for sale in Normandy. There was also a question of attracting bullion into the country. English wool-exporters were required to bring back bullion in proportion to the amount of wool they took abroad, and merchant strangers coming to England to deliver a certain amount of bullion to the mint.

Thus the direction of the flow of bullion was becoming a matter of prime concern for governments on the grounds, put to the Estates General of France in 1484, that 'money is to the body politic what blood is in the human body' and that the measure of a nation's wealth was the stock of precious metals within it. This view led to control of overseas payments in order to secure an inflow of bullion, persuaded Edward III to test the claims of alchemists that they could make gold and turned the eyes of Edward IV and Louis XI to Africa, the great source of gold, with the object of diverting from the infidel 'wealth and other things precious'. In England the theoretical discussion was taken a step further. In 1381–2

sundry experts were brought together at the wish of parliament to discuss
the shortage of money in the country due to the feebleness of currencies
abroad which led to the export of English coin. They declared that it was
essential that foreign merchandise should be allowed into England only
up to the value of the exports of home-produced goods. Thenceforward
the argument that exports should balance imports was seldom absent
from discussions about trade, and a number of attempts were made to
give it practical effect. In 1390 alien merchants were to buy English goods
at least of half the value of goods they imported, and in 1402 all importing
merchants were to bestow the proceeds of their trading on English goods
for export. The balance of trade theory helped to inspire the anti-Italian
policy of fifteenth-century England, and by that time it was also being
heard in France. It was an argument used by Louis XI for establishing the
silk industry in his country, for seeking to capture the spice trade from
the Italians, and probably prompted his sumptuary legislation designed
to curb the demand for imported luxuries. The monetary situation was
thus an adjunct to other forces leading to the adoption of protectionist
policies, not only to satisfy private interests but to safeguard *la chose
publique*.

It was, however, but one force among many leading to increased
government concern about trade. In France commercial restoration was
part of the work of reconstruction to which Charles VII and Louis XI set
their hands. War and civil war had driven foreign traders from the fairs of
France and completed the diversion of the great north–south trade route
to the seaways converging on the ports of the Low Countries and the
land-ways converging on Geneva. At the same time, French participation
in the Mediterranean trade had been reduced practically to nothing.
Peace permitted an attempt to recapture the transit trade which had been
an important feature of the economy of France. The fairs of Lyons were
re-established as distributing centres for the goods of northern France,
of Languedoc and the Mediterranean. Fairs were established at Rouen
to draw trade away from the Low Countries, and attempts were made to
situate on French territory the staple for English wools. These ventures
were only partially successful. England was not to be detached from the
Low Countries. Trade barriers between France and Flanders compelled
the Flemish to switch from French wheat to Hanseatic rye. The French
cloth industry, deprived of wool from Bruges, never secured a hold on
that of England. Norman traders, therefore, more and more turned south
for their trading contacts, to Brittany and Portugal and Spain: thus their
faces were turned to the Atlantic horizons which were soon to expand so
quickly. The intentions of King Louis, however, can hardly be held accountable for that.

His dominant intention was to make France once again a meeting place of trade routes, in the light of his conviction that 'fairs and markets enrich the country' and that wealth would accrue from 'multiplying' traffic and merchandise within the kingdom.[1] Even his Mediterranean policy is only in part exceptional. Between 1444 and 1482 a series of trading companies was organized in the Mediterranean by Jacques Cœur and later entrepreneurs to capture the spice trade from the Italians. Charles VII and Louis XI gave intermittent support in the form of trade monopolies in the Mediterranean theatre and financial subventions from the Estates of Languedoc. Yet Pierre Doriole in 1471 envisaged this policy as one which would bring even the English to France to buy spices, thus linking Mediterranean enterprise with attempts to restore the great international fairs to French soil. Nor was Louis single-minded in sponsoring these trading companies: they also enabled him to exert pressure on Venice and Provence and to dispose of a Mediterranean marine to support his political objectives in that region. It is typical that in 1476 the 'Galleys of France' were diverted from the spice trade to provision the armies in Roussillon. The whole scheme, moreover, came under continuous fire. No one wanted to pay a monopoly price for spices. The Estates of Languedoc desired that all should be free to seek the produce of the province. The privileges of the Mediterranean companies were also in the last analysis incompatible with the attempt to make the fairs of Lyons, dependent as they were on the Italian overland trade in spices, into great international marts. In consequence Louis finally abandoned the whole scheme of a Mediterranean company in 1482, and his surrender was underlined in 1484 by the uncompromising declaration of the Estates General in favour of freedom of trade.

In France, then, government support was only to a limited extent enlisted on the side of native trading interests and failed to establish those interests in a permanently organized form. In England, on the other hand, native traders during the later Middle Ages captured a major share in overseas trade. Towards the end of Edward IV's reign the Staplers controlled 27% of English exports and the Merchant Adventurers 38% of exports from and more than two-thirds of the imports into England. This was partly a result of the cramping of England's trade to the narrow seas where English interests were particularly strong, but the more effective organization of native traders also contributed to this end. In this government policy played a considerable part, particularly in the case of the Company of the Staple.

In its final form the English staple system involved most of the exports of wool and hides passing through a single centre overseas and the management of the trade in these commodities by a monopolistic company. The system appealed to the kings of England because foreign rulers

[1] R. Gandilhon, *Politique économique de Louis XI*, 217.

valued the presence of the staple in their lands and it could be placed to suit diplomatic ends; and because it served the purposes of a financial system in which wool export taxes were one of the main pillars. It was administratively convenient to levy these taxes at a single foreign centre, for evasion of them by smuggling was perhaps made somewhat more difficult. At the same time, the payment of customs was exacted at the point where merchants had ready money at their disposal from the sale of their cargoes and where the proceeds could be disbursed to finance military operations or maintain an English base (such as Calais became) across the Channel. Moreover, by putting the trade into the hands of a monopolistic company, the Crown was enabled 'to tax monopoly profits by means of a heavy export duty and raise loans from the merchants on the security of that duty'.[1] Monopoly rights, therefore, were the price the Crown had to pay the commercial interests involved if they were to play the fiscal role allotted to them. Naturally enough any staple system, and especially the foreign staple favoured by the Crown and the great export merchants, evoked opposition. The up-country wool dealers preferred home staples to which all exporters would have access; the growers, faced with falling prices, and the alien merchants had no desire for any staples at all. The system only emerged, therefore, out of much controversy. Before 1337 there were a number of experiments with both home and foreign staples, but it was not until after that date that the staple system was established as one of the methods of financing the Hundred Years War. Between 1337 and 1353 Edward III maintained a staple in the Low Countries, served by a ring of capitalist merchants, as part of the machinery to scale up wool taxes, raise loans on the security of those taxes and turn into money his loans and taxes in wool. In consequence the traders excluded from the ring and the growers alarmed at tumbling prices combined against him, and Edward secured the maintenance of the export taxes in 1353 only by sacrificing the monopolists. Staples were set up in English towns, and alien merchants were given the sole right to export wool and were allowed to buy up-country side by side with denizens. But this was too patently to 'the great profit of aliens', and by 1363 the native exporters had secured the restitution of a quasi-monopolistic company and the removal of the staple to Calais. There it normally remained for the rest of the Middle Ages. The trade to Italy was the only significant branch of the wool trade outside the Staple Company's control. Early in Richard II's reign the Italians and Catalans were allowed to ship wool direct and to buy freely in England for the purpose: at the beginning of the fifteenth century they were in fact shipping about one-fifth of English wool exported. Elsewhere the Staplers' monopoly was fairly complete. In return the government was always turning to them for loans on security of the customs,

[1] E. Power, *The Wool Trade in Medieval English History*, 88.

and it was doubtless inevitable that in due course the administration of the wool custom should be entrusted to the company.[1]

The very monopoly of the Staplers, however, contributed to the running down of wool exports, and by the mid-fifteenth century England was an exporter of cloth rather than wool. Here too an English company, the Merchant Adventurers, eventually secured the dominant position, and the way was being prepared for this in the fifteenth century and even before. The final establishment of a staple at Calais and of an organized company of wool exporters helped to give a separate identity to the group of English merchants trading directly to the Low Countries, whose business was more and more the export of English cloth and importing general merchandise from the great entrepôt cities of that region. This group had been acquiring a growing share in this trade ever since Flemish shipping had begun to decline in the late thirteenth century; and within the general body of English merchants engaged in it the London element, closely associated with the Mercers' Company, eventually captured the main positions. It was these Londoners who eventually secured recognition of themselves as the Merchant Adventurers of England *par excellence*. Their predominance in what became, in the fifteenth century, the main artery of English commerce, owed far less than did that of the Staplers in the wool trade to government artifice. The earliest privileges of English traders to the Low Countries were obtained from the princes of those lands, and the first dealings of English kings with them were simply the confirmation of such privileges. Henry IV gave his approval to the rights enjoyed by English merchants, trading both to the Baltic and to the Low Countries, to have their own assemblies and to choose their own governors; and Edward IV's charter to the group trading in the Low Countries was for the most part a reaffirmation of the privileges conceded by his Lancastrian predecessors. It was only during the reign of Henry VII that a measure of government approval was given to the trend which was turning the Netherlands trade into the preserve of a monopolistic London company.

Thus, in England, government policy had either favoured or not obstructed the growing prominence of the English trader in English overseas commerce. This commerce, furthermore, was closely linked with a native industry using mainly native raw materials, and this probably explains the coherence and relative effectiveness of the economic interests which in the fifteenth century imposed protectionist policies upon the Crown. In France, on the other hand, the attempt to create a Mediterranean company was designed to capture an import rather than an export trade, and proved incompatible with the interests of the agricultural and industrial classes of Languedoc and of the distributing trades in Lyons and

[1] This is fully treated in chap. VII, part iv.

the clientele they served. There was no French export commodity which integrated economic interests as cloth did those of England. French economic policy after the Hundred Years War, when not designed to secure diplomatic ends or to buttress royal power, was simply a policy of restoration: an attempt to revive the entrepôt activities which had once been centred in the fairs of Champagne. To some extent this was a policy which had been rendered anachronistic by the growth of sea-borne commerce. It was to be rendered more anachronistic still when the discovery of the Cape route and of the New World revolutionized commercial horizons.

E. *Conclusion*

The fact remains, none the less, that the range of government economic policies had increased immensely since the thirteenth century. Governments could now make very large claims in this field. In an ordinance for the Parisian pastry-cooks in 1406 Charles VI alleged that he possessed the right to 'dispose and order the estates, trades, crafts and other activities in which our subjects are engaged day by day for the common good and their own sustenance, so that by good governance ... each may be preserved, maintained and conserved by our edicts ... whereby each of them can remain and live in good tranquillity and peace under us'. In practice, of course, government control was neither so comprehensive nor so continuous, but the fact that such a proclamation could be made is still significant. Ever since the revival of commerce in the eleventh and the twelfth centuries, governments had begun to frame economic policies. By furthering economic activity they maximized their financial resources. By acting as patrons of commerce they diversified the range of goods available and multiplied the outlets for the produce of their own lands. They served the interests of all great buyers of goods by founding and controlling markets. These policies, which may perhaps be called 'policies of plenty', were a strand in the policies of governments right down to the end of the Middle Ages.

They were not, however, the only strand. The acquisition of powers of economic direction was part of the process of 'state-building' which, with many reverses, characterized the centuries between the tenth and the sixteenth. The kings of France at the end of the Middle Ages had scarcely completed the territorial unification of their realm, which still bore plain upon it the signs of its piecemeal acquisition. Even in France, however, much had been done to curtail the autonomy of infra-state authorities and harness them to the monarchy. England was even more precocious in achieving a degree of centralization. In the process powers of taxation were acquired which gave the Crown a direct interest in a wider range of economic activities and provided a firmer basis for the royal authority. The power of the economic weapon in external affairs had been recognized: economic controls became an adjunct of diplomacy and statecraft, and sometimes their slave. At the same time economic statecraft began to feel the impact of other forces. The crises of the later Middle Ages provoked demands from below for the regulation of prices, wages, the conditions of labour and of marketing, and of the shares in the commercial cake. In England, particularly, something like a 'popular' economic programme obtained very general currency. Protectionist ideas born in the town market-place broadened into a doctrine akin to economic nationalism, and its protagonists found in parliament a vehicle for presenting it effectively. In the wake of this programme a series of other ideas began to emerge: bullionist and balance of trade theories and a pervasive nationalism to which government and people alike found it wise to pay lip-service. In France similar notions were abroad; but they lacked the deep roots they had in the economic structure of England. They seem in consequence more forced and more exotic and to have been less effective for the time being in shaping the French economy and French economic policies.

The impregnation of government policies, therefore, 'with a national as well as a dynastic spirit', and efforts to 'stimulate and co-ordinate economic activity and develop the general wealth' are features of the later Middle Ages.[1] At the same time the detailed history of the period displays constant vacillation, rapid changes of front, edicts promulgated which were never executed. It is tempting to describe government policy as 'pure and simple empiricism',[2] for opportunism certainly ranked high amongst the motives of kings. Attempts to develop the wealth of the nation had often no further object than to ensure that this wealth was put at the disposal of the State. This in turn is merely one aspect of the subordination of economic well-being to grander schemes of internal consolidation and foreign affairs, which made economic policy the handmaid of politics or the momentary and half-hearted accommodation of governments to the insistent demands of subjects. However, it is not only in the Middle Ages that economic desiderata have been sacrificed on the altar of political necessity, or that governments have found it wise to temporize without much conviction with powerful interests. The fact remains that, in the later Middle Ages, something like a set of economic ideas emerged which inspired a set of economic policies, though in a period of beginnings the effectiveness with which they were prosecuted was perhaps inevitably limited. Government policies, moreover, had to be executed by officials widely scattered and remote from close super-

[1] E. Coornaert, *Annales de l'université de Paris*, VIII (1933), 414 ff.
[2] J. Calmette, *L'élaboration du monde moderne*, 92.

vision. Royal officials and the officials of towns and gilds and country districts were doing remarkable work in the later Middle Ages, but it cannot be claimed that they were adequate for all the tasks which were heaped upon them. The prosecution of comprehensive policies to co-ordinate economic activities was still to a great extent precluded by the institutional equipment of which governments disposed. Nevertheless, the administrative groundwork was being laid for the mercantilist age, a work of preparation comparable with the expanding habit of governmental intervention and the emergence of a system of ideas which gave coherence and direction to it.

III. *The Low Countries*

(I) INTRODUCTION

It is, in general terms, somewhat hazardous to speak of 'economic policies' in connection with the Middle Ages. This applies even more particularly in the Low Countries than it does elsewhere. Before the Burgundian period this part of Europe did not constitute a political entity, but was divided into a number of territorial principalities, feudally dependent some upon the Empire and some upon France. Their small extent and the limited range of the interests at work in each of them were hardly likely to move princes to take account of economic considerations in drawing up their political schemes. Doubtless we must differentiate somewhat between the various provinces. Flanders, certainly, was more thickly populated than its neighbours, its political structure was stronger, and its economic life (particularly its trade and industry) was more intensive. It also numbered amongst its rulers some remarkable princes, and most notably Philip of Alsace, who were distinguished amongst their contemporaries for the lead they gave in this department of statecraft. For these reasons, examples drawn from the history of Flanders must inevitably bulk large in what follows.

At the same time it is important to note that, in some respects, the very fact that regions like Brabant or Holland developed economically much later than Flanders gave rise in itself to economic policies in these two principalities for which no equivalent is to be found in Flanders. Their rulers endeavoured, by positive intervention, to stimulate the growth of forms of commerce and industry of which they had been able to observe the beneficial effects in Flanders, though there they had arisen through the free play of economic forces.

The limited range of economic policies in medieval principalities is also explicable in large degree by the lack of financial resources at the disposal of the heads of territorial states. As Henri Pirenne very rightly observed: 'The prince's revenues were inadequate to meet the expenditure which public interest demanded. His resources, which were derived for the most part from the various issues of his domain, were almost entirely absorbed in maintaining his court and in his personal expenses... Apart from [a few occasional expenses and payments] there is no sign of a budget, no possibility of allotting funds to deal with the problems created by the development and growing complexity of social and economic life.'

Finally, a few measures with a bearing on economic affairs are not in themselves enough to warrant our attributing to a ruler a genuine economic policy. Particularly in the principalities of the Low Countries, where the ruler was faced by communities, social classes, towns, etc. with powerful economic interests, his acts which have an economic bearing were often prompted by these communities and were sometimes imposed by them upon him against his will. His decision between two alternatives might be no more than a matter of opportunism; and often enough, when previous measures were repealed, this was not because the prince's views on economic affairs had altered in the interval but because the political circumstances had changed.

Before turning to a systematic treatment of the problem, one other introductory matter calls for treatment here: the principal landmarks, so far as the subject under discussion is concerned, under the successive counts of Flanders and, from 1384, the dukes of Burgundy.

The first territorial prince of the Low Countries who adopted a quite well co-ordinated set of measures in the economic field was probably Charles the Good, count of Flanders (1119–27). At the same time, what we are concerned with here are essentially ephemeral measures, promulgated to deal with relatively short-term difficulties arising out of the famine of the years 1125–6. Because they were ephemeral we can hardly properly describe these measures as constituting an 'economic policy'. They deserve attention none the less because of their early date, because they were exceptional in medieval Europe (as Curschmann's study of famines in the Middle Ages makes clear) and because of the grasp of economic facts which some of them display. They can be divided into two categories, the first of which is hardly relevant to the subject with which we are concerned here. Count Charles, as any other great landowner would have done, out of pity for his subjects in their distress, ordered stocks of food and clothing held in the main centres of his domains to be distributed to them. His actions in this respect were simply those of a private individual. At the same time, however, he used his authority as head of the Flemish territorial state to impose—or at least to attempt to impose—certain measures of an economic character designed to alleviate the scourge of famine. He laid it down that agricultural producers were to sow half their lands with beans and peas, with the object of obtaining a supply of food from these leguminous crops during the weeks preceding the new grain harvest. He forbade the brewing of beer so that all the oats available could be used for bread. He ordered that, in addition to the normal penny loaf, halfpenny loaves should be made so that even the poorest would be able to buy. Finally, he fixed maximum retail prices for wine so that, as Galbert of Bruges tells us, 'merchants would cease to import it and find more profit in exchanging their merchandise for foodstuffs with which to relieve the dearth amongst the poor'. For wine, as we know from other sources, was already imported on a large scale into Flanders, where it was in daily use amongst the wealthier sections of the community. It was the normal return freight, in fact, at least for merchants trading to France and the Rhineland.

Only in the reign of Philip of Alsace (1157/68–1191), however, do we see a ruler of a territorial state adopt a series of measures which, because of their evident object to effect changes of a permanent nature in the material life of the country, deserve to be described as an economic policy in the proper sense of the phrase. This was quite characteristic of this ruler, with his grand political designs, whose final defeat, in both the diplomatic and the military fields, was due only to the excessive boldness of his schemes. Philip's economic measures were mainly concentrated in the first half of his reign before he allowed himself to become absorbed by his ambitions in France and Palestine, and particularly in the first decade after he assumed power, during which time his father had associated him with his government and gradually handed over to him more and more of the reality of power. Some of his acts, doubtless, were inspired by the interests which benefited from them—his military and diplomatic intervention on behalf of the merchants trading to the Rhineland is a case in point. Other measures, however, like the creation of new ports near the Flemish coast, the protection accorded to the traders who peopled these new foundations, and the digging of canals in the heart of the country, appear to be attributable to his personal initiative.

The short reign of Baldwin IX (1194–1205) and the weakness of the comital authority under Joan of Constantinople (1205–44) were hardly circumstances designed to favour active state intervention in matters of trade, industry or agriculture. On Joan's death, she was succeeded by her sister, Margaret of Constantinople (1244–78). At a first glance, circumstances during her reign were scarcely more conducive to comital intervention. Closer study, however, reveals two sets of factors which helped to provoke active intervention on Margaret's part. On the one hand, the heavy financial obligations which Margaret had to face led her to take a series of fiscal steps which had their effects upon economic life; on the other, her reign saw the beginnings of the transformation of Flemish

trade from an active character to a passive one and in particular the frequenting of some Flemish ports by foreign merchants, a fact which the
public authority could not ignore.

It seems, too, that it was during Margaret's last years and more particularly during the reign of her son, Guy of Dampierre (1278–1305), that the
comital power had for the first time to take up some sort of position in relation to the serious conflict of economic interest between different
groups of its subjects. As already indicated the decisions of princes were
most frequently dictated by general political considerations. If the counts
of the house of Dampierre and particularly Louis de Male (1346–84),
whenever they could reach their decisions freely, favoured the textile industry of the smaller towns and the countryside against that of Ghent,
Bruges and Ypres, this was not because they saw in such a policy a better
means of advancing the prosperity of their county. It was merely because
they hoped by this means to strengthen the elements in the population
which constituted a counterpoise to the encroaching power of the 'three
members' of Flanders.

The accession of Philip the Bold as count of Flanders in 1384 marked
the entry of the house of Burgundy into the Low Countries; but it is only
after 1430, when his grandson Philip the Good (1419–67) had united under his control Flanders, Artois, Hainault, Holland, Zeeland, Namur,
Brabant and Limburg, that we can properly speak of a Burgundian state.
However, this ruler, and even his successors in the last third of the fifteenth century, fell far short of realizing a general economic policy which
merits the description of 'Burgundian' or 'Netherlandish'. Not only
were they troubled by the problem inherited from their predecessors of
finding a method of dealing with the internal conflicts in their various
principalities, but they also had to cope with the basic opposition of interests between the different territorial states they had united under their
rule. The attitude of the Flemish clothing towns to the import of English
textiles into the Low Countries was precisely the reverse of that of Antwerp. Likewise, ducal policy was full of hesitation and inconsistencies in
dealing with the dispute between Bruges (by the fifteenth century the
centre of 'passive' trade) and the merchants of Holland concerning the
attitude to be taken towards the Hanse. So far as the Dutch were concerned, the German merchant was a competitor they sought to expel; for
the men of Bruges he was a welcome visitor whom they went out of their
way to attract. Like their predecessors the Burgundian dukes allowed
themselves to be guided by considerations of political opportunism.
In other respects, however, it is important to note that they took steps
which imply the inspiration of pre-mercantilist notions. They succeeded, not in unifying, but at least in co-ordinating the monetary systems in force in their various principalities; and the enterprise shown by

Philip the Good in exploiting the mineral resources of his lands makes him a ruler far more 'modern' than 'medieval'.

(2) THE PRINCES AND THE TOWNS

Since the territorial princes generally subordinated their decisions with an economic bearing to general political considerations, it is important to look in the first instance at their attitude towards the towns, the essential centres of trade and industry during the Middle Ages. The dominant features of their policies in this respect have been clearly displayed by Pirenne. He has demonstrated the difference in the positions taken up by the lay and ecclesiastical princes during the early period of growth of urban centres. The bishops, compelled to reside in their cities and distrusting the desire of their subjects for autonomy, were naturally disquieted at seeing these towns develop without limit or control. The lay princes, on the other hand, did not feel the need to establish a permanent residence in or near to one or other of their towns; they were able without too much difficulty to avert possible friction, and moreover attached far greater importance than the clergy did to the advantages which accrued from an increase in urban population and wealth. It is quite characteristic that 'sworn communes' and above all 'revolutionary communes' were formed chiefly in episcopal cities (Cambrai, and to a lesser degree Utrecht, Liège, Tournai), while they are little in evidence in the lay principalities. This tendency on the part of the bourgeoisie to create for themselves organs of self-protection, so clearly manifested in the ecclesiastical cities, was canalized or rendered superfluous by the way in which the lay princes strengthened the jurisdiction of the *échevins* and adapted it to meet the wishes of their subjects.

A time came, however, even in Flanders, when urban development and desire for autonomy began to trouble the ruler of the county and provoke him to counter-measures. This reaction becomes evident under Philip of Alsace; and its most important manifestation lay in the fact that, in place of the charters granted to the towns by his predecessors, he substituted a uniform urban law which, at least in judicial matters, represented a strengthening of the count's authority. At the same time, as Pirenne rightly points out, this policy designed to safeguard and consolidate the unity of the state in no way implied that the count was opposed to the development of commerce and therefore of the bourgeoisie. On the contrary, we shall see later with what energy he defended the interests of his merchants against the foreigner, and in particular the interests of the men of Ghent in the Rhineland. He gave preferential treatment, however, to the towns of his own foundation in the vicinity of the coast, which he endowed with privileges more extensive than those possessed by the older towns; he probably felt confident of maintaining his control over them, even when they had achieved a certain degree of prosperity, and considered them as a potential counterpoise to the power of the older towns.

This princely reaction ended with the death of Philip of Alsace. For the first three-quarters of the thirteenth century Flanders was subjected to a regimen of women, which imposed few restraints upon urban autonomy. In the last years of Margaret of Constantinople (1244–78), however, the countess intervened in the social and economic struggles between the wealthier classes of the towns, composed for the most part of merchants and entrepreneurs in the textile industry, and the popular classes amongst whom weavers and fullers played the principal role. This intervention took place at a decisive turning point in the economic history of Flanders. At this moment 'active' trade was rapidly declining. The patricians were faced, not only with the centralizing policy of the countess and the claims of the artisans, but also with the competition of foreign merchants. In 1276 and the years which followed Countess Margaret intervened on the side of the cloth-workers at Douai and Ghent. The social revolt of 1280 led Guy of Dampierre, though with many reservations, to take similar steps at Bruges and Ypres. The outbreak of war between France and Flanders in 1297, and above all the victory of the Flemish at Courtrai in 1302, forced the count's hand and ensured the complete triumph, on the social and economic plane, of the artisan class.

If the count in the end reconciled himself with the wealthier classes and remained reasonably consistent in his adherence to this new attitude, his policy in this respect ceased to have economic significance. To all intents the patriciate in the course of the fourteenth century ceased to play any active role in production or exchange; it was content thenceforward to live upon its rents and interest. Large-scale commerce by that time had passed into the hands of foreign merchants and industrial enterprise had become the province of a crowd of drapers of limited substance who had risen from the ranks of the people.

In Brabant the towns developed much later than in Flanders. They could only compensate for their relative weakness by close unity amongst themselves, and they were wise enough consistently to follow this line of policy. In this way they gradually succeeded, in the course of the century from 1261 to 1356, in laying the foundations of a veritable constitution for the territory. They subjected the duke to their tutelage, particularly in financial matters, and they were in a position to dictate to him measures with an economic bearing designed to solve the problems which faced him in both the external and internal spheres.

In Holland, urban development was later even than in Brabant. The counts believed that they could make up for this tardiness of urban growth by their active intervention. They granted numerous urban charters to places which lacked urban characteristics in the proper sense, in the hope, sometimes unfulfilled and sometimes realized, that these new rights would contribute to the growth of trade and industry.

(3) FOREIGN TRADE

From a very early date, perhaps from the time when the territorial principalities of the Low Countries took shape, the merchants of this area established commercial relations with neighbouring lands, and in particular with England and the Rhineland. It seems clear that this active trade was born and grew independently of any intervention on the part of the princes. To be sure, the oldest urban charters of Flanders, like that of St Omer (1127), contained clauses in which the count promised his subjects that he would intervene on their behalf with this or that foreign ruler. These were promises, however, which had been wrested from the count, and his death prevented any action being taken on them.

With Philip of Alsace the situation changed completely. Undoubtedly he too was influenced by the grievances of his subjects; but at least he threw his military and diplomatic power into the scales with conviction and energy, the more so because during his reign the difficulties which faced his subjects in foreign lands became more serious than they had been half a century earlier.

At the very moment when Philip became co-ruler with his father, Thierry (1157), the Flemish merchants engaged in trade with the Rhineland were complaining of their treatment, both in Holland and Zeeland, on the river route they used to reach western Germany, and on their arrival at Cologne. The young count hastened to intervene on their behalf. He undertook a first war against the count of Holland and Zeeland in the very year of his accession, and then a second which was ended in 1168 by a treaty signed at Bruges which apparently gave some satisfaction to his subjects. Certainly, as things turned out, the exemption he obtained for them from tolls levied at Geervliet in Holland was not respected; but he did succeed in securing for them certain commercial privileges designed to safeguard their persons and their goods.

Philip also threw his prestige into the balance to secure the removal of obstacles in the way of his subjects' activities in the Rhineland. These arose particularly from the fact that the citizens of Cologne claimed the right to bar the Flemish merchants from proceeding further up the Rhine beyond their town. The count first made representations to Frederick I at Christmas 1165 and obtained from him a charter drafted in general terms, which met the demands made by his subjects but which was probably without practical effect. He tried again in 1173: this time the emperor, in addition to confirming their trading privileges in more precise terms, also granted to the Flemish that he would establish two fairs at Aix-la-Chapelle and two more at Duisburg, apparently in order to allow them to trade in the Rhineland while at the same time by-passing Cologne. It does not appear, however, that this solution had any success or that the fairs were ever in fact held. The count then applied to the archbishop of Cologne and secured a promise that he would act as arbitrator in the dispute between his subjects and the Flemish; but the latter derived only empty satisfaction from this arrangement, for the prelate's judgment was so equivocal that the citizens of Cologne found no great difficulty in ignoring it. In fact the count, for all his energy and good will, failed to make good the active trading rights claimed by his subjects above Cologne.

Philip of Alsace, however, was not content, at the instance of the townsmen of his lands, merely to defend their interests when these were threatened from without. He also displayed in this field of external trade a positive attitude which was apparently all his own. The fact that he created new ports in the vicinity of the Flemish coast and endowed them with commercial privileges of unusual scope has already been mentioned. The very advantages which he procured for them are proof that his object was to establish new bourgeois groups occupied essentially in trade, and foreign trade in particular. The construction of new ports seems to have become necessary at this time because the rising level of the Flemish plain made it more and more difficult for ships to reach the older ports, which were situated further up the rivers and estuaries. In this respect again the count gave evidence of his resolution. He secured possession of lands situated respectively at the mouths of the Aa and the Yser to lay out the ports of Gravelines and Nieuport—lands which had been granted half a century earlier by his predecessor, Robert II, to two Flemish abbeys. In a like manner he founded Damme, the outport of Bruges, and Biervliet, actually in Flemish Zeeland.

The identical franchises he conferred on them (though these have not been preserved for Gravelines) included two sets of privileges. In the first place the count granted to the inhabitants of these towns complete exemption from tolls throughout Flanders—no small advantage when we remember that the older cities at best were exempted from one or two tolls, paid some others at reduced rates, but met the majority in full.

The second privilege was directly concerned with overseas trade: the count forbade merchants of the older towns to exact any *droit de hanse* from the inhabitants of his new towns. This was a charge levied from their compatriots by merchants trading to a particular country, and generally constituted the entry fee to an association (likewise described by the word hanse) formed for purposes of mutual protection. The practice gave rise to abuses, and it is possible that the *droit de hanse*, fixed at a relatively high figure, had always served to keep out unwanted competitors.

It is also possible that newcomers had found the charge they were called upon to pay out of proportion to the services the association could render them. It was apparently against these abuses, for which the merchants of the older towns were responsible, that Count Philip desired to protect the men of the *novi portus*. In this instance it is most probable that he sought to combat the arbitrary conduct of the men of Ghent, who occupied the leading positions in Flemish trade to the Rhineland and endeavoured, as we know from other sources, to bring all merchants from other towns into their hanse. The new towns did not, however, flourish to the extent which Philip had anticipated, and this aspect of his economic policy did not result in outstanding success.

For the reasons given above, the counts of the thirteenth century did not continue along the lines which Philip had laid down. There are few instances, if any, of representations made by them to foreign rulers on behalf of Flemish merchants. The conduct of Margaret of Constantinople, who in 1270, in order to compel Henry III to pay the arrears of a money-fief, provoked the breakdown of commercial relations and the ruin of active Flemish trade with England, was the antithesis of an economic policy.

It is rather to Brabant that we must look to find princes who pursued a foreign policy in harmony with the commercial interests of their subjects. From the time of Henry I (1190–1235) to that of John I (1268–94) the dukes of Brabant set themselves to extend their influence eastwards and to dominate the route between their principality and Cologne. In this way they satisfied the desire of their subjects for the protection of their commercial relations with the Rhineland against the plundering activities of the petty princelings of the area between the Meuse and the Rhine.

(4) INTERNAL TRADE: THE ECONOMIC FRAMEWORK OF THE COUNTRY

The active trade carried on in the principalities of the Low Countries, and in Flanders particularly, gave rise from a very early date to a material prosperity which had an influence in turn upon the economic structure of the country. The resulting transformation was the outcome of action by both princes and the communities concerned. One of the most curious features of the county of Flanders in its early days was its lack of cohesion. Although access from outside was easy by sea, by river-routes and by land-ways, communications and trade within the county were much more difficult. The northern coastal region was at all times the seat of intense traffic; while the Scheldt valley to the south and east, as well as the southern romance region of the principality, was peppered with flourishing industrial and trading centres. But these two belts of active economic life were long separated from each other by a broad central zone which was essentially agrarian in character.

The counts apparently endeavoured to bring improvement to this situation. During the second half of the eleventh century and at the beinning of the twelfth, particularly during the reign of Robert the Frisian (1071–93), they established many new castellanies and several new chapters of canons which were called upon to render administrative services to the territorial state. It would be too much to postulate economic objectives in this, but it is none the less certain that this policy did have economic consequences. It was indeed upon this axis that Ypres came into existence as a new centre of industry destined to have a great future. In this same region, too, new fairs emerged and were grouped into a cycle (the *fiestes de Flandre*); of these, two were established in towns still of modest size (Ypres and Lille) and two others in places still rural in character (Torhout and Messines). All of these places, however, were seats of churches of canons, which could assume the responsibility for organizing these periodical gatherings of merchants.

The links between the coastal region and the Scheldt valley were likewise made closer by the improvement of old waterways and the creation of new. Canals were dug across the Flemish plain, mainly during the reigns of Philip of Alsace and Margaret of Constantinople. In addition, during the eleventh, twelfth and thirteenth centuries, the navigability of natural waterways was considerably improved by artificial means. The rivers were deepened by setting up at intervals *overdraghes* (i.e. wooden constructions blocking the course of the water and presenting an inclined plane both upstream and down) or *portes d'eau* (i.e. locks made of thick planks fastened one upon the other and fitting at their ends into a block of masonry).

Generally speaking these works were not undertaken by the princes nor did the initiative come from them. It was certainly those who used the waterways, townsmen and merchants in particular, who called for these improvements and bore the cost. At the same time, the prince's co-operation was essential in view of his rights of jurisdiction over navigable rivers. His authority had to be sought to proceed with any such work; he had the right to nominate the persons or corporate group responsible for carrying it out; and he apportioned the cost amongst those who would benefit from it.

In some instances, however, the part played by the ruler does not seem to have been quite so limited; and once again we must turn our attention to Philip of Alsace. A charter of 1183 states explicitly that he *made* a canal to be dug from Dixmude to Furnes, with the object apparently of linking the latter town with the Yser valley. This is understandable enough if we remember that twenty years earlier the count had founded the port of Nieuport near the mouth of that river and that, in 1176, he had granted privileges to the citizens of Furnes. This same charter also points to another way in which the prince took part in such operations and which was doubtless relevant even when he did not himself undertake the execution of the work. It was in fact the count who compulsorily acquired the land necessary for digging canals. The tenants of the land it crossed received compensation to an amount determined by capitalizing the annual rent they paid to the owners of the property taken over, and the tenants in turn were under obligation to indemnify the owners. We do not know, unfortunately, whether the cost of the canal from Furnes to Dixmude was borne by the communities which were expected to benefit from its construction or by the prince himself, and, if by the latter, upon what resources the count drew to carry it out.

In connection with internal trade the counts also played an important part in regulating fairs. The first *nundinae*, doubtless, had an essentially local function, their basic role being to ensure a supply of consumption goods for the towns in which they were held. From the second half of the eleventh century, at least in Flanders, some of them (like the fair at Torhout) had become merchants' meeting places of regional or even interregional importance. Consequently the counts took steps to watch over the safety of merchants coming to them and staying there. Soon certain of these fairs—especially those of Torhout, Messines, Ypres and Lille, as mentioned above—came to constitute a cycle covering the whole year. This evolution was completed in 1200 by the creation of a fair at Bruges by an edict, if not at the initiative, of Count Baldwin IX.

The dues which the counts received from the transactions carried out at the fairs made Baldwin's successors, and especially his second daughter, Margaret of Constantinople, anxious to create the most satisfactory conditions for the business done in them by minute regulation of the legal and fiscal rules under which they operated. The establishment of new fairs by the same princess at Douai, Aardenburg and Lille must also be viewed in the same light.

A comparable concern for safeguarding their fiscal resources, while at the same time furthering the commercial interests of their subjects and affording them greater legal security, dominated the policy of the princes in regard to tolls. Little is known about the origin of tolls in Flanders. It seems possible that none of them go back to Roman times, not even that at Arras, for it was simply a market due levied in the market granted in the Carolingian period to the Abbey of St Vaast (the Roman Empire, as is well known, at least in the west knew nothing of market dues). The majority of tolls on the transit of goods probably had their origin in the time of the revival of commerce, and were levied at the most frequented crossroads and ports. Many were doubtless established by the counts, and others by local lords. By the time they appear in the full light of history many of them had been subinfeudated, though this did not prevent the count from claiming the right to deal with the abuses which arose out of their collection. Comital policy regarding tolls assumed two forms: the granting of exemptions and the fixing of tariffs. The great towns endeavoured, from the time when they first secured privileges, to obtain for their inhabitants exemption, or at least preferential rates, particularly so far as tolls levied in their own territories were concerned. Often these preferential rates, once one town had gained them, became an object which other towns set themselves to obtain. The outcome was, as is well enough known, that the toll system became exceedingly complex, the result of a series of grants which successive counts were compelled by political circumstances to make. Many such concessions date from the period of governmental crisis in 1127–8, but they are not unknown even during the reign of a prince as imbued as Philip of Alsace was with the sense of his own authority. Apparently Philip was prepared to see his own revenues reduced to a certain extent in the hope of witnessing in return the expansion of the commercial activities of his subjects. As pointed out above, Philip went so far as to grant total exemption throughout all Flanders to the new towns of his own foundation, the growth of which he desired to hasten.

Down to the end of the twelfth century, apparently, the majority of tolls, whether remaining in the count's possession or granted away by him in fee, were collected at rates based upon oral tradition. In 1199, however, Baldwin IX laid down in writing the tolls which were to be levied at Ghent and Termonde, and threatened those who contravened his edict with the fate of highway robbers. But it was not until the reign of Margaret of Constantinople that this principle was generalized. She had inquests made to determine the rates at which customary charges had been levied at various points, and followed these by ordinances laying down the tariffs to be observed in the future. That of May 1271, which dealt with the Scheldt and the Scarpe, was concerned with a considerable number of tolls.

(5) INTERNAL TRADE: THE STAPLES

In the second half of the thirteenth century Flanders was rapidly transformed from an active to a passive trading country. While previously contacts with foreign lands had principally been in the hands of native merchants, the latter were more and more being supplanted by aliens. The exchange of goods thenceforward took place within the confines of Flanders itself, and mainly in the ports at which overseas merchants came to land. The merchant class of the Flemish towns found its very existence threatened, but the new dispensation seems to have brought prosperity to a large proportion of the population and the counts from the very start took steps to encourage foreign traders to come to their dominions. Margaret of Constantinople in 1262 granted privileges to the merchants of La Rochelle, St Jean d'Angély, Niort and the neighbouring towns who frequented the port of Gravelines. It soon appeared, however, that there was a natural tendency for trade to concentrate upon Bruges and its outports on the banks of the Zwin. Again Countess Margaret favoured the alien merchants conforming to this trend, particularly by alleviating the burden of tolls (1252). About the same time she seems to have been disposed to allow the establishment of a German colony at Damme or in its neighbourhood (1253), though this scheme proved abortive. But even without encouragement from the ruler a 'staple' in the broad sense of a market developed on the Zwin, in so far as trade tended to concentrate there owing simply to the geographical and economic advantages the location possessed. There was no compulsion for goods to pass through the staple (*Stapelzwang*); at best the counts were in a position to intervene in order to designate a place (Bruges or one of its outports) at which trade in a particular commodity passing along the Zwin should take place.

Things were very different in Holland where Dordrecht, from the last quarter of the thirteenth century, was making great efforts to set itself up in rivalry to Bruges as a centre of passive trade and a market for traders from outside the Low Countries. Dordrecht, admirably situated near the mouths of the Meuse and the Rhine and on waterways leading to the sea, to the interior of Holland and to Flanders and Brabant, became at an early date a centre for the transhipment of merchandise. This natural development was furthered by measures taken by the count: *c.* 1260–70, at a time when his other towns were of little economic significance, he laid down that goods of any importance carried by water should be measured there. He also grasped the opportunity of profiting from the damage inflicted upon Flemish commerce by the rupture of Anglo-Flemish relations in 1270 and the years which followed. He granted privileges to merchants coming from the lands to the east of the Zuider Zee in 1276, and to those of northern Germany, and Hamburg especially, in order to divert them from Bruges for the benefit of Dordrecht. We must add to this policy the count's attempt at the same time to attract weavers to the port on the Merwede in order to ensure for the foreign trader a return cargo produced on the spot.

For a short time Florence V even succeeded in diverting to Dordrecht the English wool staple (1294–5). This protectionist policy of the counts reached its highest point when the *de facto* staple in the town was transformed into a compulsory institution during the brief reign of the young

Count John I, at a time when he was under the wardship of John d'Avesnes, the future Count John II. During this period, merchants coming down the Merwede or Lek were obliged to offer their goods for sale at Dordrecht. Thus the town became a compulsory market for dealings between the Rhineland and middle Meuse on the one hand, and Zeeland, Flanders, western Brabant and England on the other. The count's object was not simply to stimulate trade in his dominions and thus augment their prosperity. By concentrating trade at Dordrecht, he also made it easier to administer the tolls to which he was entitled on the many branches of the great rivers. It was, finally, probably also at this time that he established, again at Dordrecht, an institution which the sources call *wissel* (exchange) which, according to the persuasive hypothesis of Professor J. F. Niermeyer, was designed officially to regulate the price and quality of goods. By so doing it must have rendered, at least indirectly, great service to trade, especially by reducing the possibility of frauds.

The exceptional position of Dordrecht and the special regulations which applied to it led to a conflict of interests between it and the other trading towns of northern Holland, the rise to prominence of which is one of the features of the fourteenth century. This conflict was closely linked with the political struggles between the well-known factions of the Hoeken and the Kabeljauwen, which lasted throughout the fourteenth and fifteenth centuries. The attitude of the count towards Dordrecht was often determined by the control which one or other of these factions exercised over him. Thus the regent Albert, from the time he took over the direction of government, persuaded the German Hanse, at that time in difficulties at Bruges, to move their factory to Dordrecht (1358–60). This happy state of affairs lasted only for the brief period required by the Flemish to capitulate to the terms set by the Hansards for their return to Bruges, while at almost the same moment Albert on his side was brought to an agreement with the other Dutch towns which were jealous of Dordrecht's privileges. Thirty years later, it is true, the circumstances of 1358 recurred and Albert, who became count at this moment (1389), again came to an agreement with the Hansards for the removal of their factory and staple in the Low Countries from Bruges to Dordrecht. This new interlude lasted only from 1389 to 1392: once more Dordrecht proved no more than second best so far as the German merchants were concerned. Soon after they had departed, anti-Dordrecht feeling reappeared more powerfully than ever, and a comital edict in 1394 exempted a great number of the Dutch towns from staple obligations. The issue again came to the front in the first half of the fifteenth century. Thus the council of Holland in 1432 and again in 1446 recognized the staple rights of Dordrecht as a result of disputes which had been provoked by the towns of Guelders.

Y

Like the count of Holland, the duke of Brabant encouraged the de-velopment in his dominions of an active centre of trade, Antwerp, to which city in all probability the staple of English wool was moved from Dordrecht in 1295, since John II gave privileges to the Englishmen trad-ing there in 1296. He augmented these privileges in 1305 and renewed them in 1315; and in the same year extended them to the Hansards, Florentines and Genoese. This policy produced quite tangible results and, by about the middle of the fourteenth century, Antwerp would have been well on the way to becoming a serious rival of Bruges but for the fact that Louis de Male, count of Flanders, at war with his sister-in-law Joan of Brabant and her husband Wenceslas, seized possession of Ant-werp and Malines in 1356. The counts of Flanders had not up to this time adopted a line of economic policy designed to favour Bruges as a centre of passive trade. Louis de Male, however, took advantage of his conquest to aid Bruges indirectly by ruining its rival. Cut off from its hinterland, the duchy of Brabant, Antwerp was deprived besides of the staples of fish, salt and oats which it had possessed up to this time, but which now passed to Malines. It was not until the beginning of the fifteenth century, when, like Flanders, Brabant in its turn came under the control of the dukes of Burgundy, that Antwerp was reunited to Brabant. Thereafter the curve of its prosperity resumed its natural upward course.

(6) INDUSTRY

The textile industry in Flanders developed with such vigour that any in-tervention on the part of the counts may well have seemed quite super-fluous. It was the obvious results of the spontaneous development of the great clothing centres which moved Joan of Constantinople in 1224 to promise exemption from *taille* to the first fifty 'foreigners' who estab-lished themselves in Courtrai for the purpose of carrying on cloth-work-ing. But this was quite an exceptional measure, explicable only in terms of the countess's wish to favour a town which was closely dependent upon her. More interesting is the fact that, while the larger clothing towns built markets for themselves with their own funds, the princes as-sisted in meeting the cost of such construction in the less important centres, at least to the extent of granting them the necessary sites. Even more than in Flanders this was the case in Brabant, where the cloth in-dustry was less developed and the dukes deliberately applied themselves to making up this leeway.

From the end of the thirteenth century rulers began to be faced by problems arising out of the competition between the urban textile in-dustry and that of the smaller places and of the countryside. As has already been pointed out, however, their policy was dictated by motives which were political rather than economic. The industry of the great towns was always the basis of the prosperity of the region, yet at the same time their power was the prime obstacle to the absolute authority of the princes. A policy which favoured the growth of a cloth industry competing with that of Bruges, Ghent or Ypres was, so far as the counts of Flanders were concerned, one which generated new support against the forces opposed to the count's authority. On the other hand, their hands were sometimes forced. Whenever the count found himself at the mercy of the great towns, the latter compelled him to enact measures ensuring them a monopoly of manufacture or at least a specially favoured position in that part of the principality over which they claimed ascendancy.

This happened for the first time during the struggle between the counts of Flanders and the kings of France from 1297 to 1320. Ghent succeeded in obtaining successively in 1297, 1302 and 1314 prohibitions, first upon holding a cloth staple, tentering cloth and dyeing cloth or wool within an area of three leagues around it; secondly upon bringing into the city cloth woven or fulled elsewhere; and finally upon all textile manufacture within a radius of five leagues. Bruges and Ypres exacted favours similar to this last of the Ghent privileges from the young Louis de Nevers at his accession and before his authority was firmly established. Likewise when this same prince at the end of his reign relinquished power, in fact if not in law, to James van Artevelde, he had also to resign himself to sanctioning the destruction of the cloth industry of Langemark to the advantage of Ypres and that of the castellany of the Franc to the advantage of Bruges.

Each time the counts recovered their authority, however, they seem regularly to have shown sympathy for the endeavours of the small towns and country districts to develop a woollen industry. This is particularly true of Louis de Male, whose surviving acts include the concession of rights to carry on textile manufacture in Menin (1351), Oudenburg (1353), Roeselare (Roulers, 1357), Wervik (1359), La Gorgue (1359), Tielt (1359), Gistel (1365) and Hondschote (1374). During his reign, again, Ypres, unable to subjugate Poperinghe by force, had to resign itself to bringing its rival before the count's council; we do not know what the decision was in this case, but it is certain that the expansion of clothmaking at Poperinghe was not checked.

Indeed, while Ghent and Bruges had succeeded in eliminating textile manufacture from their rural hinterland, Ypres, the weakest of the three 'members of Flanders', failed to prevent the small towns and villages around it from raising their heads once more and resuming competition with unabated vigour. This same problem, in the fifteenth century, faced the dukes of Burgundy. Presumably purely opportunist reasons persuaded Philip the Good to grant to Ypres the privilege of 1428, which forbade cloth manufacture, save for purely local consumption, in the castellanies of Ypres, Warneton, Cassel and Bailleul. No doubt he was too preoccupied with a multitude of problems of foreign policy to be able to resist at this juncture pressure from his Flemish subjects. These measures enacted by the duke at the request of the men of Ypres were directed primarily against the cloth industry at Neuve Église, a village to the south of the city under the jurisdiction of a private lady—a fact which enabled it to resist them with greater vigour than if it had been directly dependent upon the duke. Neuve Église, the industry of which was to display remarkable vitality in the future, decided to appeal to the Parlement of Paris. The king of France, at war at this very moment with his vassal Philip the Good, hastened to take the side of this village in distress against the town protected by the duke. In the outcome, however, the latter ceased to be concerned about the decaying industry of the third town of Flanders: when in 1446, eleven years after peace had been made between the duke and the king, the latter gave provisional licence for the villages to make cloth as they had done before 1428, Philip the Good made no serious attempt to oppose this decision. The problem again raised its head after the death of Charles the Bold and particularly after that of Mary of Burgundy, when in 1483 the king of France (now Louis XI) renewed, ironically enough, the privileges granted to Ypres in 1428 in order to win the good will of the 'members of Flanders'. In despite of this, however, the country drapery continued its expansion.

(7) MONETARY PROBLEMS

In view of their dependence on either France (Flanders) or the Empire (the principalities of lower Lotharingia), the princes of the Low Countries enjoyed no minting rights save through grant or delegation: they could not, therefore, dispose of these rights in the fullest sense. In fact, however, the principalities to the east of the Scheldt, in imperial territory, soon acquired their freedom in this respect. As for Flanders, it attained a large independence at an early date and quickly built up a solid organization at a time when the royal power in France was still weak. It had, however, from the end of the twelfth century, to take account of the growth of Capetian power, and active intervention in particular on the part of Philip the Fair (1285–1314). The latter sought to impose upon Flanders the currency regulations he made for the rest of France, a policy harmful to the interests of Flemish trade. In like manner the kings of France attempted to limit the minting powers of the counts to a 'black silver' currency; but they got over this difficulty by striking 'white silver' and gold coins at their mints in imperial Flanders (i.e. in that part of their principality which they did not hold of the French king) and at the same time allowing the circulation of this coinage throughout their dominions. Louis de Male (1346–84) was the first count who ceased to be disturbed by these pretensions on the part of his suzerain, as he was also the first to mint exclusively a currency completely different, not only in type but also in value, from the money of France.

In the thirteenth century his predecessors had adopted as their 'black silver' currency the money of Paris, which therefore became the basis for the Flemish money of account. Several of the principalities of lower Lotharingia, which from the beginning of the thirteenth century fell under strong French influence, adopted as their money of account the money of Tours. All these currencies, whether real or of account, underwent modifications of value of the same degree and according to the same rhythm as the corresponding royal moneys. At the beginning of the Hundred Years War, however, when the French Crown began a new series of mutations, Flanders ceased to follow in the wake of the kingdom: while the ratio of 12:1 between its *livre de gros* and its *livre parisis* which had been normal for some time was maintained, the weight and alloy of the actual coins in circulation and on which the money of account was based ceased to correspond with those of the money of France, with the result that the moneys of account of France and Flanders (both *livres de gros* and *livres parisis*) also ceased to coincide. This independence of its monetary system symbolizes to some degree the political independence of Flanders from France.

In like manner we may say that, under Philip the Good, the unification or at least co-ordination of the monetary systems of the principalities of the Low Countries was symbolic of their territorial unification under his sceptre. The duke of Burgundy, by the reform of 1433–4, provided a common currency, so far as 'white silver' and gold were concerned, for Flanders, Brabant, Holland, Zeeland and Hainault. Only the 'black silver' currency continued to differ from principality to principality. As for a common money of account, that of Flanders was extended to the other territories.

We must also ask what motives guided the princes of the Low Countries who, particularly in the fourteenth century, had recourse to devaluation and debasement of their money. Was it simply a matter of necessity that they should follow the example of their neighbours and in particular that of the kings of France? Doubtless we must give considerable weight to this factor; but must we also believe, as some have been inclined to assert, that by gradually reducing the intrinsic value of their coinage rulers were concerned to produce a kind of inflation and thereby to exercise a stimulating effect upon business tendencies? Up to the present not a shadow of proof has been adduced to support this point of view. On the contrary, it seems clear that Louis de Male at least was, in this connection, moved solely by a desire for gain. It is possible to calculate the number of gold and silver coins struck during his reign as amounting to 15 and 135 millions respectively—i.e. quantities far in excess of real needs. These enormous quantities were doubtless the outcome of a large number of re-coinages of the same volume of bullion. It was successive depreciations, and purchases stimulated by the attraction of ever higher prices for the mark (made possible by the progressive reduction of its intrinsic value), which always brought bullion back again to the mints. These continuous alterations allowed a reasonably high seignorage to be charged for minting; and the results of this policy can be assessed from the fact that mint profits during certain years represented from one-sixth to one-fifth of the revenues of Louis de Male.

Philip the Bold, who followed Louis, continued the monetary policy pursued by his father-in-law, at least at the beginning of his reign. He succeeded in this way, not only in feeding his treasury, but also in sowing such confusion in the monetary system of the duchess of Brabant that the ground was virtually prepared for the absorption of the Brabançon currency into that of Flanders. Between Philip the Bold and his grandson Philip the Good there is a striking contrast. In addition to the unification of currencies, the latter's reign also brought monetary stability at least for reasonably long periods (e.g. from 1434 to 1466 for the silver currency). The cost of this new attitude in monetary policy, so much desired by his subjects, was a slowing down of minting and consequently a diminution of the revenue derived from seignorage. But the 'great duke of the west' disposed of other resources sufficiently large to enable him to adopt this course.

It is interesting to note that in another respect the dukes of Burgundy appear to have guarded their prerogatives in monetary matters with a jealous care. As R. de Roover has clearly demonstrated, the changers of the fourteenth century and especially those of Bruges had, in their capacity as bankers, from one point of view created money: in accepting deposits for their clients and making transfers for them, they operated in fact with cash balances which represented no more than a fraction of their liabilities. Did the ducal counsellors grasp the fact that the changers were thus, in a way, usurping the monetary powers which belonged to the duke? It is possible that they did, and this may explain the ordinances of Philip the Good (1433), Charles the Bold (1467) and Maximilian of Austria (1489) prohibiting the activities of banker-changers and even of bankers pure and simple.

The princes, indeed, had from the very beginning regarded everything connected with exchange operations as part of their prerogative in the matter of money. The office of changer could only be exercised in virtue of a grant from them, which was subject to their regulation and conceded in return for payment. At Bruges, at the beginning of the thirteenth century, there were five exchanges granted out as fiefs. During that century, with the expansion of financial activity in the mart of Bruges, about fifteen others were added and let out at a fee-farm rent. Things were different at Ghent: there the count had granted away his rights to the town, which received the profits which would have gone to him. With a few exceptions (as when the Lombards were vested with the exchanges in 1281) the office of managing the exchanges was normally entrusted to denizens. Apart from their primary function, i.e. petty exchange, the changers were also given a responsibility which they exercised on the prince's behalf and which enabled him to secure the enforcement of his monetary edicts. While they were bound to exchange according to a prescribed tariff currencies the circulation of which was permitted, they were also obliged to purchase prohibited currencies (at prices depending on their bullion content) in order to supply the mints. They bound themselves loyally to carry out this duty by an oath normally taken before the city authorities in the presence of a representative of the prince. In principle, as burgesses, the changers were subject to the jurisdiction of the magistrates of their town. The princes, however, endeavoured continuously to bring them under their own jurisdiction: it is in this light that we must view the edict of Charles the Bold ordering all new changers to relinquish their burgess-ship.

The intervention of the princes in the money-lending activities carried on by the Lombards was likewise, though less obviously, connected with their prerogatives in monetary matters. An example was set apparently by Guy of Dampierre, count of Flanders, who authorized the Lombards in 1281 to settle in a certain number of his towns. This course of action is explicable, no doubt, in terms of his financial needs, but it also displays a certain boldness. If he restricted usury to the Lombards alone and to certain types of transaction, if he subjected the conduct of such business to the payment of a sum agreed upon, he authorized usury none the less and thereby trespassed upon the province of the Church which in principle exercised a sole competence in this regard. The payments which the prince received had their counterpart in the privileged status granted to the Lombards, which was not extended to the other Italians settled in his lands, such as the members and the agents of the great commercial companies.

(8) EXPLOITATION OF THE SOIL

The fact that the territorial princes of the Low Countries had usurped the regalian rights over unoccupied lands along the sea coasts, on heaths, etc., enjoyed by kings at an earlier date, meant that each new extension of the cultivated area was only possible as a result of their intervention. This can be discussed most conveniently in connection with Flanders and Holland.

In the first of these counties the exploitation of a belt of polders, which steadily took shape along the coast after a last inundation in the tenth century, goes back to a very early time; but the methods are only known to us from the reign of Philip of Alsace. Unoccupied lands were either brought under cultivation by the domanial administration of the count himself, or distributed in large blocks to the abbeys and chapters of his land, who undertook to till them. The latter obtained from the count every facility for carrying out the works necessary to this end, and in particular for digging the canals required for drainage. As in other spheres, active participation by the count ceased after the death of the energetic Philip of Alsace and was only resumed with vigour under Margaret of Constantinople. Under pressure of her financial needs this princess alienated a large quantity of previously uncultivated land on condition that in future an annual rent would be paid for it. The very act of subjecting this land to a rent imposed upon those who acquired it the obligation of bringing it into cultivation. The participation of the ruler in the extension of the cultivated area is found throughout medieval times. Thus, in the mid-fifteenth century, Philip the Good was engaged in restoring the dykes of the polders along the south bank of the western Scheldt. He entrusted the direction of this work to the heads of certain Flemish abbeys with property in the district, and empowered them to raise the funds they required by taxing the owners of submerged property.

In Holland, too, the count took part in the work of colonizing and exploiting the soil, from as early as the eleventh century, by establishing manorial centres in lands previously waste. He also intervened in a more indirect manner by ceding vast areas of peat land to entrepreneurs who undertook in their turn to establish colonists upon them.

The control and supervision of the lands along the coast, reclaimed from the sea and always in danger of returning to it, demanded a special administration. In the Carolingian period, the count, as the local royal official, was invested with this authority; he delegated it normally to a subordinate official (*schout*). After the formation of the principalities, at least in the northern part of the Low Countries, the local communities (*buurschappen*) seem from the first to have undertaken the administration of sea-defences. The prince's role was limited originally to protecting their works. There soon emerged on a local scale administrative institutions charged with the task of constructing water-defences (*waterschappen*), and then judicial bodies presided over by a *schout* and *heemraden*, which were responsible for inspecting waterways and dykes. Finally, institutions with a regional competence (*hoofdwaterschappen*) were created, which were invested by the count with extensive powers and which were in particular charged with the carrying out of works of more than merely local importance. These *hoofdwaterschappen* gave birth in turn to a judicial institution, the *hoogheemraadschappen*, with a competence extending over the same district. In maritime Flanders, in the associations called *wateringen* and in the *dijkgraven* (who were officials appointed by the count), we have the elements of similar institutions.

Governments likewise played a part, though a very variable one, in the exploitation of the subsoil. Among the regalian rights which territorial princes assumed for themselves were proprietary claims to the wealth which lay beneath the soil. This problem has been systematically studied only for the old duchy of Limburg on the borders of modern Germany, Belgium and the Netherlands. This region was rich in minerals, of which the most valuable was calamine, a mixture in which zinc carbonate is the most important constituent. Philip the Good took an interest in its exploitation, granting concessions and affording facilities to new entrepreneurs. Originally he took a part in the enterprise by providing the site and the timber required for working it; but later he was satisfied, as were his successors, merely to farm out the mines. At any rate, at the very end of the Middle Ages, the dukes of Burgundy in this respect at least took on the appearance of mercantilist rulers.

IV. *The Baltic Countries*

(1) GOVERNMENT FINANCE

The history of government finance in the countries of the Baltic area in the later Middle Ages suffers generally from a lack of sources. It is normally impossible to express economic realities for this area in statistical terms. Financial records were poor from the beginning and have been preserved only in a fragmentary fashion; but even if they had been preserved without loss, they would probably still have told only an unsatisfactory tale of what really happened. It is not before the period of centralized royal governments that we first have the chance of surveying financial development with any degree of certainty. Even at this stage, however, although some figures are available, they are scarcely ever of a sort which would permit safe deductions about the rise and fall of revenue.

For our knowledge of government finance we are consequently thrown back for the most part upon legal and political documents and what we know of the political circumstances of the time. Such material, clearly, provides only glimpses of economic conditions and hints about the crucial economic problems of government. On the other hand, it does reveal the relationship between needs and resources—the activities of kings and dukes and their counsellors which called for expenditure, and the measures they took to obtain some sort of financial balance. It is in any case impossible to estimate the taxable capacity of a medieval people; at least in the political sources we get evidence of the limits of its willingness to pay taxes. So the history of government finance in the medieval states of northern Europe is the history of state administrations wrestling with economic difficulties of which we only now and then get a clear view.

A. *The Economic Background*

In the period from the eleventh to the thirteenth century the countries of Scandinavia and on the shores of the Baltic became members of European society and civilization. Poland and the Scandinavian countries, and later the border countries on the southern and eastern Baltic, were won over to Christianity. Only Lithuania remained heathen after 1300. German, Danish and Swedish colonization carried with it not only the Christian religion, but also the ways of living, the social organization and the economy of central and western Europe, into areas sparsely populated by Slav, Baltic and Finnish tribes. The gradual incorporation of all this part of Europe into the economic community of Catholic civilization is the major trend which underlies all the varied aspects of its economic and financial history.

Part of this development was the bringing of new land into cultivation from the forests of all these countries. New settlements were established on the light, sandy soils, which a more primitive agrarian technique or a drier climate had previously excluded from the boundaries of cultivation. In Scandinavia this movement gradually created whole new populated districts, which in Norway and Sweden ate into the barriers of virgin woodland that had separated the largely independent provinces. In Poland it created new communities under German law. In the areas east of the Elbe it was one of the principal vehicles of German colonization, and was closely connected with and in some respects dependent upon the growth of German cities. On both sides of the gulfs of Finland and Bothnia, the rather more sporadic and agricultural Swedish colonization was a prolongation of the general movement for settling the forest lands, and went hand in hand with the intensified maritime enterprise of the Scandinavian countries in the age of medieval economic expansion.

Socially this movement created a large number of small tenements, less subject to the influence of the nobility than those in the older settled areas. In the non-feudal countries the new settlers were free landholders; in the feudal countries their land was under the control of kings or princes rather than that of the local nobles. In either case, agrarian expansion in northern Europe furthered financial centralization, for the free Scandinavian peasantry, both politically and economically, provided the material upon which the representatives of the Crown could work. In the general development of society in all these newly Europeanized countries, the movement of settlers out into the less fertile areas counterbalanced the normal dependence of men upon the privileged estates.

The period in question was also the great era of town foundation in northern Europe. The Hanseatic cities of the Wendish, Prussian and Baltic coasts became the great centres of trade and cultural exchange in this part of the world. Under their influence, the towns of the Danish coast (especially along the Sound), those along the coasts of Norway and Sweden, and also those of the interior of Germany, Poland and Scandinavia, flourished and grew. The stimulus given by these towns to the economic and social life of the countries in which they lay can hardly be over-estimated. On the other hand, it is difficult to assess their importance in the history of government finance. The larger towns, members of the Hanseatic League, were self-governing political units which, by investment outside their walls, contributed indirectly to the resources of the territorial princes, and sometimes contributed directly in the form of tribute or military aid; at the same time they lived and acted as independent political communities side by side with the monarchical states. The smaller towns, which acknowledged membership of a territorial state and obeyed the laws of their overlord, were modest in size and of limited fiscal importance. Even though charges on trade provided rulers with much-needed cash revenue and the financial capacity of the towns represented a reserve of credit of the greatest importance at moments of crisis, this does not alter the fact that the territorial states of northern Europe during the Middle Ages were predominantly agrarian in character. Nor does it alter the fact that government finance depended mainly upon the countryside. Lordship over large towns might be all-important financially; lordship over the smaller towns did not count for much.

Two basic features of economic development should also be remembered as a background to the history of economic policy in this region. The first is that the colonizing movement continued during the fourteenth and fifteenth centuries, thus making these centuries a period of continuing economic expansion, even though the same signs of agrarian difficulties and economic stagnation as in western Europe are found in the older cultivated districts. The further east we look, the more marked is the expansive character of economic life in the later Middle Ages. The second fact is that this part of Europe continued to be generally backward, which accentuated the importance of even small amounts of liquid capital in the hands of a prince or a lord. Relatively the northern countries gained in importance in the common life of the Christian world during this period, but they still held rather a peripheral position as outposts of civilization.

B. *The Early Kingdoms of Poland and Scandinavia*

There was from the beginning of the thirteenth century a striking contrast between the small feudal principalities of north Germany and Poland on the one hand, and the vast, sparsely populated Scandinavian kingdoms on the other. Obviously the former were the normal and the latter the abnormal political units in Europe in the high Middle Ages. Finally, the state of the Teutonic Order was a unique form of political organization, modelled on the non-territorial organization of the international orders of chivalry.

Denmark, Norway and Sweden had come into existence as unified kingdoms in the eleventh century, and the kingdom of Poland, too, flourished politically for a time; the other Baltic states of later times, on the other hand, had not yet been formed. At the same time, the picture of early consolidation in the Scandinavian viking kingdoms, and also in Poland, is to a considerable degree an illusory one. Very little is known about the economic basis of government under such kings as Sven Forkbeard of Denmark, Olaf Haraldsson of Norway or Olof Eriksson of Sweden; but certain deductions are possible from their political activities and from archaeological data. Their political activity and authority depended directly on their military power, which tended to vary between extremes of strength and weakness from one year to another. They also took desperate risks in their attempts to gain control over the North Sea and Baltic trade routes. Olaf Tryggvason of Norway was killed in one such attempt; Olaf Haraldsson and Amund of Sweden challenged Cnut the Great in Scania and not in their own home waters. Danish excavations at Trelleborg, Aggersborg and other viking 'bourgs' show that the warriors of the Danish kings of this age were concentrated in great fortified camps near the central seaways. The viking kings must have had their troops—or at least the pick of them—strictly organized as a permanent force under regulations similar to those which are implied by accounts of the law of the 'hird' of Cnut the Great a century later. These troops, like mercenary soldiers of all periods, must have been paid in cash and fed by regular supplies from the country around their camps. The kings obtained cash by levying tribute or by piracy along the trade routes; and supplies were probably delivered rather as 'protection' paid to gangsters than as taxes in our sense of the word. The system worked so long as kings could dispose of supplies of cash; when these failed they fell easy victims to rivals or rebellious chieftains. In short, the viking kingdoms of Norway, Denmark and Sweden were concentrations of sea-power rather than territorial dominions, and their fiscal organization was that of a self-supplying body of mercenary troops rather than a properly constituted state. They were composed of a host of peasant communities held together by but few institutional bonds. At periods of dynastic change in the eleventh and twelfth centuries, Scania, Seland and Jutland easily fell apart and acclaimed different Danish kings; more than one king ruled at the same time in Sweden proper—in the Mälar valley and in Västergötland; and Norway was divided into completely independent coasts and valleys, nominally dominated by a royal family, some of whose members, each with the name of king, resided in different parts of the country. These provincial kings had little of the glory of pirate emperors like Erik the Victorious, Sven Forkbeard or Harald the Hardminded; but at least they were rooted in the territorial organization of society.

There are remarkable parallels between the earliest Polish kingdom and the viking kingdoms of Scandinavia, though Poland was less primitive and more densely peopled. Poland was unified by Mesco I at about the same time as Denmark and probably Sweden. There may have been direct connection between viking military organization and that of Mesco's warriors; at least vivid traditions in Norse sagas tell of a fortified viking camp at the mouth of the Oder at the end of the tenth century, i.e. at a time when the first Polish king was becoming master of this region. But Norse influence in early Poland should not be exaggerated. Mesco and Boleslav I were neither viking leaders nor viking puppets. At the same time, the military force which kept the tribal units of early Poland together was an organized royal guard, numbering 3,000 men and paid in cash 'from the market places' according to the Arab writer, Ibrahim ibn Jacub. The later chronicle of Gallus Anonymus tells us that Boleslav the Valiant drew his warriors from Poznan, Gniezno and the 'castle of Wloclawek'. As Poznan and Gniezno were the two centres of the kingdom and both had castles at this period, we may assume that Mesco and Boleslav ruled with the support of a mercenary army, established at centres of trade and paid for by levies on trade in much the same manner as were the viking 'hirds'.

Regular taxation cannot be assumed for this early period in either Scandinavia or Poland. The earliest taxes in Scandinavia, like the Polish *narzaz*, were paid in kind, as was natural enough in view of the agrarian economy of the region. On the other hand the military budgets of the viking and early Polish kings were based upon payments in cash or unminted silver. We may conclude that these kingdoms flourished as by-products of the trade of north-eastern Europe round the year 1000, and withered as the main trade routes shifted in the course of the eleventh century. Political life reverted to the more natural provincial units, which were kept together by dynastic tradition, sometimes by the exigencies of external policy, and everywhere by ecclesiastical organization—established in Poland in the tenth and eleventh centuries and in Scandi-

navia in the eleventh and twelfth. A more stable economic basis for
government was gradually built up, rooted in the rural communities of
the provinces and tribes.

The Polish kingdom disappeared in the eleventh century: it succumbed to the centrifugal force of tribal feudalism within and the political
pressure of the German Empire from without. For a time the tribal duch-
ies represented the largest political units of Poland until the Grand Duke
Boleslav Wrymouth, just before the middle of the twelfth century,
created the nucleus of a Polish state in his own central grand duchy with
its capital at Cracow. The kingdoms of Denmark, Norway and Sweden
continued to exist during this period, but politically they were weak. In
the peasant communities of these countries no form of feudalism had
taken root and, with the temporary exception of the Danish earldom of
Schlesvig, they lay outside the influence of the Empire. The Scandinavian
kings, therefore, were faced with less powerful opposition than the
Polish rulers. In the latter's sphere of influence in the Baltic region, progressively subjected to German colonization, no real monarchical
authority was recognized. The only change was that local chieftains were
replaced by German counts.

How far the social life of the Baltic countries in the tenth and eleventh
centuries made any normal demands for the regular exercise of a central
authority is problematical. In times of peace the Scandinavian kings exercised a kind of supreme judicial and police power, but their exercise of
this function could clearly be interrupted for longer or shorter periods.
When the Polish kingdom disappeared, there is no sign that these social
functions of the ruler were greatly missed. The real and urgent task of
kings at this period was leadership in war. Where no supreme military
authority was permanently recognized, the problems of war finance
had to be solved by lesser authorities. In such circumstances, it was
more difficult to justify the need for a properly organized state financial system.

In feudal Poland the traditional tribal society was transformed under
influences from the neighbouring countries of Moravia, Bohemia and
Germany. Imperial pressure on Poland inevitably made it necessary for
the Polish princes to create military resources comparable to those of the
dukes and margraves west of the indeterminate frontier. The forces of
the first Piast kings were based on castles built to replace the older tribal
fortresses, and their castellans were appointed governors of the surrounding territories. Gradually the country was divided into districts controlled from the castles. To them were attached *opoles*, serf villages,
peopled to a large extent by prisoners of war, who thus represented valuable spoils of victory for the prince. The *opoles* provided the labour
force required by the castles in their character of military and administra-

tive centres; in them lived the farm workers, artisans, fishermen, miners, etc. of the state. A shortage of serfs in the *opoles* seems to have been endemic. This organization seems to have been adequate to permit the castellans to carry out their governmental and judicial duties, but the great mercenary armies of the earlier kings could not be replaced by the small and scattered garrisons of castles of a feudal type. The original duty of all free men to man and defend the fortresses of the land was transformed into one of making a contribution to their maintenance. The Polish armies of the feudal age became armies of knights, cavalrymen drawn from the privileged classes and exempted from common public obligations. The privileges of the knights were established by 1200, though it is impossible to pin down the date of their origin more precisely. As a military force this cavalry was composed of the mail-clad lords of the larger estates, who led the provincial forces in war and co-operated politically with the ecclesiastical aristocracy to check any tendency on the part of the princes to establish a real authority over their subjects.

In the absence of reliable statistics, it is of course impossible to estimate the strength or weakness of the dukes of Silesia, Cracow, etc. in relation to their own nobility. Everything depended on the size of the force of paid soldiers the princes were able to maintain, and the extent to which they could buy the service of knights. We know something of their sources of revenue, but not the relative importance of different sources or the relation of their revenues to their needs. The political results in twelfth- and early thirteenth-century Poland, however, are evident enough: the central power was weak and constantly on the retreat in face of German pressure on the west and on the north.

The oldest Polish tax, the *narzaz*, was paid originally in cattle and pigs, but in the thirteenth century in corn. The *stroza* was a charge in lieu of garrison duty in the castles, and the *stan* replaced the obligation to feed the prince and his court when they visited the district. These and similar less important taxes were clearly designed for the sustenance of the prince and his men in their castles, and probably allowed little scope for extraordinary government action. They could hardly develop into an adequate central financial system, and the same is true of revenue from judicial administration and similar sources. Moreover, the proceeds of these taxes fell off in the thirteenth century in consequence of the immunities conceded to the privileged classes.

Town revenues, market dues and mint profits may have offered the princes a better opportunity to buy services with hard cash. The extent to which this was true must have depended on the volume of trade. There is no possibility of setting a figure to revenue drawn from these sources or of evaluating the opportunities it opened up; but the expansion of the grand duchy of Boleslav seems to point to a tendency in the early twelfth century to establish administrative districts dependent upon important trading centres. In this respect, the separation of Silesia from Poland and the loss of the Baltic ports to the Teutonic Order not only demonstrated Poland's political weakness but also prolonged it.

Feudal Poland, then, was an agrarian land with a social structure modelled on that of the more economically developed European states but relatively poor in supplies of liquid resources created by trade. In some respects the same is true of the Scandinavian countries, despite the part they played in the eastward colonizing movement. They were distinguished, so far as the economic basis of government is concerned, in that they were seafaring, and not inland, nations. In the latter government is swayed mainly by the ambitions of princes; in a seafaring country it is much more a matter of general interest.

When the period of 'crusading' and colonization began in the Baltic region in the twelfth century, the Danish state of the Valdemars was the leading power. Its economic system provided a model for Sweden and Norway; it was rather an original system, for it was based fundamentally on the principle of political and military co-operation on the part of peasant communities organized in self-governing provinces.

Scandinavian military forces, since the viking period, had consisted of fleets of 'long ships' manned by warriors who rowed them and fought on board or on land according to circumstances. In principle all men owning land had to contribute to maritime expeditions. Danish, Swedish and Norwegian provincial laws, most of them codified in the thirteenth century, show that all of these countries were divided into districts each of which had to equip one 'long ship'. As these sources are comparatively late and derive from a time when maritime expeditions of the traditional sort were out of date, we must be careful not to exaggerate the antiquity of the organization they describe. According to the laws, the free peasantry of a district was responsible for maintaining, equipping, provisioning and manning a ship. This responsibility was a communal one, for the ship only came under the command of a royal captain in time of war. In fact, however, this picture probably departs as far from reality as the general one given in the laws of a society of free and equal peasants governing themselves communally under the leadership of men chosen only for the confidence they commanded. The Danish chroniclers of the age of the Valdemars and the contemporary Norse sagas make it clear that the ships and men of the bishops and magnates were of decisive importance. Even in the laws we get evidence that the peasant communities, at least in Denmark, were not expected to own their 'long ships'. The provincial aristocracy certainly provided not only the leaders but also the backbone of the *ledung* or naval contingents. They were, of course, not paid for their services, but the success of an expedition largely depended upon their political engagement in it. They owned their own ships and furnished the crews for them; they were, like their viking ancestors, more or less habitually engaged in trade and seafaring; and they took the lead in the affairs of their districts in peace and war. Thus we may assume that their followers were not only men of their households, but of whole districts; and that their authority was the effective force behind the communal obligations of all free men in naval expeditions. Valdemar I could have founded neither a dynasty nor the beginnings of a Baltic empire without the support of the powerful noble family of the Hvides; and the rival royal dynasties in Sweden and the pretenders to the Norwegian throne were no less dependent upon the good will of aristocratic factions, whose interests could never be ignored.

If the Scandinavian kings were to achieve military emancipation from the noble families, who really governed the rural communities of the provinces, they needed to acquire resources of their own. They disposed of royal estates scattered over their dominions—vast agglomerations of tenements unsuited to regular exploitation under central control or to serve as the basis for an effective and loyal local administration. This meant that kings had to ride round their country with their followers, consume the stores accumulated on their estates, and to a certain extent rely on the hospitality of the local inhabitants. Thus, under favourable circumstances, the king was master of that part of the country where he was residing for the time being, but the people of the rest of the land could be confident that in the meantime they would not feel the weight of his authority. Without an effective administrative system, based on a regular royal revenue, the king could never control the whole country at any one time. This was a general problem in feudal Europe in the early Middle Ages, but in Scandinavia it operated in a distinctive form of society with a very limited range of economic opportunity.

The first known attempt by a Scandinavian king to substitute a tax for the general obligation of service in the fleet was made by St Cnut of Denmark in 1086, in an endeavour to allay rebellion in parts of his land at a time when a viking expedition to England was being organized. The details are unknown, but a later chronicler emphasizes the point that Cnut's demand was a novel one. It led to a general rebellion and the king's death at the hands of his enraged subjects. He may have wished to revive the viking garrison at Aggersborg, where his fleet was ordered to assemble; and also to create a military force of some other sort to hold his people down. At any rate, the project was premature, and the outcome clearly shows that the king lacked the means to carry it out. More than a century later, about 1213, Cnut's plan was finally put into effect in Denmark; and Norway and Sweden followed this example in the 1260's or 1270's. This reform, however, implying the establishment of regular taxation, was carried out in quite a different social milieu from that in which St Cnut had planned to revive the Anglo-Danish viking empire.

In the twelfth century German colonization reached the Baltic and German feudalism began to exercise a strong influence upon the Scandinavian peoples. In the first instance this influence was naturally strongest in the field of military organization and the outward forms of upper-class life. Heavy cavalry was introduced into Danish warfare in 1134 when Erik Emune, with a mounted mercenary army, crushed the combined forces of King Niels and the Church at a single blow at Fotevik. During the whole of the twelfth century, however, this kind of warfare could be only of incidental or secondary importance in Denmark. The king, the bishops and some magnates were able to retain small forces of mounted men, but generally speaking resources were lacking for this expensive type of retinue. Still, following upon the appearance of these mounted forces, came the first castles of a continental type which were able to house permanent garrisons.

During Barbarossa's rule over the Empire, Denmark began to win a position as the leading power east of the Elbe, a development culminating in the reign of Valdemar II the Victorious, whose supremacy over the German territorial princes in this region was recognized. In Holstein, as in Mecklenburg, a normal system of taxation had come into being in the course of the twelfth century, as an outcome of a general claim to levy taxes made by the emperors, but of which their territorial vassals had been the main beneficiaries. The main tax, the *petitio* (in German *bede* or *grevenscat*), appears originally to have been connected with the position of the prince as the judicial head of his dominions and probably took the form at first of hospitality afforded to the count when he visited a district to hold his court. This system and the terminology associated with it were exported eastwards from the older German territories west of the Elbe. In the last decades of the twelfth century the tax was sufficiently recognized for the count of Holstein to grant exemption from it to churches. The counts of Ratzeburg and Schwerin had also made good their right to levy it in the late 1190's and in 1200. It formed part of that feudal order of society which spread eastwards with German colonization, but to the Danish overlord of the lands beyond the Elbe it would also appear to be a more advanced method of organizing the resources of the state than the non-feudal order of his own country, based upon the co-operation of the provincial leaders. When moreover, at the beginning of the thirteenth century, the grandiose policies of the Danish king involved military clashes with German feudal armies, an urgent need arose for a military reorganization that would enable the king to pay for a cavalry force equal to that of the German chivalry.

So the common obligation of the Danish people to equip and man the *ledung* fleet was transformed into a system of ordinary taxes, paid chiefly in corn or other natural products. The large payments received in oats are clear evidence for the use of one of the taxes, the *stud*, for feeding the king's horses. Exempted from these taxes were the men who served the king as mounted warriors at their own expense, and who were thus marked off from the common people as a privileged nobility.

The social consequences of this reform, however, were not limited to this process of differentiation. The *ledung* organization had been based upon the principle of communal action. Groups of peasants, probably in most cases village communities, had been the basic units in the traditional division of the country for this purpose, each of them responsible for manning one oar of the 'long ship'. The new system of taxation had to be based on individuals, each economically capable of being regarded as a unit for purposes of paying taxes. In northern Germany the hide (*mansus, hufe*, in the Scandinavian languages *bol*) had been the basic unit for assessing the *bede*. The hide also became a land measure in Denmark; in Sweden and Norway it had the general connotation of a family holding; while in certain parts of Finland in the later Middle Ages it was used as a unit of taxation. In connection with the commutation of Danish *ledung* obligations into taxes, a new assessment of the land was felt to be necessary; it was given a money valuation which bore a fixed relationship to its purchase price and rent. This taxation of the land helped to bring land onto the market: in that sense it was a reform which mainly furthered the interests of the Church and the nobility. This may be regarded as the price demanded by the old aristocracy in the peasant communities for accepting the commutation of the *ledung*, by which the king gained in military power and the aristocracy lost its independent control over the provinces. Perhaps the Church gained even more than the nobility from the system of land taxation. The fixed assessments of their lands took on the air of a *justum pretium*, officially unchangeable, at a time of rapid agricultural expansion. This period, too, saw a great enlargement of ecclesiastical estates in Scandinavia.

When Sweden and Norway half a century later, after a lengthy period of slow adjustment, finally followed the Danish example and commuted the *ledung* into a general tax (except in Västergötland in Sweden, where no *ledung* obligation existed, and the new tax replaced the duty of feeding the king's followers visiting the province) it was, as in Denmark, the political result of an alliance between the monarchy and the Church. As in Denmark again, the peasant communities paid the price economically and politically. Their traditional leaders, the great landowners, coalesced with the king's followers to form a new privileged nobility which soon found many interests in common with the clergy. At the same time the Scandinavian landed nobility was never transformed into a class of feudal

landlords of the continental sort. All through the Middle Ages there existed links of mutual loyalty, based on equality before the law, between the
nobility and the peasantry of the various provinces—more marked in
Norway and Sweden than in Denmark, where geographical conditions
did not impose the same degree of separatism. Thus the basis of Scandinavian government was never a strictly feudal one.

C. *Feudal Decentralization in Thirteenth- and Fourteenth-century Scandinavia*

In the thirteenth century the Danes subjugated the Esthonians, and the
Swedes the Finnish tribes west of Lake Ladoga. These conquests, like the
stabilization of Norwegian dominion over the Scottish isles and Iceland,
were manifestations of the *ledung* fleets still in action. These could still get
the upper hand over sufficiently primitive, divided or otherwise weak
adversaries. But in the 1220's the greatest power of Scandinavia, the Denmark of Valdemar II, met a crushing defeat at the hands of a coalition of
small German princes headed by the counts of Schwerin and Holstein.
The weakness of the Scandinavians in heavy cavalry, by comparison with
the Germans, was demonstrated for the first time. King Valdemar's resources in men and money, which the new financial system had been
meant to assure, had proved inadequate.

A new system was introduced after the defeat at Bornhöved—a feudal
system. Several peripheral Danish provinces (Schleswig, Halland, the islands of Als and Langeland) were given as hereditary fiefs to King Valdemar's legitimate sons and his bastards. After the thirteenth century only
Schleswig remained a separate duchy, but all the same, the system meant
the division of the country into smaller units which had to organize individually their finances and military resources. In the kingdom proper
little more appears to have been expected of the castellans than the fulfilment of the military duty of maintaining and equipping a certain number of soldiers in their castles and following the king with these men when
required. The political result was the king's dependence upon the fidelity
of his vassals when he needed their service.

The economic reason for the decentralization of Denmark implied by
the feudal experiment was the acute shortage of ready money in the
Scandinavian countries. One instance illustrates what this shortage meant
in terms of military weakness. In 1275 the Swedish duke, Magnus Bir-
gersson, rebelled against his brother, King Valdemar of Sweden, and
obtained aid from King Erik Glipping of Denmark in the form of 100
armed men *cum omni bellico apparatu* for a cash payment of 6,000 marks.
To obtain this sum he had to mortgage one of Sweden's richest districts,
including its only western port, Lödöse. The 100 men gave Magnus vic-

tory, whereupon he tried to avoid payment of the sum he had offered and even made war against Denmark to this end. The latent strength of the Scandinavian peoples, the strength which made their expansion and colonization to the east of the Baltic possible, depended upon the agrarian improvements of this period. At the same time, the amount of surplus wealth from the land of Denmark or Sweden which the Crown was in a position to exploit fell far short of meeting the cost of an army of the latest European model. The nobleman ruling a district as a castellan could afford to keep a handful of soldiers out of peasant taxes, but it was impossible for the king to squeeze money out of the castellans to feed and pay a central military force.

The political conduct of the Scandinavian kings at the end of the thirteenth and beginning of the fourteenth centuries clearly shows their indifference to control over land and their intense interest in control over trade and the resources they could derive from it. Erik Menved of Denmark built up a phantom empire in north-western Germany, but struggled to keep in his own hands only the protectorate over the Hanse towns (Lübeck especially) and the customs of the international market at Skanör. The violent inter-Scandinavian war which raged throughout his reign, centring on the internal opposition in Denmark of the party of the Outlaws to the party of the king, seems to have been rooted in a fight over different ways of controlling maritime trade in the Skagerrak, Kattegat, Sound and the Belt. Norway, ruled by King Erik the Priesthater or rather by his advisers, made a desperate effort to maintain by force Norwegian dominance in home waters against the German Hanse. The Swedish duke, Erik Magnusson, made a brilliant and daring bid to create a new Scandinavian state out of Norway, the western provinces of Sweden and Danish Halland—obviously in order to prosecute the struggle for control over the trade going westwards by sea. His elder brother and opponent, King Birger of Sweden, risked his throne in an unsuccessful expedition to Gotland to subdue the Swedish Hanseatic town of Visby.

During this long period of war, many castles were built and garrisoned. The maintenance of these new castles still further strained government finances, for effective royal control and financial resources were continuously shrinking. From a military point of view, this meant that the forces of the Scandinavian countries were put increasingly on the defensive. In the thirteenth century employment of foreign mercenary troops had been a somewhat desperate throw to avert disaster; in the fourteenth century desperation became the rule, first in Denmark and later in Sweden. The counts of Holstein had already played the part of condottieri in Scandinavian wars in the 1270's, and in the 1330's they gradually took Denmark over on mortgage for unpaid military services. In the 1370's the duke of Mecklenburg interfered in Sweden's dynastic troubles, conquered the country in virtue of his military superiority and made his son king of Sweden.

The economic realities behind these events can be discerned in the continual disputes about new taxes, imposed as temporary expedients and then demanded again and again. They can also be read in the cold figures of the accounts of two Swedish fiefs held by a knight of Mecklenburg, which in the years 1365-6 were in the hands of King Albrecht. Although one of the fiefs was in the mining district of Dalecarlia, one of Sweden's chief financial resources, the account shows a loss of more than 9,000 Swedish marks. Out of this sum, 6,500 marks represented military expenses incurred during war by thirty soldiers. It is also evident, however, that the income in kind, which represented the greater part of the taxes paid by the peasantry, lay outside effective royal control and was never subjected to proper audit. The castellans were free to make what profit they liked from trading with the proceeds of the taxes; and this explains the eagerness of the castellans to retain their positions which, on the face of it, seem to involve such heavy financial burdens for them. Under such conditions the difficulty for kings of exercising effective financial administration over the castles and their territories is obvious enough.

The small German princes profited from their nearness to the great Hanse towns. They and their nobility were a military force of considerable importance in northern Europe, and they gained wealth by making war their profession. Their superiority was the superiority of German trading capital and, to some extent, that of a feudal society in a period of agricultural boom. They did not balance their budgets much better than the Scandinavian kings: the dukes of Mecklenburg, for instance, largely mortgaged their income from the *bede* at the very time when they were building up their power in the fourteenth century. On the other hand, their war machine worked. The limited extent of their territories was in itself a source of strength at a time when military effectiveness first and last depended on the loyalty of vassals. The prince's and the knight's common interest in the exploitation of conquered lands did the rest.

D. *The Establishment of the Teutonic Order*

In the thirteenth century, when the Polish dukes were fighting for hegemony in the absence of any central authority in that kingdom, and when the Scandinavian countries were experimenting with feudal decentralization, a new and vigorous major power made its appearance in the Baltic area. This was the state of the Teutonic Order. Until its defeat by the Poles and Lithuanians at Tannenberg in 1410, it was the best organized and best endowed power in the region.

Our knowledge of its financial organization is limited by the fact that its surviving fiscal records are comparatively late in date. A clear picture only becomes available for the years around 1400, when we have to deal with the results of a long process of development. These sources, however, permit us to draw some conclusions about the character of the financial system of the Order as far back as the thirteenth century and at the beginning of the fourteenth.

The Order, in its purpose and organization, was a militant power in a much stricter sense than any of its neighbours. It preserved the original features of the orders of chivalry which had fought for Christianity in the Holy Land. A network of castles belonged to the Order, each of which was governed by a *komthur*, who was responsible for the management of an annexed territory and maintained the 'brothers' in the castle from its revenues. Decentralization and great independence for the individual *komthurs* were characteristic of the system, which was designed to operate over vast regions of varying economic structure. The unity of the brotherhood was meant to be of a spiritual character, with an elected Grand Master as the executive authority and a Grand Chapter of the Order as its representative assembly.

When the Teutonic Order concentrated its missionary warfare on Germany's north-eastern frontier, it conquered Prussia and (in succession to the Order of the Sword in Livonia) took over the Livonian dioceses. By imperial privilege it became master of the state composed of these subjugated territories. Naturally this gave the Order its solid base, though it maintained in principle its character as a supra-national order of chivalry with castles and *komthurs* elsewhere in the Empire than in the Prussian-Livonian area. The Grand Master acquired the position of a feudal prince and the Grand Chapter, through which the collective will of the Order was in the main expressed, faded gradually into honorary passivity. Instead, the local *komthurs* and especially the 'grand *komthur*' of Königsberg, who managed and controlled the revenues of the Order, gradually came to hold the key political and financial positions. The local *komthurs* collected the *bede* and rents for land, and used with great freedom for their own purposes these payments in kind which were made to them. They were all responsible, however, to the central authorities in the Order, of whom the treasurer audited their accounts and appropriated the surpluses of local budgets for common purposes.

What were the special sources of strength which gave the Order its power? It may be assumed that the collection of taxes and rents from subjects of non-German nationality would be fairly ruthless, though the amounts known to have been paid by individuals do not seem to have been extraordinarily heavy as compared with other north German states. Nevertheless, the political conduct of the Order proves that it controlled financial resources exceeding those of its neighbours. It not only kept up an efficient army, but was able to buy the Danes out of Esthonia in 1346. At the end of the fifteenth century, the treasury of the Order played its part in international finance, although its Christian ideals prohibited it from taking usury of any kind. The budget of the Order must have shown a favourable balance and it must have enjoyed opportunities of investing its income. The semi-clerical nature of its organization may explain some of its discipline and the speed of communication which enabled a highly developed central control to be exercised over local revenues; but this does not explain the existence of these resources themselves.

A primary cause of the early strength of the Order was a spiritual asset, which in this age could almost have a money value set upon it: the readiness to fight loyally and the military competence of a chivalric brotherhood. The Grand Master got for nothing a military force which would have involved any contemporary ruler in heavy charges. One consequence of the spiritual authority of the government of the Order was the preservation of older and stricter rules of succession to fiefs. In Prussia down to the end of the Middle Ages they passed by inheritance only to men capable of serving in person, enabling a much firmer hold to be kept on vassals than elsewhere. The fact that the Baltic territories fell to it by conquest made it easy for the government of the Order to establish regalian rights over mills, inns, the trade in amber. This gave it control over day-to-day transactions amounting in aggregate to large sums of money, though probably difficult to supervise effectively.

An important reason for the resources of which the Order disposed may have been the integration of the Prussian Hanseatic towns into its financial system. These towns emerged as large trading centres later than their Wendish and Saxon sisters, and the Order was able from the beginning to secure recognition of its overlordship. The Grand Master received a share of the important Hanseatic customs duty, the *pfundzoll*, levied in these Prussian towns. He was also owner of the mint situated in Thorn, which served him as a bank. Although he had to pay close attention to the wishes of the towns in exercising his minting rights, his possession of them clearly conferred economic power. The towns also contributed to the *usrichtungen* (equipping of important military expeditions) which are thought to have been one of the principal means of centralizing the Order financially. The political co-operation of the towns was a prerequisite for the Order's own commercial activities which will receive mention later, and which in their turn must largely explain the Order's capital resources. The political loyalty of the towns clearly counted tremendously in the financial balance as a guarantee of credit, and when this failed in the fifteenth century political disaster was not far away.

At the end of the fourteenth century the power of the Order was at its height. Its administration had been turned into that of a highly central-

ized state. To the outside world it was a greater power than the new united kingdom of Poland-Lithuania, and its influence was far-reaching. It
interfered in the internal affairs of Lithuania and tried to annex the island
of Gotland from the piratical survivors of the Mecklenburg dynasty in
Sweden. The decline which followed was sudden, and must be viewed in
connection with the development of the other Baltic powers in the
decades round 1400. It was part of the general recession of the smaller
German powers after the peak of their military superiority in the fourteenth century. This in turn was a result of the new capacity displayed by
the larger non-German kingdoms of the north to grapple with the problems of financial disintegration.

E. *The Re-emergence of Poland and the Decline of the Teutonic Order*

In the course of the thirteenth and fourteenth centuries Poland slowly
developed economically, and its new sources of wealth were subjected to
fiscal exploitation. The older forms of taxation were commuted into
money payments. Underlying these developments was the expansion of
corn growing and of the corn trade. Agrarian progress and assarting from
the woodland were turning Poland into the granary it was to be in the
future. Markets grew into towns, and a new social class of merchants
made grain an article of commerce of the first importance. Down to the
fifteenth century, when Polish grain was established as a major commodity of international trade, there was a steady growth in the capital
resources of the country.

In the political field, this growing wealth of the Polish countryside intensified the decentralizing tendencies of the thirteenth century as the resources of the nobility and local princes expanded. In the fourteenth century, however, when the kingdom of Poland was re-established, the
Crown found methods of exploiting the wealth of the nation in the interests of the central power. The reign of Casimir the Great was epoch-
making in this respect. A prerequisite of financial centralization was the
establishment of a network of local officials, the *starosts*, each governing
his own district as full representative of the king. Supported by the burghers of the towns and by the nobility (some of whom had been brought to
heel while others were attracted by the royal policy, which offered the
chance of military glory and the annexation of the Ruthenian provinces
to the south-east), King Casimir was in a position to lay financial burdens
on his subjects.

In the first place, the new and efficient administrative system enabled the
revenues from the royal domains, for which money rents were established, to be collected effectively. In particular, the mills of the domain
were developed into a well organized service. A measure of the king's

political strength was the establishment of extraordinary taxes which were nominally freely granted. A corn tax (the *poradlne*) was imposed on the bishops and knights, and particularly on the monasteries, whose estates were twice as heavily taxed as those of the ecclesiastical and lay aristocracy. The free towns, too, agreed to pay a voluntary *poradlne* as proof of their willingness to co-operate politically. By strictly regulating trade routes King Casimir made the customs administration effective, and income from this source naturally expanded with the expansion of trade within the country. An important role was played by the royal monopoly of mining, especially salt mining, which besides its financial importance gave the king a hold over his subjects through his control over a vitally important article of consumption. The central financial administration also developed in order to keep pace with the problems presented by the control of the local network and the management of the revenues flowing into the centre. The treasury at Cracow became the grand treasury of the kingdom, and was ordered by Casimir to make all its payments in cash. The king's treasurer also became master of the mint, which was re-formed and used to establish a good domestic currency.

This rapid development and strict centralization, of course, was only partly a spontaneous result of a rising national income. Its stability can be measured by the fact that, after the authoritarian reign of King Casimir, the estates of Poland regained political control over extraordinary taxation. Domanial revenues (monopolies, ordinary charges and customs, and the profits of the mint) were carefully distinguished from revenues which could only be raised with the consent of the estates and which became in consequence of diminishing importance.

In the country districts the hide was the basic unit of assessment for the *poradlne*. In the towns one of the extraordinary taxes of the fifteenth century, the *szos*, was levied on the basis of a valuation of the burgher's real and personal estate, indicating a thorough assessment of taxable property and thus an efficient fiscal system.

Although the hold of the Crown upon its subjects slackened at the end of the fourteenth century, the resources of the Polish monarchy made an expansive foreign policy possible. The union of Poland and Lithuania in 1389 removed a rival on Poland's eastern frontier and at the same time put the considerable military resources of the Lithuanian empire at the king's disposal. These combined forces were strong enough to win a great victory over the Teutonic Order in 1410. Although the union with Lithuania created for the Crown new problems in relation to the Russians and the Tartars, it also greatly increased the power of Poland. Economically the potential resources of the less developed partner were laid open to Polish penetration, with immediate effect upon the economic resources of the state. It should be stressed, however, that the union was very largely a result of the pressure of the Order upon both partners. By it the balance of military power was transformed, and this in itself brought great fiscal advantage to Poland.

Casimir the Great organized the cavalry forces of the nobility into a military instrument of royal policy. This was a political operation, achieved in the main by insisting strictly on the performance of services by the privileged *szlachta* and by constituting a privileged nobility composed of cavalrymen without landed endowment, whose social prestige depended only upon their military service to the Crown. This reform was inspired by the example of Poland's powerful enemy at the beginning of the fourteenth century, Bohemia. Another southern neighbour, Hungary, provided the model for the organization of the fighting forces of the nobility into 'banners'. Combined with the Lithuanian army, the Polish mounted nobility won the decisive victory of 1410. Already at Tannenberg, however, mercenary soldiers fought in the Polish ranks, and in the course of the fifteenth century, as the new military art of combining cavalry with infantry was introduced into Baltic warfare, the military power of Poland increasingly depended upon the ability of the royal treasury to produce a normal budget surplus in ready cash.

To sustain their ambitious foreign policy, the kings of the Jagellon dynasty were normally able to meet these demands upon their treasury: indeed, up to a point, this was the condition of maintaining their political independence of the nobility. At the same time, they were able in emergency to raise extraordinary supplies in a country where economic life was expanding, and this at a time of general agrarian and commercial stagnation in western and central Europe. The Thirteen Years War in the middle of the century gave Poland a much desired outlet to the Baltic, when the Prussian towns chose as their sovereign for the future the king of their Polish hinterland.

During this era of Polish expansion the Teutonic Order declined politically and economically. This German state had reached the limits of its resources, and by the beginning of the fifteenth century financial strain had become chronic. It could not raise additional revenues to pay for the mercenary troops it required, and even the new and expensive diplomacy of this period demanded too much of its treasury. The very organization of the Order represented an obsolete military pattern. When the towns, which represented the new and expanding forces of society, chose to follow their own political aims, the Order was doomed in its struggle with Poland.

The political renaissance of Poland was, as always in such cases, the outcome of a complex of forces. Much was due to shrewd and fortunate political planning. But in the long run the representatives of the Polish state rode on the wave of economic expansion in the plains between the

Carpathians and the Baltic. The expansion of Poland followed the inland trade routes. The creation of new wealth, drawn from its cornlands, was the basic condition for Poland's political development.

F. *The Scandinavian Kingdoms in the Later Middle Ages*

In 1389 Queen Margaret of Denmark and Norway, in alliance with the leaders of the Swedish aristocracy, defeated the army of the Mecklenburgian King Albrecht and took the king himself prisoner. The foundations of the Scandinavian union of the later Middle Ages were laid.

The repelling of German infiltration into the Danish and Swedish kingdoms was almost exclusively an achievement of Margaret's political genius. At first she could count on Norway alone, and Norway was at this time by far the weakest of the three Scandinavian kingdoms. It had depended from the very beginning upon sea-power and sea communications; and, when trade in Norwegian waters passed into German hands and the Norwegian aristocracy lost its grip upon maritime commerce, it was not only the aristocracy which almost disappeared from the historical scene. The whole country seemed to dissolve into self-centred and rural mountain valleys, in which few people had even the slightest interest in what was happening in the outside world. There were no forces making for combination in political or economic affairs. Only the Church, with its limited resources, and a handful of landowning noblemen could represent a united Norway, and the interests even of the nobility were now limited to their own provinces. No political figure of the first order could possibly take a hand in the high policy of the later fourteenth century with only Norwegian support.

Margaret had to establish her power in Denmark in order to acquire sufficient political resources. Her father, Valdemar IV of Denmark, had been able to reunite the country by buying out the Holsteiners. He was able to do this because the people, under the leadership of the aristocracy, had felt themselves so oppressed by foreign rule that they spontaneously paid for liberation. If Valdemar succeeded in this design, his efforts to build up an autocratic authority sustained by a steady cash revenue led to disaster. He tried to make the international trade in the Sound and at the great fish mart of Skanör a principal object of taxation; but his policy united the Hanseatic towns from Holland to Prussia against him, and at his death they had annexed the three castles on the Sound which were in a position to dominate the trade routes.

Margaret's policy was to impose her will on one country by holding over it the threat of another. She allied herself with the traditional enemy of Denmark, the count of Holstein, who got the duchy of Schlesvig as reward; and in this way frightened the Danish aristocracy into obedience.

She forced the nobility to accept a new system of administration for the management of the castles and their districts, involving annual account to the royal treasury; and she introduced a new type of official, the bailiffs, who were often recruited from the ranks of immigrant German noblemen. When she had conquered Sweden the ambitious aristocracy of that country had to bow before her Danish resources. She organized a strong financial administration in Sweden: the taxes were simplified, made permanent and assessed in money instead of in kind. There, the bailiffs were often recruited from the lesser nobility of Denmark. Finally, about 1400, she carried through a large-scale resumption of estates of which the Crown had been deprived in both Denmark and Sweden in the latter half of the fourteenth century.

Thus, in Margaret's reign, a centralized and effective financial administration was created. Its resources are indicated by the fact that the island of Gotland was repurchased for cash from the Teutonic Order in 1408 without the imposition of special taxation. Centralization, however, was the work of an autocratic regime, and not the result of the appearance of new sources of wealth in the Scandinavian countries. On the contrary, the agrarian regression of the period seriously affected Denmark and Norway and to a lesser extent Sweden; this may have weakened the position of the aristocracy in relation to the Crown, but it also narrowed the basis for royal taxation. Taxes in money rather than in kind imposed a great burden upon Sweden, and were one cause of the great rebellion there in 1434. When war broke out against Holstein in the reign of Erik of Pomerania, the royal army of the three kingdoms proved unsatisfactory, though their fleet held the seas against the Hanseatic towns in the later 1420's. In the long run, the financial regime of Margaret and Erik was almost as unrealistic as Valdemar IV's attempt to base his rule upon the taxation of trade, for it over-estimated the resources of their subjects. It was swept away in the great rising against Erik of Pomerania in the years 1434–9. A decentralized system was re-established along with the dominance of the aristocracy in Denmark and Sweden.

In the latter part of the fifteenth century, however, a general trend towards centralization re-appeared in these two countries, although it seemed impossible to create any generally accepted basis for a united Scandinavian kingdom. Two rival kings, Christian I of Denmark and Karl Knutsson of Sweden, tried to establish new extraordinary taxes. In Denmark Christian succeeded, but Karl Knutsson was deposed by an almost unanimous rebellion in 1457. Christian, who was elected king of Sweden by the rebel aristocracy, had to face in his turn the strength of the opposition forces and was driven out of Sweden when he imposed a new tax for war. His hold over Denmark and Norway, however, remained firm in spite of economic troubles which were a target for propaganda on the part of his enemies. He inherited Holstein and Schlesvig from his uncle, the last duke of the old Holstein dynasty, and this acquisition solved a good many vital Danish problems. At the same time it removed a powerful enemy from his southern border, added to the military strength of Denmark and made available the wealth of the Holsatian aristocracy for exploitation by the Danish king. A number of Holsatian noblemen acted as Christian's bankers, for the fact that they lived in the hinterland of Hamburg and Lübeck had enabled them to accumulate resources equalling those of the merchants of these Hanseatic centres. Intensified cattle-breeding for export spread from the duchy into northern Jutland; herring fishing in the Limfjord expanded and there was a marked increase in wealth throughout the whole of Danish society. The first kings of the Oldenburg dynasty favoured the Danish towns with privileges and prohibitions, and received some return in the form of charges on trade. Of these, customs duties on sea-borne trade in the Sound (introduced in 1429) were of special importance: as trade expanded between the Baltic countries and western Europe so did the revenue accruing to the Danish treasury. Clearly the customs on the Sound in the fifteenth century were not an unduly heavy burden on commerce, or they would have aroused greater political contention than they did; but they must still have represented a considerable gain to Denmark.

Soon after the union of Denmark with Holstein, Christian I attacked the most powerful and troublesome of the Danish noble families, the Totts, and forced its members to take refuge in Sweden. From that time onwards the nobility served him and his son, King Hans, loyally and well. It seems that, during the reigns of the first Oldenburgs, fiefs ceased to be held in return for service, the holders accounting thenceforward for the proceeds of their offices to the king. Clearly, the interest of the nobility in the decades around 1500 became more and more centred on agricultural improvement. The knights and squires gained in higher land values some compensation for what they had lost in the form of control over financial administration.

We must not overstress the centralized character of Danish royal finance. Central institutions were still primitive and no real administrative treasury was created. Royal leadership of the aristocracy depended more on harmony of interests than on the subjugation of the nobility as a class. But the signs of an expansion in the resources of the central government are clear enough.

In Sweden parallel developments are even more obvious—the more so as no new territory was added to the possessions of the Swedish Crown. It seemed as though the aristocracy had triumphed in its fight for an almost republican independence of all monarchical power when the regent Sten Sture, backed by the Danish Tott family and the majority of the

Swedish nobility, inflicted a crushing defeat on King Christian and his Danish army at Brunkeberg in 1471. But the army of the regent represented new forces in Swedish society: the mine owners of Dalecarlia, the merchants of Stockholm and the cattle-breeding nobility of the border provinces, who had hitherto played a secondary role in Swedish political life. Many of the representatives of these new forces, moreover, whose appearance is significant of the capitalist development of contemporary Europe, were not unwilling to give permanent co-operation to a strong central government in Sweden. By cleverly combining territories under direct government administration and economically complementary to each other, Sten Sture succeeded in establishing the financial basis for a government disposing of sufficient troops of its own not to be totally dependent upon the good will of aristocratic factions. This work was pursued with caution until the third of the Swedish regents, the younger Sten Sture, felt himself strong enough to undertake a major struggle against the Church and Christian II of Denmark simultaneously. It ended in his defeat and death, but it is none the less certain that the national kingdom of the Vasas was built on the financial foundations laid by the Stures.

In both Sweden and Denmark growing commercial activity, canalized in the later fifteenth century by active commercial legislation, was one of the social prerequisites of financial centralization. The cattle, meat, butter and fish of the Scandinavian countries, and especially the iron and copper ores of Sweden, found their way into the European market. There are numerous indications that in the fifteenth century these countries took a marked step on the way from a natural to a monetary system of exchanges. At all events it is clear that the rising commercial centres like Copenhagen and Malmö in Denmark, and Stockholm and Viborg in Sweden, played a greater role financially than they had done in the past. This is particularly true of the mining districts of central Sweden.

Another prerequisite of financial centralization was the transformation of the nobility from a dominant military class into a class of rural entrepreneurs and landowning state functionaries. The new methods of warfare in this age made castles of the medieval type almost useless as strongholds. The military system of a country could no longer be limited to a certain number of local garrison forces. Money was needed to pay for mercenary troops and artillery. This automatically involved a transformation of the revenue system. Government revenues had to be received in the form of cash, and expended by the central authority, if there was to be any government at all. The central theme of the political history of Denmark and Sweden in the century beginning in 1450 was the alliance of the aristocracy and the Crown against the Church. By this alliance both parties secured the avoidance of serious social disturbance. It simplified the military budget, which no longer had to bear the charge of a continuous struggle for power within the country. This in turn, by contrast with the older dispensation, enabled financial surpluses to be created.

There remains the problem of why no similar development took place in the third Scandinavian country, Norway. It was the poorest of the three, though it did not entirely lack resources: the rise of Bergen as an important centre of trade and fishing and the increasing predominance of Oslo in south-eastern Norway are evidence enough of this. But the economic resources of Norway, themselves limited, had never been combined with national political leadership. Trade was dominated by Germans from Rostock and Lübeck, who had no wish to make any sacrifices to increase the internal strength of the country, for this in the first place would threaten their own position. The resources of the small Norwegian aristocracy were too limited to enable them to oppose effectively the king in Copenhagen. There was no economic specialization, as there was in Sweden, which led to exchange between the different provinces— a development which underlay the financial reforms of the Stures. The very geographical structure of Norway made a national rallying of political forces almost impossible. In consequence, there were at times local rebellions but never a national revolt; there were provincial leaders but no national regents. Norway was integrated into the Danish dominion; the Orkneys and the Shetlands were sold to Scotland by Christian I, Iceland was neglected and Greenland was forgotten.

At the end of the Middle Ages, therefore, the financial organization of the Danish and Swedish states was still relatively primitive; but financial reform had made available the resources which were to make possible the later imperialistic policies of these two countries in the Baltic.

G. *Conclusions*

The history of government finance in the Baltic countries during the later Middle Ages follows no simple lines of development. There are, however, some general threads in a complicated pattern. One is the culmination and the decline of the power of the German feudal states, which had flourished in virtue of their centralized financial institutions and military efficiency in the age of feudal cavalry. Another is the late concentration and political resurrection of the Polish and Scandinavian monarchies. In their struggle against the Germans, these monarchies won political victories through dynastic unions. Their further stabilization, however, was due to the use of new sources of capital and credit, chiefly due to the growth of an international trade in foodstuffs and metal ores in northern Europe.

There is a similarity of rhythm in the financial development of Poland and Scandinavia, which was not synchronized but equally not unmarked by a common trend. After a period of harsh and autocratic prosecution of the royal interests in the fourteenth century, which was countered by aristocratic opposition, government finances were reorganized in the fifteenth century by king and aristocracy working together in a quieter and more stable manner. This general trend was due in the main to changes in the conditions of military organization, and the financial and social consequences which these changes entailed. Military expenditure came to dominate the budgets of all the northern countries; and while the military problems were settled in different ways in different countries, generally speaking the appearance of mercenary infantry and artillery accelerated the development towards financial centralization. It ought perhaps to be stressed once again that government finance in this age was, as a rule, as much influenced by the technical, administrative and political factors described here as it was by the general development of economic life.

(2) GOVERNMENTS AND TRADE

A. *The Achievement of Hanseatic Supremacy in the Baltic*

It may well be asked in general terms to what extent there existed economic policies in the Baltic countries as distinct from those financial policies which were central and eternal preoccupations for medieval governments. In fact, for the period before 1400, we must accept the fact that the territorial states in this region had scarcely anything that can be described as a trade or monetary policy in the modern sense. The feudal states of medieval Germany had to show some respect for Hanseatic interests, which they could sometimes exploit but never direct. The Scandinavian monarchies at some moments gave backing to the wishes of their trading subjects; the latter, however, seldom showed themselves capable of national action, but appear as a rule in the form of local groups with specialized interests in particular trade routes. The coinage in the main served fiscal purposes and the need of a legal currency for the economic transactions of the ruling classes. There were attempts at a price policy in the fifteenth century, but these, too, were subordinated in the territorial states to fiscal points of view.

Amongst the German and Scandinavian powers, the Hanse towns and the Teutonic Order alone displayed a constant regard for trading interests. This was natural enough in view of the fact that upon trade depended the very existence of the Hanse towns as independent political entities, and because the Order depended economically to so great an extent upon the trade passing through the towns of Prussia. This is not to imply that these two powers had to face no opposition in prosecuting their commercial policies. What is true, however, is that the other powers displayed

AA

little initiative in this respect before 1400, and their reactions to Hanseatic initiative lacked consistency.

In order to understand the background of this behaviour, we must first take account of the erroneous character of the generally accepted view of the beginnings of medieval trade and commercial policy in the Baltic. The Germans did not organize this trade from the beginning or explore the great east–west trade route in the Baltic. Since the viking age the initiative in Baltic trade had belonged to the Scandinavians, who in the twelfth century kept communications open between the Anglo-Norman west and Novgorodian Russia, which had old Scandinavian connections. Several Scandinavian maritime towns grew up in the twelfth century, among them Visby, trading capital of the Baltic, which seems to have been founded chiefly as a Swedish centre of intenational communications. These Scandinavian towns were not towns in the normal western European sense, but rather concentrations of population with both a rural and a seafaring character. The leaders of Scandinavian trading expeditions were rather the provincial aristocratic families than urban merchants.

About 1200 the Germans rather suddenly assumed the initiative in the Baltic trade. As far as we can see this was in no way a result of political artifice, though the eagerness of Henry the Lion of Saxony to sustain the young town of Lübeck certainly created a base for German economic expansion. It was, on the contrary, due to economic development, probably accelerated by the German revolution in ship-building represented by the 'cog'. From the beginning of the thirteenth century German merchant houses and German colonists gained a firm footing in the non-German towns on the Baltic and on the west coast of Scandinavia. From now on the Hanseatic towns, governed by merchants according to commercial interests, adopted a policy of expansion to secure a stronger hold on trade and the trade routes.

The Hanseatic towns, headed by Lübeck, had the general object of obtaining privileges for their citizens which would enable them to trade in each country on terms as nearly equal as possible to those enjoyed by native traders. In particular, of course, they tried to safeguard their independent rights in the focal markets on the trade route between Novgorod and Bruges. The most important of these was the fair of Scania at Skanör, and Valdemar the Victorious in 1201 was able to subdue the city of Lübeck by imprisoning its merchants at this fair. The fall of Valdemar's empire after the battle of Bornhöved in 1227 was a prerequisite of Lübeck's political independence and the prosecution of its commercial policy. King Valdemar allowed the citizens of Lübeck to hold their own court, applying the law of Lübeck, at the Skanör market. In the mid- and later thirteenth century, Lübeck and the other Wendish towns were able to secure their exemption from native customs governing wreck of sea in the Scandinavian countries, and their right to the salvage from wrecked vessels.

In the early 1250's (probably in 1252), Earl Birger of Sweden guaranteed to the citizens of Lübeck by treaty complete exemption from duties in Swedish ports. Lübeck had been supporting a rebel faction in Sweden, and these privileges were the price paid by Earl Birger for its future neutrality In the years which followed other Hanse towns obtained privileges in Sweden modelled on those conceded to Lübeck. In this way the Hanseatic towns achieved an economic supremacy in the Swedish ports, and especially in the new town of Stockholm from which the export of Swedish iron and copper was controlled. The tactics of Lübeck are typical of the mode of operation adopted by its merchant rulers. When civil war divided any of the states bordering on the Baltic, the Hansards were able to sell economic support to one or other of the factions in return for enlarged privileges. When King Abel of Denmark had driven his brother, King Erik, from the throne in 1250, he adjusted the duties at Skanör in the following year to the advantage of the *Umlandsfahrer* (i.e. merchants using the Sound) while some other Hanse towns received the same privilege of holding courts at Skanör as Lübeck had. When Erik Glipping in 1282 was forced to concede the 'Danish Magna Carta' at Nyborg to his aristocratic parliament, he had to promise amongst other things to abolish all uncustomary burdens on foreign merchants. Next year he had to co-operate with the Wendish towns against the chief opponent of their commercial policy at this time—Norway.

Of the Scandinavian nations only the Norwegians kept up real competition with the Hanse towns on the sea in the thirteenth century. The reason for this was the well-developed trade connections between the Norwegian ports and the North Sea countries, especially England, which made Norway relatively independent of the Wendish Hanse towns and their political leader, Lübeck. In the decade before 1250 the Norwegians kept the Germans out of Bergen, the port for the extensive cod-fisheries off the west coast of Norway; while in 1250 King Haakon Haakonsson was in a position to make peace with Lübeck on the basis of reciprocal rights for each other's merchants. In the thirty years which followed, however, Germans from the Baltic towns seem to have got a firm footing in Bergen and other Norwegian ports. In 1282 the royal government of Norway reacted against the threat of German domination by forbidding foreigners who did not import corn or flour from exporting butter, hides or cod. The conflict thus opened developed in 1284 into naval war. The Norwegian earl, Alf Erlingsson, captured a number of German ships; a Hanseatic-Danish blockade cut off Norway's grain supply and closed the Sound to Norwegian shipping. In 1285 Norway had to give up the fight, acknowledge the commercial liberties previously enjoyed by foreign merchants and pay heavy damages. After this the Germans slowly but surely obtained control of Bergen's trade in stock-fish, as well as the trade in animal products at Oslo and Tönsberg.

It is interesting to note how the blockade of the Sound served the purpose, not only of starving Norway out, but also of closing the great east–west trade route to others than German merchants. The *umlandsfahrer* towns of Kampen and Zwoll thanked Lübeck for its resolute initiative in keeping the Gotlanders out of the North Sea as well as the Norwegians, Flemish and Frisians out of the Baltic. The trading peasant-sailors of the island of Gotland, and especially the Scandinavian merchant colony of Visby, were the only dangerous rivals to the Hansards in the Baltic and were engaged almost exclusively on the trade route from Novgorod to England and Bruges. We cannot say how effectively the blockade worked in cutting this vital artery of trade for the Gotlanders, for other events in the 1280's contributed to their decline. The rapidly growing German colony at Visby, which was recognized as a member of the Hanse, got the upper hand in the town. King Magnus in 1285 took advantage of his strong position as arbiter between Norway and the German towns and incorporated Gotland into Sweden. In 1288 Visby launched a war against rural Gotland, probably with the backing of Lübeck and the other Wendish towns. Again King Magnus intervened and forced the victorious burghers of Visby to swear obedience to him. After this Gotland and Visby ceased to exist as independent commercial powers. Lübeck took an unchallenged lead in Baltic maritime trade, and in the fourteenth century the German families of Visby began to move back to Lübeck. In the Novgorod *skra* of 1296 members of the German trade organization of this port were forbidden to enter into association with, or undertake commission trade for, Walloons, Flemings or Englishmen. These potential rivals were to be excluded from the Russian market once and for all.

The policy of Lübeck and its satellites during this period displays a pattern of skilful manœuvre directed to the single end of securing control of trade in the Baltic and on the west coasts of Scandinavia. Of the Scandinavian kingdoms only Norway put up any political resistance to the Hanse. In Denmark and Sweden proper (i.e. excluding Gotland) the impulse to co-operate with the German merchants seems to have been stronger than that to oppose them. It is possible that the Swedish efforts, between 1292 and 1323, to conquer the mouth of the Neva were inspired by the conscious economic (and not merely fiscal) objective of securing control over the trade to Novgorod. Certainly the sea-minded Swedish aristocracy seems to have been deeply involved in the enterprise. But internal disintegration in Sweden and Russian resistance checked this expansion, and Hanseatic voyages to Novgorod, limited by the Swedish authorities in the 1290's, were freed from restrictions once more. One early result of this Swedish 'crusade' was the removal from Visby to Lübeck in 1293 of the appeal court of the association of Hanseatic voyagers to Novgorod.

Clearly, so far as furthering trade interests was concerned, the political organization of the free Hanse towns was far more effective than that of the surrounding territorial states. This was the unique objective of Hanseatic external policy, while the royal or ducal governments had to play a game complicated by dynastic entanglements, greed for military glory, social privileges and territorial disintegration. It is no wonder that the Scandinavian rulers had to accept German control of maritime trade, whatever grounds of complaint their subjects had. Politically speaking, however, the Hanse towns were weak in one respect: if they had an overwhelmingly strong territorial neighbour they had to submit to his policy. Thus, during the era of Danish expansion during the reign of Erik Menved, Lübeck lost the political initiative from which it had reaped such advantages in the later thirteenth century. This weakness was to some extent overcome when, in the years 1356–77, the earlier rather loose co-operation between the Hanse towns developed into the powerful and well organized Hanseatic League, which proved its military strength by its victory over Valdemar Atterdag of Denmark. This strength depended on sea-power: for war on land the burghers of the Hanse towns still had to call upon allies—the king of Sweden, the duke of Mecklenburg, the counts of Holstein or the rebellious nobility of Jutland.

The extent to which Hanse policy and especially that of Lübeck was dominated by a commercial viewpoint is particularly clear in the decades after the victorious peace of Stralsund. The Hanse had gained a position which would have enabled it to interfere in Danish domestic policy and to maintain military control over the towns and castles of the Sound, which had been given to it in pledge. Yet it did neither: the confirmation of all its trading privileges in Denmark and Norway and unbroken peace at sea proved more important ambitions than any position as political arbiter or king-maker. Only when territorial lords threatened the safety of the Hanse towns themselves did they have recourse to the normal devices of medieval diplomacy. Hence the co-operation between Lübeck and Margaret of Denmark when the house of Mecklenburg seemed to have grown too powerful; hence the alliance between Lübeck and Holstein against Erik the Pomeranian. The same forces estranged the Prussian Hanseatic towns from the Teutonic Order, when the Grand Master and his stewards developed commercial interests of their own which diverged from those of the Hanse.

B. *The Commercial Policy of the Teutonic Order*

The Teutonic Order had, in the history of commercial policy, a unique position amongst the Baltic powers in view of the fact that it was at one and the same time a territorial state and a member of the Hanseatic group. This position became more and more notable as Prussian trade expanded rapidly in the later fourteenth century, and the Order itself took on the appearance of a gigantic commercial house overshadowing the merchants of the Prussian towns, which were likewise growing at a rapid rate.

The prerequisite for this position assumed by the Order was the combination of its efficient fiscal system and its political control over the towns in its territory. Its surplus revenue in the form of grain and the state monopoly of amber constituted its initial trading capital, on the basis of which the Grand Stewards of Königsberg and Marienburg established a well organized commerce extending over the Baltic and the North Sea. The need for grain in England and Flanders, and the favourable conditions for corn export thus created, stimulated the Order's trade. Gradually this came to embrace all the main commodities of Prussian export: wax, copper and furs as well as grain and amber. Of imports, chiefly salt, cloth and spices, the Order itself was by far the largest consumer.

In its political relations with the nations with which it dealt, the Order maintained a position of highly practical duplicity, appearing sometimes as a trading partner and sometimes as a sovereign power with the international responsibilities that implied. It had permanent factors in Lübeck, Bruges, England and Scotland for the purpose of acting as branch managers, but always able to pull diplomatic strings when required. The Order could throw into the scales its spiritual prestige, its weight as a power of military importance and, through the Prussian towns, the machinery of the Hanseatic League. The difficulty of playing this complicated game arose from the limited range of manœuvre that was possible if the spiritual powers, state sovereigns or the leading Hanse towns were not to be affronted. In 1383, for instance, the Grand Master reacted against piracy in the southern part of the North Sea by forbidding sailings from the Prussian ports. The non-Prussian Hanse towns, anxious to get their ships out of Prussian waters, protested against this ban. Again in 1388 a Hanse assembly proclaimed a blockade of Flanders to force the duke of Burgundy to pay certain indemnities. The duke appealed to the Grand Master to act as a mediator, which he did for several years without much success; but during these years at least some Prussian ships sailed to Flanders despite the blockade and despite the Grand Master's promises of solidarity with the Hanse. The Grand Master's duplicity was thus clearly demonstrated, though probably it was impossible for him to take sides for political reasons. In its relations with England, the Order maintained a sharper policy than the Hanse in face of the attack on Hanseatic privileges during the reign of Richard II; for both the Order itself and the Prussian towns had less to lose from a commercial conflict with England than the majority of the Hanse towns. The conflict even caused the Grand Master during the years 1386–8 to prohibit the export from Prussia of all articles in heavy demand in England, a measure which also affected the Hanse towns outside Prussia and which was basically aimed at preventing a clandestine export via the Wendish towns.

Tension between the Order and the western Hanseatic group over the Novgorod trade in the 1390's raised issues of more general interest. The Prussians did not belong to the Hanse groups allowed by the League to sail to Novgorod; they had to travel overland if they wished to reach this commercial focus of the eastern Baltic area. From 1380 to the beginning of the fifteenth century the Prussian towns and the Grand Master were claiming equality with the Wendish and Livonian towns in the trade to Novgorod. The League met this claim with shifty excuses, delays and objections, and it had not been granted when in 1398 the Prussians got privileges and a new market in Lithuania and thus lost much of their interest in the Novgorod trade. In this instance the political machinery of the Hanse worked to preserve an existing pattern of trade. It served the Flemish interest in keeping Polish cloth out of Novgorod as well as the reluctance of Lübeck and the Livonian towns to accept new competitors in the trade of the eastern Baltic.

These tensions and disputes make it the easier to understand that the Order was a somewhat curious partner for the Hanse towns and not a particularly popular one. Even to the Prussian towns, whose interests were in many ways championed by the international policy of the Order, its combined fiscal suzerainty and commercial competition with the private merchant became distasteful. In the early years of the fifteenth century the two Grand Stewards of Königsberg and Marienburg had a capital of 100,000 Prussian marks at their disposal, an enormous sum compared with the resources of any single merchant house. This enabled the Order, for example, to build ships large enough to challenge Hanseatic shipping. Before 1406 one-third, and after 1406 two-thirds, of the *pfundzoll* levied in Prussia went to the Order, and its capital resources were thus enlarged by charges which were a burden upon the trade of the private merchant. These circumstances probably played a considerable part in the desertion of the cause of the Order by the towns after the battle of Tannenberg.

The loss of political control over the Prussian towns checked the flourishing commercial activity of the Order. Its rapid descent into permanent financial difficulties, discussed above, prevented it from re-building its commercial greatness.

C. *The Scandinavian Nations and Hanseatic Privileges in the Later Middle Ages*

Hanse policy after the peace of Stralsund continued to be directed towards the conservation of its privileges; the political methods of realizing this policy were alliances, embargoes, blockade and, in the last resort, war. This traditional policy proved effective enough so long as no serious competitors such as the Dutch or English established a firm footing on the shores of the Baltic. The commercial rivalry of the Teutonic Order proved a transient episode. Not until the fifteenth century did the European tendency towards monarchical consolidation give rise in the Scandinavian countries to economic policies governed by some glimmerings of social objectives. When this development did take place, however, the international trade monopoly of the Hanse became a subject of political debate.

The townsmen of Denmark, Norway and Sweden in the thirteenth and fourteenth centuries were in each country a privileged estate, whose existence depended upon their role as intermediaries in the commercial exchanges within the country. Restricted economically by German commercial supremacy and outshone socially by the landed aristocracy, they had only limited opportunities of making national policies reflect their special interests. This might happen when the king or the aristocracy or both discovered interests in common with the townsmen. Otherwise their privileges were conventionally recognized, but in practice little respected.

In Norway the ship-owning and sea-minded aristocracy had been the chief upholders of pre-Hanseatic trade, and had therefore worked with the Norwegian townsmen in the vain efforts to set limits to German commercial influence. After the decisive clashes of the 1280's, the royal government from time to time issued decrees designed to place obstacles in the way of the establishment of German settlements and commercial associations in Norway. In 1294 foreign merchants were forbidden to sail north of Bergen. In the next year the establishment of gilds was prohibted generally. In 1315 and 1316 the sale of cod and butter to foreigners was allowed only if they brought malt, flour and grain to Norway. In 1316 the king's bailiffs were to have first option of buying all imported goods. In 1317 foreigners were only to be allowed to trade between 14 September and 3 May with certain specially nominated merchants in each town, and then only wholesale. In 1318 King Haakon V abandoned this claim, but laid it down that foreigners were to trade only with

Norwegian merchants. This ruling was repeated in 1346 together with a ban on all retail trade and on direct trade with the peasantry outside the towns. All this proved in vain. During this half-century of prohibitive legislation the Lübeckers established their great trading factory in Bergen, attracted the fish trade of the west coast of Norway to that town and took the law into their own hands when the bailiffs proved troublesome. They had at their disposal a deadly weapon against a country permanently short of food—the grain blockade. Gradually the Norwegians gave up the fight, though they never fully consented to commercial rule by the Germans. It is significant that the disappearance of this fighting spirit coincided with a general decline in the political activity of the Norwegian nobility.

In Sweden, a general town law promulgated by King Magnus II in 1347 restricted trade to the towns and forbade foreigners to engage in retail trade or direct trade with the peasantry. The merchants of the towns of western Finland (Åbo excepted) and of Sweden north of Stockholm were obliged to sail only to Stockholm with their goods. The king's bailiffs had the first option on all the goods brought to a town for sale. The Norwegian inspiration behind these prescriptions seems clear enough; it may be remembered that Sweden and Norway were joined in a personal union under Magnus. The effort to promote the trade of Stockholm indicates a joint interest on the part of the king and the leading Swedish nobles of the Mälar provinces around the town. At the same time, the attempt by this law to protect the trading interests of the Swedish townsmen against foreign competition was more a matter of theory than practice. The domination of the Hanse towns, and of Lübeck especially, over the foreign trade of Sweden remained unchallenged whenever the country was subject to a native government. No restrictions were placed on the German gilds in Sweden, and the two big merchant gilds in Stockholm were dominated by Germans. Sweden drew profit in the main from German trade, and saw no real alternative to accepting the Hanse as a trading partner. At the same time, the need for political support from the Hanse against Denmark almost always precluded Sweden from stressing national interests in the course of discussion about privileges and customs.

It may seem strange that Denmark, the strongest of the Scandinavian kingdoms, was the last to adopt protective legislation directed against German trade—strange because Denmark felt the effects of German commercial supremacy earlier than Norway. Not until 1396 did Queen Margaret confine all trade in Denmark to the towns. The reason may be that it was not until this date that the Danish nobility was subjugated to an extent that made it incapable of defending its lucrative direct trade in cattle and foodstuffs with the Germans. On the other hand, a real concern for the welfare of the burghers of the Danish towns may lie behind Margaret's decree. The cities of Copenhagen and Malmö had experienced less German settlement and felt less Hanseatic influence than other Scandinavian towns of any importance, and they had accumulated wealth in virtue of their proximity to the market of Scania. Even if Margaret and her advisers were inspired by narrow fiscal views in their dealings with the towns, they must have seen the advantage of a rapid increase in the resources of the Danish merchants. Perhaps they may even have anticipated the possibility of gaining a new political ally.

At any rate, a concern for the interests of Danish merchants is evident in an ordinance issued by King Erik of Pomerania in 1422. Besides confining trade to the towns this edict laid down regulations for a number of handicrafts to be enforced by the city magistrates, forbade magistrates to be recruited from artisans in these crafts and strengthened the hands of the burgomasters and aldermen against the craftsmen. At the same time King Erik invited English and Dutch merchants to the new town of Landskrona, and challenged the privileges of the Hanse in 1423 by imposing new customs on trade passing the Sound. During the war which followed he fought the Hanse and for some years had the Dutch as allies. This grand policy of Erik's required all the resources of his centralized Scandinavian kingdom, and ended with his reign. But the protective policy of concentrating all trade in the towns was continued under the aristocratic regimes which followed. Probably it was enforced only against the lower classes, leaving the illegal trade carried on by the nobility quite undisturbed. At the same time, it registers the growing self-awareness of the burghers of the Danish towns.

In 1475 Christian I permitted German merchants to sail to Danish ports while forbidding Danish merchants to sail to Germany, and decreed certain facilities in the export of horses and cattle from the Danish countryside to Germany. In the same edict, however, he prohibited the Germans from wintering in Danish towns and abolished all German gilds. In 1477 the Danes were allowed to sail to Germany, but the restrictions on Germans taking up permanent residence in Denmark were continued. In 1490 King Hans renewed these restrictions in forceful terms and forbade Danish burghers 'to take the money and goods of a foreign merchant, be a commissioner for him or sell to his advantage'. In the same year he made commercial treaties with England and Holland, and in the years which followed co-operated politically with the czar of Russia, the new master of Novgorod. The plan of Christian II in 1520 to unite all Scandinavian merchants into a great trading company was a logical consequence of the growing bourgeois influence on Danish policy.

This influence is displayed in a clearer light when it is set against the commercial policy of the first Oldenburg kings in Norway. There the native nobility got Christopher of Bavaria to issue an ordinance in 1444 to restrain the tyranny of the German trading establishment in Bergen: their trade in fish was to be conducted only in Bergen and their direct hold over the fishermen from Nordland was subjected to legal restraints. It required the indignation of some leading nobles about German excesses, combined with the international weight of Christopher's Scandinavian state, to secure the proclamation of these modest principles; yet in the event the ordinance came to nothing, for the Germans protested vigorously and Christopher was afraid to risk international difficulties in order to conciliate local opinion in Norway. During the second half of the fifteenth century the king tended to take the side of the Germans in Norway, and their dominant position was not shaken until the middle of the sixteenth century. In distant Iceland, Christian I overtly allied himself with the Hamburg merchants who, with the help of the royal governors, outrivalled the English in the Iceland waters and took over the trade in stock-fish. In Iceland there were no native townsmen to claim rights of their own.

The protective tendencies evident in Scandinavian trade policy in the fifteenth century were stimulated by a growing preoccupation with revenue from customs, particularly where payment was made in silver currency. A general scarcity of silver, of course, forms a background to the economic policies both of the kings in Copenhagen and the regents in Stockholm. The government of the constitutional council in Sweden, in particular, displayed a major concern for the economic welfare of the people. At the end of the century one of the Swedish bishops drew up a programme which summarizes the economic theory of his generation. Gold and silver ought not to be hoarded; on the contrary, they should be put into circulation in the country. As much bullion as possible should be imported and as little as possible exported. As with bullion, necessary commodities should be retained within the confines of the country, while luxury imports should as far as possible be excluded. In the second half of the century both the Danish and Swedish governments endeavoured to regulate the goldsmith's craft in a somewhat draconian manner in order to establish control over the trade in gold and silver. The Swedish council in 1489 made a whole-hearted but hypocritical attempt to safeguard public morality by prohibiting the payment of soldiers in money and imported cloth—a wage policy doomed from the beginning by general political unrest. In 1493 the council issued a long and somewhat drastic ordinance concerning the country's foreign trade. It prohibited the important and flourishing cattle trade across the Danish frontier; ordered all trade with foreigners in the southern provinces to be concentrated at Kalmar, Söderköping and New Lödöse; and expressed the wish that German merchants should come to these towns and especially that they should import articles upon which customs duties had to be paid. In 1502 the old decree, which had fallen into desuetude, that goods from the Bothnian towns must be brought to Stockholm and Åbo and not sent abroad was renewed in categorical terms, on the ground that 'the country and all of us have more sustenance from Stockholm than from these small towns'.

These regulations mainly subserved the fiscal concern of the regent, Sten Sture, to bring inland trade under the control of his bailiffs. At the same time, however, they equally clearly served the interests of Sten's allies, the mine owners of Dalecarlia and the merchants of Stockholm. It would in fact have been impossible to get this policy accepted by the council if it had not been in harmony with generally accepted economic principles. Even in their dealings with the Hanse the Sture regents tried to raise the customs duties in 1480, and to decree in 1505 that Lübeck shippers must take Swedish as well as German cargoes if they wished to import goods into the country. They never dared, however, to come into open conflict with Lübeck on economic matters. Only a few members of the council, who were less concerned about a national, anti-Danish policy, advocated stronger measures against the supremacy of the Hanse. The national monarchy of Gustavus Vasa was the first government strong enough to stand up to Lübeck, though at the end of the sixteenth century Lübeck and Danzig still handled the lion's share of Sweden's international trade.

D. *Conclusions*

Medieval commercial policies in the Baltic region are from start to finish Hanseatic policies, provoking certain counter-measures on the part of the territorial states. Not until the fifteenth century did Denmark, and, in its last decades, Sweden, begin to initiate measures which emanated apparently from the commercial classes in the towns on the Sound or corresponded to the interests of the Stockholm merchants and the Swedish mine owners. The dominating commercial position of the Hanse enabled it to secure from an early date a political hold over the bourgeoisie in all the Baltic countries where German colonists acted as trading intermediaries. The lack of positive commercial policies in Scandinavia reflects the weakness of the native merchants. Not until some groups amongst them in the fifteenth century had gained sufficient strength to make their own policy, and this was met in turn by somewhat more developed economic ideas at the national government level, was the Hanse confronted with real problems in pursuing its Scandinavian policy.

V. *The Italian and Iberian Peninsulas*

(1) INTRODUCTION

One of the most difficult problems confronting the historian of economic policy in the Middle Ages is to decide what constituted in those days the field of 'economic policy'. We might define 'economic policy' today as 'public policy in respect of the economic life of a country'; but, although this definition is so wide and elastic as to be almost elusive, it still remains difficult to adapt to it the remote reality of the Middle Ages.

Thus the fact that by economic policy we commonly mean a *public* policy is a source of uncertainty when we transfer such a concept to the medieval period. In dealing with the centuries preceding our millennium, it is often difficult to say whether the monarchs of that time in taking certain measures were acting as public authorities or as individuals. It is also difficult to decide whether a study of 'economic policy' in those centuries should take into consideration the provisions made and the programmes carried out by ecclesiastical or secular lords in the administration of their own manors, since we cannot disregard the fact that feudal lords were no less public authorities than the kings or emperors. The very distinction between public and private was blurred in the minds of men before the year 1000.

Even after that time, the distinction was not at once apparent. In fields like that of finance princes and monarchs continued to behave in such a way that it is difficult to say whether they acted as public bodies or as private individuals. On the other hand, it would be difficult to deny the appellation of 'public' to institutions like the gilds and similar corporations merely because we today do not recognize certain associations of workers and entrepreneurs as public bodies. To take an example, the corporations of merchants or merchant gilds in the Italian medieval towns were empowered and obliged to supervise and maintain the thoroughfares, to scrutinize prices and wages, to deal directly with foreign governments, drawing up actual commercial treaties in the name of their own cities. More than once the action of the gild of merchants seemed to imply the affirmation, *l'état c'est moi*.[1] What often brings home the role of the corporations as public bodies is that many of the clauses of their statutes are identical with the corresponding clauses in the statutes of city communities, and that in many cities the consuls of certain gilds were considered in all respects as public functionaries.[2]

To understand what constitutes the field of economic policy, another circumstance has to be borne in mind. Nowadays in defining the main

[1] This observation is by E. Verga, *La Camera dei Mercanti di Milano* (Milan, 1914), 37.
[2] Cf. R. S. Smith, *The Spanish Guild Merchant* (Durham, N. Carolina, 1940), 8 ff.

lines of the economic policy of a country, we focus attention mainly on measures taken by central public authorities. But such procedure would undoubtedly be misleading with regard to the Middle Ages. Even in the later Middle Ages, when, in countries like Italy, Spain or France, there existed political units of considerable size, with governments which were undoubtedly centralized from the political point of view, the problems of economic control were to a great extent left in the hands of local administrators.

Other difficulties are raised by the nature and type of the problems which the 'public authorities'—once these have been defined—sought to control or solve. It must be admitted that in those centuries many measures of economic policy related to matters which today are considered marginal or totally extraneous to economic policy. This shift of emphasis is in the very essence of the historical process: in any case it not only increases the difficulty of defining economic policy for those centuries, but may also lead the economic historian to concern himself with matters which may reasonably draw upon him the suspicion that he does not know the current meaning of the term 'economic policy'. Leaving aside the questions connected with demographic policy, monetary policy and financial policy, some of which will be dealt with in other chapters of this volume, it appears that a broad treatment of economic policy in Mediterranean Europe might be grouped round its main purposes, somewhat as follows:

(1) *Promoting a balanced economy:* (*a*) supply of necessities; (*b*) stabilization of prices; (*c*) control of the supply of precious metals.
(2) *Increasing production:* (*a*) agriculture; (*b*) trade and industry.
(3) *Improving the guiding mechanism of the market:* (*a*) control of consumption; (*b*) qualitative control of production; (*c*) anti-monopoly policy.

The problems which are included in this scheme are recognized by us today as belonging to the field of economic policy, and they were without doubt among the problems which medieval authorities were aware of and with which they were particularly concerned to deal.

Naturally, not all the problems of an economic nature with which the governments of Mediterranean Europe were concerned are included in this scheme. In formulating it a choice had to be made and some topics had to be sacrificed. To give some idea of the sacrifice it will be sufficient to mention the most important matters which have been left out: the policy of state monopolies, the administration of state property, the fiscal policy with regard to inheritance, the measures for improving transport and communications, the prohibitions on the export of strategic materials, the emancipation of serfs, the measures against enclosures such as those passed by Pope Honorius, Charles II and King Robert in the south of Italy. To some of these topics some references will be made; but it must be admitted that if there were enough space all these subjects would deserve much fuller treatment.

In preferring to follow a scheme arranged according to subjects rather than chronologically, one important consideration must be that economic policy did not develop homogeneously in its various sectors. For example, while in industrial and commercial policy revolutionary changes occurred in the course of the Middle Ages, the policy governing food-supplies and prices at the end of the fifteenth century was very much as it had been in the Carolingian epoch.

Looking at the development as a whole, it is possible to distinguish three basic periods: (1) the Carolingian and feudal period; (2) the communal period; (3) the period in which the Christian kings in Spain and the various ruling princes in Italy gained the upper hand over communal or feudal power. (In discussing the various economic policies we shall have frequent occasion to avail ourselves of this basic chronological distinction.)

In the modern period, transcending the economic policy of every state, there exist one or more logical, consistent and universal systems of economic theory. This makes it possible to define the economic policy of a state, even if only approximately, as 'mercantile', 'classical', 'Keynesian' or 'welfare'. It must also be admitted that the existence of these general theories exerts a decisive influence on the economic policy of individual states, which are seen in the end to have many features in common. In the Middle Ages, however, there were no consistent general economic theories worthy of the name. It is therefore rather difficult to classify the policies of those centuries according to the 'boxes' in which economists may put the policies of modern states. On the other hand, it must be admitted that the provisions made by the individual states reveal a uniformity much greater than would be expected in the absence of general systematic theories. The reason for this is the similarity of the problems and situations which public authorities in various countries had to face, in the very similar degree of technical knowledge available to the rulers who dealt with such problems, and finally in the basic similarity of the 'European culture' which was common to them all.

(2) PROMOTING A BALANCED ECONOMY

A. *Supply of Commodities of Prime Necessity*

The greatest concern of modern governments, in the field of economic policy, has been, in the last half-century, the 'business-cycle'. The greatest bogey has been unemployment. Throughout the whole of the Middle

Ages the greatest concern of governments was the 'crop-cycle'. The greatest bogey was famine.

The system of transport and communications was far from efficient. Bulk transport throughout the year was possible only by water. In all instances it was expensive and unreliable. It was impossible to guarantee supplies to highly populated areas at any distance. If the harvest in one area failed, for the mass of the local population that usually meant famine; a famine led to unrest, economic depression, and often, since the great mass of the population was already in a state of undernourishment, it led also to those epidemics which contemporaries vaguely called 'the plague'. From the remote period of the Carolingians until after the end of the Middle Ages, the fundamental problem of economic policy was always that of avoiding or at least alleviating these recurrent disasters.

Account should also be taken of the general conditions of insecurity in which the people of the Middle Ages continually lived. Day-to-day life in a medieval city resembled life in a fortress more closely than life in a modern city. The administrators were therefore firmly convinced that a continuous control had to be exercised over the production of foodstuffs and trade in them.

It must however be admitted that, despite the continuous and age-long preoccupation with this kind of control, no noticeable progress was made in technique in the course of the Middle Ages. Substantially, the economic policy as regards provision outlined in the Carolingian capitularies or in the statutes of cities in the twelfth and thirteenth centuries was in essentials still in force in the seventeenth and eighteenth. It is no wonder that economists in the eighteenth century attacked that policy, considering it a cumbersome heritage of medieval barbarism. But if such criticism by the economists of the eighteenth century was justified when applied to their own century, it was certainly unfair when applied to an age which had to make use of a system of transport and communication which was still rudimentary and fraught with dangers.

Concern for the supply of grain was generally combined with concern for the supply of the other commodities considered necessary for the basic needs of daily life: *ad quotidianum usum necessaria*. These were wine, oil, meat, fish, vegetables and other foodstuffs, straw, candles for lighting purposes, wax for the manufacture of candles, firewood, timber and also, in the Italian cities especially, building materials. Trade in many of these goods was generally submitted to many of the controls which affected trade in grain.

The great mass of regulations devised for the control of the supply of these necessities may be divided, for the sake of simplification, into two main classes: measures taken in cases of emergency and valid only during the emergency itself, and measures of a preventive and, in some way, permanent character.

Of the first group we may quote the purchases of grain from abroad made directly by the state, the forced loans imposed on the richer citizens to permit the state to buy grain from abroad and to sell it below cost to the poorer section of the population, the granting of import bonuses and free credits to importers, the concession on the part of the state of monetary rewards to owners who sold their grain in time of famine, the census of grain in the possession of private individuals with the aim of distributing it more fairly and, finally, the threats and death penalties meted out to speculators. On the whole such measures were not very original; but it is true that there was not much scope for originality.

More interesting are the permanent regulations of a preventive character. Throughout the Middle Ages, the main object of government policy with regard to grain and other necessities was that of achieving the greatest possible self-sufficiency. This aim had been the essence of the manorial organization in the Middle Ages. It continued to inform the policy of provision in the cities and principalities also in the later centuries. There is a passage in a work by St Thomas which expresses very clearly this ideal and some of the reasons which inspired it: *dignior enim est civitassi abundantiam rerum habeat ex territorio proprio quam si per mercatores abundet. Cum hoc etiam videtur esse securius quia propter bellorum eventus et diversa viarum discrimina de facili potest impediri victualium deportatio. . .*[1] Direct manifestations of this ideal were: (1) measures aimed at increasing local agrarian production in general; (2) measures aimed at achieving the greatest possible self-sufficiency in necessities.

The first group of measures will be discussed below in the section entitled 'Increasing Production'. Here it may be appropriate to say a few words about the second group. Of these the classic prototype is the Carolingian *Capitulare de Villis*. Even if it had not that general validity which historians at one time attributed to it, nevertheless it is without doubt a clear manifestation of the prevalent mentality of the Dark Ages as regards necessities. In the following centuries we find the same spirit of *Capitulare de Villis* in the city statutes or in royal or princely decrees which obliged the landed proprietors to cultivate certain products and especially those which, being ill adapted to the local climate and consequently unreliable, did not attract private enterprise. This is instanced in the statutes of Turin, Novara, Treviso, Vercelli and of a great many other cities, which imposed on landowners the obligation of planting a certain number of olive or almond trees for every given measure of land in their possession. Autarky is by its nature the negation of all forms of specialization. When, for example, in the Lombard plain during the second half of

[1] St Thomas Aquinas, *De Regimine Principum*, lib. II, cap. iii.

the fifteenth century there was a clear tendency towards expansion in the rearing of livestock to the detriment of cereal growing, the duke of Milan, 'wishing to see his kingdom abundant in wheat', ordered that in every property the area under grass should not exceed a certain proportion in relation to the arable.[1]

Not all rulers, however, were convinced that this kind of regulation was sufficient by itself to ward off the risk of unexpected and dangerous shortages. Recourse was had, therefore, everywhere and continually to other measures: (1) the formation of public stocks and (2) a system of trade restrictions.

The more imperfect the market, the more urgent becomes the maintenance of ample stocks of goods. Throughout the whole of the Middle Ages every person who was not a pauper stored in his own house substantial reserves of grain, salted meat, salt, candles, etc. What the private individuals did the state did also. In the feudal period, it was the unfailing policy to keep ample reserves for emergencies on the manors. In the following period, the communal authorities, while concerned not to allow excessive hoarding on the part of private speculators, built up stocks, especially of grain, to be resold in times of emergency at a low price. Public and private stocks of necessities did indeed represent one of the most important forms of investment in medieval economies.

As regards trade restrictions, these aimed fundamentally at (1) prohibiting or in some way continually controlling exportation, (2) encouraging importation, (3) regulating internal trade.

The prohibitions imposed on the export of grain, meat, wine, oil, wood, wax and tallow are one of the *leitmotifs* of medieval statutes. In the majority of cases the prohibitions to export food not only are continually repeated but are specific and detailed to the point of being captious. In the statutes of the city of Novara, for instance, the prohibition on the export of oxen and cows contains the express amplification: 'whether fat or thin'. This seems the pedantry of cavilling jurists; but behind it lay the tragic terror of famine. Even regions like Lombardy, Sicily and Apulia, which, being great producers of grain, were destined to be exporters of that commodity, had a series of most complicated restrictions on exports. It is true that as in the case of the kingdom of Naples, these restrictions had a fiscal character because the 'export licences' represented one of the greatest sources of income for the Crown. But it is also true that those restrictions could be enforced to the point of holding up all exports in time of famine.

While exportation of necessities was generally prohibited or severely

[1] C. M. Cipolla, 'Ripartizione delle colture nel Pavese secondo le "misure territoriali" della metà del 500', in *Studi di Economia e Statistica*, Catania, 1950–1.

restricted, efforts of all kinds were made to encourage imports.[1] Encouragement consisted of fiscal facilities (reduction in duty or even complete
exemption), facilities of an administrative category (stamps, transit documents, carriage papers, etc. were dispensed with), and even facilities of a
juridical nature (for example, grain imported and animals used for transport could not be seized for debt). In addition, there were also more drastic and more direct measures. It was the general practice of the communes to require their subject territories to send grain and other products
of the soil exclusively to the ruling city.[2] There are even cases, such as that
of the city of Cremona, in which the commune laid down for every village of the *contado* a minimum quota of grain to be made over annually to
the city. Actually, since throughout the whole of the Middle Ages a great
many citizens had lands in the surrounding territory, most of the city
statutes were also requiring them to send the products of their land to the
city.

Venetian ships shipping grain in foreign ports were explicitly obliged
by Venetian law to bring part of it to Venice itself. The fear of famine
was such that it led to the complete disregard of the danger of an excess of
supply. When, in some years at the beginning of the fourteenth century,
Venice adopted restrictive measures relating to importation in general
because the market was gorged with stocks of unsold goods, care was
taken to lay it down with much precision that the restrictive measures
should not in any way affect the imports of fats and foodstuffs.[3]

The formation of wider political organisms, such as the kingdoms of
Spain or the Italian principalities in the late Middle Ages, did not simplify
the complicated system of restrictions and limitations on the trade in
foodstuffs. On the contrary, new complications arose. On one hand the
cities did not abate their separate prohibitions. On the other hand the new

[1] Except for special cases such as that of wine in certain districts of the Mediterranean
area.

[2] After the eleventh century the city-states in central-northern Italy and in the
Iberian peninsula asserted an oppressive politico-administrative supremacy over their
surrounding territories. Among the most obvious manifestations of their domination
were the restrictions the cities imposed on the surrounding countryside on the very
subject of the supply of necessities. Their territories could not export the produce of
the soil to anywhere except the ruling city. Even later on, in the late Middle Ages,
when larger state-units grew up, or grew stronger, in Italy and Spain the cities managed
to retain their old controls. Every city or community continued to forbid the export
of corn or other 'necessary' goods to other cities or communities, even within the same
state. Political unity made no breach in the prevailing particularism of the policy of
provision. The fear of starvation continued to have more influence than the factors
working in favour of internal integration.

[3] R. Cessi, ' "L'Officium de Navigantibus" ' e i sistemi della politica commerciale
veneziana nel sec. XIV', in *Politica ed economia di Venezia del Trecento* (Rome, 1952), 26.

central authorities did not very much welcome the traffic in foodstuffs from one city to another which might mask clandestine exports out of the state. Therefore, they in their turn organized new systems of control and imposed new restrictions. Furthermore, the formation of these new greater political units was accompanied by the rise of capital towns. The provisioning of these cities soon became a new source of concern. New restrictions were imposed in an attempt to canalize the food supply towards these new metropolitan centres. For example, in Lombardy at the end of the fourteenth century, the Duke Gian Galeazzo decreed that, if any district of his state permitted the export of cereals, these could be sent only to Milan or Pavia, the two principal cities of the duchy.[1]

Thus, with prohibition following prohibition, and restriction following restriction, there grew up that complicated system of control which the eighteenth-century economists emphatically condemned.

B. *Stabilization of Prices*

Prices were the other great problem of medieval economic policy. Public authorities were not concerned with them for the sake of statistical-economic investigations, but only in so far as they affected the cost of living. More or less instinctively, therefore, they concentrated on the prices of those goods which, to use the technical language of modern statisticians, had the greatest weight in determining the cost of living.

Many books and articles have been written on the question of what the people of the Middle Ages thought about prices and interest. Such books and articles are, however, mainly based on the study of the theories of philosophers and moralists. Practical men in the Middle Ages, however, probably saw things in a very different manner from that which may be deduced from the treatises of churchmen or moral philosophers. During the Middle Ages the rate of interest, because of the scarcity of capital and the imperfection of the credit system, tended to stay at high levels and in general fluctuated between 10 and 50% and even higher. At the same time the prices of necessities, because of the rigidity of demand and the imperfection and the insecurity of the market, continually underwent drastic fluctuations which brought about poverty, hunger and even death for large sections of the population. There is no doubt that the public authorities of the time had many other and more pressing problems to think about than the preoccupations of moralists and theologians. Philosophers were concerned with having 'just' prices. Those responsible for economic policy were concerned with having 'stable' prices. Philosophers were concerned with deciding whether interest was reprehensible or not. Those responsible for economic policy after the Dark Ages were

[1] G. Giulini, *Memorie spettanti alla storia di Milano* (Milan, 1771), XI, 421.

concerned with bringing down the rate of interest to reasonable levels.

In order to control prices, wages and rates of interest, the public authorities of the Middle Ages generally had recourse to that not very original expedient to which all rulers have had recourse ever since they have been concerned with prices: that is price-fixing. The Carolingians fixed maximum legal prices from time to time, according to circumstances, for precious metals, arms, textiles, cattle, slaves, instruments of work, and above all for foodstuffs. Later in the Middle Ages, the prices most frequently fixed were those of foodstuffs, candles, wood and building materials. Wages were also regularly the object of a maximum legal rate. In northern and central Italy, the communal authorities were careful to apply the maximum legal rate directly to wages which most affected the cost of living of the mass of the population, such as the wages of workmen employed in the milling of grain, baking of bread, public ferries, transport of wine and the slaughter of animals for butcher's meat. The control of wages was in general left to the individual corporations. In the Iberian peninsula, where until the end of the fourteenth century the corporative organization was less developed than in central and northern Italy, the kings and the authorities governing the cities exercised more frequently a direct intervention in the matter of wages. Such interventions became particularly frequent and drastic in the crisis precipitated by the plague of 1348.

With regard to the rate of interest after the Dark Ages, the practice which became general was to establish maximum legal limits above which the interest was declared to be usury and therefore illegal. King Frederick II of Sicily enforced a legal maximum of 10%. In Verona in 1228 the legal maximum was 12%. In Modena in 1270 it was fixed at 20%. In Genoa in the thirteenth century it was 20%. In Lombardy in 1390 it was 10%.

Although price-fixing was everywhere an expedient to which recourse was had continually, it must not be supposed that the people of the time had many illusions as to its efficacy or wisdom. There are explicit cases in which it is evident that the authorities were aware of the negative effects which such measures could produce. One of these cases is clause 53 in the Constitution of the city of Forli, dated 1369, in which it is declared that anyone bringing grain to the city may sell it there at whatever price he likes and to any person whatever without any limitation: *pro suo libito voluntatis cuiquumque voluerit pro illo pretio quo voluerit*. It is evident that those who presided over the compilation of this rule understood that the imposition of a maximum legal price for grain would have kept the commodity away from the market instead of attracting it, thus accentuating the evil which it was the intention to remedy. However, even where the rulers did not see so clearly, it is noticeable that other measures were generally adopted which were aimed at influencing the structural conditions of the market and at removing from the market itself those elements which could provoke or facilitate the formation of an upward spiral in prices and wages. The most common and important of such measures were those intended to: (1) prevent and destroy monopolies and combines; (2) prevent the formation of associations of wage-earners; (3) restrict competition between employers; (4) improve the distribution and marketing of necessities.

The measures relating to points 1 and 2 were particularly characteristic of the economic policy of the communes of central and northern Italy: they will be discussed below in the section devoted to the struggle against monopolies.

Concerning point 3, we may observe that in many of the statutes of the mercantile or artisan gilds, it was forbidden for one master to try to attract labour away from another by promising higher wages. It is interesting that this regulation found its way into the statutes of several cities and was continually repeated. In Spain, after the plague of 1348, a law was passed forbidding landlords to take on more than twelve men (*peones*) for labour on their lands. Thus, as regards the labour market, by limiting competition in demand for labour and trying to favour, as we shall see, competition in supply of labour, an attempt was made to forestall any upward spiral in wages.

As regards point 4, the basic principle here was the decisive prohibition of the purchase of goods of prime necessity (such as meat, grain, oil, fish, hay, etc.) for the purpose of resale: *Quod nullum possit emere granum ad revendendum; Quod nullus debeat emere pisces in nostro districto ad revendendum; Quod aliqua persona non possit emere fenum seccatum causa revendendi ad minutum vel in grosso.* Regulations like these are found repeated more or less in the same words, always with the same emphasis, in innumerable statutes and legislative regulations of cities, villages and *borgate* in the Italian and Iberian peninsulas, as well as in southern France. In attempting to arrange for the product to pass directly from the producer to the consumer, it was hoped to reduce to a minimum the incidence of the costs of distribution and at the same time to avoid the danger of manœuvres by speculators, an ever-present danger in relatively small markets supplied in a somewhat irregular manner.

Actually what the ideal of medieval authorities was in the matter of prices was indicated in the clearest manner by an expedient which was frequently adopted in those centuries, in order to control the prices of certain commodities such as meat, candles or lime. In several cities of the Iberian and Italian peninsulas, the right of selling these goods was put up to public auction. The businessman who offered to sell the commodity at the lowest price obtained the monopoly for a certain number of years; in return, during that period, he was obliged to sell the commodity, always and in all cases, whether there was a glut of it or a dearth, at the price agreed in the contract. Faced with drastic, sudden and often sinister fluctuations, which the imperfection and the insecurity of the market continually provoked, the men of the Middle Ages had one dream in matter of prices—stability.

C. *Control of the Supply of Precious Metals*

One of the points on which medieval public authorities in all countries repeatedly insisted with the utmost earnestness was the control over the trade in precious metals. The measures adopted were not very original. All that was done, in general, was to prohibit or limit severely the export of precious metals and to try to encourage their importation. The lack of originality was compensated for by the insistence with which such measures were continually repeated. What the public authorities were aiming at, when they impeded the exit of precious metals from the country and encouraged their import, is clearly indicated by the obligation laid on the importer to hand over all or part of the metal to the mint.

All this might seem to be merely the expression of a simple-minded conviction that 'wealth consists in money'. Although it would be difficult to deny that illusions which we today call 'bullionistic' were indeed widespread, it is very doubtful whether these measures for the control of precious metals can be interpreted only as an expression of an exaggerated importance placed on 'treasure'. We must be careful not to judge certain aspects of medieval economic mentality on the basis of convictions of authors of treatises written two or three centuries later, at a time when the environment had altered.

It must be borne in mind that, for the whole period from the eleventh to the fifteenth century, the supply of precious metals does not seem to have kept pace with the increasing demand for money and that the development of credit was not sufficient, generally, to balance this deflationary pressure. Both in the long and the short run, medieval societies remained under the threat of dangerous shortages of money. The policy of controlling the trade in precious metals was, therefore, chiefly the expression of a widespread and justified 'fear of shortage of money'. There was, apparently, never a clear logical realization of the relations which could arise between the supply of money, level of prices and level of production and employment. On the other hand, although men in the Middle Ages were not in a position to theorize logically about these relations, they were nevertheless instinctively aware of them.

(3) INCREASING PRODUCTION

During the Dark Ages, we find a great many regulations—how successful they were we do not know—for the protection of private property, for the punishment of those who interfered with other men's work, and for the guarantee of the safety of markets and roads. Regulations of this type are frequently found in the Carolingian capitularies. There can be no doubt that, in so far as they were successful, they must have been conducive to productivity in general; but it is doubtful if we can interpret them as an expression of a clear and conscious will to increase production. More probably they were merely expressions of a general preoccupation with the maintenance of public order. Only with regard to agriculture and communications can we find signs of a more conscious and deliberate economic policy. Particularly in the Carolingian era, measures were taken by public authorities to maintain and construct bridges and roads. As regards agriculture, there are Carolingian regulations condemning those who allow formerly cultivated land to become waste.

In relation to manufacture and commerce, the Dark Ages had no economic policy worthy of the name. In manufacture there was at the very best a widespread desire for self-sufficiency and a concern that all the tools and implements necessary for daily life should be manufactured on the manors. In commerce attempts were made to guarantee the safety of markets and fairs. At the same time, it is also clear that many rulers were never able to overcome a sense of suspicion and often of hostility towards the merchants. This in part followed from the ideas of the Church concerning mercantile activity, but was also influenced by the type of merchant characteristic of the earliest Middle Ages, who more closely resembled what we today call a racketeer or a dealer on the black market than what we now describe as a businessman. It should also be recognized that by far the most prevalent economic activity was agriculture. Trade and manufacture absorbed but a minute fraction of the available resources and no need was felt at all to organize, control or develop these marginal activities.

Things certainly changed during that process of economic growth which characterized southern Europe after the end of the tenth century. There is no doubt that the effort of public authorities to increase production became more conscious and active after the tenth century and the measures taken to this end became more numerous and complex. Many pages could be written on all those regulations which were laid down more and more frequently and which were bound to favour, at least indirectly, productive activities. Thus there were measures taken to combat piracy and brigandage, the efforts to perfect maritime and commercial law, the new regulations governing insurance, the control of indemnities, the regulations relating to shipwreck, the regulations permitting and facilitating an autonomous and more expeditious mercantile jurisdiction, the penalties against those who damaged trees and vines[1] or in general did not respect the property of others, the guarantees of continuous surveillance and maintenance of streets, bridges and ports, the regulations forbidding the seizure of cattle, ploughs and working equipment from peasants and artisans who could not pay their debts. Although all such regulations were certainly important in creating a more favourable climate for the development of productive activity, we must here concentrate on others which were particularly and directly aimed at increasing production.

Most of these concerned agriculture. In Italy an ordinance which appears most frequently in the statutes of the cities in the north and centre of the peninsula is one which makes the cultivation of the soil obligatory. If a piece of ground for one reason or another was allowed by its owner to remain uncultivated, the village community was obliged to cultivate the land at its own expense and under its own responsibility.[2] Similar to this regulation in its effects, although very much more revolutionary from the point of view of the traditional Roman concept of the right of ownership, was the Constitution passed by Sixtus IV in 1474 in which the pope granted permission, to anyone who wished to avail himself of it, to plough and sow a third of the land left uncultivated by others. This permission had to be ratified by certain judges appointed by the pope for the purpose, who also had to decide what proportion of the harvest was due to the owners.[3] In Castille, regulations were passed by virtue of which an owner who ceased to cultivate his land lost the property itself, which passed automatically to the king or to the commune. The kings of Castille, on the other hand, in order to encourage agrarian development, followed the policy of granting to anyone who redeemed uncultivated land the ownership of the land and even sometimes certain fiscal exemptions.[4]

Still with the aim of increasing production, the public authorities tried to promote a more rational distribution of land. For the greater part of the Middle Ages, throughout most of Italy, southern France and parts of Spain, landed property was held in exceedingly small fragments. Even

[1] For example, in Italy the villages themselves established special *custodes vinearum* or *custodes camporum*. For Navarre and Aragon, cf. the Acts of the Cortes of Villafranca (1218), Tortosa (1225) and of Perpignan (1350).

[2] Cf. e.g. Menchetti, 'Su l'obbligo della lavorazione del suolo nei communi medievali marchigiani', *Archivio Scialoja* (1935), 33.

[3] A. Canaletti Gaudenti, *La politica agraria ed annonaria dello Stato Pontificio da Benedetto XIV a Pio VII* (Rome, 1947), 8–9.

[4] R. Altamira, *Historia de España y de la civilización española* (Barcelona, 1913), I, 513.

when a single owner possessed a considerable property as measured by its total extent, it was often made up of small pieces of land sometimes distant from each other and inextricably intermingled with other properties. In Italy the communal authorities intervened by instituting special officials, called significantly *ingrossatori*, whose task was to do all they could to encourage, persuade or even impose adjustments of boundaries, and to arrange exchanges or sales aimed at achieving a more rational distribution of property. On the other hand, they were also aware of the dangers of an excessive concentration of landed property. In an act granting freedom to the town of Caresana (Vercelli) in 1233, for example, it was explicitly stated that, in the division of the houses and lands that had been the property of the church of St Eusebius, no head of a family might hold more than fifteen hectares of land.[1] Many of the eviction measures taken against feudal property were also inspired by the same opposition to large estates. In this way, medieval authorities sought to combat two pathological manifestations of property: large estates and excessive fragmentation.

Public authorities often intervened, although with very varying intensity in the different epochs and in different regions, in direct works of drainage and land-reclamation. One of the most striking examples of highly intelligent activity of this type is undoubtedly that of the works carried out in the Po valley by the individual Lombard communes before and after the formation of the duchy of Milan.

Although all kinds of attempts were made to stimulate the local production of agrarian produce, tariff protection for agricultural production was almost always avoided. Instances of tariffs or of prohibition of imports in order to protect local products remained extremely rare during the Middle Ages; and the few instances of such measures all relate to a single product—wine—and to certain clearly defined areas—the Iberian peninsula and southern Italy—which had a great abundance of that commodity and where the production of wine constituted the greater part of the income of the ruling classes.[2] Wherever there were forces supporting

[1] G. Donna, 'I Borghifranchi nella politica della repubblica vercellese', in *Annali dell' Accademia di Agricoltura di Torino*, LXXXVI (1942–3), 107.

[2] For the Iberian peninsula cf. R. Carande, 'Sevilla, fortaleza y mercado' in *Anuario de Historia del Derecho Español*, II (1925), 370 ff. and A. Ballestreros y Beretta, *Historia de España y sua influencia en la Historia universal* (Barcelona, 1922), III, 371 and 373. In the Italian peninsula, protective measures in favour of wine-producers can be found in Sicily. At Messina, the importation of foreign wine was prohibited in 1272 and 1294, on the ground that such importation was *civibus dampnosum eo quod ex proventibus vini vivere eos oporteat cum in aliis redditibus et proventibus eorum non habeant facultates* (*Capitoli di Messina*, 44). At Castronovo (Sicily) in 1401, a policy of compulsory price-support was enforced by which no wine could be sold for less than 4 *denarii* a quarter, and if producers could not sell their wine at that price they had either to consume it themselves or to destroy it: they were not even allowed to give it away.

possible policies of tariff protection for the local agrarian production, they were never strong enough to break down the fundamental tenet of the policy of provision: doors open to the importation of all commodities *ad quotidianum usum necessaria*.

Another important branch of agrarian policy, especially in the communes of upper Italy, was that of the conservation of forests. Many of the prescriptions laid down then for the protection of forest-land are identical with those still in force today.

A crucial point in the history of medieval agrarian policy was that of the relationship between arable and pasture. In general in the Italian peninsula the public authorities aimed at controlling stock-raising in such a way that it did not injure arable agriculture. There were, therefore, established places in which flocks could graze; there were often fixed hours and seasons in which free pasture was permitted; there were the most precise regulations concerning the damage done by flocks on cultivated land. In the kingdom of Naples in 1452, King Alfonso intimated that no baron, aiming at keeping his own lands as exclusive pasture for his own flocks, should dare to prohibit farming-tenants from cultivating those lands. In other areas a veritable war was decreed on animals which did the most damage to agriculture and in some communes it was forbidden to anyone to keep goats. One of the few areas in the Italian peninsula where the interests of pasture and stock-raising had priority over those of agriculture was the *Tavoliere* of Apulia. Very different was the situation in the Iberian peninsula. Here the owners of flocks (among whom were some of the greatest landowners and the most powerful members of the lay and ecclesiastical aristocracy) were united in a powerful association—the *Mesta*. Although the concern for the policy of provision sometimes induced the Iberian rulers to take up a position against the *Mesta* in favour of arable farming, it is certain that on the whole the *Mesta* succeeded in making its own interests predominate.[1]

Manufacture. The regulation of industry and commerce in the period which runs from the eleventh to the end of the fifteenth century falls into two clearly distinguished phases. The first extends throughout the twelfth and thirteenth centuries, the second covers the fourteenth and fifteenth centuries. The first is characterized by the prevalence of the commercial interests of the mercantile class. The second is characterized by the prevalence of the interests of the manufacturing classes. In order to understand this shift of influences and power, which is at the basis of the changes in the economic policies of the various countries, it is necessary to bear in mind the fundamental lines of the economic and social history of those centuries.

[1] Cf. J. Klein, *The Mesta: a study in Spanish Economic History*, Cambridge, Mass. 1920.

In the twelfth and thirteenth centuries, manufacturing activity was concentrated above all in certain centres which devoted themselves to specialized production. This brought about a noticeable disparity in technical skills between these few manufacturing centres and the other areas of Europe, especially in regard to certain metallurgical and textile manufactures. Upon these differences was based a remarkable division of labour between developed and under-developed areas. The spectacular growth of international trade during the twelfth and thirteenth centuries was fundamentally due to this particular situation. On the other hand, it is also important to remember that the manufacturing activity was everywhere carried on by artisans who had neither the economic nor the social power to support and stand out for protectionist policies in favour of their products. In the more developed centres, there generally existed in those centuries an enormous disparity between the economic, social and political position of the mercantile class and that of the artisans. The scene was undoubtedly dominated by the merchant.[1]

In the under-developed countries, commercial policy was usually dominated by the prince or the king. Often it was confined to establishing fairs and markets, endowing them with particular privileges or protection or to granting particular fiscal privileges to this or that port, to this or that community of merchants, to this or that type of commerce. Sometimes the rulers tried to attract foreign merchants, granting them monopolies or privileges of a fiscal nature with the hope of attracting them as well as their capital. Or alternatively, they adopted policies hostile to foreigners, banishing or imprisoning foreign merchants with the aim of avoiding competition for the few local merchants whose position was in need of protection. A country often passed from one to the other of these antithetical policies with extreme nonchalance.

In the developed countries, where economic ideas were also more developed, commercial policy was more complex and organic. Such policy consisted in establishing commercial treaties, in instituting consulates abroad, in obtaining guarantees and fiscal, economic or juridical privileges for their merchants, in securing reduction or abolition of duties or tolls, and so on. In general this policy was directly dictated and directed by the gilds of merchants themselves.

The overwhelming preponderance of mercantile interests in the twelfth and thirteenth centuries had, however, one important limitation.

[1] The pre-eminence of the 'merchants' over the other groups of businessmen and artisans is clearly reflected in the very phraseology used in the statutes and charters of the time. For instance, in the statute of the merchants of Pavia of 1295, the various corporations of the city are continually spoken of as *pertinentibus seu spectantibus comuni mercationis* or, even more baldly, *paraticis seu artibus collegio mercatorum*. Cf. A. Damiani, 'La giurisdizione dei consoli del Collegio dei Mercanti di Pavia', in *Boll. Soc. Pavese di Storia Patria*, II (1902), 17.

Where mercantile interests were in conflict with the efforts to maintain a stabilized economy, it was the latter ideal which always prevailed; and mercantile policy was always and everywhere placed second in relation to the policy of provision, to the policy of stabilizing prices and to the policy of controlling the supply of precious metals.

There is no doubt that the striking differences in the levels of technical skills between the various areas of western Europe, and in the prevalence of the mercantile classes in the twelfth and thirteenth centuries, limited the rise and development of protectionist measures in favour of manufacture, while on the other hand it encouraged measures and institutions favourable to international trade. This situation, however, did not continue beyond the end of the thirteenth century. From the end of the thirteenth century onwards many of the areas, which in the preceding period had remained relatively under-developed, entered a period of rapid expansion. As we shall see later, in the majority of cases there was a conscious effort to industrialize. At the beginning of the fourteenth century, the conviction was widespread that industry spelled welfare. In a Tuscan statute of 1336 statements may be read which might have been written by the most modern upholders of industrialization in the twentieth century: *ab experto cognoscitur civitates et terre gentibus replentur et abundant divitiis si in eis ministerium et ars lane frequentantur et augmentantur.*[1] The effort of new countries to develop their own manufactures resulted inevitably in the adoption of protective measures to encourage the 'infant industries'. On the other hand, the industrial development and the adoption of protectionist policies on the part of the 'new' countries meant dangerous competition and the closing of markets for many manufactures of the 'old' countries, which were not slow to register symptoms of economic unease. At the beginning of the fourteenth century, the wool industry of Pisa underwent a crisis as a result of the development and competition of the wool industry in Florence. The wool industry in Florence showed signs of crisis from the middle of the fourteenth century and still more in the fifteenth century as a result of the expansion of the wool industry in other areas of Mediterranean Europe, and particularly in Lombardy and Catalonia. The silk industry in Lucca also entered on a crisis in the course of the fourteenth century in consequence of the growth of the silk industry at Bologna, Genoa, Venice and, later, at Milan.[2] Faced with the

[1] P. Silva, 'Intorno all'industria e al commercio della lana in Pisa', in *Studi Storici*, XIX (1911).

[2] Many modern economic historians have over-generalized the crisis of these 'old centres' of economic activity and drawn the conclusion of a general economic decline of Mediterranean Europe in the late Middle Ages (see, for example: R. S. Lopez, 'The Trade of Medieval Europe: the South', *Camb. Econ. Hist.* II, 338–45). Such a view is indeed an over-simplification, and it certainly fails to give due weight to the great development of 'new' areas during the fourteenth and fifteenth centuries.

competition of the new centres of production, it was inevitable that the old centres should seek in protectionist measures the panacea they hoped would solve their difficulties. In other words, the filling of the gap between the levels of technical and organizational skills of the various areas in Europe removed one of the basic conditions of an accentuated international division of labour, in the same way as the 'filling of the gap' between Great Britain and the rest of the world after 1870 practically marked the end of commercial liberalism.

Actually the rise of protectionist policies in the course of the fourteenth and fifteenth centuries was fostered also by another set of circumstances. In some Italian cities, various sectors of manufacture underwent important organizational changes after the thirteenth century. The structure of the firms developed in a capitalistic direction. In some cities a new class of 'industrial entrepreneurs' grew up and increased in number; these new entrepreneurs tended to become distinct both from the merchants (from whom they bought the raw materials) and from the workmen (whom they employed). Overcoming the resistance of the merchants these entrepreneurs succeeded in various cities in forming their own gilds. Following in their wake, the artisans and workers, to whom the merchants in the past had always denied the right of association, succeeded in joining together in gilds. An excellent example of all this development is provided by the city of Milan. Up to the end of the thirteenth century the corporation of the merchants had held unchallenged supremacy, as the powerful champion of mercantile interests. With the opening of the fourteenth century, however, the entrepreneurs *facientes laborare lanam* organized themselves in a new and independent gild. After 1351, textile workmen also formed their own autonomous gilds.[1]

Such was the development characteristic of many centres of northern and central Italy. In the Iberian peninsula, and particularly in Catalonia, Valencia and Aragon, the economic, political and social situation was totally different. Yet, there also, there were forces pushing in the same direction. After a period of hostility towards the old *cofradie* which had lasted for a good part of the thirteenth century and which was accentuated after the plague of 1348, the monarchs of Castille and Aragon adopted a policy of supporting the gilds, which, in the meantime, were assuming a more distinctly economic function and nature (*gremios*). The fifteenth century saw the triumph of the artisan gilds throughout Spain.

Altogether, throughout Mediterranean Europe, there was in the course of the fourteenth and fifteenth centuries a noticeable regrouping and an undoubted strengthening through corporative organization of the manufacturing interests, both of the entrepreneurs and of the workers. In the

[1] Cf. C. Santoro, *La Matricola dei mercanti di lana sottile di Milano*, Milan, 1940, introduction.

difficult situation of international competition and of the search for a new equilibrium the strengthening of those interests favoured the shift of economic policy towards protectionist and discriminatory tendencies.

It is necessary also to remember that in central and northern Italy, the territorial principalities were gradually replacing the city communes as the prevailing form of political organization. At the same time in Spain the royal power was emerging, strengthening its control over the country. Both the Spanish monarchs and the Italian princes cherished the conviction that the establishment within their states of all kinds of manufacture greatly added to their power and prestige. Such was the dawn of mercantilist aspirations; in every case they were aspirations to autarky which naturally led to protectionist measures.

All these political, social and economic circumstances can well account for the outbreaks of protectionism in southern Europe throughout the fourteenth and fifteenth centuries.

A very frequent measure then adopted was the imposition of duties in order to protect the local product from foreign competition. Very often, however, the tariff was not considered a sufficient protection and public authorities resorted easily to absolute prohibitions to import or sell foreign manufactures on the home market. Measures of this type had been extremely rare in the twelfth and thirteenth centuries,[1] but they became very frequent in the fourteenth and fifteenth. Pisa, in 1305, began to prohibit the importation of semi-finished woollen goods. In 1310, this regulation was reinforced and, in 1336, the importation was prohibited not only of semi-finished but also of finished products, that is of foreign woollen cloth.[2] At Florence, prohibitions to import *panni forestieri fatti et fabricati extra civitatem et districtum Florentiae* are already found in the statutes of 1317 and 1319. In 1397 these measures were reinforced and, to use the expression of Doren, there was erected a veritable 'tariff wall'

---

[1] They were confined especially to the ship-building and the cotton industries. The reasons for the protection given to ship-building were often of a political and military character rather than economic; which may explain why protectionist policy was born in this sector long before its time. The commonest form the policy took was state subsidies to ship-builders. 'Navigation laws' were also common, and they appeared as early as the fourteenth century (see e.g. the orders of Jaime I to Barcelona of 1227 and 1286).

Among the reasons for the early protection of the cotton industry, it will be remembered that that industry was generally carried on under the direct control of the 'merchants'. E. Heckscher, *Mercantilism* (London, 1935), II, 139, cites the case of measures at Parma in 1211 prohibiting the importation of fustians. At Pavia, another great producing centre of fustians, there were laws in existence in 1295 (which themselves reproduced rules that had already been in force for a long time) forbidding *retaliatores* at Pavia to sell foreign fustians (A. Damiani, *op. cit.*).

[2] *Statuti inediti della città di Pisa dal XII al XIV secolo*, ed. F. Bonaini (Florence, 1854), III; P. Silva, *Intorno all'industria e al commercio della lana*, passim.

against importation into Florentine territory of foreign woollen goods. In 1458, there was a specific prohibition of the import of cloth from Italy or southern France, and also a stricter control of the transit trade.[1] Milan, in 1415, began by prohibiting cloth from Turin and Perlasca. Then in 1420 it forbade the shops in the cities of the district and duchy of Milan to stock or sell any woollen cloth which had not been made in the territories subject to the duke. Only certain types of woollen cloth which did not compete with local industries were allowed. Prohibitions of this kind were repeated in 1454, 1460, 1471, 1474, 1476 and so on. In Milan again, as far as the silk industry is concerned, in July 1452 there was an embargo on *drappi di seta, oro e argento forestieri*, and this prohibition was repeated several times in the course of the century.[2]

At Genoa in the fifteenth century it was forbidden to import for resale any manufactured silk from abroad, with the sole exception of taffeta and satin and of the products of the Genoese colonies.[3] In Catalonia the importation of red-dyed cloth began to be subjected to heavy customs duty in 1365, for the protection of the Catalonian dyeing industry. In 1413 more drastic measures for the protection of all the various sections of the textile industry were taken by imposing heavy duties on the importation of foreign textiles generally. In 1422 the Cortes, meeting at Barcelona, forbade the importation of foreign woollen and silk fabrics 'for sale or wearing'. An additional declaration by the authorities of Barcelona, on the other hand, exempted semi-manufactured textile products of foreign origin from any prohibition or duty when imported into the country for finishing. Severer prohibitions were made again in 1438, 1443, 1452 and in 1456. In 1481 heavy duties were also imposed on the importation of tin, copper, iron and steel products.[1]

Closely related to this group of measures were regulations, such as those made at Venice in the second half of the fifteenth century, ordering all public officials to wear only clothes of Venetian manufacture, and at Barcelona in 1438 and 1443 under which the inhabitants were forbidden to wear clothes manufactured abroad.

[1] A. Doren, *Die Florentiner Wollentuch Industrie von XIV. bis zum XVI. Jahrhundert* (Stuttgart, 1901), 418 ff.; A. Doren, *Storia economica dell'Italia nel Medio Evo* (Padua, 1937), 517.

[2] For all this, see C. M. Cipolla, 'L'evoluzione economica del Milanese 1350–1500', in *Storia di Milano (fondaz. Treccani)*, ix (Milan, 1956).

[3] H. Sieveking, 'Studio sulle finanze genovesi nel Medioevo e in particolare sulla casa di S. Giorgio', *Atti Soc. Ligure di Storia Patria*, xxxv (1905), 176–7.

[4] Cf. A. de Capmany y de Montpalau, *Memorias historicas sobre la marina, comercio y artes de la antigua civicad de Barcelona* (Madrid, 1779), i, 242–3 and i, part iii, 29; J. Ventallo Vintro, *Historia de la industria lanera catalana: monografía de sus antiguos gremios* (Tarrasa, 1904), 436–8; Ch. Verlinden, 'Draps des Pays-Bas et du Nord de la France en Espagne au XIV Siècle', in *Le Moyen Âge*, third series, viii (1937), 11.

When we speak today of 'protectionism' we mainly mean protection against competition by 'foreign' countries. The measures just referred to come well within our present-day conception of protectionism. But medieval states were internally much less integrated than modern states. Medieval protectionism, therefore, did not only have an international aspect. The towns often tried their best to prevent competing manufactures growing up in the surrounding country. Measures of this kind were particularly common in the regions and periods in which cities formed small autonomous states exercising political domination over their surrounding countryside. Between the end of the thirteenth and the middle of the sixteenth centuries, the cities of northern and central Italy furnish numerous examples of such a policy. Curiously enough, the emergence of central power in states also often led to protective measures for the benefit of one city against competition from other cities of the same principality or kingdom. The Sforza dukes in the second half of the fifteenth century forbade all the subjects of the state of Milan to import 'foreign' woollen and silk cloth into Milan, the capital city; and the meaning of 'foreign' included cloth manufactured in other cities in the state. King Martin of Aragon went further still and decreed the actual destruction of certain cloth factories in the Contado di Ampurias, to protect those of Castello.

Other manifestations of a policy of development by protection are found in the measures taken in various states during the fourteenth and fifteenth centuries to increase and improve the supply of the factors of production in the principal manufactures. Whether for each of the three production-factors (labour, capital and raw materials) separately or for all three of them collectively and with varying emphasis on one or another according to circumstances, the aim was always to facilitate imports and discourage exports. So far as labour was concerned, the emigration of skilled artisans was generally prohibited while immigration was favoured. Foreign artisans who settled in the state to practise their trade would be promised exemptions from taxation or even (as in Catalonia) from military service. Similarly, measures were also taken to encourage the imports, and discourage the exports, of capital. In Bologna, considerable facilities were granted in 1288 to importers of silk spindles, while their export was absolutely prohibited. The export of tools for working coral was prohibited in Catalonia in 1422, 1446 and 1482 and anyone attempting to export them was threatened with heavy penalties. Measures on the same lines were taken, in far greater number, in order to improve the supply of raw materials: imports were actually facilitated by abolishing or reducing import duties while exports were discouraged by imposing export duties or even by absolute prohibitions. Measures of this kind were adopted in respect of the raw materials of the textile

CC

industry especially. Among the numerous examples that could be quoted, we may record the imposition of export duty on unworked wool in Venice in 1281, the issuing of regulations in Castile in 1462 prohibiting the export of more than two-thirds of the wool clip for any given year, the granting of facilities by King Jaime II in 1309 to importers of raw materials in Catalonia, and the reliefs from taxation granted to importers of unworked silk in Naples in 1350 and in Milan in 1442. Often semi-manufactured products were treated as raw materials, as for example when, in 1414, 1425 and 1444, in order to promote the Milanese cotton industry, first the Visconti and then the Sforza dukes prohibited the export of semi-manufactured fustians, so that the whole cycle of manufacture would have to be performed within the state.

In order to improve both the quantity and the quality of the local supply of raw material for the local cloth manufacturers various rulers favoured the importation of sheep of special breeds. We know of the importation of Berber sheep into the kingdom of Naples in the time of Charles I of Anjou and of Spanish sheep in the time of Alfonso I of Aragon. We know, too, of the importation of Spanish sheep into Lombardy in the time of Lodovico il Moro and of the importation into Spain of selected sheep from north Africa in the times of Peter IV of Aragon and Cardinal Ximenes. On the other side, in Spain the strictest rules were laid down by the national Cortes in 1313, 1315, 1322 and 1339 prohibiting the export of sheep from Spain.

In the silk industry, the regulations made in Lombardy in the second half of the sixteenth century obliging landowners to plant a certain number of mulberry trees to a given acreage of land were also made with the similar object of increasing the supply of raw material available for the silk manufacturers of Milan.

In addition to their efforts to increase the supply of the production-factors, governments readily granted exemptions or reliefs from taxation, or even loans or credit facilities, in favour of those manufactures they wanted to develop. Exemptions from, or reductions of, export duty were readily granted at Genoa in the fifteenth and sixteenth centuries in order to promote those manufactures which depended greatly on the export trade; and in Florence a law made in 1489 laid down that, in order to stimulate building, new houses should be exempt from all taxes for forty years. In 1350 King Ferdinand granted a Venetian master-craftsman a loan of a thousand scudos free of interest on condition that he set up a textile factory in Naples for making silk cloth.

The efforts to expand the supply of factors of production or the measures granting fiscal or credit facilities did not always turn out to be sufficient to achieve the result desired. Government learned quickly that 'it is more easy to bring a horse to the water than to make it drink'.

Therefore more direct action was often advocated and resorted to. At Spoleto in 1321 a foreign artisan was called in because the administration wanted to get woollen manufacture going in the town, and they gave him a salary at the public expense *ad faciendum pannos in civitate Spoleti*. Similarly, in 1442, Duke Filippo Visconti, wanting to start silk-cloth manufacture in Milan, sent for the Florentine master, Ser Pietro di Bartolo, and granted him a monthly salary to open a silk-works in the Lombard town.

In a large number of the instances we have referred to we do not know whether the measures taken were successful. Some we know remained dead letters. Others, such as Ser Pietro di Bartolo's summons to Milan, achieved their object and gave rise to flourishing new industries.

On the whole, if we assume that at least a part of the measures referred to in this chapter were successful, we could, in spite of the complete absence of statistics, be led to suppose that, from the beginning of the fourteenth century, the ratio between the volume of international trade in manufactured goods and the volume of production of manufactured goods in southern Europe may have moved progressively in favour of production.

(4) IMPROVING THE MECHANISM OF THE MARKET

Leaving aside the exceptional cases of measures taken in times of war, siege and pestilence (which are common to all peoples and all periods of history), a general policy worthy of this name, directed to control consumption, made its appearance only toward the end of the thirteenth century and spread widely throughout Mediterranean Europe in the course of the fourteenth and fifteenth centuries. Naturally, consumption was a matter of concern even before those centuries. But generally those who concerned themselves with the subject were pedagogues and moralists such as the monk of St Gall, whose fundamental interest was with the destiny of souls. Actually, before the fourteenth century, there was no great need for legislation limiting consumption because consumption was automatically limited by the prevailing poverty.

The fact that a policy of control of consumption should begin to appear towards the end of the thirteenth century, and spread in the fourteenth and the fifteenth centuries, was closely bound up with the fact that, between the middle of the thirteenth and the end of the fifteenth centuries, the income of large sections of the urban population expanded enough to permit a remarkable growth of extravagant private expenditure. Dante made a famous comparison between the level of consumption of his own time and that of previous generations in Tuscany. Galvano Flamma and Giovanni de Mussis in an extraordinarily colourful and detailed way bore witness to the same developments in Lombardy; and we have other evidence for nearly all the other regions of Mediterranean Europe. Further proof is afforded, unequivocally, by the buildings, the furniture, the clothes and the pictures of the time which have come down to us. Sumptuary laws sought to control conspicuous consumption, above all in feminine apparel, in feasting, especially at weddings and christenings, in funeral ceremonies and in dowries. Regulations are to be found in the statutes of many cities, in the fourteenth and fifteenth centuries, that women were not to wear certain materials and were not to adorn themselves with certain jewels considered too luxurious (pearls especially); that more than a certain number of guests were not to assemble for the occasion at weddings or christenings, at which not more than a certain number of courses were to be served at the feast; that when his daughter married a father was not to give her more than a certain sum as dowry or the husband was not to give the bride presents above a certain value. There are laws extant forbidding the dressing of the dead in luxurious clothing before burial; and finally, although they are a good deal rarer, laws seeking to limit extravagant expenditure on the conspicuous embellishment of private mansions. In some cases, as at Genoa in 1402, in preference to the prohibition of the use of certain luxury articles such as pearls, *ad valorem* taxes were imposed on these articles.[1]

Most of those regulations were often avoided by the people without difficulty. However, the very fact that they existed and the motives behind them are significant enough for the history of economic thought and economic policy. In seeking an explanation of why governments went to so much trouble in their anxiety to put these controls into effect, one can easily be led to emphasize ethical and religious motives. There is no doubt that when writers like Dante, Galvano Flamma and Giovanni de Mussis wrote their philippics against the growth and spread of 'conspicuous consumption', they were inspired above all by motives of an ethical and religious nature. Such motives must certainly have been present also in the minds of the rulers of the period. The very preambles of the sumptuary laws hold sufficient proof of that, for they are apt to contain references to *timor Dei* or declarations that *pro certo Deus graviter offenditur* by certain kinds of expenditure. However, it would be rather misleading to overlook other motivations. In the preamble to the Venetian sumptuary law of 1360 it is stated that: *fiunt multe vanitates et expense inordinate circa sponsas et alias mulieres et dominas . . . proinde status noster redditur minus fortis quia pecunia que deberet navigare et multiplicare de tempore in tempore jacet mortua et convertitur in vanitatibus et expensis predictis.*[2]

---

[1] H. Sieveking, *Studio sulle finanze genovesi*, 174.

[2] G. Bistort, *Il Magistrato alle pompe nella Repubblica de Venezia* (Venice, 1912), 66, note 2.

Similarly, in the preamble to the Genoese sumptuary law of 1449 it is stated that *poiva etiamde intender ogni homo de mezzam intellecto che redugandose a stao moderao e honesto, grande quantitae de monea, la qual se tegneiva morta e occupa' in vestimenta e joie, convertendose in mercantia poiva addur graindi fructi e grainde utilitae.*[1] In other words, in both these cases conspicuous consumption was regarded as harmful because it withdrew capital from productive activity and sterilized wealth.

In other cases we find a different argument expressed. Sumptuary measures were included in the fourteenth-century statutes of Cremona because *multe et intollerabiles expense facte fiunt quotidie per homines civitatis, quorum occasione persepe consumpti remanserunt et hodie remanent quod non est tolerandum ne civitas depauperetur.*[2] In the statutes of Messina, at the end of the thirteenth century, there was an explicit declaration that the purpose of the measures of a sumptuary nature was to avoid the risk that *homines civitatis depauperationis et totalis inopie periculis subiacent.*[3] Other similar quotations could be adduced. The *leitmotif* is always the same: rich citizens should not be allowed to ruin themselves, because if the rich became impoverished the state would also become impoverished. As the thirteenth-century statutes of Treviso declare: *ad decus spectare civitatis et gloriam locupletes habere subiectos.*[4] The objection might be made that the expenditure on the part of the rich—even though foolish—represented the income of the poor and that the impoverishment of the one class represented the enrichment of the other. Yet if careful consideration is given to the general economic situation of the times, to the fundamental scarcity of capital in medieval society, to the insufficiency of saving and to the high rates of interest prevailing, it is difficult to find substantial fault with the argument of the medieval authorities. We can question the logic and the sophistication of their way of reasoning and presenting the argument. But we cannot question the fundamental soundness of their concern to safeguard great private fortunes when capital formation was dangerously scarce. Even modern economists admit that 'only a rich society can afford to be egalitarian'.

All these were measures concerned with the quantitative aspects of production and consumption. Others were devoted to the qualitative control of production. Today it is generally admitted that the quality of certain products that are put on the market ought to be a concern of the state. Nevertheless, not only are we also convinced that such control ought to be limited to a few specific products only, such as pharmaceuticals and foodstuffs, but above all nobody would dream of thinking that

[1] L. T. Belgrano, *Della vita privata dei Genovesi*, Genoa, 1875.
[2] *Statuta Civitatis Cremonae* (Cremona, 1578), cap. 463.
[3] *Capitoli e Privilegi di Messina*, ed. C. Giardina (Palermo, 1937), 46.
[4] *Statuti del Comune di Treviso*, ed. G. Liberali (Venice, 1951), II, 283.

controls of this kind ought to represent one of the most important purposes of the economic policy of a modern state. For us today economic policy has much more important tasks than devoting attention to laws of adulteration; and our views on the subject of the quality of the greater part of the products put onto the market still follow more or less the stream of thought of the radical manufacturers in Great Britain in the nineteenth century, who opposed the enactment of adulteration laws on the principle of *caveat emptor*.

In the Middle Ages, men's thinking seems to have been diametrically opposite. If we must base our judgment of the relative importance attached in those days to the various sectors of economic policy upon the frequency and persistence with which one or another sector was the subject-matter of legislation, we must come straight to the conclusion that, for the man of the Middle Ages, the problem of the control of the quality of products followed immediately, in order of importance, after that of the control of the supply of goods *ad quotidianum usum necessaria*.

From the *Liber Praefecti* it appears that fraudulent practices were already a major matter of concern to the authorities of Constantinople. In Carolingian Europe *admonitiones* were common to sellers *sive in civitatibus sive in monasteriis* to keep honest weights and measures and not to sell their wares by night (except for travellers' victuals) so as to prevent the seller being tempted to take advantage of the darkness to cheat over the weight and quality of his wares. There were also strict rules and regulations made to prevent frauds in the manufacture of gold and silver articles. But it was, above all, with the great economic development of western Europe after the eleventh century that the laws against adulteration reached their most extraordinary popularity. It is safe to assert that between the thirteenth and the sixteenth centuries all the major trades and industries became subject to detailed rules and regulations designed to guarantee to the consumer the good quality of products. An extraordinarily large number of regulations was made laying down, with the most pedantic minuteness of detail, what the quality should be of the most important products in everyday life: wine offered for sale was to be pure with no water in it; bread was to be made of good flour sifted in the prescribed manner; candles were to be of good wax without resin or tallow; candle-wicks were to be of good cotton; ginger, saffron, indigo and pepper were to be unadulterated; the baking of tiles and bricks must be done the prescribed number of times and they were to have been washed in the prescribed ways; textiles had to be made of prescribed fibres, dyed with prescribed dyes, and woe betide anyone who dared to mix ox or goat hair, or anything of that sort, with wool or cotton. A fine example of the point that could be reached with all these finicking regulations is provided by the rules voted by the town council of Barcelona in 1330, which laid down the exact number of rivets to be put in breastplates; or the rules also made in Barcelona in 1438, which extended to no fewer than thirty chapters, on the method of manufacturing wool imported from England. All these instances come from urban statutes. Rural statutes were also concerned with the quality of rural work and often it was laid down how many times the land was to be ploughed, how the furrows were to be marked out and how many times the vines were to be hoed. On the whole both urban and rural statutes give the modern reader the impression of technical handbooks rather than collections of laws.

Yet the medieval authorities were not content with fixing, with minute attention to detail, the quality of the material of the principal manufactured products. They also went to great trouble to lay down types and measurements. Roof-tiles and bricks had to be of specified shapes and sizes, loaves of bread had to be of a specified weight, pieces of stuff had to conform to standardized measurements and the statutes of Bologna went so far as to prescribe a standard model for horseshoes.

In order to secure the observance of all these various regulations and to help save the consumer from being cheated, there were numerous other rules and regulations governing the sale of goods. Thus, for example, besides the continual checking of weights and measures, there were rules requiring fish and cheese to be exposed for sale on the market stalls and not kept in sacks, and the different qualities of butchers' meat to be displayed on the stalls separately; while the slaughter of beasts before dawn was prohibited. Certain products were obliged to carry special seals or marks, others to be inspected by public officials before being offered for sale and others, again, might only be sold at the hours and places appointed for the market.

In their vigilance over the good quality of products the government and gild authorities gave one another mutual support. Many regulations on the quality of products were contained in the statutes of individual gilds as well as in the statutes of the communes. However, governments generally concerned themselves above all with the quality of goods *ad quotidianum usum necessaria*: namely, foodstuffs, candles and building materials. Since (as we will see below) producers of, and traders in, commodities *ad quotidianum usum necessaria* were not allowed to set themselves up in gilds, there were no corporative controls on the quality of these commodities. Where anti-monopolistic policy had created a vacuum, the governmental authorities had therefore to take over the controls.

There is no doubt that the action of the governmental authorities and of the gilds alike sprang from a common motive: a particular conception of economic morality. But it would be difficult to deny that governmental authorities and corporations had, respectively, also other and different motives. The governmental authorities' concern for the quality of goods *ad quotidianum usum necessaria* shows a desire to protect the interests of the great mass of consumers; whereas the control exercised by the gilds over the quality of the commodities produced by their members was fundamentally aimed to prevent certain types of competition among producers who were members of the same gilds. Whatever the motives, the attitude was the same: *caveant consules*.

Finally there was the anti-monopoly policy. It would not be impossible to find very early in western Europe movements of a vaguely anti-monopolistic nature. If we agree that, from the economic point of view, the feudal lord was nothing but a great monopolist (with the monopoly, within the manor, of milling, baking, selling bread, wine and salt, and so on) we should conclude that the struggle against feudalism from the eleventh to the thirteenth centuries partook also of the nature of a struggle against monopolies. In fact there are cases in which the revolt against certain feudal lords was caused by the desire to destroy certain of their monopolistic rights. Yet it would be dangerous to carry such an interpretation too far.

The measures taken by Alfonso X in 1255 in Castille and León banning the *confraderías* were indeed the expression of a conscious anti-monopoly policy; as also were the still more drastic ones taken by Pedro IV in 1349 in Aragon and Pedro I in 1351 in Castille in order to stop the upward movement of prices and wages after the Black Death.[1]

But it was in the urban republics of north and central Italy, especially during the thirteenth, fourteenth and fifteenth centuries, that a general anti-monopolistic consciousness and an organic anti-monopoly policy developed on a great scale. It is, indeed, indicative of the profound economic insight possessed by a people who were then accomplishing a spectacular economic development that they clearly heeded the mischief inherent in monopolistic and restrictive practices. There is no doubt that in north and central Italy a general opinion grew in those centuries which was very much hostile to all sorts of *monopolia*, *raxe* and *conspiraciones*, even if we have also to remember that various interests then came into play to influence the nature, the forms and even the existence of the anti-monopoly policies in particular places.

In order to give a methodical account of the history of those policies it will be necessary first to outline the measures generally adopted, and then the branches of the economy and the times in which they were applied. In this connection it should be remembered that the organization of production was centred around the gilds. Whatever may have been the ultimate purposes of these associations it is certain that their most im-

---

[1] J. Una y Sarthou, *Las asociaciones obreras en España* (Madrid, 1900), 124; A. Ballestreros y Beretta, *Historia de España*, III, 371; C. Verlinden, 'La grande peste de 1348 en Espagne', *Revue belge de philologie et d'histoire*, XVIII (1938), 114 and 133.

mediate goal was to limit competition and facilitate agreements among the members of the same association. It cannot be surprising, therefore, that the gilds were one of the favourite targets of anti-monopoly policy.

The most common anti-monopoly measures can be grouped as follows:

(1) *Prohibitions and declarations of a general nature against monopolies and restrictive practices of all kinds.* In Florence in 1290 it was laid down for example: *quod universitas alicuius artis civitatis Florentiae non imponat modum vel certam formam seu certum pretium hominibus sue artis de mercantilis et rebus sue artis vendendis vel exercendis.*[1] In 1299 the statutes of Cremona threatened grave penalties for *quelibet persona, collegium vel universitas que fecerit vel tractaverit monopolium in civitate vel districtu.*[2] In 1369 the statutes of Forli declared *quod nullus ordo vel eius consules possint ordinare, precipere vel mandare alicui de suo ordine quod non possit vendere cui voluerit et emere a quo placuerit; et quelibet possit emere a quo voluerit et vendere cui sibi placuerit.*[3]

(2) *Prohibitions forbidding businessmen or workers of particular sectors of the economy to associate in corporations.* We shall discuss below some instances of this type of legislation.

(3) *Declarations of freedom of work,* whereby (a) the gilds were obliged to admit any person wishing to enter them; or (b) anyone could practise his trade even though he was not a member of any gild. In Pavia in 1295, for example, the consuls of the wool-beaters and weavers were forbidden to charge foreign artisans who came to practise their trade in Pavia admission dues;[4] and it was laid down in about 1340 at Alessandria that *pro magna et evidente utilitate communis* all the artisans' corporations might consider themselves abolished, *casse, irrite et nullius valoris*; and that any person, from any place, might come and practise his trade freely—*et facere et exercere artem suam ubicumque voluerit.*[5]

(4) *Prohibitions forbidding the members of a given gild or a given economic group to enter into agreements to fix prices or to control the supply of goods or services on the market.* In Venice at the beginning of the thirteenth century tailors had to swear publicly to make *nullum ordinamentum vel compagniam tam de pretio custure draporum vel emptione draporum*;[6] and in 1288 the

---

[1] A. Doren, *Le arti fiorentine* (Florence, 1940), II, 1116, note 2.

[2] *Statuta Civitatis Cremonae* (no. 236).

[3] 'Statuto di Forli dell'anno 1369', ed. E. Rinaldi, in *Corpus Statutorum Italicorum,* v (Rome, 1913), 113 (no. 93).

[4] A. Damiani, 'La giurisdizione dei consoli del Collegio dei Mercanti di Pavia', *loc. cit.*

[5] *Codex Statutorum Magnificae Comunitatis atque Diocesis Alexandrina* (Alessandria, 1547), 389.

[6] *I Capitolari delle arti veneziane sottoposte alla giustizia e poi alla giustizia vecchia dalle origini al 1330,* ed. G. Monticolo (Rome, 1896), I, 25.

statutes of Bologna provided that the heads of the gild of apothecaries: *non possint aliquibus rebus pertinentibus ad dictam artem precium taxare, nec possint interdicere alicui quominus possit quilibet de ipsa societate ire ad egrotos et etiam ad sanos causa medendi.*[1]

(5) *Individual measures taken to counter specific monopolies or cartels.* An instance of this was the resolution of the Greater Council of Venice in 1297 against a butchers' cartel and the resolution of 1358 against an agreement among cotton importers.[2]

When, why and how these various measures were brought into use depended on the complex interplay of the interests of contending economic and social groups. Broadly speaking, we should distinguish between two chronological periods: the communal period and the period of the *signori*.

In the first period the entire story is dominated by two major factors: on the one side, the eternal, continuous, tremendous fear of famine and starvation; on the other, the power and the interests of the *mercatores* of the times, the true masters of the medieval Italian communes. These two distinct factors gave rise to two distinct streams of anti-monopoly policy.

The first stream flowed logically alongside the general policy of subsistence. It expressed itself in those measures directed at preventing the formation of bottlenecks of a monopolistic kind in the supply of commodities and services *ad quotidianum usum necessaria.* As has already been stated, the expression *ad quotidianum usum necessaria* comprised foodstuffs (corn, cereals in general, bread, wine, oil, fish, etc.), candles, hay, straw, building materials, firewood and so on. Consequently, provisions of an anti-monopolistic character concerning the producers of, and dealers in, these articles are constantly found in the statutes of the Italian cities of those centuries. Most frequently associations were forbidden among bakers, millers, innkeepers, builders, tile and lime manufacturers and so on. One of the earliest examples of such a policy can be found in some statutes of Pavia of the twelfth century, which ordered *quod calcinaroli unius calcinarie non habeant societatem vel communicacionem cum calcinarolis alterius calcinarie;*[3] while a nice example of a long and detailed list of dealers in commodities *ad quotidianum usum necessaria* who were forbidden to form themselves into associations is provided by the 1288 statutes of Bologna, which laid down *quod pistores, fornarii, tabernarii, aburatores, brentatores, molendinarii, victurales, ortolani, barberii, lardaroli,*

---

[1] 'Statuti di Bologna dell'anno 1288', ed. G. Fasoli and P. Sella, in *Studi e Testi*, 1939, II, bk 12, No. 21.

[2] G. Luzzatto, 'Sindacati e cartelli nel commercio Veneziano dei secc. XIII e XIV', in *Studi di Storia Economica Veneziana* (Padua, 1954), 196–7.

[3] R. Soriga, 'Il memoriale dei consoli del comune di Pavia', in *Bollettino Società Pavese di Storia Patria*, XIII (1913), 114.

formaglarii, . . . tricoli vel tricole erbarum, fructum vel pullorum, palee, feni vel lignaminum non possint inire vel facere aut contrahere aliquam societatem vel habere ministrales, consules vel rectores aut capitaneum.[1]

There is no doubt that in the sector of the supply of foodstuffs and similar goods the anti-monopoly policy tried to protect the interests of the consumers. But the same cannot certainly be said of the other stream of anti-monopoly policy. As has already been mentioned above this other stream had its source in the overwhelming power of the 'merchants' who dominated the larger cities of medieval Italy. These groups did actually succeed in imposing a drastic legislation which banned any sort of association or collective agreements among workers and especially among those workers who were connected with textile industry (the key sector of manufacture in those days). In the majority of the most developed Italian cities associations were thus banned, among beaters, drawers, spinners, clippers, weavers, shearers, combers, washers and dyers.[2] *Septa, conniurationes, rassa, conspirationes* and *dogana* were all declared illegal; and artisans were altogether refused the right even to join together in religious or humanitarian associations, *sub quocumque nomine fraternitatis vel alio etiam sub religionis pretextu vel velamento nec funerorum vel oblationum causa vel nomine*, for fear that once they met the workers might make *coniurationes.*[3] The object of these measures was, consistently and exclusively, to prevent collective action on the part of the workers for controlling the supply of labour or imposing collective bargains on wages. Such a policy was rather unfair, as not only was the right of association not denied to the employers but also no measures were taken to prevent collective agreements among the masters on the subject of wages. On the contrary, the town statutes often reproduced the gild rules under which one employer was not to try to take away labour from another

---

[1] 'Statuti di Bologna', *op. cit.*, bk 12, no. 24.

[2] Generally these workers, who were denied the right to form their own associations, were obliged to remain under the authority and jurisdiction of the associations of the 'merchants', or else they were allowed to elect rectors or stewards for themselves—provided that they only elected men who were members of the merchants' corporations. A typical example is provided by the Statutes of Bologna of 1288. In book 12, rubric no. 23, it was laid down that the authorities of the commune ought to support and *manutenere in bono statu* the three societies—'of arts and arms, of exchange, and of commerce'; in other words, the associations of the nobles of high finance and of big business. By the next heading, all dealers in necessities and all workers in the wool trade (*tessarii pannorum, battarii, tintores, lavatores lane*) were forbidden to have associations of their own. Rubric no. 3 of the same book provided that those *qui faciunt artem lane in civitate Bononie vel burgis habeant et habere possint castaldiones et rectorem dum tamen sint de societatibus artium et merchadancie populi Bononie . . . sub quibus castaldionibus subsint omnes qui exercunt artem lane.*

[3] A. Doren, *Le arti fiorentine*, 1, 208 and 210; N. Rodolico, *I Ciompi* (Florence, 1945), 26.

employer by promising higher wages. Moreover the communal authorities never called into question the validity of the gild statutes fixing maximum wages for the workers in accordance with agreements entered into by the employers among themselves. By enforcing antimonopolistic measures on the side of the supply of labour and allowing collective agreements and restrictive practices on the side of the demand for labour, a strong pressure was thus exerted to avoid any substantial increase in the level of wages.

There is no doubt that this state of affairs lasted, in practice, until at least the middle of the fourteenth century or thereabouts. Down to that time the workers were too weak socially and economically to offer opposition to such a regime. But the combined effects of economic growth and the Black Death inevitably led to unrest of a revolutionary nature. It was in the middle of the fourteenth century that the workers' reaction began, especially in the cities that were industrially most advanced. Just at the same time important changes were taking place on the political scene also. The *comuni* were developing into more or less tyrannical *signorie* and the new *signori* came to represent a new important element in the interplay of different interests and different groups. The *signori* actually acted in obedience rather to political than to economic considerations. Their actions varied from case to case; but they always conformed to the fundamental principle of strengthening the weakest classes, weakening the most powerful, and maintaining themselves by a machiavellian balance of power between the various classes and the various groups in the state. In the majority of cases that meant seeking to weaken the merchants' gilds or other associations of employers, and conversely promoting the formation, or aiding the development, of gilds of workers and artisans. A classic example of such policy is furnished by the rule of the duke of Athens at Florence. Even if other instances are not all equally extreme, with a few exceptions the direction was still more or less the same. A powerful restraint was imposed by the constant fear of shortages in the supply of goods *ad quotidianum usum necessaria* and butchers, bakers, millers and so on were consequently still forbidden to form themselves into gilds or else, if they were allowed to do so, they were looked upon with constant suspicion and were kept under constant control. There were cases, too, where it was sought to oppose and forbid gild organizations because of particular political conditions. But on the whole it must be admitted that the corporative system gained ground under the new *signori*. The merchants' gilds lost control over the economic and social life of the towns, but new gilds came into existence in large numbers: gilds of employers and of workers in very many sectors of the economy. The working classes were the principal gainers from this trend. Independently of the advantages or disadvantages it entailed for any given class or social order, it must further be admitted that the spread of the corporative organization meant much more rigidity throughout the entire economic system. The consequences were to become apparent in all their seriousness in the seventeenth and eighteenth centuries when the peoples of the Mediterranean were to face the competition of new industrial societies.

CHAPTER VII

Public Credit, with Special Reference to North-Western Europe

I. *Introductory: Main Features and Phases*[1]

Scholars have been inclined in the past to regard the entire medieval period as a primitive stage in the development of public credit. In part this was the legacy of views expressed most clearly in the second half of the nineteenth century by Bruno Hildebrand (1864) and his followers who treated the Middle Ages as a time when credit could play at best only a minor part. These basic assumptions are today discarded by historians.[2] But one particular argument much used in the past deserves more detailed comment. Some older scholars had attached great importance to the fact that the debts of medieval rulers were, almost invariably, regarded as the personal obligations of the reigning sovereigns. They maintained that it is, therefore, impossible to speak of a true national or state debt under medieval conditions. Continuity, it was stressed, could only come with the introduction of modern funded debt. Only the municipalities have been exempted from this charge of backwardness, because they sold annuities, and they have even been hailed as the true creators of public credit.

It is quite legitimate and valuable to stress the contrasts between the medieval and the modern forms of public borrowing. But it would be misleading to apply to the medieval public credit this particular test. The presence or absence of the funded debt cannot be a valid criterion of the importance of the credit transactions of the territorial rulers at any time or place in medieval Europe. The treatment of the debts of medieval rulers as personal obligations of the princes who contracted them was an inevitable consequence of the prevailing, purely personal, conception of sovereign power. But the practical consequences of this must not be exaggerated. In reality, rulers repeatedly assumed responsibility for the debts of their predecessors. For example, shortly after the death of Louis

[1] Mr M. M. Fryde is responsible for the section on Germany. Mr M. M. and Mr E. B. Fryde jointly wrote the general introduction and the introduction to the section on towns. The rest of the chapter, dealing with England, France and the Netherlands, is the work of Mr E. B. Fryde.

[2] A von Kostanecki, *Der öffentliche Kredit im Mittelalter* (Leipzig, 1889); B. Kuske, *Das Schuldenwesen der deutschen Städte im Mittelalter* (Tübingen, 1904); J. Landmann, 'Zur Entwicklungsgeschichte der Formen und der Organisation des öffentlichen Kredites', *Finanzarchiv*, XXIX (1912); M. Postan, 'Credit in Medieval Trade', *Econ. Hist. Rev.* I (1928).

IX of France, his son and successor, Philip III, writing from north Africa, ordered the government at Paris to repay both his own debts and those of his father.[1] The testament of Edward III of England makes a clear distinction between his personal debts and the liabilities incurred for the needs of the realm and for his wars. He willed that his successors should repay the latter 'as they were bound to do according to God's law and their consciences'.[2] There is no evidence that the temporary character of princely obligations deterred financiers from advancing money to medieval governments. Their chances of securing repayment from rulers always depended on purely practical considerations. In the relations of princes with financiers there was often complete continuity from one reign to the next, just as there was continuity in most other routine matters. Casual lenders ran greater risks because their services might be less highly prized, but wholesale repudiations of the obligations of previous rulers were rare.

Like all other businessmen, voluntary lenders to rulers expected a profit. They advanced loans on condition that a satisfactory amount of interest would be paid and they expected their princely clients to shield them from anti-usury regulations. But even in the case of loans to the princes it would be wrong to deny all practical importance to the anti-usury legislation. Thus, it is significant that in the formal contracts between financiers and governments, as well as in other public documents connected with princely loans, illicit interest was rarely mentioned and all kinds of devices were used to disguise its presence.

It would be mistaken to attribute the heavy indebtedness of many medieval rulers to their alleged irresponsibility in financial matters. This might explain a few isolated cases, but cannot account for the vast bulk of medieval government borrowing. The ordinary revenues of the majority of the medieval rulers often barely sufficed for their everyday needs and did not allow them to accumulate substantial reserves. They could not even ensure a continuous supply of money for the central government all through the year. Very exalted personages were at times reduced to dire straits. Thus, when in 1274 Duke Robert II of Burgundy had to travel to Lyons to meet his brother-in-law, the French king, he could not depart for a while because the *bailli* of Dijon and the mayor of Beaune, two of the chief cities of his duchy, had both refused to lend the necessary money. The duke's trusted secretary, who was also his chief creditor, had to be summoned to the court and induced to lend 200 *li. tur.* (about 1% of the ordinary Burgundian revenue in 1278) before Duke

---

[1] Ch. V. Langlois, *Le règne de Philippe III le Hardi* (Paris, 1887), 387.

[2] *Debita nostra . . . racione regni seu guerrarum nostrarum contracta, ad que heredem et successorem nostrum, ipsiusque heredes et successores, ex lege Dei et consciencie fore intendimus obligatos.*

Robert could proceed on his journey.[1] An even more striking example can be adduced from the last years of Emperor Maximilian I; though dating from the post-medieval period, it deserves quoting because it illustrates well a state of affairs repeatedly encountered also in the Middle Ages. On two occasions in 1518 Jacob Fugger had to advance loans to Maximilian because His Majesty had nothing to eat.[2] These moments of distress, from which no medieval ruler was wholly immune, gave rise to numerous petty loans.

War imposed an excessively heavy strain on the finances of most medieval states. The cost of warfare went on increasing throughout the Middle Ages. Already in the twelfth century mercenary troops had to be employed repeatedly by the more powerful rulers. Later on, as the result of the commutation of feudal knight service and of other changes in military forces, armies came to consist predominantly of paid troops. As a result, the ordinary revenues of most medieval rulers usually proved quite inadequate in war time. The collection of the extraordinary war taxes required much time and it was often easier to borrow first in the hope that future taxes might ultimately repay the loans. Thus, borrowing was unavoidable in every serious war or other prolonged emergency.

The maintenance of diplomatic relations with other rulers and the payment of subsidies to foreign allies or agents required expenditure in foreign countries, which could be promptly financed only out of loans. Purchase of supplies on credit for princely courts was the rule. There is abundant evidence of this practice from the thirteenth century onwards. For all these reasons, *occasional* government borrowing was a constant feature of medieval life.

Some of the abler and more ambitious medieval princes grasped also the advantages of a more regular use of borrowing. At this point, we must distinguish two different phases in the development of medieval public credit in north-western Europe. The dividing line between them should be placed somewhere in the middle of the thirteenth century. In the first and earlier phase borrowing by rulers was still rare and loans were contracted by them only in exceptional circumstances. The beginning of the period of more intensive use of credit by the western rulers roughly coincided with the time of the greatest prosperity in medieval Europe. Credit facilities improved in England, France and the Netherlands in the second half of the thirteenth century and this was matched by an increase in the demand for credit among the rulers in those countries. The leading states were also undergoing a profound transformation. An earlier type

---

[1] H. Jassemin, *Le Mémorial de Robert II, Duc de Bourgogne (1273–85)* (Paris, 1933), 9–13.

[2] *Nichts zu essen gehabt hätte*, quoted in R. Ehrenberg, *Das Zeitalter der Fugger* (Jena, 1922), I, 100.

of state, lacking an elaborate administration and depending mainly on the political support and unpaid military service of the feudal vassals of its sovereign, was disappearing. It was being superseded by better organized and more centralized kingdoms and principalities, in which not only mercenary armies but also salaried officials played an increasingly vital role.

By the late thirteenth century the rulers of the more developed countries had achieved a considerable measure of efficiency, but their finances remained a weak point. Permanent ordinary revenues either did not increase at all or were expanding too slowly. Frequent taxation was becoming a necessity, but to tax their subjects was one of the hardest things for medieval governments. In the late thirteenth century taxes were still regarded as something extraordinary and the need to seek consent for them was a source of weakness to rulers. At this stage, regular borrowing from important financiers helped to tide the more important states over the difficult period of fiscal reform during which western society was adjusting itself to the painful necessity of taxation.

The frequency and intensity of government borrowing varied greatly between different states, just as it was subject to constant changes within each country. Divergencies were particularly great between medieval Germany and the countries further to the west. The kings of England and France, as well as the rulers of some of the most advanced French and Belgian principalities, found it both desirable and possible to make a fairly regular use of credit. The available financial resources could be most effectively mobilized by governments accustomed to close collaboration with important lenders. By the second half of the thirteenth century the systematic and continuous borrowing practised in some western states began to resemble the use of credit by modern governments. It was only through loans contracted on the security of future revenues that the whole machinery of state functioned smoothly in the England of Edward I or the France of Philip the Fair.

The German emperors were in quite a different position. Their German revenues had never been adequate. From the time of Otto I to the reign of Frederick II they had sought additional resources in Italy, the one European region where in that period money was comparatively abundant.[1] But this invaluable source of income disappeared with the collapse of the Hohenstaufen dynasty. The revenues from the royal domains and

---

[1] G. Deibel, 'Die italienischen Einkünfte Kaiser Friedrich Barbarossas', *Neue Heidelberger Jahrbücher*, n.s. 1932; *idem*, 'Die finanzielle Bedeutung Reichs-Italiens für die Staufische Herrscher', *Savigny Zeitschrift für Rechtsgeschichte*, Germ. Abteilung, liv (1934); Th. Mayer, 'Geschichte der Finanzwirtschaft vom Mittelalter bis zum Ende des 18. Jahrhunderts', in Gerloff-Neumark, *Handbuch der Finanzwissenschaft*, I (2), (1952), 241–2.

DD

the regalian rights in Germany were much impaired already by 1250, and most of what remained was dissipated during the long interregnum in the third quarter of the thirteenth century. Thus, at the very time when powerful centralized states were being organized in France and England, the material resources of the German kingship became utterly inadequate. The German emperors of the fourteenth and the fifteenth centuries have been justifiably described as 'beggar-kings'.[1] The frank confession of Rudolf of Habsburg in 1282 that 'there is at present no money in our treasury'[2] could have been repeated frequently by almost all his medieval successors on the imperial throne. There was no scope for organizing a central financial administration, and an effective system of imperial taxation was out of question. Many princes of the Empire similarly suffered from a chronic and desperate lack of funds. The emperors and the other German princes tried to raise loans wherever they could, but the scantiness of their assets made large-scale borrowing difficult. A considerable proportion of the imperial revenues and the regalian rights was, in the later Middle Ages, constantly pledged away to creditors and the situation of many other princes, both secular and ecclesiastical, was similar.

Frequent borrowing from professional lenders was an expensive device. It increased in the long run the need for extraordinary taxes and could be a source of political weakness. In the eyes of some western European rulers its undoubted advantages offset its heavy cost and other drawbacks. Some princes, in any case, had no choice: rulers whose ambitions outran their incomes tried to find in borrowing a way of living regularly beyond their means. But it is not surprising that regular borrowing did not find favour with every ruler. Some of the richest, who could best afford to do without it, became more impressed by the drawbacks than the advantages. Others, including most German emperors and princes, could not afford it or could not enlist the help of sufficiently wealthy or accommodating lenders. Many failed to grasp its potentialities.

Because most medieval rulers disposed of rather slender financial resources, greater risks attached to the use of credit than would menace more opulent modern governments. It did not require much to plunge the majority of medieval princes into excessive indebtedness. But it would be quite misguided to treat the presence of large debts as an invariably pathological symptom. Where rulers could confidently anticipate sizable revenues, borrowing could become a source of lasting strength. Wise and efficient use of credit lies behind some of the most successful achievements of medieval history.

[1] J. Landmann in *Finanzarchiv*, XXIX (1912), 7.
[2] A. Werminghoff, *Die Verpfändungen der mittel- und niederrheinischen Reichsstädte während des 13. und 14. Jahrhunderts* (1893), 7.

The reasons why medieval rulers wanted to borrow money are clear, but it is less obvious why men wanted to lend to such dangerous clients. Some loans were 'forced'—mere disguised taxes—but usually there was just enough chance of ultimate repayment to make them more bearable than outright levies of taxes. These compulsory loans differed widely in scope. In Germany and in France municipalities were frequently brought under contribution. Royal and princely officials were peculiarly liable to demands of this sort, while some loans were limited to a small number of selected, rich individuals. Men of some standing and local influence were often fairly ready to lend in the hope of government favour. Thus, the line between forced loans and voluntary loans became easily blurred. Outside France, forced loans were not, however, of outstanding import-ance in the Middle Ages. In England they became fairly common only in the later fourteenth and fifteenth centuries.

Every section of the propertied classes was represented among the voluntary lenders. Non-business lenders, especially monasteries and the military orders, were of outstanding importance only in the initial phase. In the course of the thirteenth century merchants and other businessmen became the main voluntary creditors of governments in England, France and the Netherlands.[1]

In dealing with the motives of the business lenders it might be best to concentrate on the more important financiers, who, after all, mattered most. Large-scale business meant trading in many countries. The good will of foreign rulers had to be purchased and preserved. In the face of competition from native merchants, special privileges might have to be sought. As a firm acquired important assets in a foreign country, it be-came increasingly dependent on the continued tolerance of the local ruler. 'When a [business] house got to a certain critical size, it *had* to help out princes or lose gains already made. It had wealth too great to jettison, placed where the prince could take it.'[2] Native merchants were exposed to even greater pressures, and motives of loyalty and obedience to their sovereign had particularly strong influence on them.

It would be misleading, however, to stress solely the negative reasons for lending to rulers. Firms reckoned on much profit while the going was good. Interest on loans was only one of the returns that the regular banker of a prince expected. He could also count on exemptions, privileges, pro-tection against extortions or violence and even diplomatic support in other countries. Medieval rulers had at their disposal yet another valu-able bait; they could confer titles of nobility on their bankers. Thus one of the greatest English financiers, William de la Pole, craved the purely

[1] The development of public credit was somewhat different in Germany.
[2] R. L. Reynolds, 'Origins of modern business enterprise: medieval Italy', *Journal of Economic History*, XII (1952), 365.

military title of a banneret, and received this high distinction, the only merchant ever to do so. Several important creditors of the French Crown were ennobled in the fourteenth and fifteenth centuries.

Once a firm plunged deeply into financial business with a ruler, withdrawal was difficult. To recover previous advances and safeguard ultimate chances of profits, the banker had to continue lending. If things were going badly with his princely client, he had to be helped more than ever. So good money might have to be thrown away after bad. Frequently the final results were catastrophic. Some princes could not, indeed, resist the temptation of plundering and ruining perfectly solvent creditors as an alternative to repaying their loans. Several eminent bankers of the French kings suffered this fate. But some firms and individual financiers escaped all these perils and managed to amass and preserve great fortunes.

Medieval rulers contracted numerous 'short-term loans'. There was usually a succession of not very large loans, obtained at fairly frequent intervals. The repayment of previous debts, many of them quite recent, proceeded simultaneously with the contracting of new debts, often destined to be equally short-lived. The modern alternative of funded debt was known to medieval rulers but, for practical reasons, most of them did not try to sell annuities. They were familiar enough, at least from the twelfth century, with the idea of paying regular, annual pensions for services rendered. By the early thirteenth century, all the more important rulers were paying out of their ordinary revenues regular annuities to relatives, foreign allies, influential magnates and military retainers. Vassals were being acquired through payment of money-fiefs in place of grants of land. But rulers could not afford to repay loans in this manner, for their permanent revenues were already sufficiently burdened with permanent charges of other sorts. Besides, the more important businessmen, on whom governments had to depend for larger loans, were not interested in buying rent charges in any quantity. In any case, men would rather buy them from towns than from rulers. Few medieval princes could be trusted to pay annuities for a long period to a mere moneylender. It is significant that the princes of the Netherlands, who sold rents quite frequently in the fourteenth and fifteenth centuries, usually, though not invariably, acted through the intermediary of the leading towns of their dominions.

The great worry of the creditors of princes was how to make sure that their mighty clients would honour their debts at all, as there was no effective way of compelling them to do so. Recourse to judicial proceedings against a ruler in his own state was normally out of question. Reprisals against the goods and persons of his subjects abroad were sometimes instigated by disappointed creditors. The popes gave vigorous support to the Italian firms employed as the papal cameral merchants, and sometimes even excommunicated the defaulting prelates or princes. But the creditors of governments could never enjoy complete security. The most elaborate guarantees could be of little avail if their princely clients could not or would not pay.

Important lenders, and especially the regular bankers of rulers, frequently required no special guarantees. General promises of repayment sufficed. They felt fairly secure that the debts to them, both principal and interest, would not be repudiated so long as they continued to lend money. In any case, their advances were apt to be very large and it would have been difficult to find adequate material securities that could have fully guaranteed them against losses. In view of the substantial size of their loans, considerable sums had to be allotted for repayment. Often specified taxes or tolls were earmarked for this purpose. But this does not mean that they were pledged to the lender. The main object was not to provide the lenders with cast-iron guarantees, but to make practical arrangements for the repayment of their important loans. In England, after 1275, each new grant of taxes was at once assigned wholly, or in part, to the royal creditors. When a new uniform duty on exported wool was created in England in 1275, it was forthwith entrusted to the company of the Riccardi, the king's chief bankers at that time. It remained at their exclusive disposal for the next nineteen years, and, in return, they advanced loans whenever the government required money. These arrangements reveal medieval public credit at its best and most useful. They were advantageous to both parties, endured for a long time and contributed to the financial stability of an efficient government.

The assigning of revenues must be sharply distinguished from the farming of revenues. Unlike the assignee, the farmer did not have to account for everything he had received, but merely owed a fixed rent; anything over and above this charge constituted his gain. Medieval rulers often farmed their revenues because trained and trustworthy officials, who could be entrusted with honest collection, were not available in sufficient numbers. Also this was one of the main ways of conferring favours on magnates and officials. Most farmers were expected to anticipate occasionally their future receipts through advances to the prince. Such overdrafts frequently seem to have been free of interest, though there were compensating advantages in gaining and preserving the prince's favour. Thus an element of credit was always present in this oldest and most common of medieval financial arrangements: the use of credit by medieval rulers is at least as old as their possession of regular monetary revenues. The creation of permanent indirect taxes in the later Middle Ages, with a constant and regular yield, added to the amount of revenue capable of being anticipated in this fashion.

One main purpose of the arrangements described hitherto was to facilitate the collection of revenues. The provision of overdrafts was only a subsidiary item in the case of lesser farms of princely assets. Wealthy and influential financiers, who were given farms of important revenues for the express purpose of encouraging them to make large and continuous advances to the government, belong to a different category. Farms of this sort were more important as instruments of government borrowing than as a method of administering the revenue. The special profits of the farmers became part of the price paid by a ruler for their loans. The danger was that, as farms were renewed, he might have to sacrifice an increasingly large part of his income. There was also a risk that the annual rent due to the government might become anticipated for several years ahead by the advances of the farmers. In this way, the most valuable sources of income might pass out of the control of a prince on terms that became increasingly unsatisfactory. The extensive farming of taxes was thus, sometimes, a symptom of bad management and could be a cause of serious financial weakness.

In the early Middle Ages (until *c.* 1200) borrowing secured by the pledge of land was probably the most common form of loan, often from ecclesiastical lenders. The need for the pledging of property diminished in England and France as the incomes of rulers expanded, and as professional lay lenders became important enough to make borrowing from ecclesiastics unnecessary. Businessmen in those countries liked, best of all, to secure temporary control over taxes and tolls due to their princely clients. They were usually willing to lend on the security of valuables, which could be easily removed and sold. Unlike the ecclesiastical lenders, they were reluctant to accept land as security. This was particularly true of businessmen operating in a foreign land, as was the case with so many of the most important creditors of western princes: they did not want to acquire land abroad.

In France, as in several other states, the pledging of the domain lands of the sovereign was hampered by ideas about its supposed inalienability, which were current from the late thirteenth century onwards.[1] A formal legal expression was given to these doctrines in the French royal decree of July 1318, which was followed by a sequestration of all the grants made by the two previous kings.[2] This policy was never consistently enforced in France, but the prohibition from alienating royal property was invoked on some occasions in the fifteenth century to compel the restitution of pledged estates, and its existence may have discouraged some creditors

[1] Ch. V. Langlois, *Le règne de Philippe III le Hardi* (Paris, 1887), 185.
[2] Ch. V. Langlois, 'Les registres perdus des archives de la chambre des comptes de Paris', *Notices et extraits des manuscrits de la bibliothèque nationale et autres bibliothèques*, XL (1917), 110–23.

from seeking pledges of land. In any case, the French Crown had recourse to such pledging only in very abnormal circumstances. Loans on the security of mortgaged property remained much longer a common resort of rulers in Germany. This practice persisted, indeed, in the Empire far beyond the Middle Ages.[1] Estates, regalian rights, towns and even entire districts were repeatedly pledged. These transactions resulted in some important permanent transfers of territory and political influence.

In Germany and the Netherlands, princes often had to accept onerous personal obligations towards their creditors. These might include a stipulation that, in cases of default, the princely borrower would be obliged to take up residence in the creditor's native town and would remain there until the debt was settled. Alternatively, a fixed number of the advisers or knights of a ruler might become hostages for the debts of their master. The kings of France and England were much too powerful to have to endure such humiliating contracts in their own lands. But during his campaigns in the Netherlands Edward III of England had repeatedly to pledge the persons of his leading prelates and magnates. In 1340-1 the earls of Derby and Northampton spent several months in custody at Malines and Louvain as hostages for Edward's debts, and the king's inability to procure their speedy release was one of the causes of his furious attack on the financial mismanagement of his officials in England. Examples of the detention of the rulers themselves can be adduced from Germany. Thus in April 1295 the three Wittelsbach dukes of Bavaria were being jointly detained for debt at Regensburg.[2]

Some of the most peculiar credit transactions in medieval history arose out of the pledging of valuables by rulers. Numerous royal and princely crowns on various occasions found their way into the hands of moneylenders, or were even partly dismantled so that jewels detached from them could be pawned. In 1340 five of the various crowns of Edward III of England and his wife were distributed between Bruges and Antwerp, Trier and Cologne. Precious relics often shared the same fate. This was one practical justification for the vast collection of valuables that every medieval ruler tried to amass. The German kings and princes, because of the distrust they inspired in prospective creditors, were forced to pledge valuables particularly often.[3] Outside Germany, the importance of these

[1] The town of Wismar was pledged to the duchy of Mecklenburg-Schwerin as late as 1803. C. Schröder, 'Die Schwedische Verpfändung Wismars an Mecklenburg-Schwerin, 1803', *Jahrbücher und Jahrberichte des Vereins für Mecklenburgische Geschichte und Altertumskunde* (Schwerin), lxxvii (1912), 177–240.

[2] J. F. Bhömer, *Regesta Imperii*, vi (*Die Regesten des Kaiserreichs unter Rudolf, Adolf, Albrecht, Heinrich VII, 1273–1313*), new ed. by V. Samanek (Innsbruck, 1948), 3 Abteilung, 3 Lieferung, no. 595 (pp. 199–200).

[3] E.g. King Rudolf pledged his crown to the archbishop of Cologne, King Ruprecht pawned the crown jewels to the Jews of Nuremberg. R. Knipping, *Die Regesten der*

transactions must not be exaggerated. Except in the earliest times, they were an irregular and abnormal feature, more typical of casual dealings with lenders than of regular borrowing from a ruler's habitual bankers. Petty money-lenders were much more likely to demand such pledges than prominent financiers.

To a student of the *forms* of public credit the end of the fifteenth century does not represent any significant dividing date. But important changes were occurring at the turn of the fifteenth and the sixteenth centuries in the European economy and in the power of the leading states, which might fittingly mark the end of the present survey. The countries of western and central Europe were again entering upon a period of renewed economic prosperity. Spain emerged as a great power, the Habsburgs inherited the Burgundian lands and England became again a strong state under Edward IV and Henry VII. The rise of these 'new monarchies' opened up a fresh period in the use of credit by European states: enormous loans were contracted by the leading powers in the first half of the sixteenth century, surpassing anything encountered in the Middle Ages. Thus Emperor Charles V in the course of thirty-seven years (1519–56) borrowed 39,000,000 ducats!

II. *The Beginnings*

Until the late twelfth century information about borrowing by rulers is scanty. Potential lenders, disposing of sizable resources, were fairly rare: they included other rulers, richer magnates, bishops and more important monasteries, and occasionally merchants and moneyers, both Christian and Jewish. The rulers were as yet in no position to borrow frequently, nor did they probably wish to do so. The scarcity of information does therefore, to some degree, reflect a real paucity of princely loans in the earlier Middle Ages. But in dealing with this obscure period it is unwise to attach too much significance to purely negative evidence. Until the more important rulers decided to keep regular records of their own (between *c.* 1150 and 1200 in most cases), most of our information about loans must come from ecclesiastical sources. Naturally, the chroniclers usually mentioned only the loans that resulted in permanent acquisitions of property by their churches. As for the original deeds, they were only preserved in the archives of churches if they concerned loans raised on mortgage and if the pledged land was never redeemed by the owner. Advances that were repaid, advances that were not secured by mortgages and loans supplied by lay lenders have left little trace. Our knowledge of the early borrowing is therefore bound to be one-sided.

Erzbischöfe von Köln im Mittelalter, III (2) (1901–15), 57 ff.; *Deutsche Reichstagsakten unter König Ruprecht*, V (1885), no. 283, art. 26, 32.

In emergencies princes have always tried to borrow, unless they could seize and keep what they needed. It is impossible to tell whether the repeated seizures of the treasures of churches by the West Frankish kings in the second half of the ninth century were followed by any restitutions.[1] In the eleventh and twelfth centuries the growing wealth of townsmen was brought under forced contribution. We know of these payments from the charters prohibiting such exactions which numerous towns in all parts of France ultimately secured from their lords.[2] The charter granted to Abbeville in 1184 is particularly explicit. It stipulated that the citizens should not be forced to lend to their lords unless pledges were offered to them or unless they wished to make advances of their own free will.[3]

In the early Middle Ages loans secured by the pledge of land were probably the commonest. Pledging of valuables is the only other alternative security encountered in the records of this early period. It might be worth while to give a sample of some of the first known cases of *voluntary* lending to rulers. Between 957 and 970 the countess of Carcassonne and her sons engaged two large domains to Jewish lenders for a loan of 50 *li*.[4] The Emperor Henry III borrowed in 1044, on the security of an estate, 20 pounds of gold and a considerable quantity of silver from the bishop of Worms. Henry also pledged a crown to the abbey of Hersfeld.[5] Examples multiply in the second half of the eleventh century. Archbishop Anno II of Cologne (1056–75) had to contract considerable loans from the Jews.[6] The Emperor Henry IV repeatedly borrowed from cathedral churches and abbeys. But voluntary advances to rulers did not become fairly common for another hundred years.

Most of the early loans appear to have been contracted for exceptional reasons. Furthermore, one gets the impression that, even in emergencies, the possibility of raising loans played at first a relatively minor part in the schemes of princes. The case of Richilda, countess of Flanders and Hainault, is instructive. In 1071 she was driven out of Flanders by a rebellion. She turned for help to the bishop of Liège and recognized him as the overlord of her hereditary possession of Hainault. In return, she received the enormous sum of 100 lb. of gold and 175 marks of silver. It is most unlikely that Richilda could have procured this huge amount by

---

[1] E. Lesne, *Histoire de la propriété ecclésiastique en France*, III (Lille, 1936), 159–60.

[2] Several texts and more important references are conveniently assembled in C. Stephenson, *Mediaeval Institutions* (ed. B. D. Lyon, Cornell U.P., 1954), 5 ff.

[3] *Ibid.* p. 10: *nec credent michi nec alicui dominorum sine vadimonio nisi ex propria voluntate.*

[4] J. de Malafosse in *Annales du Midi*, LXIII (1951), 118–19.

[5] G. Waitz, *Verfassungsgeschichte des deutschen Volkes*, VIII (1878), 238; H. Weirich (ed.), *Urkundenbuch der Reichsabtei Hersfeld*, I (1936), no. 100 (p. 179).

[6] *Monumenta Germaniae Historica*, S.S. XI, 502, no. 164; G. Bauernfeind, *Anno II, Erzbischof von Köln* (Munich, 1929).

borrowing. She could never have repaid a loan of this size, for she could not even redeem, later on, some of the properties pledged in the same emergency to monasteries.

The financing of the First Crusade provides another interesting example. Many magnates and ordinary knights set out on the proceeds of mortgages or other types of loan. But few of the leading princes needed or wished to borrow much. The most powerful or richest leaders, like Robert II of Flanders or Stephen of Blois, do not appear to have required any loans. It is possible that Raymond IV of Toulouse mortgaged some possessions, but the only heavy borrowers among the princely crusaders were two rather weak men whose personal rule had been inefficient. Duke Robert of Normandy raised 10,000 marks by pledging the duchy to his brother, King William Rufus of England. If William had not accidentally died, it is unlikely that Robert would have easily recovered Normandy. Godfrey of Bouillon, the future king of Jerusalem, was unsure about his position as duke of Lower Lorraine. His doubts about his future prospects in his homeland may explain why he was willing to raise money by extensively mortgaging and alienating his properties. The details of his financial transactions throw welcome light on the difficulties of raising a considerable loan at this period. Godfrey pledged the great allodial estate of Bouillon to Otbert, bishop of Liège, one of the most powerful prelates in the Empire, for 1,300 marks of silver and 3 marks of gold. The cathedral church of Liège was partly stripped of its valuables. Even the gold covering the shrine of St Lambert, its patron saint, was taken away. However, the resources of a single ecclesiastical institution seldom sufficed to provide a sizable loan. The bishop of Liège had to exercise his right to take the treasures belonging to the other churches of the diocese. In spite of the protests of the monks, the dependent abbeys were forced to part with their most cherished valuables. Two other estates of Godfrey were sold to the bishop of Verdun, who raised the necessary money in a similar manner.

By the twelfth century, the German bishops were rulers of extensive territories and some of them rivalled in their wealth and power the more important lay dukes and counts. But, in return, much secular service was demanded from the church by the emperors. The obligation to provide considerable military contingents for the imperial expeditions was one of the principal causes of the growing indebtedness of several German bishoprics in the second half of the twelfth century. Emperor Frederick Barbarossa personally guaranteed to the lenders the repayment of some of the loans contracted for this purpose. For example, he was able, in this way, to induce the chapter of Würzburg to lend 350 marks to its bishop for the Italian campaign of 1174.[1] Borrowing became a habit with some

---

[1] *Monumenta Germaniae Historica, Leges*, II, 144.

of the greatest German prelates. In 1158 we find Archbishop Arnold of Mainz pledging the estates of a dependent nunnery to raise money for the expedition against rebellious Milan. Two years later he was killed in an uprising of his subjects enraged by his financial exactions.[1] The next archbishop, Christian I, one of Frederick's best commanders in Italy, plunged deeply into debt. A survey drawn up in 1183 by his successor revealed a gravely encumbered inheritance.[2] It was the same at Cologne. Rainald of Dassel succeeded in 1158 to an impoverished archbishopric and had to redeem various revenues mortgaged by his predecessor.[3] As Frederick's chancellor and chief adviser, Rainald enjoyed exceptional opportunities for enrichment, but his successor, Philip I, though an able administrator, had to borrow throughout his episcopate. In 1174 he had to pledge the customs and the mint at Cologne to its citizens to raise the large loan of 1,000 marks needed for the Italian campaign of that year. Philip, apparently, came to regard borrowing as a fairly normal expedient. He was even prepared to contract loans in order to purchase additional property for his see.[4]

Bishops and monasteries were chiefly drawn into lending by their desire to acquire more land. The pledged property was in all probability usually treated as a *mortuum vadium* (mortgage): the income from it was not used to reduce the debt but constituted the lender's gain. The lender could, therefore, often expect a prolonged tenure of the pledged land. Above all, there was frequently a chance that the borrower might be altogether unable to redeem his property and would thus make it possible for a lender to acquire land very cheaply, for property was, as a rule, pledged for less than it would have fetched in a genuine sale (on average 55 to 60% of sale value in late twelfth-century Normandy).

Until the last decades of the twelfth century bishops and monasteries provided a large proportion of the recorded loans to rulers. But it would be wrong to assume that, as a group, they were becoming professional lenders or that they were systematically diverting their surplus revenues to investment in loans. Indeed, they themselves had sometimes to borrow in order to oblige friendly landowners or influential rulers, who often

---

[1] K. F. Stumpf, *Acta Maguntina seculi XII* (Innsbruck, 1863), 69–72, nos. 67, 68; M. Stimming, *Die Entstehung des weltlichen Territoriums des Erzbistums Mainz* (Darmstadt, 1915), 82–3.

[2] Stumpf, *op. cit.* 114–17, no. 112; J. F. Böhmer, *Regesta archiepiscoporum Maguntinensium*, II (1886), 60–1, no. 91.

[3] T. J. Lacomblet, *Urkundenbuch für die Geschichte des Niederrheins*, I (Düsseldorf, 1840), 431; J. Ficker, *Reinald von Dassel, Reichskanzler und Erzbischof von Köln, 1156–67* (Cologne, 1850), 94–5.

[4] Lacomblet, *op. cit.* I, 318, 455, 467, 517; H. Hecker, *Die territoriale Politik des Erzbischofs Philipp I von Köln, 1167–1191* (Leipzig, 1883), 96; H. Rothert, *Westfälische Geschichte*, I (1949), 188 ff.

preferred to borrow from churchmen. Rulers found it safer to mortgage important properties to churches rather than to the leading magnates of their dominions, though the money might ultimately be derived from some of these magnates. Thus Bishop Rudolph of Liège, in order to lend the emperor 1,000 marks for the Italian campaign of 1174 on the security of the imperial properties west of the Meuse, had to borrow 230 marks from Count Rudolf of Louvain on the security of two episcopal estates.[1] It may be that religious establishments repeatedly acted merely as trusted intermediaries.

A class of substantial, or even wealthy, lay businessmen emerged in the course of the twelfth century. In Languedoc, lay lenders, both Jewish and Christian, were already very active and important in the early part of the century; they may have particularly profited from the financial difficulties of many southern churches, impoverished by excessive building enterprises. To begin with, the lay lenders supplemented rather than replaced ecclesiastical lenders. They also supplied ecclesiastics themselves with money. Perhaps loans by churchmen became more frequent in the course of the twelfth century because it was becoming easier for them to borrow in turn from professional lay usurers and merchants in the towns.[2] Thus, between 1122 and 1155 Abbot Peter the Venerable of Cluny was able to borrow over 10,000 marks of silver (equivalent to more than five years' revenue), which he raised mainly from the merchants of his own town of Cluny and from the Jews of Mâcon and Chalon. Later on, lay financiers gradually displaced bishops and monasteries as lenders to princes. This happened in France and the Netherlands by the early thirteenth century, but not to the same extent in Germany. In the thirteenth century, only one of the military orders, the Templars, was of first-rate financial importance among ecclesiastical bodies.

The principal reasons for the replacement of episcopal and monastic lenders by laymen were economic, but a change in the attitude of churchmen to usury may have hastened it. A decretal of Pope Alexander III (1163), declaring loans on mortgage to be a form of usury and forbidding ecclesiastics to practise this, had apparently little effect at first, but it may have contributed to the gradual withdrawal of monasteries from this form of business (around 1200 in Normandy) and to their preference, in the thirteenth century, for lawful forms of credit transactions, such as the purchase of perpetual rent-charges from borrowers. This was a type of loan particularly suited to the needs of lesser landowners rather than of rulers who now, increasingly, sought loans from the lay professionals.

[1] St Bormans and E. Schoolmesters, *Cartulaire de l'Église St Lambert à Liège*, I (Brussels, 1893), nos. lvi and lxii (pp. 93–4, 103–4).
[2] H. Van Werveke in *Annales d'Histoire Économique et Sociale*, IV (1932), 457–9.

In the late twelfth and early thirteenth centuries the only lay lenders easily accessible to the rulers were the townsmen of their own domains or from neighbouring regions. Hence the utmost diversity prevailed and it will be more convenient to give examples in the sections devoted to particular countries. One special group of early lenders, the Jews, should however be discussed collectively. Only in Germany did they remain important as financiers until the late Middle Ages. There were never many Jews in medieval Flanders and other more advanced parts of the Netherlands, presumably because there was no economic need for them. The period of their greatest prosperity in France and England is, perhaps, to be found in the second half of the twelfth century. They were then profiting from the general increase of prosperity in western Europe and they were not, as yet, suffering seriously from economic restrictions. In most regions of western Europe they were at this time as free to acquire and to hold land as were the Christian merchants.

In the towns of Languedoc Jews were entirely free from economic and social disabilities until the time of the Albigensian crusade. Some of the early loans contracted by the great lords of this region came from Jewish businessmen of Toulouse, Montpellier and other southern towns. In England Henry II borrowed regularly from several Jews during the middle years of his reign. His successors preferred to tax them. The same thing happened elsewhere in western Europe. As a result, Jewish loans to rulers dwindled almost everywhere outside Germany to insignificant proportions in the course of the thirteenth century. Jews were increasingly debarred from participation in wholesale trade and were confined to petty money-lending, practised under licences from the local rulers, to whom they had to pay regular taxes.

The emergence of important lay lenders opened up entirely new financial possibilities for governments. Rulers could now raise loans in ways better suited to their needs and interests: they could hope to avoid the embarrassment of mortgaging estates. For the first time frequent borrowing and even regular borrowing became possible. The earliest consequences of this change can be seen in the second half of the twelfth century. Some of the ablest monarchs ceased to regard loans as a wholly exceptional expedient. For Henry II of England borrowing was a useful device, conducive to increased efficiency. The growing cost of warfare was one of the main causes of the increased need for government borrowing. Larger and more elaborate stone castles were being built, costly to construct and to provision. Warfare became increasingly a matter of lengthy sieges and campaigns became more prolonged. Important rulers, like Henry II of England and Emperor Frederick I, frequently employed mercenary troops, including large bodies of infantry.[1] In 1186, after five

[1] J. Boussard, 'Les mercenaires au XIIe siècle. Henri II Plantagenet et les origines de

years of warfare with most of his neighbours in turn, Baldwin V of Hainault owed 41,000 *li*. (of the currency of Valenciennes). This was a large debt, but a single tax sufficed to repay most of it.[1] By the late twelfth century an element of credit was also becoming more clearly discernible in the ordinary financial arrangements of many princes. Their mints were kept in operation by bullion, supplied on credit, by merchants and money-changers. Businessmen were particularly suited to the handling of the new tolls, excises and other taxes that sprang up in this period. It was often found advisable to farm these fresh revenues to them in return for fixed payments, so that some of the resulting rents might then be borrowed in advance. As the expenditure of princes grew, the officials collecting or farming their ordinary revenues were, likewise, increasingly expected to anticipate future receipts by advances to the government when necessity arose. Such uses of credit were beginning to be taken for granted by the more important western rulers by about 1200.

III. *The Crusades and the Coming of the Italians to Northern Europe*

In most regions of north-western Europe native businessmen could not complain of much Italian competition until, roughly, the third quarter of the thirteenth century. But long before then several northern princes had come into close contact with Italian merchants in the course of crusading ventures. Money, shipping and supplies were repeatedly obtained on credit in Italian harbours and from members of the Italian colonies in the Levant. The knowledge that these superior facilities existed in the Mediterranean region profoundly influenced the attitude of rulers towards ventures in southern Europe and encouraged them to embark on expeditions that would otherwise have been doomed to almost certain failure. The conquest by Charles of Anjou of the kingdom of Sicily provides one outstanding example.

We do not hear of any borrowing from the Italian merchants by the leaders of the Second Crusade. The letters of Louis VII to Suger, his chief minister in France, mention only loans from French magnates and from the Templars. The latter appear to have acted as intermediaries in raising money for him in Syria.[2] This is one of the earliest pieces of information about the financial activities of the military orders. At first their financial

---

l'armée de métier', *Bibliothèque de l'École des Chartes*, cvi (1945–6); Grundmann, 'Rotten und Brabanzonen', *Deutsches Archiv für Geschichte des Mittelalters*, v (1942).

[1] *Chronique de Gislebert de Mons* (ed. L. Vanderkindere, 1904), 193–4.

[2] *Recueil des Historiens des Gaules et de la France*, xv, 499–502, 509; A. Luchaire, *Études sur les actes de Louis VII* (Paris, 1885), nos. 230–1, 236, 240.

operations were presumably confined to organizing transfers of money to the crusading states in the East for their own needs or to help their allies. The Hospitallers never deliberately expanded their financial activities any further, though now and then they got involved in intermittent credit transactions with rulers and churchmen. The Templars chose a different path and began to specialize in financial business. Already at the end of the twelfth century they were turning their European commanderies into banks of deposit. In the thirteenth century they were the favourite bankers of several princes. This interest in high finance ultimately contributed to their downfall, while the less business-minded Hospitallers survived and even secured a share of the landed property of the ruined Templars.

The financial history of the Third Crusade is very obscure. The Genoese were specially active in helping the French contingent and King Philip Augustus embarked from Genoa. It is possible that they also made loans to the French king in Syria. No such obscurity surrounds the part played by Italian businessmen in the Fourth Crusade. The Venetians undertook to provide the necessary shipping and they lent money to some of the leaders. The inability of the crusaders to pay for these services helped the Venetians to divert the expedition from its original objectives to an attack on Constantinople.

The story of the loans contracted by Louis IX during his crusade to Egypt and Syria is not perhaps very typical, as he had an exceptional reputation for honesty. But it does show what could be achieved in favourable circumstances. Italian businessmen were delighted to lend money to such a safe client. Some business contracts drawn up in 1253 at Genoa specifically instructed Genoese business agents in the Levant to invest in loans to the king of France the money derived from the sale of commodities in Syria. It was the safest way of remitting money back to Europe, as all the loans of Louis were repayable at the headquarters of the Templars in Paris. In 1253 Louis borrowed in Syria at least 80,000 *li. par.*[1] from some seventy different lenders. Nearly half came from seven major Genoese firms. The lenders recovered their advances through the intermediacy of other Italian merchants trading in France. We know the names of at least fifty-seven merchants of Piacenza who were employed for this purpose, and it has been plausibly suggested that the origins of the exceptionally flourishing Placentine colony in Paris may go back to these transactions.

It is uncertain when Italian merchants first began to travel regularly to northern France, but they were already frequenting the fairs of Champagne in some numbers in the last decade of the twelfth century. During the next seventy years (*c.* 1200–70), the fairs of Champagne developed

---

[1] By comparison royal revenue from the farm of *prévôtés*, one of the principal sources of Louis's income, amounted to 56,000 *li. par.* in 1256.

into a major financial centre of international importance, the earliest such centre in north-western Europe. The more important Italian firms gradually became accustomed to maintain representatives at all the fairs and many other prominent merchants came fairly regularly. This continuity in the personnel of merchants present in Champagne played a part in accustoming rulers to seek loans there. From being a centre of dealings in commodities the fairs evolved into predominantly financial institutions. In the last decades of the thirteenth century one of their chief functions was to provide a convenient meeting place where periodic financial settlements could be negotiated. A semi-permanent money market developed, where very considerable sums could be borrowed from a wide choice of lenders. Thus the Riccardi of Lucca claimed that in the days of their prosperity they could borrow at a single fair up to 200,000 *li. tur.* It is not surprising that, in the second half of the thirteenth century, rulers, bishops and towns from a wide area of northern France and the Netherlands should have repeatedly sought loans at the Champagne fairs.

The influence of the papacy did much to promote the business of the Italian merchants north of the Alps. Prelates throughout Christendom owed payments to the popes in return for securing promotion to bishoprics and abbacies (so-called 'services') or for other grants and favours. Debts were incurred by many ecclesiastics as a result of litigation at the papal court. The papacy encouraged churchmen to borrow the necessary money from the financiers at Rome, as often this was the only way of assuring speedy payment. Some German bishops were contracting such loans already in the late twelfth century. Examples abound in the surviving papal registers from the pontificate of Innocent III onwards. The need to collect these debts forced Italians to travel to the home countries of the borrowers and the papacy did what it could to help the lenders. A surviving letter of a Sienese businessman to his partners, describing his difficulties with a recalcitrant archbishop of Lyons, regards papal intervention as the only efficacious remedy.[1] Already under Innocent IV several German prelates incurred excommunication for failing to satisfy their Italian creditors. By the late thirteenth century these papal interventions on behalf of merchants were a part of normal routine and continued to prove very efficacious.[2] The papacy was particularly ready to help its regular bankers. As Gregory IX once put it, any injury to them was to be regarded as an injury to the Holy See.[3]

---

[1] A. Schulte, *Geschichte des mittelalterlichen Handels und Verkehrs zwischen West-deutschland und Italien mit Ausschluss von Venedig*, I (1900), 265 and n. I.

[2] Cf. for example, D. P. Waley, 'A Register of Boniface VIII's Chamberlain, Theoderic of Orvieto', *Journal of Ecclesiastical History*, VIII (1957).

[3] *In quorum offensu nos ipsos et Sedem Apostolicam reputamus offendi*, quoted by A. Gottlob in *Vierteljahrschrift für Sozial- und Wirtschaftsgeschichte*, I (1903), 350.

The need to employ Italian firms systematically arose out of the collection of papal taxes from churchmen throughout Europe. At first the proceeds of the various papal levies (crusading tenths, subsidies, services, etc.) were transmitted to the popes mainly by the Templars and other religious orders. But as the financial needs of the papacy increased rapidly during the prolonged struggle against the Emperor Frederick II and his sons, more regular arrangements with businessmen became desirable. In the course of the pontificate of Gregory IX (1227–41), Italian merchants came to be used habitually for this purpose and their position as the chief papal bankers was still further consolidated under his successor, Innocent IV (1243–54). Innocent's favourite firm, the Bonsignori of Siena, became one of the wealthiest merchant companies in Europe. The group of Italian firms used as the papal cameral merchants acquired the means to render to the papacy every financial service that might be demanded of them. They were mostly used to transfer money throughout western Europe, but they were also capable of advancing large loans. The conquest of the kingdom of Sicily by Charles of Anjou in 1266 would have been impossible without the loans of the Bonsignori and other firms of cameral merchants whose help was enlisted by the papacy. In a few months they advanced over 160,000 *li. par.*[1]

During the second half of the thirteenth century Italian merchants were spreading their activity to England and to most regions of northern and eastern France and the Netherlands. Trade and papal financial business drew leading Italian merchant companies to a number of new centres. Several important firms of Siena, Lucca, Florence and Piacenza became permanently established in London within a few years of the end of the English civil war in 1267. Only one Italian company was regularly employed by the English Crown in the 'seventies and the 'eighties, but a number of firms were concurrently used for the transfer of the papal funds from England. Thus fourteen firms divided between them £70,000 levied in England from a papal sexennial tenth between 1274 and 1283 (seven Florentine, four Lucchese, one each from Siena, Pistoia and Piacenza).[2] This papal business and the profitable opportunities offered by the English wool trade were probably the chief causes of their settlement in this country. It is probable that the establishment of contacts between rulers and Italian firms at the fairs of Champagne encouraged, and in some cases may have hastened, the geographic expansion of their business in France and the Netherlands.

In France, Paris was the most important of the new centres of Italian

---

[1] Two and a half times the revenue of Louis IX from the farm of *prévôtés* (64,000 *li. par.* in 1265).

[2] W. E. Lunt, *Financial Relations of the Papacy with England to 1327* (Cambridge, Mass., 1939), Appendix VI, 641–65.

activity. Italians were chiefly attracted to it by the presence within its walls of the royal court. In the late thirteenth century more Italian firms appear to have been represented in Paris than in London. Thus, after the king of France became also the lord of Champagne in 1285, two of the main centres of Italian activity in northern Europe were under direct royal control. As we shall see, French kings were not slow in exploiting these new opportunities for raising funds. The Italian business expansion touched only the western fringes of the Empire. They settled in fair numbers in the Netherlands and for a time were active in Lorraine. They became permanently established in the lands immediately to the east of the Rhône. But the visits of the Italian merchants to the Rhineland were relatively rare and they seldom penetrated further east.[1] Papal business and loans to German prelates accounted for much of this limited Italian activity in Germany.

The leading Italian firms had an incontestable superiority over merchants of north-western Europe: their business techniques were better, they controlled more capital, they belonged to a closely integrated group with branches and correspondents in all the more important commercial centres of western Europe and the Mediterranean region. All Italian firms of merchant-bankers tended to be interconnected, the bond being particularly close between the merchants from the same town. They all depended as much on credit as on their own capital and drew frequently upon the resources of each other. Within each firm the original capital came from the merchants who founded it and their associates, but as each company grew, an ever increasing proportion of its funds came from deposits of other persons, many of them not even merchants. The leading Italian firms appear to have attracted much larger deposits from non-business investors than did contemporary merchants in northern Europe. At home the leading Italian bankers belonged to the ruling class of their towns and could reckon on diplomatic and even military support from their city republics. No wonder that as soon as the important firms settled permanently in each region the more powerful and enterprising rulers tried to harness this new economic force in a regular fashion, starting thereby a new era in the history of European public credit.

While the representatives of the prominent Italian firms established themselves in the chief commercial and political centres of western Europe, many of the lesser Italian merchants and money-lenders tried to exploit more backward regions. These humbler businessmen were specially attracted by the possibilities of lending to the poorer classes or in regions where hitherto sufficient credit facilities had been lacking. In 1309

[1] J. Schneider, 'Les activités des marchands et financiers italiens dans la région lorraine aux XIIIe et XIVe siècles', *Comptes rendus des séances de l'Académie des Inscriptions et Belles Lettres* (1951), 327-30.

Italians, chiefly petty money-lenders it appears, were established in at least seventy localities in the Netherlands, exclusive of Flanders. Professional money-lenders needed licences from rulers to set up *tables de prêt*, public pawnshops. Such licences seem to have been granted fairly readily at this period, because of the annual payments that had to be made by 'the Lombards' for this privilege and also because rulers found it convenient to borrow from Italian businessmen who were completely under their control.

IV. *England*

England[1] provides one of the best-documented examples of the use of credit facilities by a medieval monarchy. There exists a fairly continuous body of evidence about royal borrowing from the reign of Henry II onwards. Three different stages can be distinguished fairly clearly in the history of public credit in medieval England. From the days of Henry II down to the middle of the thirteenth century loans normally played only a subsidiary part in the financing of the Crown. Systematic use of borrowing, as a regular method of supplementing royal resources in emergencies and of stabilizing royal finances at all times, started in the reign of Edward I. Henceforth for nearly eighty years, until the middle of the fourteenth century, the Crown was able to draw freely upon the resources of a succession of important lenders. In the second half of the fourteenth century English rulers began to experience difficulties in finding lenders who were both willing and able to advance all that was required. These difficulties increased still further under the Lancastrian dynasty and they contributed to the collapse of the royal finances in the middle of the fifteenth century. A marked improvement in the general financial position of the Crown took place under Edward IV and again under Henry VII. But it was achieved mainly through the exploitation of the royal domain lands and the prerogative rights of the Crown, and borrowing played a relatively subsidiary part in it.

(I) THE EARLY PERIOD

The first part of the story, down to Henry III's Sicilian venture, is mainly a chronicle of sporadic and unsystematic borrowing. There are, however, some exceptions and one of them is possibly to be found in the reign of Henry II. He dealt at first with a Fleming, William Cade of St Omer; there were also some substantial townsmen among Henry's English subjects, like the wealthy Londoner, Gervase of Cornhill, who in 1141 had

[1] All references in this section to unpublished sources refer to documents in the Public Record Office in London, unless otherwise indicated.

lent money to the wife of King Stephen at a crucial moment in the civil war in England. But it is unlikely that any English merchant of the time had resources comparable with those of Cade, to whom, at the time of his death around 1166, the large sum of about £5,000 was owed by a variety of debtors in Flanders, Normandy and especially England, including some very great men. Cade was a merchant as well as a financier, but a leading canonist, writing about 1200, found it suitable to choose him as the best example of an outstanding usurer, who had lent money to merchants trading in many lands.[1] Our sole evidence of Cade's dealings with Henry II consists of payments totalling some £5,600, received by Cade from various royal revenues between 1155 and 1165. In several years they ranged between £500 and £1,000. Very little is known about the precise nature of Cade's services to Henry II, but in view of Cade's other activities as a money-lender it can be reasonably conjectured that the royal payments to him were made in return for loans. Cade is certainly known to have financed the bringing of Flemish soldiers to England and he repeatedly paid for the passage between Dover and the Continent of persons connected with the Crown.[2]

Cade's disappearance from the records coincides with the first occurrence in the exchequer rolls of substantial disbursements to a number of English Jews. These payments, totalling at least £5,670 between 1165 and 1179, were probably made in return for loans.[3] The Jewish funds thus made available to Henry II were derived from the profits of money-lending to English landowners and ecclesiastics. All the leading Jewish financiers in England appear to have been closely connected with each other. Some idea of their resources is given by the sum of £15,000 owed by various borrowers to Aaron of Lincoln, one of the principal Jewish creditors of the Crown, at the time of his death in 1185.[4]

The loans from Jews largely ceased in the reigns of Henry's two sons, because there was evolved, instead, a regular system of exploiting the English Jews by taxes and fines at the will of the Crown. After a century of this regime the Jewish community in this country became so impoverished that it ceased to be of much value to the king and Edward I could expel all Jews from England in 1290 without a sense of serious financial loss.

King John, making the fullest use of the efficient machinery of government left by Henry II, was able, between 1206 and 1213, to achieve some-

---

[1] C. H. Haskins, 'William Cade', *Eng. Hist. Rev.* XXVIII (1913), 730–1.

[2] *Pipe Rolls 3–8 Henry II* (ed. Pipe Roll Society), *passim*; H. G. Richardson, 'The Chamber under Henry II', *Eng. Hist. Rev.* LXIX (1954), 605–11.

[3] *Pipe Rolls 9–25 Henry II*. Payments of £37 are recorded under 1163–4, rising sharply to £1,375 in 1165–6.

[4] J. Jacobs, 'Aaron of Lincoln', *Trans. of the Jewish Historical Society of England*, III (1899); G. Roth, *A History of the Jews in England* (Oxford, 1941), 14–16.

thing quite rare in the Middle Ages, the accumulation of a very considerable reserve treasure, amounting to at least £100,000. But John's financial independence was short-lived and his methods of achieving it contributed to the final revolt against him in 1215. The reign of his successor, Henry III, exemplifies well the financial dilemma confronting thirteenth-century monarchy. To try to achieve solvency by imitating the ruthless measures of John was likely to arouse dangerous opposition. Henry's ordinary revenue did not suffice to finance wars, but after 1237 Henry was never able to secure from the baronage grants of extraordinary aids on terms acceptable to him. Henry's wars, therefore, had to be financed by a variety of expedients, including much borrowing. Even in peaceful times the absence of reserves, the difficulties of ensuring a continuous supply of money all through the year, as well as of mobilizing resources quickly in moments of special need, involved Henry in frequent trouble and more borrowing. 'All the agitation and vexation of spirit of which we read was due to the hand-to-mouth way of living.'[1] It is true that Henry's troubles were made worse by his unpractical and spendthrift nature, but this must not obscure the fact that recurrent anticipation of revenue was in any case inevitable. In normal times there was nothing radically wrong with Henry's finances, 'Henry never complained that he was more than a year's normal revenue in arrears',[2] but in his position of political isolation, to be a year's normal revenue in arrears could be enough to paralyse the effectiveness of his government in times of crisis.

The large number and variety of royal creditors, as well as the paucity of the outstanding financiers among them, are the striking features of Henry's dealings with lenders before 1255. In England we encounter at various times during Henry's reign loans from the following: bishops and religious houses, the Templars and the Hospitallers, a few magnates, such rich Italian and other foreign merchants as happened to be active in England, as well as English townsmen, especially Londoners. It is significant that the most important lender between 1244 and 1255 was not a merchant, but the king's brother, Richard, earl of Cornwall. But he never lent more than £10,000 in any single year. Richard was a business-like man with large properties, including the lucrative Cornish tin-mines. He did not charge interest to his brother, but certain of his loans were repaid in ways calculated to assure him some gain. The most profitable of his numerous ventures is also the most significant economically. In 1247, in return for obtaining the farm of the royal mint, he undertook the recoinage of the entire English currency in order to produce improved coins.

[1] F. M. Powicke, *King Henry III and the Lord Edward*, 1 (Oxford, 1947), 305. The entire discussion of Henry's finances owes much to this work.

[2] Powicke, *op. cit.* 305.

He lent 10,000 marks (£6,666 13s. 4d.) to provide the initial stock of silver and made a profit of more than £11,000 on the whole operation. When recoinage was next attempted in 1279, important professional financiers were available to the Crown to carry out this task. It was then entrusted to Edward I's bankers, the Riccardi of Lucca, acting in conjunction with a leading London merchant, Gregory de Rokesle.

(2) THE ROYAL CREDIT SYSTEM AT ITS HEIGHT

In 1254 Henry III accepted the papal offer of the kingdom of Sicily; he was expected to finance an expedition to Italy and, in addition, to make large payments to the pope. The financial transactions that followed form a fantastic episode in Henry's reign. The papacy placed at his disposal the Tuscan companies employed as papal cameral merchants. During the next four years, before a baronial revolt in 1258 ended the whole scheme, at least £54,000 were borrowed by Henry in Italy. The same business group ultimately financed the successful conquest of Naples and Sicily by Charles of Anjou. But Henry's dealings with these bankers were doomed to financial disaster, because he did not possess in England any new resources out of which loans of this magnitude could be repaid. Nor was there the slightest chance that Henry would ever conquer the kingdom of Sicily and satisfy his creditors out of the revenues of his new domain, as Charles was able to do after 1266.

The Sicilian episode provided a practical demonstration of the great potential value of this newly arisen Italian business group. The lesson was grasped by Edward I. His experiences, during a lengthy absence abroad on crusade, in Italy and in France (1270–4)[1] confirmed him in his appreciation of the Italian financiers. After his return to England he continued to employ systematically one of the leading Italian firms who had already served him during his travels. But he did so in a way that avoided the mistakes of his father. Unlike Henry III, Edward could borrow successfully and regularly because he was able to acquire fresh sources of revenue. Administrative and constitutional changes within England played an important part in making this new development possible. The new king enforced effectively royal financial prerogatives and inaugurated in 1275, with the consent of parliament, a unified system of customs, with a duty on exported wool as its chief feature. Henceforth the customs were the revenue most often assigned to royal creditors in repayment of loans. The customs constituted the largest single source of regular royal income and the yield from them continued to increase throughout Edward's reign. In addition, until 1296 Edward I was able, when necessary, to secure

[1] Cf. wardrobe account of Philip de Willoughby, P.R.O., Pipe Roll 5 Edw. I, E. 372/121, m. 22; *Cal. Patent R. 1272–81*, 131–2.

grants of direct taxes, denied to his father between 1237 and 1269, and the yield from the levies collected before 1295 was exceptionally good. These taxes were used to extinguish larger debts that could not be repaid out of the regular revenues alone.

Thus Edward's increased use of credit facilities simply represented a more effective deployment of resources in themselves considerable. Regular borrowing, on a scale sufficiently large to increase appreciably royal resources at any given moment, became a normal feature of the royal finances. It was an expensive device, but Edward's ambitious policies were bound to be costly and this was the best method of financing them efficiently.

The English Crown chose its Italian bankers from among the most prominent firms of the time. In 1318, at a time when the ordinary revenue of Edward II probably did not surpass £30,000 a year, his main bankers, the Bardi of Florence, possessed total assets of 875,000 florins (c. £130,000). Italian firms of this stature could afford to be easy-going in their relations with royal clients. Relations between the English government and its chief lenders were often very informal. Thus Edward I's Household Ordinance of 1279 named Orlandino de Podio, at that time the head of the Lucchese company of the Riccardi in England, among eight prominent household officials entitled, when at court, to sleep in the king's wardrobe. Some of the tasks entrusted to the regular royal bankers went, indeed, considerably beyond the mere function of providing money. For example, during eight months in 1338-9, the Bardi maintained spies in Normandy and Flanders who reported to Edward III about French naval preparations.[1]

The English kings, like the popes and other European rulers, made good use of the network of branches and business correspondents possessed by the Italian firms in all the more important centres of western Europe. 'Cause the companions of your company staying at Naples to pay the equivalent of 1,000 marks sterling' begins a royal mandate to the London Bardi, when making arrangements for the bringing to England from Italy of one of the reputed murderers of Edward II. But the major part of the money demanded from these regular lenders was usually needed in England particularly for the expenses of the king's household. The distribution of the money supplied by lenders can be illustrated from the relatively peaceful and normal period between August 1328 and October 1331. During this time Edward III's government borrowed £45,548. About a third (£15,528) was provided by the Bardi for payments abroad. £21,644 were needed for the upkeep of the royal household and the Bardi also supplied the court with goods valued at £2,312.

[1] P.R.O., K.R. Exchequer Accounts Various, E. 101/127/32.

There is a good deal of information about the profits of the leading royal creditors in the first half of the fourteenth century. Agreements with lenders repeatedly stipulated that, in the words of one of them, 'the King will have regard both to the sum of money thus paid or to be paid . . . and to the damages and expenses sustained . . . by reason of this service'.[1] An informal agreement with the Frescobaldi expands this into a promise to repay 'the damages' that their firm 'will show in good faith' it had thus incurred.[2] The compensation chiefly took the form of 'gifts' of money conceded periodically to the lenders by the king, for which formal royal bonds were issued, and these were treated as part of the aggregate royal debt. On a total debt of £42,000 owed to the Bardi by Edward III, as the result of transactions with them between August 1328 and October 1331, their firm was granted 'gifts' of £11,000. This amounts to a rate of 26%. In this particular case, by February 1332 the Bardi appear to have recovered not only all their advances of the past three years but also to have been paid some 'gifts' as well. The amount of interest actually cashed by them by that date might have covered, in large part or even entirely, the cost of all the Bardi establishments in England between 1328 and 1331. In favourable circumstances profits from regular credit transactions with the Crown were thus likely to defray much of the overhead expenses of a firm's entire activities in England, including its private business as wool exporters, general merchants and financiers. The royal bankers had also important advantages over other merchants. The indirect benefits from having a specially protected and privileged position in the country were considerable. The English kings realized that it was in the royal interest that the private business of their bankers should expand and took active measures to help them. Thus Edward III, in renewing to the Bardi the invaluable privilege of using the machinery of the exchequer to enforce the collection of private debts due to them in England, stressed that their firm could not help him adequately unless they were able to collect such debts efficiently.

The history of the dealings of Edward I and his two successors with lenders, while revealing how effective government credit operations could be in medieval conditions, also illustrates the fragility of this edifice of credit. The stability and success of the first twenty years of Edward I's reign were, in some measure, due to the financial solvency which the employment of the Riccardi of Lucca helped to ensure. Their firm played a vital part in financing Edward's conquest of Wales. Edward's aggregate debts to the Riccardi amounted between 1272 and 1294 to at least £392,000, though this figure may include an element of interest. Repayment came chiefly out of Edward's new financial assets. Nearly half the

[1] *Cal. Close R. 1330–33*, 280 (agreement with the Bardi).
[2] P.R.O., Parliamentary and Council Proceedings, C. 49/4/7 (August 1309).

royal debt to them was repaid out of the customs, which were entirely in the hands of the Riccardi from 1275 to 1294. Direct taxation provided much of the remainder; from the 'fifteenth' of 1275 alone the Riccardi received £97,000.[1] Their dealings with Edward I came to an abrupt end in the summer of 1294, after the outbreak of the Anglo-French war. Edward's war measures, especially the seizure by him in June 1294 of the wool of all merchants, embarrassed the Riccardi. Simultaneously, Philip IV of France seized all the agents and assets of the Riccardi in his kingdom on the ground that their firm was helping his English enemy and he extorted a huge fine from them. These events precipitated a mass withdrawal of deposits entrusted to their firm and their credit was seriously undermined. The obvious distress of the Riccardi may have convinced Edward I that their society could be of little further use to him; at any rate, on 29 July 1294, he deprived them of control over the customs[2] and soon afterwards their assets in England were requisitioned by his orders. This happened at a time when the war with France caused the greatest crisis of Edward's reign. He was in desperate need of money. He had promised large subsidies to his continental allies and, in addition, he had to fight campaigns in Wales and Scotland. But throughout the period of his worst necessity between 1294 and 1298 he could not find a substitute for the Riccardi. The Frescobaldi of Florence, who had been active in England since the 'seventies, began to lend to Edward in 1296, but, during the next two crucial years, they were unable to provide more than c. £7,000 on the Continent,[3] where much larger sums were needed. The loans raised from other lenders abroad, including several English merchants trading in the Netherlands, did not amount to much. The later claim of the Frescobaldi, that various depositors withdrew some 50,000 florins (at least £7,500) from their firm 'because of the great loan which they had made the king in Flanders and at Florence', appears to refer to this period. Edward I was driven to finance his wars through a series of extraordinary measures which caused a serious constitutional crisis in England in 1297. His difficulties at home contributed to the failure of his expedition to the Netherlands in the same year, and the after-effects of this crisis hampered Edward for the rest of his reign.

The Frescobaldi acted as chief royal bankers between 1299 and 1311. They claimed in 1302 that, up to that time, they had advanced £32,886, while accounts rendered in 1310 reveal loans totalling at least £120,000,

[1] All the figures concerning Edward I's dealings with the Riccardi are based on a series of royal accounts with their firm which is complete except for one gap. P.R.O., Exchequer Accounts Various, E. 101/126/1; Pipe Rolls (E. 372), nos. 123, 124, 125, 133, 134 and 143.
[2] P.R.O., K.R. Memoranda Roll, E. 159/68, m. 82d.
[3] P.R.O., Exchequer Accounts Various, E. 101/126, nos. 13 and 15.

almost all of it lent since the estimate of 1302.[1] Their advances helped Edward to continue the war with Scotland, but his finances were in increasing disorder during the last decade of the reign. Since the beginning of a period of almost continuous warfare in 1294, the royal practice of purchase or seizure on credit of goods and means of transport from merchants and others had assumed huge proportions. As the king's financial difficulties deepened, payment for ordinary purchases for the court likewise increasingly lagged behind. At Edward I's death in 1307 at least £60,000 were owed by the treasurer of the king's household. Many of these debts were never satisfied. This sort of disguised bankruptcy, hitting not the king's chief bankers but multitudes of humbler men, henceforth became a recurrent feature of royal finances, especially in wartime.

The more powerful groups among the creditors were able to exert pressure. The shipowners and wine merchants of Bayonne secured control over the entire English customs between 1299 and 1302 in repayment of debts totalling £45,000.[2] The Frescobaldi fared best of all in this matter of repayment. Much of the royal revenue passed continually into their hands; customs at all harbours were under their control for eight years. At the completion of their last account with the Crown in 1310, the Frescobaldi were owed £21,635, but interest and compensation for losses accounted for £12,000 out of this total. It was not a crushing debt. The system of regular Crown borrowing from major financiers was, therefore, still working fairly well when a political revolution in 1311 temporarily destroyed it. The wealth of the Frescobaldi and their influence at court had made them many enemies. Also, in demanding their expulsion, the baronial opposition was trying to render Edward II financially helpless. Members of the society had to save themselves by a precipitate flight from England. The royal debt to them was never repaid and their expulsion from what had become the chief sphere of their activities, joined to other misfortunes on the Continent, led to a speedy bankruptcy. No wonder that the poet Giovanni Frescobaldi should later have warned his compatriots active in England, 'Do not have any dealings with the men of the court.'

The fate of the Frescobaldi did not, however, deter other Italians for long. While Edward II, threatened with imminent baronial attack, was sheltering in northern England in the early months of 1312, a Genoese, Antonio Pessagno, was willing to supply him with goods on credit and with some loans as well. After Edward's power was partly re-established

---

[1] P.R.O., Enrolled Account of the Frescobaldi, Pipe Roll, E. 372/154; Receipt and Issue Rolls for 1304–10; Warrants for Issue (Exchequer of Receipt) for the reigns of Edward I and II (E. 404/1 and E. 404/481–5); Exchequer Accounts Various, E. 101/126/9; Brit. Mus., Cottonian MS. Nero C. VIII, m. 5d.

[2] Ch. Bémont, Rôles Gascons, III (Paris, 1906), clxxi.

in the later part of 1312, Pessagno's advances increased. He was a new-comer, belonging to a family very active in the newly developed Genoese maritime trade to Flanders and England. He may have been actuated by a desire to establish his position at all costs. This could not be the motive of the great Florentine society of the Bardi, which began to lend to Edward II regularly from the autumn of 1312 onwards. Nor is it likely that in deciding to enter the royal service the Bardi were primarily influenced by a desire to secure the repayment of royal debts already owed to them, for in October 1312 these debts were not considerable.[1] Prospective profits from credit dealings with the king probably formed the main incentive. The Bardi remained the chief lenders for the rest of the reign. The value of their firm was recognized by the men who govern-ed England after the violent overthrow of Edward II in 1326, and when yet another revolution in 1330 gave personal power to Edward III, he likewise continued to employ the Bardi. They had become part of the normal arrangements of government and, like the personnel of the ad-ministration, were little affected by political upheavals.

The early years of Edward III's reign, until the outbreak of the war with France, were the last period during which the system of regular borrowing from a single great lender, or a pair of such lenders, func-tioned normally. The ordinary revenue did not usually surpass £30,000 a year. It was a period of continuous but moderate borrowing, ranging on the average between some £12,000 and £20,000 a year, involving an annual interest charge of perhaps £4,000. The customs continued to provide the most important regular security for repayment; in 1328–31, out of the total debt of some £56,000 incurred to lenders during this time, debts amounting to £21,000 were repaid from this source. The proceeds of direct taxation formed the ultimate reserve. Every few years Edward III was able to secure a grant of a lay or ecclesiastical subsidy, often the two together. Such a joint grant was likely to yield about £57,000, which would generally suffice to discharge his outstanding liabilities. The whole system depended for its proper functioning on the king's capacity to collaborate with his parliaments and with ecclesiastical convocations, but at the same time his ability to draw upon powerful lenders strength-ened his hands for dealing with parliament.

When the war with France began in 1337 high hopes were attached to the possibilities of exploiting England's chief economic asset, its mono-poly of supplying fine wool, particularly to the great industrial areas in the Low Countries. Edward III started with the initial advantage of hav-ing the full support of the Florentine bankers, which Edward I had lacked at the critical moment. Edward III also secured the help of English mer-

[1] P.R.O., Enrolled Account of the Bardi, Pipe Roll 6 Edward III (E. 372/158) and K.R. Memoranda Roll 5 Edward II, E. 159/85, m. 55 (*Recorda*, Trinity term).

chants, in part through tempting them with the possibilities of establishing
a greater measure of native control over the wool trade. While it is probably true that a crisis in royal finances comparable to that of 1337 would
have given English merchants similar opportunities at an earlier date,
Edward III was certainly dealing with an exceptionally enterprising
group of businessmen. For the first time English merchants became a
serious alternative source of credit for the Crown. The support of the
Florentine and the English financiers helped Edward III substantially in
negotiating further loans in the Netherlands and the Rhineland. No
medieval English ruler ever borrowed so much in a comparably short
time as did Edward between 1337 and 1340. The king's council was not
exaggerating when, in October 1339, it estimated royal indebtedness
at over £300,000. By 1340, however, Edward's credit sank very low.
The Bardi and the Peruzzi were exhausted after advancing more than
£125,000 in 1338–9. The great English merchant, William de la Pole of
Hull, who had raised for the king over £100,000 in the same period, in
large part by borrowing from Englishmen and foreigners in the Netherlands, refused further loans. The year ended in royal bankruptcy,
amidst a violent political crisis in England.

One of the important consequences of this episode was the serious
damage to the financial position of the Bardi and the Peruzzi. Their connection with the English Crown was known throughout Europe; in
October 1338 the Peruzzi considered it necessary to send a special ship
from Italy to their branch in Rhodes with information about the progress of the Anglo-French war, presumably to counter damaging rumours.[1] Edward III was in no position to repay speedily the large debts he
owed to the two firms and he had little inducement to help them, as their
loans virtually ceased after 1342. The Peruzzi with other Florentine firms
went bankrupt in the following year; the Bardi held out until 1346.
While financial and political difficulties in Italy were the immediate
cause of this collapse of Florentine companies, the entanglement of the
Bardi and the Peruzzi with the English king undoubtedly played an important part in weakening them. In 1345 Edward III owed the Bardi
£63,000 for advances made to him and at least £40,000 more for interest.[2] The Peruzzi appear to have been owed some £44,000 for loans and
at least £27,000 for interest.[3] The representatives of the Bardi in England
were arrested shortly before the bankruptcy of the firm and were released

[1] A. Sapori, *I libri di commercio dei Peruzzi* (Milan, 1934), 181.

[2] P.R.O., Exchequer Accounts Various, E. 101/126/3; *Cal. Patent R. 1343–45*,
467–9 and Chancery Miscellanea, C. 47/13/12; A. Beardwood, *Alien Merchants in
England 1350–1377* (Cambridge, Mass., 1931), Appendix A.

[3] P.R.O., Exchequer Accounts Various, E. 101/127/36; Pipe Roll 20 Edward III,
m. 35; Chancery Miscellanea, C. 47/13/11.

only on condition that they renounced all claims to payment of interest.[1]

No other Italian firm succeeded to the position held by the Bardi and the Peruzzi in royal service. Several other, lesser Italian financiers continued to have dealings with the Crown, but none of them was of much importance during the rest of the reign of Edward III. The disappearance of the Bardi and the Peruzzi gave English merchants the opportunity to replace them as the chief royal bankers. A succession of syndicates was organized by leading English merchants for this purpose. It looked as if a class of great English capitalists had suddenly arisen. But an analysis of the sources of their financial power should modify such an impression. With the exception of William de la Pole, Henry Picard and perhaps one or two others, the members and supporters of these syndicates were not very wealthy. The capacity of the syndicates to raise considerable sums was largely bound up with their possession of special financial and trading privileges. They lacked large initial capital resources, such as the Italian companies had normally possessed at the time of their entry into royal service. The English syndicates had, therefore, to be endowed by Edward III with assets on the security of which they might try to borrow money in England or abroad, so that they could then lend this money to the king. Thus the company headed by Walter Cheriton borrowed at least £53,000 in two and a half years. In the first place the syndicates were conceded the entire revenue from customs, for which they had to pay a fixed sum of £50,000 a year. At the increased wartime rate of duty on exported wool, this should have left them an appreciable margin of profit. Their control over the customs also facilitated borrowing. Favoured creditors could be promised exemptions from the payment of customs or allowed to export at privileged rates of duty. During certain periods the syndicates also enjoyed the monopoly of the export of wool. On various occasions in 1347–9 embargoes on the export of wool were imposed by the king at the request of Walter Cheriton and his associates, so that they might be able to buy wool more cheaply in England and resell it at higher prices abroad.

Furthermore the king tried to exploit the fact that since the outbreak of the war in 1337 a very considerable number of debts had been incurred by the Crown, both as a result of loans and purchases of goods on credit and through the failure to pay wages to soldiers and officials. The first English syndicate was organized in 1343 by a considerable group of leading merchants largely in the hope of securing the repayment of debts owed to themselves. Soon the idea arose of allowing the farmers of customs to relieve the king of other debts as well, by buying them up at a discount and securing an allowance in their farm of customs for the full face-value of the debts so redeemed. Thus, John Wesenham owed to

[1] P.R.O., Parliamentary and Council Proceedings, C. 49/7, no. 17.

the king for the farm of the customs during fifteen months (in 1345–6) £62,000. But he was allowed to contribute £20,000 out of this total in restored royal bonds, so that he was obliged to provide in cash only £42,000. The profits of the syndicates thus largely depended on the rate of discount at which they could acquire royal obligations. In 1352 the exchequer officials, in auditing the accounts connected with these transactions, accepted the testimony of several trustworthy witnesses that normally 2s. or 2s. 6d. in the pound was paid, but seldom more.[1] By conceding to lenders the right to obtain profits in this way, Edward III was avoiding the necessity of paying them much interest on their advances. Royal debts amounting to at least £80,000 were extinguished in this manner between 1343 and 1352.

The English syndicates drew their capital, in the first place, from a wide circle of English merchants. All the firms that succeeded each other between 1343 and 1351 had their headquarters in London, but Londoners were only one of the several merchant groups concerned with these schemes. William de la Pole, who was alleged by many merchants to have initiated the whole idea, was the most prominent of a group of northerners, enriched by supplying the English forces fighting against the Scots as well as by trade in Yorkshire and Lincolnshire wool. The brothers Melchebourn and John Wesenham, who played a leading part between 1343 and 1346, came from East Anglian ports. The last syndicate of Walter Cheriton and Thomas Swanland, citizens of London, frequently employed, for the purpose of transferring money to Bruges, an important group of northern wool exporters headed by John Goldbeter of York. The syndicates also borrowed money from Hanseatic and Italian merchants active in England and funds were raised on several occasions in the great money market of Bruges. The English companies thus drew on all the chief sources of capital available in north-western Europe.

For a few years these arrangements proved adequate to satisfy Edward III's immediate financial needs. The English syndicates financed the Crécy campaign in 1346 and the prolonged siege of Calais that followed. While all went well merchants were keen to secure the farm of customs and in 1346 they were outbidding each other in the offers they made to the king. The whole scheme was ruined by the epidemic of plague that reached England by the autumn of 1348. The last company of Walter Cheriton, who farmed the customs at that time, was too enfeebled by excessive commitments and unlucky speculations to weather this unexpected storm. It did not collapse at once, but it could not get out of debts incurred in 1348–9. The king ruthlessly exacted the debts owed by it and

---

[1] *Testatum est per plures fidedignos quod communiter libra empta fuit pro IIs. et IIs. VId. et raro ad plus.* P.R.O., K.R. Customs Accounts, E. 122/158/37.

ts final bankruptcy ruined several important merchants as well as many lesser men. For the time being the great financiers were largely discredited. Their ruthless exploitation of the licences to redeem royal bonds had made them very unpopular and serious frauds were discovered. Such was the dislike of the way in which the syndicates had exploited their control over the wool trade, that in 1353 parliament prohibited altogether the export of wool by Englishmen to prevent the renewal of similar monopoly schemes, so that, for a few years, the trade passed wholly into the hands of foreign exporters.

(3) THE ROYAL CREDIT SYSTEM IN DECLINE

The discrediting and ruin of the English syndicates had lasting consequences. While important English financiers were not wholly lacking in the second half of Edward III's reign, most leading English businessmen were now afraid to become too closely involved in dealings with the Crown. There was also the discouraging realization that the open pursuit of profit out of lending to the king involved unwelcome publicity and unpopularity, and made a merchant very vulnerable to prosecution by the Crown once his usefulness was ended. The behaviour of Henry Picard of London illustrates well the more cautious attitude of English financiers. He was one of the wealthiest merchants of his time and he had derived much profit in the past from the operations of Wesenham and Cheriton. But by remaining always in the background, he escaped being involved in the ruin of Cheriton's associates and continued to avoid dangerous commitments thereafter. A Londoner, Richard Lyons, found comparatively little support in his attempt to revive the farm of the customs in the last years of Edward III's reign. He agreed to advance loans on the security of the customs in return for permission to redeem old royal debts. A group of leading Londoners strongly opposed him. Lyons possessed little capital of his own and his loans were partly financed by certain courtiers and magnates who hoped to share in his profits. This was one of the features of the scheme that obviously lent itself to charges of corruption. During the political crisis of 1376 Lyons's alleged malpractices figured prominently in the parliamentary proceedings. He was put on trial and convicted; his fate served as a fresh warning of the dangers inherent in large-scale financial dealings with the Crown. The cautious attitude of the majority of English merchants is well illustrated by an incident in the parliament of 1382. To a request for a large loan on the security of the customs, the merchants there present replied that they neither wished nor dared to lend in this manner, for fear that they might suffer the fate of Pole, Cheriton and other promoters of the syndicates who, as the merchants put it, for having advanced money to the king 'for a little gain', were later maliciously prosecuted and some were 'utterly destroyed'. Most foreign merchants gradually learnt the same lesson. For the sixty years of the Lancastrian rule in England, the surviving exchequer receipt rolls record loans from aliens amounting to no more than £26,500, and part of this money was advanced only under duress.

After 1352 Edward III had to manage his affairs without regular borrowing from important financiers. Fortunately for Edward, his other resources were now considerably larger than they had been at the beginning of his reign. The great epidemic of 1348–9 had no disastrous effect on royal revenue. The export of wool soon returned to its former high level and already in the fiscal year 1350–1 the customs yielded £78,900. Money received from the ransoms of war captives helped to save Edward from financial embarrassment after the return of peace in the 'sixties. Under these conditions borrowing could be reduced to the role of a casual expedient; purchase of supplies for the household on credit remained, of course, a constant feature. But credit arrangements which were adapted to a period of financial ease proved wholly inadequate when the financial position of the royal government deteriorated, as it did during the minority of Richard II and again under the Lancastrians. It was then that the inability of the Crown to secure help from outstanding professional financiers began to be seriously felt.

The reluctance of merchants to deal with the Crown was only one of the causes of the difficulties experienced by Edward III's successors in raising loans. General economic changes were affecting adversely the Crown's capacity to borrow and its ability to find substantial lenders. During the fifty years between the Black Death and the deposition of Richard II, English wool exports declined by about a third and they were further reduced by more than a half during the sixty years of the Lancastrian rule. Consequently, between 1350 and 1430, the royal income from the customs was halved and the amount of royal revenue that could be *regularly* anticipated was much reduced. Cloth began to replace wool as the most important English export. But English cloth, unlike wool, had to remain cheap if it was to be sold abroad successfully and no attempt was ever made in the Middle Ages to impose heavy duties on it. These changes in the structure of the English trade, in conjunction with transformations in the agrarian economy of the country, produced a decline in the wealth of the English merchants. Englishmen now controlled the bulk of the declining wool trade, but English wool exporters were fewer in number and appear to have possessed smaller resources than their predecessors before the outbreak of the Hundred Years War. In the first half of the fifteenth century the export trade in cloth did not, as yet, lend itself easily to monopoly arrangements of the sort that had allowed Edward III to borrow heavily from the wool merchants. 'Indeed the whole age is that of merchants tuned to a lower scale.'[1] Deprived of the support of foreign merchants, the English Crown had to depend on loans from its own subjects, but in the fifteenth century none of them, with the exception of some prelates and magnates, could lend very much.

This dependence of the English kings in the later fourteenth and the fifteenth centuries on borrowing from native lenders, drawn from all sections of the propertied classes, was bound to affect their relations with all the groups whose political support they needed. It is, therefore, very important to know whether satisfactory remuneration was normally promised to the native lenders. Unfortunately, evidence is almost wholly lacking. Very occasionally it is possible to show that a merchant was granted special trading privileges in return for his loans. It has been suggested that royal bonds given to these native lenders frequently credited them with more than they had actually advanced, in which case the sums entered as loans on the exchequer receipt rolls, our main source of information, are a record of what the king owed and not what he had really borrowed.[2] This is possibly a correct description of what may have been done in several cases. When we find a wealthy London alderman, like the famous mercer, Richard Whittington, credited in exchequer records with £13,700 as a result of ten different loans, spread over the years 1400 to 1413, we are probably justified in assuming that he derived some advantage from these transactions. But it is improbable that all lenders were treated alike in this matter of profit. In any case, many Crown creditors were far more preoccupied with the dangers of loss than with the possibilities of financial gain. Throughout the fourteenth and the fifteenth centuries the royal debts habitually surpassed the revenues available for their repayment and each creditor had to use all his influence and ingenuity to assure for himself preferential treatment in order to receive anything at all. Even very important men might have much difficulty in securing, within reasonable time, the integral payment of the sums owed to them.

All medieval governments were inclined to be unscrupulous when dealing with their creditors. But there seems to be some justification for the view that the attitude of the English Crown to royal debts deteriorated in the late Middle Ages. Edward III did, at least, express in his will the hope that his successor would assume responsibility for the debts incurred for the needs of the State, as opposed to his personal debts which were to be settled by his executors. Richard II's high-handed proceedings in the last two years of his reign seem to have aroused apprehension among

[1] E. Power, *The Wool Trade in English Medieval History* (Oxford, 1941), 121.

[2] K. B. McFarlane, 'Loans to the Lancastrian Kings: the problem of inducement', *Cambridge Historical Journal*, IX, no. 1 (1947). The discussion of this problem in A. Steel, *The Receipt of the Exchequer, 1377–1485*, 18–20, is unsatisfactory.

FF

sections of the propertied classes, and his opponents made it one of the
charges against him that he had never intended to repay the loans contracted during those years. Yet Henry IV, though he tried to profit from
this propaganda, made no attempt to honour the debts of the monarch
whom he had deposed. The Lancastrians displayed a short-sighted attitude to the problem of maintaining royal credit. Henry V failed to pay
most of the debts of his father. By 1422 the executors of Henry IV's will
had only received £4,000 towards the payment of his debts, out of the
25,000 marks (£16,666) promised in 1413. During the minority of Henry
VI, there were long delays before adequate provision was made for satisfying the creditors of his grandfather and father.[1] The resulting distrust of
royal promises was at the root of the inability of the Lancastrian kings to
raise sufficient loans.

The king's recurrent need of hasty borrowing to make urgent payments was well described during a governmental inquiry in 1362. 'Sometimes money to make payments must be borrowed of men in the said
city [of London] and elsewhere and payment hastily made ... for divers
the king's business and for taking journeys ... as well after noon as before,
and sometimes by night.'[2] Much of this business fell into the hands of the
Londoners. This may have been one of the more lasting effects of the
episode of the English syndicates, which accustomed the Crown to the
raising of money through the London business community. Londoners
were more likely to secure repayment than most other lenders, because
they had exceptional opportunities for becoming familiar with exchequer officials and their methods. Whittington was one of the very few
persons who recovered from Henry IV the loans he had advanced to
Richard II. Some of the most important Londoners lent money fairly
often under Richard II and the first two Lancastrian kings, but no single
loan ever exceeded £4,000. Individual Londoners and the municipality
of London together contributed between 33% and 40% of all the loans
recorded on the exchequer receipt rolls in the reign of Richard II and
more than half of the loans recorded there under Henry IV.

The permanent establishment of the exchequer and other departments
of the central government in London after 1338 and their continued presence there, at a time when royal income and expenditure were higher
than ever in the past, presented Londoners with enhanced opportunities
for a variety of profitable dealings with the Crown. Simple money-
lending to the government was only one of several possible types of business and probably not the most lucrative. There were complicated dealings in connection with the ransoms of royal prisoners and some Londoners advanced considerable sums to the important captives, like King

[1] J. S. Roskell, *The Commons in the Parliament of 1422* (Manchester, 1954), 118–20.
[2] *Cal. Close R. 1364–68*, 119.

John of France.[1] Some of the London financiers engaged in the lucrative business of buying up, at a discount, the assignments on future revenues given to royal creditors by the exchequer. The recipients of these assignments not infrequently preferred to receive some ready cash from these middlemen, rather than to face the uncertainties and delays of collecting personally the money promised them by the government. The business of supplying on credit precious metals to the royal mint in the Tower of London offered yet another field for profitable speculations. Londoners achieved a predominance in English foreign trade and a superiority over all other groups of English merchants only in the century following on the outbreak of the Hundred Years War. The existence in London of varied opportunities for financial business with the royal government contributed in some measure to this development. These opportunities increased as a result of the prolonged war in France, and in the late Middle Ages they were for the first time exploited mainly by Londoners rather than by foreign merchants.

In the fifteenth century, Londoners formed the most influential group among the exporters of English wool, organized into the Company of the Staple at Calais. There was, thus, a close connection between advances by Londoners and advances by the Staple in its corporate capacity. The earliest loan by the Staple, as opposed to loans by individual wool merchants, arose out of an emergency in 1407. On that occasion, the garrison of Calais mutinied and seized the accumulated wool in an effort to recover arrears of wages; the Staple had to advance £8,000 to recover the merchandise of its members. This only served to encourage a number of similar mutinies during the later years of the Lancastrian regime. The huge loan of £43,000 advanced by the Staple between 1454 and 1456, the largest it ever made, was the result of a similar occurrence. Fairly regular lending by the Staple began in 1430. One of the chief reasons was the recurrent need to bribe the Crown in order to persuade it to respect the privileges of the Staplers. After 1448, when one English possession in France after another was being lost, the need to assure the defence of Calais prompted the Staple to advance loans more generously. This was, likewise, the only object for which Londoners were still willing to lend money to the Lancastrian government.[2] In the civil war that followed soon after, the Staple lent to anybody who, for the time being, could protect Calais.

It was a source of weakness to English governments in the later fourteenth century and under the Lancastrian dynasty that, whenever they

---

[1] L. Douët d'Arcq, *Comptes de l'Argenterie des rois de France au XIVe siècle* (Paris, 1851), 235, 237–8, 270.

[2] M. I. Peake, *London and the Wars of the Roses, 1445–61* (M.A. thesis, University of London, 1925).

needed to borrow considerable sums, the money had usually to be sought, in part at least, from others than merchants. Important magnates and prelates figure prominently as lenders during this period and some of them exploited this situation for their own political ends. This is best exemplified by the story of Bishop Beaufort of Winchester. He started his career as a lender in order to extricate himself from political difficulties with his nephew, Henry V. Beaufort's loans proved indispensable during the minority of Henry VI, and he exploited this to preserve and to increase his control over the government. His aggregate loans to the Lancastrian rulers slightly surpassed £200,000. More than half of this amount was advanced between 1432 and 1444 in an effort to avert defeats in France. It is probable that Beaufort also derived financial profit from his loans. In 1421, when most of his treasure was probably in Henry V's hands, he was owed by Henry £26,000; this was the largest amount ever due to Beaufort by the Crown at any single moment. By the time of Beaufort's death in 1447, his treasure amounted to at least twice as much (roughly equalling the king's average annual revenue). Beaufort was almost invariably able to assure speedy repayment of his advances. He exploited his position as a leading royal councillor to detain permanently valuable crown jewels pledged to him for a loan. The same dependence on over-mighty subjects was characteristic of Crown finance during the subsequent years of the Wars of the Roses. Between 1452 and 1475 magnates advanced more money than any other group of lenders except the Staple: both Lancastrian and Yorkist kings were financed chiefly by their respective partisans in the civil war.

In the later fourteenth and fifteenth centuries, generalized levies of loans from municipalities and wealthier individuals throughout England became one of the normal fiscal devices. This was not wholly an innovation. But in the late Middle Ages such levies were much more frequent and important. This was the only way in which the Crown could supplement the usually inadequate sums that native merchants and magnates might be persuaded to lend. A combination of two methods was used. Requests were sent to selected persons asking them to lend specified sums. In times of special need commissions were appointed to raise loans in every county. These levies were undoubtedly unpopular. If we are to believe hostile chroniclers, a certain amount of pressure was exerted at times to induce people to contribute. For example, this was alleged to have happened during Richard II's 'tyranny'. But there is much evidence to show that men usually felt quite free to refuse to advance money or made loans only on conditions of their own choosing. Many lenders agreed to advance only their quota of a future tax. Most of the general levies of loans were only raised in anticipation of a direct tax that had already been granted by parliament.

The absence in England of permanent taxes other than customs pre-vented the growth in this country of the local bureaucracy of professional financial officials, who in France played such an important part in finan-cing the king with their loans. The French receivers of the extraordinary revenues and the more important farmers of the indirect taxes had a sufficiently permanent and assured position to be able to raise consider-able sums on the security of the revenues controlled by them, and to make large and frequent advances to the French Crown. In England no general levy of loans ever yielded as much as a single 'tenth and fifteenth' (not more than £38,000). If exceptionally important lenders, like the Staple or Beaufort, are left out of account, the Crown never raised in this man-ner above £20,000 in any single year. It may be that the reluctance of parliaments to make grants, the diminishing yield of taxes in the fifteenth century and the smallness of the sums that could be borrowed in England, all had their deep-rooted cause in the economic difficulties experienced by Englishmen in the later Middle Ages. But the purely political causes of the weakness of the Lancastrian regime must not be overlooked. It is sig-nificant that Henry V, the only able and popular ruler of the Lancastrian house, was fairly successful in securing grants of taxes and raising loans.

The absence of an efficient system of borrowing was one of the more serious weaknesses of the royal finances in the last century of the Middle Ages. Henry IV's difficulties sprang partly from his inability to borrow as much as he required. When things were at their worst, in 1402–5, com-manders of royal forces in Wales were driven to raise loans by pawning their jewels or pledging their private estates.[1] Only a small number of lenders, mostly Londoners, were willing to risk money in regular ad-vances to Henry IV. His son was much more successful in raising loans throughout the country. But Henry V's remarkable victories gave Englishmen a false sense of security. The government was unable to se-cure a single grant of direct taxation in England between 1422 and 1428. The ordinary royal revenue, which averaged about £57,000 a year around 1433, was almost entirely absorbed by the ordinary expenses of government in England. In 1433 the debt of the English government to lenders amounted to just under £20,000, while arrears of annuities and other old debts were estimated by the treasurer at £88,000.[2] The situa-tion was deteriorating, but did not yet seem hopeless; fairly low but regular taxation, while the hostilities lasted, would have made the prob-lem of financing the war manageable. The 'thirties were a period of such

---

[1] *Proceedings and Ordinances of the Privy Council of England* (ed. Sir H. Nicolas), I, 231–2, 266–74; II, 63.

[2] J. L. Kirby, 'The Issues of the Lancastrian Exchequer and Lord Cromwell's Esti-mates of 1433', *Bulletin of the Institute of Historical Research*, XXIV (1951). I owe thanks to Mr Kirby for much valuable information and advice about this period.

military disaster that it temporarily shook even parliaments into granting taxes more frequently and generously. This provided added security for loans. Beaufort alone advanced at least £91,500 between 1432 and 1442. The annual average of loans recorded on exchequer receipt rolls during this decade rose to the considerable figure of £25,000. But this exceptional effort could not be maintained. By the later 'forties the Lancastrian government had become too unpopular to be able to secure sufficient taxes. Its debts, according to one estimate, amounted in 1449 to £372,000. The business community was becoming indifferent to the fate of the regime and had lost all trust in it: the repeated refusals of Londoners to lend money to Henry VI during the last disastrous campaigns in France in 1448–53 show this very clearly. The financial bankruptcy of the Lancastrian monarchy was as complete on the eve of the Wars of the Roses as was its political collapse.

In finance, as in other matters, a fresh start was made by Edward IV. 'I purpose to lyve uppon my nowne', he told the Commons in 1467. These words expressed Edward's determination to exploit more effectively royal possessions and prerogatives. More could be expected from Crown lands, but a radical change in administrative methods was needed if royal estates were again to become the mainstay of the king's finances. Edward achieved this. It has been estimated that his brother, Richard III, may have enjoyed at his accession an annual net income of at least £25,000 from his lands alone.[1]

In his earlier years, when his needs often outran his resources, Edward IV had to borrow frequently and from a wide variety of lenders. The Londoners and the Staplers appear to have preferred Edward to the last Lancastrian governments. In agreeing to assume responsibility for Henry VI's debts to the Staplers, Edward showed that he understood clearly how indispensable the Staple's help had become for the preservation of Calais. This was formally recognized in the so-called Act of Retainer of 1466 which, with some modifications, remained in force until the loss of Calais by England in 1558. Under this arrangement the Staple assumed complete responsibility for the cost of maintaining Calais and, in return, was conceded the farm of all the revenue from the customs on wool exported to Calais. This was expected to bring in annually about £15,000. The Company was to recover gradually out of this sum the outstanding royal debts, which in 1464 amounted to £32,800. These were small sums when compared with the £240,000 supplied by Cheri-

---

[1] B. P. Wolffe, 'The management of English Royal Estates under the Yorkist Kings', *Eng. Hist. Rev.* LXXI (1956), 19–20. By comparison, net royal revenue from lands was estimated fifty years earlier, in 1433, by the king's treasurer at *c.* £8,000. See J. L. Kirby, 'The Issues of the Lancastrian Exchequer and Lord Cromwell's Estimates of 1433', *Bulletin of the Institute of Historical Research*, XXIV (1951), 132–3.

ton and his associates between 1346 and 1351, when they were farming
the customs for £50,000 a year. The revenue from the customs had
shrunk drastically during the intervening century. Even the arrangement of 1466 proved very precarious and soon broke down for a time
because of the inadequacy of revenue from the customs during a period
of disturbed trade. Edward even managed to tap effectively sources of
credit denied to his immediate predecessors. For the first time since the
reign of Richard II, sizable loans were obtained from the Italian businessmen in England. Edward established friendly relations with Gerard
Caniziani, one of the senior factors of the firm of the Medici in England.
Caniziani's willingness to lend money to the English king caused much
uneasiness to his employers, and losses on these loans were the chief cause
of the winding up of the London branch of the Medici after 1471. But
Caniziani's advances helped to tide Edward over some of the most critical
years of his life.

In the last decade of Edward's reign royal borrowing shrank to modest
proportions. Edward now felt strong enough politically to levy forced
gifts (benevolences) where his predecessors would have tried to raise
generalized 'forced' loans from their subjects. Towards the end of his
reign Edward was able to liquidate most of his debts: thus, by the time of
his death, his debt to the Staple was reduced to £2,616.[1] Small loans from
royal officials and from London merchants continued to recur, a simple
treasury expedient such as any efficient government may find useful. The
normal functioning of the exchequer and of the royal government continued to give rise to a variety of other routine credit arrangements, for
furnishing the royal mint with bullion, for purchase of supplies on credit
or for discounting government bonds and tallies of assignment. But the
collection of revenue was not connected with any specific type or group
of lenders, with the one notable exception of the custom on wool and of
the Company of the Staple responsible for collecting it. The latter was a
legacy of a bygone age, with little future before it. The most important
body of English traders at the end of the fifteenth century were the exporters of cloth. But their organization as Merchant Adventurers was
then of fairly recent origin as a national body, and its potential value as
lender was only just beginning to attract the interest of the Crown in the
days of Edward IV and Henry VII.

At the end of the fifteenth century Englishmen had less cause to complain of taxation than had the subjects of the king of France. Direct taxes
were still regarded as exceptional in the early Tudor period. Tenths and
fifteenths were still being collected on a fixed and antiquated system of
assessment that did not allow the government to tap new wealth. Other

[1] J. R. Lander, 'Edward IV: the Modern Legend and a Revision', *History*, XLI (1956),
47.

fifteenth-century experiments in direct taxation had not given rise to any satisfactory alternatives. There were no royal excise duties on articles of common consumption comparable with the French *aides* or the *gabelle* on salt. The custom on wool, once the mainstay of royal credit, now only provided for the upkeep of Calais. Other commodities, whether exported or imported, mostly paid only very slight duties, and at the beginning of the reign of Henry VII, the whole system of valuing goods and collecting customs was in urgent need of reform. A century later, in the second half of the reign of Elizabeth I, the revenue from the customs was still not very much greater than it had been in the middle of Edward III's reign, when it reached its medieval peak.[1] The axiom 'no large regular taxes, no regular borrowing' was certainly applicable to early Tudor England. For the same reason most English institutions were, as yet, comparatively little affected by the royal search for credit facilities. While the sixteenth-century French monarchy used credit in ways that can be traced back, in most essentials, to the reign of Louis XI or even earlier, in England there is a less direct connection between its history in the Middle Ages and in the Tudor and Stuart periods. The medieval cycle, based chiefly on the wool custom and on the taxation of personal property—both taxes corresponding to medieval realities—was played out by 1485.

V. *France*

The history of French public credit in the Middle Ages presents exceptional difficulties. A large proportion of the central financial archives of the French monarchy has disappeared. Very few modern works are specifically devoted to this aspect of medieval French history.

During most of the thirteenth century the chief interest centres in the credit transactions of the rulers of French feudal principalities. It is a story of utmost diversity, reflecting the economic differences between the various French provinces. In the later thirteenth century, Italian merchants partly replaced local French lenders in many regions of the country and a short period of intensive employment of Italian bankers by the French Crown occurred in the reign of Philip the Fair. But during the greater part of the fourteenth century French kings were anxious to avoid the predominance of any group of over-mighty financiers, alien or French. The temporary departure from this policy during the disastrous period of civil and foreign war in the first half of the fifteenth century was a symptom of financial weakness. Louis XI returned to the former, more independent attitude. But casual borrowing from all the wealthier classes

---

[1] The average annual revenue from customs in 1596–1603 was estimated at £85,000. Cf. A. P. Newton, 'The establishment of the Great Farm of the English customs', *T.R. Hist. S.*, 4th series, 1 (1918), 152.

of royal subjects was much more widespread and successful in medieval France than it was in England. Reliance on credit underlay many French financial arrangements in the late Middle Ages, and the desire of the Crown to assure for itself adequate credit facilities left a deep mark on French institutions and society.

(1) THE THIRTEENTH CENTURY: A GENERAL SURVEY

The earliest surviving financial account of a French king dates from 1202–3. It shows that Philip Augustus was already keeping the royal treasury in the custody of the Templars in Paris.[1] All his successors down to 1295 deposited their money in the Paris Temple and several other princes of the Capetian dynasty did likewise. The Templars not only provided a place of safe deposit for royal treasure, but also discharged the functions of royal bankers. They received money from royal officials and debtors and made payments for the king; when necessary, they executed transfers of money on the king's behalf between Paris and foreign countries where their order possessed commanderies. In the late thirteenth century, the treasurer of the Temple in Paris received from the king an annual fee of 600 *li. par.* But he was not a royal official. The king was only the most eminent of the numerous depositors who used the financial facilities provided by the Temple.

It is possible that the possession by the French Crown of what amounted to a current account with the Paris Temple enabled the French kings, from an early date, to borrow freely from the Order in moments of need. But with regard to the earlier thirteenth century this is far from certain. In the absence of French evidence, a comparison with England might be instructive. Both John and Henry III frequently used the London Temple as an additional place of deposit, subsidiary to the main royal treasury at Westminster. In spite of this, Henry III seldom borrowed from the Templars. The loans of the Paris Temple to the French Crown may have been equally rare at first. Later, however, the relations of the Templars with the sovereigns of England and France increasingly diverged. Edward I eventually ceased to use the London Temple as a place of deposit and seldom borrowed from the Templars. On the other hand, Philip the Fair owed the Temple in May 1286 the large sum of 101,000 *li. par.* (about one-sixth of the average annual receipts of the French central government in 1289–92). This debt was not wholly extinguished until the later part of 1287 and further, though smaller, 'overdrafts' recurred during the next few years. All this suggests that by the time of the accession of Philip the Fair in 1285 the practice of such overdrawing was well established.

[1] F. Lot and R. Fawtier, *Le premier budget de la monarchie française. Le compte général de 1202–1203* (Paris, 1932), 5, 12.

The French kings began to employ the Templars regularly at a time when that Order offered exceptional advantages to princely clients. They combined financial experience and efficiency with guarantees of great security. They had high social prestige as especially privileged members of the Church and as an organization composed, in its higher ranks, exclusively of men of knightly class.

Louis IX did not need to borrow from the towns of the royal domain, because he could always secure substantial gifts or aids from them, but few other contemporary French rulers could levy enough in extraordinary taxes to avoid the need of frequent borrowing. For example, the dukes of Burgundy derived considerable revenues from their city of Dijon. But just because this was one of their most dependable sources of income, they used it in the thirteenth century chiefly as a security for a long series of loans.[1] In some of the more developed regions of France capacity to borrow freely was becoming for the more important potentates the necessary condition of continued political and military power.[2] Some of the earliest examples of borrowing by the great French feudatories deserve a brief mention. The merchants of Rouen and other Norman towns contributed loans towardsthe defence of the Angevin dominions in France between 1194 and 1204. The records of the last months of John's rule in Normandy 'give the impression that the revenue must have been far exceeded by his anticipations'.[3] The government of young Henry III during the critical first decade of his reign received valuable financial aid from the citizens of La Rochelle and Bordeaux. A merchant of Cahors residing at Montpellier helped to finance Simon de Montfort during the Albigensian crusade. Around 1220 Duchess Alix of Burgundy was borrowing from the great Lyons merchant, Pons de Chaponnay, as well as from the leading men of Dijon.[4] The first recorded loans by the money-lenders of Arras to Countess Jeanne of Flanders and other neighbouring rulers date from 1223–5. The earliest surviving accounts of the rulers of Champagne (1217–19) reveal regular borrowing by the reigning Countess Blanche from Italians and merchants of Cahors. Her loans were contracted from one fair to the next and bore interest.[5]

[1] J. Richard, *Les Ducs de Bourgogne et la formation du duché du XIe au XIVe siècle* (Paris, 1954), 342–7, 363–4.

[2] G. Duby, *La société aux XIe et XIIe siècles dans la région mâconnaise* (Paris, 1953), 487–94.

[3] F. M. Powicke, *The Loss of Normandy, 1189–1204* (Manchester, 1913), 352–4. For a comprehensive list of sources see also S. R. Packard, 'The Norman communes under Richard and John 1189–1204', in *Anniversary Essays in Medieval History by Students of Charles Homer Haskins* (Boston, Mass., 1929), 244, n. 64.

[4] Richard, *op. cit.* 362–4.

[5] A. Longnon, *Documents relatifs au Comté de Champagne et de Brie, 1172–1361*, III, (Paris, 1914), 1–7.

The gradual emergence of a class of prosperous 'patricians' is one of the most striking features of the development of French towns in the thirteenth century.[1] Money-lending to public authorities provided one tempting field for the investment of the surplus capital of these important burgesses. Native French townsmen at first profited most from the increased opportunities for financial business with princes. Outside Champagne, French businessmen did not have to face much Italian competition in this risky but lucrative business until the last decades of the thirteenth century. Even then many important Italian companies were more interested in wholesale trade than in financial operations, and the major companies confined their dealings in France chiefly to the regions connected with the main currents of European trade. Several groups of French merchants, therefore, either because they were wealthier or better organized than the rest or because they were operating in regions of small interest to the leading Italian firms, managed to retain a substantial amount of the financial business with rulers.

A few detailed examples will illustrate the striking diversity in the facilities for government borrowing in different regions of France in the thirteenth century and the changes brought about by the spread of Italian business activity. The remarkable expansion in the export of wine from south-western France led to the rapid development of Bordeaux, which became one of the chief supporters of the English rule in Gascony. All the continental expeditions of King Henry III appear to have been planned on the assumption that, if supplies from England were delayed, it would be possible to borrow enough money in his French possessions. Some £10,000, or about a quarter of Henry's total expenditure during the expedition of 1242–3, were borrowed in Gascony and the adjoining regions; a not much smaller amount was raised there during his Gascon visit of 1253–4.[2] The loans from members of the ruling families of Bordeaux were specially important. Most of the royal creditors in Bordeaux were prominent merchants and exporters to England, where several of them secured, as part of their recompense, valuable trading privileges. During Henry's last stay at Bordeaux, in 1254, the citizens purchased from him a general exemption from all duties on wine throughout his dominions, with the exception of certain specified royal levies. The next generation of Gascon merchants found their opportunities for lucrative money-lending to their English lord greatly curtailed, because Edward I relied on regular borrowing from Italian firms. During Edward's visit to his French possessions in 1286–9, there was no repetition of widespread borrowing from the local merchants, because the Riccardi of Lucca supplied

[1] Ch. Petit-Dutaillis, *Les communes françaises. Caractères et évolution des origines au XVIIIe siècle* (Paris, 1947), 150–1.
[2] S. K. Mitchell, *Studies in Taxation under John and Henry III* (1914), 238–9, 260–1.

him in France with at least £95,000. The Riccardi and later the Frescobaldi of Florence were introduced into Gascony by the English kings and between 1309 and 1318 Edward II's successive Italian bankers even exercised, for a few years, complete control over the entire financial administration of the duchy.

Merchants of Arras played a leading part in the twelfth century in exporting cloth from Artois and Flanders to the fairs of Champagne and to Italy. In the course of the thirteenth century the richer Arras families turned to the less strenuous but very lucrative business of money-lending. In the second half of the century Arras rivalled the fairs of Champagne as a money-lending centre, although it mainly served a more restricted area, comprising Flanders, Hainault, Artois and Picardy. The capital at the disposal of the leading financiers of Arras was enormous for their time. The count and the municipalities of Flanders owed at the end of the thirteenth century nearly 200,000 *li. par.* to the richest Arras family, the Crespins. While the larger short-term loans to princes and municipalities came from a few outstanding men, numerous citizens of Arras subscribed to life annuities sold by the towns of northern France and Flanders. The activity of the Arras money-lenders reached its peak in the second half of the thirteenth century. This coincided with the first period of Italian predominance in the trade and international finance of north-western Europe, but there is no trace of any effective co-operation in the late thirteenth century between Arras financiers and the leading Italian firms. The area of possible mutual contacts was bound to be limited because the leading Arras financiers carried on most of their business in their native city: prospective borrowers had to send for money to Arras. Nor do we hear of any deposits entrusted to Arras money-lenders. The Arras capitalists thus represented a more primitive type of financial enterprise than the contemporary Tuscan banking companies.

In the later thirteenth century Burgundy and the Dauphiné were a less advanced region economically than Artois and Champagne. Italians began to settle in some numbers in these territories in the 'seventies. The important mercantile firms displayed little interest in these backward territories and most of the Italians who established themselves there were first and foremost money-lenders. The Florentine family of Gianfigliazzi, who figure as typical usurers in Dante's *Inferno*, found the chief field for their activity in this region. These Italian money-lenders encountered little native competition and some of them came to wield as much influence with the local rulers as the greatest Italian firms possessed at the courts of the leading European sovereigns. The existence of these new opportunities for borrowing in fact proved fatal to the needy rulers of the Imperial Free County of Burgundy and of the Dauphiné. Ultimately they were persuaded to sell their states to the French Crown, as the best

way to free themselves from debt as well as to solve their political problems. Otto IV of Franche-Comté sold his county in 1295 for 100,000 *li.
tur.*, of which half was to go to his creditors. The annexation of the county
by Philip the Fair was even in part negotiated by a Florentine financier,
Scaglia Tifi, the chief receiver and, at the same time, the main creditor of
the last count. To the local chronicler, who accurately reflects the contemporary views of his fellow-countrymen, the count's debts to 'the
Lombards' were the chief cause of the county's loss of independence.[1]
Humbert II of Dauphiné sold his state for the first time to the French king
in 1343, but reserving his right to keep it during his own lifetime. Within a few years he spent the 120,000 florins paid him under this treaty and a
further payment of 100,000 florins was necessary to induce Humbert to
hand over Dauphiné in 1349.[2]

(2) ROYAL CREDIT DEALINGS WITH PROFESSIONAL FINANCIERS (AFTER 1285)

The reign of Philip the Fair begins a new chapter in the history of French
royal borrowing. It was a period of internal reorganization and territorial
expansion, for which considerable increases in royal revenue were required. The vigorous and comprehensive manner in which Philip tried
to exploit all possible resources simultaneously marked the beginning
of a new phase in the development of strong monarchy in France.

As far as is known, Philip was the first French king to make effective
and continuous use of Italian financiers. The Florentine firm of the brothers Musciatto and Albizo Franzesi replaced the Templars as the chief
royal bankers. The latter seem to have found increasing difficulty in adjusting themselves to the growing requirements of their royal client. This
is suggested by the fact that, after 1289, the Paris Temple had to employ
the Franzesi as agents for carrying out many of the financial operations
required by Philip. After the outbreak of the war with England in 1294,
the king decided to remove the treasury completely from the Temple.
The change was effected with the help of the Franzesi, whose resources
were sufficiently large to ensure the satisfactory functioning of the treasury during the period of transition. At the end of 1295 the Franzesi were
made sole treasurers and acted in this capacity for a year, until they handed over the treasury to royal officials. It was replaced in the Temple in

---

[1] *Foeneratores destruxerunt comitem Ottonem et vocabuntur lumbardi nomine*, quoted in
L. Gauthier, *Les Lombards dans les Deux Bourgognes* (Paris, 1907), 29.

[2] J. Viard, 'La France sous Philippe VI de Valois. État géographique et militaire',
Revue des Questions Historiques, LIX (1896), 345–8; F. Arens, 'Analekten zur Geschichte des spätmittelalterlichen Geldhandels im Dauphiné', *Vierteljahrschrift für Sozial-
und Wirtschaftsgeschichte*, XXI (1928).

1303, but this return to the old usage was suddenly brought to a close with the arrest of the Templars by Philip in October 1307.

Between 1294 and his death in 1307 Musciatto Franzesi was an influential royal adviser and diplomatic agent as well as the chief royal banker. Part of the value of the Franzesi to Philip lay, apparently, in their capacity to act as intermediaries in dealings with the Italian business world. Thus in 1294 the Franzesi lent about 200,000 *li. tur.* to Philip, which they had borrowed partly in Paris and partly at the fairs of Champagne. Musciatto's capacity to provide funds wherever they might be needed in western Europe may help to explain his employment on many important foreign missions. He played an important part in the negotiations that enabled Philip in 1297 to detach from the anti-French coalition the Emperor Adolf of Nassau, to whom Musciatto paid 80,000 *li. tur.* He financed and helped to organize the attack on Boniface VIII at Anagni.

The death of the two brothers Franzesi in 1307 and the ruin of the Templars in the same year ended the period of the most intensive employment of foreign financiers by the French Crown. During much of the fourteenth century borrowing seems usually to have been regarded, by those in charge of the French finances, as a temporary expedient and not as a normal aid to the smooth financing of government. The revenues of the French Crown were exceptionally large at this period in comparison with the incomes of the English kings and other leading European rulers. By contrast with England, therefore, the French kings of the first half of the fourteenth century did not feel the same urgent need for regular borrowing from professional lenders. Thus, while the English Crown continued to employ major Italian financiers as long as it could find sufficiently wealthy lenders among them, in France the leading Italian firms ceased to act as the permanent bankers of the Crown at a time when they were still in the heyday of their financial power. Italian businessmen continued to be occasionally used by the French government for a variety of financial operations. Charles IV, for example, in 1322–5 borrowed about 150,000 *li. par.* from Italians and other merchants, but this only represented about 7% of the total receipts of the royal *Trésor* in those years.

Loans from the royal officials were beginning to become an important alternative source of credit in the early fourteenth century. Under Charles IV advances by officials already constituted more than half of the total sums borrowed in 1322–5.[1] A bureaucracy of salaried officials de-

---

[1] The evidence about royal borrowing in 1322–5 is derived from J. Viard, *Les Journaux du Trésor de Charles IV le Bel* (Paris, 1917), lxxxiv–lxxxvii, cviii–cix and *passim* and from tables in R. Fawtier, *Comptes du Trésor* (Recueil des Historiens de France, Documents Financiers, Paris, 1930), lix–lx, based on Viard.

The records of the *Trésor* for 1316 and 1329 (printed by Fawtier, *op. cit.*) suggest the

veloped in France in the thirteenth century, partly recruited from among well-to-do townsmen. This was particularly true of the receivers of *bailliages* and *sénéchaussées*, who often combined government service with private trade or money-lending. They were, naturally, very willing to lend to the Crown. Even more important, again by contrast with England, was the presence of businessmen within the French central financial administration who used their private business connections to procure money for the Crown. The absence of regular royal arrangements with professional financiers encouraged these practices because the leading officials in charge of the French finances were expected, in practice, to find ready money as best they could.

Géraud Gayte, who enjoyed the special favour of Philip V (1316–22), supplies a good example of a leading official with good business connections. Gayte was the most influential member of an important group of merchants of Clermont in Auvergne. He inherited a prosperous family business that, by its widespread activity, anticipated, to some extent, the fifteenth-century firm of Jacques Cœur. He and his brothers at first acted as royal receivers in various parts of France. Even after he had become the head of the *Chambre des Comptes*, Gayte still continued his trading operations through partners. He lent to Philip V at least 460,000 *li. tur.* by 1320 (somewhat less than the total receipts of the royal treasury in 1322). He repeatedly stated that he had to borrow from others the bulk of what he had loaned to the Crown. Philip's gift of 40,000 *li tur.* to Gayte was connected with the loans advanced by the latter,[1] one of the comparatively rare medieval instances when we have some information about the payment of interest by the French Crown to its more important creditors. The few men who attained considerable influence as lenders to the French Crown in the later Middle Ages were mostly prominent officials of this type.

The position of the more important creditors of the French Crown was always precarious under Philip the Fair and his successors in the first half of the fourteenth century. In no other country were lenders so frequently despoiled and ruined. The best-known of these incidents is the arrest of the Templars by Philip the Fair in 1307, at a time when the royal treasury was in their custody. Philip subsequently procured the dissolution of their Order by the pope and the confiscation of its property. Again, on at least

same general conclusions. In view of the loss of the royal accounts with individual lenders, which appear to have once existed among the archives of the *Chambre des Comptes*, it is impossible to tell how far the records of the *Trésor* provide a complete picture of the royal borrowing.

[1] M. Boudet, 'Étude sur les sociétés marchandes et financières au moyen âge. Les Gayte et les Chauchat de Clermont', *Revue d'Auvergne*, XXVIII (1911), 405–7 and 407, n. 1. For other gifts to Gayte see P. Lehugeur, *Philippe le Long, roi de France (1316–1322)*, II (Paris, 1931), 238–9.

five occasions between 1277 and 1349, Italian merchants were seized by the king on the pretext that they were guilty of usurious practices and they were released each time only after paying very substantial fines. The frequent political changes in France between 1314 and 1328, caused by a rapid succession of rulers, contributed to the insecurity of royal creditors. Each king revoked many of the grants of his predecessors and persecuted some of their favourites. After the death of Philip V, his protégé, Géraud Gayte, was accused of dishonest practices and died in prison. Pierre Rémy, another French merchant, who acted as treasurer under Charles IV, was executed at the beginning of the next reign.[1] Rémy's successor as treasurer, a Florentine related to the Franzesi, suffered the same fate three years later.

It is probable that these repeated royal acts of violence against important financiers had the effect of gradually restricting the Crown's choice of lenders. Some financiers were ruined or seriously impoverished, others were discouraged from becoming too deeply involved in financial dealings with the government. Simultaneously, the credit facilities readily accessible to the French Crown were being curtailed as a result of more general economic changes. The fairs of Champagne seriously declined from about 1315 onwards and an important centre of financial business gradually disappeared from the domains of the French Crown. In the second and third quarters of the fourteenth century, Bruges and Avignon were the two most important centres of Italian business activity beyond the Alps. Both were closely connected with French economic life, but they lay outside the political control of the French kings.

Thus, by the time of the outbreak of the Hundred Years War, important professional financiers able and willing to lend regularly considerable sums to the Crown were becoming somewhat scarce in France and the monarchy was becoming accustomed to manage without regular help from them. As far as we can tell from the evidence now available, the war brought no fundamental change in this respect. Edward III's successful reorganization of the English wool trade, which enabled him to increase the profits of the leading English merchants and to share in these profits through taxes and loans, could not be imitated in France. No branch of French external trade lent itself to a similar reorganization in war time. But if Philip VI of France was unable to exploit the economic resources of his state as effectively as his English rival, he enjoyed certain compensating political advantages. Between 1343 and 1350 Philip VI was able to borrow at Avignon nearly 1,000,000 florins from a friendly pope, Clement VI (considerably more than a year's ordinary royal expenditure). The bulk of this loan was received by Philip between

[1] J. Viard, 'Philippe VI de Valois. Début du règne (février–juillet 1328)', *Bibliothèque de l'École des Chartes*, XCV (1934), 263–8.

1345 and 1348, when the war with England was especially serious and costly.[1]

Philip's immediate successors John and Charles V repeatedly had to borrow from professional financiers. Sometimes large sums were involved, like the loan of 100,000 *li. tur.* contracted in 1371 by Charles V from a group of Italians at Avignon.[2] In November 1372 a government estimate of future expenditure included the repayment of loans amounting to 135,000 *li. tur.* (*c.* 8% of the total expenditure).[3] But the printed evidence about the loans contracted by Charles is very incomplete and no discussion of them can be usefully attempted at present. Attention must, instead, be directed to the growth of generalized borrowing from royal officials and other wealthier Frenchmen and to its singular extension during the Hundred Years War.

(3) BORROWING FROM OFFICIALS AND 'FORCED LOANS'

There has survived a detailed government memorandum, written in 1329, enumerating the sources of revenue that could be made available for an expected war with England: loans from French burgesses constituted the only type of borrowing worth including in these estimates.[4] Levies of loans from all the richer classes of royal subjects formed, in fact, one of the most usual types of government borrowing in fourteenth-century France. The majority of these levies were fairly localized, restricted to a selected group of officials or to a number of the more important towns. In times of serious need, recourse was repeatedly had to very widespread borrowing through special commissions sent to all parts of the realm. The earliest known general levy of this sort was attempted in 1285 by Philip III to pay for his invasion of Aragon. Next we have a unique record of a debate in 1294, after the start of the war with England, concerning the merits of this and other methods of financing that emergency.[5] The master of the Paris mint favoured the depreciation

[1] M. Faucon, 'Prêts faits aux rois de France par Clement VI, Innocent VI et le comte de Beaufort, 1345-1360', *Bibliothèque de l'École des Chartes*, XL (1879); E. Göller, 'Inventarium instrumentorum camerae apostolicae. Verzeichnis der Schuldurkunden des päpstlichen Kammerarchivs aus der Zeit Urbans V', *Römische Quartalschrift für Christliche Altertumskunde und Kirchengeschichte*, XXIII (1909).

[2] L. Delisle, *Mandements et actes divers de Charles V, 1364–1380* (Paris, 1874), no. 861 (pp. 445–6).

[3] F. Lot and R. Fawtier, *Histoire des institutions françaises au moyen âge*, II (Paris, 1958), 267.

[4] M. Jusselin, 'Comment la France se préparait à la guerre de Cent Ans', *Bibliothèque de l'École des Chartes*, LXXIII (1912), 225.

[5] Printed by F. Funck-Brentano, 'Document pour servir à l'histoire des relations de la France avec l'Angleterre et l'Allemagne sous le règne de Philippe le Bel', *Revue Historique*, XXXIX (1889).

of the coinage. Musciatto Franzesi, as a counter-proposal, suggested the levy of a general loan. As a prominent merchant and banker, he feared the dislocation of business that an alteration of the coinage would cause, and his arguments prevailed at first. Over 700,000 *li. tur.* were borrowed from all parts of the kingdom (more than a normal year's income). But six months later the depreciation of the coinage was also tried. These two ways of raising quickly large sums of money remained henceforth, for over a century, the traditional expedients of the French Crown in periods of financial difficulty.

The introduction of frequent taxation after 1337 favoured the extension of the practice of levying general loans, because there was now more revenue to anticipate. In 1413 the university of Paris estimated the annual income of the Crown from taxation at 1,200,000 *li. tur.* Lenders could be given more convincing assurances of ultimate reimbursement by being promised remissions of their quotas of future taxes until the royal debts to them were repaid. The term 'forced loans' is often applied to these widespread levies. A certain amount of pressure was undoubtedly exerted at times, and an unqualified refusal to contribute was likely to be regarded as disloyal to the king.[1] But it would be misleading to lay too much stress on the compulsory nature of such loans. Wealthy townsmen and other prominent persons had much to gain from earning and maintaining the king's good will towards them by contributing. Service to the Crown in this and connected ways furthered the rise of many families to importance and fortune. One example may suffice. Raymond Ysalguier, a leading Toulouse money-changer, administered for Philip the Fair the confiscated Jewish property in Languedoc, advanced loans to the Crown and was ennobled in 1328. In the later fourteenth century, landed property in the hands of the Ysalguiers formed the largest fortune belonging to any Toulousan family. A considerable proportion of these estates had been acquired by Raymond's sons from Philip VI and John in return for loans advanced for the war in Gascony.

There was no effective compulsion on the Crown to repay loans to non-professional lenders, though the wiser rulers understood that it was in the royal interest to honour some, at least, of these obligations in order to facilitate future borrowing. The chances of repayment varied considerably under different kings. The majority of the loans of this kind contracted by Philip the Fair do not seem to have been reimbursed in his lifetime. Charles V, another heavy borrower, tried to repay loans scrupulously. The general attitude of most Frenchmen is perhaps best conveyed by the well-informed chronicler of St Denis who, writing of the careful reimbursement of loans contracted in 1385, remarked that

---

[1] E.g. the reply of the town of Laon in 1380. See L. Mirot, *Les insurrections urbaines au début du règne de Charles VI (1380–1383)*, (Paris, 1906), 19, n. 1.

'such repayment, because unaccustomed, seemed incredible to the common people.'[1]

Compared with the loans that could be obtained from important professional financiers, borrowing from the general body of the king's subjects was a clumsy and slow method of raising money. Nevertheless this type of borrowing might often seem preferable to bargaining with powerful professional lenders, who were likely to insist on good security and certain to stipulate a considerable amount of profit for themselves. In all probability interest was rarely paid on loans contracted from non-professional lenders, unless they were important people. The known exceptions are very instructive. It is very significant that promises of interest, at the fairly high rate of 25%, on loans contracted from rich Parisians and government officials between 1415 and 1417 were treated in pleadings before the Parlement of Paris as a special measure, designed to attract lenders.[2] But the available evidence is so scanty that it is impossible to reach any firm conclusions about this problem.

The monetary 'mutations' inaugurated by Philip the Fair introduced a troublesome complication into royal credit transactions. French legislation dealing with the effects of changes in currency on existing contracts favoured debtors in the main, and the Crown, as borrower, profited from this.[3] Important lenders were sometimes able to safeguard themselves against losses from this cause. On one occasion in 1307 officials of the count of Dreux refused to receive from the king on their master's behalf 5,000 li. tur., in repayment of a loan, on the ground that payment was being offered to them in worse money than was due to the count. Thereupon new, good coins were specially minted and were transported from Paris to the count's own house near Dreux, so that he might receive them in person, all at the additional cost to the king of 192 li.[4] But the generality of lenders were frequently running the risk of being repaid in a currency the purchasing power of which was smaller than the purchasing power of the money they had originally advanced.

The existence of regular taxation created increased opportunities for government borrowing from officials connected with financial administration. A new bureaucracy sprang up, distinct from the old-established officials in charge of the ordinary finances. The receivers of the various types of *finances extraordinaires* became more important than the receivers

---

[1] *Quod ... quia non solitum, vulgaribus incredibile videbatur*, quoted in H. Moranvillé, *Étude sur la vie de Jean le Mercier* (Paris, 1888), 102.

[2] *A ceulx qui prestoient l'en bailloit le quart entierement de gain, pour laquele friandise ils prestoient*, quoted in A. Bossuat, 'Étude sur les emprunts royaux au début du XVe siècle', *Revue Historique de Droit Français et Étranger*, 4th series, XXVIII (1950), 353 and n. 2.

[3] E. Stampe, *Das Zahlkraftrecht in den Königsgesetzen Frankreichs von 1306 bis 1547*, Berlin, 1930.

[4] J. Viard, *Les Journaux du Trésor de Philippe IV le Bel* (Paris, 1940), 846–7.

of the traditional revenues and they handled much larger sums. Inevitably, both financial officials and farmers of the indirect taxes were largely drawn from the same class of prosperous townsmen. The indirect taxes were normally farmed out to those who offered the highest bids at a public auction. In the last two centuries of the Middle Ages an appreciable proportion of urban wealth was to be found in the hands of men whose chief ambition in life was to rise in social importance and to acquire still greater wealth through government service. A *noblesse de robe* was in process of formation.

In the later fourteenth century loans were sought more frequently by the king from royal officials and farmers of royal revenues than from any other category of lenders. It was a dangerous policy. As the lawyer of Thomas Orlant, a prominent Parisian money-changer and master of the royal mint, aptly put it in 1420, 'officials were accustomed and expected to lend, as they knew best how to secure repayment'.[1] All medieval governments borrowed occasionally from officials, but the systematic fashion in which French fiscal officials were compelled to lend to the Crown, and the frequency of such calls on their funds, endangered the integrity and the efficiency of the entire French financial system. While usually obtaining no remuneration for their loans, the officials themselves often had to borrow at heavy rates of interest in order to make the required advances. It is not surprising that bankruptcies of royal receivers were not uncommon. Thus Jean Chauchat of Clermont, as treasurer of Duke Jean de Berry in Languedoc, had to levy the enormous fine of 800,000 *li. tur.* imposed upon this province in 1383 as a punishment for rebellion. He was ruined by the large advances that he had made to the king before he was able to levy much of this fine, and several other businessmen of Auvergne, who had lent money to him, suffered heavy losses. By making the terms of royal service more onerous, the government encouraged malpractices. The leniency with which the *Chambre des Comptes* in the fifteenth century was apt to treat peccant officials probably sprang, in part, from the realization that, if the government wished to continue to borrow from its agents, it had to shut its eyes to their corrupt methods.[2]

---

[1] 'Ils sont acoustumé et sont tenus de prester, pour ce qu'ils scevent miex trouver maniere de soy rembourser', Bossuat, *loc. cit.* 363.

[2] H. Jassemin, *La Chambre des Comptes de Paris au XVe siècle* (Paris, 1933), 89–90, 320–2; R. Gandilhon, *Politique économique de Louis XI* (Rennes, 1941), 344–5.

(4) THE DECLINE AND REVIVAL OF THE FRENCH
MONARCHY, 1380–1483

Royal government remained relatively solvent and fairly independent of professional financiers during the first half of the reign of Charles VI, in spite of the rapacity of the princes who surrounded that helpless king and of the growing corruption of the royal administration. The outbreak of the civil war in the later years of his reign produced a rapid decline of the royal credit. Loans from royal officials and generalized levies of 'forced loans' became extremely frequent. There was also a revival of heavy borrowing from professional financiers, but these loans were not the result of a deliberate policy to strengthen royal finances through the use of credit. On the contrary, they were a symptom of weakness. The lenders showed by their behaviour that they reposed little trust in the Crown, but they were tempted to exploit the desperate need for ready money of the king and the other warring French princes. They did so ruthlessly. The university and the city of Paris complained in a petition, presented to Charles VI in February 1413, that the king's resources were being 'pillaged and devoured' by financiers who had been levying interest at the rate of 50 or 60%. The petition alleged that the king had been losing in this manner some 300,000 li. annually.[1] There was undoubtedly a substantial measure of truth in these allegations.

The Crown became entangled during this crisis with two main groups of financiers. Much was borrowed from wealthy Parisians. From about 1408 there was also a noticeable increase in the number of important posts in financial administration held by the leading Parisian money-changers, goldsmiths and dealers in luxuries. The petition of February 1413 contained the grave, but apparently justified, charge that some of these prominent officials were partners of the Parisian and foreign lenders whose extortionate demands were ruining the Crown.[2] Secondly, there was an important group of Italian Crown creditors, including in particular several Lucchese merchants. Since 1334 Lucca had been under the nominal sovereignty of the French Crown and around 1400 the Lucchese formed one of the most prosperous Italian groups in France and Flanders.

Most of the loans contracted in this period by the king had to be raised on the security of valuables. Usually the precious objects thus deposited were of considerably higher value than the loans made in exchange for them. The times were very uncertain and the lenders were trying in this

---

[1] H. Moranvillé, 'Remontrances de l'université et de la ville de Paris à Charles VI sur le gouvernement du royaume', *Bibliothèque de l'École des Chartes*, LI (1890), 428–9 (articles XXVII and XXIX).

[2] I am indebted to M. Maurice Rey for much valuable information about this period.

way to avoid losses and to make sure of a profit, irrespective of whether the loan was repaid or not. The wide prevalence of this practice was a symptom of the collapse of the royal credit. Even the king's crown had to be dismembered. The Cabochian Ordinance of 1413 ordered the return of all the pieces detached from the crown and prohibited any further transactions with them, but it remained a dead letter. By 1418 four large *fleurons* garnished with jewels had been detached from it and pledged for 73,000 *li. tur.* to an assortment of Parisian and Italian financiers. An inventory of royal jewels made in 1424 revealed that at that date only two *fleurons* still remained on the crown and that even these were not complete, for a valuable jewel, missing from one of them, was said to be somewhere at Genoa.[1] Some royal valuables appear to have been pledged without proper authority and in dubious circumstances. Thus several jewels were entrusted for about 10% of their estimated value to a prominent Lucchese, Galvano Trenta, who was one of the main bankers both of the king and of the duke of Burgundy and was receiving considerable payments of interest from them. It is not surprising that in his will, drawn up in 1421, he estimated his fortune at about 400,000 gold francs.[2]

Mere royal promises of repayment were ceasing to be of much value. The royal government even exploited the fact that more debts had been incurred than could be repaid. In 1416 the Armagnac administration, then ruling in Paris, tried to attract further loans by offering the prospective lenders licences to acquire royal bonds belonging to other persons. The government promised to repay the full face-value of the debts so redeemed. According to later statements of the lawyers acting on behalf of some of the lenders, royal bonds could be purchased for as little as 1% of their value.[3] Debts contracted by the Crown during the rule of one of the contending factions were unlikely to be honoured by the opposing party when it regained power. Henry V, as regent of France, issued an ordinance repudiating liability for the debts of the Armagnac regime. Charles VII was never willing, later on, to recognize officially the debts contracted by his opponents. Some financiers managed to survive all changes and lent to every regime in turn. Thus Michel de Laillier and other important

---

[1] *L'Ordonnance Cabochienne* (ed. A. Coville, Paris, 1891), art. 118 (pp. 59–60); A. Coville, 'La très belle couronne royale aux temps des Armagnacs et des Bourguignons', *Mélanges offerts à Nicolas Iorga* (Paris, 1933); G. du Fresne de Beaucourt, *Histoire de Charles VII*, II (Paris, 1882), 633 and n. 2.

[2] L. Mirot, 'Galvano Trenta et les joyaux de la couronne', *Bibliothèque de l'École des Chartes*, CI (1940), 144; H. Moranvillé, 'Extraits de Journaux du Trésor, 1345–1419', *ibid.* XLIX (1888), 432 (royal payment of 1,000 *li. tur.* of interest). Trenta's fortune was roughly equivalent to the annual revenue of Philip the Bold of Burgundy at the height of his power in 1400–4.

[3] A. Bossuat, 'Étude sur les emprunts royaux au début du XVe siècle', *Revue Historique de Droit Français et Étranger*, 4th series, XXVIII (1950), 353, n. 1.

Parisians connected with him, after helping to finance Bedford's campaigns, notably the siege of Orléans, played a leading part in opening the gates of Paris to Charles VII in 1436 and Laillier then became *prévôt des marchands* in Paris.[1] Men of this sort were in a position to claim that debts contracted by a royal French government were repayable by its successors irrespective of all political changes.

The civil war had at first opened up possibilities of considerable profits for the financiers, but ended by ruining many of them. A number of financiers were killed during the successive revolutions, while several others were plundered and driven into exile. The Florentines and the Genoese suffered severely at the hands of the Burgundian party in Paris in May 1418, while the Dauphin Charles was simultaneously plundering the pro-Burgundian Lucchese merchants in the territories under his control.[2] By 1420 conditions in France had become very unfavourable for large-scale business. The division of France into two hostile zones seemed to have become permanent. The currency was rapidly deteriorating, as both sides were busily minting large masses of miserable coins. The development of Paris into a leading European business centre suffered a rude setback. Among the foreign merchants the Lucchese were the hardest hit, because of their specially close connection with the French market. According to a contemporary Lucchese historian, the war in France ruined the silk industry of his native city.

The 'twenties and the 'thirties of the fifteenth century are a very obscure period in the history of French public credit. Both Charles VII and the English government in northern France were continually short of money. Such foreign merchants as still remained in France seem usually to have avoided financial dealings with the warring governments. Both Charles VII and his English opponents contracted a multitude of loans from Frenchmen. They borrowed from towns, from individual merchants, from officials, and above all from important councillors, great nobles and military commanders. Charles VII was forced on a number of occasions early in his reign to pledge royal lands in order to borrow money or in repayment of past debts, a method reminiscent of the earlier Middle Ages. Some permanent alienations resulted from this, though later on serious efforts were made to recover all lost royal domains.[3] Altogether, one has the impression of a return to an earlier age. Transfers of money were more difficult, there was no well-organized money

---

[1] A. Bossuat, 'Le rétablissement de la paix sociale sous le règne de Charles VII', *Moyen Âge*, LX (1954), 155–8.

[2] J. Calmette et E. Déprez, *Histoire Générale* (ed. G. Glotz): *Histoire du Moyen Âge*, VII (1), (1937), 345–7, 354, n. 90.

[3] Beaucourt, *op. cit.* II, 560–3, 634; III, 215–16; L. de la Trémoille, *Les la Trémoille pendant cinq siècles*, I (Nantes, 1890), 177–82, 198.

market, the resources of native Frenchmen were alone available to French rulers and often amateur lenders were more willing than professionals to advance money. The withdrawal of foreign competitors favoured French financiers. But the times were dangerous and exceptionally demoralizing. The careers of the Frenchmen who made fortunes out of the war often do not make an edifying story.[1]

Jacques Cœur, the most important of the French financiers, became a legendary figure even in his own lifetime. His rise to power occurred during the middle years of the reign of Charles VII, when the king was again strong enough to levy taxes by his own authority. Cœur's help was needed in order to organize in a more effective way regular anticipation of the expanding royal resources. Cœur had acquired sufficient credit as a merchant to become a good intermediary for this purpose between Charles VII and the business world. From 1438 to his disgrace in July 1451, Cœur acted as the royal *argentier* charged with purchases for the royal household. During those thirteen years he undertook every kind of financial task and was also a trusted royal councillor and diplomatic agent. But he managed to combine his ceaseless activity in the royal service with a flourishing commercial business of his own. He had close contacts with all the main foreign centres of international trade and had especially strong ties with Aragon and Florence. He was, therefore, much used for financing royal enterprises in the Mediterranean. But his most famous loans were made for the reconquest of Normandy in 1450. The most cautious estimates put them at some 100,000 *écus* (150,000 *li. tur.*). This is borne out by Cœur's statement, after his imprisonment, that he owed some 100,000 or 120,000 *écus* which he had borrowed from various persons on the king's behalf.

Charles VII later complained that Cœur obtained excessive gains from his loans to the Crown.[2] He was alleged to have charged interest at the rate of 15 or 20%. Certainly Cœur was repeatedly given compensation for expenses and losses incurred in transacting royal business. Gifts were made to him from time to time.[3] All these payments may have included a substantial element of interest. But Cœur's chief 'offence' probably lay elsewhere. The king owed Cœur more than he was willing to repay. The easiest way to default was to prosecute Cœur and to confiscate his property.

One of the most striking features of Cœur's business is his lack of large

[1] E.g. M. Mollat, 'Un "collaborateur" au temps de la guerre de Cent Ans. Jehan Marcel, changeur à Rouen', *Annales (Économies, Sociétés, Civilisations)*, 1 (1946).

[2] *Icelluy Jacques Cuer, meu de grant avarice . . . en nous chargant . . . très grandement* (*Journal du Procureur Dauvet*, ed. M. Mollat, 1, 9).

[3] *Les La Trémoille pendant cinq siècles*, 1 (Nantes, 1890), 148; G. du Fresne de Beaucourt, 'Rôles de dépenses du temps de Charles VII (1450–51)', *Annuaire-Bulletin de la Société de l'Histoire de France*, 1864, 132, 139–40, 142.

supplies of ready cash. His aggregate capital may have been very considerable, but at any given moment most of it was immobilized. Large stocks of textiles and other goods had to be kept in the royal *argenterie* at Tours: goods worth slightly over 20,000 *li. tur.* were found there after Cœur's fall.[1] But he invested also in every type of enterprise all over France, and for this purpose needed supplies of ready money from sources outside his business. Increasingly he came to depend for some of his working capital on royal money. He secured large assignments on various Crown revenues. More valuable still were the services of those of his agents who were also prominent fiscal officials of the Crown. They repeatedly placed royal funds under their control at Cœur's disposal. There was nothing abnormal in all this. But these practices lent some support to the accusation that Cœur was advancing usuriously to Charles VII the king's own money.

Cœur was ruined because he was no longer considered to be indispensable. The war was virtually ended. The monarchy could return to the older tradition of independence of over-mighty financiers. Louis XI certainly was not a ruler who would put up with the excessive predominance of any single banker. He employed financiers, both Italians and Frenchmen, borrowed from them in moments of need and tolerated the same mixture of public finance and private business that Cœur's career exemplifies. But, compared with Cœur or with the financiers who raised money for the early Italian wars, like Semblançay, the men employed by Louis XI had moderate resources and limited influence. Semblançay's father, Jean de Beaune of Tours, came perhaps nearest to being Louis's trusted banker. But there is no indication that he lent money regularly. His largest recorded loan to Louis amounted to 30,000 *li*. At his death in 1487 his entire property was evaluated at 22,500 *li*. (the value of Cœur's goods at Tours alone).

Many of the financial practices and habits of the sixteenth-century French governments can be traced back clearly to the reign of Louis XI. By the end of the Middle Ages the unceasing royal search for credit facilities had left a deep mark on French institutions and society. This may be the right moment for enumerating those financial arrangements that depended on credit and for estimating their importance for subsequent French history.

Louis XI had a marked preference for restricting the levy of the main direct tax (*taille*) to the countryside, while excise duties were preferably confined to the towns. A few cities had secured exemption from *taille* at an early date, but concessions of this privilege became numerous only under Louis. The king expected, in return, subsidies, gifts and interest-free loans whenever he asked the exempted towns for help. Some of the

[1] *Journal du Procureur Dauvet*, 26–96.

loans were even repaid. On one occasion a leading councillor of Louis is found advocating the reimbursement of a loan of 56,000 *li.*, previously levied in Languedoc, in order to encourage future advances.[1] It was a flexible system and it suited Louis, who collaborated with the ruling groups in towns and readily conferred titles of nobility and other privileges upon them. But the ultimate consequences were very serious. *Taille* was not an excessive burden at Louis's accession (*c.* 1,000,000 *li. tur.*), but it was more than trebled in the course of his reign and went on increasing thereafter. But henceforth the burden of it fell chiefly on the peasantry. The nobles and the clergy were not liable to it and Louis XI had extended exemption to the richest section of the Third Estate. The whole financial system of the French monarchy was permanently warped as a result of this.[2]

The dealings of Louis XI with Lyons supply a good example of his methods. In 1462 he exempted the city from *taille*. With his active assistance the fairs of Lyons became some of the most important international gatherings of merchants in Europe. But the city had to pay for all this with heavy subsidies and loans. Louis had to be satisfied at all costs. He had helped to undermine the prosperity of the rival fairs of Geneva, but he repeatedly threatened to reverse his policy. When in 1466 he opened negotiations with the count of Savoy, Geneva's suzerain, Lyons offered nearly 10,000 *li. tur.* to put an end to this threat. Louis did not borrow often from the Italians and other foreigners who now frequented Lyons in large numbers, but he knew that the municipality could borrow from them. Louis's financial demands cost Lyons, at a very conservative estimate, more than 75,000 *li. tur.*, out of which at least 42,000 *li. tur.* were advanced in loans.[3]

Systematic borrowing from royal officials was an old habit of the French monarchy. Louis XI often had recourse to it. Refusal to contribute could result in dismissal, as happened, for example, in 1465 to a *greffier* of the Parlement of Paris. The practice of the sale of offices grew, in part, out of these loans. Already in the reign of Charles VI complaints were made that men were appointed to financial offices on condition that they assumed personal responsibility for repayment of debts to specified royal creditors.[4] In the reign of Louis XI, a prospective receiver of the

---

[1] H. Sée, *Louis XI et les villes* (Paris, 1891), 145.

[2] Cf. R. Doucet, *Finances municipales et crédit public à Lyon au XVIe siècle* (Paris, 1937), 5: 'les difficultés du Trésor provenaient de ce que le système financier avait été faussé par l'exemption de la taille qui avait été accordée aux villes.'

[3] In 1458–61 Lyons's annual quota of *taille* had oscillated between 3,100 *li.* and 3,300 *li.*

[4] H. Moranvillé, 'Remontrances de l'université et de la ville de Paris à Charles VI sur le gouvernement du royaume', *Bibliothèque de l'École des Chartes*, LI (1890), 429 (article XXVIII).

king's chamber failed to get this office because he had offered to lend only 4,000 or 5,000 *fr.*, which was less than one-third of what he was required to advance.[1] The transition from demanding a loan from a new official to demanding an outright payment was not difficult. In the sixteenth century the practice of the sale of offices became one of the gravest weaknesses of the French governmental system.

Gabelles on salt were probably the most detested of all the French indirect taxes. The entire levy depended on credit. Merchants supplied salt to the royal warehouses (*greniers*) on credit and were repaid out of the proceeds of the sale to consumers. In moments of special need Louis XI imposed forced loans upon the salt merchants, at a fixed rate for each measure of salt supplied to the royal *greniers*. In some regions of France the right to transport salt was a royal monopoly, administered by a company of financiers. They advanced, in return, fixed annual loans which were repaid when the salt had been ultimately disposed of. Thus the company that possessed the monopoly of transport on the Rhône lent annually to Louis around 60,000 *li.* for this lucrative privilege. The cost of all the credit extended to the Crown by the salt merchants was passed on to the consumers in the shape of higher prices.

Since early times all French indirect taxes, tolls levied on roads and rivers, duties on foreign trade (*traites*) and internal excise duties (*aides*) had usually been farmed to businessmen. Some tax-farmers were small men who only farmed petty revenues in their own localities, but others were wealthy and influential financiers, hand in glove with royal officials who were supposed to supervise them. Abuses of all sorts flourished under this system. There was collusive bidding to keep the farms as low as possible. In spite of royal prohibitions, financiers were allowed to accumulate leases of several revenues at once. The tendencies that produced *les cinq grosses fermes* at the end of the sixteenth century and created the oligarchy of *fermiers généraux* were clearly already in evidence in the reign of Louis XI. The more important tax-farmers, by lending money to the Crown, could perpetuate their hold on the revenues they farmed and their misdemeanours were overlooked by needy governments. Besides, many of the senior financial officials were men of the same type, rich businessmen valued by the Crown as much for the money they could raise from the business community as for their personal qualities. The supervisor of the royal finances was also the chief broker for raising royal loans and might be the head or an associate of a flourishing merchant firm. The kings suspected that they were being plundered by their chief servants but no other system seemed possible. Thus, in the early sixteenth century the mother of Francis I believed that during the first eight years of his reign

[1] G. Jacqueton, *Documents relatifs à l'administration financière en France de Charles VII à François I* (Paris, 1891), 101–2.

her son had been continually robbed by the small oligarchy who controlled the royal finances.[1] In the absence of a uniform and economically sound system of taxation, royal finances were constantly in an embarrassed state. Consequently, the French Crown could secure credit only on unfavourable or even ruinous conditions and this, in turn, perpetually encouraged private profiteering within the financial administration.

VI. *The Netherlands*

The Netherlands contained some of the most populous and wealthiest areas in medieval Europe. But until the fifteenth century the whole region was excessively divided politically. The administrative development of its various principalities did not keep pace with the economic progress of the country. Even in Flanders central financial institutions developed more slowly than in the more powerful French and English monarchies. The financial organization of the other states of the Netherlands remained even more backward. A brief continuous survey of the development of public credit can be profitably attempted, at present, only in the case of Flanders. The facilities for borrowing increased in the thirteenth and fourteenth centuries faster than the power of the rulers to use them to the best advantage. The Burgundian dynasty was strong enough to make a more effective use of these ample opportunities for raising loans. It was conspicuous among medieval princes for its almost continuous borrowing. In its almost regular dependence on credit, as well as in its widespread use of the device of the sale of annuities, the Burgundian state of the fifteenth century anticipated the development of European public credit in the post-medieval period.

(1) THE NETHERLANDS BEFORE THE FORMATION OF THE BURGUNDIAN STATE

In the thirteenth century Flanders contained some of the richest cities in Europe. So long as the counts of Flanders could rely on the loyal support of the towns, they were the richest princes in the Netherlands. Loans from individual townsmen were more frequent than direct advances by municipalities, but many of these individual lenders were themselves members of the 'patrician' class who governed the Flemish cities in the thirteenth century. Some of the largest loans came, however, directly from the city governments and they repeatedly guaranteed important loans from other lenders. Above all, only the towns could provide the money for the repayment of the count's larger debts. But there was a reverse side to this

---

[1] G. Jacqueton, 'Le Trésor de l'Épargne sous François I, 1523–1547', *Revue Historique*, LV (1894), 1; *sans y pouvoir donner provision mon fils et moi feusmes continuellement desrobés par les gens de finances.*

bright picture. The ease with which considerable sums of money could be raised from the towns in 'gifts', aids and loans tempted the counts into enterprises that were beyond their personal means. The urban finances were administered with much laxity under the patrician regimes. This made it easier to satisfy the needs of the counts, especially as the ruling patricians often had a vested interest in the promotion of the loans raised for this purpose. But there was mounting discontent among the rest of the townsmen who bore the resultant burdens. In return for financial help the counts had to grant concessions to the towns and a larger measure of autonomy. As the government of the count became progressively more effective everywhere in Flanders outside the great cities, he found the independence of the latter increasingly irksome. Despite the apparent power and success of the counts, there were serious elements of weakness in the whole regime and it became increasingly unstable in the later thirteenth century. The growing financial needs of the counts and their increasing reliance on credit were one of the threats to its endurance.

Many different sources of loans were easily accessible to the counts of Flanders in the thirteenth century and they made frequent use of these exceptional facilities. The wide dispersal of the sources of credit used by the counts was already noticeable during the reign of Countess Jeanne (1202–44). At the time of her death in 1244 she owed debts in Flanders, Hainault and England, at Paris and the fairs of Champagne, in her husband's county of Savoy and elsewhere. In 1221 Jeanne owed 34,600 *li.* to Sienese and other Italian merchants for loans contracted to ransom her husband, Count Ferrand, from his French prison. When in 1227 Ferrand was at last liberated for the huge ransom of 50,000 *li. par.*,[1] the city of Ghent acted as a surety for one loan of 12,000 *li.* and was richly rewarded. In 1212 Ferrand had compelled the city to elect its magistrates annually. In 1228 all his reforms were annulled and Ghent was allowed to adopt the constitution that its leading families desired. Henceforth it was ruled by a virtually closed oligarchy (the rule of the so-called XXXIX). This is a good example of the way in which loans to the counts helped to consolidate the autonomy of the Flemish cities.

The reign of Countess Margaret (1244–78) coincided with a notable increase in facilities for borrowing in France and in the Netherlands. In contrast with her successor, Count Guy, she used them with restraint. Such evidence as survives gives the impression that Margaret was able to secure, under one pretext or another, aids and gifts from the towns whenever she needed additional resources. The money had to be asked for politely, but it was usually forthcoming. There was therefore little need to borrow from Flemish municipalities. Thus out of 32,000 *li. par.*

---

[1] By comparison, 53,700 *li. par.* were received by the French royal *Trésor* in the Candlemas term 1227 (one of the three annual *Trésor* terms).

received by Margaret from Douai between 1244 and 1268 only 1,400 *li.* were borrowed. But the Flemish cities gave valuable help as intermediaries between the countess and her other creditors. Foreign sources of credit were tapped by Margaret with increasing frequency at least from 1265 onwards. Several loans were contracted at Arras, chiefly from the two leading families, the Crespins and the Louchards. Shortly before her abdication in 1278, Margaret owed 18,600 *li.* to Arras financiers. Flemish agents were repeatedly dispatched to the fairs of Champagne with instructions to borrow. In 1278 Margaret owed at least 11,000 *li.* to several Sienese and Florentine firms, including the Bonsignori of Siena. At the time of her abdication Margaret's debts (exclusive of the money owed to the king of France) amounted to 47,000 *li. par.* This was not an exceptionally large debt. Margaret's neighbour, Count Robert of Artois, who enjoyed very similar facilities for borrowing, owed 62,000 *li. par.* in 1274.[1]

Margaret's successor, Count Guy (1278–1300), was an ambitious man, impatient of internal opposition and he became for some time the most powerful prince in the Netherlands. There are no records to show what Guy's ordinary financial resources were, but they were certainly inadequate for his ambitious schemes. Hence constant borrowing became essential and his loans reached enormous size. At first the resources of the Flemish towns seemed sufficient to secure an endless succession of loans. They could provide additional revenues out of which Guy's debts might be repaid, they could lend themselves, and they could reinforce his failing credit. But Guy expected too much. He seems to have thought that a forcible assertion of his authority might fill his coffers more quickly than a policy of continued co-operation with the patrician regimes. Ypres and Bruges were punished for outbreaks of internal disorder in 1280 by crushing fines. In the case of Bruges they amounted to over 225,000 *li. par.*[2] But Guy's opponents in the towns found support after 1285 at the court of the new French king, Philip the Fair. The count was drawn into a series of dangerous disputes with his sovereign. His lack of independent financial resources now proved one of his decisive weaknesses.

An incomplete list of Guy's debts in 1290, before his worst troubles occurred, adds up to the astounding figure of 136,500 *li.*[3] All the important creditors of Margaret reappear in it. In twelve years the debt to the Arras financiers had more than trebled and it stood at 65,100 *li.* in 1290. The debts to the Italian merchants at the fairs of Champagne and else-

[1] Exclusive of his debt of 51,000 *li. par.* to the king of France.
[2] The successive payments can be traced in L. Gilliodts-Van Severen, *Inventaire des archives de la ville de Bruges*, i (Bruges, 1871), nos. 15 ff.
[3] Equivalent to 23% of the receipts of the French royal *Trésor* in 1290 or to the average annual revenues from Normandy at this period (*c.* 142,000 *li. par.* in 1290, *c.* 134,000 *li. par.* in 1299).

where in France nearly doubled (to 21,400 *li.*). There are also some interesting new elements in the list. Italian businessmen began to settle in Flanders in considerable numbers towards the end of the thirteenth century. By 1290 Lombard pawnshops existed in several Flemish localities and the count owed them at least 6,800 *li.* in that year. The earliest Italian to fill the post of the receiver of Flanders was a Florentine, Gerard Lupichini, to whom the count owed 8,600 *li.* in 1290.

By 1294 Guy's position was desperate. His reckless borrowing and oppressive financial expedients were not due to a deliberate policy but were forced upon him. As Flemish nobles were unfriendly to him, he had to depend on hired mercenaries. His credit sank lower and lower. On a number of occasions between 1287 and 1293 various Flemish towns borrowed on his behalf at Arras without informing the lenders that the money was destined for the count.[1] The long series of loans by the Crespins to Guy (his creditors for 56,000 *li. par.* in 1290) virtually came to an end in 1292. In 1298 he was begging Pope Boniface VIII to release him from *usures* he owed to the Crespins, as he would not be able to pay them any more.[2] Borrowing through the intermediacy of Flemish cities, whose credit was somewhat better than his own, became Guy's chief recourse. Ypres borrowed for Guy 45,000 *li. par.* from the Crespins and Bruges procured for him from the same source 68,600 *li. par.* (1292–5). It is not surprising that Ypres and Bruges were in grave financial difficulties at the end of Guy's reign. The disastrous state of the municipal finances encouraged agitation against the patrician regimes, which ended in their overthrow at Ghent and Douai in 1296–7. Guy supported these revolutions in his last desperate bid for aid from the cities. In the last three years of his reign he had to rely on loans from his own subjects from every part of the county. One of Guy's most important friends at Ghent was Wouter van der Meere, a newly enriched broker, who did not belong to the old Ghent ruling class. He became Guy's most important creditor during this last crisis of the reign. The debts owed to Meere in 1299 and the early months of 1300 amounted to at least 53,000 *li. par.* It was all in vain. The old count, 'short of money and deserted by all his friends',[3] had to surrender in April 1300. Flanders was annexed to the royal domain. Borrowing can become a permanent source of power only if it is backed by substantial assets. Guy's dependence upon loans recklessly outstripped his real resources.

Until the last years of the thirteenth century the most important creditors of the princes and the municipalities of the Netherlands were to be found in northern France, at Arras, Paris and the fairs of Champagne.

---

[1] F. Funck-Brentano, *Philippe le Bel en Flandre* (Paris, 1897), 80.   [2] *Ibid.* 79–80.
[3] *Annales Gandenses* (ed. H. Johnstone, London, 1951), 11: *deficientibus expensis et ab amicis omnibus quasi derelictus.*

All this was altered during the prolonged Franco-Flemish warfare between 1297 and 1320. The financiers of Arras gradually ceased to lend. The debts of the counts and of the chief Flemish cities to them were repudiated and little could be expected henceforth by the Flemings from this quarter. The fairs of Champagne lost their international importance. But during the same period facilities for borrowing increased inside the Netherlands. Regular voyages of Catalan and Genoese merchant galleys to Bruges began in the last years of the thirteenth century. Henceforth the representatives of several leading Italian trading companies were permanently settled at Bruges.[1] Lombard pawnbrokers scattered their *tables de prêt* throughout the southern Netherlands. There was also much local capital seeking safe investment. This encouraged the princes of the Netherlands to practise the sale of annuities. They were, apparently, the first European rulers to adapt to their needs this hitherto exclusively urban device. The count of Holland was selling life-rents in 1336 and the rulers of Flanders and Brabant did so repeatedly in the third quarter of the fourteenth century. Thus there was a plentiful supply of credit facilities in the Netherlands, but the ability of rulers and municipalities to make good use of them fluctuated with their political fortunes and the degree of their financial solvency.

The long-term remedy for the financial troubles of the Belgian rulers lay in creating a system of taxation or, at least, in earning a recognition of their right to tax their subjects in moments of serious need. Borrowing, when secured by taxes, could be a useful device, but otherwise it could easily become a source of grave weakness, as in the case of Guy of Flanders. The great constitutional crisis in Brabant in 1312–14, during the minority of Duke John III, provides another clear example. His father, John II, had left large debts. In 1313 Brabantine merchants were being arrested abroad by the creditors of John II. This provoked the formation of a league of Brabantine towns. They were willing to assume responsibility for a part of the ducal debts, up to a total amount of 40,000 *li. brab.* (24,000 *li. par.*), in return for the redress of various grievances. Their demands were accepted, and in July 1314 all the ducal revenues were temporarily placed under the control of the commissioners delegated by the towns, to whom was entrusted the payment of the ducal debts. The crisis left a permanent legacy of constitutional restrictions on ducal power.[2]

Flanders passed through a far more prolonged and devastating finan-

---

[1] The Peruzzi of Florence possessed a regular branch at Bruges by 1302. Cf. A. Sapori, *Studi di Storia Economica*, 3rd ed. (Florence, 1956), I, 59, n. 4.

[2] J. Van der Straeten, *Het Charter en de Raad van Kortenberg*, II (Brussels, 1952); E. Lousse, 'Les deux chartes romanes brabançonnes du 12 juillet 1314', *Bulletin de la Commission Royale d'Histoire*, XCVI (1932).

cial crisis in the early fourteenth century. The treaty of peace with France in 1305 imposed a crushing war contribution upon the county. Between June 1305 and September 1333, Flanders paid 869,000 *li. par.* to successive French governments.[1] The cities of Flanders had to repudiate in part their old foreign debts and their credit declined seriously. The main bankrupt was in reality the count, as the Flemish cities had incurred a large part of the debt to Arras lenders on his behalf. The repudiation of debts was facilitated by the policy of the French Crown. Successive French kings willingly authorized suspension of payments to the creditors of the Flemish counts and municipalities in order to assure speedier payment of the Flemish contributions due to the royal treasury. The days when the counts could borrow large sums through the Flemish cities or on their security had gone. Hence the extreme dependence of Guy's successor, Robert III (1305–22), in his early years on Italian financiers. It was a case of regular borrowing out of necessity rather than choice, and Robert fell into the hands of some very unscrupulous Sienese. By April 1306 Robert had appointed as his receiver Thomas Fini of the Company of the Gallerani. The count was heavily in debt to this firm at the time when Fini assumed office. Robert reposed at first great trust in Fini and for a while this Sienese merchant virtually controlled the government of the county. Fini undertook to provide 500 *li. par.* a week for the expenses of the comital household. A steady supply of money was thus assured to the count. Fini busied himself with raising further loans from other Italians. The loans procured by him at the fairs of Champagne were apparently the last that the counts of Flanders ever raised there. Robert's credit at the fairs sank very low after the fall of Fini in the summer or early autumn of 1309. The assets of the merchants of Ypres were seized at the fairs of Champagne at the demand of Scaglia Tifi, to whom Robert III owed 12,000 *li. par.*[2] At the beginning of 1311 Robert claimed that he did not dare to visit France for fear of his creditors there.[3] Henceforth the count borrowed chiefly from the Italians established at Bruges.

Fini was given exceptionally wide powers of control over Flemish internal administration and his tenure of the receivership enhanced permanently the importance of that office.[4] One of his main tasks was the introduction of direct taxation designed to raise the war contributions

---

[1] By comparison, the annual receipts of the French royal treasury oscillated in 1322–9 between 477,000 *li. par.* and 839,000 *li. par.*: R. Fawtier, *Comptes du Trésor* (Paris, 1930), lix–lxiii.

[2] H. Pirenne, 'Un conflit entre le magistrat yprois et les gardes des foires de Champagne en 1309–10', *Bulletin de la Commission Royale d'Histoire*, LXXXVI (1922).

[3] Funck-Brentano, *op. cit.* 568, n. 1.

[4] R. Monier, *Les institutions centrales du comté de Flandre de la fin du IXe siècle à 1384* (Paris, 1943), 70; H. Nowé, *Les baillis comtaux de Flandre des origines à la fin du XIVe siècle* (Brussels, 1926), 132.

HH

demanded by France. Fini's dismissal may have been due to growing complaints against his extortions and corrupt methods.[1] His last account was completed on 25 September 1309. At that date the count appeared to be in debt to the Gallerani, but Fini was accused, quite justifiably it seems, of serious frauds. He managed to flee abroad, but his brother was in all probability executed by the count.

The political position of the counts of Flanders was weaker in the first half of the fourteenth century than it had been before 1294. They could no longer afford to pursue ambitious policies, independent alike of their French sovereign and of the wishes of their subjects. But the financial position of the counts gradually improved under Robert III and his successor, Louis de Nevers. The people of Flanders became accustomed to frequent taxation. The count's authority was repeatedly challenged by internal revolts, but confiscations and fines that followed their repression brought in large sums: Louis de Nevers received 300,000 li. in this way between 1328 and 1331. The regular revenue also grew, in part through the diversion to the comital treasury of annual payments originally due to the king of France. The count's regular revenue in 1332 (c. 36,000 li. par. a year) was appreciably larger than it had been in 1305. Under a wise ruler Flemish government could probably have remained solvent in the 'thirties and the presence of abundant credit facilities in the Netherlands could have been a source of strength to it. Several Italians acted as chief receivers of Flanders under Louis, including a member of the rich Florentine firm of the Peruzzi. Unfortunately, Louis de Nevers was an improvident man, quite incapable of turning the improvement in his financial situation after 1328 to lasting advantage. By 1332 he owed again 357,000 li. The potential strength of the financial position was only revealed under his astute son, Louis de Male (1346–84).

The credit operations of Edward III in the Netherlands do not, of course, belong to the history of the public credit of the Belgian princes, but they throw welcome light on the distribution of the potential Belgian lenders.[2] In 1338–40 Edward combed the Netherlands for loans. If advances by Englishmen and by Edward's habitual Italian bankers are excluded, at least £195,000 sterling (c. 624,000 li. par.)[3] were raised from other Italians, Germans and native Belgians. Lenders from Brabant were particularly important (£91,000). They included important councillors of the duke, cloth merchants and other prominent citizens of Brussels, Louvain and Malines, money-changers and pawnbrokers of Antwerp

---

[1] Cf. *Annales Gandenses* (ed. cit.), 97.

[2] E. B. Fryde, *Edward III's War Finance, 1337–41* (D. Phil. dissertation, 1947, deposited at the Bodleian Library, Oxford).

[3] Equivalent to nearly one year's normal revenue of Philip VI of France. Cf. figures for 1329 and 1349 in R. Fawtier, *Comptes du Trésor* (Paris, 1930), lxii–lxiv.

and other towns. The exact share of Flanders is harder to ascertain. The only unmistakably Flemish lenders of note were the Lombard pawn-brokers of Bruges. It is probable that the majority of the German, Italian and Catalan lenders were active in Bruges, but some may have been established at Antwerp. Bruges was certainly at that time the outstanding place in the Netherlands for negotiating loans. Whenever Edward III urgently needed money he usually sent agents to Bruges to procure it. Bruges was equally important to Edward during the long siege of Calais in 1346–7.[1]

In the fourteenth century money-lending could raise a man to great wealth in the Netherlands. Two of the lenders who helped Edward III provide good examples of this. Simon van Halen (or Mirabello) was the son of an Italian pawnbroker who had acted as receiver of Brabant. Simon became receiver of Flanders and married an illegitimate sister of the count. But he remained a partner in a chain of Flemish and Braban-tine pawnshops: one contemporary writer described him as *usuarius maximus*. In December 1339 Simon was proclaimed regent (*ruwaert*) of Flanders by the revolutionary government at Ghent. The promotion of such a man to this position would have been unthinkable in any other country of north-western Europe. Between 1336 and 1346 Simon lent money annually to Ghent and his advances were the mainstay of Arte-velde's regime. The fall of Artevelde was followed by the assassination of Simon himself.

William van Duvenvoorde represented a very different type of lender, more reminiscent of the German financier-landowners of the lower Rhineland. Early in his career he became a trusted household official of the count of Holland. He displayed a special preference for investing spare capital in loans to rulers. His known advances stretch from 1316 to 1352 and his clients included, at one time or another, most of the princes and bishops in the Netherlands. He charged interest of course: thus, in 1320 he advanced a loan to his master, William I of Holland, at 20%. But he himself had, at times, to borrow from businessmen. As his wealth in-creased, he steadily bought more land and he used his loans to rulers for the same purpose. Thus he converted a temporary grant of the lordship of Breda into a hereditary possession by remitting to the duke of Bra-bant, whose trusted councillor he was, all the ducal debts owed to him. At his death in 1353, he was the wealthiest non-princely landowner in the Netherlands. His possessions, descending in the sixteenth century to William of Orange, provided the bulk of William's immense fortune in the Netherlands.

---

[1] P.R.O. Exchequer Accounts Various, E. 101/128/3; K.R. Customs Accounts, E. 122/197/4.

(2) THE BURGUNDIAN STATE (TO 1477)

The rich financial archives of the Burgundian dynasty have been in-sufficiently studied and are still largely unpublished.[1] Thus, while it is clear that all the four Valois dukes who ruled down to 1477 borrowed frequently, when their records are fully explored it may turn out that they borrowed *almost continuously*, except perhaps for an interval of relative financial ease between *c.* 1440 and 1465. The Burgundian dynasty was certainly conspicuous among medieval princes for its steady appreciation of the value of good relations with financiers. The treatment of its chief bankers provides a welcome contrast with the more reckless proceedings of the French kings. No important lender was ever executed or brutally despoiled of everything by the Burgun-dian dukes.

The reasons for this constant borrowing are fairly clear. The Burgun-dian dukes tried to be the political equals of the major powers of Europe. Until the acquisition by Philip the Good of the greater part of the Netherlands (between 1428 and 1433), they lacked sufficient income to sustain these ambitions. Much of their borrowing represented only an anticipation of their ordinary revenues. Without such flexible means of mobilizing all their resources they could not have achieved very much. But they were trying to do more than that. They were groping after some way of living regularly beyond their inadequate income. They tried to increase it each year through loans, in the hope that taxes, foreign subsidies or some other windfall would wipe out one day the accumu-lated surplus debt, or at least would reduce it again to manageable pro-portions. It is no wonder that Burgundian borrowing exceeded at times all bounds of prudence. This happened repeatedly under the first two dukes, Philip the Bold and John the Fearless. They would have been helpless without large subsidies from the French Crown, which con-stituted about 40% of the income of Philip the Bold at the height of his power in 1400–4. The size of these subsidies depended on the influence exerted by the dukes over the French government and varied in amount as a result of the fluctuations in internal French politics. These uncertain-ties help to account for some of the excessive borrowing of Philip and John. But there are more general reasons for the recklessness displayed by the Burgundian rulers in their use of credit. All of them were in-different to purely financial considerations and, except perhaps for the founder of the dynasty, were poor administrators. Philip the Bold and John habitually incurred larger debts than was financially sound, because

---

[1] Since this was written M. Mollat has used these records to calculate that loans contracted by Philip the Good totalled *c.* 2,760,000 *li. tur.* and that Charles the Bold borrowed *c.* 1,970,000 *li. tur.*: *Revue Historique*, CCXIX (1958), 314–16.

their political schemes required this. The third duke, Philip the Good, according to his court biographer, disdained to have anything to do with financial administration and was not interested in knowing the size of his revenue.[1] Nevertheless, he was the first solvent member of his house, because he had the good fortune to acquire sufficiently large and valuable new possessions. His successor, Charles, was indifferent to all considerations of prudence in finance, as in any other matters.

The Burgundian dynasty acquired most of its possessions by marriage, inheritance or conquest. But there were also purchases. Of particular importance was the acquisition by Philip the Bold of claims to the duchy of Limburg and other Brabantine lands east of the Meuse. In this eastern portion of the Netherlands somewhat backward forms of credit transactions still flourished, based on mortgaging of land as was usual in medieval Germany. At the death of Duke Wenceslas of Brabant in 1383, almost all the Brabantine possessions east of the Meuse were in the hands of his creditors. The lenders were no mere merchants, but leading vassals of the duke who, like other German *raubritter*, had accumulated much wealth from war and the plundering of merchants and were eager to invest it in castles and lordships. They did not expect that the duke of Brabant would ever manage to assemble enough money to redeem his lands. But Philip the Bold, with the support of Duchess Jeanne of Brabant, bought them all out between 1387 and 1396. The necessary money was raised with considerable difficulty and after long delays; Philip had to borrow some of it on onerous terms. But the cost mattered little in view of the issues at stake. Philip's main aim was to secure the recognition of one of his sons as Jeanne's heir to all the Brabantine lands, and his purchase of the mortgaged lordships 'd'Outre-Meuse' was an important step in this direction. It prepared the way for the ultimate acquisition of Brabant by the Burgundian dynasty.

The Burgundian state consisted of very diverse territories. In each there existed some long-established facilities for governmental borrowing and some traditional contacts with particular business centres. The Burgundian dukes simultaneously exploited all the varied possibilities for borrowing that their position gave them. In the duchy of Burgundy Philip the Bold inherited a backward financial system and mediocre revenues which averaged around 70,000 *li. tur.* a year under Philip. Use of credit was limited chiefly to loans from petty Lombard pawnbrokers, supplemented by semi-compulsory levies from ducal officials and richer townsmen. But in the fifteenth century the dukes borrowed, through the intermediacy of local middlemen from Burgundy, at the fairs of Geneva. The dependence of the first two dukes on French subsidies has already been

[1] J. Bartier, *Légistes et gens de finances au XVe siècle. Les conseillers des Ducs de Bourgogne, Philippe le Bon et Charles le Téméraire* (Brussels, 1955), 164 and n. 2.

noted. They had to preserve at all costs their influence in France. Maintenance of close contacts with leading Parisians was an important feature of their policy. Thus, both out of business convenience and for political reasons, the dukes ranked among the foremost customers of Paris merchants and money-lenders. For example, in 1403 Philip the Bold owed 60,000 *li. tur.* to a group of leading Parisians for commodities and loans (16% of the receipts of the Burgundian receiver-general in that year). Many Paris businessmen had valuable interests at Bruges as well as in France and they were naturally inclined to deal, as much as possible, with the lord of Flanders.

By his acquisition in 1384 of Artois and Flanders Philip nearly trebled his income (*c.* 183,000 *li. tur.* from the two counties in 1386–7).[1] His predecessor in Flanders, Count Louis de Male, had carefully safeguarded and expanded his prerogative sources of revenue, and he managed to derive a considerable additional income from various bargains with the towns and from taxation. Indirectly, his financial success was based largely on credit, because Flemish towns could only meet his frequent financial demands by borrowing. Louis de Male himself did not borrow overmuch. He was not, it seems, particularly dependent on any one single lender but exploited all the varied sources of credit that existed at Bruges and elsewhere in Flanders. Besides contracting short-term loans, Louis also sold life-rents secured by revenues due from the towns. The receivers of Flanders were now mainly Flemings, but they were expected to make advances to the count, just as their foreign predecessors used to do. The more important Flemish tolls were farmed to a succession of Italians. Philip continued to use the same credit facilities, but did so less moderately and wisely. Most of the foreigners frequenting Bruges were probably not very keen on lending money to the local ruler. It was an Italian merchant established at Bruges who wrote in 1399 to his associates: 'No one ever becomes embroiled with great lords without losing his feathers in the end.' The business community of Bruges could only be tapped effectively through the intermediacy of one of its more influential and trusted members. Hence the regular employment by Philip of a firm of Italian merchant-bankers, the Rapondi of Lucca. Dino Rapondi supplied the Burgundian government with goods and money for over forty years and proved during that long period an exceptionally accommodating creditor. He became Philip's *maître d'hôtel* in 1384 and, until his death in 1415, he remained a trusted councillor of the Burgundian dukes. The best-known incident of his career was his contribution to the ransoming of John the Fearless after John's capture by the Turks in the rout of Nicopolis. On Rapondi's request and security several Genoese made preliminary advances that helped to procure John's release. A three months'

---

[1] H. Van Werveke in *Trans. R. Hist. Soc.*, 1949, 123 (given there as 146,245 *li. par.*).

visit to Italy by Rapondi, in the course of which he advanced 131,000 *li. tur.* to John at Venice, sufficed to complete other necessary arrangements for John's return home. The payments of interest, gifts and special privileges showered on Dino Rapondi by the dukes made him into one of the richest merchants in Europe.

The income of Philip the Bold (1363–1404) rose from *c.* 100,000 *li. tur.* at the start of his career to some 500,000 *li. tur.* in his last years.[1] But, nevertheless, Philip was seldom free for long from serious financial embarrassments and some of his most cherished schemes were delayed by lack of funds. He borrowed continually, but could not always manage to procure all that was needed. Philip died heavily in debt. His widow renounced her right to her share of the inheritance to avoid responsibility for his liabilities. His successor could not prevent the seizure of all the contents of l'Hôtel d'Artois, the ducal residence in Paris, at the suit of Philip's creditors.[2] A loan from Dino Rapondi paid for Philip's funeral.

The ducal finances deteriorated still further under John the Fearless (1404–19). He was a bad administrator, indifferent to details. Also he was not allowed to inherit most of his father's pension from the French king, and Burgundian revenue declined at once by nearly 100,000 *li. tur.* a year. These money troubles added an element of desperation to John's policy and may have largely determined his decision to kill Louis d'Orléans, whom he regarded as the main obstacle both to his general plans and to his financial demands. In the absence of any adequate study of John's finances, it is impossible to arrive at any precise estimate of the amounts he borrowed during the ensuing civil war. In 1410–11, the first period of open warfare, his known loans amounted to at least 200,000 *li. tur.*, which would correspond to roughly a quarter of his income in those two years. Even incomplete estimates of this sort are not possible for the remaining years of John's life. But it is certain that, until the end, he remained desperately short of money. The disastrous effects of the civil war on the credit of all the protagonists have been mentioned in an earlier section. John could at least rely on a larger number of professional lenders than his opponents. The support of the Rapondi secured for him the help of the majority of the Lucchese and many Parisian financiers remained faithful to the Burgundian party.[3] A vast quantity of Burgundian jewels had to be pledged to money-lenders. At his death John

---

[1] Cf. E. Perroy, 'Feudalism or principalities in fifteenth century France', *Bulletin of the Institute of Historical Research*, XX (1945), 184.

[2] J. Calmette and E. Déprez, *Histoire Générale* (ed. G. Glotz): *Histoire du Moyen Âge*, VII (1), (1937), 543, n. 92.

[3] L. Mirot, *Une grande famille parlementaire aux XIVe et XVe siècles: les d'Orgemont* (Paris, 1913), 140–1.

left a mass of debts. Repayment of some of them was delayed for several decades.

The character of the Burgundian state altered considerably under Philip the Good. His acquisitions in the Netherlands could yield at least as much income as did the older possessions of his house. In the second half of Philip's reign his revenues reached, in some years, the remarkably high totals of the last years of his grandfather (400,000 to 500,000 *li. tur.*), but this time there were no French subsidies and it all came from the Burgundian possessions alone. With his new territories Philip acquired valuable fresh facilities for borrowing. Antwerp attracted, as yet, fewer Italians than Bruges, but it was increasingly frequented by English and German merchants. Loans from them became of outstanding importance, however, only after the death of Charles the Bold. The practice of selling hereditary and life annuities had long been familiar, particularly to the governments of Brabant and Hainault, and under Philip issues of new ducal annuities occurred most frequently in those two provinces. The dukes usually sold these rents through the intermediacy of the municipal governments. The duke handed over to the municipalities revenues sufficient to cover the yearly cost of the new annuities, while the towns sold the rents so secured in their own names. Thus the great domain of Mons, contributing about one-sixth of the total domanial revenues of Philip in Hainault, was in his time used almost exclusively to pay rents issued on his behalf by the towns of Valenciennes and Mons. The Burgundian government could afford to assign a part of its income in this way because it disposed of extensive revenues elsewhere.

The administration of the Burgundian finances was much tainted with corruption.[1] One important cause of abuses was the weakness of the ducal credit. Delays in the repayment of government debts led to illicit speculation in ducal obligations. A special commission had to be appointed in March 1404, shortly before the death of Philip the Bold, to investigate this evil. It was alleged that ducal officials were buying up Philip's debts (*cédules et mandements d'argent*) at a discount, paying sometimes a half, sometimes a third, or even a quarter of their face value. The same abuses recurred under Philip the Good and were prohibited by a ducal ordinance of 1454, though apparently again without much effect. As in contemporary France, the persistent need for government borrowing from officials was one of the main reasons why these and other malpractices continued to flourish with relative impunity. Thus Odot Molain, the leading financier in the duchy of Burgundy and a ducal councillor, for nineteen years possessed the monopoly of supplying with salt all the ducal *greniers* in Burgundy. In 1448 he was heavily fined for illicit dealings in

---

[1] Bartier, *op. cit.* 156: *Nous pensons . . . que dans l'état bourguignon la prévarication était un mal profondément enraciné et que les ducs n'ont iamais tenté sérieusement de détruire.*

salt; but in 1453 Duke Philip was again humbly begging Molain for loans and promising to satisfy any requests that the financier and his partners might make.[1]

Except perhaps in his earliest years, Philip the Good did not borrow very much from any single banker. For many years his credit was none too good. When in 1452–3 he desperately needed money to put down the revolt of Ghent, he found it necessary to borrow through the intermediacy of Molain. The latter was specifically paid interest (10%) for the expenses he might incur at Geneva and elsewhere in raising the money. Foreign merchants at the fairs of Geneva clearly preferred to deal with a professional financier like Molain rather than to lend directly to Duke Philip. Some of the leading financiers had become very distrustful of rulers in general. The Medici were in Philip's time the most important Italian firm represented at Bruges, but as long as Cosimo de' Medici was head of the firm (1429–64) all the branches abroad were firmly restrained from dealing with princes, except when Cosimo permitted them. The next head of the Medici bank, Piero (1464–9), would have liked to pursue the same policy, but he was unable to control properly the new manager of the Bruges branch, Tommaso Portinari, who was a personal friend of Duke Charles of Burgundy. Pointed reminders that dealings with rulers had brought many merchants into trouble[2] had no effect on Portinari. He was even able to persuade Piero's successor, Lorenzo, to relax in 1471 the ban on lending to the Burgundian government 'because of the good qualities of this illustrious prince [Charles] and because of the many favours received from him through his friendship for Tommaso Portinari'. An upper limit was stipulated beyond which Portinari was not to lend to the government, but even this safeguard disappeared from a fresh contract concluded between Lorenzo and Portinari in 1473, and by 1477 the original limit had been surpassed by at least 40,000 *li. tur.* Portinari for a while enjoyed great influence at the Burgundian court. Various valuable ducal assets were entrusted to him in partial satisfaction of his large loans; he farmed the toll at Gravelines, levied on English wool imported from Calais, and a tax on imported alum. But at the time of Charles's death in January 1477 the duke owed the Medici 9,500 *li. gros* (114,000 *li. tur.*), which his successors were in no position to repay speedily. The Bruges branch was not yet bankrupt, but Lorenzo could not afford to sink any more money into it. Losses on the London and Bruges branches up to 1478 were estimated by Lorenzo at 70,000 ducats. So the Bruges branch was wound up in 1480.

Few medieval rulers wasted a great inheritance so quickly as did

---

[1] Bartier, *op. cit.* 167.
[2] Cf. Piero's letter in 1469 quoted by R. de Roover in 'Lorenzo il Magnifico e il tramonto del Banco dei Medici', *Archivio Storico Italiano*, CVII (1949), 176–7.

Charles the Bold. He spent money freely in pursuit of grandiose ambitions. It was the pledging to Charles, for a loan of 50,000 *Rh. fl.*, of all the rights of Sigismund of Tirol in Alsace that chiefly brought him into the fatal conflict with the Swiss. Charles had inherited a large reserve from his father, but it was all spent within the first five years of his rule. The Estates General of the Netherlands were induced to grant him heavy taxes. Charles's average annual revenue was nearly twice as large as the average income of his father during the last ten years of his rule (a yearly average of 366,000 *li. tur.* for Philip and of 693,000 *li. tur.* for Charles).[1] Money was borrowed everywhere. The loans from the Medici became specially important after 1470. Other native and foreign merchants in the Netherlands and Burgundy were also brought under contribution. Chancellor Hugonet told the Estates General that about 400,000 *li.* (a year's normal revenue) had been raised in 1472 from the sale of annuities.[2] Charles even authorized forced sales of rents if no voluntary buyers could be found.[3] Cases of forcible borrowing multiplied. In July 1473 the duke suddenly revoked all the special licences to Lombard pawnbrokers throughout the Netherlands and seized their establishments. The sole purpose of the operation was to force the Lombards to advance a large loan (14,000 *écus* lent by the holders of 45 pawnshops), whereupon they were all allowed to resume business. The account of the chief ducal receiver for 1475 contains a long list of officials who contributed 12,000 *li. tur.* to a forced loan in that year. In Burgundy the chief financial officials at Dijon declared in 1474 that they no longer knew how they could raise further loans. Towards the end of Charles's reign financial difficulties became crippling. The desertion of some of his mercenary forces in 1476 was due in part to lack of pay. But Charles was not yet financially ruined at the time of his final defeat. According to Commynes, during the last campaign outside Nancy he could still draw on a large store of money kept within easy reach at the castle of Luxembourg.[4] Considerable fresh resources could have been procured from the Netherlands. This was, at least, the opinion of Commynes. There was also the great collection of ducal jewels which could be pledged to lenders and were so used by Charles's daughter in the critical years after his death. The credit of the Burgundian dynasty had never sunk so low as in the early months of 1477. Yet Mary of Burgundy and her husband had only to maintain themselves in power for their credit with businessmen to revive.

[1] J. Bartier in *Algemene Geschiedenis der Nederlanden*, III (Utrecht, 1951), 293.

[2] *Environ 400 mille livres procedans des vendicions des rentes a la cherge et par engaigement de son demaine*, printed in J. Cuvelier, etc. (ed.), *Actes des États Généraux des anciens Pays-Bas*, I (Brussels, 1948), 186.

[3] L. J. A. Diegerick, *Inventaire analytique et chronologique des chartes et documents appartenant aux archives de la ville d'Ypres*, IV (1859), nos. 1032, 1035, 1036.

[4] Philippe de Commynes, *Mémoires*, II (ed. J. Calmette, Paris, 1925), 150.

Charles's reckless career did no lasting damage to the financial prospects of the Burgundian government in the Netherlands. And, within a few decades Antwerp became the chief business centre of north-western Europe, the place where not only its own Habsburg sovereigns but many other princes habitually sought relief from their financial troubles.

VII. Germany

(1) INTRODUCTORY

From the beginning of the thirteenth century the constitutional development of Germany diverges rapidly from that of the increasingly centralized other leading powers of the West. After 1250 no German king combined in a lasting fashion German with Italian resources, previously a mainstay of Hohenstaufen power, and the royal revenues from Germany, never adequate, were further drastically reduced through the dissipation during the great Interregnum (1250–72) of the bulk of the Hohenstaufen domains. The attempts of Rudolf of Habsburg to recover royal lands and prerogatives achieved some success, but the resulting improvement did not endure. The continued weakness of the monarchy after 1273 prevented the creation of central administrative and financial institutions such as the English and French kings developed. The autonomy of the German princes, already safeguarded in the privileges granted under Frederick II in 1220 and 1231–2,[1] became permanently established during the Interregnum. Germany came to consist of some 300 'territories' whose rulers were virtually independent *domini terrae*. It is only in some of the principalities that a centralized organization appeared at a late date and haltingly.

The material endowment of the monarchy was exposed after 1273 to further attrition through lack of dynastic continuity. At each royal election the votes of the electors had to be bought by exorbitant concessions, and loans needed for payments to the electors had to be secured by pledging royal property. The financial resources of the German kingship failed to expand and even tended to contract. In wealth, and even in administrative efficiency, the German kings were overshadowed by the more powerful princes of the Empire.

After 1272 only those German kings who controlled valuable principalities could attain some degree of financial stability, and several of them, like Louis IV of Bavaria (1314–47), disposed of resources 'ludicrously

---

[1] For recent attempts to reconsider the existing views on the influence of these privileges, see K. Hampe, *Deutsche Kaisergeschichte in der Zeit der Salier und Staufer* (10th ed. by F. Baethgen, 1949), 286 ff.; H. Mitteis, 'Zum Mainzer Reichslandfrieden', in *Rechtsidee in der Geschichte* (1957), 416–17.

inadequate to sustain a kingly activity'.[1] Frequent borrowing was thus a necessity.

The mediocre development of the royal and princely finances in late medieval Germany is sometimes attributed to the relative backwardness of the German economy.[2] In the sphere of public credit there is, certainly, one striking economic contrast between Germany and the countries further west. While in England and France the expansion of princely borrowing in the late thirteenth century was connected with the influx of Italian financiers, Germany was almost entirely neglected by Italian businessmen. This probably had some bearing on the persistence in Germany of the types of public borrowing that elsewhere were not of paramount importance after the middle of the thirteenth century.

Loans raised on the security of pledged property and princely prerogatives remained extremely common in Germany throughout the Middle Ages.[3] Before 1250 the German kings had been reluctant to pledge royal property on a large scale, but during the great Interregnum this became the habitual method of raising money and every subsequent medieval German king had to resort to it. German rulers frequently had to borrow not from merchants but from fellow-princes, prelates or nobles, and these eminent creditors were particularly attracted by the chances of increasing thereby their territorial power. The pledging of domains and governmental powers was the normal sort of security demanded by one German ruler from another in all sorts of circumstances (treaties, marriage alliances, war indemnities, etc.) and it is often difficult to distinguish between pledges for debts arising out of loans and the mortgaging of property for other reasons.[4]

Two types of pledges were known in medieval Germany, the property gage (substanzpfand) and the usufruct gage (nutzungspfand). The property gage in its older form involved the physical transfer of the pledged land to the creditor, and the pledges made by the German kings were of this sort. The royal possessions mortgaged by the sovereign remained legally the property of the Reich, but had to be incorporated into the territory

---

[1] H. S. Offler, 'Empire and Papacy: the last struggle', *Trans. R. Hist. Soc.*, 1956, 31.

[2] The belief in a relative economic backwardness of Germany and of the finances of its rulers is not shared by all the leading German authorities. These views had been criticized by G. von Below (attacking Lotz) in *Weltwirtschaftliches Archiv*, 1919, 72 ff. and by A. Dopsch, *V.f.Soz.u.W.G.* XIV (1918), 509 ff. A more sober approach is to be found in E. Bamberger, 'Die Finanzverwaltung in den deutschen Territorien des Mittelalters, 1200–1500', *Zeitschrift für die gesamte Staatswissenschaft*, LXXVII (1923), 168–255. For a recent well-balanced discussion see Th. Mayer in Gerloff–Neumark, *Handbuch der Finanzwissenschaft*, I (1952), 236 ff.

[3] H. Niese, *Die Verwaltung des Reichsgutes im 13. Jahrhundert* (1905), 168 ff., 243 ff. 262 ff.; H. Planitz, *Das deutsche Grundpfandrecht* (1936), 85.

[4] For a discussion of the evidence, Planitz, *op. cit.*

of the creditor; the royal subjects inhabiting them were ordered to take an oath of allegiance and to do homage to their new temporary lord. It was normally stipulated that the income from the pledged possessions should not be deducted from the debt, but to avoid the charge of usury the revenues were sometimes donated to the creditor. The Hohenstaufen emperors could dispose of the properties belonging to the Reich only with the consent of the German princes, but after 1250 this rule ceased to be strictly observed. Other territorial rulers could, in consequence of the privileges of 1220 and 1230-1, dispose freely of their possessions, and their transactions were modelled on the royal practice. A veritable riot of princely pledging was only checked to some extent in the late Middle Ages by the opposition of the provincial Estates.

The mortgaging of the imperial cities (*Reichsstädte*) by the Crown to the princes was especially important because these towns formed the most valuable part of the royal endowments. In order to retain their direct connection with the Crown the cities themselves often preferred to repay the debts in respect of which they had been mortgaged. The pledging of the *Reichstädte* could thus become a form of forced loan from the towns.

In addition to the pledging of territories, towns and estates, the German kings and other princes also frequently engaged profitable regalian rights, especially the tolls and the mints. The tax on the Jews (*Judensteuer*) was often pledged and sometimes even the persons of the Jews, with all the profits that might be derived from them. Thus on 25 June 1349 Charles IV pledged to the city of Frankfurt all the Jews resident there for a debt of 15,200 heller pounds. The pawning of valuables by the German princes was also very frequent.

While loans secured by immovable or movable pledges predominated, most other contemporary forms of borrowing were also practised in Germany. The issuing to creditors of letters obligatory unsupported by other guarantees was common, particularly by ecclesiastical princes, and these documents circulated freely. Like the towns, the princes, particularly of western Germany, also sold annuities on a fair scale from the first half of the fourteenth century onwards.

(2) ROYAL CREDIT OPERATIONS

The outstanding fact about the finances of the German emperors in the second half of the twelfth century was their reliance on large revenues from Italy.[1] The recovery of regalian rights in the Italian kingdom gave Frederick I an additional annual income estimated at *c.* 30,000 pounds and

[1] See especially the works of G. Deibel: 'Die italienischen Einkünfte Kaiser Friedrich Barbarossas', *Neue Heidelberger Jahrbücher* (N.F. 1932) and 'Die finanzielle Bedeutung Reichs-Italiens für die staufischen Herrscher des zwölften Jahrhunderts', *ZRG.* LIV (1934).

further substantial sums were secured from miscellaneous sources. Royal revenues from Germany were much smaller than those derived by the Hohenstaufen from Italy. Frederick I needed considerable sums for his wars and for his mercenary troops.[1] We have referred elsewhere to the loan contracted by him in 1174 at Liège and to the recurrent heavy borrowing by some of the leading German prelates in order to fulfil their military obligations in Italy. Loans were also contracted by the Hohenstaufen from Italian lenders. Thus in 1190 a legate of Henry VI borrowed 1,000 marks of silver (by weight of Cologne) from the bishop of Volterra on the security of various revenues.

In the civil war between Philip of Swabia and Otto IV both sides started hostilities well endowed with treasure, but were later compelled to borrow extensively.[2] The pledging of royal estates, revenues and regalian rights anticipated on a smaller scale the practices of the later German monarchs, but no really massive mortgaging of royal property occurred in Germany until the reign of Conrad IV (1250–4).

Frederick II was the richest secular ruler of his time. His Italian possessions, which provided the bulk of this wealth, and his credit operations there fall outside the scope of this chapter. He was fully prepared repeatedly to raise short-term loans,[3] repayable by assignments on the regular Sicilian revenues. Some of the loans contracted in Italy came from his German subjects.[4] An incomplete list of Frederick's revenues from Germany in 1241 enumerates sources of income totalling some 7,700 marks.[5] The royal agents administering these revenues lent considerable sums to the emperor. Some of these men were clearly very wealthy. After Wolf of Hainault was dismissed from the office of *scultetus* and imprisoned for extortions, Frederick in 1236 recovered from him 16,000 marks.[6]

Frederick's successor, Conrad IV, deliberately sacrificed his German assets. He inaugurated the policy of mass pledging of royal properties in 1251 in preparation for his expedition to Italy.[7] The remainder of the royal possessions was largely dissipated during the great Interregnum.

---

[1] H. Grundmann, *DA.* v (1942).

[2] Böhmer–Ficker, *Regesta Imperii*, v, nos. 53, 227.

[3] E.g. E. Winkelmann, *De regni Siculi administratione, qualis fuerit regnante Frederico II* (1859), 31–2.

[4] Böhmer–Ficker, *Regesta Imperii*, v, nos. 2609, 2713, 3107.

[5] K. Zeumer, 'Zur Geschichte der Reichssteuern im früheren Mittelalter', *HZ*, LXXXI (1898), 24–45; B. Hilliger, 'Die Reichssteuerliste von 1242', *HV.* XXVIII (1934) giving the estimate of 7,700 marks; Hilliger's evaluation criticized recently by G. Kirchner, 'Die Steuerliste von 1241', *ZRG.* LXX (1953).

[6] For comparison, the dowry of Isabella of England, married to Frederick II in 1235, amounted to 30,000 marks.

[7] Böhmer–Ficker, *Regesta Imperii*, v, nos. 4553, 4559, 4562, 4563a.

Conrad's opponent, the anti-king William of Holland, had very slender resources and depended mainly on papal subsidies.[1] In Germany he was forced to pledge imperial properties and some of his debts were repaid only by his successor, Richard of Cornwall. Richard was a wealthy man and his occasional borrowing was due to purely temporary difficulties. He derived the bulk of his resources, however, from England.

In electing Rudolf of Habsburg in 1273 the electors chose a very experienced and practical man who made the fullest use of the limited resources left to him. He inaugurated his reign by a determined attempt to recover alienated royal possessions. He increased the annual tax paid by the imperial towns (*stura*), which in 1241 represented approximately two-thirds of the royal revenues, and raised its yield even in his early years to over 8,000 silver marks (probably more than the issues of his hereditary possessions in south-western Germany). Furthermore on several occasions he imposed extraordinary taxes on the *Reichsstädte* which yielded much more than the annual *stura*. The proceeds were used, among other things, to repay his debts.[2] Rudolf was prepared to borrow on a considerable scale to achieve important results. For the crucial campaign of 1276 against Ottokar II of Bohemia Rudolf not only received a large subsidy (12,000 marks) from Pope Gregory X, but also borrowed from Gregory on the security of the town of Kaiserwerth a further 3,000 marks.[3]

By his conquest of Austria Rudolf more than doubled his revenue and acquired also long-established credit facilities. Ottokar's leading financial agent, Konrad von Tulln, continued to administer the Austrian revenues for the Habsburgs and to advance considerable loans on their security with the help of other wealthy Austrian and Bavarian townsmen. Sometimes, as in the year June 1281 to June 1282, Tulln's advances were double the revenues he received during the same period. In October 1282, after six years of such borrowing, the Habsburgs owed Tulln and his associates 15,070 marks and had to pledge valuable properties to them.[4] Leading Viennese businessmen succeeded Tulln as heads of the Austrian finances and chief government creditors. Rudolf was repeatedly forced to pledge royal domains and regalian rights, and it has been estimated that in this way in the course of his reign he diminished the annual royal revenues by at least 5,000 marks. While his pledgings of Austrian revenues represented mostly short-term credit operations,

---

[1] For details see O. Hintze, *Das Königtum Wilhelms von Holland* (1885), 137.

[2] Böhmer–Redlich, *Regesta Imperii*, VI (I) (1898), nos. 2423, 2426–7.

[3] *Ibid.* nos. 438b, 450, 505.

[4] Texts in E. von Schwind and A. Dopsch, *Ausgewählte Urkunden zur Verfassungs-Geschichte der deutsch-österreichischen Erblande im Mittelalter* (1895). Cf. Böhmer–Redlich, *Regesta Imperii*, VI (I), nos. 1280, 1326–7, 1330, 1738–9, 1742.

some of the alienations of the royal domains proved much more enduring.

In preferring Adolf of Nassau to another Habsburg, the electors were deliberately choosing a prince with very mediocre private resources and his election was bound to lead to further alienations of royal revenues. Adolf had to pledge extensive possessions to the electors to pay for their votes. Further mortgaging of royal revenues followed during his reign and his resources would have remained very insufficient if he had not received subsidies first from Edward I of England (£40,000)[1] and later from Philip IV of France (£20,000).

The replacement of Adolf in 1298 by Albrecht I of Austria gave Germany a much wealthier king, practical in financial matters and exceptionally frugal, who inherited a sound financial position in Austria and was able to maintain it. The most important event in the reign of his successor, Henry of Luxembourg, was his expedition to Italy. Henry's financial arrangements set the pattern for all subsequent Italian ventures of the German kings in the fourteenth century. The resources brought by him from Germany only sufficed to launch the enterprise, which thereafter had to be maintained entirely out of the subsidies furnished by his Italian allies (Pisa alone supplied 230,000 florins in 1310–12). Because of this continuous help Henry did not experience serious financial hardship in Italy, even though the large sums needed for his army involved him in temporary embarrassments. Early in 1312 he had even to pledge his crown. But the loans contracted between March 1312 and February 1313 (9,600 florins) represented only 5% of his total receipts in that period (191,500 florins). He had to borrow sometimes on rather costly terms (15 to $26\frac{2}{3}$% in 1312–13), but fortunately he was able to liquidate several debts fairly quickly.

The reign of his successor, Louis IV, was marred by persistent poverty. His own inheritance (Upper Bavaria) provided only slender revenues. In his early years as duke he had frequently been forced to borrow from every type of local Bavarian lender; his creditors included the townsmen of Augsburg and Landshut, a syndicate of rich citizens of Regensburg, the Jews of Augsburg and the Bavarian monasteries.[2] The credit facilities accessible to him were quite inadequate to pay for his election and this had to be purchased by wholesale pledging of the royal revenues to the electors. To the archbishop of Trier were due 22,000 marks and he received in pledge the towns of Boppard and Wesel. The debt to John of Bohemia was 10,000 marks, secured by the town of Cheb and other pos-

---

[1] P.R.O. Pipe Roll, E. 372/144 m. 31 and K.R. Exchequer Accounts Various, E. 101/308/18.

[2] For the Regensburg syndicate see note 334 of L. Rockinger in G. von Lerchenfeld, *Die altbayerischen landständischen Freibriefe* . . . (Munich, 1853).

sessions. The pledges to the archbishop of Mainz included the important *Reichsstadt* of Oppenheim.[1]

It has been said of Louis IV that 'his lack of money was chronic and desperate to a degree which sets him apart from most of his contemporaries'. This hampered him at every crucial point. Thus, his Italian venture resembled Henry VII's expedition in its total dependence on the subsidies of friendly Italian princes, and poverty was one cause of his failure to achieve any lasting results in Italy. Louis's charters and other records teem with references to loans and to alienations of royal assets.[2] Planitz justifiably remarked of Louis that he developed the art of pledging to real virtuosity. He left a greatly depleted royal inheritance.

Unlike Louis, Charles IV disposed of considerable revenues in his hereditary possessions, especially in the kingdom of Bohemia. He skilfully used his wealth to make or consolidate territorial acquisitions such as the part of the Upper Palatinate adjoining Bohemia. The succession of his family to the electorate of Brandenburg was secured in 1373 at the enormous cost of around 500,000 florins.

Charles relates in his autobiography that when he first assumed the government of Bohemia in 1333 on behalf of his spendthrift father, John of Luxembourg, he 'found that kingdom desolate. Not a castle . . . that was not pledged, so that I had nowhere to lodge except in houses in cities like any other citizen. . . I recovered all sorts of other pawned goods alienated from the kingdom.'[3] It was the same in John's other possessions at the end of his rule, though some of John's last debts were incurred in procuring the German crown for Charles in 1346. At the time of John's death, later in the same year, he was heavily in debt to his chief lieutenant and receiver in Luxembourg, Arnoul d'Arlon, and the cost of John's funeral had to be defrayed out of this financier's advances. In spite of these initial difficulties Charles achieved solvency by his orderliness, interest in financial details and frugal tastes.

Charles's two Italian ventures illustrate well his interest in turning everything to financial profit. The initial preparations involved him in some financial embarrassment. Thus, for his second expedition (1368–9), he had to borrow 11,000 florins from the archbishop of Mainz and 3,000 florins at Nuremberg.[4] In Italy he was amply supplied by his allies, but money reached him irregularly and he had to borrow at certain times. He

---

[1] See especially H. Gradenwitz, *Beiträge zur Finanzgeschichte des deutschen Reiches unter Ludwig dem Bayer* (1908), 7 ff.

[2] Böhmer, *Regesta Imperii*, VII (Frankfurt, 1839, with supplements 1–3 published 1841–63), *passim*.

[3] Quoted from the translation in B. Jarrett, *The Emperor Charles IV* (London, 1935), 46–7. The text of *Vita Karoli IV ab ipso conscripta* is reprinted in *Fontes Rerum Bohemicarum* (1871–84), III.

[4] Böhmer–Huber, *Regesta Imperii*, VIII, no. 4616.

was even forced to pledge his crown at Perugia for 1,620 florins, redeeming it only through a further loan from Sienese bankers.[1] But he returned from both expeditions with large treasures. In 1354–5 he may have received in Italy as much as 560,000 florins, in 1368–9 around 307,000 florins.

Charles was particularly concerned with preserving and increasing the revenues in his hereditary dominions. He attached less value to the royal resources in Germany, which probably did not yield much above 30,000 florins a year[2] and which he was quite ready to mortgage. The aggregate value of the possessions pledged by him in Germany in the course of thirty-two years of his reign has been estimated at around 2,000,000 florins, a considerable part being permanently alienated. Charles's readiness to sacrifice regalian rights aroused strong opposition among the Reichsstädte, for they feared permanent mediatization. The enormous sums needed by Charles to acquire Brandenburg led both to the imposition of extraordinary taxes on the Reichsstädte (200,000 florins in 1373–5) and to the pledging of four Swabian imperial cities to Margrave Otto of Brandenburg. The alarm aroused by these threats to urban liberties turned into armed opposition in 1376 after Charles's son, Wenzel, had been elected king. The Swabian towns justifiably feared that the emperor had purchased the good will of the electors by further pledgings. A league of fourteen towns sprang up which Charles had to recognize and to which he had to promise, among other things, not to pledge Reichsstädte.

Charles's son and successor, King Wenzel, possessed very considerable revenues, mainly from Bohemia. His financial administration was efficient, though unscrupulous, and loans were for him only an occasional expedient.

The reign of Wenzel's rival and successor, Rupert of the Rhenish Palatinate, again clearly demonstrated that the financial resources of the German monarchy were by themselves utterly inadequate. It has been estimated that during the ten years of his reign (1400–10) Rupert's total income from royal revenues and prerogatives amounted to between 175,000 and 250,000 guldens, the lower figure being probably nearer the truth.[3] In his first months Rupert already incurred debts totalling at least 16,000 guldens in order to prosecute the war against Wenzel[4] and his Italian campaign of 1401 was conducted from the outset in the face of

[1] Quellen und Forschungen aus dem Gebiete der Geschichte, 1 (1930), 289; 'Cronaca Senese di Neri di Donato', in L. A. Muratori, Rerum Italicarum Scriptores, xv, 199.

[2] Th. Mayer in Handbuch der Finanzwissenschaft, ed. W. Gerloff and F. Neumark, 1 (1952), 242, correcting the over-optimistic estimate of Nuglische (c. 65,500 florins).

[3] O. Schmidt, Die Reichseinnahmen Ruprechts von der Pfalz (1912), 97 ff. A register of Rupert's camera for the period 11 July 1401–4 August 1407 is printed in Deutsche Reichstagsakten, v (1885), no. 168, continued in vi (1888), no. 435 and in v, no. 283.

[4] Deutsche Reichstagsakten, v, 15.

grave difficulties. The Florentines refused to give their promised help until he reached Italy, and various German merchants defaulted on a promised loan of 50,000 guldens. Rupert managed to borrow at least another 50,000 guldens from various sources,[1] including the margravine of Baden (14,000 guldens) and the merchants of Amberg, Rupert's capital. His subsequent letters from Italy show that he was much troubled by the burden of debts left behind in Germany,[2] but the sums assembled by September 1401 did not even suffice to pay his army and a part of his forces had to be dismissed before the expedition started. The Milanese defences completely foiled Rupert. Thereupon the Florentines interrupted payments and the German army largely disbanded for lack of pay. The Venetians refused either to subsidize Rupert or to lend him money, and in December he had to pawn his golden crown and other valuables to raise a few thousand ducats.[3] A renewed Florentine promise of subsidies induced the king to postpone his departure, but his forces were now too small and the Florentines soon lost interest. With great difficulty Rupert borrowed the money for his return journey from the merchants of Nuremberg and through the intermediacy of his followers at Venice; his credit stood too low to permit direct borrowing there.

Rupert had to keep borrowing for the rest of his reign, and his need for money drove him into harsh and unpopular measures, out of keeping with his ordinary, well-intentioned policies. He angered the towns by repeated taxation and he seemed unable to keep his promise never to pledge the *Reichsstädte* for royal debts. After his return from Italy he borrowed the dowry of his son's wife in order to repay his most pressing debts and pledged as security the town of Oppenheim and other royal property.[4] In 1405 it was feared that he was intending to secure the marriage portion of his daughter, betrothed to the duke of Austria, on imperial towns coveted by the Habsburgs. This brought to a head urban discontent and Rupert's princely opponents were able to combine with the Swabian towns against him; Rupert died deeply in debt. In his will he ordered the sale of his crown and jewels to repay numerous debts to various petty creditors—artisans, shopkeepers and artists.[5]

No scruples embarrassed Rupert's able successor, Sigismund of Luxembourg. During most of his reign he did not effectively control any extensive German lands of his own and the German royal revenues could not furnish sufficient money for his ambitious schemes. Sigismund was, how-

---

[1] *Ibid.* IV (1882), no. 384 n. 4; V, p. 16 and especially Oberndorff and Krebs, *Regesta der Pfalzgrafen am Rhein 1214–1508*, II (1939), *passim*.

[2] *Deutsche Reichstagsakten*, V, no. 8, 34–5.   [3] *Ibid.* V, no. 168, art. 37, 41.

[4] *Regesten der Pfalzgrafen*, II, no. 1240 and *Deutsche Reichstagsakten*, V, 361–2. See also A. Vosselmann, *Die reichstädtische Politik König Ruprechts von der Pfalz* (1904), 65–6.

[5] *Regesten der Pfalzgrafen*, II, no. 6254.

ever, unduly disparaging when he complained in 1412 that he was receiving annually no more than 13,000 guldens from Germany.[1] He cleverly used his position as arbitrator in internal disputes and freely took bribes.[2] Thus in 1414 the city of Cologne, in order to gain his support against its archbishop, paid him 30,000 florins: 25,000 florins as a loan and the rest as a 'gift'. At a later stage Cologne lent a further 9,000 florins, while the archbishop paid Sigismund 18,000 florins. In some periods Sigismund was able to secure considerable income from extraordinary sources. Between his imperial coronation in May 1433 and the end of 1434 he received approximately 150,000 florins[3] mainly from the German towns and the Jews. He was, however, far too reckless and extravagant, and oscillated between periods of lavish expenditure and utter penury.

Throughout his reign Sigismund was borrowing. His shabby financial expedients and habitual failure to repay debts brought him into great disrepute. An entry in Nuremberg's municipal accounts provides a revealing commentary on Sigismund's bad reputation. The city, on being approached in 1437 for a loan of 4,000 guldens, sent 2,000 and received royal letters obligatory for this amount; in the municipal account the payment was, however, entered as a gift[4] because repayment was not expected. The surprising thing is that throughout his reign Sigismund continued to find lenders. His leading officials were ready to lend, knowing that Sigismund was willing to shut his eyes to the corrupt practices that were rampant in his administration. Kaspar Schlick, Sigismund's chancellor, lent in 1437, with another chancery official, 1,500 Rhenish guldens.[5] Albrecht II, Sigismund's son-in-law and successor, owed Schlick at the end of his reign (October 1439) 20,000 guldens.[6] It has been estimated

---

[1] Deutsche Reichstagsakten, VII, 181. For the need to treat this statement with scepticism see A. Nuglisch, 'Das Finanzwesen des deutschen Reiches unter Kaiser Sigismund', JNOS. III Folge (1901), 146.

[2] He was publicly accused of this in 1433 at the Council of Basle by Cardinal Cervantes. Cf. the report of Aeneas Sylvius Piccolomini printed in Deutsche Reichstagsakten, XI, no. 55 (pp. 168–70).

[3] Quidde's estimate in the introduction to vol. XI of Deutsche Reichstagsakten (1898), xxxiii–xliv.

[4] Deutsche Reichstagsakten, XII (1901), no. 163; P. Sander, Die reichstädtische Haushaltung Nürnbergs . . . (1902), 618.

[5] Regesta Imperii, XI, nos. 12021, 12144. For the enormous bribes received by these two officials from the Venetians in 1437 see Deutsche Reichstagsakten, XII, no. 124, art. 5 and no. 133, art. 2; for other examples ibid. pp. xl–xlii and nos. 101, 130, 132, 134 and vol. XI, xliii–xliv. For Schlick see especially Allgemeine deutsche Biographie, XXXI (Leipzig, 1890), 505–10 and A. Zechel, 'Studien über Kaspar Schlick', Quellen und Forschungen aus dem Gebiete der Geschichte, XV (1939).

[6] O. Hufnagel, 'Caspar Schlick als Kanzler Friedrichs III', Mitteilungen des Instituts für österr. Geschichtsforschung, VIII Ergänzungsband (1911), 277–8.

that between 1415 and 1439 Sigismund's chief financial minister, his *camerarius* Konrad von Weinsberg, lent to these two rulers 40,000 guldens.[1]

An incomplete list of Sigismund's loans secured on royal possessions totals 390,000 florins, very much less than was procured in this way by his father, Charles IV, in a reign of comparable length. The decline of the royal property and the increasing resistance of the *Reichstädte* to pledging may partly account for this difference. This figure does not include the pledgings of Sigismund's family lands. His royal crown was pawned during the Council of Constance and later on at Nuremberg for 15,000 Rhenish guldens. Within three days of its recovery on 3 May 1434 it was again pledged with other valuables to the burghers of Basle for 5,100 guldens.[2]

Albrecht II, dying after a reign of only nineteen months, left behind enormous debts. In November 1441, his outstanding liabilities were estimated by a commission of the Austrian Estates at 300,000 guldens.[3] Albrecht had owed much money as duke of Austria, but he incurred particularly large debts during his brief royal rule. The mercenary army used by Albrecht for fighting the Turks in 1439 was clamouring for pay after his death. The accounts of Ulrich Eizing, the head of the Austrian finances, for the period from 20 March 1437 to 14 April 1440 reveal a deficit of over 12,000 lb. of Viennese pfennigs, which had to be met out of his own resources.

Albrecht's relative and successor, King Frederick III, was exceedingly harassed by this encumbered inheritance. As guardian of Albrecht's son, he was responsible for the Austrian liabilities. There were prolonged negotiations with the Austrian Estates for financial help.[4] In 1441 they refused to accord all the financial help Frederick requested and at one time he was openly defied by an association of Albrecht's creditors led by Eizing and supported by some 150 members.[5] Chancellor Schlick was one of the most aggrieved creditors. The settlement of these claims delayed for two years Frederick's royal coronation in Germany.

Frederick was a cold, indolent, unenterprising man, averse to ambitious and costly undertakings, thrifty to the point of avarice, and quite unscrupulous in his financial methods. He acquired many of the pos-

[1] *Deutsche Reichstagsakten*, xv (1914), xxv–lxxviii (a detailed list of loans p. lxxvii).

[2] *Regesta Imperii*, xi, pp. xlii, 291–2, 313.

[3] A. F. Kollar, *Analecta monumentorum omnis aevi Vindobonensia* (Vienna, 1762), ii, 992–1004.

[4] For Frederick's debts in 1439–41 and his dealings with the Austrian Estates see Kollar, *op. cit.* and sources in Chmel, *Regesta chronologico-diplomatica Friderici III* . . . (Vienna, 1859).

[5] Kollar, *op. cit.* ii, 878; Chmel, *Regesta*, nos. 271, 276–7 and Chmel, *Geschichte Kaiser Friedrichs III* . . . ii, 106 ff. 121 ff.

sessions of Albrecht's impecunious widow by lending her money.[1] His expedition to Italy in 1452 for the imperial coronation was treated as a business enterprise, during which titles and concessions were freely sold.[2] Nevertheless, through much of his reign he was harassed by lack of money and borrowed constantly. His financial troubles sometimes assumed grotesque proportions. Thus in the summer of 1473 he could not leave Augsburg because he owed 1,730 florins to various shopkeepers and craftsmen there. A delegation from Cologne, who needed his help against Charles of Burgundy, offered to repay these debts, but as they did not have sufficient money with them, the local folk would not allow Frederick to depart and forcibly held up his horses. A loan from the municipality of Augsburg finally released the emperor. Frederick left, however, a considerable treasure at his death in 1493.

The reign of his son Maximilian I falls outside the chronological limits of this chapter but it marked the beginning of a new phase in the credit dealings of the Habsburg emperors. In return for granting to the Fuggers and other south German financiers mining concessions in the Tyrol, Maximilian was able to secure far larger loans than any of his predecessors. It was estimated by Archduke Ferdinand that in 1523 Maximilian's debts, with the addition of some liabilities of Charles V, amounted to about 1,000,000 guldens. The great importance of these new credit facilities was strikingly demonstrated after Maximilian's death. Charles V owed his imperial election partly to the large sums placed at his disposal by his bankers, in all 851,918 guldens, of which 543,585 guldens came from the Fuggers. With justice Jacob Fugger could write to Charles in 1523, in a letter protesting at the slow repayment of these loans, that without this help his Imperial Majesty could not have secured the Roman Crown.[3]

(3) CREDIT OPERATIONS OF GERMAN PRINCES

No account of the development of public credit in medieval Germany would be complete without some discussion of the credit operations of the territorial princes. In some principalities the mortgaging of princely resources was so widespread as to ruin utterly the credit of the rulers. The presence of these debts played an important part in shaping the constitutional development of many principalities and in accentuating the tendency towards a division of power between the rulers and the Estates representing the chief classes of their subjects. This 'dualism' had its constitutional basis in the royal decision of 1 May 1231 which prohibited the

---

[1] Kollar, *op. cit.* II, 843, 851; Chmel, *Regesta*, nos. 92, 98–9, 166, 174, 238, 243.
[2] Chmel, *Regesta*, nos. 2794–5, 2854 ff.
[3] Quoted in Ehrenberg, *Das Zeitalter der Fugger* (3rd ed. 1922), I, 111–12.

princes from enacting new laws unless they were approved by the notables in their territory.[1] It was only very rarely that the princes dared to
impose extraordinary taxes without the consent of the Estates. Thus two
separate financial powers developed: the 'cameral' administration of the
ruler had to reconcile itself to the existence of separate extraordinary
revenues controlled by the Estates and available to the prince only under
special conditions. The Estates also tried to check the pledging of princely
revenues and sometimes insisted on the need for their consent to such
transactions.

Many German rulers were far from certain of securing grants of taxes
on every request. Until a relatively late date the idea that the ruler's subjects were responsible for the debts of their prince was alien to the inhabitants of German principalities. Attempts to secure taxes for the repayment of debts often met with scant sympathy and painful criticism;
therefore princes often tried to manage without the help of the Estates.
Heavy borrowing was often the only possible alternative, but usually the
Estates had to be called in ultimately to rescue their ruler. Gradually the
Estates were forced to recognize that the debts of the prince and his predecessors were the debts of the principality and to shoulder the burden
of repaying them. In several territories this led in the sixteenth century to
the creation of separate treasuries for the administration of the debt, supplied and supervised by the Estates (*Landschaft* in Bavaria, *Kreditwerk* in
Brandenburg, *Obersteuerkollegium* in Saxony, etc.). In the later fifteenth
century a more centralized and orderly financial system was introduced
in several principalities by a number of remarkable rulers, but the 'dual'
authority of princes and Estates persisted in most territories until at least
the seventeenth century. It should be added, however, that several principalities, including some of the larger ones, lacked strong Estates, and that
even in the territories where these assemblies were most influential their
power never overshadowed for very long the authority of the rulers.

The German principalities were very slow in developing a central
system of accounting. Most of them were fairly small and the need for
more effective and elaborate fiscal methods was not strongly felt. Except
in the Tyrol and a few other territories, regular accounting and the systematic keeping of written records for all financial transactions did not
properly develop before the middle of the fifteenth century. In the electorates of Brandenburg and Saxony even at that late date no written receipts were given to the collectors of the revenues and only very summary records of income and expenditure were kept by their rulers. The
frequency of uncoordinated assignments on every source of revenue
was an inevitable feature of these backward arrangements, but it would
be mistaken to seek here the main cause of the financial difficulties that

[1] *Monumenta Germaniae Historica, Leges*, II, no. 305, p. 420.

plagued most of the princes. The chief cause of their troubles was the habit of living beyond their means.

The rudimentary character of the financial records kept by the German princes greatly hampers the student of their credit operations. While the functioning of the financial administration is often tolerably well known, a satisfactory continuous history of their finances and borrowing is seldom possible.[1] This has drastically narrowed our choice of detailed examples. Only certain episodes could be selected, derived mainly from the electorates and other important principalities.

The financial history of the Habsburg territories during the periods when their rulers were kings of Germany has been already discussed. Ducal debts in Austria did not become unmanageable until the second half of the fourteenth century. From the time of Rudolph IV, a remarkable but over-ambitious and spendthrift prince, financial difficulties were frequent. One of the consequences was the rise to power of the Estates of Austria and Tyrol; the heavy debts of the Habsburgs played an important part in this process.

Rudolph's brothers, Leopold III and Albrecht III, inherited from him in 1365 a debt of 60,000 guilders and rapidly added to it by ambitious territorial acquisitions; thus in 1369 they paid 116,000 florins to the duke of Bavaria to end his claims to the Tyrol. By 1370 drastic remedies were necessary. The revenues and the entire administration of the Austrian lands were handed over for four years to a consortium headed by Albrecht's *Hofmeister*, Hans von Liechtenstein zu Nikolsburg. This syndicate undertook to provide the dukes annually with 17,000 lb. of Viennese pfennigs, while the remainder of the Austrian revenues was to be used to repay debts.[2]

The most important development in the use of credit by the Habsburg rulers at the end of the fifteenth century was their continuous relationship with the Augsburg financiers. The way for this was prepared by the non-royal branch of the dynasty ruling in Tyrol. The career of Sigismund, the last ruler of the Tyrolese line (1427–96), was one long series of financial crises. His pledging of the Habsburg possessions in Alsace to Charles of Burgundy was the prime cause of Charles's disastrous war with the Swiss. In the Tyrol, Sigismund's extravagance led to the sale or pledging of the bulk of his possessions. In 1485 he owed 73,000 guilders to three different financiers and in November 1487 he agreed to hand over for three years the entire financial administration to a special council set up by the Tyrolese Estates. His most valuable asset was the Tyrolese

---

[1] These difficulties are admirably discussed in F. Ernst, *Eberhard im Bart. Die Politik eines deutschen Landesherrn am Ende des Mittelalters* (1933), 65–6.

[2] Schwind and Dopsch, *op. cit.* no. 125. For a list of the outstanding debts at the end of 1373, see Fr. Kurz, *Österreich unter Herzog Albrecht III*, I (1827), 248.

silver mines. The right to exploit them was pledged in 1487 to the Fuggers. In the course of the next two years, by making further large advances to Sigismund (150,000 florins in 1488), their firm became the virtual master of the mines. In March 1490 Sigismund sold the Tyrol to Maximilian I, who soon began to ask the Fuggers for further loans in exchange for the prolongation of their control over the mines.

The power of the electors of Brandenburg was at its peak at the end of the thirteenth century, but with the dying out of the Ascanian dynasty in 1320 three different families ruled the electorate in turn during the succeeding century. The financial resources of the margraves dwindled alarmingly as most of their possessions were sold or pledged, chiefly to the local nobles. Lack of cash compelled the electors to resort frequently to forced requisitions of goods on credit (conquisitio), a practice also widely prevalent outside Brandenburg, and it usually led to a rapid accumulation of debts.

The impecuniousness of the Wittelsbach margraves led to the sale of the electorate to Emperor Charles IV in 1373. The survey compiled by his orders in 1375 reveals clearly the enormous reduction of the elector's prerogatives and possessions through pledging and the consequent increase in the power of the nobles. The disintegration of the domains continued under the Luxembourgs. In 1402 Sigismund pledged the entire New Mark to the Teutonic Knights, from whom it was recovered only in 1455. When Frederick I Hohenzollern (1415–40) undertook the government of Brandenburg he found nine-tenths of the sources of revenue either pledged or entirely alienated. Frederick I was unable to recover the bulk of margravial properties and he left a colossal debt of 1,000,000 guldens. Effective financial reforms came only under Albrecht III Achilles (1470–86).[1] Frugal in his habits he managed to increase annual revenue both in Brandenburg (up to 50,000 guldens) and in his south German possessions (up to 90,000 guldens). He clashed with the provincial Estates and the towns in 1472–3 over his demand for aid to repay the debts of his predecessors, and for the first time in the history of the electorate made the Estates responsible for the debts of the margraves. New excises and taxes granted by the Estates enabled Albrecht to reduce his debts and to leave a reserve estimated at c. 400,000 guldens. Conflicts with the towns over taxes recurred under his son John Cicero (1486–99), but this urban opposition was effectively silenced by a display of force. The rule of Albrecht and John thus marked a decisive stage in the subjection of the towns to the elector. The dependence of the margraves on the Estates endured much longer because their debts again reached staggering proportions in the sixteenth century.

[1] E. W. Kanter, 'Markgraf Albrecht Achilles von Brandenburg', *Quellen und Untersuchungen zur Geschichte des Hauses Hohenzollern*, x (1911).

It is seldom that the credit operations of a German prince can be studied in as much detail as in the case of Albrecht III, called Animosus, of Saxony (1485–1500).[1] Earlier the system of forced borrowing of supplies was much used, despite its drawbacks. From the middle of the fourteenth century the dukes farmed out taxes, but in the absence of proper central control this did not produce any real improvement. Serious reform of the fiscal administration was delayed until the 1460's when a central financial official, a *Landrentmeister*, was at last appointed. But in the time of Duke Albrecht the real heads of the finances were not the successors of this official (the *Kammerschreiber*, with smaller powers), but the businessmen whom he employed as tax-farmers and who, without being strictly ducal officials, came to control the entire ducal revenue. A merchant of Leipzig, Jacob Blasbalg, acted as Albrecht's chief financier in 1487–90. He was succeeded by his widow, herself a daughter of a wealthy mayor of Friedberg, and in 1491 by her second husband, Georg von Wiedebach. Blasbalg and Wiedebach were the duke's bankers. They were willing to provide money speedily for urgent needs, they covered deficits and used their personal credit to negotiate loans for him.

Between 1488 and 1497 Albrecht's yearly receipts averaged 73,000 guilders and in ordinary years, when there was no need for much borrowing, his revenue oscillated between 54,000 and 66,000 guilders. The annual expenditure during the same period averaged 69,643 guilders, but fluctuated more considerably because of the expenses incurred by Albrecht in the service of the Habsburgs in Hungary and the Netherlands. During these nine years 32% of his entire expenditure arose out of his campaigns in the Netherlands (202,034 out of the total of 628,788 guilders). In November 1496 Emperor Maximilian I and his son Philip owed the duke of Saxony 375,928 guilders and Philip discharged his share of the debt by ceding Frisia to Albrecht in 1498.

In years without warfare Albrecht could manage without loans and his commitments in the Netherlands occasioned most of his heavier borrowing. When in 1490–1 his foreign expenses dwindled into insignificance he could devote 24% of his expenditure to the repayment of debts. The annual debt charge paid by Albrecht was thus reduced to the lowest figure it ever attained (1,367 guilders). The recurrence of heavy commitments abroad in 1491–2 (44,367 guilders spent in the Netherlands) drove Albrecht again to large-scale borrowing. His loans in that fiscal year accounted for 21% of his receipts and, in spite of this, there was a deficit of 8,057 guilders which Wiedebach had to cover. The same alternating pattern recurred in the later years of Albrecht's rule.

The larger loans were mostly raised through the municipality of Leipzig and, to a lesser extent, through the other Saxon towns. The munici-

[1] A. Puff, *Die Finanzen Albrechts des Beherzten* (1911), is the fundamental authority.

palities sold redeemable annuities in their own names and advanced the proceeds to the duke. The annual rent-charges were paid by the ducal *camera* to the towns, which in turn satisfied the holders of the annuities. Large loans were also contracted directly from some leading families of the duchy and from ecclesiastics; thus 4,500 guilders were borrowed in 1496-7 from the bishop of Meissen, on which interest was paid at 5% *per annum*.

In financial matters the German episcopal principalities closely resembled the territories ruled by the lay princes. Efficient central financial administration was usually lacking. The bishops, drawn predominantly from the upper nobility, were often immersed in ambitious political schemes and family feuds. Their finances were frequently in deplorable condition for secular reasons. The financial troubles of the prelates were also aggravated by the expenses connected with their initial promotion, particularly by payments to the popes. Such payments were easily financed by loans supplied by the papal cameral merchants, but the papacy vigorously supported the demands of its bankers for repayment. In trying to meet their financial obligations the German bishops needed the help of their cathedral chapters and diocesan clergy, but these demands often led to quarrels with these groups as well as with the Estates of their principalities. The operation of all these factors can be illustrated from the history of the three Rhenish archbishoprics, whose financial troubles repeatedly influenced the general history of Germany.

Liabilities incurred at the papal court were already haunting the archbishops of Cologne in the early years of the thirteenth century. Engelbert I (1216-25) was for two years denied the archiepiscopal pallium by the pope because of his inability to repay the debts of his three predecessors, totalling 16,000 marks sterling.[1] The conflicts of his successor, Henry von Molenark, with the chapter and city of Cologne were partly due to his debts and the city and the chapter secured in 1231-2 formal exemptions from liability for the archiepiscopal debts.[2] This continued indebtedness made the successive archbishops specially dependent on the good will of the papacy. Conrad von Hochstaden (1238-61), one of the most powerful medieval archbishops of Cologne, was able to support without excessive embarrassment his heavy liabilities only because, as the leader of the anti-Hohenstaufen party in Germany, he was indispensable to the popes. During his initial visit to Italy in 1239 Conrad incurred a debt of 4,740 marks to Sienese merchants. He was excommunicated for non-repayment, but absolved by Innocent IV in 1244 and the papacy sanc-

---

[1] R. Knipping (ed.), *Regesten der Kölner Erzbischöfe*, III (1909), nos. 107, 122, 168, 194, 198; Ficker, *op. cit.* 320-4.

[2] L. Ennen and G. Eckertz, *Quellen zur Geschichte der Stadt Köln*, II, nos. 125, 127, 160; C. A. Ley, *Kölnische Kirchengeschichte* (2nd ed. 1917), 222.

tioned special taxes in the province of Cologne for the discharge of Conrad's obligations. The Sienese were still unsatisfied in 1258 and a papal arbitrator cancelled the interest due from Conrad up to this time (at 12% *per annum*).

The financial difficulties of the archbishops of Cologne help to explain the large sums demanded by them for their electoral vote in the royal elections from 1257 onwards. Conrad von Hochstaden received 8,000 marks from Richard of Cornwall in that year. Albrecht I promised 8,000 marks in 1298 to Archbishop Wigbold for his vote. The king's failure to surrender one of the imperial towns pledged to the archbishop as a security for this debt was one of the causes of Wigbold's subsequent war against Albrecht. Archbishop Walram von Jülich (1332–49) in 1346, in order to obtain the means to redeem some mortgaged possessions of his see, obtained from John and Charles of Luxembourg a promise to pay nearly 100,000 *li.* to Walram's chief creditors: his brother, the margrave of Jülich, and the latter's advisers, and the influential Rhineland knight, Reinhert von Schönau. Payment was to be made in part on the day fixed for the royal election. The Luxembourgs had also to promise Walram 100,000 marks of silver as compensation for losses suffered by the previous archbishops; revenues from the Jews and from the town and county of Dortmund had to be pledged to the archbishop as security. When at the end of his reign Charles IV wanted to assure the election of his son Wenzel as king of Germany he was able to buy the compliance of Archbishop Frederick von Saarwerden (1370–1414), who had succeeded to an impoverished see and was saddled with a debt of 120,000 florins to the papal *camera* as the price of his promotion to Cologne, for non-payment of which he had been suspended and excommunicated in 1376.[1] Charles IV, by promising a substantial subsidy, secured his vote and an undertaking to crown Wenzel.

The career of an outstanding fourteenth-century archbishop of Trier, Baldwin of Luxembourg (1307–54), provides an interesting contrast with the desperate financial shifts of his contemporaries at Cologne. Baldwin was, indeed, an exception in his own province, for the majority of the medieval archbishops of Trier experienced the same financial tribulations as their electoral colleagues at Cologne and Mainz. Baldwin's episcopate shows what could be achieved by able administration and intelligent use of professional financiers. The state of affairs found by Baldwin on his accession could hardly have been worse. His predecessor, Diether von Nassau, shortly before his death (1307) had been reduced to such penury[2]

---

[1] Lacomblet, *Urkundenbuch für die Geschichte des Niederrheins*, III, nos. 627, 704, 718.

[2] See especially *Gesta Trevirorum*, ed. J. H. Wyttenbach and M. F. J. Müller, II (Trier, 1838), cap. ccxix, p. 185: *ecclesiam suam . . . debitisque gravatam, dilapidatam, impignoratam, dissipatam relinquendo.*

that he attempted to seize the property of his cathedral chapter and of the diocesan clergy. Baldwin himself could not at first pay the *servitia* due to the papacy (7,834 guilders, customary for Trier) and had to borrow 80,000 guilders from his brother, Count Henry of Luxembourg, to get out of his initial debts.[1] In return, he played a decisive part in promoting Henry's election to the German kingship. Gradually Baldwin restored his finances. The most original feature of his administration was his dependence on the Jews. From 1323 onwards three Jews succeeded each other at the head of his financial administration: Muskin (1323–36), Jacob Daniels and, after 1341, his son-in-law Michels. The accounts of Baldwin's treasury were kept in Hebrew and were later translated into Latin. These Jewish agents were sometimes able to borrow money for Baldwin without special security or pledging property, though his credit was not always equally good.[2] After the massacres of German Jews in 1349 Baldwin was compelled to rely mainly on the Lombards. By the end of his life he amassed an enormous treasure, reputed to amount to 300,000 guilders. Baldwin's wealth contributed to the election of his grand-nephew, Charles of Luxembourg, as king in 1346. He lent for this purpose 36,333 florins to buy the vote of the archbishop of Cologne.

Dietrich von Mörs of Cologne (1414–63) was typical of the warlike prelates who occupied so many German sees in the later Middle Ages. Unlike his immediate predecessors, he was on good terms with the city of Cologne and repeatedly borrowed from it. Both the city and the cathedral chapter sold annuities to raise loans for Dietrich. He waged a number of savage wars with neighbours which left him overwhelmed with debts.[3] At the end of Dietrich's episcopate, as his successor, Rupert von der Pfalz, complained later, there was hardly a single property or revenue that had not been diminished by pledging and assignments. Rupert's disastrous rule was largely the result of the deplorable situation inherited by him in 1463. A loan from the city of Cologne allowed Rupert to pay for the pallium, but he had to postpone, until 1471, the journey to the imperial court for investiture with the 'regalia', as he could not afford the expense. In consequence, the normal functioning of criminal justice at Cologne had to be suspended for a time and hundreds of untried prisoners accumulated in the city jail. As the Estates of his principality and the cathedral chapter would not help to repay his debts, Rupert proceeded to seize his pledged properties. His creditors tried in

---

[1] A. Dominicus, *Baldewin von Lützelburg, Erzbischof und Kurfürst von Trier* (1862), 52; *Regesta Papae Clementis V* (9 vols., 1884–92), nos. 2783, 2790.

[2] M. Hoffmann, *Der Geldhandel der deutschen Juden während des Mittelalters bis zum Jahre 1350* (1910), 117–18.

[3] For his numerous credit transactions see Lacomblet, *op. cit.* IV, *passim.*

1468 to organize resistance[1] but were defeated by Rupert with the aid of his brother, the count palatine of the Rhine. By 1471 Rupert's position was desperate. His soldiers were unpaid and he had drifted into conflict with the city and cathedral chapter of Cologne, whose repeated requests for the repayment of debts were ignored. Rupert's violence made matters worse and the chapter, after appealing to the emperor, appointed in 1473 an administrator of the archiepiscopal office and property.[2] Rupert's appeal for help to Duke Charles of Burgundy led to the Burgundian invasion and the long siege of Neuss which ruined the finances of the city of Cologne.

The requirement that a newly elected archbishop must pay the papacy for his pallium had been a major cause of financial embarrassment to all the German archbishops since the thirteenth century, but nowhere had it such momentous consequences as at Mainz at the end of the Middle Ages. Opposition to the exorbitant size of these payments had in 1461 led to the deposition of Archbishop Diether von Isenburg and to a bitter war, in the course of which the city of Mainz was sacked and lost its autonomy. An acute financial crisis occurred for the same reason in the early sixteenth century. Three successive archbishops of Mainz died in ten years, so that Albrecht von Hohenzollern, on his election in 1514, was saddled with the debts of several predecessors as well as with his own obligations to the papacy. At the beginning of Albrecht's episcopate these debts and the value of pledged properties amounted together to the colossal sum of 1,200,000 florins. Albrecht had been chosen largely because, more than any other candidate, he seemed capable of paying for his pallium without imposing a fresh tax on the clergy of the province. He tried to solve his problems by borrowing from the Fuggers.[3] On the morrow of his election they agreed to pay the pope 29,400 Rhenish florins and for a further payment of 14,000 florins to Pope Leo X, likewise advanced by the Fuggers, Albrecht procured a concession for the sale of indulgences in the provinces of Mainz and Magdeburg. He hoped to repay out of the proceeds his debts to the Fuggers, increased in the meantime to 48,236 florins (including interest). Tetzel, the seller of the indulgences, was accompanied by a representative of the Fuggers. Tetzel's activities provoked the famous protest of Luther at Wittenberg with all its momentous consequences. But as far as Albrecht was concerned, the whole transaction was a financial success. By September 1518 his debt to the Fuggers was reduced to 6,192 florins. In 1519 he received from Charles V for his electoral vote 103,000 guilders, twice as much as the expenses of his own promotion to the electorate of Mainz.

[1] Lacomblet, *op. cit.* IV, no. 340.   [2] *Ibid.* IV, no. 363.
[3] A. Schulte, *Die Fugger in Rom, 1495–1523* (1904), I, pp. 93–141 and II, nos. 54, 62, 71, 84, 108, 113.

VIII. *The Towns of Northern Europe*

In the thirteenth century the municipalities of France and the Netherlands were able to borrow without much interference from their sovereigns. When kings and other territorial rulers began to impose frequent taxes they tried to restrict local taxation for purely urban purposes and assumed supervision over the municipal finances. Municipal borrowing continued, but in the fourteenth and fifteenth centuries it was mainly occasioned by the fiscal demands of the French Crown and other princes. A reverse development occurred in Germany. Some German towns, forming part of the territorial principalities, continued to be controlled and exploited by their rulers. The imperial cities (*Reichstädte*) and the 'free cities' (*Freistädte*), which comprised most of the important towns, gradually achieved almost complete freedom in financial matters and borrowed mainly for their own needs.

(1) INTRODUCTORY

Special interest attaches to the credit transactions of the medieval cities because they developed forms of public credit that anticipated the funded debt of the modern states. Several German scholars, including Georg von Below,[1] B. Kuske, W. Lotz and J. Landmann, have even assumed in the past that the towns were pioneers in developing public borrowing and that their practice greatly influenced the territorial rulers. This view is still held today with special reference to medieval Germany[2] and it finds some partial confirmation in the special circumstances of that country, but it is not applicable to England and France, where borrowing by the territorial rulers started before the appearance of self-governing municipalities, retained great importance throughout the Middle Ages and was not influenced by the forms of municipal credit until a late date.

The general causes of frequent borrowing by medieval public authorities have already been discussed, but certain special reasons for municipal borrowing require further comment. The men who governed the medieval towns were both taxpayers and potential investors in loans to their cities. In all municipalities, whether controlled by narrow oligarchies, as was usually the case everywhere in the thirteenth century, or by governments more responsive to the demands of the whole citizen body, there was a tendency to solve current financial troubles by contracting

---

[1] In 'Die städtische Verwaltung des Mittelalters als Vorbild der späteren Territorialverwaltung', *Historische Zeitschrift*, N.F., XXXIX (1895).

[2] Th. Mayer, 'Geschichte der Finanzwirtschaft vom Mittelalter bis zum Ende des 18. Jahrhunderts', in *Handbuch der Finanzwissenschaft*, ed. Gerloff–Neumark, I (2) (1952), 267, 272; H. Mitteis, *Die deutsche Rechtsgeschichte*, 3rd ed. (1954), 137–8.

debts. This avoided, or at least postponed, the necessity for harsh taxation and permitted the spreading of the resulting liabilities over a long period. The oligarchic regimes were, however, more inclined to pile up large debts quickly, partly because this provided scope for profitable investment by the richer citizens.[1] Cologne provides a particularly clear example. Under the patrician regime, which lasted until a revolution in 1396, direct taxes were almost entirely absent and large annuities were sold to a relatively small number of wealthy individuals; after the revolution opportunities for investment in city funds were for the first time thrown open to the mass of small investors.[2]

The influence of the legal status of the municipalities on their credit operations has been much discussed. A careful distinction must be preserved between the benefits accruing from political autonomy and the effects of the corporate status of the self-governing towns. The autonomous municipalities were likely to incur considerable financial liabilities and consequently needed to borrow on a large scale. They acquired valuable permanent assets and were able to tax their inhabitants as often as they wished; hence they were able to contract loans freely. Any restriction of financial autonomy by the sovereign at once affected municipal borrowing. Thus, when in the fourteenth century the French Crown imposed limitations on the right of the towns to tax themselves freely, this curtailed their power to borrow and encouraged the contraction of loans secured on permanent city revenues independent of royal control.

The view that the city funds offered special attraction to investors because the municipalities were corporate bodies[3] requires much qualification. The principle that a fully developed corporate personality assumes a collective liability that discharges the liabilities of its members (*quod universitas debet singuli non debent*), which forms the essence of the modern corporation, was largely ignored by the foreign creditors of medieval municipalities.[4] The strongest weapon of the medieval investor in city funds against a defaulting municipality was to arrest such of its inhabitants as happened to be within his reach and to procure compensation from their ransoms and the sale of their goods. Only a stranger could do this, and citizens of a foreign town could sometimes enlist official support of their own city government for such seizures. Any town might be a victim, irrespective of whether it was an autonomous corporation or

[1] For detailed examples in France and the Netherlands see below.

[2] R. Knipping, 'Das Schuldenwesen der Stadt Köln im 14. und 15. Jahrhundert', *Westdeutsche Zeitschrift für Geschichte und Kunst*, XIII (1894), especially 340–3; F. Lau, *Entwicklung der kommunalen Verfassung und Verwaltung der Stadt Köln bis zum Jahre 1396* (1898), 556.

[3] See especially the works of Kuske and Landmann quoted in the bibliography and Otto von Gierke, *Das deutsche Genossenschaftsrecht* (1863–1913), II and III.

[4] Even Gierke admits this, *op. cit.* II, 770.

not. This habit of reprisal was mitigated by inter-urban treaties,[1] but it persisted beyond the Middle Ages. It explains why men preferred to lend to other towns than their own and why a large part of the debt of many towns was owed to strangers: for example, about 60% of the annuities of Mainz in 1444 and about half the debt of Douai in the early Burgundian period.

Municipal borrowing started at a time when the notion of a corporation was still vague. In France, by the second half of the thirteenth century, the royal officials evolved precise doctrines about corporate municipalities and applied them with consistency. In the corporate towns the civic authorities contracted loans in the name of the commune, while in other localities the representatives of the inhabitants had to borrow in their own names, which did not prevent them, however, from borrowing considerable sums.[2] Some communes lost their corporate character because of overwhelming debts and the arrangements imposed upon them by the Crown were shaped by the contemporary ideas about corporate liability. In Germany those ideas had equally great practical importance, but in the absence of a single unifying influence, such as the monarchy provided in France, they developed less uniformly and cannot be discussed here.

The sale of annuities constituted the most usual form of medieval municipal borrowing in Germany,[3] the Netherlands and northern France. The French towns south of the Loire pose a puzzling problem. There is no published evidence of the sale of annuities by any medieval municipality in southern France, though by the middle of the fourteenth century this practice was well established in Catalonia,[4] with which Languedoc had strong legal and cultural affinities. The contrast in the forms of municipal borrowing between northern and southern France cannot be satisfactorily explained at present.

While the sale of annuities was the most distinctive feature of the

[1] E.g. Cologne signed such treaties with Soest, Liège, Deventer and Nuremberg.

[2] J. Carolus-Barré, 'Les institutions municipales de Compiègne au temps des gouverneurs-attournés, 1319–1692', Bulletin Philologique et Historique du Comité des Travaux Historiques et Scientifiques, 1940–1, 36, 45–6; J. Delaville le Roulx, Registres des Comptes Municipaux de la Ville de Tours, I (1878), 3–4, 12–13, 196. See also J. Flammermont, 'Histoire de Senlis pendant la seconde partie de la guerre de Cent Ans, 1405–1441', Mémoires de la Société de l'Histoire de Paris et de l'Ile de France, V (1878), 200, 257, 272–3.

[3] The annuities were for a long time treated as a purely German institution. This was disproved by W. Endemann, Studien in der romanisch-kanonistischen Wirtschafts- und Rechtslehre . . . , II (1883), 104–5.

[4] For Catalonia see A. P. Usher, The Early History of Deposit Banking in Mediterranean Europe, I (Cambridge, Mass., 1943), 151ff., 356–60; and J. Broussolle, 'Les impositions municipales de Barcelone de 1328 à 1462', Estudios de Historia Moderna, V (Barcelona, 1955).

municipal finances in north-western Europe, all towns were also familiar with other types of loans. It is possible that at first only short-term loans were contracted and that the sale of annuities started at a slightly later period, but by the middle of the thirteenth century, both forms of loans already existed side by side in several localities. Like the territorial rulers, the towns resorted in moments of difficulty to forced loans and they were usually able to secure from their citizens advances *sine usura*. Thus only 9 out of 146 short-term loans contracted by Cologne between 1370 and 1392 bore interest.[1] Payment of interest was only inevitable in dealings with professional money-lenders and loans from them tended to be more costly for the towns than the sale of annuities.

There existed two main types of medieval annuities: life annuities and perpetual annuities. Both kinds developed out of older legal practices rooted in the pre-feudal and early feudal society and in its agrarian economy. Life annuities were gradually evolved in the special conditions of town life out of the ecclesiastical institutions of *precaria oblata* and *precaria remuneratoria* which had previously developed in the countryside during the early Middle Ages.[2] Similarly, the perpetual annuity gradually developed in the towns out of the non-urban perpetual grants.

The municipal annuities were a special adaptation of the annuities sold by private persons and ecclesiastical institutions. The towns sold both life and perpetual annuities. In either case, in return for a payment of a single lump sum to the town, a person was entitled to receive from the municipality annual payments for a period defined by the terms of the annuity. A single-life annuity guaranteed payments for the rest of the *rentier's* life, while an annuity for several lives (usually not exceeding three) was payable during the lifetime of the investor and specified relatives. A perpetual annuity was payable to the investor, his heirs and successors in perpetuity. Faced with the increasing burden of rent charges, most municipalities gradually resorted, however, to the practice of redemption, which modified the distinctive characteristics of the two original main types of annuities and blurred somewhat the difference between them.

---

[1] Knipping, *loc. cit.* p. 350.

[2] The historical stages of this development were traced by W. Arnold, *Zur Geschichte des Eigentums in den deutschen Städten* (Basle, 1861), 95 ff.; A. Heusler, *Institutionen des deutschen Privatrechts* (Leipzig, 1886), II, 169 ff.; P. Viollet, *Histoire du droit civil français* (Paris, 1893), 680–95; B. Kuske, *Das Schuldenwesen der deutschen Städte im Mittelalter* (Tübingen, 1904), 12–24. Recently, however, O. Cremer and H. Planitz have questioned the derivation of the life annuities from *precaria* and considered that they developed out of the perpetual annuities: O. Cremer, *Der Rentenkauf im mittelalterlichen Köln* (Würzburg, 1936), 103 ff.; H. Planitz, *Grundzüge des deutschen Privatrechts* (Berlin, 1931), 115 and *Deutsche Rechtsgeschichte* (Graz, 1950), 164. The development of life annuities as an instrument of rudimentary life insurance in the early Middle Ages still awaits a proper study.

The towns were specially anxious to avoid the accumulation of perpetual annuities. From the late thirteenth century several municipalities in northern France and the Netherlands reserved the option to redeem them. At Cologne, one of the most important sellers of municipal annuities, they were already redeemable around 1300 and the practice spread elsewhere in Germany, sanctioned in several cases by decrees of territorial rulers or imposed by town legislation. Thus, Goslar procured such a decree from King Rudolf in 1283 and Rudolf IV of Austria ordered in 1360 the redemption of perpetual annuities at Vienna.[1] The perpetual annuities were turned in the later Middle Ages into a species of short-term debt and in this form became the favourite of city governments.[2]

The redemption of the life-rents aroused more opposition, perhaps partly because this type of annuity often attracted a particular kind of lender seeking security rather than speculative investments. In northern France and the Netherlands it became usual for towns to claim the right to redeem life annuities unless the act of sale specifically prohibited this. Thus, Douai sold in the last decade of the fourteenth century two types of life annuities, one of which was non-redeemable, but yielded a lower rate of interest. In German towns, redemption of life annuities was fairly common in the fifteenth century, but never universal: thus at Nuremberg it occurred only in exceptional circumstances.

The sale of annuities did not spring up as a device for circumventing the canonistic prohibition of usury. In the Middle Ages it was treated as an act of sale or purchase (*vente de rente*, *Rentenkauf*) and, as such, was absolutely lawful. The Church, long accustomed to various forms of *census* and *precaria*, did not object to the creation of annuities in the initial stages of their development and, indeed, ecclesiastical establishments did much to popularize them. When, later on, the selling of annuities became very common and some writers on Canon Law began to demand restrictive measures, the Church, for reasons which cannot be discussed here, could not bring itself to condemn these transactions. The main medieval attempt to regulate the sale of annuities occurred in 1425 when Pope Martin V declared them lawful, subject to certain limiting conditions which made little practical difference. The purchase of annuities thus remained an entirely lawful form of credit transaction and this favoured the extension of the practice in the later Middle Ages.

In many towns the rate of interest on life annuities did not vary with the age of the buyer, but cases are known when this was taken into consideration. At Aire-sur-Lys in Artois the rate of interest offered in 1399

---

[1] Max Neumann, *Geschichte des Wuchers* (Halle, 1865), 234 ff.; Kuske, *op. cit.* 35 ff.; E. K. Winter, *Rudolf IV von Österreich* (Vienna, 1936), II, 161–85.

[2] E.g. at Cologne in the fifteenth century. Louis XI of France also preferred this type of municipal loan.

to a man of fifty-eight was twice as high as rates paid on annuities sold in that year to children. Most towns tried, of course, to check the transfer of life annuities through the substitution of one person for another: this was, for example, wholly prohibited at Lille in 1291.[1] The rents for several lives always gave a lower annual return than the single-life variety and the lowest rates of all were paid on the perpetual annuities, which were, however, freely transferable from an early date.

The rates of interest on all types of municipal annuities were fairly high in the second half of the thirteenth century, but tended to decline subsequently. For example, in the Netherlands, 12½% was commonly paid on the life-rents of the thirteenth century, but 10 to 8% became usual in the more important towns by the early fifteenth century. The rates on the perpetual annuities declined there in the same period from 10% to an average of 6¼ to 6⅔%. Important divergences developed, however, between the leading business centres and the more backward communities. In Germany 10% was the most common rate on the life annuities in the later Middle Ages. But it was usually higher in the towns of the less developed regions of eastern Germany, averaging there between 12 and 13⅓%. On the other hand a great city like Cologne paid 8⅓% at certain periods, as did Lüneburg, specially connected with the Hanseatic port of Lübeck. A deterioration in the financial situation of a town was likely to raise the rate of interest on new issues of annuities. As a result of the growing indebtedness of the towns in the Burgundian state, they were forced to offer better terms to attract investors: by the later fifteenth century there was a widespread return to rates ranging between 10 and 12%. Similarly, Dortmund in Westphalia, partly ruined by a war in 1374, had to pay at the end of the fourteenth century the high rate of 11 to 12⅓% on its life annuities.[2]

The municipal annuities found a ready market because they satisfied important needs. Life annuities in particular, bearing a higher rate of interest than the perpetual annuities and less liable to redemption than the latter, were an important form of insurance, providing an old-age pension for the investor or helping to make some provision for his dependants. It would be an exaggeration to say that they provided the only readily accessible outlet for the medium and small investors,[3] but they

[1] R. Monier, ed., *Le Livre Roisin. Coutumier Lillois de la fin du XIIIe siècle* (Paris and Lille, 1932), 43 (no. 58).

[2] For rates of interest in German towns see Arnold, *op. cit.* 235–9, 245–6; Max Neumann, *op. cit.* 266–73. Some of Neumann's figures had been criticized by H. Albers, *Die Anleihen der Stadt Bremen vom 14. bis zum 18. Jahrhundert* (1930), 109 ff. and A. v. Brandt, *Der Lübecker Rentenmarkt von 1320–50* (1935), 18–19.

[3] Cf. the criticism of such views, with special reference to the German evidence, by H. Reincke, 'Die alte Hamburger Stadtschuld der Hansezeit (1300–1563)', in A. v. Brandt and W. Koppe, *Städtewesen und Bürgertum als geschichtliche Kräfte* (1953), 490 ff.

were regarded as an unusually secure investment, especially when sold by the rich and well-governed towns. To lessen risks still further, lenders dispersed their purchases among several towns. Thus in 1408 Heinrich Topler, burgomaster of Rotenburg, was receiving rents from some 120 localities.[1] We have already discussed one reason why lenders preferred to invest in the annuities of foreign towns. It should be added that this not only gave them better chances of reprisal in case of non-payment, but also assured for them more considerate treatment at all times. Thus, when in 1392 the municipality of Arras carried out a compulsory conversion of life-rents into less valuable perpetual annuities, it was careful to exempt strangers.

All classes of society invested in municipal annuities. The tendency of some oligarchic regimes to favour investment by a more restricted group has already been noted, but such attempts occurred only in certain towns and were seldom effective for very long. One way of achieving restriction was to offer for sale only annuities of fairly high value. As a reaction to such restrictive policies, the more popular regimes sometimes created special facilities for lesser investors. For example, at Cologne after the anti-patrician revolution of 1396 the new government inaugurated sales of very small rents, as low as between one and five guldens, which attracted some very humble people.

(2) THE FRENCH TOWNS

The distinctive feature of northern France in the thirteenth century was the presence there of numerous communes which, until the last decades of the century, possessed a very considerable measure of autonomy. During most of the thirteenth century they did not require any special royal licences for the levy of taxes and for the contraction of loans. All the communes, whether royal or seignorial, had considerable financial responsibilities and became easily involved in frequent borrowing. The sale of municipal annuities was, in France, restricted mainly to this group of northern communes. The towns of central France, while enjoying a measure of self-government, usually lacked the wide autonomy in financial matters possessed by the communes and much less evidence is available about their municipal loans.

By the middle of the thirteenth century, the ordinary revenues of most French towns barely sufficed even for normal purposes and all the extra-ordinary expenditure had to be met out of new types of resources. Frequent direct taxation (*taille*) became unavoidable and all the municipalities developed the habit of anticipating these levies through borrowing. In the reports submitted to Louis IX in 1260 several communes of

---

[1] B. Kuske, *Köln, der Rhein und das Reich* (Graz, 1956), 114.

northern France attributed their financial troubles chiefly to the crusade of 1248 and to other costly royal policies (six aids between 1248 and 1260). In 1262, when these communes began to render accounts to the royal government, very few municipalities were entirely free from financial embarrassments, though apparently no important town was threatened, as yet, by imminent bankruptcy. In that year nine of the more important towns of Picardy and Vermandois owed a total of 52,000 *li. par.* in short-term debts (including 26,000 *li. par.* borrowed at interest). Ten lesser localities owed about 11,500 *li. par.* In addition, these nineteen towns together paid annually some 10,500 *li. par.* to holders of life annuities. The total capital invested in the municipal loans of this region may have amounted to about one-third of the annual revenue of Louis IX at this time.[1] The wide geographic distribution of the lenders is equally striking. As early as 1232, Troyes, the capital of Champagne, owed over 1,000 *li. par.* for life annuities sold to citizens of Arras, Peronne, Laon and Rheims. The list of non-citizen creditors of eight minor Picard municipalities in 1259-60 includes lenders from at least twelve towns of Picardy, Vermandois, Artois, southern Flanders and western Champagne. Wealthy personages from Douai and Arras were buying annuities of many towns, including small places like Chambly, Montreuil and Roye.

The reigns of Philip IV and his sons were a critical age in the history of the French communes. Several towns lost their autonomous institutions altogether, while the remainder came under more frequent supervision by royal officials. There was, in fact, no place in an increasingly centralized and efficient monarchy for numerous semi-independent communes. The growth of municipal indebtedness was only one of several threats to the survival of a vigorous urban self-government, but in several communes it proved to be the fatal weakness.

The growing financial claims of the monarchy continued to be an important cause of the progressive deterioration of urban finances, but there were also deep-seated causes of trouble within the towns themselves. A town could avoid heavy borrowing and could try to pay its way mainly through raising taxes. This would necessitate a combination of permanent indirect taxes and of fairly frequent levies of heavy direct *tailles*. In such a financial system loans would be a mere supplement. But most French towns in the later thirteenth century were controlled by an oligarchy of wealthy businessmen and property owners who were op-

---

[1] Based on documents printed or summarized in Ch. Dufour, 'Situation financière des villes de Picardie sous Saint Louis', *Mémoires de la Société des Antiquaires de Picardie*, xv (1858); J. de Laborde, *Layettes du Trésor des Chartes*, III (Paris, 1875), 513-69; A. Giry, *Documents sur les relations de la royauté avec les villes en France de 1180 à 1314* (Paris, 1885); Borrelli de Serres, *Recherches sur divers services publics du XIIIe au XVIIe siècle*, I (1895), 103-6.

posed to all direct taxes assessed on income or property. In some larger towns, like Amiens, the great centre of trade in woad, the patriciate did not permit the levy of any direct taxes as long as it maintained itself in power. The alternative favoured at Amiens, and also in some important Flemish cities, was the levy of excises, which fell relatively more lightly on the rich than on the poorer citizens. But preference for excises, which could not yield as much as the direct taxes, made frequent borrowing unavoidable. The cost of the resulting interest charges was borne by the taxpayers in general, in a form which bore hardest on the poorer inhabitants. Where direct taxes persisted, they were not always equitably assessed and there was much tax evasion by members of the wealthy ruling class. Thus many of the oligarchic regimes were unable or unwilling to solve their financial difficulties by introducing adequate taxation and were apt quickly to pile up huge debts. These same wealthy citizens stood most to profit from the opportunities for investment in municipal annuities and loans; as rulers of their towns in some cases they actively encouraged municipal borrowing. For example, the total indebtedness of Arras was increased by two of its leading magistrates in the space of nine months in 1303 by over 15,000 *li. par.* This was done at a time when there was apparently no real need for heavy borrowing. The money for the loans was furnished largely by these two *scabini* themselves and, after drawing interest on these advances, they secured repayment of principal out of the proceeds of a fresh sale of life annuities. They again subscribed together with their friends to these annuities. Throughout they acted through intermediaries, as magistrates were not supposed to make profitable investments in the town funds during their term of office.

Financial malpractices existed in several towns under the patrician rule and added to the growing exasperation of the citizens at the heavy cost of these debt-ridden regimes. Beaumanoir, in a famous passage, refers to instances of serious disorders in towns, where the poorer inhabitants were forced to bear an excessive share of fiscal burdens and, ignoring the possibilities of obtaining redress by lawful methods, launched murderous attacks on their rulers. The history of financial maladministration at Senlis, where Beaumanoir acquired his experience as a royal *bailli*, fully bears out his unfavourable comments on the shortcomings of municipal governments. There were chronic deficits at Senlis and heavy debts. There is evidence of serious abuses including the embezzlement by officials of the funds earmarked for payments of life annuities (652 *li. par.* for annuities payable in 1306–9). No wonder that the bulk of the inhabitants welcomed a royal inquiry, which resulted in 1320 in the suppression of the autonomous commune and in stern measures for the repayment of its debts. At least four other towns ceased to be communes between 1318 and 1329 because of similar financial difficulties. Other municipalities avoided the loss of communal status only through painful financial reforms. At Noyon this even involved a period of complete bankruptcy. Noyon was a poorer locality than other neighbouring towns of comparable size and its revenues (800 *li. par.* in 1260) were wholly inadequate. The burdens imposed upon the town by the French Crown were out of all proportion to its resources. In 1279 the inhabitants asked the king for protection from arrest for the debts of the town, as otherwise they could not trade freely. Noyon then paid annually 4,200 *li. par.* in life annuities and owed also 16,000 *li. par.* of other debts. A final settlement was imposed by the Crown in 1291. Part of the interest-bearing debt was repudiated and payments of annuities were partially suspended. The personal responsibility of all the citizens of a commune for the debts of their town was reaffirmed in a striking fashion; all the movables of the citizens and their immovable property outside the town could be forcibly sold in order to repay the debts of Noyon.

The increase in the royal control over the financial administration of French towns had important repercussions on their credit transactions. Their freedom to contract loans became gradually restricted. Until the last decades of the fourteenth century there is no documentary evidence that royal permission was needed for the sale of life annuities. But throughout the fourteenth century the municipal taxes normally required royal sanction. As the towns could not usually repay loans or pay annuities without the aid of taxation, this imposed, in an indirect way, an effective limitation on their capacity to borrow freely. Only the sale of perpetual annuities, which were normally secured on the ordinary and permanent urban revenues, remained entirely free from all restrictions by the royal government. Douai, a Flemish city temporarily annexed by the French kings, developed for this reason in the fourteenth century the sale of perpetual rents. The towns of the old French royal domain stuck to their earlier habit of selling life annuities. Thus a royal attorney treated the sale of life annuities as a normal custom of Picardy (1401).[1]

The existence of effective royal supervision also promoted a regime of moderation in municipal finances in several other ways. The drastic reforms of city finances ordered by the Crown in several localities in the reigns of Philip the Fair and his sons produced a lasting improvement. While the rich governing class retained in many towns much of its former importance, the days of its irresponsible rule were over. The improvement in the municipal finances can be well illustrated by a comparison between the budgets of Douai in 1295–6, the last financial year of unrestricted patrician rule, and in 1326–7. Between those two dates both revenue and expenditure declined by three-quarters (from over

[1] Quoted by E. Maugis in *Mémoires de la Société des Antiquaires de la Picardie*, XXXIII (1898), 195, n. 3.

40,000 *li. par.* in 1295–6 to *c.* 10,000 *li. par.* in 1326–7). At the end of 1327 the short-term debt amounted to one-fifth of the comparable debt in 1296 and the annual cost of the municipal life annuities declined by nearly 40% during the same period. In a normal year of the new regime, like 1326–7, Douai not only did not need to contract any loans, but was even able to liquidate a portion of the existing debt.

The outbreak of the Hundred Years War ended this period of financial ease. The requirements of local defence, as well as the incessant demands of the Crown, involved towns in every part of the French kingdom in ruinous expenditure and heavy borrowing. In this emergency the presence or absence of autonomous institutions became of subsidiary importance. At Tours, which enjoyed only a very restricted measure of self-government, the representatives of the town contracted loans and sold rents in their own names in order to provide money for fortifications and other necessities. Amiens, which until 1383 was one of the most independent French communes, claimed in 1401 that, since the reign of Philip VI, it had paid to the Crown and spent on fortifications and soldiers some 280,000 *li.* which had to be raised from the sale of life-rents.[1] The same thing was happening in southern France. At Toulouse in the early fifteenth century the sums required for each instalment of the subsidies due to the king were borrowed from wealthy merchants and money-changers. Royal exactions were the chief cause of the indebtedness of the French towns in the late Middle Ages.

By the end of the fourteenth century the old distinction between the communes and other less privileged municipalities had lost much of its former practical importance. Almost all the French towns were, by then, under close royal supervision and the Crown tended to treat them alike in all essential matters. Henceforth all the towns raised loans mainly in order to satisfy the requirements of the royal government. The king determined how much each town might be allowed to borrow and even the methods of contracting municipal loans became a matter for royal regulations. For example, Louis XI appears to have been opposed to the sale of life annuities by the towns and Amiens was compelled by him to switch over to the sale of perpetual, but redeemable, annuities. The financial history of the French towns in the last century of the Middle Ages can only be profitably discussed, therefore, as part of the general history of the royal finances. The fortunes of the towns became so inseparably linked with the development of the main fiscal policies of the Crown that it seemed best to deal with this last part of the story in the general section on fifteenth-century France.

---

[1] *De quoy et pourquoy paier a falu vendre rentes à vie*, quoted by E. Maugis, *loc. cit.* 196–7.

(3) THE TOWNS OF THE NETHERLANDS

A. *Flemish Towns (Thirteenth to Fourteenth Centuries)*

The first phase in the history of Flemish municipal credit might be called the age of the patrician regimes and ended with their overthrow in 1297. Its main features were the same as in the towns of northern France in the second half of the thirteenth century. City budgets were excessively inflated. There was much suspicion of financial corruption and municipal debts were growing apace. The demands of the Flemish counts for money singularly aggravated this bad financial situation. The subsidies granted to Count Guy (1278–1300), and the loans contracted on his behalf by the towns, were the main cause of the virtual bankruptcy of Ghent, Bruges and Ypres in the last years of the thirteenth century.

In 1279 the Flemish towns were compelled by Count Guy to render public accounts for the first time. Because of the absence of such compulsion earlier on, little is known about the municipal loans contracted previous to that date. The sale of annuities was practised by Bruges[1] and Douai from at least the 1260's. Ghent was paying 1,600 *li. par.* to holders of life annuities in 1275. Both life and perpetual annuities were familiar to Flemish municipal governments in the second half of the thirteenth century. In 1294 the funded debt of Ghent was divided nearly equally between these two types of rents: perpetual rents involved an annual debt-charge of 2,046 *li. par.*, and 2,900 *li. par.* were paid on life-rents. It has been pointed out by H. Van Werveke that both these forms of annuities show at Ghent a clear influence of French models, which might suggest that the practice of the sale of annuities may have reached Ghent from northern France.[2] The inhabitants of Arras and other French towns were the chief buyers of the annuities offered for sale by the Flemish municipalities. The leading financiers of Arras advanced the bulk of the enormous short-term loans contracted by the Flemish cities between 1278 and 1297 on behalf of Count Guy. In 1299 Bruges owed for this reason 110,000 *li. par.* to the Crespins of Arras. This debt included a substantial amount of interest. It was usual for Arras financiers to charge, on average, from 14 to 16% on their loans. Each time an unrepaid debt was renewed, which might happen once a year, it could be augmented by the addition of the unpaid arrears of interest. This befell Bruges several times. Ghent had suspended payments to its creditors by 1294. In that year its debt amounted to just over 100,000 *li. par.*, involving an annual interest and rent-charge of at least 10,600 *li. par.*

The grave financial crisis through which Flanders passed in the early

---

[1] L. Gilliodts-Van Severen, *Inventaire des archives de la ville de Bruges*, I, no. 8 (pp. 6–7).
[2] H. Van Werveke, *De Gentsche Stadsfinanciën in de Middeleeuwen* (1934), 283, 289–90.

decades of the fourteenth century has already been described. The down-fall of the patrician regimes at the end of the thirteenth century certainly did not inaugurate an era of financial ease in the cities, but it at least made possible a less spendthrift administration of the municipal finances. At a time when Ghent's ordinary annual revenue could seldom have exceeded 20,000 *li. par.*, that city was forced to pay at least 177,000 *li. par.* to the counts of Flanders and the kings of France in the space of thirty-five years (1302–37). In the same period Bruges paid about 291,000 *li. par.* to these rulers and Ypres paid a good deal more than Ghent. The partial repudiation of the older Flemish debts to the financiers of Arras alone made these new burdens bearable. Several of the weaker Flemish towns tried to maintain good relations with Arras financiers; Ypres resumed by 1312 payments of life annuities due to its Arras creditors.[1] Bruges and Ghent persisted in their refusal to honour their past obligations. Some of the claims against Ghent passed into the hands of Pope John XXII, but that city preferred to endure between 1321 and 1330 a papal interdict rather than to pay the entire debt. Gradually many of the creditors despaired of repayment. During the 'thirties both Ghent and Bruges managed to repurchase several old debts for a fraction of their full value.

This resort to partial bankruptcy after 1302 seriously weakened the credit of the Flemish cities and hampered the sale of the municipal an-nuities. Short-term loans could sometimes be obtained from the Italians trading in Flanders, at a stiff price. But even this was not always easy in the early fourteenth century. The large payments made by the Flemish towns between 1302 and 1337 to the king and the count had to be financed mainly out of indirect taxes and forced loans imposed upon their own inhabitants. The revolution at Ghent at the end of 1337 and the growing likelihood of another war with France put an end at Ghent and Bruges to all further negotiations with the old creditors. This second repudiation of past obligations was a necessary prelude to the extra-ordinary efforts made by Ghent, under the leadership of Van Artevelde, to control and defend Flanders. As usually happens in times of revolution, sound financial methods were abandoned. Maintenance of good credit was sacrificed for the sake of immediate lightening of financial burdens by partial bankruptcy. Between 1337 and 1346 sizeable deficits were in-curred each year at Ghent. In years of exceptional military efforts the city's expenditure was three times as large as in peace time. Annual forced loans from the citizens and borrowing from Flemish financiers connected with the new regime (especially the regent of Flanders, Simon van Halen) provided the necessary money. In 1346–7 the short-term debt

[1] G. Des Marez and E. de Sagher, *Comptes de la ville d'Ypres*, I (Brussels, 1909), 296, 303–4, 329, 366, 376.

(21,500 *li. par.*) was compulsorily converted into life-rents and through this new measure of disguised bankruptcy the annual deficit was reduced again to reasonable proportions, for the first time for a decade.

A temporary decline in the importance of annuities, as opposed to other forms of municipal credit, can be clearly discerned in the leading Flemish towns in the first half of the fourteenth century. Lack of confidence among the would-be investors was presumably the main cause. In the thirteenth century the Flemish towns had not sold life annuities to their own citizens but only to outsiders. After 1297 it became difficult to find foreign purchasers for such rents. Thus an attempt of Ghent in 1326 to sell them at Brussels, in Brabant, met with a rebuff. Thereafter, for twenty years, Ghent made no attempt to sell life annuities abroad. When such sales were resumed in 1346, Count Louis de Male was requested to guarantee them. Ypres had to seek in 1352 royal protection to prevent the arrest of its citizens at Lille for unpaid arrears of its municipal annuities. Elsewhere in the Netherlands, where conditions were stabler, the towns continued to sell annuities; this was so, for example, at Brussels, the capital of Brabant. Indeed, even the Flemish municipal annuities came back into favour with investors in the third quarter of the fourteenth century, after the return of internal peace to Flanders in the reign of Louis de Male.

The presence within Flanders of the great money market of Bruges gave the leading Flemish towns exceptional opportunities for short-term borrowing. The municipality of Bruges made particularly frequent use of these facilities. A few specially important examples may suffice. In 1328 Bruges borrowed 20,000 *li. par.* from the Peruzzi of Florence in order to discharge heavy obligations towards Count Louis de Nevers. In 1357 Bruges agreed to pay his successor, Louis de Male, 66,000 *li. par.* to redeem an annual rent-charge of 3,000 *li.* The city forthwith borrowed 20,000 *li. par.* from the foreign merchants present within its walls and repaid them later by doubling the municipal excise duty. In time of civil war, in 1379-80, Bruges even imposed forced loans on its cosmopolitan business community.[1]

B. *The Belgian Towns in the Burgundian Period*

The Burgundian dukes maintained close control over the financial administration of the towns in their dominions. The levy of taxes and the sale of life-rents by municipalities required ducal consent. As in contemporary France, this control was designed to safeguard the financial resources of the municipalities, so that the prince might derive the maximum benefit from them. The requirements of the Burgundian govern-

[1] L. Gilliodts-Van Severen, *Inventaire des archives de la ville de Bruges*, II, 347-53.

ment were the chief cause of the serious indebtedness of the towns of the Netherlands in the last century of the Middle Ages. Between 1390 and 1413 almost every payment due from Bruges to the dukes was made through the intermediacy of the main ducal bankers, the Rapondi. Dino Rapondi advanced the money directly to the duke as soon as the tax was imposed, and recovered his loans later on from Bruges, together with a suitable amount of interest. Other Flemish municipalities likewise had to avail themselves frequently of Dino's services. These loans from important businessmen involved the use of forms of credit familiar to professional merchants, but not habitually employed in municipal credit transactions outside the Netherlands. Bruges and the other Flemish municipalities which borrowed from the Rapondi gave these financiers bills of exchange drawn on other European commercial centres. These bills included an element of interest fluctuating with the credit of each municipality and the current commercial exchange rates. On loans advanced by Dino Rapondi to Bruges this oscillated between 12 and 28%. The Rapondi in this way were assuring prompt payment of taxes to the dukes at an extra charge to the urban taxpayers.

The towns of French Flanders and Artois regularly sold life annuities in order to satisfy the Burgundian government. Douai was heavily in debt for this reason at the end of the fourteenth century. Arras was nearly bankrupt in 1392 and was forced to convert a part of its life annuities into perpetual rents bearing a much lower rate of interest. The heavy debts incurred by Ghent on behalf of the Burgundian rulers figure among the complaints presented to Duke Philip the Good; these grievances contributed to Ghent's growing hostility towards the ducal government, culminating in the revolt of 1450.[1] The town of Namur, previous to its annexation by Philip the Good in 1421, had a balanced budget. It first began to sell life annuities in order to provide subsidies for its new Burgundian master. Until 1436 Namur was still in a position to redeem speedily most of the annuities sold for this purpose. Thereafter its financial situation steadily deteriorated.

The Burgundian rule increased the indebtedness of the towns, but it was not unfavourable to the interests of the wealthier townsmen. They stood to gain most from the increased opportunities to invest in municipal annuities. At Douai and other towns, by the late fourteenth century, the annuities were being sold in larger units than had been usual in the past (change from sales in silver to sales in gold currency). Consequently only the richer investors could afford to buy them. The contrast between the impoverishment of the municipalities and the enrichment of their leading citizens might be well illustrated from the example of Lille under Philip the Good. Lille was Philip's favourite residence and the ducal

[1] L. P. Gachard, *Rapport . . . . sur les archives de Dijon* (Brussels, 1843), 143–4.

financial administration had its headquarters there. The town was governed by an oligarchy of wealthy citizens, with the families of the local money-changers in the lead. These Lille changers were much employed on lucrative government business. For example, they were used as agents for the disposal of the annuities offered for sale by the duke. Under Philip they were the wealthiest citizens of Lille and a few were even ennobled. The municipality under their control was always ready to lend money to the government. The changers themselves often lent to the town for this purpose. When Philip towards the end of his life wanted to build a new palace at Lille, the city readily advanced a large part of the necessary funds and raised the money from taxes 'on the inhabitants of this town who profit from the presence of our lord'. But while individual citizens grew richer, the town sank ever deeper in debt. For a long time annual deficits were covered up by further borrowing, but by the end of Philip's life Lille's finances were in a deplorable state.[1]

(4) THE GERMAN TOWNS

The majority of the more important German towns had been, from the second half of the thirteenth century, free from subjection to powerful territorial rulers. Regular royal or princely taxation, which in France and the Burgundian state permanently unbalanced urban budgets in the later Middle Ages, was not an important cause of financial embarrassment to the leading German cities. The German towns never attained, however, the complete independence of the Italian city republics. The occasional financial demands of German rulers continued to be a recurrent cause of fiscal emergency in several self-governing municipalities. In the later Middle Ages there was a constant menace of private war or brigandage in many parts of Germany and towns suffered severely from the persistent hostility of the nobles. To the ordinary expenses of municipal administration were thus added the costs of conducting an independent foreign policy and of maintaining urban armies. While the German towns were spared the fiscal burdens that the more powerful western states continuously imposed upon townsmen, they lacked the effective protection against attacks by predatory neighbours which the English and French kings normally guaranteed. Several German towns were financially crippled by wars against the turbulent powers around them.

The towns which in the middle of the thirteenth century were under the direct control of the German kings (*königliche Städte*) became later imperial cities (*Reichsstädte*) and were characterized by a special status. They were subject to no territorial ruler other than the king and, in practice, enjoyed a very wide measure of autonomy. In the later Middle Ages,

[1] R. Marquant, *La vie économique à Lille sous Philippe le Bon* (Paris, 1940), 27.

their greatest fear was that they might be mediatized. This was most likely to happen as the result of kings pledging their rights in the *Reichstädte* and royal credit operations thus became a matter of lively concern to the imperial cities. Several towns tried to obtain the privilege of immunity from mediatization (*privilegia de non alienando ab imperio*). Many of the episcopal and princely towns gradually achieved self-government, in some cases through revolt, more often by buying out their lords' regalian and domanial rights in the urban territory: power to fill the office of bailiff and other administrative posts, and control over minting, tolls and other taxes. These rights were often, in the first place, only pledged to the cities, but the chronic disorder of princely finances usually precluded their redemption. Several of the leading episcopal cities (e.g. Cologne, Augsburg, Mainz) came to be classified as 'free towns' (*Freie Städte*) because of their unusually extensive liberties and, with the *Reichsstädte*, were later known as *Freie Reichsstädte*. Some of the towns belonging to the lay princes (*Landesherrliche Städte*) managed to attain even greater independence than the imperial cities, but they lived in dread of losing their privileges, while many towns never obtained liberty or lost it. Out of some 3,000 urban communities in Germany in the later Middle Ages only a small minority lost their original agrarian character and developed a really urban economy; only twenty to twenty-five towns may have had above 10,000 inhabitants. In the struggle for autonomy the possession or the lack of appreciable financial resources could be of decisive importance. The poorer towns, the great majority, were the least successful in improving their status, and the impoverishment of an autonomous city might encourage a revival of its lord's claims. Thus the financial bankruptcy of Mainz prepared the way for the overthrow of its independence by the archbishop in 1462.

Most self-governing German cities were gradually forced to accept loans as a frequent financial expedient, and several even came to regard continuous borrowing as normal and indispensable. In some cases, though this was generally a sign that things had got out of hand, existing debt-charges could be maintained only out of further borrowing. Many German municipalities, particularly if they were governed by the patricians, avoided direct taxation as far as possible. Whenever this happened very frequent borrowing was the main alternative.

The absence of budgeting has been regarded by many German scholars as an important cause of the excessive indebtedness of the municipalities. The instability of the political and military situation made financial planning particularly impracticable.[1] When special circum-

---

[1] See especially W. Stieda, 'Städtische Finanzen im Mittelalter', *JNOS*. 3rd series, XVII (1899), 47; B. Kuske, *Das Schuldenwesen der deutschen Städte im Mittelalter* (1904), 5–9; J. Landmann in *Finanzarchiv*, XXIX (1912), 12 ff.

stances warranted it, as at Cologne in 1395,[1] municipal governments
were able to draw up estimates or surveys of their financial position, but
fluctuations in expenditure were normally too incalculable to make
orderly budgeting worth while. L. Schönberg, in particular, stressed this
uncertainty, rather than the carelessness or irresponsibility, of municipal
governments as one of the leading causes of their recurrent heavy borrowing.[2]

Oppressive and unevenly distributed taxation provoked much unrest
in the German towns. The growth of indebtedness was often the consequence of an unsatisfactory system of taxes and aggravated still further
the pressure of taxation on the urban population. There was a succession
of urban uprisings in which the craft gilds usually played the leading role
and which often resulted in permanent changes of regime. While some
of these revolts occurred as early as the first half of the fourteenth century
(at Speyer in 1327, at Strasbourg in 1332, at Zürich in 1336), it is noticeable that they became more frequent after the plague of 1348. As recent
research has clearly shown, that disaster marked the beginning of a decline in the economic life of medieval Germany, though not every
region was equally affected, the southern towns apparently suffering
less severely than others. There were revolts at Nuremberg (1348),
Cologne (1364, 1370, 1396), Frankfurt (1355, 1364–5), Augsburg
(1370), Lübeck (1383) and elsewhere, in which the demands of the artisans for just distribution of taxation played an important part in the agitation that led to these uprisings. Growing debts were also important in
exacerbating dissatisfaction with the financial system; in some cases,
indeed, the demand for special taxes, designed to reduce debts, actually
precipitated uprisings.

During the epidemic of 1348 massacres and plunder of Jews occurred
in many German towns and several municipalities thus got rid of part of
their debts. Another mass spoliation of Jews took place in 1385 in the
towns of southern Germany with the encouragement of King Wenzel.[3]
The debts of numerous Swabian municipalities to the Jews were annulled
altogether, while the debts of private persons were cut by 25% and the
right to collect the remainder was transferred to the town governments.
Thus the city of Nuremberg, besides getting rid of its own debts, acquired
a claim on the burgrave of Nuremberg for 8,000 florins, from which he
freed himself only by surrendering to the town his court and the revenues
from the customs. The consent of Wenzel to the operation cost the towns

[1] R. Knipping, Die Kölner Stadtrechnungen des Mittelalters, xxii and 141, 159, 187.
[2] Die Technik des Finanzhaushaltes der deutschen Städte im Mittelalter (1910).
[3] Deutsche Reichstagsakten, I, nos. 272 ff.; K. Hegel, Deutsche Städtechroniken, I,
113–24; O. Stobbe, Die Juden in Deutschland während des Mittelalters (3rd ed. 1923),
134–40; A. Süssmann, Die Judenschuldentilgungen unter König Wenzel I (1907).

only 40,000 florins, representing only a small share of the total gains obtained by the townsmen. The success of this operation encouraged Wenzel to repeat it in 1390, so that by the beginning of the fifteenth century the importance of Jewish loans to the German municipalities had seriously declined.

With the appearance in 1879 of an essay by R. Sohm it became common in Germany to regard the medieval town governments as banking institutions, providing facilities for safe deposit and investment that were allegedly lacking otherwise. Sohm drew these too far-reaching generalizations from Schönberg's study of Basle's finances and his view was also influenced by the belief, widely held when he wrote, that the towns, because of their corporate character, were alone capable of becoming satisfactory credit institutions. Recent studies have disproved the idea that there was little scope for investing in private enterprises in Germany in the later Middle Ages,[1] but it remains true that modest investors seem often to have preferred to place their money in municipal funds rather than in private ventures. The preference for municipal loans was specially noticeable in the fifteenth century, and some of the more democratic governments that were set up in several German towns in the later fourteenth and fifteenth centuries, for political and social reasons, encouraged lending by small investors. Sometimes they felt compelled to accept all the loans offered by the citizens even if the money was not actually needed by the town.

The popularity of municipal loans among the German investors is closely bound up with the prevalence of the sale of rents. While the Jews and other professional lenders frequently preferred to advance short-term loans, municipal annuities found a ready market among every section of the German propertied classes, nobles and clergy as well as townsmen. Life annuities, in particular, were highly prized as a form of insurance, providing an old-age pension for the investor or helping to provide for his dependants. This need for security, and for forms of investment yielding a steady return over long periods, amply accounts for the attractiveness of the municipal annuities. The existence in Germany of numerous self-governing towns, and the frequency with which they borrowed, accustomed lenders to expect that whenever they had spare capital they would be presented with a wide choice of urban borrowers and could minimize risks by distributing their purchases over many towns. Thus Heinrich Topler, the burgomaster of Rotenburg, was in 1408 receiving rents from about 120 localities.

While there existed considerable local divergencies, certain general

[1] See especially H. Reincke, 'Die alte Hamburger Stadtschuld der Hansezeit (1300–1563)', in A. von Brandt and W. Koppe (eds.), *Städtewesen und Bürgertum als geschichtliche Kräfte* (1953), pp. 490 ff.

trends in German urban borrowing stand out. The early sources show much short-term borrowing, often on fairly onerous terms. Gradually the sale of annuities became predominant and the municipalities accumulated experience in the flexible use of different types of annuities. Life annuities, besides being popular with the German buyers, were attractive to city administrators because of the speculative possibilities of profit whenever investors died speedily. But this type of annuity was not normally redeemable and it always bore high rates of interest (often fixed quasi-permanently at 10%). For these reasons several towns ceased to sell them in any quantities and perpetual rents replaced them as the favourite instrument of municipal credit. They bore lower rates of interest and, once it was fully accepted that they were freely redeemable, they could be changed at will by the town governments from long-term investments into short-term loans. By the early fifteenth century the rate of interest on perpetual annuities was lowered in all the more important German centres to c. 3 to 5%. But, while cheaper types of borrowing became common, the overall indebtedness of the towns tended to increase and became a major problem.

Cologne, Nuremberg, Basle and Hamburg provide the best illustrations of credit operations of German towns. In Cologne, the greatest German town, borrowing played an exceptionally important part and an unusually elaborate system of city debt was gradually evolved. Until the last quarter of the thirteenth century Cologne lacked autonomy. The city was finally freed from responsibility for archiepiscopal debts only by a privilege of King Rudolf in 1274[1] and its political independence was securely established only in 1288. The earliest evidence concerning borrowing by Cologne dates from 1228-9: the city was then repaying at the fairs of Champagne loans contracted from Sienese merchants.[2] Considerable short-term loans were contracted from citizens of Cologne in 1275 (a debt of 2,704 marks to 9 citizens).[3] It can be assumed that life annuities were already sold by Cologne in the thirteenth century,[4] and perpetual annuities made their appearance by c. 1300. The first surviving register of annuities dates from 1351 and reveals a well-organized system of public credit. Until the revolution of 1396, Cologne was ruled by an oligarchy of rich patricians who financed its government almost entirely out of indirect taxes, chiefly excises, supplemented by borrowing at diffi-

---

[1] O. Redlich, *Rudolf von Habsburg* (1903), 222-3. For Cologne's earlier efforts to achieve this (1231, 1236, 1258) see L. Ennen and G. Eckertz, *Quellen zur Geschichte der Stadt Köln* (1860-79), II, 125, 127, 160 and 287 (II, par. 1).

[2] Ennen and Eckertz, *op. cit.* II, 116, nos. 107-8.   [3] *Ibid.* III, nos. 109, 113.

[4] R. Knipping, 'Das Schuldenwesen der Stadt Köln im 14. und 15. Jahrhundert', *Westdeutsche Zeitschrift für Geschichte und Kunst*, XIII (1894), 346. Our account of public credit at Cologne is mainly based on this article and Knipping's edition of *Kölner Stadtrechnungen des Mittelalters*, 2 vols. (Bonn, 1897-8).

cult moments. Between 1351 and 1370 the sale of life annuities (at 10%) was the predominant form of public borrowing and the debt to the holders of annuities more than trebled (102,560 marks in 1370). This produced a shift to less costly forms of borrowing. Short-term loans, partly free of interest, were successfully raised at Cologne from a relatively small number of rich lenders. Out of the aggregate total of 768,948 marks borrowed for a restricted period between 1370 and 1392, as much as 76% was procured locally at Cologne. The loans raised abroad chiefly took the form of perpetual, but redeemable, annuities, sold at variable rates (chiefly 5 to 5½% in 1381–92). It was assumed that these annuities, despite their name, would be speedily redeemed and, because of their temporary character, they were not even entered in the register of annuities. They were chiefly sold at Lübeck, Mainz and Augsburg. On the eve of the revolution of 1396 the finances of Cologne were in a fairly sound state, but the burdensome indirect taxation pressed heavily on the bulk of the population.

The overthrow of the rule of the patriciate in that year produced a marked change in credit policy. Widespread investment in life annuities was encouraged. In 1418, for example, 83,632 marks were borrowed from 425 persons. Humble people, including craftsmen and domestic servants, appeared for the first time among lenders, buying small annuities for as little as 1 to 5 guldens. The municipal treasury of Cologne developed into a kind of savings bank.

During the greater part of the fifteenth century (before 1474) the credit of Cologne stood fairly high. The city could borrow cheaply and much ingenuity was displayed in varying the terms of the annuities. Money was saved through successful conversions. Redeemable life annuities were introduced for the first time in 1416. The municipality successfully exploited the depreciation of the silver coinage in which the annuities were paid to rentiers. The rate of interest on perpetual annuities declined from 5% in the early fifteenth century to 4% or even 3% after 1450. Cologne's annual debt-charge gradually diminished from 35,134 marks in 1432 to only 23,846 marks in 1462.

The war against Charles of Burgundy in defence of Neuss, in 1474–5, irretrievably undermined Cologne's solvency. It had to borrow much more in two years (1,301,000 marks in 1474–6) than it had raised from loans during the preceding fifty (878,000 marks in 1432–73). Higher rates of interest had to be offered; the funded debt alone rose in 1477 to 1,754,000 marks and the annual debt-charge amounted in that year to 121,000 marks. The worst was still to come. The ruling rich merchants still preferred to rely exclusively on indirect taxes and tried to meet the increased cost of debt by raising more revenue from excise duties. This provoked a violent agitation in the autumn of 1481. The lesser craftsmen, the more radical wing of the opposition, demanded among other things a suspension in the payment of annuities. This helped to split the movement, as it frightened numerous citizens who had invested their small savings in city funds. The union of the more moderate elements with the rich governing class led to the crushing of the revolt early in 1482. Thereafter the debt continued to mount and by 1512 reached the staggering sum of 3,243,000 marks. In December of that year came the inevitable revolution. The municipal government was entirely changed, some of the former magistrates were executed and far-reaching reforms were attempted. Fiscal changes included the imposition of a property tax and the reduction of interest rates on the existing annuities. It was decreed that, in future, municipal borrowing should require the consent of the whole community. The great seal of Cologne, with which all the city obligations had to be sealed, was placed under the control of twenty-three craft gilds.

The surviving municipal accounts of Nuremberg[1] start in 1377. Some of the information concerning borrowing is given in Table IV as a detailed example of the steady expansion in the need for credit experienced by the leading German cities.

Between 1377 and 1385 direct taxation formed the mainstay of the city's budget, the funded debt, consisting exclusively of the life annuities (at 10%), was of moderate size and there was little fresh borrowing. The spoliation of the Jews in 1385 yielded large immediate returns. Nuremberg cancelled its own debts of 7,000 florins and acquired 80,000 florins, but lost the annual tax on Jews; in the subsequent years direct taxation began to be avoided and there was a sharp increase in borrowing. Nuremberg started in 1388 to sell redeemable perpetual annuities and within a few years the funded debt roughly doubled.

The next considerable expansion in the city's indebtedness occurred in the second quarter of the fifteenth century. Nuremberg then completed its control over the urban territory by buying for 137,611 *li.* from the burgrave of Nuremberg, Frederick of Hohenzollern, the castle with all the rights and revenues pertaining to it. This resulted in an unprecedented increase of borrowing in 1426-7. The annual debt-charge more than doubled between 1426 and 1429. It would have increased even faster if Nuremberg had not in 1427 resumed the sale of perpetual annuities bearing only 4 to 5% interest compared with 10% paid on life annuities. Between 1431 and 1440 the city did not have to face any fresh emergencies, but it was too heavily in debt to be able to balance its budget. During this decade Nuremberg devoted on average 35·7% of its total expenditure to annuities and the debt-charge constituted the largest single item in its

---

[1] Based on P. Sander, *Die reichstädtische Haushaltung Nürnbergs dargestellt auf Grund ihres Zustandes von 1431 bis 1440* (1902).

Table IV. Debts of Nuremberg 1377–1458

Year	New Borrowing		Total Receipts	Total Expenditure	Annual Rent-charge		Total Funded Debt	
	Particular Years	Averages			Particular Years	Averages	Particular Years	Averages
1377	229		17,241	16,832	4,745*		47,452	38,896
1381–7						3,889*		75,773
1388–92						6,789		87,061
1393–6						7,462		
1406	5,520		18,471	31,642	6,707		82,431	60,602
1418–22						6,060*		
1423–5						5,216*		52,167
1426	27,534		59,855		4,868*		48,680	
1427	73,974		136,362	169,594	6,011		73,320	
1428–32		27,501				12,128		182,657†
1433–7		18,169				20,978		292,363†
1438–42		11,477				25,526		333,243
1458	10,590			59,070			733,360	

All the figures in Nuremberg's new heller pounds.
* Years when only life annuities paid.
† Years when the debt from perpetual annuities preponderated over debt from life annuities.

annual spending. The city could no longer satisfy its creditors without contracting fresh loans each year. Borrowing amounted on average to 33·9% of yearly revenue and surpassed the receipts from any other source (direct taxation provided 20·2% and excise duties on liquors 21·2%). Between 1427 and 1442 the funded debt more than quadrupled. It more than doubled again by 1458, partly as result of the costly war with the Hohenzollerns in the middle of the century. Nuremberg was, however, prosperous enough to expand adequately its other revenues (its annual income was 130,000 li. in 1469). In the first half of the sixteenth century the city even accumulated a large reserve fund which allowed it to dispense with borrowing in ordinary years. This reserve amounted to 1,048,000 li. in 1548 (more than twice the annual revenue at that time).[1]

From an early date the finances of Basle were based on a well-organized system of taxation. The city borrowed continuously (e.g. every year between 1365 and 1483) and its wars were financed largely out of loans, but the municipal budget was never allowed to become permanently unbalanced. To keep its indebtedness within safe limits, Basle repeatedly resorted to extraordinary taxation, including direct taxes on persons and property. Periods of peace and prosperity were systematically used to reduce the debt. All the main forms of municipal credit were employed, but the sale of annuities predominated. Handled prudently, as a supplement but not a substitute for taxation, borrowing was a source of strength to Basle and never of disaster.

The fluctuations in borrowing between periods of peace and of emergency can be traced in considerable detail. In the last decade of the fourteenth century the debt of Basle was still fairly low. The financial situation was then improving. After 1394 the rate of interest on redeemable perpetual annuities did not again rise above 6⅔%, and it declined to 5½–5% after 1402. The annual debt-charge declined from c. 6,500 li. in 1393–4 to c. 6,000 li. in 1395–6. In a period of warfare between 1424 and 1428[2] the debt-charges rose to more than double these figures, partly because the city had to sell a considerable amount of life annuities (at 10%); the debt-charge stood at 14,255 li. in 1429–30. In that year, out of the total expenditure of 40,000 li. some 33,000 li. were spent on redeeming debts and on interest. Between 1430 and 1443 Basle enjoyed peace, the ordinary revenue increased considerably and the debt was steadily reduced. By 1442–3 the annual debt-charge was brought down to 7,302 li. The so-

[1] Sander, op. cit. 862–5. In comparing the figures quoted above allowance must be made for the reduced purchasing power of money in the sixteenth century.

[2] Urkundenbuch der Stadt Basel (ed. R. Wackernagel, Thommen and Huber), 11 vols. (Basle, 1890–1910), VI, 191, 198, 210, 230, 276; H. Boos, Urkundenbuch der Landschaft Basel (1881), 788; G. Schönberg, Finanzverhältnisse der Stadt Basel (1879), 14 ff., 90, 150–67.

called war of St Jacob, in which Basle had to protect its independence against the Habsburgs, imposed a heavy strain on the municipal resources. It was financed mainly out of loans and slightly over 100,000 *li*. was borrowed between 1443 and 1450, while repayment of debts virtually ceased. After the return of peace vigorous efforts were again made to stabilize the city budget and several special taxes were imposed. Borrowing balanced by steady repayment continued throughout the 'fifties. A similar pattern recurred during the briefer emergency (1473–6) of the Burgundian war. Again, there was recourse to heavy borrowing, while repayment was suspended, but after the hostilities were over the debt was gradually reduced through the levy of extraordinary taxes.

Similar moderation in the use of credit prevailed in the other leading Swiss cities of Bern and Zürich. Like Basle they were occasionally faced with grave financial liabilities and found themselves loaded with debt. But like Basle they were able to extricate themselves without courting financial ruin and entered the sixteenth century relatively free from debt. In 1492 Bern's debt totalled only 7,700 florins. Zürich's indebtedness at one time in 1389 rose to as much as 60,000 florins, but more typical of the normal situation at Zürich are the figures for 1440. The debt-charge amounted then to about 20% of the city's expenditure, a substantially lighter burden than the debt-charges borne by Basle and Nuremberg at the same date. Yet its rate of interest on annuities declined more slowly than in the most advanced German towns. Between 1386 and 1415 Zürich paid between 16⅔ and 9% on life-rents, though later the rate settled at the more normal average of 11 to 10%. Similarly as much as 10% was paid on redeemable perpetual annuities in the middle of the fourteenth century. By 1404 this declined to 5% but did not diminish further.

Space prevents the detailed discussion of most other German towns whose financial affairs have been studied by historians, such as Worms, Aachen, Dortmund or Brunswick. But the financial history of Mainz deserves retelling as an example of political decline resulting from excessive indebtedness and financial mismanagement. Although financial difficulties led to the craft gilds being represented on the city council from 1332, serious internal strife was avoided until 1411. In that year payments of annuities accounted for 48% of the total expenditure[1] and this deplorable situation provoked a popular revolution. The new municipal government set up in 1411 was prohibited from selling fresh annuities without the permission of the gilds. The financial position continued, however, to deteriorate. In 1436–7 as much as 75% of the city's expenditure went to creditors and arrears of overdue debt were accumulating.[2]

---

[1] The surviving medieval accounts of Mainz are summarized and discussed by C. Hegel, *Die Chroniken der mittelrheinischen Städte. Mainz*, I (2), (1882), 91 ff.

[2] For accounts of 1436–7 see *ibid*. I, 90–2 and II, 80.

Mainz experienced growing difficulties in finding buyers for its annuities and had to pay higher rates of interest: in the 1430's it was offering 5% on the perpetual rents instead of 3 or 4% paid formerly. Mainz could no longer meet its annual debt-charges without contracting fresh loans each year. The city was obviously heading towards bankruptcy. In 1444 a special committee was set up to seek a solution. The city council admitted the existence of an aggregate debt of 373,184 guilders (249,418 guilders of perpetual annuities, 95,000 guilders of life annuities at 10%, and the rest short-term debts and unpaid arrears). The committee recommended stringent economies and reforms, but on 30 July 1444 a revolt broke out and a new council was set up, representing the gilds. The new administration proved, however, as helpless as all its predecessors. In 1448, as a last desperate remedy, it asked the archbishop and the clergy for a loan of 21,000 guilders. This was refused and Mainz then declared itself bankrupt. The major part of the debt was due outside the city (c. 60% in 1444) and its creditors had Mainz put under the ban of the Empire, excommunicated by the pope and put under an interdict by its archbishop.

In the end, deserted by the wealthier burghers and impoverished, it was on 28 October 1462 captured and partly burnt by Adolf of Nassau (one of the two rival archbishops of Mainz). Several hundred citizens were exiled, its independence was ended and it became part of the electoral principality.

It remains to conclude the account of urban finance in Germany by a summary of the credit transactions of the leading Hanseatic port of Hamburg. A comparable wealth of evidence about public borrowing has not survived for any other German city.[1] Municipal annuities were being sold at Hamburg as early as 1251. At first, their payment was secured by urban property or revenues specially earmarked for this purpose, but the need for this ceased to be felt by the middle of the fourteenth century. The annuities were recorded in a special city register and from the early fifteenth century a supplementary recognizance was also issued; these *Kammerbriefe*, as they were called, became after 1453 the sole evidence of debt. The recognition of debt was made by all the members of the city council collectively,[2] but, in contrast to many other German towns (e.g. Cologne, Nuremberg, Bremen, Lüneburg), individual councillors were never required to give additional personal guarantees and their individual

---

[1] H. Reincke, 'Die alte Hamburger Stadtschuld der Hansezeit (1300–1563)', in A. von Brandt and W. Koppe, *Städtewesen und Bürgertum als geschichtliche Kräfte* (1953), 489. The accounts for the period 1350–1562 are in K. Koppmann (and others), *Kämmereirechnungen der Stadt Hamburg*, 10 vols. (Hamburg, 1869–1951).

[2] *Nos consules debemus. . .* is the usual form of the Latin documents.

responsibility for repayment was never invoked.[1] The absence of such additional precautions was a signal tribute to the long-enduring solidity of Hamburg's credit. Some of the annuities issued at Hamburg at the end of the Middle Ages continued, in fact, to be paid until very recent times. The same thing happened at Bremen where several annuities dating from the beginning of the sixteenth century were converted into a modern currency in the early nineteenth century and remained valid until 1859.

Between 1350 and 1500 Hamburg's indebtedness increased steadily. It totalled 6,000 marks (of Lübeck currency) in 1350, involving a debt-charge of 401 marks, doubled by 1400 and in 1500 amounted to 57,753 marks and a debt-charge of 3,580 marks. If allowance is made for the intervening depreciation in the value of silver currency, it can be estimated that Hamburg's debt roughly trebled between 1350 and 1500. At no stage, however, did the debt-charge absorb a disproportionate part of the revenue, averaging no more than 16% of total receipts in 1461–96 and representing a still lighter burden earlier on.

Until about 1370 loans were contributed exclusively by the citizens and the ecclesiastical establishments of Hamburg: the city councillors and their families, orphans and widows, and the hospitals formed the main categories of creditors. Bremen likewise depended in the fourteenth century mainly on the loans from its own citizens.[2] At Hamburg after 1426, however, as a result of a costly war with Denmark, there was an influx of capital from Lübeck, possibly due in part to a shift in interest among Lübeck merchants from active commerce to less venturesome investments in municipal loans. Between 1370 and 1400 Lübeck financiers became the main creditors of Lüneburg. Between 1426 and 1453 they lent 47,000 marks to Hamburg, mostly by investing in its perpetual annuities, and at times controlled more than half of the debt of Hamburg. Foreign lenders from Lübeck and other Hanseatic cities (e.g. Lüneburg, Stade, Wismar) similarly came to predominate in the fifteenth century among the creditors of Bremen.

[1] Reincke, *op. cit.* 495.
[2] Bremen's known loans from 1357 onwards are listed by H. Albers, *Die Anleihen der Stadt Bremen vom 14. bis zum 18. Jahrhundert* (Veröffentlichen aus dem Staatsarchiv der freien Hansestadt Bremen, III, 1930), 109 ff.

CHAPTER VIII
Conceptions of Economy and Society

The Empire which collapsed in 476 left a rich legacy of economic and social thought which survived its political structure and remained untouched by historical accident. This inheritance consisted primarily of moral principles, derived from the Gospels and defined by the Fathers, and of habits of thought formed in the Roman world.

In East and West alike, Christianity had flowered among peoples accustomed to certain economic and social institutions deemed natural or commonly accepted and regulated by laws: for example, property and slavery. It did not reject outright the learned or popular view of these traditional institutions, but it introduced a conception of man and of human relationships which modified and threatened existing customs and, indeed, the very foundations of society. By their commentaries upon the Scriptures, by their enlargements upon precepts and counsels, the Doctors, and especially Ambrose and Augustine, established the whole programme of a new system of ethics, the fiats and the interdicts of which were already sanctioned by popes and councils.

Thus, as early as the end of the fifth century, the fundamental conceptions about economy and society had been enunciated in Christian literature and in the imperial legal codes. The barbarian and feudal periods were to do no more than preserve this accumulated wealth of ideas, which came to sudden fruition at the time of the twelfth-century renaissance and the scholastic period.

In a broad introduction we shall trace the external history, as represented by the environment and sources; then consider successively the conceptions of economy and of society before summing up, in conclusion, the principal repercussions of these conceptions upon the practice of nations.

I. *Environment and Sources*

For six centuries the West modified its economy and its social hierarchy but little. The open economy of the Empire was replaced, from the time of the barbarian invasions and the later Moslem expansion, by a closed economy with a static technique. There is no great social distinction between the great Merovingian proprietor and the feudal lord; the status of the peasants, who comprised the overwhelming majority of the population, and that of the urban artisans were to all intents and purposes firmly fixed. The occasions for expressing an opinion upon economy and society were rare. A few conciliar canons, a few rulings by territorial princes upon the everlasting problems of usury and domestic organization, represent the sum total of the views expressed by Church and State in that early period of this unchanging, school-less, prophet-less world.

The eleventh century saw the beginning of a general revolution in the organization of society. Contacts between East and West, and between the various regions of the West, were re-established on a wider basis, through the medium of more numerous and more active fairs and markets and of maritime and overland business agencies; ships and caravans began to move more freely and more frequently; banks and associations were founded, and methods of effecting payments were perfected. As a result a profound modification occurred in the social structure: the merchant rose alongside the warrior, the burgher alongside the noble.

The re-awakening of the human mind resulted in the reconstitution of the ancient heritage, as represented by the writings of the Fathers, the Justinian compilations, and Aristotelian philosophy; it led to the collection of all the canonical and legal rulings, to the birth and multiplication of the universities, and to an efflorescence of literature. From now on, the Greek, Roman and Christian thought of the Ancient World, together with the medieval precepts, became completely available to teachers who had before them collections of texts, the content of which, in so far as it relates to economic and social questions, we must note. A brief account of these fundamental works and of the principal masters who utilized them is essential.

The decretals of the popes, the canons of Church councils and the *sententiae* of the Fathers were available in the *Concordia discordantium canonum* (soon called the *Decretum*) which, composed by Gratian about 1140, became from the middle of the twelfth century onwards the canonists' manual. It comprised a treatise on ordination in 101 distinctions giving rules about the clergy; thirty-six causes divided into questions dealing with the status of persons (clerks, monks, married people) and with possessions (temporal, ecclesiastical, usury), and a *De consecratione*, which is of little concern here. The new decretals were collected in what may be called codes by Gregory IX (1234), Boniface VIII (*Sextus*, 1298), Clement V (*Clementinae*, 1317), in which many sections deal with economic questions (methods of acquiring property, contracts, inheritance) and with social questions (clerks, monks, married people).

These two collections were commented upon by numerous teachers: among the 'decretists' may be mentioned especially Huguccio (*c.* 1190) and John the Teuton, who compiled about 1216 the *Glossa ordinaria* (that

found in the manuscripts and ancient editions); and among the decretal-
ists, Innocent IV (d. 1254), Hostiensis (d. 1270) and their contemporary
Bernard of Parma, whose gloss became standard.

Shortly after the *Concordia* was published, Peter Lombard produced
the *Libri quattuor sententiarum* which was quickly adopted as the theologians' manual; it became the subject of commentaries by all the great
masters, outstanding among whom are Thomas Aquinas (d. 1274) and
Duns Scotus (d. 1308). The most conspicuous writings are those of
Thomas Aquinas and, in particular, his *Summa theologica*.

The scriptural commentators came upon texts relating to wealth and
usury and to the status of classes and professions; these texts supported
the conclusions of the theologians occupied with dogma or morals. But
contrary to general belief, the theologians and the scriptural commentators were not the only ones engaged in formulating economic and
social doctrines.

The revival of Roman law in the twelfth century resuscitated in the
schools all the texts of the Justinian *Corpus juris civilis* in which the
economic and social structure occupied an important place. We shall
quote several works by the Bolognese masters who were prominent between 1150 and 1250: Bazianus, Azo whose *Summa* was ranked with the
Codex, Accursius, author of the great *Glossa* accompanying the various
parts of the *Corpus*. We shall have recourse to the dialecticians of Orleans
and Italy: Jacques de Revigny, Cino da Pistoia, Bartolo di Sassoferrato.
Philosophers like Buridan, as well as the theologians, made use of the
Politics and the *Nicomachean Ethics*.

In addition to these commentaries upon the basic manuals—the Bible,
and canonical *Corpus*, the *Ethics* and Justinian's *Corpus*, the Lombard's
Sententiae, and the *Summa theologica*—many works relate to, or take into
account, the economic and social system. One could profitably explore
the innumerable collections of *Quaestiones*, *Consilia*, *Disputationes*, in
which many subjects are treated by the way; all the *Summae* which, like
that of Hostiensis, bring together the principles in the sections of the
Corpus; all the valuable confessors' manuals and all the monographs (of
which the most important will be mentioned). Finally, various learned
'polygraphs', writers of comprehensive treatises alive to the problems of
their day, composed works in which theology and law joined forces to
usher in the studies of political and social economy and even the studies
of the technique of finance and trade; among them, in the fourteenth
century, are Henry of Langenstein, Henry of Oyta, Nicholas Oresme.

Thus, from the end of the thirteenth century onwards, economic and
social doctrines rapidly developed in well-known circumstances which
can be summarized under three heads.

The expansion of international trade entailed a technical and universal law, the idea of which had been lost sight of since the decay and ruin of the Empire. In the universities which had just sprung up the basic manuals, derived from ancient texts newly restored to honour, provided moral principles and legal rulings capable of meeting the needs of the time. These needs were strongly felt by a Church anxious on the one hand to inculcate moral principles in a world so much influenced by the spirit of trade and, on the other, to preserve its own immense patrimony; they were felt, too, by the young states, grappling with all the problems of organizing a financial system and maintaining equilibrium between social groups.

Reasons both spiritual and temporal combined with causes at once intellectual and practical; never had conditions been so favourable for the emergence of an intellectual system. Yet the medieval Doctors never conceived the idea of a general theory nor of a didactic exposition of economic problems. Various elements scattered among their works can be systematized, however, under the headings of doctrines of wealth, the acquisition of property, lawful gain and social status.

II. *Doctrines of Wealth*

The one thing which immediately struck the Doctors' minds, and indeed their eyes, was the inequality of wealth and its resulting moral consequences. Theologians and Romanists were, very often, of the same opinion in the beginning and the end of their work. They disputed about the lawfulness of its foundations, that is, about property and ownership; about the distribution of property, the cause of misery and opulence; and about its disposal, at once the source of avarice and prodigality.

The apparently communistic tradition of the Fathers was perpetuated among the standard writers. *Natura omnia omnibus in commune profudit*, Saint Ambrose had written. *Communis usus omnium quae sunt in hoc mundo* is the message attributed by the pseudo-Isidore to Clement of Rome. Gratian reproduces this passage only with the ultimate purpose of recommending to clerks the cenobitic life, but throughout the Middle Ages the maxim was expounded in the schools. It reappears in the commentaries of Duns Scotus and indicates that the only foundation for individual appropriation is the positive law which provides the means of defending private property.

Generally speaking, the traditional view from Plato to Augustine, which favoured common property and which Gratian follows, was practically left aside by the decretists. These, as early as the end of the eleventh century, voiced the opinion that nature was not really concerned with the problem of private property, except in case of famine, when all goods were to be put at the disposal of the community.

The *Glossa ordinaria* proposes two explanations of the pseudo-Clementine text: either it relates only to those who voluntarily embrace poverty, or else it is to be understood as a general precept, comprehensible in the primitive Church but liable to disturb the public order of the twelfth-century Church. A more moderate view authorizes ownership of necessities, considering anything over and above as a theft practised to the detriment of the human community. Rufinus, translating one of Basil's homilies, expresses this opinion which Gratian reproduces as one of Ambrose's. The decretists twisted its meaning, holding that the *Glossa ordinaria* restricts the obligation to share food to times of need (i.e. of famine), beyond which no limits are set to possession.

These views, all of them positive, seemed very superficial to the theologians, who, engaged though they were in the same way, did not adopt quite the same form of argument. Thomas Aquinas raises the question of the rights of man over things. Is not God the universal Master? What property does man bring with him at birth? And how may he own objects whose nature he cannot change? These objections, while they acknowledge the overall mastership of God, do not exclude the idea that He has granted to man the power of making use of things. It is even a good thing that man should administer and dispose of them in his own right, since we are all more careful of our own possessions, and joint-possession gives rise to confusion and quarrels. Nature undoubtedly commits all property to the community of mankind, but apportionment does but add to, not contradict, the natural law. And what the state of innocence might have permitted has become impossible through the Fall. God retains the supreme mastership and man participates correspondingly in it.

This radical distinction made between the law of primeval mankind and the possibilities of a fallen humanity (where it is a question of experience that private property must be established for the good of peace, order and activity) was commended by great masters such as Alexander of Hales and Albert the Great. It amounts to a justification of private property by the common law of nations and by a secondary natural law, inspired by the requirements of reason, as they appear in an imperfect world; but without going so far as to lay down detailed and precise rules for the distribution of wealth.

Not only does individual ownership appear to be lawful, but no limit is set to its amount: inequality of apportionment results from the inequality of family origins, from individual success and from luck. Far from shocking the Doctors, inequality seemed to them both natural and ordained by Providence. Its causes were beyond criticism and no one would think of seeking a justification for lawful inheritance or for encouraging remunerative production, or of excluding honest good fortune.

The moralists never considered self-enrichment as a laudable aim nor its attainment as a divine reward. On the contrary, indeed, they condemn avarice, which is an immoderate desire to amass and preserve wealth. But the vast differences of economic station left them cold. More than that: they offered an opportunity for the practice of the capital Christian virtue of charity, a virtue which might be said to justify poverty since it provided the occasion for its practice in the perilous domain of Mammon. Poverty itself was virtuous when it was practised voluntarily in conformity with scriptural counsels. Self-deprivation for the profit of the Church (and to enable it to attain its prescribed ends) was the ideal proposed or implied by the Doctors.

On the other hand, the doctrine of the absolute poverty of a Christ, who, possessing neither communal nor private property, might be deemed to offer a model for Christians, was condemned by Pope John XXII. To their theological audacity the theoreticians added a whiff of revolution. The first victim of their victory would have been the Church. So the Church spoke out accordingly. Its conservative principles and its spiritual programme led, just as temporal interests did, to the continued and undisputed acceptance of unequal wealth in Christendom.

General opinion is less preoccupied with the principle of possession than with the use to which the things possessed are put. In themselves, riches are neither a good nor evil thing. Since they are the means of acting for better or for worse it is the manner of their employment which is to be judged. Whoever considers them as an end in themselves and delights in laying up treasure commits the second of the capital sins; whoever squanders them on sensual pleasures incurs his own damnation. But he who distributes them in alms is justified. To desire temporal goods to sustain the temporal life with a view to attaining eternal life by the practice of the virtues is not only permitted by God but has His approbation. Wealth is a means and not an end, allowing Man to attain the most desirable of all ends. The theologians therefore profess a theory which is inspired by purely spiritual ideas, yet which results in the justification of wealth which is used generously and in the accumulation of income and capital.

III. *The Acquisition of Property*

The theologians came closer to realities in their reflections upon the methods of acquiring wealth: its legitimate sources, the process of exchange and the assessment of values.

They argued that wealth ought desirably to be the outcome of work, which allows a man to earn what is necessary for his subsistence. Every man must submit to this divine law of work, the neglect of which, being the capital sin of sloth, lays him open to many vices. All exertion deserves reward. All earnings have their justification in human effort. According to St Thomas Aquinas, man is under the obligation to do manual work when he has no other means of subsistence. If he can choose, let him make his choice from among those honest occupations which are profitable to the social groups of which he is a member.

The general organization of work is subject to the common weal: this supreme law dictates the order of priorities. The first need is food. Agriculture therefore takes precedence. It is God's institute that man shall earn his bread by the sweat of his brow. It is to agriculture that the prince is to give his main support in the hierarchy of the *artes possessivae*. Tilling and grazing come first, proclaim the Doctors in unison, and also fishing and hunting. House-building ranked only second but assured for architecture its honourable place. All occupations required by the life of a community were thought to be lawful and commended: for example, the craftsmen who produce furniture, or the practitioners of medicine and the law, who were deemed to be at the service of health and justice. Some approval was also given to the work of the administration, whose task was the ordering of the whole system.

The attitude to trade was more complex. The theologians were wary of condemning trade: there is a laudable type of commerce (*commutatio laudabilis*) which provides the supplies a town requires. Inasmuch as it ensures so necessary a service it escapes all censure: it came into the category of the *artes pecuniariae* required by the nature of things.

Nevertheless the simple transfer of a commodity not modified or improved by work was viewed with suspicion by the theologians, who were afraid of speculation. Is it right, they asked, to resell an article unaltered more dearly than it has been bought? The offence lies in the intention of making money without due cause. There is no offence if the profit was, so to speak, involuntary; for example, because it resulted from a rise in prices or was justified by the risks of holding goods for a long period, or if it is intended for a necessary and honest end such as the relief of the poor or the support of a family. In such cases, the dangers of greed—which concentrates men's thoughts on temporal things and provokes fraudulent practices, specious untruths and the blasphemies of the loser and the bankrupt—were avoided.

Thus it was not trade which the Doctors condemned but the injustices and vices to which it gave rise. The economy necessary for the subsistence of nations was naturally permitted and encouraged. But the feverish activity of trading transactions, far from being considered as the open road to prosperity for the adventurous or for Providence's favourites, seemed to place men's souls in jeopardy. St Thomas Aquinas wanted each country to produce sufficient to avoid the necessity of importing goods.

The attitude to trade as such was not the only problem which commerce presented to the theologians. They were also concerned with the methods and instruments of trade. Producers and merchants exchanged their work or their goods for things and, more frequently, for money. The Church and the Doctors were obliged to pronounce upon the methods and means they used.

The methods are represented by contracts and agreements. The Roman technique of sale and hire was adopted by the Doctors. But their care for truth lent support to the need for simplicity in commerce. The canonists taught that simple contracts are binding in themselves. For the Roman maxim that the *nudum pactum* (that is to say, the simple understanding between parties) is not a basis for claims, John the Teuton, completing a doctrinal trend started by Huguccio, substituted the opposite maxim. His reason is that he who does not carry out his promise is guilty of falsehood. Whether he is on oath or not, a Christian's word must be kept. What the Doctors are penalizing—and the legislator is silent here—is sin, not the obligation inherent in assent. The Romanists' reaction was, so to speak, functional. Yet, from Accursius onwards, there was hesitation on their part and a search for compromise. The canonists themselves were divided over the sanction question, and even over the scope of the new principle, which was, however, supported by natural equity and moral theology. In fact, it gradually permeated ecclesiastical and commercial law, and the future was on its side. It had the twofold merit of binding men by their declared intentions, without any formal obligation, and at the same time of facilitating commercial operations under the ultimate protection of the confessor and the ecclesiastical authority. The ethics of the Church, so strict on this point, ensured the development of a free economy.

As for money, the necessary instrument of payments, it rests with every sovereign power to ensure its production. But it was the Church's function to uphold Christian ethics and its own interests: hence its severity against forgers and its distrust of changes in money values. Popes and councils, canonists and theologians co-operated with kings and officials in repressing crime, and with Romanists and jurists in discussing the effects of every debasement of the coinage. The feudal conception left rulers the freedom of fixing the weight, fineness and circulation of the currency. Because of its aversion to taxation, the populace accepted monetary mutations as an alternative source of princes' incomes. The Church, however, suffered by the consequent diminution of the revenues it derived from rents, pious bequest or Peter's pence. At the first Lateran Council (1123) it reacted by excommunicating counterfeiters, and Boniface VIII (*Ausculta fili*, article 9) later accused Philip the Fair of this crime. A celebrated decretal of Innocent III had laid down rules governing monetary fluctuations, stigmatizing as fraudulent coins struck below the legal weight: Innocent IV, in his commentary, allowed a reduction of this weight with the people's consent, but even then only if it was a question of an internal operation which would not injure foreigners. Nevertheless, the idea that money is something quite distinct from *merchandise*, that it is a measure and that its weight, fineness and value should be fixed by the prince according to currency requirements, was ultimately to prevail. 'The prince', wrote Oresme, 'is proprietor and lord of the money circulating within his estate and domain.' Not only has he the monopoly in striking money but he is also the authority which determines its value. The publicists exploited for the sovereign's profit the nominalism which Romanists like Odofredus or canonists like Durandus had, by subtle distinctions, introduced into the exegesis of civil law, forgetting on this point the claims of equity.

Weights and measures were more exposed than was coinage to deceitful practices which could entail dangerous consequences. The Doctors supported the measures of inspection taken by the public authorities to check frauds and to ensure standard measures. Roman law had inflicted on the users of false measures exemplary punishments which went as far as transportation for life. In the Carolingian period, penitentials and councils multiplied the penalties. An article of the *Concordia* of 813, to which Burchard attaches a penance of thirty days on bread and water, is reproduced in the Decretals of Gregory IX. This text and the triad of the *Digest* served as a basis for reaffirmations of the doctrine.

The major difficulty was that of fixing the value of work and things. It was a problem which had arisen before the triumph of Christianity, but one which was resolutely dealt with from the legal aspect only in the patristic period and systematically treated only from the scholastic period onwards.

Greeks and Romans had laid down some basic principles. The *Nicomachean Ethics* emphasized that parties to a contract must possess equal consideration under it and desire equal benefit from it. A constitution of Diocletian, too, authorized the rescission of sale if the agreed price is less than half the *justum pretium*. The Fathers had established the religious grounds of all the decisions reached by philosophy and the law: namely, the doctrine of commutative justice which, in social intercourse, fixes the responsibility of man before God. The task of the classical writers on theology and law was to co-ordinate these traditions: they taught a theory of exchange and prices.

The commentaries on the *Nicomachean Ethics* scarcely did more than develop the Aristotelian idea of reciprocal services in the *contractus communicativi*. Albertus Magnus sketches the form of this *contrapassum*: a builder is to receive from the shoemaker a stock of footwear equivalent in value to the house he has built for that craftsman, and not an arbitrary sum which may enrich (without cause) one of the two parties. This is simply an affirmation of the equivalence of the services which leaves the problem of the computation of the values unresolved.

How is the value of the house and of the shoes to be determined in the only common measure, that of legal currency? The idea of an intrinsic value deriving from the nature of the things themselves was not much help. It was better to have recourse to the form of valuation current in the market, to public or corporative tariffs. These, in fact, did not interfere, except in cases of collusion or economic crises, the doctrine of scholastics being much more favourable to free competition than is commonly admitted. This valuation itself depended on conditions difficult to define precisely. The producer could put forward his time and the difficulty of his work: all parties concerned in an exchange of services could invoke the standard of living of people of their class, the usefulness of the reciprocal services, the scarcity of the things involved, or, if it was a question of wages, the scarcity and skill of the technicians. In such a manner subjective elements ultimately entered into the reckoning, as Aquinas explicitly recognizes in his chapter dealing with selling. This criterion, which in sum justified profit at a rate depending on the time, the place and the parties, led to many and various interpretations in Buridan's time. The chief point which was considered as a basis for a fair appraisal was not (as too many people have taught) the necessity for the producer to keep his own standing (*statum suum continuare*) but the need of the purchasers, the demand: St Albert the Great and St Thomas merely repeat Aristotle's *Ethics*; and calls for help uttered by consumers were emphasized by Bernardino of Siena and Antoninus of Florence. They aimed at checking any attempts made by sellers to impose an arbitrary price. The only constant is the affirmation of the *aequitas juris naturalis*. Whatever the contract, the main preoccupation of the theologians was to prevent excess.

Canonists and Romanists supported them by their constant effort to repair the consequences of wrongs and of fluctuations in the value of money. The flexibility of values in exchange which the theologians themselves admitted did not authorize either fraud or excess profit. These two vices were checked by both laws. A decretal of Pope Alexander III allows a vendor who receives less than half the just price a choice between cancelling the contract and receiving a supplement, which will re-establish the legality of the transaction: for example, if the article worth 100 has been sold for 25, the vendor will obtain either a cancellation or a second payment of 25. The principle which, with some exceptions, was confirmed was easily extended to the purchaser and was one which, in its application, gave rise to variations only in the method of computation.

The frequent devaluations posed the problem of forward payments. How was a loan of 100 pounds to be repaid in the event of a 20% decline in the value of the pound? At the rate of 100 or of 125 pounds? Two traditions confronted one another: on the one hand, the Roman concept of intrinsic values which would have answered 125 pounds, and, on the other, feudal nominalism. In a celebrated *questio*, Pillius had opted *c.* 1182 for the former: *tempus dationis inspicitur, tempora primitiva servari debent*. He applies the maxim also to all contracts, adducing numerous texts from the *Digest* and the idea of a tacit condition. The same reply had been given in respect of payments in kind by Bulgarus (question 107) and by the first Bolognese Doctors. In short, the Romanists followed the tradition which was to be expressed by Azo's gibe: *Eadem mensura vel moneta debetur quae erat tempore contractus*.

The canonists hesitated. Nevertheless, Huguccio prepared the way for the intrinsic interpretation, which was later to be sanctioned by Innocent III and Gregory IX. It was the money current at the time of the contract which was owed by the debtor and, if that money has been changed, the exact equivalent.

IV. *Lawful Incomes*

Despite all prohibitions, capital, whether in land or money, could not lie unproductive: the great problem for the Church was to lay down what operations were permissible.

In the economic sphere, the main preoccupation of the medieval Church was to prevent usury, which was *Quodcumque sorti accedit*: everything received by a lender over and above the capital lent. Such was St Ambrose's definition, which is taken up by Gratian. From ancient times, interest-bearing loans had been the subject of a number of celebrated condemnations: the Old Testament forbade the practice among the Israelites; Aristotle had taught that money does not beget money. St Luke (vi. 34–5) reports one of Christ's sayings which apparently forbids interest (in the Latin version: *mutuum date nil inde sperantes*).[1] The practice

[1] The fortune of the text from Deuteronomy begins with St Jerome and St Ambrose. Cf. B. N. Nelson, *The Idea of Usury* (Princeton, 1949). Aristotle had little influence, the text of St Luke being called as evidence only from the end of the twelfth century. Cf. J. T. Noonan, *The Scholastic Analysis of Usury* (Cambridge, Mass., 1957), 12, 14, 20.

of usury was forbidden to the clergy by the Council of Nicaea (325), and to the faithful by Pope Leo I. At the same time, the Church Fathers found abundant justification for its prohibition in the name of charity and love of one's neighbour, and the Christian emperors began to impose limitations upon the rate of interest. During the early centuries of the Middle Ages, this tradition of antagonism was supplemented by conciliar canons and papal decisions, and all the more rightly so in view of the fact that the closed economy of the barbarian period allowed only the most unjustifiable form of usury, that practised at the expense of a needy neighbour borrowing necessaries or the means of work.

Gratian accepted the canonical and patristic inheritance in the two distinctions 46 and 47 and later in the whole of cause 14 of the *Decretum*. Peter Lombard limited himself to transcribing or summarizing various fragments from the Fathers. These placid inventories were drawn up in a world in which capital had once again assumed a function essential for the promotion of the major undertakings of trade by sea and land. Shipowners, manufacturers, bankers, all required considerable capital which they could not get from philanthropists content with the choice either of making the fortunes of others without a share themselves or of losing everything without any compensation. A relaxation of the rules might have been expected. It was the contrary which happened.

Popes and councils, being powerful enough to react against general temptation, adhered to the moral principles themselves rather than to adaptations of those principles, for this they feared might open the way to abuses. Could the Doctors be relied upon to tone down the severity of the law? It was at this moment that they received not only a complete translation of the works of Aristotle, but also the stern commentary made upon those works by the Rabbis and the Arabs. They inclined to severity rather than to indulgence.

There is abundant literary and documentary evidence of this attitude. A chapter-heading *De Usuris* is expanded in Book III of the collection of *Decretals*. Every literary *genre* was employed as a framework for the canonists' reflections. These reflections never had the breadth of the theological dissertations, the model for which was afforded by St Thomas Aquinas in his *Summa theologica*, in which usury occurs in the treatise on justice, *Secunda Secundae*, question 78. The penitentials and the confessors' *Summae* provided abundant guidance for matters of conscience. Finally, many monographs were devoted to usury, the oldest of them being the *De usuris* of Giles of Lessines, composed between 1276 and 1285 (Opus 73 in the Roman edition of the *Opera* of St Thomas, Giles's master, to whom it was attributed until recently). In the second quarter of the fifteenth century, Bernardino of Siena and Antoninus of Florence took to a point of perfection the moral theology of usury.

The Romanists, commenting upon laws which had never contested the principle of usury, found themselves in a delicate position and their opposition or their concessions must be indicated.

They start from the view that all profit not justified by work is suspect. The normal opportunity for usury is the loan for consumption. The nature of the additional payment levied, whether thing or service, is immaterial: the professor who advances a few pence to his students so that they may follow his course and who stipulates certain benefits for his own advantage compromises himself as much as a miller who makes a loan to a baker in order to build up a connection. Every additional payment is usury: the terminology of the fourth Lateran Council (*immoderatas usuras*) does not imply that there was any fair rate for such payment. On the contrary: the mere desire of obtaining a supplementary payment, the hope of profit, is deemed sufficient to make a man guilty and liable to the punishments of conscience. The only concession made to the lender is that of receiving a spontaneous present.

Such severity was based upon the Scriptures, rigorously interpreted: the Deuteronomic prohibition against requiring anything from one's brothers now applied to every Christian and the saying reported by Luke dispelled all ambiguity.[1] Justice and reason confirmed this radical opposition. How could it be assumed that a man might sell the right of user of a property, after the ownership of it had been transferred? Or that a man might exploit the functions of the bailee, the only true reason for a return on things lent, as happened so patently in the case of money-lending? The requirements of public order increased the positive justification: the lazy waxed fat on usury, the industrious were ruined by it, and it destroyed the harmony secured by work.

Usury, which was a mortal, enduring and inexcusable sin, brought in interest, the status and use of which were discussed by the theologians: most of the Doctors did not allow that it might be converted into alms.

This whole doctrine was rounded off by the threat of exemplary punishments. The sentence of excommunication passed upon the usurer prohibited his receiving the sacraments and even, according to many Doctors, prevented his entering a church; burial in consecrated ground would be forbidden to him, and likewise prayers for the repose of his soul; a cleric would be suspended from office and benefice. Civil disqualifications were inflicted upon the man guilty of this offence and the Church asked the secular authorities (who had a joint competence in the

[1] Capitani thinks the common foundations for doctrines of usury and just price are to be looked for in the twofold ideal of *aequitas* and *caritas*. Cf. 'Sulla questione dell' usura nel Medio Evo', *Bollettino dell'Istituto storico italiano per il Medio Evo* (1958), 551. According to Albert the Great and Pope Innocent IV, and to the common feeling of theologians, it suffices, for the foundation of that doctrine, to call on the duty of love.

prosecution) to place their power at its service. Full restitution, except by arrangement, was exacted, the terms of which were complicated by a calculation of the profits resulting from the usury and often by a 'realization' of property acquired by means of the capital lent.[1] All those involved were to answer for their fault, whether they were members of a domestic or social group, partners and collaborators, beneficiaries and protectors. The direct participants were required to make reparation.

Such severity, which interfered with business and impeded all those who derived avowed or unavowed profit therefrom, was bound to give rise to many objections on the part of those against whom it was directed. Also, as far as the transactions themselves were concerned, it inevitably encouraged fraud on the part of borrowers as well as suspicion on the part of the Church.

The question arose as to whether Jews, Lombards and Cahorsins came under the canonical prohibition. It had to be recognized that formal decretals and indulgences treated them as neutrals even within the papal states. The papacy was less tolerant about transactions which cloaked, or seemed to cloak, usury. Alexander III forbade mortgage and credit sales at increased prices; Innocent III forbade false repurchase as a disguise of interest and Gregory IX the 'sea loan'. Theologians and canonists discussed partnership without participation in losses, the 'dry exchange' and the *mohatra* contract, which Rome was eventually to condemn.

Thus the tendency was towards severity. Economic life, ecclesiastical interests and even the law itself demanded some relaxation, and some relaxation was introduced for contingencies.

The prohibition of usury, however, was no bar to lawful additional payments which were justified by some cause unconnected with the spirit of speculation. The jurists contrasted the pursuit of profit, which was a vice, with the fair compensation for loss: *prohibemur sumere usuram causa lucri captandi, non autem vitandi damni*, writes John the Teuton, a disciple of the Romanist Azo, who had taught the same doctrine. Romanists, canonists and theologians were in agreement on this principle. Let us refer to the expression *Quod interest*. This was supposed to mean a just indemnity, which the *Digest*, and the Code as well, had carefully distinguished from usury. The word *interesse* seems to have been coined by Azo, and introduced into the canonical terminology by one of his pupils called Laurent of Spain. The common gloss took it from Laurent, and made it part of common terminology.

No general doctrine of *interesse* was built up, but a series of cases was elaborated, the oldest of which is the case of the warrantor who is

---

[1] In fact, the doctrine of the Church was not without efficiency. Cf. R. E. de Roover, 'Restitution in Renaissance Florence', in *Studi in onore di A. Sapori*, 775–89.

obliged to borrow with interest in order to fulfil his obligation: equity demands that no such damage be inflicted upon him. Interest on overdue payments did no more than repair a wrong. *Damnum emergens* and *lucrum cessans* called for compensation and punishment.

Often the contracting parties made provision for this. A stipulation of penalty in the case of non-payment on the due date of the sum lent was valid, provided that its true aim was to prompt the debtor to fulfil his obligation and not to establish, after the alleged terminal date, a disguised form of usury. A fraudulent intention concealed in a man's heart could be presumed if a penalty was fixed proportionate to the period of waiting and, more obviously, from the creditor's profession of money-lender. In equity the penalty must be calculated according to the injury suffered by the fact of the delay: certain canonists grant the judge power to reduce it; others allow that a figure exceeding the injury suffered may be admitted if the intention of compulsion is duly proved.

Even without any agreement, interest attributable to the delay of payment was due in all operations in good faith, such as the four consensual contracts, or cases where continuous charge was involved, as in tutelage, stewardship or upkeep of a household. On this latter point, the canonists invoked a decretal of Pope Innocent III, which conformed to Roman law. On the other hand they were reluctant to follow the Romanists' opinion that in strictly legal contracts interest was due from the date of the *litis contestatio*.

In all cases reparation was to be as exact as possible. Thus, the vendor who retains a revenue-bearing commodity should pay the equivalent of the revenues received from the date he should have received the purchase price. Much more delicate was the determination of the *lucrum cessans*. The very conception of *lucrum cessans* was a subject of constant discussion. Hostiensis was the first to admit that charity makes it an obligation to compensate a dealer who, in perfect good faith and far from usury, lends a sum of money which is retained for so long that it handicaps his own business. The thesis was adopted by the Asti *Summa*, but a stern opposition by some theologians was to go on until the end of the Middle Ages.

Linked with usury was the problem of profit. Profit derived by money-changers and bankers presented the moralists with a delay problem. Transfers from one currency to another, whether effected in coin (*change manuel*) or by bills of exchange (*change tiré*), were an opportunity for usurious speculations because of the fluctuations in the exchange-rates and their lack of uniformity (for example, the florin was worth more in Florence than in Rome).[1] Nevertheless, the *cambium* was a necessity for the Apostolic Chamber no less than for those who frequented

[1] R. de Roover, 'Cambium ad Venetias: Contribution to the History of Foreign Exchange', in *Studi . . . Sapori*.

fairs. Theologians and canonists insisted upon the application of common rules in the fixing of currency values. In spite of reservations and limitations they generally admitted a premium was justified by the money-changer's time and trouble and the risks attending carriage.

According to the Romanists, the depositing of money in a bank justified an interest charge, which was in fact sanctioned by the *actio depositi*: the canonists refrained from granting legal recognition to an operation so similar to the *mutuum*.

Not only banking but also the lending of money itself could justify profit. The deed of partnership is a frequent case in point. Every act of financial participation entailed a risk, for which compensation was provided by the eventual profit; and, since the partner retained the ownership of the sum invested, there was no question whatever of a *mutuum*. This opinion of St Thomas was well received by the theologians and canonists who, having no fundamental text to explain either in the *Corpus* or in the *Sententiae*, left the better-equipped Romanists the task of setting out the technique in their glosses or in their special treatises. The famous law *Pro socio* (*Digest*, XVII 2.63) offered a basis for their reasoning. Sleeping partnership (*commendite*), so widespread from the twelfth century onwards, was thus approved. The *contractus trinus*, which appears in the fifteenth century, raised more difficulties: it consists of three contracts simultaneously passed between the same parties: first a sleeping partnership, where one brings his money, the other one his work; next, an insurance against all risks, whereby a guarantee is given to the capitalist in exchange for a percentage of his eventual profit; and last, the sale by the capitalist for a fixed sum to be paid to him each year of his chances of profit above a certain level. The theologian John Major called it: *societas, assecuratio, venditio incerti lucri pro lucro certo*. Such a contract was to be discussed by Doctors and pronounced upon by popes only in modern times.

To the same order of transaction belonged the annuity, a common way of obtaining a fixed income. The owner of property alienated it against a perpetual annuity, the title to which could be negotiated by its vendor. Did not this operation, which was very common in all regions enjoying customary law (*coutumes*) and especially so in the towns, smack of usury? Innocent IV denied it, provided that the annuity did not exceed the income normally derived from an estate of a value equal to the sum handed over by the recipient of the annuity: it was a question of a sale in which the price was spread over a period. The controversy lasted until the day when two Bulls of 1425 and 1455 (inserted in the *Extravagantes Communes*) brought it to a summary end.

Personal annuities, which were also called floating annuities (*rentes volantes*) could be set up from the fourteenth century onwards and were charged as an expense against the totality of a patrimony. They are not the subject of any special discussion. As far as doctrine is concerned, their fate seems linked with that of ground-rents.

Doctrine went further; it even permitted, nay encouraged, certain loans at interest. It had to accept the fact that the Italian cities made perpetual annuitants out of contributors to forced loans whom they could not reimburse. The creditors could plead coercion as an excuse; moreover, they ran the risk of never seeing again the sums which, had they been free to do so, they could have earmarked for legally profitable transactions.

Why should not the Church try, in the interest of needy Christians, what in the public interest the cities were permitted to do? So the Franciscans reasoned when establishing mutual credit institutions in the *Monts de Piété*. In the face of sharp criticism, they justified the interest they exacted from the borrower, which was 10% at first, on the grounds of general expenses, the usefulness of the loan, responsibility for the pledge, and explained it as a hiring-out of services. Two œcumenical councils ratified the institution; the principles which authorized it opened the door to more liberal transactions.

The economic doctrines of the Middle Ages were influenced by contrary tendencies. On the one hand, a moral tradition, bequeathed by antiquity and adapted by Christianity, curbed men's freedom to transact business and even to possess goods; on the other, commercial activity and the irrepressible desire for profit called for latitude, tolerance and relaxation. An ever-increasing firmness in the statement of principles was accompanied by an increasing flexibility in the comprehension of facts. To what extent did social doctrines inspire or suffer this dualism? This is a question we must now examine.

V. *Social Status*

Medieval economic doctrines were influenced by medieval conceptions of society; on the other hand, they themselves greatly influenced these conceptions. The two theoretical systems are closely linked but are sufficiently distinct for one to speak of the interaction of the one upon the other. Let us look in turn at the organization of the family, at the social dichotomies and, lastly, at public institutions.

The economy of the Middle Ages was for a long time based on the family in the double sense that it was organized within the framework of the home and was directed to satisfying domestic needs. Now, the household dwelt beneath the law of the Church which fixed the conditions of its birth, its government and its demise. It is therefore correct to affirm that theology and the law governing family life dominated the whole system of economic activity.

For centuries, the formal act of marriage was fixed by local laws and customs. Towards the end of the twelfth century, the papacy imposed everywhere the rule that simple consent creates the marriage bond: this is one aspect of the reaction against formalism which upset all organized systems. Being indissoluble and monogamous, Christian marriage ensured a series of stable and unified units for the economy, at the same time as the law and doctrine of conjugal relationships tended to increase the number of offspring, or, in other words, the supply of hereditary labour.

By favouring joint ownership by man and wife, and by its insistence on the dowry, the Church determined the economic basis of the household. By declaring the needs of the family to be the norm for prices, the theologians made the value of things depend on the size of the home.

Thus, according to clerical thought, the family occupied an essential place in the economy no less than in the social order.

Conversely, economic doctrines had repercussions upon the conceptions of family life. Thus, the popularity of pious legacies could, in certain countries like Poland, hasten the division of property among the members of the family and thus, by creating economic independence, furnish the justification for a breaking-up of the group, and even for a certain individualism. In the opposite direction, the repression of usury affirmed a solidarity within the family which the severity of punishment perhaps tended to weaken.

The conservative nature of economic doctrines had its exact counterpart in the doctrine of social dichotomies. Freedom provided the first criterion. When they teach the natural law of personal freedom, both jurists and theologians appear to jeopardize the conception of an economy founded in large measure upon respect for servile labour. This conservatism, however, may be said to have curbed the liberal doctrines which had their basis in the Gospels. There were thus two conflicting principles, which had to be, and were in part, reconciled. Medieval views of social differentiation had their roots in several features of medieval life and correspondingly in several branches of medieval doctrine. In the Middle Ages, social differentiation resulted from the Church's constitution, from one's place in the secular hierarchy, from personal liberty, and from the degree of power or poverty.

The Church was divided into clerks and laymen; monks and nuns belong to another category. Many laws and commentaries laid down the status within the economic system of the clergy, whose number increased from the twelfth century onwards and who controlled a considerable portion of the wealth of society.

According to strict doctrine they had to abstain from all worldly business, not merely from menial labour but also from anything which could take them away from service at the altar. But, since they were also strictly required to manage their benefices well, laws and commentaries bound them to turn to the profit of the ecclesiastical patrimony, that is to say of the rural economy, resources diverted from the cupidity of the individual. The theory of the temporal power of the Church and all the legislation connected with it affected the economy as much as the law did, and had implications for the life of the world no less than for the life of the Church.

Inalienability, immunity, appropriation: the fundamental status of that enormous patrimony which was always growing bound the clergy to the management of great estates. The ecclesiastical body, unified and disciplined by the combination of two elaborate laws (the Roman and the Canon Law), was diversified by wealth as much as by hierarchy. From wealth to poverty, there were many degrees: the bishop of Lincoln was the owner of a large estate when many chaplains were on short commons. The benefice system, which was intended to provide all clerics with a fair standard of living, led to the establishment of an autonomous society divided into aristocracy, middle class and proletariat.

In the secular hierarchy, nobles and commoners faced each other like two different races of men whose status was fixed by custom and doctrine. Noble rank, acquired in the eleventh century by the knightly accolade or by the acquisition of a fief, became hereditary in the twelfth century and was extended by royal concessions. The *bellatores*, like the *oratores*, constituted a marginal class as far as the secular economy was concerned. The noble was not allowed to take up any work which would bring him profit, under penalty of losing his status for derogation of rank. His role in the production of wealth would therefore be nil unless he exercised a function as protector which, at least in theory, would guarantee freedom to work.

The prohibitions and injunctions which governed the economic role of the noble were defined and justified by the Doctors. In their commentaries upon the *Codex*, and in the opinions they drew up, they specified the forbidden occupations: above all the manual arts, but also the notarial profession. Theologians and moralists stressed the duty of affording military and pecuniary aid to dependants. They generally relate this social function, however, to the existence of another social stratum, that characterized by weakness. To the *potentes* they oppose the *miserabiles personae*.

Weakness could result from physical decay and from social loneliness, but more frequently it sprang from material poverty. The sick and the infirm, widows and orphans, together with the poor, who alone concern us here, are all the subject of constant solicitude in the Bible. This solicitude was echoed by the Christian emperors in several constitutions which prepared the way for the general theory of the *miserabiles personae*. This received its fullest development from the Fathers, who formulated the doctrine of social interdependence which by and large consolidated the economic system.

Biblical commentators, canonists, Romanists find in the Scriptures, in the *Decretum* and in the Justinian *Corpus* many texts for commentary regarding the distinction and relationships between rich and poor (those who, according to the ordinary gloss of the *Digest*, did not possess fifty gold *sous*). No Doctor doubted that the *Corpus Christianorum* was normally composed of rich and poor: and this was a solid foundation for a liberal economy. Nevertheless, theologians and canonists, in order to ensure the subsistence of the poor (and to maintain social distances at the same time) recommended almsgiving, which the law of the Church enjoined, and the founding of charitable institutions. Thus a modest corrective was applied to the unequal distribution of incomes, itself a safeguard for the inequality of possession.

The co-ordination of men divided by so many barriers was the work of those in authority and of organized bodies. It offered a subject for theological and legal considerations, both of which were influenced by economic doctrines and influenced them in their turn.

We have already seen something of the repercussions of economic ideas upon political ideas in the chapter on trade. State policy in the economic sphere was the subject of Chapter III, Book II, of the *De Regimine Principum*, in which St Thomas recommends the construction of towns in fertile places so that their food may be produced by the surrounding countryside and the influx of foreign merchants consequently restricted. It rests with the prince to choose the site: in connection with this problem of town-planning, St Thomas expressed his opinion in concrete form upon the production and circulation of wealth, an opinion inspired at once by practical and by moral considerations.

The attitudes adopted in regard to the economy have already given us an inkling of theory concerning the professions. Some of them are honourable, some suspect, some tolerated: but in this hierarchy there are necessarily many gradations which will enable a true value to be placed upon excessively radical formulae which have passed naturally into maxims. The views of the Church were perhaps not always those of the State; nor were opinions unanimous within the Church, *a fortiori* the Doctors of the canon and civil law often differing between themselves.

Views were affected by an order of dignity derived from criteria other than the order (which interests us here much more) of usefulness.

We may leave aside the clerical profession, which surpasses all others and which, by setting man apart from the world, sets him among the non-producers. Yet one must distinguish between the holders of larger benefices, whose whole output lies in the realm of the intellect, and holders of minor ones who, unable to live on their benefice, did manual work and thus constituted a true plebeian class, which deserves and needs a special study. Yet again, cognizance must be taken of the mass of clerks who belonged to the clergy only by their tonsures. With these reservations, it may be taken that the cleric abstained from productive work.

Contrariwise, it was the productive function of the farmer and the artisan which sets them in the front rank of the secular population. All trades, however, do not enjoy the same prestige. Among the lists of professions forbidden to the clerk a discrimination, or rather a number of discriminations, can be seen. In the synodal statutes of Arras c. 1275, fullers, weavers, tanners, dyers, shoemakers are considered to be engaged in *inhonesta mercimonia*. In the Liège statutes of 1298 the trades of fuller, shoemaker, weaver, miller, perfumer are forbidden, and, sixty years later in the statutes of Englebert de la Marck, those of brewer, carpenter, tanner, baker, smith. About the same period (1366) the synodal statutes of Tournai authorized the profession of shoemaker and smith. As Génicot observes, it would be extremely interesting to note all these lists which shed light upon the esteem enjoyed by each trade: the criterion was no doubt the prestige resulting from personal independence and levels of earnings.

No profession was more suspect than that of the merchant. The scriptural, moral and economic reasons for this suspicion are known to us. The profession of merchant was, however, a necessary one and protected by the Church no less than by the State. What the moralists feared, as we have seen, was speculation, and to avoid this risk the clergy was required to abstain from all forms of trading; the same circumspection was recommended in confession. The layman, however, could be a merchant, on condition that he observed all the rules relating to prices and profits.

Although the Church refrained from legislating on the craft gilds it maintained towards the confraternities an attitude at once benevolent and mistrustful, which was translated into both law and doctrine. The whole theory of the *universitates* and *collegia* legitimized and strengthened the unity of the gilds. When Innocent IV or Baldus discussed the principle of the legal status of these groups they were concerned only with the legal problem, but at the same time they reduced the obstacles standing in the way of the working of bodies on whom depended the organization of labour and the levels of prices.

What was the practical effect of all these official and private doctrines? Writers are divided: some hold them to be but a slight encumbrance, others believe them a crushing burden; some consider as a tissue of vain ideas what others would call a living law. Between these extremes one may strike a happy mean. It would seem that jurists and theologians consolidated ideas on property, encouraged the fixing of prices and wages, checked usury and increased respect for the various trades and occupations; that their ideas on the distribution of wealth, on the dangers of trade, on the non-productive function of money and on economic policy could not halt the trends of the world. It lies with the historians of institutions and facts to measure the influence of ideas which we have only been concerned to present in their variety. If we look at the medieval economy as a whole, we cannot but notice the manifest predominance of deontology over ontology: scientific curiosity plays a very small part by comparison with moral concern.

APPENDIX

Coinage and Currency

Roman-Barbarian Continuity

The collapse of the Roman Empire in the West was so prolonged a process that to expect to find any cataclysmic change in the coinage would be unreasonable. No such violent change or lengthy cessation of coinage occurred except in Britain. After the Roman departure no further coin entered the country, and within a generation, by about A.D. 435, coin had ceased to be used as a medium of exchange. Not until the latter part of the seventh century were coins again used in Britain other than as jewellery. Elsewhere continuity was maintained. The barbarian 'allies' took over the Roman mints which continued to strike in the names of the emperors.

The coinage of the late Roman Empire reflected its economic decrepitude. On the one hand there was a highly valued gold coin, the solidus, introduced by Constantine, of fine gold, weighing 24 siliquae (about 4·48 gm.), together with its half, the semissis, and third, the tremissis or triens. On the other hand there was the heavy copper follis, revived by Anastasius I in 498 as a coin of forty nummi, and its poor relations down to the nummus. Between were the sparsely issued silver siliquae and half-siliquae, twenty-four siliquae being worth a solidus. The magnificent gold coinage served for imperial gifts and the payment of subsidies to imperial 'allies' such as the 50,000 solidi paid by Maurice Tiberius to Chilperic in 584. It was only of importance within the Empire because taxes had to be paid in gold. The prolific bronze coinage was of use only for the multiplicity of small local payments. Neither was of much use in commerce, and the small silver coinage came to an end under Justinian (527–65).

It is not precisely clear at what date the barbarians took over the Roman mints, but this probably occurred under Clovis (484–511) among the Franks, and under Alaric II (484–507) among the Visigoths. Over the next half-century trientes in the names of Anastasius, Justin and Justinian were issued by various Merovingian kings in northern Gaul and by Visigothic kings from such mints as Bordeaux, Toulouse and Narbonne, without giving any indication of their real issuers. The small bronze coinage, on the other hand, as issued by the Burgundian Godemar (524–34), or by Thierry and Theodebert of Austrasia (511–34 and 534–48), Childebert of Paris (511–58) and Clothair I (511–61), did bear some indication of its true issuers, but such issues came to an end about the middle of the sixth century. No further bronze or copper coins were struck in western

Europe until the end of the fifteenth century, save in ninth-century Northumbria, Norman Sicily and thirteenth-century Hungary.

At the end of the fifth century and the beginning of the sixth century there was struck in Gaul a small series of poor copies of late Roman silver coins ranging from Valentinian to Anastasius. Surviving examples weigh from 0·907 down to 0·3 gm., but they were probably intended as half-siliquae, although their prototypes weighed from 1·04 to 1·25 gm. This was followed by a very limited number of small coins, issued in the names of the Merovingian kings Thierry I, Theodebert, Clothair I and Sigebert I. Surviving examples of these weigh from 0·55 gm. down to as little as 0·25 gm., but they also were probably intended as half-siliquae, being imitations of the much heavier half-siliqua of Justinian. At about the same time copies in the name of Justinian were being struck in the Rhineland. The minting of silver ceased for about three-quarters of a century in both the west and the east about the middle of the sixth century. In the east it was resumed by Heraclius (610–41) and in the west by Caribert II of Aquitaine (629–31).

The first of the barbarians to have the audacity to put his own name on gold coins was Theodebert I of Austrasia, an action which brought forth bitter comment in Procopius's *De Bello Gothico*. Neither of his two immediate successors issued coins in their own names, although some of the solidi and trientes in the name of Theodebert may have been issued by them. From the reign of Sigebert (561–75) and his brother Gontran (561–92) onwards, however, the minting of coins bearing the name of their true issuer became regular in the Frankish kingdoms of northern Gaul, although issues in the names of the emperors continued in Provence down to Heraclius. The Visigothic kings from Leovigild (572–86) similarly struck trientes in their own names. There was a similar time-lag among the Lombard kings who maintained the Italian mints in operation after their conquest in the years following 568, but did not issue in their own names until Cunincpert (680–700). Thus for periods of up to a century, the various barbarian rulers struggled to keep alive the fiction that western Europe was still a part of the Roman Empire before daring to proclaim on their gold coinage that they had created new and independent kingdoms.

It was basically an uncommercial coinage of gold that the barbarians had inherited. Their solidi, whether in the name of the emperors or themselves, were, initially at any rate, as good as those issued from mints under direct imperial control, and were used for the same purposes, prestigious gifts and taxation. Their bronze and silver, before it was given up in the middle of the sixth century, was rather poorer than its imperial prototypes and did not serve well for commercial purposes. After the disappearance of bronze and silver coinage only gold remained, and in

NN

this too there were difficulties. It became more usual to strike the triens than the solidus. The Escharen hoard, deposited near Nijmegen about 600, contained fifty-four trientes, but only eleven solidi and of these five were of Byzantine rather than barbarian origin. The triens also was dropping in weight. The Byzantine prototype weighed 8 siliquae (about 1·5 gm.), but the seventh-century triens issued in the south of France in the name of the emperor was of a new, lower, weight, 7 siliquae (about 1·3 gm.). In the latter part of the century and the early part of the next, the weight sank still further, only being stabilized by the Merovingians about 630 at 1·23 gm. The size of the issues involved may be judged from the fact that all the surviving specimens of the triens of the Bonn mint were struck from one pair of dies. The Merovingians set up mints additional to those they had inherited from the Romans in all parts of their kingdoms, but there was a certain amount of concentration in the valleys of the Meuse and the Rhine (the routes to Frisia) and, after the Lombard invasion of Italy, in Provence.

The Merovingians also struck a new silver denarius alongside the gold triens. The future lay with the denarius rather than with the declining Roman triens, for the Merovingian denarius was the ancestor of the Carolingian denier and the whole range of medieval penny coinages. Except in Italy the triens came to an end during the latter part of the seventh century. The Merovingians ceased striking it under Dagobert II (674–79), the Anglo-Saxons probably at the end of the century. In Spain the last Visigothic trientes of Achila II (c. 710–14) were succeeded only by a very sparse issue of dinars by the conquering Ummayads. The minting of gold then ceased in Spain until the tenth century. In northern Italy the issue of trientes, by the Lombards and by Charlemagne, continued until about 790, but in the south the issue of gold coins of various sorts continued intermittently as the only gold coinage in western Europe until the thirteenth century.

There is some reason to suppose that although we may be technically correct today in speaking of these pieces as trientes, using the Byzantine solidus for comparison, yet at the time they were known as solidi. It has therefore been suggested that for a short time in seventh-century Merovingian Gaul a relationship existed in which one pound (weight of silver) =twenty solidi (gold trientes)=240 denarii (silver coins), and that it was from this period that the familiar relationship of pounds, shillings and pence arose. On the demise of the triens as a coin, and the decline in the weight of the denier, the relationship remained as a convenient means of counting coins. A shilling meant a dozen coins, and a pound meant a score of dozens.

The Denier

The silver penny or denier, the minting of which began in the seventh-century Merovingian and Anglo-Saxon kingdoms, was for over five centuries not merely the characteristic coin of western Europe but virtually the only coin in use.

Evidence for the Merovingian denarius is based on a restricted number of coin hoards, and, whilst it is not possible to estimate the actual quantities minted, they do not seem to have been large. The issue of these pieces seems to have been mainly concentrated in the mints of northern Gaul, and apart from a single known royal issue, by Charibert II (629–31), was entirely struck by feudatories in the period of late Merovingian collapse. The majority of issuers were ecclesiastical, whether bishops like St Lambert of Lyons (680–90) or abbeys such as St Denis or St Martin of Tours. A certain number of issuers were, however, laymen, such as Ebroin, mayor of the palace of Neustria (659–81), or Ansedert and his two fellow patricians of Marseilles. The denarius of the middle and late seventh century was modelled so exactly on the triens that they can only be distinguished by the metal. In the early eighth century the types were reduced almost entirely to legends and monograms. These deniers were thick, dumpy objects as opposed to the thinner, broader penny struck from the mid-eighth century onwards.

The end of the gold coinage in the seventh century saw the closure of many mints which had been striking gold only, whilst some of those which had also been striking silver appear to have remained in uninterrupted operation until the Carolingian period. It is difficult to be certain of this because the majority of the pieces do not distinguish their issuers as individuals, but merely as the bishop of Clermont or the abbey of St Maxentius, and hence cannot be dated exactly.

The most prolific issues of the period were the contemporary pennies of England and Frisia, known as sceattan or sceats. These were obviously closely related to the Merovingian denier and were minted in enormous quantities between the end of the seventh and the third quarter of the eighth centuries. Sceats were used on both sides of the North Sea indiscriminately and sprang from the prosperous trade of the northern Netherlands. This trade had already made the mints of Frisia and the valleys of the Meuse and Rhine amongst the larger issuers of trientes in the previous century, and was to make the mint of Duurstede the most prolific issuer of deniers in the succeeding century.

It is not clear what weight standard was intended for either the Merovingian denier or the Anglo-Frisian sceatta. When in 755 Pepin reformed the coinage he said that he was increasing the weight of the coin by stipulating that no more than 22s. (i.e. 264 deniers) should be made from the pound, whereas, he said, as many as 25s. (i.e. 300 deniers) had in the past been struck from the pound. If the pound at this time weighed 327 gm., which is by no means certain, Pepin implied that he was raising the weight of the denier from 1·08 gm. to 1·24 gm. It has been inferred from this that Merovingian deniers were intended to weigh 1·08 gm., but the surviving examples disprove this hypothesis, for the majority of them weigh between 1·2 gm. and 1·3 gm.—one is even as heavy as 1·37 gm. It would seem that Pepin was merely over-stating his case in order to make his own 'reform' look more impressive. It would seem clear that Merovingian deniers had been struck on a standard of 264 to the pound (i.e. 1·24 gm.) or even occasionally of 240 to the pound (i.e. 1·36 gm.). Pepin's reform can thus be seen as merely a restoration, after a temporary lapse, rather than a great improvement.

Pepin's reform of 755 did, however, alter the appearance of the coins, for although they were of the same weight and the same value as hitherto, the new deniers were struck on thinner, broader flans of some ¾ inch in diameter. It has been suggested that the thinner, broader flan was adopted under the influence of the contemporary silver dirhem of Ummayad Spain which was also struck on a thin, broad flan. In Byzantium a thinner, broader flan was similarly introduced for the miliaresion by Leo III (717–40), also under the influence of the dirhem.

Pepin's reform applied primarily to mints under royal control, but the non-royal mints, mainly in ecclesiastical hands, gradually turned from the issue of the smaller to the broader denier, and once more placed the royal title on their issues. An increasing number of new mints were opened at the same time. Those at Duurstede close to Frisian trade, and Melle close to a rich vein of silver, were extraordinarily prolific in their issues.

The issue of the broader, thinner deniers was not confined to Gaul. They were struck in all parts of the Carolingian Empire—in Spain at such mints as Barcelona and Ampurias, and in Italy at such mints as Lucca, Pisa, Milan and Pavia.

In England the issue of the new pennies commenced somewhere about 775–80 in Kent, where the sub-reguli Heahbert and Ecgbehrt opened a mint at Canterbury, which was taken over about 783/4 by Offa of Mercia. It was this new thin, broad denier rather than the smaller, thicker sceatta which served as the model for the later pennies of all the Anglo-Saxon kingdoms, apart from Northumbria, where pieces of the smaller, thicker module, in copper, continued to be minted for much of the ninth century.

By the opening of the ninth century the larger part of western Europe was using a penny coinage. Within the Empire the denier was issued at a known weight and fineness under the strict control of the counts. With the break-up of the Empire in the ninth and particularly the tenth centuries, fragmentation of issue began to occur once more. The counts who were intended to protect imperial interests began to strike for themselves, although naturally not at first solely under their own names. Mint-owning monasteries, such as St Martin of Tours or St Martial, struck deniers in their own names. The whole range of Frankish bishops, whether endowed with comital powers or not, opened mints for themselves. The imperial right of coinage was naturally feudalized at the same time as other regalian rights, either by imperial grant or by usurpation; but since it remained, in theory at least, an imperial or royal prerogative, it was equally natural that the lords who controlled the individual mints should for long refrain from the exclusive use of their own names on the pennies, and should issue instead pennies bearing the name of the current emperor or king or the name of some long-dead emperor. Very many of these post- or sub-Carolingian deniers were anonymous, bearing neither the name of the emperor nor of the feudatory. The date at which the feudatory took to using his own name on the coinage varied according to the particular circumstances. For example, as early as 876–80 Bruno, duke of the Saxons, issued an obol in his own name together with that of King Louis, whilst as late as 984–6 Heribert, count of Vermandois, was still using on his deniers the name of Lothair, with whom he was allied, as well as his own. On the other hand, Hugh, count of the Lyonnais (936–48), was already omitting the king's name from his deniers.

In these circumstances, new dies were copied slavishly from those previously in use. The consequence was that certain types became immobilized and degenerated—for example Carolingian monograms continued to appear in gradually less and less recognizable forms on deniers from all parts of France until the eleventh or even the twelfth century, whilst the obverse head became at times grotesque with over-copying, for example the notorious *tête chartrain* on the pennies of Chartres and neighbouring mints of the eleventh century. Similarly the tenth-century temple became transformed on the deniers of St Martin of Tours, first into a church porch flanked by towers and then into a castle by the time that the minting of deniers tournois was taken over by Philip Augustus in 1205. The process of degeneration in Italy and in Germany was considerably less extreme.

As dukes of France the Capetians minted deniers like any other late Carolingian feudatory, and the title of king made little difference to their issues which, until the reign of Louis VII, remained variable and indistinguishable from those of their feudal neighbours. More important at this stage were the deniers with something of an international circulation issued in the name of the counts of Champagne by the great fair towns, Troyes, Chalons and above all Provins. The denier of Provins formed the basis of a money of account which became the standard not only at Provins but for the whole of Champagne and all its fairs, and even for the Barrois and Lorraine also.

In late Anglo-Saxon England the denier or penny was perhaps more closely controlled than anywhere else in western Europe during the whole of the Middle Ages. The coinages of the various other Anglo-Saxon kingdoms had come to an end during the Scandinavian onslaught of the ninth century and the coinage of Wessex remained alone, apart from a variety of Danish and Hiberno-Norse penny coinages of not dissimilar type in northern England. With the West Saxon reconquest a uniform coinage was imposed on the whole of England, with only slight regional deviations, as for example in the mints of the north-west. The mint towns had originally been few in number and the bulk of the coinage had been issued at Canterbury and London, but during the tenth century the coinage rapidly increased in quantity and the number of mints increased more than correspondingly. Under Aethelstan it was stipulated that every borough should have a mint, but this was not a case of extreme decentralization, for the dies were cut for the whole country either in a series of regional workshops or in London, and very strict royal control of the coinage was maintained. Over the next generation the number of mints increased prodigiously, although the extreme of one mint to every borough was never quite achieved. In 973 Edgar tightened royal control of the coinage still further by ordering that every six years the complete coinage was to be reminted and the previous issue demonetized. This remarkable policy was actually put into execution, and during the reign of Edward the Confessor the lifetime of a coinage was reduced to three years. The contrast with the Continent, where an immobilized type might be issued with greater and greater degeneration for three centuries, is astonishing. The large number of mints proved invaluable for these frequent total remintings, and there is some evidence to suggest that an attempt was made to ensure that no one should be more than fifteen miles distant from a mint. These re-coinages implied a very considerable measure of royal authority, also implied by the fact that the Anglo-Saxon pennies were of token value rather than of intrinsic value. They fluctuated quite considerably in weight and fineness from one issue to the next and yet their value remained constant, since it derived not from their intrinsic worth but from the word of the king.

Elsewhere in western Europe the value of the denier depended entirely on its silver content or supposed silver content. The Normans, coming from a bad feudal coinage, adopted the Anglo-Saxon system in its entirety. It continued to function, with its triennial change and its basis on royal credit, albeit with a declining number of mints, until the reign of Henry I. The anarchy of Stephen's reign saw, for the only time in England, the emergence of a feudal coinage and the shattering of royal credit. The feudal coinage was on a very limited scale and the only permanent survival was the national coinage of Scotland. After Stephen's reign it was no longer possible to validate the coinage by the authority and credit of the monarchy. Henry II abandoned the hope of restoring a triennial change in the coinage and commenced the series of coinages of fixed and known type lasting for many years. He saw to it that, if the coinage had to be based on the intrinsic value of the coin, it should be good, known and stable. Broadly speaking, until the first debasement of silver coinage in 1344–51 the silver content of the silver penny remained constant, a fact which was in large measure responsible for the high reputation enjoyed by the medieval English coinage. The change in attitude resulting from the adoption of coinage based on its *valor intrinsecus* was reflected in the practice of the English Exchequer which less and less accepted coin *per numero*. A penny was no longer a penny because the king said so, it was a penny because, and only if, it contained a pennyworth of silver. Hence the Exchequer came more frequently to accept coin by weight or preferably blanched.

In Ottonian Germany the feudal confusion existing in France was much less apparent. Certain great ecclesiastics such as the archbishop of Cologne issued on their own, but the majority of issues were in the name of and by the authority of the emperor. The Carolingian system survived much better in the Empire than in France. Coinage reached eastern Europe via the Ottonian Empire in the eleventh century. Deniers were struck for the first time in Hungary, for example, under Stefan I (997–1038).

In Scandinavia coin was not minted until the tenth century. Large quantities of foreign coin, particularly Anglo-Saxon, found their way into Scandinavia during the tenth century either by way of loot or overseas trade or in the form of Danegeld. This coined money was thought of in terms of weight. Hence broken pieces of silver could very well be mixed with coin, and Anglo-Saxon pennies mixed with middle-eastern dirhems. During the second half of the tenth century coined silver came to be regarded more highly than uncoined silver. Consequently copies were minted of the coins most available, particularly the pennies of Aethelred II of England. From imitation of English coin, with either the name of the king of England or with blundered and incoherent inscriptions, there was little distance to the creation of an indigenous coinage, albeit with types based on those of others.

Louis VII, by issuing the denier parisis, made a first attempt at re-creating a non-feudal coinage in France, and started to exercise the rights over the coinage inherent in the title of king. Surviving examples of the new denier weigh between 0·85 and 1·28 gm. This issue of a national coinage, initially effective only in the royal domain, was accompanied by the closure over the next generation of a number of feudal mints as they fell into royal hands. The next considerable extension of royal money in France was made by Philip Augustus who, on conquering the Angevin lands, took over the mint of the abbey of St Martin at Tours and commenced striking deniers tournois on his own account. Surviving examples of royal deniers tournois of Philip Augustus weigh between 0·78 and 1·01 gm., significantly less than the deniers parisis. Philip Augustus finally suppressed the issue of local coinages in his name, and allowed only deniers tournois and parisis to be used in the royal domain. St Louis insisted that these royal deniers should circulate freely throughout France, whilst the pieces of the great feudatories were to be limited to circulation in the fief in which they were issued. The task of unifying the coinage had been made easier by the fact that the number of minor seigneurial coinages had already been considerably reduced by the activities in this direction of the great feudatories themselves. The denier tournois tended initially to circulate in western France and the denier parisis in northern France.

Whilst the Capetians were valiantly struggling to build up a national coinage out of feudal chaos, and whilst the English coinage was being refounded on a basis of sound weight and fineness, the coinage of the Empire broke down and fell almost entirely into seigneurial hands as the imperial authority declined, from the close of the Salian dynasty onwards through the twelfth and thirteenth centuries. In this confusion and breakdown two distinct types of coin came to be issued. Feudatories in the western parts of the Empire (Frisia, the Rhineland, Lotharingia, Bavaria and parts of Franconia and Swabia) continued to issue ordinary silver deniers, whilst those in the east (along the Baltic, in Saxony and the remainder of Franconia and Swabia) struck paper-thin pfennige or deniers commonly called bracteates. These were struck from very thin plates of silver, the design being hollow on the under side and convex on the upper. They are considerably lighter than the normal deniers and of very slight intrinsic value. In Poland, Silesia and Bohemia, also, the minting of bracteates replaced that of the heavier denier in the last quarter of the twelfth century and the first years of the thirteenth. Bracteates similarly replaced the heavier denier in Hungary under Bela IV (1235-70). The number of issuers in the thoroughly fragmented Empire of the thirteenth century seemed as infinite, and many of them as insignificant, as the wave of feudal denier-strikers in post-Carolingian France. Order eventually came out of the chaos by the creation of monetary unions in the fourteenth century, for example in the Rhineland or among the Hanseatic cities. Amongst the confusion of deniers there were a considerable number of imitations of the English penny, particularly in

Westphalia in the first and second decades of the thirteenth century, and in the Rhineland in the middle years of the century. The former copied the English short-cross penny and have been associated with John's subsidies to Otto IV, and the latter copied the English long-cross penny and have been associated with Richard of Cornwall's bid for the imperial throne. The Low Countries, technically within the confines of the Empire, but always very largely independent, were equally the scene of a riotous confusion of seigneurial minting, although with time the considerable principalities such as Flanders (only partially within the Empire) or Brabant engrossed much of the minting. The Low Countries were an area peculiarly prone to imitation of foreign coins, or the coins of the other principalities in the Low Countries, as will be seen more clearly in the period of issues of gold and larger silver, but during the last years of the thirteenth century and the first of the fourteenth century the great vogue was for imitation of the sterlings of Edward I of England.

Although there was so great a degree of fragmentation in the issue of deniers in tenth- and eleventh-century France, or in Germany and the Low Countries of the twelfth and thirteenth centuries, it must not be thought that the currency in use changed at every political frontier across Europe. Apart from the fact that the concept of a frontier is anachronistic, it must be emphasized that a different coinage for every minor seigneury did not mean a different currency for each. Only in England was there a successful attempt to ensure that the local currency was exclusively of local coinage. The kings of France from Philip Augustus onwards may have attempted this, but they failed, and elsewhere it was hardly attempted. The currency of any principality or city consisted not only of the local coinage, but also of a possibly even larger number of deniers from neighbouring territories and cities, together with a few pieces that had travelled considerable distances.

The circulating medium of western Europe from the eighth to the thirteenth century did not consist exclusively of silver deniers, for a certain, very restricted, number of Byzantine gold nomismata and Islamic gold dinars also circulated. The extent to which these were used has been the subject of much speculation, but it appears that, in Italy at least, Byzantine gold solidi circulated commonly so long as the Byzantine mint at Syracuse remained open—up to 878—and for some considerable time afterwards. North of the Alps, however, the situation was different, and, except in the extreme south of France, the bezant was a rare piece. Literary sources would lead one to believe that gold, although not used in France or Germany, was widely used in England, at least in the tenth century, but there is some reason to suppose that its use was more restricted than documents would at first sight suggest. Sums of money expressed in bezants would seem to have been frequently paid in deniers: the Pipe Roll of 1178/9, for example, indicates that a sum of 20 bezants was discharged by payment of 40s., i.e. 480 silver pennies.

The use of the dinar was even rarer than that of the bezant. A very limited number of dinars of the Caliphate found their way into western Europe in the eighth century; one such was the prototype for Offa's dinar. Islamic gold coins hardly circulated again until after the tenth century, when the dinars of Moslem Spain and the taris of Moslem Sicily found their way into the hands of their Christian neighbours in northern Spain and in Italy, among whom they found imitations in the eleventh-century dinars of Barcelona, the taris of Salerno and Amalfi and the twelfth-century alfonsini of Castille.

The term *mancus* or *mangon*, used in Italy and England from the last decades of the eighth to the end of the eleventh century, has caused some confusion. It would appear to have been applied primarily to the light-weight solidus of Byzantine Italy and only secondarily in Christian Spain from the tenth century to the Ummayad and Almoravid dinars.

The Groat

The use of the penny or denier alone could be, and on occasion was, inconvenient. The very size of a hoard found at Brussels, over 150,000 pennies, bears witness to the difficulties of making large payments by the middle of the thirteenth century. The price rise during that century had necessitated the payment of larger and larger numbers of coin, and the general process of debasement meant that the denier was no longer of its pristine size, fineness and weight. Compare for example the Carolingian denier weighing 1·4 gm. with the deniers of Lucca or Pisa of the second half of the twelfth century, which were among the best in Italy, but only contained 0·6 gm. of silver. Fifty years later this had been cut to 0·25 gm.

It is not surprising that Venice, riding high on a wave of economic prosperity and having just received 51,000 marks of silver for transporting the Fourth Crusade, should be the first, in or about 1202, to issue a larger piece. The new piece, the grosso or matapan, was struck of much finer silver than the deniers, it was 0·965 fine, and weighed 2·18 gm. The type was Byzantine in inspiration, the enthroned Christ in Glory and the two reverse figures being derived from the contemporary solidus or nomisma. At first it was valued at 24 of the old deniers, an indication of how small the old denier had become and how inadequate it was for the needs of internal commercial transactions, let alone long-distance trade.

The example of Venice was followed rapidly by Verona, which as early as 1203 was also issuing a grosso, a larger silver piece. In this case it was tied, initially at least, to the pre-existing denier and was made to equal twelve of them; in other words the soldo veronese had become, temporarily at least, a real coin rather than a convenient accounting multiple. When about 1237 Florence also issued a grosso, this was likewise made equal to the soldo; and the same occurred in Milan about the middle of the century.

In the south of Italy the grosso, designed to serve the duchy of Apulia, was known as a ducat. The term ducat spread northwards and for a time the Venetian matapan was also known as a ducat. The Angevin successors to the Hohenstaufen in the kingdom of Naples produced a grosso, known as the gigliato or carlino, which had a very long life. It was first issued by Charles II (1285–1309) and continued to be minted until the beginning of the sixteenth century. Similar gigliati were also struck by the Angevins in Provence and Hungary and by the kings of Cyprus.

The striking of larger silver outside Italy did not occur until 1266 when St Louis issued the gros tournois. This was a much larger coin than the Venetian matapan. It weighed 4·22 gm. as against 2·18 gm., but like the grossi of Verona, Florence and Milan it was designed to be worth twelve of the pre-existing deniers. The gros tournois was, for a short time, the sou tournois, but in 1290 Philip IV brought this equivalence to an end by reducing the weight of the denier tournois and revaluing the gros tournois at $13\frac{1}{8}$ deniers tournois. From then on the gros, or its successor the blanc, continued in France, although its relationship with the money of account, which continued to be based on the deniers, tournois and parisis, was subject to considerable variation.

From France the minting of larger silver pieces spread rapidly. The croat of Aragon and the maravedi de plata of Castille were among the first pieces to draw their inspiration from the French gros tournois.

The various principalities of the Low Countries were also quick in taking up the innovation. In the expanding conditions of thirteenth- and early fourteenth-century Netherlands trade and industry a larger silver piece was invaluable. Florence V (1266–96) in Holland, John I (1268–94) in Brabant, Hugh of Chalon (1295–1301) in Liège and John of Namur (1302–3) in Flanders all struck grooten modelled on the French gros tournois.

In the Empire many princes, and towns, struck groschen in imitation of the French gros tournois in the earlier part of the fourteenth century. These imitators were mainly in western Germany, particularly such Rhineland princes as the archbishop of Cologne, but even two of the emperors—Louis of Bavaria and Charles IV—were among their number. Among the more distant imitators were the kings of Bohemia, who, from 1300, issued the derivative grossus pragensis or Prague groat.

In Hungary the inspiration for a larger silver coinage was drawn direct from Italy. Charles Robert (1308–42), grandson of Charles II of Naples, swept away the bracteates of the previous half-century and introduced a groschen based on the Neapolitan gigliatos.

In France the fine gros was replaced from the mid-fourteenth century by the considerably less fine blanc, whilst in the Empire at the same time the fine groschen were replaced by the less fine weisspfennig, witte or albus. Among the most prominent issuers of weisspfennige were the electors and other Rhineland princes who, by a series of agreements from 1354 onwards, established a Münzverein or monetary union by which they issued pieces of common standard and type. These weisspfennige, sometimes known as raderalbus, had a very considerable circulation, principally in the western parts of the Empire. In Bohemia, on the other hand, the type of the Prague groat remained unaltered until the mid-sixteenth century, although both its weight and fineness declined. These Prague groats had a very considerable circulation throughout the Empire, particularly in the eastern parts of it, although countermarks indicate that they circulated to the west as far as the Rhine and into Holland, and to the east they were imitated in Poland by Casimir the Great. In the Baltic and northern Germany the Hanseatic cities used the coin of their customers to a certain extent, although they were not inconsiderable issues of witte by the Wendish Münzverein, an organization dating from 1379 and similar to the Rhenish Munzverein, although between leagued cities rather than leagued princes.

In England Edward I attempted to follow the example of St Louis and issued a groat which was somewhat less fine but considerably heavier. Since the penny sterling had not deteriorated so much as the denier tournois, the new groat was worth only four old pennies while the gros tournois was the equivalent of twelve old deniers. The attempt was unsuccessful, and England did not receive a permanent large silver coinage until Edward III in 1351 successfully reintroduced the groat, almost one hundred and fifty years after the Venetians had commenced the process of using larger silver coin, and at the same time as France and the Empire were declining from fine gros into baser blancs and albus. Since there was no major debasement or monetary mutation in late medieval England, the groat retained the value of fourpence sterling and no secondary system of money of account based on the groat came into existence as occurred in Venice and Flanders. As with the Prague groats, the type of English groats remained immobilized until the sixteenth century, but unlike the Prague groat, the English groat, or stoter as it was known in the Netherlands, declined in weight rather than fineness, and that only by about a third.

One of the features of the later Middle Ages was that, whilst the new fine gros and groschen declined into blancs and albus, the old deniers often became billon, with a very nominal silver content. The mites of Brabant between 1468 and 1474 contained only one ninety-sixth part silver. Apart from England, where even the halfpennies and farthings were of good silver, all small change, like the Venetian soldini, consisted of this terrible *monnaie noire*. This black money was effectively token coinage, for the cost of manufacture so greatly surpassed the cost of the raw materials that the face value of the coins bore no relation to the intrinsic value of the metal of which they were made. Since it was so expensive to manufacture in relation to its face value, mint masters were averse to minting *monnaie noire* and there was always an insufficient quantity struck. The continually reiterated complaints of a dearth of money were almost always occasioned by the chronic lack of small change.

There were no further additions to the range of silver coinage until the last third of the fifteenth century when the German gulden groschen, later the taler, and the Italian testone revolutionized the currency. England was again somewhat behindhand, not issuing testoons until 1544 (although there had been a limited issue under Henry VII) or crowns until 1551.

The Florin

In southern Italy and Spain the use of gold as currency never entirely ceased, and the minting of gold continued, somewhat hesitantly, throughout the earlier Middle Ages.

Byzantine and Beneventan solidi and trientes were minted in Sicily and southern Italy up to the second half of the ninth century. During the Moslem occupations, taris or quarter-dinars, similar to those of north Africa, were struck in Sicily. From the mid-tenth to the late twelfth century derivative taris were struck at Salerno and the mint at Amalfi also produced taris from the mid-eleventh century to the reign of the Emperor Frederick II. It was therefore into a society used to gold coinage that Frederick II in 1231 launched his famous augustale from the Messina and Brindisi mints. It proved to be the precursor rather than the prototype of the gold coinages of western Europe in the later Middle Ages. This splendid piece, based on classical models, was imitated only by Charles I of Anjou. The gold coinages of western Europe drew their inspiration from the coins of trading cities rather than from those of this pre-Renaissance prince.

Save in the ninth century the minting of gold coins was maintained continuously in Moslem Spain. These were supplemented in Christian Spain in the eleventh century by derivative mancusi de oro from Barcelona, and in the twelfth and early thirteenth century by dinars and double dinars from Castille, Leon and Portugal.

Minting of gold coins continued not only in Spain, Islamic and Christian, southern Italy and Sicily, but also in north Africa, so that the western basin of the Mediterranean was largely surrounded by dinar-issuing countries. It was therefore natural that cities such as Genoa or Florence, whose trade was largely carried on in the western Mediterranean, should use the dinar to a considerable extent. In the twelfth and thirteenth centuries a problem was posed, especially to such trading cities, by the declining standard of the dinar, for it was rapidly becoming unusable for commercial purposes. A replacement for the dinar was needed. The flamboyant augustale proved impractical, but in 1252 Genoa commenced the issue of the gold genovino, and later in the same year Florence began to issue the florin. Both genovino and florin weighed about three and a half grams, which was considerably more than the contemporary almohade dinar, and both were nominally of fine gold, whereas the dinar had become very much debased.

The genovino and its quarter, the quartarolo, seem to have been largely used in commercial transactions in the western Mediterranean, hitherto the province of the dinar and tari, although they were also used in the Levant. The florin on the other hand travelled along the increasingly important trade routes into northern and western Europe and became the prototype of most later European gold coinage.

Meanwhile in the eastern basin of the Mediterranean the bezant was becoming increasingly less useful for commercial purposes. It had kept its fineness and weight until the early eleventh century, but had then become very erratic. The Latin Empire in Constantinople minted no solidi although the exiled Byzantines kept minting gold after a fashion at Nicaea. After the Palaeologue restoration solidi were once more struck in Constantinople, but they were unsatisfactory for trade. Venice from 1284 struck a replacement coinage, the zecchino or gold ducat (as opposed to the matapan or silver ducat). It was the same weight as the genovino and the florin, and was also of fine gold.

The florin and the ducat had their great international vogue in two distinct areas, the one in western Europe, the other in the Levant. Whereas the florin found imitators, a sign of considerable circulation, in Aragon, France, the Low Countries, the Holy Roman Empire and Hungary, the ducat was principally imitated in the Latin orient.

In the wake of international gold coinages there sprang up national gold coinages, although with some difficulty. In 1257 Henry III attempted to issue a gold penny in England, but nothing came of it, and in 1266 St Louis attempted to issue an écu, but with equally little success. It would be pleasant to be able to associate the issue of these coins with English and French connections with the gold-using areas of Europe. The proposed Sicilian expedition of Henry III and the crusades of St

Louis would provide such links. Northern Europe, in general, was not yet ready to use, let alone issue, gold coin. The time-lag in the striking of gold between southern and northern Europe was not so considerable as the parallel time-lag in the adoption of larger silver coinage.

It was not until 1290 that Philip IV of France managed to establish the first successful national gold coinage. He altered the coinage so frequently that it is perhaps not at first sight clear what were his principal types; but these would appear to have been the masse, the chaise and the agnel. The chaise, or clincquart as it was known in the Netherlands, was of nominally fine gold, and initially weighed the same as two Florentine florins or French royals. The type, the king enthroned, was to be used very considerably throughout the fourteenth and into the fifteenth century. The agnel or mouton also derived its name from its type—the paschal lamb—and also had a considerable vogue during the fourteenth and early fifteenth centuries as the type not only for royal issues but also for imitations, particularly in the Low Countries. Another type which had considerable vogue was the cavalier or franc à cheval minted by the French kings from 1360 onwards. This was initially associated with the ransom payable to England for King John, and weighed the half of an English noble. This was a piece which had great popularity not only in the fourteenth century, but also in the fifteenth when revived by Philip the Good of Burgundy.

The French gold coinage found its standard type at last in 1385 in the écu, a coin which continued to be issued with some modification until the reign of Louis XIV. Initially the écu à la couronne or crown weighed 4·079 gm. and was of nominally fine gold and was valued at a livre tournois. The value gradually rose, and the weight and fineness gradually sank, so that when Louis XI slightly modified the écu by issuing the écu au soleil of gold 0·963 fine and weighing 3·496 gm., it was an improvement. The Lancastrian kings of France, Henry V and Henry VI, issued from 1421 to 1449 the salut, of nominally fine gold and weighing half an English noble. It was issued in far greater quantities than the Valois écu and for a short time it looked as if it might supplant it. As the fortunes of war and politics turned in favour of the Valois the supremacy of the écu as the national coin of France was reasserted.

In England a national gold coinage was later in its establishment. After a false start with abortive issues of florins and leopards, Edward III from 1344 minted the noble of fine gold. This was valued at 6s. 8d. sterling (half of a mark and one-third of a pound), and remained of the same fineness and value from 1344 to 1464, although its weight was reduced by over a fifth during that period. The obverse type, the king standing in a ship, has frequently been supposed to relate to the English naval victory at Sluys in 1340. The noble was one of the largest gold pieces of the

Middle Ages and retained throughout its century and a quarter of existence a particular esteem for goodness. Like the French chaise, mouton and cavalier it was much imitated, again principally in the Low Countries, notably by the counts of Flanders of the house of Burgundy. These Flemish nobles became something of a menace in the 1390's when they began to circulate in England, since they were slightly lighter and of somewhat lesser fineness than their English prototype.

In 1464 the noble was replaced by the ryal or rose-noble, sometimes known in the Low Countries as the sun-noble, which was valued at 10s. sterling and weighed 7·78 gm., and was a variation of the noble. A new piece, the angel, was introduced at 6s. 8d.

Burgundy, a hopeful aspirant in the fifteenth century for the status of a national state, issued a national coinage for the Low Countries. In 1433 a Philippus was introduced by Philip the Good for concurrent issue in Flanders, Brabant, Holland, Hainault and Namur—although the issues of Namur never in fact materialized. This was of the same fineness and weight as the contemporary French salut, but quite unlike in type, being a revival of the franc à cheval type, for which reason it became known as the cavalier or rider. In 1454 this was replaced by the leeuw or lion, which was of an entirely independent standard, and was replaced in its turn by the florin of St Andrew, which derived its standard and its general type from the electoral Rhinegulden. It lasted as the principal coin of the Netherlands through four reigns from Philip the Good to Philip the Handsome.

In the Empire the Rhineland electors, the archbishops of Cologne, Mainz and Trier, and the count palatine were among the most prolific issuers of florins. The electors, and from time to time other Rhineland princes, bound themselves by a series of monetary conventions to issue florins of like type, fineness and weight. By the first of these conventions, that of 1354, they agreed to issue florins of $23\frac{1}{2}$-carat gold, sixty-six of which were to be struck from the Cologne mark of metal. This was in effect the same standard as that of the Florentine florin. The fineness of these Rhineland florins or Rhinegulden rapidly dropped, but was stabilized from 1419 to 1490 at 19 carats. Whilst the fineness was stabilized in the fifteenth century the weight dropped very slightly. When issue of these gulden finally ceased in 1626 they were struck of $18\frac{1}{2}$-carat gold, at the rate of seventy-two to the Cologne mark. In the fifteenth century the Rhinegulden were used very greatly in commerce not only in the valley of the Rhine, but throughout Germany and the Low Countries. They found imitators not only in the Burgundian florins of St Andrew, but also in the florins issued in the name of such emperors as Sigismund and Frederick III by imperial free cities like Frankfurt and Nördlingen.

Whilst western Germany had to be content with a standard for its coinage of only 19-carat gold, central Europe retained a coinage of fine gold. The Hungarian ducat, gulden or florin of St Ladislas, backed by the Transylvanian gold mines, maintained parity with the Venetian ducat from the early fourteenth into the sixteenth century.

Whilst national coinages might or might not weaken, largely according to political stresses and strains, the great coinages of international commerce, the Florentine florin and the Venetian ducat, remained unchanged, and continued to sprout new progeny when further national coinages were set up. The standard adopted for the Portuguese cruzado in 1457, backed by the newly accessible African gold, was that of the florin.

Money of Account

In most parts of late medieval Europe, and in many places up to the eighteenth or even the nineteenth century, a dichotomy existed in the functions of money. On the one hand money of account was the *measure of value*, whilst on the other, the actual coin was the *medium of exchange* and the *store of wealth*.

Money of account derived its name from its function. As a measure of value it was used almost exclusively for accounting purposes. Most financial transactions were first determined and expressed in money of account, although payments were naturally made subsequently in coin. Coin itself was valued as a commodity in terms of money of account, and, like any other commodity, its value frequently varied. This variation of the value of coin in terms of money of account has been the cause of much confusion of thought about the nature of money of account. This confusion of thought has resulted in the expression of a differing concept of money of account by practically every writer on medieval money. *Quot homines tot sententiae.*

With the decline of the denier at different rates in different places in the eleventh and twelfth centuries a standard of reference was needed for the wide variety of deniers that might be circulating in any region in addition to the indigenous coinage. Such a need was particularly felt in such regions as Champagne on account of the fairs. With the introduction in the thirteenth century of the fine silver groat and the gold florin in addition to the often base denier, a common denominator became necessary to express the varying values of gold, silver and billon coins, as well as those of other commodities. Money of account supplied both these needs.

Although the necessity for money of account did not arise until the twelfth and, more seriously, the thirteenth century, the form taken by money of account dated from a much earlier period. As early as the eighth, and probably the seventh, century the system of pounds and

oo

shillings had been in use. With regional modifications the relationship of twelve deniers or pennies to the sou or shilling, and of twenty shillings to the livre or pound, had gradually become established throughout western Europe. As has been seen, this was basically a system of counting coins rather than a system of money. A shilling meant a dozen coins, and a pound meant a score of dozens. Marc Bloch maintained that the sou and the livre, before the thirteenth century were no more than *unités numériques*.

In some cases the development of money of account was facilitated by a transitional stage in which the new coins neatly represented the old multiples of deniers. The grossi of Verona, Florence, Milan and Montpellier and the gros tournois were originally intended to be sous, containing twelve times as much silver as their respective deniers, but they soon ceased to fulfil this function. Similarly the Florentine florin was originally intended to represent the Florentine lira, but was soon elevated in official value to 29 soldi. The English noble succeeded where others had failed. It was designed as the third of the pound sterling and remained as such for well over a century.

The habit of counting coins in dozens and scores of dozens was so ingrained that when a new coin did not coincide neatly with a multiple of the pre-existing coins, a new system of pounds, shillings and pence was automatically constructed on the basis of the new coin. In Venice, after the creation of the matapan, two concurrent systems of money of account came into use, the one based on the old little (piccolo) denier, the other on the new great (grosso) denier. There was no firm relationship between the two systems of accounting, for whereas the base denaro of the lira, soldo and denaro piccolo system sank further and further in quality, eventually becoming undisguised copper in the late fifteenth century, the denaro of the £ s. d. grosso system very largely conserved its fineness and weight. The original relationship of 24 lire piccolo to one lira grosso remained tolerably stable for over half a century. In 1265 the lira grosso still equalled only 27 lire piccolo, but from then on the decline was rapid. In 1269 the lira grosso was equal to 28 lire piccolo, and by 1282 it was equal to 32 lire piccolo.

Whereas at Venice two divergent systems of money of account came into existence based on different coins, in other places the newer gros ousted the older deniers so completely that methods of accounting based on the denier either ceased, or continued to be used only on the basis of a notional relationship between the defunct denier and the surviving gros. This occurred in Flanders early in the fourteenth century when the new groot penning supplanted the Flemish denier parisis and the Flemish sterling. The groot was held to be worth three of the old sterlings and twelve of the old deniers parisis, and the systems of account based on the groot, the sterling and the denier parisis were thereafter fossilized in this relationship. All three moneys of account were thus in reality tied to the groot.

Not only were new systems of money of account constructed using the larger silver pieces as deniers, but others were built up using the gold pieces as livres. Both the Florentine florin and the electoral Rhinegulden became pounds of account. Unfortunately for simplicity of comprehension, both the florin and the Rhinegulden as coins became in time detached from their namesakes as pounds of account. In Florence the lira a fiorini came to mean 29 soldi, or rather 348 denari, instead of an actual gold florin, whose value, in lire a fiorini, continued to rise as the Florentine denaro was further debased. In the Netherlands the Rhinegulden was commercially current in the 1440's at 40 Flemish groats, and in the 1450's officially current at that rate and so became equated in men's minds with the pound of 40 groats. Although by 1467 the Rhinegulden had officially become worth 42 Flemish groats and by 1488 90 Flemish groats, it still remained in use, into the sixteenth century, as the name of the pound of 40 groats. This was a strange fossilized system, for its denier did not exist, its sou was for a considerable time the stuiver or patard and its livre was for a short time the Rhinegulden, yet it attached itself to monetary reality by its fixed relationship to the Flemish groat. Similar fossilized systems existed elsewhere. In France the system of livre, sou and denier parisis, based, until its disappearance in 1365, on the denier parisis, continued in use for at least another century and a half, keeping contact with reality by the fossilization of the mid-fourteenth-century relationship of 5 : 4 with the denier tournois. In Flanders the system of livre, sou and denier parisis was kept in contact with reality, as has already been seen, through the perpetual equivalence of the Flemish sou parisis to the Flemish groat. After 1433 there was no independent Brabançon coinage, yet the Brabançon money of account continued to be used; it was also kept in contact with reality by the fossilization of its relationship with the Flemish money of account as it had been in 1433, when 3 Brabançon livres equalled 2 Flemish livres. Thereafter Brabançon money of account was based on the Flemish groat.

The misnomer 'imaginary money' has often been applied to late medieval money of account, perhaps because the real coin on which the money of account was resting was not always evident on first inspection, as in the cases cited above. To untangle the maze of moneys of account which were created in the last 250 years of the Middle Ages is beyond the scope of this brief survey, but it may be taken as axiomatic that on closer inspection a historical explanation may be found for the existence of each money of account, and that such a historical explanation will indicate to which real coin the system continued to be attached.

International and National Coinages

The variety of coins in use in later medieval Europe was very great, but a few generalizations may be made. In general only gold coins travelled long distances whilst silver coins circulated only within what one recent writer has called *coinage provinces*. These *coinage provinces* are usually definable in terms of economics and geography and within each one may expect to find that the silver coins issued by all the mints in that area, on whatever authority, mixed indiscriminately in circulation. This situation with regard to silver coin was a survival from the denier period.

The larger silver coins of the later Middle Ages were used for the payment of wages, for example of mercenary soldiers, payment of rent and for the settlement of the purchases of everyday life, whilst the denier sank to the level of small change and the gold coinage remained largely for international commerce and government expenditure. Gold coins might therefore travel long distances, but again a distinction should be drawn between national and international coinages. National coinages, such as the English noble or the French écu, were designed for use in England and France and, except in the Low Countries, were seldom found outside the country of issue. International coinages such as the florin and the ducat were designed for long-distance commerce and were used as much outside Florence and Venice as within these cities.

The two most highly developed commercial and industrial areas of medieval Europe, northern Italy and the Low Countries, expressed (in monetary matters) in diametrically opposite ways their economic sophistication. The one sent out its own distinctive gold coinages to all parts of Europe, whilst the other drew its gold currency from all parts of Europe. Until the Burgundian unification of the Netherlands there was no distinctive gold coinage issued in the Low Countries. Each independent prince issued his own, nearly always on the standard and after the type of some foreign gold coin which was circulating in large quantities, such as the Florentine florin, the French chaise and mouton and the English noble. If, however, the variety of gold coin circulating in the Low Countries was greater than elsewhere it was not so cumbersome a variety as might appear at first sight, for many of the pieces in use, although of different issuers and types, conformed to the same standards of weight and fineness. The principal standard was one which in the fifteenth century was common to the Florentine florin, the Venetian ducat, the genovino, the papal florin, the Hungarian and Bohemian ducats, the Portuguese cruzado, the Spanish excelente, the Plantagenet-French salut, the English half-noble and the Burgundian rider. All were over 0·989 fine gold and of weights between 3·5 and 3·63 gm. In any commercial transaction therefore all these coins were interchangeable one with another.

Although the range of pieces in use was greater in the Low Countries than elsewhere, a very considerable variety of gold coins circulated together in any part of late medieval Europe except England. The entry of foreign coin into England was prevented by the vigilant action of Royal Exchanges at Canterbury or London, of the mint at Calais and of the local authorities in seaports like Sandwich.

The following table is designed to give a list of the coins most commonly in use in the Middle Ages. It provides brief details of their country and period of origin and of some of their copies. It also indicates their fineness, weight and value and some of the names under which they were current.

Table V. *Medieval Money: a list of coins most commonly in use in the Middle Ages, together with details of their country and period of origin, their fineness and weight, their value and the names under which they were current.*

Imperial Gold

Solidus	Byzantine Empire—Constantine I onwards.
or Solidus Aureus	Nominally fine gold, initially at least 0·98 fine. Wt. 24
or Solidus Aureus	siliquae (4·48 gm.). Retained original fineness and weight to
Nummus	eleventh century, both in erratic decline for next three cen-
or Nomisma	turies. Principal mint: Constantinople.
or Hyperperon	Half = semissis; third = tremissis or triens (1·49 gm.).
or Perper	Byzantine mints in southern Italy issued solidi and trientes on
or Bezant	lighter weight standard.
or Mancus	
or Mangon	

Barbarian Gold

Visigoths
Triens

In names of Emperors Anastasius, Justin and Justinian; issued by Alaric II (484–507) to Leovigild (568–86).
In names of kings from Leovigild (from about 575) to Achila II (c. 710–14). Fineness and weight near Byzantine triens until last quarter seventh century.

Merovingians
Solidus
and Triens

In names of Emperors Anastasius, Justin, and Justinian; issued by Clovis (484–511) until, in northern Gaul, Theodebert I of Austrasia (534–48), and in Provence, Heraclius (610–41).
In names of kings from Theodebert I to Dagobert II (674–9). Weight in sixth century on two standards: solidus at 24 and 21 siliquae (4·48 and 3·92 gm.) and triens at 8 and 7 siliquae (1·49 and 1·306 gm.); of the seventh century surviving trientes weigh mostly 1·15–1·3 gm. Most solidi from Provence.

Lombards
Triens

In names of emperors from c. 571 onwards.
In names of kings from Cuninepert (680–700) to Charlemagne (until about 790). Fineness and weight initially near Byzantine triens, but by Charlemagne 0·39 fine, wt. 0·972 gm.

Anglo-Saxons

Triens
or Thrymsa
Mainly issued in last quarter of seventh century, only identi-
fiable ruler Peada. Mints Canterbury and London. Wt. surviving examples 1·25–1·35 gm. Value thought to be one
shilling.

Islamic

Dinar
or Saracen Perper
Issued by Ummayad and Abbasid Caliphs from Damascus
mint. Nominally fine, wt. 4·25 gm.

Copies
Dinar of Offa of Mercia (post 774) wt. 4·276 gm.

Dinar
or Marobotin
or Mancus
Issued by Ummayads in Spain. Abd-al-Rahman III to Sulaij-
man (928–1013). Fineness and weight of surviving dinars vary
greatly: fineness 0·79–0·98; wt. 3·43–4·71 gm. Also by
Almoravides (wt. 3·88 gm.) and Almohades (wt. 2·32 gm.).

Copies
Mancusi de oro of Berengar Raymond I and Raymond
Berengar I, counts of Barcelona (1018–76). Dinars (and
doblas) of late twelfth- and early thirteenth-century Castille,
issued initially by Alfonso VIII from 1172 at Toledo. Also
known as alfonsini and marobotini.

Tari
Quarter-dinar issued in Ummayad Spain, north Africa and
Moslem Sicily.

Copies
Taris of Salerno (946–1194) and Amalfi (1042–1220+).

Dirhems
Issued throughout Ummayad Caliphate. Early eighth century
Spain: 0·95–0·99 silver; wt. c. 2·81 gm. Late tenth- and early
eleventh-century Spain: 0·73–0·78 silver; wt. 3·11–3·13 gm.
Under Almoravides wt. 2 gm.; under Almohades wt. 1·5 gm.

Penny Coinage

Penny = penning = pfennig = denarius = denaro = denier = dinero = dinhero.
Halfpenny = obolus = obole = medaglia = maille.
Farthing = ferling = pogesa = pougeoise.
12 pennies = shilling = scilling = skillingr = solidus = sou = soldo = sueldo.
240 pennies = pound = pfund = pond = libra = lira = livre.

Merovingians

Denier
or Denarius
In name of Caribert II of Aquitaine (629–31) and of many
ecclesiastics and some lay feudatories during the remainder of
the seventh and first half eighth century. Majority of surviving
examples weigh 1·2–1·3 gm. Probable standard 1·24 gm.

Carolingians

Denier
Replaced Merovingian denier from 755.
755 wt. 1·24 gm.; post-c. 790 wt. 1·7 gm. After end of Carolingians, issue continued in Gaul with immobilized types, into
eleventh century.

France
Feudal deniers issued throughout Gaul after break up of
Carolingian Empire.

Denier Provinois
Minted at Provins in the name of the Count of Troyes and then
of the Count of Champagne (end tenth century—post 1265).
Basis of money of account for Champagne, Barrois and
Lorraine. From 1210 of same standard as denier tournois.

Denier Tournois
Issued by Abbey of St Martin of Tours, from tenth century to
1204. Wt. declining 1·2–0·95 gm.

Capetians
Denier   Local types, undifferentiable from other feudal deniers. From Hugh Capet to Philip Augustus (987–1223). Surviving examples wt. 0·8–1·62 gm.

Denier Parisis   Louis VII–Charles V (1137–1380—last issue 1365).
or Peregin   Louis VII: wt. surviving examples 0·85–1·28 gm.
Charles V: fineness 0·159; wt. 1·275 gm.

Denier Tournois   From Philip Augustus onwards (1204–1649).
or Torneso   Philip Augustus: wt. surviving examples 0·78–1·01 gm.
Charles VIII (1483 issue): fineness 0·079; wt. 1·019 gm.

Italy   Denari on Carolingian standard issued by or in name of Carolingians, native kings of Italy and German emperors, Otto I to Henry V (962–1125).

Rome   Denari issued jointly in names of pope and emperor from Leo III and Charlemagne.

Republic of Venice   Denari issued from Louis the Pious, without imperial title from end ninth century.

Pisa   Minting rights granted to city by Frederick Barbarossa. Denari among best in Italy, but by second half twelfth century wt. 0·6 gm.; and by first half thirteenth century wt. 0·25 gm.

Empire   Imperial deniers or pfenningen theoretically on Carolingian standard, i.e. 240 to pound, or from twelfth century 160 to mark of Cologne (i.e. 1·46 gm.).
In practice: pfennig at Trier 1160, wt. 0·97 gm.
    pfennig of Luxembourg early thirteenth century, wt. 0·73 gm.
    bracteate pfennig at Minden 1265, fineness 0·8; wt. 0·67 gm.

Hungary   Deniers from Stefan I (1008–38) onwards.
Bracteate deniers Bela IV (1235–70) to Otto (1305–7).

Anglo-Saxons and Frisians
Sceat   From the end of the seventh to the third quarter of the eighth
or Sceatta   century. Also Kings of Northumbria, Eadberht (737–58) to
or Penny   Osberht (849–67) and Archbishops of York Eanbold (796–807+) to Wulfhere (854–900).

England
Penny   c. 775/80–1156/7. Issued from c. 775–80 Heaberht and Ecgberht,
or Sterling   Kings of Kent, and c. 784–5 Offa King of Mercia onwards. Fineness and weight fluctuated considerably from issue to issue. Wt. within limits 1·0–1·8 gm.
1156/7–1279:
'Tealby' coinage (1156/7–80)   fineness 0·925
Short-cross pennies (1180–1247)   wt. 1·46 gm.
Long-cross pennies (1247–78)
1279 onwards: fineness 0·925; declining wt.:
Edward I 1·44 gm.; Henry VII 0·78 gm.

Copies   Of Anglo-Saxon pennies in large numbers in Scandinavia, particularly of Aethelred II;
Of short-cross pennies in Westphalia;
Of long-cross pennies in the Rhineland;
Of sterlings of Edward I–III in the Low Countries.

Stray Gold

Carolingian	Louis the Pious—Solidus—Aachen(?)—816–18; wt. 4·4 gm., i.e. as Byzantine solidus, a little heavier than Abbasid dinar.
Copies	In ninth-century Frisia and by Wigmund, Archbishop of York (837–54), wt. 4·42 gm.
Anglo-Saxon	Offa of Mercia—Dinar—post 774—wt. 4·276 gm.
	Edward the Elder—Gold Penny—wt. 4·536 gm.
	Aethelred II—Gold Penny—1003–9—wt. 3·336 gm.
	Edward the Confessor—Gold Penny—wt. 3·514 gm.
	Henry III—Gold Penny—1257—nominally fine; wt. 2·915 gm. = that of two silver pennies; valued at 20d. sterling.

Larger Silver

Grossus denarius = great coin = grosso = gros = groschen = groat = groot.

Venice

Matapan or Grosso	First issued by Doge Enrico Dandolo, c. 1202; wt. 2·18 gm.; 0·965 fine. Original value 26.9d. piccoli.

Verona

Grosso	First issued 1203, originally valued at Veronese soldo.

Florence

Grosso	First issued 1237, originally valued at Florentine soldo.

Milan

Grosso or Ambrosino	Issued from about mid-thirteenth century, originally valued at Milanese soldo.

Naples

Grosso or Gigliato or Carlino	Charles II (1285–1309) to Louis XII of France (King of Naples 1501–4). Weight fairly constant. Wt. surviving examples Charles II 3·75–3·95 gm.; Louis XII 3·4–3·6 gm.
Copies	Hungary from Charles Robert (1308–42) onwards. Provence from Robert (1309–43) onwards. Cyprus from Henry II (1288–1324) onwards. Emirates of Mentesche and Aidin in Asia Minor.

France

Gros tournois or grossus tornensis	St Louis to Charles VI. Fineness 0·958. 1266–1322 wt. 4·219 gm. 1329–64 wt. declining to 2·549 gm. Valued at sou tournois 1266–90.
Copies	Almost entirely fourteenth century. French feudatories, principalities of the Low Countries and the Rhineland and Holy Roman emperors.
Blanc	Issued from 1364 in place of gros.

Bohemia

Grossus pragensis or Prager-Groschen or Prague groat	From 1300 to mid-sixteenth century. Initially struck at 60 to mark (i.e. 3·75 gm.).

England

Groat or Stoter	Edward I, isolated issue 1279: fineness 0·925; wt. 5·767 gm. Edward III onwards, from 1351, 0·925 fine; declining in weight: 1351: 4·665 gm.; under Henry VII: 3·11 gm. Valued throughout at 4d. sterling.
Copies	Scotland from 1357.

Empire
  Rhineland   Weisspfennig or Albus struck by electors and other Rhineland princes under a series of agreements commencing 1354.
  Hanseatic League Witte or Albus minted by six Wendish towns—Hamburg, Lübeck, Lüneburg, Rostock, Stralsund and Wismar—under a series of monetary conventions commencing 1379.

Gold
Italy
  Augustale   Frederick II—1231—Messina and Brindisi mints. Fineness 0·854; wt. 5·3 gm.
  Genovino   Genoa, from 1252; nominally fine; wt. 3·56 gm.; valued
  or Genoino   initially at 8s. Also quartarolo or quarter-florin; cf. tari or
  or Genoese florin   quarter-dinar.
  Florin   Florence 1252–1533; nominally fine; wt. 3·536 gm.
  or Fiorino d'oro   1252–1422 Fiorino d'oro stretto.
                   1422–1533 Fiorino d'oro largo.
    Copies   France, Low Countries, Rhineland, Austria, Hungary.
  Ducato d'oro   Venice 1284–c. 1840; nominally fine (0·997 by assay); wt.
  or Ducat   3·559 gm.
  or Zecchino
  or Sequin
    Copies   Rome, Latin Orient, Moslem Orient, India.
                   Gold florins also issued by Perugia (from 1259), Lucca (by 1275) and Milan before end of thirteenth century.
  Papacy   Florins at Avignon from 1322, later at Rome.
Hungary
  Florins of   From Charles Robert (1308–42) onwards; nominally fine;
  St Ladislaus   wt. 3·536 gm.
  or Ducats   Also double ducat Mathias Corvinus (1458–90) and triple ducat (1453–7).
Empire
  Emperors   Imperial gulden or florins from Louis of Bavaria (1314–47).
  Bohemia   Florins, ducats or gulden from 1325.
  Hanseatic League Issue of Gulden governed by same monetary conventions as Witten.
  Rhineland   Rhinegulden, florins of the Rhine, electoral florins or gulden, issued under monetary conventions 1354–1626. Declining in weight and fineness.
                   1354: fineness 0·979; wt. 66 to mark of Cologne (i.e. 3·536 gm.).
                   1419: fineness 0·79; wt. 66⅔ to mark of Cologne (i.e. 3·51 gm.).
                   1626: fineness 0·77; wt. 72 to mark of Cologne (i.e. 3·24 gm.).
France
  Ecu   St Louis, 1266, nominally fine; wt. 4·196 gm.; value 10 sous tournois.
  Petit Royal   Philip IV from 1290; nominally fine; wt. 3·547 gm.
  or Florin
  Masse   Philip IV from 1296; double of royal or florin.
  Chaise   Philip IV from 1303; double of royal or florin.
  or Clinkaert

Mouton
or Agnel

Philip IV from 1311.

Franc à cheval
or Cavalier

John II, from 1360; nominally fine; wt. 3·885 gm., i.e. same as English half-noble; original value 30s. tournois.

Ecu

Charles VI–Louis XIV:
1385: nominally fine; wt. 4·079 gm.
Ecu à la couronne or crown 1388–1475: nominally fine; wt. in 1388: 3·99 gm.
Ecu au soleil from 1475: 0·963 fine; wt. in 1475: 3·496 gm.

Salut

Charles VI–Henry VI; nominally fine.
1421–3 wt. 3·885 gm. 1423–49 wt. 3·495 gm.

England
Noble

Edward III–Edward IV. Valued at 6s. 8d. sterling.
Nominally fine.
1344–6 wt. 8·972 gm. 1346–51 wt. 8·331 gm.
1351–1412 wt. 7·776 gm. 1412–64 wt. 6·998 gm.

Copies

Scotland, Aquitaine, Flanders.

Rose-noble
or Ryal

From 1464; valued at 10s. sterling, nominally fine; wt. 7·776 gm.

Angel

From 1464; valued at 6s. 8d. sterling, nominally fine, wt. 5·184 gm.

Burgundy or Burgundian Netherlands
Philippus
or Cavalier
or Rider

Philip the Good, 1433–51; valued in 1433 at 4s. groot of Flanders; fineness 0·992; wt. 3·63 gm.

Lion
or Leeuw

Philip the Good, 1454–60; valued in 1454 at 5s. groot of Flanders; fineness 0·958; wt. 4·25 gm.

Florin of St Andrew
or St Andriesgulden

Philip the Good to Philip the Handsome, 1466–96; valued in 1466 at 3s. 5d. groot of Flanders; fineness 0·792; wt. 3·4 gm.

Portugal
Cruzado

From 1457; fineness 0·989; wt. 3·78 gm.

Spain
Excelente

From 1497; fineness 0·989; wt. 3·78 gm.

Bibliographies

EDITORS' NOTE

In accordance with the established practice of the Cambridge series of histories, the bibliographies printed below are selective and incomplete. Their purpose is not to list all the publications bearing directly or indirectly on the subject, but to enable the readers to study some of the topics in greater detail. As a rule, books and articles superseded by later publications have not been included, and references to general treatises indirectly relevant to the subject-matter of individual chapters have been reduced to the minimum. As most of the chapters are not new pieces of research, but summaries and interpretations of knowledge already available in secondary literature, references to original sources have either been left out altogether or have been confined to the principal and most essential classes of evidence.

Within the limits set by these general principles, the individual contributors were given the freedom of composing and arranging bibliographies as they thought best. The 'layout' of the bibliographical lists, therefore, varies from chapter to chapter. The editors did not even find it desirable to insist on a uniform method of abbreviating the references to learned periodicals, since the same learned periodicals may be referred to more frequently in some bibliographies than in others. The authors were asked to make their own decisions about abbreviations, and to explain them, if necessary, in prefatory notes to their bibliographies. The prefatory notes will also explain the other special features of the separate lists of authorities.

CHAPTER I
The Rise of the Towns
ABBREVIATIONS

AHES.　　Annales d'histoire économique et sociale
VSWG.　　Vierteljahrschrift für Sozial- und Wirtschaftsgeschichte
ZRG. Germ.　Zeitschrift der Savigny-Stiftung für Rechtsgeschichte: Germanistische
　　　　　Abteilung

AMMANN, H. 'Die schweizerische Kleinstadt in der mittelalterlichen Wirtschaft.' *Festschrift für W. Merz.* Aarau, 1928.
—— 'Huy an der Maas in der mittelalterlichen Wirtschaft.' *Städtewesen und Bürgertum.* Lübeck, 1953.
—— 'Vom Städtewesen Spaniens und Westfrankreichs im Mittelalter.' *Studien zu den Anfängen des europäischen Städtewesens.* Lindau–Constance, 1958.
ARNOLD, W. *Zur Geschichte des Eigenthums in den deutschen Städten.* Basle, 1861.
ARNOULD, M. A. *Les dénombrements de foyers dans le comté de Hainaut (XIVe–XVIe siècle).* Brussels, 1956.
AUBIN, H. *Vom Altertum zum Mittelalter.* Munich, 1949.
BELOCH, J. *Bevölkerungsgeschichte Italiens.* 2 vols. Berlin, 1937–9.
BLOCKMANS, F. *Het Gentsche stadspatriciaat tot omstreeks 1302.* Antwerp–The Hague, 1938.
BONENFANT, P. 'L'origine des villes brabançonnes et la «route» de Bruges à Cologne.' *Revue belge de philologie et d'histoire,* XXXI (1953).
BÜCHER, K. *Die Bevölkerung von Frankfurt am Main im 14. und 15. Jahrhundert.* Tübingen, 1886.
BÜTTNER, H. 'Studien zum frühmittelalterlichen Städtewesen in Frankreich, vornehmlich im Loire- und Rhonegebiet.' *Studien zu den Anfängen des europäischen Städtewesens.* Lindau–Constance, 1958.
CARO, G. 'Die wirtschaftliche Tätigkeit der Juden im frühen Mittelalter.' *VSWG.* X (1912).
CIPOLLA, C., DHONDT, J., POSTAN, M. M. and WOLFF, PH. 'Moyen âge. Rapport collectif.' *Comité international des sciences historiques. International Committee of Historical Sciences. IXe Congrès International des Sciences Historiques. I. Rapports.* Paris, 1950.
COVILLE, A. *Recherches sur l'histoire de Lyon du Ve siècle au IXe siècle (450–800).* Paris, 1928.
CUVELIER, J. *Les dénombrements de foyers en Brabant (XIVe–XVIe siècle).* 2 vols. Brussels, 1912–13.
DES MAREZ, G. *Étude sur la propriété foncière dans les villes du moyen-âge et spécialement en Flandre.* Ghent–Paris, 1898.
DHONDT, J. 'Développement urbain et initiative comtale en Flandre au XIe siècle.' *Revue du Nord,* XXX (1948).
—— 'L'essor urbain entre Meuse et Mer du Nord à l'époque mérovingienne.' *Studi in onore di Armando Sapori,* I. Milan, 1957.
DOLLINGER, PH. 'Le chiffre de la population de Paris au XIVe siècle. 210.000 ou 80.000 habitants?' *Revue Historique,* CCXVI (1956).
—— 'Patriciat noble et patriciat bourgeois à Strasbourg au XIVe siècle.' *Revue d'Alsace,* XC (1950–1).
—— 'Le patriciat des villes du Rhin supérieur et ses dissensions internes dans la première moitié du XIVe siècle.' *Schweizerische Zeitschrift für Geschichte,* III (1953).
DOLLINGER-LÉONARD, YVETTE. 'De la cité romaine à la ville médiévale dans la région de la Moselle et de la Haute-Meuse.' *Studien zu den Anfängen des europäischen Städtewesens.* Lindau–Constance, 1958.
DOPSCH, A. *Wirtschaftliche und soziale Grundlagen der europäischen Kulturentwicklung von Cäsar bis auf Karl den Grossen.* 2 vols. Vienna, 1923–4.
DOREN, A. *Italienische Wirtschaftsgeschichte,* I. Jena, 1934.

DUPONT, A. *Les cités de la Narbonnaise Première depuis les invasions germaniques jusqu'à l'apparition du consulat.* Nîmes, 1942.

ENNEN, EDITH. *Frühgeschichte der europäischen Stadt.* Bonn, 1953.

ESPINAS, G. *Les origines du capitalisme.* 1. *Sire Jehan Boinebroke, patricien et drapier douaisien (?-1286 environ).* Lille, 1933.

—— *Les origines du capitalisme.* 2. *Sire Jean de France, patricien et rentier douaisien. Sire Jacques le Blond, patricien et drapier douaisien (seconde moitié du XIIIe siècle).* Lille, 1936.

FENGLER, O. 'Quentowic, seine maritime Bedeutung unter Merowinger und Karolinger.' *Hansische Geschichtsblätter,* XXXIV (1907).

FLACH, J. *Les origines de l'ancienne France, Xe et XIe siècles,* II. Paris, 1893.

GANSHOF, F. L. *Étude sur le développement des villes entre Loire et Rhin au moyen âge.* Paris–Brussels, 1944.

—— 'Note sur les ports de Provence du VIIIe au Xe siècle.' *Revue Historique,* CLXXXIII (1938).

GÉNESTAL, R. *La tenure en bourgage. Étude sur la propriété foncière dans les villes normandes.* Paris, 1900.

HAHN, B. *Die wirtschaftliche Tätigkeit der Juden im fränkischen und deutschen Reich bis zum 2. Kreuzzug.* Diss. Freiburg, 1911.

HAMM, E. *Die Städtegründungen der Herzöge von Zähringen in Südwestdeutschland.* Freiburg i. Br., 1932.

HARTMANN, L. M. 'Die wirtschaftlichen Anfänge Venedigs.' *VSWG.* II (1904).

HEMMEON, M. D. *Burgage tenure in medieval England.* Cambridge (Mass.)–London, 1914.

HEYNEN, R. *Zur Entstehung des Kapitalismus in Venedig.* Stuttgart, 1905.

HOLWERDA, I. H. *Dorestad en onze vroegste middeleeuwen.* Leyden, 1929.

HUIZINGA, J. 'Burg en kerspel in Walcheren.' *Mededeelingen der Koninklijke Akademie,* LXXX, ser. B; nr 2. Amsterdam, 1935.

JANKUHN, H. *Haithabu. Eine germanische Stadt der Frühzeit.* 3rd ed. Neumünster, 1956.

—— 'Die frühmittelalterlichen Seehandelsplätze im Nord- und Ostseeraum.' *Studien zu den Anfängen des europäischen Städtewesens.* Lindau–Constance, 1958.

JASTROW, J. *Die Volkszahl deutscher Städte zu Ende des Mittelalters und zu Beginn der Neuzeit.* Berlin, 1886.

JOHANSEN, P. 'Die Kaufmannskirche im Ostseegebiet.' *Studien zu den Anfängen des europäischen Städtewesens.* Lindau–Constance, 1958.

JORIS, A. 'Les origines commerciales du patriciat hutois et la charte de 1066.' *La Nouvelle Clio,* III (1951).

JÜRGENS, O. *Spanische Städte. Ihre bauliche Entwicklung und Ausgestaltung.* Hamburg, 1926.

KEYSER, E. *Deutsches Städtebuch.* 3 vols. Stuttgart–Berlin, 1939, 1941, 1952.

LAVEDAN, P. *Histoire de l'urbanisme.* 1: *Antiquité. Moyen âge.* Paris, 1926.

LESTOCQUOY, J. *Patriciens du moyen-âge. Les dynasties bourgeoises d'Arras du XIe au XVe siècle.* Arras, 1945.

—— *Les villes de Flandre et d'Italie sous le gouvernement des patriciens (XIe–XVe siècles).* Paris, 1952.

LOPEZ, R. 'Aux origines du capitalisme génois.' *AHES.* IX (1937).

LOT, F. *Recherches sur la population et la superficie des cités remontant à l'époque gallo-romaine.* 2 vols. Paris, 1945–6, 1950.

LUCHAIRE, A. *Les communes françaises à l'époque des Capétiens.* 2nd ed. Paris, 1911.

LUZZATTO, G. 'Les activités économiques du patriciat vénitien (Xe–XIVe siècles).' *AHES.* IX (1937).

MAISSIET DU BIEST, J. 'Le chef-cens et la demi-liberté dans les villes du nord avant le développement des institutions urbaines (Xe–XIIe siècles).' *Revue d'histoire du droit français et étranger,* 4e série, VI (1927).

MAITLAND, F. W. *Township and Borough.* Cambridge, 1898.

MENGOZZI, G. *La città italiana nell'alto medio evo.* 2nd ed. Florence, 1931.

MOLS, R. *Introduction à la démographie historique des villes d'Europe du XIVe au XVIIIe siècle.* 3 vols. Louvain, 1954–6.

PETIT-DUTAILLIS, CH. *Les communes, caractères et évolution, des origines au XVIIIe siècle.* Paris, 1947.

Petri, F. 'Die Anfänge des mittelalterlichen Städtewesens in den Niederlanden und dem angrenzenden Frankreich.' *Studien zu den Anfängen des europäischen Städtewesens.* Lindau–Constance, 1958.

Pfeiffer, G. *Das Breslauer Patriziat im Mittelalter.* Breslau, 1929.

Pirenne, H. *Les anciennes démocraties des Pays-Bas.* Paris, 1910. Reprinted in: *Les villes et les institutions urbaines,* I. Paris–Brussels, 1939. English translation: *Belgian Democracy. Its early History.* Manchester, 1915.

—— 'Les dénombrements de la population d'Ypres au XVe siècle (1412–1506).' *VSWG.* I (1903). Reprinted in: Pirenne, H. *Histoire économique de l'Occident médiéval.* 1951.

—— 'Le mouvement économique et social au moyen âge, du XIe au milieu du XVe siècle.' *Histoire générale,* publiée sous la direction de G. Glotz, 2e section, VIII (1933). Reprinted in: Pirenne, H. *Histoire économique de l'Occident médiéval.* Bruges, 1951. English translation: *Economic and Social History of Medieval Europe.* London, 1936.

—— 'L'origine des constitutions urbaines.' *Revue Historique,* 1893–5. Reprinted in: *Les villes et les institutions urbaines,* I. Paris–Brussels, 1939.

—— 'Les périodes de l'histoire sociale du capitalisme.' *Bulletin de l'Académie Royale Belgique,* Classe des Lettres (1914). Reprinted in: Pirenne, H. *Histoire économique de l'Occident médiéval.* 1951. English translation: 'The stages in the social history of capitalism.' *American Historical Review,* XIX (1914).

—— 'Les villes flamandes avant le XIIe siècle.' *Annales de l'Est et du Nord,* I (1905). Reprinted in: *Les villes et les institutions urbaines,* I. Paris–Brussels, 1939.

—— *Les villes et les institutions urbaines.* 2 vols. Paris–Brussels, 1939. (Reprint of all Pirenne's studies about the history of towns.)

—— *Les villes du moyen âge. Essai d'histoire économique et sociale.* Brussels, 1927. Reprinted in: *Les villes et les institutions urbaines,* I. Paris–Brussels, 1939. First published in English: *Medieval Cities. Their Origins and the Revival of Trade.* Princeton University Press, 1925.

—— 'Villes, marchés et marchands au moyen âge.' *Revue Historique,* LXVII (1898). Reprinted in: *Les villes et les institutions urbaines,* I. Paris–Brussels, 1939.

—— 'Les villes du nord et leur commerce.' *Les villes et les institutions urbaines,* I. Paris–Brussels, 1939. First published in English: 'Northern Towns and their Commerce.' *Cambridge Medieval History,* VI (1929).

Planitz, H. 'Frühgeschichte der deutschen Stadt.' *ZRG. Germ.* LXIII (1943).

—— *Die deutsche Stadt im Mittelalter.* Graz–Cologne, 1954.

Püschl, A. *Das Anwachsen der deutschen Städte in der Zeit der deutschen Kolonialbewegung.* Berlin, 1910.

Rietschel, S. *Die Civitas auf deutschen Boden bis zum Ausgang der Karolingerzeit.* Leipzig, 1894.

—— 'Die Entstehung der freien Erbleihe.' *ZRG. Germ.* XXII (1901).

—— *Markt und Stadt in ihrem rechtlichen Verhältnis.* Leipzig, 1897.

Rolland, P. 'De l'économie antique au grand commerce médiéval. Le problème de la continuité à Tournai et dans la Gaule du Nord.' *AHES.* VII (1935).

Rörig, F. *Hansische Beiträge zur deutschen Wirtschaftsgeschichte.* Breslau, 1928.

—— *Die europäische Stadt und die Kultur des Bürgertums im Mittelalter.* Göttingen, 1955. First, but incompletely, published in: *Propyläen-Weltgeschichte,* IV. Berlin, 1932.

—— 'Unternehmerkräfte im flandrisch-hansischen Raum.' *Historische Zeitschrift,* CLIX (1939).

Rohwer, B. *Der friesische Handel im frühen Mittelalter.* Kiel, 1937.

Rousseau, F. 'La Meuse et le pays mosan en Belgique.' *Annales de la société archéologique de Namur,* XXXIX (1930). Also separately: Namur, 1930.

Sabbe, E. 'Quelques types de marchands du IXe et Xe siècles.' *Revue belge de philologie et d'histoire,* XIII (1934).

Sanchez-Albornoz, Cl. *Estampas de la vida de León durante el siglo X.* 3rd ed. Madrid, 1934.

Sayous, A. E. 'Aristocratie et noblesse à Gênes.' *AHES.* IX (1937).

Schipper, I. 'Anfänge des Kapitalismus bei den abendländlichen Juden im früherem Mittelalter bis zum Ausgang des 12. Jahrhunderts.' *Zeitschrift für Volkswirtschaft, Sozialpolitik und Verwaltung,* XV (1906).

SCHLESINGER, W. 'Städtische Frühformen zwischen Rhein und Elbe.' *Studien zu den Anfängen des europäischen Städtewesens.* Lindau–Constance, 1958.

SCHMOLLER, G. 'Die Bevölkerungsbewegung der deutschen Städte von ihrem Ursprung bis im 19. Jahrhundert.' *Festschrift O. Gierke.* Weimar, 1911. Reprinted in SCHMOLLER, G. *Deutsches Städtewesen in älterer Zeit.* Bonn, 1922.

STEPHENSON, C. *Borough and Town. A Study of Urban Origins in England.* Cambridge (Mass.), 1933.

Studien zu den Anfängen des europäischen Städtewesens. Vorträge und Forschungen, IV. Herausgegeben vom Institut für geschichtliche Landesforschung des Bodenseegebietes in Konstanz, geleitet von Theodor Mayer. Lindau–Constance, 1958.

TAIT, J. *The Medieval English Borough. Studies in constitutional History.* Manchester, 1936.

TORRES BALBAS, L., CERVERA, L., CHUECA, F. and BIDAGOR, P. *Resumen histórico del urbanismo en España.* Madrid, 1954.

UNGER, W. S. 'De oudste Nederlandsche bevolkingsstatistiek.' *De Economist* (1913).

VAN DE WEERD, H. 'Les fouilles de Tongres de 1934 et 1935.' *L'Antiquité Classique,* IV (1936).

VAN WERVEKE, H. *Gand. Esquisse d'histoire sociale.* Brussels, 1946.

—— 'De opbloei van handel en nijverheid.' *Algemene Geschiedenis der Nederlanden,* II (1950).

—— 'De steden. Ontstaan en eerste groei.' *Algemene Geschiedenis der Nederlanden,* II (1950).

—— 'De steden. Rechten, instellingen en maatschappelijke toestanden.' *Algemene Geschiedenis der Nederlanden,* II (1950).

VERCAUTEREN, F. *Étude sur les civitates de la Belgique Seconde.* Brussels, 1934.

—— 'Marchands et bourgeois dans le pays mosan aux XIe et XIIe siècles.' *Mélanges Rousseau* (1958).

—— 'De wordingsgeschiedenis der Maassteden in de hoge middeleeuwen.' *Verslag van de algemene vergadering van het Historisch Genootschap verenigd met Bijdragen en Mededelingen,* lxxi (1957).

La Ville. Première partie: Institutions administratives et judiciaires. Deuxième partie: Institutions économiques et sociales. Recueils de la Société Jean Bodin, VI, VII (1954–5).

VOGEL, W. 'Ein seefahrender Kaufmann um 1100.' *Hansische Geschichtsblätter,* XVIII (1912).

—— 'Wik-Orte und Wikinger. Eine Studie zu den Anfängen des germanischen Städtewesens.' *Hansische Geschichtsblätter,* LX (1935).

VOLLMER, G. *Die Stadtentstehung am unteren Niederrhein.* Bonn, 1952.

VON BELOW, G. *Deutsche Städtegründung im Mittelalter, mit besonderer Hinsicht auf Freiburg i. Breisgau.* Freiburg i.B., 1920.

—— *Probleme der Wirtschaftsgeschichte.* Tübingen, 1926.

VON KLOCKE, F. *Patriziat und Stadtadel im alten Soest.* Lübeck, 1927.

VON PETRIKOVITS, H. 'Das Fortleben römischer Städte an Rhein und Donau.' *Studien zu den Anfängen des europäischen Städtewesens.* Lindau–Constance, 1958.

VON WINTERFELD, LUISE. 'Gründung, Markt- und Ratsbildung deutscher Fernhandelsstädte, Westfalen, Hanse, Ostseeraum.' *Veröffentlichungen des Provinzialinstituts für Westfalische Landes- und Volkskunde,* I (7). Münster, 1955.

—— *Handel, Kapital und Patriziat in Köln bis 1400.* Lübeck, 1925.

WOLFF, PH. *Les «estimes» toulousaines des XIVe et XVe siècles.* Toulouse, 1956.

CHAPTER II

The Organization of Trade

There is no point in giving a list of titles which would largely duplicate the bibliographies for chapters IV and V in volume II of *The Cambridge Economic History of Europe.* It seems preferable to provide the reader with a bibliographical guide which will include works that have appeared too recently to be mentioned in the above lists.

The best general treatise on business organization remains the work of Professor N. S. B. Gras, *Business and Capitalism,* New York, 1939. It is now supplemented with regard to the Italian merchants in the Middle Ages by two books: Yves Renouard, *Les hommes d'affaires italiens au moyen âge*, Paris, 1949; Armando Sapori, *Le marchand italien au moyen âge* (École pratique des Hautes Études: VIe Section, Affaires et Gens d'Affaires, 1), Paris, 1952. The latter volume has an extensive bibliography. Most recent of all is an invaluable selection of documents translated into English and edited by Robert S. Lopez and Irving W. Raymond, *Medieval Trade in the Mediterranean World*, New York, 1955. Its bibliography complements that of Sapori. Attention should also be called to a collection of essays containing a translation of Sapori's article on the culture of the medieval merchant and Luzzatto's study on the coexistence in the Middle Ages of large mercantile companies and small merchants: Frederic C. Lane and Jelle C. Riemersma (eds), *Enterprise and Secular Change*, London, 1953. A very useful report discussing the *status quaestionis* of many problems connected with medieval trade is that written for the international congress held in Rome (1955): Michel Mollat, Paul Johansen, Michael M. Postan, Armando Sapori, Charles Verlinden, 'L'économie européenne aux deux derniers siècles du moyen âge', *Relazioni del X Congresso internazionale di Scienze storiche*, VI (Florence, 1955), 803–957. The discussion of the report will be found in *Atti* (Rome, 1957), 369–414.

Professor Sapori's essays on medieval trade are now available in a new and enlarged edition: *Studi di storia economica (Secoli XIII–XIV–XV)*, 3rd enlarged ed. Florence: Sansoni, 1955. Those of Professor Gino Luzzatto have also been published in a volume of collected essays: *Studi di storia economica veneziana*. Padua, 1954. The same is true of the studies of Miss Eleanora Carus-Wilson, *Medieval Merchant Venturers, Collected Essays*. London: Methuen & Co. 1954.

The following anniversary and memorial volumes contain articles of interest on the organization of medieval trade:

Studi in onore di Armando Sapori. Milan, 1957. Of special interest are the studies of M. M. Postan on 'Partnerships in English medieval commerce', and Frederic C. Lane on 'Fleets and Fairs: the Functions of the Venetian Muda'.
Studi in onore di Gino Luzzatto. 4 vols. Milan, 1950.
Städtewesen und Bürgertum als geschichtliche Kräfte. Gedächtnisschrift für Fritz Rörig. Lübeck, 1953.

A recent biography of a medieval merchant is that of Iris Origo, *The Merchant of Prato, Francesco di Marco Datini, 1335–1410*. New York and London, 1957. A monograph on an important business firm is that of Raymond de Roover, *The Medici Bank, Its Organization, Management, Operations, and Decline*. New York, 1948. An enlarged Italian edition, to be published under the title of *Il Banco dei Medici, 1397–1494*, is in preparation.

On the organization of the Italian companies, the latest study is that of Raymond de Roover, 'The Story of the Alberti Company, 1302–1348, as revealed in its Account Books.' *The Business History Review*, XXXII (1958), 14–59. A book on Pisan trade, industry and urban development has just appeared: David Herlihy, *Pisa in the Early Renaissance, a Study of Urban Growth*. New Haven: Yale University Press, 1958.

On the organization of trade in Genoa there is the important series of the *Documenti e studi per la Storia del Commercio e del Diritto Commerciale Italiano*, first published under the editorship of Federico Patetta and Mario Chiaudano and continued under the joint editorship of Italian and American scholars. The cartularies of all the Genoese notaries of the twelfth century have been published in their entirety and several of those of the thirteenth century have already appeared.

CHIAUDANO, MARIO (ed.). *Cartolare di Giovanni Scriba, 1154–1164* (Documenti e Studi, I–II). Turin, 1935.
CHIAUDANO, M. and MOROZZO DELLA ROCCA, R. (eds). *Oberto Scriba de Mercato, 1186–1190* (Documenti, XI and XVI). Turin, 1938–40.
EIERMANN, J. E., KRUEGER, H. G. and REYNOLDS, R. L. (eds). *Bonvillano, 1198* (Documenti, XV). Turin, 1939.
HALL-COLE, M. W., KRUEGER, H. G. and REYNOLDS, R. L. (eds). *Guglielmo Cassinese, 1190–1192* (Documenti, XII–XIII). Turin, 1938.

HALL-COLE, M. W., KRUEGER, H. G., REINERT, R. G. and REYNOLDS, R. L. (eds). *Giovanni di Guiberto, 1200–1211* (Documenti, XVII–XVIII). Turin, 1939–40.

KRUEGER, H. G. and REYNOLDS, R. L. (eds). *Lanfranco, 1202–1226* (Notari Liguri del secolo XII e del XIII, I–III). Genoa, 1952–4.

The series also includes a collection of Venetian and Sicilian notarial contracts, most of them prior to 1200:

LOMBARDO, A. and MOROZZO DELLA ROCCA, R. (eds). *I documenti del commercio veneziano nei secoli XI–XIII* (Documenti e Studi, XIX–XX). Turin, 1940.

——— (eds). *Nuovi documenti del commercio veneto del secolo XI–XIII* (Deputazione di storia patria per le Venezie). Venice, 1953.

ZENO, R. (ed.). *Documenti per la storia del diritto marittimo nei secoli XIII e XIV* (Documenti e Studi, VI). Turin, 1936.

One should also consult the notarial acts of Venetian notaries in Crete:

LOMBARDO, A. (ed.). *Documenti della colonia veneziana di Creta*, I: *Imbreviature di Pietro Scardon, 1271* (Documenti, XXI). Turin, 1942.

MOROZZO DELLA ROCCA, R. (ed.). *Benvenuto di Brixano, notaio in Candia, 1301–1302* (Fonti per la storia di Venezia, Sez. III: Archivi notarili). Venice, 1950.

On Italian account books, the best bibliographical list is that of Professor Sapori in his introductions to the account books of the Peruzzi and of the Alberti which he edited:

I libri di commercio dei Peruzzi. Milan, 1934.
I libri degli Alberti del Giudice. Milan, 1952.

Since the publication of the last list, Umberto Dorini and Tommaso Bertelè (eds) have published the full text of the account book of a Venetian merchant in Constantinople, a few years before the capture of the city by the Turks (1436–9): *Il libro dei conti di Giacomo Badoer* (Il Nuovo Ramusio, III). Rome: Libreria dello Stato, 1956. This volume will be followed by another containing essays by various specialists.

The field of medieval Italian accounting in general has been the subject of very important publications and new discoveries:

CASTELLANI, ARRIGO (ed.). *Nuovi testi fiorentini del Dugento* (Autori classici e documenti di lingua pubblicati dell'Accademia della Crusca). Florence, 1952.

DE ROOVER, RAYMOND. 'The Development of Accounting prior to Luca Pacioli according to the Account Books of Medieval Merchants.' *Studies in the History of Accounting*, ed. A. C. Littleton and B. S. Yamey. London: Sweet & Maxwell, 1956.

MELIS, FEDERIGO. *Storia della Ragioneria*. Bologna, 1950.

ZERBI, TOMMASO. *Le origini della partita doppia: Gestioni aziendali e situazioni di mercato nei secoli XIV e XV*. Milan, 1952.

On French account books, a useful bibliography is appended to Jean Schneider, *Le livre de comptes des merciers messins Jean Le Clerc et Jacquemin de Moyeuvre, 1460–1461*. Metz, 1951. The only book dealing with business organization and accounting in Holland is that of N. W. Posthumus, *De Oosterse handel te Amsterdam: Het oudste bewaarde koopmansboek van een Amsterdamse vennootschap betreffende de handel op de Oostzee, 1485–1490*. Leyden, 1953. It is partly based on the accounts of an Amsterdam partnership toward the end of the fifteenth century.

For other countries, a useful guide is still:

DE ROOVER, RAYMOND. 'Aux origines d'une technique intellectuelle: la formation et l'expansion de la comptabilité à partie double.' *Annales d'histoire économique et sociale*, IX (1937), 171–93, 270–98. This article is not entirely superseded by the one cited above.

On medieval banking, recent important publications are:

DE ROOVER, RAYMOND. *Money, Banking, and Credit in Mediaeval Bruges: Italian Merchant-Bankers, Lombards, and Money-Changers*. Cambridge (Mass.), 1948.

DE ROOVER, RAYMOND. 'New Interpretations of the History of Banking.' *Journal of World History*, II (1954), 38–76.

—— *L'évolution de la lettre de change (XIVe–XVIIIe siècles)*. Paris, 1953.

INCARNATI, LAMBERTO. *Banca e Moneta dalle Crociate alla Rivoluzione francese*. Rome, 1949.

LOPEZ, ROBERTO S. *La prima crisi della banca di Genova (1250–1259)* (Università commerciale Luigi Bocconi, Istituto di storia economica, serie I, vol. XI). Milan, 1956.

USHER, ABBOTT PAYSON. *The Early History of Deposit Banking in Mediterranean Europe* (Harvard Economic Series, LXXV). Cambridge (Mass.), 1943.

On insurance, bibliographical guidance may be obtained from Florence Edler (de Roover)'s article:

'Early Examples of Marine Insurance.' *Journal of Economic History*, V (1945), 172–200.

The important recent contributions to the history of consular organization are:

LAZZARESCHI, EUGENIO (ed.). *Libro della Communità dei mercanti lucchesi in Bruges*. Milan, 1949. Cf. Raymond de Roover, 'La communauté des marchands lucquois à Bruges de 1377 à 1404.' *Annales de la Société d'Émulation de Bruges*, LXXXVI (1949), 23–89.

MASI, G. *Statuti delle colonie fiorentine all'estero (secoli XV–XVI)*. Milan, 1941.

On Italians abroad, the outstanding recent publication is:

RUDDOCK, ALWYN A. *Italian Merchants and Shipping in Southampton, 1270–1600*. Southampton, 1951.

On French economic history, a series of important monographs have appeared recently:

Histoire du commerce de Marseille (published by the Chamber of Commerce of Marseilles under the direction of Gaston Rambert, director of the École supérieure de Commerce): vol. I, *L'Antiquité*, by Raoul Busquet; *Le Moyen Âge jusqu'en 1291*, by Régine Pernoud; vol. II, *De 1291 à 1423*, by Edouard Baratier; *De 1423 à 1480*, by Félix Reynoud; vol. III, *1480–1599*, by Raymond Collier and Joseph Billioud. Paris, 1949–57.

MOLLAT, MICHEL. *Les affaires de Jacques Cœur: Journal du Procureur Dauvet*. 2 vols. (École pratique des Hautes Études: VIe Section, Affaires et Gens d'affaires. Nos. 2 and 2 bis.)

—— *Le commerce maritime normand à la fin du moyen âge*. Paris, 1952.

SCHNEIDER, JEAN. *La ville de Metz aux XIIIe et XIVe siècles*. Nancy, 1950.

WOLFF, PHILIPPE. *Commerces et marchands de Toulouse (vers 1350–vers 1450)*. Paris, 1954.

For the Hansa, a good synthesis is available in:

PAGEL, KARL. *Die Hansa*. Berlin, 1942.

The following monographs are also useful:

KOPPE, WILHELM. *Lübeck-Stockholmer Handelsgeschichte im 14. Jahrhundert*. Neumünster i.H. 1933.

ROPP, G. BARON VON DER. *Kaufmannsleben zur Zeit der Hanse* (Pfingstblätter des Hansischen Geschichtsvereins, no. 3). Leipzig, 1907.

WINTERFELD, LUISE VON. *Tidemann Lemberg. Ein Dortmunder Kaufmannsleben aus dem 14. Jahrhundert* (Hansische Volkshefte, no. 10). Bremen, n.d.

—— *Hildebrand Veckinchusen. Ein hansischer Kaufmann vor 500 Jahren* (Hansische Volkshefte, no. 18). Bremen, n.d.

On South Germany:

BASTIAN, FRANZ. *Das Runtingerbuch (1383–1407) und verwandtes Material zum Regensburger-südostdeutschen Handel- und Münzwesen*. 3 vols. Regensburg, 1935–44.

MÜLLER, K. OTTO. *Quellen zur Handelsgeschichte der Baumgartner von Augsburg, 1480–1570* (Deutsche Handelsakten des Mittelalters und der Neuzeit herausgegeben durch die Historische Kommission bei der Bayerischen Akademie der Wissenschaften, IX). Wiesbaden, 1954.

The studies of Hedwig Fitzler on Portuguese joint-stock companies of the fifteenth and sixteenth centuries (*Vierteljahrschrift für Sozial- und Wirtschaftsgeschichte*, XXIV (1931), 282–98; XXV (1932), 209–50) have been shown to be an invention. Cf. Virginia Rau and B. W. Diffis, 'Alleged fifteenth-century Portuguese joint-stock companies and the articles of Dr Fitzler.' *Bulletin of the Institute of Historical Research*, XXVI (1953), 181–99. In the fifteenth century, Portugal took the lead in geographical discoveries, but certainly not in the development of new forms of business organization, as Dr Fitzler claims.

CHAPTER III

Markets and Fairs

I. General Works

HUVELIN, P. *Essai historique sur le droit des marchés et des foires.* Paris, 1897.
ALLIX, A. 'Les foires: étude géographique.' *La Géographie*, XXIX (1923).

II. Fairs and Markets in the Early Middle Ages[1]

LAMBRECHTS, P. 'Le commerce des Syriens en Gaule du Haut-Empire à l'époque mérovingienne.' *L'antiquité classique*, VI (1937).
VERLINDEN, C. *L'esclavage dans l'Europe médiévale*, I: *Péninsule ibérique, France.* Bruges, 1955.
VERCAUTEREN, F. 'Cataplus et catabolus.' *Bulletin Ducange*, II (1925).
PIRENNE, H. 'Le cellarium fisci.' *Bulletin de l'Académie Royale de Belgique*, 5th ser., XVI (1930).
LEVILLAIN, L. 'Études sur l'abbaye de Saint-Denis à l'époque mérovingienne.' *Bibliothèque de l'École des Chartes*, XCI (1930).
KLETLER, P. *Nordwesteuropas Verkehr, Handel und Gewerbe im frühen Mittelalter.* Vienna, 1925.
POELMAN, H. A. *Geschiedenis van den handel van Noordnederland gedurende het merovingisch en karolingisch tijdperk.* Amsterdam, 1908.
CARLI, F. *Storia del Commercio italiano: il mercato nell'alto medio evo.* Padua, 1934.

III. Urban Markets

GANSHOF, F. L. *Étude sur le développement des villes entre Loire et Rhin au moyen âge.* Paris–Brussels, 1943.
VAN DE WALLE, A. L. J. *Historisch en archeologisch onderzoek van het portus Eename.* Handelingen van de Maatschappij voor Geschied en Oudheidk.te Gent, I (1944).
PROU, M. 'Une ville-marché au XIIe siècle. Étampes.' *Mélanges Pirenne*, II. Brussels, 1926.
SÁNCHEZ ALBORNOZ, CL. *Estampas de la vida en León hace mil años.* 3rd ed. Madrid, 1934.
VERLINDEN, CH. 'L'histoire urbaine dans la péninsule ibérique.' *Rev. belge de Philologie et d'Histoire*, XV (1936).
VALDEAVELLANO, L. G. DE. 'El mercado. Apuntes para su estudio en León y Castilla durante la edad media.' *Anuario de historia del derecho español*, VIII (1931).
RÖRIG, F. 'Der Markt von Lübeck' in *Hansische Beiträge zur deutschen Wirtschaftsgeschichte.* Breslau, 1928.

IV. The Fairs

LEVILLAIN, L. 'Essai sur les origines du Lendit.' *Revue historique*, CLV (1927).
DHONDT, J. 'Bijdrage tot het cartularium van Meesen (1065–1334).' *Bulletin de la Commission royale d'histoire de Belgique*, CVI (1941).
BOURQUELOT, F. *Étude sur les foires de Champagne aux XIIe, XIIIe et XIVe siècles.* Paris, 1865.
BASSERMANN, E. *Die Champagnermessen. Ein Beitrag zur Geschichte des Kredits.* Tübingen, 1911.

[1] Works and articles are listed in the order in which the subjects treated occur in the chapter.

BAUTIER, R. 'Les registres des foires de Champagne. À propos d'un feuillet récemment découvert.' *Bulletin philologique et historique*, 1942–3; published separately, Paris, 1945.

BAUTIER, 'Les foires de Champagne. Recherches sur une évolution historique.' *Recueils de la Société Jean Bodin*, v: *La Foire*. Brussels, 1953.

REYNOLDS, R. L. 'Genoese trade in the late twelfth century, particularly in cloth from the fairs of Champagne.' *Journal of Economic and Business History*, III (1931).

POIGNANT, S. *La foire de Lille. Contribution à l'étude des foires flamandes au moyen âge.* Lille, 1932.

DES MAREZ, G. *La lettre de foire à Ypres au XIIIe siècle. Contribution à l'étude des papiers de crédit.* Brussels, 1907.

TOUSSAINT, P. *Les foires de Chalon-sur-Saône des origines au XVIe siècle.* Dijon, 1910.

AMMANN, H. *Die Deutschen in mittelalterlichen Frankreich.* I. *Deutschland und die Messen der Champagne.* II. *Die Deutschen auf den Messen von Chalon an der Saone und in Burgund.* Deutsches Archiv für Landes- und Volksforschung, III (1939) and V (1941).

BOREL, F. *Les foires de Genève au XVe siècle.* Geneva, 1892.

AMMANN, H. *Freiburg und Bern und die Genfer Messen.* Langensalza, 1921.

—— 'Genfer Handelsbücher des 15. Jahrhunderts.' *Anzeiger für schweizerische Geschichte* (1920).

BRÉSARD, M. *Les foires de Lyon aux XVe et XVIe siècles.* Paris, 1914.

DIETZ, A. *Frankfurter Handelsgeschichte*, I. Frankfurt, 1910.

AMMANN, H. 'Die Friedberger Messen.' *Rheinische Vierteljahrsblätter*, XV–XVI (1950–1).

SCHULTE, A. *Geschichte der grossen Ravensburger Handelsgesellschaft, 1380–1530*, I. Stuttgart–Berlin, 1923.

AMMANN, H. 'Die Zurzacher Messen im Mittelalter.' *Taschenbuch der historischen Gesellschaft des Kantons Aargau* (1923).

—— 'Neue Beiträge zur Geschichte der Zurzacher Messen.' *Ibid.* (1929).

—— 'Die deutschen und schweizerischen Messen des Mittelalters.' *Rec. de la Soc. J. Bodin*, v: *La Foire*. Brussels, 1953.

LAENEN, J. *Geschiedenis van Mechelen tot op het einde der Middeleeuwen.* 2nd ed. Malines, 1934.

SLOOTMANS, C. *De Bergen-op-Zoomsche jaarmarkten en de bezoekers uit Zuid-Nederland.* Sinte Geertruidbronne, 1935.

BLOCKMANS, F. *Van wanneer dateren de Antwerpse jaarmarkten?* XVIIe Vlaamse Filologencongres, Louvain, 1947, résumé.

VAN HOUTTE, J. A. 'La genèse du grand marché international d'Anvers à la fin du moyen âge.' *Revue belge de Phil. et d'Histoire*, XIX (1940).

—— 'Les foires dans la Belgique ancienne.' *Rec. de la Soc. J. Bodin*, v: *La Foire*. Brussels, 1953.

SNELLER, Z. *Deventer, die Stadt der Jahrmärkte.* Weimar, 1935.

FEENSTRA, R. 'Les foires aux Pays-Bas septentrionaux.' *Rec. de la Soc. J. Bodin*, v: *La Foire*. Brussels, 1953.

CHRISTENSEN, A. 'La foire de Scanie.' *Ibid.*

ZDEKAUER, L. *Fiera e mercato in Italia sulla fine del medio evo.* Macerata, 1920.

LUZZATTO, G. 'Vi furono fiere a Venezia?' *Rec. de la Soc. J. Bodin*, v: *La Foire*. Brussels, 1953.

ESPEJO, C. and PAZ, J. *Las antiguas ferias de Medina del Campo.* Madrid, 1912.

RAU, V. *Subsidios para o estudo das feiras medievais portuguesas.* Lisbon, 1943.

CHAPIN, E. *Les villes de foires de Champagne des origines au début du XIVe siècle.* Paris, 1937.

CHAPTER IV

The Economic Policies of Towns

The number of works directly and solely concerned with the economic policies of medieval towns is small. On the other hand a list of those works which refer to the subject or which give pertinent information would be unmanageably large. It has been necessary to be highly selective as far as this second group of works is concerned, but it is hoped that the following list, though far from exhaustive, will at least be representative.

ABBREVIATIONS

Annales   *Annales d'Histoire Économique et Sociale*, later: *Annales d'Histoire Sociale, Mélanges d'Histoire Sociale, Annales (Économies, Sociétés, Civilisations)*
HG.   *Hansische Geschichtsblätter*
RB.   *Revue Belge de Philologie et d'Histoire*
VSWG.   *Vierteljahrschrift für Sozial- und Wirtschaftsgeschichte*
ZRGG.   *Zeitschrift der Savigny-Stiftung für Rechtsgeschichte: Germanistische Abteilung*

A. GENERAL WORKS

1. Economic History

BELOW, G. VON. *Probleme der Wirtschaftsgeschichte. Eine Einführung in das Studium der Wirtschaftsgeschichte.* 2nd ed. Tübingen, 1926.
DOBB, M. H. *Studies in the Development of Capitalism.* London, 1946.
HALPERIN, J. 'Les transformations économiques aux XIIe et XIIIe siècles.' *Revue d'histoire économique et sociale,* XXXVIII (1950).
HAUSER, H. *Les débuts du capitalisme.* Paris, 1927.
HECKSCHER, E. F. *Mercantilism.* (English translation.) 2 vols. London, 1934.
KULISCHER, J. *Allgemeine Wirtschaftsgeschichte des Mittelalters und der Neuzeit.* Vol. I: Das Mittelalter. Munich and Berlin, 1928.
PERROY, E. 'A l'origine d'une économie contractée. Les crises du XIVe siècle.' *Annales,* IV (1949).
PIRENNE, H. 'Les périodes de l'histoire sociale du capitalisme.' *Bulletin de l'Académie Royale de Belgique: Classe des Lettres,* V (1914).
—— *Economic and Social History of Medieval Europe.* (English translation.) London, 1936.
POSTAN, M. M. and RICH, E. E. (eds). *The Cambridge Economic History of Europe,* II. Cambridge, 1952.
RÖRIG, F. *Mittelalterliche Weltwirtschaft. Blüte und Ende einer Weltwirtschaftsperiode.* Kieler Vorträge, XL. Jena, 1933.
SCHMOLLER, G. *The Mercantile System and its Historical Significance.* New York, 1896.
SOMBART, W. *Der moderne Kapitalismus. Historisch-systematische Darstellung des gesamteuropäischen Wirtschaftslebens von seinem Anfangen bis zur Gegenwart,* I. 5th ed. Munich and Leipzig, 1922.

2. Towns

LESTOCQUOY, J. *Les villes de Flandre et d'Italie sous le gouvernement des patriciens (XIe–XVe siècles).* Paris, 1952.
MAUNIER, R. *L'origine et la fonction économique des villes. Étude de morphologie sociale.* Paris, 1910.
PERNOUD, R. *Les villes marchandes aux XIVème et XVème siècles.* Paris, 1948.
PIRENNE, H. *Les villes et les institutions urbaines.* 2 vols. Paris and Brussels, 1939.
RÖRIG, F. *Die europäische Stadt im Mittelalter.* Göttingen, 1955.

SAPORI, A. 'Villes et classes sociales au moyen âge.' *Rapport au IXe Congrès International des Sciences Historiques, Paris, 28 août–3 septembre, 1950*, section IV, Histoire Sociale. Paris, 1950.

SPANGENBERG, H. 'Territorialwirtschaft und Stadtwirtschaft. Ein Beitrag zur Kritik der Wirtschaftsstufentheorie.' *Historische Zeitschrift*, Beiheft XXIV, 1932. Munich and Berlin, 1932.

WEBER, M. 'Die Stadt.' *Grundriss der Sozialökonomik*, III, 2. Tübingen, 1925.

3. Trade, Industry, etc.

ARIAS, G. 'La base delle rappresaglie nella costituzione sociale del medioevo.' *Atti del Congresso di Scienze Storiche, Roma, 1–9 aprile, 1903*, IX. Rome, 1904.

BOURQUELOT, F. 'Études sur les foires de Champagne, sur la nature, l'étendue et les règles du commerce qui s'y faisait aux XIIIe et XIVe siècles.' *Mémoires présentés par divers savants à l'Académie des Inscriptions de France*, 2e série, v. Paris, 1865.

CHAPIN, E. *Les villes de foires de Champagne des origines au début du XIVe siècle.* Paris, 1937.

COORNAERT, E. 'Les ghildes mediévales (Ve–XIVe siècles). Définition, Évolution.' (1st article.) *Revue Historique*, CXCIX (1948).

GOLDSCHMIDT, L. 'Universalgeschichte des Handelsrechts.' *Handbuch des Handelsrechts*, I (I). 3rd ed. Stuttgart, 1891.

HEYD, W. *Geschichte des Levantehandels im Mittelalter.* 2 vols. Stuttgart, 1879.

HOUTTE, J. A. VAN. 'Les courtiers au moyen âge.' *Revue historique de droit français et étranger*, 4e série, XV (1936).

HUVELIN, P. *Essai historique sur le droit des marchés et des foires.* Paris, 1897.

KELLER, R. VON. 'Freiheitsgarantien für Person und Eigentum im Mittelalter.' *Deutschrechtliche Beiträge*, XIV (I). Heidelberg, 1939.

KLETLER, P. *Nordwesteuropas Verkehr, Handel und Gewerbe im frühen Mittelalter.* Deutsches Kultur, Historische Reihe, II. Vienna, 1924.

LA RONCIÈRE, C. DE. *La découverte de l'Afrique au moyen âge.* 3 vols. Cairo, 1925–7.

MAS LATRIE, L., COMTE DE. 'Du droit de marque ou de représailles au moyen âge.' *Bibliothèque de l'École des Chartes*, 6e série, II (1866).

McLAUGHLIN, T. D. 'The teachings of the canonists on usury (XII, XIII and XIV centuries).' *Medieval Studies*, I (1939), II (1940).

MICKWITZ, G. *Die Kartellfunktionen der Zünfte und ihre Bedeutung bei der Entstehung des Zunftwesens. Eine Studie in spätantiker und mittelalterlicher Wirtschaftsgeschichte.* Societas Scientiarum Fennica: Commentationes Humanarum Litterarum, VIII (3). Helsinki, 1936.

MONROE, A. E. *Early Economic Thought.* Cambridge (Mass.), 1924.

NAUDE, W. *Die Getreidehandelspolitik der europäischen Staaten vom 13. bis zum 18. Jahrhundert.* Acta Borussica. Berlin, 1896.

REHME, P. 'Geschichte des Handelsrechts.' *Handbuch des gesamten Handelsrechts herausgegeben von Victor Ehrenberg*, I. Leipzig, 1913.

SABBE, E. 'Quelques types de marchands des IXe et Xe siècles.' *RB.* XIII (1934).

SAYOUS, A. E. 'Le capitalisme commercial et financier dans les pays chrétiens de la Méditerranée occidentale depuis la Première Croisade jusqu'à la fin du moyen âge.' *VSWG.* XXIX (1936).

SCHAUBE, A. 'Handelsgeschichte der romanischen Völker des Mittelmeergebiets bis zum Ende der Kreuzzüge.' *Handbuch der mittelalterlichen und neueren Geschichte*, Abt. III. Munich and Berlin, 1906.

SIEVEKING, H. 'Der Kaufmann im Mittelalter.' *Schmollers Jahrbuch für Gesetzgebung, Verwaltung und Volkswirtschaft* (1928).

STRIEDER, J. *Studien zur Geschichte Kapitalistischer Organisationsformen; Monopole, Kartelle und Aktiengesellschaften im Mittelalter und zu Beginn der Neuzeit.* 2nd ed. Munich, 1925.

TROELTSCH, E. *The Social Teachings of the Christian Churches.* (English translation.) London, 1931.

B. Local and Regional Studies

1. Works with the emphasis on the interrelationships between different towns or different regions

AGATS, A. *Der Hansische Baienhandel.* Heidelberg, 1904.

ARAUZ DE ROBLES, C. *Cataluña y el Mediterraneo.* Madrid, 1930.

ARIAS, G. *I trattati commerciali della Repubblica fiorentina, secolo XIII.* Florence, 1901.

BAECHTOLD, H. *Die schweizerische Volkswirtschaft in ihren Beziehungen zu Deutschland.* Frauenfeld, 1927.

BAHR, K. *Handel und Verkehr der deutschen Hanse in Flandern während des vierzehnten Jahrhunderts.* Leipzig, 1911.

BEARDWOOD, A. *Alien Merchants in England, 1350 to 1377; their legal and economic position.* The Medieval Academy of America: monographs, 3. Cambridge (Mass.), 1931.

BRATIANU, C. J. *Recherches sur le commerce des Génois dans la Mer Noire au XIIIe siècle.* Paris, 1929.

—— 'Les Vénitiens dans la Mer Noire au XIVe siècle après la deuxième guerre des Détroits.' *Échos d'Orient,* XXXII (1934).

BYRNE, E. H. 'Genoese trade with Syria in the twelfth century.' *American Historical Review,* XXV (1920).

CARABELLESE, F. *Le relazioni commerciali fra la Puglia e la Repubblica di Venezia del secolo X al secolo XV.* 2 vols. Trani, 1897.

CARO, G. *Genua und die Mächte am Mittelmeer (1257–1311).* 2 vols. Halle, 1895, 1899.

CESSI, R. 'Le relazioni commerciali fra Venezia e le Fiandre nel secolo XV.' *Nuovo Archivio Veneto,* n.s., XXVII, 1914.

—— *La Repubblica di Venezia e il problema adriatico.* Padua, 1943.

—— *Le colonie medievali in oriente.* Bologna, 1942.

CHONE, H. 'Die Handelsbeziehungen Kaiser Friedrichs II zu den Seestädten Venedig, Pisa, Genua.' *Historische Studien herausgegeben von Ebering,* XXXII. Berlin, 1902.

DOEHAERD, R. *Les relations commerciales entre Gênes, la Belgique et l'Outremont d'après les archives notariales génoises aux XIIIe et XIVe siècles.* Institut Historique Belge de Rome; Études d'Histoire Économique et Sociale, II–IV. Brussels, 1941.

DUDAN, B. *Il dominio veneziano nel Levante.* Bologna, 1938.

DUPONT, A. *Les relations commerciales entre les cités maritimes du Languedoc et les cités méditerranéennes d'Espagne et d'Italie du Xe au XIIe siècle.* Nîmes, 1942.

ESPINAS, G. *Une guerre sociale interurbaine dans la Flandre Wallonne au XIIIe siècle; Douai et Lille, 1284–1285.* Bibliothèque de la Société d'Histoire du Droit des Pays Flamands, Picards et Wallons, I. Paris and Lille, 1930.

FINOT, J. *Étude historique sur les relations commerciales entre la Flandre et l'Espagne au moyen âge.* Paris, 1899.

—— *Étude historique sur les relations commerciales entre la Flandre et la Republique de Gênes au moyen âge.* Paris, 1906.

FLENLEY, R. 'London and Foreign Merchants in the reign of Henry VI.' *English Historical Review,* XXV (1910).

FRICCIUS, W. 'Der Wirtschaftskrieg als Mittel hansischen Politik im 14. und 15. Jahrhundert in Flandern und in den Niederlanden.' *HG.* LVII–LVIII (1932–3).

GARNELO, B. *Relaciones entre España y Italia durante la Edad Media.* Real Monasterio del Escorial, 1927.

GIUSEPPI, M. S. 'Alien merchants in England in the fifteenth century.' *Transactions of the Royal Historical Society,* n.s., IX (1895).

GOETZ, L. K. 'Deutsch-Russische Handelsverträge des Mittelalters.' *Hansische Geschichtsquellen,* N.F., V. Lübeck, 1922.

GORIS, J. A. 'Étude sur les colonies marchandes méridionales (Portugais, Espagnols, Italiens) à Anvers, de 1488 à 1567. Contribution à l'histoire des débuts du capitalisme moderne.' *Recueil de Travaux publiés par les Membres des Conférences d'Histoire et de Philologie de l'Université de Louvain,* série 2, IV. Louvain, 1925.

HAMPE, K. *Der Zug nach dem Osten.* Leipzig and Berlin, 1935.

JANSSENS DE BISTHOVEN, R. *La loge des Génois à Bruges.* Genoa, 1915.

KERLING, N. J. M. *Commercial relations of Holland and Zeeland with England from the late 13th century to the close of the Middle Ages.* London, 1954.

KIPARSKY, V. 'Fremder im Baltendeutsch.' *Mémoires de la Société Néo-Philologique*, XI. Helsingfors, 1936.

KLEENTJENS, J. 'Les relations économiques des Pays Bas avec la Pologne aux XIVe et XVe siècles.' *Revue du Nord* (1935).

KOHLER, J. 'Handelsverträge zwischen Genua und Narbonne im 12. und 13. Jahrhundert.' *Berliner juristische Beiträge zum Civilrecht, Handelsrecht und Strafprozess und vergleich. Rechtswissen., herausgegeben von J. Kohler*, III. Berlin, 1903.

KOPPE, W. 'Lübeck-Stockholmer Handelsgeschichte im 14. Jahrhundert.' *Abhandlungen zur Handels- und Seegeschichte*, II (1953).

KUSKE, B. 'Die Handelsbeziehungen zwischen Köln und Italien im späteren Mittelalter.' *Westdeutsche Zeitschrift für Geschichte und Kunst*, XXVII (1908).

LAURENT, H. *Un grand commerce d'exportation au moyen âge: la draperie des Pays Bas en France et dans les pays méditerranéens, XIIe–XVe siècle.* Paris, 1935.

—— 'Les relations commerciales entre les villes brabançonnes et les foires françaises au moyen âge.' *Actes du 1er Congrès national français des sciences historiques.* Paris, 1928.

LENEL, W. *Die Entstehung der Vorherrschaft Venedigs an der Adria.* Strasbourg, 1897.

—— 'Un trattato di commercio tra Venezia e Imola dell'anno 1099.' *Nuovo Archivio Veneto*, n.s., XVI. Venice, 1908.

LOPEZ, R. S. *Storia delle colonie genovesi nel Mediterraneo.* Bologna, 1938.

—— 'Le relazioni commerciali fra Genova e la Francia nel Medioevo.' *Cooperazione Intellettuale*, VI. Rome, 1937.

LUZZATO, G. 'I più antichi trattati tra Venezia e le città Marchigiane; 1141–1345.' *Nuovo Archivio Veneto*, serie 2, IX (1). Venice, 1906.

MALOWIST, M. 'Le développement des rapports économiques entre la Flandre, la Pologne et les pays limitrophes du XIIIe au XIVe siècle.' *RB.* X (1931).

MAS LATRIE, L., COMTE DE. *Documents sur les relations diplomatiques et commerciales de la France avec la République de Venise pendant les siècles XIII–XV.* Collection des documents inédits. Paris, 1880.

—— *Relations et commerce de l'Afrique septentrionale ou Magreb avec les nations chrétiennes au moyen âge.* Paris, 1886.

MOREL, P. *Les Lombards dans la Flandre française et le Hainaut.* Lille, 1908.

NALDINI, L. 'La politica coloniale di Pisa nel Medioevo.' *Bollettino Storico Pisano*, n.s., VIII (1939), 1–3.

NICOLAU D'OLWER, L. *L'expansió de Catalunya en la Mediterrània oriental.* Barcelona, 1926.

NORDMANN, C. 'Oberdeutschland und die deutsche Hanse.' *Pfingstblätter des Hansischen Geschichtsvereins*, XXVI. Weimar, 1939.

ÖHLMANN, E. 'Die Alpenpässe im Mittelalter.' *Jahrbuch für schweizerische Geschichte*, V (1878).

ÖSTERREICH, H. 'Die Handelsbeziehungen der Stadt Thorn zu Polen.' *Zeitschrift des Westpreussische Geschichtsvereins*, XLII (1900).

PLANITZ, H. *Köln und die nordfranzösischen und belgischen Städte.* Cologne, 1940.

POWER, E. E. and POSTAN, M. M. (eds). *Studies in English Trade in the Fifteenth Century.* London, 1933.

REINCKE, H. 'Die Deutschlandfahrt der Flandrer während der hansischen Fruhzeit.' *HG.* LXVII–LXVIII (1942–3).

—— 'Kölner, Soester, Lübecker und Hamburger Recht in ihren gegenseitigen Beziehungen.' *HG.* LXIX (1950).

REPARAZ, G. DE. *Catalunya a les mars.* Barcelona, 1930.

REYNOLDS, R. L. 'The Market for Northern Textiles in Genoa, 1179–1200.' *RB.* VIII (1929).

—— 'Merchants of Arras and the Overland Trade with Genoa, Twelfth Century.' *RB.* IX (1930).

ROBERTI, M. 'I trattati fra Venezia e Padova anteriori al dominio ezzeliniano.' *Nuovo Archivio Veneto*, XVI. Venice, 1908.

ROTHHARDT, H. 'Der Kampf Lübecks gegen die Ausübung des Strandrechtes im Ost-seeraum.' *Diss. Rechts- und Staatswiss. Halle-Wittenberg.* Würzburg, 1938.

RUDDOCK, A. A. *Italian Merchants and Shipping in Southampton, 1270–1600.* Southampton, 1951.

SABBE, E. 'Les relations économiques entre l'Angleterre et le Continent au haut moyen âge.' *Le Moyen Âge,* LVI (1950).

SAYOUS, A. E. *Le commerce des Européens à Tunis depuis le XIIe siècle jusqu'à la fin du XVIe.* (Bibliothèque d'Histoire Coloniale.) Paris, 1929.

—— 'Le commerce et la navigation des Génois au XIIe et XIIIe siècles.' *Annales* (1931).

SCHANZ, G. *Englische Handelspolitik gegen Ende des Mittelalters und besonderer des Zeitaltesr der beiden ersten Tudors, Heinrich VII und Heinrich VIII.* 2 vols. Leipzig, 1880, 1881.

SCHEFFEL, P. H. *Verkehrsgeschichte der Alpen.* 2 vols. Berlin. 1908, 1914.

SCHULTE, A. *Geschichte des mittelalterlichen Handels und Verkehrs zwischen Westdeutschland und Italien, mit Ausschluss von Venedig.* 2 vols. Leipzig, 1900.

SIMONSFELD, A. *Der 'fondaco dei tedeschi' in Venedig und die deutschvenetianischen Handels-beziehungen. Quellen und Forschungen.* 2 vols. Stuttgart, 1887.

STEIN, W. 'Über den Umfang des spätmittelalterlichen Handels der Hanse in Flandern und in den Niederlanden.' *HG.* XLIII (1917).

—— 'Der Streit zwischen Köln und Flandern um die Rheinschiffahrt im 12. Jahrhundert.' *HG.* XVII (1911).

STIEDA, W. 'Hansisch-Venetianische Handelsbeziehungen im 15. Jahrhundert.' *Festschrift der Universität Rostock.* Halle, 1894.

STURLER, J. DE. *Les relations politiques et les échanges commerciaux entre le duché de Brabant et l'Angleterre au Moyen Âge; l'étape des laines anglaises en Brabant et les origines du développement du port d'Anvers.* Paris, 1936.

TYLER, J. T. *The Alpine Passes in the Middle Ages.* Oxford, 1930.

2. *Works with the emphasis on one town or region*

(a) *The British Isles*

ASHLEY, W. J. *An Introduction to English Economic History and Theory.* 2 vols. London, 1892, 1893.

BALLARD, A. (ed.). *British Borough Charters, 1042–1216.* Cambridge, 1913.

—— and TAIT, J. (eds). *British Borough Charters, 1216–1307.* Cambridge, 1923.

BATESON, M. (ed.). *Borough Customs.* 2 vols. Selden Society Publications, XVIII (1904) and XXI (1906).

BIRD, R. *The Turbulent London of Richard II.* London, 1949.

BLAND, A. E., BROWN, P. A. and TAWNEY, R. H. *English Economic History. Select Docu-ments.* London, 1914.

BRODNITZ, G. 'Die Stadtswirtschaft in England.' *Jahrbuch für Nationalökonomie und Statistik,* CII (1914).

CARUS-WILSON, E. M. *Medieval Merchant Venturers. Collected Studies.* London, 1954.

COLBY, C. W. 'The growth of oligarchy in English towns.' *English Historical Review,* V (1890).

CUNNINGHAM, W. *The Growth of English Industry and Commerce.* Vol. I, The Middle Ages. 4th ed. Cambridge, 1905.

GRAS, N. S. B. *The Evolution of the English Corn Market from the twelfth to the eighteenth century.* Cambridge (Mass.), 1915.

—— *The Early English Customs System.* Harvard Economic Studies, XVIII. Cambridge (Mass.) and London, 1918.

GROSS, C. *The Gild Merchant.* 2 vols. London, 1890.

JONES, G. P. 'Trading in Medieval Caernarvon.' *Transactions of the Caernarvonshire His-torical Society,* X (1950).

LIPSON, E. *An Introduction to the Economic History of England.* Vol. I, The Middle Ages. 5th ed. London, 1929.

LOBEL, M. D. *The Borough of Bury St Edmunds; a Study in the Government and Development of a Monastic Town.* Oxford, 1935.

MEYER, E. 'English Craft Gilds and Borough Governments of the Later Middle Ages.' *University of Colorado Studies*, XVII (1929–30).

O'SULLIVAN, W. *The Economic History of Cork City from the Earliest Times to the Act of Union*. Cork, 1938.

TAIT, J. *The Medieval English Borough: Studies on its Origins and Constitutional History*. (University of Manchester Publications, Historical Series, 70.) Manchester, 1936.

THRUPP, S. L. *The Merchant Class of Medieval London*. University of Chicago Press, 1948.

TRENHOLME, N. M. 'The English Monastic Boroughs.' *University of Missouri Studies*, II (3) (July 1927).

UNWIN, G. *The Gilds and Companies of London*. London, 1908.

—— *Studies in Economic History: the Collected Papers of George Unwin*. London, 1927.

(b) *Germany, Switzerland and the North*

AHRENS, R. 'Die Wohlfahrtspolitik des Rostocker Rats bis zum Ende des 15. Jahrhunderts.' *Beiträge zur Geschichte der Stadt Rostock*, XV. Rostock, 1927.

AMMANN, H. 'Die schweizerische Kleinstadt in der mittelalterlichen Wirtschaft.' *Festschrift für W. Merz*. Aarau, 1928.

—— 'Das schweizerische Städtewesen des Mittelalters in seiner wirtschaftlichen und sozialen Ausprägung.' *Recueils de la Société Jean Bodin*, VII: *La Ville; 2e partie: Institutions économiques et sociales*. Brussels, 1955.

BAECHTOLD, H. 'Der norddeutsche Handel im XII. und beginnenden XIII. Jahrhundert.' *Abhandlungen zur Mittleren und Neueren Geschichte*, XXI. Berlin and Leipzig, 1910.

BELOW, G. VON. 'Über Theorien der wirkschaftlichen Entwicklung der Völker, mit besonderer Rücksicht auf die Stadtwirtschaft des deutschen Mittelalters.' *Historische Zeitschrift*, LXXXVI (1901).

—— 'Territorium und Stadt. Aufsätze zur deutschen Verfassungs-, Verwaltungs- und Wirtschaftsgeschichte.' *Historische Bibliothek*, II. 2nd ed. Munich and Berlin, 1923.

BOSCH, R. *Der Kornhandel der Nord-, Ost- und Innerschweiz und der ennetbirgischen Vogteien im 15. und 16. Jahrhundert*. Zurich, 1913.

DAENELL, E. *Die Blütezeit der deutschen Hanse. Hansische Geschichte von der zweiten Hälfte des XIV. bis zum letzten Viertel des XV. Jahrhunderts*. 2 vols. Berlin, 1905, 1906.

DIETZ, A. *Frankfürter Handelsgeschichte*. 4 vols. Frankfurt, 1910–25.

GAENSCHALZ, E. 'Die Nahrungspolitik der Stadt Erfurt bis zum Jahre 1664.' *Mitteilungen des Vereins für die Geschichte und Altertumskunde von Erfurt*, XLVII. Erfurt, 1931.

GÖNNENWEIN, O. 'Das Stapel- und Niederlagsrecht. Quellen und Darstellungen zur hansischen Geschichte,' *Hansische Geschichtsverein*, N.F., XI. Weimar, 1939.

GROSS, L. 'Stadt und Markt im späteren Mittelalter.' *ZRGG*. XLV. Weimar, 1925.

HAFEMANN, M. *Das Stapelrecht, eine rechtshistorische Untersuchung*. Leipzig, 1910.

HANSEN, J. 'Beiträge zur Geschichte des Getreidehandels und der Getreidepolitik Lübecks.' *Veröffentlichungen zur Geschichte der Freien und Hansestadt Lübeck*, I (I). Lübeck, 1912.

HERZOG, A. 'Die Lebensmittelpolitik der Stadt Strassburg im Mittelalter.' *Abhandlungen zur Mittleren und Neueren Geschichte*, XII. Berlin, 1909.

HIRSCH, T. 'Danzigs Handels- und Gewerbsgeschichte unter der Herrschaft des deutschen Ordens.' *Preisschriften gekront und herausgegeben von der fürstlich Jablonowskischen Gesellschaft zu Leipzig*, VI. Leipzig, 1858.

HÖLBAUM, K., KUNZE, K. and STEIN, W. *Hansisches Urkundenbuch*. (Verein für Hansische Geschichte.) Halle and Leipzig, 1876–1907.

HOLLIHN, G. 'Die Stapel- und Gästepolitik Rigas in der Ordenzeit (1201–1562). Ein Beitrag zur Wirtschaftsgeschichte Rigas in der Hansezeit.' *HG*. LX (1935).

ILGENSTEIN, E. 'Handels- und Gewerbsgeschichte der Stadt Magdeburg im Mittelalter bis zum Beginn der Zunftherrschaft (1330).' *Geschichtsblätter für Stadt und Land Magdeburg*. Magdeburg, 1908.

INAMA-STERNEGG, K. T. VON. *Deutsche Wirtschaftsgeschichte*. 6 vols. Leipzig, 1909.

JOSET, C. J. 'Les villes au pays de Luxembourg (1196–1383).' *Université de Louvain; Recueil de Travaux d'Histoire et de Philosophie*. 3e série, v. Brussels and Louvain. 1940.

KEYSER, E. *Danzigs Geschichte*. Danzig, 1921.

KLAIBER, L. 'Beiträge zur Wirtschaftspolitik oberschwäbische Reichsstädte im ausgehenden Mittelalter.' *VSWG*. Beiheft X (1927).

KULISCHER, J. *Russischer Wirtschaftsgeschichte*, I. Jena, 1925.

KUSKE, B. 'Handel und Handelspolitik am Niederrhein vom 13. bis 16. Jahrhundert.' *HG*. (1909).

—— *Quellen zur Geschichte des Kölner Handels und Verkehrs im Mittelalter*. Publikationen der Gesellschaft für rheinische Geschichtskunde, XXIII. 4 vols. Bonn, 1917–34.

MEYER, J. 'Die Entstehung des Patriziats in Nürnberg.' *Mitteilungen des Vereins für Geschichte der Stadt Nürnberg*, XXVII (1928).

NIITEEMAA, V. 'Deutsche städtische Getreidehandelspolitik vom 15.–17. Jahrhundert, mit besonderer Berücksichtigung Stettins und Hamburgs.' *Staats- und sozialwissenschaftliche Forschungen, herausgegeben von G. Schmoller*, VIII (5). Leipzig, 1889.

PLANITZ, H. 'Kaufmannsgilde und städtische Eidgenossenschaft in niederfränkischen Städten im 11. und 12. Jahrhundert.' *ZRGG*. LX (1940).

—— 'Der Fremdenarrest.' *ZRGG*. XXXIX–XL (1918–1919).

—— 'Über hansisches Handels- und Verkehrsrecht.' *HG*. XXXI (1924).

—— 'Handelsverkehr und Kaufmannsrecht im fränkischen Reich.' *Festschrift E. Heyman* (1940).

RIETSCHEL, S. *Markt und Stadt in ihren rechtlichen Verhältnis. Ein Beitrag zur Geschichte der deutschen Stadtverfassung*. Leipzig, 1897.

RÖRIG, F. *Vom Werden und Wesen der Hanse*. Leipzig, 1940.

—— *Hansische Beiträge zur deutschen Wirtschaftsgeschichte*. Veröffentlichungen der Schleswig-Holsteinischen Universitätsgesellschaft, XII. Breslau, 1928.

RUNDSTEDT, H.-G. VON. 'Die Regelung des Getreidehandels in den Städten Südwestdeutschlands und der deutschen Schweiz im spätern Mittelalter und im Beginn der Neuzeit.' *VSWG*. Beiheft XIX. Stuttgart, 1930.

RUTKOWSKI, J. *Histoire Économique de la Pologne avant les Partages*. Institut d'Etudes slaves de l'Université de Paris. Bibliothèque Polonaise, I. Paris, 1927.

SACHS, C. L. 'Metzgergewerbe und Fleischversorgung der Reichsstadt Nürnberg bis zum Ende des 30-jährigen Krieges.' *Mitteilungen des Vereins für Geschichte der Stadt Nürnberg*, XXIV. Nuremberg, 1922.

SCHNEIDER, J. 'Les villes allemandes au moyen âge: les institutions économiques.' *Recueils de la Société Jean Bodin*, VII: *La Ville; 2e partie: Institutions économiques et sociales*. Brussels, 1955.

SCHULTZE, A. 'Über Gästerecht und Gastgerichte in den deutschen Städten des Mittelalters.' *Historische Zeitschrift*, CI (1908).

SIMSON, P. *Geschichte der Stadt Danzig*. 3 vols. Danzig, 1913–18.

SOMMERLAD, T. *Die Rheinzölle im Mittelalter*. Halle, 1894.

STEIN, W. *Beiträge zur Geschichte der deutschen Hanse bis um die Mitte des 15. Jahrhunderts*. Giessen, 1899–1900.

—— 'Handels- und Verkehrsgeschichte der deutschen Kaiserzeit.' *Abhandlungen zur Handels- und Seegeschichte*, X. Berlin, 1922.

STOLZ, K. 'Die Wiener Nahrungs- und Genussmittelpolitik im Mittelalter.' *Mitteilungen des Vereins für Geschichte der Stadt Wien*, VIII. Vienna, 1928.

STOLZ, O. 'Zur Entwicklungsgeschichte des Zollwesens innerhalb des alten Deutschen Reiches.' *VSWG*. XLI (1954).

STRIEDER, J. *Zur Genesis der modernen Kapitalismus. Forschungen zur Entstehung der grossen bürgerlichen Kapitalvermögen am Ausgang des Mittelalters und zu Beginn der Neuzeit, zunächst in Augsburg*. 2nd ed. Munich and Leipzig, 1935.

ZEUMER, K. 'Die deutschen Städtesteuern, insbesondere die städtischen Reichssteuern im 12. und 13. Jahrhundert.' *Staats- und sozialwissenschäftliche Forschungen, herausgegeben von Gustav Schmoller*, I (2). Leipzig, 1878.

(c) France, Belgium and Holland

ARASKHANIANTZ, A. 'Die französische Getreidehandelspolitik bis zum Jahre 1780.' *Staats- und sozialwissenschaftliche Forschungen, herausgegeben von Gustav Schmoller*, IV (3). Leipzig, 1882.

BARATIER, E. and REYNAUD, F. *Histoire du Commerce de Marseille de 1291–1480.* Paris, 1951.

BIGWOOD, G. 'Gand et la circulation des grains en Flandre du XIVe au XVIIIe siècle.' *VSWG.* IV (1905).

—— 'Le régime juridique et économique du commerce de l'argent dans la Belgique du moyen âge.' *Mémoires de l'Académie Royale de Belgique, Classe des Lettres* (etc.), 2e série, XIV (1–2). Brussels, 1921–2.

—— 'La politique de la laine en France sous les règnes de Philippe le Bel et ses fils.' *RB.* XVI (1936).

BLOCKMANS, FR. *Het Gentsche Stadspatriciaat tot omstreeks 1302.* Rijksuniversiteit te Gent, Werken uitgeven door de Faculteit van de Wijsbegeerte en Letteren, LXXXV. Antwerp, 1938.

CUVELIER, J. 'Les institutions de la ville de Louvain au moyen âge.' *Mémoires de l'Académie Royale de Belgique, Classe des Lettres* (etc.), 2e série, XI (7). Brussels, 1935.

DECHESNE, CL. *Histoire économique et sociale de Belgique.* Paris and Liège, 1932.

DES MAREZ, G. 'Étude sur la propriété foncière dans les villes du moyen âge et spéciale-ment en Flandre.' *Recueil des Travaux publiés par la Faculté de Philosophie et Lettres de l'Université de Gand,* XX. Ghent, 1898.

—— *Les luttes sociales en Flandre au moyen âge.* Brussels, 1900.

—— 'L'organisation du travail à Bruxelles au XVe siècle.' *Mémoires de l'Académie Royale de Belgique, Classe des Lettres.* Brussels, 1904.

DOEHAERD, R. 'Au temps de Charlemagne et les Normands; ce qu'on vendait et com-ment on le vendait dans le bassin parisien.' *Annales,* II (1947).

DOGNON, P. *Les institutions politiques et administratives du Pays de Languedoc du XIIIe siècle aux guerres de religion.* Toulouse, 1895.

EHRENBERG, R. 'Maklers, Hosteliers und Börse in Brugge vom XIII. bis zum XVI. Jahrhundert.' *Zeitschrift für das gesamte Handelsrecht,* XXX (1885).

ESPINAS, G. *Les finances de la Commune de Douai des origines au XVe siècle.* 3 vols. Paris, 1902.

—— *La draperie dans la Flandre française au moyen âge.* 2 vols. Paris, 1923.

—— *La vie urbaine de Douai au moyen âge.* 4 vols. Paris, 1913.

—— *Recueil de documents relatifs à l'histoire du droit municipal en France des origines à la Révolution; Artois,* I. (Société d'histoire du droit.) Paris, 1934.

—— *Le droit économique et social d'une petite ville artésienne à la fin du moyen âge, Guines.* Paris, 1949.

—— and PIRENNE, H. *Recueil de documents relatifs à l'histoire de l'industrie drapière en Flandre.* 4 vols. Brussels, 1906–24.

FAGNIEZ, G. *Documents relatifs à l'histoire de l'industrie et du commerce en France au moyen âge.* 2 vols. Paris, 1898, 1900.

GERMAIN, A. C. *Histoire du Commerce de Montpellier au moyen âge.* 2 vols. Montpellier, 1861.

GIRY, A. *Documents sur les relations de la royauté avec les villes en France de 1180 à 1314.* Paris, 1885.

—— *Les Établissements de Rouen.* 2 vols. (Bibliothèque de l'École des Hautes Études.) Paris, 1883, 1885.

—— *Histoire de la ville de Saint-Omer et de ses institutions jusqu'au XIVe siècle.* (Biblio-thèque de l'École des Hautes Études.) Paris, 1877.

GODARD, J. 'Contributions à l'étude de l'histoire du commerce des grains à Douai, du XIVe au XVIIe siècle.' *Revue du Nord,* XXVII (1945).

HÄPKE, R. 'Brügges Entwicklung zum mittelalterlichen Weltmarkt.' *Abhandlungen zur Verkehrs- und Seegeschichte,* I. Berlin, 1908.

HAYEM, J. *Mémoires et Documents pour servir à l'Histoire du Commerce et de l'Industrie en France.* Paris, 1922.

JANSMA, T. S. 'Scheepvaarpolitiek van Amsterdam in de tweede helft van de vijftiende eeuw.' *Jaarboek van het Genootschap Amstelodamum,* XLVII (1955).

KURTH, G. *La cité de Liège au moyen âge.* 3 vols. Brussels, 1909.

LAURENT, H. 'Le Hanse des XVII villes.' *Revue Historique du droit français et étranger,* LIX (1935).

LESTOCQUOY, J. 'Patriciens du moyen âge. Les dynasties bourgeoisies d'Arras du XIe au XVe siècle.' *Mémoires de la Commission Départementale des Monuments Historiques du Pas-de-Calais*, V (1). Arras, 1945.

LINDEN, H. VAN DER. *Histoire de la constitution de la ville de Louvain au moyen âge*. Université de Gand; Recueil des Travaux publiés par la Faculté de Philosophie et Lettres, VII. Ghent, 1892.

—— *Les Gildes marchandes dans les Pays Bas au moyen âge*. Université de Gand: Recueil des Travaux publiés par la Faculté de Philosophie et Lettres, XV. Ghent, 1896.

MARQUANT, R. *La vie économique à Lille sous Philippe le Bon*. Paris, 1940.

MOLLAT, M. *Le commerce maritime normand à la fin du moyen âge*. Paris, 1952.

PIRENNE, H. *Histoire de Belgique*. 7 vols. 2nd ed. Brussels, 1902–32.

ROLLAND, P. *Les origines de la commune de Tournai: histoire interne de la seigneurie épiscopale tournaisienne*. Brussels, 1931.

ROOVER, R. DE. *Money, Banking and Credit in Medieval Bruges*. Cambridge (Mass.), 1948.

SAYOUS, A. E. 'Le commerce terrestre de Marseille au XIIIe siècle.' *Revue Historique*, CLXIII (1930).

—— 'Le commerce de Nice avec l'intérieur.' *Annales*, I (1939).

SCHNEIDER, J. *La ville de Metz aux XIIIe et XIVe siècles*. Nancy, 1950.

—— *Recherches sur la vie économique de Metz au XVe siècle; le livre de comptes des merciers messins Jean le Clerc et Jacquemin de Moyeuvre (1460–1461). Introduction*. Metz, 1951.

THOMAS, L. J. *Montpellier, ville marchande; histoire économique et sociale*. Montpellier, 1936.

UNGER, W. S. *De levensmiddeln voorziening der hollandsche steden in de middeleeuwen*. Amsterdam, 1916.

USHER, A. P. *The History of the Grain Trade in France, 1400–1710*. Harvard Economic Studies, IX. Cambridge (Mass.), 1913.

VERCAUTEREN, F. *Luttes sociales à Liège (XIIIme et XIVme siècles)*. Brussels, 1943.

WERVEKE, H. VAN. *De Gentsche Stadsfinancien in de Middeleeuwen*. Brussels, 1934.

—— *Gand. Esquisse d'histoire sociale*. Brussels, 1946.

—— 'Industrial Growth in the Middle Ages: the Cloth Industry in Flanders.' *Economic History Review*, 2nd ser. IV (1954).

—— 'Der Flandrische Eigenhandel in Mittelalter.' *HG*. LXI (1936).

WOLFF, PH. 'Les luttes sociales dans les villes du Midi français, XIIIe–XVe siècles.' *Annales*, II (1947).

—— *Commerces et marchands de Toulouse*. Paris, 1954.

(d) Spain and Portugal

AUNÓS PÉREZ, A. *El Derecho Catalán en el siglo XIII*. Barcelona, 1926.

CAPMANY Y DE MONTPALAU, A. DE. *Memorias históricas sobre la marina, comercio y artes de la antigua ciudad de Barcelona*. 4 vols. Madrid, 1779–92.

ESPEJO, C. and PAZ, J. *Las antiguas ferias de Medina del Campo*. Madrid, 1912.

FONT RIUS, J. M. 'Origenes del régimen municipal de Cataluña.' *Anuario de Historia del Derecho Español*, XVI (1945).

GOGINHO, V. M. *História econômica e social da expansão portuguesa*, I. Lisbon, 1947.

HAMILTON, E. J. *Money, Prices and Wages in Valencia, Aragon and Navarre, 1351–1500*. Cambridge (Mass.), 1936.

MIRET I SANS, J. 'Les represálies a Catalunya en l'edat mitjana.' *Revista juridica de Cataluña*, XXXI (1925).

OLIVER, B. *Historia del Derecho en Cataluña, Mallorca y Valencia*. 4 vols. Madrid, 1876–81.

PENELS, L. 'Die Handelsgerichtordnung von Barcelona aus dem fünfzehnten Jahrhundert.' *Zeitschrift für das gesamte Handels- und Konkursrecht*, LXXXV. Stuttgart, 1921.

SMITH, R. S. *The Spanish Gild Merchant, 1250–1700*. Durham, N.C., 1940.

USHER, A. P. *The Early History of Deposit Banking in Mediterranean Europe*, I. Cambridge (Mass.), 1943.

VALDEAVELLANO, L. G. DE. *El Mercado. Apuntes para su estudio en León y Castilla durante la Edad Media*. Madrid, 1952.

VALLS I TABERNER, F. *Estudis d'Historia jurídica catalana*. Barcelona, 1929.

(e) Italy

ARIAS, G. *Il sistema della costituzione economica e sociale italiana nell'età dei Comuni.* Turin, 1905.

BARBIERI, G. *Economia e politica nel Ducato di Milano, 1386–1535.* Milan, 1938.

—— *Ideali economici degli italiani all'inizio della età moderna.* Milan, 1940.

BAUER, C. 'Venezianische Salzhandelspolitik bis zum Ende des 14. Jahrhunderts.' *VSWG.* XXIII (1930).

BOÜARD, M. DE. 'Problèmes des subsistances dans un état mediéval: le marché et le prix des céréales au royaume angevin de Sicile (1266–1282).' *Annales,* X (1938).

CARLI, F. *Storia del commercio italiano.* 2 vols. Padua, 1934, 1936.

CASSANDRO, G. I. 'Le rappresaglie e il fallimento a Venezia nei secoli XIII–XVI.' *Documenti e Studi per la Storia del Commercio e del Diritto Commerciale Italiano pubblicati sotto la Direzione di F. Patetta e M. Chiaudano.* Turin, 1938.

CESSI, R. *Storia della Repubblica di Venezia.* 2 vols. (Biblioteca Storica, XXIII, XXVI.) Milan and Messina, 1944, 1946.

—— 'La regolazione delle entrate e delle spese.' (Introduction to) *Documenti finanziari della Repubblica di Venezia editi a cura della Commissione per gli atti delle Assemblee Costituzionali Italiane,* I (I). Padua, 1925.

—— and ALBERTI, A. *La politica mineraria veneziana.* Rome, 1924.

CIPOLLA, C. M. 'The Trends in Italian Economic History in the Later Middle Ages.' *Economic History Review,* 2nd ser. II (1949).

DAVIDSOHN, R. *Geschichte von Florenz.* 4 vols. Berlin, 1896–1927.

—— *Forschungen zur älteren Geschichte von Florenz.* 4 vols. Berlin, 1896–1908.

—— 'Der florentiner Welthandel des Mittelalters.' *Weltwirtschaftliches Archiv,* XXX (I). Jena, 1929.

DOREN, A. *Studien aus der florentiner Wirtschaftsgeschichte.* 2 vols. Stuttgart and Berlin, 1901, 1908.

—— 'Italienische Wirtschaftsgeschichte.' *Handbuch der Wirtschaftsgeschichte, herausgegeben von G. Brodnitz,* I. Jena, 1934.

HEINEMANN, L. VON. *Zur Entstehung der Stadtverfassung in Italien.* Leipzig, 1896.

HEYNEN, R. 'Zur Entstehung des Kapitalismus in Venedig.' *Münchner Volkswirtschaftlicher Studien,* LXXI. Stuttgart and Berlin, 1905.

KRETSCHMAYR, H. *Geschichte von Venedig,* I. Gotha, 1905.

LOPEZ, R. S. 'Studi sull'economia genovese nel medio evo.' *Documenti e Studi per la Storia del Commercio e del Diritto Commerciale Italiano,* VIII. Turin, 1936.

—— 'Aux origines du capitalisme génois.' *Annales,* IX (1937).

LUZZATO, G. *Storia economica d'Italia.* I: *Antichità e medioevo.* Rome, 1949.

—— *I prestiti della repubblica di Venezia.* Padua, 1929.

—— 'Il debito pubblico nel sistema finanziario dei secoli XIII–XV.' *Nuova Rivista Storica,* XIII (1929).

—— 'L'economia di guerra di un grande Comune del Trecento.' *Rivista di Storia Economica,* I (1940).

—— 'Les noblesses: les activités économiques du Patriciat vénitien.' *Annales,* IX (1937).

—— 'Piccoli e grandi mercanti nelle città italiane del Rinascimento.' *Saggi di storia e teoria economica in onore e memoria del professore Giuseppe Prato.* Turin, 1931.

OTTOKAR, N. *Il comune di Firenze alla fine del dugento.* Florence, 1926.

PEYER, H. C. *Zur Getreidehandelspolitik oberitalienischer Städte im 13. Jahrhundert.* Veröffentlichungen des Instituts für Österreichische Geschichtsforschung, XII. Vienna, 1950.

PÖHLMANN, R. 'Die Wirtschaftspolitik der florentiner Renaissance und das Prinzip der Verkehrsfreiheit.' *Preisschriften . . . der fürstlich Jablonowskischen Gesellschaft zu Leipzig,* XXI. Leipzig, 1878.

PLESNER, J. *L'émigration de la campagne à la ville libre de Florence au XIIIe siècle.* Copenhagen, 1934.

RENOUARD, Y. *Les hommes d'affaires italiens du moyen âge.* Paris, 1949.

RODOLICO, N. 'The struggle for the right of association in fourteenth-century Florence.' *History,* VII (April 1922–Jan. 1923).

RODOLICO, N. 'Il sistema monetario e le classi sociali nel medioevo.' *Rivista Italiana di Sociologia*, VIII (1904), 4.

SALVATORELLI, L. 'L'Italia comunale.' *Storia d'Italia*, ed. Mondadori, IV. Milan, 1940.

SALVEMINI, G. *Magnati e Popolani in Firenze dal 1280 al 1295.* Pubblicazioni del R. Istituto di Studi Superiori Pratici e di Perfezionamento in Firenze, Sezione di Filosofia e Filologia. Florence, 1899.

SAPORI, A. *Studi di storia economica (secoli XIII–XIV–XV).* 2 vols. Florence, 1955.

SIEVEKING, H. *Genueser Finanzwesen mit besonderer Berücksichtigung der Casa di San Giorgio.* Freiburg i.Br., 1898–9.

—— 'Die kapitalistische Entwicklung in den italienischen Städten des Mittelalters.' *VSWG.* VII (1909).

SILBERSCHMIDT, W. 'Die Bedeutung der Gilde, insbesondere der Handelsgilde für die Entstehung der italienischen Städtefreiheit.' *ZRGG.* LI. Weimar, 1931.

TAFEL, G. L. FR. and THOMAS, G. M. *Urkunden zur älteren Handels- und Staatsgeschichte der Republik Venedig mit besonderer Rücksicht auf Byzanz und die Levante vom 9. bis zum Ausgange des 15. Jahrhunderts, 814–1499.* Fontes Rerum Austriacarum, XII–XIV. Vienna, 1856–7.

VERGOTTINI, G. DE. *Arti e popolo nella prima metà del Secolo XIII.* Milan, 1943.

VITALE, V. 'Economia e commercio a Genova nei secoli XII e XIII.' *Rivista Storica Italiana*, IV (1937).

YVER, G. *Le commerce et les marchands dans l'Italie méridionale du XIIIe et du XIVe siècle.* Bibliothèque des Écoles Françaises d'Athènes et de Rome, LXXXVIII. Paris, 1903.

CHAPTER V

The Gilds

Since limitations of space preclude the complete bibliography of sources and studies bearing on urban economic development for which the subject logically calls, a selection has been made from editions of town and gild records and from secondary work that deals with gilds, on the basis of relevance to the problems raised in the article. Reference is made to special bibliographies already available. It is worth noting that some of the best work on gilds occurs in introductions to printed records.

I. GENERAL STUDIES OF GILD DEVELOPMENT

VON BELOW, G. 'Die Motive der Zunftbildung im deutschen Mittelalter.' *Historische Zeitschrift*, CIX (1912), 23–48.

BÜCHER, K. 'Mittelalterliche Handwerksverbände.' *Zeitschrift für die gesamte Staatswissenschaft*, LXXVII (1922).

COORNAERT, E. 'Des confréries Carolingiennes aux gildes marchandes.' *Mélanges d'histoire sociale*, II (1942).

DOREN, A. 'Der heutige Stand der Frage nach der Entstehung der Zünfte.' *Mitteilungen der deutschen Geschichte zur Erforschung vaterlicher Sprache und Altertümer in Leipzig*, X (5) (1912), 92–4.

EBERSTADT, R. *Der Ursprung des Zunftwesens.* 2nd ed. Leipzig, 1915.

JECHT, H. 'Die gesellschaftliche Struktur der mittelalterlichen Städte.' *Vierteljahrschrift für Sozial- und Wirtschaftsgeschichte*, XIX (1926), 48–85.

KELTER, E. 'Die Wirtschaftsgesinnung des mittelalterlichen Zunftlers.' *Schmollers Jahrbuch* (1932), 749–75.

KEUTGEN, F. *Aemter und Zünfte.* Jena, 1903.

LOPEZ, R. S. 'Continuità e adattamento nel medio evo: Un millennio di storia delle associazioni di monetieri nell'Europa meridionale', in *Studi in Onore di Gino Luzzatto*. Milan, 1950.

MICKWITZ, G. *Die Kartellfunktionen der Zünfte und ihre Bedeutung bei der Entstehung des Zunftwesens.* Societas scientiarum Fennica, Comm. hum. Litt. VIII (3). Helsinki, 1936.

THRUPP, S. L. 'Medieval Gilds Reconsidered.' *Journal of Economic History*, II (1942), 164–73.

II. ITALY AND SPAIN

Excellent bibliographies in *The Cambridge Economic History*, II, 526, 537–49, 559–60, and in A. Sapori, *Le Marchand Italien au Moyen Âge*, Paris, 1952, 24–34, 99–105.

1. *General and Regional*

BOFARULL Y DE SARTORIO, M. *Gremios y Cofradías*. Colección de documentos inéditos del archivo de la corona de Aragón, XL, XLI (1870, 1910).

CAVALLARI, V. ' "Guadiare se sub gastaldione", ricerche sulla trasformazione del ministerium curtense nell'arte medievale.' *Studi Storici Veronesi*, I (1947), 24–40.

CESSI, R. 'L'organizzazione di mestere e l'arte della lana del Polesine nel secole XIV e XV.' *Nuovo Archivio Veneto*, series 3, XIV (1908), 222–50.

DOREN, A. *Deutsche Handwerker und Handwerkerbruderschaften im mittelalterlichen Italien*. Berlin. 1903.

FONT RIUS, J. M. *Origenes del regimen municipal de Cataluña*. Madrid, 1946.

HARTMANN, L. M. 'Zur Geschichte der Zünfte im frühen Mittelalter.' *Zeitschrift für Sozial- und Wirtschaftsgeschichte*, III (1895).

KLEIN, J. 'Medieval Spanish Gilds', in *Facts and Factors in Economic History. Essays in Honor of E. F. Gay*. Cambridge (Mass.), 1932.

LEICHT, P. S. *Operai, Artigiani, Agricoltari in Italia del secolo VI al XVI*. Milan, 1946.

LÉVI-PROVENÇAL, E. 'La vie économique de l'Espagne musulmane au Xme siècle.' *Revue Historique*, CLXVII (1931).

LOPEZ, R. S. 'An Aristocracy of Money in the early Middle Ages.' *Speculum*, XXVIII (1953).

LUZZATTO, G. 'Piccoli e grandi mercanti nelle città italiane del Rinascimento', in *Saggi di storia e teoria economica in onore e ricordo di Giuseppe Prato*. Turin, 1931. Also in abridged translation in Lane and Riemersma (eds), *Enterprise and Secular Change*. Homewood, Illinois, 1953.

MANUCCI, F. L. 'Della società d'arti e mestieri durante il secolo XIII.' *Giornale storico e letterato della Ligiura*, VI (1905).

RUMEU DE ARMAS, ANTONIO. *Historia de la previsión social en España*. Madrid, 1944.

SÁNCHEZ-ALBORNOZ, C. *Ruina y extinción del municipio romano en España*. Buenos Aires, 1943.

VISCONTI, A. 'Il "collegium pistorum" nelle fonti giuridiche romane e medievali.' *Rendiconti dell'Istituto Lombardo*, ser. 2, LXIV (1931), 517–34.

2. *Sources and Studies Relating to Particular Towns*

Leges Muncipales. Historiae Patriae Monumenta, XVI. Turin, 1876.

Bologna

FRANCHINI, V. 'La funzione economica di talune arti nel secolo XIII in Bologna.' *Rivista internazionale delle scienze sociale*, ser. 3 (1) (1930).

GAUDENZI, A. *Statuti delle Societa del popolo di Bologna*. 2 vols. Rome, 1889, 1896.

Ferrara

SIMEONI, L. 'Il documento ferrarese del 1112 della fondazione dell'arti dei callegari.' *Rendiconti dell'Istituto di Bologna*, classe di scienza morali, ser. 3, VII (1932–3), 56–71.

Florence

Fonti sulle Corporazioni Medioevali (a cura di Storia Patria per la Toscana), continuing series.

GARGIOLLI, G. (ed.). *L'arte della seta in Firenze: trattato del secolo XV*. Florence, 1868.

Milan
PAGANI, G. 'Alcune notizie delle antiche corporazioni Milanesi d'arti e mestieri.' *Archivio Storico Lombardo*, ser. 2, IX (1892).

Modena
FRANCHINI, V. *Lo Statuto della corporazione dei fabbri del 1244.* Modena, 1914.

Parma
MICHELI, G. 'Le corporazioni parmensi d'arti e mestieri.' *Archivio storico per le provincie parmensi*, v. Parma, 1903.

Pavia
SORIGA, R. (ed.). 'Honorantiae civitatis Papiae.' *Bollettino della Società Pavese di storia patria*, XIV (1914).
VACCARI, P. 'Classi e movimenti di classi in Pavia nell'XI secolo.' *Ibid.* n.s. I (1946), 29–41.

Pisa
BONAINI, F. *Statuti inediti della città di Pisa del secolo XII al XIV.* 3 vols. Florence, 1854–7.

Pistoia
BERLAN, F. *Statuti di Pistoia del secolo XII.* Bologna, 1882.
ZDEKAUER, L. *Statutum potestatis communis Pistorii.* Milan, 1888.

Sarzana
'Statuti di Sarzan.' *Monumenta di Storia Patria delle provincie Modenesi*, IV (1893).

Siena
POLIDORI, F. L. *Statuti Senesi.* 3 vols. Bologna, 1863–77.

Venice
MONTICOLO, G. *I capitolari delle arti Veneziane.* (Istituto Storico Italiano.) 3 vols. Rome, 1896–1914.

Verona
CAMPAGNOLA, B. *Liber iuris civilis urbis.* Verona, 1728.

Vicenza
POZZA, F. 'Le corporazioni d'arti mestieri a Vicenza.' *Nuovo Archivio Veneto*, ser. 2, X (1895).

III. FRANCE AND THE LOW COUNTRIES

See *The Cambridge Economic History*, II, 531–6, 549–52.

1. General and Regional

D'ALANZIER, L. 'Statuts des merciers du Languedoc en 1395.' *Annales du Midi*, LXII (1950).
BOISSONADE, P. *Essai sur l'organisation du travail en Poitou.* 2 vols. Poitiers, 1900.
COORNAERT, E. *Les corporations en France avant 1789.* Paris, 1941.
CREPIN, H. *La liberté du travail dans l'ancienne France.* Vézelay, 1937.
EBERSTADT, R. *Das französische Gewerberecht und die Schaffung staatlicher Gesetzgebung und Verwaltung in Frankreich vom dreizehnten Jahrhundert bis 1581.* Leipzig, 1899.
ESPINAS, G. *Les origines de l'association.* 2 vols. Lille, 1941–2.
GOURON, A. *La réglementation des métiers en Languedoc au moyen âge.* Études d'histoire économique, politique et sociale, XXII. Paris–Geneva, 1958.

LEMPEREUR, L. 'Les chevaliers merciers du Rouergue.' *Mémoires de la société des lettres de l'Avrevron*, XXII (1928).

LESTOCQUOY, J. 'Le commerce des œuvres d'art au moyen âge.' *Mélanges d'histoire sociale*, III (1943).

SCHNEIDER, J. 'Note sur quelques documents concernant les cités lorraines au moyen âge.' *Revue Historique de la Lorraine*, LXXXVII (1950).

VAN WERVEKE, H. *De medezeggenschap von Knapen (gezellen) in de middeleawsche Ambachten*. Mededelingen van de Koniglijke Vlaamse Academie voor Wetenschappen, Letteren en Schone Kunsten van Belgie, Klasse der Letteren, V, no. 3. Brussels, 1943.

—— *Ambachten en Erfelijkeit*. Mededelingen van de Koniglijke Vlaamse Academie voor Wetenschappen, Letteren en Schone Kunsten van Belgie, Klasse der Letteren, IV, no. 1. Brussels, 1942.

—— 'Les corporations flamandes et l'origine des corporations de métiers.' *Revue du Nord*, XXXII (1950).

WYFFELS, C. *De vorsprong der ambachten in Vlaanderen en Brabant*. Mededelingen van de Koniglijke Vlaamse Academie voor Wetenschappen, Letteren en Schone Kunsten van Belgie, Klasse der Letteren, XIII, no. 13. Brussels, 1951.

2. Sources and Studies Relating to Particular Towns

Petitions and charters of gilds in many towns are contained in *Ordonnances des rois de France*, 21 vols. 1723–1849.

Amiens

MAUGIS, E. 'La saietterie à Amiens, 1480–1587.' *Vierteljahrschrift für Social- und Wirtschaftsgeschichte*, V (1907).

THIERRY, A. *Recueil des monuments inédits de l'histoire du tiers état*. Paris, 1850, 1853.

Arras

ESPINAS, G. 'La corporation des boulangers-pâtissiers d'Arras,' *Revue d'histoire économique et sociale*, XX (1932).

Ath

VERRIEST, L. *Les bouchers d'Ath et leur charte de confrérie (1437)*. Brussels, 1942.

Beauvais

LABANDE, L. *Histoire de Beauvais et de ses institutions communales jusqu'au commencement du XVme siècle*. Paris, 1892.

Bourges

BOYER, H. 'Histoires des corporations et confréries d'arts et métiers de la ville de Bourges.' *Mémoires de la société historique, scientifique et littéraire du Cher*, II. Bourges, 1933.

Brussels

BONEUFANT-FEYTMANS, A. 'La corporation des orfèvres de Bruxelles au moyen âge.' *Bulletin de la commission royale d'histoire belgique* (1950).

FAVRESSE, F. 'Les débuts de la nouvelle draperie bruxelloise appelée aussi draperie légère.' *Revue belge de philologie et d'histoire*, XXVIII (1950).

—— 'Comment on choisissait les Jurés de Métier à Bruxelles pendant le moyen âge.' *Revue belge de philologie et d'histoire*, XXXV (1957).

Chartres

ACLOQUE, G. *Les corporations d'industrie et le commerce à Chartres du XIe siècle à la révolution*. Paris, 1917.

Dijon
CHAPUIS, A. 'Les anciennes corporations Dijonnaises.' *Mémoires de la société bourguignonne de géographie et d'histoire*, XXII (1906).
LABAL, P. 'Le monde des métiers dans le cadre urbain 1430 à 1550.' *Annales de Bourgogne*, XXII (1950).
—— 'Artisans dijonnais d'autrefois, 1430–1560.' *Ibid.* XXIII (1951).

Dinant
BORMANS, S. (ed.). *Cartulaire de la Commune de Dinant*, III, IV. Namur, 1882; vol. VIII, ed. D. Brouwers, 1908.
PIRENNE, H. 'Les marchands-batteurs de Dinant au XIVe et au XVe siècle.' *Zeitschrift für Sozial- und Wirtschaftsgeschichte*, III (1904), reprinted in Pirenne, *Histoire économique de l'occident médiéval* (1951).
—— 'Notice sur l'industrie du laiton à Dinant.' *Ibid.* pp. 613–17.

Eu
DECK, S. *Une commune normande au moyen âge. La ville d'Eu. Son histoire, ses institutions (1151–1475)*. Paris, 1924.
LEGRIS, A. (ed.) *Le livre rouge d'Eu*. Rouen, 1911.

Evreux
GIFFORD, A. *Ordonnances de Jean d'Ableiges pour les métiers d'Evreux*. Caen, 1913.

Ghent
HUYTTENS, J. *Les corporations Gantoises*. Ghent, 1861.

Gisors
PASSY, L. *Le Livre des métiers de Gisors au XVIe siècle*. Pontoise, 1907.

Guines
ESPINAS, G. *Le droit économique et social d'une petite ville artésienne à la fin du moyen âge*. Vol. IV of *Les origines du capitalisme*. Lille, 1949.

Liège
BORMANS, S. *Le bon métier des tanneurs de l'ancienne cité de Liège*. Liège, 1863.
HANSOTTE, G. and MASSART, R. *Règlements et privileges des XXXIII métiers de la cité de Liège*. Liège, 1950.
LEJEUNE, J. *La formation du capitalisme moderne dans la principauté de Liège au XVIe siècle*. Liège, 1934.
—— *Liège et son pays: naissance d'une patrie*. Liège, 1948.
PONCELET, E. *Le bon métier des merciers de la cité de Liège*. Liège, 1908.
VAN SANTBERGEN, R. *Les bons métiers des meuniers*. Bibliothèque de philosophie et lettres de l'Université de Liège, fasc. CXV.

Lille
DESCAMPS, J. *Histoire de la corporation des orfèvres de Lille*. Lille, 1926.
DUBOIS, L. *Le régime de la brasserie à Lilles 1279–1789*. Lille, 1912.

Limoges
LYON, E. *La corporation des maîtres boulangers de la ville de Limoges*. Limoges, 1907.

Lyons
GUIGNE, C. 'Les pelletiers de Lyon.' *Bibliothèque historique du Lyonnais*, I (1886), 53–9.

Marseilles
PERNOUD, R. (ed.). *Les statuts municipaux de Marseille*. Monaco, 1949.
REYNAUD, J. *Les auffiers marseillais*. Marseilles, 1929.

Malines

CONINCK, H. 'Le livre des apprentis de la corporation des peintres et des sculpteurs de Malines.' *Bulletin du cercle archéologique, littéraire et artistique de Malines*, III (1903).

VAN DOORSLAER, G. 'L'ancienne industrie du cuivre à Malines.' *Ibid.* XX (1910).

JOOSEN, H. 'Documents relatifs à l'histoire de l'industrie drapière à Malines.' *Bulletin de la commission royale d'histoire*, XCVIII (1938).

Metz

SCHNEIDER, J. *La ville de Metz aux XIII et XIV siècles*. Nancy, 1950.

Montbéliard

NARDIN, L. and MAUVEAUX, J. *Histoire des corporations d'arts et métiers des ville et comté de Montbéliard*, I. Paris, 1910.

Mulhouse

COUTILLARD, R. *La corporation des bouchers à Mulhouse*. Strasbourg, 1937.

RISCH, P. *Histoire de la boucherie à Mulhouse du XIIIe siècle à nos jours*. Mulhouse, 1935.

Namur

BORMANS, S. (ed.). *Cartulaire de la commune de Namur*, III. Namur, 1876.

GOETSTOWERS, J. B. *Les métiers de Namur*. Louvain, 1908.

Narbonne

PORT, C. *Essai sur l'histoire du commerce maritime de Narbonne*. Paris, 1854.

Noyon

LEFRANC, A. *Histoire de la ville de Noyon et de ses institutions jusqu'à la fin du XIIIe siècle*. Paris, 1887.

Paris

COORNAERT, E. 'Notes sur les corporations parisiennes au temps de Saint Louis.' *Revue historique*, CLXXVII (1936).

GALLION, W. *Der Ursprung der Zünfte in Paris*. Berlin, 1910.

LESPINASSE, R. and BONNARDOT, F. (eds). *Le Livre des métiers d'Étienne Boileau*. Paris, 1879.

—— *Les métiers et corporations de la ville de Paris*. 3 vols. Paris, 1886–97.

MOREL, O. *La grande chancellerie royale et l'expédition des lettres royaux 1328–1400*. Paris, 1900.

DE VILLEFOSSE, R. H. 'La grande boucherie de Paris.' *Bulletin de la société de l'histoire de Paris et de l'Ile de France*, LV (1928), 39–73.

Poitiers

BOISSONADE, P. and AUDOUIN, E. *Recueil de documents concernant la commune et la ville de Poitiers*, I. Poitiers, 1923.

Rheims

DEMAISON, L. 'Documents sur les drapiers de Reims au moyen âge.' *Bibliothèque de l'École des Chartes*, LXXXIX (1928), 5–39.

VARIN, P. *Archives administratives de la ville de Reims*, I. Paris, 1839.

Rouen

GIRY, A. *Les établissements de Rouen*. Paris, 1883.

St Omer

GIRY, A. *Histoire de la ville de Saint-Omer et de ses institutions jusqu'au XIVe siècle*. Paris, 1877.

D'HERMANSART, P. 'Les anciennes communautés d'arts et métiers à Saint-Omer.' *Mémoires de la société des antiquaires de la Morinie*, XVI, XVII. St Omer, 1879, 1881.

Senlis
FLAMMERMONT, J. *Histoire des institutions municipales de Senlis.* Paris, 1887.

Sens
TURLAN, J. *La commune et le corps de ville de Sens (1146–1789).* Paris, 1942.

Strasbourg
HATT, J. *Une ville du XVe siècle, Strasbourg.* Strasbourg, 1929.
SCHMOLLER, G. *Die Strassburger Tucher- und Weberzunft. Urkunden und Darstellung.* Strasbourg, 1879.

Toul
SCHNEIDER, J. 'Note sur l'organisation des métiers à Toul au moyen âge', in *Mélanges d'histoire du moyen âge dédiés à la mémoire de Louis Helphen.* Paris, 1951.

Toulouse
ESPINAS, G. 'Métiers, associations et confréries: l'exemple des naypiers de Toulouse.' *Annales d'histoire sociale,* VIII (1945).
MULHOLLAND, M. A. (ed.). *Early Gild Records of Toulouse.* New York, 1941.
WOLFF, PH. 'Les bouchers de Toulouse du XIIe au XVe siècle.' *Annales du Midi,* LXV (1953).

Ypres
DES MAREZ, G. 'L'évolution corporative et le contrat d'apprentissage à Ypres, à la fin du XIIIe siècle.' *Bulletin de la société historique et philologique* (1905, 1906).
—— 'L'apprentissage à Ypres à la fin du XIIIe siècle.' *Revue du Nord,* II (1911).

IV. GERMANY, SWITZERLAND AND CENTRAL EUROPE

See *Cambridge Economic History,* II, 531–6, 552–4.

1. *General and Regional*

AMMANN, H. 'Die schweizerische Kleinstadt in der mittelalterlichen Wirtschaft', in *Festschrift für Walter Merz.* Aarau, 1928.
DIEHLING, F. *Zunftrecht: Eine Rechtsquellenstudie mit besonderer Berücksichtigung des Schneiderhandwerks.* Heidelberg, 1932.
GHIULEA, N. 'Les corporations de métiers en Roumanie.' *Revue d'histoire économique et sociale,* XII (1924).
EHEBERG, K. *Über das ältere deutsche Munzwesen und die Hausgenossenschaften, besonders in volkswirtschaftliche Beziehungen.* Leipzig, 1879.
KÖHNE, C. 'Studien über die Entstehung der Zwangs- und Bannrechte.' *Zeitschrift der Savigny-Stiftung für Rechtsgeschichte, Germanistische Abteilung,* XXVIII (1907).
LENTZE, H. *Der Kaiser und die Zunftverfassung.* Breslau, 1933.
MENDL, B. *Sbornik venovany Jaroslava Bidlovi.* Prague, 1928.
PABST, H. *Die ökonomische Landschaft am Mittelrhein vom Elsass bis zur Mosel im Mittelalter.* Marburg, 1930.
PETERKA, O. *Das Gewerberecht Bohmens in XIV. Jahrhundert.* Vienna, 1909.
POPELKA, F. 'Geschichte des Handwerks in Obersteiermark bis zum 1527.' *Vierteljahrschrift für Sozial- und Wirtschaftsgeschichte,* XIX (1926).
RÜTIMEYER, E. 'Stadtherr und Stadtburgerschaft in den rheinischen Bischofsstädten.' *Vierteljahrschrift für Sozial- und Wirtschaftsgeschichte,* Beiheft XIII (1928).
SCHMIEDER, E. *Geschichte des Arbeitsrechts im deutschen Mittelalter.* Leipzig, 1939.
SCHÜNEMANN, K. *Die Entstehung des Stadtwesens in Südosteuropa.* Breslau, 1929.
SEEGER, H. J. *Westfalens Handel und Gewerbe vom 9. bis zum Beginn des 14. Jahrhunderts.* Berlin, 1926.

2. Sources and Studies Relating to Particular Towns

Baden
AMMANN, H. *Die Stadt Baden in der mittelalterlichen Wirtschaft*. Aarau, 1952.

Brandenburg
JEROCH, F. W. *Die Innungsverfassung der Stadt Brandenburg vom 13. bis zum 18. Jahrhundert.* Brandenburg, 1927.

Brunswick
HAUSELMANN, L. *Urkundenbuch der Stadt Braunschweig*, I. Brunswick, 1863.
SCHULZE, A. *Die Kleinschmiedergilde zu Braunschweig*. Berlin, 1935.
STALMANN, M. *Beiträge zur Geschichte der Gewerbe in Braunschweig*. Wernigerode, 1907.

Bremen
HOYER, K. 'Das Bremer Brauereigewerbe.' *Hansische Geschichtsblätter*, XIX (1913).
THIKÖTTER, E. *Die Zünfte Bremens im Mittelalter*. Bremen, 1930.

Breslau
MENDL, W. 'Breslau zum Beginn des 15. Jahrhunderts.' *Zeitschrift des Vereins für Geschichte und Altertum Schlesiens*, VI (1929), 154–85.

Cologne
KOEBNER, R. *Die Anfänge des Gemeindewesens der Stadt Köln*. Bonn, 1922.
VON LOESCH, H. (ed.). *Die Kölner Zunfturkunden nebst anderen Kölner Gewerbeurkunden bis zum Jahre 1500*. 2 vols. Bonn, 1907.
SEELIGER, G. 'Zur Entwicklungsgeschichte der Stadt Köln.' *Westdeutsche Zeitschrift für Geschichte und Kunst* (1911).

Dortmund
LENZ, P. 'Die Entwicklung des Dortmunder Brauwesens.' *Beiträge zur Geschichte Dortmunds und der Grafschaft Mark*, XXXIII (1926).
OTTE, J. 'Untersuchungen über die Bevölkerung Dortmunds im 13. und 14. Jahrhunderts.' *Ibid.*
VON WINTERFELD, L. 'Die Dortmunder Wantschneidergesellschaft.' *Ibid.* XXIX (1922).

Eger
SIEGL, K. (ed.). *Die Egerer Zunftordnungen*. Prague, 1909.

Erfurt
NEUBAUER, TH. 'Wirtschaftsleben im mittelalterlichen Erfurt.' *Vierteljahrschrift für Sozial- und Wirtschaftsgeschichte*, Beiheft XII (1914).

Freiberg i. Sa.
SCHULZE, F. *Die Handwerkerorganisation in Freiberg i. Sa. bis zum Ende des 16. Jahrhunderts.* Freiberg i. Sa. 1920.

Freiburg
FLAMM, H. *Die wirtschaftliche Niedergang Freiburgs-im-Breisgau*. (Volkswirtschaftliche Abhandlungen der Badischen Hochschulen, Bd VIII, Ergänzungsband 3.) Karlsruhe, 1905.

Fulda
HOHMANN, J. *Das Zunftwesen der Stadt Fulda*. Fulda, 1909.

Goslar
BODE, G. (ed.). *Urkundenbuch der Stadt Goslar*. 4 vols. Halle, 1893 ff.

FRÖHLICH, K. 'Die Verfassungsentwicklung von Goslar im Mittelalter.' *Zeitschrift der Savigny-Stiftung für Rechtsgeschichte, Germanistische Abteilung*, XLVII (1927), 287–486.

Hamburg
FEHRING, M. *Das Amt der Tischler in Hamburg*. Hamburg, 1928.
WELTER, J. *Studien zur Geschichte des hamburgischen Zunftwesens im Mittelalter*. Berlin, 1896.

Hildesheim
DOEBNER, R. (ed.). *Urkundenbuch der Stadt Hildesheim*. 8 vols. Hildesheim, 1881–1901.
HARTMANN, M. 'Geschichte der Handwerkerverbände der Stadt Hildesheim im Mittelalter.' *Beiträge für die Geschichte Niedersachsens und Westfalens*, 1. Hildesheim, 1905.
TUCKERMANN, W. *Das Gewerbe der Stadt Hildesheim bis zur Mitte des 15. Jahrhunderts*. Tübingen, 1906.

Kotor
SINDIK, I. *Komunalus uredjeuje Kotora od druge polovine XII do pocetka stoleca*. Belgrade, 1950.

Lüneburg
BODEMANN, E. (ed.). *Die älteren Zunfturkunden der Stadt Lüneburg*. Hanover, 1883.

Lübeck
STIEDA, W. 'Studien zur Gewerbegeschichte Lübecks.' *Mitteilungen des Vereins für Lübeckische Geschichte und Altertumskunde*. 1887.

Memmingen
WESTERMANN, A. 'Zur Geschichte der Memminger Weberzunft und ihrer Erzeugnisse im 15. and 16. Jahrhundert.' *Vierteljahrschrift für Sozial- und Wirtschaftsgeschichte*, Beiheft XII (3–4) (1914), 385–403, 567–92.

Nuremberg
SCHÖNLANK, B. 'Zur Geschichte altnürnbergischen Gesellenwesens.' *Jahrbüchern für National-Oekonomie*, N.F., XIX (1889).

Riga
STIEDA, W. and METTIG, G. (eds). *Schragen der Gilden und Aemter der Stadt Riga bis 1621*. Riga, 1896.

Rostock
LEPS, C. 'Das Zunftswesen der Stadt Rostock bis um die Mitte des 15. Jahrhunderts.' *Hansische Geschichtsblätter*, LVIII–LIX (1933–4), 122–56, 177–242.

Schweidnitz
WEBNER, F. *Zunftkämpfe in Schweidnitz bis zum Ausgang des Mittelalters*. Breslau, 1907.

Siegen
BECK, I. L. *Geschichte der Nassauischen Eisenindustrien*. Marburg, 1937.

Speyer
WAGNER, G. *Munzwesen und Hausgenossen in Speyer*. Speyer, 1931.

Stettin
BLÜMCKE, O. 'Die Handwerkszünfte im Mittelalterlichen Stettin.' *Baltische Studien*, XXXIV (1884).

Ulm
NÜBLING, E. *Ulms Handel und Gewerbe im Mittelalter*. Ulm, 1900.

Vienna
EULENBERG, F. 'Die Wiener Zunftwesen.' *Zeitschrift für Sozial- und Wirtschaftsgeschichte*, I (1893).

Wismar
BRUGMANN, F. *Das Zunftwesen der Seestadt Wismar bis zum Beginn des 17. Jahrhunderts.* Rostock, 1935.
TESCHEN, F. 'Die Böttcher in den wendischen Städten, besonders in Wismar.' *Hansische Geschichtsblätter*, XXX (1925), 67–127.
—— *Geschichte der Seestadt Wismars.* Wismar, 1929.

V. BRITAIN, IRELAND AND SCANDINAVIA

See *Cambridge Economic History*, II, 531–6, 560–1.

1. *General and Regional*

BENDIXON, B. E. *De tyske Haandverkere paa norsk grund i meddelalderen.* Videaskabs-Selsabet Skrifter, II, Hist. philos. Kl., nr. 2. Christiania, 1912.
BUGGE, A. 'The Earliest Guilds of Northmen in England, Norway and Denmark', in *Sproglige og historiske Afhandlinger viede Sophus Bugges Minde.* Christiana, 1908.
—— 'Deutsche Handwerker im mittelalterlichen Norwegen.' *Vierteljahrschrift für Sozial- und Wirtschaftsgeschichte*, X (1912).
—— 'Altschwedische Gilden.' *Ibid.* XI (1913).
CUNNINGHAM, W. 'The Formation and Decay of Craft Gilds.' *Transactions of the Royal Historical Society*, n.s., III (1886), 371–92.
KNOOP, D. and JONES, G. P. *The Mediaeval Mason.* Manchester, 1933.
NYROP, C. *Danmarks Gilde og Lavsskraaer fra Middelderen*, I. Copenhagen, 1895.
SCHÜCK, A. *Studier rörande det svenska stadsväsen, dets uppkomst och äldsta utveckling.* Stockholm, 1926.
SMITH, T. and L. T. *English Gilds.* Early English Text Society, original series, XCL (1870).

2. *Sources and Studies Relating to Particular Towns*

Beverley
LEACH, A. F. *Beverley Town Documents.* Selden Society, 1900.

Bristol
BICKLEY, F. B. (ed.). *The Little Red Book of Bristol*, I. Bristol, 1900.
PERRY, R. 'The Gloucestershire Woollen Industry 1100–1696.' *Transactions of the Bristol and Gloucestershire Archaeological Society*, LXVI (1947).

Bury St Edmunds
LOBEL, M. D. *The Borough of Bury St Edmunds.* Oxford, 1934.

Coventry
GILL, C. *Studies in Midland History.* Oxford, 1930.
HARRIS, M. D. (ed.). *The Coventry Leet Book.* Early English Text Society, original series, XXXIV–XXXVI, CXXXVIII (1907–13).
—— *Life in an old English Town.* London, 1898.

Dublin
WEBB, J. J. *The Guilds of Dublin.* Dublin, 1929.

Helston
HENDERSON, C. 'The rules of a cobblers' gild at Helston in 1517', in Rowse and Henderson (eds). *Essays in Cornish History.* Oxford, 1935.

London
See bibliography in G. Unwin, *The Gilds and Companies of London,* revised edition. London, 1938.

BIRD, R. *The Turbulent London of Richard II.* Manchester, 1948.
JONES, P. E. *The Worshipful Company of Poulters.* Oxford, 1939.
KNOOP, D. and JONES, G. P. 'The London Masons' Company.' *Economic History,* III (1939).
SABINE, E. L. 'Butchering in Medieval London.' *Speculum,* VIII (1933).
THRUPP, S. L. *The Merchant Class of Medieval London.* Chicago, 1948.

Norwich
HUDSON, W. *Leet Jurisdiction in the City of Norwich.* Selden Society, V (1892).
HUDSON, W. and TINGEY, J. C. *The Records of the City of Norwich.* 2 vols. 1906–10.

Winchester
BIRD, W. H. B. *The Black Book of Winchester.* Winchester, 1925.
FURLEY, J. S. *The City Government of Winchester from the Records of the XIVth and XVth Centuries.* Oxford, 1923.

York
RAINE, A. (ed.). *York Civic Records,* II (1941). Yorkshire Archeological Society, CIII.
SELLERS, M. (ed.). *York Memorandum Book,* II. Surtees Society, 1915.

CHAPTER VI

The Economic Policies of Governments

II. FRANCE AND ENGLAND

The following abbreviations have been used:

AHES.	*Annales d'histoire économique et sociale*
AM.	*Annales du Midi*
BEC.	*Bibliothèque de l'École des Chartes*
BEHE.	Bibliothèque de l'École des Hautes Études
BIHR.	*Bulletin of the Institute of Historical Research*
Coll. des documents inédits	Collection des documents inédits relatifs à l'histoire de France
Coll. de textes	Collection de textes pour servir à l'étude et l'enseignement de l'histoire
EcHR.	*Economic History Review*
EHR.	*English Historical Review*
MA.	*Le Moyen Âge*
Rev. Belge	*Revue belge de philologie et d'histoire*
RH.	*Revue historique*
RHDF.	*Revue historique du droit français et étranger*
TRHS.	*Transactions of the Royal Historical Society*
VSWG.	*Vierteljahrschrift fur Sozial- und Wirtschaftsgeschichte*

The author wishes to acknowledge his indebtedness to Dr E. B. Fryde for much advice and assistance.

1. *Selected Printed Sources*

BALLARD, A. *British Borough Charters, 1042–1216.* Cambridge, 1913.
—— and TAIT, J. *British Borough Charters, 1216–1307.* Cambridge, 1923.
BEUGNOT, A. A. *Les Olim, ou registres des arrêts rendus par la cour du roi.* 4 vols. Coll. des documents inédits. Paris, 1839–48.

BIBLIOGRAPHIES 635

BORETIUS, A. and KRAUSE, V. *Capitularia Regum Francorum*. 2 vols. Monumenta Germaniae Historica: Leges. Hanover, 1883, 1897.
BOUTARIC, E. *Actes du parlement de Paris*. 2 vols. Paris, 1863, 1867.
Calendar of Close Rolls, 1272–1485. London, 1893 ff.
Calendar of Patent Rolls, 1232–1485. London, 1891 ff.
Calendar of State Papers (Venetian), I. London, 1864.
CARUS-WILSON, E. M. *The Overseas Trade of Bristol in the Later Middle Ages*. Bristol Record Society Pubns, VII. Bristol, 1937.
Close Rolls, 1227–72. London, 1902–38.
FAGNIEZ, G. *Documents relatifs à l'histoire de l'industrie et du commerce en France*. 2 vols. Coll. de textes, XXII and XXXI. Paris, 1898 and 1900.
FAWTIER, R. *Comptes du Trésor, 1296–1477*. Recueil des historiens de France: documents financiers, II. Paris, 1930.
GROSS, C. and HALL, H. *Select Cases concerning the Law Merchant*. 3 vols. Selden Society pubns, XXII, XLVI, XLIX. London, 1908–32.
HARDY, T. D. *Rotuli Litterarum Clausarum*. 2 vols. London, 1833, 1844.
—— *Rotuli Litterarum Patentium*. London, 1835.
HOHLBAUM, K., KUNZE, K. and STEIN, W. *Hansisches Urkundenbuch*. Verein für Hansische Geschichte. Halle and Leipzig, 1876–1907.
JACQUETON, G. *Documents relatifs à l'administration financière en France de Charles VII à François Ier (1443–1523)*. Coll. de textes. Paris, 1891.
KUNZE, K. *Hanseakten aus England, 1275 bis 1412*. Hansische Geschichtsquellen, VI. Verein für Hansische Geschichte. Halle, 1891.
LIEBERMANN, F. *Die Gesetze der Angelsachsen*. 3 vols. Halle, 1903–16.
LOT, F. and FAWTIER, R. *Le premier budget de la monarchie française: le compte général de 1202–3*. BEHE. fasc. CCLIX. Paris, 1932.
MASSELIN, J. *Journal des États Généraux de France tenus à Tours en 1484 sous le règne de Charles VIII*. Trans. Bernier, A. Coll. des documents inédits. Paris, 1835.
NICOLAS, N. H. *Proceedings and Ordinances of the Privy Council of England, 10 Richard II—33 Henry VIII*. 7 vols. London, 1834–7.
Ordonnances des rois de France de la troisième race, I–XIX. Paris, 1723 ff.
Patent Rolls, 1216–32. 2 vols. London, 1901, 1903.
Rotuli Parliamentorum. 6 vols. London, n.d.
RYMER, T. *Foedera, conventiones, literae . . . inter reges Angliae et alios quosvis imperatores, reges, pontifices et principes. . .* 7 vols. London, 1816–69.
Statutes of the Realm, I–II. London, 1810, 1816.
TEULET, A. etc. *Layettes du Trésor des Chartes*. 5 vols. Paris, 1863–1909.
WARNER, G. (ed.). *The Libelle of Englyshe Polycye*. Oxford, 1926.
WRIGHT, T. *Political Poems and Songs relating to English History from the Accession of Edward III to the Reign of Henry VIII*. 2 vols. Rolls Series. London, 1859, 1861.
VIARD, J. *Journaux du Trésor de Charles IV le Bel*. Coll. des documents inédits. Paris, 1917.
—— *Journaux du Trésor de Philippe IV le Bel*. Coll. des documents inédits. Paris, 1940.
—— *Journaux du Trésor de Philippe VI de Valois*. Coll. des documents inédits. Paris, 1889.

2. Secondary Authorities

(a) General Works

ASHLEY, W. J. *Surveys, Historical and Economic*. London, 1900.
—— *Introduction to English Economic History and Theory*. 2 vols. London, 1909.
BLOCH, M. *Esquisse d'une histoire monétaire de l'Europe*. Cahiers d'Annales, no. IX. Paris, 1954.
—— *Les caractères originaux de l'histoire rurale française*. Paris, 1931.
—— 'Les mutations monétaires et les dettes.' *AHES*. VI (1934).
—— 'L'or au moyen âge.' *AHES*. IV (1932).
BOISSONADE, G. *Life and Work in Medieval Europe*. Trans. Power, E. London, 1927.
BOURRILLY, V. L. and BUSQUET, R. *La Provence au moyen âge: histoire politique, l'église, les institutions (1112–1481)*. Marseilles, 1924.

BROOKE, G. C. *English Coins from the Seventh Century to the Present Day*. London, 1932.

Cambridge Economic History of Europe, I, ed. Clapham, J. H. and Power, E.; II, ed. Postan, M. M. and Rich, E. E. Cambridge, 1941, 1952.

CHÉNON, E. *Histoire générale du droit français public et privé des origines à 1815*. 2 vols. Paris, 1926–9.

CHOMEL, V. and EBERSOLT, J. *Cinq siècles de circulation internationale vue de Jougne: un péage jurassien du XIIIe au XVIIIe siècle*. Paris, 1951.

COORNAERT, E. *Les corporations en France avant 1789*. Paris, 1941.

—— 'Les ghildes médiévales.' *RH*. CXCIX, 1948.

CUNNINGHAM, W. *The Growth of English Industry and Commerce*, I. Cambridge, 1915.

DECLAREUIL, J. *Histoire générale du droit français des origines à 1789*. Paris, 1925.

DOGNON, P. *Les institutions politiques et administratives du pays de Languedoc du XIIIe siècle aux guerres de religion*. Toulouse, 1895.

EBERSTADT, R. *Das französische Gewerberecht und die Schaffung staatlicher Gesetzgebung und Verwaltung in Frankreich vom 13. Jahrhundert bis 1581*. Staats- und Sozialwissenschaftliche Forschungen, ed. Schmoller, G., XVII (2). Leipzig, 1899.

ESMEIN, A. *Cours élémentaire d'histoire du droit français*. Paris, 1895.

FAGNIEZ, G. *Études sur l'industrie et la classe industrielle à Paris au XIIIe et XIVe siècle*. BEHE. fasc. XXXIII. Paris, 1877.

FEAVERYEAR, A. E. *The Pound Sterling: a History of English Money*. London, 1932.

GAUTHIER, L. *Les Lombards dans les Deux-Bourgognes*. BEHE. fasc. CLVI. Paris, 1907.

GONNARD, R. *Histoire des doctrines monétaires dans ses rapports avec l'histoire des monnaies*. 2 vols. Paris, 1935.

GRAS, N. S. B. *The Early English Customs System*. Harvard Economic Studies, XVIII. Cambridge (Mass.), 1918.

—— *The Evolution of the English Corn Market*. Harvard Economic Studies, X. Cambridge (Mass.), 1926.

GROSS, C. *The Gild Merchant*. 2 vols. Oxford, 1890.

HEATON, H. *The Yorkshire Woollen and Worsted Industries*. Oxford Historical and Literary Studies, X. Oxford, 1920.

HECKSHER, E. F. *Mercantilism*. Trans. Shapiro, M. 2 vols. London, 1935.

HOLDSWORTH, W. S. *A History of English Law*, I–III. London, 1931–6.

HUISMAN, G. *La juridiction de la municipalité parisienne de S. Louis à Charles VII*. Bibliothèque d'histoire de Paris. Paris, 1912.

HUVELIN, P. *Essai historique sur le droit des marchés et des foires*. Paris, 1897.

LAURENT, H. *Un grand commerce d'exportation au moyen âge: la draperie des Pays-Bas en France et dans les pays mediterranéens (XIIe–XVe siècle)*. Paris, 1935.

LAVISSE, E. (ed.). *Histoire de France depuis les origines jusqu'à la Révolution*, I–IV. Paris, 1900–3.

LEVASSEUR, E. *Histoire du commerce de la France*, I. Paris, 1911.

LIPSON, E. *Economic History of England*, I. London, 1945.

LOGNON, A. *La formation de l'unité française*. Paris, 1922.

LOT, F. and FAWTIER, R. *Histoire des institutions françaises au moyen âge*, I–II. Paris, 1957–8.

MACPHERSON, D. *Annals of Commerce, Manufacture, Fisheries and Navigation*, I. London, 1805.

MATHOREZ, J. *Les étrangers en France sous l'ancien régime*. 2 vols. Paris, 1921.

MOYNE DE LA BORDERIE, A. LE. *Histoire de Bretagne*. 5 vols. Paris, 1896–1913.

NAUDE, W. *Die Getreidehandelspolitik der Europäischen Staaten vom 13. bis zum 18. Jahrhundert*. Acta Borussica. Berlin, 1896.

OLIVIER-MARTIN, F. *Histoire du droit français des origines à la Révolution*. Paris, 1950.

—— *L'organisation corporative de la France d'ancien régime*. Paris, 1938.

PIGEONNEAU, H. *Histoire du commerce de la France*, I. Paris, 1885.

PIRENNE, H. *Histoire de Belgique*, I–III. Brussels, 1909–12.

—— *Histoire économique de l'occident médiéval*. Bruges, 1951.

—— *Les villes et les institutions urbaines*. 2 vols. Paris, 1939.

POLLOCK, F. and MAITLAND, F. W. *The History of English Law*. 2 vols. Cambridge, 1923.

RAMSAY OF BAMFF, J. H. *A History of the Revenues of the Kings of England, 1066–1399.* 2 vols. Oxford, 1925.

Recueils de la Société Jean Bodin, v: *La Foire.* Brussels, 1953. vi: *La ville: institutions administratives et judiciares.* Brussels, 1954.

RUDDOCK, A. A. *Italian Merchants and Shipping in Southampton, 1270–1600.* Southampton Record Series. Southampton, 1951.

SAINT-LÉON, E. M. *Histoire des corporations de métiers depuis leurs origines jusqu'à leur suppression en 1791.* Paris, 1922.

SAPORI, A. *Le marchand italien au moyen âge.* Paris, 1952.

SCHANZ, G. *Englische Handelspolitik gegen Ende des Mittelalters.* 2 vols. Leipzig, 1881.

SÉE, H. *Histoire économique de la France: le moyen âge et l'ancien régime.* Paris, 1939.

STURLER, J. DE. *Les relations politiques et les échanges commerciaux entre le duché de Brabant et l'Angleterre au moyen âge.* Paris, 1936.

VIOLLET, P. *Histoire des institutions politiques et administratives de la France.* 3 vols. Paris, 1898.

VUITRY, A. *Études sur le régime financier de la France avant la Révolution de 1789.* 3 vols. Paris, 1878–83.

(b) The Early Middle Ages

BLOCH, M. 'Comment et pourquoi finit l'esclavage antique.' *Annales,* II (1947).

—— *La société féodale: la formation des liens de dépendance.* Paris, 1939.

—— *La société féodale: les classes et le gouvernement des hommes.* Paris, 1940.

BOLIN, S. 'Mohammed, Charlemagne and Ruric.' *Scandinavian Economic History Review,* I (1953).

BRÉHIER, L. 'Les colonies d'Orientaux en Occident au commencement du moyen âge.' *Byzantinische Zeitschrift,* XII (1903).

DENNETT, D. C. 'Pirenne and Muhammad.' *Speculum,* XXIII (1948).

DHONDT, J. *Études sur la naissance des principautés territoriales en France.* Rijksuniversiteit te Gent: Werken uitegeven door de Faculteit van de Wijsbegeerte en Letteren. Bruges, 1948.

DOEHAERD, R. 'Ce qu'on vendait et comment on le vendait dans le bassin parisien.' *Annales,* II (1947).

—— 'Les réformes monétaires carolingiennes.' *Annales,* VII (1952).

DOPSCH, A. *Die Wirtschaftsentwicklung der Karolingerzeit.* 2 vols. Weimar, 1912.

—— *The Economic and Social Foundations of European Civilization.* London, 1937.

DUPONT, A. *Les cités de la Narbonnaise Première depuis les invasions germaniques jusqu'à l'apparition du consulat.* Nîmes, 1942.

GANSHOF, F. L. *Feudalism.* Trans. Grierson, P. London, 1952.

—— 'Observations sur la localisation du Capitulare de Villis.' *MA.* LV (1949).

GRIERSON, P. 'Carolingian Europe and the Arabs: the Myth of the Mancus.' *Rev. Belge,* XXXII (1954).

HALPHEN, L. *Charlemagne et l'empire carolingien.* Paris, 1947.

—— *Études critiques sur l'histoire de Charlemagne.* Paris, 1921.

—— *Le comté d'Anjou au XIe siècle.* Paris, 1906.

HASKINS, C. H. *Norman Institutions.* Harvard Historical Studies, XXIV. Cambridge (Mass.), 1918.

HIMLY, F. J. 'Y a-t-il emprise musulmane sur l'économie des états européens du VIIIe au Xe siècle?' *Schweizerische Zeitschrift für Geschichte,* V (1955).

JONES, A. H. M. 'Inflation under the Roman Empire.' *EcHR.* ser. 2, V (1953).

KLEINCLAUSZ, A. *Charlemagne.* Paris, 1934.

LAURENT, H. 'Marchands du palais et marchands d'abbayes.' *RH.* CLXXXIII (1938).

LE GENTILHOMME, P. 'Notes de numismatique merovingienne.' *Revue numismatique* (1937, 1938).

LEVILLAIN, L. 'Essai sur les origines de Lendit.' *RH.* CLV (1927).

—— 'Études sur l'abbaye de S. Denis à l'époque merovingienne.' *BEC.* LXXXII (1921), LXXXVI (1925), LXXXVII (1926), XCI (1930).

—— 'Notes sur l'immunité merovingienne.' *RHDF.* (1927).

LEWIS, A. R. *Naval Power and Trade in the Mediterranean, A.D. 500–1100.* Princeton (N.J.), 1951.

LOMBARD, M. 'L'or musulman du VIIe au XIe siècle.' *Annales,* II (1947).

—— 'Mahomet et Charlemagne: le problème économique.' *Annales,* III (1948).

LOPEZ, R. S. 'Mohammed and Charlemagne: a Revision.' *Speculum,* XVIII (1943).

—— 'Relations Anglo-Byzantines du VIIe au Xe siècle.' *Byzantion,* XVIII (1948).

LOT, F. *Études sur le règne de Hugues Capet et la fin du Xe siècle.* BEHE. fasc. CXLVII. Paris, 1903.

——*La fin du monde antique et le début du moyen âge.* Paris, 1951.

—— *L'impôt foncier et la capitation personnelle sous le Bas-Empire et à l'époque franque.* BEHE. fasc. CCLIII. Paris, 1928.

MAITLAND, F. W. *Domesday Book and Beyond.* Cambridge, 1921.

NEWMAN, W. M. *Le domaine royal sous les premiers Capétiens (987–1180).* Paris, 1937.

PIGANIOL, A. *L'empire chrétien, 325–395. Histoire romaine,* ed. Glotz, G., IV. Paris, 1947.

PIRENNE, H. *Mahomet et Charlemagne.* Paris, 1937.

SABBE, E. 'Quelques types de marchands des IXe et Xe siècles.' *Rev. Belge,* XIII (1934).

—— 'Les relations économiques entre l'Angleterre et le continent au haut moyen âge.' *MA.* LVI (1950).

—— 'L'importation des tissus orientaux en Europe occidental au haut moyen âge.' *Rev. Belge,* XIV (1935).

STENTON, F. M. *Anglo-Saxon England.* Oxford, 1943.

TOUR, IMBART DE LA. 'Des immunités commerciales accordées aux églises du VIIe au IXe siècle.' *Études d'histoire du moyen âge dédiées à Gabriel Monod.* Paris, 1896.

VERCAUTEREN, F. *Études sur les civitates de la Belgique Seconde.* Mémoires de l'Académie Royale de Belgique. Brussels, 1934.

(c) The Twelfth and Thirteenth Centuries

BALLARD, A. *The Domesday Boroughs.* Cambridge, 1904.

BIGWOOD, G. 'La politique de la laine en France sous les règnes de Philippe le Bel et ses fils.' *Rev. Belge,* XV (1936) and XVI (1937).

—— 'Un marché de matières premières: laines d'Angleterre et marchands italiens vers la fin du XIIIe siècle.' *AHES* II (1930).

BLOCH, M. *Rois et serfs: un chapitre d'histoire capétienne.* Paris, 1920.

BORRELLI DE SERRES, L. L. *Recherches sur divers services publics du XIIIe au XVIIIe siècles.* 3 vols. Paris, 1895–1909.

BOUSSARD, J. *Le comté d'Anjou sous Henri Plantagenet et ses fils (1151–1204).* BEHE. fasc. CCLXXI. Paris, 1928.

BOUTARIC, E. *La France sous Philippe le Bel.* Paris, 1861.

BUGGE, A. 'The Norse Settlements in the British Islands.' *TRHS.* ser. 4, IV (1921).

CAROLUS-BARRÉ, L. 'Le gouvernement communal d'après le «Livre de Jostice et de Plet».' *RHDF.* 4th ser. XIX (1941).

COORNAERT, E. 'Notes sur les corporations parisiennes au temps de S. Louis d'après le Livre des Métiers d'Étienne Boileau.' *RH.* CLXXVII (1936).

CRUMP, C. G. and HUGHES, A. 'The English Currency under Edward I.' *Economic Journal,* V (1895).

DELISLE, L. 'Les revenus de la Normandie au XIIe siècle.' *BEC.* X (1848), XII (1849), XIV (1852).

—— *Mémoire sur les opérations financières des Templiers.* Paris, 1889.

DEPT, G. *Les influences anglaise et française dans le comté de Flandre au début du XIIIe siècle.* Ghent, 1928.

—— 'Les marchands flamands et le roi d'Angleterre, 1154–1215.' *Revue du Nord,* XII (1926).

DIEUDONNÉ, A. 'Les variations monétaires sous Philippe le Bel.' *MA.* IX (1905).

FAWTIER, R. *L'Europe occidentale de 1270 à 1328. Histoire du moyen âge,* ed. Glotz, G., VI (i). Paris, 1940.

FUNCK-BRENTANO, F. 'Document pour servir à l'histoire des relations de la France avec l'Angleterre et l'Allemagne sous le règne de Philippe le Bel.' *RH.* XXXIX (1889).

GRUNZWEIG, A. 'Les incidences internationales des mutations monétaires de Philippe le Bel.' *MA.* LIX (1953).

HOYT, R. S. 'Royal Demesne, Parliamentary Taxation and the Realm, 1294–1322.' *Speculum,* XXIII (1948).

—— 'Royal Taxation and the Growth of the Realm in Medieval England.' *Speculum,* XXV (1950).

—— *The Royal Demesne in English Constitutional History.* Ithaca (N.Y.), 1950.

LANGLOIS, C. V. *Le règne de Philippe III le Hardi.* Paris, 1887.

LESAGE, G. *Marseille angevine: recherches sur son évolution administrative, économique et urbaine . . . (1264–1348).* Bibliothèque des Écoles françaises d'Athènes et de Rome, fasc. CLXVIII. Paris, 1950.

LIMOUZIN-LAMOTHE, R. *La commune de Toulouse et les sources de son histoire, 1120–1249.* Toulouse, 1932.

LUCHAIRE, A. *Les communes françaises.* Paris, 1890.

—— *Manuel des institutions françaises: période des Capétiens directs.* Paris, 1892.

LUNT, W. E. 'Clerical tenths levied in England by papal authority during the reign of Edward II.' *Anniversary Essays in Medieval History by Students of C. H. Haskins,* ed. Taylor, C. H. Boston, 1929.

—— *Financial Relations of the Papacy with England to 1327.* Medieval Academy of America. Cambridge (Mass.), 1939.

MARSH, F. B. *The English Rule in Gascony 1199–1259, with special reference to the Towns.* Ann Arbor (Michigan), 1912.

MILLER, E. 'The State and Landed Interests in Thirteenth-Century France and England.' *TRHS.* ser. 5, II (1952).

MITCHELL, S. K. *Studies in Taxation under John and Henry III.* Yale Historical Publications, II. New Haven, 1914.

—— *Taxation in Medieval England.* Yale Historical Publications, XV. New Haven, 1951.

MOLINIER, A. 'La commune de Toulouse et Philippe III.' *BEC.* XLIII (1882).

MUNDY, J. H. *Liberty and Political Power in Toulouse, 1050–1230.* New York, 1954.

PACKARD, S. R. 'The Norman Communes under Richard I and John.' *Anniversary Essays in Medieval History by the Students of C. H. Haskins,* ed. Taylor, C. H. Boston, 1929.

PAINTER, S. *The Reign of King John.* Baltimore, 1949.

PETIT-DUTAILLIS, C. *Les communes françaises: caractères et évolution des origines au XVIIIe siècle.* Paris, 1947.

—— and GUINARD, P. *L'essor des états d'occident.* Histoire du moyen âge, ed. Glotz, G. IV (2). Paris, 1944.

PICQUET, J. *Les Templiers: étude sur leurs opérations financières.* Paris, 1939.

PLUCKNETT, T. F. T. *The Legislation of Edward I.* Oxford, 1949.

POOLE, R. L. *The Exchequer in the Twelfth Century.* Oxford, 1912.

PRESTWICH, J. O. 'War and finance in the Anglo-Norman state.' *TRHS.* ser. 5, IV (1954).

RICHARD, J. *Les ducs de Bourgogne et la formation du duché du XIe au XIVe siècle.* Publications de l'université de Dijon, fasc. XII. Paris, 1954.

ROON-BASSERMANN, E. VON. 'Die ersten Florentiner Handelsgesellschaften in England.' *VSWG.* XXXIX (1952).

SOUTHERN, R. W. *The Making of the Middle Ages.* London, 1953.

STEPHENSON, C. *Borough and Town: a Study of Urban Origins in England.* Medieval Academy of America. Cambridge (Mass.), 1933.

STRAYER, J. R. 'Economic conditions in the county of Beaumont-le-Roger, 1261–1313.' *Speculum,* XXVI (1951).

—— *The Administration of Normandy under St Louis.* Medieval Academy of America. Cambridge (Mass.), 1932.

—— *The Royal Domain in the Bailliage of Rouen.* Princeton, 1936.

—— and TAYLOR, C. H. *Studies in Early French Taxation.* Harvard Historical Monographs, XII. Cambridge (Mass.), 1939.

TAIT, J. *The Medieval English Borough.* Manchester, 1936.

TRABUT-CUSSAC, J. P. 'Bastides ou forteresses? Les bastides de l'Aquitaine anglaise.' *MA.* LX (1954).

TRABUT-CUSSAC, J. P. 'Les coutumes ou droits de douane perçus à Bordeaux sur les vins et les marchandises par l'administration anglaise, 1252–1307.' *AM.* LXII (1950).

WILLARD, J. F. *Parliamentary Taxes on Personal Property, 1290 to 1334.* Medieval Academy of America. Cambridge (Mass.), 1934.

(d) The Later Middle Ages

BARATIER, E. and REYNAUD, F. *Histoire du commerce de Marseille, 1294–1480.* Paris, 1951.

BEARDWOOD, A. 'Alien merchants and the English Crown in the later Fourteenth Century.' *EcHR.* II (1929–30).

—— *Alien Merchants in England: their Legal and Economic Position, 1350–1377.* Medieval Academy of America. Cambridge (Mass.), 1931.

BRIDBURY, A. R. *England and the Salt Trade in the Later Middle Ages.* Oxford, 1955.

BRIDGE, J. S. C. *A History of France from the Death of Louis XI*, I. Oxford, 1921.

BRIDREY, E. *La Théorie de la monnaie au XIVe siècle: Nicole Oresme.* Paris, 1906.

CALLERY, A. 'Les douanes avant Colbert et l'ordonnance de 1664.' *RH.* XVIII (1882).

CALMETTE, J. *L'élaboration du monde moderne.* Paris, n.d.

—— and PÉRINELLE, G. *Louis XI et l'Angleterre, 1461–1483.* Paris, 1930.

CARUS-WILSON, E. M. *Medieval Merchant Venturers.* London, 1954.

COLE, C. W. *French Mercantile Doctrines before Colbert.* New York, 1931.

COORNAERT, E. 'La politique économique de la France au début du règne de François Ier.' *Annales de l'université de Paris,* VIII (1933).

COVILLE, A. *Les états de Normandie: leurs origines et leur développement au XIVe siècle.* Paris, 1894.

—— 'Les finances des ducs de Bourgogne au commencement du XVe siècle.' *Études d'histoire du moyen âge dédiées à Gabriel Monod.* Paris, 1896.

DIEUDONNÉ, A. 'La monnaie royale depuis la réforme de Charles V jusqu'à la restauration monétaire par Charles VII.' *BEC.* LXXII (1911), LXXIII (1912).

DODU, G. 'Le roi de Bourges.' *RH.* CLIX (1928).

DOGNON, P. 'La taille en Languedoc de Charles VII à François Ier.' *AM.* III (1891).

DOUCET, R. 'Les finances anglaises en France à la fin de la guerre de cent ans, 1413–35.' *MA.* XXVII (1926).

—— *Les institutions de la France au XVIe siècle.* 2 vols. Paris, 1948.

DUPONT-FERRIER, G. *Études sur les institutions financières de la France à la fin du moyen âge.* 2 vols. Paris, 1930–2.

—— 'Histoire et signification du mot «aides» dans les institutions financières de la France, spécialement aux XIVe et XVe siècles.' *BEC.* LXXXIX (1928).

—— 'Les origines des elections financières en France aux XIVe et XVe siècles.' *BEC.* XC (1929).

—— *Les origines et le premier siècle de la Cour du Trésor.* BEHE. fasc. CCLXVI. Paris, 1936.

FEBVRE, L. 'Activité politique ou histoire économique à propos de Louis XI.' *Annales d'histoire sociale,* III (1941).

FLENLEY, R. 'London and Foreign Merchants in the reign of Henry VI.' *EHR.* XXV (1910).

FRYDE, E. B. 'Edward III's wool monopoly of 1337: a fourteenth-century royal trading venture.' *History,* n.s., XXXVII (1952).

—— 'Loans to the English Crown, 1328–31.' *EHR.* LXIX (1955).

—— 'Materials for the study of Edward III's credit operations, 1327–48.' *BIHR.* XXII (1949), XXIII (1950).

GANDILHON, R. *Politique économique de Louis XI.* Rennes, 1941.

GIRARD, A. 'La guerre monétaire (XIVe–XVe siècles).' *Annales d'histoire sociale,* II (1940).

GODARD, J. 'Contribution à l'étude de l'histoire du commerce des grains à Douai du XIVe au XVIIe siècle.' *Revue du Nord,* XXVII (1945).

HARSIN, P. *Les doctrines monétaires et financières en France du XVIe au XVIIIe siècle.* Paris, 1928.

HAUSER, H. *Les débuts du capitalisme.* Paris, 1931.

—— *Ouvriers du temps passé (XVe–XVIe siècles).* Paris, 1899.

—— *Travailleurs et marchands dans l'ancienne France.* Paris, 1920.

HUBRECHT, G. 'Les consequences juridiques des mutations monétaires dans la législation et la jurisprudence françaises des XIVe et XVe siècles.' *RHDF.* (1933).

JASSEMIN, H. 'La Chambre de Comptes et la gestion des deniers publics au XVe siècle.' *BEC.* XCIII (1932).

JENKINSON, H. and BROOME, D. M. 'An Exchequer statement of receipts and issues, 1339–40.' *EHR.* LVIII (1943).

JUSSELIN, M. 'Comment la France se préparait à la guerre de cent ans.' *BEC.* LXXIII (1912).

KERLING, N. J. M. *Commercial Relations of Holland and Zeeland with England from the late Thirteenth Century to the Close of the Middle Ages.* Leiden, 1954.

KIRBY, J. L. 'The financing of Calais under Henry V.' *BIHR.* XXIII (1950).

—— 'The issues of the Lancastrian Exchequer and Lord Cromwell's estimates of 1433.' *BIHR.* XXIV (1951).

KRAMER, S. *The English Craft Gilds and the Government.* Columbia University Studies in History, XXIII (4). New York, 1905.

LABANDE, E. R. 'L'administration du duc d'Anjou en Languedoc (1365–80).' *AM.* LXII (1950).

LARENAUDIE, M. J. 'Les famines en Languedoc au XIVe et XVe siècles.' *AM.* LXIV (1952).

LESAGE, G. 'La circulation monétaire en France dans la seconde moitié du XVe siècle.' *Annales,* III (1948).

MAÎTRE, L. 'Le budget du duché de Bretagne sous le règne de François II.' *Annales de Bretagne,* V (1889–90).

MIROT, L. *Les insurrections urbaines au début du règne de Charles VI (1380–1383).* Paris, 1905.

MOLLAT, M. *Le commerce maritime normand à la fin du moyen âge.* Paris, 1952.

MORANVILLÉ, H. 'Rapports à Philippe VI sur l'état de ses finances.' *BEC.* XLVIII (1887), LIII (1892).

NEWTON, A. P. 'The King's Chamber under the early Tudors.' *EHR.* XXXII (1917).

PERROY, E. 'À l'origine d'une économie contractée: les crises du XIVe siècle.' *Annales,* IV (1949).

—— 'La fiscalité royale en Beaujolais aux XIVe et XVe siècles.' *MA.* XXIX (1928).

—— *La guerre de cent ans.* Paris, 1945.

—— 'Wage Labour in France in the Later Middle Ages.' *EcHR.* (1955).

PICARDA, E. *Les marchands de l'eau: hanse parisienne et compagnie française.* BEHE. fasc. CXXXIV. Paris, 1901.

POCQUET DU HAUT-JUSSÉ, B. A. 'Dons du roi aux grands feudataires: les ducs de Bourgogne.' *RH.* CLXXXIII (1938).

—— 'Le compte de Pierre Gorremont, receveur-général du royaume (1418–20).' *BEC.* XCVIII (1937).

POSTAN, M. M. 'Some social consequences of the Hundred Years War.' *EcHR.* XII (1942).

POWER, E. *The Wool Trade in English Medieval History.* Oxford, 1941.

—— 'The wool trade in the reign of Edward IV.' *Cambridge Historical Journal,* II (1926).

—— and POSTAN, M. M. *Studies in English Trade in the Fifteenth Century.* London, 1933.

PUTNAM, B. H. *The Enforcement of the Statute of Labourers.* Columbia University Studies in History. New York, 1908.

QUINN, D. B. 'Edward IV and Exploration.' *The Mariner's Mirror,* XXI (1935).

RAMSAY of Bamff, J. H. *Lancaster and York: a Century of English History.* 2 vols. Oxford, 1892.

RONCIÈRE, C. DE LA. 'Première guerre entre le protectionnisme et le libre-échange.' *Revue des questions historiques,* LVIII (1895).

SCOFIELD, C. L. *The Life and Reign of Edward IV.* 2 vols. London, 1923.

SÉE, H. *Louis XI et les villes.* Paris, 1891.

SPONT, A. 'La gabelle du sel en Languedoc au XVe siècle.' *AM.* III (1891).

—— 'La taille en Languedoc de 1450 à 1515.' *AM.* II (1890).

—— 'L'équivalent en Languedoc de 1450 à 1515.' *AM.* III (1891).

STAMPE, E. *Das Zahlkraftrecht in den Königsgesetzen Frankreichs von 1306 bis 1547.* Berlin, 1930.

STEEL, A. B. *The Receipt of the Exchequer, 1377–1485.* Cambridge, 1954.

TOUT, T. F. and BROOME, D. M. 'A national balance-sheet for 1362–3.' *EHR.* XXXIX (1924).

UNWIN, G. *Finance and Trade under Edward III*. Manchester, 1918.

VIARD, J. 'La guerre de Flandre (1328).' *BEC*. LXXXIII (1922).

—— 'Les ressources extraordinaires de la royauté sous Philippe VI de Valois.' *Revue des questions historiques*, XLIV (1888).

VIVIER, R. 'La grande ordonnance de février 1351: Les mesures anticorporatives et la liberté de travail.' *RH*. CXXXVIII, 1921.

—— 'Une crise économique au milieu de XIVe siècle.' *Revue d'histoire économique et sociale*, VIII (1920).

WARD, G. F. 'The early history of the Merchants Staplers.' *EHR*. XXXIII (1918).

WOLFF, P. *Commerces et marchands de Toulouse (1350–1450)*. Paris, 1954.

ZELLER, G. *Les institutions de la France au XVIe siècle*. Paris, 1948.

—— 'Louis XI, la noblesse et la marchandise.' *Annales*, I (1946).

III. THE LOW COUNTRIES

DE ROOVER, R. *Money, Banking and Credit in mediaeval Bruges*. Cambridge (Mass.), 1948.

DE SAGHER, H. E. *Recueil de documents relatifs à l'histoire de l'industrie drapière en Flandre. Deuxième partie. Le Sud-Ouest de la Flandre depuis l'époque bourguignonne*, I. Brussels, 1951.

DHONDT, J. 'Développement urbain et initiative comtale en Flandre au XIe siècle.' *Revue du Nord*, XXX. Lille–Arras, 1948.

ESPINAS, G. and PIRENNE, H. *Recueil de documents relatifs à l'histoire de l'industrie drapière en Flandre. Première partie. Des origines à l'époque bourguignonne*. 4 vols. Brussels, 1906–23.

FOCKEMA ANDREAE, S. J. *Het hoogheemraadschap van Rijnland. Zijn recht en zijn bestuur van de vroegste tijd tot 1857*. Leyden, 1934.

GALBERT DE BRUGES, *Histoire du meurtre de Charles le Bon, comte de Flandre*, ed. Pirenne, H. Paris, 1891.

HAEPKE, R. *Brügges Entwicklung zum mittelalterlichen Weltmarkt*. Berlin, 1908.

LAURENT, H. *La loi de Gresham au moyen âge. Essai sur la circulation monétaire entre la Flandre et le Brabant à la fin du XIVe siècle*. Brussels, 1933.

MARÉCHAL, J. *Bijdrage tot de geschiedenis van het bankwezen te Brugge*. Bruges, 1955.

NIERMEYER, J. F. 'Dordrecht als handelsstad in de tweede helft van de veertiende eeuw.' *Bijdragen voor Vaderlandsche Geschiedenis en Oudheidkunde*, 8th ser., III–IV. The Hague, 1941–2.

—— *De wording van onze volkshuishouding*. The Hague, 1946.

PIRENNE, H. *Mediaeval Cities. Their Origins and the Revival of Trade*. Princeton, 1925.

—— *Les anciennes démocraties des Pays-Bas*. Paris, 1910. Reprinted in: PIRENNE, H. *Les villes et les institutions urbaines*, I. Paris–Brussels, 1939.

—— 'La Hanse flamande de Londres.' *Bulletin de l'Académie royale de Belgique*, 3rd ser., XXXVII. Classe des Lettres. Brussels, 1899. Reprinted in: PIRENNE, H. *Les villes et les institutions urbaines*, II. Paris–Brussels, 1939.

—— 'Les «overdraghes» et les «portes d'eau» en Flandre au XIIIe siècle, à propos d'une charte inédite provenant des archives de la ville d'Ypres.' *Essays in Medieval History presented to Thomas Frederick Tout*. Manchester, 1925. Reprinted in PIRENNE, H. *Histoire économique de l'Occident médiéval*. Bruges, 1951.

STEIN, W. 'Der Streit zwischen Köln und Flandern um die Rheinschiffahrt im 12. Jahrhundert.' *Hansische Geschichtsblätter*, XVII (1911).

VAN HOUTTE, J. A. 'Les foires dans la Belgique ancienne.' *Recueils de la société Jean Bodin*, V: *La Foire*. Brussels, 1953.

VAN WERVEKE, H. 'Currency Manipulation in the Middle Ages: the Case of Louis de Male, count of Flanders.' *Transactions of The Royal Historical Society*, 4th ser. XXXI. London, 1949.

—— ' "Hansa" in Vlaanderen en aangrenzende gebieden.' *Handelingen Société d'Émulation* XC. Bruges, 1953.

—— 'De economische politiek van Filips van de Elzas (1157–68 tot 1191).' *Mededelingen van de Koninklijke Vlaamse Academie voor Wetenschappen, Letteren en Schone Kunsten, Klasse der Letteren*, XIV (3). Brussels, 1952.

YANS, M. *Histoire économique du duché de Limbourg sous la Maison de Bourgogne. Les forêts et les mines.* Brussels, 1938.

IV. THE BALTIC COUNTRIES

ANDERSSON, INGVOR M. *Erik Menved och Venden.* Lund, 1954.

ARUP, E. *Danmarks Historie,* I–II. Copenhagen, 1925–32.

BOLIN, S. 'Hallandslistan i king Valdemars jordebok.' *Scandia,* II (1929).

—— *Ledung och frälse.* Lund, 1934.

—— *Skånelands historia,* II. Lund, 1932.

VON BRANDT, A. 'De äldsta urkunderna rörande tysk-svenska förbindelser.' *Svensk Historisk Tidskrift,* LXXIII (1953).

BRENNECKE, A. 'Die ordentlichen direkten Staats-Steuern Meklenburgs im Mittelalter.' *Jahrbücher des Vereins für meklenburgische Geschichte und Altertumskunde,* LXV (1900).

BUGGE, A. *Den norske sjöfarts historie,* I. Christiana, 1923.

CHRISTENSEN, AKSEL E. *Kongemagt og Aristokrati.* Copenhagen, 1945.

CHRISTENSEN, WILLIAM. *Unionskongerne og Hansestaederne 1439–1466.* Copenhagen, 1895.

DAENELL, E. *Die Blütezeit der deutschen Hanse,* I–II. Berlin, 1905–6.

DOVRING, F. *De stående skatterna på jord 1400–1600.* Lund, 1951.

ENGSTRÖM, STEN. *Bo Jonsson I.* Uppsala, 1935.

ERSLEV, KR. *Erik af Pommern.* Copenhagen, 1901.

—— *Valdemarernes Storhedstid.* Copenhagen, 1898.

TEN HAAF, R. *Deutschordensstaat und Deutschordensballeien.* Göttingen, 1951.

HAMMARSTRÖM, I. *Finansförvaltning och varuhandel 1504–1540.* Uppsala, 1956.

HASSELBERG, G. *Studier rörande Visby stadslag och dess källor.* Uppsala, 1953.

JOHNSEN, O. A. *Noregsveldets undergang.* Christiana, 1924.

KLEIN, A. *Die zentrale Finanzverwaltung im Deutschordensstaate Preussen am Anfang des XV. Jahrhunderts.* Staats- und Sozialwissenschaftliche Forschungen hrsgg. von G. Schmoller und M. Sering, XXIII (2). Leipzig, 1904.

KOSSMANN, E. O. *Die deutschrechtliche Siedlung in Polen.* Leipzig, 1937.

KRUMBHOLTZ, R. 'Die Finanzen des Deutschen Ordens unter dem Einfluss der Polnischen Politik des Hochmeisters Michael Küchmeister.' *Deutsche Zeitschr. für Geschichtswissenschaft hrsgg. von L. Quidde,* VIII (1892).

KUMLIEN, KJ. *Sverige och hanseaterna.* Kungl. Vitterhets-, Historie- och Antikvitetsakademiens Handlingar, LXXXVI. Stockholm, 1953.

LÖNNROTH, E. 'Slaget på Brunkeberg och dess förhistoria.' *Scandia,* XI (1938).

—— *Statsmakt och statsfinans i det medeltida Sverige.* Gothenburg, 1940.

MALOWIST, M. *Le commerce de la Baltique et le problème des luttes sociales en Pologne aux XVe et XVIe siècles.* La Pologne au Xe congrès international des sciences historiques à Rome. Warsaw, 1955.

MÜLLER, K. O. 'Das Finanzwesen der Deutschordensballei Elsass–Schwaben–Burgund im Jahre 1414.' *Historisches Jahrbuch hrsgg. im Auftrage der Görres-Gesellschaft,* XXXIV (1913).

NIITEMAA, V. *Das Strandrecht in Nordeuropa im Mittelalter.* Helsinki, 1955.

RENKEN, F. *Der Handel der Königsberger Grosschäfferei des deutschen Ordens mit Flandern um 1400.* Weimar, 1937.

REUTER, H. 'Die ordentliche Bede der Grafschaft Holstein.' *Zeitschr. der Gesellschaft für Schleswig-Holsteinische Geschichte,* XXXV (1905).

RÖRIG, F. 'Reichssymbolik auf Gotland.' *Hansische Geschichtsblätter,* Sonderdruck LXIV. Weimar, 1940.

—— *Vom Wesen und Werden der Hanse.* Leipzig, 1940.

ROSÉN, J. *Kronoavsöndringar under äldre medeltid.* Lund, 1949.

VON RUNDSTEDT, H. G. *Die Hanse und der Deutsche Orden in Preussen bis zur Schlacht bei Tannenberg.* Weimar, 1937.

SCHÄFER, D. *Die Hansestädte und König Waldemar von Dänemark.* Jena, 1879.

SCHREINER, J. *Hanseatene og Norges nedgang.* Oslo, 1935.

SEMKOWICZ, W. 'Methodisch-kritische Bemerkungen über Herkunft und Siede-lungsverhältnisse der polnischen Ritterschaft im Mittelalter.' *Bulletin intern. de l'Académie des Sciences de Cracovie*, Résumé 4 (1912).

STEINMANN, PAUL. 'Die Geschichte der mecklenburgischen Landessteuern und der Landesstände bis zu der Neuordnung des Jahres 1555.' *Jahrbücher des Vereins für mecklenburgische Geschichte und Altertumskunde*, LXXXVIII (1924).

STEINNES, A. *Gamal skatteskipnad i Noreg*, I–II. Oslo, 1930–3.

TECHEN, F. 'Über die Bede in Mecklenburg bis zum Jahre 1385.' *Jahrbücher des Vereins für mecklenburgische Geschichte und Altertumskunde*, LXVII (1902).

TYMIENIECKI, K. 'Processus créateurs dans la formation de la société polonaise au moyen âge.' *Bull. intern. de l'Académie polonaise des sciences et des lettres*. Résumé 37 (1919–20).

WEIBULL, C. *Sverige och dess nordiska grannmakter under den tidigare medeltiden*. Lund, 1921.

WEIBULL, L. 'S:t Knut i Österled.' *Scandia*, XVII (1946).

WOJCIECHOWSKI, Z. *L'état polonais au moyen âge. Histoire des institutions*. Paris, 1949.

YRWING, H. *Gotland under äldre medeltid*. Lund, 1940.

—— *Kungamordet i Finderup*. Lund, 1954.

V. THE ITALIAN AND IBERIAN PENINSULAS

ALTAMIRA, R. *Historia de España y de la civilización española*, I and II. Barcelona, 1913.

ARIAS, G. *Il sistema della costituzione economica e sociale italiana nell'età dei Communi*. Turin–Rome, 1905.

BALLESTREROS Y BERETTA, A. *Historia de España y sua influencia en la Historia universal*. Barcelona, 1922.

—— *Sevilla en el siglo XIII*. Madrid, 1913.

BARBADORO, B. *Le finanze della Repubblica fiorentina*. Florence, 1929.

BARBIERI, G. *Economia e politica nel Ducato di Milano (1386–1535)*. Milan, 1936.

BENIGNI, V. *Die Getreidepolitik der Päpste, 1420–1471*. Berlin, 1898.

BESTA, E. *Dell'indole degli Statuti locali del Dogado Veneziano e di quelli di Chioggia in particolare*. Turin, 1898.

BIANCHINI, L. *La storia delle finanze del Regno di Napoli*. 3 vols. Naples, 1834–5.

BISCARO, G. 'Gli estimi del comune di Milano nel secolo XIII.' *Archivio Storico Lombardo*, XIII (1928), 343.

BISTORT, G. *Il magistrato alle pompe nella Repubblica di Venezia*. Miscellanea di Storia Veneta, ser. 3, v. Venice, 1912.

BOGNETTI, G. 'Note per la storia del passaporto e del salvacondotto.' *Studi giuridici dell'Università di Pavia*, XVI–XVIII (1933).

BONARDI, A. 'Il lusso di altri tempi (Pistoia). Studio storico con documenti inediti.' *Miscellanea di Storia Veneta*, ser. 3, II (1909).

BRATIANU, A. *Recherches sur le commerce des Génois dans la Mer Noire au XIIIe siècle*. Paris, 1929.

BRUNETTI, M. 'Venezia durante la peste del 1348.' *Ateneo Veneto*, XXXII (1909).

CAGGESE, R. *Roberto d'Angiò e i suoi tempi*. Florence, 1922.

CANALETTI GAUDENTI, A. *La politica agraria ed annonaria dello Stato Pontificio da Benedetto XIV a Pio VII*. Rome, 1947.

CANTINI, L. *Legislazione toscana 1532–1775*. 32 vols. Florence, 1800–8.

CARANDE, R. 'Sevilla, fortaleza y mercado.' *Anuario de Historia del Derecho Español*, II. Madrid, 1925.

CEDILLO, CONDE DE. *Contribuciones y impuestas en León y Castilla durante la Edad Media*. Madrid, 1896.

CESSI, R. *Politica ed economia di Venezia nel Trecento*. Rome, 1952.

CIAMPI, S. *Statuti suntuari ricordati da G. Villani circa il vestiario delle donne, dei regali e i banchetti . . . ordinati dal Comune di Pistoia negli anni 1332–1333*. Pisa, 1815.

CIBRARIO, L. *Della economia politica del Medio Evo*. Turin, 1842.

CIPOLLA, C. M. 'Ripartizione delle colture nel Pavese secondo le "misure territoriali" della metà del Cinquecento'. *Studi di Economia e Statistica dell'Università di Catanài*. Catania, 1950–1.

CIPOLLA, C. M. 'L'economia Milanese, 1350–1500', in *Storia di Milano* (Fond. Trecconi), VII. Milan, 1955.

COGNETTI DE MARTIIS, S. 'I due sistemi della politica commerciale veneziana.' *Biblioteca dell'Economista*, ser. 4, I. Turin, 1900.

COLMEIRO, M. *Historia de la Economía política en España*. Madrid, 1863.

CUSUMANO, V. *La teoria del commercio dei grani in Italia*. Bologna, 1877.

DALLARI, U. 'Lo statuto suntuario di Bologna del 1401 e il registro delle vesti bollate.' *Atti e Memorie della R. Deputazione di Storia Patria per le Province della Romagna*, ser. 3, VII (1889).

DAL PANE, L. 'La politica annonaria di Venezia.' *Giornale degli Economisti ed Annali di Economia*, n.s., V (1–2) (1943–6), 331–3.

DAMIANI, A. 'La giurisdizione dei consoli del Collegio dei Mercanti di Pavia.' *Bollettino Soc. Pavese di Storia Patria*, II. Pavia, 1902.

DE CAPMANY Y DE MONTPALAU, A. *Memorias históricas sobra la marina, comercio y artes de la antigua ciudad de Barcelona*. 4 vols. Madrid, 1779–92.

DE HINOJOSA, E. *Estudios sobre la historia del derecho español*. Madrid, 1903.

DEL GIUDICE, G. 'Una legge suntuaria inedita del 1290.' *Atti della Accademia Pontoniana*, XVI. Naples, 1886.

DONNA, G. 'I Borghifranchi nella politica della repubblica vercellese.' *Annali dell'Accademia di Agricoltura di Torino*, LXXXVI (Turin, 1942–3), 89–152.

DOPSCH, A. *Naturalwirtschaft und Geldwirtschaft in der Weltgeschichte*. Vienna, 1930.

DOREN, A. *Storia economica dell'Italia nel Medio Evo*. Padua, 1937.

—— *Le arti fiorentine*. Florence, 1940.

FABRETTI, A. 'Statuti ed ordinamenti suntuari intorno al vestire degli uomini e delle donne in Perugia dall'anno 1266 al 1536, raccolti e annotati da. . .' *Memorie della R. Accademia delle Scienze di Torino*, ser. 2, XXXVIII (1888).

FABRONI, G. *Dei provvedimenti annonari*. Florence, 1804.

FANFANI, A. 'Aspetti demografici della politica economica nel Ducato di Milano.' *Saggi di Storia Economica Italiana*. Milan, 1936.

FANFANI, P. *La legge suntuaria fatta dal Comune di Firenze l'anno 1355 e volgarizzata nel 1356 da Ser Andrea Lancia, stampata ora per la prima volta per cura di . . . con note e dichiarazioni*. Florence, 1851.

FANO, N. 'Ricerche sull'arte della lana a Venezia nel XIII e XIV secolo.' *Archivio Veneto*, ser. 5, XVIII (1936).

FIUMI, E. 'Fioritura e decadenza dell'economia fiorentina: politica economica e classi sociali.' *Archivio Storico Italiano*, CXVII (1959).

GADDI, L. *Per la storia della legislazione e delle istituzioni mercantili lombarde*. Milan, 1893.

GARUFI, C. A. 'La giurisdizione annonaria municipale nei secoli XIII e XIV.' *Archivio Storico Siciliano*, XXII (1897).

GENNARDI, L. *Terre communi e usi civici in Sicilia*. Documenti per servire alla storia della Sicilia. Palermo, 1911.

GLENISSON, J. 'Une administration médiévale aux prises avec la disette.' *Le Moyen Âge*, ser. A, VI. Paris, 1951.

INVERNIZZI, C. 'Gli Ebrei a Pavia.' *Bollett. Soc. Pavese di Storia Patria*, V. Pavia, 1905.

KLEIN, J. *The Mesta: a Study in Spanish Economic History*. Cambridge (Mass.), 1920.

LANDRY, A. *Essai économique sur les imitations des monnaies dans l'ancienne France de Philippe le Bel et Charles VII*. Paris, 1910.

LEICHT, P. S. *Corporazioni romane e arti medievali*. Turin, 1937.

LOISEL, S. *Essai sur la législation économique des Carolingiens*. Caen, 1904.

LOPEZ, R. S. 'Du marché temporaire à la colonie permanente. L'évolution de la politique commerciale au Moyen Âge.' *Annales (Économies, Sociétés, Civilisations)*, IV (4) (1949), 389–405.

LUCAS, H. S. 'The great European famine of 1315–16–17.' *Speculum*, October 1930.

LUZZATTO, G. *Storia economica—l'Età Moderna*. Padua, 1938.

—— *I prestiti della Repubblica di Venezia*. Vol. I, ser. III: 'Documenti finanziari della Repubblica di Venezia.' Padua, 1929.

—— *Studi di storia economica veneziana*. Padua, 1954.

LUZZATTO, G. 'Sindacati e cartelli nel commercio veneziano dei secoli XIII e XIV' in *Studi di storia economica veneziana* (Padua, 1954), 195–200.

MARCHETTI, A. 'Su l'obbligo della lavorazione del suolo nei comuni medievali marchigiani.' *Archivio Vittorio Scialoja per le consuetudini giuridiche agrarie e le tradiz. popolari italiane*, II, fasc. 1 (Florence, 1935), 18–41.

MAYER, E. *Historia de las instituciones sociales y políticas de España y Portugal durante los siglos V al XIV*. Madrid, 1925.

MERRIMAN, R. B. *The rise of the Spanish empire*. New York, 1918.

MICKWITZ, G. *Die Kartellfunktionen der Zünfte und ihre Bedeutung bei der Entstehung des Zunftwesens*. Helsinki, 1936.

MONTICOLO, G. Preface to *I Capitolari delle arti veneziane*, 1. Fonti per la Storia d'Italia. Rome, 1896.

MOTTA, E. *Ebrei a Como e in altre città del Ducato di Milano*. Como, 1885.

NAUDE, W. *Die Getreidehandelspolitik und Kriegsmagazinverwaltung Branderburg–Preussens bis 1740*. Acta Borussica, Berlin, 1901.

NEWETT, M. 'The Sumptuary Law of Venice in the 14th and 15th Centuries.' *Historical Essays by Members of Owens College, Manchester*, edited by T. F. Tout and J. Tait. London, 1902.

PAVESI, A. *Memorie per servire alla storia del commercio dello Stato di Milano*. Como, 1778.

PEYER, H. C. *Zur Getreidehandelspolitik oberitalienischer Städte im 13. Jahrhundert*. Veröffentlichungen des Instituts für Österreichische Geschichtsforschung. Vienna, 1950.

PIERRO, M. 'Le leggi suntuarie e la politica demografica nel Medioevo.' *Politica Sociale* (Jan./Feb. 1930).

POEHLMANN, E. *Die Wirtschaftspolitik der florentiner Renaissance*. Leipzig, 1868.

POGGI, E. *Cenni storici delle leggi dell'agricoltura*. Florence, 1848.

RODOLICO, N. *La democrazia fiorentina nel suo tramonto*. Bologna, 1905.

ROMANO, G. 'A proposito di un passo di Agnello Ravennate.' *Bollettino Soc. Pavese di Storia Patria*, X. Pavia, 1910.

ROSCHER, W. *Über Kornhandel und Theurungspolitik*. 3rd ed. Stuttgart–Tübingen, 1852.

ROSSI, B. 'La politica agraria dei comuni dominanti negli Statuti della Bassa Lombardia.' *Scritti giuridici in memoria di A. Arcangeli*, II (Padua, 1939), 403–36.

SAGREDO, A. 'Sulle consorterie delle arti edificatorie in Venezia.' *Archivio Storico Italiano*, ser. 2, VI (1857).

SÁNCHEZ ALBORNOZ, C. 'La primitiva organización monetaria de León y Castilla.' *Anuario de historia del derecho español*, V (1928).

SAPORI, A. 'L'usura nel Duecento a Pistoia' in *Studi di storia economica*, 3rd ed. 2 vols. 1955.
—— 'I mutui dei mercanti fiorentini del Trecento e l'incremento della proprietà fondiaria' in *ibid*.
—— 'L'interesse del danaro a Firenze nel Trecento' in *ibid*.
—— *Le marchand italien au Moyen Age*. Paris, 1952.

SCHAUBE, A. 'Die Anfänge der venetianischen Galerenfahrten nach der Nordsee.' *Hist. Zeitschrift*, ser. 3, V (1908), 28–89.

SIEVEKING, H. *Studio sulle finanze genovesi nel Medioevo e in particolare sulla case di S. Giorgio*. Atti Soc. Ligure St. Patria, XXXV, part I (Genoa, 1905), part II (Genoa, 1906).

SILVA, P. *Intorno all'industria e al commercio della lana in Pisa*. Studi Storici, XIX. Pisa, 1911.

SIMEONI, L. *Gli antichi statuti delle arti veronesi a cura di . . .* Venice, 1914.

SMITH, R. S. *The Spanish Guild Merchant*. Durham, N. Carolina, 1940.

SORIGA, R. 'Il memoriale dei Consoli del Comune di Pavia.' *Bollettino Soc. Pavese di Storia Patria*, XIII. Pavia, 1913.

TRAMOYERES BLASCO, L. *Instituciones gremiales: su origen y organización en Valencia*. Valencia, 1889.

UNA Y SARTHOU, J. *Las asociaciones obreras en España*. Madrid, 1900.

VENTALLO VINTRO, J. *Historia de la industria lanera catalana: monografía de sus antiguos gremios*. Tarrasa, 1904.

VERGA, E. 'Le leggi suntuarie milanesi: Gli statuti dal 1396 al 1498.' *Archivio Storico Lombardo*, ser. 3, IX (1898).

VERLINDEN, C. 'La grande peste de 1348 en Espagne.' *Revue belge de philologie et d'histoire*, XVIII. Brussels, 1938.

YVER, G. *Le commerce et les marchands dans l'Italie méridionale au XIII et au XIV siècle*. Bibliothèque des Écoles françaises d'Athènes et de Rome publiée sous les auspices du Ministère de l'instruction publique, fasc. 88. Paris, 1903.

ZANELLI, A. 'Di alcune leggi suntuarie pistoiesi dal XIV al XVI secolo.' *Archivio Storico Italiano*, ser. 5, XVI (1895).

CHAPTER VII

Public Credit, with Special Reference to North-Western Europe

An attempt has been made to give a comprehensive bibliography of works specially concerned with public credit in northern Europe or with particular lenders. Printed sources and works on general history, public finance and on businessmen are listed in the bibliography only if they have been used extensively. Unpublished sources and works containing only incidental references to credit transactions are mentioned in the footnotes to the main text. Notes have been also added on matters of special importance or interest.

The following abbreviations have been used:

AHES.	*Annales d'Histoire Économique et Sociale*, later, *Annales d'Histoire Sociale, Mélanges d'Histoire Sociale* and *Annales (Économies, Sociétés, Civilisations)*
AHR.	*American Historical Review*
BECh.	*Bibliothèque de l'École des Chartes*
BCRH.	*Bulletin de la Commission Royale d'Histoire*
BIHR.	*Bulletin of the Institute of Historical Research*
EcHR.	*Economic History Review*
EHR.	*English Historical Review*
JNOS.	*Conrads Jahrbücher für Nationalökonomie und Statistik*
P.R.O.	Public Record Office (London)
RBPH.	*Revue Belge de Philologie et d'Histoire*
RH.	*Revue Historique*
RHDr.	*Revue Historique de Droit Français et Étranger*
TRHS.	*Transactions of the Royal Historical Society*
VSWG.	*Vierteljahrschrift für Sozial- und Wirtschaftsgeschichte*

I. GENERAL

(a) General Works on Credit

BIGWOOD, G. *Le régime juridique et économique du commerce de l'argent dans la Belgique du moyen âge.* 2 vols. Brussels, 1921-2.

EHRENBERG, R. *Das Zeitalter der Fugger. Geldkapital und Kreditverkehr im 16. Jahrhundert.* 2 vols. 3rd ed. Jena, 1922.

KUSKE, B. 'Die Entstehung der Kreditwirtschaft und des Kapitalverkehrs.' *Kölner Vorträge hersg. von der Wirtschafts- und Sozialwissenschaftlichen Fakultät der Universität Köln*, I (1927) (reprinted in B. Kuske, *Köln, der Rhein und das Reich*. Cologne, 1956).

LANDMANN, J. 'Zur Entwicklungsgeschichte der Formen und der Organisation des öffentlichen Kredites.' *Finanzarchiv*, XXIX (1912).

—— 'Geschichte des öffentliches Kredites.' *Handbuch der Finanzwissenschaft* (ed. W. Gerloff and F. Neumark), III. 2nd ed. Tübingen, 1958.

LOTZ, W. *Finanzwissenschaft*. 2nd ed. Berlin, 1931.

MAYER, T. H. 'Geschichte der Finanzwirtschaft vom Mittelalter bis zum Ende des 18. Jahrhunderts.' *Handbuch der Finanzwissenschaft*, 2nd ed. (ed. Gerloff–Neumark), 1. Tubingen, 1952.

POSTAN, M. M. 'The Financing of Trade in the Later Middle Ages.' M.Sc. Thesis, University of London, 1926.

—— 'Credit in medieval trade.' *EcHR*. I (1928).

SAPORI, A. *Studi di storia economica*. 2 vols. 3rd ed. Florence, 1956.

(*b*) *General Works on the Economic and Institutional Background*

BAUTIER, R. H. 'Les foires de Champagne. Recherches sur une évolution historique.' *Recueils de la Société Jean Bodin*, V: *La Foire*. Brussels, 1953.

BLOCH, M. *Esquisse d'une histoire monétaire de l'Europe*. Paris, 1954.

BOURQUELOT, F. 'Études sur les foires de Champagne et de Brie . . . aux XIIe, XIIIe et XIVe siècles.' *Mémoires présentés par divers savants à l'Académie des Inscriptions et Belles-Lettres*, 2nd ser. V. 2 vols. Paris, 1865.

ENDEMANN, W. *Studien in der romanisch-kanonistischen Wirtschafts- und Rechtslehre bis gegen Ende des siebzehnten Jahrhunderts*. 2 vols. Berlin, 1874–83.

GIRARD, A. 'Un phénomène économique: la guerre monétaire (XIVe–XVe siècles).' *Annales d'Histoire Sociale*, II (1940).

LAURENT, H. *Un grand commerce d'exportation au moyen-âge. La draperie des Pays Bas en France et dans les pays méditerranéens (XIIe–XVe siècle)*. Paris, 1935.

McLAUGHLIN, T. P. 'The teaching of the canonists on usury (XII, XIII and XIV centuries).' *Mediaeval Studies*, I–II (1939–40).

NELSON, B. N. *The idea of usury. From tribal brotherhood to universal otherhood*. Princeton, 1949.

PIRENNE, H. *Histoire économique de l'occident médiéval*. Bruges, 1951.

REYNOLDS, R. L. 'Origins of modern business enterprise. Medieval Italy.' *Journal of Economic History*, XII (1952).

SCHAUBE, A. *Handelsgeschichte der romanischen Völker des Mittelmeergebiets biz zum Ende der Kreuzzüge*. Munich and Berlin, 1906.

SCHNEIDER, F. 'Das kirchliche Zinsverbot und die kuriale Praxis im 13. Jahrhundert.' *Festgabe für Heinrich Finke*. Münster, 1904.

SCHULTE, A. *Geschichte des mittelalterlichen Handels und Verkehrs zwischen Westdeutschland und Italien mit Ausschluss von Venedig*. 2 vols. Leipzig, 1900.

SCZANIECKI, M. *Essai sur les fiefs-rentes*. Paris, 1946.

(*c*) *The influence of the Papacy on Credit* (*main general works*)

BAUER, C. 'Die Epochen der Papstfinanz.' *Historische Zeitschrift*, CXXXVIII (1929).

GOTTLOB, A. *Die päpstlichen Kreuzzugs-Steuern des 13. Jahrhunderts*. Heiligenstadt, 1892.

—— 'Päpstliche Darlehnsschulden des 13. Jahrhunderts.' *Historisches Jahrbuch*, XX (1899).

—— 'Kuriale Prälatenanleihen im 13. Jahrhundert.' *VSWG*. I (1903).

—— *Die Servitientaxe im 13. Jahrhundert. Eine Studie zur Geschichte des päpstlichen Gebührenwesens*. Stuttgart, 1903.

JORDAN, E. *De mercatoribus camerae apostolicae saeculo XIII*. Rennes, 1909.

KIRSCH, J. P. *Die päpstlichen Kollektorien in Deutschland während des XIV. Jahrhunderts*. Quellen und Forschungen hersg. von der Görres-Gesellschaft, IV. Paderborn, 1894.

LUNT, W. E. *Papal revenues in the middle ages*. 2 vols. New York, 1934.

—— *Financial relations of the Papacy with England to 1327*. Cambridge (Mass.), 1939.

RENOUARD, Y. *Les relations des papes d'Avignon et des compagnies commerciales et bancaires de 1316 à 1378*. Paris, 1941.

SAMARAN, CH. and MOLLAT, G. *La fiscalité pontificale en France au XIVe siècle*. Paris, 1905.

(d) Particular Groups of Lenders

ARIAS, G. *Studi e documenti di storia del diritto.* Florence, 1901. (The Bonsignori of Siena.)

CARO, G. *Sozial- und Wirtschaftsgeschichte der Juden im Mittelalter und in der Neuzeit.* 2 vols. Frankfurt, 1920–4.

CHIAUDANO, M. 'I Rothschild del Dugento: la Gran Tavola di Orlando Bonsignori.' *Bull. Senese di Storia Patria,* n.s. VI (1935).

DAVIDSOHN, R. *Forschungen zur Geschichte von Florenz.* 4 vols. Berlin, 1896–1908.

DELISLE, L. 'Mémoire sur les opérations financières des Templiers.' *Mémoires de l'Institut National de France, Académie des Inscriptions et Belles-Lettres,* XXXIII (1889).

DENHOLM-YOUNG, N. 'The merchants of Cahors.' *Medievalia et Humanistica,* IV (1946).

FLINIAUX, A. 'La faillite des Ammannati de Pistoia et le Saint-Siège.' *RHDr.* 4th ser. III (1924).

JORDAN, E. 'La faillite des Bonsignori.' *Mélanges Paul Fabre: Études d'histoire du moyen âge.* Paris, 1902.

PIQUET, J. *Des banquiers au moyen âge. Les Templiers. Étude de leurs opérations financières.* Paris, 1939.

PITON, C. *Les Lombards en France et à Paris.* 2 vols. Paris, 1892–3 (an outdated work).

PRUTZ, H. *Die geistlichen Ritterorden. Ihre Stellung zur kirchlichen, politischen, gesellschaftlichen und wirtschaftlichen Entwicklung des Mittelalters.* Berlin, 1908.

RENOUARD, Y. *Les hommes d'affaires italiens du moyen âge.* Paris, 1949.

ROOVER, R. DE. *The Medici Bank.* New York, 1948.

—— 'Lorenzo il Magnifico e il tramonto del Banco dei Medici.' *Archivio Storico Italiano,* CVII (1949).

SAYOUS, A. E. 'Les opérations des banquiers en Italie et aux foires de Champagne pendant le XIIIe siècle.' *RH.* CLXX (1932).

SCHNEIDER, G. *Die finanziellen Beziehungen der florentinischen Bankiers zur Kirche von 1285 bis 1304.* Leipzig, 1899. Staats- und socialwissenschaftliche Forschungen herausg. von Gustav Schmoller, XVII (I) (Heft 73).

WOLFF, P. 'Le problème des Cahorsins.' *Annales du Midi,* LXII (1951).

YVER, G. *Le commerce et les marchands dans l'Italie méridionale au XIIIe et au XIVe siècle.* Paris, 1903.

(e) The Towns and the Sale of Rents

(See also the sections on towns under particular countries)

ARNOLD, W. *Zur Geschichte des Eigentums in den deutschen Städten.* Basle, 1861.

BROUSSOLLE, J. 'Les impositions municipales de Barcelone de 1328 à 1462.' *Estudios de Historia Moderna.* Barcelona, 1955.

CAUWÈS, P. 'Les commencements du crédit public en France; les rentes sur l'hôtel de ville au XVIe siècle.' *Revue d'économie politique,* IX–X (1895–6).

COMBES, J. 'La constitution de rente à Montpellier au commencement du XVe siècle.' *Annales de l'Université de Montpellier et du Languedoc-Roussillon,* II (1944).

ESPINAS, G. *Les finances de la commune de Douai des origines au XVe siècle.* Paris, 1902.

FRYDE, M. M. 'Z badań nad dziejami kredytu publicznego w średniowieczu. Kredyt miast.' *Ekonomista,* III. Warsaw, 1935.

GÉNESTAL, R. *Rôle des monastères comme établissements de crédit étudié en Normandie du XIe à la fin du XIIIe siècle.* Paris, 1901.

JACK, A. F. *An introduction to the history of life assurance.* New York, 1912.

JANOWICZ, A. *Kupno renty. Studyum historyczno-prawne.* Lwów, 1883.

KUSKE, B. *Das Schuldenwesen der deutschen Städte im Mittelalter.* Tübingen, 1904.

LEFEBVRE, CH. *Observations sur les rentes perpétuelles dans l'ancien droit français.* Paris, 1914.

MAREZ, G. DES. *Étude sur la propriété foncière dans les villes du moyen âge et spécialement en Flandre.* Ghent, 1898.

PETOT, P. 'La constitution de rente aux XIIe et XIIIe siècles dans les pays coutumiers.' *Publications de l'Université de Dijon,* I. Paris, 1928.

PIRENNE, H. *Les villes et les institutions urbaines.* 2 vols. Brussels, 1939.

Stieda, W. 'Städtische Finanzen im Mittelalter.' *JNOS.* lxxii (1899).

Trenerry, C. F. *The Origins and Early History of Insurance including the Contract of Bottomry.* 1926.

Usher, A. P. *The Early History of Deposit Banking in Mediterranean Europe,* i. Cambridge (Mass.), 1943.

Van Werveke, H. *De Gentsche Stadsfinanciën in de Middeleeuwen.* Brussels, 1934.

(*f*) *The Earliest Period and the Crusades*

Bridrey, E. *La condition juridique des croisés et le privilège de Croix.* Paris, 1900.

Deibel, G. 'Die italienischen Einkünfte Kaiser Friedrich Barbarossas.' *Neue Heidelberger Jahrbücher,* n.s. 1932.

—— 'Die finanzielle Bedeutung Reichs-Italiens für die Staufische Herrscher des zwölften Jahrhunderts.' *Zeitschrift der Savigny-Stiftung für Rechtsgeschichte, Germ. Abt.* liv (1934*)*.

Delisle, L. 'Mémoire sur les opérations financières des Templiers.' *Mémoires de l'Institut National de France, Académie des Inscriptions et Belles-Lettres,* xxxiii (1889).

Duby, G. *La société aux XIe et XIIe siècles dans la région mâconnaise.* Paris, 1953.

Génestal, R. *Rôle des monastères comme établissements de crédit étudié en Normandie du XIe à la fin du XIIIe siècle.* Paris, 1901.

Gottlob, A. *Die päpstlichen Kreuzzugs-Steuern des XIII. Jahrhunderts.* Heiligenstadt, 1892.

Jordan, E. *Les origines de la domination angevine en Italie.* Paris, 1909.

Lestocquoy, J. 'Les usuriers du début du Moyen Age.' *Studi in onore di Gino Luzzatto,* i. Milan, 1949.

Malafosse, J. de. 'Contribution à l'étude du crédit dans le Midi aux Xe et XIe siècles: les sûretés réelles.' *Annales du Midi,* lxiii (1951).

Prutz, H. *Kulturgeschichte der Kreuzzüge.* Berlin, 1883.

Sayous, A. E. 'Les mandats de Saint Louis sur son Trésor et le mouvement international des capitaux pendant la septième croisade.' *RH.* clxvii (1931).

Schaube, A. 'Die Wechselbriefe König Ludwigs des Heiligen von seinem ersten Kreuzzuge und ihre Rolle auf dem Geldmarkte in Genua.' *JNOS.* xv (1898).

Servois, G. 'Emprunts de Saint Louis en Palestine et en Afrique.' *BECh.* 4th ser., iv (1858).

Van Werveke, H. 'Monnaie, lingots ou marchandises? Les instruments d'échange aux XIe et XIIe siècles.' *AHES.* iv (1932).

—— 'Le mort-gage et son rôle économique en Flandre et en Lotharingie.' *RBPH.* viii (1929).

Vercauteren, F. *Étude sur les Civitates de la Belgique Seconde: contribution à l'histoire urbaine du nord de la France de la fin du IIIe à la fin du XIe siècle.* Brussels, 1934.

—— 'Note sur l'origine et l'évolution du contrat de mort-gage en Lotharingie du XIe au XIIIe siècle.' *Miscellanea Historica in honorem Leonis van der Essen,* i. Brussels, 1947.

II. England

1. *Sources*

Anonimalle Chronicle (ed. V. H. Galbraith). Manchester, 1927.

Bond, E. A. 'Extracts from the Liberate Rolls relative to Loans supplied by Italian Merchants to the Kings of England in the Thirteenth and Fourteenth Centuries.' *Archaeologia,* xxviii (1840).

Broome, D. M. (ed.). 'The Ransom of John II, King of France, 1360–1370.' *The Camden Miscellany,* xiv. R.H.S. London, 1926

Calendar of Close Rolls (P.R.O.).

Calendar of Fine Rolls (P.R.O.).

Calendar of Patent Rolls (P.R.O.).

Devon, F. (ed.). *Issue Roll of Thomas de Brantingham, Bishop of Exeter . . . 44 Edward III, 1370.* Rec. Com. London, 1835.

KUNZE, K. (ed.). *Hanseakten aus England, 1275 bis 1413. Hansische Geschichtsquellen*, VI. Halle a.S. 1891.

MILLS, M. H. (ed.). 'The Pipe Roll for 1295 (Surrey Membrane).' *Surrey Record Society*, XXI (1924).

NICHOLS, J. (ed.). *Collection of all the Wills . . . of the Kings and Queens of England . . .* London, 1780.

NICOLAS, Sir N. H. (ed.). *Proceedings and Ordinances of the Privy Council of England.* 6 vols. Rec. Com. London, 1834–7.

PALGRAVE, Sir F. (ed.). *Antient Kalendars and Inventories of the Treasury of H.M. Exchequer.* 3 vols. Rec. Com. London, 1836.

Pipe Roll Society Publications (Pipe Rolls and Memoranda Rolls).

Red Book of the Exchequer (ed. H. HALL). 3 vols. R.S. London, 1897.

Rôles Gascons (ed. F. MICHEL and C. BÉMONT). 4 vols. *Documents inédits sur l'histoire de France.* Paris, 1885–1906.

Rotuli Parliamentorum. 6 vols. London, 1783.

SHARPE, R. R. (ed.). *Calendar of Letters from the Mayor and the Corporation of the City of London, circa 1350–70.* London, 1885.

—— (ed.). *Calendar of the Letter-Books of the City of London (A–L).* London, 1899–1912.

WILLARD, J. F. and JOHNSON, H. C. (eds). 'Surrey Taxation Returns.' *Surrey Record Society*, XVIII (1922).

2. Modern Works

(a) General

BALDWIN, J. F. *The King's Council.* Oxford, 1913.

BEARDWOOD, A. *Alien Merchants in England, 1350 to 1377. Their Legal and Economic Position.* Cambridge (Mass.), 1931.

CHRIMES, S. B. *An Introduction to the Administrative History of Medieval England.* Oxford, 1952.

LUNT, W. E. *Financial Relations of the Papacy with England to 1327.* Cambridge (Mass.), 1939.

McFARLANE, K. B. 'England: the Lancastrian Kings, 1399–1461.' *Cambridge Medieval History*, VIII. Cambridge, 1936.

MORRIS, W. A., STRAYER, J. R. and WILLARD, J. F. *The English Government at Work, 1327–1336*, I and II. Cambridge (Mass.), 1940–7.

POSTAN, M. M. 'The Financing of Trade in the Later Middle Ages.' M.Sc. Thesis, University of London, 1926.

—— 'Revisions in Economic History: the Fifteenth Century'. *EcHR.* IX (1939).

—— 'Some Social Consequences of the Hundred Years War.' *EcHR.* XII (1942).

—— 'Italy and the economic development of England in the middle ages.' *Journal of Economic History*, XI (1951).

POWER, E. and POSTAN, M. M. (eds). *Studies in English Trade in the Fifteenth Century.* London, 1933.

POWER, E. *The Wool Trade in English Medieval History.* Oxford, 1941.

SCOFIELD, C. L. *The Life and Reign of Edward the Fourth.* 2 vols. London, 1923.

STEEL, A. *Richard II.* Cambridge, 1941.

STURLER, J. DE. *Les relations politiques et les échanges commerciaux entre le Duché de Brabant et l'Angleterre au moyen âge.* Paris, 1936.

TOUT, T. F. *Chapters in the Administrative History of Medieval England.* 6 vols. Manchester, 1920–33.

(b) Financial History

CRAIG, Sir JOHN. *The Mint. A History of the London Mint from A.D. 287 to 1948.* Cambridge, 1953.

GRAS, N. S. B. *The Early English Customs System.* Cambridge (Mass.), 1918.

GRAY, H. L. 'The First Benevolence.' *Facts and Factors in Economic History. Essays presented to E. F. Gay.* Cambridge (Mass.), 1932.

KIRBY, J. L. 'The Issues of the Lancastrian Exchequer and Lord Cromwell's Estimates of 1433.' *BIHR.* XXIV (1951).

Lyon, B. D. 'The Money Fief under the English Kings, 1066–1485.' *EHR.* LXVI (1951).

Mills, M. H. 'Exchequer Agenda and Estimate of Revenue, Easter Term, 1284.' *EHR.* XL (1925).

Mitchell, S. K. *Studies in Taxation under John and Henry III.* New Haven (Conn.), 1914.

—— *Taxation in Medieval England.* New Haven (Conn.), 1951.

Newhall, R. A. 'The War Finances of Henry V and the Duke of Bedford.' *EHR.* XXXVI (1921).

Ramsay, Sir J. H. *A History of the Revenues of the Kings of England, 1066–1399.* 2 vols. Oxford, 1925.

Steel, A. *The Receipt of the Exchequer, 1377–1485.* Cambridge, 1954.

Tout, T. F. and Broome, D. M. 'A National Balance Sheet for 1362–3.' *EHR.* XXXIX (1924).

Unwin, G. (ed.). *Finance and Trade under Edward III.* Manchester, 1918.

Willard, J. F. 'The Taxes upon Movables of the Reigns of Edward I, Edward II and Edward III.' *EHR.* XXVIII–XXX (1913–15).

—— *Parliamentary Taxes on Personal Property 1290 to 1334. A Study in Medieval English Financial Administration.* Cambridge (Mass.), 1934.

Wolffe, B. P. 'The Management of English Royal Estates under the Yorkist Kings.' *EHR.* LXXI (1956).

(c) Arrangements for Borrowing and Repayment

Fryde, E. B. 'Materials for the Study of Edward III's Credit Operations, 1327–48.' *BIHR.* XXII–XXIII (1949–50).

—— 'Loans to the English Crown, 1328–31.' *EHR.* LXX (1955).

Harriss, G. L. 'Fictitious Loans.' *EcHR.* 2nd ser. VIII (1955).

—— 'Preference at the Medieval Exchequer.' *BIHR.* XXX (1957).

Jenkinson, H. 'Exchequer Tallies.' *Archaeologia,* LXII (1911).

—— 'Medieval Tallies, Public and Private.' *Archaeologia,* LXXIV (1925).

Kingsford, C. L. 'An Historical Collection of the Fifteenth Century.' *EHR.* XXIX (1914). (Forced loans under Henry V.)

Kirby, J. L. 'The Financing of Calais under Henry V.' *BIHR.* XXIII (1950).

McFarlane, K. B. 'Loans to the Lancastrian Kings: the Problem of Inducement.' *Cambridge Historical Journal,* IX (1947).

Mills, M. H. 'Adventus Vicecomitum, 1272–1307.' *EHR.* XXXVIII (1923). (Assignments by tally.)

Sayles, G. O. 'A Dealer in Wardrobe Bills.' *EcHR.* III (1931).

Steel, A. 'The Practice of Assignment in the Later Fourteenth Century.' *EHR.* XLIII (1928).

—— 'The Negotiation of Wardrobe Debentures in the Fourteenth Century.' *EHR.* XLIV (1929).

—— 'The Marginalia of the Treasurer's Receipt Rolls, 1349–99.' *BIHR.* VII–VIII (1929–30).

—— 'Mutua per talliam, 1377–1413.' *BIHR.* XIII (1935).

Willard, J. F. 'An Early Exchequer Tally.' *Bulletin of the John Rylands Library,* VII (1923).

—— 'The Crown and its Creditors, 1327–33.' *EHR.* XLII (1927).

(d) Particular Transactions and Lenders

Barber, M. 'John Norbury (c. 1350–1414): an Esquire of Henry IV.' *EHR.* LXVIII (1953).

Bromberg, B. 'The Financial and Administrative Importance of the Knights Hospitallers.' *Economic History,* IV (1940).

Ehrle, F. 'Process über den Nachlass Clemens V.' *Archiv für Literatur und Kirchengeschichte,* V (1889).

Ferris, E. 'The Financial Relations of the Knights Templars to the English Crown.' *AHR.* VIII (1902–3).

Fryde, E. B. 'Edward III's War Finance 1337–1341.' D.Phil. Thesis, University of Oxford, 1947.

—— 'Edward III's Wool Monopoly of 1337: a Fourteenth-century Royal Trading Venture.' *History,* n.s. XXXVII (1952).

FRYDE, E. B. 'The English Farmers of the Customs, 1343–1351.' *TRHS*. 5th ser. IX (1959).

HANSEN, J. 'Der englische Staatskredit unter König Eduard III (1327–77) und die hansischen Kaufleute.' *Hansische Geschichtsblätter*, XVI (1910).

HASKINS, C. H. 'William Cade.' *EHR*. XXVIII (1913).

HUGHES, D. *A Study of Social and Constitutional Tendencies in the Early Years of Edward III.* London, 1915. (1337–41.)

JACOBS, J. 'Aaron of Lincoln.' *Transactions of the Jewish Historical Society of England*, III (1896–8).

JAMES, M. K. 'A London Merchant of the Fourteenth Century.' *EcHR*. 2nd ser. VIII (1956).

JENKINSON, H. 'A Money-lender's Bonds of the Twelfth Century.' *Essays in History Presented to R. L. Poole*. Oxford, 1927.

JENKINSON, H. and STEAD, M. T. 'William Cade, a financier of the Twelfth Century.' *EHR*. XXVIII (1913).

JOHNSON, C. 'A Financial House in the Fourteenth Century' (the Frescobaldi). *Transactions of St Albans and Hertfordshire Architectural and Archaeological Society*, I (1901–2).

McFARLANE, K. B. 'Henry V, Bishop Beaufort and the Red Hat, 1417–21.' *EHR*. LX (1945).

—— 'At the Death-bed of Cardinal Beaufort.' *Studies in Medieval History Presented to F. M. Powicke*. Oxford, 1948.

NAPIER, H. A. *Historical Notices of the parishes of Swyncombe and Ewelme*. Oxford, 1858. (Materials concerning William de la Pole.)

PLUCKNETT, T. F. T. 'The Impeachments of 1376.' *TRHS*. 5th ser. I (1951).

RE, E. 'La Compagnia dei Riccardi in Inghilterra e il suo fallimento alla fine del secolo decimoterzo.' *Archivio de la Società Romana di Storia Patria*, XXXVII (1914).

RENOUARD, Y. 'Édouard II et Clément V d'après les Rôles Gascons.' *Annales du Midi*, LXVII (1955).

RHODES, W. E. 'Italian Bankers in England and their Loans to Edward I and Edward II.' *Historical Essays by Members of Owens College*. Manchester, 1902.

ROON-BASSERMANN, E. VON. 'Die ersten Florentiner Handelsgesellschaften in England.' *VSWG*. XXXIX (1952).

ROTH, C. *A History of the Jews in England*. Oxford, 1941.

SANDYS, A. 'The Financial and Administrative Importance of the London Temple in the Thirteenth Century.' *Essays in Medieval History Presented to Thomas Frederick Tout*. Manchester, 1925.

SAPORI, A. *La crisi delle compagnie mercantili dei Bardi e dei Peruzzi*. Florence, 1926.

—— *La compagnia dei Frescobaldi in Inghilterra*. Florence, 1947.

SAYLES, G. O. 'The English Company of 1343.' *Speculum*, VI (1931).

WHITWELL, R. J. 'Italian Bankers and the English Crown.' *TRHS*. n.s. XVII (1903).

WINTERFELD, L. VON. 'Tidemann Lemberg. Ein Dortmunder Kaufmannsleben aus dem 14. Jahrhundert.' *Hansische Volkshefte*, Heft 10. Bremen, 1926.

(e) London

BIRD, R. *The Turbulent London of Richard II*. London, 1949.

DAVIS, E. J. and PEAKE, M. I. 'Loans from the City of London to Henry VI, 1431–49.' *BIHR*. IV (1926–7).

PEAKE, M. I. 'London and the Wars of the Roses, 1445–61.' M.A. Thesis, University of London, 1925.

MEAD, J. DE C. 'The Financial Relations between the Crown and the City of London, Edward I–Henry VII.' M.A. Thesis, University of London, 1936.

THRUPP, S. L. *The Merchant Class of Medieval London*. Chicago, 1948.

TOUT, T. F. 'The Beginnings of a Modern Capital: London and Westminster in the Fourteenth Century.' *Proceedings of the British Academy*, XI (1924).

WEINBAUM, M. *London unter Eduard I und Eduard II*. Stuttgart, 1933.

WILLIAMS, G. A. 'Social and Constitutional Tendencies in Thirteenth-century London.' M.A. Thesis, University of Wales (Aberystwyth), 1952.

III. FRANCE

1. *Sources*

DELAVILLE LE ROULX, J. (ed.). *Registres des comptes municipaux de la ville de Tours, 1358–1380*. 2 vols. Tours, 1878–81.

DELISLE, L. (ed.). *Mandements et actes divers de Charles V, 1364–1380*. Paris, 1874.

DOUCET, R. (ed.). *L'État des Finances de 1523*. Paris, 1923.

DOUËT D'ARCQ, L. (ed.). *Comptes de l'Argenterie des rois de France au XIVe siècle*. Société de l'histoire de France. Paris, 1851.

FAWTIER, R. (ed.). *Comptes du Trésor (1296, 1316, 1384, 1477)*. Recueil des Historiens de France. Documents Financiers, II. Paris, 1930.

FUNCK-BRENTANO, F. 'Document pour servir à l'histoire des relations de la France avec l'Angleterre et l'Allemagne sous le règne de Philippe le Bel.' (1294–7.) *RH*. XXXIX (1889).

GIRY, A. (ed.). *Documents sur les relations de la royauté avec les villes en France de 1180 à 1314*. Paris, 1885.

JOHNSON, C. (ed.). *The 'De Moneta' of Nicholas Oresme and English Mint Documents*. London, 1956.

LANGLOIS, CH. V. (ed.). *Inventaires d'anciens comptes royaux dressés par Robert Mignon sous le règne de Philippe de Valois*. Recueil des Historiens de France. Documents Financiers, I. Paris, 1899.

LA TRÉMOILLE, L. DE. *Les la Trémoille pendant cinq siècles*. Vol. I: *Guy VI et Georges, 1343–1446*. Nantes, 1890.

Layettes du Trésor des Chartes (ed. A. TEULET, J. DE LABORDE, E. BERGER, H. F. DELABORDE). 5 vols. Paris, 1863–1909.

MOLLAT, M. (ed.). *Les affaires de Jacques Cœur. Journal du Procureur Dauvet*. 2 vols. Paris, 1952–3.

MORANVILLÉ, H. 'Rapport à Philippe VI sur l'état de ses finances.' *BECh*. XLVIII (1887).

——— 'Extraits de Journaux du Trésor, 1345–1419.' *BECh*. XLIX (1888).

PROU, M. and D'AURIAC, J. (eds). *Actes et comptes de la commune de Provins de l'an 1271 à l'an 1330*. Provins, 1933.

SALMON, A. (ed.). *Philippe de Beaumanoir: «Coutumes de Beauvaisis»*. 2 vols. Paris, 1899–1900.

VIARD, J. (ed.). *Les Journaux du Trésor de Philippe VI de Valois suivis de l'Ordinarium Thesaurii de 1338–39*. Paris, 1899.

——— (ed.). *Les Journaux du Trésor de Charles IV le Bel*. Paris, 1917.

——— (ed.). *Les Journaux du Trésor de Philippe IV le Bel*. Paris, 1940.

2. *Modern Works*

(a) *General Works and Financial History*

BEAUCOURT, G. DU FRESNE DE. *Histoire de Charles VII*, II–V (1422–53). Paris, 1882–90.

BORRELLI DE SERRES, L. L. *Recherches sur divers services publics du XIIIe au XVIIe siècle*. 3 vols. Paris, 1895–1909.

BRIDREY, E. *La théorie de la monnaie au XIVe siècle. Nicole Oresme*. Paris, 1906.

COVILLE, A. *Les Cabochiens et l'ordonnance de 1413*. Paris, 1888.

DELACHENAL, CH. *Histoire de Charles V*. 5 vols. Paris, 1909–31.

DIEUDONNÉ, A. 'La monnaie royale depuis la réforme de Charles V jusqu'à la restauration monétaire par Charles VII, spécialement dans ses rapports avec l'histoire politique.' *BECh*. LXXII–LXXIII (1911–12).

DOGNON, P. *Les institutions politiques et administratives du Pays de Languedoc du XIIIe siècle aux guerres de religion*. Toulouse, 1895.

DOUCET, R. 'Le gouvernement de Louis XI.' *Revue des Cours et Conférences*, XXV (1924).

——— 'Les finances anglaises en France à la fin de la Guerre de Cent Ans, 1413–1435.' *Moyen Âge*, XXXVI (1926).

——— *Les institutions de la France au XVIe siècle*. 2 vols. Paris, 1948.

DUPONT-FERRIER, G. *Études sur les institutions financières de la France à la fin du moyen âge.* 2 vols. Paris, 1930–2.

GANDILHON, R. *La politique économique de Louis XI.* Rennes, 1940.

LANGLOIS, CH. V. 'Registres perdus des archives de la Chambre des Comptes de Paris.' *Notices et Extraits des Manuscrits de la Bibliothèque Nationale,* XL (1917). (Specially useful for the period 1314–28.)

LEHUGEUR, P. *Philippe le Long, roi de France (1316–1322),* II: *Le mécanisme du gouvernement.* Paris, 1931.

LOT, F. and FAWTIER, R. *Histoire des institutions françaises au moyen âge.* 2 vols. Paris, 1957–8.

OLIVIER-MARTIN, F. *Histoire de la coutume de la prévôté et vicomté de Paris.* 3 vols. Paris, 1922.

—— *Histoire du droit français des origines à la Révolution.* 2nd ed. Paris, 1951.

SCHMIDT, B. 'Die Anfänge der französischen Staatsschulden.' *Finanzarchiv,* XXXV (1918).

STAMPE, E. *Das Zahlkraftrecht in den Königsgesetzen Frankreichs von 1306 bis 1547.* Berlin, 1930.

STRAYER, J. R. and TAYLOR, C. H. *Studies in early French Taxation.* Cambridge (Mass.), 1939.

VIARD, J. 'Un chapitre d'histoire administrative, les ressources extraordinaires de la royauté sous Philippe VI de Valois.' *Revue des Questions Historiques,* XLIV (1888).

VIOLLET, P. *Histoire des institutions politiques et administratives de la France,* III. Paris, 1903.

VÜHRER, A. *Histoire de la dette publique en France.* 2 vols. Paris, 1886.

VUITRY, A. *Études sur le régime financier de la France avant la révolution de 1789: Philippe le Bel et ses trois fils, les trois premiers Valois (1285–1380).* 2 vols. Paris, 1883.

(b) Arrangements for borrowing and repayment

BOSSUAT, A. 'Étude sur les emprunts royaux au début du XVe siècle. La politique financière du connétable Bernard d'Armagnac.' *RHDr.* 4th ser. XXVIII (1950).

—— 'La rétablissement de la paix sociale sous le règne de Charles VII.' *Moyen Âge,* LX (1954). (Parisian lenders and the validity of contracts concluded during the civil war.)

JACQUETON, G. 'Le Trésor de l'Épargne sous François I, 1523–1547.' *RH.* LV (1894).

POCQUET DE HAUT JUSSÉ, B. A. 'Le compte de Pierre Gorremont, receveur général du royaume (1418–20).' *BECh.* XCVIII (1937). ('Forced loans' in Paris.)

RICHARD, J. M. 'Instructions données aux commissaires chargés de lever la rançon du Roi Jean.' *BECh.* XXXVI (1875). (Instructions for a levy of a 'forced loan'.)

ROUX, P. *Les fermes d'impôts sous l'ancien régime.* Paris, 1916.

(c) Particular transactions and lenders

BEAUCOURT, G. DU FRESNE DE. 'Le procès de Jacques Cœur.' *Revue des Questions Historiques,* XLVII (1890).

BENGY-PUYVALLÉE, M. DE. 'Le livre d'affaires d'un marchand berrichon au XVe siècle.' (Michau Dauron.) *Mémoires de la Société des Antiquaires du Centre,* XL (1921).

BIGWOOD, G. 'Les financiers d'Arras. Contribution à l'étude des origines du capitalisme moderne.' *RBPH.* III–IV (1924–5).

BOCK, F. 'Musciatto dei Francesi.' *Deutsches Archiv für Geschichte des Mittelalters,* VI (1943).

BOUDET, M. 'Étude sur les sociétés marchandes et financières au moyen âge. Les Gayte et les Chauchat de Clermont.' *Revue d'Auvergne,* XXVIII–XXIX (1911–12).

CHIAPPELLI, L. 'Una lettera mercantile del 1330 e la crisi del commercio italiano nella prima metà del Trecento.' *Archivio Storico Italiano,* 7th ser. I (1924).

CLEMENT, P. *Jacques Cœur et Charles VII.* 2nd ed. Paris, 1873.

COVILLE, A. 'La très belle couronne royale aux temps des Armagnacs et des Bourguignons.' *Mélanges offerts à Nicolas Iorga.* Paris, 1933.

FAUCON, M. 'Prêts faits aux rois de France par Clement VI, Innocent VI et le comte de Beaufort, 1345–1360.' *BECh.* XL (1879).

FUNK, A. L. 'Confiscation of Lombard debts in France, 1347–58.' *Medievalia et Humanistica,* VII (1952).

LANGLOIS, CH. V. 'Notices et documents relatifs à l'histoire de France au temps de Philippe le Bel.' (Brothers Franzesi.) *RH.* LX (1896).

LEHOUX, F. 'Le duc de Berri, les Juifs et les Lombards.' *RH.* CCXV (1956).

LESTOCQUOY, J. *Patriciens du moyen-âge. Les dynasties bourgeoises d'Arras du XIe au XVe siècle.* Arras, 1945.

—— 'Deux familles de financiers d'Arras. Louchard et Wagon.' *RBPH.* XXXII (1954).

MARSH, F. B. *English Rule in Gascony, 1199–1259.* Ann Arbor, 1912. (Gascon loans to English kings.)

MIROT, L. *Une grande famille parlementaire aux XIVe et XIVe siècles: les d'Orgemont.* Paris, 1913. (Parisian financiers under Charles VI.)

'Études Lucquoises':

—— 'La colonie lucquoise à Paris du XIIIe au XVe siècle.' *BECh.* LXXXVIII (1927).

—— 'La société de Raponde, Dine Raponde.' *Ibid.* LXXXIX (1928).

—— 'Origine de Spifame. Barthélemi Spifame.' *Ibid.* XCIX (1938).

—— 'Galvano Trenta et les joyaux de la couronne.' *Ibid.* CI (1940). (Important for the reign of Charles VI.)

MOLLAT, M. 'Un «collaborateur» au temps de la Guerre de Cent Ans. Jehan Marcel, changeur à Rouen.' *AHES.* XVIII (1946).

—— 'Les opérations financières de Jacques Cœur.' *Revue de la Banque,* XVIII (1954).

—— 'Une équipe; les commis de Jacques Cœur.' *Hommage à Lucien Febvre: éventail de l'histoire vivante,* II. Paris, 1954.

—— 'Les affaires de Jacques Cœur à Florence.' *Studi in onore di A. Sapori,* II. Milan, 1957.

PRUTZ, H. *J. Cœur von Bourges. Geschichte eines patriotischen Kaufmanns aus dem 15. Jahrhundert.* Berlin, 1911.

SPONT, A. *Semblançay (?–1527). La bourgeoisie financière au début du XVIe siècle.* Paris, 1895.

TERROINE, ANNE. 'Études sur la bourgeoisie parisienne: Gandoufle d'Arcelles et les compagnies placentines.' *AHES.* XVII (1945).

VALOIS, N. 'Notes sur la révolution parisienne de 1356–58: la revanche des frères Braque.' *Mémoires de la Société de l'Histoire de Paris et de l'Ile de France,* X (1883).

WOLFF, P. 'Une famille du XIIIe siècle au XVIe siècle: les Ysalguier de Toulouse.' *AHES.* XIV (1942).

(d) Towns

BERTIN, P. *Une commune flamande-artésienne. Aire-sur-Lys des origines au XVIe siècle.* Arras, 1946.

BESNIER, G. 'Finances d'Arras (1282–1407).' *Recueil de Travaux offert à Clovis Brunel,* I. Paris, 1955.

BOULET-SAUTEL, M. 'Les villes de Centre.' *Recueils de la Société Jean Bodin,* VI: *La Ville (1e partie), Institutions administratives et judiciares.* Brussels, 1954.

CAILLET, L. *Étude sur les relations de la commune de Lyon avec Charles VII et Louis XI (1417–1483).* Lyon–Paris, 1909.

CAROLUS-BARRÉ, M. 'Les institutions municipales de Compiègne au temps des gouverneurs-attournés (1319–1692).' *Bulletin Philologique et Historique du Comité des Travaux Historiques et Scientifiques* (1940–1).

CAUWÈS, P. 'Les commencements du crédit public en France; les rentes sur l'hôtel de ville au XVIe siècle.' *Revue d'économie politique,* IX–X (1895–6).

CHAPIN, E. *Les villes de foires de Champagne.* Paris, 1937.

CHÉNON, E. 'De la personnalité juridique des villes de commune d'après le droit français du XIIIe siècle.' *Tijdschrift voor Rechtsgeschiedenis,* IV (1923).

DÉNIAU, J. *La commune de Lyon et la guerre bourguignonne, 1417–1435.* Lyon, 1934.

DOUCET, R. *Finances municipales et crédit public à Lyon au XVIe siècle.* Paris, 1937.

DUBRULLE, H. *Cambrai à la fin du Moyen Âge.* Lille, 1903.

DUFOUR, CH. 'Situation financière des villes de Picardie sous saint Louis.' *Mémoires de la Société des Antiquaires de Picardie,* XV. Amiens, 1858.

ESPINAS, G. *Les finances de la commune de Douai des origines au XVe siècle.* Paris, 1902.

FLAMMERMONT, J. 'Histoire de Senlis pendant la seconde partie de la guerre de Cent Ans (1405–1441).' *Mémoires de la Société de l'Histoire de Paris et de l'Ile de France,* V (1878).

—— *Histoire des institutions municipales de Senlis.* Paris, 1881.

GIRY, A. *Les établissements de Rouen.* 2 vols. Paris, 1883–5.

LEFRANC, A. *Histoire de la ville de Noyon et de ses institutions jusqu'à la fin du XIIIe siècle.* Paris, 1887.

LUCHAIRE, A. *Les communes françaises.* 2nd ed. Paris, 1911.

MAUGIS, E. 'Essai sur le régime financier de la ville d'Amiens du XIVe à la fin du XVIe siècle (1356–1588).' *Mémoires de la Société des Antiquaires de Picardie,* XXXIII. Amiens, 1899.

MIROT, L. *Les insurrections urbaines au début du règne de Charles VI (1380–1383). Leurs causes, leurs conséquences.* Paris, 1906.

PETIT-DUTAILLIS, CH. *Les communes françaises. Caractères et évolution des origines au XVIIIe siècle.* Paris, 1947.

RICHARD, J. M. 'Une conversion de rentes à Arras en 1392.' *BECh.* XLI (1880).

SÉE, H. *Louis XI et les villes.* Paris, 1891.

WOLFF, P. 'Les luttes sociales dans les villes du Midi français, XIIIe–XVe siècles.' *AHES.* XIX (1947).

—— *Commerces et marchands de Toulouse (vers 1350–vers 1450).* Paris, 1954.

IV. THE NETHERLANDS AND THE BURGUNDIAN STATE

1. *Sources*

CUVELIER, J., DHONDT, J. and DOEHAERD, R. (eds). *Actes des États Généraux des Anciens Pays-Bas,* I (1427 à 1477). Brussels, 1948.

DEHAISNES, C. (ed.). *Inventaire-sommaire des archives départementales antérieurs à 1790. Nord,* IV. Lille, 1881.

DES MAREZ, G. and DE SAGHER, E. (eds). *Comptes de la ville d'Ypres de 1267 à 1329.* 2 vols. Brussels, 1909–13.

DIEGERICK, I. L. A. *Inventaire analytique et chronologique des chartes et documents appartenant aux archives de la ville d'Ypres.* 7 vols. Bruges, 1853–68.

GACHARD, L. P. *Rapport sur les documents concernant l'histoire de Belgique qui existent dans les dépôts littéraires de Dijon et de Paris.* 1e partie, *Archives de Dijon.* Brussels, 1843.

GAILLARD, V. 'Inventaire analytique des chartes des comtes de Flandre autrefois déposées au château de Rupelmonde.' *BCRH.* 2nd ser. VI–VII (1854–5).

GILLIODTS-VAN SEVEREN, L. *Inventaire des archives de la ville de Bruges.* 7 vols. Bruges, 1871–8.

GRUNZWEIG, A. (ed.). *Correspondance de la filiale de Bruges des Medici,* I. Brussels, 1931.

LIMBURG-STIRUM, T. DE (ed.). *Cartulaire de Louis de Male, comte de Flandre, 1348–58.* 2 vols. Bruges, 1898–1901.

PROST, B. and H. (eds). *Inventaires mobiliers et extraits des comptes des ducs de Bourgogne de la maison de Valois (1363–1477).* 2 vols. Paris, 1902–13.

QUICKE, F. (ed.). 'Documents concernant la politique des ducs de Brabant et de Bourgogne dans le duché de Limbourg et les terres d'Outre Meuse pendant la seconde moitié du XIVe siècle (1364–96).' *BCRH.* XCIII (1929).

QUICKE, F. and LAURENT, H. (eds). 'Documents pour servir à l'histoire de la maison de Bourgogne en Brabant et en Limbourg (fin du XIVe siècle).' *BCRH.* XCVII (1933).

VUYLSTEKE, J. (ed.). *Cartulaire de la ville de Gand. Comptes de la ville et des baillis de Gand, 1280–1336.* Ghent, 1900.

VUYLSTEKE, J. and PAUW, N. DE (eds). *Rekeningen der stad Gent. Tijdvak van Jacob van Artevelde (1336–49).* 5 vols. Ghent, 1874–85.

2. *Modern Works*

(a) *General Works*

BARTIER, J. *Charles le Téméraire.* Brussels, 1944.

BONENFANT, P. *Philippe le Bon.* 3rd ed. Brussels, 1955.

HIRSCHAUER, CH. *Les États d'Artois de leurs origines à l'occupation française, 1340–1640,* I. Paris, 1923.

LEMEERE, E. *Le grand conseil des ducs de Bourgogne de la maison de Valois.* Brussels, 1900.

MONIER, R. *Les institutions centrales du comté de Flandre de la fin du IXe siècle à 1384.* Paris, 1943.

NIERMEYER, J. F. and VAN WERVEKE, H. (eds with others). *Algemene Geschiedenis der Nederlanden,* II–III. Utrecht, 1950–1.

PIRENNE, H. *Histoire de Belgique,* I (5th ed. 1929) and II (4th ed. 1947).

POCQUET DU HAUT-JUSSÉ, B. A. 'Jean sans Peur. Son but et sa méthode.' *Annales de Bourgogne,* XIV (1942).

QUICKE, F. and LAURENT, H. *Les origines de l'état bourguignon: l'accession de la maison de Bourgogne aux duchés de Brabant et de Limbourg, 1383–1407,* I. Brussels, 1939.

STURLER, J. DE. *Les relations politiques et les échanges commerciaux entre le duché de Brabant et l'Angleterre au moyen âge.* Paris, 1936.

(b) Financial History

BARTIER, J. 'Un discours du chancelier Hugonet aux États Généraux de 1473.' *BCRH.* CVII (1942).

——— *Légistes et gens de finances au XVe siècle. Les conseillers des Ducs de Bourgogne, Philippe le Bon et Charles le Téméraire.* Brussels, 1955.

BRUWIER, M. 'Notes sur les finances hennuyères à l'époque bourguignonne.' *Moyen Âge,* LIV (1948).

COVILLE, A. 'Les finances des ducs de Bourgogne au commencement du XVe siècle.' *Études d'histoire du moyen âge dédiées à Gabriel Monod.* Paris, 1896.

JASSEMIN, H. 'Le contrôle financier en Bourgogne sous les derniers ducs capétiens (1274–1353).' *BECh.* LXXIX (1918).

KAUCH, P. 'Le trésor de l'épargne, création de Philippe le Bon.' *RBPH.* XI (1932).

LIÈVRE, L. *La monnaie et le change en Bourgogne sous les Ducs Valois.* Dijon, 1929.

MARTENS, M. *L'administration du domaine ducal en Brabant au moyen âge, 1250–1406.* Brussels, 1954.

MIROT, L. 'Jean sans Peur de 1398 à 1405 d'après les comptes de sa chambre aux deniers.' *Annuaire-Bulletin de la Société de l'Histoire de France,* LXXIV (1938).

MONIER, R. *Les institutions financières du comté de Flandre du XIe siècle à 1384.* Paris, 1948.

POCQUET DU HAUT-JUSSÉ, B. A. 'Dons du roi aux grands feudataires. Les ducs de Bourgogne, Philippe le Hardi et Jean sans Peur.' *RH.* CLXXXIII (1938).

——— 'Les dons du roi aux ducs de Bourgogne, Philippe le Hardi et Jean sans Peur (1363–1419). Le don des aides.' *Annales de Bourgogne,* X (1938).

——— 'Les dons du roi aux ducs de Bourgogne, Philippe le Hardi et Jean sans Peur (1363–1419).' *Mémoires de la Société pour l'Histoire du Droit et des Institutions des anciens pays bourguignons, comtois et romands,* VI–VII (1939–41).

RIANDEY, P. *L'organisation financière de la Bourgogne sous Philippe le Hardi.* Dijon, 1908.

THOMAS, P. 'Le registre de Guillaume d'Auxonne.' *Revue du Nord,* X (1924).

VAN WERVEKE, H. 'Currency manipulation in the middle ages: the case of Louis de Male, count of Flanders.' *TRHS.* 4th ser. XXXI (1949).

——— 'Les charges financières issues du traité d'Athis (1305).' *Revue du Nord,* XXXII (1950).

(c) Particular Transactions and Lenders

BARTIER, J. 'L'ascension d'un marchand bourguignon au XVe siècle. Odot Molain.' *Annales de Bourgogne,* XV (1943).

BERNAYS, E. and VANNÉRUS, J. *Histoire numismatique du comté, puis duché de Luxembourg et de ses fiefs.* Brussels, 1910.

BIGWOOD, G. *Le régime juridique et économique du commerce de l'argent dans la Belgique du moyen âge.* 2 vols. Brussels, 1921–2.

——— 'Un relevé de recettes tenu par le personnel de Thomas Fini, receveur général de Flandre.' *Mélanges d'Histoire offerts à Henri Pirenne,* I. Brussels, 1926.

BIVIER, A. and MIROT, L. 'Prêts consentis au duc et à la duchesse de Bourgogne en Nivernais et en Donziais de 1384 à 1386.' *BECh.* CIII (1942).

CUMONT, C. 'Un officier monétaire du XIVe siècle, Nicolas Chavre.' *Gazette Numismatique Française,* I (1897).

CUVELIER, J. *Les origines de la fortune de la maison d'Orange-Nassau. Contribution à l'histoire du capitalisme au moyen âge.* (William van Duvenvoorde.) Brussels, 1921.

DELAVILLE LE ROULX, J. *La France en Orient au XIVe siècle.* (The crusade of 1396.) 2 vols. Paris, 1886.

FRIS, V. 'Note sur Thomas Fin, receveur de Flandre (1306–9).' *BCRH.* LXIX (1900).

GAUTHIER, L. *Les Lombards dans les Deux Bourgognes.* Paris, 1907.

LAENEN, J. 'Usuriers et Lombards dans le Brabant au XVe siècle.' *Bulletin de l'Académie Royale d'Archéologie de Belgique,* IV (1904).

—— 'Les Lombards à Malines, 1295–1457.' *Bulletin du Cercle Archéologique, Littéraire et Artistique de Malines,* XV (1905).

MIROT, L. 'Études Lucquoises: la société de Raponde, Dine Raponde.' *BECh.* LXXXIX (1928).

MOREL, P. *Les Lombards dans la Flandre française et le Hainaut.* Lille, 1908.

POCQUET DU HAUT-JUSSÉ, B. A. 'Le retour de Nicopolis et la rançon de Jean sans Peur.' *Annales de Bourgogne,* IX (1937).

STENGERS, J. *Les Juifs dans les Pays-Bas au moyen âge.* Brussels, 1950.

VANNÉRUS, J. 'Les Lombards dans l'ancien pays de Luxembourg.' *Bull. de l'Institut Historique Belge de Rome,* XXVII (1952).

VERCAUTEREN, F. 'Note sur les opérations financières de Charles Quint dans les Pays-Bas en 1523.' *RH.* CLXXI (1933).

—— 'Document pour servir à l'histoire des financiers lombards en Belgique (1309).' *Bulletin de l'Institut Historique Belge de Rome,* XXVI (1950–1).

(d) Towns

BIGWOOD, G. 'Les émissions de rentes de la ville de Namur au XVe siècle.' *Annales de la Société Archéologique de Namur,* XXXVI (1923).

BLOCKMANS, F. 'Peilingen nopens de bezittende klass te Gent omstreeks 1300.' *RBPH.* XV–XVI (1936–7).

—— *Het Gentsche Stadspatriciat tot omstreeks 1302.* Antwerp, 1938.

ESPINAS, G. *Les finances de la commune de Douai des origines au XVe siècle.* Paris, 1902.

FAVRESSE, F. *L'avènement du régime démocratique à Bruxelles pendant le moyen âge (1306–1423).* Brussels, 1932.

HÄPKE, R. *Brügges Entwicklung zum mittelalterlichen Weltmarkt.* Berlin, 1908.

MARECHAL, J. 'Bruges, centre du commerce de l'argent aux derniers siècles du moyen âge.' *Revue de la Banque,* XIV (1950).

MARQUANT, R. *La vie économique à Lille sous Philippe le Bon.* Paris, 1940.

RICHEBÉ, A. 'Note sur la comptabilité en Flandre avant la fin du XVIe siècle.' *Annales du Comité Flamand de France,* XXII (1895).

ROOVER, R. DE. *Money, Banking and Credit in Mediaeval Bruges.* Cambridge (Mass.), 1948.

VAN WERVEKE, H. *De Gentsche Stadsfinanciën in de Middeleeuwen.* Brussels, 1934.

V. GERMANY

ABBREVIATIONS

ADB.: Allgemeine Deutsche Biographie

DA.: Deutsches Archiv für Geschichte des Mittelalters

Gierkes Untersuchungen: Untersuchungen zur deutschen Staats- und Rechtsgeschichte, Herausgegeben von Otto von Gierke

HV.: Historische Vierteljahrschrift

HZ.: Historische Zeitschrift

Jhb. f. Nat. u. Stat.: Jahrbücher für Nationalökonomie und Statistik

Kuske, I: BRUNO KUSKE. 'Das Schuldenwesen der deutschen Städte im Mittelalter.' *Zeitschrift für die gesamte Staatswissenschaft,* Ergänzungsheft XII (Tübingen, 1904)

Kuske, II: BRUNO KUSKE. 'Die Entstehung der Kreditwirtschaft und des Kapitalverkehrs' (in *Kölner Vorträge* Hsg. von der Wirtschafts- und Sozialwissenschaftlichen Fakultät der Universität Köln,* I. Leipzig, 1929. Reprinted in Bruno Kuske, *Köln, der Rhein und das Reich. Beiträge aus fünf Jahrzehnten Wirtschaftsgeschichtlicher Forschung.* Cologne–Graz, 1956)

Landmann, I: J. LANDMANN. 'Zur Entwicklungsgeschichte der Formen und Organisation des öffentlichen Kredites.' *Finanzarchiv*, XXIX (1912).

Landmann, II: J. LANDMANN. 'Der öffentliche Kredit' (in W. Gerloff and F. Neumark, *Handbuch der Finanzwissenschaft*, III. 2nd ed. Tübingen, 1958).

Miög.: Mitteilungen des Instituts für österreichische Forschung.

Sb. Ak.: Sitzungsberichte der Akademie der Wissenschaften.

Schmollers Forschungen: Staats- und sozialwissenschaftliche Forschungen herausgegeben von Gustav Schmoller.

Schmollers Jahrbuch: Jahrbuch für Gesetzgebung, Verwaltung und Volkwirtschaft.

Veröff.: Veröffentlichungen.

V. f. Soz. u. WG.: Vierteljahrschrift für Sozial- und Wirtschaftsgeschichte.

Ztschr.: Zeitschrift.

Z. f. Soz. u. WG.: Zeitschrift für Sozial- und Wirtschaftsgeschichte.

ZRG. Germ. Abt.: Zeitschrift der Savigny-Stiftung für Rechtsgeschichte, Germanistische Abteilung.

I. Sources

An exhaustive bibliography of sources has not been provided here for reasons of space. A detailed (complete) list of sources pertaining to the Empire, territories, bishoprics, abbeys and towns may be found in DAHLMANN-WAITZ, *Quellenkunde der Deutschen Geschichte* (9th ed. 1931), in Jahresberichte für Deutsche Geschichte (16 vols. 1927–42; new ser. 1952 sqq.) and in HOLTZMANN-RITTER, *Die Deutsche Geschichtswissenschaft im 2. Weltkrieg* (2 vols. 1951). Certain important sources will be found among the books and articles listed in the separate sections of this bibliography. The most important general sources, i.e. those transcending the limits of particular regions or towns, are as follows:

Deutsche Reichstagsakten. (Ältere Reihe), herausgegeben von der Historischen Kommission bei der Kgl. Akademie der Wissenschaften.

I–III (unter König Wenzel, 1376–1400), hg. von J. Weizsäcker. Munich, 1866–77.

IV–VI (unter König Ruprecht), hg. von J. Weizsäcker. Gotha, 1882–8.

VII–XII (unter Kaiser Sigmund). Munich–Gotha, 1878–1906.

XIII–XIV (unter König Albrecht). Gotha–Stuttgart, 1908–35.

XV–XVI, XVII (I) (unter Kaiser Friedrich III, 1440–4). Gotha-Stuttgart, 1912–39.

BÖHMER, J. F. *Regesta Imperii 1246–1313*, Stuttgart, 1844. 2 *additamenta*, 1849–57. New, not yet completed, edition of Böhmer's *Regesta* contains for the period concerned the following publications:

v. *Die Regesten des Kaiserreichs unter Philipp, Otto IV, Friedrich II, Heinrich, Konrad IV, Heinrich Raspe, Wilhelm und Richard, 1198–1272*, hg. von J. Ficker und E. Winkelmann. 3 Bde in 5 Abt. Innsbruck, 1881–1901.

VI. *Die Regesten des Kaiserreichs unter Rudolf, Adolf, Albrecht, Heinrich VII, 1273–1313*. I Abt. *1273–1291*, hg. von O. Redlich. Innsbruck, 1898 sq. 2 Abt. *1291–1298*, hg. von V. Samanek. Innsbruck, 1933–48.

VIII. *Die Regesten des Kaiserreichs unter Karl IV, 1346–1378*, hg. von A. Huber. Innsbruck, 1877. *Additamenta*, 1889.

XI. *Die Urkunden Kaiser Sigmunds, 1410–1437*, hg. von W. Altmann. 2 Bde. Innsbruck, 1896–1900.

CHMEL, J. *Regesta Chronologico-diplomatica Ruperti regis Romanorum 1400–1410*. Frankfurt a. M. 1834.

——— *Regesta Chronologico-diplomatica Friderici III, Romanorum imperatoris*. Vienna, 1859.

Die Chroniken der deutschen Städte vom 14. bis ins 16. Jh., hg. von der Historischen Kommission bei der Bayerischen Akademie der Wissenschaften. 36 vols. Leipzig-Stuttgart, 1862–1931.

Fontes rerum Austriacarum. Österreichische Geschichtsquellen. Abt. I: *Scriptores.* Abt. 2: *Diplomataria*, hg. von der Historischen Kommission der Kgl. Akademie der Wissenschaften in Wien. 68 vols. Vienna, 1855 sq.

Von Oberndorff, L. Graf. *Regesten König Ruprechts* (=*Regesten der Pfalzgrafen am Rhein, 1214–1508*, hg. von der Badischen Historischen Kommission, II Band. *Additamenta* von M. Krebs. Innsbruck, 1912–39).

2. *General Works Relevant to the Study of German Finances and Public Credit*

(*a*) *General Histories, Works of Reference*

Barraclough, G. *The Origins of Modern Germany.* 2nd ed. Oxford, 1952.

Bechtel, H. *Wirtschaftsgeschichte Deutschlands.* 1 vol. 2nd ed. Munich, 1957.

Below, G. von. *Der deutsche Staat des Mittelalters*, I. 2nd ed. Leipzig, 1925.

—— *Territorium und Staat.* 2nd ed. Munich–Leipzig, 1923.

Bihlmeyer, K. and Tüchle, H. *Kirchengeschichte*, II: *Das Mittelalter.* 13th ed. Paderborn, 1952.

Bosl, K. *Staat, Gesellschaft, Wirtschaft im deutschen Mittelalter* (in Gebhardt, B. *Handbuch der deutschen Geschichte*, I. 8th ed. Stuttgart, 1954).

Caro, G. *Sozial- und Wirtschaftsgeschichte der Juden im Mittelalter und in der Neuzeit.* I, 2nd ed. Frankfurt a.m. 1924; II, Leipzig, 1920.

Conrad, H. *Deutsche Rechtsgeschichte*, I: *Frühzeit und Mittelalter.* Karlsruhe, 1954.

Fehr, H. *Deutsche Rechtsgeschichte.* 6th ed. Berlin–Leipzig, 1954.

Feine, H. E. *Kirchliche Rechtsgeschichte. Auf der Grundlage des Kirchenrechts von Ulrich Stutz*, I: *Die Katholische Kirche.* 3rd ed. Weimar, 1955.

Hartung, F. *Deutsche Verfassungsgeschichte vom 15. Jahrhundert bis zur Gegenwart.* 6th ed. Stuttgart, 1954.

Heimpel, H. 'Deutschland im späteren Mittelalter.' *Handbuch der deutschen Geschichte*, I, part 5. Constance, 1956.

Inama-Sternegg, K. T. von. *Deutsche Wirtschaftsgeschichte.* 3 parts in 4 vols. (I vol. 2nd ed. 1909), Leipzig, 1879–1901.

Kelter, E. 'Das deutsche Wirtschaftsleben des 14. und 15. Jahrhunderts im Schatten der Pestepidemien.' *Jahrb. f. Nationalökon. u. Statistik*, CLXV (1953).

Keutgen, F. *Der deutsche Staat des Mittelalters.* Jena, 1918.

Kisch, G. *The Jews in Medieval Germany. A Study of their Legal and Social Status.* Chicago, 1949.

Kötzschke, R. *Grundzüge der deutschen Wirtschaftsgeschichte bis zum 17. Jhdt.* 2nd ed. Leipzig–Berlin, 1923.

Kulischer, J. *Allgemeine Wirtschaftsgeschichte des Mittelalters und der Neuzeit*, I: *Das Mittelalter.* 2nd ed. Munich, 1958.

Lamprecht, K. *Deutsche Wirtschaftsgeschichte im Mittelalter.* 3 parts in 4 vols. Leipzig, 1885–6.

Lütge, F. 'Das 14/15. Jahrhundert in der Sozial- und Wirtschaftsgeschichte.' *Jahrb. f. Nationalökon. u. Statistik*, CLXII (1950).

—— *Deutsche Sozial- und Wirtschaftsgeschichte. Ein Überblick.* Berlin–Göttingen–Heidelberg, 1952.

Mayer, Th. *Deutsche Wirtschaftsgeschichte des Mittelalters.* Leipzig, 1928.

Mitteis, H. *Deutsches Privatrecht.* 3rd ed. Munich–Berlin, 1958.

—— *Deutsche Rechtsgeschichte.* 5th ed. Munich–Berlin, 1958.

Nabholz, H., Muralt, L. von, Feller, R. and Dürr, E. *Geschichte der Schweiz*, I. Zürich, 1932.

Parkes, J. W. *The Jew in the Medieval Community, a Study of his Political and Economic Situation.* London, 1938.

Planitz, H. *Deutsche Rechtsgeschichte.* Graz, 1950.

Postan, M. M. 'Die wirtschaftlichen Grundlagen der mittelalterlichen Gesellschaft.' *Jahrb. f. Nationalökon. u. Statistik*, CLXVI (1954).

Scherer, J. E. *Die Rechtsverhältnisse der Juden in den deutsch-österreichischen Ländern.* Leipzig, 1901.

Schulte, A. *Geschichte des Mittelalterlichen Handels und Verkehrs zwischen Westdeutschland und Italien mit Ausschluss von Venedig.* 2 vols. Leipzig, 1900.

—— *Der deutsche Staat, Verfassung, Macht und Grenzen, 919–1914.* Stuttgart–Berlin, 1933.

SIEVEKING, H. *Wirtschaftsgeschichte*. Berlin, 1935.

STOBBE, O. *Die Juden in Deutschland*. 3rd ed. Berlin, 1923.

WAITZ, G. *Verfassungsgeschichte des deutschen Volkes*, 8 vols. Kiel–Berlin, 1844–78. Reprinted, 1953–6.

WERMINGHOFF, A. *Geschichte der Kirchenverfassung Deutschlands im Mittelalter*, I. Hanover–Leipzig, 1905.

—— *Verfassungsgeschichte der deutschen Kirche im Mittelalter*. 2nd ed. Leipzig–Berlin, 1913.

(b) *The Empire*

ASCHBACH, J. *Geschichte Kaiser Sigmunds*. 4 vols. Hamburg, 1838–45.

CHMEL, J. *Geschichte Kaiser Friedrichs III und seines Sohnes Maximilian I*. 2 vols. Hamburg, 1840–3.

DENHOLM-YOUNG, N. *Richard of Cornwall*. Oxford, 1947.

FINKE, H. *König Sigmunds reichsstädtische Politik von 1410–1418*. (Diss. Tübingen.) Bocholt, 1880.

GIESEBRECHT, W. VON. *Geschichte der deutschen Kaiserzeit*. 6 vols. Leipzig–Brunswick, 1855–95 and various editions.

HELMOLT, H. F. *König Ruprechts Zug nach Italien*. (Diss. Leipzig.) Jena, 1892.

HEUPEL, W. *Der Sizilische Grosshof unter Kaiser Friedrich II. Eine verwaltungsgeschichtliche Studie*. (Schriften des Reichsinstituts für altere deutsche Geschichtskunde. Monumenta Germaniae Historica, 1940.) Reprinted Stuttgart, 1952.

HINTZE, O. *Das Königtum Wilhelms von Holland*. Eingeleitet von J. Weizsäcker. (Historische Studien, 15.) Leipzig, 1885.

HÖFLER, C. *Ruprecht von der Pfalz genannt Clem. Römischer König, 1400–1410*. Freiburg, 1861.

HUFNAGEL, O. *Caspar Schlick als Kanzler Friedrichs III*. (Miög. VIII Erg. Band, 1911.) Vienna, 1911.

KEMPF, J. *Geschichte des deutschen Reiches während des grossen Interregnums, 1245–1273*. Würzburg, 1893.

KRONES, FR. 'Schlick Kaspar.' *ADB*. XXXI, 2 vols.

LINDNER, TH. *Geschichte des deutschen Reiches unter König Wenzel*. 2 vols. Brunswick, 1875–80.

OFFLER, H. S. 'Empire and Papacy. The last Struggle.' *TRHS*. fifth series, VI (1956).

PIRCHAN, G. *Italien und Kaiser Karl IV in der Zeit seiner 2. Romfahrt*. 2 vols. (Quellen und Forschungen aus dem Gebiete der Geschichte.) Prague, 1930.

REDLICH, O. *Rudolf von Habsburg. Das deutsche Reich nach dem Untergange des alten Kaisertums*. Innsbruck, 1903.

ROTH, F. W. E. *Geschichte des Römischen Königs Adolf I von Nassau*. Wiesbaden, 1879.

SCHNEIDER, FR. *Kaiser Heinrich VII*. 3 parts. Greiz, 1924–8.

—— *Kaiser Heinrich VII, Dantes Kaiser*. 2nd ed. Stuttgart, 1943.

SIMONSFELD, H. *Jahrbücher des deutschen Reiches unter Friedrich I*, 1: *1152–1158*. Leipzig, 1908.

STENGEL, E. E. 'Avignon und Rhens. Forschungen zur Geschichte des Kampfes um das Recht am Reich in der 1. Hälfte des 14. Jhdts.' *Quellen und Studien zur Verfassungsgeschichte des deutschen Reiches im Mittelalter und Neuzeit*, VI (1). Weimar, 1930.

ULMANN, H. *Kaiser Maximilian I*. 2 vols. Stuttgart, 1884–91.

Vita Caroli IV ab ipso conscripta, 1346. Reprinted in *Fontes Rerum Bohemicarum*, III. Prague, 1882.

VOSSELMANN, A. *Die reichstädtische Politik König Ruprechts von der Pfalz*. Paderborn, 1904.

WERUNSKY, E. *Geschichte Kaiser Karls IV und seiner Zeit*. 3 vols. Innsbruck, 1880–92.

WINDECKE, E. *Kaiser Sigismunds Buch* (in *Scriptores rerum Germanicarum praecipue Saxonicarum*, ed. J. B. Menckenius. Leipzig, 1728; later edition by W. Altmann under the title *Denkwürdigkeiten zur Geschichte des Zeitalters Kaiser Sigmunds*. Berlin, 1893).

WINKELMANN, E. *De regni Siculi administratione, qualis fuerit regnante Frederico II, Romanorum imperatore, Ierusalem et Siciliae rege*. (Dissertatio Inauguralis, Berlin, 1859.) (Important for financial history.)

—— *Philipp von Schwaben und Otto IV von Braunschweig*. 2 vols. Leipzig, 1873–8.

WINKELMANN, E. *Geschichte Friedrichs II und seiner Reiche*. 2 vols. Berlin, 1863 and Reval, 1865.
—— *Kaiser Friedrich II*. 2 vols. Leipzig, 1889–97.
WOSTRY, W. 'König Albrecht II (1437–1439).' *Prager Studien aus d. Gebiet der Geschichtswissenschaft*, XII/XIII. Prague, 1906–7.
ZECHEL, A. 'Studien über Kaspar Schlick.' *Quellen und Forschungen aus dem Gebiete der Geschichte*, XV. Prague, 1939.

(c) *The Territories*

AUBIN, H. *Die Verwaltungsorganisation des Fürstbistums Paderborn im Mittelalter*. (Abh. zur Mittelalt. und Neueren Gesch. Heft 26.) Berlin, 1911.
AUBIN, H. and others. *Geschichte des Rheinlandes von den ältesten Zeit bis zur Gegenwart*. 2 vols. Essen, 1922.
BIRCK, M. *Der Kölner Erzbischof Dietrich II im Streit mit dem päpstlichen Stuhle*. Mühlheim, 1878.
CARDAUNS, H. *Konrad von Hochstaden*. Cologne, 1880.
CARSTEN, F. L. *The Origins of Prussia*. Oxford, 1954.
DOMINICUS, A. *Baldewin von Lützelburg, Erzbischof und Kurfürst von Trier*. Coblenz, 1862.
DROYSEN, J. G. *Geschichte der preussischen Politik*. 5 parts in 14 vols. Berlin, 1855–86; 2nd ed. vols. I–IV, Berlin, 1868–72.
EGGER, J. *Geschichte Tirols von den ältesten Zeiten bis in die Neuzeit*. 3 vols. Innsbruck, 1872–8.
ENNEN, L. 'Friedrich von Saarwerden, Erzbischof von Köln.' *ADB*. VIII, 538.
ERNST, F. *Eberhard im Bart. Die Politik eines deutschen Landesherrn am Ende des Mittelalters*. Stuttgart, 1933. (Valuable for the history of princely finances.)
FICKER, J. *Reinald von Dassel, Reichskanzler und Erzbischof von Köln, 1156–1167*. Cologne, 1850.
—— *Engelbert der Heilige, Erzbischof von Köln und Reichsverweser*. Cologne, 1853.
GUNDLACH, F. *Die Hessischen Zentralbehörden von 1247 bis 1604*. 3 vols. (Veröff. der Histor.-Komm. für Hessen und Waldeck, XVI.) Marburg, 1930–2.
HANTSCH, H. *Die Geschichte Österreichs*, I. 3rd ed. Vienna, 1951.
HAVEMANN, W. *Geschichte der Lande Braunschweig und Lüneburg*. 3 vols. Göttingen, 1853–7.
HECKER, H. *Die territoriale Politik des Erzbischofs Philipp I von Köln (1167–1191)*. (Historische Studien, X, 1883.) Leipzig, 1883.
HEINEMANN, O. VON. *Geschichte Braunschweigs und Hannovers*. 3 vols. Gotha, 1882–92.
HENNES, J. H. *Albrecht von Brandenburg, Erzbischof von Mainz und Magdeburg*. Mainz, 1858.
HERKERT, O. *Landesherrliches Beamtentum der Markgrafschaft Baden im Mittelalter*. (Diss. Freiburg.) Freiburg i. Br., 1910.
HUBER, A. *Geschichte Österreichs*, I, II, III, IV. Gotha, 1885 sq.
HUBER, A. and DOPSCH, A. *Österreichische Reichsgeschichte*. 2nd ed. Vienna, 1901.
ISAACSOHN, S. *Geschichte des preussischen Beamtentums vom Anfang des 15. Jhdts. bis auf die Gegenwart*, I. Berlin, 1873.
KANTER, E. W. 'Markgraf Albrecht Achilles von Brandenburg.' *Quellen und Untersuchungen zur Geschichte des Hauses Hohenzollern*, X. Berlin, 1911.
KEUSSEN, H. 'Walram von Jülich, Erzbischof von Köln.' *ADB*. XL, 773.
KÖTZSCHKE, R. and KRETSCHMAR, H. *Sächsische Geschichte*, I. Dresden, 1935.
KREUTZKAMPF, P. F. *Die Territorialpolitik des Kölner Erzbischofs Heinrich von Virneburg, 1306–1332*. (Diss. Cologne.) Bigge-Ruhr, 1933.
LEY, C. A. *Kölnische Kirchengeschichte von der Einführung des Christentums bis zur Gegenwart*. 2nd ed. Essen, 1917.
MAY, J. *Kurfürst Kardinal und Erzbischof Albrecht II von Mainz und Magdeburg*. 2 vols. Munich, 1865–75.
MENZEL, K. *Diether von Isenburg, Erzbischof von Mainz, 1459–1463*. Erlangen, 1868.
MEYER, H. B. 'Hof- und Zentralverwaltung der Wettiner in der Zeit einheitlicher Herrschaft über die Meissnisch-Thüringischen Lande 1248–1379.' *Leipziger Studien aus dem Gebiet der Geschichte*, IX (3). Leipzig, 1902.

PFEIL, F. *Der Kampf Gerlachs von Nassau mit Heinrich von Virneburg um das Erzstift Mainz.* (Diss. Strassburg). Darmstadt, 1910.

PÖSCHL, A. *Bischofsgut und Mensa episcopalis. Ein Beitrag zur Geschichte des kirchlichen Vermögensrechts.* 3 vols. Bonn, 1908–12.

PRIESACK, J. *Die Reichspolitik des Erzbischofs Balduin von Trier in den Jahren 1314–1328.* Göttingen, 1894.

PRUTZ, H. *Preussische Geschichte*, I. Stuttgart, 1900.

RATHJE, J. *Die Behördenorganisation im ehemals Kurkölnischen Herzogtum Westfalen.* (Diss. Heidelberg.) Kiel, 1905.

RIEZLER, S. *Geschichte Bayerns*. 8 vols. Gotha, 1878–1914. *Register* by Widemann, J. Munich, 1932.

ROSENTHAL, E. *Geschichte des Gerichtswesens und der Verwaltungsorganisation Baierns,* I *(1180–1598).* Würzburg, 1889.

ROTHERT, H. *Westfälische Geschichte*, I. Gütersloh, 1949.

SAUERLAND, H. V. *Der Trierer Erzbischof Diether von Nassau in seinen Beziehungen zur päpstlichen Kurie.* (Annalen des Historischen Vereins für den Niederrhein, Heft 68.) Cologne, 1899.

SCHOTTE, W. *Fürstentum und Stände in der Mark Brandenburg unter Regierung Joachims I.* (Veröff. des Vereins für Geschichte der Mark Brandenburg.) Leipzig, 1911.

SCHWIND, E. VON and DOPSCH, A. *Ausgewählte Urkunden zur Verfassungs-Geschichte der Deutsch-Österreichischen Erblande im Mittelalter.* Vienna, 1895.

SPANGENBERG, H. *Hof- und Zentralverwaltung der Mark Brandenburg im Mittelalter.* (Veröff. des Vereins für Geschichte der Mark Brandenburg.) Leipzig, 1908.

—— 'Landesherrliche Verwaltung, Feudalismus und Ständetum in den deutschen Territorien des 13. bis 15. Jahrhunderts.' *HZ.* CIII (1909).

—— 'Territorialwirtschaft und Stadtwirtschaft. Ein Beitrag zur Kritik der Wirtschaftsstufentheorie.' *HZ.* Beiheft (1932).

STENGEL, E. E. *Baldewin von Luxemburg. Ein grenzdeutscher Staatsmann des 14. Jhdts.* Weimar, 1937.

STIMMING, M. *Die Entstehung des weltlichen Territoriums des Erzbistums Mainz.* Darmstadt, 1915.

WALDEYER, K. J. *Walram von Jülich, Erzbischof von Köln und seine Reichspolitik.* 2 parts, Bonn, 1890–1.

WEISS, J. *Berthold von Henneberg, Erzbischof von Mainz (1484–1504). Seine kirchenpolitische und kirchliche Stellung.* Freiburg i. Br., 1889.

WINTER, E. K. *Rudolf IV von Österreich.* 2 vols. Vienna, 1934–6.

WINTTERLIN, F. *Geschichte der Behördenorganisation in Württemberg.* 2 vols. Stuttgart, 1902–6.

(d) The Towns

ARNOLD, W. *Verfassungsgeschichte der deutschen Freistädte im Anschluss an die Verfassungsgeschichte der Stadt Worms.* 2 vols. Hamburg-Gotha, 1854.

—— *Zur Geschichte des Eigentums in den deutschen Städten.* Basle, 1861.

BELOW, G. VON. *Entstehung der deutschen Stadtgemeinde.* Düsseldorf, 1889.

—— *Ursprung der deutschen Stadtverfassung.* Düsseldorf, 1892.

—— 'Die städtische Verwaltung des Mittelalters als Vorbild der späteren Territorialverwaltung.' *HZ.* N.F. XXXIX (1895).

BEUTIN, L. 'Italien und Köln.' *Studi in Onore Armando Sapori,* I. Milan, 1957.

BEYERLE, F. 'Zur Typenfrage in der Stadtverfassung.' *ZRG. Germ. Abt.* L (1930).

BOOS, H. *Geschichte der Rheinischen Städtekultur von ihren Anfängen bis zur Gegenwart mit besonderer Berücksichtigung der Stadt Worms.* 2nd ed. Berlin, 1897–1901.

DAENELL, E. *Die Blütezeit der deutschen Hanse. Hansische Geschichte von der 2. Hälfte des 14. bis zum letzten Viertel des 15. Jahrhunderts.* 2 vols. Berlin, 1906.

ENNEN, E. *Frühgeschichte der europäischen Stadt.* Bonn, 1953.

ENNEN, L. *Geschichte der Stadt Köln.* 5 vols. Cologne, 1863–80.

FEINE, H. E. 'Der Goslarische Rat bis zum Jahre 1400.' *Gierkes Untersuchungen,* CXX. Breslau, 1913.

FELLER, R. *Geschichte Berns*, I. 2nd ed. Bern, 1949.

FINK, G. 'Die Frage des Lübeckischen Patriziats im Lichte der Forschung.' *Ztschr. des Ver. für Lübische Gesch. und Altertumskunde*, Jhg. 1937–1938, Heft 2.

FRÖHLICH, K. 'Die Verfassungsentwicklung von Goslar im Mittelalter.' *ZRG. Germ. Abt.* XLVII (1927).

HEER, F. 'Augsburgs Bürgertum im Aufstieg Augsburgs zur Weltstadt (1275–1530).' *Augusta, 955–1955*. Munich, 1955.

HEGEL, K. *Städte und Gilden der germanischen Völker im Mittelalter*. 2 vols. Leipzig, 1891.

HOFFMANN, M. *Geschichte der Freien und Hansastadt Lübeck*. 2 vols. Lübeck, 1899–1902.

KEUSSEN, H. *Die Kölner Revolution von 1396, ihre Begründung und Darstellung*. Cologne, 1888.

KEUTGEN, F. *Urkunden zur Städtischen Verfassungsgeschichte*. Berlin, 1901.

KIRCHOFF, P. *Die Dortmunder Fehde von 1388–1389*. (Dortmunder Beiträge, XVIII.) Dortmund, 1910.

KRACAUER, I. *Geschichte der Juden in Frankfurt 1150–1824*, I. Frankfurt a.M., 1925.

KUSKE, B. *Quellen zur Geschichte des Kölner Handels und Verkehrs im Mittelalter*. 4 vols. Bonn, 1918–34.

LARGIADER, A. *Geschichte der Stadt und Landschaft Zürich*, I. Zürich, 1945.

LAU, F. *Entwicklung der kommunalen Verfassung und Verwaltung der Stadt Köln bis zum Jahre 1396*. Bonn, 1898.

LAUER, E. 'The South German Reichstädte in the late Middle Ages', in *Medieval and Historiographical Essays in Honour of James Westfall Thompson*. Chicago, 1938.

MEIER, P. J. *Die Stadt Goslar*. Stuttgart-Berlin, 1926.

MEINERT, H. *Frankfurts Geschichte*. Frankfurt, 1949.

MUNDY, J. H. and RIESENBERG, P. *The Medieval Town*. Princeton, 1958.

NABHOLZ, H. 'Die Anfänge der hochmittelalterlichen Stadt und ihrer Verfassung als Frage der Forschungsmethode betrachtet' (in Nabholz, H. *Ausgewählte Aufsätze zur Wirtschaftsgeschichte*. Zürich, 1954).

NEUMANN, H. *Die Geschichte Berlins*. 2 vols. Berlin, 1927.

NUGLISCH, A. 'Die wirtschaftliche Leistungsfähigkeit deutscher Städte im Mittelalter.' *Ztschr. für Sozialwissenschaft*, IX (1906).

PETERS, E. *Das grosse Sterben 1350 in Lübeck und seine Auswirkungen auf die wirtschaftliche und soziale Struktur der Stadt*. (Diss. Berlin.) Berlin, 1939.

PLANITZ, H. 'Zur Geschichte des Städtischen Meliorats.' *ZRG. Germ. Abt.* LXVII (1950).
—— *Die deutsche Stadt im Mittelalter*. Graz-Cologne, 1954.

PREUSS, H. *Die Entwicklung des deutschen Städtewesens*, I: *Entwicklungsgeschichte der deutschen Städteverfassung*. Leipzig, 1906.

Recueils de la Société Jean Bodin, VI and VII: *La Ville* (1954 and 1955): articles of J. Schneider on 'Les villes allemandes' (urban credit operations discussed in vol. VI).

REINECKE, W. *Geschichte der Stadt Lüneburg*. 2 vols. Lüneburg, 1933.

RÖRIG, F. *Vom Werden und Wesen der Hanse*. 3rd ed. Leipzig, 1943.
—— *Die europäische Stadt und die Kultur des Bürgertums im Mittelalter*. 2nd ed. Göttingen, 1955.

ROTHERT, H. *Geschichte der Stadt Osnabrück im Mittelalter*. 2 vols. Osnabrück, 1938.

RÜBEL, K. *Geschichte der Frei- und Reichsstadt Dortmund*. 2nd ed. Dortmund, 1906.
—— *Geschichte der Grafschaft und der Freien Reichsstadt Dortmund*, I. Dortmund, 1917.

SANDER, P. *Geschichte des Städtewesens*. (Bonner Staatswissenschaftliche Untersuchungen, Heft VI.) Bonn-Leipzig, 1922.

SCHMOLLER, G. *Deutsches Städtewesen in älterer Zeit*. (Ibid. Heft V.) Bonn-Leipzig, 1922.

SCHNEIDER, J. *La ville de Metz aux XIIIe et XIVe siècles*. Nancy, 1950.

SCHULTE, A. *Geschichte der grossen Ravensburger Handelsgesellschaft, 1380–1530*. 3 vols. Stuttgart-Berlin, 1923.

SCHUMANN, E. *Verfassung und Verwaltung des Rates in Augsburg von 1276 bis 1368*. Rostock, 1905.

SIEVEKING, H. 'Die mittelalterliche Stadt. Ein Beitrag zur Theorie der Wirtschaftsgeschichte.' *V. f. Soz. u. WG.* II (1904).

SPIESS, W. *Braunschweig. Die Verfassung und Verwaltung der mittelalterlichen Stadt.* Hildesheim, 1949.

STEINBACH, F. *Geschichtliche Grundlagen der kommunalen Selbstverwaltung in Deutschland.* (Rheinisches Archiv, xx.) Bonn, 1932.

WACKERNAGEL, R. *Geschichte der Stadt Basel*, I. Basle, 1907.

WALTER, F. *Wien. Die Geschichte einer deutschen Grosstadt an der Grenze.* 3 vols. Vienna, 1940–4.

WINTERFELD, L. VON. *Handel, Kapital und Patriziat in Köln bis 1400.* (Pfingstblatt des Hansischen Geschichtsvereins, xvi.) Lübeck, 1925.

—— *Gründung, Markt und Ratsbildung deutscher Fernhandelsstädte. Westfalen, Hanse Ostseeraum.* Münster, 1955.

—— *Geschichte der freien Reichs- und Hansestadt Dortmund.* 2nd ed. Dortmund, 1956.

ZIMMERMANN, H. (ed.). *Geschichte der Stadt Wien.* 4 vols. Vienna, 1897–1911.

ZORN, W. *Augsburg. Geschichte einer deutschen Stadt.* Augsburg, 1956.

3. Financial History

(a) General Works

BAUER, C. 'Mittelalterliche Staatsfinanz und internationale Hochfinanz.' *Historisches Jahrbuch der Görres Gesellschaft* (1930).

BEYERLE, F. 'Die ewigen Renten des Mittelalters.' *V. f. Soz. u. WG.* IX (1911).

EHRENBERG, R. *Das Zeitalter der Fugger. Geldkapital und Kreditverkehr im 16. Jahrhundert.* 3rd ed. Jena, 1922.

ENGEL, A. and SERRURE, R. *Traité de numismatique du Moyen Âge.* 3 vols. Paris, 1890–1905.

FRIEDENSBURG, F. *Deutsche Münzgeschichte.* Leipzig, 1912.

—— *Münzkunde und Geldgeschichte der Einzelstaaten des Mittelalters und der Neueren Zeit.* Munich–Berlin, 1926.

GEBHART, H. *Die deutschen Münzen des Mittelalters und der Neuzeit.* Berlin, 1929.

GOTTLOB, A. *Aus der Camera Apostolica des 15. Jhdts.* Innsbruck, 1889.

—— *Die Servitientaxe im 13. Jhdt. Eine Studie zur Geschichte des päpstlichen Gebühren- wesens.* (Stutz's Kirchenrechtliche Abhandlungen, Heft II.) Stuttgart, 1903.

HÄPKE, R. 'Die Entstehung der grossen bürgerlichen Vermögen im Mittelalter.' *Schmollers Jahrbuch*, XXIX (1905).

JANSEN, M. *Jakob Fugger der Reiche. Studien und Quellen*, I. Leipzig, 1910.

KARAISL VON KARAIS, F. *Studien zur Entwicklung des Staatskredites unter besonderer Berück- sichtigung der Konsortiabeteiligungsform.* (Diss. Munich.) Munich, 1934.

KIRSCH, J. P. 'Die Päpstlichen Kollektorien in Deutschland während des 14. Jahrhunderts.' *Quellen und Forschungen, Görres Institut*, III (1894). Paderborn, 1894.

—— 'Die päpstlichen Annaten in Deutschland während des 14. Jahrhunderts. I. Von Johann XXII bis Innozenz VI.' *Quellen und Forschungen, Görres Institut*, IX (1903). Paderborn, 1903.

KUSKE, B. 'Die Entstehung der Kreditwirtschaft und des Kapitalverkehrs' (in *Kölner Vorträge Hsg. von der Wirtschafts- und Sozialwissenschaftlichen Fakultät der Universität Köln*, I. Leipzig, 1927, reprinted in Kuske, B. *Köln, der Rhein und das Reich. Beiträge aus fünf Jahrzehnten wirtschaftgeschichtlicher Forschung.* Cologne–Graz, 1956).

LANDMANN, J. 'Zur Entwicklungsgeschichte der Formen und Organisation des öffent- lichen Kredites.' *Finanzarchiv*, XXIX (1912).

—— 'Der öffentliche Kredit' (in *Handbuch der Finanzwissenschaft*, 2nd ed. by W. Gerloff and F. Neumark, III. Tübingen, 1958).

LOTZ, W. *Das Aufkommen der Geldwirtschaft im staatlichen Haushalt.* (Volkswirtschaftliche Zeitfragen, Heft 238.) Berlin, 1908.

—— *finanzwissenschaft.* 2nd ed. Tübingen, 1931.

LUSCHIN VON EBENGREUTH, A. *Allgemeine Münzkunde und Geldgeschichte des Mittelalters und der Neuen Zeit.* 2nd ed. Munich, 1926.

LUTZ, K. *Die geschichtliche Entwicklung der europäischen Hochfinanz vom Mittelalter bis zum beginnenden 19. Jahrhundert.* (Diss. Munich.) Munich, 1934.

LYON, B. D. *From Fief to Indenture. The Transition from Feudal to Non-Feudal Contract in Western Europe.* Cambridge (Mass.), 1957.

MANES, A. *Staatsbankerotte.* 3rd ed. Berlin, 1922.

MAYER, T. 'Geschichte der Finanzwirtschaft vom Mittelalter bis zum Ende des 18. Jahrhunderts' (in W. Gerloff and F. Neumark, *Handbuch der Finanzwissenschaft*, I. 2nd ed. Tübingen, 1952.)

PLANITZ, H. *Das deutsche Grundpfandrecht.* (Forschungen zum deutschen Recht, Beiheft IV.) Weimar, 1936.

PÖLNITZ, G. VON. *Jakob Fugger. Kaiser, Kirche und Kapital in der oberdeutschen Renaissance.* 2 vols. Tübingen, 1949–52.

—— *Anton Fugger I, 1453–1535.* Tübingen, 1958.

RIETSCHEL, S. 'Die Entstehung der freien Erbleihe.' *ZRG. Germ. Abt.* XX (1901).

ROESEL, I. *Die Reichssteuern der deutschen Judengemeinden von ihren Anfängen bis zur Mitte des 14. Jahrhunderts.* Berlin, 1910.

SCHMIED, R. *Die Formen der Kapitalbeschaffung und der Vergrösserung des Eigenkapitals der frühkapitalistischen Kaufleute und Handelsgesellschaften des 15. und 16. Jahrhunderts.* (Diss. Munich.) Berlin, 1936.

SCHNEIDER, F. 'Das kirchliche Zinsverbot und die kuriale Praxis im 13. Jahrhundert. Eine historische Skizze.' *Mélanges Finke.* Münster, 1904.

SCHULTE, A. *Die Fugger in Rom, 1495–1523.* 2 vols. Leipzig, 1904.

STEMPELL, B. VON. *Die ewigen Renten und ihre Ablösung. Zur mittleren Wirtschaftsgeschichte Deutschlands.* (Diss. Leipzig.) Borna–Leipzig, 1910.

STRIEDER, J. *Zur Genesis des modernen Kapitalismus. Forschungen zur Entstehung der grossen bürgerlichen Kapitalvermögen am Ausgange des Mittelalters und zu Beginn der Neuzeit, zunächst in Augsburg.* 2nd ed. Munich–Leipzig, 1935.

—— *Studien zur Geschichte kapitalistischer Organisationsformen. Monopole, Kartelle und Aktiengesellschaften im Mittelalter und zu Beginn der Neuzeit.* Munich, 1925.

—— 'Staatliche Finanznot als Nährboden des Kapitalismus.' *Forschungen und Fortschritte, Nachrichtenblatt der deutschen Wissenschaft und Technik*, 9 Jhg., no. 30. Berlin, 1933.

—— 'Finanznot des Staates und Entwicklung des Frühkapitalismus'. *7e Congrès International des Sciences Historiques*, II. Warsaw, 1933.

SUHLE, A. *Deutsche Münz- und Geldgeschichte von den Anfängen bis zum 15. Jahrhundert.* Berlin, 1955.

TÄUBER, W. *Geld und Kredit im Mittelalter.* Berlin, 1933.

TROE, H. *Münze, Zoll und Markt und ihre finanzielle Bedeutung für das Reich vom Ausgang der Staufer bis zum Regierungsantritt Karls IV.* Stuttgart, 1937.

VERCAUTEREN, F. 'Gilles de la Marcelle, Chanoine de Liège, Trésorier de l'Empereur Henri VII (c. 1270/80–1337).' *Studi in onore Armando Sapori*, I. Milan, 1957.

(b) The Empire

ADLER, S. *Organisation der Finanzverwaltung unter Kaiser Maximilian I.* Leipzig, 1886.

CARANDE, R. *Carlos V y sus Banqueros. La Hacienda real de Castilla.* Madrid, 1949.

CARO, G. 'Zur Geschichte der Reichsjudensteuer im 13. Jahrhundert.' *Monatsschrift für die Geschichte und Wissenschaft des Judentums*, XLVIII (1904).

DEIBEL, G. *Die italienischen Einkünfte Kaiser Friedrich Barbarossas.* Neue Heidelberger Jahrbücher, N.F. 1932.

—— 'Die finanzielle Bedeutung Reichs-Italiens für die staufische Herrscher des zwölften Jahrhunderts.' *ZRG. Germ. Abt.* LIV (1934).

FREY, K. *Das Schicksal des königlichen Gutes in Deutschland unter den letzten Staufern seit König Philipp.* Berlin, 1881.

GRADENWITZ, H. *Beiträge zur Finanzgeschichte des deutschen Reiches unter Ludwig dem Bayer.* (Diss. Erlangen.) Borna–Leipzig, 1908.

HILLIGER, B. 'Die Reichssteuerliste von 1242.' *Historische Vierteljahrschrift*, XXVIII (1934).

KIRCHNER, G. 'Die Steuerliste von 1241.' *ZRG. Germ. Abt.* LXX (1953).

KÜSTER, W. *Beiträge zur Finanzgeschichte des deutschen Reiches nach dem Interregnum*, I: *Das deutsche Reichsgut in den Jahren 1273 bis 1313 nebst einer Ausgabe und Kritik des Nürnberger Salbüchleins.* (Diss. Leipzig.) Leipzig, 1883.

NIESE, H. *Die Verwaltung des Reichsgutes im 13. Jahrhundert. Ein Beitrag zur deutschen Verfassungsgeschichte.* Innsbruck, 1905.

NUGLISCH, A. *Das Finanzwesen des deutschen Reiches unter Kaiser Karl IV.* (Diss. Strassburg.) Strassbourg, 1899.

—— 'Das Finanzwesen des deutschen Reiches unter Kaiser Sigmund.' *Jhb. f. Nat. u. Stat.* 3rd ser., XXI (1901).

PROWE, F. 'Die Finanzverwaltung am Hofe Heinrichs VII während des Römerzuges. Nach den Rechnungsberichten bei Bonainini.' *Acta Henrici VII*, I, pp. 286–346. (Diss. Berlin.) Berlin, 1888.

SCHMIDT, O. *Die Reichseinnahmen Ruprechts von der Pfalz.* (Leipziger Histor. Abhandlungen, XXX.) Leipzig, 1912.

SOMMERLAD, T. *Die Rheinzölle im Mittelalter.* Halle, 1894.

STOLZ, O. 'Zur Entwicklungsgeschichte des Zollwesens innerhalb des alten deutschen Reiches.' *V. f. Soz. u. WG.* XLI (1954).

SÜSSMANN, A. *Die Judenschuldentilgungen unter König Wenzel I.* Berlin, 1906.

VANNÉRUS, J. 'Les Lombards dans l'ancien pays de Luxembourg.' *Bulletin de l'Institut Historique de Rome,* fasc. XXVII (1952).

WETZEL, E. 'Das Zollrecht der deutschen Könige von den ältesten Zeiten bis zur Goldenen Bulle.' *Gierkes Untersuchungen,* XLIII (1893).

ZECHEL, A. 'Studien über Kaspar Schlick.' *Quellen und Forschungen aus dem Gebiete der Geschichte,* XV (1939). Prague.

ZEUMER, K. 'Die deutschen Städtesteuern, insbesondere die städtischen Reichssteuern im 12. und 13. Jhdt. Ein Beitrag zur Geschichte der Steuerverfassung des deutschen Reiches.' *Schmollers Forschungen,* I (2). Leipzig, 1878.

—— 'Zur Geschichte der Reichssteuern im früheren Mittelalter.' *HZ.* LXXXI (1898).

(c) The Territories

BAMBERGER, E. 'Die Finanzverwaltung in den deutschen Territorien des Mittelalters (1200–1500).' *Ztschr. für die Gesamte Staatswissenschaft,* LXXVII (1922–3).

CAEMMERER, V. 'Die Einnahmen des Kurfürsten Albrecht Achilles.' *Forschungen zur Brandenburgischen und Preussischen Geschichte,* XXVI (1913). Leipzig.

DOPSCH, A. 'Zur Geschichte der Finanzverwaltung Österreichs im 13. Jahrhundert.' *Miög.* XVIII (1897). Reprinted in Dopsch, A., *Verfassungs- und Wirtschaftsgeschichte des Mittelalters.* Vienna, 1928.

ERNST, V. 'Die direkten Staatssteuern in der Graffschaft Württemberg.' *Würt. Jahrbuch für Statistik und Landeskunde* (1904).

FALKE, J. 'Bete, Zins und Ungeld im Kurfürstentum Sachsen bis 1485.' *Mitteilungen d. Kgl. Sächs. Ver. für Erforschung vaterländischen Geschichtsdenkmale,* XIX, XX (1869). Dresden.

—— 'Die Steuerbewilligungen der Landesstände im Kurfürstentum Sachsen bis zum Anfang des 17. Jahrhunderts.' *Ztschr. für die gesamte Staatswissenschaft,* XXX, XXXI (1874–5). Tübingen.

HERMANN, J. *Die Mainzer Servitienzahlungen.* (Archiv für Hessische Geschichte und Altertumskunde.) Darmstadt, 1904.

HOFFMANN, M. *Der Geldhandel der Juden während des Mittelalters bis zum Jahre 1350.* Schmollers Forschungen, CLII. Leipzig, 1910.

KNIES, H. 'Ursprung der ersten Mainzer Kirchensteuer.' *Festschrift Schroe.* Mainz, 1934.

KOGLER, F. *Das landesfürstliche Steuerwesen in Tirol bis zum Ausgange des Mittelalters.* (Archiv für Österr. Geschichte, XC.) Vienna, 1901.

KOSTANECKI, A. VON. 'Der öffentliche Kredit im Mittelalter. Nach Urkunden der Herzogtümer Braunschweig und Lüneburg.' *Schmollers Forschungen,* IX (1). Leipzig, 1889.

KOTELMANN, A. 'Die Finanzen des Kurfürsten Albrecht Achilles.' *Ztschr. für Preussische Geschichte und Landeskunde,* III (1886).

LIEBE, O. 'Die rechtlichen und wirtschaftlichen Zustände der Juden im Erzstift Trier.' *Westdeutsche Ztschr. für Geschichte und Kunst,* XII (1893). Trier.

LUSCHIN VON EBENGREUTH, A. *Umrisse einer Münzgeschichte der altösterreichischen Lande im Mittelalter.* Vienna, 1909.

MEYER, H. B. 'Hof- und Zentralverwaltung der Wettiner in der Zeit einheitlicher Herr-schaft über die Meissnisch-Thüringischen Lande, 1248–1379.' *Leipziger Studien aus dem Gebiete der Geschichte*, IX (3). Leipzig, 1902.

PUFF, A. *Die Finanzen Albrechts des Beherzten.* (Diss. Leipzig.) Leipzig, 1911.

SAUERLAND, H. V. 'Trierische Taxen und Trinkgelder an der päpstlichen Kurie während des späteren Mittelalters.' *Westdeutsche Ztschr. für Geschichte und Kunst*, XVI. Trier, 1897.

SCHAPPER, G. *Die Hofordnung von 1470 und die Verwaltung am Berliner Hofe zur Zeit Kurfürst Albrechts im historischen Zusammenhange behandelt.* (Veröff. des Vereins für Geschichte der Mark Brandenburg.) Leipzig, 1912.

SCHMOLLER, G. 'Die Epochen der preussischen Finanzpolitik.' *Schmollers Jahrbuch*, N.F. I (1877).

—— *Preussische Verfassungs-, Verwaltungs- und Finanzgeschichte.* Berlin, 1921.

SCHWICKERATH, W. *Die Finanzwirtschaft der deutschen Bistümer.* (Beiträge zur kirchlichen Verwaltungswissenschaft, 1.) Breslau, 1942.

STOLZ, O. 'Über die ältesten Rechnungsbücher deutscher Landesverwaltungen.' *Histor. Vierteljahrschrift*, XXIII (1926).

(d) The Towns

ALBERS, H. *Die Anleihen der Stadt Bremen vom 14. bis zum 18. Jahrhundert.* (Veröff. aus dem Staatsarchiv der freien Hansestadt Bremen, III.) Bremen, 1930.

BEYERLE, K. 'Die Anfänge des Kölner Schreinswesens.' *ZRG. Germ. Abt.* LI (1931).

BRANDT, A. VON. *Der Lübecker Rentenmarkt von 1320–1350.* (Diss. Kiel.) Düsseldorf, 1935.

BRUNNER, O. *Die Finanzen der Stadt Wien von den Anfängen bis ins 16. Jahrhundert.* (Studien aus dem Archiv der Stadt Wien, I–II.) Vienna, 1929.

BUCHNER, H. *Zur Entwicklung des städtischen Kredits in Deutschland im Mittelalter und im 16. Jahrhundert.* (Diss. Munich.) Munich, 1925.

BÜCHER, K. 'Der öffentliche Haushalt der Stadt Frankfurt im Mittelalter.' *Ztschr. für die gesamte Staatswissenschaft*, LII (1896). Tübingen. Reprinted in Bücher, K. *Beiträge zur Wirtschaftsgeschichte.* Tübingen, 1922.

CREMER, O. *Der Rentenkauf im mittelalterlichen Köln. Nach Schreinsurkunden des 12. bis 14. Jahrhundert (mit Urkundenanhang).* (Diss. Cologne.) Würzburg, 1936.

ERLER, A. *Bürgerrecht und Steuerpflicht im mittelalterlichen Städtewesen.* Frankfurt a.M. 1939.

FAHLBUSCH, O. 'Die Finanzverwaltung der Stadt Braunschweig seit dem Grossen Aufstand im Jahre 1374 bis zum Jahre 1425.' *Gierkes Untersuchungen*, CXVI. Breslau, 1913.

FOLTZ, M. *Beiträge zur Geschichte des Patriziats in den deutschen Städten vor dem Ausbruch der Zunftkämpfe.* (Diss. Marburg.) Marburg, 1899.

FRANKE, G. *Lübeck als Geldgeber Lüneburgs. Ein Beitrag zur Geschichte des städtischen Schuldenwesens im 14. und 15. Jahrhundert.* (Abhandlungen zur Handels- und Seege-schichte, N.F. IV.) Neumünster, 1935.

FREY, W. 'Beiträge zur Finanzgeschichte Zürichs im Mittelalter.' *Schweiz. Studien zur Geschichtswissenschaft*, III (1). Zürich, 1911.

GÄTJEN, B. *Der Rentenkauf in Bremen.* (Veröff. aus dem Staatsarchiv der freien Hansestadt Bremen, Heft 1.) Bremen, 1928.

GOBBERS, J. 'Die Erbleihe und ihr Verhältnis zum Rentenkauf im mittelalterlichen Köln des 12–14. Jahrhunderts.' *ZRG. Germ. Abt.* IV (1883).

GOERLITZ, T. 'Die Haftung des Bürgers und Einwohners für Schulden der Stadt und ihrer Bewohner nach Madgeburger Recht.' *ZRG. Germ. Abt.* LVI (1936).

HARMS, B. 'Die Steuern und Anleihen im öffentlichen Haushalt der Stadt Basel 1361–1500. Ein Beitrag zur mittelalterlichen Finanzstatistik.' *Ztschr. für die gesamte Staatswissenschaft*, LXIII (1907).

HARTWIG, J. 'Der Lübecker Schoss bis zur Reformationszeit.' *Schmollers Forschungen*, XXI (6). Leipzig, 1903.

HEFENBROCK, M. *Lübecker Kapitalsanlagen in Mecklenburg.* (Diss. Kiel.) Heide, 1929.

HEIDENHAIN, M. E. *Städtische Vermögenssteuern im Mittelalter.* (Diss. Leipzig.) Leipzig, 1906.

JAEGER, G. *Die Entwicklung der Eigentumsübertragung an städtischen Grundstücken in Bremen.* (Veröff. aus dem Staatsarchiv der freien Hansestadt Bremen, Heft 1.) Bremen, 1928.

KENTENICH, G. *Trierer Stadtrechnungen des Mittelalters.* (Trierer Archiv, Ergänzungsheft IX.) Trier, 1908.

KLEINAU, H. *Der Grundzins in der Stadt Braunschweig bis 1350.* (Leipziger Rechtswiss. Studien, XL.) Leipzig, 1929.

KNIPPING, R. *Die mittelalterlichen Rechnungen der Stadt Köln.* (Mitteilungen aus dem Stadtarchiv von Köln, XXIII.) Cologne, 1893.

——— 'Das Schuldenwesen der Stadt Köln im 14. und 15. Jahrhundert.' *Westdeutsche Ztschr. für Geschichte und Kunst*, XIII. Trier, 1894.

——— 'Ein mittelalterlicher Jahreshaushalt der Stadt Köln (1379).' *Festschrift für G. von Mevissen.* Cologne, 1895.

KUSKE, B. 'Das Schuldenwesen der deutschen Städte im Mittelalter.' *Ztschr. für die Gesamte Staatswissenschaft*, Ergänzungsheft, XII. Tübingen, 1904.

LEIBER, E. *Das kanonische Zinsverbot in deutschen Städten des Mittelalters.* (Diss. Freiburg.) Überlingen, 1926.

LUSCHIN VON EBENGREUTH, A. 'Wiens Münzwesen, Handel und Verkehr im späteren Mittelalter' (in Zimmermann, H. *Geschichte der Stadt Wien*, II. Vienna, 1905).

MACK, H. 'Die Finanzgeschichte der Stadt Braunschweig bis zum Jahre 1374.' *Gierkes Untersuchungen*, XXXII. Breslau, 1889.

MEYER, C. 'Der Haushalt einer deutschen Stadt im Mittelalter.' *V. f. Soz. u. WG.* 1 (1903).

MITTAG, H. *Zur Struktur des Haushalts der Stadt Hamburg im Mittelalter.* (Diss. Kiel.) Leipzig, 1914.

NABHOLZ, H. *Beitrag zum Steuerwesen der Stadt Zürich in der 2. Hälfte des 14. Jahrhunderts.* (Auszug aus der Einleitung zu der Edition der Züricher Steuerrödel des 14. und 15. Jahrhunderts.) Zürich, 1918.

PAULI, K. W. *Die sogenannten Wichboldsrenten oder die Rentenkäufe des Lübischen Rechts.* (Abhandlungen aus dem Lübischen Rechte, IV.) Lübeck, 1865.

PLANITZ, H. 'Das Grundpfandrecht in den Kölner Schreinskarten.' *ZRG. Germ. Abt.* LIV (1934).

POTTHOFF, H. 'Der öffentliche Haushalt Hamburgs im 15. und 16. Jahrhundert.' *Ztschr. des Vereins für Hamburg. Geschichte*, XVI (1). Hamburg, 1911.

RACHEL, H., PAPRITZ, J. and WALLICH, P. *Berliner Grosskaufleute und Kapitalisten*, 1. Berlin, 1934.

REINCKE, H. 'Die alte Hamburger Stadtschuld der Hansezeit, 1300–1563' (in A. von Brandt and W. Koppe, *Städtewesen und Bürgertum als geschichtliche Kräfte.* Lübeck, 1953).

RÜBEL, K. *Dortmunder Finanz- und Steuerwesen. Das vierzehnte Jahrhundert.* Dortmund, 1892.

SANDER, P. *Die reichstädtische Haushaltung Nürnbergs 1431 bis 1440.* Leipzig, 1902.

SCHINDLER, K. 'Finanzwesen und Bevölkerung der Stadt Bern im 15. Jahrhundert.' *Ztschr. für Schweizer Statistik*, XXXVI. Bern, 1900.

SCHONBERG, G. *Finanzverhältnisse der Stadt Basel im XIV. und XV. Jahrhundert.* Tübingen, 1879.

SCHÖNBERG, L. *Die Technik des Finanzhaushaltes der deutschen Städte im Mittelalter.* (Münchener Volkswirtschaftliche Studien, CIII.) Stuttgart–Berlin, 1910.

SCHWARZ, D. W. H. *Münz- und Geldgeschichte Zürichs im Mittelalter.* Aarau, 1940.

SCHWÖRBEL, L. *Die Rechnungsbücher der Stadt Köln, 1351–1798.* (Mitteilungen aus dem Stadtarchiv von Köln.) Cologne, 1892.

SEHRING, W. *Die finanziellen Leistungen der Reichsstädte unter Ruprecht von der Pfalz.* (Sammlung Wissenschaftlicher Arbeiten, XXXVI.) Langensalza, 1916.

SOHM, R. 'Städtische Wirtschaft im fünfzehnten Jahrhundert.' *Jhb. f. Nat. u. Stat.* XXXIV (1879).

STIEDA, W. 'Städtische Finanzen im Mittelalter.' *Jhb. f. Nat. u. Stat.* 3rd ser., XVII (1899).

STÜVE, C. 'Das Finanzwesen der Stadt Osnabrück bis zum Westfälischen Frieden.' *Mitteilungen des Vereins für Geschichte und Landeskunde von Osnabrück*, XI. Osnabrück, 1886.

—— 'Verzeichnis der Renten der Stadt Osnabrück, 1347.' *Mitteilungen des Vereins für Geschichte und Landeskunde von Osnabrück*, XVI. Osnabrück, 1891.

USINGER, R. 'Der Haushalt der Stadt Hamburg im 14. Jahrhundert.' *HZ*. XXIV (1870).

WACKERNAGEL, J. 'Städtische Schuldscheine als Zahlungsmittel im 13. Jahrhundert.' *V. f. Soz. u. WG.* Beiheft II (1924).

WELTI, F. E. 'Die Tellbücher der Stadt Bern aus dem Jahre 1389.' *Archiv des Historischen Vereins des Kantons Bern*, XIV. Bern, 1895.

—— 'Die ältesten Bernischen Stadtrechnungen.' *Archiv des Historischen Vereins des Kantons Bern*, XIV. Bern, 1895.

—— *Die Stadtrechnungen von Bern aus den Jahren 1375–1384.* Bern, 1896.

WERMINGHOFF, A. 'Die Verpfändung der Mittel- und Niederrheinischen Reichsstädte während des 13. und 14. Jahrhunderts.' *Gierkes Untersuchungen*, XLV. Breslau, 1893.

ZEDERMANN, F. *Die Einnahmequellen der deutschen Städte im Mittelalter.* (Diss. Würzburg.) Erlangen, 1911.

CHAPTER VIII

Conceptions of Economy and Society

I. GENERAL SOURCES

1. Laws

Corpus juris canonici. Edited by E. Friedberg. 2 vols. (I *Decretum*, II *Decretales*.) Leipzig, 1879–81.

Corpus juris civilis. Edited by T. Mommsen, W. Kroll, P. Krueger and R. Schoell. Berlin, 1928–9.

2. Ideas

(a) Theology

Peter Lombard. *Libri IV Sententiarum* (*c.* 1153). Quaracchi, 1916.

St Thomas Aquinas. *Opera omnia.* Rome, 1882 sqq.

STEGMÜLLER, F. 'Repertorium . . . Lombardi commentariorum.' *Römische Quartalschrift*, XLV (1937), 85–360.

(b) Canonists

Huguccio (*c.* 1190). *Summa Decretorum.* (Manuscript.)

Innocent IV. *Apparatus in Quinque Libros Decretalium* (*c.* 1251). Venice, 1578.

Henry de Segusia (Hostiensis). *Summa Decretalium* (*c.* 1253). Lyons, 1578.

—— *Lectura* (*c.* 1270).

Glossae ordinariae Decreti et Decretalium.

KUTTNER, ST. *Repertorium der Kanonistik (1140–1234).* Vatican City, 1937.

SCHULTE, FR. VON. *Die Geschichte der Quellen und Literatur des kanonischen Rechts.* I: *Von Gratian bis auf Papst Gregor IX.* II: *Von Papst Gregor IX bis zum Konzil von Trient.* Stuttgart, 1875 and 1877.

(c) Moralists

Summae confessorum. Cf. A. van Hove. *Prolegomena . . .* Rome, 1945.

St Antoninus of Florence. *Summa* (middle fifteenth century), in *Opera Omnia*, I. Florence, 1741.

St Bernardino of Siena. *Opera omnia.* Ed. J. de la Haye. Venice, 1745.

(d) Romanists

Azo. *Summa* and *Lectura* (beginning thirteenth century).
Accursius. *Glose ordinaire du Corpus* (*c.* 1230).
Bartolus (died 1347). *Opera omnia.* 10 vols.

CALASSO, FR. *Medio evo del diritto.* 1: *Le Fonti.* Milan, 1954.
SAVIGNY, F. VON. *Geschichte des römischen Rechts im Mittelalter,* 2nd ed. 7 vols. 1834–51.

(e) Customary Codes

BEAUMANOIR, PH. DE. *Coutumes de Beauvaisis* (*c.* 1280). Ed. A. Salmon. Paris, 1899.

(f) Publicists

The De Moneta of Nicholas Oresme, ed. C. Johnson. London, 1956.

II. GENERAL WORKS

ASHLEY, W. *An Introduction to English economic history and theory.* I, 1892; II, 1893, London.
BRANTS, V. *Esquisse des théories économiques professées par les écrivains des XIIIe et XIVe siècles.* Louvain, 1895.
ENDEMANN, W. *Studien in der romanisch-kanonistische Wirtschafts- und Rechtslehre.* Berlin, I, 1874; II, 1883.
FANFANI, A. *Le origini dello spirito capitalistico in Italia.* Milan, 1933.
JOURDAIN, CH. *Mémoire sur les commencements de l'économie politique dans les écoles du moyen âge.* (Académie des Inscriptions et Belles Lettres.) Paris, 1874.
O'BRIEN, G. *An essay on medieval economic teaching.* London, 1920.
SAPORI, A. *Studi di storia economica.* 3rd ed. Florence, 1955.
SCHREIBER, E. *Die Volkswirtschaftlichen Anschauungen der Scholastik seit Thomas von Aquin.* Jena, 1913.
SCHUMPETER, J. A. *History of economic analysis.* New York, 1954.
TROELSCH, E. *The social Teachings of the Christian Churches.* Transl. O. Wyon. London, 1931.
TRUGENBERGER, A. E. *San Bernardino da Siena. Considerazioni sullo sviluppo dell'etica economica cristiana nel primo Rinascimento.* Bern, 1951.

III. SPECIAL STUDIES

1. *Wealth*

BRUNET, R. 'La propriété privée chez saint Thomas.' *Nouvelle Revue théologique,* XI (1934), 914–27 and 1002–41.
GIET, ST. 'De trois textes de Gratien sur la propriété.' *Studia Gratiana,* III (Bologna, 1954), 319–32.
LEITMAIER, CH. 'Das Privateigentum im Gratianischen Dekret.' *Studia Gratiana,* III (1954), 361–74.

2. *Exchange*

(a) Contracts and Agreements

FEDELE, PIO. 'Considerazioni sull'efficacia dei patti nudi nel diritto canonico.' *Annali della R. Università di Macerata* (1937).
LE BRAS, G. 'La concorde des droits savants dans le domaine des contrats.' *Annales de la Faculté de Droit d'Aix-en-Provence* (1950).
ROUSSIER, J. *Le fondement de l'obligation contractuelle dans le droit classique de l'Eglise.* Thèse de la Faculté de Droit. Paris, 1933.

(b) Money

HUBRECHT, G. *Quelques observations sur l'évolution des doctrines concernant les paiements monétaires du XIIème au XVIIIème siècle.* Festgabe Simonius. Basle, 1955.
STAMPE, E. *Das Zahlkraftrecht der Postglossatorenzeit.* Berlin, 1933.
TAUBER, W. *Geld und Kredit im Mittelalter.* Berlin, 1933.

(c) The Just Price

BALDWIN, J. W. 'The medieval Theories of the just price. The twelfth and thirteenth Centuries.' (Unpublished doctoral dissertation.) Baltimore, 1956.

HAGUENAUER, S. 'Das justum pretium bei Thomas von Aquin.' *Vierteljahrschrift für sozial- und wirtschaftgeschichte*, XXIV. Stuttgart, 1931.

ROOVER, R. DE. 'The Concept of the Just Price. Theory and Economic Policy.' *Journal of Economic History*, XVIII, 1958.

TARDE, A. DE. *L'idée du juste prix*. Paris, 1907.

3. *Usury and interest*

CAPITANI, O. 'Sulla questione dell'usura nel medio evo (A proposito del volume di J. T. Noonan).' *Bollettino dell'Istituto storico italiano per il Medio Evo* (Rome, 1958), 537–66.

DUMAS, G. 'Intérêt et usure.' *Dictionnaire de droit canonique*, 1951.

HAMELIN, A. M. *Le Tractatus de usuris de maître Alexandre d'Alexandrie*. Montreal, 1955.

JOHNSTON, H. L. 'Medieval Teachings on the morality of Usury.' (Unpublished doctoral dissertation.) University of Toronto, 1938.

KNOLL, A. *Der Zins in der Scholastik*. Innsbruck, 1933.

LE BRAS, G. 'Usure.' *Dictionnaire de Théologie catholique*, XV. Paris, 1950.

MACLAUGHLIN, T. 'The teaching of the canonists on Usury.' *Medieval Studies*, I (1939) and VI (1944).

NELSON, B. N. *The Idea of Usury*. Princeton, 1949.

NOONAN, J. T. *The Scholastic Analysis of Usury*. Cambridge (Mass.), 1957.

4. *Social Theory*

BERRY, M. 'Les professions civiles dans le Décret de Gratien.' (Unpublished doctoral dissertation of the Faculté de Droit of Paris.) 1956.

BLOCH, M. *La société féodale*. I: *La formation des liens de dépendance*. II: *Les classes et le gouvernement des hommes*. L'évolution de l'humanité, XXXIV and XXXIV bis. Paris, 1939 and 1940.

GÉNICOT, L. 'Clercs et laïques au diocèse de Liège à la fin du moyen âge.' *Revue d'histoire du droit* (1955), 42–52.

LESTOCQUOY, J. 'Inhonesta mercimonia.' *Mélanges Halphen* (1951), 411–15.

APPENDIX
Coinage and Currency

The best bibliography of medieval coinage is provided by:

GRIERSON, PHILIP. *Coins and Medals, a Select Bibliography*. Historical Association, London, 1954.

For publications since 1952 consult the bibliographies in the Medieval relazioni to the *Congresso Internazionale di Numismatica*, i (Rome, 1961), 211–394.

The following bibliography is intended to indicate some of the more recent or more important books and articles.

BLOCH, M. *Esquisse d'une Histoire Monétaire de l'Europe*. Cahiers des Annales, Paris, 1954.

—— 'Le problème de l'or au Moyen Age', *Annales d'Histoire Economique et Sociale*, V (1933), 1–34.

CIPOLLA, C. M. *Money, Prices and Civilization in the Mediterranean World*. Princeton, 1956.

DIEPENBACH, W. 'Der Rheinische Münzverein', *Kultur und Wirtschaft im Rheinischen Raum, Festschrift zu Christian Eckert*. Mainz, 1949.

EINAUDI, L. 'Teoria della moneta imaginaria nel tempo da Carlomagno alla Rivoluzione francese', *Rivista di storia economica*, i (1936), 1–35. An English translation appears in *Enterprise and Secular Change*, ed. F. C. Lane and J. C. Riemersma. London, 1953.

ENGEL, A. and SERRURE, R. *Traité du Numismatique du Moyen Age*, 3 vols. Paris, 1891–1905.

ENNO VAN GELDER, H. and HOC, M. *Les Monnaies des Pays-Bas Bourguignons et Espagnols 1434–1713*. Amsterdam, 1960.

EVANS, A. 'Some Coinage Systems of the Fourteenth Century', *Journal of Economic and Business History*, iii (1930–1), 481–96.

FARRES, O. GIL. *Historia de la Moneda Española*. Madrid, 1959.

FRIEDENSBURG, F. *Münzkunde und Geldgeschichte der Einzelstaaten*. Munich, 1928.

LE GENTILHOMME, P. 'Le monnayage et la circulation monétaire dans les royaumes barbares en Occident (V^e–VIIIe siècles)', *Revue Numismatique*, 5th series, vii (1943), 46–112 and viii (1944–45), 13–59.

GRIERSON, PHILIP. *Numismatics and History*. Historical Association, London, 1951.

——'Commerce in the Dark Ages; A Critique of the Evidence', *Transactions of the Royal Historical Society*, 5th series, ix (1959), 123–40.

——'The Myth of the Mancus', *Revue Belge de Philologie et d'Histoire*, xxxii (1954), 1059–74.

JESSE, W. *Der Wendische Münzverein*. Lubeck, 1928.

JESSE, W. *Quellenbuch zur Münz- und Geldgeschichte des Mittelalters*. Halle, 1924.

KENT, J. P. C. 'From Roman Britain to Saxon England', *Anglo-Saxon Coins, Studies presented to Sir Frank Stenton* (London, 1961), pp. 1–22.

LAFAURIE, J. *Les Monnaies des rois de France*, 2 vols. Paris–Bâle, 1951–6.

LUSCHIN VON EBENGREUTH, A. *Allgemeine Münzkunde und Geldgeschichte*. 2nd ed. Munich, 1928.

OMAN, C. *The Coinage of England*. Oxford, 1931.

PEGOLOTTI, F. B. *La Pratica della Mercatura*, ed. A. Evans. Mediaeval Academy of America, 1936.

VAN WERVEKE, H. 'Monnaie de compte et monnaie réelle', *Revue Belge de Philologie et d'Histoire*, xiii (1934), 123–52.

INDEX

Aachen, 551
Aardenburg, 182, 199, 224–5, 226
Aaron of Lincoln, 452
Abbeville, 301, 441
Abbeys
  St Bertin, 9
  St Géry, 9
  Hersfeld, 441
  St Martin, 584
  St Omer, 9
  Stavelot-Malmédy, 120
  St Vaast, 9, 19
Abel, King of Denmark, 387
Acciaiuoli company, size of staff, 85, 86
  (table)
Accounts, 91–3
  settlement of, 110–11
Act of Retainer (1466), 470
Administrators, professional, 433
Adolf of Nassau, Archbishop of Mainz, 552
Adolf of Nassau, German Emperor, 478, 512
Aegean, the, 62, 64
Aethelred II, 298, 299, 583
Africa, north coast of, 64, 590
Aggersborg, 364, 369
Agrarian policy
  in England, 306–7, 324
  in France, 306–7
  in the Iberian peninsula, 409–11, 423
  in Italy, 409–11
  in the Low Countries, 341–2, 359–61
  in Poland, 377
Aigues-Mortes, 333
Aire-sur-Lys, 531
Aistulf, 10
Albania, 61
Albert, Count of Holland, 353
Alberti company, 77, 90
  account-books of, 91, 92
Albert III of Saxony, 522
Albertus Magnus, 563
Albrecht I, German Emperor, 512, 524
Albrecht II, German Emperor, 516–17
Albrecht von Hohenzollern, Archbishop of Mainz, 526
Albrecht, King of Mecklenburg, 374, 380
Albrecht III, Margrave of Brandenburg, 521
Alessandria, 168, 425
  founding of, by Lombard League, 166

Alexandria, 43, 60, 61, 63
Alexius Comnenus, Emperor of Byzantium, 61
Alfonso I, King of Aragon, 418
Alfonso X, King of Aragon, 424
Alfonso, King of Naples, 411
Alfred the Great, 10
Alix, Duchess of Burgundy, 474
Alms-giving, 573
Alpert, monk, 47
Alphonse of Poitiers, 300, 301
  domains of, 303
Alum, 88
Amalfi, 61
Amberg, 515
Ambrose, 554
Amiens, 12, 18, 241, 254, 256, 263, 272, 535, 537
Ammannati company, 71
Amsterdam, 13–14, 39
Amund of Sweden, 364
Angers, 249
Anjou, 299–300
Anno II, Archbishop of Cologne, 441
Annuities
  ecclesiastical approval of, 531
  hereditary, 504
  life, 504, 530, 534, 535, 536, 537, 538, 540, 541, 545, 546, 547, 548, 550
  market for, 532–3
  payment of, 436, 551
  permission of gilds to sell, 551
  perpetual, 530, 536, 537, 538, 547, 548, 551, 569
  personal, 569–70
  rate of interest, 531–2, 546, 548, 551, 552
  redemption of, 531
  sale of, 504, 506, 509, 522–3, 525, 529–30, 531, 534–42, 545–7, 550, 552–3
  security for, 552
  transferability of, 532
  see also Life-rents, Perpetual rents
Anti-combination laws, 204–5
Anti-monopoly policy, in Italy, 424–8
Antwerp, 39, 104, 123, 133, 142, 149, 150, 227, 288, 325, 332, 354, 439, 498, 504, 507
Apulia, 402, 411
Aquitaine, 300
Aragon, 269, 414, 424, 481, 488, 587, 590
Arezzo, 34
d'Arlon, Arnoul, 513